ISBN 978-0-656-60530-9
PIBN 11336457

English
Français
Deutsche
Italiano
Español
Português

www.forgottenbooks.com

Mythology Photography **Fiction**
Fishing Christianity **Art** Cooking
Essays Buddhism Freemasonry
Medicine **Biology** Music **Ancient
Egypt** Evolution Carpentry Physics
Dance Geology **Mathematics** Fitness
Shakespeare **Folklore** Yoga Marketing
Confidence Immortality Biographies
Poetry **Psychology** Witchcraft
Electronics Chemistry History **Law**
Accounting **Philosophy** Anthropology
Alchemy Drama Quantum Mechanics
Atheism Sexual Health **Ancient History**
Entrepreneurship Languages Sport
Paleontology Needlework Islam
Metaphysics Investment Archaeology
Parenting Statistics Criminology
Motivational

Illustrated Album

.. OF ..

Biography

———OF———

Southwestern Minnesota

CONTAINING BIOGRAPHICAL SKETCHES OF HUNDREDS OF PROMINENT OLD
SETTLERS AND REPRESENTATIVE CITIZENS, WITH A REVIEW OF THEIR LIFE
WORK, THEIR IDENTITY WITH THE GROWTH AND DEVELOPMENT OF THIS
REGION; AND REMINISCENCES OF PERSONAL HISTORY AND PIONEER LIFE.

History of Minnesota,

EMBRACING AN ACCOUNT OF EARLY EXPLORATIONS, ORGANIZATION, A REVIEW OF THE
POLITICAL HISTORY, AND A CONCISE HISTORY OF THE
INDIAN OUTBREAK OF 1862.

Presidents of the United States,

EMBRACING BIOGRAPHICAL SKETCHES AND A FULL-PAGE PORTRAIT OF EACH.

ILLUSTRATED.

CHICAGO:
OCCIDENTAL PUBLISHING COMPANY
1889

"Biography is the only true history."—EMERSON.

COPYRIGHT, 1889,
BY
OCCIDENTAL PUBLISHING CO.
CHICAGO, ILL.

———————

PRINTED AND BOUND BY
DONOHUE & HENNEBERRY,
CHICAGO.

CONTENTS

PRESIDENTS OF THE UNITED STATES.

HISTORY OF MINNESOTA.

Southwestern Minnesota

DESCRIPTIVE AND HISTORICAL INTRODUCTORY.

BIOGRAPHICAL.

ILLUSTRATIONS.

GEORGE WASHINGTON.

EORGE WASHING-TON, the "Father of his Country" and its first President, 1789–'97' was born February 22, 1732, in Washington Parish, Westmoreland County, Virginia. His father, Augustine Washington, first married Jane Butler, who bore him four children, and March 6, 1730, he married Mary Ball. Of six children by his second marriage, George was the eldest, the others being Betty, Samuel, John, Augustine, Charles and Mildred, of whom the youngest died in infancy. Little is known of the early years of Washington, beyond the fact that the house in which he was born was burned during his early childhood, and that his father thereupon moved to another farm, inherited from his paternal ancestors, situated in Stafford County, on the north bank of the Rappahannock, where he acted as agent of the Principio Iron Works in the immediate vicinity, and died there in 1743.

From earliest childhood George developed a noble character. He had a vigorous constitution, a fine form, and great bodily strength. His education was somewhat defective, being confined to the elementary branches taught him by his mother and at a neighboring school. He developed, however, a fondness for mathematics, and enjoyed in that branch the instructions of a private teacher. On leaving school he resided for some time at Mount Vernon with his half brother, Lawrence, who acted as his guardian, and who had married a daughter of his neighbor at Belvoir on the Potomac, the wealthy William Fairfax, for some time president of the executive council of the colony. Both Fairfax and his son-in-law, Lawrence Washington, had served with distinction in 1740 as officers of an American battalion at the siege of Carthagena, and were friends and correspondents of Admiral Vernon, for whom the latter's residence on the Potomac has been named. George's inclinations were for a similar career, and a midshipman's warrant was procured for him, probably through the influence of the Admiral; but through the opposition of his mother the project was abandoned. The family connection with the Fairfaxes, however, opened another career for the young man, who, at the age of sixteen, was appointed surveyor to the immense estates of the eccentric Lord Fairfax, who was then on a visit at Belvoir, and who shortly afterward established his baronial residence at Greenway Court, in the Shenandoah Valley.

Three years were passed by young Washington in a rough frontier life, gaining experience which afterward proved very essential to him.

In 1751, when the Virginia militia were put under training with a view to active service against France, Washington, though only nineteen years of age, was appointed Adjutant with the rank of Major. In September of that year the failing health of Lawrence Washington rendered it necessary for him to seek a warmer climate, and George accompanied him in a voyage to Barbadoes. They returned early in 1752, and Lawrence shortly afterward died, leaving his large property to an infant daughter. In his will George was named one of the executors and as eventual heir to Mount Vernon, and by the death of the infant niece soon succeeded to that estate.

On the arrival of Robert Dinwiddie as Lieutenant-Governor of Virginia in 1752 the militia was reorganized, and the province divided into four districts. Washington was commissioned by Dinwiddie Adjutant-General of the Northern District in 1753, and in November of that year a most important as well as hazardous mission was assigned him. This was to proceed to the Canadian posts recently established on French Creek, near Lake Erie, to demand in the name of the King of England the withdrawal of the French from a territory claimed by Virginia. This enterprise had been declined by more than one officer, since it involved a journey through an extensive and almost unexplored wilderness in the occupancy of savage Indian tribes, either hostile to the English, or of doubtful attachment. Major Washington, however, accepted the commission with alacrity ; and, accompanied by Captain Gist, he reached Fort Le Bœuf on French Creek, delivered his dispatches and received reply, which, of course, was a polite refusal to surrender the posts. This reply was of such a character

as to induce the Assembly of Virginia to authorize the executive to raise a regiment of 300 men for the purpose of maintaining the asserted rights of the British crown over the territory claimed. As Washington declined to be a candidate for that post, the command of this regiment was given to Colonel Joshua Fry, and Major Washington, at his own request, was commissioned Lieutenant-Colonel. On the march to Ohio, news was received that a party previously sent to build a fort at the confluence of the Monongahela with the Ohio had been driven back by a considerable French force, which had completed the work there begun, and named it Fort Duquesne, in honor of the Marquis Duquesne, then Governor of Canada. This was the beginning of the great "French and Indian war," which continued seven years. On the death of Colonel Fry, Washington succeeded to the command of the regiment, and so well did he fulfill his trust that the Virginia Assembly commissioned him as Commander-in-Chief of all the forces raised in the colony.

A cessation of all Indian hostility on the frontier having followed the expulsion of the French from the Ohio, the object of Washington was accomplished and he resigned his commission as Commander-in-Chief of the Virginia forces. He then proceeded to Williamsburg to take his seat in the General Assembly, of which he had been elected a member.

January 17, 1759, Washington married Mrs. Martha (Dandridge) Custis, a young and beautiful widow of great wealth, and devoted himself for the ensuing fifteen years to the quiet pursuits of agriculture, interrupted only by his annual attendance in winter upon the Colonial Legislature at Williamsburg, until summoned by his country to enter upon that other arena of which his fame was to become world wide.

It is unnecessary here to trace the details of the struggle upon the question of local self-government, which, after ten years, culminated by act of Parliament of the port of Boston. It was at the instance of Virginia that a congress of all the colonies was called to meet at Philadelphia September 5, 1774, to secure their common liberties—if possible by peaceful means. To this Congress Colonel Washington was sent as a delegate. On dissolving in October, it recommended the colonies to send deputies to another Congress the following spring. In the meantime several of the colonies felt impelled to raise local forces to repel insults and aggressions on the part of British troops, so that on the assembling of the next Congress, May 10, 1775, the war preparations of the mother country were unmistakable. The battles of Concord and Lexington had been fought. Among the earliest acts, therefore, of the Congress was the selection of a commander-in-chief of the colonial forces. This office was unanimously conferred upon Washington, still a member of the Congress. He accepted it on June 19, but on the express condition he should receive no salary.

He immediately repaired to the vicinity of Boston, against which point the British ministry had concentrated their forces. As early as April General Gage had 3,000 troops in and around this proscribed city. During the fall and winter the British policy clearly indicated a purpose to divide public sentiment and to build up a British party in the colonies. Those who sided with the ministry were stigmatized by the patriots as "Tories," while the patriots took to themselves the name of "Whigs."

As early as 1776 the leading men had come to the conclusion that there was no hope except in separation and independence. In May of that year Washington wrote from the head of the army in New York: "A reconciliation with Great Britain is impossible. . . . . When I took command of the army, I abhorred the idea of independence; but I am now fully satisfied that nothing else will save us."

It is not the object of this sketch to trace the military acts of the patriot hero, to whose hands the fortunes and liberties of the United States were confided during the seven years' bloody struggle that ensued until the treaty of 1783, in which England acknowledged the independence of each of the thirteen States, and negotiated with them, jointly, as separate sovereignties. The merits of Washington as a military chieftain have been considerably discussed, especially by writers in his own country. During the war he was most bitterly assailed for incompetency, and great efforts were made to displace him; but he never for a moment lost the confidence of either the Congress or the people. December 4, 1783, the great commander took leave of his officers in most affectionate and patriotic terms, and went to Annapolis, Maryland, where the Congress of the States was in session, and to that body, when peace and order prevailed everywhere, resigned his commission and retired to Mount Vernon.

It was in 1788 that Washington was called to the chief magistracy of the nation. He received every electoral vote cast in all the colleges of the States voting for the office of President. The 4th of March, 1789, was the time appointed for the Government of the United States to begin its operations, but several weeks elapsed before quorums of both the newly constituted houses of the Congress were assembled. The city of New York was the place where the Congress then met. April 16 Washington left home to enter upon the discharge of his new duties. He set out with a purpose of traveling privately, and without attracting any public attention; but this was impossible. Everywhere on his way he was met with thronging crowds, eager to see the man whom they regarded as the chief defender of their liberties, and everywhere he was hailed with those public manifestations of joy, regard and love which spring spontaneously from the hearts of an affectionate and grateful people. His reception in New York was marked by a grandeur and an enthusiasm never before witnessed in that metropolis. The inauguration took place April 30, in the presence of an immense multitude which had assembled to witness the new and imposing ceremony. The oath of office was administered by Robert R. Livingston, Chancellor of the State. When this sacred pledge was given, he retired with the other officials into the Senate chamber, where he delivered his inaugural address to both houses of the newly constituted Congress in joint assembly.

In the manifold details of his civil administration, Washington proved himself equal to the requirements of his position. The greater portion of the first session of the first Congress was occupied in passing the necessary statutes for putting the new organization into complete operation. In the discussions brought up in the course of this legislation the nature and character of the new system came under general review. On no one of them did any decided antagonism of opinion arise. All held it to be a limited government, clothed only with specific powers conferred by delegation from the States. There was no change in the name of the legislative department; it still remained "the Congress of the United States of America." There was no change in the original flag of the country, and none in the seal, which still remains with the Grecian escutcheon borne by the eagle, with other emblems, under the great and expressive motto, " *E Pluribus Unum.*"

The first division of parties arose upon the manner of construing the powers delegated, and they were first styled "strict constructionists" and "latitudinarian constructionists." The former were for confining the action of the Government strictly within its specific and limited sphere, while the others were for enlarging its powers by inference and implication. Hamilton and Jefferson, both members of the first cabinet, were regarded as the chief leaders, respectively, of these rising antagonistic parties which have existed, under different names, from that day to this. Washington was regarded as holding a neutral position between them, though, by mature deliberation, he vetoed the first apportionment bill, in 1790, passed by the party headed by Hamilton, which was based upon a principle constructively leading to centralization or consolidation. This was the first exercise of the veto power under the present Constitution. It created considerable excitement at the time. Another bill was soon passed in pursuance of Mr. Jefferson's views, which has been adhered to in principle in every apportionment act passed since.

At the second session of the new Congress, Washington announced the gratifying fact of "the accession of North Carolina" to the Constitution of 1787, and June 1 of the same year he announced by special message the like "accession of the State of Rhode Island," with his congratulations on the happy event which "united under the general Government" all the States which were originally confederated.

In 1792, at the second Presidential election, Washington was desirous to retire; but he yielded to the general wish of the country, and was again chosen President by the unanimous vote of every electoral college. At the third election, 1796, he was again most urgently entreated to consent to remain in the executive chair. This he positively refused. In September, before the election, he gave to his countrymen his memorable Farewell Address, which in language, sentiment and patriotism was a fit and crowning glory of his illustrious life. After March 4, 1797, he again retired to Mount Vernon for peace, quiet and repose.

His administration for the two terms had been successful beyond the expectation and hopes of even the most sanguine of his friends. The finances of the country were no longer in an embarrassed condition, the public credit was fully restored, life was given to every department of industry, the workings of the new system in allowing Congress to raise revenue from duties on imports proved to be not only harmonious in its federal action, but astonishing in its results upon the commerce and trade of all the States. The exports from the Union increased from $19,000,000 to over $56,000,000 per annum, while the imports increased in about the same proportion. Three new members had been added to the Union. The progress of the States in their new career under their new organization thus far was exceedingly encouraging, not only to the friends of liberty within their own limits, but to their sympathizing allies in all climes and countries.

Of the call again made on this illustrious chief to quit his repose at Mount Vernon and take command of all the United States forces, with the rank of Lieutenant-General, when war was threatened with France in 1798, nothing need here be stated, except to note the fact as an unmistakable testimonial of the high regard in which he was still held by his countrymen, of all shades of political opinion. He patriotically accepted this trust, but a treaty of peace put a stop to all action under it. He again retired to Mount Vernon, where, after a short and severe illness, he died December 14, 1799, in the sixty-eighth year of his age. The whole country was filled with gloom by this sad intelligence. Men of all parties in politics and creeds in religion, in every State in the Union, united with Congress in "paying honor to the man, first in war, first in peace, and first in the hearts of his countrymen."

His remains were deposited in a family vault on the banks of the Potomac at Mount Vernon, where they still lie entombed.

OHN ADAMS, the second President of the United States, 1797 to 1801, was born in the present town of Quincy, then a portion of Braintree, Massachusetts, October 30, 1735. His father was a farmer of moderate means, a worthy and industrious man. He was a deacon in the church, and was very desirous of giving his son a collegiate education, hoping that he would become a minister of the gospel. But, as up to this time, the age of fourteen, he had been only a play-boy in the fields and forests, he had no taste for books, he chose farming. On being set to work, however, by his father out in the field, the very first day converted the boy into a lover of books.

Accordingly, at the age of sixteen he entered Harvard College, and graduated in 1755, at the age of twenty, highly esteemed for integrity, energy and ability. Thus, having no capital but his education, he started out into the stormy world at a time of great political excitement, as France and England were then engaged in their great seven-years struggle for the mastery over the New World. The fire of patriotism seized young Adams, and for a time he studied over the question whether he should take to the law, to politics or the army. He wrote a remarkable letter to a friend, making prophecies concerning the future greatness of this country which have since been more than fulfilled. For two years he taught school and studied law, wasting no odd moments, and at the early age of twenty-two years he opened a law office in his native town. His inherited powers of mind and untiring devotion to his profession caused him to rise rapidly in public esteem. ·

In October, 1764, Mr. Adams married Miss Abigail Smith, daughter of a clergyman at Weymouth and a lady of rare personal and intellectual endowments, who afterward contributed much to her husband's celebrity.

Soon the oppression of the British in America reached its climax. The Boston merchants employed an attorney by the name of James Otis to argue the legality of oppressive tax law before the Superior Court. Adams heard the argument, and afterward wrote to a friend concerning the ability displayed, as follows: "Otis was a flame of fire. With a promptitude of classical allusion, a depth of research, a rapid summary of historical events and dates, a profusion of legal authorities and a

John Adams

prophetic glance into futurity, he hurried away all before him. *American independence was then and there born.* Every man of an immensely crowded audience appeared to me to go away, as I did, ready to take up arms."

Soon Mr. Adams wrote an essay to be read before the literary club of his town, upon the state of affairs, which was so able as to attract public attention. It was published in American journals, republished in England, and was pronounced by the friends of the colonists there as "one of the very best productions ever seen from North America."

The memorable Stamp Act was now issued, and Adams entered with all the ardor of his soul into political life in order to resist it. He drew up a series of resolutions remonstrating against the act, which were adopted at a public meeting of the citizens of Braintree, and which were subsequently adopted, word for word, by more than forty towns in the State. Popular commotion prevented the landing of the Stamp Act papers, and the English authorities then closed the courts. The town of Boston therefore appointed Jeremy Gridley, James Otis and John Adams to argue a petition before the Governor and council for the re-opening of the courts; and while the two first mentioned attorneys based their argument upon the distress caused to the people by the measure, Adams boldly claimed that the Stamp Act was a violation both of the English Constitution and the charter of the Provinces. It is said that this was the first direct denial of the unlimited right of Parliament over the colonies. Soon after this the Stamp Act was repealed.

Directly Mr. Adams was employed to defend Ansell Nickerson, who had killed an Englishman in the act of impressing him (Nickerson) into the King's service, and his client was acquitted, the court thus establishing the principle that the infamous royal prerogative of impressment could have no existence in the colonial code. But in 1770 Messrs. Adams and Josiah Quincy defended a party of British soldiers who had been arrested for murder when they had been only obeying Governmental orders; and when reproached for thus apparently deserting the cause of popular liberty, Mr. Adams replied that he would a thousandfold rather live under the domination of the worst of England's kings than under that of a lawless mob. Next, after serving a term as a member of the Colonial Legislature from Boston, Mr. Adams, finding his health affected by too great labor, retired to his native home at Braintree.

The year 1774 soon arrived, with its famous Boston "Tea Party," the first open act of rebellion. Adams was sent to the Congress at Philadelphia; and when the Attorney-General announced that Great Britain had "determined on her system, and that her power to execute it was irresistible," Adams replied: "I know that Great Britain has determined on her system, and that very determination determines me on mine. You know that I have been constant in my opposition to her measures. The die is now cast. I have passed the Rubicon. Sink or swim, live or die, with my country, is my unalterable determination." The rumor beginning to prevail at Philadelphia that the Congress had independence in view, Adams foresaw that it was too soon to declare it openly. He advised every one to remain quiet in that respect; and as soon as it became apparent that he himself was for independence, he was advised to hide himself, which he did.

The next year the great Revolutionary war opened in earnest, and Mrs. Adams, residing near Boston, kept her husband advised by letter of all the events transpiring in her vicinity. The battle of Bunker Hill came on. Congress had to do something immediately. The first thing was to choose a commander-in-chief for the—we can't say "army"—the fighting men of the colonies. The New England delegation was almost unanimous in favor of appointing General Ward, then at the head of the Massachusetts forces, but Mr. Adams urged the appointment of George Washington, then almost unknown outside of his own State. He was appointed without opposition. Mr. Adams offered the resolution, which was adopted, annulling all the royal authority in the colonies. Having thus prepared the way, a few weeks later, viz., June 7, 1776, Richard Henry Lee, of Virginia, who a few months before had declared that the British Government would abandon its oppressive measures, now offered the memorable resolution, seconded by Adams, "that these United States are, and of right ought to be, free and independent." Jefferson, Adams, Franklin, Sherman and Livingston were then appointed a committee to draught a declaration of independence. Mr. Jefferson desired Mr. Adams to draw up the bold document, but the latter persuaded Mr. Jefferson to perform that responsible task. The Declaration drawn up, Mr. Adams became its foremost defender on the floor of Congress. It was signed by all the fifty-five members present, and the next day Mr. Adams wrote to his wife how great a deed was done, and how proud he was of it. Mr. Adams continued to be the leading man of Congress, and the leading advocate of American independence. Above all other Americans, he was considered by every one the principal shining mark for British vengeance. Thus circumstanced, he was appointed to the most dangerous task of crossing the ocean in winter, exposed to capture by the British, who knew of his mission, which was to visit Paris and solicit the co-operation of the French. Besides, to take him-

self away from the country of which he was the most prominent defender, at that critical time, was an act of the greatest self-sacrifice. Sure enough, while crossing the sea, he had two very narrow escapes from capture; and the transit was otherwise a stormy and eventful one. During the summer of 1779 he returned home, but was immediately dispatched back to France, to be in readiness there to negotiate terms of peace and commerce with Great Britain as soon as the latter power was ready for such business. But as Dr. Franklin was more popular than he at the court of France, Mr. Adams repaired to Holland, where he was far more successful as a diplomatist.

The treaty of peace between the United States and England was finally signed at Paris, January 21, 1783; and the re-action from so great excitement as Mr. Adams had so long been experiencing threw him into a dangerous fever. Before he fully recovered he was in London, whence he was dispatched again to Amsterdam to negotiate another loan. Compliance with this order undermined his physical constitution for life.

In 1785 Mr. Adams was appointed envoy to the court of St. James, to meet face to face the very king who had regarded him as an arch traitor! Accordingly he repaired thither, where he did actually meet and converse with George III.! After a residence there for about three years, he obtained permission to return to America. While in London he wrote and published an able work, in three volumes, entitled: "A Defense of the American Constitution."

The Articles of Confederation proving inefficient, as Adams had prophesied, a carefully draughted Constitution was adopted in 1789, when George Washington was elected President of the new nation, and Adams Vice-President. Congress met for a time in New York, but was removed to Philadelphia for ten years, until suitable buildings should be erected at the new capital in the District of Columbia. Mr. Adams then moved his family to Philadelphia. Toward the close of his term of office the French Revolution culminated, when Adams and Washington rather sympathized with England, and Jefferson with France. The Presidential election of 1796 resulted in giving Mr. Adams the first place by a small majority, and Mr. Jefferson the second place.

Mr. Adams's administration was conscientious, patriotic and able. The period was a turbulent one, and even an archangel could not have reconciled the hostile parties. Partisanism with reference to England and France was bitter, and for four years Mr. Adams struggled through almost a constant tempest of assaults. In fact, he was not truly a popular man, and his chagrin at not receiving a re-election was so great that he did not even remain at Philadelphia to witness the inauguration of Mr. Jefferson, his successor. The friendly intimacy between these two men was interrupted for about thirteen years of their life. Adams finally made the first advances toward a restoration of their mutual friendship, which were gratefully accepted by Jefferson.

Mr. Adams was glad of his opportunity to retire to private life, where he could rest his mind and enjoy the comforts of home. By a thousand bitter experiences he found the path of public duty a thorny one. For twenty-six years his service of the public was as arduous, self-sacrificing and devoted as ever fell to the lot of man. In one important sense he was as much the "Father of his Country" as was Washington in another sense. During these long years of anxiety and toil, in which he was laying broad and deep, the foundations of the

greatest nation the sun ever shone upon, he received from his impoverished country a meager support. The only privilege he carried with him into his retirement was that of franking his letters.

Although taking no active part in public affairs, both himself and his son, John Quincy, nobly supported the policy of Mr. Jefferson in resisting the encroachments of England, who persisted in searching American ships on the high seas and dragging from them any sailors that might be designated by any pert lieutenant as British subjects. Even for this noble support Mr. Adams was maligned by thousands of bitter enemies! On this occasion, for the first time since his retirement, he broke silence and drew up a very able paper, exposing the atrocity of the British pretensions.

Mr. Adams outlived nearly all his family. Though his physical frame began to give way many years before his death, his mental powers retained their strength and vigor to the last. In his ninetieth year he was gladdened by the popular elevation of his son to the Presidential office, the highest in the gift of the people. A few months more passed away and the 4th of July, 1826, arrived. The people, unaware of the near approach of the end of two great lives— that of Adams and Jefferson—were making unusual preparations for a national holiday. Mr. Adams lay upon his couch, listening to the ringing of bells, the waftures of martial music and the roar of cannon, with silent emotion. Only four days before, he had given for a public toast, "Independence forever." About two o'clock in the afternoon he said, "And Jefferson still survives." But he was mistaken by an hour or so; and in a few minutes he had breathed his last.

2

THOMAS JEFFER-
son, the third Presi-
dent of the United
States, 1801–'9, was
born April 2, 1743,
the eldest child of
his parents, Peter
and Jane (Randolph) Jef-
ferson, near Charlottes-
ville, Albemarle County,
Virginia, upon the slopes
of the Blue Ridge. When
he·was fourteen years of
age, his father died, leaving a widow and eight
children. She was a beau-
tiful and accomplished
lady, a good letter-writer, with a fund of
humor, and an admirable housekeeper. His
parents belonged to the Church of England,
and are said to be of Welch origin. But
little is known of them, however.

Thomas was naturally of a serious turn
of mind, apt to learn, and a favorite at
school, his choice studies being mathematics and the classics. At the age of seventeen he entered William and Mary College,
in an advanced class, and lived in rather an
expensive style, consequently being much
caressed by gay society. That he was not
ruined, is proof of his stamina of character.
But during his second year he discarded
society, his horses and even his favorite
violin, and devoted thenceforward fifteen
hours a day to hard study, becoming ex-
traordinarily proficient in Latin and Greek
authors.

On leaving college, before he was twenty-
one, he commenced the study of law, and
pursued it diligently until he was well
qualified for practice, upon which he
entered in 1767. By this time he was also
versed in French, Spanish, Italian and Anglo-Saxon, and in the criticism of the fine
arts. Being very polite and polished in his
manners, he won the friendship of all whom
he met. Though able with his pen, he was
not fluent in public speech.

In 1769 he was chosen a member of the
Virginia Legislature, and was the largest
slave-holding member of that body. He
introduced a bill empowering slave-holders
to manumit their slaves, but it was rejected
by an overwhelming vote.

In 1770 Mr. Jefferson met with a great
loss; his house at Shadwell was burned,
and his valuable library of 2,000 volumes
was consumed. But he was wealthy
enough to replace the most of it, as from
his 5,000 acres tilled by slaves and his
practice at the bar his income amounted to
about $5,000 a year.

In 1772 he married Mrs. Martha Skelton,
a beautiful, wealthy and accomplished

Th. Jefferson

young widow, who owned 40,000 acres of land and 130 slaves; yet he labored assiduously for the abolition of slavery. For his new home he selected a majestic rise of land upon his large estate at Shadwell, called Monticello, whereon he erected a mansion of modest yet elegant architecture. Here he lived in luxury, indulging his taste in magnificent, high-blooded horses.

At this period the British Government gradually became more insolent and oppressive toward the American colonies, and Mr. Jefferson was ever one of the most foremost to resist its encroachments. From time to time he drew up resolutions of remonstrance, which were finally adopted, thus proving his ability as a statesman and as a leader. By the year 1774 he became quite busy, both with voice and pen, in defending the right of the colonies to defend themselves. His pamphlet entitled: "A Summary View of the Rights of British America," attracted much attention in England. The following year he, in company with George Washington, served as an executive committee in measures to defend by arms the State of Virginia. As a Member of the Congress, he was not a speech-maker, yet in conversation and upon committees he was so frank and decisive that he always made a favorable impression. But as late as the autumn of 1775 he remained in hopes of reconciliation with the parent country.

At length, however, the hour arrived for draughting the "Declaration of Independence," and this responsible task was devolved upon Jefferson. Franklin, and Adams suggested a few verbal corrections before it was submitted to Congress, which was June 28, 1776, only six days before it was adopted. During the three days of the fiery ordeal of criticism through which it passed in Congress, Mr. Jefferson opened not his lips. John Adams was the main champion of the Declaration on the floor of Congress. The signing of this document was one of the most solemn and momentous occasions ever attended to by man. Prayer and silence reigned throughout the hall, and each signer realized that if American independence was not finally sustained by arms he was doomed to the scaffold.

After the colonies became independent States, Jefferson resigned for a time his seat in Congress in order to aid in organizing the government of Virginia, of which State he was chosen Governor in 1779, when he was thirty-six years of age. At this time the British had possession of Georgia and were invading South Carolina, and at one time a British officer, Tarleton, sent a secret expedition to Monticello to capture the Governor. Five minutes after Mr. Jefferson escaped with his family, his mansion was in possession of the enemy! The British troops also destroyed his valuable plantation on the James River. "Had they carried off the slaves," said Jefferson, with characteristic magnanimity, "to give them freedom, they would have done right."

The year 1781 was a gloomy one for the Virginia Governor. While confined to his secluded home in the forest by a sick and dying wife, a party arose against him throughout the State, severely criticising his course as Governor. Being very sensitive to reproach, this touched him to the quick, and the heap of troubles then surrounding him nearly crushed him. He resolved, in despair, to retire from public life for the rest of his days. For weeks Mr. Jefferson sat lovingly, but with a crushed heart, at the bedside of his sick wife, during which time unfeeling letters were sent to him, accusing him of weakness and unfaithfulness to duty. All this, after he had lost so much property and at the same time done so much for his country! After her death he actually fainted away, and remained so long insensible that it was feared he never would recover! Several weeks passed before he could fully recover his equilibrium. He was never married a second time.

In the spring of 1782 the people of England compelled their king to make to the Americans overtures of peace, and in November following, Mr. Jefferson was reappointed by Congress, unanimously and without a single adverse remark, minister plenipotentiary to negotiate a treaty.

In March, 1784, Mr. Jefferson was appointed on a committee to draught a plan for the government of the Northwestern Territory. His slavery-prohibition clause in that plan was stricken out by the proslavery majority of the committee; but amid all the controversies and wrangles of politicians, he made it a rule never to contradict anybody or engage in any discussion as a debater.

In company with Mr. Adams and Dr. Franklin, Mr. Jefferson was appointed in May, 1784, to act as minister plenipotentiary in the negotiation of treaties of commerce with foreign nations. Accordingly, he went to Paris and satisfactorily accomplished his mission. The suavity and high bearing of his manner made all the French his friends; and even Mrs. Adams at one time wrote to her sister that he was "the chosen of the earth." But all the honors that he received, both at home and abroad, seemed to make no change in the simplicity of his republican tastes. On his return to America, he found two parties respecting the foreign commercial policy, Mr. Adams sympathizing with that in favor of England and himself favoring France.

On the inauguration of General Washington as President, Mr. Jefferson was chosen by him for the office of Secretary of State. At this time the rising storm of the French Revolution became visible, and Washington watched it with great anxiety. His cabinet was divided in their views of constitutional government as well as regarding the issues in France. General Hamilton, Secretary of the Treasury, was the leader of the so-called Federal party, while Mr. Jefferson was the leader of the Republican party. At the same time there was a strong monarchical party in this country, with which Mr. Adams sympathized. Some important financial measures, which were proposed by Hamilton and finally adopted by the cabinet and approved by Washington, were opposed by Mr. Jefferson; and his enemies then began to reproach him with holding office under an administration whose views he opposed. The President poured oil on the troubled waters. On his re-election to the Presidency he desired Mr. Jefferson to remain in the cabinet, but the latter sent in his resignation at two different times, probably because he was dissatisfied with some of the measures of the Government. His final one was not received until January 1, 1794, when General Washington parted from him with great regret.

Jefferson then retired to his quiet home at Monticello, to enjoy a good rest, not even reading the newspapers lest the political gossip should disquiet him. On the President's again calling him back to the office of Secretary of State, he replied that no circumstances would ever again tempt him to engage in anything public! But, while all Europe was ablaze with war, and France in the throes of a bloody revolution and the principal theater of the conflict, a new Presidential election in this country came on. John Adams was the Federal candidate and Mr. Jefferson became the Republican candidate. The result of the election was the promotion of the latter to the Vice-Presidency, while the former was chosen President. In this contest Mr. Jefferson really did not desire to have either office, he was "so weary" of party strife. He loved the retirement of home more than any other place on the earth.

But for four long years his Vice-Presidency passed joylessly away, while the partisan strife between Federalist and Republican was ever growing hotter. The former party split and the result of the fourth general election was the elevation of Mr. Jefferson to the Presidency! with Aaron Burr as Vice-President. These men being at the head of a growing party, their election was hailed everywhere with joy. On the other hand, many of the Federalists turned pale, as they believed what a portion of the pulpit and the press had been preaching—that Jefferson was a " scoffing atheist," a "Jacobin," the "incarnation of all evil," " breathing threatening and slaughter!"

Mr. Jefferson's inaugural address contained nothing but the noblest sentiments, expressed in fine language, and his personal behavior afterward exhibited the extreme of American, democratic simplicity. His disgust of European court etiquette grew upon him with age. He believed that General Washington was somewhat distrustful of the ultimate success of a popular Government, and that, imbued with a little admiration of the forms of a monarchical Government, he had instituted levees, birthdays, pompous meetings with Congress, etc. Jefferson was always polite, even to slaves everywhere he met them, and carried in his countenance the indications of an accommodating disposition.

The political principles of the Jeffersonian party now swept the country, and Mr. Jefferson himself swayed an influence which was never exceeded even by Washington. Under his administration, in 1803, the Louisiana purchase was made, for $15,000,000, the " Louisiana Territory " purchased comprising all the land west of the Mississippi to the Pacific Ocean.

The year 1804 witnessed another severe loss in his family. His highly accomplished and most beloved daughter Maria sickened and died, causing as great grief in the stricken parent as it was possible for him to survive with any degree of sanity.

The same year he was re-elected to the Presidency, with George Clinton as Vice-President. During his second term our relations with England became more complicated, and on June 22, 1807, near Hampton Roads, the United States frigate Chesapeake was fired upon by the British man-of-war Leopard, and was made to surrender. Three men were killed and ten wounded. Jefferson demanded reparation. England grew insolent. It became evident that war was determined upon by the latter power. More than 1,200 Americans were forced into the British service upon the high seas. Before any satisfactory solution was reached, Mr. Jefferson's Presidential term closed. Amid all these public excitements he thought constantly of the welfare of his family, and longed for the time when he could return home to remain. There, at Monticello, his subsequent life was very similar to that of Washington at Mt. Vernon. His hospitality toward his numerous friends, indulgence of his slaves, and misfortunes to his property, etc., finally involved him in debt. For years his home resembled a fashionable watering-place. During the summer, thirty-seven house servants were required! It was presided over by his daughter, Mrs. Randolph.

Mr. Jefferson did much for the establishment of the University at Charlottesville, making it unsectarian, in keeping with the spirit of American institutions, but poverty and the feebleness of old age prevented him from doing what he would. He even went so far as to petition the Legislature for permission to dispose of some of his possessions by lottery, in order to raise the necessary funds for home expenses. It was granted; but before the plan was carried out, Mr. Jefferson died, July 4, 1826, at 12:50 P. M.

JAMES MADISON, the fourth President of the United States, 1809–'17, was born at Port Conway, Prince George County, Virginia, March 16, 1751. His father, Colonel James Madison, was a wealthy planter, residing upon a very fine estate called "Montpelier," only twenty-five miles from the home of Thomas Jefferson at Monticello. The closest personal and political attachment existed between these illustrious men from their early youth until death.

James was the eldest of a family of seven children, four sons and three daughters, all of whom attained maturity. His early education was conducted mostly at home, under a private tutor. Being naturally intellectual in his tastes, he consecrated himself with unusual vigor to study. At a very early age he made considerable proficiency in the Greek, Latin, French and Spanish languages. In 1769 he entered Princeton College, New Jersey, of which the illustrious Dr. Weatherspoon was then President. He graduated in 1771, with a char-

acter of the utmost purity, and a mind highly disciplined and stored with all the learning which embellished and gave efficiency to his subsequent career. After graduating he pursued a course of reading for several months, under the guidance of President Weatherspoon, and in 1772 returned to Virginia, where he continued in incessant study for two years, nominally directed to the law, but really including extended researches in theology, philosophy and general literature.

The Church of England was the established church in Virginia, invested with all the prerogatives and immunities which it enjoyed in the fatherland, and other denominations labored under serious disabilities, the enforcement of which was rightly or wrongly characterized by them as persecution. Madison took a prominent stand in behalf of the removal of all disabilities, repeatedly appeared in the court of his own county to defend the Baptist nonconformists, and was elected from Orange County to the Virginia Convention in the spring of 1766, when he signalized the beginning of his public career by procuring the passage of an amendment to the Declaration of Rights as prepared by George Mason, substituting for "toleration" a more emphatic assertion of religious liberty.

James Madison

In 1776 he was elected a member of the Virginia Convention to frame the Constitution of the State. Like Jefferson, he took but little part in the public debates. His main strength lay in his conversational influence and in his pen. In November, 1777, he was chosen a member of the Council of State, and in March, 1780, took his seat in the Continental Congress, where he first gained prominence through his energetic opposition to the issue of paper money by the States. He continued in Congress three years, one of its most active and influential members.

In 1784 Mr. Madison was elected a member of the Virginia Legislature. He rendered important service by promoting and participating in that revision of the statutes which effectually abolished the remnants of the feudal system subsistent up to that time in the form of entails, primogeniture, and State support given the Anglican Church; and his "Memorial and Remonstrance" against a general assessment for the support of religion is one of the ablest papers which emanated from his pen. It settled the question of the entire separation of church and State in Virginia.

Mr. Jefferson says of him, in allusion to the study and experience through which he had already passed:

" Trained in these successive schools, he acquired a habit of self-possession which placed at ready command the rich resources of his luminous and discriminating mind and of his extensive information, and rendered him the first of every assembly of which he afterward became a member. Never wandering from his subject into vain declamation, but pursuing it closely in language pure, classical and copious, soothing always the feelings of his adversaries by civilities and softness of expression, he rose to the eminent station which he held in the great National Convention of 1787; and in that of Virginia, which followed, he sustained the

new Constitution in all its parts, bearing off the palm against the logic of George Mason and the fervid declamation of Patrick Henry. With these consummate powers were united a pure and spotless virtue which no calumny has ever attempted to sully. Of the power and polish of his pen, and of the wisdom of his administration in the highest office of the nation, I need say nothing. They have spoken, and will forever speak, for themselves."

In January, 1786, Mr. Madison took the initiative in proposing a meeting of State Commissioners to devise measures for more satisfactory commercial relations between the States. A meeting was held at Annapolis to discuss this subject, and but five States were represented. The convention issued another call, drawn up by Mr. Madison, urging all the States to send their delegates to Philadelphia, in May, 1787, to draught a Constitution for the United States. The delegates met at the time appointed, every State except Rhode Island being represented. George Washington was chosen president of the convention, and the present Constitution of the United States was then and there formed. There was no mind and no pen more active in framing this immortal document than the mind and pen of James Madison. He was, perhaps, its ablest advocate in the pages of the *Federalist*.

Mr. Madison was a member of the first four Congresses, 1789-'97, in which he maintained a moderate opposition to Hamilton's financial policy. He declined the mission to France and the Secretaryship of State, and, gradually identifying himself with the Republican party, became from 1792 its avowed leader. In 1796 he was its choice for the Presidency as successor to Washington. Mr. Jefferson wrote: "There is not another person in the United States with whom, being placed at the helm of our affairs, my mind would be so completely at rest for the fortune of our political bark." But Mr. Madison declined to be a candiaate. His term in Congress had expired, and he returned from New York to his beautiful retreat at Montpelier.

In 1794 Mr. Madison married a young widow of remarkable powers of fascination —Mrs. Todd. Her maiden name was Dorothy Paine. She was born in 1767, in Virginia, of Quaker parents, and had been educated in the strictest rules of that sect. When but eighteen years of age she married a young lawyer and moved to Philadelphia, where she was introduced to brilliant scenes of fashionable life. She speedily laid aside the dress and address of the Quakeress, and became one of the most fascinating ladies of the republican court. In New York, after the death of her husband, she was the belle of the season and was surrounded with admirers. Mr. Madison won the prize. She proved an invaluable helpmate. In Washington she was the life of society. If there was any diffident, timid young girl just making her appearance, she found in Mrs. Madison an encouraging friend.

During the stormy administration of John Adams Madison remained in private life, but was the author of the celebrated " Resolutions of 1798," adopted by the Virginia Legislature, in condemnation of the Alien and Sedition laws, as well as of the " report" in which he defended those resolutions, which is, by many, considered his ablest State paper.

The storm passed away; the Alien and Sedition laws were repealed, John Adams lost his re-election, and in 1801 Thomas Jefferson was chosen President. The great reaction in public sentiment which seated Jefferson in the presidential chair was largely owing to the writings of Madison, who was consequently well entitled to the post of Secretary of State. With great ability he discharged the duties of this responsible office during the eight years of Mr. Jefferson's administration.

As Mr. Jefferson was a widower, and neither of his daughters could be often with him, Mrs. Madison usually presided over the festivities of the White House; and as her husband succeeded Mr. Jefferson, holding his office for two terms, this remarkable woman was the mistress of the presidential mansion for sixteen years.

Mr. Madison being entirely engrossed by the cares of his office, all the duties of social life devolved upon his accomplished wife. Never were such responsibilities more ably discharged. The most bitter foes of her husband and of the administration were received with the frankly proffered hand and the cordial smile of welcome; and the influence of this gentle woman in allaying the bitterness of party rancor became a great and salutary power in the nation.

As the term of Mr. Jefferson's Presidency drew near its close, party strife was roused to the utmost to elect his successor. It was a death-grapple between the two great parties, the Federal and Republican. Mr. Madison was chosen President by an electoral vote of 122 to 53, and was inaugurated March 4, 1809, at a critical period, when the relations of the United States with Great Britain were becoming embittered, and his first term was passed in diplomatic quarrels, aggravated by the act of non-intercourse of May, 1810, and finally resulting in a declaration of war.

On the 18th of June, 1812, President Madison gave his approval to an act of Congress declaring war against Great Britain. Notwithstanding the bitter hostility of the Federal party to the war, the country in general approved; and in the autumn Madison was re-elected to the Presidency by 128 electoral votes to 89 in favor of George Clinton.

March 4, 1817, Madison yielded the Presidency to his Secretary of State and intimate friend, James Monroe, and retired to his ancestral estate at Montpelier, where he passed the evening of his days surrounded by attached friends and enjoying the merited respect of the whole nation. He took pleasure in promoting agriculture, as president of the county society, and in watching the development of the University of Virginia, of which he was long rector and visitor. In extreme old age he sat in 1829 as a member of the convention called to reform the Virginia Constitution, where his appearance was hailed with the most genuine interest and satisfaction, though he was too infirm to participate in the active work of revision. Small in stature, slender and delicate in form, with a countenance full of intelligence, and expressive alike of mildness and dignity, he attracted the attention of all who attended the convention, and was treated with the utmost deference. He seldom addressed the assembly, though he always appeared self-possessed, and watched with unflagging interest the progress of every measure. Though the convention sat sixteen weeks, he spoke only twice; but when he did speak, the whole house paused to listen. His voice was feeble though his enunciation was very distinct. One of the reporters, Mr. Stansbury, relates the following anecdote of **Mr. Madison's** last speech:

"The next day, as there was a great call for it, and the report had not been returned for publication, I sent my son with a respectful note, requesting the manuscript. My son was a lad of sixteen, whom I had taken with me to act as amanuensis. On delivering my note, he was received with the utmost politeness, and requested to come up into Mr. Madison's room and wait while his eye ran over the paper, as company had prevented his attending to it. He did so, and Mr. Madison sat down to correct the report. The lad stood near him so that his eye fell on the paper. Coming to a certain sentence in the speech, Mr. Madison erased a word and substituted another; but hesitated, and not feeling satisfied with the second word, drew his pen through it also. My son was young, ignorant of the world, and unconscious of the solecism of which he was about to be guilty, when, in all simplicity, he suggested a word. Probably no other person then living would have taken such a liberty. But the sage, instead of regarding such an intrusion with a frown, raised his eyes to the boy's face with a pleased surprise, and said, ' Thank you, sir ; it is the very word,' and immediately inserted it. I saw him the next day, and he mentioned the circumstance, with a compliment on the young critic."

Mr. Madison died at Montpelier, June 28, 1836, at the advanced age of eighty-five. While not possessing the highest order of talent, and deficient in oratorical powers, he was pre-eminently a statesman, of a well-balanced mind. His attainments were solid, his knowledge copious, his judgment generally sound, his powers of analysis and logical statement rarely surpassed, his language and literary style correct and polished, his conversation witty, his temperament sanguine and trustful, his integrity unquestioned, his manners simple, courteous and winning. By these rare qualities he conciliated the esteem not only of friends, but of political opponents, in a greater degree than any American statesman in the present century.

Mrs. Madison survived her husband thirteen years, and died July 12, 1849, in the eighty-second year of her age. She was one of the most remarkable women our country has produced. Even now she is admiringly remembered in Washington as "Dolly Madison," and it is fitting that her memory should descend to posterity in company with that of the companion of her life.

AMES MONROE, the fifth President of the United States, 1817–'25, was born in Westmoreland County, Virginia, April 28, 1758. He was a son of Spence Monroe, and a descendant of a Scottish cavalier family. Like all his predecessors thus far in the Presidential chair, he enjoyed all the advantages of education which the country could then afford. He was early sent to a fine classical school, and at the age of sixteen entered William and Mary College.. In 1776, when he had been in college but two years, the Declaration of Independence was adopted, and our feeble militia, without arms, amunition or clothing, were struggling against the trained armies of England. James Monroe left college, hastened to General Washington's headquarters at New York and enrolled himself as a cadet in the army.

At Trenton Lieutenant Monroe so distinguished himself, receiving a wound in his shoulder, that he was promoted to a Captaincy. Upon recovering from his wound, he was invited to act as aide to Lord Sterling, and in that capacity he took an active part in the battles of Brandywine, Germantown and Monmouth. At Germantown he stood by the side of Lafayette when the French Marquis received his wound. General Washington, who had formed a high idea of young Monroe's ability, sent him to Virginia to raise a new regiment, of which he was to be Colonel; but so exhausted was Virginia at that time that the effort proved unsuccessful. He, however, received his commission.

Finding no opportunity to enter the army as a commissioned officer, he returned to his original plan of studying law, and entered the office of Thomas Jefferson, who was then Governor of Virginia. He developed a very noble character, frank, manly and sincere. Mr. Jefferson said of him: "James Monroe is so perfectly honest that if his soul were turned inside out there would not be found a spot on it."

In 1782 he was elected to the Assembly of Virginia, and was also appointed a member of the Executive Council. The next year he was chosen delegate to the Continental Congress for a term of three years. He was present at Annapolis when Washington surrendered his commission of Commander-in-chief.

With Washington, Jefferson and Madison he felt deeply the inefficiency of the old Articles of Confederation, and urged the formation of a new Constitution, which should invest the Central Government with something like national power. Influenced by these views, he introduced a resolution

James Monroe

that Congress should be empowered to regulate trade, and to lay an impost duty of five per cent. The resolution was referred to a committee of which he was chairman. The report and the discussion which rose upon it led to the convention of five States at Annapolis, and the consequent general convention at Philadelphia, which, in 1787, drafted the Constitution of the United States.

At this time there was a controversy between New York and Massachusetts in reference to their boundaries. The high esteem in which Colonel Monroe was held is indicated by the fact that he was appointed one of the judges to decide the controversy. While in New York attending Congress, he married Miss Kortright, a young lady distinguished alike for her beauty and accomplishments. For nearly fifty years this happy union remained unbroken. In London and in Paris, as in her own country, Mrs. Monroe won admiration and affection by the loveliness of her person, the brilliancy of her intellect, and the amiability of her character.

Returning to Virginia, Colonel Monroe commenced the practice of law at Fredericksburg. He was very soon elected to a seat in the State Legislature, and the next year he was chosen a member of the Virginia convention which was assembled to decide upon the acceptance or rejection of the Constitution which had been drawn up at Philadelphia, and was now submitted to the several States. Deeply as he felt the imperfections of the old Confederacy, he was opposed to the new Constitution, thinking, with many others of the Republican party, that it gave too much power to the Central Government, and not enough to the individual States.

In 1789 he became a member of the United States Senate, which office he held acceptably to his constituents, and with honor to himself for four years.

Having opposed the Constitution as not leaving enough power with the States, he, of course, became more and more identified with the Republican party. Thus he found himself in cordial co-operation with Jefferson and Madison. The great Republican party became the dominant power which ruled the land.

George Washington was then President. England had espoused the cause of the Bourbons against the principles of the French Revolution. President Washington issued a proclamation of neutrality between these contending powers. France had helped us in the struggle for our liberties. All the despotisms of Europe were now combined to prevent the French from escaping from tyranny a thousandfold worse than that which we had endured. Colonel Monroe, more magnanimous than prudent, was anxious that we should help our old allies in their extremity. He violently opposed the President's proclamation as ungrateful and wanting in magnanimity.

Washington, who could appreciate such a character, developed his calm, serene, almost divine greatness by appointing that very James Monroe, who was denouncing the policy of the Government, as the Minister of that Government to the republic of France. He was directed by Washington to express to the French people our warmest sympathy, communicating to them corresponding resolves approved by the President, and adopted by both houses of Congress.

Mr. Monroe was welcomed by the National Convention in France with the most enthusiastic demonstrations of respect and affection. He was publicly introduced to that body, and received the embrace of the President, Merlin de Douay, after having been addressed in a speech glowing with congratulations, and with expressions of desire that harmony might ever exist between the two nations. The flags of the two republics were intertwined in the hall of the convention. Mr. Monroe presented the American colors, and received those of France in return. The course which he pursued in Paris was so annoying to England and to the friends of England in this country that, near the close of Washington's administration, Mr. Monroe, was recalled.

After his return Colonel Monroe wrote a book of 400 pages, entitled "A View of the Conduct of the Executive in Foreign Affairs." In this work he very ably advocated his side of the question; but, with the magnanimity of the man, he recorded a warm tribute to the patriotism, ability and spotless integrity of John Jay, between whom and himself there was intense antagonism ; and in subsequent years he expressed in warmest terms his perfect veneration for the character of George Washington.

Shortly after his return to this country Colonel Monroe was elected Governor of Virginia, and held that office for three years, the period limited by the Constitution. In 1802 he was an Envoy to France, and to Spain in 1805, and was Minister to England in 1803. In 1806 he returned to his quiet home in Virginia, and with his wife and children and an ample competence from his paternal estate, enjoyed a few years of domestic repose.

In 1809 Mr. Jefferson's second term of office expired, and many of the Republican party were anxious to nominate James Monroe as his successor. The majority were in favor of Mr. Madison. Mr. Monroe withdrew his name and was soon after chosen a second time Governor of Virginia. He soon resigned that office to accept the position of Secretary of State, offered him by President Madison. The correspondence which he then carried on with the British Government demonstrated that

there was no hope of any peaceful adjustment of our difficulties with the cabinet of St. James. War was consequently declared in June; 1812. Immediately after the sack of Washington the Secretary of War resigned, and Mr. Monroe, at the earnest request of Mr. Madison, assumed the additional duties of the War Department, without resigning his position as Secretary of State. It has been confidently stated, that, had Mr. Monroe's energies been in the War Department a few months earlier, the disaster at Washington would not have occurred.

The duties now devolving upon Mr. Monroe were extremely arduous. Ten thousand men, picked from the veteran armies of England, were sent with a powerful fleet to New Orleans to acquire possession of the mouths of the Mississippi. Our finances were in the most deplorable condition. The treasury was exhausted and our credit gone. And yet it was necessary to make the most rigorous preparations to meet the foe. In this crisis James Monroe, the Secretary of War, with virtue unsurpassed in Greek or Roman story, stepped forward and pledged his own individual credit as subsidiary to that of the nation, and thus succeeded in placing the city of New Orleans in such a posture of defense, that it was enabled successfully to repel the invader.

Mr. Monroe was truly the armor-bearer of President Madison, and the most efficient business man in his cabinet. His energy in the double capacity of Secretary, both of State and War, pervaded all the departments of the country. He proposed to increase the army to 100,000 men, a measure which he deemed absolutely necessary to save us from ignominious defeat, but which, at the same time, he knew would render his name so unpopular as to preclude the possibility of his being a successful candidate for the Presidency.

The happy result of the conference at Ghent in securing peace rendered the increase of the army unnecessary; but it is not too much to say that James Monroe placed in the hands of Andrew Jackson the weapon with which to beat off the foe at New Orleans. Upon the return of peace Mr. Monroe resigned the department of war, devoting himself entirely to the duties of Secretary of State. These he continued to discharge until the close of President Madison's administration, with zeal which was never abated, and with an ardor of self-devotion which made him almost forgetful of the claims of fortune, health or life.

Mr. Madison's second term expired in March, 1817, and Mr. Monroe succeeded to the Presidency. He was a candidate of the Republican party, now taking the name of the Democratic Republican. In 1821 he was re-elected, with scarcely any opposition. Out of 232 electoral votes, he received 231. The slavery question, which subsequently assumed such formidable dimensions, now began to make its appearance. The State of Missouri, which had been carved out of that immense territory which we had purchased of France, applied for admission to the Union, with a slavery Constitution. There were not a few who foresaw the evils impending. After the debate of a week it was decided that Missouri could not be admitted into the Union with slavery. This important question was at length settled by a compromise proposed by Henry Clay.

The famous "Monroe Doctrine," of which so much has been said, originated in this way: In 1823 it was rumored that the Holy Alliance was about to interfere to prevent the establishment of Republican liberty in the European colonies of South America. President Monroe wrote to his old friend Thomas Jefferson for advice in the emergency. In his reply under date of October 24, Mr. Jefferson writes upon the supposition that our attempt to resist this European movement might lead to war:

"Its object is to introduce and establish the American system of keeping out of our land all foreign powers; of never permitting those of Europe to intermeddle with the affairs of our nation. It is to maintain our own principle, not to depart from it."

December 2, 1823, President Monroe sent a message to Congress, declaring it to be the policy of this Government not to entangle ourselves with the broils of Europe, and not to allow Europe to interfere with the affairs of nations on the American continent; and the doctrine was announced, that any attempt on the part of the European powers "to extend their system to any portion of this hemisphere would be regarded by the United States as dangerous to our peace and safety."

March 4, 1825, Mr. Monroe surrendered the presidential chair to his Secretary of State, John Quincy Adams, and retired, with the universal respect of the nation, to his private residence at Oak Hill, Loudoun County, Virginia. His time had been so entirely consecrated to his country, that he had neglected his pecuniary interests, and was deeply involved in debt. The welfare of his country had ever been uppermost in his mind.

For many years Mrs. Monroe was in such feeble health that she rarely appeared in public. In 1830 Mr. Monroe took up his residence with his son-in-law in New York, where he died on the 4th of July, 1831. The citizens of New York conducted his obsequies with pageants more imposing than had ever been witnessed there before. Our country will ever cherish his memory with pride, gratefully enrolling his name in the list of its benefactors, pronouncing him the worthy successor of the illustrious men who had preceded him in the presidential chair.

John Quincy Adams.

OHN QUINCY ADAMS, the sixth President of the United States, 1825-'9, was born in the rural home of his honored father, John Adams, in Quincy, Massachusetts, July 11, 1767. His mother, a woman of exalted worth, watched over his childhood during the almost constant absence of his father. He commenced his education at the village school, giving at an early period indications of superior mental endowments.

When eleven years of age he sailed with his father for Europe, where the latter was associated with Franklin and Lee as Minister Plenipotentiary. The intelligence of John Quincy attracted the attention of these men and received from them flattering marks of attention. Mr. Adams had scarcely returned to this country in 1779 ere he was again sent abroad, and John Quincy again accompanied him. On this voyage he commenced a diary, which practice he continued, with but few interruptions, until his death. He journeyed with his father from Ferrol, in Spain, to Paris. Here he applied himself for six months to study; then accompanied his father to Holland, where he entered, first a school in Amsterdam, and then the University of Leyden. In 1781, when only fourteen years of age, he was selected by Mr. Dana, our Minister to the Russian court, as his private secretary. In this school of incessant labor he spent fourteen months, and then returned alone to Holland through Sweden, Denmark, Hamburg and Bremen. Again he resumed his studies under a private tutor, at The Hague.

In the spring of 1782 he accompanied his father to Paris, forming acquaintance with the most distinguished men on the Continent. After a short visit to England, he returned to Paris and studied until May, 1785, when he returned to America, leaving his father an embassador at the court of St. James. In 1786 he entered the junior class in Harvard University, and graduated with the second honor of his class. The oration he delivered on this occasion, the "Importance of Public Faith to the Well-being of a Community," was published—an event very rare in this or any other land.

Upon leaving college at the age of twenty he studied law three years with the Hon. Theophilus Parsons in Newburyport. In 1790 he opened a law office in Boston. The profession was crowded with able men, and the fees were small. The first year he had

J. Q. Adams

no clients, but not a moment was lost. The second year passed away, still no clients, and still he was dependent upon his parents for support. Anxiously he awaited the third year. The reward now came. Clients began to enter his office, and before the end of the year he was so crowded with business that all solicitude respecting a support was at an end.

When Great Britain commenced war against France, in 1793, Mr. Adams wrote some articles, urging entire neutrality on the part of the United States. The view was not a popular one. Many felt that as France had helped us, we were bound to help France. But President Washington coincided with Mr. Adams, and issued his proclamation of neutrality. His writings at this time in the Boston journals gave him so high a reputation, that in June, 1794, he was appointed by Washington resident Minister at the Netherlands. In July, 1797, he left The Hague to go to Portugal as Minister Plenipotentiary. Washington at this time wrote to his father, John Adams:

"Without intending to compliment the father or the mother, or to censure any others, I give it as my decided opinion, that Mr. Adams is the most valuable character we have abroad; and there remains no doubt in my mind that he will prove the ablest of our diplomatic corps."

On his way to Portugal, upon his arrival in London, he met with dispatches directing him to the court of Berlin, but requesting him to remain in London until he should receive instructions. While waiting he was married to Miss Louisa Catherine Johnson, to whom he had been previously engaged. Miss Johnson was a daughter of Mr. Joshua Johnson, American Consul in London, and was a lady endowed with that beauty and those accomplishments which fitted her to move in the elevated sphere for which she was destined.

In July, 1799, having fulfilled all the purposes of his mission, Mr. Adams returned. In 1802 he was chosen to the Senate of Massachusetts from Boston, and then was elected Senator of the United States for six years from March 4, 1804. His reputation, his ability and his experience, placed him immediately among the most prominent and influential members of that body. He sustained the Government in its measures of resistance to the encroachments of England, destroying our commerce and insulting our flag. There was no man in America more familiar with the arrogance of the British court upon these points, and no one more resolved to present a firm resistance. This course, so truly patriotic, and which scarcely a voice will now be found to condemn, alienated him from the Federal party dominant in Boston, and subjected him to censure.

In 1805 Mr. Adams was chosen professor of rhetoric in Harvard College. His lectures at this place were subsequently published. In 1809 he was sent as Minister to Russia. He was one of the commissioners that negotiated the treaty of peace with Great Britain, signed December 24, 1814, and he was appointed Minister to the court of St. James in 1815. In 1817 he became Secretary of State in Mr. Monroe's cabinet in which position he remained eight years. Few will now contradict the assertion that the duties of that office were never more ably discharged. Probably the most important measure which Mr. Adams conducted was the purchase of Florida from Spain for $5,000,000.

The campaign of 1824 was an exciting one. Four candidates were in the field. Of the 260 electoral votes that were cast, Andrew Jackson received ninety-nine; John Quincy Adams, eighty-four; William H. Crawford, forty-one, and Henry Clay, thirty-seven. As there was no choice by the people, the question went to the House of Representatives. Mr. Clay gave the vote of Kentucky to Mr. Adams, and he was elected.

The friends of all disappointed candidates now combined in a venomous assault upon Mr. Adams. There is nothing more disgraceful in the past history of our country than the abuse which was poured in one uninterrupted stream upon this high-minded, upright, patriotic man. There was never an administration more pure in principles, more conscientiously devoted to the best interests of the country, than that of John Quincy Adams; and never, perhaps, was there an administration more unscrupulously assailed. Mr. Adams took his seat in the presidential chair resolved not to know any partisanship, but only to consult for the interests of the whole Republic,

He refused to dismiss any man from office for his political views. If he was a faithful officer that was enough. Bitter must have been his disappointment to find that the Nation could not appreciate such conduct.

Mr. Adams, in his public manners, was cold and repulsive; though with his personal friends he was at times very genial. This chilling address very seriously detracted from his popularity. No one can read an impartial record of his administration without admitting that a more noble example of uncompromising dignity can scarcely be found. It was stated publicly that Mr. Adams' administration was to be put down, "though it be as pure as the angels which stand at the right hand of the throne of God." Many of the active participants in these scenes lived to regret the course they pursued. Some years after, Warren R. Davis, of South Carolina, turning to Mr. Adams, then a member of the House of Representatives, said:

"Well do I remember the enthusiastic zeal with which we reproached the administration of that gentleman, and the ardor and vehemence with which we labored to bring in another. For the share I had in these transactions, and it was not a small one, *I hope God will forgive me, for I shall never forgive myself.*"

March 4, 1829, Mr. Adams retired from the Presidency and was succeeded by Andrew Jackson, the latter receiving 168 out of 261 electoral votes. John C. Calhoun was elected Vice-President. The slavery question now began to assume pretentious magnitude. Mr. Adams returned to Quincy, and pursued his studies with unabated zeal. But he was not long permitted to remain in retirement. In November, 1830, he was elected to Congress. In this he recognized the principle that it is honorable for the General of yesterday to act as Corporal to-day, if by so doing he can render service to his country. Deep are our obligations to John Quincy Adams for his services as embassador, as Secretary of State and as President; in his capacity as legislator in the House of Representatives, he conferred benefits upon our land which eclipsed all the rest, and which can never be over-estimated.

For seventeen years, until his death, he occupied the post of Representative, towering above all his peers, ever ready to do brave battle for freedom, and winning the title of "the old man eloquent." Upon taking his seat in the House he announced that he should hold himself bound to no party. He was usually the first in his place in the morning, and the last to leave his seat in the evening. Not a measure could escape his scrutiny. The battle which he fought, almost singly, against the pro-slavery party in the Government, was sublime in its moral daring and heroism. For persisting in presenting petitions for the abolition of slavery, he was threatened with indictment by the Grand Jury, with expulsion from the House, with assassination; but no threats could intimidate him, and his final triumph was complete.

On one occasion Mr. Adams presented a petition, signed by several women, against the annexation of Texas for the purpose of cutting it up into slave States. Mr. Howard, of Maryland, said that these women discredited not only themselves, but their section of the country, by turning from their domestic duties to the conflicts of political life.

"Are women," exclaimed Mr. Adams, "to have no opinions or actions on subjects relating to the general welfare? Where did the gentleman get his principle? Did he find it in sacred history,—in the language of Miriam, the prophetess, in one of the noblest and sublime songs of triumph that ever met the human eye or ear? Did the gentleman never hear of Deborah, to whom the children of Israel came up for judgment? Has he forgotten the deed of Jael, who slew the dreaded enemy of her country? Has he forgotten Esther, who, by her *petition* saved her people and her country?

"To go from sacred history to profane, does the gentleman there find it 'discreditable' for women to take an interest in political affairs? Has he forgotten the Spartan mother, who said to her son when going out to battle, 'My son, come back to me *with* thy shield, or *upon* thy shield?' Does he remember Cloelia and her hundred companions, who swam across the river under a shower of darts, escaping from Porsena? Has he forgotten Cornelia, the mother of the Gracchi? Does he not remember Portia, the wife of Brutus and the daughter of Cato?

"To come to later periods, what says the history of our Anglo-Saxon ancestors? To say nothing of Boadicea, the British heroine in the time of the Cæsars, what name is more illustrious than that of Elizabeth? Or, if he will go to the continent, will he not find the names of Maria Theresa of Hungary, of the two Catherines of

Prussia, and of Isabella of Castile, the patroness of Columbus? Did she bring 'discredit' on her sex by mingling in politics?"

In this glowing strain Mr. Adams silenced and overwhelmed his antagonists.

In January, 1842, Mr. Adams presented a petition from forty-five citizens of Haverhill, Massachusetts, praying for a peaceable dissolution of the Union. The pro-slavery party in Congress, who were then plotting the destruction of the Government, were aroused to a pretense of commotion such as even our stormy hall of legislation has rarely witnessed. They met in caucus, and, finding that they probably would not be able to expel Mr. Adams from the House drew up a series of resolutions, which, if adopted, would inflict upon him disgrace, equivalent to expulsion. Mr. Adams had presented the petition, which was most respectfully worded, and had moved that it be referred to a committee instructed to report an answer, showing the reason why the prayer ought not to be granted.

It was the 25th of January. The whole body of the pro-slavery party came crowding together in the House, prepared to crush Mr. Adams forever. One of the number, Thomas F. Marshall, of Kentucky, was appointed to read the resolutions, which accused Mr. Adams of high treason, of having insulted the Government, and of meriting expulsion; but for which deserved punishment, the House, in its great mercy, would substitute its severest censure. With the assumption of a very solemn and magisterial air, there being breathless silence in the audience, Mr. Marshall hurled the carefully prepared anathemas at his victim. Mr. Adams stood alone, the whole pro-slavery party against him.

As soon as the resolutions were read, every eye being fixed upon him, that bold old man, whose scattered locks were whitened by seventy-five years, casting a withering glance in the direction of his assailants, in a clear, shrill tone, tremulous with suppressed emotion, said:

"In reply to this audacious, atrocious charge of high treason, I call for the reading of the first paragraph of the Declaration of Independence. Read it! Read it! and see what that says of the rights of a people to reform, to change, and to dissolve their Government.'

The attitude, the manner, the tone, the words; the venerable old man, with flashing eye and flushed cheek, and whose very form seemed to expand under the inspiration of the occasion—all presented a scene overflowing in its sublimity. There was breathless silence as that paragraph was read, in defense of whose principles our fathers had pledged their lives, their fortunes and their sacred honor. It was a proud hour to Mr. Adams as they were all compelled to listen to the words:

"That, to secure these rights, governments are instituted among men, deriving their just powers from the consent of the governed; and that whenever any form of government becomes destructive of those ends, it is the right of the people to alter or abolish it, and to institute new government, laying its foundations on such principles and organizing its powers in such form as shall seem most likely to effect their safety and happiness."

That one sentence routed and baffled the foe. The heroic old man looked around upon the audience, and thundered out, "Read that again!" It was again read. Then in a few fiery, logical words he stated his defense in terms which even prejudiced minds could not resist. His discomfited assailants made several attempts to rally. After a conflict of eleven days they gave up vanquished and their resolution was ignominiously laid upon the table.

In January, 1846, when seventy-eight years of age, he took part in the great debate on the Oregon question, displaying intellectual vigor, and an extent and accuracy of acquaintance with the subject that excited great admiration.

On the 21st of February, 1848, he rose on the floor of Congress with a paper in his hand to address the Speaker. Suddenly he fell, stricken by paralysis, and was caught in the arms of those around him. For a time he was senseless and was conveyed to a sofa in the rotunda. With reviving consciousness he opened his eyes, looked calmly around and said, " *This is the end of earth.*" Then after a moment's pause, he added, " *I am content.*" These were his last words, and he soon breathed his last, in the apartment beneath the dome of the capitol —the theater of his labors and his triumphs. In the language of hymnology, he "died at his post;" he " ceased at once to work and live."

Andrew Jackson

NDREW JACKSON, the seventh President of the United States, 1829–'37, was born at the Waxhaw Settle-ment, Union Coun-ty, North Carolina, March 16, 1767. His parents were Scotch-Irish, natives of Carrickfergus, who came to America in 1765, and settled on Twelve-Mile Creek, a tributary of the Catawba. His father, who was a poor farm laborer, died shortly before Andrew's birth, when his mother removed to Waxhaw, where some relatives resided.

Few particulars of the childhood of Jackson have been preserved. His education was of the most limited kind, and he showed no fondness for books. He grew up to be a tall, lank boy, with coarse hair and freckled cheeks, with bare feet dangling from trousers too short for him, very fond of athletic sports, running, boxing and wrestling. He was generous to the younger and weaker boys, but very irascible and overbearing with his equals and superiors. He was profane—a vice in which he surpassed all other men. The character of his mother he revered; and it was not until after her death that his predominant vices gained full strength.

In 1780, at the age of thirteen, Andrew, or Andy, as he was called, with his brother Robert, volunteered to serve in the Revolutionary forces under General Sumter, and was a witness of the latter's defeat at Hanging Rock. In the following year the brothers were made prisoners, and confined in Camden, experiencing brutal treatment from their captors, and being spectators of General Green's defeat at Hobkirk Hill. Through their mother's exertions the boys were exchanged while suffering from smallpox. In two days Robert was dead, and Andy apparently dying. The strength of his constitution triumphed, and he regained health and vigor.

As he was getting better, his mother heard the cry of anguish from the prisoners whom the British held in Charleston, among whom were the sons of her sisters. She hastened to their relief, was attacked by fever, died and was buried where her grave could never be found. Thus Andrew Jackson, when fourteen years of age, was left alone in the world, without father, mother, sister or brother, and without one dollar which he could call his own. He soon entered a saddler's shop, and labored diligently for six months. But gradually, as health returned, he became more and more a wild, reckless, lawless boy. He gambled, drank and was regarded as about the worst character that could be found.

He now turned schoolmaster. He could teach the alphabet, perhaps the multiplication table; and as he was a very bold boy, it is possible he might have ventured to teach a little writing. But he soon began to think of a profession and decided to study law: With a very slender purse, and on the back of a very fine horse, he set out for Salisbury, North Carolina, where he entered the law office of Mr. McCay. Here he remained two years, professedly studying law. He is still remembered in traditions of Salisbury, which say:

"Andrew Jackson was the most roaring, rollicking, horse-racing, card-playing, mischievous fellow that ever lived in Salisbury. He did not trouble the law-books much."

Andrew was now, at the age of twenty, a tall young man, being over six feet in height. He was slender, remarkably graceful and dignified in his manners, an exquisite horseman, and developed, amidst his loathesome profanity and multiform vices, a vein of rare magnanimity. His temper was fiery in the extreme; but it was said of him that no man knew better than Andrew Jackson when to get angry and when not.

In 1786 he was admitted to the bar, and two years later removed to Nashville, in what was then the western district of North Carolina, with the appointment of solicitor, or public prosecutor. It was an office of little honor, small emolument and great peril. Few men could be found to accept it.

And now Andrew Jackson commenced vigorously to practice law. It was. an important part of his business to collect debts. It required nerve. During the first seven years of his residence in those wilds he traversed the almost pathless forest between Nashville and Jonesborough, a distance of 200 miles, twenty-two times. Hostile Indians were constantly on the watch, and a man was liable at any moment to be shot down in his own field. Andrew Jackson was just the man for this service—a wild, daring, rough backwoodsman. Daily he made hair-breadth escapes. He seemed to bear a charmed life. Boldly, alone or with few companions, he traversed the forests, encountering all perils and triumphing over all.

In 1790 Tennessee became a Territory, and Jackson was appointed, by President Washington, United States Attorney for the new district. In 1791 he married Mrs. Rachel Robards (daughter of Colonel John Donelson), whom he supposed to have been divorced in that year by an act of the Legislature of Virginia. Two years after this Mr. and Mrs. Jackson learned, to their great surprise, that Mr. Robards had just obtained a divorce in one of the courts of Kentucky, and that the act of the Virginia Legislature was not final, but conditional. To remedy the irregularity as much as possible, a new license was obtained and the marriage ceremony was again performed.

It proved to be a marriage of rare felicity. Probably there never was a more affectionate union. However rough Mr. Jackson might have been abroad, he was always gentle and tender at home; and through all the vicissitudes of their lives, he treated Mrs. Jackson with the most chivalric attention.

Under the circumstances it was not unnatural that the facts in the case of this marriage were so misrepresented by opponents in the political campaigns a quarter or a century later as to become the basis of serious charges against Jackson's morality which, however, have been satisfactorily attested by abundant evidence.

Jackson was untiring in his duties as

United States Attorney, which demanded frequent journeys through the wilderness and exposed him to Indian hostilities. He acquired considerable property in land, and obtained such influence as to be chosen a member of the convention which framed the Constitution for the new State of Tennessee, in 1796, and in that year was elected its first Representative in Congress. Albert Gallatin thus describes the first appearance of the Hon. Andrew Jackson in the House:

"A tall, lank, uncouth-looking personage, with locks of hair hanging over his face and a cue down his back, tied with an eel skin; his dress singular, his manners and deportment those of a rough backwoodsman."

Jackson was an earnest advocate of the Democratic party. Jefferson was his idol. He admired Bonaparte, loved France and hated England. As Mr. Jackson took his seat, General Washington, whose second term of office was just expiring, delivered his last speech to Congress. A committee drew up a complimentary address in reply. Andrew Jackson did not approve the address and was one of twelve who voted against it.

Tennessee had fitted out an expedition against the Indians, contrary to the policy of the Government. A resolution was introduced that the National Government should pay the expenses. Jackson advocated it and it was carried. This rendered him very popular in Tennessee. A vacancy chanced soon after to occur in the Senate, and Andrew Jackson was chosen United States Senator by the State of Tennessee. John Adams was then President and Thomas Jefferson, Vice-President.

In 1798 Mr. Jackson returned to Tennessee, and resigned his seat in the Senate. Soon after he was chosen Judge of the Supreme Court of that State, with a salary of $600. This office he held six years. It is said that his decisions, though sometimes ungrammatical, were generally right. He

did not enjoy his seat upon the bench, and renounced the dignity in 1804. About this time he was chosen Major-General of militia, and lost the title of judge in that of General.

When he retired from the Senate Chamber, he decided to try his fortune through trade. He purchased a stock of goods in Philadelphia and sent them to Nashville, where he opened a store. He lived about thirteen miles from Nashville, on a tract of land of several thousand acres, mostly uncultivated. He used a small block-house for a store, from a narrow window of which he sold goods to the Indians. As he had an assistant his office as judge did not materially interfere with his business.

As to slavery, born in the midst of it, the idea never seemed to enter his mind that it could be wrong. He eventually became an extensive slave owner, but he was one of the most humane and gentle of masters.

In 1804 Mr. Jackson withdrew from politics and settled on a plantation which he called the Hermitage, near Nashville. He set up a cotton-gin, formed a partnership and traded in New Orleans, making the voyage on flatboats. Through his hot temper he became involved in several quarrels and "affairs of honor," during this period, in one of which he was severely wounded, but had the misfortune to kill his opponent, Charles Dickinson. For a time this affair greatly injured General Jackson's popularity. The verdict then was, and continues to be, that General Jackson was outrageously wrong. If he subsequently felt any remorse he never revealed it to anyone.

In 1805 Aaron Burr had visited Nashville and been a guest of Jackson, with whom he corresponded on the subject of a war with Spain, which was anticipated and desired by them, as well as by the people of the Southwest generally.

Burr repeated his visit in September, 1806, when he engaged in the celebrated combinations which led to his trial for treason. He was warmly received by Jackson, at whose instance a public ball was given in his honor at Nashville, and contracted with the latter for boats and provisions. Early in 1807, when Burr had been proclaimed a traitor by President Jefferson, volunteer forces for the Federal service were organized at Nashville under Jackson's command; but his energy and activity did not shield him from suspicions of connivance in the supposed treason. He was summoned to Richmond as a witness in Burr's trial, but was not called to the stand, probably because he was out-spoken in his partisanship.

On the outbreak of the war with Great Britain in 1812, Jackson tendered his services, and in January, 1813, embarked for New Orleans at the head of the Tennessee contingent. In March he received an order to disband his forces; but in September he again took the field, in the Creek war, and in conjunction with his former partner, Colonel Coffee, inflicted upon the Indians the memorable defeat at Talladega, Emuckfaw and Tallapoosa.

In May, 1814, Jackson, who had now acquired a national reputation, was appointed a Major-General of the United States army, and commenced a campaign against the British in Florida. He conducted the defense at Mobile, September 15, seized upon Pensacola, November 6, and immediately transported the bulk of his troops to New Orleans, then threatened by a powerful naval force. Martial law was declared in Louisiana, the State militia was called to arms, engagements with the British were fought December 23 and 28, and after re-enforcements had been received on both sides the famous victory of January 8, 1815, crowned Jackson's fame as a soldier, and made him the typical American hero of the first half of the nineteenth century.

In 1817-'18 Jackson conducted the war against the Seminoles of Florida, during which he seized upon Pensacola and executed by courtmartial two British subjects, Arbuthnot and Ambrister——acts which might easily have involved the United States in war both with Spain and Great Britain. Fortunately the peril was averted by the cession of Florida to the United States; and Jackson, who had escaped a trial for the irregularity of his conduct only through a division of opinion in Monroe's cabinet, was appointed in 1821 Governor of the new Territory. Soon after he declined the appointment of minister to Mexico.

In 1823 Jackson was elected to the United States Senate, and nominated by the Tennessee Legislature for the Presidency. This candidacy, though a matter of surprise, and even merriment, speedily became popular, and in 1824, when the stormy electoral canvas resulted in the choice of John Quincy Adams by the House of Representatives, General Jackson received the largest popular vote among the four candidates.

In 1828 Jackson was triumphantly elected President over Adams after a campaign of unparalleled bitterness. He was inaugurated March 4, 1829, and at once removed from office all the incumbents belonging to the opposite party—a procedure new to American politics, but which naturally became a precedent.

His first term was characterized by quarrels between the Vice-President, Calhoun, and the Secretary of State, Van Buren, attended by a cabinet crisis originating in scandals connected with the name of Mrs. General Eaton, wife of the Secretary of War; by the beginning of his war upon the United States Bank, and by his vigorous action against the partisans of Calhoun, who, in South Carolina, threatened to nullify the acts of Congress, establishing a protective tariff.

In the Presidential campaign of 1832

Jackson received 219 out of 288 electoral votes, his competitor being Mr. Clay, while Mr. Wirt, on an Anti-Masonic platform, received the vote of Vermont alone. In 1833 President Jackson removed the Government deposits from the United States bank, thereby incurring a vote of censure from the Senate, which was, however, expunged four years later. During this second term of office the Cherokees, Choctaws and Creeks were removed, not without difficulty, from Georgia, Alabama and Mississippi, to the Indian Territory; the National debt was extinguished; Arkansas and Michigan were admitted as States to the Union; the Seminole war was renewed; the anti-slavery agitation first acquired importance; the Mormon delusion, which had organized in 1829, attained considerable proportions in Ohio and Missouri, and the country experienced its greatest pecuniary panic.

Railroads with locomotive propulsion were introduced into America during Jackson's first term, and had become an important element of national life before the close of his second term. For many reasons, therefore, the administration of President Jackson formed an era in American history, political, social and industrial. He succeeded in effecting the election of his friend Van Buren as his successor, retired from the Presidency March 4, 1837, and led a tranquil life at the Hermitage until his death, which occurred June 8, 1845.

During his closing years he was a professed Christian and a member of the Presbyterian church. No American of this century has been the subject of such opposite judgments. He was loved and hated with equal vehemence during his life, but at the present distance of time from his career, while opinions still vary as to the merits of his public acts, few of his countrymen will question that he was a warmhearted, brave, patriotic, honest and sincere man. If his distinguishing qualities were not such as constitute statesmanship, in the highest sense, he at least never pretended to other merits than such as were written to his credit on the page of American history—not attempting to disguise the demerits which were equally legible. The majority of his countrymen accepted and honored him, in spite of all that calumny as well as truth could allege against him. His faults may therefore be truly said to have been those of his time; his magnificent virtues may also, with the same justice, be considered as typical of a state of society which has nearly passed away.

ARTIN VAN BU-
REN, the eighth
President of the
United States, 1837-
'41, was born at Kin-
derhook, New York,
December 5, 1782.
His ancestors were of Dutch
origin, and were among the
earliest emigrants from Holland to the banks of the
Hudson. His father was a
tavern-keeper, as well as a
farmer, and a very decided
Democrat.

Martin commenced the study
of law at the age of fourteen, and took an
active part in politics before he had reached
the age of twenty. In 1803 he commenced
the practice of law in his native village.
In 1809 he removed to Hudson, the shire
town of his county, where he spent seven
years, gaining strength by contending in
the courts with some of the ablest men
who have adorned the bar of his State.
The heroic example of John Quincy Adams
in retaining in office every faithful man,
without regard to his political preferences,
had been thoroughly repudiated by General Jackson. The unfortunate principle
was now fully established, that "to the
victor belong the spoils." Still, this principle, to which Mr. Van Buren gave his ad-

herence, was not devoid of inconveniences.
When, subsequently, he attained power
which placed vast patronage in his hands,
he was heard to say: "I prefer an office
that has no patronage. When I give a man
an office I offend his disappointed competitors and their friends. Nor am I certain of
gaining a friend in the man I appoint, for,
in all probability, he expected something
better."

In 1812 Mr. Van Buren was elected to
the State Senate. In 1815 he was appointed·
Attorney-General, and in 1816 to the Senate
a second time. In 1818 there was a great
split in the Democratic party in New York,
and Mr. Van Buren took the lead in organizing that portion of the party called
the Albany Regency, which is said to have
swayed the destinies of the State for a
quarter of a century.

In 1821 he was chosen a member of the
convention for revising the State Constitution, in which he advocated an extension of
the franchise, but opposed universal suf-
frage, and also favored the proposal that
colored persons, in order to vote, should
have freehold property to the amount of
$250. In this year he was also elected to
the United States Senate, and at the conclusion of his term, in 1827, was re-elected,
but resigned the following year, having
been chosen Governor of the State. In
March, 1829, he was appointed Secretary of

State by President Jackson, but resigned in April, 1831, and during the recess of Congress was appointed minister to England, whither he proceeded in September, but the Senate, when convened in December, refused to ratify the appointment.

In May, 1832, Mr. Van Buren was nominated as the Democratic candidate for Vice-President, and elected in the following November. May 26, 1836, he received the nomination to succeed General Jackson as President, and received 170 electoral votes, out of 283.

Scarcely had he taken his seat in the Presidential chair when a financial panic swept over the land. Many attributed this to the war which General Jackson had waged on the banks, and to his endeavor to secure an almost exclusive specie currency. Nearly every bank in the country was compelled to suspend specie payment, and ruin pervaded all our great cities. Not less than 254 houses failed in New York in one week. All public works were brought to a stand, and there was a general state of dismay. President Van Buren urged the adoption of the independent treasury system, which was twice passed in the Senate and defeated in the House, but finally became a law near the close of his administration.

Another important measure was the passage of a pre-emption law, giving actual settlers the preference in the purchase of public lands. The question of slavery, also, now began to assume great prominence in national politics, and after an elaborate anti-slavery speech by Mr. Slade, of Vermont, in the House of Representatives, the Southern members withdrew for a separate consultation, at which Mr. Rhett, of South Carolina, proposed to declare it expedient that the Union should be dissolved; but the matter was tided over by the passage of a resolution that no petitions or papers relating to slavery should be in any way considered or acted upon.

5

In the Presidential election of 1840 Mr. Van Buren was nominated, without opposition, as the Democratic candidate, William H. Harrison being the candidate of the Whig party. The Democrats carried only seven States, and out of 294 electoral votes only sixty were for Mr. Van Buren, the remaining 234 being for his opponent. The Whig popular majority, however, was not large, the elections in many of the States being very close.

March 4, 1841, Mr. Van Buren retired from the Presidency. From his fine estate at Lindenwald he still exerted a powerful influence upon the politics of the country. In 1844 he was again proposed as the Democratic candidate for the Presidency, and a majority of the delegates of the nominating convention were in his favor; but, owing to his opposition to the proposed annexation of Texas, he could not secure the requisite two-thirds vote. His name was at length withdrawn by his friends, and Mr. Polk received the nomination, and was elected.

In 1848 Mr. Cass was the regular Democratic candidate. A schism, however, sprang up in the party, upon the question of the permission of slavery in the newly-acquired territory, and a portion of the party, taking the name of "Free-Soilers," nominated Mr. Van Buren. They drew away sufficient votes to secure the election of General Taylor, the Whig candidate. After this Mr. Van Buren retired to his estate at Kinderhook, where the remainder of his life was passed, with the exception of a European tour in 1853. He died at Kinderhook, July 24, 1862, at the age of eighty years.

Martin Van Buren was a great and good man, and no one will question his right to a high position among those who have been the successors of Washington in the faithful occupancy of the Presidential chair.

WILLIAM HENRY HARRISON, the ninth President of the United States, 1841, was born February 9, 1773, in Charles County, Virginia, at Berkeley, the residence of his father, Governor Benjamin Harrison. He studied at Hampden, Sidney College, with a view of entering the medical profession. After graduation he went to Philadelphia to study medicine under the instruction of Dr. Rush.

George Washington was then President of the United States. The Indians were committing fearful ravages on our Northwestern frontier. Young Harrison, either lured by the love of adventure, or moved by the sufferings of families exposed to the most horrible outrages, abandoned his medical studies and entered the army, having obtained a commission of ensign from President Washington. The first duty assigned him was to take a train of pack-horses bound to Fort Hamilton, on the Miami River, about forty miles from Fort Washington. He was soon promoted to the rank of Lieutenant, and joined the army which Washington had placed under the command of General Wayne to prosecute more vigorously the war with the Indians. Lieutenant Harrison received great commendation from his commanding officer, and was promoted to the rank of Captain, and placed in command at Fort Washington, now Cincinnati, Ohio.

About this time he married a daughter of John Cleves Symmes, one of the frontiersmen who had established a thriving settlement on the bank of the Maumee.

In 1797 Captain Harrison resigned his commission in the army and was appointed Secretary of the Northwest Territory, and *ex-officio* Lieutenant-Governor, General St. Clair being then Governor of the Territory. At that time the law in reference to the disposal of the public lands was such that no one could purchase in tracts less than 4,000 acres. Captain Harrison, in the face of violent opposition, succeeded in obtaining so much of a modification of this unjust law that the land was sold in alternate tracts of 640 and 320 acres. The Northwest Territory was then entitled to one delegate in Congress, and Captain Harrison was chosen to fill that office. In 1800 he was appointed Governor

W. H. Harrison

of Indiana Territory and soon after of Upper Louisiana. He was also Superintendent of Indian Affairs, and so well did he fulfill these duties that he was four times appointed to this office. During his administration he effected thirteen treaties with the Indians, by which the United States acquired 60,000,000 acres of land. In 1804 he obtained a cession from the Indians of all the land between the Illinois River and the Mississippi.

In 1812 he was made Major-General of Kentucky militia and Brigadier-General in the army, with the command of the Northwest frontier. In 1813 he was made Major-General, and as such won much renown by the defense of Fort Meigs, and the battle of the Thames, October 5, 1813. In 1814 he left the army and was employed in Indian affairs by the Government.

In 1816 General Harrison was chosen a member of the National House of Representatives to represent the district of Ohio. In the contest which preceded his election he was accused of corruption in respect to the commissariat of the army. Immediately upon taking his seat, he called for an investigation of the charge. A committee was appointed, and his vindication was triumphant. A high compliment was paid to his patriotism, disinterestedness and devotion to the public service. For these services a gold medal was presented to him with the thanks of Congress.

In 1819 he was elected to the Senate of Ohio, and in 1824, as one of the Presidential electors of that State, he gave his vote to Henry Clay. In the same year he was elected to the Senate of the United States. In 1828 he was appointed by President Adams minister plenipotentiary to Colombia, but was recalled by General Jackson immediately after the inauguration of the latter.

Upon his return to the United States, General Harrison retired to his farm at North Bend, Hamilton County, Ohio, sixteen miles below Cincinnati, where for twelve years he was clerk of the County Court. He once owned a distillery, but perceiving the sad effects of whisky upon the surrounding population, he promptly abandoned his business at great pecuniary sacrifice.

In 1836 General Harrison was brought forward as a candidate for the Presidency. Van Buren was the administration candidate; the opposite party could not unite, and four candidates were brought forward. General Harrison received seventy-three electoral votes without any general concert among his friends. The Democratic party triumphed and Mr. Van Buren was chosen President. In 1839 General Harrison was again nominated for the Presidency by the Whigs, at Harrisburg, Pennsylvania, Mr. Van Buren being the Democratic candidate. General Harrison received 234 electoral votes against sixty for his opponent. This election is memorable chiefly for the then extraordinary means employed during the canvass for popular votes. Mass meetings and processions were introduced, and the watchwords "log cabin" and "hard cider" were effectually used by the Whigs, and aroused a popular enthusiasm.

A vast concourse of people attended his inauguration. His address on that occasion was in accordance with his antecedents, and gave great satisfaction. A short time after he took his seat, he was seized by a pleurisy-fever, and after a few days of violent sickness, died April 4, just one short month after his inauguration. His death was universally regarded as one of the greatest of National calamities. Never, since the death of Washington, were there, throughout one land, such demonstrations of sorrow. Not one single spot can be found to sully his fame; and through all ages Americans will pronounce with love and reverence the name of William Henry Harrison.

OHN TYLER, the tenth President of the United States, was born in Charles City County, Virginia, March 29, 1790. His father, Judge John Tyler, possessed large landed estates in Virginia, and was one of the most distinguished men of his day, filling the offices of Speaker of the House of Delegates, Judge of the Supreme Court and Governor of the State.

At the early age of twelve young John entered William and Mary College, and graduated with honor when but seventeen years old. He then closely applied himself to the study of law, and at nineteen years of age commenced the practice of his profession. When only twenty-one he was elected to a seat in the State Legislature. He acted with the Democratic party and advocated the measures of Jefferson and Madison. For five years he was elected to the Legislature, receiving nearly the unanimous vote of his county.

When but twenty-six years of age he was elected a member of Congress. He advocated a strict construction of the Constitution and the most careful vigilance over State rights. He was soon compelled to resign his seat in Congress, owing to ill health, but afterward took his seat in the State Legislature, where he exerted a powerful influence in promoting public works of great utility.

In 1825 Mr. Tyler was chosen Governor of his State—a high honor, for Virginia had many able men as competitors for the prize. His administration was signally a successful one. He urged forward internal improvements and strove to remove sectional jealousies. His popularity secured his re-election. In 1827 he was elected United States Senator, and upon taking his seat joined the ranks of the opposition. He opposed the tariff, voted against the bank as unconstitutional, opposed all restrictions upon slavery, resisted all projects of internal improvements by the General Government, avowed his sympathy with Mr. Calhoun's views of nullification, and declared that General Jackson, by his opposition to the nullifiers, had abandoned the principles of the Democratic party. Such was Mr. Tyler's record in Congress.

This hostility to Jackson caused Mr. Tyler's retirement from the Senate, after his election to a second term. He soon after removed to Williamsburg for the better education of his children, and again took his seat in the Legislature.

John Tyler

In 1839 he was sent to the National Convention at Harrisburg to nominate a President. General Harrison received a majority of votes, much to the disappointment of the South, who had wished for Henry Clay. In order to conciliate the Southern Whigs, John Tyler was nominated for Vice-President. Harrison and Tyler were inaugurated March 4, 1841. In one short month from that time President Harrison died, and Mr. Tyler, to his own surprise as well as that of the nation, found himself an occupant of the Presidential chair. His position was an exceedingly difficult one, as he was opposed to the main principles of the party which had brought him into power. General Harrison had selected a Whig cabinet Should he retain them, and thus surround himself with councilors whose views were antagonistic to his own? or should he turn against the party that had elected him, and select a cabinet in harmony with himself? This was his fearful dilemma.

President Tyler deserves more charity than he has received. He issued an address to the people, which gave general satisfaction. He retained the cabinet General Harrison had selected. His veto of a bill chartering a new national bank led to an open quarrel with the party which elected him, and to a resignation of the entire cabinet, except Daniel Webster, Secretary of State.

President Tyler attempted to conciliate. He appointed a new cabinet, leaving out all strong party men, but the Whig members of Congress were not satisfied, and they published a manifesto September 13, breaking off all political relations. The Democrats had a majority in the House; the Whigs in the Senate. Mr. Webster soon found it necessary to resign, being forced out by the pressure of his Whig friends.

April 12, 1844, President Tyler concluded, through Mr. Calhoun, a treaty for the annexation of Texas, which was rejected by the Senate; but he effected his object in the closing days of his administration by the passage of the joint resolution of March 1 1845.

He was nominated for the Presidency by an informal Democratic Convention, held at Baltimore in May, 1844, but soon withdrew from the canvass, perceiving that he had not gained the confidence of the Democrats at large.

Mr. Tyler's administration was particularly unfortunate. No one was satisfied. Whigs and Democrats alike assailed him. Situated as he was, it is more than can be expected of human nature that he should, in all cases, have acted in the wisest manner; but it will probably be the verdict of all candid men, in a careful review of his career, that John Tyler was placed in a position of such difficulty that he could not pursue any course which would not expose him to severe censure and denunciation.

In 1813 Mr. Tyler married Letitia Christian, who bore him three sons and three daughters, and died in Washington in 1842. June 26, 1844, he contracted a second marriage with Miss Julia Gardner, of New York. He lived in almost complete retirement from politics until February, 1861, when he was a member of the abortive "peace convention," held at Washington, and was chosen its President. Soon after he renounced his allegiance to the United States and was elected to the Confederate Congress. He died at Richmond, January 17, 1862, after a short illness.

Unfortunately for his memory the name of John Tyler must forever be associated with all the misery of that terrible Rebellion, whose cause he openly espoused. It is with sorrow that history records that a President of the United States died while defending the flag of rebellion, which was arrayed against the national banner in deadly warfare.

JAMES K. POLK.

AMES KNOX POLK, the eleventh President of the United States, 1845-'49, was born in Mecklenburg County, North Carolina, November 2, 1795. He was the eldest son of a family of six sons and four daughters, and was a grand-nephew of Colonel Thomas Polk, celebrated in connection with the Mecklenburg Declaration of Independence.

In 1806 his father, Samuel Polk, emigrated with his family two or three hundred miles west to the valley of the Duck River. He was a surveyor as well as farmer, and gradually increased in wealth until he became one of the leading men of the region.

In the common schools James rapidly became proficient in all the common branches of an English education. In 1813 he was sent to Murfreesboro Academy, and in the autumn of 1815 entered the sophomore class in the University of North Carolina, at Chapel Hill, graduating in 1818. After a short season of recreation he went to Nashville and entered the law office of Felix Grundy. As soon as he had his finished legal studies and been admitted to the bar, he returned to Columbia, the shire town of Maury County, and opened an office.

James K. Polk ever adhered to the political faith of his father, which was that of a Jeffersonian Republican. In 1823 he was elected to the Legislature of Tennessee. As a "strict constructionist," he did not think that the Constitution empowered the General Government to carry on a system of internal improvements in the States, but deemed it important that it should have that power, and wished the Constitution amended that it might be conferred. Subsequently, however, he became alarmed lest the General Government become so strong as to undertake to interfere with slavery. He therefore gave all his influence to strengthen the State governments, and to check the growth of the central power.

In January, 1824, Mr. Polk married Miss Mary Childress, of Rutherford County, Tennessee. Had some one then whispered to him that he was destined to become President of the United States, and that he must select for his companion one who would adorn that distinguished station, he could not have made a more fitting choice. She was truly a lady of rare beauty and culture.

In the fall of 1825 Mr. Polk was chosen a member of Congress, and was continu-

James K. Polk

ously re-elected until 1839. He then withdrew, only that he might accept the gubernatorial chair of his native State. He was a warm friend of General Jackson, who had been defeated in the electoral contest by John Quincy Adams. This latter gentleman had just taken his seat in the Presidential chair when Mr. Polk took his seat in the House of Representatives. He immediately united himself with the opponents of Mr. Adams, and was soon regarded as the leader of the Jackson party in the House.

The four years of Mr. Adams' administration passed away, and General Jackson took the Presidential chair. Mr. Polk had now become a man of great influence in Congress, and was chairman of its most important committee—that of Ways and Means. Eloquently he sustained General Jackson in all his measures—in his hostility to internal improvements, to the banks, and to the tariff. Eight years of General Jackson's administration passed away, and the powers he had wielded passed into the hands of Martin Van Buren; and still Mr. Polk remained in the House, the advocate of that type of Democracy which those distinguished men upheld.

During five sessions of Congress Mr. Polk was speaker of the House. He performed his arduous duties to general satisfaction, and a unanimous vote of thanks to him was passed by the House as he withdrew, March 4, 1839. He was elected Governor by a large majority, and took the oath of office at Nashville, October 14, 1839. He was a candidate for re-election in 1841, but was defeated. In the meantime a wonderful revolution had swept over the country. W. H. Harrison, the Whig candidate, had been called to the Presidential chair, and in Tennessee the Whig ticket had been carried by over 12,000 majority. Under these circumstances Mr. Polk's success was hopeless. Still he canvassed the State with his Whig competitor, Mr. Jones, traveling in the most friendly manner together, often in the same carriage, and at one time sleeping in the same bed. Mr. Jones was elected by 3,000 majority.

And now the question of the annexation of Texas to our country agitated the whole land. When this question became national Mr. Polk, as the avowed champion of annexation, became the Presidential candidate of the pro-slavery wing of the Democratic party, and George M. Dallas their candidate for the Vice-Presidency. They were elected by a large majority, and were inaugurated March 4, 1845.

President Polk formed an able cabinet, consisting of James Buchanan, Robert J. Walker, William L. Marcy, George Bancroft, Cave Johnson and John Y. Mason. The Oregon boundary question was settled, the Department of the Interior was created, the low tariff of 1846 was carried, the financial system of the Government was reorganized, the Mexican war was conducted, which resulted in the acquisition of California and New Mexico, and had far-reaching consequences upon the later fortunes of the republic. Peace was made. We had wrested from Mexico territory equal to four times the empire of France, and five times that of Spain. In the prosecution of this war we expended 20,000 lives and more than $100,000,000. Of this money $15,000,000 were paid to Mexico.

Declining to seek a renomination, Mr. Polk retired from the Presidency March 4, 1849, when he was succeeded by General Zachary Taylor. He retired to Nashville, and died there June 19, 1849, in the fifty-fourth year of his age. His funeral was attended the following day, in Nashville, with every demonstration of respect. He left no children. Without being possessed of extraordinary talent, Mr. Polk was a capable administrator of public affairs, and irreproachable in private life.

ACHARY TAY- LOR, the twelfth President of the United States, 1849–'50, was born in Orange County, Virginia, September 24, 1784. His father, Richard Taylor, was Colonel of a Virginia regiment in the Revolutionary war, and removed to Kentucky in 1785; purchased a large plantation near Louisville and became an influential citizen; was a member of the convention that framed the Constitution of Kentucky; served in both branches of the Legislature; was Collector of the port of Louisville under President Washington; as a Presidential elector, voted for Jefferson, Madison, Monroe and Clay; died January 19, 1829.

Zachary remained on his father's plantation until 1808, in which year (May 3) he was appointed First Lieutenant in the Seventh Infantry, to fill a vacancy occasioned by the death of his elder brother, Hancock. Up to this point he had received but a limited education.

Joining his regiment at New Orleans, he was attacked with yellow fever, with nearly fatal termination. In November, 1810, he was promoted to Captain, and in the summer of 1812 he was in command of Fort Harrison, on the left bank of the Wabash River, near the present site of Terre Haute, his successful defense of which with but a handful of men against a large force of Indians which had attacked him was one of the first marked military achievements of the war. He was then brevetted Major, and in 1814 promoted to the full rank.

During the remainder of the war Taylor was actively employed on the Western frontier. In the peace organization of 1815 he was retained as Captain, but soon after resigned and settled near Louisville. In May, 1816, however, he re-entered the army as Major of the Third Infantry; became Lieutenant-Colonel of the Eighth Infantry in 1819, and in 1832 attained the Colonelcy of the First Infantry, of which he had been Lieutenant-Colonel since 1821. On different occasions he had been called to Washington as member of a military board for organizing the militia of the Union, and to aid the Government with his knowledge in the organization of the Indian Bureau, having for many years discharged the duties of Indian agent over large tracts of Western

Zachary Taylor

country. He served through the Black Hawk war in 1832, and in 1837 was ordered to take command in Florida, then the scene of war with the Indians.

In 1846 he was transferred to the command of the Army of the Southwest, from which he was relieved the same year at his own request. Subsequently he was stationed on the Arkansas frontier at Forts Gibbon, Smith and Jesup, which latter work had been built under his direction in 1822.

May 28, 1845, he received a dispatch from the Secretary of War informing him of the receipt of information by the President "that Texas would shortly accede to the terms of annexation," in which event he was instructed to defend and protect her from "foreign invasion and Indian incursions." He proceeded, upon the annexation of Texas, with about 1,500 men to Corpus Christi, where his force was increased to some 4,000.

Taylor was brevetted Major-General May 28, and a month later, June 29, 1846, his full commission to that grade was issued. After needed rest and reinforcement, he advanced in September on Monterey, which city capitulated after three-days stubborn resistance. Here he took up his winter quarters. The plan for the invasion of Mexico, by way of Vera Cruz, with General Scott in command, was now determined upon by the Government, and at the moment Taylor was about to resume active operations, he received orders to send the larger part of his force to reinforce the army of General Scott at Vera Cruz. Though subsequently reinforced by raw recruits, yet after providing a garrison for Monterey and Saltillo he had but about 5,300 effective troops, of which but 500 or 600 were regulars. In this weakened condition, however, he was destined to achieve his greatest victory. Confidently relying upon his strength at Vera Cruz to resist the enemy for a long time, Santa Anna directed his entire army against Taylor to overwhelm him, and then to return to oppose the advance of Scott's more formidable invasion. The battle of Buena Vista was fought February 22 and 23, 1847. Taylor received the thanks of Congress and a gold medal, and "Old Rough and Ready," the sobriquet given him in the army, became a household word. He remained in quiet possession of the Rio Grande Valley until November, when he returned to the United States.

In the Whig convention which met at Philadelphia, June 7, 1848, Taylor was nominated on the fourth ballot as candidate of the Whig party for President, over Henry Clay, General Scott and Daniel Webster. In November Taylor received a majority of electoral votes, and a popular vote of 1,360,752, against 1,219,962 for Cass and Butler, and 291,342 for Van Buren and Adams. General Taylor was inaugurated March 4, 1849.

The free and slave States being then equal in number, the struggle for supremacy on the part of the leaders in Congress was violent and bitter. In the summer of 1849 California adopted in convention a Constitution prohibiting slavery within its borders. Taylor advocated the immediate admission of California with her Constitution, and the postponement of the question as to the other Territories until they could hold conventions and decide for themselves whether slavery should exist within their borders. This policy ultimately prevailed through the celebrated "Compromise Measures" of Henry Clay; but not during the life of the brave soldier and patriot statesman. July 5 he was taken suddenly ill with a bilious fever, which proved fatal, his death occurring July 9, 1850. One of his daughters married Colonel W. W. S. Bliss, his Adjutant-General and Chief of Staff in Florida and Mexico, and Private Secretary during his Presidency. Another daughter was married to Jefferson Davis.

ILLARD FILL-
MORE, the thir-
teenth President
of the United
States, 1850-'3, was
born in Summer
Hill, Cayuga
County, New York, Janu-
ary 7, 1800. He was of
New England ancestry, and
his educational advantages
were limited. He early
learned the clothiers' trade,
but spent all his leisure time
in study. At nineteen years
of age he was induced by
Judge Walter Wood to abandon his trade
and commence the study of law. Upon
learning that the young man was entirely
destitute of means, he took him into his
own office and loaned him such money as
he needed. That he might not be heavily
burdened with debt, young Fillmore taught
school during the winter months, and in
various other ways helped himself along.

At the age of twenty-three he was admitted to the Court of Common Pleas, and
commenced the practice of his profession
in the village of Aurora, situated on the
eastern bank of the Cayuga Lake. In 1825
he married Miss Abigail Powers, daughter
of Rev. Lemuel Powers, a lady of great
moral worth. In 1825 he took his seat in
the House of Assembly of his native State,
as Representative from Erie County,
whither he had recently moved.

Though he had never taken a very
active part in politics his vote and his sympathies were with the Whig party. The
State was then Democratic, but his cour-
tesy, ability and integrity won the respect
of his associates. In 1832 he was elected
to a seat in the United States Congress.
At the close of his term he returned to his
law practice, and in two years more he was
again elected to Congress.

He now began to have a national reputation. His labors were very arduous. To
draft resolutions in the committee room,
and then to defend them against the most
skillful opponents on the floor of the House
requires readiness of mind, mental resources
and skill in debate such as few possess.
Weary with these exhausting labors, and
pressed by the claims of his private affairs,
Mr. Fillmore wrote a letter to his constituents and declined to be a candidate for re-
election. Notwithstanding this communi-

Millard Fillmore

cation his friends met in convention and renominated him by acclamation. Though gratified by this proof of their appreciation of his labors he adhered to his resolve and returned to his home.

In 1847 Mr. Fillmore was elected to the important office of comptroller of the State. In entering upon the very responsible duties which this situation demanded, it was necessary for him to abandon his profession, and he removed to the city of Albany. In this year, also, the Whigs were looking around to find suitable candidates for the President and Vice-President at the approaching election, and the names of Zachary Taylor and Millard Fillmore became the rallying cry of the Whigs. On the 4th of March, 1849, General Taylor was inaugurated President and Millard Fillmore Vice-President of the United States.

The great question of slavery had assumed enormous proportions, and permeated every subject that was brought before Congress. It was evident that the strength of our institutions was to be severely tried. July 9, 1850, President Taylor died, and, by the Constitution, Vice-President Fillmore became President of the United States. The agitated condition of the country brought questions of great delicacy before him. He was bound by his oath of office to execute the laws of the United States. One of these laws was understood to be, that if a slave, escaping from bondage, should reach a free State, the United States was bound to do its utmost to capture him and return him to his master. Most Christian men loathed this law. President Fillmore felt bound by his oath rigidly to see it enforced. Slavery was organizing armies to invade Cuba as it had invaded Texas, and annex it to the United States. President Fillmore gave all the influence of his exalted station against the atrocious enterprise.

Mr. Fillmore had serious difficulties to contend with, since the opposition had a majority in both Houses. He did everything in his power to conciliate the South, but the pro-slavery party in that section felt the inadequency of all measures of transient conciliation. The population of the free States was so rapidly increasing over that of the slave States, that it was inevitable that the power of the Government should soon pass into the hands of the free States. The famous compromise measures were adopted under Mr. Fillmore's administration, and the Japan expedition was sent out.

March 4, 1853, having served one term, President Fillmore retired from office. He then took a long tour through the South, where he met with quite an enthusiastic reception. In a speech at Vicksburg, alluding to the rapid growth of the country, he said:

" Canada is knocking for admission, and Mexico would be glad to come in, and without saying whether it would be right or wrong, we stand with open arms to receive them; for it is the manifest destiny of this Government to embrace the whole North American Continent."

In 1855 Mr. Fillmore went to Europe where he was received with those marked attentions which his position and character merited. Returning to this country in 1856 he was nominated for the Presidency by the " Know-Nothing " party. Mr. Buchanan, the Democratic candidate was the successful competitor. Mr. Fillmore ever afterward lived in retirement. During the conflict of civil war he was mostly silent. It was generally supposed, however, that his sympathy was with the Southern Confederacy. He kept aloof from the conflict without any words of cheer to the one party or the other. For this reason he was forgotten by both. He died of paralysis, in Buffalo, New York, March 8, 1874.

FRANKLIN PIERCE.

RANKLIN PIERCE, the fourteenth President of the United States, was born in Hillsborough, New Hampshire, November 23, 1804. His father, Governor Benjamin Pierce, was a Revolutionary soldier, a man of rigid integrity; was for several years in the State Legislature, a member of the Governor's council and a General of the militia.

Franklin was the sixth of eight children. As a boy he listened eagerly to the arguments of his father, enforced by strong and ready utterance and earnest gesture. It was in the days of intense political excitement, when, all over the New England States, Federalists and Democrats were arrayed so fiercely against each other.

In 1820 he entered Bowdoin College, at Brunswick, Maine, and graduated in 1824, and commenced the study of law in the office of Judge Woodbury, a very distinguished lawyer, and in 1827 was admitted to the bar. He practiced with great success in Hillsborough and Concord. He served in the State Legislature four years, the last two of which he was chosen Speaker of the House by a very large vote.

In 1833 he was elected a member of Congress. In 1837 he was elected to the United States Senate, just as Mr. Van Buren commenced his administration.

In 1834 he married Miss Jane Means Appleton, a lady admirably fitted to adorn every station with which her husband was honored. Three sons born to them all found an early grave.

Upon his accession to office, President Polk appointed Mr. Pierce Attorney-General of the United States, but the offer was declined in consequence of numerous professional engagements at home and the precarious state of Mrs. Pierce's health. About the same time he also declined the nomination for Governor by the Democratic party.

The war with Mexico called Mr. Pierce into the army. Receiving the appointment of Brigadier-General, he embarked with a portion of his troops at Newport, Rhode Island, May 27, 1847. He served during this war, and distinguished himself by his bravery, skill and excellent judgment. When he reached his home in his native State he was enthusiastically received by

Franklin Peirce

the advocates of the war, and coldly by its opponents. He resumed the practice of his profession, frequently taking an active part in political questions, and giving his support to the pro-slavery wing of the Democratic party.

June 12, 1852, the Democratic convention met in Baltimore to nominate a candidate for the Presidency. For four days they continued in session, and in thirty-five ballotings no one had received the requisite two-thirds vote. Not a vote had been thrown thus far for General Pierce. Then the Virginia delegation brought forward his name. There were fourteen more ballotings, during which General Pierce gained strength, until, at the forty-ninth ballot, he received 282 votes, and all other candidates eleven. General Winfield Scott was the Whig candidate. General Pierce was elected with great unanimity. Only four States—Vermont, Massachusetts, Kentucky and Tennessee—cast their electoral votes against him. March 4, 1853, he was inaugurated President of the United States, and William R. King, Vice-President.

President Pierce's cabinet consisted of William S. Marcy, James Guthrie, Jefferson Davis, James C. Dobbin, Robert McClelland, James Campbell and Caleb Cushing.

At the demand of slavery the Missouri Compromise was repealed, and all the Territories of the Union were thrown open to slavery. The Territory of Kansas, west of Missouri, was settled by emigrants mainly from the North. According to law, they were about to meet and decide whether slavery or freedom should be the law of that realm. Slavery in Missouri and other Southern States rallied her armed legions, marched them into Kansas, took possession of the polls, drove away the citizens, deposited their own votes by handfuls, went through the farce of counting them, and then declared that, by an overwhelming majority, slavery was established in Kansas. These facts nobody denied, and yet President Pierce's administration felt bound to respect the decision obtained by such votes. The citizens of Kansas, the majority of whom were free-State men, met in convention and adopted the following resolve:

"*Resolved,* That the body of men who, for the past two months, have been passing laws for the people of our Territory, moved, counseled and dictated to by the demagogues of other States, are to us a foreign body, representing only the lawless invaders who elected them, and not the people of this Territory; that we repudiate their action as the monstrous consummation of an act of violence, usurpation and fraud unparalleled in the history of the Union."

The free-State people of Kansas also sent a petition to the General Government, imploring its protection. In reply the President issued a proclamation, declaring that Legislature thus created must be recognized as the legitimate Legislature of Kansas, and that its laws were binding upon the people, and that, if necessary, the whole force of the Governmental arm would be put forth to inforce those laws.

James Buchanan succeeded him in the Presidency, and, March 4, 1857, President Pierce retired to his home in Concord, New Hampshire. When the Rebellion burst forth Mr. Pierce remained steadfast to the principles he had always cherished, and gave his sympathies to the pro-slavery party, with which he had ever been allied. He declined to do anything, either by voice or pen, to strengthen the hands of the National Government. He resided in Concord until his death, which occurred in October, 1869. He was one of the most genial and social of men, generous to a fault, and contributed liberally of his moderate means for the alleviation of suffering and want. He was an honored communicant of the Episcopal church.

AMES BUCHANAN, the
fifteenth President of the
United States. 1857–'61,
was born in Franklin
County, Pennsylvania,
April 23, 1791. The
place where his father's
cabin stood was called
Stony Batter, and it was
situated in a wild, romantic
spot, in a gorge of mountains, with towering sum-
mits rising all around. He
was of Irish ancestry, his
father having emigrated in
1783, with very little property, save his own strong arms.

James remained in his secluded home for
eight years enjoying very few social or
intellectual advantages. His parents were
industrious, frugal, prosperous and intelligent. In 1799 his father removed to Mer-
cersburg, where James was placed in
school and commenced a course in English,
Greek and Latin. His progress was rapid
and in 1801 he entered Dickinson College
at Carlisle. Here he took his stand among
the first scholars in the institution, and was
able to master the most abstruse subjects
with facility. In 1809 he graduated with
the highest honors in his class.

He was then eighteen years of age, tall,
graceful and in vigorous health, fond of
athletic sports, an unerring shot and en-
livened with an exuberant flow of animal
spirits. He immediately commenced the
study of law in the city of Lancaster, and
was admitted to the bar in 1812. He rose
very rapidly in his profession and at once
took undisputed stand with the ablest lawyers of the State. When but twenty-six
years of age, unaided by counsel, he successfully defended before the State Senate
one of the Judges of the State, who was
tried upon articles of impeachment At
the age of thirty it was generally admitted
that he stood at the head of the bar, and
there was no lawyer in the State who had
a more extensive or lucrative practice.

In 1812, just after Mr. Buchanan had
entered upon the practice of the law, our
second war with England occurred. With
all his powers he sustained the Government, eloquently urging the rigorous prosecution of the war; and even enlisting as a
private soldier to assist in repelling the
British, who had sacked Washington and
were threatening Baltimore. He was at
that time a Federalist, but when the Constitution was adopted by both parties,
Jefferson truly said, "We are all Federalists; we are all Republicans."

The opposition of the Federalists to the
war with England, and the alien and sedi-

James Buchanan

tion laws of John Adams, brought the party into dispute, and the name of Federalist became a reproach. Mr. Buchanan almost immediately upon entering Congress began to incline more and more to the Republicans. In the stormy Presidential election of 1824, in which Jackson, Clay, Crawford and John Quincy Adams were candidates, Mr. Buchanan espoused the cause of General Jackson and unrelentingly opposed the administration of Mr. Adams.

Upon his elevation to the Presidency, General Jackson appointed Mr. Buchanan, minister to Russia. Upon his return in 1833 he was elected to a seat in the United States Senate. He there met as his associates, Webster, Clay, Wright and Calhoun. He advocated the measures proposed by President Jackson of making reprisals against France, and defended the course of the President in his unprecedented and wholesale removals from office of those who were not the supporters of his administration. Upon this question he was brought into direct collision with Henry Clay. In the discussion of the question respecting the admission of Michigan and Arkansas into the Union, Mr. Buchanan defined his position by saying:

" The older I grow, the more I am inclined to be what is called a State-rights man."

M. de Tocqueville, in his renowned work upon " Democracy in America," foresaw the trouble which was inevitable from the doctrine of State sovereignty as held by Calhoun and Buchanan. He was convinced that the National Government was losing that strength which was essential to its own existence, and that the States were assuming powers which threatened the perpetuity of the Union. Mr. Buchanan received the book in the Senate and declared the fears of De Tocqueville to be groundless, and yet he lived to sit in the Presidential chair and see State after State, in accordance with his own views of State

rights, breaking from the Union, thus crumbling our Republic into ruins; while the unhappy old man folded his arms in despair, declaring that the National Constitution invested him with no power to arrest the destruction.

Upon Mr. Polk's accession to the Presidency, Mr. Buchanan became Secretary of State, and as such took his share of the responsibility in the conduct of the Mexican war. At the close of Mr. Polk's administration, Mr. Buchanan retired to private life; but his intelligence, and his great ability as a statesman, enabled him to exert a powerful influence in National affairs.

Mr. Pierce, upon his election to the Presidency, honored Mr. Buchanan with the mission to England. In the year 1856 the National Democratic convention nominated Mr. Buchanan for the Presidency. The political conflict was one of the most severe in which our country has ever engaged. On the 4th of March, 1857, Mr. Buchanan was inaugurated President. His cabinet were Lewis Cass, Howell Cobb, J. B. Floyd, Isaac Toucey, Jacob Thompson, A. V. Brown and J. S. Black.

The disruption of the Democratic party, in consequence of the manner in which the issue of the nationality of slavery was pressed by the Southern wing, occurred at the National convention, held at Charleston in April, 1860, for the nomination of Mr. Buchanan's successor, when the majority of Southern delegates withdrew upon the passage of a resolution declaring that the constitutional status of slavery should be determined by the Supreme Court.

In the next Presidential canvass Abraham Lincoln was nominated by the opponents of Mr. Buchanan's administration. Mr. Buchanan remained in Washington long enough to see his successor installed and then retired to his home in Wheatland. He died June 1, 1868, aged seventy-seven years.

BRAHAM LIN-
COLN, the sixteenth
President of the
United States, 1861-'5,
was born February
12, 1809, in Larue
(then Hardin) County,
Kentucky, in a cabin on Nolan
Creek, three miles west of
Hudgensville.   His parents
were Thomas and Nancy
(Hanks) Lincoln.   Of his ancestry and early years the little
that is known may best be
given in his own language: " My
parents were both born in Virginia, of un-
distinguished families—second families, perhaps I should say. My mother, who died
in my tenth year, was of a family of the
name of Hanks, some of whom now remain
in Adams, and others in Macon County,
Illinois. My paternal grandfather, Abraham Lincoln, emigrated from Rockbridge
County, Virginia, to Kentucky in 1781 or
1782, where, a year or two later, he was
killed by Indians—not in battle, but by
stealth, when he was laboring to open a
farm in the forest. His ancestors, who were
Quakers, went to Virginia from Berks
County, Pennsylvania. An effort to iden-
tify them with the New England family of
the same name ended in nothing more definite than a similarity of Christian names in
both families, such as Enoch, Levi, Mor-
decai, Solomon, Abraham and the like.
My father, at the death of his father, was
but six years of age, and he grew up, literally, without education. He removed from
Kentucky to what is now Spencer County,
Indiana, in my eighth year. We reached
our new home about the time the State came
into the Union. It was a wild region, with
bears and other wild animals still in the
woods. There I grew to manhood.

" There were some schools, so called, but
no qualification was ever required of a
teacher beyond ' readin', writin', and cipher-
in' to the rule of three.' If a straggler, supposed to understand Latin, happened to
sojourn in the neighborhood, he was looked
upon as a wizard. There was absolutely
nothing to excite ambition for education.
Of course, when I came of age I did not
know much. Still, somehow, I could read,
write and cipher to the rule of three, and
that was all. I have not been to school
since. The little advance I now have upon
this store of education I have picked up
from time to time under the pressure of
necessity. I was raised to farm-work, which

Your forever as ever
A. Lincoln

I continued till I was twenty-two. At twenty-one I came to Illinois and passed the first year in Macon County. Then I got to New Salem, at that time in Sangamon, now in Menard County, where I remained a year as a sort of clerk in a store.

"Then came the Black Hawk war, and I was elected a Captain of volunteers—a success which gave me more pleasure than any I have had since. I went the campaign, was elated; ran for the Legislature the same year (1832) and was beaten, the only time I have ever been beaten by the people. The next and three succeeding biennial elections I was elected to the Legislature, and was never a candidate afterward.

"During this legislative period I had studied law, and removed to Springfield to practice it. In 1846 I was elected to the Lower House of Congress; was not a candidate for re-election. From 1849 to 1854, inclusive, I practiced the law more assiduously than ever before. Always a Whig in politics, and generally on the Whig electoral tickets, making active canvasses, I was losing interest in politics, when the repeal of the Missouri Compromise roused me again. What I have done since is pretty well known."

The early residence of Lincoln in Indiana was sixteen miles north of the Ohio River, on Little Pigeon Creek, one and a half miles east of Gentryville, within the present township of Carter. Here his mother died October 5, 1818, and the next year his father married Mrs. Sally (Bush) Johnston, of Elizabethtown, Kentucky. She was an affectionate foster-parent, to whom Abraham was indebted for his first encouragement to study. He became an eager reader, and the few books owned in the vicinity were many times perused. He worked frequently for the neighbors as a farm laborer; was for some time clerk in a store at Gentryville; and became famous throughout that region for his athletic

7

powers, his fondness for argument, his inexhaustible fund of humerous anecdote, as well as for mock oratory and the composition of rude satirical verses. In 1828 he made a trading voyage to New Orleans as "bow-hand" on a flatboat; removed to Illinois in 1830; helped his father build a log house and clear a farm on the north fork of Sangamon River, ten miles west of Decatur, and was for some time employed in splitting rails for the fences—a fact which was prominently brought forward for a political purpose thirty years later.

In the spring of 1851 he, with two of his relatives, was hired to build a flatboat on the Sangamon River and navigate it to New Orleans. The boat "stuck" on a mill-dam, and was got off with great labor through an ingenious mechanical device which some years later led to Lincoln's taking out a patent for "an improved method for lifting vessels over shoals." This voyage was memorable for another reason—the sight of slaves chained, maltreated and flogged at New Orleans was the origin of his deep convictions upon the slavery question.

Returning from this voyage he became a resident for several years at New Salem, a recently settled village on the Sangamon, where he was successively a clerk, grocer, surveyor and postmaster, and acted as pilot to the first steamboat that ascended the Sangamon. Here he studied law, interested himself in local politics after his return from the Black Hawk war, and became known as an effective "stump-speaker." The subject of his first political speech was the improvement of the channel of the Sangamon, and the chief ground on which he announced himself (1832) a candidate for the Legislature was his advocacy of this popular measure, on which subject his practical experience made him the highest authority.

Elected to the Legislature in 1834 as a

"Henry Clay Whig," he rapidly acquired that command of language and that homely but forcible rhetoric which, added to his intimate knowledge of the people from which he sprang, made him more than a match in debate for his few well-educated opponents.

Admitted to the bar in 1837 he soon established himself at Springfield, where the State capital was located in 1839, largely through his influence; became a successful pleader in the State, Circuit and District Courts; married in 1842 a lady belonging to a prominent family in Lexington, Kentucky; took an active part in the Presidential campaigns of 1840 and 1844 as candidate for elector on the Harrison and Clay tickets, and in 1846 was elected to the United States House of Representatives over the celebrated Peter Cartwright. During his single term in Congress he did not attain any prominence.

He voted for the reception of anti-slavery petitions for the abolition of the slave trade in the District of Columbia and for the Wilmot proviso; but was chiefly remembered for the stand he took against the Mexican war. For several years thereafter he took comparatively little interest in politics, but gained a leading position at the Springfield bar. Two or three non-political lectures and an eulogy on Henry Clay (1852) added nothing to his reputation.

In 1854 the repeal of the Missouri Compromise by the Kansas-Nebraska act aroused Lincoln from his indifference, and in attacking that measure he had the immense advantage of knowing perfectly well the motives and the record of its author, Stephen A. Douglas, of Illinois, then popularly designated as the "Little Giant." The latter came to Springfield in October, 1854, on the occasion of the State Fair, to vindicate his policy in the Senate, and the "Anti-Nebraska" Whigs, remembering that Lincoln had often measured his strength with

Douglas in the Illinois Legislature and before the Springfield Courts, engaged him to improvise a reply. This speech, in the opinion of those who heard it, was one of the greatest efforts of Lincoln's life; certainly the most effective in his whole career. It took the audience by storm, and from that moment it was felt that Douglas had met his match. Lincoln was accordingly selected as the Anti-Nebraska candidate for the United States Senate in place of General Shields, whose term expired March 4, 1855, and led to several ballots; but Trumbull was ultimately chosen.

The second conflict on the soil of Kansas, which Lincoln had predicted, soon began. The result was the disruption of the Whig and the formation of the Republican party. At the Bloomington State Convention in 1856, where the new party first assumed form in Illinois, Lincoln made an impressive address, in which for the first time he took distinctive ground against slavery in itself.

At the National Republican Convention at Philadelphia, June 17, after the nomination of Fremont, Lincoln was put forward by the Illinois delegation for the Vice-Presidency, and received on the first ballot 110 votes against 259 for William L. Dayton. He took a prominent part in the canvass, being on the electoral ticket.

In 1858 Lincoln was unanimously nominated by the Republican State Convention as its candidate for the United States Senate in place of Douglas, and in his speech of acceptance used the celebrated illustration of a "house divided against itself" on the slavery question, which was, perhaps, the cause of his defeat. The great debate carried on at all the principal towns of Illinois between Lincoln and Douglas as rival Senatorial candidates resulted at the time in the election of the latter; but being widely circulated as a campaign document, it fixed the attention of the country upon the former, as the clearest and most convincing exponent of Republican doctrine.

Early in 1859 he began to be named in Illinois as a suitable Republican candidate for the Presidential campaign of the ensuing year, and a political address delivered at the Cooper Institute, New York, February 27, 1860, followed by similar speeches at New Haven, Hartford and elsewhere in New England, first made him known to the Eastern States in the light by which he had long been regarded at home. By the Republican State Convention, which met at Decatur, Illinois, May 9 and 10, Lincoln was unanimously endorsed for the Presidency. It was on this occasion that two rails, said to have been split by his hands thirty years before, were brought into the convention, and the incident contributed much to his popularity. The National Republican Convention at Chicago, after spirited efforts made in favor of Seward, Chase and Bates, nominated Lincoln for the Presidency, with Hannibal Hamlin for Vice-President, at the same time adopting a vigorous anti-slavery platform.

The Democratic party having been disorganized and presenting two candidates, Douglas and Breckenridge, and the remnant of the "American" party having put forward John Bell, of Tennessee, the Republican victory was an easy one, Lincoln being elected November 6 by a large plurality, comprehending nearly all the Northern States, but none of the Southern. The secession of South Carolina and the Gulf States was the immediate result, followed a few months later by that of the border slave States and the outbreak of the great civil war.

The life of Abraham Lincoln became thenceforth merged in the history of his country. None of the details of the vast conflict which filled the remainder of Lincoln's life can here be given. Narrowly escaping assassination by avoiding Balti-more on his way to the capital, he reached Washington February 23, and was inaugurated President of the United States March 4, 1861.

In his inaugural address he said: "I hold, that in contemplation of universal law and the Constitution the Union of these States is perpetual. Perpetuity is implied if not expressed in the fundamental laws of all national governments. It is safe to assert that no government proper ever had a provision in its organic law for its own termination. I therefore consider that in view of the Constitution and the laws, the Union is unbroken, and to the extent of my ability I shall take care, as the Constitution enjoins upon me, that the laws of the United States be extended in all the States. In doing this there need be no bloodshed or violence, and there shall be none unless it be forced upon the national authority. The power conferred to me will be used to hold, occupy and possess the property and places belonging to the Government, and to collect the duties and imports, but beyond what may be necessary for these objects there will be no invasion, no using of force against or among the people anywhere. In your hands, my dissatisfied fellow-countrymen, is the momentous issue of civil war. The Government will not assail you. You can have no conflict without being yourselves the aggressors. You have no oath registered in heaven to destroy the Government, while I shall have the most solemn one to preserve, protect and defend it."

He called to his cabinet his principal rivals for the Presidential nomination — Seward, Chase, Cameron and Bates; secured the co-operation of the Union Democrats, headed by Douglas; called out 75,000 militia from the several States upon the first tidings of the bombardment of Fort Sumter, April 15; proclaimed a blockade of the Southern posts April 19; called an extra session of Congress for July 4, from which he asked and obtained 400,000 men and $400,000,000 for the war; placed McClellan at the head of the Federal army on General Scott's resignation, October 31; appointed Edwin M. Stanton Secretary of War, January 14, 1862, and September 22, 1862, issued a proclamation declaring the freedom of all slaves in the States and parts of States then in rebellion from and after January 1, 1863. This was the crowning act of Lincoln's career—the act by which he will be chiefly known through all future time—and it decided the war.

October 16, 1863, President Lincoln called for 300,000 volunteers to replace those whose term of enlistment had expired; made a celebrated and touching, though brief, address at the dedication of the Gettysburg military cemetery, November 19, 1863; commissioned Ulysses S. Grant Lieutenant-General and Commander-in-Chief of the armies of the United States, March 9, 1864; was re-elected President in November of the same year, by a large majority over General McClellan, with Andrew Johnson, of Tennessee, as Vice-President; delivered a very remarkable address at his second inauguration, March 4, 1865; visited the army before Richmond the same month; entered the capital of the Confederacy the day after its fall, and upon the surrender of General Robert E. Lee's army, April 9, was actively engaged in devising generous plans for the reconstruction of the Union, when, on the evening of Good Friday, April 14, he was shot in his box at Ford's Theatre, Washington, by John Wilkes Booth, a fanatical actor, and expired early on the following morning, April 15. Almost simultaneously a murderous attack was made upon William H. Seward, Secretary of State.

At noon on the 15th of April Andrew Johnson assumed the Presidency, and active measures were taken which resulted in the death of Booth and the execution of his principal accomplices.

The funeral of President Lincoln was conducted with unexampled solemnity and magnificence. Impressive services were held in Washington, after which the sad procession proceeded over the same route he had traveled four years before, from Springfield to Washington. In Philadelphia his body lay in state in Independence Hall, in which he had declared before his first inauguration "that I would sooner be assassinated than to give up the principles of the Declaration of Independence." He was buried at Oak Ridge Cemetery, near Springfield, Illinois, on May 4, where a monument emblematic of the emancipation of the slaves and the restoration of the Union mark his resting place.

The leaders and citizens of the expiring Confederacy expressed genuine indignation at the murder of a generous political adversary. Foreign nations took part in mourning the death of a statesman who had proved himself a true representative of American nationality. The freedmen of the South almost worshiped the memory of their deliverer; and the general sentiment of the great Nation he had saved awarded him a place in its affections, second only to that held by Washington.

The characteristics of Abraham Lincoln have been familiarly known throughout the civilized world. His tall, gaunt, ungainly figure, homely countenance, and his shrewd mother-wit, shown in his celebrated conversations overflowing in humorous and pointed anecdote, combined with an accurate, intuitive appreciation of the questions of the time, are recognized as forming the best type of a period of American history now rapidly passing away.

ANDREW JOHNSON, the seventeenth President of the United States, 1865-'9, was born at Raleigh, North Carolina, December 29, 1808. His father died when he was four years old, and in his eleventh year he was apprenticed to a tailor. He never attended school, and did not learn to read until late in his apprenticeship, when he suddenly acquired a passion for obtaining knowledge, and devoted all his spare time to reading.

After working two years as a journeyman tailor at Lauren's Court-House, South Carolina, he removed, in 1826, to Greenville, Tennessee, where he worked at his trade and married. Under his wife's instructions he made rapid progress in his education, and manifested such an intelligent interest in local politics as to be elected as "workingmen's candidate" alderman, in 1828, and mayor in 1830, being twice re-elected to each office.

During this period he cultivated his talents as a public speaker by taking part in a debating society, consisting largely of students of Greenville College. In 1835, and again in 1839, he was chosen to the lower house of the Legislature, as a Democrat. In 1841 he was elected State Senator, and in 1843, Representative in Congress, being re-elected four successive periods, until 1853, when he was chosen Governor of Tennessee. In Congress he supported the administrations of Tyler and Polk in their chief measures, especially the annexation of Texas, the adjustment of the Oregon boundary, the Mexican war, and the tariff of 1846.

In 1855 Mr. Johnson was re-elected Governor, and in 1857 entered the United States Senate, where he was conspicuous as an advocate of retrenchment and of the Homestead bill, and as an opponent of the Pacific Railroad. He was supported by the Tennessee delegation to the Democratic convention in 1860 for the Presidential nomination, and lent his influence to the Breckenridge wing of that party.

When the election of Lincoln had brought about the first attempt at secession in December, 1860, Johnson took in the Senate a firm attitude for the Union, and in May, 1861, on returning to Tennessee, he was in imminent peril of suffering from popular violence for his loyalty to the "old flag." He was the leader of the Loyalists' convention of East Tennessee, and during the following winter was very active in organizing relief for the destitute loyal refugees from that region, his own family being among those compelled to leave.

By his course in this crisis Johnson came prominently before the Northern public, and when in March, 1862, he was appointed by President Lincoln military Governor of Tennessee, with the rank of Brigadier-General, he increased in popularity by the vigorous and successful manner in which he labored to restore order, protect Union men and punish marauders. On the approach of the Presidential campaign of 1864, the termination of the war being plainly foreseen, and several Southern States being partially reconstructed, it was felt that the Vice-Presidency should be given to a Southern man of conspicuous loyalty, and Governor Johnson was elected on the same platform and ticket as President Lincoln; and on the assassination of the latter succeeded to the Presidency, April 15, 1865. In a public speech two days later he said: "The American people must be taught, if they do not already feel, that treason is a crime and must be punished; that the Government will not always bear with its enemies; that it is strong, not only to protect, but to punish. In our peaceful history treason has been almost unknown. The people must understand that it is the blackest of crimes, and will be punished." He then added the ominous sentence: "In regard to my future course, I make no promises, no pledges." President Johnson retained the cabinet of Lincoln, and exhibited considerable severity toward traitors in his earlier acts and speeches, but he soon inaugurated a policy of reconstruction, proclaiming a general amnesty to the late Confederates, and successively establishing provisional Governments in the Southern States.

These States accordingly claimed representation in Congress in the following December, and the momentous question of what should be the policy of the victorious Union toward its late armed opponents was forced upon that body.

Two considerations impelled the Republican majority to reject the policy of President Johnson: First, an apprehension that the chief magistrate intended to undo the results of the war in regard to slavery; and, second, the sullen attitude of the South, which seemed to be plotting to regain the policy which arms had lost. The credentials of the Southern members elect were laid on the table, a civil rights bill and a bill extending the sphere of the Freedmen's Bureau were passed over the executive veto, and the two highest branches of the Government were soon in open antagonism. The action of Congress was characterized by the President as a "new rebellion." In July the cabinet was reconstructed, Messrs. Randall, Stanbury and Browning taking the places of Messrs. Denison, Speed and Harlan, and an unsuccessful attempt was made by means of a general convention in Philadelphia to form a new party on the basis of the administration policy.

In an excursion to Chicago for the purpose of laying a corner-stone of the monument to Stephen A. Douglas, President Johnson, accompanied by several members of the cabinet, passed through Philadelphia, New York and Albany, in each of which cities, and in other places along the route, he made speeches justifying and explaining his own policy, and violently denouncing the action of Congress.

August 12, 1867, President Johnson removed the Secretary of War, replacing him by General Grant. Secretary Stanton retired under protest, based upon the tenure-of-office act which had been passed the preceding March. The President then issued a proclamation declaring the insurrection at an end, and that " peace, order, tranquility and civil authority existed in and throughout the United States." Another proclamation enjoined obedience to the Constitution and the laws, and an amnesty was published September 7, relieving nearly all the participants in the late Rebellion from the disabilities thereby incurred, on condition of taking the oath to support the Constitution and the laws.

In December Congress refused to confirm the removal of Secretary Stanton, who thereupon resumed the exercise of his office; but February 21, 1868, President Johnson again attempted to remove him, appointing General Lorenzo Thomas in his place. Stanton refused to vacate his post, and was sustained by the Senate.

February 24 the House of Representatives voted to impeach the President for "high crime and misdemeanors," and March 5 presented eleven articles of impeachment on the ground of his resistance to the execution of the acts of Congress, alleging, in addition to the offense lately committed, his public expressions of contempt for Congress, in " certain intemperate, inflammatory and scandalous harangues" pronounced in August and September, 1866, and thereafter declaring that the Thirty-ninth Congress of the United States was not a competent legislative body, and denying its power to propose Constitutional amendments. March 23 the impeachment trial began, the President appearing by counsel, and resulted in acquittal, the vote lacking one of the two-thirds vote required for conviction.

The remainder of President Johnson's term of office was passed without any such conflicts as might have been anticipated. He failed to obtain a nomination for re-election by the Democratic party, though receiving sixty-five votes on the first ballot. July 4 and December 25 new proclamations of pardon to the participants in the late Rebellion were issued, but were of little effect. On the accession of General Grant to the Presidency, March 4, 1869, Johnson returned to Greenville, Tennessee. Unsuccessful in 1870 and 1872 as a candidate respectively for United States Senator and Representative, he was finally elected to the Senate in 1875, and took his seat in the extra session of March, in which his speeches were comparatively temperate. He died July 31, 1875, and was buried at Greenville.

President Johnson's administration was a peculiarly unfortunate one. That he should so soon become involved in bitter feud with the Republican majority in Congress was certainly a surprising and deplorable incident; yet, in reviewing the circumstances after a lapse of so many years, it is easy to find ample room for a charitable judgment of both the parties in the heated controversy, since it cannot be doubted that any President, even Lincoln himself, had he lived, must have sacrificed a large portion of his popularity in carrying out any possible scheme of reconstruction.

ULYSSES SIMPSON GRANT, the eighteenth President of the United States, 1869-'77, was born April 27, 1822, at Point Pleasant, Clermont County, Ohio. His father was of Scotch descent, and a dealer in leather. At the age of seventeen he entered the Military Academy at West Point, and four years later graduated twenty-first in a class of thirty-nine, receiving the commission of Brevet Second Lieutenant. He was assigned to the Fourth Infantry and remained in the army eleven years. He was engaged in every battle of the Mexican war except that of Buena Vista, and received two brevets for gallantry.

In 1848 Mr. Grant married Julia, daughter of Frederick Dent, a prominent merchant of St. Louis, and in 1854, having reached the grade of Captain, he resigned his commission in the army. For several years he followed farming near St. Louis, but unsuccessfully; and in 1860 he entered the leather trade with his father at Galena, Illinois.

When the civil war broke out in 1861, Grant was thirty-nine years of age, but entirely unknown to public men and without any personal acquaintance with great affairs. President Lincoln's first call for troops was made on the 15th of April, and on the 19th Grant was drilling a company of volunteers at Galena. He also offered his services to the Adjutant-General of the army, but received no reply. The Governor of Illinois, however, employed him in the organization of volunteer troops, and at the end of five weeks he was appointed Colonel of the Twenty-first Infantry. He took command of his regiment in June, and reported first to General Pope in Missouri. His superior knowledge of military life rather surprised his superior officers, who had never before even heard of him, and they were thus led to place him on the road to rapid advancement. August 7 he was commissioned a Brigadier-General of volunteers, the appointment having been made without his knowledge. He had been unanimously recommended by the Congressmen from Illinois, not one of whom had been his personal acquaintance. For a few weeks he was occupied in watching the movements of partisan forces in Missouri.

September 1 he was placed in command of the District of Southeast Missouri, with headquarters at Cairo, and on the 6th, without orders, he seized Paducah, at the mouth of the Tennessee River, and commanding the navigation both of that stream and of

the Ohio. This stroke secured Kentucky to the Union; for the State Legislature, which had until then affected to be neutral, at once declared in favor of the Government. In November following, according to orders, he made a demonstration about eighteen miles below Cairo, preventing the crossing of hostile troops into Missouri; but in order to accomplish this purpose he had to do some fighting, and that, too, with only 3,000 raw recruits, against 7,000 Confederates. Grant carried off two pieces of artillery and 200 prisoners.

After repeated applications to General Halleck, his immediate superior, he was allowed, in February, 1862, to move up the Tennessee River against Fort Henry, in conjunction with a naval force. The gunboats silenced the fort, and Grant immediately made preparations to attack Fort Donelson, about twelve miles distant, on the Cumberland River. Without waiting for orders he moved his troops there, and with 15,000 men began the siege. The fort, garrisoned with 21,000 men, was a strong one, but after hard fighting on three successive days Grant forced an "Unconditional Surrender" (an alliteration upon the initials of his name). The prize he captured consisted of sixty-five cannon, 17,600 small arms and 14,623 soldiers. About 4,000 of the garrison had escaped in the night, and 2,500 were killed or wounded. Grant's entire loss was less than 2,000. This was the first important success won by the national troops during the war, and its strategic results were marked, as the entire States of Kentucky and Tennessee at once fell into the National hands. Our hero was made a Major-General of Volunteers and placed in command of the District of West Tennessee.

In March, 1862, he was ordered to move up the Tennessee River toward Corinth, where the Confederates were concentrating a large army; but he was directed not

to attack. His forces, now numbering 38,-000, were accordingly encamped near Shiloh, or Pittsburg Landing, to await the arrival of General Buell with 40,000 more; but April 6 the Confederates came out from Corinth 50,000 strong and attacked Grant violently, hoping to overwhelm him before Buell could arrive; 5,000 of his troops were beyond supporting distance, so that he was largely outnumbered and forced back to the river, where, however, he held out until dark, when the head of Buell's column came upon the field. The next day the Confederates were driven back to Corinth, nineteen miles. The loss was heavy on both sides; Grant, being senior in rank to Buell, commanded on both days. Two days afterward Halleck arrived at the front and assumed command of the army, Grant remaining at the head of the right wing and the reserve. On May 30 Corinth was evacuated by the Confederates. In July Halleck was made General-in-Chief, and Grant succeeded him in command of the Department of the Tennessee. September 19 the battle of Iuka was fought, where, owing to Rosecrans's fault, only an incomplete victory was obtained.

Next, Grant, with 30,000 men, moved down into Mississippi and threatened Vicksburg, while Sherman, with 40,000 men, was sent by way of the river to attack that place in front; but, owing to Colonel Murphy's surrendering Holly Springs to the Confederates, Grant was so weakened that he had to retire to Corinth, and then Sherman failed to sustain his intended attack.

In January, 1863, General Grant took command in person of all the troops in the Mississippi Valley, and spent several months in fruitless attempts to compel the surrender or evacuation of Vicksburg; but July 4, following, the place surrendered, with 31,-600 men and 172 cannon, and the Mississippi River thus fell permanently into the hands of the Government. Grant was made a

Major-General in the regular army, and in October following he was placed in command of the Division of the Mississippi. The same month he went to Chattanooga and saved the Army of the Cumberland from starvation, and drove Bragg from that part of the country. This victory overthrew the last important hostile force west of the Alleghanjes and opened the way for the National armies into Georgia and Sherman's march to the sea.

The remarkable series of successes which Grant had now achieved pointed him out as the appropriate leader of the National armies, and accordingly, in February, 1864, the rank of Lieutenant-General was created for him by Congress, and on March 17 he assumed command of the armies of the United States. Planning the grand final campaign, he sent Sherman into Georgia, Sigel into the valley of Virginia, and Butler to capture Richmond, while he fought his own way from the Rapidan to the James. The costly but victorious battles of the Wilderness, Spottsylvania, North Anna and Cold Harbor were fought, more for the purpose of annihilating Lee than to capture any particular point. In June, 1864, the siege of Richmond was begun. Sherman, meanwhile, was marching and fighting daily in Georgia and steadily advancing toward Atlanta; but Sigel had been defeated in the valley of Virginia, and was superseded by Hunter. Lee sent Early to threaten the National capital; whereupon Grant gathered up a force which he placed under Sheridan, and that commander rapidly drove Early, in a succession of battles, through the valley of Virginia and destroyed his army as an organized force. The siege of Richmond went on, and Grant made numerous attacks, but was only partially successful. The people of the North grew impatient, and even the Government advised him to abandon the attempt to take Richmond or crush the Confederacy in that way; but he

never wavered. He resolved to "fight it out on that line, if it took all summer."

By September Sherman had made his way to Atlanta, and Grant then sent him on his famous "march to the sea," a route which the chief had designed six months before. He made Sherman's success possible, not only by holding Lee in front of Richmond, but also by sending reinforcements to Thomas, who then drew off and defeated the only army which could have confronted Sherman. Thus the latter was left unopposed, and, with Thomas and Sheridan, was used in the furtherance of Grant's plans. Each executed his part in the great design and contributed his share to the result at which Grant was aiming. Sherman finally reached Savannah, Schofield beat the enemy at Franklin, Thomas at Nashville, and Sheridan wherever he met him; and all this while General Grant was holding Lee, with the principal Confederate army, near Richmond, as it were chained and helpless. Then Schofield was brought from the West, and Fort Fisher and Wilmington were captured on the sea-coast, so as to afford him a foothold; from here he was sent into the interior of North Carolina, and Sherman was ordered to move northward to join him. When all this was effected, and Sheridan could find no one else to fight in the Shenandoah Valley, Grant brought the cavalry leader to the front of Richmond, and, making a last effort, drove Lee from his entrenchments and captured Richmond.

At the beginning of the final campaign Lee had collected 73,000 fighting men in the lines at Richmond, besides the local militia and the gunboat crews, amounting to 5,000 more. Including Sheridan's force Grant had 110,000 men in the works before Petersburg and Richmond. Petersburg fell on the 2d of April, and Richmond on the 3d, and Lee fled in the direction of Lynchburg. Grant pursued with remorseless energy, only stopping to strike fresh blows, and Lee at last found himself not only out-fought but also out-marched and out-generaled. Being completely surrounded, he surrendered on the 9th of April, 1865, at Appomattox Court-House, in the open field, with 27,000 men, all that remained of his army. This act virtually ended the war. Thus, in ten days Grant had captured Petersburg and Richmond, fought, by his subordinates, the battles of Five Forks and Sailor's Creek, besides numerous smaller ones, captured 20,000 men in actual battle, and received the surrender of 27,000 more at Appomattox, absolutely annihilating an army of 70,000 soldiers.

General Grant returned at once to Washington to superintend the disbandment of the armies, but this pleasurable work was scarcely begun when President Lincoln was assassinated. It had doubtless been intended to inflict the same fate upon Grant; but he, fortunately, on account of leaving Washington early in the evening, declined an invitation to accompany the President to the theater where the murder was committed. This event made Andrew Johnson President, but left Grant by far the most conspicuous figure in the public life of the country. He became the object of an enthusiasm greater than had ever been known in America. Every possible honor was heaped upon him; the grade of General was created for him by Congress; houses were presented to him by citizens; towns were illuminated on his entrance into them; and, to cap the climax, when he made his tour around the world, "all nations did him honor" as they had never before honored a foreigner.

The General, as Commander-in-Chief, was placed in an embarrassing position by the opposition of President Johnson to the measures of Congress; but he directly manifested his characteristic loyalty by obeying Congress rather than the disaffected Presi-dent, although for a short time he had served in his cabinet as Secretary of War.

Of course, everybody thought of General Grant as the next President of the United States, and he was accordingly elected as such in 1868 "by a large majority," and four years later re-elected by a much larger majority — the most overwhelming ever given by the people of this country. His first administration was distinguished by a cessation of the strifes which sprang from the war, by a large reduction of the National debt, and by a settlement of the difficulties with England which had grown out of the depredations committed by privateers fitted out in England during the war. This last settlement was made by the famous "Geneva arbitration," which saved to this Government $15,000,000, but, more than all, prevented a war with England. "Let us have peace," was Grant's motto. And this is the most appropriate place to remark that above all Presidents whom this Government has ever had, General Grant the most non-partisan. He regarded the Executive office as purely and exclusively *executive* of the laws of Congress, irrespective of "politics." But every great man has jealous, bitter enemies, a fact Grant was well aware of.

After the close of his Presidency, our General made his famous tour around the world, already referred to, and soon afterward, in company with Ferdinand Ward, of New York City, he engaged in banking and stock brokerage, which business was made disastrous to Grant, as well as to himself, by his rascality. By this time an incurable cancer of the tongue developed itself in the person of the afflicted ex-President, which ended his unrequited life July 23, 1885. Thus passed away from earth's turmoils the man, the General, who was as truly the "father of this regenerated country" as was Washington the father of the infant nation.

RUTHERFORD BIRCH-ARD HAYES, the nineteenth President of the United States, 1877-'81, was born in Delaware, Ohio, October 4, 1822. His ancestry can be traced as far back as 1280, when Hayes and Rutherford were two Scottish chieftains fighting side by side with Baliol, William Wallace and Robert Bruce. Both families belonged to the nobility, owned extensive estates and had a large following. The Hayes family had, for a coat of-arms, a shield, barred and surmounted by a flying eagle. There was a circle of stars about the eagle and above the shield, while on a scroll underneath the shield was inscribed the motto, "Recte." Misfortune overtaking the family, George Hayes left Scotland in 1680, and settled in Windsor, Connecticut. He was an industrious worker in wood and iron, having a mechanical genius and a cultivated mind. His son George was born in Windsor and remained there during his life.

Daniel Hayes, son of the latter, married Sarah Lee, and lived in Simsbury, Connecticut. Ezekiel, son of Daniel, was born in 1724, and was a manufacturer of scythes at Bradford, Connecticut. Rutherford Hayes, son of Ezekiel and grandfather of President Hayes, was born in New Haven, in August, 1756. He was a famous blacksmith and tavern-keeper. He immigrated to Vermont at an unknown date, settling in Brattleboro where he established a hotel. Here his son Rutherford, father of President Hayes, was born. In September, 1813, he married Sophia Birchard, of Wilmington, Vermont, whose ancestry on the male side is traced back to 1635, to John Birchard, one of the principal founders of Norwich. Both of her grandfathers were soldiers in the Revolutionary war.

The father of President Hayes was of a mechanical turn, and could mend a plow, knit a stocking, or do almost anything that he might undertake. He was prosperous in business, a member of the church and active in all the benevolent enterprises of the town. After the close of the war of 1812 he immigrated to Ohio, and purchased a farm near the present town of Delaware. His family then consisted of his wife and two children, and an orphan girl whom he had adopted.

It was in 1817 that the family arrived at Delaware. Instead of settling upon his

Sincerely
R.B.Hayes

farm, Mr. Hayes concluded to enter into business in the village. He purchased an interest in a distillery, a business then as respectable as it was profitable. His capital and recognized ability assured him the highest social position in the community. He died July 22, 1822, less than three months before the birth of the son that was destined to fill the office of President of the United States.

Mrs. Hayes at this period was very weak, and the subject of this sketch was so feeble at birth that he was not expected to live beyond a month or two at most. As the months went by he grew weaker and weaker so that the neighbors were in the habit of inquiring from time to time "if Mrs. Hayes's baby died last night." On one occasion a neighbor, who was on friendly terms with the family, after alluding to the boy's big head and the mother's assiduous care of him, said to her, in a bantering way, "That's right! Stick to him. You have got him along so far, and I shouldn't wonder if he would really come to something yet." "You need not laugh," said Mrs. Hayes, "you wait and see. You can't tell but I shall make him President of the United States yet."

The boy lived, in spite of the universal predictions of his speedy death; and when, in 1825, his elder brother was drowned, he became, if possible, still dearer to his mother. He was seven years old before he was placed in school. His education, however, was not neglected. His sports were almost wholly within doors, his playmates being his sister and her associates. These circumstances tended, no doubt, to foster that gentleness of disposition and that delicate consideration for the feelings of others which are marked traits of his character. At school he was ardently devoted to his studies, obedient to the teacher, and careful to avoid the quarrels in which many of his schoolmates were involved. He was always waiting at the school-house door when it opened in the morning, and never late in returning to his seat at recess. His sister Fannie was his constant companion, and their affection for each other excited the admiration of their friends.

In 1838 young Hayes entered Kenyon College and graduated in 1842. He then began the study of law in the office of Thomas Sparrow at Columbus. His health was now well established, his figure robust, his mind vigorous and alert. In a short time he determined to enter the law school at Cambridge, Massachusetts, where for two years he pursued his studies with great diligence.

In 1845 he was admitted to the bar at Marietta, Ohio, and shortly afterward went into practice as an attorney-at-law with Ralph P. Buckland, of Fremont. Here he remained three years, acquiring but limited practice, and apparently unambitious of distinction in his profession. His bachelor uncle, Sardis Birchard, who had always manifested great interest in his nephew and rendered him assistance in boyhood, was now a wealthy banker, and it was understood that the young man would be his heir. It is possible that this expectation may have made Mr. Hayes more indifferent to the attainment of wealth than he would otherwise have been, but he was led into no extravagance or vices on this account.

In 1849 he removed to Cincinnati where his ambition found new stimulus. Two events occurring at this period had a powerful influence upon his subsequent life. One of them was his marriage to Miss Lucy Ware Webb, daughter of Dr. James Webb, of Cincinnati; the other was his introduction to the Cincinnati Literary Club, a body embracing such men as Chief Justice Salmon P. Chase, General John Pope and Governor Edward F. Noyes. The marriage was a fortunate one as everybody knows. Not one of all the wives of our Presidents was more universally admired, reverenced and beloved than is Mrs. Hayes, and no one has done more than she to reflect honor upon American womanhood.

In 1856 Mr. Hayes was nominated to the office of Judge of the Court of Common Pleas, but declined to accept the nomination. Two years later he was chosen to the office of City Solicitor.

In 1861, when the Rebellion broke out, he was eager to take up arms in the defense of his country. His military life was bright and illustrious. June 7, 1861, he was appointed Major of the Twenty-third Ohio Infantry. In July the regiment was sent to Virginia. October 15, 1861, he was made Lieutenant-Colonel of his regiment, and in August, 1862, was promoted Colonel of the Seventy-ninth Ohio Regiment, but refused to leave his old comrades. He was wounded at the battle of South Mountain, and suffered severely, being unable to enter upon active duty for several weeks. November 30, 1862, he rejoined his regiment as its Colonel, having been promoted October 15.

December 25, 1862, he was placed in command of the Kanawha division, and for meritorious service in several battles was promoted Brigadier-General. He was also brevetted Major-General for distinguished services in 1864. He was wounded four times, and five horses were shot from under him.

Mr. Hayes was first a Whig in politics, and was among the first to unite with the Free-Soil and Republican parties. In 1864 he was elected to Congress from the Second Ohio District, which had always been Democratic, receiving a majority of 3,098. In 1866 he was renominated for Congress and was a second time elected. In 1867 he was elected Governor over Allen G. Thurman, the Democratic candidate, and re-elected in 1869. In 1874 Sardis Birchard died, leaving his large estate to General Hayes.

In 1876 he was nominated for the Presidency. His letter of acceptance excited the admiration of the whole country. He resigned the office of Governor and retired to his home in Fremont to await the result of the canvass. After a hard, long contest he was inaugurated March 5, 1877. His Presidency was characterized by compromises with all parties, in order to please as many as possible. The close of his Presidential term in 1881 was the close of his public life, and since then he has remained at his home in Fremont, Ohio, in Jeffersonian retirement from public notice, in striking contrast with most others of the world's notables.

JAMES A. GARFIELD, twentieth President of the United States, 1881, was born November 19, 1831, in the wild woods of Cuyahoga County, Ohio. His parents were Abram and Eliza (Ballou) Garfield, who were of New England ancestry. The senior Garfield was an industrious farmer, as the rapid improvements which appeared on his place attested. The residence was the familiar pioneer log cabin, and the household comprised the parents and their children—Mehetable, Thomas, Mary and James A. In May, 1833, the father died, and the care of the household consequently devolved upon young Thomas, to whom James was greatly indebted for the educational and other advantages he enjoyed. He now lives in Michigan, and the two sisters live in Solon, Ohio, near their birthplace.

As the subject of our sketch grew up, he, too, was industrious, both in mental and physical labor. He worked upon the farm, or at carpentering, or chopped wood, or at any other odd job that would aid in support of the family, and in the meantime made the most of his books. Ever afterward he was never ashamed of his humble origin, nor forgot the friends of his youth. The poorest laborer was sure of his sympathy, and he always exhibited the character of a modest gentleman.

Until he was about sixteen years of age, James's highest ambition was to be a lake captain. To this his mother was strongly opposed, but she finally consented to his going to Cleveland to carry out his long-cherished design, with the understanding, however, that he should try to obtain some other kind of employment. He walked all the way to Cleveland, and this was his first visit to the city. After making many applications for work, including labor on board a lake vessel, but all in vain, he finally engaged as a driver for his cousin, Amos Letcher, on the Ohio & Pennsylvania Canal. In a short time, however, he quit this and returned home. He then attended the seminary at Chester for about three years, and next he entered Hiram Institute, a school started in 1850 by the Disciples of Christ, of which church he was a member. In order to pay his way he assumed the duties of janitor, and at times taught school. He soon completed the curriculum there, and then entered Williams College, at which he graduated in 1856, taking one of the highest honors of his class.

Afterward he returned to Hiram as President. In his youthful and therefore zealous piety, he exercised his talents occasionally as a preacher of the Gospel. He was a man of strong moral and religious convictions, and as soon as he began to look into politics, he saw innumerable points that could be improved. He also studied law, and was admitted to the bar in 1859. November 11, 1858, Mr. Garfield married Miss Lucretia Rudolph, who ever afterward proved a worthy consort in all the stages of her husband's career. They had seven children, five of whom are still living.

It was in 1859 that Garfield made his first political speeches, in Hiram and the neighboring villages, and three years later he began to speak at county mass-meetings, being received everywhere with popular favor. He was elected to the State Senate this year, taking his seat in January, 1860.

On the breaking out of the war of the Rebellion in 1861, Mr. Garfield resolved to fight as he had talked, and accordingly he enlisted to defend the old flag, receiving his commission as Lieutenant-Colonel of the Forty-second Regiment of the Ohio Volunteer Infantry, August 14, that year. He was immediately thrown into active service, and before he had ever seen a gun fired in action he was placed in command of four regiments of infantry and eight companies of cavalry, charged with the work of driving the Confederates, headed by Humphrey Marshall, from his native State, Kentucky. This task was speedily accomplished, although against great odds. On account of his success, President Lincoln commissioned him Brigadier-General, January 11, 1862; and, as he had been the youngest man in the Ohio Senate two years before, so now he was the youngest General in the army. He was with General Buell's army at Shiloh, also in its operations around Corinth and its march through Alabama. Next, he was detailed as a member of the general court-martial for the trial of General Fitz-John Porter, and then ordered to report to General Rosecrans, when he was assigned to the position of Chief of Staff. His military history closed with his brilliant services at Chickamauga, where he won the stars of Major-General.

In the fall of 1862, without any effort on his part, he was elected as a Representative to Congress, from that section of Ohio which had been represented for sixty years mainly by two men—Elisha Whittlesey and Joshua R. Giddings. Again, he was the youngest member of that body, and continued there by successive re-elections, as Representative or Senator, until he was elected President in 1880. During his life in Congress he compiled and published by his speeches, there and elsewhere, more information on the issues of the day, especially on one side, than any other member.

June 8, 1880, at the National Republican Convention held in Chicago, General Garfield was nominated for the Presidency, in preference to the old war-horses, Blaine and Grant; and although many of the Republican party felt sore over the failure of their respective heroes to obtain the nomination, General Garfield was elected by a fair popular majority. He was duly inaugurated, but on July 2 following, before he had fairly got started in his administration, he was fatally shot by a half-demented assassin. After very painful and protracted suffering, he died September 19, 1881, lamented by all the American people. Never before in the history of this country had anything occurred which so nearly froze the blood of the Nation, for the moment, as the awful act of Guiteau, the murderer. He was duly tried, convicted and put to death on the gallows.

The lamented Garfield was succeeded by the Vice-President, General Arthur, who seemed to endeavor to carry out the policy inaugurated by his predecessor.

CHESTER A. ARTHUR.

HESTER ALLEN ARTHUR, the twenty-first Chief Executive of this growing republic, 1881-'5, was born in Franklin County, Vermont, October 5, 1830, the eldest of a family of two sons and five daughters. His father, Rev. Dr. William Arthur, a Baptist clergyman, immigrated to this country from County Antrim, Ireland, in his eighteenth year, and died in 1875, in Newtonville, near Albany, New York, after serving many years as a successful minister. Chester A. was educated at that old, conservative institution, Union College, at Schenectady, New York, where he excelled in all his studies. He graduated there, with honor, and then struck out in life for himself by teaching school for about two years in his native State.

At the expiration of that time young Arthur, with $500 in his purse, went to the city of New York and entered the law office of ex-Judge E. D. Culver as a student. In due time he was admitted to the bar, when he formed a partnership with his intimate friend and old room-mate, Henry D. Gardiner, with the intention of practicing law at some point in the West; but after spending about three months in the Western States, in search of an eligible place, they returned to New York City, leased a room, exhibited a sign of their business and almost immediately enjoyed a paying patronage.

At this stage of his career Mr. Arthur's business prospects were so encouraging that he concluded to take a wife, and accordingly he married the daughter of Lieutenant Herndon, of the United States Navy, who had been lost at sea. To the widow of the latter Congress voted a gold medal, in recognition of the Lieutenant's bravery during the occasion in which he lost his life. Mrs. Arthur died shortly before her husband's nomination to the Vice-Presidency, leaving two children.

Mr. Arthur obtained considerable celebrity as an attorney in the famous Lemmon suit, which was brought to recover possession of eight slaves, who had been declared free by the Superior Court of New York City. The noted Charles O'Conor, who was nominated by the "Straight Democrats" in 1872 for the United States Presidency, was retained by Jonathan G. Lemmon, of Virginia, to recover the negroes, but he lost the suit. In this case, however, Mr. Arthur was assisted by William M. Evarts, now United States Senator. Soon afterward, in 1856, a respectable colored woman was ejected from a street car in New York City. Mr. Arthur sued the car company in her behalf and recovered $500 damages. Immediately afterward all the car companies in the city issued orders to their employes to admit colored persons upon their cars.

Mr. Arthur's political doctrines, as well as his practice as a lawyer, raised him to prominence in the party of freedom; and accordingly he was sent as a delegate to the first National Republican Convention. Soon afterward he was appointed Judge Advocate for the Second Brigade of the State of New York, and then Engineer-in-Chief on Governor Morgan's staff. In 1861, the first year of the war, he was made Inspector-General, and next, Quartermaster-General, in both which offices he rendered great service to the Government. After the close of Governor Morgan's term he resumed the practice of law, forming first a partnership with Mr. Ransom, and subsequently adding Mr. Phelps to the firm. Each of these gentlemen were able lawyers.

November 21, 1872, General Arthur was appointed Collector of the Port of New York by President Grant, and he held the office until July 20, 1878.

The next event of prominence in General Arthur's career was his nomination to the Vice-Presidency of the United States, under the influence of Roscoe Conkling, at the National Republican Convention held at Chicago in June, 1880, when James A. Garfield was placed at the head of the ticket. Both the convention and the campaign that followed were noisy and exciting. The friends of Grant, constituting nearly half the convention, were exceedingly persistent, and were sorely disappointed over their defeat. At the head of the Democratic ticket was placed a very strong and popular man; yet Garfield and Arthur were elected by a respectable plurality of the popular vote. The 4th of March following, these gentlemen were accordingly inaugurated; but within four months the assassin's bullet made a fatal wound in the person of General Garfield, whose life terminated September 19, 1881, when General Arthur, *ex officio*, was obliged to take the chief reins of government. Some misgivings were entertained by many in this event, as Mr. Arthur was thought to represent especially the Grant and Conkling wing of the Republican party; but President Arthur had both the ability and the good sense to allay all fears, and he gave the restless, critical American people as good an administration as they had ever been blessed with. Neither selfishness nor low partisanism ever characterized any feature of his public service. He ever maintained a high sense of every individual right as well as of the Nation's honor. Indeed, he stood so high that his successor, President Cleveland, though of opposing politics, expressed a wish in his inaugural address that he could only satisfy the people with as good an administration.

But the day of civil service reform had come in so far, and the corresponding reaction against "third-termism" had encroached so far even upon "second-term" service, that the Republican party saw fit in 1884 to nominate another man for President. Only by this means was General Arthur's tenure of office closed at Washington. On his retirement from the Presidency, March, 1885, he engaged in the practice of law at New York City, where he died November 18, 1886.

Grover Cleveland

GROVER CLEVELAND, the twenty-second President of the United States, 1885—, was born in Caldwell, Essex County, New Jersey, March 18, 1837. The house in which he was born, a small two-story wooden building, is still standing. It was the parsonage of the Presbyterian church, of which his father, Richard Cleveland, at the time was pastor. The family is of New England origin, and for two centuries has contributed to the professions and to business, men who have reflected honor on the name. Aaron Cleveland, Grover Cleveland's great-great-grandfather, was born in Massachusetts, but subsequently moved to Philadelphia, where he became an intimate friend of Benjamin Franklin, at whose house he died. He left a large family of children, who in time married and settled in different parts of New England. A grandson was one of the small American force that fought the British at Bunker Hill. He served with gallantry throughout the Revolution and was honorably discharged at its close as a Lieutenant in the Continental army. Another grandson, William Cleveland (a son of a second Aaron Cleveland, who was distinguished as a writer and member of the Connecticut Legislature) was Grover Cleveland's grandfather. William Cleveland became a silversmith in Norwich, Connecticut. He acquired by industry some property and sent his son, Richard Cleveland, the father of Grover Cleveland, to Yale College, where he graduated in 1824. During a year spent in teaching at Baltimore, Maryland, after graduation, he met and fell in love with a Miss Annie Neale, daughter of a wealthy Baltimore book publisher, of Irish birth. He was earning his own way in the world at the time and was unable to marry; but in three years he completed a course of preparation for the ministry, secured a church in Windham, Connecticut, and married Annie Neale. Subsequently he moved to Portsmouth, Virginia, where he preached for nearly two years, when he was summoned to Caldwell, New Jersey, where was born Grover Cleveland.

When he was three years old the family moved to Fayetteville, Onondaga County, New York. Here Grover Cleveland lived until he was fourteen years old, the rugged, healthful life of a country boy. His frank, generous manner made him a favorite among his companions, and their respect was won by the good qualities in the germ which his manhood developed. He attended the district school of the village and was for a short time at the academy. His father, however, believed that boys should be taught to labor at an early age, and before he had completed the course of study at the academy he began to work in the village store at $50 for the first year, and the promise of $100 for the second year. His work was well done and the promised increase of pay was granted the second year.

Meanwhile his father and family had moved to Clinton, the seat of Hamilton College, where his father acted as agent to the Presbyterian Board of Home Missions, preaching in the churches of the vicinity. Hither Grover came at his father's request shortly after the beginning of his second year at the Fayetteville store, and resumed his studies at the Clinton Academy. After three years spent in this town, the Rev. Richard Cleveland was called to the village church of Holland Patent. He had preached here only a month when he was suddenly stricken down and died without an hour's warning. The death of the father left the family in straitened circumstances, as Richard Cleveland had spent all his salary of $1,000 per year, which was not required for the necessary expenses of living, upon the education of his children, of whom there were nine, Grover being the fifth. Grover was hoping to enter Hamilton College, but the death of his father made it necessary for him to earn his own livelihood. For the first year (1853-'4) he acted as assistant teacher and bookkeeper in the Institution for the Blind in New York City, of which the late Augustus Schell was for many years the patron. In the winter of 1854 he returned to Holland Patent, where the generous people of that place, Fayetteville and Clinton, had purchased a home for his mother, and in the following spring, borrowing $25, he set out for the West to earn his living.

Reaching Buffalo he paid a hasty visit to an uncle, Lewis F. Allen, a well-known stock farmer, living at Black Rock, a few miles distant. He communicated his plans to Mr. Allen, who discouraged the idea of the West, and finally induced the enthusiastic boy of seventeen to remain with him and help him prepare a catalogue of blooded short-horn cattle, known as " Allen's American Herd Book," a publication familiar to all breeders of cattle. In August, 1855, he entered the law office of Rogers, Bowen & Rogers, at Buffalo, and after serving a few months without pay, was paid $4 a week—an amount barely sufficient to meet the necessary expenses of his board in the family of a fellow-student in Buffalo, with whom he took lodgings. Life at this time with Grover Cleveland was a stern battle with the world. He took his breakfast by candle-light with the drovers, and went at once to the office where the whole day was spent in work and study. Usually he returned again at night to resume reading which had been interrupted by the duties of the day. Gradually his employers came to recognize the ability, trustworthiness and capacity for hard work in their young employe, and by the time he was admitted to the bar (1859) he stood high in their confidence. A year later he was made confidential and managing clerk, and in the course of three years more his salary had been raised to $1,000. In 1863 he was appointed assistant district attorney of Erie County by the district attorney, the Hon. C. C. Torrance.

Since his first vote had been cast in 1858 he had been a staunch Democrat, and until he was chosen Governor he always made it his duty, rain or shine, to stand at the polls and give out ballots to Democratic voters. During the first year of his term as assistant district attorney, the Democrats desired especially to carry the Board of Supervisors. The old Second Ward in which he lived was Republican ordinarily by 250 majority, but at the urgent request of the party Grover Cleveland consented to be the Democratic candidate for Supervisor, and came within thirteen votes of an election. The three years spent in the district attorney's office were devoted to assiduous labor and the extension of his professional attainments. He then formed a law partnership with the late Isaac V. Vanderpoel, ex-State Treasurer, under the firm name of Vanderpoel & Cleveland. Here the bulk of the work devolved on Cleveland's shoulders, and he soon won a good standing at the bar of Erie County. In 1869 Mr. Cleveland formed a partnership with ex-Senator A. P. Laning and ex-Assistant United States District Attorney Oscar Folsom, under the firm name of Laning, Cleveland & Folsom. During these years he began to earn a moderate professional income; but the larger portion of it was sent to his mother and sisters at Holland Patent to whose support he had contributed ever since 1860. He served as sheriff of Erie County, 1870–'4, and then resumed the practice of law, associating himself with the Hon. Lyman K. Bass and Wilson S. Bissell.

The firm was strong and popular, and soon commanded a large and lucrative practice. Ill health forced the retirement of Mr. Bass in 1879, and the firm became Cleveland & Bissell. In 1881 Mr. George J. Sicard was added to the firm.

In the autumn election of 1881 he was elected mayor of Buffalo by a majority of over 3,500—the largest majority ever given a candidate for mayor—and the Democratic city ticket was successful, although the Republicans carried Buffalo by over 1,000 majority for their State ticket. Grover Cleveland's administration as mayor fully justified the confidence reposed in him by the people of Buffalo, evidenced by the great vote he received.

The Democratic State Convention met at Syracuse, September 22, 1882, and nominated Grover Cleveland for Governor on the third ballot and Cleveland was elected by 192,000 majority. In the fall of 1884 he was elected President of the United States by about 1,000 popular majority, in New York State, and he was accordingly inaugurated the 4th of March following.

BENJAMIN HARRISON.

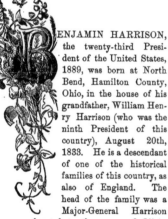

ENJAMIN HARRISON, the twenty-third President of the United States, 1889, was born at North Bend, Hamilton County, Ohio, in the house of his grandfather, William Henry Harrison (who was the ninth President of this country), August 20th, 1833. He is a descendant of one of the historical families of this country, as also of England. The head of the family was a Major-General Harrison who was devoted to the cause of Oliver Cromwell. It became the duty of this Harrison to participate in the trial of Charles I. and afterward to sign the death warrant of the king, which subsequently cost him his life. His enemies succeeding to power, he was condemned and executed October 13th, 1660. His descendants came to America, and the first mention made in history of the Harrison family as representative in public affairs, is that of Benjamin Harrison, great-grandfather of our present President, who was a member of the Continental Congress, 1774–5–6, and one of the original signers of the Declaration of Independence, and three times Governor of Virginia. His son, William Henry Harrison, made a brilliant military record, was Governor of the Northwest Territory, and the ninth President of the United States.

The subject of this sketch at an early age became a student at Farmers College, where he remained two years, at the end of which time he entered Miami University, at Oxford, Ohio. Upon graduation from said seat of learning he entered, as a student, the office of Stover & Gwyne, a notable law firm at Cincinnati, Ohio, where he applied himself closely to the study of his chosen profession, and here laid the foundation for the honorable and famous career before him. He spent two years with the firm in Cincinnati, at the expiration of which time he received the only inheritance of his life, which was a lot left him by an aunt, which he sold for $800. This sum he deemed sufficient to justify him in marrying the lady of his choice, and to whom he was then engaged, a daughter of Dr. Scott, then Principal of a female school at Oxford, Ohio.

After marriage he located at Indianapolis, Indiana, where he began the practice of law. Meeting with slight encouragement he made but little the first year, but applied himself

Benj. Harrison

closely to his business, and by perseverance, honorable dealing and an upright life, succeeded in building up an extensive practice and took a leading position in the legal profession.

In 1860 he was nominated for the position of Supreme Court Reporter for the State of Indiana, and then began his experience as a stump speaker. He canvassed the State thoroughly and was elected.

In 1862 his patriotism caused him to abandon a civil office and to offer his country his services in a military capacity. He organized the Seventieth Indiana Infantry and was chosen its Colonel. Although his regiment was composed of raw material, and he practically void of military schooling, he at once mastered military tactics and drilled his men, so that when he with his regiment was assigned to Gen. Sherman's command it was known as one of the best drilled organizations of the army. He was especially distinguished for bravery at the battles of Resacca and Peach Tree Creek. For his bravery and efficiency at the last named battle he was made a Brigadier-General, General Hooker speaking of him in the most complimentary terms.

While General Harrison was actively engaged in the field the Supreme Court declared the office of Supreme Court Reporter vacant, and another person was elected to fill the position. From the time of leaving Indiana with his regiment for the front, until the fall of 1864, General Harrison had taken no leave of absence. But having been nominated that year for the same office that he vacated in order to serve his country where he could do the greatest good, he got a thirty-day leave of absence, and during that time canvassed the State and was elected for another term as Supreme Court Reporter. He then started to rejoin his command, then with General Sherman in the South, but was stricken down with fever and after a very trying siege, made his way to the front, and participated in the closing scenes and incidents of the war.

In 1868 General Harrison declined a reelection as Reporter, and applied himself to the practice of his profession. He was a candidate for Governor of Indiana on the Republican ticket in 1876. Although defeated, the brilliant campaign brought him to public notice and gave him a National reputation as an able and formidable debater and he was much sought in the Eastern States as a public speaker. He took an active part in the Presidential campaign of 1880, and was elected to the United States Senate, where he served six years, and was known as one of the strongest debaters, as well as one of the ablest men and best lawyers. When his term expired in the Senate he resumed his law practice at Indianapolis, becoming the head of one of the strongest law firms in the State of Indiana.

Sometime prior to the opening of the Presidential campaign of 1888, the two great political parties (Republican and Democratic) drew the line of political battle on the question of tariff, which became the leading issue and the rallying watchword during the memorable campaign. The Republicans appealed to the people for their voice as to a tariff to protect home industries, while the Democrats wanted a tariff for revenue only. The Republican convention assembled in Chicago in June and selected Mr. Harrison as their standard bearer on a platform of principles, among other important clauses being that of protection, which he cordially indorsed in accepting the nomination. November 6, 1888, after a heated canvass, General Harrison was elected, defeating Grover Cleveland, who was again the nominee of the Democratic party. He was inaugurated and assumed the duties of his office March 4, 1889.

HISTORY

OF

◁MINNESOTA.▷

HISTORY OF MINNESOTA.

CHAPTER I.

LOCATION, TOPOGRAPHY AND GENERAL REMARKS.

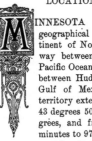

MINNESOTA is located in the geographical center of the continent of North America — midway between the Atlantic and Pacific Oceans, and also midway between Hudson's Bay and the Gulf of Mexico. It embraces territory extending from latitude 43 degrees 50 minutes, to 49 degrees, and from 89 degrees 29 minutes to 97 degrees 5 minutes west longitude. As to its area, it can only be estimated, as portions of the State are as yet unsurveyed; but as near as can be arrived at, the area is 85,531 square miles, or about 53,760,000 acres. In size Minnesota is the fourth State in the Union. From its southern boundary to the northern is about 400 miles, and from the most eastern to the extreme western point about 354 miles. In altitude it appears to be one of the highest portions of the continent, as the headwaters of the three great river systems are found in its limits — those of streams flowing northward to Hudson's Bay; eastward to the Atlantic Ocean, and southward to the Gulf of Mexico.

Nearly three-quarters of the surface of the State is made up of rolling prairie, interspersed with frequent groves, oak openings and belts of hardwood timber, watered by numerous lakes and streams, and covered with a warm, dark soil of great fertility. The balance, embracing the elevated district immediately west of Lake Superior, consists mainly of the rich mineral ranges on its shores, and of the pine forests which extend over the upper Mississippi country, affording extensive supplies of timber. But a very small portion is broken, rocky or worthless land; nearly all is arable. But few States are so well watered as Minnesota, and the numerous rivers and water-courses give excellent drainage. A number of the rivers — the Mississippi, the Minnesota, the St. Croix, the St. Louis, the Red and the Red Lake rivers — are navigable, and nearly all of the balance afford water power. The lakes of Minnesota are among its principal physical characteristics. The estimate of 10,000 lakes in the State is not an unreasonable one.

With all these natural advantages, favorable climate and rich soil, Minnesota has become one of the most successful agricultural States in the Union, and stock-raising and dairying is rapidly becoming a leading industry. Lumbering is also carried on very extensively, and the manufacturing branch is rapidly becoming large. While at first it was supposed that this State was destitute of valuable minerals, recent discoveries prove to the contrary. Inexhaustible supplies of the best iron ore exist, and are now being mined and exported in large quantities. Silver veins have also been found near the boundary line; copper ore has also been found, and it is known that plumbago and gold quartz exist. Building material, granite, brownstone, limestone, sandstone and brick and potter's clay are abundant.

A few words as to railroads and history relating to their construction will also be interesting. Twenty-five years ago (1862), there were only ten miles of railway in operation in the State. At the close of 1885 there were 6,721 miles in operation. The general government has granted to railroads within this State 12,151,527 acres of land, and the State has given 1,811,750 acres of swamp and other lands, making a total of 13,933,277 acres of land within the State given to railroads, valued on the average at $5 per acre, making $69,666,385 thus given. In addition, local, county and State bonds have been given them amounting to over $6,680,000, making in lands and cash a total gift of $76,496,385, or about $19,345 for every mile completed. There is material in these facts for an extended political essay, and they certainly furnish food for thought.

In concluding these general remarks it may justly be said that the outlook for the State is most gratifying. Its population is rapidly increasing, and its taxable wealth increasing in similar ratio. Every year sees an enormous area of its rich soil brought under cultivation, while there are still millions of acres awaiting the plow of the settler.

The following table of census returns will show the growth of the State as to population: 1850, population 6,077; 1860, population 172,023; 1865, population 250,099; 1870, population 439,706; 1875, population 597,407; 1880, population 780,773, and in 1885 the population was 1,117,798.

CHAPTER II.

HISTORY OF MINNESOTA—FROM 1660 TO 1887.

THE first exploration by whites of the territory which now comprises the State of Minnesota dates back early into the seventeenth century. It is claimed by good authority that Jean Nicolet (pronounced Nicolay), one of Champlain's interpreters, was the first to spread knowledge of the country west of Lake Michigan. As early as 1635 he set foot upon the western shores of Lake Michigan, and traded near Green Bay, also roaming over various portions of Wisconsin at about that time. In December of the same year he returned to Canada. It is very doubtful whether Nicolet ever set foot on Minnesota soil, although it is certain that his visit to the country west of Lake Michigan. was the means of spreading knowledge of this country, and of the aborigines of Minnesota. It was said of him that he penetrated far distant countries, and in a letter bearing date of 1640, it is stated that "if he had proceeded three days more on a river which flows from that lake (Green Bay), he would have found the sea." The death of this explorer occurred at Three Rivers in 1640.

After Nicolet's visit to Wisconsin, for a quarter of a century history brings no trace of any explorations concerning this region. At the end of this time, in 1660, the first white men of whom there is any reliable record, set foot on Minnesota soil. They were Medard Chouart, called Grosselliers, and Pierre d'Esprit, who was known as Sieur Radisson. Both were Frenchmen who had come to Canada when young men to engage in the fur trade. About the middle of that century several important changes had been made in the location of Indian tribes. The Hurons and their allies, the Ottawas, after successive battles, had drifted to the west of Lake Michigan. In former times they had been located in the St. Lawrence region. Finally reaching the Mississippi they found the Iowa River. Later, returning to the Mississippi, they settled upon an island in the river near where the city of Hastings is now located; but becoming involved in battles with the Sioux, we finally find the Hurons located about the headwaters of the Chippeway, and the Ottawas on the shores of Lake Superior, near where Bayfield is now situated. It was to trade with the Indians that the two Frenchmen mentioned, Grosselliers and Radisson, made their trip to this wild region. They passed the winter of 1659–60 among the Sioux villages in the Mille Lacs country, and the following spring and summer was spent in the region of Lake Superior. In August, 1660, they returned to Montreal, and their report of the country they had visited created much excitement. Within a few weeks an exploring and trading party was formed, and accompanied by six Frenchmen and two priests, one of whom was the Jesuit, Rene Menard, they again started westward, and on the 15th of October, 1660, they reached the Ottawa settlement on the shores of Lake Superior. The objects of this party were various, some bent on exploration, others on trading, while Father Menard went as a missionary. Grosselliers (pronounced Grosay-ya) and Radisson, accompanied by others, pushed on through the country to the northwest of Lake Superior and at length reached Hudson's Bay. They returned to Montreal in May, 1662. The names of all the members of this party have not been preserved. Groselliers and Radisson proceeded to Paris, thence to London, where they were well received by the nobility and scientific men. A vessel was fitted out and placed at their disposal, in the hope of finding a northwest passage to Asia. In June, 1668, they left England and made an extended voyage, reaching a tributary of Hudson's Bay and returning to England, where, in 1670, the famous trading corporation, the "Hudson's Bay Company," was chartered.

Now to return to the venerable Father Menard, who had been left among the Ottawa Indians on the shores of Lake Superior in October, 1660. For nearly a year he lived there in a cabin built of fir branches. In the summer of 1661 he decided to visit the Hurons, who had fled eastward from the Sioux of Minnesota and were located among the woods of northern Wisconsin, as stated. He was accompanied by one Frenchman, whose name has been lost in the mist of years. They became separated, and Father Menard was lost, as Perrot says, "in the labyrinth of trees." This was the last ever positively known of him, although his breviary and cassock were said afterward to have been found among the Sioux Indians. Whether this good and venerable man starved or was murdered or captured by the Indians will forever be shrouded in mystery.

These were the earliest explorations of the Northwest of which any record has been left, but after that period this region was visited by various parties at long intervals, and many interesting documents have been preserved giving accounts of their journeys and discoveries.

About the year 1665 several French trad-

ers and the Jesuit, Allouez, visited the country off the western shore of Lake Superior. Early in 1679 we find Daniel G. Du Luth west of Lake Michigan, and it is believed he planted the French arms on Minnesota soil. His records state that "on July 2d he caused his Majesty's arms to be planted in the great village of the Nadousioux, called Kathio, and at Songaskicous and Houetbatons, one hundred and twenty leagues distant from the former." Rev. E. D. Neill in his thorough work relating to early explorers of Minnesota, locates this as being "one hundred and twenty leagues beyond Mille Lacs." Du Luth states that at one point on Minnesota soil he found upon a tree this legend: "Arms of the King cut on this tree in the year 1679." He established several posts, carried on trading with the Indians, and was probably the most prominent of the early explorers. Later he was stationed near Lake Erie and died in 1710. His reports furnish much interesting information regarding the early explorations in the Northwest.

La Salle was given a commission by the King of France in 1678 to "explore the West," and do limited trading. He visited various parts of the Northwest. His jealousy of Du Luth appears to form a considerable portion of his official reports, but it is stated on good authority that he wrote the first description of the upper Mississippi Valley, August 22, 1682, some months before the publication of Father Hennepin's first work, "Description de la Louisiane." He must, however, have obtained his information from one of Hennepin's men.

Father Louis Hennepin's explorations and adventures through the Northwest form an interesting chapter in the earlier history of this region. He was a native of Ath, an inland town of the Netherlands, and had early assumed the robes of priesthood. In 1676 he came to Canada, and two years later was ordered to join the La Salle exploring expedition. A ship was rigged, and on August 7th, 1679, its sails caught the breezes of Lake Erie — the first European vessel launched on the great lakes. La Salle conducted his expedition to Green Bay, thence along the coast of Lake Michigan, and about the middle of January, 1680, landed it on an eminence near Lake Peoria, on the Illinois River, where he commenced the erection of Fort Crevecœur. On the last of February of the same year, Father Hennepin, in company with Michael Accault (Ako) and Angelle, left the fort to ascend the Mississippi River. On the 11th of April, 1680, after having reached a point north of the Chippewa River, they were met and taken charge of by a party of over a hundred Sioux Indians. They then proceeded with the Indians to their villages, nearly sixty leagues north of St. Anthony falls. They remained with the Indians some time, being well treated, and on the 25th of July, 1680, they were met by Du Luth, who was accompanied by his interpreter, Faffart, and several French soldiers. They then proceeded to Mille Lacs, arriving, according to Father's Hennepin writings, on the 11th of August, 1680. In the latter part of September they started to return to the French settlement, passing by St. Anthony falls. Father Hennepin published two works relating to his discoveries, the first, "Description de la Louisiane," in 1836; the second, "The New Discovery," in 1697. These works called forth much criticism, as there can be no doubt Hennepin greatly magnified his own importance, and exaggerated his services and discoveries. For instance, he claims to have descended the Mississippi River to the Gulf of Mexico, before proceeding northward, then returned and proceeded on to the St. Anthony falls. This in the face of his own stated facts — leaving Fort Crevecœur the last of February, he claims to have made this wonderful trip, and arrived two miles south of where the city of St. Paul is now located, late in April, giving the 11th of April as the date of their capture by the Indians. However this may be, Father Hennepin's work was not in vain, and his memory is entitled to the credit for that which he did. His publications hastened and facilitated exploration, and his failing — if such it was — should be treated with charity. La Salle speaks of him highly, but charitably says, "it was his failing to magnify those adventures which concerned him."

During 1684, Nicholas Perrot and Le Sueur visited Lake Pepin, and the following winter the French traded with the Indians on Minnesota soil. Perrot had been appointed by the governor of Canada as the commandant for the West, and was accompanied by twenty men. Upon his arrival he caused a stockade to be built on the east bank of Lake Pepin, which bore his name for many years. He discovered a number of lead mines, and his name figures conspicuously in the history of the early French explorations and frontier work. Perrot remained for some time after building the fort, then, in 1686, returned to Green Bay. He passed much time in collecting allies for the expedition against the Iroquois in New York, and in the spring of 1687, was with Du Luth and Tonty with the French and Indian allies in the expedition against the Senecas of the Genesee Valley in New York. The following year he was sent with a company of Frenchmen to reoccupy the post on Lake Pepin, in Minnesota, and it was in 1689 that Perrot, in the presence of Father Joseph James Marest, a Jesuit, Boisguiblot, a trader on the Wisconsin and Mississippi, and Le Seur, made a formal record of taking possession of the Sioux country in the name of the King of France.

Le Sueur, who accompanied Perrot in his first trip to Lake Pepin in 1684, was intimately connected with that explorer's movements. In 1692 Le Sueur was sent by Gov. Frontenac, of Canada, to the extremity of Lake Superior to maintain peace between the Indian tribes. Entering the Sioux country, in 1694, he established a post upon a prairie island, nine miles below where Hastings is now located. He was accompanied by Penicaut and others. Here they established a fort and storehouse and passed the winter, as game was very abundant. On July 15, 1695, Le Sueur went back to Montreal accompanied by a party of Ojibways, and the first Dakotah brave that ever visited Canada. Le Sueur then visited France, and in 1697 received a license to open certain mines that were supposed to exist in Minnesota. The ship in which he was returning was captured by the English, and he was taken to England; when released he returned to France and secured a new commission, but it was afterward suspended. Fortunately, D'Ilberville, a kinsman of Le Sueur, was appointed governor of the new territory of Louisiana, and in December, 1699, Le Sueur arrived from France with thirty workmen to proceed to the mines. During the next year he ascended the Minnesota River with his expedition, and in October, 1700, built a fort on the Blue Earth River, which he named L'Huillier. This was occupied by Le Sueur's men until 1702, when it was abandoned because of the hostility of the Indians. Charlevoix, who visited the valley of the lower Mississippi in 1722, says that "Le Sueur spent at least one winter in his fort on the banks of the Blue Earth, and that in the following April he went up to the mine, *about a mile above*, and in twenty-two days they obtained more than 30,000 pounds of the substance—lead." Le Sueur estimated the Sioux Indians at that time as being four thousand families.

In 1703 a little volume was published in France and England by Baron La Hontan, giving an account of his "travels," in which he claimed to have penetrated and pursued explorations through the territory which now forms Minnesota, farther than any of his predecessors. He states that he found a river tributary to the Mississippi, and describes a journey of 500 miles up this stream, which he named Long River. His wonderful story was believed at the time and the river was placed upon the early maps; but in later years it was discredited and is now by the closest students and ablest historians treated as fabulous.

In September, 1727, Fort Beauharnois was erected and a French post established on the shores of Lake Pepin, under the directions of Sieur de la Perriere. An extensive trade was carried on with the Indians here, and it was occupied for a number of years. In 1728 Veranderie, who had been placed in command of a post on Lake Nepigon, began laying plans for finding a communication with the Pacific Ocean. An expedition was fitted out which left Montreal in 1731, under the management of his sons and a nephew, De la Jemeraye, he not joining the party until 1733. A fourth son joined the expedition in 1735. In the autumn of 1731, the party reached Rainy Lake, at the foot of which a post, called Fort St. Pierre, was erected. The next year they reached Lake of the Woods, and established Fort St. Charles on its southwest bank. A few miles from Lake Winnepeg they established a post on the Assinaboine, and a fort was established on the Maurepas (Winnepeg) River. In June, 1736, while twenty-one of the expedition were encamped on an isle in the Lake of the Woods, they were surprised by a band of Sioux Indians hostile to the French allies, and all were killed. The island on this account is called Massacre Island. The remaining portion of the expedition progressed as best they could. October 3, 1738, they built an advanced post called Fort la Reine on the Assinaboine River.

They came in sight of the Rocky Mountains on the 1st of January, 1743, and, on the 12th, ascended them. In 1744, after planting a leaden plate of the arms of France in the upper Missouri country, they returned, reaching Minnesota soil late in June, and after establishing several posts in the extreme northern frontier country they finally returned to Montreal. Expeditions were afterward fitted out, one of which again reached the Rocky Mountains, but the clash of arms between France and England put an end to the explorations so far as the French were concerned.

In 1763, by the treaty of Versailles, France ceded Minnesota east of the Mississippi to England and west of it to Spain. In 1766 Capt. Jonathan Carver, the first British subject, although a native of Connecticut, visited the Falls of St. Anthony. He spent some three years among the different tribes of Indians in the upper Mississippi country; found the Indian nations at war and succeeded in making peace between them. As a reward for his good offices, it is claimed that two chiefs of the Sioux, acting for their nation, at a council held with Carver at a great cave, now within the corporate limits of St. Paul, deeded to Carver a vast tract of land on the Mississippi River, extending from the Falls of St. Anthony to the foot of Lake Pepin, on the Mississippi, thence east one hundred miles; thence north one hundred and twenty miles; thence west to the place of beginning. This pretended grant, however, was examined by our government and totally ignored.

At the beginning of the present century there were no white men in Minnesota, except the few engaged in the fur trade, and the posts were chiefly held by the Northwest Company, which corporation in 1794 erected a stockade at Sandy Lake. In 1802 we find William Morrison trading at Leech Lake, and two years later at Itasca. In the meantime,

in 1796, the laws of the ordinance of 1787 had been extended over the Northwest, and on May 7, 1800, that part of Minnesota east of the Mississippi had become a part of Indiana by the division of Ohio. On the 20th of December, 1803, that part of Minnesota west of the Mississippi, for forty years in the possession of Spain as a part of Louisiana, was ceded to the United States by Napoleon Bonaparte, who had just obtained it from Spain. In 1804 Upper Louisiana Territory was constituted. During the following year the United States for the first time sent an officer to Minnesota, in the person of Lieut. Z. M. Pike, who established government relations and obtained the Fort Snelling reservation from the Dakotahs. He remained here for some time, but the war of 1812 coming on postponed the military occupation of the upper Mississippi by the United States for several years. Pike afterward fell in battle at York, in Upper Canada.

In 1817 the Earl of Selkirk, a nobleman, visited the Scotch colony on the Red River, established in 1812, and created quite an excitement on the part of some of the United States authorities. The same year Mayor Stephen H. Long, of the United States Engineer Corps, visited Minnesota and made a report recommending the bluff at the junction of the Minnesota and Mississippi rivers as a site for a fort.

In 1819 Minnesota east of the Mississippi River became a part of Crawford County, Mich. During the same year Fort Snelling was established and the site of Mendota was occupied by the United States troops, under Col. Leavenworth. Major Taliaferro was appointed Indian agent.

During the year 1820 much of interest transpired on Minnesota soil. Early in the spring Jean Baptiste Faribault brought Leavenworth's horses from Prairie du Chien. On the 5th of May Col. Leavenworth established summer quarters at Camp Coldwater,

(Hennepin County). In July Gov. Cass, of Michigan, visited the camps. In August Col. Joshia Snelling succeeded Leavenworth in command, and on the 20th of September the corner-stone of Fort Snelling (then Fort St. Anthony) was laid. On the 15th of April the superintendent of farming for Earl Selkirk left Prairie du Chien, having purchased seed wheat; he ascended the Minnesota River to Big Stone Lake, where the boats were placed on rollers, dragged a short distance to Lake Traverse, and reached Pembina June 3. This year the first marriage in Minnesota occurred, Lieut. Green to a daughter of Capt. Gooding. The first birth of a white child in the State occurred this year, a daughter to Col. Snelling; died the following year.

In 1821 Fort St. Anthony (Snelling) was sufficiently completed to be occupied by troops. During this year a sawmill was constructed at St. Anthony Falls for the use of the garrison under the supervision of Lieut. McCabe.

Nothing of particular interest transpired during 1822. In 1823, however, the first steamboat, the Virginia, arrived at the mouth of the Minnesota River on the 10th of May, and created consternation among the Indians. Beltrami, the Italian, during the same year explored the northernmost sources of the Mississippi, and Maj. Long, of the United States army, visited the northern boundary by way of the Minnesota and Red rivers. Millstones for grinding flour were sent to St. Anthony to be placed in the sawmill.

In 1824 Gen. Winfield Scott visited Fort St. Anthony, and at his suggestion the name was changed to Fort Snelling.

After this time events crowd rapidly one after the other to fill in the time. From 1825 on, the arrival of steamboats became more frequent. During this year a heavy flood visited the Red River, and a portion of the colony were driven to Minnesota and settled near Fort Snelling.

In 1832 Schoolcraft explored the sources of the Mississippi River, and during the following year Rev. W. T. Boutwell established the first mission among the Ojibways on Leech Lake. About the same time E. F. Ely opened a mission school at Atkins, a trading post on Sandy Lake.

That portion of Minnesota lying west of the Mississippi River was attached to Michigan in 1834. During this year Gen. H. H. Sibley settled at Mendota as agent for the fur company, and Samuel W. and Gideon H. Pond, missionaries among the Sioux, arrived. They were followed the next year by T. S. Williamson, J. D. Stevens and Alexander G. Huggins, and in June, 1835, a Presbyterian Church was organized at Fort Snelling. Late the same year Maj. J. L. Bean, in accordance with the treaty of 1825, surveyed the Sioux and Chippeway boundary line as far as Otter Tail Lake.

In 1836 the Territory of Wisconsin was organized, embracing all of Minnesota east of the Mississippi River; that territory west of the river being attached to Iowa. A number of steamboats arrived during this year, a passenger on one of them being the distinguished French astronomer, Jean N. Nicollet.

In 1837 Gov. Dodge, of Wisconsin, made a treaty at Fort Snelling with the Ojibways, by which the latter ceded all their pine lands on the St. Croix and its tributaries; a treaty was also effected at Washington with a deputation of Dakotahs for their pine lands east of the Mississippi. These treaties led the way to the first actual settlements in the State. The treaty was ratified by Congress in 1838. At about this time Franklin Steele made a claim at St. Anthony Falls; Pierre Parrant took a claim and built a cabin on the present site of St. Paul; Jeremiah Russell and L. W. Stratton made the first claim at Marine in the St. Croix Valley. During the year 1838 a steamboat arrived at Fort Snelling with J. N. Nicollet and J. C.

Fremont on a scientific expedition. Development begins in the St. Croix Valley. The next year the chapel of "St. Paul" was built and consecrated, giving the name to the capital of the State.

Henry M. Rice arrived at Fort Snelling in 1840, others came and in November, 1841, St. Croix County was established with "Dakotah" designated as the county-seat.

On the 10th of October, 1843, a settlement was commenced on the present site of the city of Stillwater, and the erection of a saw-mill was immediately commenced. The names of the town proprietors were: John McKusick, from Maine; Calvin Leach, from Vermont; Elam Greeley, from Maine and Elias McKeane, from Pennsylvania.

Dr. E. D. Neill in his " Explorers and Pioneers of Minnesota," says that in 1846 "the site of St. Paul was chiefly occupied by a few shanties, owned by ' certain lewd fellows of the baser sort,' who sold rum to the soldiers and Indians." On the 6th of August, 1846, the Wisconsin enabling act was passed.

In 1847 St. Croix County was detached from Crawford County, Wis., and reorganized for civil and judicial purposes with Stillwater as the county-seat. The town of St. Paul was surveyed and platted, and recorded in St. Croix County. During this year the Wisconsin constitutional convention was held.

On the 29th of May, 1848, Wisconsin was admitted to the Union, leaving Minnesota (with its present boundaries) without a government, and on the 26th of the following August a convention was held at Stillwater to take measures for a separate territorial organization. On the 30th of October, 1848, Henry H. Sibley was elected delegate to Congress, and he was admitted to a seat January 15, 1849. March 3d, 1849, a bill was passed organizing Minnesota Territory, and on the 19th of the same month territorial officers were appointed. June 1st Gov. Ramsey issued a proclamation declaring the territory organized, and on September 3d the first territorial Legislature assembled. In 1851 the capital of the State was permanently located, as was also the penitentiary. In June, 1854, the first line of railway was completed to St. Paul.

On the 23d of February, 1857, an act passed the United States Senate, to authorize the people of Minnesota to form a constitution, preparatory to their admission to the Union. In June a constitutional convention was held, and the State constitution was framed. This was adopted on the 13th of October, 1857, and a full list of State officers was elected. On the 11th of May, 1858, the President approved of the bill admitting the State, and Minnesota was fully recognized as one of the United States of America. The first State officers were sworn in on the 24th of May.

From this time on we can only briefly review the most important events that have transpired. A great tide of immigration had set in early in the "fifties," which rapidly filled up portions of the State, until in 1857 a census gave the State a total population of 150,037. During that year, however, real estate speculation reached a climax, and the terrible financial panic occurred which greatly retarded the settlement.

In 1858 the State loan of $250,000 was negotiated; five million loan bill was passed, being voted on April 15; great stringency in money market.

During 1859 the hard times continued to intensify. "Wright County War" occurred; "Glencoe" and "Owatonna" money was issued; work on the land grant roads ceased; collapse of the five million scheme; first export of grain that fall; hard political struggle, in which the Republicans triumphed.

Another warm political-canvass occurred in 1860; the census taken this year gave the State a total population of 172,123.

In 1861 war cast its gloom over the country; on April 13th the President's proclamation for troops was received; the first regiment recruited at once, and June 22d it embarked at Fort Snelling for the seat of war.

In 1862 occurred the memorable Sioux outbreak; August 17th, massacre at Acton; August 18th, outbreak at Lower Sioux Agency; 19th, New Ulm attacked; 20th, Fort Ridgely attacked; 25th, second attack on New Ulm; 30th, Fort Abercrombie besieged; September 1st, the bloody affair at Birch Coolie; 19th, first railroad in Minnesota in operation, between St. Paul and Minneapolis; 22d, battle of Wood Lake; 26th, captives surrendered by the Indians at Camp Release; military commission tried 321 Indians for murder, 303 condemned to die; December 26th, thirty-eight hung at Mankato.

In 1863 Gen. Sibley conducted an expedition to the Missouri River; July 3d; Little Crow was killed; July 24th, battle of Big Mound; 26th, battle of Dead Buffalo Lake; July 28th, battle of Stony Lake.

In 1864 the civil war was still in progress, and large levies for troops were made in Minnesota; expedition to Missouri River, under Sully; inflation of money market; occasional Indian raids.

In 1865 the war closed and peace returns; Minnesota regiments return and are disbanded; in all, 25,052 troops were furnished by the State; census showed 250,000 inhabitants.

After the close of the war, and from 1866 until 1872, "good times" prevailed; immigration was very heavy, and real estate and all values were inflated. The western portion of the State received many settlers. Railway construction was very active.

In 1873 the famous grasshopper raid began throughout the western part of the State, and continued about five seasons. January 7–8–9 of this year, a terrible storm swept over the State, in which seventy persons perished. In September of the same year, the financial "panic of 1873" began.

In 1874 and 1875 nothing of especial importance occurred.

On the 7th of September, 1876, an attack was made on the Bank of Northfield by a gang of armed outlaws from Missouri; three of the latter were killed, and three were captured.

In 1877 biennial sessions amendment was adopted.

In 1878 (May 2), three flouring mills at Minneapolis exploded, and eighteen lives lost.

On November 15th, 1880, a portion of the hospital for the insane, at St. Peter, was destroyed by fire; eighteen inmates were burned to death, seven died subsequently of injuries and fright, and six were missing. Total loss was $150,000.

In 1881 the State capitol at St. Paul was destroyed by fire.

In 1884 the State prison, located at Stillwater, was partly burned.

In 1886 (April 14), a cyclone swept over St. Cloud and Sauk Rapids, demolishing scores of buildings, and killing about seventy people.

CHAPTER III.

THE INDIAN MASSACRE.

THE outbreak of the Indians in 1862 furnishes one of the most interesting chapters in Minnesota's history. At the time of this sad tragedy there were scattered throughout the State various bands of Sioux Indians, a powerful and warlike nation. They included the Medawakontons (or Village of the Spirit Lake); Wapatons, (or Village of the Leaves); Sissetons (or Village of the Marsh), and Wapakutas (or Leaf Shooters). These four tribes, numbering about six thousand and·two hundred persons, comprised the entire annuity Sioux of Minnesota. All these Indians had from time to time, from the 19th of July, 1815, to the date of the massacre in 1862, received presents from the government, by virtue of various treaties of amity and friendship. From the time of the treaty of St. Louis in 1816, these tribes had remained friendly to the whites, and had by treaty stipulations parted with all the lands to which they claimed title in Iowa; all on the east side of the Mississippi River, and all on the Minnesota River in Minnesota, except certain reservations. One of these reservations lay upon both sides of the Minnesota ten miles on either side of that stream, from Hawk River on the north to Yellow Medicine River on the south side, thence westerly to the head of Big Stone Lake and Lake Traverse, a distance of about one hundred miles. Another of these reservations commenced at Little Rock River on the east and a line running due south from its mouth, and extending up the river westerly to the eastern line of the reserva-

tion first named, at the Hawk and Yellow Medicine rivers. The last also had a width of ten miles on each side of the Minnesota River.

Early in 1858 a scheme was devised by the authorities at Washington for the civilization of these annuity Indians. A civilization fund was provided, to be taken from their annuities and expended in improving the lands of such as should abandon their tribal relations and adopt the habits and modes of life of the whites. To all such, lands were assigned in severalty, eighty acres to the head of each family, on which should be erected the necessary farm buildings, and farming implements and cattle furnished him. At the time of the outbreak about one hundred and seventy-five Indians had taken advantage of the provisions of this treaty and become "farmer Indians." A great majority of the Indians, however, disliked the idea of taking any portion of their general fund to carry out the civilization scheme. Those who retained the blanket, called "blanket Indians," denounced the measure as a fraud, as it was slowly but surely destroying what was, to them, their God-given right to the chase. The result, in brief, of this civilization scheme was this: After the chase was over the "blanket Indians" would pitch their tents about the homes of the "farmer Indians" and proceed to eat them out of house and home, and when the ruin was complete, the "farmer" with his wife and children, driven by necessity, would again seek temporary subsistence in the chase. During their absence the "blanket Indians" would commit whatever destruction of fences or tenements their desires or necessities would suggest. In this way the annual process continued, so that when the "farmer Indian" returned to his desolate home in the spring to prepare again for a crop, he looked forward to no different results for the coming winter. It will thus be seen that the civilization scheme was an utter failure.

The treaty referred to, of 1858, had opened for settlement a vast frontier country of the most attractive character in the valley of the Minnesota River, and on the streams putting into the Minnesota on either side, such as Beaver Creek, Sacred Heart, Hawk and Chippewa rivers, and some other small streams, there were flourishing settlements of white families. Within this ceded tract, ten miles wide, were the scattered settlements of Birch Coolie, Patterson Rapids, and others as far up as the upper agency at Yellow Medicine, in Renville County. The county of Brown adjoined the reservation, and was at that time settled mostly by Germans. Here was also the flourishing town of New Ulm, and further on was a thriving settlement on the Big Cottonwood and Watonwan. Other counties, Blue Earth, Nicollet, Sibley, Meeker, McLeod, Kandiyohi, Monongalia and Murray, together with others somewhat removed from the direct attack of the Indians, as Wright, Stearns and Jackson, and even reaching on the north to Fort Abercrombie, thus extending from Iowa to the valley of the Red River of the North, were severally involved in the consequences of the warfare of 1862. This extended area had a population estimated at over fifty thousand.

Early in the fifties complaints began to be made by the Indians, and dissatisfaction began to be manifest. By the treaty of Traverse des Sioux, dated July 23, 1851, between the United States and the Sissetons and Wapatons, $275,000 was to be paid their chiefs, and a further sum of $30,000 was to be expended for their benefit in Indian improvements. By the treaty of Mendota, dated August 5, 1851, the Medawakantons and Wapakutas were to receive the sum of $200,000, to be paid to their chief, and a further sum of $30,000. These several sums amounting in the aggregate to $550,000, these Indians, to whom they were payable, claim they were never paid, except perhaps a small portion expended in improvements. This led to great dissatisfaction, of which the government was fully apprised. Several parties were at different times sent out by the Indian department of the government to investigate into the causes, but the rascality of the agents and officers who had defrauded the Indians had been carefully covered up, and as usual in such cases the guilty parties were exculpated. This was one of the leading and most important causes which led to the massacre of 1862.

Another cause of irritation among these annuity Sioux arose out of the Spirit Lake massacre of 1857—known as the Inkpadutah massacre. Inkpadutah was an outlaw of the Wapakuta band of Sioux Indians, and his acts were entirely disclaimed by the "annuity Sioux." He had committed murder in his own tribe some twenty years previous, and since had led a wandering and marauding life about the headwaters of the Des Moines River and westward to Dakota. Finally his outrages reached a climax, when early in 1857 with a few of his followers, he proceeded to murder every family in the little settlement about Spirit Lake, Iowa, except four women whom they bore away captives. From there they went to the Springfield settlement (on the present site of Jackson, Minn.), where they murdered seventeen people, making a total of forty seven persons killed. They then retreated westward. Shortly after the massacre at Springfield (now Jackson) a company of regular soldiers under Capt. Bee was stationed at that place, and had the officer been a zealous or capable one might easily have overtaken and punished them. As stated the "annuity Sioux" disclaimed the acts of this outlaw; but for a time the government refused to pay the annuities until they should deliver up the murderers. In a short time, however, the government let the matter drop, and continued to pay the annuities as before. Some thought that this was a great error, and that the Indians mistook it for a sign of weakness.

However that may be, as time went on the Indians became more and more insolent, and Little Crow, together with a few leaders among the annuity Sioux, from the time the government ceased its efforts to punish Inkpadutah, began to agitate and plan the great conspiracy to drive the whites from the State of Minnesota. Little Crow was one of the "farmer Indians," whose headquarters was a short distance above the Lower Agency, who is credited with being the leader in the outbreak against the whites.

The antecedent exciting causes of this massacre are numerous. The displaced agents and traders find the cause in the erroneous action of the government, resulting in their removal from office. The statesman and the philosopher may unite in tracing the cause to improper theories as to the mode of acquiring the right to Indian lands. The former may locate the evil in our system of treaties, and the latter in our theories of government. The philanthropist may find the cause in the absence of justice which we exhibit in all our intercourse with the Indian races. The poet and the lovers of romance in human character find the true cause, as they believe, in the total absence of all appreciation of the noble, generous, confiding traits peculiar to the native Indian. The Christian teacher finds apologies for acts of Indian atrocities in the deficient systems of mental and moral culture. Each of these

different classes are satisfied that the great massacre of August, 1862, had its origin in some way intimately connected with his favorite theory.

Maj. Thomas Galbraith, Sioux agent, says, in writing of the causes which led to the massacre: "The radical, moving cause of the outbreak is, I am satisfied, the ingrained and fixed hostility of the savage barbarian to reform and civilization. As in all barbarous communities in the history of the world, the same people have, for the most part, resisted the encroachments of civilization upon their ancient customs, so it is in the case before us. Nor does it matter materially in what shape civilization makes its attack. Hostile, opposing forces meet in conflict, and a war of social elements is the result — civilization is aggressive, and barbarism stubbornly resistant. Sometimes, indeed, civilization has achieved a bloodless victory, but generally it has been otherwise. Christianity, itself, the true basis of civilization, has, in most instances, waded to success through seas of blood. . . . Having stated thus much, I state, as a settled fact in my mind, that the encroachments of Christianity, and its handmaid, civilization, upon the habits and customs of the Sioux Indians, is the cause of the late terrible Sioux outbreak. There were, it is true, many immediate inciting causes, which will be alluded to and stated hereafter, but they are subsidiary to, and developments of, or incident to, the great cause set forth. . . . But that the recent Sioux outbreak would have happened at any rate, as a result, a fair consequence of the cause here stated, I have no doubt.

"Now as to the existing or immediate causes of the outbreak : By my predecessor a new and radical system was inaugurated; practically, and in its inauguration, he was aided by the Christian missionaries and by the government. The treaties of 1858 were ostensibly made to carry this new system into effect. The theory, in substance, was to break up the community system which obtained among the Sioux, weaken and destroy their tribal relations, and individualize them, by giving them each a separate home. . . . On the 1st day of June, A. D. 1861, when I entered upon the duties of my office, I found that the system had just been inaugurated. Some hundred families of the annuity Sioux had become novitiates, and their relatives and friends seemed to be favorably disposed to the new order of things. But I also found that, against these were arrayed over five thousand 'annuity Sioux,' besides at least three thousand Yanktonais, all inflamed by the most bitter, relentless and devilish hostility.

"I saw, to some extent, the difficulty of the situation, but I determined to continue, if in my power, the civilization system. To favor it, to aid and build it up by every fair means, I advised, encouraged, and assisted the farmer novitiates; in short I sustained the policy inaugurated by my predecessor, and sustained and recommended by the government. I soon discovered that the system could not be successful without a sufficient force to protect the 'farmer' from the hostility of the 'blanket' Indians.

"During my term, and up to the time of the outbreak, about 175 had their hair cut and had adopted the habits and customs of the white men.

"For a time, indeed, my hopes were strong that civilization would soon be in the ascendant. But the increase in the civilization party and their evident prosperity, only tended to exasperate the Indians of the 'ancient customs,' and to widen the breach. But while these are to be enumerated, it may be permitted me to hope that the radical cause will not be forgotten or overlooked; and I am bold to express this desire, because, ever since the outbreak, the public journals of the country, religious and secular, have teemed with editorials by and communications from 'reliable individuals,' politicians, philanthropists, philosophers and hired 'penny-a-liners,' mostly mistaken and sometimes willfully and grossly false, giving the cause of the Indian raid."

Maj. Galbraith enumerates a variety of other exciting causes of the massacre, which our limit will not allow us to insert in this volume. Among other causes, . . that the United States was itself at war, and that Washington was taken by the negroes. . . But none of these were, in his opinion, the cause of the outbreak.

The Major then adds:

"Grievances such as have been related, and numberless others akin to them, were spoken of, recited, and chanted at their councils, dances and feasts, to such an extent that, in their excitement, in June, 1862, a secret organization known as the 'Soldiers' Lodge' was founded by the young men and soldiers of the lower Sioux, with the object, as far as I was able to learn through spies and informers, of preventing the 'traders' from going to the pay-tables, as had been their custom. Since the outbreak I have become satisfied that the real object of this 'Lodge' was to adopt measures to 'clean out' all the white people at the end of the payment."

Whatever may have been the cause of the fearful and bloody tragedy, it is certain that the manner of the execution of the infernal deed was a deep-laid conspiracy, long cherished by Little Crow, taking form under the guise of the "Soldiers' Lodge," and matured in secret Indian councils. In all these secret movements Little Crow was the moving spirit.

Now the opportune moment seemed to have come. Only thirty soldiers were stationed at Fort Ridgely. Some thirty were all that Fort Ripley could muster, and at

Fort Abercrombie, one company under Capt. Van Der Hork was all the whites could depend upon to repel any attack in that quarter. The whole effective force for the defense of the entire frontier, from Pembina to the Iowa line, did not exceed 200 men. The annuity money was daily expected, and no troops except about one hundred men at Yellow Medicine, had been detailed, as usual, to attend the anticipated payment. Here was a glittering prize to be paraded before the minds of the excited savages. The whites were weak; they were engaged in a terrible war among themselves; their attention was now directed toward the great struggle in the South. At such a time, offering so many chances for rapine and plunder, it would be easy to unite at least all the annuity Indians in one common movement. Little Crow knew full well that the Indians could easily be made to believe that now was a favorable time to make a grand attack upon the border settlements.

A memorable council convened at Little Crow's village, near the lower agency, on Sunday night, August 3, previous to the attack on Fort Ridgely, and precisely two weeks before the massacres at Acton. Little Crow was at this council, and he was not wanting in ability to meet the greatness of the occasion. The proceedings of this council, of course, were secret. The council matured the details of the conspiracy. It appears that the next day, August 4, a party of ninety-six Indians in war paint and fully armed, rode up to Fort Ridgely and requested permission to hold a dance and feast in the fort. They were allowed to hold the dance outside the fort, but Sergeant Jones, with singular foresight, mounted a howitzer charged with shell and canister-shot and guarded the entrance, having it pointed toward the Indians. After finishing the dance the red-skins left without making the attack, which had undoubtedly been medi-tated. Only thirty soldiers occupied the post at Fort Ridgely, and this was deemed amply sufficient for times of peace.

On the same day a great many Indians were encamped about the Upper Agency. They were afraid they would not get their annuity money, which had not arrived as yet. They had been complaining bitterly of starvation, and on this day made an attack on the warehouse, carrying off a great deal of flour and other provisions. The matter, however, was finally adjusted, and the agent issued rations, promising to distribute their money as soon as it should arrive. None of the Indians, however, were punished for their attack on the supply house.

We now come to the massacre itself, the first blow of which fell upon the town of Acton, in Meeker County, about thirty-five miles northeast of the Lower Sioux Agency. On Sunday, August 17, 1862, six Sioux Indians brutally murdered a man named Jones, with his wife and a daughter, and a man named Webster and Howard Baker.

On the next day, Monday, the massacre at the Lower Agency occurred, where many were killed and fearfully mutilated. A few escaped and made their way to the eastern settlements. The Indians declared it to be their intention to kill or drive off all the whites to the east of the Mississippi River, and to spare none. All that day the work of plunder went on at the lower agency, and when the stores and dwellings had been emptied, they were fired. So complete was the surprise and so sudden and unexpected the terrible blow that not a single one of the host of savages was slain. In thirty minutes from the time the first gun was fired not a white person was left alive. All were either weltering in their gore or had fled in fear and terror from that place of death. It seems that hundreds of the Indians had gathered here and then dispersed through the scattered settlements for their murderous work.

On the same morning—of August 18—the massacre began on the north side of the Minnesota River, from Birch Coolie to Beaver Creek and beyond, and the region was strewn with the mutilated bodies of the dead and dying men, women and children. So the terrible warfare continued, murdering and burning ; none were allowed to escape who could possibly be discovered. The outbreak extended over a vast scope of country, and the Indians numbered well up into the thousands. The entire length of the Minnesota and its tributaries, and out into Dakota, together with all the western part of this State was the scene everywhere of a carnival of blood. The counties affected have already been named.

On the 18th of August the Indians attacked New Ulm, and after several battles and skirmishes were defeated. A few days later the whites evacuated the town and moved toward Mankato.

On the 18th of August the battle at Lower Agency Ferry was fought.

On the 20th, seeing they were foiled in their attack on New Ulm, they made a furious assault on Fort Ridgely. A number of whites were killed and wounded, but the Indians were defeated. The attack was renewed on the 22d and another severe battle occurred, which was ended by night coming on.

Numerous engagements were also fought in the northern part of the State.

Throughout all the Minnesota River country many women and children were taken prisoners. In the meantime companies had been raised and were everywhere following up the Indians and guarding the various posts at which the settlers had gathered. These various companies had also picked up a great many wounded found on the prairies, and also buried the dead. On the 1st of September,

Company A, Sixth Regiment Minnesota Volunteers, under Capt. H. P. Grant, fought the battle of Birch Coolie, a most terrible and bloody engagement. The noble little band of soldiers were relieved on September 3, by an advance movement of Col. Sibley's forces at Fort Ridgely. The signal defeat of Little Crow at this battle, in effect, ended the efforts of the Indians in subduing the whites on the border. After this battle all of the Indian forces under Little Crow began a retreat up the valley of the Minnesota toward Yellow Medicine; and on September 16, Col. Sibley, with his whole column, moved in pursuit of the fleeing foe, and on the 23d they came up with the Indians and defeated them in the battle of Wood Lake. This put an end to the hopes of Little Crow. On the same day as the battle of Wood Lake, the Wapeton band of Indians surrendered later and turned over to Col. Sibley all the captives — 107 whites and 162 half-breeds. This place has since been known as "Camp Release."

After the disaster at Wood Lake, Little Crow retreated in the direction of Big Stone Lake, with those who remained with him. The chief was never captured, but is said to have been killed at Scattered Lake in 1863. Col. Sibley continued to pursue the deserting Indians, and demanded the surrender of all bands. By the 8th of October, 1862, prisoners had come in and surrendered to the number of 2,000. Scouting parties were sent over various parts of the West, and, until all danger of further depredations was past, soldiers were stationed at all of the frontier posts and settlements.

A military commission was soon after inaugurated to try the parties charged with murder of white persons. On the 5th of November, 1862, 321 Indians and their allies were found guilty, and 303 were recommended for capital punishment, and the others for imprisonment. They were immediately removed under a guard of 1,500 men to South Bend, on the Minnesota River, to await further orders from the government. The final decision of the President was rendered on the 17th of December, 1862, ordering that forty of these be hung on Friday, December 26. One of these died a short time before the day set, and one other, a half breed, had his sentence commuted to imprisonment for life just before the fatal day. As to the other thirty-eight the sentence was executed at Mankato on the day set.

On the 16th of February, 1863, the treaties before that time existing between the United States and these "annuity Indians" were abrogated and annulled, and all lands and rights of occupancy, and all annuities and claims then existing in favor of said Indians, were declared forfeited. Thus ended the saddest chapter of Minnesota's history.

CHAPTER IV.

TERRITORIAL AND STATE OFFICERS.

THE first governor of the Territory of Minnesota was Alexander Ramsey, who served from June 1, 1849, to May 15, 1853. Willis A. Gorman succeeded him, and held the office until April 23, 1857. Samuel Medary was the next territorial governor, and held the office until the State officers were sworn in, May 24, 1858.

The first secretary of the Territory was Charles K. Smith, who served from June 1, 1849, until October 23, 1851, when Alexander Wilkin qualified and held the office until May 15, 1853. Joseph Travis Rosser was the next, and served until April 23, 1857. Charles L. Chase, the last territorial secretary, qualified on the date last named and served until succeeded by the newly chosen secretary of state, May 24, 1858.

The office of territorial treasurer was first filled by Calvin A. Tuttle, who served from November 3, 1849, to July 2, 1853. George W. Prescott came next and retained the position until February 24, 1854. Succeeding him Charles E. Leonard served until May 7, 1857, when George W. Armstrong was appointed and served until the State officers qualified, May 24, 1858.

J. E. McKusick was the first territorial auditor, qualifying November 3, 1849, and serving until November 30, 1852. A. Van Vorhees succeeded him and held the office until the 15th of May, 1853, when Socrates Nelson qualified. January 17, 1854, Julius Georgii took charge of the office and served until succeeded by the State auditor, May 24, 1858.

During the existence of the Territory of Minnesota, Lorenzo A. Babcock and then Lafayette Emmett were the only ones to hold the office of attorney general. The first named served from June 1, 1849, until May 15, 1853, and the latter from 1853 until May 24, 1858.

In territorial times there were no district judges, but the justices of the supreme court attended to all judicial matters now within the jurisdiction of the district bench. The first chief justice of the territorial supreme court was Aaron Goodrich, who served from June 1, 1849, to November 13, 1851, when Jerome Fuller was appointed and presided until December 16, 1852. Henry Z. Hayner was next appointed, but never presided at a term of court. William H. Welch was appointed April 7, 1853, and served until May 24, 1858.

David Cooper and Bradley B. Meeker were the first associate justices, and served from June 1, 1849, until April 7, 1853. Their successors were Andrew G. Chatfield and Moses G. Sherburne, who retained the positions until April, 1857, and were followed by R. R. Nelson and Charles E. Flandrau, who served until the State officers qualified.

The clerks of the territorial supreme court were: James K. Humphrey, Andrew J. Whitney and George W. Prescott, in the order named. The reporters were: William Hollinshead, Isaac Atwater, John B. Brisbin, M. E. Ames and Harvey Officer.

Henry H. Sibley was the first delegate from the Territory to Congress, serving from January 15, 1849, to March 4, 1853. Henry

M. Rice was the second, serving from December 5, 1853, to March 4, 1857, when he was succeeded by W. W. Kingsbury, who qualified December 7, 1857, and whose term expired May 11, 1858.

The governors of the State of Minnesota, in their order have been as follows: Henry H. Sibley, from May 24, 1858, to January 2, 1860; Alexander Ramsey, to July 10, 1863; Henry A. Swift, to January 11, 1864; Stephen Miller, during 1864–5; William R. Marshall, during 1866–7–8–9; Horace Austin, during 1870–1–2–3; Cushman K. Davis, during 1874–5; John S. Pillsbury, during 1876–7–8–9–80–81; Lucius F. Hubbard, during 1882–3–4–5–6, and A. R. McGill, the present governor, who assumed the duties of the office January 5, 1887.

The lieutenant governors since the organization of the State have been as follows: William Holcomb, from May 24, 1858, to January 2, 1860; Ignatius Donnelly, to March 3, 1863; Henry A. Swift, to July 10, 1863; Charles D. Sherwood, during 1864–5; Thomas H. Armstrong, during 1866–7–8–9; William H. Yale, during 1870–1–2–3; Alphonzo Barto, during 1874–5; James B. Wakefield, during 1876–7–8–9; C. A. Gillman, during 1880–1–2–3–4–5–6, and A. E. Rice, who qualified January 4, 1887.

The office of secretary of State has been filled successively by the following gentlemen: Francis Baasen, from May 24, 1858, to January 2, 1860; James H. Baker, to November 17, 1862; David Blakely, to January 8, 1866; Henry C. Rogers, during the years 1866–7–8–9; Hans Mattson, during 1870–1; S. P. Jennison, during 1872–3–4–5; John S. Irgens, during 1876–7–8–9; Fred. Von Baumbach, during 1880–1–2–3–4–5–6, and Hans Mattson, during 1887–8.

The State treasurers have been as follows: George W. Armstrong, from May 24, 1858, to January 2, 1860; Charles Scheffer, during 1860–1–2–3–4–5–6–7; Emil Munch, during 1868–9–70–1; William Seeger, from January 5, 1872, to February 7, 1873; Edwin W. Dyke, to January 7, 1876; William Pfaender, during 1876–7–8–9; Charles Kittelson, during 1880–1–2–3–4–5–6, and Joseph Bobleter, the present treasurer, who was elected for 1887–8.

The auditors of State have been as follows: W. F. Dunbar, from May 24, 1858, to January 1, 1861; Charles McIlrath to January 13, 1873; O. P. Whitcomb, to January 10, 1882, and W. W. Braden, who is the present incumbent of the office.

The office of attorney general has been filled as follows: Charles H. Berry, served from May 24, 1858, to January 2, 1860; Gordon E. Cole, served during 1860–1–2–3–4–5; William Colville, during 1866–7; F. R. E. Cornell, during 1868–9–70–1–2–3; George P. Wilson, during 1874–5–6–7–8–9; Charles M. Start, from January 10, 1880, to March 11, 1881; W. J. Hahn, to January 5, 1887, and Moses E. Clapp, the present attorney general.

The present board of railroad commissioners is made up of Horace Austin, John L. Gibbs and George L. Becker. Those who have composed the board in the past were: A. J. Edgerton, W. R. Marshall, J. J. Randall, J. H. Baker and S. S. Murdock.

Edward D. Neill was the first superintendent of public instruction for Minnesota. He was appointed in March, 1860, and on the 1st of July, 1861, was succeeded by B. F. Crary. From 1862 to 1867 the secretary of State was *ex-officio* superintendent, but on April 1, 1867, M. H. Dunnell was appointed superintendent, and served until August, 1870, when he was succeeded by H. B. Wilson. April 3, 1875, David Burt was appointed superintendent, and retained the office until succeeded by the present incumbent, D. L. Kiehl, who was appointed September 1, 1881.

The office of insurance commissioner has been held in turn by Pennock Pusey, A. R. McGill and Charles Shandrew; the last named gentleman having been appointed January 6, 1887, is the present commissioner.

The commissioners of statistics have been as follows: J. A. Wheelock, Pennock Pusey, C. F. Solberg, J. B. Phillips, T. M. Metcalf, J. P. Jacobson, F. Sneedorff, Oscar Malmros, A. F. Nordin, Victor Hjortsberg and Herman Stockenstrom.

The following is a list of the gentlemen who have filled the office of adjutant-general: Alex. C. Jones, W. H. Acker, John B. Sanborn, Oscar Malmros, John Peller, H. P. Van Cleve, M. D. Flower, H. A. Castle, H. P. Van Cleve, A. C. Hawley, C. M. McCarthy and F. W. Seeley.

JUDICIARY.

The first chief justice of the supreme court of the State was Lafayette Emmett, who was sworn in May 24, 1858, and served until January 10, 1865. Thomas Wilson succeeded him and served until July 14, 1869, when he was succeeded by James Gilfillan.

Christopher G. Ripley was the next, holding the position from January 7, 1870, until April 7, 1874, when he was followed by S. J. R. McMillan, who served until March 10, 1875. At that time James Gilfillan became chief justice, and is the present incumbent.

The following statements will show the associate justices, together with the date of qualification of each: Charles E. Flandrau and Isaac Atwater served from May 24, 1858, to July 6, 1864; S. J. R. McMillan from July 6, 1864, to April 7, 1874; Thomas Wilson from July 6, 1864, to January 10, 1865; George B. Young from April 16, 1874, to January 11, 1875; F. R. E. Cornell from January 11, 1875, to May 23, 1881, and Greenleaf Clark from March 14, 1881, to January 12, 1882. The present associate justices are John M. Berry, who first qualified January 10, 1865; D. A. Dickinson, since June 27, 1881; William Mitchell, since March 14, 1881, and C. E. Vanderburgh, since January 12, 1882.

As to district courts, the State is now divided into thirteen districts.

CHAPTER V.

REPRESENTATION IN THE UNITED STATES CONGRESS, AND THE CREATION OF COUNTIES.

SENATORS. The first United States Senators from Minnesota were James Shields and Henry M. Rice, who took the oath of office May 11, 1858. The former was succeeded on March 4th, 1860, by Morton S. Wilkinson, who served the full term. Daniel S. Norton was sworn in to succeed Wilkinson, March 4, 1867, and died while in office, July 14, 1870. O. P. Stearns was appointed, and served out the few weeks left of the term. William Windom came next, and retained the office until March 12, 1881, when he was succeeded by A. J. Edgerton, who resigned, however, in October of the same year, and William Windom was again chosen, serving until succeeded by one of the present Senators, D. M. Sabin, March 4, 1883.

Henry M. Rice, who was mentioned as a colleague of James Shields, served as United States Senator from May 11, 1858, to March 4, 1863, when Alexander Ramsey succeeded him, and retained the position until March 4, 1875. S. J. R. McMillan became United States Senator on the day last named, and occupied the position for two full terms — twelve years — being succeeded March 4, 1887, by Cushman K. Davis, one of the present Senators.

REPRESENTATIVES IN CONGRESS.

The territorial delegates have already been spoken of. When the State of Minnesota was organized, it was entitled to two representatives in the House of Representatives of the United States. This state of affairs continued until 1871, when a reapportionment was made, and the State was allowed three members of the House. At that time the State was divided into three congressional districts — No. 1, embracing the southern, No. 2 the central, and No. 3 the northern portion of the State. In 1881 another apportionment was made, by which the State secured five Representatives. This is the present status of the representation. The State is divided into five congressional districts, as follows: The first district includes Houston, Fillmore, Mower, Freeborn, Steele, Dodge, Olmsted, Winona and Wabasha counties; the second district includes Faribault, Blue Earth, Waseca, Watonwan, Martin, Cottonwood, Jackson, Murray, Nobles, Rock, Pipestone, Lincoln, Lyon, Redwood, Brown, Nicollet, Yellow Medicine, Lac qui Parle, Sibley and Le Sueur counties; the third district embraces Goodhue, Rice, Swift, Dakota, Scott, Carver, McLeod, Meeker, Kandiyohi, Renville and Chippewa counties; the fourth district includes Washington, Ramsey, Hennepin, Wright, Pine, Kanabec, Anoka, Chisago, Isanti and Sherburne counties, and the fifth district includes Mille Lacs, Benton, Morrison, Stearns, Pope, Douglas, Stevens, Big Stone, Traverse, Grant, Todd,

Crow Wing, Aitkin, Carlton, Wadena, Otter Tail, Wilkin, Cass, Becker, Clay, Polk, Beltrami, Marshall, Hubbard, Kittson, Itasca, St. Louis, Lake and Cook counties.

The following is a list of the various gentlemen who have represented Minnesota in the lower house of Congress, with the years during which they served. With one or two exceptions, the term of office began and closed March 4th.

W. W. Phelps, 1858-9; J. M. Cavenaugh, 1858; William Windom, 1860-1-2-3-4-5-6-7-8; Cyrus Aldrich, 1860-1-2; Ignatius Donnelly, 1864-5 6-7-8; M. S. Wilkinson, 1869-70; E. M. Wilson, 1869-70; John T. Averill, 1871-2-3-4; M. H. Dunnell, from 1871 to 1883; H. B. Straight, 1874-5-6-7-8; William S. King, 1876; J. H. Stewart, 1878; Henry Poehler, 1879-80; H. B. Straight, 1881-2-3-4-5-6; W. D. Washburn, 1879-80-1-2-3-4; Milo White, 1883-4-5-6; J. B. Wakefield, 1883-4-5-6; Knute Nelson, 1883-4-5-6-7-8; J. B. Gilfillan, 1885-6; Thomas Wilson, 1887-8; John Lind, 1887-8; John L. McDonald, 1887-8; Edmund Rice, 1887-8.

CREATION OF COUNTIES.

In this connection we present a list of the counties of Minnesota, together with the date on which they were created by the territorial or State Legislatures, viz.:

Aitkin, May 23, 1857,	Marshall, February 25, 1879,
Anoka, May 23, 1857,	Martin, May 23, 1857,
Becker, March 18, 1858,	Meeker, February 23, 1856,
Beltrami, F'bru'ry 28, 1866,	Mille Lacs, May 23, 1857,
Benton, October 27, 1849,	Morrison, Febr'ry 25, 1858,
Big Stone, F'br'ry 20, 1862,	Mower, February 20, 1855,
Blue Earth, March 5, 1853,	Murray, May 23, 1857,
Brown, February 20, 1855,	Nicollet, March 5, 1853,
Carlton, May 23, 1857,	Nobles, May 23, 1857,
Carver, February 20, 1855,	Norman, Nov'mb'r 29, 1881,
Cass, September 1, 1851,	Olmsted, February 20, 1855,
Chippewa, F'br'ry 20, 1862,	Otter Tail. March 18, 1858,
Chisago, September 1, 1851,	Pine, March 31, 1856,
Clay, March 2, 1862,	Pipestone, May 23, 1857,
Cook, March 9, 1874,	Polk, July 20, 1858,
Cottonwood, May 23, 1857,	Pope, February 20, 1862,
Crow Wing, May 23, 1857,	Ramsey, October 27, 1849,
Dakota, October 27, 1849,	Redwood, February 6, 1862,
Dodge, February 20, 1855,	Renville, February 20, 1855,
Douglas, March 8, 1858,	Rice, March 5, 1853,
Faribault, F'br'ry 20, 1855,	Rock, March 23, 1857,
Fillmore, March 5, 1853,	St. Louis, March 1, 1856,
Freeborn, F'br'ry, 20, 1855,	Scott, March 5, 1858,
Goodhue, March 5, 1853,	Sherburne, Feb'y 25, 1856
Grant, March 6, 1868,	Sibley, March 5, 1853,
Hennepin, March 6, 1852,	Stearns, February 20, 1855,
Houston, Feb'ry 23, 1854,	Steele, February 20, 1855,
Hubbard, Feb'y 26, 1883,	Stevens, February 20, 1860,
Isanti, February 13, 1857,	Swift, March 4, 1870,
Itasca, October 29, 1849,	Todd, February 20, 1862,
Jackson, May 23, 1857,	Travers, February 20, 1862,
Kanabec, March 13, 1858,	Wabasha, October 27, 1849,
Kandiyohi, March 20, 1858,	Wadena, July 11, 1858,
Kittson, February 25, 1879,	Waseca, February 27, 1857,
Lac qui Parle, Nov. 3, 1871,	Washington, Oct. 27, 1849,
Lake, March 1, 1856,	Watonwan, Nov. 6, 1860,
Le Sueur, March 5, 1853,	Wilkin, March 6, 1868,
Lincoln, March 6.1873,	Winona, February 23, 1849.
Lyon, November 2, 1869,	Wright, February 20, 1855,
McLeod, March 1, 1856,	Yellow Medicine, November 3, 1871.

SOUTHWESTERN

MINNESOTA

DESCRIPTIVE AND HISTORICAL

INTRODUCTORY

Descriptive and Historical Introductory

T IS with wonder and amazement that one contemplates the results of "Time's" wonder-working hand. The rapid civilization and development of the Northwest within a period that is almost within the memory of our children even, is the marvel of the age. This is especially true of that territory which comes properly within the scope of this work — Southwestern Minnesota —or the counties of Lincoln, Pipestone, Rock, Murray Nobles. Cottonwood, Jackson Martin and Faribault, This belt of counties has gained the reputation of being one of the most fertile and promising regions of the Northwest — has been termed "the fertile blue-grass region of Minnesota;" widely advertised as being blessed with "the soil of the river bottoms and climate of the mountains," and the name of being "the home of the cereals," the yields of wheat having usually been enormous. And these praises are not very extravagant. But it is an established fact that as years roll by, and as decades bury former decades, localities seem to change as to the yielding qualities of their soil, and this is to a certain extent the case with Southwestern Minnesota. Exclusive wheat raising is gradually giving way to diversified farming, or mixed farming and stock raising, although as yet wheat yields large returns. This has been the case in all the older States. The reputations which localities bear ever shift and vary according to the occupation and even temperament of the people, the success of their undertakings, or as the discovery of new Eldorados bedim and lessen the brilliancy of their former greatness. The writer distinctly remembers the time when the Genesee Valley of the noble. "Empire State" was the garden spot of the world, so far as wheat raising was concerned, and was supposed to be the only native "home of the cereal." But through succeeding decades this has been entirely changed. The center of the wheat belt rapidly moved westward, stopping for a time in

Ohio, then in Illinois, and finally, to-day, it rests over a belt of country which includes Western Minnesota and the two Dakotas. And who shall say where it will next land?

The soil of Southwestern Minnesota has fitted this region for almost every department of agricultural industry. It is a rich, black loam, underlaid with a sub-soil, which absorbs and retains moisture in such a manner as to have made this region famed for its capabilities in withstanding the effects of either drought or excellent rainfall. It is admirably adapted to raising all cereals, and corn is one of the staple products. Wheat is as yet the banner crop, and the yields of this cereal have at times been marvelous. All other products do remarkaly well, and in later years, as indicated above, diversified farming has been radily taking the place of exclusive wheat raising. Southwestern Minnesota is supplied with an abundance of pure, wholesome water, which makes it at once a desirable and profitable stock-raising locality. For some years past the intelligent class of agriculturists have been devoting much attention to this important industry, and to-day Southwestern Minnesota is second to no portion of the State in the assessed valuation of its cattle, proportionate to its settlement. Blooded and high grade stock are by no means rare in any portion of this region, and yearly more and more attention is devoted to this department. No portion of the United States, or world, for that matter, is better adapted by nature for raising stock, for the soil is very prolific in the production of both tame and indigenous grasses, furnishing the best of pasturage, and an abundance of rich, nutritious wild hay can be had merely for the labor of cutting and caring for it.

The surface of the land is made up of rolling prairies, which are interspersed with natural and domestic groves, and the scenery is magnificent. The country is dotted with lakes, and the drainage afforded by the numerous rivers, creeks and rivulets is almost perfect. These lakes are of pure, limpid water, bordered by sandy beaches and hemmed in by natural groves. Almost without exception they abound with fish, while their shores and the adjacent prairies are the resorts of game of almost every description. This portion of Minnesota is the "home of the sportsman and hunter," and each year thousand of pleasure seekers visit the resorts of this region, to fish in the clear depths of the beautiful lakes, to hunt, or for rest and recreation. The climate of Southwestern Minnesota is excellent. The clear, dry atmosphere and pure fresh air from off the countless miles of prairie have justly given it the reputation of being among the most healthy portions of the globe.

For many years prior to the first actual settlement in the western counties in Southwestern Minnesota, there is no question but that the soil was frequently trod by the foot of the white man. The abundance of game which infested this region drew hunters and trappers regularly to its lakes, and many of them took claims here and afterward made permanent settlements. The Indians for ages had made this portion of the State a hunting and camping ground, and, could they speak, each tree could, no doubt, tell some wild tale of Indian adventure. Wild game of almost every description—bear, elk, deer, etc.—abounded in those days, and many of these animals have only passed from these grounds recently. Many of the older settlers report that they frequently saw deer, elk and bear in the first days of their settlement here, and not a few have been seen and killed in recent years.

In 1856 there was a great tide of emigration "toward the setting sun" from the Eastern States, and a great proportion of the present area of Minnesota grew rapidly in population This tide of emigration continued through the following year, but then came on the panic of 1857, and the influx of settlers almost completely ceased. Times were very hard all through the country, and especially was this condition of affairs felt in the Northwest. It was at about the beginning of this rush of settlers that the first settlements were made in what is properly termed Southwestern Minnesota. In 1855-57 settlers found their way to and made settlements in territory which now forms Faribault, Martin, Jackson and Cottonwood counties, and in some of these counties substantial settlements were begun; villages were platted, counties were organized, and civilization took its first advancing stride in these localities. A few of the settlers of these years are left, especially in Faribault county, but death has sadly thinned their ranks. In Jackson and Cottonwood counties thriving settlements were begun, but in 1857 there occurred the "Inkpadutah Massacre," when the Indians under the leadership of Inkpadutah ruthlessly murdered settlers at Spirit Lake, Iowa, and others along the Des Moines River in Jackson and Cottonwood counties, Minnesota. This proved to be a serious blow to the growth and development of this region. The counties named were depopulated, everything was abandoned, and the pioneers fled for their lives. After this, those counties lying west of Faribault county remained almost wholly devoid of inhabitants for several years. Troops, however, were soon stationed through this region, and as soon as confidence was again established the settlement commmenced again, and early in the "sixties" many settlers had again found homes in Jackson, Cottonwood and Murray counties, and counties lying east of them. Other events, however, transpired to still further delay the development of Southwestern Minnesota. Following close upon the Inkpadutah massacre and the financial panic of 1857, came the outbreak of the Civil War in 1861, and in August, 1862, was inaugurated the terrible Sioux Indian outbreak, which depopulated the western part of Minnesota and crimsoned the fair soil with the blood of so many innocent men, women and children. Fiendish atrocity, blood-curdling cruelty and red-handed murder ran riot, and the growth of Minnesota received a set-back from which it took many years to fully recover. After the inauguration of this fiendish warfare, the western frontier line receded eastward, and the greater portion of Southwestern Minnesota was again left in the midst of the hostile Indian country, and for many months no white man trod its soil. After the settlements in the eastern part of the State had partially recovered from the first rude shock of the Indian outbreak, which fell like a thunderbolt from a clear sky, steps were at once taken to defend the exposed settlements, to conquer the redskins and drive them back. At that time the Civil War was in progress, and a majority of the able-bodied settlers were in the South fighting for the flag and the Union. It therefore required some time to muster troops and place them in advantageous positions to cope with the wily red foe, and in the meantime the Indians carried on their brutal warfare, murdering men, women and children and burning as they went. After considerable delay the Indians were driven back, soldiers were placed all through this western country, and the prairies were constantly patrolled by companies which were detailed for this service. The redskins were soon subdued, but for a number of years the settlers on the extreme frontier lived in a state of constant fear and anxiety, not knowing at what time the massacre might break out afresh. Through these causes soldiers were kept on the frontier for some time, and many of these soldiers afterward found homes in Southwestern Minnesota, not a few having selected their claims while here in the service. When peace was again established on the border, settlements again began, and the frontier line moved westward very rapidly. Immediately after the close of the war all of the Northwest began a very rapid development, and especially was this the case in Southwestern Minnesota, as all counties in this portion of the State grew rapidly in population, a great many of the settlers being men who had been in the service; and it is to-day questionable whether any portion of the United States has an equal proportion of veterans of the war among its inhabitants as has Southwestern Minnesota. When the war closed railroads began reaching out and interlocking through the Northwest, and this seems to have been the starting point of such an era of rapid growth and development as has been the marvel of the times. Railroads reached Southwestern Minnesota late in the "sixties," and early in the "seventies" they were constructed through and beyond these counties. After that thousands upon thousands of settlers crowded into this favored region, selected farms and began improvements. Cities and villages sprung up as if by magic, substantial farms were opened, tasty and comfortable dwellings, churches and school houses soon dotted the prairie in all directions, and the waving fields of golden grain bespoke the wonderful prosperity which prevailed. The financial panic of 1873 caused a slight depression here, but as the settlement was so new, and was made up of an excellent class of men, the drawback was not a very serious one. The yields of crops were so enormous and the prospects so flattering that a majority of the farmers in preparing for more convenient and extensive operations, incurred indebtedness which they otherwise would have refrained from, and they thereby made an unforeseen calamity harder to bear. Thus,

in the midst of present prosperity, and the most flattering prospects for the future, the grasshoppers swarmed down upon the crops of the settlers, annihilating and destroying almost every vestige of the growing crops, leaving the farmers destitute. This began in 1874, and continued for three years, proving even a more disastrous set-back to the country than the Indian massacre. Times were very hard during those days. Unable to draw support and sustenance from the soil, thousands of the settlers left, while others, unable or unwilling to leave and abandon their claims, engaged in trapping, and it can be truthfully said that for several years "fur was legal tender" in this region. Money was very scarce. There was no sale for personal property, and after the first blow fell the only sale for land was in mortgaging it to Eastern capitalists, and nearly all the Eastern money was withdrawn after the first year. But finally the grasshoppers left or ceased coming and again Southwestern Minnesota resumed its onward march.

Nothing has since occurred to seriously interrupt the growth, development and prosperity. Like all new countries there have been years of slight depression and occasionally a partial failure of crops, but they are the exception to what has been the rule in the history of Southwestern Minnesota. And the native energy and enterprise of the inhabitants soon overcame the obstacles, and as success has always followed a reverse, the onward march has been resumed with more satisfactory results than before; and to-day, taken as a whole, Southwestern Minnesota is one of the most prosperous and promising regions of the whole Northwest.

Contemplate the changes that have been made here, and one can not but wonder at the marvelous results that have been accomplished within so short a period of time. Turn back, as it were, the leaves of Time's great book to a period only a little more than a quarter of a century ago, and what a contrast. Then all was as nature had formed it. The broad and rolling prairies were as green then as now; in summer a perfect paradise of verdure, with its variegated hues of flowers and vegetation; in winter a dreary snow-mantled desert. Selected as a camping and hunting ground by the Sioux, with that wonderful appreciation of the beautiful which nature has made an instinct in the savage, scarcely a sign of habitation or civilization existed. It was the home of the red man, and the freedom of bird and beast reigned supreme. To-day, what a contrast! Cities and villages, the peer of those which have been centuries in building, have sprung up as if by magic; civilization and progress are apparent on every hand; comfortable and elegant dwellings are everywhere visible; schools and churches adorn the former barren prairie; and the result is a prosperous land, filled with an enterprising, intelligent and happy people, and the iron horse, swifter than the nimble deer, treads the pathway so recently the trail of the red man.

The early settlers in this region, as in all other localities in pioneer days, experienced many hardships and disadvantages, but as a rule, they are to-day in comfortable circumstances, and have been well repaid for their industry, tenacity and enterprise. The excellent class of improvements attest their general prosperity. Some of the most magnificent farms on the continent are found in this region—some devoted to exclusive grain raising, others to mixed farming and to stock raising. No portion of the country is better adapted to stock raising and general farming, and the intelligent class of farmers who have located here devote much of their attention to these lines, although wheat raising as yet is the leading occupation of the husbandman.

It has been the endeavor in this volume to gather and place in enduring form, a history of the lives of many of those who have aided in the growth and development of Southwestern Minnesota; to preserve the lives of many of the old settlers and their recollections of pioneer days, together with biographies of many of the prominent and representative citizens, who are to-day, or have in the past, been identified with business interests or the growth and development of the various localities. Years roll by so rapidly that time is already fast thinning the ranks of those who were the forerunners of civilization in the Northwest, and it will be but few years until our children and our children's children will succeed the present generation, and take the places of those who are now the leading factors. It is for the purpose of gathering the history of the life work of the present citizens before it is too late, and placing it in an enduring form, that this ALBUM has been compiled, as an heirloom to posterity; so that when, in years to come, some future historian takes up the pen to write of the Northwest and its past, he will not have to depend upon the uncertainty of tradition, but will have in authentic and enduring form a review of the lives of hundreds of those who took part and aided in the early progress and development of SOUTHWESTERN MINNESOTA.

BIOGRAPHICAL

BIOGRAPHICAL

HON. JOHN CLARK is a retired capitalist, who resides in Windom, Cottonwood county, Minnesota. He is a native of Unity, New Hampshire, where he was born December 8, 1825.

The parents of the subject of our sketch were Robert and Sophia (Silsby) Clark, natives of Axworth, New Hampshire. The father was engaged extensively in farming and was perhaps one of the most successful farmers in his locality, having accumulated considerable means. Robert Clark's father was also named Robert, and was a native of Londonderry, New Hampshire, a farmer by occupation and of Scotch descent. The founders of the American branch of this family left the old country on account of religious persecution and located in the northern part of Ireland, from whence with sixteen other families they came to the United States, locating in Londonderry, New Hampshire. On the Silsby side this family are of English descent. The subject of our sketch was one of nine children, seven of whom grew to manhood and four of whom are now living—Mrs. Eustis, of Minneapolis; John, Eliza (now Mrs. Dickerson, of Massachusetts), and Amanda (now Mrs. Fairbanks, of Massachusetts).

Until he was nineteen years of age the subject of our sketch remained with his parents on the old homestead and was given good educational advantages and took a course of study in an academical institution in his native State. At nineteen he engaged in selling goods throughout the New England States, following that line of business for six years. He then removed to Ashland, Massachusetts, where for twenty-eight years he had the distinction of being the largest dealer in hardware and tinware. He did a remarkably large business and employed thirty men on the road selling his goods throughout the New England States. In 1877 he sold out his extensive manufacturing interests and came to Windom, Minnesota, where he located in the spring of 1878. He purchased two sections of land and also considerable village property, and erected the hotel known as the "Clark House." This he operated for one and a half years, then rented the same until 1886, when he sold out. This has been and is the leading hotel of Windom. Our subject has been engaged quite extensively in farming, and this year has eight hundred acres in small grain. He has built several fine buildings in the village of Windom. He has expended somewhat over four thousand dollars in various improvements in the village, and platted an addition to Windom in 1876 calling it "Clark's addition." Mr. Clark has always taken an active part in matters of a public nature, and has acceptably filled various official positions. In 1864 he was elected a member of the legislature of Massachusetts, and served on the finance committee. In 1886, while residing in Windom, he was elected a member of the upper house, or senate, of the legislature of Minnesota. In this capacity he served his constituents faithfully and well. He has been president of the village board for four years and for the same length of time was chairman of the board of county commissioners. He has always taken an active part in matters which pertain to the development and strengthening of the financial interests of Windom and has aided liberally both by word and means in the furtherance of various plans for internal improvements. He built the county court house and was also instrumental in the construction of several combination bridges across the Des Moines river. In politics the subject of our sketch affiliates with the republican party and has become one of the leading local representatives of that organization. He is a member of the Masonic fraternity and is one of Windom's leading and wealthiest citizens.

Mr. Clark was married in the year 1860 to Miss Hannah A. Stearns, a native of Hopkinton, Massachusetts. This lady was a daughter of Alanson Stearns, a prominent citizen of the place just named. She is a lady of much culture and is held in high esteem by all who know her.

HON. ANDREW CLARKSON DUNN, one of the first settlers of Winnebago City, and the pioneer lawyer of Fairbault county, Minnesota, was born in New York City on the 9th of October, 1834. He is the son of Nathaniel Dunn, for forty years an eminent educator and the first principal of the Wilbraham Academy of Massachusetts, and for many years professor of chemistry in Rutger Female College in New York City. The Dunns are an old Maine family and of Scotch and English descent. The maiden name of Andrew's mother was Charlotte Tillinghast, the family being quite prominent in Rhode Island, to which State they came from England in about 1642. Our subject's father is still living in New York City, at the bale old age of eighty-nine years. He has always followed the life of an author and public educator, and has risen to high eminence in his profession. The mother was a lady of high literary attainments, was also a professional educator, and died in 1838. In the father's family there were three children, two of whom are now living—Mary (now Mrs. Rushmore, of New York City) and Andrew C.

The subject of our sketch was educated by his father and commenced reading law when about fourteen years of age with Edward Sandford, Esq., and also with Judge Campbell, of New York City, and for some time taught school at Fordham, New York, before coming to Minnesota in April, 1854. After coming to Minnesota he was admitted to the bar in the autumn of that year at a term of the territorial supreme court held at St. Paul. He practiced in the legal profession for a few months at Sauk Rapids, and then located in St. Paul, and was there in practice between one and two years.

Mr. Dunn was one of the original proprietors of Winnebago City, locating the land on which the city is built in 1856 at the United States land-office at Chatfield, Minn., and building the first house on the site. He assisted in the organization of the county into townships, under an appointment from Governor Sibley. At the time the city was laid out there were not a hundred people in Faribault county, and there was but one house between this place and Albert Lea, a distance of forty miles. Strolling Indians of the Sioux and Winnebago tribes were much more numerous than white men. The nearest post-office was at Mankato, thirty-five miles to the north. Directly west the nearest post-office was on the Pacific coast. Provisions were drawn from Independence, Iowa, a distance of 140 miles. Mr. Dunn also helped to lay out the village of Sauk Rapids, in 1854, and assisted in surveying the site for the present prosperous city of St. Cloud.

Mr. Dunn was secretary of the first State senate, which convened on the 2d of September, 1857, and which finally adjourned on the 12th of August, 1858, having in the interim a rest of a few weeks. This position brought him in contact with the leading men of Minnesota at that period, and he is well posted as to the status of Minnesota's statesmen of twenty years ago. He was chief clerk of the house of representatives in 1864-5-6, and was one of the clerks in the house in the old territorial days. He was a member of the lower house of the legislature in 1881-82, and was one of the managers on the part of the house of representatives in the trial of the impeachment of Judge E. St. Julian Cox. He has also held various local offices, having been county attorney for two or three terms, and has done much valuable work on the local school board. By this record it will be seen that Mr. Dunn has been prominent in the political affairs of the State, and in these places has occupied a high place among his fellows.

In politics Mr. Dunn was a democrat in early life, was a war democrat while civil strife reigned at the South, and since then has acted with the republican party. He is one of the stanch supporters of that party in the State. He is a member of the Masonic fraternity, of the degree of Knights Templar, and is a member of the Methodist Episcopal church, in which society he has been superintendent of the Sunday-school for the past seventeen years.

Mr. Dunn has gradually built up an extensive law practice, and has long stood at the head of the Faribault county bar. Not only this, but his practice in recent years has brought him in contact with the most learned members of the profession in the State, and he is acknowledged and recognized as being one of the leading lawyers of Minnesota. Thoroughly learned in the law, always a student as well as a practitioner; with not only a quick but a comprehensive mind, earnest in his convictions, able in his assertion of them; devoted to the interests intrusted to his keeping, he has few superiors as a well equipped practitioner, an able advocate and a thorough lawyer. In speaking Mr. Dunn is ready, forcible and yet graceful, not only entertaining his listeners, but impressing upon them his own convictions. His legal business is extensive and lucrative, and a considerable portion of his attention professionally is taken up with railroad work. In connection with his legal duties he is also operating a farm of 640 acres, and is engaged in raising grain, horses and cattle.

On the 1st of January, 1859, Mr. Dunn was married to Miss Diana Jane Smith, a daughter of Colonel B. F. Smith of Blue Earth county, Minnesota. Mr. and Mrs. Dunn have three living children—Mary T., Alice H. and Andrew Paul. Mary T. married Professor F. A. Molyneaux, now of California. She has one son, Francis A.

❧

ERBERT J. MILLER is the editor and publisher of the Rock County *Herald*. He located in Luverne in 1879, and has since made that place his residence.

Mr. Miller is a native of Deerfield, Wisconsin, where he was born July 13, 1855. His parents were Hon. William H. and Ann L. (Gee) Miller, the former a native of Maine and the latter born in England. The mother came to America with her parents when she was a child. The father learned the trade of tanning and boot and shoe making in early life, and followed those occupations until he was about thirty years of age. Then, in 1852, he removed to Wisconsin and became one of the pioneers of Dane county, where he engaged in farming. He was a man of excellent character and of the highest integrity, and was elected a member of the Wisconsin legislature in the sessions of 1862–63 and 1863–64. He continued his residence in Dane county, Wisconsin, until 1878, but in the meantime had removed from Deerfield to the town of Stoughton in 1867, in which latter place he had opened a boot and shoe store, continuing in that line until 1878. In the last named year he removed to Florida, settling in the village of Bronson, for the benefit of his health. He made that place his home until his death, which occurred in May, 1879. The mother died at Deerfield,

Wisconsin, in 1858. The father was a man of the highest integrity of character and was esteemed and respected by all who knew him. He was honored in life and mourned in death. In the father's family there were nine children. The mother of the subject of this sketch was a lady of high education and for many years was a correspondent of the Boston *Cultivator*. The parents were both members of the Methodist Episcopal church in which society they always took an active interest. They were consistent Christian people and the father held various offices in that church society to which he was a large contributor throughout his life.

Until he was sixteen years of age our subject remained at home on the farm and received his early training as a farmer's boy, attending the district schools. At sixteen he entered the high school at Stoughton and graduated from that institution two years later. He then entered the University of Wisconsin with the class of 1879, and for four years pursued the course of study prescribed in the ancient classical course. For the most part he earned all means required to pay his expenses at college by teaching school, but before completing his course he was compelled for pecuniary reasons to leave the university and engaged in newspaper work at Reinbeck, Iowa. He continued in this line of occupation for two years and in the spring of 1879 he came to Luverne, where he has since resided, with the exception of six months, which were spent on the editorial staff on the Minneapolis *Evening Journal*. During his entire residence in Luverne he has been connected with the Rock County *Herald* of which prosperous and popular newspaper he is the editor and proprietor. Besides being connected with this newspaper enterprise, he is also connected with other financial concerns of the city, and has served as one of the directors of the First National Bank for some time. He has also served four terms as president of the village.

The subject of our sketch was married in the year 1887, to Miss Lillian Crane, of Stoughton, Wisconsin. She was a daughter of Edwin and Elzada (Stoughton) Crane. Two children have blessed this union—Edna Z. and Ella B.

Mr. Miller has always affiliated with the republican party, and his newspaper is conducted as the exponent of the principles of that party. He is one of the ablest newspaper writers in Southern Minnesota, and has built up an enviable reputation for liberal and progressive thought, and fearlessness in the presentation of all those matters which he has deemed right, and for the public benefit. By careful attention to the details of his profession he has built up a large patronage and enjoys the confidence of a large circle of friends. He has interested himself considerably in the various civic societies of the city, and, besides belonging to the Independent Order of Odd Fellows, is master of the local Masonic lodge. His political affiliations with the republican party have been of the most cordial character, and our subject has been honored in various ways by being elected to positions of honor and responsibility. He was one of the delegates to the national convention which met in Chicago, Illinois, in 1888. He was one of the representatives of the Second Congressional district of the State of Minnesota, and was a member of the committee on credentials of the national convention. Mr. Miller has interested himself to a considerable extent in landed property in Rock county, and at present owns 320 acres in Denver township. He is building a fine residence in the city, and also constructed a fine two-story brick newspaper office. His newspaper establishment is one of the best in Minnesota. Mr. Miller is loyal and determined in his adherence to the right

and to his friends, and is one of the most important factors in the development and growth of the social and financial interests of Luverne.

HON. ALEXANDER FIDDES is perhaps one of the most favorably known citizens of Jackson county, Minnesota. He is at present engaged in the hardware business and is the postmaster of Jackson. He is a native of Scotland, and was born in Campsie, Sterlingshire, March 15, 1840, his parents being James and Jessie (Nesbit) Fiddes, natives of the same country.

Alexander Fiddes resided in the village of his birth and assisted his parents in various employments, and attended the public school until he was seventeen years of age. He then cut loose from home influence, and went to Glasgow, where he served a five years' apprenticeship, learning engineering. He then went to sea as engineer on a steamship, and for four years cruised among the East India islands, went to China, to Rangoon in Burmah, and during the war between England and Abyssinia was engaged in carrying troops and dispatches between India and Abyssinia. He was for three years chief engineer for the Bombay and Bengal Steamship Company. The company with which he was engaged sold the ship in which he was employed to the Persians, with the agreement with our subject that he was to remain with the ship for six months, and at the expiration of that time he left the ship at Bagdad on the river Euphrates. He had spent in all some seven years in the seafaring life, and in going from Bagdad to Bombay, went from thence up the Red sea to Suez, thence crossed the desert to Alexandria, and taking ship went down the Mediterranean sea to Marseilles, thence to Paris and London, and on to his home in Campsie, Scotland. On reaching this place he learned that two of his brothers had gone to Canada and concluded to try his fortune in the new country, so he followed them, stopping but a brief time in the country to which they had gone, and from thence in 1869, came to Jackson county, landing in the village of Jackson. In the fall of that year he was married, and shortly afterward engaged in the general mercantile business in company with his wife's brother, James Hunter. This partnership was continued until the fall of 1872, when it was dissolved and our subject engaged in the hardware business, which he has followed ever since.

Mr. Fiddes was married, September 16, 1869, to Miss Agnes Hunter, daughter of James and Agnes (Cook) Hunter, natives of Scotland. Agnes Hunter was born in Perthshire, Scotland, in 1840. Mr. and Mrs. Fiddes have had the following named children — Jessie N., James H., John S., David H. and Alexander T.

A gentleman of the highest character, possessed of an excellent education and a wide knowledge of men and the world, no man in this county has taken a more prominent place in general matters than has the subject of our sketch. He has interested himself heartily in all matters pertaining to the building up of his village and of the entire county, and has rendered valuable aid in the affairs of local government. In the fall of 1877 he was elected to the legislature from his district, which comprised the territory of six counties. He was elected again in 1884, and in both instances served his constituents with rare fidelity and success. He has been a republican in politics throughout his career here, and is one of the leading spirits of that organization. He has been treasurer of the school board for some twelve years, president of the village council for three or four years, postmaster from 1877 to 1885, and again appointed June 28, 1889. When he started out in life for himself he had no means whatever, and nothing to de-

pend upon but his own efforts, and by constant and systematic labor he has accumulated wealth single-handed. He has a fine store, well supplied with a large and costly stock of goods, owns an excellent farm of four hundred acres one and a half miles from the village, under good cultivation and provided with comfortable buildings. He owns several valuable lots in the village, and where he lives his fine dwelling stands in the suburbs of the village on a tract of five acres.

THOMAS A. BLACK is the president of the Pipestone County Bank, at Pipestone City, one of the strongest financial institutions of the county. This gentleman is also vice-president of the State Bank of Slayton, Murray county, Minnesota. The Pipestone County Bank was incorporated May 11, 1883, with a capital of $25,000, which was increased to $50,000 the following year, and the State Bank at Slayton was established in 1884.

The subject of our sketch is a native of Philadelphia, Pennsylvania, where he was born September 29, 1853. He is a son of James and Esther (Service) Black, the former a native of County Antrim, Ireland, and the latter a native of Cazenovia, New York, the mother being of Scotch-Irish ancestry. At twenty-five years of age the father came to America and settled in Philadelphia where he remained throughout life engaged in mercantile business. His death occurred in 1865. The father was a man of considerable influence among the Scotch-Irish people who at that time were the dominating element in the city of Philadelphia. After the father's death, the wife and children moved back to Cazenovia, the birthplace of the mother. This village was made her home until her death, which occurred in 1887. In this family there were four children, only two of whom are now living—our subject and James S., now a hydraulic engineer in Redlands, San Bernardino county, California.

The children in the Black family were given good · educational advantages in the schools of Cazenovia, New York, the birthplace of the mother of the family. Our subject received his education at the Cazenovia seminary. During his school life he taught school for some time in his own district. After completing his school course he accepted a position in E. S. Card & Co.'s bank in Cazenovia, New York, this being in August, 1873. He remained with this firm in the banking business for four years. In the fall of 1873 he came west on a prospecting tour, traveling over Wisconsin, Illinois, Iowa and Minnesota. After some time spent in this manner, he returned to Cazenovia and made arrangements for a removal to the West. His first move was to West Union, Iowa, where he engaged in loaning money for eastern capitalists, making that city his home until 1878. In that year he accepted a position in Webster City, Iowa, as teller and book-keeper in the First National Bank. After remaining a short time engaged in the bank, he engaged in the drug business, in which he continued about two years. At the end of that period he sold out his interest in the* store, and returning to the First National Bank, accepted the position he had occupied on coming to the city. He continued his connection with that institution until coming to Pipestone in 1883. On arriving in the city he, in company with several others, purchased the Pipestone County Bank, and the following year built the present commodious and elegant bank block, on the corner of Hiawatha and Olive streets, at the cost of over six thousand dollars. This building is well constructed, and is built of the famous red jasper stone. Besides his city interests, our subject owns considerable outside property, among these being several excellent farms in this county. He is secretary and treasurer of the Minnesota Percheron Horse Company, of Cazenovia village, six miles from Pipestone city. Mr. Black named this town in honor of the birthplace of his mother. At that place this company owns a farm of three thousand acres of land, and also about a hundred head of fine blooded horses. The farm is excellently improved, is all fenced, and contains some excellent farm buildings. The town plat of Cazenovia is located on this farm. The company employ constantly about fifteen men in taking care of their imported horses. Our subject is also interested financially in the red pipestone quarry in company with J. M. Poorbaugh. This company is now opening a tract of one hundred acres from which to quarry their stone. They have a large force of men employed, are daily shipping large quantities of their building stone to Eastern cities, where it meets with a ready sale owing to its rarity, beauty and practical qualities. Mr. Black is also secretary of the Jasper Improvement Company, of the village of Jasper, Pipestone county, which company owns twelve hundred acres of land on which is located the Jasper town site. Here also is found valuable quarrying stone. This latter company has also opened extensive quarries near the village of Jasper, and employs a large number of men. The company is composed of J. M. Spicer, E. A. Sherman, J. M. Poorbaugh, E. W. Davies and T. A. Black.

The subject of our sketch was married, in 1880, to Miss Georgia Bass, of Benton Harbor, Michigan. Miss Bass' birthplace and early home was Fort Wayne, Indiana, where she received her training and education. This lady was a daughter of Colonel Sion and Eliza M. (George) Bass. Mr. and Mrs. Black have been blessed with two children—Jennie and Thomas Bass.

The subject of our sketch has long affiliated with the republican party, and of recent years has become quite prominent in the local affairs of that organization. In political movements and in the affairs relating to the government of the county and city in which he lives, he takes a prominent and active position and has held several official positions. For some three years he has been a member of the school board and interested himself actively in all educational matters, being secretary of the school board. He has also been a member of the village council and has been elected to the position of mayor of the city. In religious matters he is also actively interested and is trustee of the Presbyterian and Episcopal societies. Throughout his business career, our subject has been remarkably successful. He is a man of careful, systematic habits, is of a conservative turn of mind and all matters with which he is connected are materially benefited when the management thereof is left to his care. He is a man of excellent character, enterprising, and no one in the city has been more liberal in rendering aid to public projects than Mr. Black. He is intelligent and progressive, and any project, however new, that has for its tendency the development of the financial welfare of the city invariably meets with his sanction and earnest endorsement. He is a man of the highest integrity of character, and it is a common saying among the citizens of Pipestone, that the word of T. A. Black is as good as his bond. It is therefore seen that Mr. Black has built up for himself an enviable reputation as regards business ability and integrity. No worthy man has come for financial or other aid without being granted assistance, if such was in the power of our subject. In all public matters he has been actively interested since making his location in the county, and perhaps no man has accomplished more in the development of the city than he has. Being at the head of one of the soundest financial institutions of the county, and being possessed of large means and extensive general knowledge, he occupies a prominent place among the leaders in the affairs of Pipestone county.

ON. JUSTIN P. MOULTON is engaged in the real estate business in Worthington, Minnesota, and is also operating extensive farming enterprises. He was born in Gilbertsville, Otsego county, New York, July 4, 1828. His parents were Samuel and Sidna (Hendricks) Moulton, natives of Massachusetts.

Mr. Moulton was educated in the district schools and was attending the Gilbertsville academy at the time of the death of his father, which occurred in 1840. At fourteen our subject started in life for himself; learned tanning and the boot and shoe business in Homer, Courtland county, New York, serving an apprenticeship for four years. For several years he served as foreman for the firm, then became a partner and engaged in the business until 1855. He then sold out, came to Winona county, Minnesota, helped to lay out and name the town of Saratoga, put up a dwelling, kept hotel for several years, and also engaged in the mercantile business. He built the first frame house in the village and resided there until 1861, when he went to the village of Marion, Olmsted county, and engaged in the mercantile business until 1862; then rented a hotel and operated the same until 1864. Mr. Moulton purchased and moved onto a farm four miles south of the city of Rochester, and a year later moved into that city for the purpose of giving his children an education in the high schools. From 1865 our subject was head salesman and book-keeper in a large wholesale boot and shoe house. In the fall of 1874 he was appointed receiver of the

United States land office at Worthington, and moved his family to that place in January, 1875. Our subject held this important position until July 1881, then resigned on account of ill-health. In the meantime he purchased several farms and had several hundred acres under cultivation. On resigning his public office, he moved to one·of his farms for a short time, then returned to the·city and assisted in the organization of the Minnesota Loan and Investment Company, with George D. Dayton, president; our subject, vice-president; George O. Moore, secretary, and George W. Wilson, counsel; authorized capital, $1,-000,000; capital stock paid in, $100,000.

Mr. Moulton was married in Preble, Courtland county, New York, April 30, 1851, to Miss Mary B. Clark, daughter of Gardner K. and Lucy (Bement) Clark. Miss Clark was born in· Spencer, Tioga county, New York, August 2, 1828. Her father was a minister in the Congregational church, and came to Minnesota at an early day. Mr. and Mrs. Moulton have had two children— Justin Frank and Flora, the latter being now the wife of C. J. Smallwood, a train dispatcher at Omaha, Nebraska, where he has held the position for eight years. Justin Frank was accidentally killed in Rochester, April 13, 1867. While boating with two other boys on a lake, he went to the forward end of the boat to push aside the branches of some willow trees, and while in the act, his gun was accidentally discharged and he was killed instantly.

Affiliating throughout his life with the republican party, Mr. Moulton has held numerous positions of trust and responsibility. In the fall of 1861 he was elected county commissioner in Olmsted county, and in the fall of .1862 was elected to the State legislature and served two terms. In 1863, he was appointed deputy provost marshal and deputy United States marshal. Of the minor offices, he has been justice of the peace and member of the school board and city council. He is a member of the Congregational church, and of the Ancient Free and Accepted Masons, of Rochester. He resides on his farm two miles from town, and does an extensive real estate business in the village.

Mr. Moulton is a self-made man. Starting in life with nothing, and throughout it all having depended upon his own resources and his own energy, business prudence and sagacity have won him a comfortable fortune. Enterprising, intelligent, and progressive, every enterprise calculated to benefit his locality receives his earnest support and encouragement. In all public matters he is, and has always been one of the leaders, and his name is indissolubly associated with the history of the growth and development, and also the political history of Southern Minnesota. A man of high moral character, and strictest business integrity, the word of J. P. Moulton is recognized as being as good as a bond.

ALBERT C. MATTHEWS, a reliable and respected citizen and prominent business man of Lake Benton, Minnesota, is the successor of Messrs. Matthews & Kimball, proprietors of the private bank at Lake Benton, Minnesota. This institution is one of the strongest financial institutions in the county and enjoys a large patronage. Mr. Matthews' bank transacts general banking business as well as foreign and domestic exchange, and all collections sent to him receive careful attention. Albert C. Matthews was born near Indianapolis, Morgan county, Indiana, October 17, 1832. His parents were George and Mary ·(Coble) Matthews, natives of Ohio and Tennessee, respectively. The mother was of German descent and the father traced his ancestry to Wales and

England. The father was a millwright by trade and was a well-to-do citizen in Indiana.

The subject of our sketch received a good education in his early life and learned the trade of millwrighting from his father. During all his spare time he assisted his father until he was eighteen years of age, when he removed to Wapello, Iowa, where for seven or eight months he found employment in a large mill. Removing thence he went to Mineral Point, Wisconsin, where he remained until the spring of 1852. At this time, being struck with the gold fever, he concluded to go to California, and so, buying an ox team, he started overland to reach the gold fields. He was five months and four days on the journey, and when he arrived in California he engaged in mining for eighteen months. He was not very successful, however. Gold did not appear at every touch of the pick-ax, as he had heard it did. So, becoming disgusted with this kind of work, he concluded to engage in employment at his trade. Going to Shasta City, he was employed in repairing a large mill, and also built two new ones, remaining in that locality for some three years. At the end of this time he returned to his home in Wisconsin, where he found work at his trade and built a large steam mill at Mineral Point. He engaged in millwriting and working at the carpenter's trade until 1859, when he commenced buying wheat and all kinds of farm produce and also hides, shipping his purchases to Chicago, where he found a ready market. November 19, 1862, he enlisted as fourth sergeant in Company B, Thirty-fourth Wisconsin Infantry. This regiment was enlisted for nine months, and our subject continued in the service for ten months and twenty-two days, and was discharged as orderly sergeant. On his return from the service he was given a recruiting officer's commission, and he recruited a company of thirty-two men and took them to Milwaukee and with them enlisted. He was then commissioned as lieutenant of Company G, Thirty-fifth Regiment Wisconsin Volunteer Infantry. He was sent South in command of his company, and engaged with the Rebels in Louisiana. He participated in two severe battles in that State and in all the engagements of the Mobile campaign, and assisted in the reduction of Spanish Fort and Fort Blakeley. He had charge of fifty men in putting in mortars and guns at several important places, and in all his active service proved a faithful and efficient officer and soldier. At the capture of Mobile his corps was sent up the Tombigbee river, where, after a sanguinary battle he captured a large number of Rebel soldiers. After the close of the Mobile campaign our subject was sent into Texas, and was at Maximilian's siege of Matamoras. He saw much severe service, and was mustered out as captain with his regiment at Madison, Wisconsin. His promotion to the rank of captain was dated August 21, 1865. Although being a participant in many of the severest battles and engagements of the war, and passing through many hair-breadth escapes, he succeeded in coming out of the war without a scratch or injury. He brought his army equipments home with him, and, as during the years of the rebellion, he is now ready to serve his country in every time of need. On being mustered out of the service he went to Portage, Wisconsin, and built a large mill fourteen miles north of that city. He operated this mill until fall, and then went into Portage and found employment in a sash and blind factory, continuing at that occupation for a year. He then went to Baraboo, and helped build a saw-mill and furniture factory for a Baraboo manufacturing company. He also engaged in contracting and building, and put up some of the finest dwelling-houses in the city. He remained there during twelve years, during five years of which time he purchased and operated a catalogue nursery. This, however, was not a profitable investment and he lost considerable money. In June, 1879, he came to Lincoln county, Minnesota, and prospected over the country for several days, after which he returned to La Crosse, where he had established a nursery delivery headquarters. He remained attending to the delivery and setting up of his nursery supplies, and in January, 1880, returned to Lincoln county and took up a pre-emption, on a part of which is now the village of Lake Benton. He has continued his residence in the county ever since, and has been engaged to some extent in farming. On locating here he opened up a set of abstract books and engaged in the real estate business, in which he is still occupied. Perhaps no citizen in Lake Benton is equally interested, financially, in the improvement and development of the village as our subject. He is connected with several important business enterprises, and is one of the best known and most public-sprited men in that part of the county. He owns the Matthews' Bank, a general store, and is engaged in operating three large farms, one of which he has under his direct supervision, the others being rented. He has been interested in the culture of various kinds of fruits since coming to the county, and has now 1,400 apple trees growing, and also 1,600 currant bushes, one hundred goosebery bushes, 250 raspberry bushes, all in excellent shape, and exemplifying the fact that fruit can be successfully grown in Minnesota. He has one of the finest farms in the county, containing 240 acres in one body, on which is about thirty acres of timber and 115 acres under cultivation. He has provided it with excellent buildings, and the visitor can not help being struck with the evidences of prosperity and thrift exhibited on the farm.

The subject of our sketch since coming to the county has occupied a prominent and influential position in the multiplicity of business interests with which he has been more or less associated and connected. He is a man of excellent business qualifications, and whatever enlists his assistance is almost sure of meeting with success. Careful and systematic in all details, the general outcome of all matters is assuredly desirable and profitable. With these qualifications he combines a conservative disposition, a clear head and a character of the highest integrity. He is well known all over the county, and in fact all over southern Minnesota. He is a man of the highest honor, and is respected by all with whom he has to do. In affairs pertaining to local government he has taken active part, and has held various official positions. He has been justice of the peace for five years, deputy clerk of the court for nineteen months, and in the fall of 1885 was elected clerk of the court, which position he held one term. He is at present on his second term as president of the village council and has been a member of the school board for five years. Civic matters also demand and obtain a considerable portion of his attention. He was instrumental in the organization of the lodge of Independent Order of Odd Fellows in Lake Benton and also at Pipestone. He became a member of that order, joining North Bend lodge, No. 262, at North Bend, Wisconsin.

Albert C. Matthews was married to his present wife, formerly Susan Olmem, in 1883, and they have one son, Archie George. By a former marriage Mr. Matthews had the following-named children — Stephen E., Asher, Flora, Ann, L. A., A. C., Minnie, Grant and Mattie.

❖•❄❰❮❯❱❄•❖

HON. M. N. LELAND is one of the leading citizens of Wells, Minnesota, and, indeed, of Faribault county, in which Wells is situated. Mr. Leland is a native of Branch county, Michigan, where he was born in the year 1849. His parents are Hon. Elijah and Julia (Sherwood) Leland, the former a native of Vermont and the latter born in New York State.

The father of our subject was reared on a farm, and resided in the State of his nativity engaged in farming until thirty years of age. He then settled in Branch county, Michigan, where for years he was an extensive farmer and one of the most prominent citizens. He was elected to the lower house of the legislature for two terms, and also served by election during one session of the senate. He was an active, public-spirited citizen, and served the republican party, with which he affiliates, in various capacities, having been sent as a delegate to a number of State conventions. He lived a useful life and passed away, January 10, 1863, at the age of sixty years. The mother died July 2, 1857, at forty-three years of age. The parents were members of the Presbyterian church, and the father was a deacon in that society for many years. They had a family of seven children, four of whom are now living—Warren was a soldier in the Rebellion, and served in Company G, Fourth Regiment Michigan Cavalry. He died September 6, 1865, aged thirty-one years, and holding the office of second lieutenant, having been in the service for two years. He lost his health during the war and died in Michigan from the effects of hard service. Elijah, Jr., was born in 1859 and died at twenty-one years of age. Somers is now engaged in the agricultural implement business in Quincy, Michigan; he also served in the Union army for a period of three years. Imogene, now Mrs. A. D. Hall of Chicago, Illinois, died in January, 1878. Sidney C., served in the army of the Union for four years and is now a resident of Toledo, Tama county, Iowa, where he is engaged in the practice of law and where for a number of years he was clerk of the courts;

Murat N., our subject, and William S., a general salesman for a wholesale house in Chicago, Illinois.

Hon. M. N. Leland was reared as a farmer's boy until he was fourteen years old. Educational advantages up to that time were somewhat limited and were received in the common schools. At this age he was sent to the Quincy high school in Michigan and attended that institution for two years. Then for three years he went to Coldwater, Michigan, and attended a high school there, after which he engaged in clerking in a dry goods store in that city for two years. In 1870 he came to Wells on a brief visit to his sister, then a resident of that place. While on this visit he purchased a stock of goods at Rochester, Minnesota, and shipped them to Wells, where he became the second merchant of the place, and where he has since continued in business. He built his present good store building in 1880. It is 50x80 feet and well provided with all modern conveniences and improvements. He has a fine stock of goods and keeps a large force of clerks to wait on his increasing trade. He has not been tied completely to his own private affairs, but has shown considerable public spirit in the establishment and operation of various enterprises which have tended to build up the welfare of the village. He assisted in the organization of the Wells Creamery Company and now is president of the company. This company operates three creameries, one at Easton, one at Alden and the third at Wells.

The political history of Faribault county would be incomplete without a mention of the subject of our sketch. He has been one of the wide-awake supporters and agressive leaders of the republican party in the county. He stands high in that party throughout the State, and wherever he has been in official capacity he has proven himself an efficient and capable officer. He was elected to the

State legislature in 1884 and served his constituents with ability for one term. He has been a delegate to several State conventions and was a delegate to the national convention in Chicago in 1888 and was one of the warm supporters of General Harrison. In local matters he is always actively interested and is treasurer of the Farmers' Co-operative Association and president of the village board of trade and also of the school board, and has held and now holds various other positions. He is a warm-hearted, genial, liberal-spirited gentleman, a warm friend and an energetic business man. In his financial affairs he is cautious and conservative and has accumulated considerable means. He is a member of the Masonic fraternity and also a Sir Knight Templar.

Mr. Leland was married October 25, 1870, to Miss Libbie E. Townsend, of Coldwater, Michigan. This lady was a daughter of Madison G. Townsend, now a resident of Chicago. Mr. and Mrs. Leland have been blessed with five children—Blanche, Muret N., Virginia, Carmen and Rosamond.

HON. CHRISTOPHER HOLMES SMITH, late member of the Minnesota legislature, and for years a prominent citizen of Cottonwood county, is at present a resident of Worthington, Nobles county. He was born in Windsor county, Vermont, July 14, 1834.

The parents of the subject of this sketch were Stephen and Sarah (Glazier) Smith, the former a native of New York and the latter born in Manchester, Vermont. Both of his great-grandfathers were participants in the successful struggle for independence. Our subject's grandfather, Christopher, after whom he was named, served in the War of 1812, participating in the Plattsburg campaign of 1813–14.

Mr. Smith received an academic education at Chester and Weston, Vermont, and in Twinsburgh, Ohio. In 1854 he left his native State, and, going to Bedford, Cuyahoga county, Ohio, made that his home until in April, 1856, when he went to Richland county, Wisconsin. For ten years prior to 1860, he was engaged in farming and in teaching school. In that year he quit the pursuits just named and entered upon the duties of the office of county clerk, and held that position for two years. On the expiration of that term he was elected treasurer of his county, and held the position for seven years, and during the latter part of his term he was also engaged in the real estate business. In March, 1872, Mr. Smith came to Minnesota, and was one of the first settlers of Windom, Cottonwood county, that village being made the county seat in November of the same year. While a resident of Windom, our subject was engaged considerably in buying and selling land, and became one of the most prominent citizens of the county, being almost constantly the incumbent of some important office. He held the position of county treasurer of Cottonwood county for six years, was a member of the lower house of the State legislature in 1877, and a member of the senate in 1878. While in the house, Mr. Smith was chairman of the committee on rules, and while in the senate, was a member of the committee on towns and counties, railroads, education and two or three other committees of minor importance. In all his work in the legislature Mr. Smith considered well the best interests of the State at large and the welfare of his constituents. On the same day he was elected to the legislature, Mr. Smith received the appointment of receiver of the United States land office at New Ulm, but as his acceptance of that position would leave his district of counties without a representative, he concluded not to accept the receivership.

Mr. Smith is a republican in politics, and as may be inferred from the many important positions he has held, is a favorite of his party. In religious sentiment he is a Universalist. He is a Royal Arch Mason and a Knight Templar, and for seven consecutive years was master of Prudence Lodge, No. 97, at Windom.

Our subject was appointed receiver of the United States land office at Worthington, Nobles county, Minnesota, in March, 1881, and took possession of the office June 1. He continued administering the affairs of the receivership until September, 1885, when his successor was appointed. On the death of ex-Governor Miller, in 1881, Mr. Smith was appointed field agent for the St. Paul & Sioux City Railroad Company and had charge of fifty town sites. Our subject held this important position for five and a half years and during this time handled some fifty thousand dollars per year for the company.

Since 1886 Mr. Smith has engaged principally in the real estate business, occasionally mixing in politics, finding it almost impossible to throw off old associates and habits acquired while a leader in the political events of the State. He is a director of the Minnesota Loan and Investment Company, of Worthington; vice-president of the bank of Beaver Creek, Rock county; is a member of the board of education, and has been mayor of the village for three terms.

On the 8th of March, 1857, Mr. Smith was married to Miss Elizabeth A. Freeman, of Richland county, Wisconsin. She was born in Montgomery, New York, September 29, 1836, and was the daughter of Morris and Mary (Snell) Freeman. This union has been blessed with one child—Grace E. They have adopted two children—Lillie J. (now Mrs. J. H. Kennedy, of Seattle, Washington Territory), and Bessie B., now eleven years old.

HON. JAMES McHENCH is the present efficient and popular treasurer of Martin county, Minnesota. He resides in Fairmont, the county seat. He was born in Schoharie county, New York, March 10th, 1824, and has the purest of Scotch blood running in his veins, both parents, Captain William and Ann (Ferguson) McHench, being of Scotch descent. John McHench, the grandfather of our subject, came from the old country in early life and settled in the State of Massachusetts, where his son William was born and from whence they afterward removed to Broom, now Gilboa, Schoharie county, New York, where the grandson, our subject, was born, and where, on the same farm, both the father and grandfather died. John McHench was a soldier in the Revolutionary War and did valuable service in gaining independence for the colonies. Captain William McHench served in the War of 1812, during which he had command of a company on Long Island.

All the intellectual training our subject ever had besides that obtained by private study, was acquired in the primitive schoolhouses of early days before he was seventeen years of age. On attaining that age he commenced teaching school and followed that profession for fifteen consecutive winters, engaging in agricultural pursuits during the balance of the time. In May, 1856, he went to Wabasha county, Minnesota, and pre-empted 160 acres of land on Greenwood prairie. He opened up a farm and added to it from time to time until he owned 600 acres, nearly all of which he improved. He has since sold the greater part of it. He also became the owner of 800 acres of land in Martin county, which was purchased in 1878. His Wabasha farm is one of the best in that region and is stocked with from forty to eighty head of cattle, fifty to seventy-five hogs, and about a dozen horses. Our subject is a fancier of fine horses and cattle, and deals largely in raising animals of good grade. He keeps continually posted in the experiments and progressive movements of the day, and tries to be thoroughly scientific in all his business engagements. He has excellent foresight, and is continually anticipating the market price of cattle and grain, always selling at the right time and obtaining the most money for his various products.

By reason of his extensive farming interests, Mr. McHench was prevented from going to the battle-field during the Civil War, but he gave to the Union cause his warmest sympathy and pecuniary aid. He also held a captain's commission in the home guards, or militia of the town in which he lived, during the war.

The older settlers of the counties of the southern part of Minnesota who have remained here as a rule have become thrifty and prosperous. Coming into the State at an early day, before the territory had taken on Statehood, they made good selections of lands, and being men of push and energy, they have opened up large and valuable farms, most of them being thoroughly improved and provided with buildings of the best class and well-stocked. These early settlers and pioneer farmers are now in good circumstances and are surrounded with the manifestations of prosperity and success. Among these enterprising and wealthy agriculturists is the subject of our sketch. He is engaged principally in farming, and has also turned considerable of his attention to the raising of good stock. Intelligent and business-like in all his ventures, being possessed of indomitable will and perseverance, he has gathered to himself a comfortable fortune. He has also been identified with all the better interests of the region in which he settled, and especially in the affairs pertaining to the general welfare of Martin county. He is public spirited

and is one of the most liberal citizens in giving his time and means toward the furtherance of public enterprises. He has served his fellow-citizens in various official capacities, superintendent of schools, justice of the peace, etc., and has at all times proven an honorable and painstaking officer. He has served at different times on the board of town supervisors, being chairman of that body for some time, and was a member of the State Agricultural Society for seventeen or eighteen years, through which time, and indeed, ever since, he has taken an active interest in every move which tended to the development of the great and wealthy North Star State. He was elected as a member of the State senate for the session of 1877, in which year he commenced his duties as chairman of the committee on agriculture. He also served in the following session of the senate and was the chairman of the committee on insane asylums, and during each of these meetings of the legislature served on two or three other committees. During his service as senator, Mr. McHench was brought in contact with some of the leading and representative citizens of the State of Minnesota. By these gentlemen he was looked upon with great respect, and was honored for his excellent judgment in legislative matters and for the close and careful attention he gave to his various duties. The political affiliations of the subject of our sketch are with the republican party. In 1852 he voted the whig ticket, but from the organization of the republican party has given it his warm and earnest support. In religious belief he was formerly a member of the Christian church. He cherishes his faith most sacredly, is a constant church-goer, and is a liberal supporter of the various churches. On coming to Martin county, in 1878, he took a homestead of 160 acres near Fairmont, and made that his home until the spring of 1889, when he moved into the village. In the fall of 1882 he was elected treasurer of Martin county, and has held that position ever since, now serving his third term.

On the 17th day of April, 1889, James McHench was united in marriage with Miss Nellie Daniels. She was the daughter of Reuben G. and Susana Daniels, and was born in Waterloo, De Kalb county, Indiana, February 1, 1859.

JOHN HUTTON is perhaps one of the wealthiest and most influential citizens of Windom, Cottonwood county, Minnesota. He is engaged in the general mercantile business, and also carries on a large trade in grain and wool. He came to the village April 1, 1872, and engaged in his present business.

Mr. Hutton is of Scotch birth, and first saw the light of day in Scotland in the year 1835. His parents were Robert and Isabel (Wilson) Hutton, natives of Scotland. The father was a shepherd by occupation, and was a man of high character.

The subject of our sketch was reared in his native land as a shepherd boy until he was sixteen years of age. He then came to America, first settling in St. Lawrence county, New York, where he engaged in farming for about a year. He then attended the St. Lawrence schools, and remained in the State until 1860, when he started on a prospecting trip to Pike's Peak and Montana. He was engaged in mining in the western country until the fall of 1867. He then went to Colorado and Idaho for a brief stay, and soon returned to New York State, and engaged in the mercantile business in Ogdensburg. In 1873 he came west and located in the village of Windom, Cottonwood county, Minnesota. Being possessed of considerable means, he has made numerous investments throughout the county and also in village property. He has been careful and prudent in all his business ventures, and has met with merited financial success. In his business relations no man is looked upon with greater regard than is the subject of our sketch. He has built up a large and profitable trade, and is respected as an honest and upright business man. He has purchased considerable land and built an elevator in the village. He assisted in the establishment of the Windom Bank, of which he was president for some time. He is now vice-president of that institution. He has always assisted liberally in the development of any project which tended toward the advancement and improvement of his village, and has proven himself one of the most generous and public-spirited of its citizens. In politics he affiliates with the Republican party, and is an influential member of the Masonic fraternity.

Mr. Hutton was married, in 1873, to Miss Nellie Carmichael, of Johnstown, New York. This lady died at Pomona, California, in March, 1886, leaving four children—Jennie B., Nellie D., E. May and Jessie F. Prior to her death Mrs. Hutton had been an invalid for two years, and had gone to California for a brief sojourn on account of her health. In October, 1888, Mr. Hutton was married to Miss C. J. Carmichael, a sister of his first wife.

WILLIAM H. DAWSON, a prominent business man of Slayton, Minnesota, is the son of John W. and Evaline C. (Beeman) Dawson, natives, respectively, of Illinois and Pennsylvania. He was born in Clark county, Illinois. October 15, 1853, near the old homestead of his grandfather, Daniel Dawson, a farmer, and into whose home the family of John W. went to live when the subject of this sketch was but a few weeks old. When he was two or three years of age his father moved to a farm a short distance from the grandfather's house. Every few days Grandpa Dawson would ride over and take William on his horse behind him, take him home and keep the lad until his father or mother came after him. When William was about seven years old the father gave his consent for William to take up his permanent residence with his grandparents, as the old people were so fond of him. This he did, continuing in the home of his grandfather until fifteen years of age, at which time his grandfather died, when he returned to his father, who resided then in Kankakee county, Illinois. Remaining here one summer, he then returned to Crawford county, and went to school in winter, and engaged in work as a farm hand the following summer. The following winter he did chores for his board and went to school again, and the next summer engaged in teaching. For one year thereafter, he followed agricultural pursuits, and then went to Robinson, Illinois, where he clerked in a general store for nine months. Returning then to his father's farm, he continued thereon until he was twenty-three years of age, when he was married, after which he engaged in teaching school during the winters and worked on a small farm that he had purchased, during the summers for some four years. At the end of this time he sold out his interests in that locality, and moved into the city of Kankakee, Illinois, and engaged in clerking in a clothing house for nine months. One year thereafter was spent in the wholesale and retail grocery establishment of Major R. J. Hanna, of Kankakee, Illinois. He then concluded to engage in business for himself, so, forming a partnership with H. A. Magruder, they opened a clothing and gents' furnishing goods store under the firm name of Magruder & Dawson. They did a remarkably good business, and in two years doubled their capital. At the end of these two years our subject sold out his interests to his partner and engaged in clerking for him for one year. He then came to Murray county, Minnesota, in the employ of A. Boysen, of Chicago, for whom he was selling lands. He continued in the employ of this gentleman from August, 1885, until November, and made seven trips between Illinois and Minnesota, bringing settlers out to and locating them on farms in Murray county. In February, 1886, he came to Slayton, and built a house, to which he moved his family in the month of March, and on June 7, 1886, he purchased the interest of Mr. Quaintance in the hardware business of Barker & Quaintance. The firm is now Barker & Dawson.

Mr. Dawson was married in Kankakee county, Illinois, September 20, 1876, to Miss Amanda J. Lancaster, a native of Kankakee county, where she was born July 20, 1859. Her parents were Hugh and Elizabeth (Magruder) Lancaster, natives of Virginia. Mr. and Mrs. Dawson have been blessed with the following children—Flora Agnes, Charles Arthur, Oscar O. and Lillian O.

On starting out in life for himself, Mr. Dawson had no one to look to for help, the parents being in limited circumstances, and, commencing with empty hands, he had to carve his own way in the world. Looking back over his life, one may see that the success which has come to him has not been the result of fortune or luck, but has been hewn out of the hard rocks of life which surrounded him on every side. His triumphs have been the result of earnest, systematic, thorough toil, and now he looks back over a life well spent in useful business pursuits, crowned with success and good fortune. Wherever he has been, his influence has been felt on the side of right, and he has striven in every department of his busy life to render aid to the many business projects which have arisen in his different homes for the upbuilding and improvement of the general welfare. He has held various official positions, among them being that of village recorder, township clerk and justice of the peace. He is now serving his third term as secretary of the Murray County Agricultural and Mechanical Fair Association. His life is not so busy but that he finds time to engage to a considerable extent in religious work. He is superintendent of the Methodist Sunday-school, and accomplishes great good in this line. He organized the first local camp of Modern Woodmen of America organized in the State of Minnesota, having been deputy head consul of that organization while a resident of the State of Illinois. He was a charter member of King's Forest Camp of Modern Woodmen of America, No. 134, at Kankakee, Illinois, and feels a just pride in the fact that he is the founder of so grand an order in the great State of Minnesota. He surrendered his membership with the above mentioned camp to become a charter member of Minnesota Camp, No. 169, of Slayton, Minnesota, which is the pioneer camp of the State. He afterward organized Fulda Camp, No. 487, at Fulda, Minnesota. Both of these camps are living monuments of his ambition to do good, and reflect credit upon their founder. He has been for several years an active member of the Independent Order of Odd Fellows, having become a past grand in the State of Illinois, holding his membership in Howard Lodge, No. 218. Having missed very few meetings of his lodge for several years, he felt quite at a loss on coming into a village where no lodge existed, and in the spring of 1888 he succeeded in getting four others to join him in a petition for a charter and became a charter member of Charity Lodge, No. 136, Independent Order of Odd Fellows, at Slayton, Minnesota, of which he is now the acting past grand, and which he represented this year in the State Grand Lodge. Notwithstanding his great love for these orders and matters of public interest, he does not forget to let his family interest him more than all else. He is very fond of children birds, flowers, and works of art, and my informant says, "There is no doubt that he has more friends among the little folks of the village than any man in town."

Below we append a short sketch of the grandmother of Mr. Dawson, taken from the St. Louis *Globe:*

"The oldest person, and one well known in Crawford county, Illinois, is Mrs. Esther Dawson, of the village of Hutsonville, who reached the advanced age of ninety-four years, the 18th of June, 1889. Her maiden name was Esther Wells, and she was born near Raleigh, North Carolina, June 18, 1795. She was the daughter of Stephen and Esther Wells, natives of North Carolina. When Esther was a little girl they moved to Orange county, Indiana, where she lived until her marriage to John Fulton, by whom she had four children, only one of whom is living at the present writing—Mrs. Charles Williard, now of Hutsonville, Illinois. Mr. and Mrs. Fulton moved to Illinois in a very early day, settling in Crawford county on the site of the present little village of Hutsonville. When they moved there the country was covered with unbroken forests, and heavy timber extended miles upon miles in every direction. The shrill cries of the forest birds and the howls of the wild beasts could be heard on every hand, while the lawless Indians wandered all through the woods in small bands. These and many other dangers and hardships threatened on every hand, but the hardy pioneers suffered but little injury and patiently worked and watched and waited for the dawn of prosperity which gradually came and which now has attained to high noonday. In October, 1827, Mr. Fulton died, and somewhat over a year later his widow married Daniel Dawson. By this latter marriage there were four children— Nancy (now Mrs. William R. Cox), William W., John W. (who married Evaline C. Beeman), and Henry C. Mrs. Esthur Dawson is five feet five inches in height, and although having attained such an extremely old age, is but slightly bent. Her eyesight is very good, and the only point in which she suffers a little inconvenience is the fact of having slightly defective hearing. She is still able to move about and indeed makes a practice of getting exercise by walking. She is a rapid walker and thinks nothing of walking to the postoffice, a mile distant, and during the summer of 1888 walked this distance some half dozen times. The Dawson family has produced some of the most loyal, patriotic and intelligent citizens that the West has had, and every member of the family, and especially the pioneers of whom we have just spoken, is held in the highest esteem by the citizens of Crawford county, Illinois."

———◦—◦—◦—❮❮❰❁❱❯❯—◦—◦—◦———

DWIN W. DAY is the present efficient register of deeds of Pipestone county, Minnesota. He is now serving his second term as the incumbent of that office, and is peculiarly well fitted to fill the same with the highest efficiency. Our subject was born in Granville, New York, November 14, 1832. His parents were Captain Lanson and Phœbe (Whitney) Day, both natives of New York. The father was a hatter by trade, and followed that line of occupation until he was about thirty years of age, at which time he turned his attention to agricultural pursuits, operating a farm of some two hundred acres. He continued in this line of business, also raising sheep and cattle, until within a few years of his death, when he turned his attention principally to keeping bees. He was a man of extensive general knowledge, and was considered an authority in all matters pertaining to the bee industry; having a perfect acquaintance with the nature and habits of the bee he was enabled to adapt himself to their keeping, and made an eminent success in a financial way. In the last year of his life, in 1865, he cleared five hundred dollars from this industry. So attached was he to this line of occupation that they caused a bee-hive to be graven on his tombstone. His death occurred in 1865. The mother died in 1842. In the father's family there were nine children, three of whom are now living—Eliza (now Mrs. Jason Miller, of Woodstock, Illinois), our subject and Mary C. (now Mrs. Sim, of Winona, Minnesota). The grand-parents of the subject of our sketch were Luther and Meribah (Smith) Day, both natives of Massachusetts. The grandfather was a blacksmith by trade and followed that occupation throughout a long life. He was a great religious worker, and was a deacon in the Presbyterian church for many years. These people removed to Granville, New York, in early life, and made that their home until their death. They had one son—Lanson, the father of the subject of our sketch. The great-grandfather of our subject was Noah Day, who was without doubt a native of England, and who came to America with three brothers in about 1650. He settled in Massachusetts with one of his brothers, one locating in Connecticut, and one in New-Hampshire. Captain Lanson Day, the father of the subject of our sketch, was a great worker in all church enterprises, and was a consistent member of the Presbyterian church. He took great interest in the work of the Sunday-school, and gave that department of church work a great amount of study and attention throughout his life. He received the title of captain by reason of his being a captain of the State militia for a great many years. Besides his religious and social work he also interested himself largely in the temperance movement and did all in his power to promulgate the principles of temperance and sobriety. He was also a great singer, and taught his sons to sing temperance songs. They would then attend temperance meetings and interest and enlighten the audience by their singing. Phœbe Whitney, our subject's mother, was a daughter of Isaac and Mary (Gould) Whitney, both of whom were natives of Connecticut. This lady's parents were extensively engaged in farming in their native State, and moved to Granville, New York, in an early day, where her father lived until his death, which occurred in 1838. The wife, Mary (Gould) Whitney, is probably of the parent stock of the same family as Jay Gould, of New York, and it is interesting to note that the Whitney family, of social renown in New York City, also trace their family history to the same line of English ancestry. Her parents reared a family of seven children. They were people of prominence and influence in social and religious circles, and were members of the Presbyterian church.

The youthful days of the subject of our sketch were spent by him on the home farm, where he remained with his parents until fourteen years of age. During this time he had, at every opportunity, attended the public schools, and had up to this age received a fair common school education. He afterward was given the advantages of a thorough course of instruction at Granville Academy, where he finished his education and became thoroughly fitted for the honorable duties which have fallen to him throughout his career. He commenced teaching school at seventeen years of age, and later worked for two years in Warren county, New York, for the American Tract Society. In 1855 he went to Elmira, New York State, and for two years engaged as bookkeeper for his step-brother, B. G. Carpenter. In 1857 he started westward, locating finally at Saratoga, Winona county, Minnesota, where, during the first winter, he taught school in what was known as

the "Harvey district." In company with his brother, George F., he purchased land in that township and engaged in farming for some two years. Then his health failed and he accepted a position in J. A. Austin's store at Saratoga, in which he remained for some three years. In 1862 he was elected clerk of the township and held that position during a period of thirteen years. During this time he engaged somewhat in farming, and in February, 1864, he enlisted with his brother in Company K, Ninth Regiment Minnesota Volunteer Infantry. He only served five months, however, and was discharged at the end of that time at Benton Barracks, Missouri, on account of physical disabilities. He then returned to his home in Minnesota and continued farming and engaged in other pursuits until coming to Pipestone county in 1878. He became one of the early settlers in Osborn township, and located on 160 acres of land. There was but one other family in the township when he located therein. He at once interested himself in the public affairs of his town and was largely instrumental in the organization of the township and school district, being elected first township clerk. On the organization of the county he was appointed first justice of the peace by the county commissioners. In 1879 he was appointed county superintendent of schools, in which capacity he served exceedingly well for nine months, at which time he was elected to the office, serving two terms thereafter; in all, four years and nine months. In the fall of 1886 he was elected register of deeds, which office he now holds. Throughout his career in this county he has been thoroughly alive to the needs of the county government, and has interested himself financially and otherwise in giving to the citizens of the county and township a thorough and efficient government. Besides the office already mentioned, he has also held the position of township supervisor, which office he held for three years, and also that of assessor in which position he acted for two years in Winona county. His life has not all been sunshine and prosperity since coming to Pipestone county, but, with others, he has met with financial backsets and other misfortunes. On the 17th of June, 1882, a cyclone destroyed his home property, entailing upon him a loss of about a thousand dollars. He lost nearly everything on his farm, his house, corn cribs, granary and all farming utensils being entirely destroyed. In spite of these misfortunes he has retained courage and kept sturdily at work, has rebuilt his financial fortunes and is now in good circumstances. Mr. Day was united in marriage, in 1859, to Miss Harriet E. Ingalls, of Saratoga, Winona county, Minnesota, where she was reared and educated. This lady was a daughter of Henry and Mary (Bisbee) Ingalls, both of whom were natives of New York. In the early days her parents came to Minnesota and became among the pioneer settlers of Winona county, where they lived until their death. They had a family of four daughters: Anna H. (now Mrs. George F. J. Day), Jane R. (now Mrs. H. H. Straw), Harriet E. (now Mrs. E. W. Day). and Lydia A. (now Mrs. W. F. Brann). Mr. and Mrs. Day have a family of five sons and one daughter, namely—George W., a teacher and farmer; Lanson H., a book-keeper for the Chicago, Milwaukee & St. Paul railway, in Chicago; Winnifred L., Evan A., Earnest C. and Edith.

In politics the subject of our sketch affiliates with the republican party, having had faith in that institution for many years. Himself and family are members of the Congregational church of Edgerton, which society he organized, and of which he is one of the leading deacons. He takes an especial pride in Sunday-school work, and has given many years of his life to study and prepara-

tion in this particular line. For fifteen years he was Sunday-school superintendent in Winona, Edgerton and Pipestone. He also takes an intelligent interest in all musical matters, being a fine singer, and having led the choir in Saratoga and Edgerton for many years. In his business affairs Mr. Day's character is beyond reproach, and with whomsoever he has had business transactions he has always been found to be prompt, reliable and trustworthy.. He is a man of strong character, broad ideas, and has a large circle of warm friends.

HON. DAVID SECOR is the president of the Faribault County Bank, which was established in Winnebago City in January, 1887. The leading men of this financial institution are Messrs. Secor Brothers, Law & Plummer, the headquarters of the last named members of the firm being at Forest City, Iowa.

The place of the nativity of the subject of our sketch is found in Putnam county, New York, where he was born January 6th, 1836. His parents were Alson and Sarah C. (Knapp) Secor, also natives of Putnam county, New York. The father was a farmer by occupation, and followed the same throughout his life, dying in 1868. The mother died in 1881. The father was a prominent and influential citizen in his native county, and was one of its associate justices, having held various other offices during his life with great efficiency. He was a democrat in politics, and took an active share in the local affairs of that organization. The mother was a member of the Presbyterian church in early life, and later associated her religious interests with the Methodist Episcopal church. They had a family of eleven children, ten of whom are now living—John was a resident of Brooklyn, New York, and died in July, 1889; Abbie J., of Forest City, Iowa;

Catherine, now Mrs. O. W. Fowler, of West Chester county, New York; David, of whom this sketch treats; Carrie, now Mrs. Sherman, of Peekskill, New York; Eugene, now engaged in the banking and real estate business in Forest City, Iowa; Mary E., the wife of L. G. Banister, a leading attorney of Des Moines, Iowa; Phœbe A., of Peekskill, New York; Julia, now the wife of D. Champlin, a hardware merchant of Indianola, Iowa, and Leonard H., a farmer residing near Forest City, Iowa. Egbert Secor died at forty years of age and was burried at Peekskill, New York.

. Until twenty years of age, David Secor resided with his parents on the farm. He attended the district schools in Putnam county, New York, and came west in May, 1856, locating for a short time in Iowa City, Johnson county, Iowa. He then went to the western part of Linn county, same State, where he worked for a mason by the name of Leonard Hill at mason work. During the winter months he attended college, and remained engaged as just described until the spring of 1859. He then located in Mason City, where he engaged in mason work during the summer and taught school during the winter. After one year he located in Forest City and engaged in contracting and building. He purchased a farm of 140 acres adjoining the town plat, and in about 1862 engaged in the real estate business. He became quite prominent in public affairs and was soon after elected county treasurer and recorder, holding the two offices until they were separated by act of legislature. He was re-elected to the office of treasurer and was its incumbent for six years. In 1882, having been quite successful in his various financial enterprises, he embarked in the banking business in Forest City under the firm name of Secor, Law & Plummer. This firm is still doing business in Forest City and is also interested in banks at Lake Mills,

Winnebago county, Iowa, and at Garner, Hancock county. In 1886 our subject came to Winnebago City for the purpose of beginning a banking business. His plans were perfected and the bank organized in January, 1887. The present excellent bank building was built in 1887. It is 42x66 feet, two stories high, one-half of the ground floor being occupied by a hardware store and a rear room occupied by the post-office. The bank is located in the room in the corner.

Throughout his life Mr. Secor has been one of the most prominent public men in the locality in which he has lived. He took an active interest in political affairs in the State of Iowa and held some of the most important offices in the gift of his fellow-citizens. He was a member of the Iowa State legislature for four years and was a register of the State land office for some length of time. For nine years he held the office of postmaster at Forest City and held various positions in that village, among them being that of mayor. He has always been actively interested in all matters which tended to develop the local financial affairs, and has associated himself in various business organizations, in all of which his counsels and executive ability have been utilized to the benefit of his associates and of the business in which he engaged.

Mr. Secor was not without a feeling of patriotism and of loyalty for his country's interests on the breaking out of the War of the Rebellion. He was a stanch unionist and enlisted in Company C, Second Iowa Infantry, being engaged in a number of battles and skirmishes and participating in General Sherman's famous march to the sea. He was taken sick and spent some six months in various hospitals, his life being despaired of several different times. On his discharge he returned to his business in Iowa In politics Mr. Secor affiliates with the republican party. He is a loyal member of the Grand Army of the Republic and Masonic fraternities, and also of the Congregational church.

Mr. Secor was first married in 1862 to Miss Samantha E. Van Curen, by whom he had three children—Elsworth E., a real estate agent; Stanley S., a farmer, and Myrtle, now Mrs. Regan, of Iowa.

The second marriage of Mr. Secor occurred in 1878, when he wedded Miss Jennie Lyons. This union has been blessed with two children—Joy and Ruth.

DAVID P. SEARLES resides on section twenty-two, Shaokatan township, Lincoln county, Minnesota. His farm is under good cultivation and is a valuable piece of property.

The subject of our sketch was born in St. Lawrence county, New York, on the 22d day of May, 1850. He is the son of Philemon and Permelia M. (Covey) Searles. The father was a native of New York and the mother a native of Vermont. The parents lived on a farm and followed agricultural pursuits. There were two children in the father's family, David being the youngest. The father died in June, 1851, and the mother passed from this life in June, 1879. Both the parents spent their lives in the State of New York.

Our subject assisted in supporting his mother until he was eighteen years of age. Up to this time he had attended school at every opportunity and had obtained a good common school education. At eighteen he took exclusive control of the farm and continued its operation for three years. Then he and his brother, Elihu E., operated the farm together for one year, and David, our subject, purchased land in an adjoining town. One year later he sold out to his brother and mother and came West, spending a year in Illinois and Wisconsin. He then returned to New York and purchased the farm which he had sold the year before, and operated the same until October, 1879. Passing then on toward the West he spent a couple of months in Illinois and Wisconsin, and in February, 1880, came to Lincoln county, Minnesota, from whence he went to Redwood county, and from thence to Marshall, Lyon county, prospecting through this region. He next moved to Lincoln county and purchased the right to the farm on which he now lives. Returning to Illinois he spent a month, and then returned to his farm in Lincoln county, where he has resided ever since. In politics the subject of our sketch affiliates with no particular party. He is a man of independent spirit and thinks for himself and votes for the best adapted and most available candidate for the position as he understands the men and measures. During his early life he received a thorough classical education, and was well-equipped for any line of life into which he might be called. He is an influential member of the Ancient Order United Workmen, and is respected and esteemed by all his neighbors as a kind and considerate gentleman and public spirited citizen.

Mr. Searles was married January 7, 1871, to Celestia M. Cook. This lady was a native of St. Lawrence county, New York, and is a daughter of Samuel and Mira M. (Palmer) Crook, both natives of Vermont. The father was a millwright and also a wheelwright by occupation, and died in 1886. The mother still lives and is residing with her daughter, Mrs. Searles. Mr. and Mrs. Searles have one child, Milton D.

DANIEL WEBSTER McNAIR, a prosperous farmer and leading citizen of Jackson, county, Minnesota, resides on section four of Alba township. He is a native of Erie county, Pennsylvania, where he was born December 25, 1839. His parents,

D. D. and Evaline (Moody) McNair, were both natives of Pennsylvania. Our subject spent his early life in the home of his parents, received a good common-school education, and assisted his father in various kinds of labor. In the fall of 1862 he joined the Union army, enlisting in Company F, Thirteenth Regiment, Wisconsin Volunteer Infantry, under Captain Stephens. He was appointed regimental wagon-master and filled the position for seven months, when he was detached and appointed brigade wagon-master. Later he became division wagon-master, and after holding that position for a time was appointed on Captain Dutton's staff, that officer being quartermaster of the district of Northern Alabama. Our subject was general superintendent of the quartermaster's department under Captain Dutton for one and a half years. At the end of that time he was ordered to join the Fourth Corps, which was stationed at Galveston, Texas. He went to New Orleans and reported to General Strang and was put on duty as a secret detective of the river transportation force. After holding this position for some time he returned to Galveston, Texas, and remained there until the Fourth Corps was mustered out of the service. There was then a call for old soldiers and our subject veteranized, serving thereafter one and a half years, making in all a total service in the army of four years. He was discharged at Galveston, Texas, and the regiment was disbanded at Madison, Wisconsin, where he received his final discharge papers. After the war he spent a number of years in the South, residing in Tennessee, Mississippi and Alabama, a considerable portion of the time being spent in Memphis, Tennessee, where he was engaged in making cotton-seed oil. In 1876 he came to Jackson county, Minnesota, and purchased a farm, on which he now lives. He returned to the South, and remained a few years, but

improved his farm, erecting buildings and putting his land under good cultivation. His next move was to New York City, where he engaged in canning fruit and vegetables for seven years. At the end of that time he returned to Jackson county, and settled on his farm in Alba township. On first coming to this county, in 1876, Mr. McNair found almost an unbroken, uninhabited prairie. Since that time houses have been built in various locations, settlers have planted trees, cultivated their lands, and this part of Jackson county has become one of the most admirable and productive farming regions in the country. Our subject has a fine grove of trees, which is only one among the many scattered here and there over the prairie. He has made good improvements, has a comfortable and commodious dwelling house, large barns and other outbuildings.

Mr McNair was married, in the year 1866, to Miss Angeline Crunk, a native of Huntsville, Ala. This union has been blessed with three children—Frank D., Hattie L. and Fred F.

The subject of our sketch has been eminently successful in all his business operations and his various other enterprises, and has accumulated considerable means. He does not spend his entire time on the farm, but has a winter residence in the village of Heron Lake, where he resides during the cold season and to give his children educational advantages. In the summer he moves to his farm, and superintends its management. He has an exellent stock farm, has a number of fine horses, cattle and sheep. In politics Mr. McNair affiliates with the republican party, is an enthusiastic and conscientious worker for its principles, takes an active interest in matters pertaining to the general welfare, and is highly esteemed for his loyal citizenship and integrity of character. He is a member of the Grand Army of the Republic, B. F. Sweet Post, No. 149, of Heron Lake.

CHARLES CHENEY DREW. Probably no man has been more intimately associated with the business interests of Southwestern Minnesota than the gentleman whose name heads our present article, and his name is indissolubly connected with the history of the growth and development of the counties in which he has operated. At the present time he is a resident of Luverne, Rock county, Minnesota, but carries on business in the furniture line at Pipestone.

Charles Cheney Drew's ancestors were among the pioneers of New England, having settled upon those rugged shores early in Colonial times. Records which have been preserved in the family carry the lineage back through five generations, including our present subject. This brings us back to Levi Drew, of whom but little is known except that he removed from Connecticut, and located at Madbury, New Hampshire. He married and reared a family of the following children—Levi, Andrew, Daniel, Ephraim and Girl Drew. The oldest son, Levi Drew, moved from Madbury to New Hampton, New Hampshire. He married and became the father of the following named children—William, Joseph, Betsey, Zachies and Benjamin. About all these children were born at Holderness, New Hampshire. The second son, Joseph Drew, was the grandfather of our present subject. Joseph Drew was born at Holderness, New Hampshire, August 10, 1772, and died April 17, 1833. He married Betsy Wallace, who was born July 25, 1773, and died January 26, 1871. Their marriage was blessed with the following named children—Levi, Merribah, Nathaniel, Enoch W., Andrew B., Josiah, Asa, Aseneth and Henry. The oldest son, Levi, was the father of Charles C. He was born April 20, 1800, and died July 13, 1850. He married Rhoda Ames, who was born July 4, 1796, and died in September, 1852. They became the parents of six children, as follows—Nathan LaFayette, who was born July 30, 1824; Charles C., our subject, who is mentioned at length later; Levi Burleigh, who was born May 17, 1827, (deceased) ....; Daniel Kelly, born November 20, 1828, died July 13, 1851; Rhoda Elizabeth, born March 24, 1830, and Amanda M., born October 27, 1833.

We now come down to the history of Charles Cheney Drew, whose name heads our present article. He was born at Holderness, New Hampshire, October 24, 1825. His early life was spent in his native State, where he received his education and learned the carpenter's trade. He remained at Holderness until 1836, then removed to Plymouth, in the same county, and made that his home for the succeeding fourteen years. At the expiration of that time he settled in Holderness village, where he worked at the carpenter's trade with his father, until the death of the latter. Shortly after, in 1852, he was married, and in 1854 moved to Nashua, and worked at his trade in Nashua, Boston, and Chelsea. In March, 1856, Mr. Drew settled at Oshkosh, Wisconsin, and engaged in the lumbering business. In 1860 his saw mill burned, causing a loss of all his accumulations up to that time. He at that time owned an interest in the first circular-saw mill built in that city. He continued in the lumbering business until 1870, when he removed to Charles City, Iowa, and remained there for several years, visiting, meanwhile, California, Boston, and other places, and also devoting some attention to the logging business on the Chippewa river, in Wisconsin. In 1876 he removed with his family to Rock county, Minnesota, where he has since lived. He engaged in the furniture trade, and also carried on other important business ventures. In 1880 he opened a branch store at Pipestone, which he still conducts, and erected the first stone store building in that county.

In 1880, with his son-in-law, Frank Smith, he engaged in the banking business at Edgerton, and continued this until May, 1884. He has since been identified with various other enterprises; he built the fine "Jasper front" block on Main street, Luverne, and has taken an active interest in all matters pertaining to the development of all material and financial interests of this locality. He is also engaged to some extent in farming, and operates four large, well-improved farms in Pipestone and Rock counties. He is a stockholder in the Rock County *News*, which paper he helped to establish in 1888. In politics he affiliates with the prohibition party, and, with his wife, belongs to the Baptist church, of which he has been a trustee for over twenty years. He is an influential member of the Odd Fellows' fraternity, and in all his relations, whether of a business or of a social nature, he holds the high respect and esteem of his fellow citizens.

Charles C. Drew was married, June 1, 1852, to Sarah Frances Ferson, and their marriage has been blessed with three children—Inez Isabella, Zillah Estella and Jennie Lendamine. Inez Isabella, who still resides at Luverne, was born March 20, 1857. December 25, 1877, she married Frank Smith, of Stillwater, Minnesota, who died April 9, 1886. They became the parents of three children—Cleon Drew Smith, born November 19, 1879; Frank Dayton Smith, born March 3, 1882, and died January 30, 1886, and Forest C. C. Smith, born March 1, 1884. Zillah Estella Drew was born August 30, 1860. She married William Henry Wilson, of Ogdensburg, New York, December 24, 1881. They were married at Luverne, Minnesota, where they still live. They have one child, Charles Drew Wilson, born October 1, 1882. Jennie Lendamine was born September 12, 1863. She married Walter M. Savage, of Canada, December 24, 1885. They have two children—Edith Evangeline Savage, born February 2, 1887, and Walter Merle Savage, born March 18, 1889. They were married in Luverne and removed to Watertown, Dakota, where they still reside.

We can not close this article without an appropriate mention of Mrs. Drew's ancestry. She is a descendant of the MacPhersons, who were originally from the highland counties of Scotland, where they formed a part of the famous "Clan Chattan." Families of this name emigrated to the north of Ireland to escape religious persecution at the hands of the Catholics. For some years their residence was in Ireland, but at length the Catholics in that country commenced persecutions which led to the famous siege of Londonderry, after which they determined to seek in the New World a home for themselves and children, where they could worship God unmolested. Numbers came to the then new settlement of New England, among whom was (first) Paul MacPherson, from the Parish Dumbe, County Derry, in Ireland. He landed in Boston, Massachusetts, in 1732 with his son William. The year following the rest of the family came over, consisting of his daughter Elizabeth, and sons James, Samuel, Joseph and Henry. It is believed that his wife had died previous. They settled in Chester, New Hampshire, where they lived until the sons married and new homes became necessary, and William, the eldest, went to Londonderry, New Hampshire, where he died, leaving a son and daughter. James went to New Boston, New Hampshire, where he died, leaving a family, most of whom afterward went to Ohio. Samuel and Henry went to Frencestown, New Hampshire. Both had families whose descendants are still, many of them, in New England. Joseph settled in Deering, New Hampshire. He had two sons whose descendants may be found in Illinois, Michigan and New York. The daughter, Elizabeth, married Sam Dickey, of Chester, where they died, leaving a large family. Of the next generation, Samuel MacPherson married Patty Weatherspoon, of Chester. Their children were Elizabeth, John, Martha, Joshua, James, Margaret and Mary. They came to Francestown about 1777. [Third generation.] Their son James married Mary Starrett, a daughter of David and Mary (McClintock) Starrett, November 27, 1786. Their children were Rebecca, Margaret, John, Samuel, David S., Moses B., David, Levi and Leonard. [Fourth generation.] One of their sons, John, was the father of Mrs. Drew. It was during his generation that the name was changed from MacPherson to Ferson. John MacPherson was born March 11, 1792, and died July 17, 1872, at Francestown, New Hampshire. He was married, January 19, 1819, to Lucy Woods, of Francestown, New Hampshire. She was born November 28, 1798, and died February 3, 1885. Their marriage was blessed with ten children as follows—Lucy Maria, Mary Sophia, John Leonard, Clarissa Ann, James Starrett, Levi Pratt, Sarah Frances, Julia Antoinette, Lendamine Antoinette and Mary Sophia. Their history, in brief, in the order named, is as follows— Lucy Maria, was born July 23, 1820; married Granville Rideout, of Nashua, New Hampshire, April 1, 1841, and settled at that place, where she died and where her husband and family still live. Mary Sophia was born in 1822, and died at Francestown, in October, 1840. John Leonard was born December 8, 1823; he first married Mary Branch, of Maine, who died in 1854, and in 1855 he married Lenora Sabin; they emigrated to Oshkosh, Wisconsin, where they still live. Clarissa Ann was born January 1, 1826; married Amos Fletcher, of Maine, in 1847; they still live at Nashua, New Hampshire. James Starrett was born July 23, 1827; he married Augusta Willard, of Canada, in 1850; they live in Minneapolis,

Minnesota. Levi Pratt was born in 1829, and died in 1837. Sarah Frances, who is now Mrs. C. C. Drew, was born May 15, 1831. Julia Antoinette was born November 16, 1833, and died May 14, 1837. Lendamine Antoinette was born November 30, 1838; she married William Wallace, of Nashua, New Hampshire, in 1853; they still live in that place. Mary Sophia was born June 6, 1842, and died February 23, 1847.

GIDEON W. HILES is a member of the firm of Holer & Hiles, dealers in lumber, lath, shingles, sash, doors, moldings, fence posts, and all kinds of building materials, in St. James, Watonwan county, Minnesota. Mr. Hiles is a native of Dryden, Tompkins county, New York, where he was born June 21, 1852.

Our subject is the son of Jacob and Flavilla (West) Hiles, natives of New Jersey and Connecticut, respectively. The parents came to New York State when quite young and the father engaged in farming and lumbering and also owned a grist mill which he operated a few years. The parents resided in Tompkins county until their death, that of the father occurring in 1871, and that of the mother in 1881. They had two children—Jonn W. and Gideon W. The grandparents of our subject were John and Cynthia (Griswold) Hiles, the former a native of New Jersey and the latter born in New York. The grandfather was a lumber merchant throughout his life.

The subject of our sketch attended school until he was twenty-two years of age, and also assisted to a great extent in work on the home farm. For three years he found employment in a meat market in the village of Dryden and then operated a farm in Tompkins county for some three years. In 1881 he came to Minneapolis, Minnesota, and worked for John Martin & Co., lumbermen, for one year. This firm then sent Mr. Hiles to Devil's Lake, Dakota, to establish a lumber yard. This he did and continued its operation during one season. He was the sent to Angus, Boone county, Iowa, where he took charge of the company's lumber office and continued in the business four years. The yard was then sold out and our subject returned to Minneapolis, where he remained until the spring of 1887. At this time he came to St. James and purchased his present lumber yard of J. S. Anderson. He continued the business until February, 1888, when he took in his present partner, to whom he sold a one-half interest in the business.

Mr. Hiles was married in 1883 to Miss Alice B. Lemont, of Tompkins county, New York, where she was reared and educated. This lady was a daughter of A. B. Lemont, a prominent citizen of New York.

Mr. Hiles is a man of good business qualifications, and, by careful attention to the various details of his work, has built up an extensive and profitable trade. He is public spirited and active in all matters pertaining to the general welfare, and is a member of the village council. In politics he affiliates with the democratic party and is a member of the Masonic fraternity.

CHARLES P. DAVIS is one of the leading citizens and most well-to-do farmers of Germantown township, Cottonwood county, Minnesota. He was born in Le Sueur county, Minnesota, February 23, 1860. His parents, Isaac and Catharine (Pettis) Davis, were natives of Canada and Ohio, respectively. They came to Minnesota in an early day, locating in Le Sueur county. They were leading citizens of that locality.

The subject of our sketch received his early training on a farm, and at twenty-one years of age, after his marriage, he rented a farm in Le Sueur county and engaged in agricult-

ural pursuits for some two years. Then, in order to better his condition, he came to Germantown township, Cottonwood county, and purchased a farm of one hundred acres on section 10. Here our subject has erected a very fine frame dwelling-house two stories high and 28x28 feet, nicely painted and provided with modern conveniences. He has a good barn 28x40 feet on the place, and everything is kept up in very good order. Our subject has seventy-five acres under cultivation on his own farm and has also about seventy-five acres sown to grain on railroad land adjoining. He has four horses and thirty-four head of cattle and is exceedingly well-to-do. On coming to the county he had but ten dollars in money, and whatever he is worth to-day has been accumulated by hard work and perseverance.

October 5, 1880, Mr. Davis was married in Mankato, Minnesota, to Miss Emma Dellaughter, daughter of William and Mary (Robins) Dellaughter, natives of Pennsylvania and Maryland, respectively. This lady was born in Le Sueur county, Minnesota, February 7, 1863. This union has been blessed with three children—Newton, Walter and Blanche. The subject of our sketch is a man of wide influence and takes an active part in political matters of the township. He is at present township clerk, justice of the peace and treasurer of School District No. 60, and has also been treasurer of his township. Being considered one of the most prominent men in the township, his assistance is demanded in all matters of a public nature, and this is cheerfully given, as our subject feels the need of improvement in local politics. Our subject has a nice home, a hospitable and pleasant family, and is considered one of the leading and most prominent men in the township of Germantown.

HON. ORRIN W. FREEMAN is one of the leading lawyers of Nobles county, Minnesota, and is located in the village of Adrian. He is the son of Abner and Carolie (Rogers) Freeman, both of whom were natives of Maine. Our subject was born in Milo, Maine, July 28, 1850. His father was the station agent at Milo, and also owned and operated an extensive farm, and was largely interested in the mercantile business in the town.

The principal part of our subject's early life was spent in school, and at eighteen years of age he entered the Maine Wesleyan Seminary, at Readfield, Maine, from which institution he graduated, and also became a graduate of the Maine State Seminary, at Lewiston, in 1879–80. He attended the law department of the University of Michigan, from which he became a graduate. Previous to this he had for some time studied law with W. P. Young, Esq., of Milo, Maine, and was admitted to the bar in Piscataquis county in 1878. He practiced law in his native State until 1887. He then came West for the purpose of finding a permanent location. He came to Adrain, and since that time has been actively engaged in the practice of his profession.

Mr. Freeman's native and acquired abilities have made him a man of much prominence wherever he has resided. While living in Maine he took an active part in public affairs, and was elected to various positions of trust and responsibility. While in Milo, his boyhood's home, he held the positions of collector, town treasurer, selectman and chairman of the town board. In 1885 and 1886 he served in the Maine legislature, and was a member of the committee on the revision of the State statutes; was also a member of the committee on business of the house, on bills of third reading and on ways and bridges. He has always been a stanch republican in politics, and is to-day making his influence felt in the affairs of that party in Nobles county.

After coming to Adrian, our subject went to Worthington, and spent a short time during the summer with George W. Wilson, Esq., and was admitted to the Minnesota bar in the fall of 1887. Returning to Adrian he applied himself to the building up of his now extensive and lucrative practice. He is a public-spirited man, and has taken an active part in the affairs pertaining to the welfare of the village. He was elected justice of the peace of Adrian in the spring of 1889. In the summer of 1889 he was elected one of the directors of the Adrian school district, and was chosen president of the board. He is a member of the Ancient Free and Accepted Masons, of Milo, Maine, of the St. John commandery of Bangor, same State, and of the Independent Order of Odd Fellows, Dirego lodge, of Milo.

Mr. Freeman was married in Milo, Maine, in 1873, to Miss Fannie Staples, adopted daughter of Hosea and Rachel Staples, natives of the State just named, and in which State, at Bradford, Miss Staples was born in 1855. June 12, 1888, Mrs. Freeman died in Milo, Maine, leaving the following named children—Elroy A. and Callie S. Elroy is living with his father and Callie is with our subject's mother in Milo.

W. F. MYERS is the proprietor of the Wells Bank, of Wells, Minnesota. He came to the village in 1883, and prior to this time was in the banking business in New York City, and also in Syracuse, New York. On coming to the village of Wells he purchased an interest in the Bank of Wells, and for some time this institution was operated under the firm name of Watson & Myers. In 1887 our subject became sole owner of this bank.

Mr. Myers is a native of New York City, where he was born in the year 1853. His parents were James and Mary (Wright) Myers, natives of the State of New York.

His father was engaged in the wholesale dry goods business in New York City for a period of fifty years, and is now a resident of Newburg, New York, where he is living a retired life. James Myers was the son of Peter Myers, a native of New York State, Mary Wright s father was Benjamin Wright, an extensive farmer in New York.

The subject of our sketch received his education in the Brooklyn Polytechnic. After graduating therefrom, he engaged as a clerk in a bank in New York City for some four years. During that time he made a thorough study of the details of the banking business, and in 1873 he was appointed paying teller for the State Bank of Syracuse. He held this position for four years, and then returned to New York City and remained until coming to Wells in 1883. He is perhaps one of the largest landed proprietors in the county, and owns a number of farms through Southern Minnesota. He built his present bank building in 1886 on the corner of First and C streets. It is brick, forty by seventy-four feet and and two stories high. In 1883 he built a beautiful residence and provided it with all modern improvements. He is largely interested in various other financial projects; is the treasurer of the Wells Creamery Company, which operates three creameries, at Wells, Easton and Alden. He is vice president of the board of trade of the village, a director in the Farmer's Co-operative Association, and has taken an active interest in all matters of a public nature. He is largely interested in the hay pressing business, having started the first plant of that kind in the village. He is independent in politics, and affiliates with no particular party, believing that the best ends of government are served by supporting the men best fitted for. the various positions. Mr. Myers is a man of the highest business integrity, and is one of the prominent and substantial men of the county and State.

Mr. Myers was married in 1876 to Miss Mary Hovey, of Syracuse, New York. She was a daughter of Alfred and Frances Hovey. Her father was engaged in the banking business at Syracuse, New York, for a number of years. Mr. and Mrs. Myers have been blessed with five children—Ruth, Paul N., Margaret, Rawdon and Donald.

CHARLES WINZER is a leading farmer of Weimer township, Jackson county, Minnesota. He resides on section 26, having homesteaded his present place of 160 acres in 1869. He was the first man to take a claim and remain in the township. He assisted largely and was instrumental in the organization of the township in 1872, the first meeting being held on section 22. Our subject was elected the first chairman of the township board of supervisors, holding the office one year, and from that time taking an active part in the public affairs of the township.

Mr. Winzer was born in Saxe-Weimar, Germany, June 14, 1845. He received his early training in his native land, and at seventeen years of age came to the United States. Soon after coming to this country he enlisted in the One Hundred and Seventy-third New York Infantry. He participated in numerous battles, and was wounded in the engagement at Port Hudson, May 27, 1863. He was in the hospital some nine months, and was then, on account of his wound, transferred to the Invalid Corps, and, being of good musical ability, was transferred to the band of the famous Twenty-second V. R. C., and so served out the balance of his time. After the war had closed he was honorably discharged at Columbus, Ohio. After his discharge he removed to Fond du Lac, Wisconsin, and was there married and stayed some six months.

He then went to Chicago, and remained in that city until 1869, engaged in the grocery business. In that year he came to his present place in Jackson county, Minnesota, where he has since lived.

Mr. Winzer was married in the year 1866, to Miss Ida M. Peter, a native of Germany. This union has been blessed with five children—Charles, Earnest, Minnie, Dasie and Lena.

In politics the subject of our sketch has affiliated with the Republican party, and has taken an active interest in all matters pertaining to the public welfare since coming to the township. He has held various official positions, among them being that of chairman of the board of supervisors; supervisor, which position he held for six years; town clerk, two years; justice, four years, etc. He belongs to the Grand Army of the Republic, and is senior commander of the local post. He is also a member of the Odd Fellows and United Workmen. Our subject resides in a beautiful home on the shores of Heron lake, and has one of the most delightful places in the county. It is becoming quite popular as a summer resort, many hunters and tourists finding a brief lodgment there during the hunting season. On his register are found the names of sporting men from all over the world. Mr. Winzer is a genial, warm-hearted gentleman, and is highly thought of by all who know him.

JUDGE GEORGE W. WILSON, one of the most prominent members of the bar of Southwestern Minnesota, and one of the leading attorneys of Worthington, Nobles county, Minnesota, was born at Newport, Adams county, Ohio, October 2, 1844. His parents, Robert M. and Margaret A. (Plummer) Wilson, were natives of Ohio, and farmers by occupation.

The subject of our sketch was reared on the farm in Ohio, and resided with his parents until he was nineteen years of age. He then commenced teaching school, having up to this time obtained a good education in the public institutions of learning. He taught school some two years, and in the meantime engaged in the study of law. He was married in 1865, and then engaged in the mercantile business in Hamersville, Ohio, until 1870, and during this time he continued his law studies. In 1870 he sold his business and was admitted to the bar in Georgetown. He immediately removed to Olathe City, Kansas, where he opened a law office, and also, in company with his brother, engaged in the mercantile business, the brother being the manager of the same, and our subject furnishing one-half of the money for its operation. In the fall of 1871 he sold his interest in the store to his brother, but still continued in the practice of his profession, making his home in Olathe until the spring of 1880. At this time he came to Minnesota to find a new location for the benefit of his wife's health. He settled in Worthington, and has made that place his home ever since.

Wherever Mr. Wilson has resided he has taken an active part in public matters, and has with credit and efficiency held various official positions. He held the office of municipal judge for three terms while in Olathe, Kansas; he was postmaster of Hamersville, Ohio, during Andrew Johnson's presidency, and resigned the office on his removal to Kansas. In the fall of 1880 Mr. Wilson was elected county attorney of Nobles county, and held the position for two terms. In politics he affiliates with the republican party. Since coming to Minnesota, our subject's business has steadily increased, and he now enjoys a large and lucrative practice, and is recognized as one of the most capable and successful practitioners in this part of the State.

Mr. Wilson was married in Hamersville,

Ohio, September 21, 1865, to Miss Eliza D. Powell, a daughter of Adam Powell. She was born in Brown county, Ohio, and died in Olathe, Kansas, leaving one child, George W. E. C., nine months old. Mr. Wilson was married again in Olathe, April 25, 1875, to Miss Lillie J. Washington, who was born in Loudoun county, Virginia, in 1855. She was the daughter of Samuel E. and Sarah Washington, natives of Virginia, and lineal descendants of General Washington. Mr. and Mrs. Wilson have two children—Irma Vista and Blanch.

CAPTAIN W. W. MURPHY is perhaps one of the best known and most prominent farmers of Madelia township, Watonwan county, Minnesota. He was born in Westmoreland county, Pennsylvania, July 27, 1837.

Captain Murphy's parents were Joseph and Matilda (McIsaac) Murphy, natives, respectively, of Pennsylvania and Scotland. The father was a large farmer and was engaged extensively in general farming. In early days he affiliated with the democratic party, but at the organization of the republican party joined hands with the principles promulgated by the latter organization. The father died in 1878; the mother is still living in Pennsylvania. In the father's family there were eight children—Captain W. W., H. M., Captain George H., Robert who was killed at the second battle of Bull Run while a member of the Eleventh Regiment Pennsylvania Volunteer Infantry; Maria (deceased), Samuel D., Mary and Paul. Five of the brothers were in the Union army at the same time. · Their grandfather served as a soldier during the Revolutionary War.

Until sixteen years of age the subject of our sketch remained with his parents. He then went to California during the gold excitement and remained seven years. He was moderately successful in his mining operations. On the breaking out of the war he returned to the East and in August, 1862, enlisted in Company G, Fourteenth Pennsylvania Cavalry. He was soon promoted to the rank of first lieutenant and later became captain of Company D, Fourteenth Regiment. He served for three years and three months and was one of the most gallant soldiers in the Union army. He was taken prisoner at Mimm's Flat and was held in captivity by the rebels for three and a half months, a portion of this time being spent in Libby prison. Previous to his capture he had been in prison a few days, but had made his escape. He was wounded at the battle of Piedmont, Virginia, under General David Hunter. He received a severe sabre cut across the head and left wrist. He was also shot in the left elbow while on the Salem raid in Virginia, under General W. W. Averill. Our subject participated in seven severe battles and seventeen lighter engagements, besides numerous raids and skirmishes. He served the Union cause bravely and faithfully, and received the commendations of his superior officers. After being discharged at Leavenworth, Kansas, he went to Pittsburgh, Pennsylvania, and in 1866 came west, traveling through Indiana, Illinois, Wisconsin and Iowa, and finally coming to Watonwan county, Minnesota, where he selected a tract of land which he soon purchased. He has since purchased additional land, and now has a splendid farm. His place adjoins the village of Madelia, and is in a high state of cultivation. He has a beautiful grove of trees, and is engaged extensively in raising cattle and horses and general farming.

A sketch of Captain Murphy would be incomplete without a brief recital of his actions during the excitement attendant on the raid of the Younger brothers through Southern Minnesota. Captain Murphy took seven men from Madelia and captured

James, Robert and Cole Younger and Charles Pitts. The Younger boys had fled into a dense thicket of underbrush six miles west of Madelia, and had fortified themselves against attack. Captain Murphy discovered their hiding place and advanced with his men, and continued firing persistently until the bandits were shot almost to pieces and called out to cease firing. Captain Murphy ordered the men to advance. Bob Younger was the only one of the number captured who could walk. He was relieved of his belt and arms by Captain Murphy, and was assured of protection from further injury. Pitts was killed, and Cole and Jim Younger survived their wounds through the care and attention of their captors. The captives were taken to the Flanders House in Madelia, and Captain Murphy and his brave men stood guard to keep off would-be lynchers. During the firing in the brush Captain Murphy was hit by a shot in the right side, the ball striking a briar pipe in his vest pocket and lodging in his pistol belt. The capture of these Northfield robbers was due to the generalship and bravery of Captain Murphy.

Mr. Murphy was married in 1866 to Miss Inez Atkin, a native of Ripon, Wisconsin. They have had a family of seven children— Ralph E., Georgie E., Marion L., Charles F., Florence M., Richard H. O. and Roscoe.

No man in the county takes a more active part in public matters than does Captain Murphy. He is a man of high character, liberal and public spirited, and is esteemed both as a man and citizen throughout the entire county. He has held various official positions, among them being that of justice of the peace, which position he has held for the last sixteen years. In the fall of 1871 he was elected to the lower house of the legislature, and while in that capacity served his constituents with rare fidelity and ability. In politics he affiliates with the republican party. He is a member of the Masonic and Grand Army of the Republic fraternities. He organized Mitchell Post, Grand Army of the Republic, at Madelia, and was its first commander, and is now assistant inspector and assistant deputy commander on the department staff. He has been statistical correspondent of the Agricultural Department at Washington for the last twenty-two years, and local correspondent of the Smithsonian Institution for the last twenty years. He well deserves to be classed among the most prominent and influential citizens of Southwestern Minnesota.

FRANCIS STONE LIVERMORE is a resident of Fairmont, Martin county, Minnesota, where he deals in farm machinery of all kinds, wagons, buggies, sewing machines, etc. His parents were Rufus Livermore and wife, both of whom were natives of Massachusetts. The mother died when our subject was about two years of age, in 1836, and the father married Lucinda Kenyon, and resided on a farm in the State of New York until 1853, when they removed to Columbia county, Wisconsin. They purchased a farm near Fountain Prairie, and still reside in that place.

Francis S. Livermore was born in Tioga county, New York, March 17, 1834. He received his early training and education in his native county, and resided with his father on the farm in that State until 1853, when he came with them to Columbia county, Wisconsin. Four years after this our subject was married and rented a farm, on which he resided until October 1, 1861. He then enlisted in Company B, Eleventh Wisconsin Infantry, serving until February, 1864, at the expiration of his enlistment. In February of that year he again enlisted, and served until the close of the war, being mustered out of the service September 29, 1865.

He served faithfully and gallantly in the Union army, and participated in the following named battles—Bayou Cache, Arkansas Post, Grand Caton, Waufield, Kane River, Chickasaw Bayou, Lane's prairie, Milliken's Bend, Gibson, Black River, Vicksburg, Jackson, Champion Hills, Fort Morgan, Spanish Fort, Blakely, Mobile, and a great number of skirmishes and smaller battles. He was engaged with his company in the siege of Vicksburg from May 19 to July 4, and in consequence of wounds received was in the hospital for four weeks at Mound City, Illinois, being with his regiment during the entire service, with the exception of this short time spent on the sick roll. After his honorable discharge he returned to Fountain Prairie, Wisconsin, and one month later went to Osage, Iowa, where he remained during the winter of 1865-66. The following spring he removed to Martin county, Minnesota, and settled on a homestead which is now inside the limits of the village of Fairmont. He has owned this farm ever since and has resided thereon, engaged somewhat in farming, and also for the last ten years being engaged in other business in the village, leaving the management of his farm to his sons. Throughout his history in this county he has taken an active part in all public matters, and has held some of the most important offices within the gift of his fellow citizens. For six successive years he held the office of judge of probate; in 1879 was appointed by the governor to fill an unexpired term in the county treasurer's office. In 1886 he was elected county attorney, and held that position for two years. He has held all the township offices, all the school offices, and was village attorney from 1886 to 1888. In 1888 he engaged in the machinery business and has been successful in building up a large trade.

On the 2d day of June, 1857, Mr. Livermore was united in marriage to Miss Hannah Meulich. Miss Meulich was born in Over-

witchdidt, Germany. Mr. and Mrs. Livermore have been blessed with the following-named children—Carrie L., George S., Charles H., Francis S., William R. and Eddie Jay.

JESSE A. MAXWELL is the editor and proprietor of the Murray County *Pioneer* at Currie, Minnesota. He has been at the head of this newspaper enterprise since July 1, 1880, and has met continually with merited success in his chosen field of journalism. This newspaper is the oldest in the county, its first publication being issued January 24, 1878, and is the most popular newspaper in the county. Mr. Maxwell, throughout his history in this county, has been perhaps one of the most active and public spirited of its citizens. He has held various official positions, among them being that of justice of the peace, which position he holds at present, and in which he has officiated since 1880. He has also been secretary of the Murray County Agricultural Society for eight years, and has been secretary of the Old Settlers' Association since its organization. He is at present secretary of the Minnesota Northern Railway Company. He is a member of the Masonic fraternity, of which he has been warden, and is at present a steward. He is also an active worker in the temperance cause, and is a member of the Good Templars' society, having been associated with this organization since 1866. He has passed through all the ranks and degrees of this association, and has held the various offices from chief templar to outside guard. He is also a member of the Grand Army of the Republic, and has been since 1866.

The subject of our sketch was born in Van Buren county, Iowa, July 17, 1848. His parents were Harrison and Nancy (Ellis) Maxwell, both of whom were natives of Illinois.

The father was a tailor by trade, and after a brief stay in Iowa about the time of the birth of our subject, went to Cuba, Illinois, and there engaged in general merchandising. He is now engaged in farming in Mason county of that State. The father was an exemplary citizen, and with his family was a member of the Protestant Methodist church. The mother died in 1859. In the father's family there were seven children that grew to man and womanhood—V. H., Armilda, Henry C., J. A., J. N., R. F. and Cinderilla.

The early training and education of the subject of our sketch was received in Illinois, principally in Mason county. He first came to Murray county in 1868, where his home has been ever since, but there being no schools he spent several winters attending the public schools in Steele county, and at Owatonna high school in 1876. Our subject's life has not been devoid of its evidences of patriotism, for on the breaking out of the war, although not old enough to join the army, his bosom was fired with patriotic feelings. Toward the close of the war, as soon as he could possibly pass muster, in 1865, he enlisted in answer to the president's last call for volunteers in Company K, Eleventh Illinois Cavalry. While in the service he was stricken with the small-pox at Memphis, Tennessee, and on this account was discharged. After his discharge he returned to Illinois, remaining there until coming to Murray county. In politics Mr. Maxwell believes in the principles of the republican party, and ably conducts his paper in defense of that organization. He has taken an interest in public matters, and his aid has been oftentimes enlisted in various public enterprises, which tended to the improvement and development of his locality. Being one of the early settlers of Murray county he has watched its growth with feelings of pride caused from the fact that he was an important factor in the county's development, and its better history.

He made his location in the county for the sake of his health, having become an invalid from diseases contracted in the service. For five years after making his location he did not enjoy good health, but of recent years he has been mending, and now enjoys much better health, but not as good as he had before entering the service. He has held various official positions in the county, having been deputy county treasurer two years, and deputy county auditor for some time. Mr. Maxwell is a pleasant gentleman, an able editor and a warm friend. He is highly respected by all who know him (who have not crossed "pens" with him).

———————

SQUIRE S. G. HODGE is one of the leading business men, being engaged in the drug trade at Delavan, Faribault county, Minnesota. He is a native of Perry county, Ohio, where he was born in the year 1836. His parents, Daniel F. and Eliza (Bugh) Hodge, were natives, respectively, of New Jersey and Ohio. The father was a clothier by occupation, and engaged in that line for several years in Ohio. In 1848 he removed to Wisconsin and engaged in farming. In the fall of 1864 he came to Faribault county, Minnesota, and settled in the township of Lura. He purchased a farm of 160 acres and improved the same, making it his residence until 1877. He then came to the village of Delavan and remained until his death, which occurred in November, 1887. The mother is now residing in the village. The father was a member of the Disciples church, and in politics was a stanch republican. He had a family of eight children, six of whom are now living—John, Samuel, Mary, William, Jacob and Joseph.

The subject of our sketch was well educated in the schools of Ohio and Wisconsin. At eighteen years of age he commenced teaching school, and occupied his time for several years in Wisconsin. For two years he was deputy postmaster of Watoma, in that State, and was town clerk and town treasurer until he left in 1864. For two years he engaged in the insurance business, and on coming to Minnesota engaged in farming for several years. He owned a farm of 160 acres in Lura township, and traded this for the same number of acres in the township of Minnesota Lake, and engaged in farming in that township until 1874, when he opened a drug store in Delavan, which business he has continued ever since. He has taken an active part in all matters pertaining to the welfare of the village, and has held various official positions. In the spring of 1889 he was elected member of the village council. In politics he affiliates with the republican party, is an Odd Fellow, and is one of the prominent and substantial merchants of the village and county. He owns a fine farm in Goodhue, Centre township, Goodhue county, this State, besides owning property in the village in which he lives.

Mr. Hodge was married in the year 1870 to Miss Janet Bailey. She died, and our subject was married to Mrs. Kate G. Savage, widow of Albert Savage, deceased, and daughter of William and Margaret (Van Cleek) White, the former a native of Ireland, and the latter born in New York. In 1848 her father removed to Wisconsin, where he resided until his death. The mother now resides in Delavan. Mr. and Mrs. Hodge have three children—Mary, Katie and Daisy.

ANDREW G. T. BROUN, a well informed and able attorney of Sherburne, Martin county, Minnesota, is the son of Archibald and Madeline (Miekle) Broun, natives of Scotland. Our subject was born in Edinburgh, of that country, December 18, 1866. His father was a prominent advocate of Edinburgh. Our subject was reared in the city of his birth and attended school in the Edinburgh collegiate school, being given exceptional advantages in that institution. When seventeen years of age he came to America, and first located in the vicinity of Fairmont, Minnesota, finding employment for about eighteen months on a farm. At the end of that time he concluded that farming was not the occupation he had dreamed it was, and so, taking his father's advice, he commenced the study of law, entering the office of H. W. Sinclair, Esq., of Fairmont, Minnesota. Continuing his studies assiduously until in June, 1888, he was admitted to the bar before a term of court at which Judge Severance presided. After this for three months he was assistant cashier in the Martin County Bank, in which institution he had been employed for three months prior to his admission to the bar. At the end of the time just referred to, our subject came to Sherburne and opened a law, collection and insurance office. He also engaged in the real estate business, and in that line has made a number of profitable investments, not only for himself but for his clients. He is village attorney of Sherburne and is one of its most esteemed citizens.

EDWARD ROBINSON, a prosperous farmer of Lincoln county, Minnesota, lives in section thirty-four, in Verdi township. He was born in the State of New York, October 18, 1826. His parents were John and Betsey Robinson, natives of Ohio. The father was a wagon-maker by trade, and was an influential citizen.

The subject of our sketch left the parental roof at the age of ten years, and employed his time in working on a farm for two years. He then found employment at various kinds of labor for some years, and then became a pilot on the Delaware river. He followed this occupation for some twenty years. In July, 1862, Mr. Robinson enlisted in Company E, One Hundred and Ninth Regiment New York Volunteer Infantry, and served his country faithfully and bravely until the close of the rebellion, in 1865. He participated in a great many hard-fought battles, among them being the battle of the Wilderness, all the battles of the campaign against Petersburgh, North Iron River, Cold Harbor Spottsylvania Court House, Velo House, and many other battles and skirmishes of minor importance. He was twice wounded, once by a musket-ball and again by a piece of shell. As the result of these wounds he was in the City Point hospital for some six weeks. After the war was over he came westward to the State of Iowa, and for four years resided, in the vicinity of Davenport. From that city he removed to Black River Falls, Wisconsin, where he made his home some four or five years, going thence to Trempealeau, in the same State, where he engaged in farming until in August, 1878. At this last date he came to Lincoln county, Minnesota, and settled on the homestead where he now lives. He commenced active operations and during the first few months of his residence there, broke forty acres of land and made other improvements. For a short time during the summer he returned to Wisconsin, returning to his farm to gather his harvest. In the fall he came to his homestead and made a permanent location.

The subject of our sketch was married October 12, 1851, to Miss Eunice Burrows. This union has been blessed with nine children, seven of whom are now living—Ambrose, Charles, Harriet, Edward, Frank, Fred and Lucy.

Although pressed on all sides with straitened circumstances in his youthful days, the subject of our sketch has been able to acquire a fair common-school education, which has been considerably augmented by careful study and close observation throughout his life. He is a man of large intelligence, of careful business habits, and is one of the prominent and influential citizens of the township. In politics he affiliates with the republican party, and is an active participant in all matters pertaining to the welfare of that organization. In local governmental matters he takes an active part and ably assists in the management of various official affairs.

WILLIAM ALBERT FUNK, one of the ablest attorneys of Jackson county, Minnesota, resides in Lakefield. He is the son of Abraham and Margaret (Hutchinson) Funk, the former a native of Virginia, and the latter born in Ohio. William is a native of La Salle county, Illinois, where he was born February 25, 1854. His parents were farmers by occupation, and were influential citizens of Illinois for a number of years, residing at present at Odell, Illinois.

The subject of this sketch was reared as a farmer's boy, but was given good educational advantages. At eleven years of age his parents moved to Odell, Livingston county, Illinois, where he attended the high school until he was fifteen years of age. He then commenced work, in the summer months, on the farms in that county, and attended school during the winters in Odell and Piper City. When he was nineteen years of age he commenced teaching school and studying law, following this plan until he was twenty-one years old. He was then admitted to the bar before the supreme court of Ottawa, Illinois, in September, 1875. Soon after he formed a partnership with his brother, J. H. Funk, in the village of Odell. His brother was the county attorney, and our subject continued with him, doing an excellent business, until November, 1877. He then went to Marseilles, Illinois, and engaged in practice for six months, after which he removed to Streator, and made that his location until March, 1887. At this time he started for Minnesota, and located in Lakefield, adjoining which he owns a splendid farm, where he has been engaged in practice ever since.

A man of progressive ideas, studious and painstaking in all his legal work, the subject of our sketch has built up a large and lucrative practice, and has established himself firmly in the good-will and esteem of his fellow-citizens. He is a man of excellent qualities, and in former places has held various official positions with the greatest success. While in Streator, Illinois, he held the position of alderman from the Fourth Ward of that city, and, being elected in the spring of 1883, held the office for two years; was made chairman of the city republican committee in 1884, and continued in that position until he left the city. Since coming to Jackson county he has taken an active part in the affairs of the republican party, and in the fall of 1888 was nominated for county attorney by the republican convention. He made an excellent run, and was beaten by but one hundred votes, his opponent being an old, tried, and very prominent attorney, T. J. Knox. Mr. Funk was president of the first council of Wakefield, which office he resigned early in 1888, and was then appointed corporation counsel. Our subject being a young man of good character and sterling abilities, and a prominent political worker, will soon rank among the foremost citizens of the county, and will, no doubt, ere long, be called upon to officiate in important positions in the county government.

Mr. Funk was married in Ransom, Illinois, October 29, 1879, to Miss Nellie Douglass, daughter of A. N. and Janet (Lathrop) Douglass, natives of New York. Miss Douglass was born in Genesee county in that State, May 7, 1861. This union has been blessed with the following-named children—William Douglass, Nettie Margaret and Leslie Albert.

MAJOR D. E. RUNALS, is one of the foremost citizens and influential ex-soldiers of Osborn township, Pipestone county, Minnesota. At present he resides on a fine farm on section 34. He first came to Pipestone county, October 20, 1876, and made entry on a tree claim in the southeast quarter of section 22, June 18, 1877, also homesteaded land in Battle Plain township, in Rock county, and later purchased a farm in Murray county, this State. He lived on the homestead in Rock county until 1879, when he rented his place there and moved to Pipestone county. Prior to this time our subject had been engaged for a few years in locating government and railroad lands in Rock and Pipestone counties. In this business Mr. Runals was associated with Messrs. Hadley and Kniss. Locating in the section now a part of Battle Plain township, Rock county, he became the originator of the petition for the organization of this township, and was instrumental in giving it the name it now bears. The township was named Battle Plain because of the fact that some years before an Indian battle had taken place on section 16. The first settler of that township was Charles B. Rolph, who located on a timber claim and pre-emption in the north half of section 28, May 21, 1874. John Boyes, another early settler, located in the northwest quarter of section 12, in 1875. David Hendershott located in section 4, in the same year, and his son Daniel located a farm on the same section. David Hendershott is now dead and the son, Daniel, is living in Nebraska. Mr. Runals took a prominent position among the early settlers of Battle Plain township, and was elected its first town clerk. He held the office of town clerk for some two and a half terms. He was a man of much push and energy, and was one of the very best qualified men for official position that could be found in the township. In 1879 Major Runals removed to the village of Edgerton, Pipestone county, and assisted in platting that village and in making the first improvements. The first dwelling-house in Osborn township was built by Alonzo D. Kingsbury, who was the first actual resident, the village of Edgerton being located on a part of his land on section 28. The first child born in the village was Kittie Finnigan, and Frank Kingsbury was the first white child born in Osborn township. During the first days of the existence of Edgerton, James Headrick put up the first store building, which was used by Mr. Crandall for mercantile purposes. Thomas E. Fitzgerald was another merchant who soon after built a store building and opened in business, and also built a residence in the village. The third building erected in the village was erected by Major Runals, and used for a postoffice and boarding-house. The next building was a hotel constructed by S. McLain, the size of the house being 12x16 feet. Later, William Lockwood built a small store 12x16 feet. Besides the gentlemen already named, the other business men were J. B. Barlow, Jr., hardware merchant; George W. Knee, who erected a store building on the east side of Main street, which was occupied by Charles W. Ask for mercantile purposes. Mr. Runals was one of the leaders in all public movements in Osborn township, and originated the petition for the location of the postoffice, and the appointment of the postmaster in the township, April 16, 1879, A. D. Kingsbury being the first postmaster, with his office located on section 28, our subject being the deputy. Mails were not very heavy in those early days, and it is curious to note that from April 17th until October 30th, 1879,

twenty-five letters and twelve postal cards had found their way into the postoffice, this being the extent of the business done during the first six months of the existence of the office. Mr. Runals was the second notary public in the entire county, and was the first notary in the township.

The subject of our sketch was born in (East) Burlington, Bradford county, Pennsylvania, May 1, 1843. He was the son of Abner and Cassandra (Thomas) Runals, the second marriage of both parents, the father a native of Concord, New Hampshire, and the mother being born in Bucks county, Pennsylvania. The father was a miller and millwright by occupation, and continued in these lines of business throughout his life, his death occurring in April, 1860. The mother died at Granville, Pennsylvania, when our subject was about nine years of age. In the father's family (second marriage) there were two children—our subject and Mary Ann, who died in infancy.

The subject of our sketch remained with his father in Bradford county, Pennsylvania, receiving his early training and education until he was about eleven years of age, when the father and son removed to Carimona, Fillmore county, Minnesota, where our subject set type on the first issue of the paper called the *Fillmore County Pioneer*, in the fall of 1855. Mr. Runals followed the printing business for about three months, and then commenced attending school in Fillmore county, continuing his studies throughout the winter term. Later he engaged on two different papers as typesetter, one called the *Transcript*, and the other the *Telegraph*, working for a short time on these papers, or until they ceased to exist. He then found work on a farm for about six months, removing at the end of this period to Forestville, in the same county. He then removed to Decorah, Iowa, and found employment setting type on the Decorah *Journal*, continuing in the employ of that paper until it was discontinued. He then returned to Forestville, and took care of his father until the latter's death, which occurred in April, 1860. Shortly after the death of his father, he commenced working out by the month, and did chores during the winter, and attended school until the breaking out of the war, in 1861. In that year our subject enlisted in Company A, Second Regiment Minnesota Volunteer Infantry, as a drummer. Shortly after he was transferred to the ranks, and made orderly for the commanding officer of the regiment. Later he was promoted to the office of regimental postmaster, this not occurring until after he was severely wounded at the battle of Chickamauga, which took place September 19, 1863, a minnie ball passing entirely through his left breast. Our subject saw much severe fighting during his military life, and was engaged in a number of hard-fought battles, several of them being as follows: Battle of Perryville, Kentucky; siege of Corinth, Mississippi, he being the first Union soldier to enter the works and town when evacuated by the Confederates; Tallahoma, Chickamauga and battles of the Atlanta campaign; battle of Kenesaw Mountain, Resaca, Jonesboro, Ayersboro and Bentonville, and several other engagements and skirmishes of lesser note. Mr. Runals was discharged at Louisville, Kentucky, in July, 1865. After his discharge he removed to Osage, Iowa, and for two terms attended the seminary in that city. Then, in company with R. B. Brown, he went to Poughkeepsie, New York, and entered Eastman's Business College, from which institution he graduated in 1866. After his graduation he came to Minnesota and engaged as clerk and book-keeper in a general store at Forestville, in Fillmore county for a period of one year. He then married and removed

to Anson, Wisconsin, where he engaged as clerk in the store of Gilbert Bros. & Co. A few months later, upon the urgent solicitation of a friend, he canceled his engagement with this firm, who reluctantly consented to a change. He next turned his attention to patent rights, and, with his old schoolmate, R. B. Brown, took charge of the selling of territory for B. Taylor, the inventor of a garden hoe and cultivator, and grain register. Continuing in this line for a short time, he then turned his attention to teaching school in Forestville township, Fillmore county, Minnesota, where he continued some two terms. He then concluded to turn his attention to agricultural pursuits and located on land in the same township, and operated it for about a year. Then he again turned his attention to teaching and presided over a term of school in what is familiarly known as the Baldwin school-house. After this term was concluded, he started out on a prospecting tour through Nevada and Idaho, and while in these localities he engaged in various employments, part of the time being clerk in a mining store and also in a hotel. For a time he prospected in and about Winnemucca, and later worked in the depot of the Central Pacific Railroad, same place. He next associated himself with George W. Garside, and found employment on a government survey through Highrock cañon and Soldier Meadows. On his return from this expedition he went to Columbia, Esmeralda county, Nevada, and became book-keeper for R. Nadeau & Company, "freighters." The company selling out that summer, he found employment as clerk for P. L. Traver, with whom he continued in the same town for about two months, when urgent business caused him to return to Minnesota, and eventually to make a tour of the New England States. Returning to Illinois, he visited with his brother for a time, and afterward again started on a trip to the Rocky Mountains, returning to Minnesota at the close of this expedition, and finding employment at various occupations for a period of two years. At the end of this time he removed to Rock county, Minnesota, and became one of the early settlers, as was stated in the opening lines of this biography.

January 1, 1867, the subject of our sketch was married to Miss Eliza S. Baldwin, a native of Essex county, New York, where she was born, March 21, 1848. This marriage was dissolved by legal proceedings, April 5, 1879. September 16, 1882, Major Runals was married, in the house in which he now lives, to Miss Sarah J. Chapman, who was born March 28, 1846, in Salem, Kenosha county, Wisconsin. This lady received her early training and was given an excellent education in the county in which she was born. She attended the high school in Kenosha city, and graduated therefrom in 1867. She commenced her experience as a teacher before her graduation, however, and at the age of sixteen taught her first term of school; she taught twelve terms of school in Fillmore county, these terms having been taught in but two districts, teaching in all about thirty terms of school. Mrs. Runals homesteaded the place on which the family now live, on section 34, in 1880, and resided on the same until her marriage, before which she was engaged in teaching school in the vicinity of her home. Mrs. Runals is a daughter of Robert and Jane Chapman, farmers by occupation, and both of whom are now dead. Mr. Runals had one child by his first wife—Kenneth A., born September 4, 1868.

The subject of our sketch is one of the leading and most influential republicans in Pipestone county, and wields a strong influence in the councils of that party. He is a leading member of the Grand Army of the Republic, and was first senior vice-commander of U. S. Grant Post, No. 80, which position he held for one term. He was also appointed assistant inspector of the State department Grand Army of the Republic, and continued as incumbent of that office for one term. His ability as an executive officer and as a business man have been recognized in many ways during his residence in Rock and Pipestone counties, and in every instance he has proven his capability, and has administered the duties of the various offices with credit and honor. He was justice of the peace of the township for one term and was afterward elected once and appointed twice to the position, but refused to qualify. While holding that position he proved himself a man of excellent judgment and judicial knowledge.

It is well to notice here, before closing this sketch of Mr. Runals, the importance of his service during the war. He was placed in many difficult and trying circumstances, but was faithful to the Union cause in every duty, serving in different capacities with rare fidelity and patriotism. During the latter part of the war he was ordered to report for duty to General W. H. Slocum, commanding left wing Army of Georgia, where he remained from March 6, 1865, until June 10, same year, when the army was being disbanded, rendering excellent service. Major Runals is decidedly a man of action, and in whatever line of work he is called to render assistance his deportment is characterized by push and energy.

He has led a checkered active life, but through it all has commanded the esteem and confidence of all those with whom he has had to do. He has been quite successful in his business operations and has accumulated considerable means. He is a warm friend, a loyal citizen, a strong advocate of temperance and is respected by all with whom he has to do.

HEMAN A. CONE is the present efficient county treasurer of Cottonwood
county, Minnesota. He is a native of Vermont, where he was born in the year 1839.

Mr. Cone is the son of Randall and Polly
(Carpenter) Cone, natives of Vermont. The
father was engaged to some extent in farming, but by trade was a boot and shoe maker.
He was a man of excellent qualifications,
and was highly respected. He had a family
of seven children, three of whom are now
living—Seymour R., Cornelia S. and Heman A.

The subject of our sketch spent his early
life beneath the parental roof. When he
was twelve years of age his father died, and
our subject was obliged to work to provide
for himself means upon which to live. He
found employment on a farm, and continued
that line of work for some two years, after
which two years were spent at the tannery
trade. Again he returned to farming,
spending two years thereat. He then engaged in raising and selling nursery stock.
He continued this line of business for some
three years, and then entered the Connecticut Literary Institution at Suffield, continuing his studies therein for one year. In
1861 he enlisted in Company C, First Connecticut Heavy Artillery. He served in the
Union army four and one-half years, and
held the office of corporal, for one year
acting as ordnance sergeant. Among
the battles in which our subject participated were those of Hanover Court House,
Fair Oaks, siege of Yorktown, Malvern
Hill, Bermuda Hundred, under General Butler, and the siege of Petersborough. These
were the more important engagements in
which our subject participated. He served
his country gallantly and faithfully and was
discharged in 1865. He soon returned to
Connecticut and again engaged in the nursery business, going, after a year and a half,
to Appleton, Wisconsin, where he worked at

fire insurance for two years. In 1870 he
located in Cottonwood county, Minnesota,
took a pre-emption in the township of Springfield and a homestead in Amo township. He
proved up on the land and continued thereon
some two years. In 1872 he was elected by
the unanimous choice of the people as register of deeds. He held that position for six
years, and was then appointed as postmaster
of Windom, receiving his commission from
President Grant. He held the position some
seven years and was then appointed deputy
county treasurer, being elected to that office
in the fall of 1886. He was re-elected in
1888. Wherever he has been Mr. Cone has
taken an active interest in matters of a public nature and has held various official positions, among them being that of justice of
the peace of the village of Windom, etc. He
is a leading member of the republican party
and is also connected with the Masonic,
Grand Army of the Republic and Ancient
Order of United Workmen fraternities. He
has a valuable and comfortable home in the
village and is one of the prominent and most
substantial citizens of this part of the county.

Mr. Cone was married in 1867 to Miss
Priscilla A. Jopson, a native of Massachusetts. Mr. and Mrs. Cone have been blessed
with three children—Frank S., Benjamin A.
and Edna.

EZRA P. BARKER, a leading hardware
merchant of the village of Slayton,
Murray county, Minnesota, was born in
Chester, Middlesex county, Connecticut, September 6, 1837. His parents were Elihu and
Cynthia (Baldwin) Barker, natives of Connecticut. The father was a carpenter and
joiner by trade, and when our subject was
seven years of age his parents moved to
Peru, Illinois, where his father died in 1848.

The early education of Ezra P. Barker
was received in the State of Illinois. Soon

after his father's death he went to Stone Church, Genesee county, New York. Here he resided with his grandmother until 1856, assisting an uncle in work on the old farm. Here he was given good educational advantages, and in 1856 went to La Salle, Illinois, where he learned the tinner's trade, remaining in that village until 1863. At this time he removed to Wenona, same State, and opened a hardware store and tin shop for himself. He continued in this business until 1880, when he sold out, went to Mendota, same State, and opened in the line in which he had been previously engaged. In 1885 he sold out his interests in Illinois, and came to Slayton, Minnesota, where he again engaged in the hardware business. His first visit to Slayton was in 1882, where he put up a store building in 1883, and soon after returned to Illinois. During three summers he spent a few months in Slayton, and in 1885 brought his family to the village, where he has since resided.

Mr. Barker was married in West Randolph, Vermont, March 25, 1864, to Miss Maria Morton, who was born in Vermont, March 13, 1839. She was the daughter of John and Mary (Sanford) Morton, natives of Vermont. Mrs. Barker died May 25, 1880, leaving one child, Willis E., born November 2, 1865, who married Jennie Taylor, of Mendota. The subject of our sketch was again married, in Wenona, Illinois, June 21, 1881, to Miss Louisa Robbins, who was born in Springfield, Otsego county, New York, July 12, 1848. She was the daughter of Joseph and Emma (Bates) Robbins, natives, respectively, of Massachusetts and England. This latter union has been blessed with one child, Emma Bertelle, born in Mendota, Illinois, September 16, 1884.

The subject of our sketch has been an active participant in all matters of a public nature, and has accomplished as much as any other citizen in the village toward building up and bringing about the present excellent financial condition of local affairs. He is a man of much public spirit, and is an upright and intelligent citizen, and is highly esteemed by all who know him. Among the offices which he has held throughout his life may be named that of alderman in the village of Wenona, treasurer of the fair association, and village trustee in Slayton for two years, and various other local and minor offices, thus showing that our subject has taken an active part in political affairs. He is a member of the Independent Order of Odd Fellows and the Modern Woodmen of America. When our subject started out in life he had but $150. By careful use of this and by watching his opportunities and making conservative investments, he had accumulated, in January, 1880, a large amount of property. He sold his business interests in January, 1880, for $10,000 in cash. Coming to Slayton, he engaged in the hardware business in partnership with Mr. Quaintance, with whom he continued until 1886, when Mr. Dawson purchased Mr. Quaintance's share of the business, and the business is now operated under the firm name of Barker & Dawson. In connection with their hardware business they also manufacture all kinds of tinware, and carry a large and costly supply of excellent goods.

WILLIAM H. BRADLEY. This gentleman represents one of the largest and most important mercantile establishments in Lake Benton, Lincoln county, Minnesota. He located in the village in 1885, and has since been engaged in operating his extensive business. His parents were Lemi and Urania (Hart) Bradley, both natives of New York. They were farmers by occupation, and resided in their native State where the father died.

William H. Bradley was born in Tompkins county, New York, March 13, 1854. His early life was spent with his parents on the farm, and his early education was received in the district schools. When he was about thirteen years old his mother moved into the village of Groton, the father having died some years before. On moving into that place our subject commenced clerking in a general store when he was seventeen years of age, up to which time he had attended the district schools. He continued his clerkship for two years, and then went to Auburn, New York, and found employ ment as clerk in a dry goods store. Continuing in that city one year, in 1874 he came to Lincoln county, Minnesota, on a hunting and fishing expedition. His health had been poor up to this time, and this trip was made for the purpose of recuperation. He spent the entire summer in hunting, and in the fall went to Minneapolis, finding employment in that city in a dry goods store, where he remained somewhat over a year. He then returned to his native State and remained until the winter of 1875-76, when he returned to Lincoln county and took a homestead, on which he lived a short time. This was in the spring of 1876, and the year previous the country had been scourged by grasshoppers and the ground was full of grasshopper eggs. Our subject remained until these insects began hatching out, and he then concluded that it would not be profitable to remain during the summer, so he went to Minneapolis and found employment as a clerk in a cigar store during the summer, and through the following winter he clerked in a hotel. In the spring of 1877 he returned to his claim in Lincoln county and kept "bachelor's hall" for four years, improving the farm and proving up in 1883. He continued his residence on the farm until June, 1885, when he traded it for a dwelling, a store building, and also a stock of

groceries, in the village of Lake Benton. He moved to that place shortly after, and has ever since been engaged in that line. Since coming to the city he has identified himself intimately with the affairs of local government, and has held the office of town clerk. He is a man of excellent business principles, has a fine stock of goods and an extensive trade. His business transactions have always been characterized by uprightness and fair dealing, and he has made friends of all with whom he has had business relations.

Mr. Bradley was married in Lake Benton, May 22, 1883, to Miss Fannie Fletcher, who was born in Winona county, Minnesota. She was the daughter of Alexander and Rose (Gilbert) Fletcher, the former a native of New York and the latter a native of England. This marriage has been blessed with two children—Lemi and Bernice.

ISAAC L. HART. This gentleman is the proprietor and publisher of the *Pipestone County Star*, the pioneer newspaper of Pipestone county, Minnesota. This journal was established June 19,1879, and by its successful management Mr. Hart has grown in popularity and influence, and his paper has become the leading newspaper in the county. Having entered the newspaper business at a very early age, the gentleman whose name appears at the head of this sketch has become a master of the art in which he is at present engaged, and understands the business in all its manifold details. He has therefore built his paper on a strong foundation and, understanding how best to push its management, has caused it to gain in popularity and favor among the people and has built up a large subscription list and other patronage.

The place of the nativity of the subject of our sketch is found in the State of New York, where he was born August 9, 1843. He is the son of Elijah and Margaret (Stanton) Hart, both of whom are natives of New York State. The father made a business of manufacturing fire-engine hose and followed that occupation in New York until 1850, at which time he removed to Chicago, Illinois. For some years he followed the old business in that city, but later entered the steam fire department, where he continued some years. He is still a resident of Chicago and is at present employed in the city water works. The mother died in January, 1887. In the father's family there were nine children, three of whom are now living—Martha I., Isaac L. and John S. Martha I. married Robert V. Shurley and is at present living in Chicago. She has two children—Henry and Winnie, the latter now Mrs. George Leslie, of Chicago. John S. still resides in that city.

The school education of the subject of our sketch was of comparatively light character, but, being an eager reader and a careful observer throughout his life, he has acquired an excellent and extensive fund of general knowledge, and has in this way become a self-educated man. His business, too, has been of such a character as to give him an excellent chance to obtain a large knowledge of practical things and an acquaintance with the events of current history. When nine years of age he entered the office of the Chicago *Times* as an apprentice, serving seven years, and at the end of that period he engaged in the office of the *Evening Journal*, and continued his employment there until the breaking out of the War of the Rebellion. August 7, 1862, he enlisted in Company C, Seventy-second Illinois Infantry, and continued serving in the Union army until March 21, 1864, when he was discharged. Immediately after his discharge he entered the treasury department at Natchez, Mississippi, where he was employed until September of the same year. At that

time he returned to his home in Chicago, Illinois. The war experience of our subject was of the severest and most exciting nature. He was engaged in a number of the most sanguinary battles of the Civil War, among them being Champion Hills, Black River, siege of Vicksburg, and all the skirmishes and battles of the Yazoo river expedition, in which his regiment was under the command of General McPherson. He was stricken down with small-pox at Natchez, Mississippi, and confined to the hospital over two months. During this time his life was despaired of a number of times, but he recovered, and at the close of the war he returned to his friends and family in Chicago. In that city he continued working at his trade until 1871, when he came to Iowa, settling at Eldora, Hardin county, where he established the Eldora *Herald*. He continued the operation of that journal until 1879, when he sold out and came to Pipestone county, where he established his present paper, which was the first newspaper in the county, and it has met with fine success. He built his present office, 25x60 feet, in 1883. It is constructed out of the famous jasper stone. This stone is of the finest kind of building material and makes a beautiful and elegant looking building. The first office was built by our subject on Olive street in 1879, at which time his office was 18x40 feet, and was then the best frame structure in the county. In 1881 Mr. Hart built a fine residence on Maine street. It is one of the best in the city, the grounds being beautifully ornamented with shade trees of various kinds.

Editor Hart was married in 1865 to Miss Mary E. Gardner, of Chicago, Illinois, where she was reared and educated. She was the daughter of Charles and Ellen Gardner. Mr. and Mrs. Hart have been blessed with six children—Gardner E., now a partner with his father in the *Star* office; Lillian G.,

Mabel G., Charles G., Ralph G. and Kittie E. In political affairs the subject of our sketch has taken a prominent part since settling in Pipestone county. He has not only taken an active part in all matters which pertain to the welfare of the government of the State and county but is also deeply interested in whatever pertains to the welfare of Pipestone City and vicinity. He is tied to no party, but being of an independent spirit, fearless in opinions, and out-spoken through his paper in all things which seem to him right and just, he conducts the *Star* on an independent basis. It may be said of him that this course has made him more friends than otherwise, as all men of sound principles and good judgment look with favor upon independence and fearlessness in politics. Our subject has served his constituency well and ably in several positions of honor and responsibility. For one term he held the office of judge of probate and was village recorder for the same length of time, and was also secretary of the school board for three years. He is a leading and influential Mason and Odd Fellow, and is adjutant of Simon Mix Post, Grand Army of the Republic, of Pipestone City. In all matters which pertain to the social and financial development of his adopted city he takes an increasing interest, and is always willing to render aid in any manner possible.

SIMON HUNTINGTON is an influential and prosperous farmer of Mountain Lake township, Cottonwood county, Minnesota. He was born in Vergennes, Vermont, December 19th, 1825. At this early day Vergennes was the only city in the present territory of Vermont and had about three hundred inhabitants.

The subject of our sketch is the son of Jonathan and Sally (Hickox) Huntington, the father a native of Massachusetts and the mother a native of Connecticut. The father was a carpenter by occupation and followed that business until fifty-eight years of age. He then purchased a farm and engaged in farming during the balance of his life.

Simon Huntington resided with his parents on the farm throughout his early life and received a good common school education. He was married in 1849 and continued to live with his parents for three years thereafter. In 1852 he removed to Winnebago county, Illinois, where he purchased a farm on which he lived for four years. Removing thence he engaged in the mercantile business in Clayton county, Iowa, where he remained four years. He then sold out and went on the road for a Milwaukee wholesale house, continuing traveling for that company until 1878. In 1872, however, he moved his family to Cottonwood county to a claim that he had taken in 1871. He had three claims, a pre-emption, a tree claim and a homestead, and has obtained deeds for the pre-emption and homestead. The tree claim he has turned over to his daughter Eliza. Our subject continued traveling until 1878, and then came to his farm, since which time he has devoted his time to agricultural pursuits. He has made fine improvements on his place, and has about three hundred acres under cultivation, and has devoted considerable of his attention to raising fine stock and dairying. He has a herd of finely graded Durham cattle, the admiration of all his fellow-townsmen—also a flock of one thousand sheep, of the finest in the county. Our subject has always taken an active interest in matters pertaining to the public welfare, and has held various official positions. He has been justice of the peace for several years, has been school treasurer or director ever since he settled in the township, and has held various other positions. He is a leading republican, and is a member of the Congregational church. His experience with farming during the first few years of his ownership of the lands in Cottonwood county, was not very cheerful, as for three years during the grasshopper raids he did not raise enough grain to pay expenses. With the exception of this time he has been quite successful and has accumulated considerable means. Mr. Huntington is a man of excellent qualities, genial, frank and open-hearted, and is respected by all who know him. He is a man of good business capabilities, and is a wise counselor in all matters pertaining to private as well as public welfare. He is a stockholder and one of the board of directors of the Cottonwood County Bank, recently organized at Windom.

Mr. Huntington was married in St. Albans, Vermont, January 30, 1849, to Miss Louisa M. Kellogg, a native of Vermont, where she was born in June, 1826. This lady was the daughter of Simon H. and Louisa (Evarts) Kellogg. Mr. and Mrs. Huntington have been blessed with the following-named children — Ebenezer C., Eliza C., Sarah L., Charles K. and Nellie S., all living except Sarah L. and Nellie S. Ebenezer married Julia Knowlton, and resides in the village of Windom. A sketch of this gentleman is given in another department of this work. Charles married Frankie Clark, a daughter of DeWitt and Sarah (Lack) Clark, of Lemars, Iowa. He now resides at Seneca, Nebraska, and is in the employ of the Chicago, Burlington & Quincy Railroad as station agent, a business he has followed since he was seventeen years of age. Eliza C. is unmarried, resides with her parents on the farm, and by industry and economy has accumulated considerable property in her own name. Mr. Huntington having arrived at an age when it is desirable to have less care on his hands desires to sell this property, and offers it for sale at low figures, and on long time, at a low rate of interest. There is no better opening anywhere in the country for a young man of energy to locate, where he can make a fortune in a few years.

━━━◦━≫━❰❁❱━◦━━━

JOHN H. WELCH is the present efficient and popular postmaster of Winnebago City, Faribault county, Minnesota. The place of his nativity is found in Niagara county, New York, where he was born March 21, 1833. His parents were Nathan and Amy (Lake) Welch, the former a native of New York and the latter born in Connecticut. The father was engaged extensively in farming throughout his life and died in the year 1835. The mother died in 1875. Of four children in the father's family three are now living—Daniel L., Wheaton A. and John H. Wheaton A. is principal of one of the ward schools in Brooklyn, New York. The grandfather of our subject was William Welch, a native of Connecticut and of English descent. He was a farmer by occupation. The father of our subject's mother was Daniel Lake, a native of Connecticut, where he was engaged in farming throughout the most of his life.

The subject of our sketch spent his early days on the home farm where he received a good common school education. He was given the advantages of a course in the high school at Lockport, New York, from which he graduated. He remained with his parents until twenty-one years of age and then removed to Wisconsin where he spent three years in civil engineering on the Milwaukee and St. Paul and the Milwaukee and Beloit railroads. In 1857 he came to Faribault county and took a pre-emption in the township of Verona, four miles southwest of Winnebago City. He broke a portion of this land and made other valuable improvements, moving thereon in 1861 after his marriage. Shortly after his removal to the farm, however, in May, 1861, he was appointed by

President Lincoln as register of the United States land office at Chatfield. In October this office was moved to Winnebago City to which place our subject also came. He held the position until the fall of 1866, when he engaged in the hardware business, continuing in the same until 1887. He was appointed postmaster of Winnebago City by President Harrison in 1889, which position he now occupies. Mr. Welch has been one of Winnebago City's most prominent citizens and has become largely interested in city property. He purchased an interest in Easton's addition to the village, which proved a valuable investment. He built the large brick block in which is now the Winnebago City opera house. He owns a good house on Moulton street. In public matters Mr. Welch has always taken an active interest and has held some of the most important local offices. He has been chairman of the board of supervisors, township clerk and village recorder. He was also president of the village for some time, and was a member of the village board of education.

Mr. Welch was married in 1859 to Miss Martha J. Hazeltine, of Dodge county, Wisconsin, and daughter of William and Sarah (Blesset) Hazeltine, natives of England. Her parents came to America before their marriage and resided at Utica, New York, for several years. The father finally moved to Madison county, New York, where, for about nineteen years, he was engaged in the boot and shoe business. They then removed to Dodge county, Wisconsin, and engaged in farming. The father died in 1880 and the mother in 1883. In the Hazeltine family there were seven children, six of whom are now living— William B., Elizabeth (now Mrs. DeGarmo), Laura A. (now Mrs. Andrews), Martha J. (now Mrs. Welch), George S. and Burdett B. Mr. and Mrs. Welch have been blessed with three children—Herbert N., Frances A.

(now Mrs. Dr. Beebe, a leading dentist of Winnebago City), and Fallie E. The wife and children are all members of the Presbyterian church, in which society they are all most prominent and influential workers.

In all matters tending to the welfare and improvement of Winnebago City and vinicity, Mr. Welch has always proved a valuable factor. He has always sanctioned and given material aid in the development of all financial matters which tended to the better establishment of the business of Winnebago, and in the organization of various societies he has rendered valuable aid. In politics he has for years been a stanch republican and cast his first vote for John C. Fremont, in 1856. He is a man of excellent business qualities, is genial, warm-hearted and generous, and is highly esteemed by all who know him.

THEOPHILUS E. HILLS is a resident of the village of Heron Lake, Jackson county, Minnesota. He is one of the most influential citizens of the county and is engaged in the banking business. He was born near Oskaloosa, Mahaska county, Iowa, in March, 1844, his parents being Riley E. and Melissa (Pierce) Hills. The father was a native of the State of New York and the mother was born in New Jersey. The father of our subject was a farmer by occupation, and died in 1859; the mother died in 1848. Our subject was one of two children, his only brother, Wesley, dying in 1848.

Up to seventeen years of age our subject assisted his father on the farm and attended the district schools. He then enlisted in Company I, Thirty-fourth Regiment Illinois Volunteer Infantry, under E. N. Kirk. The principal battles in which his regiment was engaged were Shiloh, siege of Corinth, Stone River, siege of Atlanta, and all the skirmishes and battles of the "march through Georgia." Our subject served faithfully and was always on duty during his entire service, being discharged July 12, 1865, at Chicago. He then went to Monmouth, of that State, and attended school for nine months. Then, entering the Eastman Business College, of Chicago, he remained three months, and was then married and engaged in farming in Carroll county, Illinois. After one year's stay he removed to Ogle county and engaged in agricultural pursuits until the fall of 1870. His next move was to Red Oak, Montgomery county, Iowa, where he remained until the spring of 1874. Returning then to the State of Illinois he resided for a time in Lake county and also in Ogle county, and then removed to Sheldon, Iowa, where he engaged in the furniture business until November, 1885, at which time with A. A. Beebe and S. S. Striker as partners the Cherokee County Bank at Meriden, Cherokee county, Iowa, was opened. He continued in that place for some time, and then, in 1886, started a bank in Heron Lake, Minnesota.

No man in the village has taken a more active interest in the welfare of the locality than has the subject of this sketch. All matters pertaining to the business welfare of the village have met with his earnest support, and he is always willing to lend a helping hand for the development of the resources of Jackson county. He has built up an enviable reputation for integrity of character and uprightness in business methods, and is highly esteemed as an exemplary citizen. He is a member of the Knights of Pythias and of the B. F. Sweet Post, No. 149, Grand Army of the Republic, of Heron Lake, in which he is now holding the office of commander for the second term. Politically he affiliates with the republican party.

On the 9th day of July, 1867, Mr. Hills was married to Miss Emily E. Beebe, daughter of N. W. Beebe and a native of Ogle county, Illinois. She was one of a family of nine children, of whom the following are living—Mary J., Emily E., Nathaniel W., Charles E., Alice A. and Earnest E.

ROBERT HYSLOP, one of the leading and most influential citizens of the village of Currie, Murray county, Minnesota, is engaged as a dealer in dry goods and groceries. He has a fine stock of general merchandise, and is doing an extensive business. He was born January 14, 1860, in Olmsted county, Minnesota.

The subject of our sketch is the son of Hon. John and Lucy F. (Kelley) Hyslop, the father being a native of Scotland and the mother a native of New Hampshire. The father came to the United States in about 1851, locating in New Jersey, where he engaged in farming for about three years. He then came to Olmsted county, where he was one of the pioneer settlers, and where he became one of the prominent and influential citizens. He took a prominent part in public affairs, and was twice elected as a representative in the State legislature. He was finely educated in his native land, and was a devout member of the Presbyterian church. The mother was reared in the State of New Hampshire. She is also a consistent member of the Presbyterian church, and is still living. There were nine children in the father's family, six of whom are now living—Robert, Mary, John, Jennie, Emma and Lucy.

Until he was about twenty years of age Robert Hyslop gave his time principally to obtaining an education in the county in which he was born. Then, in 1878, he came to Murray county, locating on a farm in Murray township, on section 19, on land purchased of the railroad company. Making this his home for about three years, he then moved into the village of Currie, and engaged as clerk in Neil Currie's store. For some eight years he continued his employment with this gentleman, and then took charge of the co-operative store. The subject of our sketch has taken a prominent part in public affairs since taking up his residence in Murray county. He has filled the offices of township treasurer and township clerk, which latter position he has held for four years. In politics the subject of our sketch affiliates with the democratic party. He is a member of the Presbyterian church, of which he is a trustee. He has thoroughly identified himself with every project which tended to improve the financial condition of the village in which he lives, and he has become one of Currie's representative citizens. He has an extensive trade in his line, and has the best store in the village.

HARLES HEILIG is a prominent farmer of Pipestone county, who lives on section 8, Altona township. He was born in Dodge county, Wisconsin, February 25, 1856.

The parents of the subject of our sketch were George and Sophia (Heinowsky) Heilig, the father being a native of France, and the mother born in Prussia. Mr. Heilig, Sr., was a carpenter by trade, and continued his residence in his native land until 1847, in which year he came to America, and located in Dodge county, Wisconsin. He was one of the pioneer settlers of that locality, and worked at his trade there until 1853. Then he purchased a farm and engaged in agricultural pursuits in Dodge county until 1864. In the latter year he removed to Minnesota, locating in Olmsted county, where he engaged in farming until his death, which occurred November 17, 1869.

Charles Heilig remained beneath the parental roof, assisting upon the home farm and attending the district schools, until he was seventeen years of age. Then, in 1878, with his mother and the rest of the family,

he came to Altona township, where he now lives. Our subject came a short time previous to the arrival of the rest of the family, his arrival being on May 1, and that of the rest of the family on the 17th of the same month. He at once took the claim where he now lives, his mother locating a claim on section 10. Our subject's mother built the second house in the township, and the family have all continued their residence there, engaged in farming up to the present time.

In early life the subject of our sketch received a good common-school education and was well prepared to enter upon the duties of the life into which he might be called. He has assisted in a very large measure in the development of the various public projects which have agitated the minds of the citizens of Altona township. He has affiliated with the republican party and has efficiently acted in several official capacities. He has been township treasurer for two terms and assessor for one term and is the present town clerk, as which he has officiated for three years. On coming to the township he had but very little means with which to commence. He had a horse and wagon and this was about the extent of his worldly possessions. He located on the farm, however, and commenced actively improving it and has accumulated considerable means. This has all come as a result of hard work and continual and careful attention to the various details of his farming operations.

Mr. Heilig was married August 5, 1885, to Miss Mina M. Smith, who was born in Dover township, Olmsted county, Minnesota, in 1866. Her father was a native of New York and her mother of Canada. This marriage has been blessed with two children—Laura M., born April 30, 1886, and Charles A., born September 22, 1887, both of whom are living.

R. BENJAMIN H. HINKLY is one of the most prominent resident citizens of Luverne, Minnesota, and is the president of the Rock County Bank. He has been actively engaged in various important business enterprises since making his settlement in the county early in 1888. He accepted his present position as president of the Rock County Bank in May, soon after making his location. The doctor is a native of Tompkins county, New York, where he was born July 19, 1824.

He is the son of Horace and Laura (McIntyre) Hinkly, natives, respectively, o Albany and Tompkins counties, New York. The father was engaged in farming, which line of occupation he followed through the most of his life. In 1832 he removed to the State of Ohio, settling in Fitchville, Huron county, where he remained until his death. He was a man of considerable means and exerted a wide influence in the locality in which he lived.

The life of the subject of our sketch was spent on the home farm until he was twenty-one years of age. He received a thorough high-school education in Huron county, Ohio, and also attended the Cleveland College of Medicine. In 1852 Dr. Hinkly crossed the plains to California, going overland with mules and horses and arriving at "Hangtown" or Placerville, July 23. They were about the first to arrive there. Sickness, cholera and death seemed to rage along the route, but only two out of their train of fifty persons died. One train, which had previously left the same town they did, lost one-fourth of their number and did not arrive until in September. Our subject remained in Eldorado county, California, and vicinity, about three years, mining, trading and practicing his profession. He then, in 1855, returned by way of the sea; was shipwrecked with the "Golden Age" on the island of Te-Caro, but after

three days was picked up by the "John L. Stephens" and carried to Panama and from there took a vessel to New York, arriving at his home in Ohio, in May, 1855, having been absent over three years.

Dr. Hinkly graduated from the Cleveland College of Medicine in 1855, and, after completing his medical course, removed to the State of Iowa, locating in Clermont, Fayette county, in 1856. Here he became one of the pioneers of that region, and continued in the practice of his profession until 1876. In that year he removed to Lansing, Michigan, and engaged in business for about a year, after which he took a trip to Europe, visiting Ireland, England, France, Switzerland, Germany, Holland, Brussels and Scotland, and the World's Exposition at Paris. After visiting friends in the East for a short time after his return from the old country, and after an absence of one year, he returned to Fayette county, Iowa. After going to Michigan in 1876, the doctor practically retired from the active practice of his profession, but occasionally called in that line upon a friend. He has been giving his attention to various financial enterprises in which he has been associated with business friends in the State of Iowa and in Luverne. He is a large stockholder in the Fayette County National Bank, of Fayette, Iowa, and is also a stockholder in the savings bank of the same place, being president of the latter institution. He is also a stockholder in several other banks in Iowa. He became interested in the Rock County Bank, on its organization, as a stockholder, and is now the president of the same. The following are the names of the organizers of the Rock County Bank: William Jacobson, O. P. Miller, J. K. Thompson, W. H. Wilson, Ezra Rice, R. B. Hinkly, W. R. Kinnard, William Larabee, Frank Larabee, B. H. Hinkly and Daniel Stone. Soon after the organization of the bank the stockholders built a very fine building, which cost $7,200. The doctor has purchased a very fine residence in the city, and has large landed interests in Southern Minnesota and in the State of Iowa.

The subject of our sketch was married, in 1857, to Miss Emma C. Bryant, a daughter of S. S. and Elizabeth Bryant, of Albion, Michigan. Dr. and Mrs. Hinkly have had a family of five children, one of whom died in infancy and one at three years of age. The names of the others are—Ray B., who has been cashier of the Rock County Bank since its organization; Frank L. and Fred M.

In politics the subject of our sketch affiliates with the republican party, and throughout his career he has been intimately associated with all movements tending to the renovation of politics and the building up and strengthening of good government. He has held several positions in the various localities in which he has lived, and in every instance has proven his efficiency and thoroughness as an official. He is a member of the Masonic fraternity and a Knight Templar, and for many years has held some of the most important offices of the lodge. He is a man of stanch character, a loyal citizen and is respected by all who know him. Careful and systematic in his business relations, he has accumulated large means, and, being of a liberal disposition and generous spirited, he has largely assisted in the building up and development of the various towns in which he has lived.

❖

ILLIS A. CHAPMAN is publisher and proprietor of the St. James *Journal*, the only newspaper published at the county seat of Watonwan county, Minnesota. Mr. Chapman is a native of Coles county, Illinois, where he was born September 19, 1853. He is the son of Dr. Newton W. and Mary J. (Bragg) Chapman, the former a native of Indiana, the latter of Virginia. Dr. Chapman practiced medicine in Sangamon, Coles and Douglas counties, Illinois, and now resides at Tuscola, in the last named county. He entered the Union army in May, 1862, enlisting in the Fifty-fourth Illinois Volunteer Infantry as assistant surgeon, at Mattoon, Illinois. In December of the same year he was transferred to the Sixteenth Illinois Cavalry, and served as physician and surgeon through the war, having charge at one time of hospital No. 23 at Nashville, Tennessee. He was wounded once and was twice taken prisoner, once in Tennessee by General Pillow's forces, and later in Virginia by General Longstreet's forces, was paroled the first time, and escaped the second. He was with Sherman in all his battles from Chattanooga to Atlanta; was discharged from the service May 12, 1865.

The subject of our sketch became an apprentice in the Tuscola (Illinois) *Journal* office on September 29, 1868, when fifteen years old, and has followed the printing business since that time, becoming part proprietor of the above paper in 1873, and later became full owner. In July, 1877, he sold out and removed to Minnesota, settling at St. James and establishing his present paper. The first issue appeared March 20, 1878. He built his printing establishment in 1883, on Main street, and has a fine residence, which cost some three thousand dollars, at the west end of Main street. The subject of our sketch is a believer in the principles promulgated by the republican party, and his paper is conducted along these lines. Mr. Chapman is a man of excellent principles, and through his paper forcibly advocates all matters that he deems right. In public matters our subject has always taken an active part, and is now serving on his sixth year as village recorder.

Editor Chapman was married in December, 1880, to Miss Lilla M. Clark, daughter of S. C. Clark, of St. James. Three children have blessed this union, namely—Severance W., Lawrence H. and Merrill B.

———⋅✠⋅⟨✦⟩⋅✠⋅———

PHILO KENDALL, one of the leading prosperous farmers of Lake Benton township, Lincoln county, Minnesota, located on a pre-emption in July, 1874. He was one among the very first settlers of the township and assisted substantially in the early foundation of the civil government. He was one of the first supervisors of the township and served for two years in that position. The officers of the board were Arthur Morris and S. G. Jones, the latter being clerk. Mr. Kendall is at present director of school district No. 43. He has always taken an active interest in local affairs and has done all in his power to assist in the building up and developing of his locality. When he came to his place he found fifteen acres broken, which he planted to corn. This crop was destroyed by grasshoppers in 1874, and in 1875 our subject sowed considerable grain and lost his harvest by reason of grasshopper raids. In 1876 he put in a crop on his entire farm and reaped about half a crop. In 1877 he had grain in on five different places besides his own. This year the harvest bid fair to be of fine quality and the yield was expected to be about thirty-five bushels per acre. Within a week of cutting time, however, as the result of a long period of dry weather, his crops were destroyed. He did not reap a sufficient harvest to pay the expenses of putting in the seed. In order to support his family he had to work out for different adjoining farmers and also to hunt through the winter, in all kinds of weather. In 1878 he had a very fair crop, but lost twelve hundred bushels of grain by wind and weather. He had this grain in the stack, but on account of the setting in of winter early in October the stacks were blown down and covered

with snow. In 1879 he rented his place and again met with misfortune in his crops, and did not reap as many bushels of grain as he sowed. Since that time his crops have been very fair, and during the last two or three years he has reaped a profitable harvest. Regardless, however, of these discouragements of his farm life, he has overcome all obstacles, and has by thrift and economy been gradually growing in prosperity, until now he is in comfortable circumstances, and is one of the most well-to-do and prosperous farmers in the township.

The subject of our sketch was born in Essex county, New York, December 19, 1835. He received his early training and education in his native State and in Walworth county, Wisconsin, to which place his parents removed in about 1838. The family resided in Walworth county for about eleven years, and then removed to Fond du Lac county, where our subject continued for about two years. He then found employment on the Wisconsin river and continued in various lines of occupation for fifteen years along the river. He then engaged in farming for about a year, and after that came to Brown county, Minnesota, where he purchased some land and followed agricultural pursuits for three years. Again the spirit of migration took possession of our subject, and he removed to Ransom county, Dakota, where he tried farming for two years. During this time he met with continual hardship and disappointment. Both of these years he was eaten out by grasshoppers and had to support his family by trapping. After these two years were expired he went to Jimtown, Stutsman county, where he engaged in farming for two years, meeting with the same experience as before, being eaten out by the grasshoppers during both seasons. Here again he had to support his family by trapping, and finally growing disheartened by his misfortunes there, he concluded to return to Minnesota. He then made his location on his present place, where he has since resided. While living in Stutsman county, Mr. Kendall served as one of the first justices of the peace in that county.

The subject of our sketch was married June 9, 1861, to Mary Bowden, a native of Walworth county, Wisconsin, where she remained until she was six years old. Removing thence she located with her parents in Fond du Lac county, where she received her training and education. Mr. and Mrs. Kendall have six living children—Miranda, Myrtie, Fernando, Nellie, Victor and Grace. The names of those deceased are William, Lucy, Effie, Walter and Genna. Miranda married C. R. Gould, and is a resident of section 20, Hope township, Lincoln county. Myrtie married Sidney Dickson, a farmer near Oaks, Dicky county, Dakota.

The subject of our sketch has passed through many thrilling experiences during his early settlement in Dakota and Minnesota. Hardships and misfortunes doubtless come to every pioneer's life, but with our subject these circumstances were especially distressing. Two or three instances of his early experiences may be of interest to the general reader. While in Ransom county, Dakota, there were only five other families besides that of our subject in the entire county, and these were sixty miles from the nearest outposts of civilization. The nearest postoffice was Abercrombie, some sixty miles distant, and it was only about twice a year that these people received any mails. One winter the subject of our sketch started for the mill to obtain flour and provisions, and was caught out in a veritable Dakota blizzard. He had to camp out in the storm during two days and one night, and suffered untold agony from the intense cold. The second winter he attempted to do this same thing. The snow

was about four feet deep, and when our subject got about four miles from Fort Abercrombie, out on the plains, a terrific northwester came up, and he had to seek the first shelter he could find and stop for a short time. Within eighty rods of him lay a man and fifteen-year-old boy in the side of a snowbank. They were both badly frozen. The boy had both legs amputated, and died three days later. Our subject thought that he could find his way along the route, and so started out again, determined to accomplish his journey without any further stopping, or perish in the attempt, as his family were nearly out of provisions. He had considerable trouble to force his ox-team along on account of the fiercely-driving snow. The blizzard was so thick about him that he could not see a rod ahead of his team, and much of the distance he had to find the road by probing through the snow with a large stick until he found the solid track. In this way he succeeded in worrying along for thirty miles, and after an absence of four weeks returned home with flour and provisions. These are merely instances of some of the thrilling experiences through which our subject passed. There have been numerous other hair-breadth escapes, and untold experiences of privations. The instances given were but passing events in those days, and it would give the reader much surprise to hear recounted all the trying circumstances through which our subject passed in the early days. Since making his location in Lincoln township our subject has built up an enviable reputation for honesty and systematic business life. He has been quite successful of late years, and has surrounded himself with the evidences of prosperity and good circumstances. In politics he affiliates with the republican party, and assists in the religious work of the Methodist Episcopal church.

JAMES COWIN, a leading citizen of Adrian, Nobles county, Minnesota, is engaged in the grain and lumber business. He is the son of William and Ann (Garrett) Cowin, natives of the Isle of Man, on which island our subject was born July 25, 1843.

The home ties of the subject of our sketch were not severed until 1867, when he came to the United States, stopping in Dodgeville, Wisconsin, for about a month. Removing thence he went to Marquette, Michigan, and resided there until April, 1868, and then started for Colorado. He traveled on the cars as far as possible, leaving them near Cheyenne, where he found one thousand railroad employes and frontiersmen gathered together for protection against the Indians, who had driven them from their work along the frontier. Our subject here took the stage to Denver, and from thence went to Black Hawk, where he was engaged in mining and contracting and superintending for some six years. He visited various places in the mining region, spending his time in Central City, Caribo, Georgetown and other places, and during that time crossing the plains some seven or eight times by way of Smoky Hill and the Pacific route. During these days he saw many exciting times, experienced hardships, and passed through many dangers. On one of his trips across the plains his train was stopped for about an hour by the passing of a herd of buffalo, estimated by the hunters as containing some fifteen thousand animals. He saw acres of buffalo hides spread on the ground to dry by the hunters who scoured the plains in search of this valuable game. In 1872 our subject spent some six months in Milwaukee visiting friends, and later, in 1874, he went to Bigelow, Nobles county, Minnesota, and formed a partnership with S. D. Tennis in the grain and fuel business. Before a year had expired our subject purchased his partner's interest and operated the business alone until 1878, in the meantime,

however, adding a stock of lumber. In 1878 he moved to Adrian and engaged in his former business, which he has followed ever since. For a time after coming to the village he also engaged in selling farm machinery, but gave that up after a year or so. He still owns and operates his grain and fuel business in Bigelow, and in connection with these lines is also engaged to some extent on buying and selling real estate. He owns over eight hundred acres of land in the county and rents all of it but one large farm near the village, which he superintends himself. He also owns ten or twelve village lots, a store building on Main street, and also a neat residence, where he now lives.

Mr. Cowin has always taken an interest in political matters and is a stanch supporter of the republican party. He has held various local offices, such as township supervisor, village councilman, and has been a member of the board of county commissioners for some five years. He is a member of the Ancient Free and Accepted Masons, Lodge No. 11, of Black Hawk, Colorado, and also of the Ancient Order of United Workmen, Lodge No. 76, of Adrian.

On the 14th day of March, 1883, he was married to Miss Rhoda C. Moberly, at Adrian, Minnesota. She was the daughter of L. B. and Susan S. (Owen) Moberly, natives of Kentucky, and was born in Davis county, that State, on November 18, 1859. Mr. and Mrs. Cowin have the following named children—James, Jr., Edith Bland and Alton Bard. Mrs. Cowin is a lady of refinement and is one of the leading members of the Baptist church of Adrian.

———◦—◦◦◦◦◦—◦———

DR. DANIEL STRAW, a leading physician and surgeon of Wells, Minnesota, came to this village in 1870, and has since been engaged in the practice of his profession. The doctor is a native of Piscataquis county, Maine, where he was born May 17, 1847. His parents, David and Caroline (Ayer) Straw, were also natives of Maine, where the father was engaged in the practice of law. David R. Straw was born in 1795, and died at Guilford, Maine, in 1876. He was a graduate of Brown University, of Providence, Rhode Island, and was a man of considerable prominence in the locality in which he lived. He was a thorough lawyer and an able practitioner. The mother is still living and is a resident of Guilford, Maine. In the father's family there were eleven children, seven of whom are now living—David R., Agnes M., William O., Gideon M., Carrie A., Henry and Dr. Daniel.

Our subject's grandfather was a native of Maine, where he was engaged in farming. The grandfather was the son of an Englishman who came to this country in an early day and settled in the State in which our subject was born. Our subject's mother's father was Dr. Moses Ayer, a native of Maine, and the son of a farmer of that State. This family was of English descent, as was also the other side of the house.

The early life of our subject was spent in the schools of his native State. Very early he exhibited a desire for the practice of medicine, and commenced studying toward that end in 1867, at Gilmanton, New Hampshire, with Dr. Nahum Wight. He remained with this physician for some three years and then entered Dartmouth College, taking a thorough course and graduating from that institution in 1869. He afterward returned home and remained a year, after which he came to Wells, Minnesota, where he has since been engaged in the practice of his profession.

Dr. Straw was married, in 1871, to Miss Florence Watson, of Boston, Massachusetts. This union has been blessed with four children—Florence, Fred, Henry and Constance.

The subject of our sketch is one of the ablest physicians and surgeons in Southern Minnesota, and since his location here, in 1870, he has by his thorough application to this profession, and by earnest and conscientious work, built up an extensive and lucrative practice. His professional calls sometimes take him into all parts of Faribault county, and even into adjoining counties for a distance of many miles. He has always taken an interest in public affairs and belongs to the State Medical Society. He is the physician and surgeon for the Chicago, Milwaukee & St. Paul Railroad Company, and is now a member of the United States pension board of that district. In politics he affiliates with the democratic party and is a member of the Masonic fraternity. He owns a beautiful home in the village, surrounded with shade and ornamental trees. As a physician, citizen, and neighbor, Dr. Straw is held in high esteem by all who know him.

WILLIAM W. ZUEL, one of the most prosperous and influential farmers of Springfield township, Cottonwood county, Minnesota, resides on section 14. His native place is found in Fulton county, New York, where he was born August 25, 1842.

The parents of the subject of our sketch were Robert and Elizabeth Zuel, natives of Scotland. In early life the father was engaged in operating a flour mill and a saw mill, and later in life followed the occupation of farming. He came to Will county, Illinois, in the spring of 1843, where he died in 1848. The mother died in 1847. In the father's family there were nine children, two of whom are now living.

The subject of our sketch was six years of age when his parents died, and for six years thereafter he resided with different farmers in the vicinity of the place where his parents had lived. In 1857 he commenced clerking in a grocery store, continuing thereat for one year, and then re-engaging in farm work. In April, 1861, he enlisted in a local com_pany to serve in the Union army, under the three months' call, but was not called out, and so the company was disbanded. Our subject returned to farming until the 1st of November, 1861, when he enlisted in Company F, Sixty-fourth Illinois Infantry, known as the Yates Sharpshooters. He enlisted as a private, and was first under fire at New Madrid, Missouri, and again at Island No. 10, under General Pope, for three weeks. His regiment was then ordered down the river to Fort Pillow; after arriving there orders came to return to Pittsburg Landing, on the Tennessee river, and soon after serving at the siege of Corinth, Mississippi. The company was then attached to the division which pursued the Rebels to Booneville, and was then ordered back under General Rosecrans to become guard at his headquarters near Corinth camp, at Clear Creek. He participated in the severe battle of Iuka, September 19, 1862, where he had his canteen shot away. His next engagement was in the battle of Corinth, Mississippi, October 3 and 4, 1862. From that time on, for a brief period, he participated in numerous light skirmishes in serving on outpost duty eight miles from Corinth. Some time was spent during the fall of that year in skirmishing with Roddy's cavalry. In the latter part of 1863 our subject's division went to Pulaski, Tennessee, where he enlisted in a veteran corps. He was then granted a furlough and went home on a visit. He reported for duty at Ottawa, Illinois, when his regiment was ordered to Decatur, Alabama, and joined General Sherman's army, and participated in the Atlanta campaign. His next move was to go with his division to Rockyface Ridge, Dallas, Resaca, and other points in Georgia, thence to Kenesaw Mountain, where he participated

in sharp fighting for several days, especially on June 27th, and on the 4th of July, 1864. July 20th witnessed the sanguinary battle at Peach Tree Creek, near Atlanta, and from this time on fighting continued until Atlanta was captured. At the battle of Atlanta, Georgia, the day that General McPherson was shot and killed, our subject was struck with a musket ball in the right side at the beginning of the battle. The shock of the shot threw him to the ground, but he recovered and started back toward the rear, moving sturdily on until he fainted from loss of blood. This was between one and two o'clock in the afternoon, and he lay on the battle-field until nearly night before he was picked up by the ambulance wagon. He was carried back to the field hospital and placed under trees. About this time the Rebels commenced throwing shells at this locality, and all who were able retreated from the place. Our subject, not being able to retreat, remained for some time before he was found and removed to the field hospital near Marietta, remaining there until September 18th. As soon as he was able to be moved he was put on board a freight train and sent North, being granted a furlough of twenty days. At the expiration of his furlough he joined the army at Snake Creek Gap, Georgia. Not being able to march with his regiment, he was ordered back to Chattanooga, Tennessee, and was there during the exciting times of the second election of President Lincoln. He remained there two weeks, and then joined Sherman's army, and had command of his company during that famous march to the sea. He served until the close of the war, and then came northward with his company through Columbia, South Carolina; Raleigh, North Carolina; Virginia, and on to Washington, District of Columbia, where he participated in the grand review. He was then ordered to Louisville, Kentucky, where he was mustered out of the United

States service, and then ordered to Chicago, Illinois, where he was paid off, and the regiment disbanded. He came home bearing the commission of captain of Company C, to which he had been appointed June 2, 1865. For gallant conduct he was promoted to the various ranks as follows— March 23, 1864, he was made second lieutenant of Company F ; October 10, 1864, he was appointed first lieutenant of Company C, and in June of the following year became captain of that company. In August, 1865, our subject came to Minnesota and located in Mankato, Blue Earth county, where he engaged in the livery business until 1867. He then operated a farm for some time near Garden City, and in May, 1871, came to Cottonwood county, and located his claim, where he now lives. In 1872 he moved his family to his new location, and has made that his home ever since.

Mr. Zuel was married to Henrietta Francisco in November, 1867. She died in June, 1874. In November, 1875, Mr. Zuel was married to Cyrena A. Williams. Mr. Zuel has a family of three children, whose names are as follows—Robert W., Archibald S. and Grace E.

The subject of our sketch is one of the most public-spirited and highly respected citizens of Springfield township, and has made his influence felt in the local affairs of the republican party, with which he affiliates. His gallant service during the war entitles him to the high position which he holds in the Grand Army of the Republic. He is also a member of the Ancient Free and Accepted Masons. He has held many official positions, among them being that of township treasurer three years, and also chairman of the board of township supervisors.

———————

WILLIAM O. KING is a prosperous farmer and stock-raiser located on section 6, Delafield township, Jackson

county, Minnesota. Mr. King was born in the State of Wisconsin, December 20, 1854.

The parents of the subject of this sketch were William and Catherine (Chadderdon) King. The father was a native of the State of New York, where he was reared and educated. When a young man he came to Dodge county, Wisconsin, where he learned the carpenter's trade and engaged thereat for many years. In 1857 he located in Belle Plaine township, Scott county, Minnesota, and made that his home for some five or six years. He then settled in Le Sueur county, Minnesota, where he resided until his death, which occurred in 1873. The father was an intelligent and talented man and was local preacher in the Methodist Episcopal church for many years. He was a man of great piety and was possessed of a charitable and lovable disposition. He had a host of warm friends, who deeply mourn his death.

The mother of our subject was a native of the State of New York, where she was reared and educated. She was the daughter of Jonathan Chadderdon, a farmer by occupation. She now resides in Jackson county on a farm of eighty acres adjoining that of our subject, and where she located in 1879. Through her life, since sixteen years of age, she has been engaged in teaching, and has taught school in Jackson county for some five or six years.

William O. King was one of five children; the names of his brothers and sisters were—Henry, Hubert, Horace Greeley, Sophie E. and Mary C. Horace G. died in Windom at nineteen years of age. William O. was reared in Minnesota, receiving a common school education in Scott and Le Sueur counties. He also attended the Northfield College for some time, and, returning to Le Sueur county, was married in 1879. In 1882 he came to his present location in Jackson county.

January 12, 1879, Mr. King was married

to Miss Luella Bolser, a native of Jennings county, Indiana, where she was born September 24, 1862. This lady was the daughter of Henry Bolser, a native of Ohio, and a farmer by occupation. Her father died in Jennings county, Indiana, in 1862, while a member of the local home guards. He was an exemplary citizen, and a member of the Church of the Disciples. The mother's name was Eveline Thomas, who was reared in Kentucky and Indiana, and is still living. In the Bolser family there were fourteen children, six of whom are now living—Rachel, Jeannette, Derothy, Harriet, Henry and Luella. The last named—wife of the subject of our sketch—completed her education in Le Sueur county, Minnesota. Mr. and Mrs. King have two children—Eveline and Clara.

The subject of our sketch is one of the leading citizens of his township, and is deeply interested in both the moral growth and financial development of his locality. Mr. King was fairly educated, and has taught several terms of school in Jackson and Cottonwood counties. November 9, 1880, Mr. King was ordained as a preacher in the Church of the Disciples, and has been following that vocation in connection with his farming ever since. He has charge of two other appointments besides the one in the vicinity of his farm. Mr. King is a man of deep piety and is highly esteemed, both as a man and a citizen.

DWARD S. MILLS, of Worthington, Minnesota, was born in Cattaraugus county, New York, November 17, 1827. His parents were Samuel H. and Anna (Carpenter) Mills, the latter's father having been a soldier in the Revolutionary War. Samuel H. Mills, his father, was a lumberman, engaged in manufacturing, rafting and selling lumber at the different towns on the Allegheny and Ohio rivers. He was taken sick and died at Cincinnati, in 1828. The subject of this sketch was carefully reared and educated by an excellent Christian mother, and at the best schools which the country afforded at that day, following in due time the occupation of his father as a lumberman, rafting, boating and selling lumber on the rivers mentioned, and on the Mississippi as far down as Vicksburg. Eventually he made Memphis, Tennessee, the principal selling point, establishing a permanent business there in 1858 and 1859. At the commencement of the War of the Rebellion, in 1861, he had a large stock of lumber and coal on hand, and up to that time had been doing an extensive and lucrative business. At that time he had to choose between abandoning his property and leaving the country, or staying with it and aiding the cause of the Rebellion; without the slightest hesitancy he decided to leave. The crisis came like a cyclone. There was not time for preparation, no possibility of settling or arranging business. Yankees must go or take the oath of allegiance to the Southern Confederacy. With hundreds of others he left Memphis the same day that the first gun was fired off Fort Sumter, and on the last train that was allowed to go North. His family had gone before him to the old home in Western New York. He took a very active interest in the preparations of the Union army for the overthrown of the Rebellion. He helped to recruit and organize the One Hundred and Fifty-fourth Regiment New York Volunteer Infantry, was chosen captain of Company I, and was with his regiment in Virginia during a part of 1862 and 1863, in the Eleventh Army Corps, under the command of Generals Sigel, Burnside and Hooker. On account of financial embarrassment, caused by reverses and losses above referred to, and the burning of a planing mill and sash factory at a later date, friends who were surety insisted on his leaving the service as soon as there was a possibility of recovering, or of getting settlement for abandoned property at Memphis. He had enlisted and accepted a position in the regiment with a tacit understanding that he should be permitted to do so if his own financial interests and that of his friends seemed to require it. His resignation was accepted in time for him to be at Memphis when the city was retaken by the Union forces. The lumber which he had left there and people indebted to him were scattered and gone. Enough, however, was realized to relieve his friends from embarrassment, fifty barrels New Orleans molasses, a few bales of cotton and a half interest in a steamboat were taken in part payment. For several years he was engaged in handling coal and lumber on the rivers, buying mostly at Cincinnati and delivering at points below. In the spring of 1866 he had a contract to carry cotton from Albany and Columbus, Georgia, to Appalachicola bay, Florida. His boat, only a light river craft, was navigated safely down the Gulf coast from the mouth of the Mississippi river to the bay. He continued doing a general freighting and passenger business on the Appalachicola river for nearly four years. He then closed up the business and returned to New York State. In 1871 he came to Minnesota, settled on the northwest quarter of section 32, township 101, range 40 (Bigelow township), Nobles county, in March, 1872. He was elected auditor of Nobles county in the fall of 1879, and removed to Worthington, where he now resides, in the spring of 1880. He was re-elected auditor for four successive terms, as an independent candidate, and held the office for nine years by mutual support of both political parties.

Mr. Mills was married in Cattaraugus county, New York State, February 7, 1855, to Helen M. Horton, daughter of Sylvester J. and Emily (Strong) Horton.

She was born November 16, 1833, in Cattaraugus county, New York. Mr. Mills' family consists of five children—Horton S., born in March, 1856, married at Bigelow, Minnesota, to Delilah Hevener. Three daughters bless the union—Ella M., Maud L. and Sarah A. They now reside at Millbank, Dakota. Henry E., born May 31, 1858, in Cattaraugus county, New York, married at Fulda, Minnesota, to Alice Christman. They have two children living—Gertrude A. and Agnes. Mary B., died February 23, 1882. Grace L. died February 1, 1889, at Minneapolis, Minnesota. Anna D., born April 27, 1862, in Cattaraugus county, New York, married at Bigelow, December 25, 1879, to Hugh Mitchell. They reside on their farm in Bigelow township, and have two children, John E. and Mary M., living, besides Nettie, who died September 15, 1889. Mary H., born June 6, 1866, in Cattaraugus county, New York, married June, 27, 1888, to Elbert Christman, of Minneapolis, where they now reside. Addie L., born August 30, 1877, at Bigelow, Minnesota.

FRED BUSSEY is located on the northwest quarter of section 8, Fountain Prairie township, where he is engaged in general farming and stock raising. He located in Pipestone county in May, 1879, entering his land as a homestead and becoming one of the first settlers of the township. He assisted in the organization of the civil township in June, 1879, the first meeting being held on the southwest quarter of section 28. Mr. Bussey was born in Chicago, Illinois, in 1857, his father being Fred Bussey, a native of Germany. The parents are still living, engaged in farming in Wisconsin. In the father's family there are eight living children —Fred, Clara, Charles, Lewis, Emma, Julius, Christian and Elizabeth. Two children are dead; William died when quite young, and a babe, unnamed, died in infancy.

When the subject of our sketch was between three and four years of age, his parents left Chicago, and removed to Milwaukee, Wisconsin, where they remained about a year. Leaving that city they went to Winona, Winona county, Minnesota, where our subject lived with his parents about twelve years, receiving in that city a good common school education. In 1871 he removed to Buffalo county, Wisconsin, from whence, after a few years' residence, he removed to Jackson county, same State, and engaged in farming for about two years. Then for a year or two he traveled extensively over the Northwest, prospecting for a permanent location, finally making his settlement on his present place, as was stated in the opening lines of this sketch.

Mr. Bussey was married June 18, 1875, to Miss Lisetta Smith, who was born in Washington county, Wisconsin, where she was reared and educated until she was twelve years of age. At that age she removed with her parents to Trempealeau county, same State, where she received a good common school educaion. Mr. and Mrs. Bussey have four children—Frederick, Lily, Nettie and Claude, all of whom are residing with their parents.

The subject of our sketch is a man of much energy and push, and has accomplished considerable success on his farm. He has surrounded himself with pleasant and comfortable circumstances and has built good farm buildings. He has a pleasant home and an agreeable family. In politics Mr. Bussey affiliates with the democratic party and is actively engaged in the furthering of all public matters. He has held several official positions, among them being that of assessor of the township, to which office he was elected in 1885, being the present incumbent, and also holding the office of clerk of the school district No. 38. Our subject wields a strong influence for good in the township and is one of its representative citizens.

GEORGE E. FRANCISCO is the leading member of the firm of Francisco, Pride & Wing, proprietors of the Blue Earth City Roller Mills of Faribault county, Minnesota.

Mr. Francisco is a native of Johnson, Fulton county New York, where he was born in the year 1848. His parents were Hiram and Phœbe (Van Northstrand) Francisco, natives of New York. The father was a tanner by trade and also dealt largely in boots and shoes. The family came West in 1853 and settled at Kenosha, Wisconsin, where the father engaged in work at his trade. Some time later he went to Clay township, Lake county, Illinois, and engaged in farming. Removing to Iowa in 1864, he settled at Steamboat Rock, Hardin county, where he engaged in the harness and boot and shoe business. He is at present a resident of Marshalltown, Iowa, to which place he went in 1875 and where he is still engaged in his old business. In the father's family there were five children—Susan E., Harriet J., George E., Hiram S. and Charles E.

The education of the subject of our sketch was not neglected in his early life. Until seventeen years of age he was allowed to attend the district schools and obtained a thorough practical education. In 1865 he enlisted at the age of seventeen years in the One Hundred and Fifty-third Illinois Infantry and continued in the service throughout the remainder of the war. He served his country bravely and gallantly, and upon his discharge went to Steamboat Rock, Iowa, where he learned the cooper's trade. He then engaged in railroad carpentering for about a year and then went into the Eldorado railroad shops and learned the business of pattern-

making, continuing thereat until 1873. His
next move was to Wells, Faribault county,
where he found employment in the shops of
the Southern Minnesota Railroad Company as
pattern-maker. Two years were spent in
this line, and then he moved to Hokah, to
which place the Southern Minnesota shops
were removed. He continued working for
the railroad company until 1881, and then
went to Minneapolis, where he and a Mr.
Musser formed a partnership to carry on a
pattern-making business. One year later he
sold out, and accepted a position as foreman
in the Union Iron Works, of Minneapolis.

In 1885, in company with his present
partners, they purchased the business in
which he is now engaged, and in 1886
he removed to Blue Earth City. He purchased several lots in the city, and built a
fine residence.

Mr. Francisco was married in 1875 to Miss
Flora M. Cobb, a native of Michigan, and
daughter of Dr. H. D. Cobb. Two children
have blessed this union — Harry L. and
Ethel M.

The subject of our sketch is a man of strict
temperance principles, and in politics affiliates with the prohibition party. He is an
Odd Fellow, having joined this order when
twenty-one years of age, and with his wife
is a member of the Presbyterian church.
In every sense of the word Mr. Francisco is
a self-made man, having had to do for himself since twelve years of age. He has had
many peculiar experiences, and has made
a great many hazardous and yet profitable
investments. He is a man of good business
foresight, and is a good adviser. His first
experience away from home was as cook on
a lumber schooner on Lake Michigan in
1861. From this small commencement and
humble work our subject has gradually
worked his way into a fortune of comfortable dimensions, and is doing a large and
increasing business.

JUDGE JAMES A. GOODRICH is one
of the best known and most influential citizens of Jackson county, Minnesota, and is justice of the peace in the village of Jackson, where
he resides. He was born in Pittsfield, Massachusetts, May 25, 1825, and is a son of Daniel H. and Mahala (Newton) Goodrich, who
were natives of Massachusetts and farmers
by occupation. The father died about 1839,
and the mother in 1868. Daniel H. Goodrich's grandfather (on his mother's side),
Captain D. Hubbard, was one of the first
settlers of the town of Pittsfield, Massachusetts, was one of the first selectmen of that
place, and one of the sixteen "foundation"
or original members of the Congregational
church of that town. The father of Daniel
H. Goodrich was Jesse W. Goodrich, whose
father was a colonel in the British army.
One of our subject's uncles, Jesse W. Goodrich, was a lawyer and editor of Worcester,
Massachusetts, and was instrumental in
bringing out John B. Gough, the famous
temperance lecturer. Our subject's brother,
Alonzo E. Goodrich, was lieutenant-colonel
of the Thirty-seventh Massachusetts Infantry, and was selectman for the town of
Pittsfield for eleven years, or until his death.
James A.'s twin sister, J. A. Ayers, is living
with her son, a merchant of Boston. His
oldest sister, Elizabeth, died in Wisconsin in
1881. The next oldest sister, Naomi, died
in Massachusetts in 1883. The youngest sister, Charlotte, married the president of the
Pittsfield Bank, and died three months after
her marriage. James A. Goodrich's mother
was formerly Mahala Newton. Her grandfather (Captain Newton), as well as her
father and one of her brothers, were captains
in the Revolutionary War. The brother
referred to for many years represented his
district in the Massachusetts legislature.

After the death of his father, James A.
Goodrich resided with his mother on the
farm for some two years, when he adopted

a seafaring life and went on board a whaling vessel, in which he sailed four months. He visited the Azores Islands and various points along the coast of South America, his ship being condemned at St. Catharine. He then shipped on board an English merchant vessel and sailed to Valparaiso, Chili, at which place he shipped on board an American bark, and thence sailed to New York City. As a sailor he then took a trip to Cuba, returning to Philadelphia, and thence to New Bedford. At this time he changed his employment and engaged on board a whaling vessel and took a cruise of four years, visiting Kema, Celebro Island — one of the group of the East Indies — and thence cruising in search of sperm whales for five or six months. The next objective point was the port of Apia, on one of the Samoan Islands, of late so prominent in the diplomatic affairs of the United States, England and Germany. The vessel touched at different places on the Friendly Islands.

After this, in the course of three years, our subject visited many ports in the Pacific ocean. During this cruise our subject was bowsman of the harpooning boat, and his party captured forty-seven whales, the largest being of the sperm species and yielding eighty barrels of oil. On completing their cargo, which consisted of twenty-eight hundred barrels of sperm oil, the vessel sailed for New Bedford and arrived in that port after having been gone four years. Then our subject, satisfied for a time with a seafaring life, returned to his home in Massachusetts, and remained from December, 1847, until the spring of 1848, when he removed to McHenry county, Illinois, and made that his home for one year. Thence he went to Baraboo, Wisconsin, where he purchased a number of lots and put up several buildings, which, for a time, he rented. One year later he went to Richland county, Wisconsin, and there made some improvements in the build-

ing line and made that his home until 1854. Being somewhat of a roving disposition, he then started for the West, going to Nebraska and taking a claim about six miles from Omaha. He made that his home until 1857, and then removed to Washington county, Nebraska, purchased a farm of 450 acres, and made that his home for two years. During this time he was one of the most prominent citizens of the county, and held the office of probate judge. At the end of the two years he sold out and removed to Onawa, settling on a farm in the vicinity of that place, where he resided until 1878. He then sold out and came to Jackson county, Minnesota, locating on a farm two and a half miles south of Jackson village, on the Des Moines river, where he owns a fine farm of 175 acres. He improved this farm, and made it one of the most desirable farms in the county, and resided thereon for three years, when he removed to the village of Jackson. He still continued to operate his farm, however, until the fall of 1888, when he rented it.

In 1863 Judge Goodrich served in the Indian expedition, holding the position of quartermaster-sergeant, remaining in the service for one year, and took part in the battle of White Stone Hills with the Indians. During the latter part of the expedition he was commander of Company I, and served gallantly and faithfully in that position, gaining the trust and confidence of all his fellow soldiers.

November 20, 1849, the subject of our sketch was married in McHenry county, Illinois, to Miss Mary White, a daughter of Hiram and Anna (Buckner) White, natives of Canada. Her parents and uncle built the Solon mills of McHenry county, Illinois, and laid out the village of Solon, naming it in honor of their uncle's son. Mrs. Goodrich was born in Canada, in March, 1833. The children of this union are as follows—Alfred

A., died at seven years of age; Amelia and Adelia, twins, the latter dying at eighteen months of age; Alonzo, who died when six months old; Henry, deceased, aged six years; Francis Irwin, died at two months of age; Clara was born in 1861, and lives in Jackson, being now Mrs. Edward Odbert; Harriet Beecher is a teacher in the public schools of Iowa; Augusta is a teacher in the North Bend high school, Nebraska, and Leon is a farmer of Iowa. Amelia married Fred Du Brava, a merchant at North Bend, Nebraska. This family is one of the most estimable and influential in the county, and exerts a wide influence in all matters of a social nature.

Throughout his life the subject of our sketch has taken an active part in the political government of the various places in which he has lived. He has been justice of the peace for five years in Jackson, was justice for fifteen years in the State of Iowa, and also held an office on the county board of supervisors for five years. He is a man of progressive ideas, and wields a strong influence in matters pertaining to the building up and establishment of projects which tend to the development of the financial and social condition of his locality. He is an honored member of the Grand Army of the Republic post and also of the Ancient Free and Accepted Masons, having been made a member of the latter society at Onawa, Iowa, in about 1868.

MATHIAS OLSON is a member of the firm of Bisbee & Olson, general merchants, of Madelia, Minnesota. This firm is one of the most reliable mercantile institutions in Southwestern Minnesota, and is doing an extensive business. Since Mr. Olson came to the village he has taken an active part in the improvement of the city, and has done a great deal toward developing the financial interests.

Mr. Olson is a native of Norway, where he was born May 21, 1846. His parents were Ole and Annie (Olson) Torgerson, both of whom were natives of Norway. The father was a farmer by occupation, and reared a family of seven children—Torger, Jacob, Rannog, Ammond, Peter, Mathias and Mathia. The father is still living; the mother died in her native country in 1880.

Attending school in his native land until he was fourteen years of age, our subject then engaged in clerking in a general store, in which line he continued for eight years. In 1868 he came in a sailing vessel to America, landing at Quebec, whence he came to St. Peter, Minnesota. He engaged for a brief time at farming in Blue Earth county, and then worked as a common laborer on the Sioux City railroad. In 1870 he came to Madelia and clerked in the general store of Boynton & Cheeney for four years. Then, in company with Mr. Bisbee, he opened their mammoth store at Madelia. Their store building is 24x120 feet, and they keep twelve men constantly employed to facilitate the handling of their immense business. Mr. Olson has earnestly and indefatigably applied himself to the building up of his various financial interests, and the successful manner of their conduction is amply manifested in the rush of trade which this firm enjoys. Not too busy with his private interests, Mr. Olson takes an active part in public matters, and has been a member of the village council for some time. In politics he occupies an independent ground, supporting the men best fitted for the various positions. With his wife he belongs to the Lutheran church. He has a fine home in the village, and has his grounds beautifully ornamented with shade trees. He owns a fine farm of 320 acres in Riverdale township, provided with excellent buildings, and with stock of all kinds. Mr. Olson is one of the leading and most prosperous citizens of Madelia.

The subject of our sketch was married in the year 1874 to Miss Mary Olson, daughter of Ole Stenerson, formerly of Madelia. This union has been blessed with three living children—Alfred M., Stella O. and Minnie.

PROFESSOR WILLIAM McDONALD, county superintendent of schools of Martin county, Minnesota, resides in Fairmont, the county seat. He is a native of Beetown, Grant county, Wisconsin, where he was born on the farm of his parents, September 26, 1847. He was the son of Joseph and Rebecca (McDonald) McDonald, the former a native of Ireland and the latter born in Fayette county, Pennsylvania. His father died when our subject was seven years of age, and he continued to reside with his mother, assisting her on the farm and attending school until about fifteen years of age.

Being possessed of a military spirit and endowed with loyal patriotism even at that early age, he enlisted in the service of the Union army. He joined the Forty-first Regiment Wisconsin Volunteer Infantry, and served for about two years, being discharged in the fall of 1865. The first battle in which he saw service was at the raid on Memphis by General Forrest. Following this came the conflict at Tupelo, Germantown and Holly Springs. From thence the division to which our subject's regiment was attached marched to Nashville and encountered the enemy at Franklin and later at the siege of Nashville under General Schofield and A. J. Smith. After his discharge he returned home and engaged in teaching, finding a position in the school at High Ridge, Cassville township, Grant county, Wisconsin. At the close of his term Professor J. F. Thompson proffered him a position in charge of the primary department of the Cassville public schools. Our subject continued in that position for one year and then entered the normal school at Plattville, continuing therein some two years. After this period he returned to his native village, and spent six years in the profession of teaching in the schools, where he had attended when a boy. During this time he built up quite a reputation as an excellent teacher, and took an active interest in the welfare of his locality. He became identified with the Independent Order of Good Templars, of which he was elected chief several times, and also held the superintendency of the Sunday-school for some time. During the vacations he occupied his time in improving his farm and hauling pig lead from the furnace to the Cassville market. He became financially interested in the mines of this region, but, finding that it was not a profitable investment, sold his stock and continued giving his attention more fully to the profession of teaching. In 1872 he was married, and then, after a summer spent on a farm, engaged as principal of the Potosi public schools, where he continued two years. He then spent one summer engaged in farming on the McCardy farm, four miles northeast of Potosi. In the fall of 1876, he removed to Colesburgh, Iowa, and filled a three years' engagement as principal of the public schools of that place. In the year 1879 he removed to North McGregor, and was there principal of the schools for three years. He then entered the political field, becoming a candidate for county superintendent of schools against J. R. McClellan. Our subject was defeated, and soon after resigned his position as teacher in the schools and returned to Colesburgh, where he entered his old position as principal, and held the same for two years. He then went to Muscolonge, Grant county, Wisconsin, and spent a year as principal of the public schools, and followed that with one year at farming and one at mining. In the winter he taught in the Lodge district, Beetown schools, and in the spring of 1883 came to Martin county, Minnesota, and engaged in agricultural pursuits in Cedarville township, on a place owned by E. F. Wade. In September of that year he was engaged as principal of the Fairmont schools and held the position for a year, after which he returned to a farm, renting a place owned by Messrs. St. John and Clark in Rolling Green township. He also taught a term of school in district No. 50, and boarded with Uncle John Schultz, whose family, as Mr. McDonald says, were of material aid to him in gaining a foothold in Martin county. He organized and conducted several Sunday-schools, and taught one term of school in district No. 61.

In 1885 he built a residence in Fairmont, and taught in district No. 51 during the winter of 1885–86. He was elected county superintendent of schools in November, 1886, and re-elected in 1888, receiving a majority of nine hundred votes over the prohibition and independent candidates. As county superintendent he has given excellent satisfaction, and has proven himself a capable and efficient officer. He is a man of high religious character, and is a member of the First Congregational church of Fairmont. He belongs to Post No. 18, Grand Army of the Republic, and is a member of the Fairmont Chapter, Royal Arch Masons.

On the 25th day of December, 1872, Professor McDonald was married in Potosi, Grant county, Wisconsin, to Miss Mary Hall, daughter of Josiah and Fannie (Grose) Hall, both of whom were natives of England. Miss Mary was also a native of England, her birth taking place in Hastings, near London, November 22, 1849. This marriage has been blessed with the following-named children — William J., Fannie R., and Eugene, who died in infancy.

DANIEL E. WAY is a successful farmer and stock-raiser located on section 10 of Holly township, Murray county, Minnesota, where he located in 1872. He homesteaded his land and has resided thereon ever since with the exception of one year, which was spent in Spring Valley, Fillmore county. Mr. Way was one of the very first settlers of the township, and has been identified with its best interests ever since his first settlement. Among the other early settlers were James Barnes, Newton Byram, Silas Clark, Mr. Vanderworker and P. Rice. On coming to the township our subject at once identified himself with the local governmental affairs, and has held various official positions. He has been township supervisor, justice of the peace, also having held various school offices in district No. 15. He is at present treasurer of the school district, and has been treasurer of the township for the past seven years. In 1884 he was elected county commissioner and served efficiently in that position for two years. He has always taken an active interest in matters of this nature, and occupies a prominent place in his community. He has a fine farm of 320 acres, and is one of the most extensive farmers in the township.

Mr. Way was born in the province of Quebec, Canada, February 6, 1848. He resided there until he was eight years old, when, with his parents, he removed to Fillmore county, Minnesota. His father was a farmer in Canada, and is at present living in Walnut Grove, Redwood county, Minnesota, where he is postmaster and is engaged in the mercantile business.

Our subject remained with his parents until twenty-one years of age, receiving a good common-school education. He enlisted as a private in the Fourth Regiment Minnesota Volunteer Infantry and joined the Fifteenth Army Corps. His was company D, Captain Murphy. He served throughout the war and was discharged May 16, 1865, at Louisville, Kentucky. He saw considerable service and was with General Sherman in his famous march to the sea. Among the battles in which he participated was that of Altona Pass, besides many other minor battles and skirmishes. After the war was over he returned to Fillmore county, Minnesota, and remained until his marriage, which occurred in 1869, when he moved to Mower county, Minnesota, and remained two years. He then came to his present location, where he has since resided. In politics Mr. Way affiliates with the republican party and is a leading member of the Grand Army of the Republic. In all county affairs he is recognized as being a representative citizen. He is genial and warmhearted, and is one of the most influential men in the township.

Mr. Way was married in April, 1869, to Miss Artemitia Root, a native of Ohio. In childhood this lady came with her parents to Wisconsin, where she received a good education and engaged in teaching school. Her father was W. S. Root, now a farmer of Holly township, Murray county. Mr. and Mrs. Way have three children—Victor, William and Berton.

———•❖•❖⟨❖⟩•❖•———

DAVID PRATT, a farmer of Amo township, Cottonwood county, Minnesota, located on section 8 in 1873. He homesteaded his present place and has made it his home ever since. He was born in Bradford county, Pennsylvania, September 13, 1847.

The subject of our sketch remained in his native county but a brief time and then went with his parents to Grant county, Wisconsin, where he resided until eighteen years of age. In that county he received his early training and education and after reaching the age just mentioned commenced farming. His parents died about this time and he then removed to Crawford county, same State, and, purchasing a farm in partnership with his brother, engaged in farming for some two years. He then sold his share in the farm to his brother and came to Cottonwood county, Minnesota. He was one of the first settlers of the township, which was then called Georgetown, but in 1872 the name was changed to that of Amo. The first year of our subject's location in the township he broke forty acres of land and put up several hay buildings. He passed through very trying circumstances and lost considerable money through the failure of crops and also by the devastating raids of the grasshoppers. He has always taken an active part in public matters and has especially interested himself in the proper government of local affairs. He is a careful business man and by careful and direct attention to the details of his farming operations has accumulated considerable means. In politics he is a republican. He belongs to the Ancient Order of United Workmen, and is one of the representative citizens of Cottonwood county.

Mr. Pratt was married February 15, 1873, to Miss Angelina De Witt, a native of Indiana.

———•❖•❖⟨❖⟩•❖•———

DANIEL THOMPSON, a leading farmer and stock raiser of Pipestone county, Minnesota, located on a fine farm on section 30, Altona township. He was born in Canada, October 5, 1851. His parents were Edward and Grace (Cook) Thompson, both of whom were natives of Argyleshire, Scotland, the father being born in the year 1810 and the mother in 1817. The father was a farmer by occupation and leaving his native country came to Canada in 1828, settling in Beauharnois county, from whence he moved to Chateauguay county. He died in the latter county in the year 1883, on the 8th day of April. The mother is still living in Chateauguay county.

The subject of our sketch remained with his parents in his native country until March, 1871. Up to this time he had assisted in work on the home farm and had attended school at every opportunity. At the date just given he came to Minnesota, locating for six months in Otter Tail county, where he worked on a railroad. Removing thence he went to Stearns county and worked on a railroad for about ten months. Then he went to Dodge county, Minnesota, in 1872, and made that his home until 1879. During his residence in Dodge county he returned to Canada on a brief visit and for a few months remained there working at different kinds of employment in various cities. In June, 1880, he came to his present location and purchased the right on his farm and commenced farming operations. He did not make a permanent location at that date, however, but for several seasons he occupied more or less of his time in work on railroads in the western part of Minnesota.

Mr. Thompson was married April 8, 1886, to Miss Ida McKown. Mrs. Thompson died May 19, 1888. Two children were born to them, but they died shortly after their birth.

The subject of our sketch has taken a prominent position among the citizens of his township and has held various official positions, serving in every instance with efficiency and to the satisfaction of his constituents. In politics he affiliates with the democratic party. Among the offices which he has held are those of assessor, to which he was appointed in 1881 and elected in 1888 and 1889. He has also been a member of the board of supervisors and was appointed town clerk in 1886. He is a man of excellent character, thrifty and industrious, and has surrounded himself with the evidences of prosperity. He has a good farm, well provided with buildings, and is successful in his farming operations. He is widely known and respected by all with whom he has to do.

JOHN P. DETIENNE is the depot agent of the Chicago, Milwaukee & St. Paul Railroad at Sherburne, Martin county, Minnesota. He is the son of Etienne and Mary Theresa (Jissart) Detienne, natives of Belgium. Our subject was born in Brabant, Belgium, July 29, 1850, and when he was three years of age his parents emigrated to the United States, first locating in Brown county, Wisconsin.

When John P. was ten years of age his parents sent him to school at Green Bay, where he continued his studies for two years. He then returned to the farm on which he had been reared, and remained there until he was about fourteen years old, then returned to school until the age of sixteen. Then for two years he engaged in operating a meat market in Green Bay, Wisconsin, and at the end of that time became a clerk in the postoffice of that village. He continued his employment in the postoffice for six and a half years, beginning as general delivery clerk and finally working up to the position of clerk of the money order department. After leaving this business he came West. After remaining a short time he received word from his former employer that if he would return he could have the position of assistant postmaster. He did not accept this position, but continued in the employment of the railroad company. He came to Sherburne, Martin county, Minnesota, in March, 1879, and was given charge of the depot on the Southern Minnesota Railroad, this being now a branch of the Chicago, Milwaukee & St. Paul system. Throughout his connection with this company he has run a successful business, and has made himself popular with both his employers and patrons. He has been under four different division superintendents and two different general superintendents and from each of them has won strong words of approval and commendation.

Mr. Detienne is a man of strong temperance principles, and affiliates with the prohibition party. He is a member of the Independent Order of Odd Fellows and Independent Order of Good Templars.

August 8, 1876, at Green Bay, Wisconsin, our subject was married to Miss Elizabeth De Godt, daughter of Ambrose and Louise (De Chaine) De Godt, natives of Belgium. She was born in Delaware, Pennsylvania, May 10, 1853. Mr. and Mrs. Detienne have had the following-named children—Norbert, John, Albert, Harry and Hazel Lieta.

———⋅⟶⋅⟨⟨⟨⟩⟩⟩⋅⟵⋅———

SEWARD J. MOE is the efficient and popular postmaster of Lakefield, Jackson county, Minnesota. He is a son of Jens and Selma (Bronken) Moe, natives of Norway. Our subject was born in Elverum, in the kingdom of Norway, April 1, 1850. The parents came to the United States in 1852, settling at Kettle Creek, Potter county, Pennsylvania, where the mother died in about 1853. The father married again fourteen years afterward, taking to wife Martha Olson.

After the death of his mother the subject of this sketch was adopted by a man named O. Solberg, with whom he continued to live at various places, Decorah, Iowa, Freeborn, Mankato and Watonwan, Minnesota, until he was seventeen years of age. At this age he went to his father's place in Butler county, Iowa, and made that his home for about a year. He then concluded to find a location, and went to Cedar Rapids, Iowa, and commenced working as brakeman on a railroad, following that line for a year. He then became foreman of a force of men laying track, and made this his business until 1872. He then turned his attention to agricultural pursuits, came to Minnesota, rented a farm in Brown county, and resided thereon four years, the grasshoppers taking every crop. He then took a contract on the railroad between Jordan and Albert Lea, and in the fall of the same year contracted to build a division of the Fort Dodge & St. James Railroad. This work was partly completed when the company failed, and our subject lost about seven hundred dollars. He remained in Blue Earth City during the winter and in the spring of 1878 engaged on the railroad between Jackson and Winnebago City. Continuing in this employment until January 1, 1881, in the spring of that year he went to Dakota, and became foreman on a construction force for the Dakota Central Railroad Company, returning to Jackson in the fall of that year. January 1, 1882, he took up his residence in Lakefield, and was section boss for three years, after which he removed to Lamberton, and kept a hotel and also run a meat-market until the fall of 1885. He then returned to Lakefield, and engaged in the retail liquor business, continuing thereat for eighteen months. He then sold out, and about four months later was appointed postmaster of the village. His experience in the western county has been a varied one, and he has met with many hardships. In 1862, with his adopted parents, he intended to make a settlement in Watonwan county, but was driven therefrom by the Indians.

In all matters pertaining to the public welfare of the villages in which he has lived he has always taken an active part, and has held the office of justice of the peace, constable, marshal, school clerk, etc. In all these positions he has served his constituents faithfully and to their entire satisfaction. He is an influential member of the Independent Order of Odd Fellows.

Mr. Moe was married at Waterloo, Iowa, May 6, 1871, to Miss Isabel Gilbertson, daughter of Gulbrand and Carrie (Paulson) Gilbertson, natives of Norway. Mrs. Moe was born in Halland, Norway, December 24, 1849. This marriage has been blessed with the following-named children—Clarence, Howard, Albert, Minnie, Earnest, William Edward, Ida Jennie and Mabel.

———————

EORGE W. DIBBLE, who is now a leading farmer, located on section 19, Verona township, Faribault county, Minnesota, was one of the early settlers of Minnesota. He came to the State in October, 1855, and pre-empted government land in Newburg township, Fillmore county. He was there engaged in farming until the winter of 1866, when he sold his farm and engaged in running a hotel at Brownsville, Houston county. In the spring of 1870 he removed to Martin county, Minnesota, and settled in what is now Jay township, which township he gave its name. The first school meeting in the town was held at his house, he being elected school director, and his eldest daughter, Ella M., taught the first school in the township. He served as assessor of the township, and otherwise took an active part in public affairs. He remained in that county until, like hundreds of others, he was forced to leave on account of the raids of the grasshoppers. He then, in the fall of 1875, came to Verona township, Faribault county, and rented a farm on section 13, which he cultivated for six-years. At the expiration of that time he purchased his present farm of 163 acres, on section 19, and has brought it to a high state of cultivation. He is rated as one of the most substantial farmers in the county, and makes a specialty of raising fine horses.

Mr. Dibble was born in Essex county, New York, May 7, 1825. His parents were Orrin and Louise (Holt) Dibble, both of whom were natives of New Hampshire. The father was an iron and coal worker, and died in the State of New York at the age of seventy-five years. Our subject continued his residence with his parents in his native county until he was twenty-nine years of age, up to which time he had been given a good practical education. He had also spent a number of years in work in the coal and iron mines in the region in which he lived. He was then married, and later came to Minnesota, as was stated in the opening lines of this sketch.

December 2, 1852, Mr. Dibble was married to Miss Maria A. Welch, a native of Franklin county, New York, and reared and educated in Essex county. She was the daughter of Reuben C. and Sallie (Brown) Welch. Her father was a farmer and bridge-builder in Keene, New York. The mother died when our subject's wife was about thirteen years of age. After this she kept house for her father until her marriage. Mr. and Mrs. Dibble have four living children—Augustia, Eulia, Josephine and Wilber I., all married but the last named. Ella M., the eldest, died at thirty-three years of age, in Mabel, Fillmore county, in January, 1887. She was the wife of Silas C. Brace, a lumberman and also engaged in the mercantile and hardware business. She was a member of the Methodist Episcopal church and an estimable Christian lady. She died leaving three children—William G., Clayton Eugene and a babe nine days old. It was her request that her mother should have the babe, which she had so lovingly named Silas, after its papa, and the request was granted. Thus, it was loved and cared for with a zeal that no one else could give until the 4th of March, 1889, when it died of diphtheria, being then two years and two months old.

A man of good, practical education, possessed of practical ideas, energetic and as well of public spirit, our subject has always proven a valuable assistant in the management of the general affairs of the township. He is a republican in politics and wields a strong influence in that organization. He is a man of high character. He was a member of the Methodist Episcopal church for twenty-eight years. He united with the Free-Will Baptist church, of Huntley, in March, 1889.

WYATT H. BENBOW is the present efficient clerk of the district court of Cottonwood county, Minnesota. He located in the county in February, 1871. Mr. Benbow is a native of Hendricks county, Indiana, where he was born on the 2d of July, 1848.

The subject of our sketch is the son of William S. and Jemima (Beeson) Benbow, natives of North Carolina. The grandfather of our subject was William Benbow, a native of North Carolina, and a tanner by trade. He came to Indiana in an early day and engaged in farming. In 1852 he removed to Iowa, where he remained until his death. He was of English descent. Jemima Beeson was the daughter of William and Hannah (Cosner) Beeson, of German descent. Her father was a blacksmith by trade, and in connection therewith operated a farm. He was an early settler of Indiana. William S. Benbow, the father of the subject of our sketch, on coming to Indiana, engaged in farming, and died in that State in 1866. He had a family of seven children, three of whom are now living — Wyatt H., William C. and Launa J., now Mrs. John Seeley.

Mr. Benbow remained with his parents on the farm until he attained his majority, three years prior to which time, at his father's death, he had taken charge of the farm. The educational advantages furnished our subject were of a good character, and he received his training principally at a boarding-school near Lafayette, Indiana. In 1869, in company with a friend, he came to Greenleaf, Meeker county, Minnesota, where he purchased a stock of drugs and engaged in the drug business during the winter. In the spring they removed their stock to Willmar, where they operated until fall.

They then sold out and our subject went to Mankato, where he remained during the winter. In the spring Mr. Benbow came to Cottonwood county, and settled in Amo township, which he helped to organize, and which he gave its name. He settled on 160 acres of government land, improved the same and resided in the township until his election to his present office in 1886. On being elected to his office in 1886 he moved into the village of Windom and purchased a dwelling, where he now lives. Our subject has held various other official positions of minor importance, and has always proved himself an efficient and conscientious public servant. He assisted in the organization of the township of Amo and was appointed chairman of the board of supervisors. He was also clerk for some seven years, and was a member of the first county convention held in the county. In 1888, having become quite prominent in the republican ranks, to which party he belongs, he was made a delegate to the district convention. He is secretary of the Agricultural Society of Cottonwood county, and is a leading and influential member of the Masonic and Ancient Order of United Workmen societies, being recorder of the latter society. In all his relations Mr. Benbow has proven himself a reliable and trustworthy citizen, and is held in high esteem by all who know him.

Mr. Benbow was married in 1879 to Miss Diana Day, of Cottonwood county. She was the daughter of Zadock Day, one of Cottonwood county's prominent citizens. Mr. and Mrs. Benbow have been blessed with four children—William R., Dora M., Wilber D. and a babe as yet unnamed.

DAVID THORNDIKE is a reliable and prosperous farmer of Slayton township, Murray county, Minnesota, and resides on section 28. He is of English birth, and was born on the 9th day of December, 1862. The parents of the subject of our sketch were

William and Sarah L. (Dyball) Thorndike, both of whom were natives of England. The father was a sea captain, and came to America in 1866 and located in La Salle, Illinois, where he still lives. He is now engaged in mercantile pursuits. The mother died December 16, 1881. In the father's family there were four children, our subject being the oldest.

Until fourteen years of age David Thorndike lived with his parents and attended the public schools. At the age just mentioned he found employment on a news route, and continued in that occupation for eight years, when he turned his business over to his brother. In the spring of 1885 he came to Murray county and purchased the place where he now lives. He has a fine farm of 200 acres, under good cultivation, and provided with excellent farm buildings. Since coming to the township he has taken an active part in public matters, and has held various official positions. He has been road overseer for three years, clerk of the school district, poundmaster, etc. He is a man of excellent qualifications, genial and warm-hearted, and is highly respected.

Mr. Thorndike was married March 7, 1889, to Emma M. Sharp, a native of England. This lady is possessed of a fine education, and is one of the leading ladies in the township.

—————◆→◆|◆◆◆◆◆◆◆|◆←◆—————

ALBERT HEMENOVER, one of the leading and influential business men of Pipestone city, Minnesota, carries a large line of drugs and stationery. He located in the city in the spring of 1882, and at once commenced business operations. In 1886 he built his present fine business building of the famous jasper granite. This building is 24x60 feet, contains elegant store rooms, and cost somewhat over five thousand dollars. It is fitted with all the modern improvements, and is one of the handsomest buildings in the city. In Mr. Hemenover's stock is found an excellent assortment of patent medicines, stationery, wall-paper, and a full line of drugs. Besides his drug business, he has also interested himself in several other financial enterprises in the city. In company with Thomas F. Robinson and Silas E. Wharton he organized a company to do business under the name of the "Merchants' Co-operative Chemical and Spice Company," with a capital of forty thousand dollars, our subject holding the office of treasurer of the company. This institution has built up one of the principal business enterprises of Pipestone city, and is engaged in manufacturing baking powders, flavoring extracts, essences, chemicals, drugs, spices, etc.

The place of the nativity of the subject of our sketch is in Canton, Fulton county, Illinois, where he was born March 6, 1852. His parents were Andrew R. and Eliza (Collins) Hemenover, the former a native of the State of New Jersey, and the latter a native of Ohio. The father was engaged in farming in Illinois, and also was largely interested in raising Norman and Percheron horses. He was a man of large means and wielded a wide influence in the place in which he lived. When he first came to Illinois he settled in McDonough county, and in 1867 removed his family to Bloomington, Illinois, being in this place engaged in the same business that we have described above. In 1883 the father removed to Hastings, Nebraska, in which city he is now living a retired life. In the father's family there were three sons—Albert, Andrew, now engaged in general mercantile business at Doniphan, Nebraska, and Edward, a general merchant of Hanson, Nebraska.

The early days of the subject of our sketch were spent by him on the home farm, where he assisted his father in the farm work and received a good common school education.

He remained with his parents until he was twenty-two years of age, at which time he was married, and afterward engaged in farming in the eastern part of McLean county, Illinois. Five years were spent by him in the locality just mentioned, and at the end of that time he purchased a farm in Normal township, where he engaged in farming and stock raising. Remaining there but one year, he then removed to Cherokee, Iowa, where another year was spent in farming and stock raising. Selling out his interests in Iowa, he next came to Pipestone, Minnesota, and engaged in his present business. When he commenced in this line he had but very little knowledge of its details. He at once commenced studying, however, and took a thorough course of home study in the National Institute of Pharmacy; continuing diligently in this way for four years he finally was granted a diploma as a pharmacist in June, 1887. Mr. Hemenover was married to Miss G. M. Willson, of Bloomington, Illinois. One child has blessed this union—Gertrude. Mrs Hemenover was a daughter of Rev. George Willson, who received his early training and education in the East. He was a graduate of the Athens College, Ohio, and after his graduation was professor of mathematics in that institution for a number of years. He entered the Presbyterian ministry, and accepted the charge of a church at Richland, Ohio, in 1841. Remaining in that city until 1844, he then severed his connections with that church because of a change in his views on baptism. His withdrawal from the Presbyterian church was the cause of much sorrow and regret on the part of his ministerial brethren. His withdrawal, however, was accomplished in the most harmonious manner and with the best brotherly feeling. From his old synod he received a certificate of regular ordination as a minister of the gospel in good standing, and left that organ-

ization with the good-will and hearty "God-speed" of all. Having changed his views in regard to the method of baptism he finally found a church home with the Baptist society, preaching for a time at Newville, Ohio. He continued his ministerial labors in active work until 1885, in which year he retired from active duty and now resides at Bloomington, Illinois. He was a man of high education, extensive general knowledge, and was a thorough and persistent student. Besides being an able preacher, he was an author of considerable prominence, having published a work entitled "Baptismal Controversy," in 1855, and another, "The Kingdom of God," in 1887. The father was a native of Pennsylvania and was reared a farmer's boy, receiving his early training and education in the district schools. He graduated from college when twenty-one years of age. Rev. Mr. Willson married Margaret J. Taggart, a native of Belmont county, Ohio. They had a family of seven children—Sarah E., Mary J., now Mrs. Davis; William T., Mrs. Hemenover, Amelia, now Mrs. Mills; Maria I. and Georgiana. Mrs. Hemenover was educated at the State University at Normal, Illinois, and is a lady of rare social and intellectual qualities.

The subject of our sketch in politics affiliates with the republican party. Himself, wife and child attend the Baptist church, in which society Mrs. Hemenover is one of the leading workers, being the present Sunday-school superintendent. In all business matters pertaining to the financial welfare of the village, Mr. Hemenover has taken a prominent and active place. He has aided willingly, both by word and deed, in the upbuilding and development of all projects tending to the advancement of Pipestone's financial interests. He is a thorough-going, capable business man, and has built up for himself a large and enviable trade. Being a man of means and business push he has become one of the prominent business men of the city.

JOHN HENRY SHERIN is the senior member of the firm of Sherin & Foss, publishers of the *Press-News* of Winnebago City, Minnesota. This newspaper was established in 1880 and has been quite successful in building up a large subscription list and lucrative patronage.

The subject of our sketch is a native of Canada, where he was born in the year 1850. He is the son of Robert Sherin, of whom a sketch is given in another department of this work. When our subject was ten years of age the family removed to Wisconsin, where, he was given a good common school education. At an early age he commenced working at the newspaper business, being employed in the *Gazette* office at Fox Lake for some three years. He then followed the business of a journeyman printer, visiting Milwaukee, Chicago, Detroit, Rochester, Buffalo, Denver, Omaha, St. Louis, Dubuque and St. Paul. He published the *News* at Lakfield, Canada, in 1875, operating it for two years, then sold out, and in 1879 located in Winnebago City, Minnesota, purchasing an interest in the *Press*. One year later he sold out and established the *News*, and after conducting the same until 1884, consolidated it with the *Press* and named the paper the *Press-News*. This paper is independent in politics and is devoted to the interests of the locality. Mr. Sherin is an able newspaper man.

CLARK W. SMITH, a leading and influential farmer and stock raiser, is located on section 12, Fountain Prairie township, Pipestone county, Minnesota. He is also a carpenter by trade, and in connection with his farming operations he gives consid-

erable attention to contracting and building. Mr. Smith was born in the city of Philadelphia, Pennsylvania, January 31, 1833.

The parents of the subject of our sketch were Joseph and Lucy (Reynolds) Smith, both of whom were natives of Pennsylvania. The father was by occupation a carpenter, following that line of business throughout the most of his life until his death, which occurred in 1884. The mother passed to the spirit world in 1888, being at the time of her decease about seventy-nine years of age. She was an exemplary Christian and a member of the Methodist Episcopal church. In the father's family there were nine children, eight of whom grew to manhood and womanhood—Elizabeth, Owen, Clark, Breton, Cook, Charles E., Mary, George and Taylor.

The subject of our sketch remained with his parents in the city of Philadelphia until he reached the age of twenty-two years. Up to this time he had been given a good common school education, and had also learned the carpenter's trade under the direction of his father. On reaching the age of twenty-two he went to Wisconsin, and located in Vernon county, where he followed the business of his trade, and, in connection therewith, engaged somewhat in the saw-mill business and in flat-boating on the Mississippi river. Vernon county remained his home until he came to his present location in 1878.

Mr. Smith was married October 13, 1867. His wife was formerly Miss Phœbe Carpenter. She was first married September 23, 1860, to David C. Martin, who died September 13, 1863, of typhoid fever; and in 1867 she was married to Mr. Smith as stated. She had taught school for three years previous to her first marriage, and also followed this vocation for three years after the death of Mr. Martin. This lady is a native of Steuben county, New York, where she was reared and educated. Remaining in her native county until she was twenty-five years of age, she then came to Wisconsin and settled in Vernon county, where she lived at the time of her marriage to Mr. Smith. She was the daughter of Timothy and Nancy (Shaw) Carpenter. The father followed the business of farming throughout the most of his life, and died in 1883, at the age of eighty-three years. The mother is still living, being eighty-four years of age. In her father's family there were ten. children—Mary Ann, Hiram, Alva, Susan, John, Jane, Phœbe, Uriah, Caroline, Fidelia. One child died in infancy. Mr. and Mrs. Smith have been blessed with three children—Mary E., born October 21, 1868; Alva O., born February 6, 1872, and Lucy J., born January 25, 1879. Mary E. was married August 3, 1885, to Hamilton De Hart.

To illustrate to the mind of the reader what the hardships of the pioneer settler are, it may be well to give a short account of the trip of our subject from his home in Wisconsin to the place where he now resides. This journey was full of difficulties, but these are the rule, rather than the exception, in the experience of the early settlers of any locality. Mr. Smith started from his home in Vernon county, Wisconsin, May 10, 1878. He started with an ox team and wagon, and the journey occupied three long, weary, toilsome weeks. When he arrived in Pipestone county, he had but twenty dollars to commence operations with, but he was of sturdy make-up, not easily discomfited. and he at once commenced pushing his farming operations. He broke five acres of land, built a shanty, mostly out of sod, and settled down to the enjoyment of pioneer farm life. Coming from a thickly settled country it was a long time before Mr. Smith's family could become accustomed to the wildness and lonesomeness of the bleak, uninhabited prairie on which they had settled, but after a time settlers came to adjoining lands, and here and there the shanties of the pioneers

dotted the landscape. Before long it was but a few miles, or perhaps but a mile to the nearest neighbor. And then the lonesomeness of prairie life began to wear off. The second year Mr. Smith broke ten acres of land, and reaped no harvest because of the destruction of his crops by hail. However, he reaped what he had sown in like quantity as well as quality—he put in nine bushels of grain and harvested nine bushels. The following year he broke up ten acres more and was successful in raising a good crop. Since that time crops have been good and our subject has increased in prosperity steadily throughout all the succeeding years up to the present time. Mr. Smith has an excellent farm of 160 acres in a good location, beautified with a fine grove of trees of about nine acres. He has about eighty acres under cultivation and about forty acres in pasture. Having passed through the experiences of pioneer life our subject understands the needs of his locality, and throughout his residence has been active in all things which pertain to the public welfare. He attended the first meeting held for the purpose of organizing the civil township, which meeting was held at the house of Charles Sizer. In politics Mr. Smith affiliates with no particular party, believing that it is proper and best to elect to office the man, not the party. In political matters he is, therefore, an independent. He is an influential member of the Masonic fraternity.

REDERICK WILLIAM FEHRING, one of the thrifty and reliable farmers of Scandia township, Murray county, Minnesota, is the son of Frederick and Gissel (Suhr) Fehring, natives of Germany, where also our subject was born December 30, 1835, in Bulkau. Our subject remained with his parents, who were farmers in the old country, assisting them in the farm work and attending the common schools until reaching the age of fifteen and one-half years. He then learned the cabinet-maker's trade, at which he continued in his native land until twenty-eight years of age. Then, in 1864, he came to the United States, stopping first in New York city, where he worked at his trade for eight years, during which time he visited his native land three times. At the end of that time he left New York city and went to Cambridge Court House, Virginia, on a visit, and later, in 1873, came to Minnesota, where he took a homestead on the northwest quarter of section 26, Scandia township, Murray county. The same year the grasshopper raids began, and for two years no crops were raised. The third year our subject succeeded in harvesting 130 bushels of wheat, but was obliged to expend forty-two cents per bushel for threshing, without counting his exchange work. The first year of his residence on the farm Mr. Fehring boarded with a friend, but after that put up a cheap house, and, being a single man, has lived a bachelor's life on his farm ever since. He owns 160 acres of excellent land, with about seventy-five acres under cultivation. Among other property owned by our subject may be named fifteen head of cattle, besides mules and other stock. In politics Mr. Fehring has been honored by his fellow-citizens with the offices of assessor, supervisor, township treasurer, besides having been school director, school treasurer, etc. He is a man of exemplary character, and is a thrifty and industrious farmer.

———◦————◦————

JAMES G. HAMLIN is the able editor and publisher of the *Post*, of Blue Earth City, Faribault county, Minnesota. He is a native of Oneida county, New York, where he was born in the year 1847. His parents were Austin and Jane (Van Valken-

burg) Hamlin, natives, respectively, of Connecticut and New York. The father followed blacksmithing throughout most of his life, and died at seventy-six years of age. The mother died in 1888. Their children were Oscar E., James G., Erwin P., Maria A., now Mrs. E. W. Porter; Mrs. Laura L. Hickey and Mrs. Dr. E. M. Somers.

The early life of our subject was spent on the farm, and his education was received in an academy in Oneida county, New York. He enlisted in Company C, Eleventh New York Cavalry, and continued in the service for three years. He was in a great many battles, and was slightly wounded in an engagement in Louisiana. He was one of the youngest soldiers from Oneida county, and belonged to what are known as "Scott's Nine Hundred." Leaving the service, he returned home and engaged at the printers' trade in Eau Claire, Wisconsin. In 1870 he established to Hancock *Autograph* in Concord, Iowa, and continued its publication until fall, when he removed his press to Mason City, Iowa. Here he conducted a paper known as the *Express*, for one year, and then established the Albert Lea *Enterprise*, of Freeborn county, Minnesota. After two and a half years he located in Blue Earth City, and, in partnership with C. A. Ingalls, purchased the *Post*. Mr. Ingalls' interest was sold, after four years, to F. W. Drake, who, two years later, sold out to C. W. Dillman, the firm now being Hamlin & Dillman. Our subject has been editor of the paper during all this time, and has been highly successful in increasing its popularity. On taking charge of it there were but three hundred subscribers, while now the paper has fifteen hundred on its list. The *Post* is conducted in the interests of the republican party, and is a stanch supporter of everything which tends to the upbuilding of local affairs. Our subject has been quite prominent in public matters, and has held various village offices. He is a member of the Knights of Pythias and Grand Army of the Republic, and is one of the leading citizens of the town and county.

'Mr. Hamlin was married, in the year 1870, to Miss Minnie R. Sumner, of Waterford, Wisconsin, daughter of Ira M. Sumner. This union has been blessed with two children — Orpha L. and Ira H.

———◦→◦|❮❰❂❱❯|◦←◦———

WILLIAM SCHROEDER resides on section 24, Germantown township, Cottonwood county, Minnesota. He was born in Germany, July 11, 1844, and was the son of Henry and Henrietta (Krause) Schroeder, both natives of the fatherland. The mother died in July, 1854, and in 1856 the father came to the United States, locating in Winnebago county, Wisconsin, where he still lives.

The subject of this sketch was reared in his native country until about twelve years of age, and then with his father came to this country, locating in Winnebago county, Wisconsin. Up to August 3, 1862, he remained at home and received his education in the common schools of that county. He then enlisted as a private in Battery C, First Wisconsin Heavy Artillery, under Captain John R. Davis. He served until the close of the war, and was discharged at Nashville, Tennessee, September 21, 1865. He participated in the following-named battles—Mission Ridge, Lookout Mountain, and several other smaller battles and skirmishes. On being discharged, he returned to Winnebago county, Wisconsin, and remained until 1869. In that year he removed to Outagamie county, where he resided some thirteen years, engaged in farming. While in that county he occupied a prominent place among his fellow-citizens and held various official positions, among them being that of assessor, supervisor and township clerk. In 1882 he

came to Minnesota and located at Sanborn, Redwood county, where he engaged in the mercantile business in partnership with O. D. Wells, under the firm name of Wells & Schroeder. He continued in this line for some five years, also giving his attention to lumbering. In June, 1889, he located on his present farm where he now owns two hundred and eighty acres of excellent land. He also owns eighty acres in Redwood county.

Mr. Schroeder was married in January, 1870, to Miss Augusta Voss, a native of Germany, and who came to this country when eighteen years of age. Mr. and Mrs. Schroeder have six children—Wellington, Charles, Louisa, Bertha, Frank and Ida.

Mr. Schroeder is a man of much energy, and is one of the systematic and successful farmers of the county. Wherever he has been he has taken an active part in matters pertaining to the general welfare, and having held various official positions, has gained the esteem and respect of his fellow-citizens. While a resident of Redwood county, he was one of its representative citizens, and did a great deal toward building up the public enterprises. In every project tending to local development he is always willing to do his share, both in a financial sense and otherwise.

———◦→◦|❮❰❂❱❯|◦←◦———

DR. WILBER S. WEBB, one of the leading physicians of Worthington, Nobles county, Minnesota, is a native of East Troy, Walworth county, Wisconsin, where he was born August 12, 1859. His parents were Albert L. and O. E. (Wilber) Webb, natives of New York. The parents were farmers by occupation and left New York in an early day, coming to Wisconsin, where they spent the most of their lives. The father died in Clinton, Iowa, in May, 1886; the mother is still living. In the father's family there are four sons and one daughter now living—Dr. Wilber S., Adelbert D., Myron, Charles and Mary (now Mrs. A. H. Scott).

Dr. Webb was reared on a farm and remained with his parents until he was twelve or thirteen years old. He then started out to do for himself, and although he met with many discouragements, he kept sturdily at work at anything he could find to do and succeeded in giving himself a good high school education. His plan was to work at different employments during the summer and attend school during the winter months. After completing the course in the high school he engaged in teaching for about two years and then pursued the study of medicine in Clinton, Iowa, with Drs. McCormick and Smith, continuing with them from 1880 until the fall of 1882, when he entered the Northwestern Medical University of Chicago. In February, 1884, he graduated from Rush Medical College, and after receiving his diploma located in Sibley, Iowa, and formed a partnership with Dr. Neil. This partnership was continued some two years, and then our subject removed to Ellsworth, Nobles county, Minnesota, and there engaged in the practice of his profession. June 1, 1889, he came to Worthington, where he is at present engaged in practice. He is thoroughly educated and well equipped for the duties of his profession. He is a member of the board of pension examiners and has been surgeon for the Burlington Railroad for three or four years. He is a member of the Ancient Free and Accepted Masons of Adrian, and also of the Chapter of Ancient Free and Accepted Masons of Worthington.

Leaving home when quite young and having no one whatever to lean upon, the success which has crowned his efforts has been brought about as the direct result of his own independent endeavor. His lines have not always fallen in pleasant places

and he has often met with discouragements sufficient to daunt the spirit of almost any young man. Through it all, however, he has kept his face toward a high place in his chosen profession, and has succeeded by earnest and honest endeavor in building up a large practice and in planting himself firmly in a high place in his professsion.

Dr. Webb was married in Clinton, Iowa, September 22, 1884, to Miss Etta P. Bitner, a native of the State in which she was married, and born October 23, 1862. Her parents were Jacob and Mary (Harding) Bitner, the former a native of Pennsylvania and the latter born in Canada. Dr. and Mrs. Webb have two children—Lillian C. and Florence. Mrs. Webb's father was a contractor and builder in Clinton, Iowa.

<hr/>

DANIEL HEDMAN resides in Storden township, Cottonwood county, Minnesota. He is one of the leading citizens of that locality and resides on a fine farm on section 6. The place of his nativity is found in Sweden, his birth occurring August 9, 1860.

The parents of the subject of our sketch were Ole Hedman and Annie Danielson, also natives of Sweden. In April, 1869, the family emigrated to the United States, and coming to Minnesota, located in the city of Mankato for some time. From thence they removed to Cottonwood county, and located on a pre-emption, the claim on which our subject now resides. The father died in 1872; the mother is still living on the farm. In the father's family there were six children, four of whom are now living—Andrew, Lewis, Mary and Daniel.

Our subject came to America with his parents and settled with them for a time in Mankato. He received a good common-school education, and on the coming of the parents to Cottonwood county, our subject accompanied them and has since made his home in Storden township. At the age of twenty-one years he commenced farming for himself and has been engaged in agricultural pursuits ever since. He has an excellent farm and in connection with the production of grain also raises a good stock of English shire horses. His farm is well improved, and provided with good buildings, and contains a good grove of cottonwood trees. Since coming to the township our subject has taken an active interest in all matters tending to the general welfare. He is a man of good characteristics and has served his constituents ably and efficiently in various official positions. He has held various offices on the town board, and has been justice of the peace two years, and is treasurer of school district No. 42.

Mr. Hedman was married December 26, 1883, to Christina Hanson, daughter of Hans Hanson Kaste, a native of Norway. The father resided in his native land until his death; the mother is living in Dane county, Wisconsin. Miss Hanson was a native of Norway, where she was born in the year 1854. Mr. and Mrs. Hedman have three children—Annie, Hattie and Lillie.

PETER KEEGAN, a prominent farmer and stock-raiser of Holly township, Murray county, Minnesota, resides on section 32. He came to Murray county in 1878, and was one of the pioneer settlers of his township. He homesteaded his present place in 1878, and commenced making permanent improvements, building a house fourteen by twenty feet. He broke some sixty acres of land, and has now a fine farm of 240 acres. Mr. Keegan has been one of the most prominent citizens of Murray county. He has taken an active interest in public matters, and in 1886 was elected judge of probate of Murray county, being re-elected in 1888. He has also held the office of chairman of the board of supervisors, and was township clerk for five years. He has held various school offices, and has always taken an active interest in educational matters. He is a man of excellent acquired as well as natural attainments, and is highly esteemed by all his constituents.

Mr. Keegan was born in Ireland, in September, 1842, being reared in that country to the age of eight years. He then came to America with his parents and located in Brooklyn for five years. Coming West they then located in Walworth county, Wisconsin, where our subject remained some five or six years. During this time he had lived on a farm with his parents, and had been given a good common-school education. In 1864 he enlisted in Company E, Forty-second Regiment Wisconsin Volunteer Infantry and was discharged in June, 1865, at Madison, Wisconsin. His regiment was stationed most of the time at Cairo, Illinois, doing provost duty, a portion of the time on the Mississippi river. After being discharged from the service our subject returned to Wisconsin and engaged in work in the pineries during the winter months, and on the rivers during the summer months, for some four or five years. He then came to Minnesota, locating in Winona county, where he remained for two years engaged in farming. Thence he removed to Steele county, and after several years returned to Walworth county, Wisconsin, where he was married and settled on a farm for about five years. Four years were then spent in Janesville, Waseca county, Minnesota, where he engaged in the wood business. In 1878 he came to his present place, where he has since resided.

Judge Keegan was married January 6, 1869, to Miss Elizabeth McAvoy, a native of Ireland, and daughter of Daniel and Ellen McAvoy. This lady came to America with her parents in 1859, and located in Wisconsin. Mr. and Mrs. Keegan have been blessed with eight children — William, Nellie, Bertha, James, Sarah, Emma, Maggie and May. The oldest son is a resident of Tracy, Lyon county, and the oldest daughter is a teacher by profession.

Perhaps no man in the county is so well known and highly respected as Judge Keegan. He has always been public-spirited, and has assisted materially in the development of the various interests of his locality. In politics he affiliates with the republican party, and is a consistent member of the Catholic church.

JOHN KROEGER resides on section 20, Verdi township, Lincoln county, Minnesota. He is a native of Germany, where he was born November 21, 1855. His parents were John and Margaret (Otto) Kroeger, who were also natives of Germany. The father was a farmer by occupation and lived in his native land until his death, which occurred in 1855. The mother is still living in Germany.

John Kroeger spent his early life in his native country and received a good common-school education. He made his home with his parents and assisted them in work on the home farm. In 1873 he bade good-by to the associations of early life and came to the United States. Landing in New York City July 25th of that year, he passed on to Minnesota, where he found employment on various farms in Waseca county. He continued in that county until the fall of 1878, when he located on the place where he now lives in Lincoln county. He has a homestead of 160 acres of fine land. After locating his claim he returned to Waseca county and remained until the spring of 1879, at which time he returned to his claim where he has since lived. He was one among the early settlers of the township, and passed through many severe experiences. Through the winter of the deep snow, so well remembered by the early settlers of Lincoln county, our subject did not get his team out of the barn from the 10th of January until the 1st of April, so badly had the snow drifted about his buildings. Seeding was not commenced that year until the 25th of April, and then the snow had not entirely disappeared. Other circumstances combined to make our subject's early life in Lincoln county one of the most trying kind. These vexatious circumstances, however, have all been forgotten in the prosperity and successes which have come to him in the succeeding years.

Mr. Kroeger was united in the bonds of marriage November 27, 1884, to Emma B. Enke. This union has been blessed with two children—Frank A. and Elsie A.

Since locating in Verdi township Mr. Kroeger has taken a prominent part in public affairs and has held several official positions. He has been chairman of the board of supervisors for four years and holds that position at the present time. In his official capacity he has exerted a strong influence for the benefit of his locality and has proven himself an efficient and loyal citizen. In politics he affiliates with the republican party and is an influential member of the German Lutheran church. In early life he received a good common-school education, and this, in connection with good, native abilities, makes him prominent in business and social circles. He is a man of excellent character, is a loyal citizen, and always gives his earnest support to every project which tends to the upbuilding of public interests.

JOHN S. ROBERTSON, deceased. Mrs. Jennie L. Robertson is the widow of J. S. Robertson, who was in life one of the most esteemed and honored citizens of Winnebago City. Mr. Robertson was a native of Dundee, Scotland, where he was born in the year 1832. He was the son of John and Maie Robertson, natives of the same land. The father was a mechanic by occupation.

John S. Robertson remained with his parents until ten years of age, and in early life learned the trade of cabinet-making. He came to America when he was about twenty-two years of age and settled in New York City, where he lived for several years engaged in the cabinet-making business. In 1858 he came to Minnesota, first locating on a farm in Delavan township, Faribault county. He returned to New York City, and after a stay of two years came to Faribault county, bringing his family and settling at Bass Lake, where he resided nine years. He improved his farm and built one of the best houses in the township. In 1869 he sold his land and came to Winnebago City, where he engaged in the furniture business. He built a beautiful home on Main street and resided there until his death, which occurred April 23, 1889. He built a brick block adjoining his residence, where for years he carried on the most extensive furniture business in the county. He purchased considerable land in the county and dealt to some extent in real estate. During his life he held many offices of trust, and at the time of his death was president of the village council and chairman of the board of supervisors. In politics he affiliated with the republican party and was one of Winnebago's best citizens. He always stood ready to aid with money and personal effort, every public enterprise. His fellow-citizens will miss him in many ways; as he labored honestly and earnestly for the welfare of the village, and he left behind him a record both successful and honorable. In his private business he was eminently successful and although commencing without any, or at most, very small capital, he left an estate valued at from fifteen to twenty thousand dollars. He was popular with the people and his death was universally regretted. He was a member of the Blue Earth Valley lodge, No. 27, Ancient Free and Accepted Masons, which lodge took charge of the funeral arrangements. He was a member of the Mount Horeb Chapter and of the Mankato Commandery of Knights Templar. The services were attended by a large number of friends, who came bringing flowers and appropriate words to show their respect and esteem for their deceased fellow-citizen. Mr. Robertson is remembered by a host of friends as a genial, public-spirited, warm-hearted man. No good cause ever applied to him for aid without receiving some assistance. When the movement toward the completing of the Baptist college at Winnebago City was first inaugurated, Mr. Robertson rendered valuable assistance and gave five hundred dollars to aid in furthering the project. He it was who selected the site for the college, and such an earnest, active part did he take in carrying the matter on toward completion, that he was elected vice-president of the institution.

Mr. Robertson was married in the year 1859 to Miss Jennie L. Brown, a native of Terryville, near New Haven, Connecticut. She was the daughter of David and Euphemia (Hill) Brown, natives of Scotland. After their marriage the parents came to America and settled in New Haven, where the father engaged in manufacturing for a number of years. Later the family removed to Long Island and from thence came to Wabasha county, Minnesota, where they built the first house in 1853. They settled on a farm and remained but a short time when, on account of sickness, they returned to New York State, where the father soon died. In the Brown family there are three living children—James, Helen (now Mrs. Grant), and Jennie L. Mrs. Robertson is a member of the Presbyterian church, and is one of the leading spirits in the Woman's Christian Temperance Union. She is also a member of the missionary society, and is one of the most charitable and highly esteemed ladies in the village.

VICTORY G. MOTT is a leading citizen of Jackson county, Minnesota, and resides on section 22 of La Crosse township. His birthplace is found in Susquehanna county, Pennsylvania, where he first saw the light in March, 1827. His parents were Elihu and Fannie (Foster) Mott, born and reared in Hartford, Connecticut, the father a farmer by occupation, and both parents resided in Pennsylvania until their death.

Up to nineteen years of age the subject of our sketch assisted his father in work on the home farm, and was also given the advantages of a good common-school education. At the age just mentioned the father died and our subject engaged in farming and lumbering until 1849, when he removed to an adjoining county and lived on a farm for some time. He then went to Missouri and remained in that State from 1857 until 1864 engaged in farming to some extent, but working principally at the carpenter's trade. April 10, 1862, he enlisted in Company H, Ninth Missouri State Militia, under Colonel Guitar. He was discharged April 6, 1863, after having served gallantly and faithfully in the Union army. He came to Minnesota in 1864 and located for some years in Watonwan county and engaged in farming. In 1873 he came to his present location, taking 160 acres of land as a tree claim. He has been actively engaged in improving his farm, building a good house, barn and other outbuildings, and in setting out a fine grove of ten acres of trees. This is one of the finest and largest groves in Jackson county.

The subject of this sketch was married in 1847 to Miss Martha Gaston, a native of Pennsylvania. This union has been blessed with five children—Horace D., J. C., John, Maria Frances and Mary, of whom all are deceased save J. C. and Mary. J. C. now resides on a farm near that of his father.

The subject of this sketch passed through many hardships during his early settlement in Jackson county. The first serious misfortune that fell to his lot was the destruction of his crops by grasshoppers, in 1874. For several years thereafter he did not raise sufficient grain to furnish flour for his family and feed for his team. The grasshoppers, not satisfied with destroying the grain, destroyed even the trees that he had set out on his tree claim.

The subject of our sketch has been one of the most prominent citizens of the township since locating therein. He has taken an active part in matters pertaining to the local government, and has held such offices as township treasurer, assessor, and school director of district No. 35. In politics he affiliates with the republican party, is a member of the Grand Army of the Republic, B. F. Sweet Post, No. 149, at Heron Lake, and is also a consistent member of the Methodist Episcopal church. In his business ventures our subject has been quite successful, and besides farming, has turned his attention, to a large extent, to the raising of Holstein cattle and Norman horses.

RAY B. HINKLY is the gentlemanly and efficient cashier of the Rock County Bank, of Luverne, Minnesota. He made his settlement in that city in 1882, and assisted in the organization of the bank, with which he has been since connected as cashier. Besides his banking interests here he also is connected financially with institutions in adjoining counties and States. He is at present vice-president of the Security Bank, of Howard, Dakota, which he assisted to organize. The early life of our subject was spent in his native State, Iowa, where he was given excellent educational advantages, finishing his education at Oberlin College, of Ohio. When nineteen years old he engaged in the newspaper business in Clermont, Fayette county, Iowa. While in Iowa he also turned his attention to the study of law, and was admitted to the bar in 1881. Throughout the most of his life, however, he has been engaged in the banking business.

He has taken an active interest in all matters pertaining to the public welfare and the development of the city and county since making his location here, and has invested largely in local real estate.

Mr. Hinkly was married in the year 1882 to Miss May Harrington, of the State of Iowa. This lady was a daughter of William H. Harrington, a prominent resident of the same place. Mr. and Mrs. Hinkly have been blessed with three children—Laura E., William B. and Harry J.

In politics the subject of our sketch affiliates with the democratic party. He is a man of considerable means, and is looked upon as one of the most reliable and substantial citizens of the county.

ALPHONZO K. PECK is a leading citizen, and is the postmaster of the village of St. James, Minnesota. He is a native of Rock county, Wisconsin, where he was born January 26, 1848.

The parents of the subject of our sketch were Kartum K. and Lydia A. (Goddard) Peck, both natives of York, Livingston county, New York, where the father was born May 11, 1817. The parents were married in 1837. Kartum K. Peck was the son of Dr. Daniel and Polly P. (Ketchum) Peck, the former born in Sharon, Montgomery county, New York, in the year 1792, and the latter a native of Canada, where she was born June 20, 1798. Dr. Daniel Peck was married, November 20, 1814, in Rutland, Jefferson county, New York. Dr. Daniel Peck was a Baptist minister and a physician, resided in Jackson City, Michigan, where he practiced medicine until his death, which occurred January 19, 1859; his wife died March 16, 1870, at Minneapolis, Minnesota.

Kartum K. Peck, the father of the gentleman whose name appears at the head of this sketch, was for many years a teacher of writing in Wisconsin, to which State he went in about 1840. In 1852 he settled in Le Sueur county, Minnesota, and engaged in the hotel and general merchandise business. He laid out and owned the town site of lower Le Sueur. He is now a resident of Deer Creek, Otter Tail county, Minnesota. His wife died May 29, 1854. In the family there are now two living children — Nathaniel A. and Alphonzo K., the former being born February, 15, 1841, and now a resident of Deer Creek, Minnesota. Nathaniel A. was a soldier in the Union army for two years, serving in the Fourth Regiment Minnesota Volunteer Infantry. The names of the children deceased are Delevan D., born March 26, 1839, died October 11, 1864, while serving in the Union army at Pine Bluff, Arkansas; Alphonzo, born January 26, 1843, died September 12, 1843; Orlando, born February 3, 1850, died February 22, 1851; and Mary Le Sueur, the first white child born in Le Sueur county, Minnesota, the date of her birth being March 25, 1853. She married Z. E. Thomas, a merchant of Glendale. They moved to Butte, Montana, where she died December 1, 1885, leaving a daughter five days old. The father of our subject married his second wife at South Bend, Minnesota, October 19, 1854. Her name before marriage was Mrs. E. D. Ransom; she died at Faribault, Minnesota.

The subject of our sketch was educated in the public schools of the village of Le Sueur.

When fourteen years and seven months old he enlisted in Company G, Tenth Minnesota Infantry, and served three years and nine days. He was engaged in numerous severe battles, among them being Tupelo, Holly Springs, Nashville, Spanish Fort, and many skirmishes in the States of Tennessee, Louisiana, Alabama, Missouri, and Kentucky. He was with a division of the commissary department during the last few months, and was sunstruck on the march to Tupelo. For several days he was carried in an ambulance wagon, and for some time his life was despaired of. He was discharged August 24, 1865, at St. Paul. Prior to his enlistment in the Union army he served in the Indian war in 1862. He, with many others in the village of Le Sueur, volunteered to go to New Ulm and assist in overcoming the Indians. They were successful in this, and our subject returned to Le Sueur, having received a slight wound in the right leg at the battle of New Ulm, Minnesota. He then enlisted in the Tenth Minnesota, as has been stated. After the war was over and he was honorably discharged from the service, he returned to his home in Le Sueur, where he attended school for some time. He learned the carpenter's trade and engaged in work on the railroad as foreman of the bridge carpenters. He continued in this line for seven years, with his headquarters at St. James. He then engaged in the lumber business under the firm name of Peck & Simons, which partnership lasted fourteen months. Our subject then engaged in contracting and building in the village, and followed that line, employing a number of men, for several years. Besides his various interests in St. James, he has a fine farm in Jackson county, Minnesota. He also owns some Minneapolis property, and is interested in this and other localities.

Mr. Peck was married, on December 26, 1872, to Miss Sophia Chadderdon, of Belle Plaine, Scott county, Minnesota. Mr. and Mrs. Peck have had three children — Ned A., Hattie Anettie and Matie. The last named died June 20, 1884, aged eight years and seven months.

The subject of our sketch has alway associated himself with matters pertaining to the general welfare, and has always aided liberally in the development of projects tending toward the improvement of his locality. He was a member of the village council for two terms, and was re-elected in the spring of 1889. He has been commander of the John A. Logan Post, No. 64, Grand Army of the Republic, for three years, and is its present quartermaster. In politics he affiliates with the democratic party, and was appointed postmaster of St. James by President Cleveland in 1885, and still holds that position. He is a member of the Masonic fraternity, and belongs to the Blue Lodge and Chapter, being junior warden of the former, and treasurer of the latter. Mr. Peck is a man of excellent business qualifications, is cautious and conservative, and has accumulated considerable means out of his various investments. He is a man of excellent business principles, and is looked upon as one of the most upright and influential citizens of the village and county in which he resides.

Mrs. Peck (formerly Sophia Chadderdon) was born in Herman, Wisconsin, February 20, 1850. Her father, Jonathan Chadderdon, was born in Schoharie county, New York, March 10, 1808. Sophia Matice, at seventeen years of age, married him. She was born in Middleburgh, Schoharie county, New York, June 25, 1817, and died in Belle Plaine, Minnesota, December 24, 1874. Jonathan Chadderdon died in Le Sueur, Minnesota, January 20, 1884. They had a family of thirteen children — George, Catherine, Mary Ann, Peter, Henry, Samantha, Abraham, Joseph, Frances, Sophia, Charles, Lida and Edwin, all of whom are still living except George, who died in the army, and Mary Ann, who died while young.

CARL PETERSON, a prominent farmer of West Brook township, Cottonwood county, Minnesota, resides on section 26, where he is engaged in farming. Of Danish birth, he first saw the light March 27, 1752. He is the son of Sorn and Sorena (Sornson) Peterson, natives of Denmark. The father still lives in his native land, where he is engaged in farming. The mother died in Denmark in March, 1866. In the father's family there were five children.

At the age of seventeen the subject of our sketch commenced work for himself. Up to this age he had attended school and assisted his father in work on the farm. On reaching seventeen years of age he commenced working on various farms in his native land. He emigrated to America in 1879 and located in Dodge county, Minnesota, where he engaged in farming for six years. He then came to the farm on which he now lives.

Mr. Peterson married Stena Sornson, May 28, 1885. The fruits of this union have been four children—Lena, Sophia, Emma and Appa. The family are members of the Lutheran church.

Since coming to the township, our subject has engaged actively in farming and has striven hard to make his farm one of the best in the township. In connection with raising grain he has also turned his attention considerably to the raising of Norman horses. He has a fine house, surrounded by a nice grove of trees and has his farm provided with other good improvements. In politics Mr. Peterson affiliates with the democratic party, and has held various positions of trust in the locality in which he has lived. He is a man of good character and is highly respected.

FRED MOHL is engaged in the real estate, loan and insurance business at Adrian, Nobles county, Minnesota, and, although still a young man, ranks high with the substantial business men of Southwestern Minnesota. He is a Scandinavian by birth, and is the son of Charles A. and Christine (Johnson) Mohl, natives of the kingdom of Sweden. Our subject was born in Warnland, Sweden, August 31, 1860. His father was a soldier, and was a prominent citizen of his native country. They resided on a farm and there our subject was reared, being given good educational advantages until he was fifteen years of age.

At fifteen he commenced earning his own living by working for various farmers, and continuing thereat for about two years, after which he went to Christiania, Norway, from whence he came to the United States in the spring of 1876. He landed in New York City July 4th, a stranger to our habits and customs, but willing and anxious to learn, and ready to take hold of whatever opportunities presented themselves for making a livelihood. He first located in Worthington, the county seat of Nobles county, Minnesota. It was only a little while before his ready brain and keen eye became familiar with the ways of doing things in America, and he thought best to move to Adrian, where he saw more prosperity than he thought Worthington could produce. While in Worthington, he engaged to some extent in farming, hiring out on various farms in the vicinity of that place, but, owing to the grasshopper raids and to the destruction of all kinds of crops, our subject failed to get his pay that year. He went to school during the winter, and continued working on farms in summers and going to school in the winters for about four years. Two years of this time he engaged in working a farm on shares. He also purchased a relinquishment of a claim which he afterward sold.

In the spring of 1883 he came to Adrian and worked in the elevator during the fall and winter, and the following spring commenced work in the lumber yard of F. J. Porter. He continued with this gentleman until June 1, 1888, when he opened a real estate office. This was not his first venture in this line, however. While with Mr. Porter he had negotiated several real estate loans and had sold considerable land, his business increasing so rapidly that he was obliged to sever his pleasant business association with Mr. Porter in order to attend to matters pertaining to the enterprise in which he had gradually gained a strong foothold. In the spring of 1889 he sold over eight thousand acres of land.

Since becoming a citizen of the village of Adrian, Mr. Mohl has become favorably known for his extensive knowledge of the country and for his honorable methods in conducting his large and increasing business. He has constantly prospered, and while enriching himself has aided many to become owners of good property, and this at little expense to the investor. He has some very valuable lands in close vicinity to Adrian, Rushmore, Ellsworth and Worthington, and some fine lands at distances of from five to ten miles from the places named at prices within the reach of all. He has done much to build up the village and the surrounding country, and while doing this he has built up an enviable reputation for honest dealing and for courteous, gentlemanly treatment of all with whom he has come in contact. He owns and operates a fine farm in Olney township, has it well improved and provided with good buildings, and also owns a residence and two lots in the village. In politics he affiliates with the republican party, is a notary public, is secretary of the board of health and school director.

On the 12th day of November, 1888, Mr. Mohl was united in the bonds of matrimony to Miss Anna Paulson, daughter of Hans and Ellen M. (Peterson) Paulson, natives of Norway. Mrs. Mohl was born in Iowa county, Wisconsin, in 1866.

———◆•◆≡◈≡◆•◆———

ADAM H. KURTH is an influential farmer of Shaokatan township, Lincoln county, Minnesota. He has a good farm on section 8, of that township. He was born in Elgrove, Illinois, April 22, 1857. He was son of Henry, Sr., and Catharine E. (Wehnes) Kurth. A sketch of the father, who was a loyal and Christian citizen, is found in the biography of Fred H. Kurth, in another department of this work.

Adam H. Kurth followed the father's family in its various travels, locating with them in its various locations until he was twenty-one years of age. He was given a good common school education, and assisted on the home farm when not in school. At twenty-one years of age he rented his father's farm in Dakota county, Minnesota, and operated it for some two years, and during the winters of this time he purchased meat for St. Paul butchers. He came West in 1884 and rented his father's farm one year, operating this in connection with his own. He then built a house on his own farm and moved therein, where he has resided ever since. He is a man of excellent qualities, true and loyal as a citizen, and is a good friend and neighbor. In politics he affilities with the republican party, and among various official positions has held the office of constable for four years, being the present incumbent of that place.

March 11, 1880, occurred the marriage of Mr. Kurth to Kate Binder. This union has been blessed with five children—Mary M., Emma C., Ida B., George A. and Elizabeth, all of whom are living at the present time.

W. MOBERLY, the present efficient and popular treasurer of Nobles county, was born on the 26th day of April, 1847, near Owensboro, the county seat of Daviess county, Kentucky, he being the eldest of eight chilren, five boys and three girls. His parents, Lewis B. and Susan (Owen) Moberly, were natives of Kentucky his grand-parents coming orginially from Virginia. His boyhood days were spent on the farm attending the district schools during the winter months.

In the spring of 1864 his father sold the homestead and removed with his family to Clay county, Illinois, where he purchased land. Young Moberly remained on the farm until the fall of 1866, when he entered the high school at Flora, Illinois, continuing for one year. After leaving school he traveled for a patent medicine firm until the spring of 1868, when he came to Quincy, Illinois, and in July of the same year to Winona county, Minnesota. Here he remained working on the farm during the summer, and teaching school winters, varied with a few trips down the river, until the spring of 1872, when he came West, arriving at Worthington May 23, 1872. He at once filed a pre-emption claim on the southeast quarter of section 14, township 102, range 42 (Olney township). He took an active part in the township's organization, giving the township its name, and being elected the first town clerk.

On the 17th day of march—prior to his coming west—he was married to Miss Annie Campbell, of St. Charles, Minnesota. She was born at Barry, Pike county, Illinois, August 24, 1852, of Scotch parentage.

For the first four or five years after settling in Nobles county, they, in common with all the settlers, suffered greatly from the grasshopper plague, seeing crop after crop destroyed by them. To gain a support for his family, Mr. Moberly spent one winter at work in the woods, and another in Winona county teaching school.

In the spring of 1877 he sold his farm in Olney and removed to Westside township, taking a homestead on section 10, township 102, range 43, where he continued his farm work, teaching school winters, until the fall of 1883. He then sold his farm, moved to Adrian, and engaged to work for his brother-in-law, James Cowin, in the grain and lumber business. In February, 1884, he came to Worthington as deputy for Captain William Wigham, who had been elected county treasurer the previous fall, moving his family down in September following.

He filled this position until the expiration of Captain Wigham's term, when he was elected county treasurer, receiving nearly the entire vote of the county.

In the fall of 1888 he was re-elected by a large majority over the democratic and prohibition candidates.

Mr. Moberly has always taken an active part in educational and political affairs, being in politics a strong anti-saloon republican. He was town clerk most of the time that he lived in Olney and Westside townships.

He is a member of the Ancient Order United Workingmen, having been recorder of Worthington lodge, No. 65, for the past three years.

Mr. and Mrs. Moberly had six children, one dying in infancy. They are as follows—Susan M., aged 16; Lura C., 14; Russell B., 12; Archie L., 10; Maude (deceased), 10 months, and Mary D., four years old.

———◆❖❱❰❖◆———

FREDERICK M. LOUNSBERRY is a prominent farmer and stock-raiser, located on section 28, Dovray township, Murray county, Minnesota. He located on this homestead May 3, 1877, and was one of the first settlers of the township. How well he has succeeded is exemplified by the present prosperous appearance of his farm. He has been an active participant in all public matters and has held various official positions. He has been justice of the peace two years, pathmaster, president of the cemetery association, etc.

Mr. Lounsberry was born in West Chester county, New York, April 15, 1829. He made this his home for a number of years and then moved to Broome county, where he lived until twenty-five years of age, receiving a good common-school education. He remained with his parents until his marriage, and then engaged in farming and after three years went to LaCrosse county, Wisconsin, from whence after a short time he removed to Green Lake county. Here he engaged extensively in farming for fourteen years and then removed to Winnebago county, where he remained five years. Returning to Green Lake county he located in Berlin township, where he operated a farm for three years. He then came to his present place, where he has lived ever since.

The father of the subject of our sketch was Gideon Lounsberry, an extensive lumberman and farmer in New York. He was born in West Chester county and died in Broome county. The mother's maiden name was Pollie Archer, who was born in West Chester county, where she was reared and educated. She died in Broome county. In the father's family there were eleven children—William Henry, Knowlton, Margaret, Simon J., James H., Reuben A., Mary E., Frederick M., Nancy J., Rachel A. and Henrietta.

The gentleman whose name appears at the head of this sketch was married August 10, 1849, to Miss Lydia Ann Sawyer, a native of Shenango county, New York, where she was born in the year 1831. Here she was reared and educated until she was eighteen years of age. Her parents were Amos S. and Lucinda Padelford, both natives of New York, where they lived until their death. The father was a farmer by occupation, and both the parents were consistent members of the Methodist Episcopal church. In the father's family there were twelve children—Amos, Lucinda, Laura, Loanna, Sarah, Henry, Simon, Andrew, Ansel, John, Almira and Lydia. Mr. and Mrs. Lounsberry have been blessed with two children—Frederick J., who is married and now resides in the village of Slayton; and Belle, now married and a resident of Dovray township. Gideon, another son, was accidentally shot April 6, 1882. He left a wife and one son—Arthur Gideon. The wife's maiden name was Cemanthia De Vore. He was a representative young man, and before his death was a member of the board of supervisors, and belonged to the Methodist Episcopal church.

Frederick Lounsberry affiliates with the republican party in politics, and is one of the most prominent and influential citizens of this part of Murray county. He is a man of excellent qualifications, and is highly respected by all who know him. He has a pleasant home and an agreeable family.

***

HENRY P. CONSTANS is one of the most popular characters in Faribault county and is proprietor of the Constans House of Blue Earth City, Minnesota. He is a native of France, where he was born in 1834.

The subject of our sketch is the son of George and Louisa (Junker) Constans, natives of France. The father was a government official in his native land, and after the Franco-Prussian war lived a retired life in Paris until his death, which occurred in 1884. The mother died in about 1873. In the father's family there were five children—Henry V., George, now of Mankato, Minnesota; Christian, still a resident of France and captain of the Fourth Regiment of Artillery, and also aid-de-camp to General Maalsharbe; Caroline, now Mrs. Kunz, and Louisa.

The early training and education of the subject of our sketch was received in his native land, and when seventeen years of age he migrated to the United States, landing at New Orleans, from whence he went to St. Paul, remaining until 1854. He then opened the second store in the village of Shakopee, a short distance south of St. Paul, and remained in business there for two years. He then sold out and became the pioneer settler of Blue Earth City. In company with ex-Governor Wakefield, George Kingsley, Samuel Hibler and S. Spencer, he built the first log-house on the town site. They made this their residence until August. During the summer Mr. Constans built a hewn log-house two stories high and 20x40 feet, with an addition 18x24 feet. He kept hotel in this building for twelve years and then built his present commodious house. The gentlemen whose name we have just given were the proprietors of the town site of Blue Earth City and laid out 320 acres, a portion of which was afterward sold to Mr. Kingsley. They were quite liberal in holding out inducements to settlers and donated a large number of lots to parties who would build houses. They also donated one block for school purposes and one block for the court-house. Our subject at once took an active interest in public matters and especially made his influence felt in political affairs. He was appointed sheriff of the county at its organization and held the office for four years. He has been a member of the school board for some twenty years and has served for several years on the city council.

Mr. Constans was married in the year 1856 to Miss Barbara H'ebeison, of Carver county, Minnesota. She was the daughter of Christian and Barbara (Jaberg) H'ebeison, a native of Berne, Switzerland. Her father was a manufacturer of medicines and was also engaged to some extent in farming. The father and family came to America in 1854, settling in Ohio, from whence after six months, they went to Indiana, remaining two years, and from thence removed to Carver, Minnesota, where they settled on government land. Later the father moved to Carver City, where he lived until his death in 1882. The mother died in her native land in 1846. In the father's family there were five children—Christian (deceased), Maggie, now Mrs. Hostetter; Mrs. Constans, John, of Carver, and Frederick (deceased). Mr. and Mrs. Constans have a family of four children—Charles W., Henry E., George F., and Dr. Frank E. Charles W. married Elizabeth Anderson and is now a druggist of Blue Earth City. Henry E. is also a druggist of the same place. George F. is engaged in the lumber business in the City. Dr. Frank E. is now a resident of New York city. He was a graduate of Carlton College, at Northfield, Minnesota, and also of the Hahnemann Medical College at Philadelphia.

Mr. Constans is a typical landlord and is conducting one of the most successful hotel enterprises in Southern Minnesota. He is genial, open-hearted, and is one of the most hospitable of men. He has accumulated considerable means and is interested in some property in St. Paul. He is one of the prominent and substantial men of Blue Earth City and Faribault county. Mr. and Mrs. Constans are both members of the Presbyterian church, of which society our subject is an elder.

CALEB D. ASH, a retired capitalist of Madelia, Watonwan county, Minnesota, is one of the foremost men of his locality. In the development and growth of the village he has proven the right man in the right place. Self-made in every particular, he stands to-day one of the most prominent and and substantial citizens of the county.

Mr. Ash is a native of New Hampshire, where he was born October 26, 1823. His parents were Samuel and Sabina (Dexter) Ash, natives of Lisbon, Grafton county, New Hampshire. The father was a man of means and operated an extensive farm in his native State, residing in Grafton county until his death. The mother died in 1882 at the age of seventy-five years. They had a family of of eight children—Phineas, who died in 1881; Mary A., now Mrs. John Hunt, of New Hampshire; William B., who died in 1887; Caleb D., James, living in Grafton county, New Hampshire; Lara J., now Mrs. Brown of Lisbon, New Hampshire; Sarah, now Mrs. Stoddard of Carroll, New Hampshire; and Eliza, now Mrs. Joseph Haynes of the same place.

Schools, like railroads, half a century ago were few and far between, and the educational advantages of the subject of our sketch were exceedingly limited. In his locality there was a small log school house roofed over with bark, and in this primitive educational institution Mr. Ash received his first school training. After attaining sixteen years of age he worked on various farms and in the lumber woods, continuing in these different lines of employment until twenty-one years of age. He then went to Newburyport, Massachusetts, and during one summer worked in a ship-yard, in the fall coming to Boston, Lowell and Manchester, as a section hand on the Boston, Lowell & Concord railroad. After three or four months he stopped in Lowell, Massachusetts, and engaged in moving buildings until nearly spring when he came back to Lowell and engaged in the milling business, and also in moving buildings. His residence in that city was continued three years, after which he engaged in farming near the village of Bethlehem, New Hampshire. Remaining

there three years he then sold out and returned to Lowell, engaging in work on a canal for some fourteen months. He concluded to go west in 1855, and, gathering together his personal effects, started for Wisconsin, locating at Beaver Dam, and engaging as a mover of buildings for some three years. His next move was to St. Croix county, where four years were spent in farming, after which, in 1862, he removed to Winona county, Minnesota, and settled on prairie land in Saratoga township, where he purchased a large acreage and became one of the most extensive farmers in that locality. He remained in Winona county six years, and then sold out and returned to Beaver Dam, Wisconsin, where he resided three years engaged at his old trade. While there he assisted in the building of one of the largest Baptist churches in that region. In 1871 he came to Watonwan county, Minnesota, and located in the village of Madelia. He has purchased considerable business property, and owns a fine residence on Main street. He is also largely interested in farming lands, and owns an extensive acreage in Watonwan and adjoining counties. He is one of the most public-spirited and generous-hearted citizens of the county, and assists liberally in all matters pertaining to the public welfare. He has held the office of president of the Old Settlers' Association, president of the Agricultural Society and president of the school board of the village. He was president of the Minnesota Valley Bank, organized August 9, 1886, which institution he assisted in organizing. He has held various official positions, among them being that of street commissioner, marshal, etc. In politics he affiliates with the republican party, and is a member of the Odd Fellows' fraternity. He is one of the wealthiest and most substantial citizens of the village.

Mr. Ash was married at Lowell, Massachusetts, September 3, 1845, to Miss Harriet M. Haynes, of Massachusetts, daughter of J. and Lydia D. Haynes, of Sudbury, Massachusetts. Three children were born to them— George H., born April 27, 1847; Mary A., born October 27, 1850, and Charles F., born February 22, 1854. George H. married Mary Nulph, by whom he had four children— Minnie, married November 20, 1888, to Alfred J. Keeling; Jennie M., William D., and George. Mary A. married C. W. Seymour, May 3, 1869, and has the following children—Frank A., Hattie E., Charles D., Maude B., and Clifford E. Charles F. wedded Miss Belle Hamell, March 4, 1883, by whom he has had one son, Caleb D.

———◆—◁◆◆▷—◆———

CHARLES B. CHEADLE is a prosperous farmer who resides on section 22, Springfield township, Cottonwood county, Minnesota. Mr. Cheadle was born in Washington county, Ohio, August 30' 1849, and was the son of A. I. and Jemima (Witham) Cheadle, both of whom were natives of Ohio. The parents came west in 1855, and settled near Kasota, Minnesota, where they still live. They were among the early settlers of that locality, and were residents of that place during the Indian troubles in an early day. They are well-to-do and influential farmers.

Charles Cheadle left the parental home when he was twenty years of age. Up to this time he had been given good educational advantages in the district schools, and had helped his father in work on the farm. In 1870 he came to Cottonwood county, looking for a location. He walked from St. James to Mountain Lake, and located a claim on section 22, of Carson township, soon after going to New Ulm, where he worked on the railroad until fall. He then went to Mankato, Blue Earth county, and found work in the woods until the spring of the following

year. He then returned to his claim in Cottonwood county, bringing his family with him, and residing there for two years. He then removed to section 22 of Springfield township, where he has since lived. He has a good farm of 160 acres, and has it under good cultivation and well improved, with substantial buildings. He built one of the first log houses in the township, and this building is still standing on his farm.

Mr. Cheadle was married, December 17, 1862, to Mrs. Elizabeth Smith, a daughter of Robert and Harriet (Warrant) Godbolt. Her parents located in Le Sueur county, in 1862, in which year her father died. The mother died in January, 1887. The father was a shoemaker by trade, and a prominent citizen of the county. Mr. and Mrs. Cheadle have been blessed with three children, only one of whom is now living, Myrtle A. Oscar and Asa are deceased.

The subject of our sketch affiliates with the republican party in politics, and has become one of the important factors in the local affairs of that organization, having held various official positions. He belongs to the Masonic fraternity, and is a member of the Ancient Order United Workmen. His wife is a member of the Episcopal church. Mr. Cheadle is a man of high character, and is esteemed by all who know him.

———◆—◁◆◆▷—◆———

NEIL CURRIE is one of the best known citizens of Murray county, Minnesota. He is a resident of the village of Currie, of which he was the founder, and which was named in his honor. He is at present engaged in the general mercantile business, being also connected with the Murray County Bank. This bank was established in 1874 and is doing a large business. He was the first settler of the town of Currie, to which he came in 1872. He built a small store and commenced making other improvements. He has identified himself closely with all matters of a public nature and was postmaster of the village from 1873 to 1887. From 1874 to 1888 he was clerk of the district court of Murray county. He has held various official positions with honor and credit.

The place of the nativity of Neil Currie is found in Canada in the county of Lanark, where he was born Dec. 15, 1842. His father was Archibald Currie, of whom a sketch is given in another department of this work.

Neil Currie was married in October, 1866, to Miss M. Augusta Canfield, a native of the State of New York. Six children have blessed this union—Nettie J., Mabel A., Archie N., Eveline, Neil, Jr., and Hellen.

Mr. Currie is a republican in politics, and is an influential member of the Masonic fraternity, of which he is treasurer.

———— ❧ ⦿ ❧ ————

ORRIN MOTT. This gentleman is one of the reliable farmers and most influential citizens of Verdi township, Lincoln county, Minnesota. He was born in Rome, Oneida county, New York, March 22, 1852. In his father's family there were thirteen children, of whom seven were boys, Orrin, our subject, being the fourth son in order of birth.

The early life of Orrin Mott was spent beneath the parental roof, and he assisted in work on the home farm. He was given the educational advantages furnished by the district schools, and continued with his parents until he reached eighteen years of age. He then engaged in farm work for a year in the employ of a man named Kline. When this year's engagement had expired, he then started out on a trip overland, driving an ox team to the Red River country, where he located land and built a shanty, and prepared to make a permanent residence. He remained a few months, when the grasshoppers raided the entire country and destroyed so many crops that our subject became disheartened and left. He then went into the pineries, where he remained until spring. His next move was up the Wisconsin river, where he took charge of bringing a raft down the river to St. Louis. Five weeks were spent on this trip, and he then returned to his home by way of Chicago. This was shortly after the great fire in that city, and our subject well remembers the chaotic appearance of the ruins left by the devastating fire fiend. Returning to Wisconsin he worked in the harvest fields for some ten days, and then went to Minnesota, where he continued working in that line for some sixteen days, receiving as remuneration $3.50 per day and board. He stopped for some time in Dakota county, Minnesota, where he spent the fall and then returned to Wisconsin. He returned to the home of his parents and took his father's team and engaged in hauling lumber on the Black river during the winter. Then he went to Sparta and engaged at the carpenter's trade until the fall of 1877, when he was married and took a trip to Winona, Minnesota. From that point he came alone to Marshall; thence overland to what was then called Marshfield, Lincoln county. He located the land where he now lives, and soon after went back to Sparta, Wisconsin, where he remained until the following spring. He then purchased a team, and on May 1st started out with his household goods and family for his claim in Lincoln county, arriving there on the 10th of the month. He also shipped a car load of lumber, and also provisions, which he had to haul by team from Marshall, a distance of forty-five miles. He built a small shanty and made a permanent residence on his present excellent farm of 320 acres.

Mr. Mott was united in the bonds of matrimony November 2, 1877, to Frances Bailey, a very estimable lady of Melrose, Wisconsin, by whom he has had one child, Alfred H.

It is interesting to recall some of the early experiences through which Mr. Mott passed, and it is also interesting to compare the difference between his circumstances now and then. When he landed in the county he had but three dollars in money and a team and wagon. To-day he is comfortably located on a fine farm of 320 acres and has the best dwelling house and barns in the county. The passer-by sees the best evidences of comfort and prosperity on the farm of our subject. He has been a hard-working and a careful farmer and by thrift and economy has accumulated considerable means. On his farm there is living water, a spring creek running across one part of it. In this stream are to be found many different kinds of fish. In the stream our subject has indeed a great deal of piscatorial sport, having caught therein a five-pound pickerel. Perhaps no other man in the county has taken as much interest in public affairs as has our subject. Being in politics a republican he has always supported the winning side, and has himself held various official positions with honor and credit. He has been township treasurer for some two terms, school treasurer two terms, and has held other positions. He has been elected twice as trustee and treasurer of the Elkton Farmers' Alliance Warehouse Company, of Elkton, Dakota. As agent for this company he went to Minneapolis and purchased lumber for the Farmers' Warehouse at Elkton.

In his travels he has sold wheat throughout Iowa, and down the Mississippi as far as St. Louis. Perhaps no man in the township is as widely known as our subject. Some time ago he took an extensive trip, being absent from home about a month, and during this time visiting the world's exposition at New Orleans. He also took a brief tour to the old battle-fields of Lookout Mountain and Mission Ridge, going thence down the Gulf of Mexico, where he had the privilege of seeing the remnants of an old torpedo used by the Rebels in the Civil War. He is an exemplary citizen, and is widely respected.

Orrin Mott's parents were J. S. and Adeline (Soals) Mott, the father a native of Steuben county, New York, and the mother of Massachusetts. The father is still living, a resident of Monroe county, Wisconsin. The mother died March 17, 1880, at Leon, Wisconsin. J. S. Mott's parents were Elias and Lucretia Mott, the former born in New Jersey, and the latter at Albany, New York.

Our subject's grand-parents on his mother's side were Asa and Ruth Soals, who had in their veins the pure "blue blood" of the Pilgrim Fathers. Grandfather Soals was a soldier in the War of 1812, and drew a land-warrant for one hundred and twenty acres. Our subject also remembers distinctly his grandmother Soals telling him (when he was a small boy) of her father doing battle in behalf of the colonies during the Revolutionary War.

HENRY AHSENMACHER is a leading farmer of Altona township, Pipestone county, Minnesota. His excellent farm and pleasant home is located on section 20, where he has surrounded himself with the signs of prosperity and industry.

The subject of our sketch was born in Prussia, Germany, February 3, 1829, his parents being Henry and Margaret (Brauer) Ahsenmacher, both natives of Prussia. The father was a shoemaker by trade and remained in his native country throughout his life. Our subject's great-grandfather was Henry Ahsenmacher, who was born in 1697 and died in 1803, at the age of 106 years.

Henry Ahsenmacher remained with his parents, being given good educational facilities, until he was fourteen years of age, and up to this time had assisted his father in work at the shoemaker's trade. After he was fourteen years old he gave his entire time to the shoemaker's business and continued with his father until he was twenty-two years of age. In 1851 he entered the Prussian army and served until 1853, and in 1854 came to the United States, landing at New York City in November. From there he went to Chicago, where he remained a few days in order to get as nearly Americanized as possible before starting out for the farther West. He then went to Blue Island and worked at his trade for some two years. In 1857 he came to Le Sueur, Minnesota, and opened a shoe shop, which he operated until August 16, 1862. At that date he enlisted in Company G, Tenth Minnesota Volunteer Infantry and gave his services to the Union army throughout the war, being honorably discharged August 16, 1865. He had a varied military experience, and served his adopted country faithfully and honorably. He was at Mankato when the thirty-eight Indians were hanged at that place, and, as he was a bugler for the company, he mingled the bugle sound with the enthusiastic hurrah from the multitude when the drop fell at the third tap of the bass drum. He served in Minnesota during the entire Indian campaign until 1863, and then was sent to the South to participate in the strife with the Rebel forces. He was a man of good military abilities, and was made sergeant of his company, in which rank he continued throughout the war. After being discharged he returned to Le Sueur, and continued running a shoe shop until 1876. He remained in the village, however, until May, 1878, when he came to Pipestone county, driving overland by team and locating his present claim in Altona township. He built his shanty and made a few other improvements, and returned to Le Sueur to get his family. He brought them to his new location

in the spring of 1879, and has made Altona township his permanent home ever since.

Mr. Ahsenmacher was married July 25, 1859, at Le Sueur, Minnesota, to Mary Hess, a native of Cologne, Prussia. She contracted a severe cold in the winter of 1862–63 at camp while nursing her husband's sick comrades, and died May 8, 1863, of quick consumption at Le Sueur, while her husband was with his company removing the Indians to their new reservation in Dakota.

Mr. Ahsenmacher was married again, April 5, 1866, to Louise A. Kruschka. This union has been blessed with eleven children —Frank, Mary, Julia, Henry, William, Louise (deceased), Carrie (deceased), Catharine, Charles, John (deceased). and George. Louise and Carrie were killed by lightning in 1881. While asleep in the house a storm came up, and a bolt of lightning struck the house, descending through it into the cellar beneath, resulting in the death of these children. Catharine was the first white child born in Altona township, her birth being July 8, 1879.

In politics our subject affiliates with the democratic party, but is not a "free trader." He has always interested himself actively in the public affairs of his township. He has a good education, and is well fitted for the various duties which have fallen to his attention. He has 320 acres of excellent land, and is engaged in raising grain and stock. While in Le Sueur he was an influential member of the Grand Army of the Republic.

CHRISTIAN N. PETERSEN, a leading citizen of Fairmont, Minnesota, is engaged in the real estate business. The place of his nativity is found in Haderslev, Nord Sleswig, Germany, where he was born April 30, 1859. His parents were Nis C. and Magdalena (Rasmussen) Petersen.

The subject of our sketch was reared on a farm, residing with his parents, and receiving a good education in the common schools. He also studied German in a private school until he was sixteen. His mother died when he was five years of age, and about four years later his father married Christina Jhul. At sixteen years of age our subject went to Denmark, and, entering the high school at Copenhagen, pursued a course of study for three years. For one year thereafter he traveled under the instruction of Professor Segelcke in the creamery and cheese business. He traveled all over Denmark; visited Sweden and Holland and different parts of Germany to learn the various methods of conducting a creamery business. He then took charge of a creamery owned by Mr. Lobb, of Sludegaard, Funen Island, Denmark, and continued in the business in that place for a year. He then returned home on a visit, and in the spring of 1881 went to Hamburg, and from thence to New York City. Going on to Chicago, he remained a few weeks, and then went to the home of an uncle in Clinton, Iowa, with whom he remained during the summer, taking lessons in English at a private school. He then entered the employ of A. Boysen, of Chicago, selling lands in the northwestern counties of Iowa. In the fall of 1882 he came to Fairmont, where his employer owned some twenty thousand acres of land. He continued in the employ of this gentleman for about a year, and after selling nearly all his lands, formed a partnership with Mr. C. H. Bullard, and soon after took the agency for the sale of lands owned by Messrs. Fredericksen, Hansen & Drummond. They also engaged in handling real estate for other parties, and our subject has made that his business ever since, doing a general real estate, insurance, loan and collection business. In the fall of 1886 he was nominated for county auditor by the democratic party. His election, however, failed, being defeated by about eighty-three votes. As the county is strongly republican, this is an excellent record for our subject, and shows how popular he is among his fellow-citizens. The party vote of that year stood 981 republican to 465 democratic. In this instance Mr. Petersen was defeated by but eighty-three votes, after but three weeks' canvass, and his first experience in politics.

On the 16th day of November, 1887, the subject of our sketch was married to Miss Anna Feehan, daughter of Patrick and Kate (Neven) Feehan, natives of Ireland. This lady was born in Oconomowoc, Waukesha county, Wisconsin, Octocer 4, 1864. Mr. and Mrs. Petersen have one child, Alma Catharine, born February 4, 1889.

FLOYD SILVERNALE is a well-known and prominent business man of Currie, Murray county, Minnesota, where he is engaged in the milling business. He owns a one-half interest in a large mill, owned and operated under the firm name of Schneider & Silvernale. Mr. Silvernale came to Murray county in 1868 with his father, and settled on the southwest quarter of section twenty-eight, in Shetek township. He made that his home for some years. The father's name was W. F. Silvernale, a native of the State of New York, where he was reared and educated. In early life he came to Waukesha county, Wisconsin, and became one of the early settlers of that locality. In 1868 he came with his son to Murray county, where he resided until 1883, when he went to Missouri. Our subject's mother's name was Zorada (Horton) Silvernale, a native of New York, where she remained during her early life. With her parents she finally removed to the vicinity of Beaver Dam, Dodge county, Wisconsin. In the father's family there were two children—

Frances, now the wife of A. C. Fling, and our subject, Floyd. Mr. Fling resided in Currie until the spring of 1889, when he removed to Missouri. While a resident of this county he was engaged in the mercantile business, and for several terms held the office of register of deeds.

The subject of our sketch was born in the town of Genesee, Waukesha county, Wisconsin, December 16, 1853. He remained in that locality until fourteen years of age. Up to this time he had received a good education. He came to Minnesota with his people, and completed his education in Lake Crystal. Then for two years he took charge of an engine in the Omaha railroad elevator in Lake Crystal. From that time he engaged in various pursuits, and finally came to Mason township, Murray county, Minnesota, where he remained several years. He took a prominent interest in local affairs, and held various offices in that township. He then came to the village of Currie, selling out his farm and purchasing a one-half interest in the mill.

February 2, 1878, Mr. Silvernale was married to Miss Emma Thomas, a native of Winona county, Minnesota, where she received her early training and education. She was the daughter of Rufus Thomas, who came to Murray county in about 1873, and removed to Missouri in 1879. He is now deceased. During a portion of his life he lived in Winona county, where he was engaged in farming. He served in the War of the Rebellion, and was an officer in the Union army. For a time he was engaged in the mercantile business in Rushford, and from thence came to Murray county and settled on a farm. He was county auditor for some years, and was one of the leading citizens of the township. He was a man of thorough piety, and was an earnest Sunday-school worker. He took an active interest in all matters pertaining to the religious and moral welfare of his fellow-citizens. He became quite prominent in political circles, and held numerous official positions.

The subject of our sketch is doing a large and extensive trade in the milling business, and enjoys the confidence and esteem of all his patrons. He is a man of high character, excellent business abilities, is public-spirited, and whenever called to serve in any official capacity, performs his duties with credit to himself and satisfaction to his constituents.

———◆◆◆———

LARS ANDERSON. This gentleman is a leading farmer of his nationality in West Brook township, Cottonwood county, Minnesota. He is engaged in farming on section twenty-four. He is a native of Denmark, where he was born April 25, 1854. His parents, Andrew and Laura (Larson) Rasmuson, were also natives of Denmark, and are still residents of that country. They reared a family of eleven children.

Up to nineteen years of age our subject assisted his father in work on the home farm and then emigrated to the United States, first locating in Rochester, Olmsted county, Minnesota, where he worked on various farms for eight years. He then came to the place on which he now resides, taking a homestead of 160 acres. He has built good buildings on the farm, and besides raising grain has devoted considerable of his attention to producing Durham cattle and Norman horses. He has a pleasant, comfortable dwelling house, which stands in the midst of a beautiful grove of eight acres of trees. The subject of our sketch is a republican in politics, and has always taken an active part in public matters. He was a member of the township board of supervisors for two years, serving his constituents well and faithfully.

November 27, 1880, Mr. Anderson married Miss Carrie Fingerson, daughter of O. Fingerson, of Olmsted county. This union has been blessed with five children.

ATHANIEL McCOLLEY is an influential and well-to-do farmer of Delavan township, Faribault county, Minnesota, and resides on a farm on section 31. He came to the county in April, 1861, and settled first on section 4 of Prescott township. Remaining in that township until 1865, with the exception of a period of two and one-half years of service in the army, he then came to Delavan township, where he has since resided.

Mr. McColley was born in Ashtabula county, Ohio, February 4, 1840. His parents were Alexander and Polley McColley. The family left Ohio when our subject was about five years old, and removed to Milwaukee, Wisconsin, where they were among the first settlers; the farm on which they located is now covered by a portion of the city. Here the family engaged in farming enterprises for seven years, and then removed to Columbia county, locating near Portage, where our subject was reared and educated until he was twenty-one years of age. His education was completed by taking a course in the seminary at Portage, which institution he left the year before he would have graduated. The president of this institution was James McGoffin, of Tennessee, a popular and efficient educator. Soon after this our subject came to Minnesota for the benefit of his health. He located in Faribault county, where he has since lived, and where he has become one of the most prominent of its citizens.

In September of 1862 the subject of this sketch enlisted in the Minnesota Rangers as a private, and was honorably discharged in the fall of that year, after having served on the frontier. He re-enlisted in the Second Minnesota Cavalry and served until the spring of 1866, being discharged at that time at Fort Snelling. After being discharged he returned to his farm, and in connection with his farming operations taught school from 1866 to 1873. He has been a hard-working and energetic farmer, and has brought his land to a high state of cultivation and provided it with excellent and valuable improvements. His place is located two miles from Winnebago City. Mr. McColley was one of the first settlers of the township, and has always taken an active interest in its growth and prosperity. For three years he was chairman of the township board, was a supervisor for three years, assessor for nine years, and for seventeen years clerk of school district Nos. 36 and 76. For some years he has taken an active interest in State Alliance matters, and was a representative three different times to the State meeting of that body which met in St. Paul in 1884, 1885 and 1886. Mr. McColley was one of the committee of which Ignatius Donnelly was a member and chairman which presented the principles and requests of the Alliance to the State democratic and republican conventions. He has been actively interested in the furtherance of any project which would benefit the farmers of the county and State, and while a member of the State Alliance convention took active steps in various ways for the amelioration of the general condition of farmers in the Northwest. In politics Mr. McColley is a republican, and belongs to the Baptist church, and has been treasurer of that organization for nine years, and has also been clerk of the society. He belongs to the Odd Fellows, and for two years was commander of the Grand Army of the Republic post. He is secretary of the Faribault County Agricultural Society, and has been for the past five years.

Nathaniel McColley was married April 2, 1867, to Miss Frances Freer, a native of

Washington county, Wisconsin. Her parents were David and Ardilla Freer, and were farmers throughout the most of their lives. Miss Freer was educated at Blue Earth City. Mr. and Mrs. McColley · have five children—Ardilla B., Marion E., Evalina M., Alvin M. and Jessie A.

CHARLES C. WALKUP is an influential citizen of Sherburne, Martin county, Minnesota, where he engaged in the lumber business. The place of his nativity is found in Marengo, McHenry county, Illinois, where he was born September 15, 1859. His parents were George and Phœbe (Spencer) Walkup, natives, respectively, of New York and Indiana. The father was engaged in farming and cattle buying, and his life was divided between residence in town and on the farm.

Our subject spent his early life with his parents, attending the common schools, and commenced working out when he was about twelve years of age. He made his home with his parents, however, until he was about twenty-five years old, in the meantime being engaged in various employments in and about Marengo and other places to which his parents moved. When he was a small boy the parents removed to Cedar Falls, Iowa, and after remaining there for about a year and a half again moved, locating in Waverly, from whence, after a six years' residence, they moved to Osage, Iowa. Here they resided, engaged in various lines of business, for six or eight years, when they removed to Pipestone, Minnesota. Our subject remained with his parents until the fall of 1887, when he came to Sherburne and took charge of the lumber yard of C. L. Coleman. Our subject has been energetically engaged in building up the lumber interests of his employer, and has succeeded in establishing a large business. He is a man of good character, an exemplary citizen, and has taken an active part in matters of a public nature wherever he has resided. In politics he affiliates with the republican party, and was city marshal for some years while a resident of Pipestone.

Mr. Walkup was married in Pipestone, Minnesota, April 21, 1887, to Miss Elizabeth Wilson, daughter of Andrew and Isabel (Sinton) Wilson. She was born near Joliet, Illinois, in 1861. This union has been blessed with one child, Hugh S.

CALVIN RANK, one of the leading and influential merchants of Windom, Minnesota, first located in Great Bend township, Cottonwood county, in 1870. He was one of the first settlers of that township and took a pre-emption of eighty acres, which was afterward charged to a soldier's claim of 160 acres. He made numerous improvements, and drew his lumber with an ox team from Lake Crystal, seventy miles distant. He resided on his farm until in 1888, when he moved into the village and engaged in his present business. He has met with large success and has built up a large trade.

Mr. Rank is a native of Union county, Pennsylvania, where he was born December 30, 1831. His parents were Samuel and Catharine (Deffenbaugher) Rank, natives of Pennsylvania. The father was engaged in milling and farming and moved to Indiana in about 1839, settling in Miami county. He made that his home until his death, which occurred in 1853. The mother died in 1860. The father was a member of the old whig party and his wife belonged to the Lutheran church. He was a wealthy man and a prominent citizen and took an active part in all church and school matters. Of fourteen children in the father's family the following-named are living—Mary, now Mrs. Hildman; Samuel D., of Indiana;

William J., a resident of Winona county, Minnesota; Eliza, now Mrs. Moss, of Iowa; and Calvin.

The subject of our sketch was reared as a farmer's boy, being given very limited advantages for an education in his early days. He received about thirty days' schooling out of each year and the balance of the time engaged in farming and teaming. He continued at this until 1854 when he went to Green county, Iowa, and purchased one hundred acres of prairie land and forty acres of timber. He made a few improvements and returned to Indiana in 1855 and engaged in farming in that State for two years. He again came to Iowa, locating in Scott county where he engaged in farming for one year. His next move was to Kansas, from whence he went to Pike's Peak, where he took a claim and commenced mining, afterward engaging in keeping boarders. He returned some time afterward to Franklin county, Kansas, where he engaged in farming until 1860. On the breaking out of the war he found himself in a peculiar dilemma. He was a Northerner of Northern proclivities surrounded by Rebels. A third of his time was occupied with quarrels with the Rebels and he came to the conclusion that it was better for him to leave the country. So, coming to Minnesota, he stopped in Rice county, where he enlisted in Company A, Seventh Minnesota Infantry. He served eighteen months. He was in the following named sanguinary battles: Tupelo, Nashville, Spanish Fort, and a great many smaller battles and skirmishes. During a part of the time he was at Paducah, Memphis, and in Arkansas, Missouri, Tennessee and other States of the South. After his discharge he returned to Rice county, Minnesota, and engaged in farming until making his location in Cottonwood county, in 1870.

Mr. Rank was married to Miss C. Fickle of Guthrie county, Iowa, in 1855. Three children have blessed this union—Alonzo C., Edwin and Ida M. Alonzo married Emma Englehart, by whom he had three children—Bert, Harry and May. Edwin is head clerk and manager of his father's store.

The subject of our sketch is a man of excellent business qualifications and has built up a profitable trade which is steadily increasing in volume. He is progressive minded, public spirited, and is a man of high character. He affiliates with the republican party in politics, and is a member of the Independent Order of Odd Fellows and Grand Army of the Republic fraternities. Mr. and Mrs. Rank are both members of the Presbyterian church.

※ — ·▹·◁◈▷·◅· — ※

JAMES McVEY, an exemplary citizen and substantial farmer of Pipestone county, Minnesota, located on section 4, of Fountain Prairie township, in 1880. He homesteaded his present excellent farm, and commenced his operations by breaking twenty acres of land during the summer. He also built a small shanty, in which he lived for about a year and a half. At the end of that time he moved to the northeast quarter of the section on which his farm lay, and remained for about two years, during which time he farmed his own land, and the part of the quarter section to which he had moved. At the expiration of the two years just mentioned he moved back to his homestead, and has made that his home ever since. Ever since the organization of the township he has occupied a prominent and influential place in all affairs of a public nature.

The place of the nativity of the subject of our sketch is found in Carleton county, near the city of Ottawa, Canada, where he was born May 4, 1838. His parents were Stewart and Mary A. McVey, who were natives of Scotland.

Our subject remained in the country of his nativity until he was about eighteen years of age. Most of this time had been spent in work on the home farm, and in attending school whenever opportunity presented itself and he could be spared from the farm. His school privileges were furnished by the district schools of his native country, and he was able to obtain a good common-school education. When he was eighteen years of age he concluded to leave the parental home, and to take hold of life's duties for himself. Removing to St. Lawrence county, New York, he remained for six months engaged in farming, after which he went to the State of Wisconsin, where he remained until his enlistment in the Union army, at which time he was located in Wood county, where he had been engaged in the lumber business. In September, 1861, he enlisted in Company E, Twelfth Regiment, Volunteer Infantry, entering the service as a corporal. His discharge was given in November, 1864, at Chattanooga, Tennessee. This regiment was commanded by Colonel George E. Bryant until the battle of Atlanta, when Colonel Bryant took command of a brigade, and James K. Proudfit commanded the regiment until the close of the war. The war experience of our subject was full of excitement and hardships. He saw many severe battles, among them being the battles of Cold Water, Vicksburg, Canton, Atlanta and Kenesaw Mountain, besides many other battles of minor importance. He was slightly wounded at the battle of Kenesaw Mountain, but soon recovered, his injury not being of such a severe nature as to require attendance at the hospital. After his discharge at Chattanooga, in 1864, our subject returned to Wisconsin and resumed his old occupation of lumbering. He continued in the State of Wisconsin until in 1880, in which year he removed to Pipestone county, Minnesota, and made

settlement on the farm on which he now lives.

On the 18th day of August, 1867, Mr. McVey was wedded to Miss Sarah Bennett, a native of Windham county, Vermont. When she was ten years of age her parents removed to Columbia county, Wisconsin, where she received her education and early training. The marriage took place in Kilbourn City, Wisconsin. Mr. and Mrs. McVey have five children—George, Victoria, Sarah, James Garfield and Donald—all still unmarried and residing with their parents.

In politics Mr. McVey affiliates with the republican party, and since coming to the county he has held a prominent place in the counsels of this organization. His abilities as an official are of a high order, and his services have been required in numerous instances. Shortly after coming to the township, in 1881, he was elected on the township board, and held that office for one year. For four years he held the position of treasurer of school district No. 38, and, in 1882, was appointed postmaster of the McVey postoffice in Fountain Prairie township. He has held the office of roadmaster also, and is at present a member of the town board of supervisors. In the fall of 1888 he was elected one of the county commissioners, which position he holds at the present time. Ever since his location in the township our subject has been intimately identified with its best interests, and has taken an active part in all matters which pertain to the welfare of the township and county. He is a man of high character and is respected by all who know him. He has an excellent farm provided with good buildings, and has a pleasant family. Mr. McVey is an influential member of the Grand Army of the Republic and Masonic fraternities. Our subject is a member of the Episcopalian church, and his wife of the Congregational church.

ARCHIBALD CURRIE, SR., is one of the most influential citizens of the village of Currie, Murray county, Minnesota. He was one of the early settlers of the county, having made his permanent location here in 1873. Mr. Currie is now engaged in the real-estate and loan business. He came to the present site of the village of Currie because of the excellent water power, and in 1872, the year previous to his location, he built the frame of a flouring mill. In 1873 the building was completed, and O. A. Pray, of Minneapolis, put in two run of stone, our subject owning an interest in the mill until 1886. This mill was well equipped with the patent roller system, and was finally sold to Snider & Silvernale. Mr. Currie and son were the first settlers on the present site of Currie, and our subject put up the first building in the village in the fall of 1872. For some time this was occupied for a small store. This business has finally developed to large proportions, and our subject's son, Neil Currie, has entire charge. Since coming to the county Mr. Currie has been one of the most prominent citizens. For five and a half years he was county treasurer, and has held other positions of minor importance, in all of which he has proven his efficiency and worth as a business man.

The gentleman whose name appears at the head of this sketch is a native of Argyleshire, Scotland, where he was born in the year 1816. Remaining in his native land until five years of age, he then came to America with his parents, locating in Canada. Here our subject remained, receiving a good common-school education, and engaged in various kinds of employment after reaching his majority, until 1861, when he removed to Minnesota, locating in Troy, Winona county. He was engaged in the mercantile business, and during this time was one of the leading public spirits of his locality. He was also largely interested in lands in the vicinity of Troy. From Troy he went to Rushford, and there operated a store for five years. St. Charles, Minnesota, became his next location, and for four or five years he operated a mercantile business in that place. He then came to Currie, Murray county, Minnesota.

Archibald Currie was married March 1, 1842, to Miss Jane Wilson, who was born in Canada. She died May 22, 1879. Mrs. Currie was a member of the Presbyterian church, and was an exemplary Christian lady. Eleven children were the fruits of this union, eight of whom grew to man and womanhood— Neil, Jane, John, Ebenezer, Margaret, Arch, Christina and Willie. A sketch of Neil Currie is found in another department of this work.

Since coming to this county the subject of our sketch has interested himself largely in buying lands, and now owns a number of farms in Murray county and one in Pipestone county. His real estate business has been of large dimensions, and he has been doing a large and profitable business. In politics Mr. Currie affiliates with the republican party, and attends the services of the Presbyterian church, with which society he is in hearty sympathy. Perhaps no man in the county is better known than Mr. Currie, and, wherever known, he is highly respected for his sterling qualities as a true and loyal citizen and careful business man.

———◆◆◆———

GEORGE S. WAIT. This gentleman became one of the pioneers of Pipestone county in the year 1878, his settlement being made on the 5th day of May, when he homesteaded his present farm on section 30, of Elmer township. Mr. Wait was possessed of the usual energy and perseverance found among the characteristics of the pioneers of every country. He intended to make himself a pleasant and comfortable home, and if possible to surround himself with sufficient of this world's comforts to be able to enjoy his old age. His first operation was to erect a shanty some 12x24 feet, and then he commenced to turn over the prairie sod, breaking about one hundred acres the first year. In this way he laid the foundations for the competency which he has since earned. Some four years of his life were spent in this primitive shanty, and at the end of that period it was destroyed by fire, entailing upon him the loss of everything he had except one quilt. This loss, however, did not discourage Mr. Wait, and he at once commenced drawing lumber for the purpose of building a new dwelling. This house was 14x24 feet, with twelve-foot posts, and in it he lived until another calamity came to him in the shape of a cyclone, in 1882, which entirely demolished his home and destroyed nearly all his personal effects. He then built the house in which he now lives, 22x14 feet, with ten-foot posts and an addition 10x22 feet. This building he has improved and made out of it a comfortable and pleasant home. Near at hand are to be seen his farm buildings, barns, granaries, and other smaller structures such as are usually seen and needed on a well-regulated farm. He has a large commodious barn, built in 1888, 46x48 feet, with room for the accommodation of about fifty head of cattle, and from twenty to thirty head of horses. The stock owned by Mr. Wait is worthy of more extended notice. He has an excellent herd of Short-horn and Hereford cattle, well bred and thoroughly cared for. Among his horses are to be found those of the Morgan and Clydesdale stock, and most of them are finely formed and handsome animals. Since coming to the county he has been engaged in diversified farming, together with the raising of blooded stock to a considerable extent. Before the railroad was built through this region of country, Mr. Wait occupied very much of his time in driving freighting teams from Pipestone to Luverne and through to Flandreau. With the growth of prosperity in Elmer township and the adjoining country, Mr. Wait's finances have also grown, and he has accumulated considerable means, in all of his enterprises having met with merited success. It may safely be said that our subject erected the first house in the township on section 30. There was a shanty built on section 29 a short time before, but it was indeed a shanty and could not be called a dwelling house, therefore Mr. Wait undoubtedly built the first house in the township. It may also be said that he was the first to break land and commence farming in the town.

The place of nativity of our subject is to be found near Coberg, in Upper Canada, where he was born October 6, 1843. His parents were Griffin and Betsey (Sprung) Wait, the father being a native of Duchess county, New York, whence he went to Canada when a small boy. He is still living and is eighty-eight years old. Throughout his life he has been engaged in the occupation of farming. The mother was a native of Canada, where she is still alive at the age of seventy-seven years. The parents have lived long lives of usefulness, and for years have been associated with the religious work of the Methodist Episcopal Church, the father having been a member of that denomination for some seventy years. The Wait family were people of prominence during the early part of this present century and the grandfather of our subject was a soldier in the War of 1812. The parents had a family of eleven children, all of whom are living in Canada, with the exception of one daughter and the subject of our sketch. The names of these children are as follows—John Dirland, Edgar, Emily, George S., Willett, Clispy, Jennie, Christiana, Sophia, Gilbert and Wallace.

The boyhood of the subject of our sketch was surrounded with the comforts of the parental home and he was given the advantages of good educational facilities in his native county. His education was received in the common schools, in which he was well fitted for the life of busy activity in which he has been engaged for so many years. At the age of seventeen years he left home and removed to Wisconsin, locating in Madison, where he engaged in farming for some twenty-one years. He then came to Pipestone county, Minnesota, where he has lived ever since.

Mr. Wait was united in marriage, March 19, 1863, in Dane county, Wisconsin, to Miss Matilda Conustock, who was a native of Canada. At the age of twelve years she came with her parents to the State of Wisconsin, where she lived until, with her husband and family, she came to Minnesota. Mr. and Mrs. Wait have a family of eight children—Griffin R., Jennie C., Olive, Sheridan, Bernard Henry, Elgin, Pearly and Effie. Jennie and Olive are both married.

In politics Mr. Wait affiliates with the democratic party, in the councils of which organization he takes a prominent stand. By virtue of his excellent business abilities, his services have been in demand throughout his life by the citizens of the localities in which he has lived, and he has been elected to fill many official positions. Since residing in this county he has held the position of deputy postmaster for two years, the postoffice being in our subject's house. He was a member of the first township board, and was elected as judge of probate of the county in 1879, which position, however, he held but a short time. In all matters of a public nature the assistance of Judge Wait has never been asked in vain. Energetic and persevering in his own business relations, he has carried these characteristics into his whole life, whether the lines be led in public or private places. He is a man of broad ideas, liberal and generous, and has a large circle of warm friends. The maintenance of the highest degree of integrity in his own character and the life of others is his uppermost thought, and it may well be said that these characteristics have always been the dominant features of Mr. Wait's life. He is a good citizen and respected by all with whom he has to do.

PROFESSOR HIRAM E. FRENCH is the efficient and popular principal of the public schools of Pipestone City, Minnesota. He has been in charge of the schools in that city since September, 1884. At present the school is divided into five departments in which the total enrollment is 378, of which there is an average daily attendance of about 240 scholars. The professor, assisted by an able corps of five teachers, has brought these schools up to a high standard, and, in connection with the common branches, the pupils are given the advantage of a thorough course in the higher studies, being prepared for college at the end of three years.

Professor French is a native of Maquoketa, Iowa, where he was born October 23, 1851. His parents were Hiram B. and Dyanthy R. (Truax) French, the father a native of Vermont, and the mother a native of Canada. Hiram B. French was a blacksmith by trade, and in 1847 came West and settled in Maquoketa, Iowa. In the summer of 1848 he went to Canada, returning to Maquoketa in the fall with a wife. He continued plying his trade in Maquoketa until the spring of 1857, when he removed to Pleasant Grove, Minnesota, where he engaged in farming, following the same for about three years, then returning to Maquoketa, Iowa, where he engaged in the mercantile business. He made this line his principal avocation until his death, which occurred in January, 1884. The mother resides at San Jose, Calfornia, the wife of General Joseph E. Gage. In the father's family there were six children, four of whom are now living—Charles E., now a merchant of Maquoketa, Iowa; Professor Hiram E., Ella B., now Mrs. Collister, of Savannah, Illinois; and William R., now traveling agent for W. W. Kimball, of Chicago, with headquarters at South Bend, Indiana.

The early days of the subject of our sketch were passed by him in his home in Maquoketa, Iowa, where, until twelve years of age, he was given good educational advantages in the common schools. At that age he engaged in the freighting business, driving one of his father's teams to Dubuque and other places on the Mississippi river, continuing in this line of employment until he was sixteen years of age. He then attended Cornell College, in Iowa, for one year, after which, during every winter for some years, he turned his attention to teaching school, still freighting during the summer. This work of teaching winters and freighting summers he continued until he was twenty-three years of age, at which time he was offered a position in the Maquoketa graded schools. He accepted this offer and continued in these schools for four years, after which he attended the Northern Indiana Normal for several terms, and graduated therefrom in 1880. He then accepted a position as principal of the high school in Sabula, Iowa, where he remained four years. From thence he removed to Pipestone, Minnesota, in 1884, and entered upon the duties of the principalship of the public school in that place, which position he had accepted a short time before. Since coming to the village the professor has been actively engaged in aiding all projects for public improvements, beside building for himself, in 1885, a fine residence, with all the modern conveniences. He has adorned and beautified his premises with evergreens and other trees, and has made for himself and family one of the handsomest homes in the city.

Professor French was married in 1871 to Miss Lucy Eberly, a daughter of John and Mary (Hammond) Eberly, natives of Virginia. Mr. and Mrs. French have one child, Kittie M., born in Maquoketa, Iowa, May 23, 1873.

In politics the subject of our sketch affiliates with the republican party, and is an influential member of the Masonic fraternity and Ancient Order of United Workmen. Professor French was one of the organizers of the First National Bank, of which he is a stockholder and director. In all matters which pertain to the upbuilding and development of the city and county he has aided loyally with both time and money, and by his energetic manner of taking hold of these things has grown rapidly in popularity among his fellow-citizens. He is a man of wide intelligence, thoroughly and highly educated, and is well qualified for the prominent educational position he occupies in Pipestone City. In all matters of a social or educational nature he is deeply interested, and ably aids in the development of these departments in the city.

----◆◆◆◆◆----

ZADOK DAY is an influential farmer of Springfield township, Cottonwood county, Minnesota. He has a fine farm, provided with a good residence and other buildings, on section 8. He is a native of St. Lawrence county, New York, where he was born October 7, 1825.

The parents of the subject of our sketch were Nathan and Lucinda (Cook) Day, the former a native of Vermont, and the latter born in New York. The father was a lumberman by occupation, and died in St. Lawrence county, New York, in 1875. The mother died in 1840. The grand-parents of the subject of our sketch were Zadok and

Jemima (Nobles) Day, natives of Vermont. The grandfather died in about 1835.

The subject of our sketch was one of nine children, and assisted his father in work at the lumber business throughout the most of his early life, being given good educational advantages during the winter months. He remained with his father until he was about twenty-one years of age, when he took up his residence on a tract of twenty-five acres of land which was presented to him by his father. This farm was in St. Lawrence county, New York, and our subject built a house and engaged in clearing land, remaining there one year, after which he went home to take care of his father, who had been suddenly struck with blindness. About one year was spent with his father and then our subject found work on the Erie canal during the summer, after which he purchased a farm of 117 acres and followed the life of an agriculturist for five years. Then in 1854 he went to California, where he engaged in mining at Longbear, on the Uber river, for about three months. From thence he went to the American river, from whence, after one year, he went to Oregon Hill. His life in the mountains was full of many wild experiences. He visited and worked at various places, among them being Branch City, Monte Christo, Eureka, and various places along the Uber and American rivers. In 1860 he returned to New York to his old home, and from thence with his family he went to Iowa City, Iowa, going by way of the lakes to Chicago, and thence by rail to his destination. He resided in the city during the winter, and in the spring bought forty acres of land, and engaged in farming for three years. October 15, 1864, Mr. Day enlisted in Company F, Fifteenth Iowa Infantry, and was discharged in July, 1865. He served with General Sherman in the march to the sea, and saw many hardships and much severe expos-

ure, the results of which have never left him. After the close of hostilities between the north and south our subject returned to Iowa, where he settled on a farm. His health had been almost completely broken down by his war experience, and he was not able to do any of the work on the farm. He had a large family of boys, however, and to these he allotted the work of carrying on the farm business. He resided in that locality until 1875, and then came to Cottonwood county, Minnesota, locating on his present farm.

Mr. Day was married July 3, 1847, to Jennett Chapin, a native of St. Lawrence county, New York. This union has been blessed with nine children—five girls and four boys.

Since coming to the county, our subject has taken an active interest in public matters and has held various official positions. In politics he is a stanch republican, and is a man who is highly respected by all who know him. He has been a member of the township board of supervisors and also a member of the school board. He is a member of the Grand Army of the Republic and of the Good Templars' society.

ROBERT VANS AGNEW is the oldest of three brothers, owners and managers of what has been known for some years as the "Carpenter farm," located on section 5, township 104, range 37, or Weimer township, Jackson county, Minnesota. The names of these brothers are Robert R., Frank and Earnest. Robert was born in India in the year 1865 and for some years was a resident of England. In 1883 he came to the United States, located in Jackson county, Minnesota, and for a year worked at the carpenter's trade in the village of Heron Lake. He then went to Florida and started an orange grove of fifteen acres at Narcrosse, where he has now about twelve hundred orange trees in fine growing condition. In 1889 the three brothers already named purchased the Carpenter farm of 480 acres, located within three miles of Heron Lake and seven miles from Wilder, villages on the Chicago, St. Paul, Minneapolis & Omaha railroad. This farm is one of the best and most productive in Southern Minnesota. On it may be found a fine large barn and large house and all necessary buildings for the keeping of stock. Three hundred acres of the farm are broken and under cultivation and the balance of the acreage is pasture land. At present the brothers are raising grain and Short-horn cattle. This farm is now for sale, and any communication in regard to its purchase will receive prompt attention by addressing Robert Vans Agnew, Heron Lake, Minnesota.

The parents of the subject of our sketch were natives of the empire of Great Britain. The father is now located in France. He spent a few months in 1885 on the orange plantation in Florida. Frank was born in 1868 and Earnest in 1871, the latter coming to America in 1887 and the former in September, 1884. Both of these brothers remained some time in Florida caring for the orange plantation.

ROBERT SHERIN is one of the leading and influential business men of Winnebago City, Faribault county, Minnesota. He is a native of Peterborough, Canada, where he was born in 1824.

The subject of our sketch is the son of Henry and Eliza (Warren) Sherin, natives of Scotland and Ireland, respectively. They came to America when quite young, and the father in his early days was a chaplain in the English army. He was educated in the classical institutions of his native land, and was prepared for the Episcopal ministry. His entire life was spent in preaching the gospel and in teaching school, fifty years being given principally to the ministry. He died at the age of eighty-three years. The mother died at eighty-seven years of age. In the father's family there were eight children, six of whom are now living —Henry, Thomas, Robert, John, Samuel and Rebecca.

The gentleman whose name appears at the head of this sketch spent his younger days at home beneath the parental roof, receiving good educational advantages. He came to the United States in 1854, and located at St. Johns, Michigan, where he engaged in the real estate business. Prior to coming to the United States he worked for some years on various farms, and had also to some extent engaged in the harness business. He also gave somewhat of his attention to carpentering, and also to the cooper's trade, being also engaged during several years in the real estate business. On coming to St. Johns and engaging in the real estate business, he made his home there until 1860, when he removed to Fox Lake, Wisconsin, continuing in the same line in which he had engaged in St. Johns. In 1868 he came to Minnesota, locating in Faribault county and purchasing a farm two miles south of Winnebago city. He resided on this land for several years and in 1872 moved into the city of Winnebago, where he has since been engaged in the real estate business. He has made numerous valuable improvements and has assisted in the development of Winnebago city and vicinity. He built his present residence in Wallace's addition on Cleveland street.

Mr. Sherin was married in 1846 to Miss Susan McCarl, a native of Canada. This union was blessed with four children—John H., editor of the Winnebago City *Press-News*, of whom a sketch is given in another department of this work; Robert W., a farmer and real estate broker; Carrie A., now the wife of Mr. Quiggle, a druggist of Winnebago, and Milton J., a barber located at Blue Earth

City, Faribault county. John H. married Emma Postlethwaite, by whom he had two children. Robert W. married Maggie McKee, and has one child, Cecil. Carrie A., now Mrs. Quiggle, has one child, Harry S. Milton J. married Delphine Pareso, by whom he had one child, Clara H.

In politics the subject of our sketch affiliates with no particular party but believes in taking an independent course and voting for the men best fitted for the various official positions. Mr. and Mrs. Sherin are both members of the Methodist Episcopal church. The subject of our sketch has taken an active interest in public matters since coming to the village and has become one of the prominent and substantial citizens of the county.

EUGENE S. BUTMAN is a prominent well-to-do farmer of Troy township, Pipestone county, Minnesota, and resides on section 12. He has an extensive farm of some four hundred acres, and is engaged largely in raising cattle. He was born in LaCrosse county, Wisconsin, October 4, 1856.

Mr. Butman is the son of Stark and Mary J. (Lynn) Butman, both of whom were natives of Ohio. The grandfather's name was Alexander P. Butman, a native of Pennsylvania, a farmer by occupation and a prominent man in the early days in which he lived. Mr. Butman's mother was the daughter of Sylvester Lynn, a native of New York. The parents of Mr. Butman came to Wisconsin in 1852, or thereabouts, and located in LaCrosse county, and in 1858 traded the farm for land in Trempealeau county, where they still live and where they are held in high esteem, being well-to-do and influential farmers.

Until the age of twenty-three Eugene S. remained with his parents, assisting in the work on the farm and attending the district school during the months of each winter. In June, 1879, he came to Pipestone county, Minnesota, and settled on the place where he now lives. In those days there were no railroads in this part of Southwestern Minnesota, and coming to the city of Marshall, from there by team and on foot he completed his journey to his present place of residence. Having located his land and remained thereon a few days, he returned to his home in Wisconsin, and remained until in November of that year. Then returning to his land, he remained three weeks, making some light improvements, after which his absence from the farm dated until the following April. At this time he concluded to make a permanent settlement on his land, and, hiring a car, he put therein all his household goods, also four mules and two cows, and started for his future home. But eight months were spent on the farm, however, and soon after the terrible October blizzard of that year, he started with his teams and drove across the country to his old home in Wisconsin. In May, of the following year, he returned to the farm, where he has since lived. The pioneer experience through which he passed during those days of early settlement was indeed severe, and it was because of that experience that he was obliged, at times, to leave the farm and engage in other employment. His settlement, however, has been permanent since 1881.

Mr. Butman was united in matrimony January 1, 1883, to Miss Elizabeth A. M. Stellpflug, a native of Wisconsin. Three children have been born to this marriage — Mary J., Nettie L. and Leroy E., all alive at the present time.

In politics, Mr. Butman is a believer in the principles of the republican party, and has taken an active interest in local politics since coming to this county. He has held several minor official positions, and in all cases has held them with credit to himself and benefit to his constituents. In 1882 he held the office of member of the town board of trustees, and is at present treasurer of the school district, which office he has held for some seven years. He has held other positions, among them being that of pathmaster. Mr. Butman is a leading spirit among the farmers of his locality, and enjoys the respect and confidence of all who know him.

THADEUS P. GROUT is one of the most reliable and most widely respected citizens of Rock county, Minnesota. He is engaged extensively in farming, and resides in the village of Luverne. He made his location in the county in the spring of 1873, settling where he now lives and building one of the first frame dwellings in the village. He was one of the earliest settlers in this region, and has been intimately identified with the better interests of Rock county throughout his entire residence. He took one of the first timber claims taken under the "timber act." Of this claim there were 160 acres, and adjoining it he also took a homestead of the same number of acres. Later, in 1874, he purchased 160 acres on the same section, and now has 480 acres of fine farming land in one body. He has been active in improving this farm, and has branched out to a considerable extent in stock raising, being the owner of some fine Polled-Angus cattle, and a number of high-bred horses and sheep. Adjoining the city limits he now owns 240 acres of fine lands, where he carries on a large stock-raising business. He has invested considerable in county and village property, and has made considerable money in investments in farming lands in various parts of the county. His farm of 240 acres just adjoining the city limits is one in which he takes a great deal of pride, having it under his own personal supervision. It is a beautiful loca-

tion and is well supplied with excellent water. In connection with his farming enterprise, in an early day he engaged considerably in loaning money.

The subject of our sketch is a native of Jefferson county, New York, and was born at Natural Bridge in the town of Wilna, on the 7th day of February, 1837. His parents were Elijah and Eleanor (Pool) Grout, the former a native of Vermont and the latter of New York. The father was an extensive farmer in the Eastern States and came to Wisconsin in the spring of 1855, settling in the town of Fountain Prairie, Columbia county. Here he engaged in agricultural pursuits until his death, which occurred in 1860. The mother died in 1870. The parents were loyal Christian people and were exemplary members of the Methodist Episcopal church throughout the most of their lives. In the father's family there were four children—Ambrose, who enlisted in Company B, Eleventh Wisconsin Regiment, and died in the service in 1862; Eli L., an extensive farmer residing near Beaver Creek, Rock county; John E., who now lives near the old homestead in Columbia county, Wis., where he is engaged in farming, and Thadeus P.

The gentleman whose name appears at the head of this sketch received his early training as a farmer's boy, being given the educational advantages of the district schools in his native State. Later, on making a location in Wisconsin, Mr. Grout attended the Lawrence University in Outagamie county. He remained with his parents until he was twenty-one years of age, at which time he took charge of the home farm, and conducted the same from 1859 to 1873. In the latter year he sold out and came to Rock county, making a settlement, as was stated in the opening lines of this biography. Throughout his career he has taken an active interest in all matters of a public nature, and has been elected to various local offices. While in Wisconsin he was a member of the board of town supervisors, and exerted a strong influence in local governmental affairs. Since coming to Rock county he has also held positions of responsibility and trust, and in all such matters has proven a valuable acquisition to the county in which he has lived.

Mr. Grout was married in the year 1858 to Miss Jennie Ingals, of Jefferson county, New York. She was left an orphan when five years of age, and the father of our subject adopted her, and she took the family name of Grout. Mr. and Mrs. Grout have four living children—Fannie, now Mrs. Rev. P. W. Cranell, of Baldwinsville, New York; Ambrose E. and Effie L., both students at Hamline University, near Minneapolis, Minnesota, and George P.

The subject of our sketch has been one of the most enthusiastic and earnest workers in the cause of temperance in Rock county, and indeed in all Southern Minnesota. This activity is not confined to his later life, but throughout his entire career his life has been founded on strictly temperance principles, ever shunning the intoxicating cup, and has given his deepest thought and his most earnest endeavor toward the overthrowing of the infamous rum traffic. Having his mind and heart full of these principles of temperance, he has, therefore, of late years, been earnestly engaged in cooperating with the movements of the prohibition party. To him more than to any other man, perhaps, is due the present state of temperance sentiment in the southwestern part of Minnesota. Wherever he has been, at every opportunity, he has raised his voice in opposition to that base traffic which is dealing out death and destruction to so many hundreds of the flower of our nation's young manhood. Shortly after the organization of the prohibition party he joined hands with its work, and has been ever since enthusiastically promulgating the principles upon which that party is founded. For the last three years he has been a member of the prohibition State central committee, and in 1888 was a delegate to the national prohibition convention which met at Indianapolis, Indiana. For years he has been chairman of the central committee of Rock county, and his efforts and intense words in favor of temperance and that party will not soon be forgotten by the residents of the county. Early in his life he became an enthusiast on these lines and joined the Sons of Temperance in Columbia county, Wisconsin, although, to become a member of that society, the lodge had to procure a special dispensation because of his extreme youth.

Besides being such an earnest worker in the temperance cause, Mr. Grout is also one of the most ready and consistent workers on religious lines. Indeed, his enthusiasm on the temperance question is traceable to the fact that he has an intensely religious nature, and with him, being the one must necessitate being the other. For years he has associated with the work of the Methodist Episcopal church, joining that organization when he was seventeen years of age, his wife becoming a member of that church when she was fifteen years old, and both she and her husband have lived useful and exemplary Christian lives. Every church enterprise which has presented its appeal for assistance to him has met with a liberal and immediate response. He has helped to establish a number of church societies, and has assisted financially in the building of a number of churches since coming to the State of Minnesota. In Sunday-school work Mr. Grout has but few superiors. He has had a long experience as a Sunday-school superintendent and so well understands the needs of the Sabbath-school that the work prospers well in his hands.

He has been the superintendent of the Sabbath-school in Luverne about half of the time that he has been in the county, has filled that position with perfect acceptability, and has accomplished a great amount of good. When he first came to the State in 1872, on Friday, the 16th of June, there were but two sod shanties in the township near Beaver Creek. When Sunday came they had no church édifice to resort to that they might pay their devotions to the God of their fathers, so they resorted to one of the sod houses, and dedicated that for their Sunday services. Here the first Sabbath-school in the county was organized, presided over by Mr. Grout, and since then this school has been continued in that neighborhood, the people of Beaver Creek having put up a new church building:

In 1873, in company with James Gillard and Rev. E. H. Bronson, Mr. Grout and others established the first Methodist Episcopal church and Sunday-school at Luverne. This was on the 20th day of June, and since that time church work and Sunday-school enterprises have been moving forward, and the religious work commenced then has prospered, and much fruit has been gathered from the seed then sown. From time to time our subject has been president of the county Sunday-school union, and has assisted in the organization of various Sunday-schools throughout the county.

Throughout his career in Rock county our subject has been loyal to the principles of Christianity, and has shown himself to be a man in whom all might place the highest confidence. In business matters he has been quite successful, and has accumulated a large amount of means and has a pleasant and comfortable home. He is a loyal citizen, and an earnest and enthusiastic supporter of everything which tends to develop and bring prosperity to the locality in which he lives.

ALBERT C. SCRIVEN is an influential and well-to-do farmer and stock raiser of Dovray township, Murray county, Minnesota. He resides on section 34, where he settled in October, 1877. On making his settlement here he commenced making improvements, and worked hard to bring his farm up to the excellent state of cultivation which it has now attained. There were but four other settlers in the township at that time, and our subject actively associated himself with all matters of a public nature, being made chairman of the township board of supervisors for six terms. He has also occupied his attention considerably with educational matters, and has been school district treasurer for some three years. In his farming and stock-raising operations he has met with large success, and has a goodly number of fine stock horses of the Norman and English draft grades. He has also a number of Holstein and Short-horn grades of cattle. His farm is under excellent cultivation and contains about ten acres of fine timber, consisting of cottonwood, maple and white willow trees.

The subject of our sketch was born in Grafton, Rensselaer county, New York, June 29, 1830. His parents were John and Phoebe (Sanders) Scriven. The father died when our subject was four and a half years old. He was a farmer and mason by trade, and was born in Rhode Island. When about twenty years old he removed to New York, where he died December 15, 1835. The mother was a native of Rhode Island, where she was reared and educated. She died in about 1863 at seventy-six years of age. She was a consistent member of the Baptist church. In the father's family there were twelve children—John, Phoebe (deceased), Schuyler, Almira, Charles (deceased), Mary (deceased), Cynthia (deceased), Franklin, Irene, Daniel, Hannah (deceased) and Albert C.

Our subject received his early education

and training in the State of New York, and remained there until he was twenty years of age, aiding his brother in the work on the old homestead. He received a good common school education, and when twenty years of age emigrated to Tazewell county, Illinois. He soon after, in fact within a few months, came to Minnesota and first located in St. Paul. After a three months' stay, engaged in work on the farm, he returned to Illinois and remained until the following April, when he went to Winona county and resided in Whitewater township for twenty years, engaged in farming. He then came to Lyon county, Minnesota, where he lived five years, engaged in farming. During three winters, in order to obtain a livelihood, he went into the woods about Mankato, and there chopped wood. During the grasshopper raids there were no crops, and this was his only manner of obtaining a living.

Mr. Scriven was married, November 21, 1875, to Miss Maggie Talcott, a native of Walworth county, Wisconsin, where she was reared and educated. This lady is a consistent member of the Methodist Episcopal church, to which also her husband belongs. Our subject takes an active interest in religious matters, and is a steward of the church of which he is a member. He is a man of excellent qualities, and was formerly a member of the Good Templars' lodge. He is a well-to-do citizen, an intelligent, public-spirited man, and is highly respected by all who know him. In political matters he is a prohibitionist, and in daily life uses neither liquors, tobacco, tea nor coffee. He voted for General Scott for president, and affiliated with the republican party until three years ago, when he felt it a duty incumbent upon him to change, and since that time he has earnestly supported the prohibition party.

ALLEN FOOTE is a machinist by trade, and resides in the village of St. James, Minnesota, where he is in the employ of the Omaha Railroad Company. He has been engaged with his present employers since 1873, at which time he located in St. James, where he has become largely interested in village property.

Mr. Foote is a native of Geauga county, Ohio, being born in the village of Parkman, in the year 1831. He is the son of Andrew N. and Amanda A. (Phillips) Foote, natives of Schoharie county, New York. The father was engaged in the cloth business, and came to Ohio in an early day, and in 1844 located at Battle Creek, Michigan. For a number of years he was engaged as superintendent of the cloth department in the factory of W. W. Wallace. Later he engaged in farming in Eaton county, Michigan, where he resided until his death. In the father's family there were nine children, seven of whom are now living—Eleanor (now Mrs. Benum), Clark, Alvin, Henry, Allen, Edward and Martin.

The subject of our sketch resided with his parents in Parkman, Ohio, where he attended the district schools. When thirteen years of age he went to the State of Illinois, and spent some three years in the lead mines. Thence he went to Battle Creek, Michigan, and for two years found employment with his father in a woolen factory. For four years thereafter he was engaged as a fireman on the Michigan Central railroad. Two years were then spent on a farm in Hillsdale county, and in 1855 he came to Minnesota, settling in Le Sueur county on a pre-emption of 160 acres. He thoroughly improved this land and lived thereon for about seventeen years. Part of this time he was engaged as an engineer and also in putting up and repairing saw-mill engines. He served under General Sibley in the Indian war and massacre of 1862, and during part of this time was foraging for the quartermaster's department. An amusing incident is related by our subject of this time. He was sent to St. Peter to confiscate some hay stacks, but was driven away by several women, who used stones and various kinds of missiles in defense of their property. It finally took twenty-five soldiers to take one stack of hay from a few Irish women. Eleven of our subject's neighbors were also engaged in the service at this time at Birch Cooley, and a number of them were killed. When they started from home they went through the big woods toward Belle Plaine during the night in order to escape the attacks of the Indians. It was so dark that the teams were allowed to follow any course they might take. In 1873 Mr. Foote came to his present location, and was one of the first settlers of St. James. He has taken an active part in all matters of a public nature, and has held various official positions. He has been deputy sheriff of the county for four years, and has also been village marshal. He is a man of strong temperance principles, and has been grand councilman of the State lodge of Good Templars, in which society he still takes an active interest. He affiliates with the prohibition party, and with his wife belongs to the Baptist church, of which he is a trustee. He is also a member of the Masonic fraternity. Mr. Foote is a thorough master of his trade, and is one of the finest machinists along the Omaha railroad. He is a man of strong principles, and is beloved for his strict adherence to all things which he deems right.

Mr. Foote was married, in the year 1850, to Miss Sarah Herrick, of Battle Creek, Michigan. Four children have blessed this union, of whom three are now living— Emma, George E. and Charles W.

———————

P RESBURY W. MOORE is a well-to-do farmer of Springfield township, Cottonwood county, Minnesota, and resides on section 34. He was born in Vermont, July 25, 1836.

The parents of the subject of our sketch were Trueman H. and Elotia (Walker) Moore, natives of Vermont, and farmers by occupation. Trueman H. Moore was the son of James and Mary (Brown) Moore, natives of New Hampshire, James being a miller by trade. The family originally came from the northern part of Ireland and settled in New Hampshire, whence they scattered to all parts of the country. Trueman Moore and his wife died in Vermont many years ago.

The gentleman whose name appears at the head of this sketch spent his younger days under parental authority. He was given a good common-school education, and assisted in work on the home farm until nineteen years of age, when he came west, stopping for a time with a friend in McHenry county, Illinois. In the spring of 1856 he came to Minnesota, taking a claim of 160 acres in Fillmore county. He engaged in agricultural pursuits until August 15, 1864, when he enlisted in Company I, Eleventh Minnesota Volunteer Infantry. He served his country gallantry and faithfully until July 9, 1865. He then returned to his farm in Fillmore county and made that his home until 1872, when he came by team and located his present claim of 160 acres in Cottonwood county. He has seen much that would dishearten and discourage the farmers of to-day, having passed through the grasshopper raids, and having met with various financial reverses.

Mr. Moore was married, April 30, 1857, to Delina Freemire, a native of New York and a daughter of George and Eva A. (Borst) Freemire. The father is now a resident of Jackson county, Minnesota. Mr. and Mrs. Moore have had ten children, nine of whom are now living, one boy having died in infancy. The family now consists of eight girls and one boy of four years. Three of the girls are married, namely—Mrs. J. A. Moore, of Ballaton, Minnesota; Mrs. Alfred Blenkiron, of Springfield, and Mrs. F. S. Kingsburg, of Woonsocket, Dakota.

The political faith of the subject of our sketch is with the principles of the republican party. He has taken an active interest in public matters, and has been township treasurer for two or three terms, and has been township clerk for the last ten years. He belongs to the Grand Army of the Republic post, and is one of the most influential and public-spirited men in the township. He is engaged in raising grain, and has also given much of his attention to the raising of horses and cattle.

LEWIS S. NELSON, a thorough-going, public-spirited citizen of Adrian, Nobles county, Minnesota, is engaged in the practice of law and is also operating an extensive real estate, farm loan and insurance business. He is one of the influential citizens of the western part of Nobles county, and is known as a man of broad ideas and of large public spirit.

The parents of the subject of our sketch were Seward and Jennie (Hill) Nelson, natives of Norway. They came to the United States in 1842 and settled in Grundy county, Illinois, where our subject was born November 2, 1850. The parents lived on a farm and Lewis S. made his home with them until he was thirteen years old, when both the father and mother died. Then for two years he worked out for farmers and was almost wholly deprived of educational advantages until he was fifteen years old. At that age he determined to apply himself to obtaining an education, and worked on farms during summers to obtain sufficient means to support him, and attending school during the winters until he was eighteen years old. He then entered the Fowler Institute at Newark,

Illinois, and pursued a course of study until graduating from that institution in 1870. He then attended the Norwegian college at Decorah, Iowa, and studied the languages for about a year. One year was then spent in traveling over different parts of the West, during which time he visited all the territories and traveled over a vast scope of country on horseback. Returning to Illinois he taught school during one winter and engaged in farming the following summer, after which he went to Ann Arbor, Michigan, and took up a course of studies in the law department of the State University. Leaving that institution he went to Storey county, Iowa, and engaged in teaching for three terms in the high schools in Cambridge and Colo. In the spring of 1876 he was admitted to the bar in Nevada, Iowa, by Judge Bradley, who was then presiding over a term of the district court. Mr. Nelson then engaged in the practice of law in Colo and Des Moines, Iowa, continuing there until the fall of 1877, when he came to Nobles county, Minnesota, and, after stopping for a brief period, returned to Storey county, where he spent one year in the practice of his profession. The following year, in 1878, he came to Adrian, Minnesota, took a contract to sell lands for the railroad company, and made a permanent location in the county. He has sold a great amount of land, and has built up an extensive practice in law. In working up the sale of his extensive list of lands Mr. Nelson has adopted an admirable plan for giving the public an adequate idea of his prices, terms of sale, and the conditions of the various farms. He publishes and sends to all, free of charge, a neat pamphlet containing an exhaustive description and analysis of the soil, surface, crops, etc., of western Nobles county. He also gives a brief description of the village of Adrian, sets forth in truthful language the merits of his region, and gives answers to all queries likely to arise in the minds of land seekers.

Mr. Nelson is a republican in politics and has always interested himself in the general affairs of the county. He has taken an active part in political affairs and has worked hard and conscientiously to further the principles of the organization to which he belongs. In 1882 he was appointed county superintendent of Nobles county, and the following year was elected judge of probate. He has held various other local offices. He is a member of the Ancient Free and Accepted Mason Lodge, No. 175, of Adrian, of which body he is master. He is also a member of the Living Arch Chapter, No. 28, of Worthington. He is a man of much push and energy and is esteemed for his many excellent business and social qualities.

Mr. Nelson was married in Cambridge, Iowa, June 13, 1887, to Miss Clemma Chandler, daughter of Sereno and Laura (Tellotson) Chandler, natives, respectively, of Maine and Canada. Mrs. Nelson was born in Storey county, Iowa, March 17, 1856. The marriage just recorded has been blessed with the following-named children — Winnie, Pearl, Archie Lee, and Harry Chandler.

JOHN W. ORTON is a reliable and influential citizen of Diamond Lake township, Lincoln county, Minnesota. He is now located on section 8, where he is engaged in general farming and stock raising. He first homesteaded land on section 14, in Royal township of this county, in 1878. He was about the fifth settler in the township and assisted in its organization in 1879. He took a prominent part in the official affairs of the town and was the first supervisor elected in the town. He commenced operations by breaking fifteen acres of land and building a small shanty 14x18 feet and a straw barn 12x16 feet. He left Royal township and

settled in Diamond Lake township in 1882. Since locating in Diamond Lake township he has taken an active part in public matters and has held several official positions, being one of the leading citizens of the township. He was assessor for two years and is at present treasurer of school district No.16, which position he has held for six years. He is engaged largely in general farming and gives special attention to raising blooded horses of the noted Black Hawk breed.

Mr. Orton is a native of Canada, where he was born December 15, 1845. His father, George Orton, was a farmer by occupation and is still living, a resident of Drammen township, Lincoln county. The father was also a native of Canada and in early life was engaged for a number of years as a cloth dresser, later engaged in farming. He is now about sixty-seven years of age. The maiden name of the mother of our subject was Lucy Leroy, a native of Vermont. She died in 1858 and was buried in North Bangor, Franklin county, New York, She was an exemplary Christian lady and was a member of the Methodist Episcopal church. In the father's family there were six children—John W., Lucy M., Joel A., George G., Rowland L. and Rowley L., twins.

The early life of the subject of our sketch was spent in Franklin county, New York, to which place his parents moved in an early day. Here he received his early training and education, and soon after the breaking out of the war, August 21, 1862, he enlisted in Company F, One Hundred and Forty-second Regiment New York Volunteer Infantry, being detailed as a musician for eleven months. He served until the close of the war and was mustered out at Raleigh, North Carolina, while acting on detailed service. Our subject was a brave and faithful soldier and participated in the following battles: Drury's Bluff, Chapman's Farm, Battle of the Wilderness, Fort Fisher, Petersburgh, and many other smaller battles and skirmishes. Our subject saw severe service at the front and received a slight wound in the shoulder at Chapman's Farm. At the close of his military career he returned to New York and for some time assisted his father on the farm. He then spent some time in the lumber woods, from whence he went to Cleveland, Ohio, where he spent two years in learning the boiler-making trade, employed by the firm of Miller & Jameson. After this time had expired he returned to New York State and engaged for a brief period in the milling business. In 1868 he was married, and afterwards engaged in railroading, finding employment as engineer on the Ogdensburg & Lake Champlain Railroad for eight months. His health failed him, however, and he had to give up his profitable engagement with the company. He was advised by his physicians to find a location somewhere in the West. So, coming to the State of Wisconsin, he engaged in farming for seven years in Walworth county. His next move was to Lincoln county, Minnesota, where he has since lived.

July 4, 1868, Mr. Orton was married to Miss Maria L. Crinklaw, a native of Franklin county, New York, and daughter of Andrew Crinklaw, who was a mason by trade. Her father was killed by a falling tree some years ago. Miss Crinklaw was one of seven children—Emily, Maria L., Robert, Horace, Henry, James and Ella. Mr. and Mrs. Orton have been blessed with six children—George, Bertie, Clarence, Mary, Martha and Emily, all still residing at home.

Throughout his life our subject has taken an active interest in the political affairs of the various localities in which he has lived. He has affiliated with the republican party and has taken an active part in the Grand Army of the Republic. While engaged in the railroad business he was a member of the firemen's union and always took an active part in all matters which tended to improve the condition of the laboring man. He is a man of excellent business ability, and has quite a wide reputation as a musician. While in Walworth county, Wisconsin, our subject was a leading spirit in the organization of a brass band, with which he played for five years. Being one of the early settlers of Lincoln county Mr. Orton has passed through many rough experiences, and relates many interesting reminiscences of pioneer days. One of these worthy of mention is the account of the hardships attending a journey on snowshoes one winter. Our subject started from his home on the prairie to Lake Benton, a distance of twenty miles. He purchased one hundred pounds of flour, and nailing a box to his snowshoes, walked over the snow and drew this hastily formed sled over the snow-covered prairies to his home. This was one of the most severe experiences of our subject during those early days, and so exposed was he to the cold that he was confined to his bed for three days after his return home. Mr. Orton's early life in this county has been visited with many like experiences, and he could enumerate many such hardships worthy of mention in a work on pioneer history. He has, however, passed through these stages of trial and hardship, and has succeeded in laying the foundations for a competency in old age. He has accumulated considerable means, and has a pleasant and commodious home. He is a man of the highest character and good business traits, and is respected by all who know him.

———◆◆◈◆◆———

HENRY C. GRASS, ESQ., is one of the leading attorneys of Murray county, Minnesota. He, in fact, is the oldest resident lawyer in the county, making his location here in the village of Currie in July, 1878. He was born in Michigan City, Indiana, July 27, 1855, and was the son of William H. Grass, a native of the State of New York. The father emigrated to the State of Indiana in the year 1853, where he engaged in blacksmithing. He also operated a large wagon and carriage factory and became one of the prominent citizens of that State. In the fall of 1869 the father removed to Winona, Minnesota, and from thence went to St. Charles where he now lives. The father and mother are engaged in the operation of a millinery and fancy goods store. In the father's family there were two children—Henry C. and Charles E. The latter is a telegraph operator in Kansas City.

The early life of the subject of our sketch, Henry C. Grass, was spent with his parents in Indiana, and later in Winona, Minnesota, and still later at St. Charles. In these latter places he received a good English education and studied law in the office of Hon. Edwin Hill. He was admitted to the bar before the district court at Windom, July, 13, 1878. He then located in Currie, where he has been engaged in the active practice of his profession ever since.

Henry C. Grass was married October 30, 1880, to Miss Lettie A. Moore, a native of Vermont. At six years of age she removed with her parents to Chicago, from whence, after two years, she came to Minnesota, settling in Rochester, where she received her training and education. Mr. and Mrs. Grass have one child living, a boy named Charles G. Two died when quite young — Walter and Robert. Mrs. Grass died October 28, 1887, at Woodstock, Pipestone county, Minnesota. She was twenty-seven years of age, and an estimable Christian lady.

Mr. Grass was again married July 24, 1889, to Miss Alice Montana Cooper, at De Soto, Wisconsin. She was born at Radersburgh, Montana, April 15, 1869. When she was but a few weeks old her parents moved to Winona, Minnesota, and in a few months to Preston, Minnesota. When she was six years old they moved to De Soto, Wisconsin. She attended the schools of De Soto until fifteen years old, and then went to the high school at Viroqua, Wisconsin, for one year, after which she attended the First Normal School at Winona, Minnesota, for two years, and graduated at the age of eighteen years. For two years she taught the primary department of the Currie schools.

In politics Mr. Grass affiliates with the republican party, and for four years served as county attorney of Murray county, being elected the first time in 1879. He is at present a member of the school board of the village, having held that position for three years. Our subject is one of the most prominent and able attorneys of the county, and is one of Currie's representative citizens. He takes an active interest in all matters pertaining to the public welfare, and heartily supports any project tending toward development and improvement of his locality.

———————

LAURITZ MARTIN LANGE is the present efficient county attorney of Nobles county, Minnesota, and is one of the leading lawyers of Worthington, the county seat. His parents, Matthias and Julia (Brandt) Lange, were natives of Norway. Our subject was born in Drontheim, Norway, February 12, 1844. His father was an important citizen of his native land and was a man of prominence in military affairs. He was first lieutenant of artillery and was afterwards inspector of prisons.

The subject of this sketch attended a private school and also a military school in his native land until October, 1862, at which time he left home and came to the United States for the purpose of entering the Union army. He first stopped in New York City and remained five days. He then enlisted in Company C, One Hundred and Sixty-fifth Regiment New York Volunteers (Second Battalion, Duryea Zouaves). He served gallantly and faithfully in this company until September 1, 1865. He participated in the battles of Ponchitoula, Louisana, in 1863, Port Hudson, Sabine Pass, etc. In 1864 he participated in the following battles and expeditions: Sabine Cross Roads, Pleasant Hill, Kane River Crossing and Shenandoah campaign under General Sheridan. Our subject ranked as second sergeant and was known throughout the regiment as an excellent and efficient soldier. He participated in the service until September 1, 1865, and then went to New York City, where he engaged in business for a short time. In July, 1866, he enlisted at Governor's Island in the regular service and shortly afterward was assigned to Company I, Thirteenth Regiment United States Infantry, the company being stationed on the island above named for several months. They were then removed to Fort Leavenworth, Kansas, where nine months were spent, and in April, 1867, they were ordered to Montana, where the company joined the regiment; the company was stationed at Fort Shaw. This fortification was built by this regiment and was occupied by them until the fall of 1869, when our subject left the army and went to Chicago and engaged in clerking in an abstract office. Here he commenced the study of law and after removing to Dixon, Illinois, continued his studies during the years 1872–73–74. He was admitted to the bar before the supreme court of Illinois, January 8, 1875, and returned to the city of Chicago. He commenced the practice of his profession and during his residence in Chicago he became prominent in military affairs. For three or four years he was captain of the First Regiment Illinois National

Guards and made his home in Chicago until 1880. In that year he went to Caldwell, Kansas; there he engaged in the practice of his profession until May 29, 1883. At that time he came to Worthington, Minnesota, resumed the practice of law, and has made his home in the village ever since. He has been prominent in political affairs and has held the office of county attorney since 1885, at present serving his third term. He has built up an extensive and lucrative practice and is acknowledged to be one of the best attorneys in Southwestern Minnesota. During his early life he was throughly educated and well equipped both by natural and acquired endowments for the arduous duties of the profession to which he belongs.

Attorney Lange was married in Canandaigua, New York, October 3, 1873, to Miss Anna L. Comstock, daughter of Harlow L. and Jane (Ives) Comstock, natives, respectively, of Vermont and New York. Miss Comstock was born in Warsaw, New York, January 18, 1858. Mr. and Mrs. Lange have had no children of their own, but have one adopted child, Harlow C. Blair, a son of Mrs. Lange's sister, who died when he was three months old. Harlow was born June 3, 1884, his parents being David C. and Catherine (Comstock) Blair.

The subject of our sketch is prominent in Grand Army of the Republic affairs and was commander of the Upton post and judge advocate of the department of Kansas for some time. He has also been commander of the Stoddard post of Worthington and judge advocate of the department of Minnesota. He has also held various other minor positions in the Grand Army of the Republic. He is past master of the Ancient Order of United Workman lodge of Worthington, and is also a member of the Ancient Free and Accepted Masons.

FRED H. KURTH is a reliable farmer located on section 8, of Shaokatan township, Lincoln county, Minnesota. He was born in the State of Illinois, August 27, 1852. He is the son of Henry and Catharine E. (Wehnes) Kurth. The father was born in Sebra, Germany, December 6, 1822. He was the son of Henry Kurth, a farmer by occupation.

Henry, the father of our subject, in his youth assisted in work on the farm. He married Catharine E. Wehnes December 6, 1848. He engaged in different kinds of employment in his native country and came to America in 1851. He worked on a railroad, employed in and about New York City for two years and then located in Illinois. After nine years spent on a farm he came to Steele county, Minnesota, and settled on government land. His stay was brief, however. His friends prevailed on him to return to Illinois. He was one of the first settlers of Steele county and found many Indians scattered over the country. His next move was to Dakota county, Minnesota, where he purchased a farm and lived until 1878. He then came to Lincoln county, becoming one of the pioneer settlers, locating on a homestead and remaining there until his death, which was the result of an accident on the 2d of April, 1889. The facts concerning his death were about as follows: Before breakfast he sent his hired man out to burn an old straw stack about sixty rods west of the house. There was but little wind and the sky was overhung with clouds and it looked very much like rain—it was even sprinkling at the time. He desired to get the stack burned before the rain. About one o'clock the wind shifted to the west and there came up a terrific hurricane. The storm was so violent that one could see but a short distance. Particles of burning straw from the fired stack blew some fifty rods to a small piece of timothy. Here the grass was ignited and the fire ran over the meadow to the barns and stables beyond. There was a straw stack just west of the barn and the fire caught in that and the wind whirled the burning straw all around and over the barn. There were three horses in the barn, and when the fire was about eight or ten rods distant the father thought that he could save the horse nearest the door without putting himself in any danger. He went into the barn, untied the horse but could not, either by force or persuasion get the animal out of the barn. He spent a minute or two using his utmost endeavors to lead the animal out without avail, and looking toward the door he saw that the barn was enveloped in flames and also that the fire had ignited a small hay stack, on one side of the door, and on the other was a load of straw which had been hauled up at noon for bedding, and this too had caught fire. Through this arch of flame it was necessary for him to pass in order to reach safety. He hesitated a moment whether to perish in the burning barn or try to escape through the lane of fire which opened up before his eyes. With despair and a prayer for help he made a dash for his life. He succeeded in getting through the flames and ran to the house, where he commenced looking for his wife as he thought that the house would catch fire every instant. The wife could not be found as she had gone a short distance away to her son Fred's house for help. Not finding her he concluded to make the attempt to save what money he had, which was about sixty dollars and which was in a pocket-book in the house. This was procured, and he ran out of the back door and around to the front door of the house, where he was met by his son Henry, who found his father with nearly all his clothes burned from him. But little was left of his clothing but a shirt and that was on fire.

This was soon extinguished, but on examination it was found that there was no space on the father's body that was not burned almost to a crisp. He lived some thirty-two hours afterward, suffering excruciating agony; when he finally died, his family having been summoned to his bedside. He was a man of deep piety, and, although suffering intense pain, died in the triumphs of Christian faith, his last words being "Savior come." He was a man of the highest integrity and his death was deeply mourned. He left a widow and five children, all of whom are living.

Fred H. Kurth, whose name appears at the head of this sketch, made his home with his parents until he was twenty-two years of age. Until he attained his majority he attended school and also rendered assistance in work on the home farm. One year before leaving home he rented his father's farm in Dakota county and engaged in farming and then sold out all his personal property. Finding another location he again engaged in farming for two years, after which he came to Lincoln county, where he homesteaded the land where he now lives and where he was one of the first settlers. He is a man of good education and excellent business abilities, being held in high esteem as a participant in the public affairs of his township. He has held several official positions, among them being that of justice of the peace, in which position he served for two years. In politics he affiliates with the republican party. He has a fine farm of 240 acres with good buildings.

Fred H. Kurth was married March 14, 1877, to Miss Jennie Gruschus, a daughter of Henry Gruschus. This union has been blessed with four children—Albert H., Asa F., Elma E. and Janet M.

WILLIAM V. KING, the present capable auditor of Jackson county, Minnesota, is a resident of Jackson, the county seat, and is the son of John and Hannah (Hilton) King, natives of England. Our subject is also of English birth, being born at Manchester, September 26, 1831.

Mr. King resided on a farm with his parents until he was twenty-one years of age, up to which time the only schooling he received was what he obtained by private study. He had to labor hard and was confined nearly all the time at home on the farm. He seldom had a holiday, and remembers that during his early life he was thirteen years of age before he ever went to a circus. At thirteen years of age he learned to make brooms, and every evening and during the days in the winter months he had to make them at home. When twenty-one years of age he commenced teaching school, having prepared himself for this occupation by careful private study. During the winter months he followed this profession and worked at home on the farm during the summer months until he was twenty-four years old. After teaching his first winter school he took what he had earned and paid for his tuition during the spring and fall terms in an academy in Janesville, Wisconsin. The family had removed from their native land to Walworth county, Wisconsin, when our subject was nine years of age. At twenty-two Mr. King was superintendent of the village schools of La Grange, having steadily advanced in his profession and acquired a good reputation for ability in that line. He continued teaching and working for his father on the farm until he was twenty-four years of age, when he was married, and moving to a farm engaged in agricultural pursuits. This farm, which he had purchased some time before, adjoined that of his father's, and he made it his home until 1861, when he sold out and moved to Crawford county, purchased land and resided thereon until 1864. He then enlisted in September of that year in Company C, Forty-third Wisconsin Infantry, and served one year, participating in the engagements at Jacksonville, Tennessee. Soon after his enlistment he sold his farm, and on his discharge from the service he came to Minnesota, locating in Austin until the following spring. He then removed to Jackson county and took a homestead on section 28, of Wisconsin township, being one of a party of seven, all from Wisconsin, after which State the township was named. Our subject resided on his farm until 1873, when he was elected county auditor. He then sold his claim and purchased land in Hunter township, which he still owns. After being elected to his important office he removed to the village of Jackson, and served two terms. He then moved to his farm in Hunter township, and made that his home until the fall of 1879, when he was again elected auditor, and again moved to the village, and has held the office, giving excellent satisfaction, and increasing in popularity ever since.

No man in the county, perhaps, has proven as valuable and painstaking a citizen as has Mr. King. His abilities have been recognized in many different ways, and especially can this be seen from the fact that he has held most of the important offices of the county. In 1867 he was elected judge of probate and held the office for six years. He was county superintendent of schools for two years and for the same length of time: while auditor held the office of county attorney. Wherever he has been, throughout his entire life, his abilities have proven of such a high order that he has been called upon to serve his fellow-citizens in various important positions of trust and responsibility. He held various positions in Wisconsin. He was the second chairman of the board of township supervisors in his township, that civil division then comprising a territory now occupied by five townships. The first presidential vote of our subject was cast for John C. Hale, of Massachusetts, a free-soil candidate. There were only two other votes of that kind in his locality. His next presidential vote was cast for J. C. Fremont, and he has voted the republican ticket ever since. It is worthy of note that when our subject voted for Fremont, although his township had been democratic for years prior to this time, the vote stood 287 for Fremont and 27 for Buchanan, our subject being the township clerk at the time. Besides owning his fine farm Mr. King also possesses an excellent residence in the village of Jackson. He is a member of the Ancient Free and Accepted Masons, the Independent Order of Odd Fellows and the Grand Army of the Republic, and also of the P. of H., U. L. and Farmers' Alliance.

At Troy, Wisconsin, March 27, 1856, Miss Antoinette L. Porter was married to Mr. King. She was the daughter of S. S. and Cornelia (Dann) Porter, natives, respectively, of New York and Connecticut. She was born in New York City, December 12, 1835. Her father printed the first newspaper in Madison, Wisconsin. Mr. and Mrs. King have been blessed with the following-named children—William P., Selah S., Nellie G. and John L. William P. married Mary E. Trumbull, who died February 28, 1887, leaving one child, Mary G. He is now a photographer of Windom. Nellie G. married E. W. Davies, a banker of Pipestone. Selah S. resides in Jasper, Pipestone county, Minnesota, where he is postmaster and editor of the Jasper *Journal*. John L. King is with his brother, Selah S., assisting in the management of his newspaper enterprise.

JOHN BISBEE, senior member of the firm of Bisbee & Olson, is at the head of the largest mercantile establishment in Watonwan county, Minnesota, the business being located at Madelia. Besides dealing in general merchandise, the firm also handles grain.

Mr. Bisbee is a native of Oxford county, Maine, where he was born April 16, 1839. His parents were Jones and Rebecca (Robinson) Bisbee, natives of the same place. The father was a farmer by occupation, and was the son of John and Sarah (Pilbrook) Bisbee, natives of Maine. John Bisbee was a farmer, and was the son of Charles Bisbee, a native of Massachusetts and a farmer. He was a soldier in the Revolutionary War. Thomas Bisbee, the founder of this family, came from England in about 1635, and resided in Massachusetts. He was a large landholder in England, and bequeathed his property to his grandchildren. He was a member of the Massachusetts assembly. The father of the subject of our sketch was reared on a farm and followed that occupation throughout his life, becoming one of the wealthiest farmers in his locality. He died in 1875, having throughout his life affiliated with the democratic party. The mother of our subject was the daughter of Increase and Abbie (Parlin) Robinson, natives of Maine. Increase Robinson was a farmer and mill owner, and owned large tracts of land in Maine. He was of Scotch-Irish descent. Our subject's mother is now a resident of Madelia, and has reached the age of seventy-five years. Our subject had but one brother, Sylvester, who resides in Madelia.

John Bisbee was reared a farmer's boy, continuing with his parents and receiving a common-school education until he was eighteen years of age. After this time he taught several terms of school, and, locating in Massachusetts, was a clerk in a store for about a year. He went on a fishing expedition down the Gulf of St. Lawrence, spending the summer, and then returned to the Auburn Academy, where he finished his education. He then accepted a position in a wholesale boot and shoe house in New York City, continuing with the company for two and a half years. On the breaking out of the war he returned to his home in Maine and taught school and also engaged somewhat in farming up to 1865. He then came to Minnesota and settled at Garden City, Blue Earth county, where he purchased a farm and also engaged in teaching school. For four years he clerked in a general store and then came to Madelia and was employed in the store of Boynton & Cheeney for four and a half years. He then associated himself with Mathias Olson and opened their mammoth general store, in which business they have continued ever since. Our subject has also a fine farm of four hundred acres about five miles from town, and has it well stocked with fine cattle, horses, sheep and hogs. He also owns one hundred and fifty acres adjoining the town site and a beautiful home on seven and a half acres on Main street. This is one of the most delightful residence places in the village and is beautified with shade and ornamental trees. Our subject has been actively engaged in building up his mercantile business. He is careful and cautious in his investments and has accumulated considerable means. He has also taken an active interest in village and county matters and has with credit and honor filled various official positions. He is at present a member of the village council, of which he was president for some time. In politics he is a believer in the principles of the democratic party. He is a member of the Masonic fraternity and is well known and highly esteemed throughout the entire county. He is a man of large means and assists liberally in all public projects.

Mr. Bisbee was married in the year 1863 to Miss Ardelia Small, of Wilton, Maine, and daughter of Jeremiah and Mary (Merrill) Small, farmers in and natives of Maine. Mr. and Mrs. Bisbee have had twelve children—

Melvina F., J. Oscar, Samuel S., Edgar C., Albert J., Mabel A., Arthur L., Frank J., Maurice S., Elmer, Everett H. and Carroll.

JOHN ALFRED SINCLAIR, one of the leading business men of Fairmont, Martin county, Minnesota, is a native of Great Britain, born in Brampton, County Cumberland, England, October 24, 1852.

Until he was nearly seventeen years of age our subject attended school, and then commenced working in his father's dry goods store, continuing in the business until he was nineteen years of age. He then went to Langholm, Scotland, as book-keeper for his brother Thomas in a large woolen mill, continuing with him for three years, or until his father died, in 1873, when he returned home. He then went to London and entered a large dry goods store to learn more about the business, intending to enter a partnership with his brother Frederick in the operation of the store of the father. Remaining in London for about a year his health failed and he returned home. His brother H. W. was also in poor health, and they concluded to come to America. They came to this country, locating, in 1876, in Martin county, Minnesota. They worked out for a couple of years in order to recover their health and learn something of the country. Our subject then engaged in clerking in the Martin County Bank, and after a short time purchased a one-half interest in a hardware store owned by J. A. Houghtaling. He still retains his interest in that business. In 1880 he started an important enterprise in the county known as the Chain Lake Creamery, which he is still operating. When our subject commenced in the creamery business he formed a partnership with Mr. Marsten, with whom he continued for a year, and then purchased the entire plant, and has continued the operation of the business as sole pro-

prietor ever since. He operates on the "gathered cream" system, and manages an extensive business to the satisfaction of his patrons and with fair financial success to himself.

Since coming to the county, Mr. Sinclair has proven an active, public-spirited citizen, and has been a valuable factor in the establishment and building up of important business enterprises. He is president of the Martin County Agricultural Society, which position he has held for three years. He has been treasurer of the Independent Order of Odd Fellows for four years, and senior warden of the Episcopal Church for the same length of time.

Mr. Sinclair was married in Fairmont, April 9, 1885, to Henrietta Wollaston, daughter of Percy and Catharine (Mossop) Wollaston, natives of England. Miss Wollaston was born in Huyton, near Liverpool, England, December 20, 1864. Mr. and Mrs. Sinclair have two children—Harold Percy and Wilifrid.

JOHN NELSON settled in Eden township, Pipestone county, Minnesota, when there was not a house in the whole town. His settlement was made on section 34, where he still lives.

The subject of our sketch was a native of Norway, where he was born February 10, 1846. His parents were Ole and Aslaug Nelson, who were farmers by occupation and natives of Norway. When our subject was but five years of age his mother died in the old country. In 1861 the father brought his family to America, landing in the city of Quebec, whence, by way of Montreal, they went to Chicago, remaining but a few days. The family then removed to Lansing, Iowa, going to Prairie du Chien by rail, whence, by steamer, they went to Lansing. The father remained in the neighborhood of the latter named city until 1879, when he removed to Eden township, Pipe-stone county, where he is still living.

The subject of our sketch remained on his father's farm in Norway, being given the educational advantages afforded by the district school, until 1861, when, as we have already stated, the family removed to the United States, when he attended the common district school until October 5, 1863, when Mr. Nelson enlisted in Company F, Ninth Iowa Cavalry, and continued in the service until the close of the war, being mustered out February 3, 1866, at Little Rock, Arkansas. He saw much severe army service, and was for some time in the general hospital at Little Rock. On being discharged from the service he returned to Lansing, Iowa, where, after engaging in different kinds of work for about a year, he purchased his father's farm. He continued the operation of this piece of property until 1877, when he came to Pipestone county, Minnesota, settling on a claim in Eden township, where he now lives. His settlement was made in June, 1877, and this was the second claim taken in the township. He at once commenced his farming operations, broke twenty acres of land, and put up a house fourteen by sixteen feet with eight-foot posts, this being the first dwelling house in the township. Remaining on his farm until in October of that year, he then returned to Allamakee county, Iowa, where he stayed during the ensuing winter. The following spring he brought his family to Eden township, and made a permanent settlement.

The marriage of the subject of our sketch occurred October 23, 1873, when he was wedded to Miss Anna R. Okre, a native of Allamakee county, Iowa. Miss Okre was born the 16th day of February, 1855. Mr. and Mrs. Nelson have had six children, all of whom are living at the present time—Otto A., Mary J., Joseph L., Selma A., Clara L. D. and Hulda M.

Mr. Nelson has watched with interest the growth in prosperity of the township in which he lives, and has also the satisfaction of knowing that the town has grown in wealth. When he settled in the town he had but little means, while to-day he has an excellent farm, provided with good buildings, and owns considerable stock. He is an intelligent and systematic farmer, and has brought his land to a high state of cultivation. In politics he affiliates with the republican party, and at one time was a member of the Nara lodge, R. H. K., of Lansing and Village Creek, Iowa. He is a member of the Simon Mix post, No. 95, Grand Army of the Republic. In political matters Mr. Nelson takes an active interest, and his services in official positions have been required by his constituents at various times. He has been township assessor for six years, and has been a member of the board of school directors ever since the school district was organized. He is a good citizen, and a man of high character. After returning from the war he was president of the school district and a member of the school board for seven years, in Allamakee county, Iowa. In religious matters he is a member of the Lutheran church, and takes an active part in its doings.

* * *

IRA C. HILL resides in the village of Huntley, Faribault county, Minnesota, where he is engaged in the grain and machinery business, being in the employ of the Huntley Warehouse Association. He came to Faribault county in October, 1863, in company with his father, and purchased a farm on section 17, of Verona township. The father's name was Felix Hill. He followed farming throughout his life, and died in 1887. He was a native of the State of New York, where he was reared and educated. He was a man of much enterprise, and took an active interest in all public matters. He served on the township board of supervisors for one year. Our subject's mother's maiden name was Julia Ann Hover, a native of New York, and is still living. The parents were members of the Baptist church. Our subject was one of eight children—Ira C., James F., Elizabeth, Orpha, Adelbert, William, Josephine and Charles.

The subject of our sketch is a native of New York, and was born in Chemung county, March 9, 1848. He was reared in his native county until he was eight years old, at which time the family moved to Waushara county, Wisconsin. After a two year's residence they went to Green Lake county, and remained there until 1863, when they came to Minnesota, locating on section 17 of Verona township, Faribault county. January 28, 1864, Mr. Hill enlisted in the Ninth Regiment Minnesota Volunteer Infantry, at this time being but fifteen years of age. He was eager to join the service, however, and, going with his company to the front, participated in the battles of Tupelo, Old Town Creek, Nashville, Spanish Fort, Blakeley and a number of skirmishes and battles of minor importance. He was discharged as a private, in August, 1865, at Fort Snelling, having served most of the time under Captain H. B. Walker. After being discharged, Mr. Hill returned to his home in Faribault county, and remained on the home farm for some three years. He then engaged at working out at various lines of business until 1877, then engaged in farming on his farm on section 18, Verona township, until 1888, when he accepted the position he now occupies as manager of the affairs of the Huntley Warehouse Association.

On the 27th day of May, 1878, Miss Jennie Rhoades was united in marriage with Mr. Hill. She was born in Essex county, New York, in 1853, and was the daughter of Elisha Rhoades, a farmer, and one of the first settlers of Verona township, where he has

been one of its prominent citizens. During her early life Mrs. Hill was thoroughly educated, and for several years before her marriage engaged in the profession of teaching. She was educated in the high school of Winnebago City. Mr. and Mrs. Hill have two children—Felix and Susie.

The political affiliations of the subject of this sketch are with the republican party, with which organization he has associated for many years. He is a man of strong religious sentiments, and is a member of the Free-Will Baptist church, being chairman of the board of trustees, and a member of the building committee of that society. In the general affairs of the township he takes an active interest, and is now the chairman of the board of township supervisors, having been elected to that position in the spring of 1889. He is a member of the Odd Fellows fraternity, and, as a man and citizen, is looked upon with high respect by all with whom he has to do.

CHARLES E. WELD was elected county auditor of Murray county Minnesota, in the fall of 1886, and is the present incumbent of that position. He has been intimately associated with the official history of Murray county, and for three years prior to 1886 he was a member of the board of county commissioners elected from Des Moines River township.

Charles E. Weld was born in the township of Cornville, Somerset county, Maine, June 16, 1856. He was the son of Rev. William M. Weld, a clergyman of the Congregational church. The father was a native of Maine and came to Minnesota in 1857, locating in Greenwood Prairie, Wabasha county. He died in July, 1885. He was a man of scholarly attainments and was an influential and highly respected citizen. The mother of our subject was Minerva (Lawrence) Weld, a native of Boonville, Oneida county, New York. She died April 2, 1867. In the father's family there were six children.

The subject of our sketch came to Minnesota with his parents when a child. He received his education in Wabasha county, where he lived for fourteen years. His residence was then taken up at Marine Mills, in Washington county, Minnesota, where, during one winter, he went to school, and the following summer engaged in clerking in a general store owned by Walker, Judd & Veazie. After six years of profitable engagement with this firm he then clerked on a freight and passenger steamboat for the St. Croix Packet Company for two seasons; and during the winter of 1877–78 spent his time in St. Paul, attending the St. Paul Business College. In February, 1879, he came to Murray county, and became one of the early settlers of Des Moines River township, locating on section 22, where he engaged in farming and stock raising, and remained until he took charge of the office which he now fills. While living there he took an active part in public matters, and held various township and school district offices.

Mr. Weld was united in marriage, May 3, 1882, to Miss Dora J. Allen, who was born in St. Anthony Falls, now East Minneapolis. Early in life she went with her parents to Marine Mills, where she received her early training and education. Her education was completed in the high school of Minneapolis. She was a daughter of B. F. Allen, a lumberman, who is still living. He was formerly from Maine. Mr. and Mrs. Weld have been blessed with two children — Mabel and Rachel.

Our subject has proven one of the most efficient and popular officers, and has become quite prominent in the local affairs of the republican party. He has been a member of the Independent Order of Old Fellows since he was twenty-one years of age, and has held various positions of honor in that organization. He is also a member of the Modern Woodmen of America. In the administration of the affairs of his office Mr. Weld has always given entire satisfaction, by virtue of his manly and courteous bearing and also because he is possessed of excellent business qualifications. As a citizen and man he stands the peer of any in the county.

ORRIN NASON is one of the early settlers of Cottonwood county, Minn., having located here in 1869 in Springfield township. He settled on eighty acres of land and made that his home until 1873. He then moved to the present site of the village of Windom. On the organization of the county our subject was appointed county surveyor, and has held the office ever since, with the exception of three terms. After moving to the village he took a contract to carry the mail to and from Jackson, for a period of two years. He took a second contract for the same term, but soon after sold out and opened a livery stable, which he operated until 1876. He then went to Great Bend, Kansas, and occupied his time in surveying, going thence to Missouri, where he worked for a railroad company. In the spring of 1877 he entered the employ of the Minneapolis & St. Louis railroad, and was given charge of a large force of men putting in piling and building culverts between Jordan and Waterville, Minnesota. He came to Windom the same year, and in the fall was elected clerk of the county courts. He served in this capacity for nine years, and was one of the most efficient clerks that the county has ever had. He is now serving as justice of the peace and is the present surveyor of the county. He has always taken an active interest in matters of a public nature, and has been county commissioner; was also assessor of Springfield township for some time.

The subject of our sketch was born in the State of Vermont. August 1, 1835. He is the son of William and Lovina (Lyon) Nason, natives, respectively, of Connecticut and Vermont. The father was a farmer, and was in the War of 1812. He came to Minnesota in 1857 and settled in Le Sueur county, where he engaged in farming in Kasota township. He died at Windom in 1882, at the age of ninety-two years, two months and twenty days. The mother died in 1871, in Le Sueur county, being seventy-four years, nine months and twenty-nine days old. In the father's family were the following named children: Thomas C., Roswell L., both of whom served in the union army; William and seven sisters are now living—Electa A., Kesia, Ellen M., Calista, Emiline, Juliana L. and Fannie. The first child was Roswell, born in 1816. He was murdered in 1841 at Plattsburg, New York.

Our subject received the training usually given in that day, and had the privilege of attending the district school. He commenced surveying as a business in Indiana when eighteen years of age, to which State he had gone in 1853. In 1856 he came to Minnesota, locating in Le Sueur county, and engaging in farming until 1858, when he took a contract to carry the mails from Mankato to Sioux City for four years. The first mail he carried on foot, swimming the rivers and plodding along over the prairies, making but slow time on his mail route. August 19, 1862, he enlisted in Company K, Seventh Minnesota Infantry, and served three years. He engaged in the following named battles: Nashville, Spanish Fort, Blakeley, and numerous other battles and skirmishes. He was in the artillery service under General Sibley on an expedition in Minnesota and Dakota. After his discharge

from the service our subject returned to Le Sueur county, and thence to Mankato, where he engaged in photography. He remained some three years, and then came to Cottonwood county.

Mr. Nason was married, in 1866, to Miss Elizabeth A. Thomas, of Jackson, Minnesota. Mr. and Mrs. Nason have one adopted child, Clyde A , aged fourteen years.

The subject of our sketch has been quite successful in his business since coming to Windom, and owns considerable property. He still owns and rents his farm. On the north side of the square at Windom he owns a large business building, in the front part of which he has a billiard hall, and has a residence in the rear. In politics he affiliates with the democratic party, and is a member of the Masonic and Odd Fellow fraternities.

EORGE H. GURLEY is the present county treasurer of Pipestone county, Minnesota, and resides in Pipestone city, where he has gathered a large circle of friends, and where he has lived since 1880. Mr. Gurley is one of the most popular men of Pipestone county, and his abilities to execute the duties of his office have been proven beyond all doubt. He was born in St. Lawrence county, New York, April 25, 1854, his parents being William R. and Louisa H. (Wallace) Gurley. The father was a native of St. Lawrence county, and the mother a native of Essex county, New York. The father was an extensive farmer in his native State, and is still living engaged in that occupation. Throughout his life he has been a man of considerable prominence in the public affairs of his locality, and has held numerous positions of trust and responsibility. For the long period of twenty-four years he was assessor of the county in which he lived. He made a specialty of dairying and operated a large dairy for a number of years. The mother of our subject died in February, 1881. In the father's family there were four children, three of whom are now living—George H., J. Frank and William W. George H., our subject, came to Pipestone in 1880, and engaged in the hardware business. On first coming to the city he purchased business property on Olive street. William W. came to Pipestone in 1885. J. Frank is residing on and operating the home farm in New York, the father having retired from active business. The grandparents of the subject of our sketch were John S. and Nancy (Spink) Gurley, natives, respectively, of Connecticut and Rhode Island. The grandfather was a farmer by occupation, and while in early life he removed to St. Lawrence county, New York, where he resided for some fifty years. The grandfather had a family of four children, two of whom are now living—George G. and William R. The parents of the mother of the subject of our sketch were Thomas N. and Betsey (Stower) Wallace, both natives of Vermont and farmers by occupation. In the Wallace family there were ten children, five of whom are now living—Mrs. Anna Benjamin, Charles and William (twins), Edwin, Mrs. George H. Perry and John S.

The parents of the subject of our sketch were members of the Universalist church, and in that belief our subject was reared. He spent his younger days with his parents engaged in work on the home farm, and also attending the district schools at every opportunity, remaining with his parents until he was twenty-one years of age. In 1877 he came west to Minnesota, first stopping in Winnebago City, Faribault county. While in that city he clerked in a hardware store for some two years, and in 1880 returned home on a short visit. He then again came west and settled at once in Pipestone City, where he engaged in the hardware business, as has already been stated. The firm of Gurley Brothers was formed in January, 1889, and is now doing an immense business, carrying a large and valuable stock of goods in their line. Besides his business in the city, he is also interested largely in farming enterprises, and keeps some sixteen head of blooded horses. One of his farms is located within the corporate limits of Pipestone City. Soon after coming to the city he purchased lots and erected a very fine residence on French street, costing somewhat over $1,800.

Mr. Gurley was married in 1881 to Miss Amelia D. Poulin, a native of West Stockholm, New York. This lady was the daughter of Narsess and Betsey (Smith) Poulin, natives of Ontario, Canada. The parents are now living in Pipestone, to which city they came in 1888.

In politics the subject of our sketch has affiliated with the republican party for many years, and since becoming a resident of this county has occupied a prominent place in the local affairs of that organization. He has become one of the most popular men in the party, and is an important factor in its councils. He has been interested largely in the financial development of the city and has done much, both in financial and other ways, to build up the city that he has made his home.

ERMAN NELSON is one of the leading business men of Slayton, Minnesota. He is the son of Swan and Eliza (Olson) Nelson, natives of Sweden. In about 1868 the parents came to the United States, locating in Decorah, Iowa, where the father engaged in work at the carpenter's trade. In 1871 they came to Murray county, Minnesota.

Herman Nelson was born November 22, 1855, in Estersund, Sweden. He resided on a farm with his parents and attended school until he was sixteen years of age, when the family came to the United States, locating in Iowa. Our subject continued at the parental residence for about three years, after which he moved to Murray county, Minnesota, in 1872. After locating in Murray county, our subject remained with his parents for about a year assisting in work on the home farm. He then took a homestead on section 4 in Leeds township. Here he remained during the greater part of the time until 1881. The hardships through which our subject, with all the other early settlers, passed are hard to describe. It is almost impossible to fully show what a disastrous scourge the grasshoppers proved. During four years all kinds of crops were entirely destroyed, and during this time the heads of families had to go to other localities in order to support their families. In 1881 our subject sold his farm and went to the village of Hadley, where he engaged in the general mercantile business. He remained in that village until 1887, and then sold out and located in Slayton, where he put in an excellent stock of general merchandise. He is a leading merchant of the village, and is building up an extensive and profitable business. Since coming to the township he has taken an active part in public matters, and has proven his efficiency as a citizen and business man by holding various official positions. He has been treasurer of the township for some five years, and has been a member of the village council. He is an influential member of the Independent Order of Odd Fellows, and belongs to the Swedish Lutheran church of Slayton. He is a man of excellent business qualifications, and has accumulated large means. He is careful and systematic in all his transactions, and enjoys the confidence of all his business associates.

Mr. Nelson was married in Kasson, Dodge county, Minnesota, in October, 1877, to Miss Betsey Peterson, daughter of Iver Peterson, a native of the Kingdom of Norway. This lady was born in the State of Iowa, where she was reared and educated. Mr. and Mrs. Nelson have been blessed with two children—George Leonard and Sadie Isabel.

JOHN BAKER EDWARDS is at present engaged in the general mercantile business in Winnebago City, Minnesota. He is a native of England, where he was born in 1827. His parents were Michael and Hannah (Horn) Baker. The father was engaged for many years in his native land as a manufacturer of various kinds of cloth goods. He came to the United States in 1862, the mother having died in England some years before. The father engaged in active business life at cloth manufacturing in various parts of the Union during most of his days and finally retired and died at Winnebago City in 1886. In the father's family there were four children—George, Joseph, Mary and John. George and Joseph are residents of Faribault county, Minnesota, and Mary is still a resident of England.

The subject of our sketch spent the early years of his live in his native land, where he was given excellent educational advantages. In connection with other lines of occupation he taught school for many years and also learned the cloth making business. Coming to America with his wife in 1851, he settled in Grundy county, Illinois, continuing his residence there until July, 1857. He then came to Winnebago City, Faribault county, Minnesota, and located a pre-emption of 160 acres of land about a mile and a half from the village. His first improvement was the building of a log house with a bark roof and no floor. After residing in that for some time he later put up a comfortable frame dwelling-house and other out-buildings. At this time there were but few settlers in this locality and our subject and his family experienced many hardships. Although bringing some thirteen hundred dollars with him, the comforts and much less the luxuries of life could not be had. His nearest mill market was over thirty miles distant, at Mankota, Blue Earth county. Passing through these early pioneer experiences, however, our subject continued improving his farm until 1883, when he sold out. Prior to this time, however, for five years he had charge of woolen mills. For three years he had charge of the woolen mills at Mankota, and for two years at Preston. During one year he leased a woolen mill, employed thirteen men and operated a most successful business, turning out a fine quality of goods. With the exception of two years, the family resided on the farm. In 1883 Mr. Edwards removed to Winnebago City, and engaged in the mercantile business, which he has since carried on.

The subject of our sketch was married in 1851 to Miss Elizabeth Holgate, a native of Yorkshire, England. There are now six children in Mr. Edwards' family—Martha, Ninnie, Sadie, Addie, Frank and Ralph. Martha married Mr. Lot and has had six children—Edith, Roy, Harry, Ethel, Herbert and Ray. Minnie married A. J. Simon, by whom she has had three children—Ray, Fay and Olive. Sadie married G. D. Eygabroad, of Winnebago City. Addie married Judson Miner, by whom she has had two children—Paul and Estella. Rusha E., now deceased, married Mr. Sperry and died leaving two children—Maude and Guy. James, the oldest child, died at seventeen years of age.

The subject of our sketch has been quite prominent in the affairs of the republican party, of which he is a member and has held various official positions. He has been an active business man ever since locating in the county and has done much to bring Winnebago City and locality up to its present pros-

perous condition. He is a man of good character and is highly respected by all who know him.

NILS S. TAARUD is the able and efficient treasurer of Murray county, Minnesota. He was elected to that position in 1882, and at each succeeding election since then he has been reinstated in the office. He made his location in the county in 1872, and first settled in Dovray township, where he remained some ten years. He homesteaded land on section 4 of that township, and was the first actual settler. He assisted in the organization of his town, and became one of its leading citizens. He was township treasurer, and held various other positions, continuing his residence on the farm until being elected to his present office. He then moved to the village of Currie, where he has since resided. He also interested himself while in Dovray township in educational matters, and held various school offices. That township was named after the birthplace of our subject.

Nils S. Taarud was born in Dovray, in the kingdom of Norway, June 6, 1842. He resided in his native land until twenty-five years of age, up to which time he had been engaged in work on the home farm, and had attended the common schools at every opportunity. He obtained a good practical education. In 1867 he concluded to come to America. He first settled in Blue Earth county, remaining in Mankato during the first winter, and from thence going to Butternut Valley, same county, where he remained some five years engaged in farming. He then removed to Murray county and settled as stated in the opening lines of this sketch. Mr. Taarud was the son of Simon T. and Thora (Wiger) Taarud, both natives of Norway. The father died in his native land when our subject was about eighteen years of age. The mother died in 1878. In the father's family there were six children—Engebret, John, Anna, Lena, Hans and Nils.

Mr. Taarud was married December 11, 1872, to Christina Tusty, a native of Norway, where she was reared and educated until she was eighteen years of age. She then came to the United States, locating for a time in Goodhue county, Minnesota. Mr. and Mrs. Taarud have seven living children—Simon, Charlie, Lena, Pearlie, Clara, Nellie and Emil.

The political preferences of the subject of our sketch are with the republican party. He is a man of stanch temperance principles, and was formerly a member of the temperance lodge, of which he was financial secretary for some time. He is a man of excellent business abilities, and is held in high esteem by all who know him. He has served in his present official position for a number of years, and has become popular as a public servant.

WILLIAM H. HALBERT is the cashier of the Security Bank of Luverne, Minnesota. He came to Rock county in 1872, and has since been a permanent resident. He took a homestead of 160 acres in Magnolia township, building a house of boards and sod 12x16, and improving the land until the fall of 1876. At this time he was elected register of deeds of the county and served three consecutive terms. He made a very efficient officer and served his constituency with honor and credit. He was then appointed to serve out the unexpired term of W. O. Croford as county auditor, and after that time had expired he was elected to the position for two successive terms. At this time he declined a third nomination which was tendered him, and gave his attention to his other business enter-

prises, which had been demanding his care for some time. He assisted in the organization of the First National Bank, one of the most important financial institutions of the city, and, in January, 1887, accepted the position of cashier, serving about one year. Then, in company with several others, he organized the Security Bank of Luverne, of which he has since been cashier. Throughout his career in this county he has held numerous positions of trust and responsibility. While a resident of Magnolia township he served as town clerk for two terms, was chairman of the board of supervisors for two terms, and was clerk of the school board throughout his entire residence in the town. Since coming to the village of Luverne he has taken an active interest in educational matters, and for some time was clerk of the school board. In 1882 he was elected mayor of the city, and served one term, declining a renomination. In March, 1886, he was appointed by the governor of Minnesota captain of the State militia, and organized Company F, Third Regiment, at Luverne, of which he is now captain.

The gentleman whose name appears at the head of this sketch was born in Erie county, Pennsylvania, August 3, 1840. His parents, James and Sallie M. (Eastman) Halbert, were natives of Otsego county, New York. The father followed the occupation of farming, and moved to Pennsylvania in 1837. In 1843 the family moved to McHenry county, Illinois, where they settled on a farm and where the father remained until his death, which occurred in 1857. The mother is still a resident of the State of Illinois. In the father's family there were eight children, five of whom are now living —Lydia, now Mrs. Giles; Louise, now Mrs. Johnson; William H., Thomas, a farmer of Phillips county, Kansas, and James W., now engaged in farming in Washington Territory.

William H. Halbert was reared on a farm, where his younger days were spent with his parents. He received a limited common-school education in the districts schools, and a short time before becoming twenty-one years of age enlisted in Company I, Eighth Illinois Cavalry, as a private. He served three years and one month, and after being in the army for two years was made corporal of his company. He participated in all of the battles of the Army of the Potomac from 1861 until the battle of Petersburg, and served on duty all of this time with the exception of about fifteen days. In December, 1863, he was granted a furlough of fifteen days, just mentioned, for meritorious conduct in an engagement in which he had participated. He was slightly wounded at the battle of the Wilderness and severely wounded at Muddy Branch, Maryland, at which latter place he had his right foot broken by his horse falling on him. This latter accident laid him up for some twelve months. After his return from the service he taught school some two terms. Shortly after this he was married and moved to Grundy county, Iowa, where he purchased a farm and engaged in agricultural pursuits for four years, and then sold out and came to Rock county, Minnesota. He was one of the organizers of Magnolia township, and was one of the officers that started the building of the first school house in the township. He became a man of considerable prominence, and was widely known throughout Southern Minnesota. Because of his influence and well-known excellent qualities for such line of work he was appointed by the State authorities as one of the three commissioners who laid out and built the road from Worthington to the Dakota line in 1873.

Mr. Halbert was married to Miss Ellen Van Hoesen, of Huntly Grove, Illinois, and daughter of R. C. Van Hoesen. This lady died in 1880. In 1881 our subject was married to Miss Della E. Gilham, a daughter of Josiah Gilham, of Luverne. Mr. Halbert has had a family of three children—William E., who died at four years of age; Jessie O., and Beatrice E.

In political and civic matters our subject takes a prominent place and is intimately associated with several of the leading organizations. He affiliates with the republican party, and has been a member of the Masonic fraternity for twenty-three years, having served in that organization as secretary for three terms, junior warden three terms, senior warden two terms, worshipful master four terms, and is now serving his third term as deputy district grand master. He is an influential member of the Grand Army of the Republic, and is commander of John A. Dix post, No. 96, at Luverne, which he helped to organize. In all matters tending to the growth and prosperity of the city he has taken an active interest, and has materially aided with moral and financial support. He is treasurer of the Rock County Loan and Building Association, which he helped to organize. Having come to the county in an early day, he has also become intimately identified with the Old Settlers' society of Rock county, of which he is the present treasurer. He lives in an elegant residence in the city, and has a pleasant and agreeable family. He is public-spirited, broad-minded, and has been one of the most important factors in bringing about the present state of growth and development to which Luverne has attained. As a citizen he is loyal in his adherence to the principles of right government, and as a friend and benefactor he has gained an enviable reputation. His financial career has been one of the most successful and praiseworthy in the county, and he has planted himself firmly in the esteem and confidence of his fellow-citizens.

THOMAS H. REYNOLDS is a prominent citizen of Verdi township, Lincoln county, Minnesota. He is engaged in general farming and stock raising on section 26 of that township.

Mr. Reynolds was born in England, March 20, 1835, and is the son of William and Hannah (Hancock) Reynolds, also natives of England. The father was a builder by occupation, and resided in his native land until his death. Thomas H. remained under parental authority, reaping the benefits of his father's life and experience, and being given a good common school education until he reached the age of eighteen years. He attended school until he was thirteen years of age, and then learned the grocery and pro vision business. His first location was in the grocery and provision business in Romsey, Hampshire, England. He clerked there for about one year and then went to Dorchester, county Dorset, where he lived for three years, engaged in clerking. Thence he removed to Weymouth, same county, and engaged in the grocery business for himself. He remained in his native land until June, 1873, at which time he came to America, first locating in Glyndon, Minnesota. Remaining in that village until in September, he then removed to Minneapolis, which city was made his home until the fall of 1878. He then came by rail to the village of Marshall, Lyon county, whence he took a team and drove across the country to section 26, Verdi township, where he located his present homestead. He lived on the homestead until early in 1888, when he purchased a farm adjoining, to which he moved. He now owns 320 acres of fine land. During his early life spent in Lincoln county he saw much hardship attending his pioneer life. His only market for all kinds of grain was at Marshall, forty-five miles distant, and during the winter it was impossible to go to that point, which was also their milling

point. Our subject and family, as well as many other settlers, were obliged to live on boiled wheat, the weather being so intensely cold that it was impossible to go to mill to obtain flour. During that winter he had no team, and many a time has Mr. Reynolds walked to Lake Benton village and brought back supplies on his shoulders. These were hard times, but they have been forgotten in the good results and prosperity which has come of late years to our subject as well as to other settlers.

The subject of our sketch was married, February 9, 1864, to Caroline Harvey. She was born in County of Essex, and was the daughter of Charles and Elizabeth (Clay) Harvey. Her parents were natives of England, and were farmers by occupation. Mr. and Mrs. Reynolds have been blessed with six children—Caroline E., Ellen H., Charles W., Frederick H., Thomas C. and Mary E.

Ever since coming to Verdi township Mr. Reynolds has participated in public matters and has held several official positions, among them being that of township clerk, in which position he is now serving on his fifth term. In politics he believes in the principles of the republican party, and has always cast his ballot for the man supported by that party. He is a man of irreproachable character, loyal and true in his citizenship, and is esteemed by a wide circle of friends. His farm is under good cultivation, and he has it provided with excellent farm buildings.

＊－－＊－ ＞◆◈◆＜ －◆－＊－－

CHARLES W. HILDRETH is a leading citizen of Worthington, Nobles county, Minnesota. He was born in Wellsborough, Tioga county, Pennsylvania, April 21, 1822. His parents were Luther R. and Belinda (Butler) Hildreth, natives of New Hampshire. The mother died when our subject was four months old.

After his mother's death our subject was taken to live with her parents, and at this time his father left the country, and he has never heard from him since. Charles W. resided with his grandparents until he was ten years of age, when he commenced working for farmers in his locality. He followed this occupation until he was fourteen years old, and then went to the woods and engaged in lumbering, following that occupation until the spring of 1861. At the age of twenty, in 1842, the accidental discharge of a rifle so wounded our subject in his arm that he had to have it amputated above the elbow. This has disabled him throughout life, and he has not been able to do the work of other men. For twenty years he was engaged as a raftsman, and was one of the most successful men in that line on the river. So successful was he during this time that fifty dollars would cover all the loss that ever occurred to all the fleets he piloted. In the spring of 1861 he started down the river, but owing to the low stage of the water he was obliged to turn his attention elsewhere. He went to Milwaukee, Wisconsin, arriving June 1, 1861, and remained in Wisconsin until the spring of 1868, during which time he was agent and operator for the railroad company. He then went to Lyon county, Minnesota, and located on section 17, ten miles southwest of the village of Marshall. Here he met with many reverses, being burned out twice and having his crops destroyed by the grasshoppers for four years.

For three falls and winters he engaged in dealing with the Indians, buying furs, etc. The first year of his location in the county he took a trip from where Pipestone now stands and at that time there was not a white man living in the entire county. This trip was made in company with a half-breed. Here our subject saw the Indians worshiping the great red rock which they believed the Great Spirit had sent for their special use. Passing on to where the city of Sioux Falls now stands, our subject there found a company of sixty soldiers and the country was devoid of white settlers. Thence Mr. Hildreth went to Yankton, and for sixty miles saw neither white man nor house. Arriving at Yankton, a little frontier settlement of five hundred inhabitants, he learned that Yankton was originally called Yankhonkton, "milky water." From thence our subject went up the Missouri river to the Sontee agency, where there were seven thousand Indians. His object in making this trip was to learn where the best trapping grounds were and to learn how to find them. Succeeding in this object he went up the river to Fort Thompson and then started homeward across the country to Madeira on the Sioux reservation. Thence he went to Lake Benton, and from that point went home after a long and weary, but successful trip into the Indian country. After the trapping season opened our subject's time was spent in buying furs of the Indians and carrying supplies to them. He passed many a night on the prairie in the terrible storms usually called blizzards. During these storms he kept himself from freezing by tramping around his sled and occasionally giving his team a handful of hay, thus keeping his attention on some occupation and driving sleep from his weary eyelids. The anxiety of Mr. Hildreth at these times can hardly be conceived of, especially his anxiety for his family at home, who were forty miles from other settlers. At one time Mr. Hildreth was out for three days and nights on his way home during one of those severe storms. He stopped on his way at a house where a lady was alone and out of provisions, and gave her enough to last her until her husband's return. For twelve years our subject continued his residence on his claim, and then, as ill-fortune would have it, the government canceled his papers in favor of the Winona & St. Peter

Railroad Company. Our subject had gone to the expense of building a mill, and was about to finish it and put in mill machinery, but in the fall of 1870 his house, barn, mill, and all his effects were destroyed by fire. These many hardships, and especially the destruction of his crops by grasshoppers, set our subject to thinking, and he framed a law which allowed those who had been on their claims during grasshopper times to be given all time after filing, whether on their claims or not. In the spring of 1880 Mr. Hildreth left his claim and went to Nobles county, and spent one year about five miles from Worthington, where he took care of a thousand sheep. In the fall of 1880 he was herding these sheep on the prairie when a severe storm swept over the country on the 15th of October. Many of these sheep were lost and our subject had much trouble in reaching home. In the spring of 1881 he moved to Worthington and took a herd of cattle and kept them through the summer, and the next winter he traveled through Dakota in the employ of the Bank of Worthington, looking after timber land at Lake Tetonkahal. He succeeded in selling these lands and returned to Worthington Febuary 14th, and for the next three years was engaged in buying and selling cattle. He then became the proprietor of the McManus hotel in Worthington, operating the same for one year at a loss of two hundred dollars. Since that time he has not been engaged in active business.

Mr. Hildreth has been quite prominent in political matters, has been village justice of the peace, court commissioner, and has held various other positions of trust. His first vote was cast for Henry Clay for president, and for years he has affiliated with the republican party. He is a member of the Knights of Labor fraternity.

Mr. Hildreth was married in Wellsboro, Pennsylvania, February 14, 1850, to Electa Butler, a daughter of Hartford and Matilda Butler, the former a native of New Hampshire and the latter born in Scotland. Mrs. Butler was born in Tioga village, Pennsylvania, in March, 1825. Mr. and Mrs. Hildreth have had the following named children—Luther, Ida M. and Flora B. Luther perished in a severe snowstorm in Minnesota; Ida M. married Henry B. Nichols; Flora B. married Herbert Chase.

ANDREW JOHNSON is one of the reliable and thrifty farmers of Leeds township, Murray county, Minnesota. He resides on a fine farm on section 32. Mr. Johnson was born in Norway, February 8, 1864. He is the son of Olaus and Ellen (Kongsmod) Johnson, natives of Norway. The father was a farmer by occupation in his native land and came to America in 1868, settling with his family in Winneshiek county, Iowa, where he lived on a rented farm until 1874. In that year he came to Murray county, Minnesota, and now resides on section 8 of Leeds township. The mother died in 1881. There were ten children in the father's family, Andrew, our subject, being the third child.

During the most of his early life, in fact until he was twenty-one years of age, the subject of our sketch attended the district school and assisted in work on his parents' farm. On attaining his majority he purchased the farm where he now lives and where he has since been engaged in general farming. He is a single man at the present writing. He has taken an active part in political affairs and has served in various official positions with fidelity and credit. He has been a member of the board of supervisors for two years, assessor for three years, and clerk of the school district for six years. In politics he affiliates with the republican party and is a consistent member of the Lutheran church. He was one of the pioneer settlers of his township, and having been through many trials, hardships and misfortunes, is now prepared to enjoy the prosperity and successes which come to him year by year. He is a man of good business qualifications, excellent character, and is highly respected.

CHARLES H. BULLARD is a real estate dealer of Fairmont, Martin county, Minnesota. His parents were Calvin and Mary A. (Gleason) Bullard, both natives of Massachusetts.

The subject of our sketch was born in Worcester, Massachusetts, May 4, 1833. He was given a good common school education and engaged in business with his father in the State of New York until 1858, when they sold out and the father moved to Kingston, New Jersey, where he purchased a farm and engaged in agricultural pursuits. Our subject remained in New York until July, 1861, when he enlisted in Company H, First New York (Lincoln) Cavalry. He continued in the service of the Union army until July, 1865, when he was mustered out of the service with his company. He was with his regiment during the entire war and was always in active service—his regiment from September, 1861, until Johnston's surrender in April, 1865, always had pickets out against the enemy. His regiment was all through the peninsular campaign in 1862, was at the battle of Antietam, from which the regiment was ordered to join General Kelley's forces in West Virginia. December 25, 1862, he was with the forces that captured Martinsburg and joined General Milroy at Winchester January 1, 1863. He remained with these forces until being driven out by the rebel forces under General Lee, June 13, 1863. His company and one other were detailed to guard

the wagon train when on its way to Winchester. Being cut off by the Rebels the train took the road to Martinsburg, thence to Hagerstown, Maryland. Sergeant Bullard was left at the toll gate south of Martinsburg with seven men with orders to hold the gate until relieved. When finally ordered back they found themselves entirely surrounded by the enemy, but it being nearly dark the Rebels mistook them for their own scouts and they safely passed through their lines. They could not rejoin their company, so they fell back to Williamsport, Maryland, which place they reached about midnight. The wagon train was in the park there, but was soon started out on the road to Chambersburg, Pennsylvania, after which the exhausted troopers lay down to rest. At daylight they were driven out of their bivouac by the Rebels and continued their retreat to Hagerstown, where they found Captain Boyd of Company C, their regiment, with some sixty of his men. Bullard decided to join Boyd and continued with him until they reached Harrisburg, Pennsylvania, with the train, without the loss of a single wagon, where, by the order of the general commanding the department, he and his little squad were attached to Boyd's company during the campaign. This little force of less than seventy men were all the force Cauch had that had seen service between the Rebel army and Harrisburg, and more arduous duty troops never performed than was done by these rough riders during those eventful three weeks previous to Gettysburg and during Lee's retreat. Boyd was promoted to colonel of the Twenty-first Pennsylvania Cavalry and Lieutenant Knowles to lieutenant-colonel for their services in that campaign. They were both gallant men and deserved it, and every non-commissioned officer in Boyd's company received a commission, and the privates were correspondingly promoted. Soon after Gettysburg his company was detailed as body-guard of General

French, commander of the Third Army Corps. In the fall of 1863 his company was ordered to join the regiment in the Shenandoah Valley, where they remained participating in the various expeditions until General Sheridan took command of the Valley in 1864, at which time the regiment and brigade were attached to Custer's division, taking part in all the battles of that year in the Valley as well as in the devastation of that historical section in the fall of that year. February 28, 1865, Sheridan's forces left the Valley, to join Grant before Petersburg, by way of Waynesborough, Charlottesville and North Anna river to White House landing, thence to Petersburg, the trip occupying nearly six weeks. They immediately left the latter place for Five Forks, circling the right flank of Lee's army; thence to Sailors' Creek and Appomattox Station and Court House, where Lee surrendered April 9, 1865, where the company was detailed as body-guard for General Merritt, commissary of prisoners. After the prisoners were paroled the regiment returned to Petersburg, learning on the way of the assassination of President Lincoln. From Petersburg Sheridan's cavalry was sent to reinforce General Sherman, who confronted Johnston, who refused to surrender but did so as Sheridan's forces were crossing the line into Carolina. The command then returned to Petersburg and soon after to Washington, where they took part in the grand review, the First New York (Lincoln) Cavalry leading the column. The regiment was soon after sent to New York and on July 7, 1865, was paid off and discharged from service. Mr. Bullard well remembers the review of the troops by the President at the close of the war and thinks it the grandest, most impressive congregation ever gathered together in the country. The troops were three days passing the grand stand. Our subject was in all the battles of the seven days' fight around Rich-

mond in June and July, 1862, was at Antietam, Gettysburg, Winchester, Cedar Creek, Fisher's Hill, Waynesborough, Dinwiddie Court House, Five Forks, Sailor's Creek, Appamattox Station and Court House, besides two or three hundred other fights and skirmishes. In 1864 for nearly three weeks his regiment and brigade were constantly in line of battle, exchanging shots with the Rebels from three to four times a day and some days it reached the proportions of a pitched battle. He was hit by Rebel bullets eight different times, one bullet taking off all the beard from the point of his chin, just drawing the blood, and was knocked insensible by a volley at close range from a concealed regiment of Rebel infantry during a charge at the battle of Winchester, but in spite of his dangerous position and exposure he received no very severe wounds. After his discharge Mr. Bullard went to Columbia county, Wisconsin, and there joined his wife. He commenced work on a threshing machine; met with an accident by which his foot was badly crushed, causing him to be confined to his bed for some six months. He remained in Wisconsin until in May, 1866, and then came to Minnesota, settling on a homestead of 160 acres six miles northeast of the village of Fairmont. Residing on this place for seven years he engaged in farming to a large extent, but also gave considerable of his attention to the duties of various offices to which he was elected. In the fall of 1867 he was elected sheriff of the county, but refused to serve. He was elected again in the fall of 1868 and entered upon the discharge of the duties of that office. He was re-elected in 1870, again in 1872 and again in 1874. He resigned his office January 1, 1875, on account of other business. He resided on his farm until 1873 and then moved to the village of Fairmont, the county seat, and in partnership with Frank A. Day established the Martin County *Sentinel*, July 4, 1874. This partnership was continued until 1880, when our subject sold his interest to Mr. Day, who still operates the paper. Our subject then engaged in the real estate business exclusively, which line he has followed ever since. In 1883 he was appointed postmaster, and in October, 1885, another man was appointed who was more in harmony with the political ideas of the party then in power.

Throughout his entire military career Mr. Bullard showed his efficiency and capability, not only as a soldier in the ranks, but as a sergeant in command of his company, having been several times complimented by his superior officers. At the battle of Waynesborough, in March, 1865, he captured the Rebel General Early's headquarters wagon with a large amount of correspondence, together with one large and one small map of the country around Richmond. This map proved of great service as, by its aid, he piloted the regiment out of danger, and doubtless saved it from capture. This map was one made by Rebel engineers, and was strictly accurate. The large one was loaned by our subject to General Capehart, commanding the brigade, who promised to return it but never did. Mr. Bullard still possesses a small portion of this official correspondence, including an autograph letter from General Lee to General Early, and the small map. He also has a revolver, holster and belt, which he captured from Colonel McDonald, commander of Virginia forces at Lexington, Virginia, on Hunter's raid to Lynchburg, Virginia, in 1864. Mr. Bullard is a member of the Grand Army of the Republic, Post No 18, of Fairmont, in which he has held every office, and of which he is the present adjutant. He is first lieutenant of Company D, Second Regiment Minnesota National Guards.

Mr. Bullard was married in New York City, on June 24, 1854, to Miss Margaret Rowland, daughter of Robert Rowland, a native of Wales. This lady was born in Remson, Oneida county, New York, in the year 1835. Mr. and Mrs. Bullard have been blessed with the following-named children—George A. and C. Frederick. George A. was a graduate of the Iowa Law School, and was admitted to the bar. Afterward he became a conductor on the Southern Minnesota and also the Chicago, St. Paul, Minneapolis & Omaha railways. He was accidentally killed October 7, 1885, by falling from his train. C. Frederick Bullard married Marillia Snow, a daughter of E. S. Snow, and is engaged in farming near Fairmont. They have the following children—Leliah, Hazel and Floyd.

Ever since coming to the county our subject's qualifications as a business man have been recognized by his fellow-citizens, and he has been called upon to serve in various official capacities. In every instance he has served with credit to himself and to the satisfaction of his constituents. He has been justice of the peace, court commissioner, county commissioner, and has held some office ever since locating in the county. He is a man of good character, and is highly respected by all.

CAROLUS PETERSON is a leading farmer of Highwater township, Cottonwood county, Minnesota, and resides on section 30. He settled on this section in 1867, and has resided in the county ever since. Mr. Peterson is a native of Helgeland, Norway, born May 26, 1827, his parents being Peder Olson and Ellen Tamine Coldevin. The parents were farmers, and the father died in his native country some years ago. The father had a family of eight children.

In 1866 the subject of our sketch concluded to try his fortune in the new world. So, taking ship, he came to the United States, and stopped one winter in Dakota county, Minnesota. Early in 1867 our subject came to his present location, and became one of the first settlers of Highwater township.

The early experience of our subject in Cottonwood county was full of interesting as well as trying circumstances. Neighbors there were none, the nearest settler to the east being thirty-two miles distant; markets were hardly accessible, the nearest place for obtaining provisions and selling grain being at New Ulm, fifty-two miles away, and the trip to that place occupying five days and over. Later Windom became the marketing point, and was much more easily reached. Mr. Peterson built the first house in the township in 1867, and lived in the same for three years. The first year he broke up some land, put up some hay, and, for the first few years, in connection with light farming, he engaged in trapping. After 1868 our subject raised a number of excellent crops, in some instances harvesting as high as thirty bushels to the acre.

The subject of our sketch was married on June 8, 1853, to Miss Anna Hanson, a native of Norway. Mr. and Mrs. Peterson have three living children—H. H., Susie and Anna. The son is now married and resides in Storden township, this county, where he is engaged in farming. Those deceased in the family were Anton M., who died June 11, 1888, at twenty-five years and eight months of age, a young man of exemplary and lovable character, and a member of the Lutheran church; Peter, who died at nine years of age; Susanna, who died aged one year; Anton, who died at six years of age, and Ellen Tomena, who married Andrew Ferring and died in May, 1880, leaving two children—Adolph and Ellen Tomena. She was a member of the Lutheran church.

Since coming to the township our subject has been one of its active citizens. He has heartily participated in all affairs pertaining to the general welfare and has held various official positions with credit and efficiency. He has held the office of supervisor for three years, being one of the first to hold that position in the township. He has been elected to the same office several times since, has been township treasurer and treasurer of the school district. In politics Mr. Peterson affiliates with the republican party. He is a man of strong moral character and belongs to the Lutheran church, of which he has been trustee and treasurer.

———▸━◦━❮❰❱❯━◦━◂———

FRASER MACKAY is the owner and proprietor of the Pipestone Roller Flouring Mills, at Pipestone City, Minnesota. This is one of the largest and most important business enterprises in the county, and is deserving of the immense patronage which it now claims and enjoys. Mr. Mackay came to Pipestone in 1882, and purchased five acres of land just east of the main part of the city, within the corporate limits. He first built a mill and put in two run of stone (French buhr), and operated the same until 1885, at which time he entirely remodeled and changed his mill, putting in the patent roller process. He has now four double rollers, and one six-roll feed mill driven by a forty-horse steam power. He has an extensive local trade, and also ships his goods in large quantities into adjacent and distant counties. He is otherwise financially interested in the welfare of Pipestone, being a stockholder in the First National Bank, and owning a fine dwelling, which he built near his mill in 1888. He owns other dwelling houses in the city, and has to-day from twelve to fourteen thousand dollars' worth of property.

The subject of our sketch was born in Scotland, February 15, 1841. His parents were Thomas and Rebecca (Battey) Mackay, both natives of Ireland. The father was a weaver by trade, and was also engaged to some extent in coal mining. He died in 1871. The mother passed from this life in about 1843. Of the father's family there are two children living—Anna (now Mrs. French), and our subject.

Mr. Mackay's early education, as far as school advantages were concerned, was somewhat neglected. The circumstances of his parents were such as to a large extent preclude his attendance at school. What early education he acquired was therefore the result of his own study, but, being of a studious turn and determined to learn, he advanced quite rapidly and gathered an extensive knowledge of general matters. He learned the multiplication table while working at the cotton mill in England, to which country he had gone when quite young. From the time he was ten years of age until he was eighteen he worked in the coal mines, but then, as he did not like the business, he quit it and secured a position firing and attending a pumping engine at the coal mines. He next engaged in firing and attending an engine at a cotton spinning and weaving mill in Blackburn, England. Becoming convinced that his education had been neglected, and feeling the need of it, he attended the Literary, Scientific and Mechanical Institute for four years, working daytime and attending school evenings. During the "cotton famine," in 1883, he obtained a position as engineer in a large flouring mill, where he studied the art of making flour for three years. He then concluded to come to America, and, landing here, he settled at Chicago, Illinois, where he engaged as an engineer with a Mr. Chapin, remaining, however, but a short time in that gentleman's employ. From thence he removed to Wilmington, Illinois, and found work in the coal mines, and after continuing thereat for some time removed to Boone county, Iowa. Here, for some five years, he divided his attention between work in the coal mines and in a small flouring mill. He raised the first coal with steam power in Boone county. At the end of that time he moved to the country and settled on a homestead of eighty acres of prairie land, remaining there part of the time milling and part of the time on the farm, until coming to Pipestone, in 1882. He at once commenced operations, as has already been stated, and succeeded in building up a fine business, his being the only flouring mill in the county.

The marriage of the subject of our sketch occurred in the year 1860, at which time he was wedded to Miss Jane E. Legget, a native of England and a daughter of James and Eliza (Gettenba) Legget. Mrs. Mackay has two sisters living now—Mrs. McCaw, and Susanna (now Mrs. D. Falls). Mr. and Mrs. Mackay have a family of six children—Thomas, Elizabeth, James A., William J., Rebecca and Nellie. Elizabeth is now Mrs. Patterson, of Kossuth county, Iowa. She has three children; their names are Charles W., Howard F. and George. Thomas is engaged with his father in the mill, and James A. is learning telegraphy.

The subject of our sketch has been one of the most prominent workers in public matters in the county, and has aided materially in the up-building of Pipestone City. Being of a liberal spirit and possessed of means, he has contributed largely in a financial way toward the development of the business of his adopted town. He also aids willingly in every project which tends to the up building of the social or moral development of the community and has accomplished a great deal in making the city and county what they are to-day. In politics our subject affiliates with the republican party, in whose principles he has had strong faith for a number of years. Mr. Mackay is a man of excellent character, possessed of broad ideas, generous and public-spirited, and has a host of friends throughout the city and county.

CHARLES H. FORBES, one of the leading farmers and stock raisers of Faribault county, Minnesota, is a resident of section 9, Verona township. He came to the county in 1857, locating on his present place where he now owns 145 acres of excellent land. The place of his nativity is found in Wattsburgh, Erie county, Pennsylvania, where he was born August 8, 1833. The parents of our subject were Benjamin and Julia Ann (Nims) Forbes. The father was born in Vermont, and leaving home at the age of fourteen years, went to the State of New York, in which State he engaged in shoemaking and also followed the business of a tanner and currier, and in 1838, going to Racine county, Wisconsin, he engaged in shoemaking and also in agricultural pursuits. In 1857 he removed to Faribault county, Minnesota, and there lived until his death, at seventy-seven years of age, in 1882. Throughout his life he was a member of the Methodist Episcopal church and was a broad-minded and liberal citizen. The mother was a native of the State of New York and was a daughter of Ruel Nims, a mechanic by trade. She died in 1866, after having been many years an exemplary member of the Methodist Episcopal church. In the father's family there were seven children—Benjamin Franklin, Charles H., Julia Ann, Charlotte, Mary, Emma and Theodore. Julia, Charlotte and Theodore are deceased.

When he was two years of age our subject's family removed to Geauga county, Ohio, locating in the town of Newberry, where they remained some three years. Removing thence they settled in Racine county Wisconsin, from whence, after a period of seven years, they went to Fond du Lac county, making that their home until 1857. In the Wisconsin public schools our subject received a thorough common-school education, completing the same at eighteen years of age. After this he learned the carpenter's

trade, and engaged in that occupation until coming to his farm in Verona township in 1857. Since coming to the county, however, he has not given his entire attention to farm work, but has worked more or less at the mason's and carpenter's trades.

Mr. Forbes was one of the first settlers of the township, and passed through the grasshopper raids and various other backsets during the early times. While the grasshoppers were devastating the country our subject was engaged in farming and also in keeping bees. He lost his crops, but his fifty-four swarms of bees made a large quantity of honey, for which he obtained twenty-five cents per pound. He remembers well the Indian scare of 1862, at which time he sent his wife to Wisconsin and himself engaged in carpenter work in that State for one year. At the end of this time he again returned with his family to his farm. He has been a hard working and industrious farmer, and has surrounded himself with the evidences of prosperity and success.

Mr. Forbes was married, in November, 1859, to Miss Arrsteen Franklin, a native of Cattaraugus county, New York. She was born in the town of Leon, and resided with her parents in that place until she was eight years of age. Then they removed to Fond du Lac county, Wisconsin, where she received her education. She was a daughter of Ichabod Franklin, a farmer and influential citizen of Fond du Lac county. Mr. and Mrs. Forbes have two children—Willie Eugene and Ella. Emily died at three years of age.

The subject of our sketch has always taken an active part in the local affairs pertaining to the government of the township and county, and has served in various official positions. He has been chairman of the board of supervisors for two years, treasurer of school district No. 81 for six years, and has always been one of the representative and substantial men of the county. His political faith is in the principles of the republican party. Formerly he was a member of the Free Will Baptist church, of which society he was deacon for two years. His wife is still a member of that society.

—◆—❧❈❧—◆—

THOMAS L. JENNESS is a leading merchant and is engaged in the furniture business at Windom, Cottonwood county, Minnesota. He made his location in the county in 1878, and for some time engaged in work at the carpenter and joiner's trade. After two years he built his present place and engaged in the cabinet and furniture trade on Tenth street and Third avenues. He is the only cabinet-maker and furniture dealer in the village and carries the largest stock in the county.

The subject of our sketch is a native of Orange county, Vermont, where he was born September 27, 1836. He is the son of Thomas and Clarrissa (McGlothlin) Jenness, the former a native of Vermont and the latter a native of Massachusetts. The father was a farmer by occupation and in 1855 removed to Vernon county, Wisconsin, where he remained until his death, which occurred in 1868. The mother is now a resident of Windom. There are four living children in the father's family—John S., Thomas L., Robert R., and Abbie A., now Mrs. Masterson.

The subject of our sketch remained with his parents in the State of his nativity until fifteen years of age. He assisted in work on the home farm, and was given the educational advantages furnished by the district schools. At fifteen he hired out to work on adjoining farms, and continued in that line of business until coming with the father and family to Wisconsin in 1855. Soon after, in company with his brother, John S., he went to Menomonee and commenced working in a saw mill owned by Knapp, Stoughton & Co. After a year had passed thus he went to Waubeek, where they assisted in the building of a large steam saw-mill. They also built several other buildings in the neighborhood, and worked at building and contracting until the breaking out of the war. Then our subject enlisted in Company I, Twelfth Wisconsin Infantry as a private. He served three years and two months, and was slightly wounded in the left leg at the battle of Baker's Creek. He was engaged in a great many battles, among them being that of Vicksburg, under the command of Sherman. Being mustered out of the service at Chattanooga, he returned home by way of Louisville, Kentucky, where he was paid off. Returning to Vernon county, he purchased a piece of land and resided thereon for five years. In company with James Wagner he purchased a steam saw-mill and operated this business in connection with his farming during these five years. In 1871 he sold out all his interests in Wisconsin and went to Sibley, Iowa, where he settled on a soldier's homestead of 160 acres. He resided on this place raising stock and grain until 1878, when he came to Cottonwood county.

The subject of our sketch was married in 1858 to Miss Ann E. Masterson, of Vernon county, Wisconsin. She was the daughter of John and Maria Masterson, prominent farmers of Vernon county. Six children have blessed this union, five of whom are living— Thomas E., John W., Charles L., Josephine, and Stella.

In politics Mr. Jenness affiliates with the republican party, and, by virtue of his gallant service in the Union army, is an influential member of the Grand Army of the Republic. He is receiver of the Ancient Order United Workmen lodge of Windom. Mr. Jenness is a man of good business qualifications, and has built up an extensive and profitable business since locating in Windom. He is a man of good character, and is held in high esteem by all who know him.

LORAIN MASON is one of the early settlers and best known citizens of Mason township, Murray county, Minnesota. He resides on an excellent farm on section 12. Mr. Mason is a native of Jo Daviess county, Illinois, where he was born October 16, 1842. He was the son of Milo D. and Mary A. (Brown) Mason, both of whom were natives of Vermont. In the State of his nativity the father was engaged for many years as a stage driver, and after he came west engaged in the freighting business between points in Iowa. Later the father came to Minnesota and took land in Murray county. In the father's family there were three children, of whom our subject was the oldest.

The gentleman whose name appears at the head of this sketch resided with his parents until attaining the age of sixteen years. Up to this time he had been given good educational advantages and followed various kinds of work, while his father followed transferring at McGregor, Iowa. After leaving home he engaged in farming for a year, and then went to St. Louis, Missouri. Here he worked for a transfer company for eight months, and in the spring of 1862, being fired with patriotic feelings, enlisted in Company B, First Missouri Cavalry. He served bravely and gallantly during the entire war, being discharged at Vicksburg, January 24, 1865. He served in the various engagements about Pea Ridge, and in the battle of Corinth was in the command of General Curtiss. He saw much severe service, and was in many hard-fought battles. After he was discharged he came to Minnesota, procured a team, and engaged with his father in freighting between Rochester and St. Paul. In the spring following he hauled freight between Rochester and Mankato and other points in the West. He continued in this occupation until the spring of 1867, when he obtained a farm and put in a large crop. In June of that year he came to Murray county in company with his father, and took the claim where he now lives. He broke a small acreage of land and then returned to his home in the eastern part of the State, remaining until after harvest. Returning to his farm in Murray county, he put up hay for his stock and returned to Mankato, harvesting and threshing his crop there, and in October returning with his family to his farm in Murray county. Since that time he has made a permanent settlement. During one winter, after coming to the county, he lived in a log house on section 1. The following spring he built a house on his own land, and into this his family moved. He made the first improvements and built the first house after the Indian outbreak. He has seen some terrible times and has passed through many bitter experiences. In order to obtain provisions during the first three years, he had to go to New Ulm and Madelia, a distance of seventy miles. Then, too, for several years he had his crops entirely destroyed by the grasshoppers. These times, however, have passed, and prosperity and success have attended his efforts.

Mr. Mason was married July 4, 1866, to Miss Ann M. Boomhawer, a native of the State of New York. This union has been blessed with six children—Eunice, Ellis, Angeline, Edgar, Laura and Lorain. Laura and Lorain are twins. Mrs. Mason is the daughter of Roswell and Angeline (Silvernale) Boomhawer, natives of New York and Pennsylvania, respectively, and now residents of Murray county. A biography of Roswell Boomhawer is given in another department of this work.

In early life our subject acquired a good common-school education, to which he has been constantly adding by careful reading and investigation through the succeeding years. In politics he affiliates with the republican party, and has taken a prominent position in the government of the county. He has been sheriff of the county for three terms and also township clerk and constable. On coming to the county he at once took hold of the various movements in a public direction and assisted in the organization of the town. He is a man of excellent business qualities and made one of the most efficient sheriffs that the county has ever had.

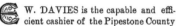

W. DAVIES is the capable and efficient cashier of the Pipestone County Bank. Mr. Davies came to the city November 15, 1876, and has since been a resident. The place of the nativity of the subject of our sketch is found in old England, where he was born April 5, 1855. His parents were John and Elizabeth (Owens) Davies, both of whom were natives of Wales. The father was a manufacturer of carriages and wagons, which trade he learned in England, serving some seven years as an apprentice in one of the English shops. Fifteen years of his life were spent in that employment after the fulfillment of his term of apprenticeship. The father was born in 1830, in Wales, and at the age of twenty-two years he was married to Elizabeth Owens. In 1857 the parents came to America, crossing the ocean in a sailing vessel, starting out from their native land on the 19th of June and landing July 27 in New York City. Thence they went to London, Canada, where they remained a short time, and then removed to Milwaukee, Wisconsin. After one year's residence in this latter place, they removed to Rock county, Wisconsin, settling in the village of Afton. In that place he followed his trade in connection with house-building for some years. He purchased a lot and

built a home for himself in the village, and also invested in other properties, remaining in that locality for about ten years. While in Rock county he occupied an influential position among his fellow citizens, and held several offices of trust and responsibility. On the 11th of May, 1869, he came to Jackson county, Minnesota, and settled on a homestead of 160 acres, which he thoroughly improved, and where he built a good dwelling house and other farm buildings. He lived on this homestead for some seventeen years, and, in this locality too, he made his influence felt in the affairs of the government of the civil division in which he lived. He held the office of town treasurer for some time, and was county judge of probate for some two years. In 1886 he moved into the village of Jackson, where he built a snug little residence, and is now living there. He had a family of five children, of whom our subject is the only one now living. The father and mother are both exemplary Christians, and are members of the Episcopal church.

The early life of the subject of our sketch was spent principally at Afton, Wis. In that village he was given fair school advantages, and on removing to Jackson with his parents in 1869, he was allowed to pursue a course of study in the graded schools in the county seat of that county. Until twenty-one years of age he remained with his parents, giving to them the benefit of his labor in work on the home farm. After attaining twenty one years he attended school some two terms, and then was engaged by J. W. Cowing as clerk in a general store in the village of Jackson. He engaged with that gentleman for one year, and then entered one of the county offices as deputy treasurer. He continued working in the treasurer's and auditor's offices for about two years, and then found employment in the management of a lumber yard of C. L.

Colman. August, 1879, Mr. Davies started the Lakefield lumber yard, and was the originator of the name of that town on the Milwaukee railroad. In August of that year he built the first building on the town site, and established the first lumber yard. He remained only three months, however, being transferred to Pipestone in November, 1879, to take charge of the interests of Mr. Colman. Our subject opened and established the lumber yard, built buildings for the purpose of storing lumber, and was manager of the business for seven years. This was the pioneer lumber yard in Pipestone City, and our subject built up an immense trade. At the end of the seven years just mentioned, Mr. Davies retired from the lumber business to accept a position as cashier of the Pipestone County Bank, the president of which is T. A. Black, a biography of whom is given in another department of this work. Mr. Davies has held the position of cashier ever since with honor to himself and satisfaction and profit to the institution with which he is connected. In 1888, in company with E. A. Sherman, J. M. Poorbaugh, T. A. Black, and J. M. Spicer, our subject purchased 1,300 acres of land on the St. Paul, Minneapolis & Manitoba railroad, and platted forty acres of it for the village of Jasper. They have since platted forty acres more, making eighty acres in all, and have named the company (which is regularly incorporated) the Jasper Improvement Company, with a paid-up capital of one hundred thousand dollars. Besides these various business enterprises, our subject has also branched out to some extent in the newspaper business and, in company with S. S. King and T. A. Black, established the Jasper *Journal*, a republican newspaper, devoted to promoting the interests of the village of Jasper and the surrounding country. Our subject has purchased considerable land in Pipestone county and in the city, and has built several impor-

tant business places. Another business venture in which our subject is reaping large profit is an extensive lumber trade at the village of Jasper, where he is engaged in that line in company with J. H. Taylor and T. A. Black. Our subject is also engaged in the mercantile business in company with L. W. Coombe in the village of Jasper, of which Mr. Coombe is the general manager.

The subject of our sketch was married in January, 1881, to Miss Nellie G. King, daughter of W. V. King, county auditor of Jackson county, Minnesota. Mr. and Mrs. Davies have two children living—Kittie A. and Burr.

The subject of our sketch is a leading Mason and Knight Templar, and is a man of excellent business capabilities, has a clear head, and is noted for guiding all financial enterprises to success. His association with some of the strongest financial institutions in the county has been of remarkable profit to himself as well as to the other members of these concerns. By his gentlemanly and courteous manner he has made many friends in his position as cashier of the Pipestone County Bank, as well as to successfully carry forward the financial affairs of that institution. Mr. Davies is a man of excellent character and is respected by all who know him.

JEFF BATHRICK is an influential business character of Winnebago City, Faribault county, Minnesota, where he handles all kinds of agricultural implements and also sewing machines.

Mr. Bathrick is a native of Racine county, Wisconsin, where he was born in 1840. He is the son of Otis and Mary F. (Miller) Bathrick, natives, respectively, of Massachusetts and Connecticut. In early life the father was engaged in the lumber and brick business, manufacturing brick for the Michigan

City light house. He settled in Indiana when twenty-five years of age, and was married in that State. On leaving that place he went to Wisconsin, settling in Racine county, and engaging in farming. Thence he went to Dane county, and engaged extensively in farming and raising stock. In 1855 he settled at Rushford, Minnesota, where he built the first store and engaged in the mercantile business. He also owned several farms, and engaged in farming. In 1857 he removed to Steele county, and purchased several farms, and remained until 1861, when he returned to Rushford to reclaim one of his farms under mortgage foreclosure. He is still living in the village of Rushford. He has been a prominent citizen of that vicinity, and has held various offices. He served in the Black Hawk War, and came by boat to Chicago with 109 militia men, 101 of whom died of cholera. The father in early life was a whig in politics, but later joined the democratic party. In the father's family there were eleven children, seven of whom are still living —Martha, Thomas, Jeff, Mary A., Milo, Emiline and Evelena.

Until twenty years of age the subject of our sketch resided with his parents on a farm. He received a good common-school education and later taught school for a brief time. November 6, 1861, he enlisted in Company B, Second Wisconsin Cavalry. He was severely injured by an accident, having his leg broken and his right ankle put out of joint. He was therefore unable to go into service with his company. He enlisted again in August, 1862, in Company D, Seventh Minnesota Infantry, serving three years. He was on detached service during most of the time as a musician stationed at Fort Abercrombie during the Indian massacre. He crossed the plains to the Missouri river in pursuit of the Indians and then returned to Fort Snelling, after which he went South with his regiment and did guard duty at St. Louis for a few months. Thence he went to. Paducah, Kentucky, thence to Memphis, Tennessee, and then over the White river into Arkansas in pursuit of General Price. The division to which his regiment belonged then crossed Missouri and reached the Missouri river at East St. Louis. Here they went on board steamer and were transferred to Nashville, where they participated in the battle of that place. His regiment followed General Hood through Tennessee to Eastport, and then went into winter quarters, remaining, however, but a short time when they were ordered to New Orleans. The company was then sent to Dauphin Island in the Gulf of Mexico, from whence they went on an expedition to the Spanish forts, where they participated in the twelve days' siege. The forts were evacuated by the Rebels at the end of that time to the Union army, who took possession, remaining twelve days. Then the company went to Montgomery, Alabama, remaining a few days, when they were sent to Selma and went into summer quarters. He was then sent to Fort Snelling, and mustered out of the service in 1865, at the close of the war. Our subject participated in a great many hard-fought battles, among them being that of Tupelo, which lasted some eight hours, and in which our subject was in the division commanded by General A. J. Smith. General Forest was in command of the Rebel forces. After the close of the war our subject returned to Rushford, Minnesota, from whence, after a few months, he went to a location about sixty miles north of Minneapolis. Here he engaged in the drug business for some time, and then went to Glencoe, McLeod county, where he engaged in the same line of business, and remained three years. From thence he removed to Minneapolis again, opening in the drug business and remaining two and a half years. He then returned to

Glencoe and opened a branch store, which he operated for three years, but in the meantime he sold his business in Minneapolis, and, after selling out at Glencoe, he commenced casting about for a location. He finally settled in Winnebago City, in the spring of 1877, and opened a drug store, continuing in that line until January 1, 1889. His present business, however, has been conducted for the last three years, it not being given his direct attention until January 1, 1889. Mr. Bathrick is a man of excellent business qualifications, and has been quite successful in accumulating considerable property. He built his drug store, a brick building of imposing proportions, in 1885. This property still belongs to him, and he also owns a fine residence on Holly street. In politics Mr. Bathrick affiliates with the republican party, and is a leading and influential member of the Masonic and Grand Army of the Republic fraternities. He is one of the solid and substantial business men of Winnebago City and vicinity.

Mr. Bathrick was married in March, 1869, to Miss Zalia L. Swain, of Monticello, Wright county, Minnesota. She was the daughter of John and Mary A. (Chance) Swain. This union has been blessed with two sons—Charley and Floyd.

--- ❖ ❖ ---

JAMES B. SHAWVER, one of the leading merchants of Luverne, Minnesota, is engaged in the hardware and agricultural implement business, and in connection with this enterprise is also engaged largely in handling live stock. He made his settlement in Rock county in the fall of 1870, in which year he settled on 320 acres of land on section 18 in Clinton township. On his first visit to the county he purchased sufficient lumber, windows, shingles, nails, and all other articles necessary for building a house 14x20 feet and eight feet high. This material was purchased at Cherokee, Iowa, 125 miles distant from Luverne. Our subject drove through from that city, bringing his materials with him on one wagon to which was driven one span of mules. This was in the month of December, and the trip occupied about three days, our subject camping out under his wagon each night. Our subject's stepfather came with him and drove through with a team and wagon loaded with household goods. With the materials thus brought from Cherokee, our subject at once commenced building the first frame house in the county, which was on section 2 of the township above named. After building his house and making other slight improvements, he returned to Le Mars, Iowa, the nearest railroad station, ninety miles distant from Luverne. Here he purchased two loads of lumber, buying out all the lumber stock which could be found in that city. He returned to his farm in Clinton township and built again in the spring of 1871. During the time he was absent from Rock county, a period of six weeks, he, with his step-father, camped out every night and slept under their wagons. After moving onto his farm of 320 acres he made that his principal abiding place for some five years, during which time he made excellent improvements and set out some twenty acres of timber. He experienced hard times during the grasshopper raids, but had sufficient means to enable him to purchase considerable land south of Luverne on the river bottom. His first purchase was of two acres of timber land, the purchase price being forty dollars per acre. He has continued purchasing land during the intervening years until now he owns a fine farm of 1,240 acres, all in one body. This property is excellently improved and is provided with fine buildings. He has occupied his attention largely with raising horses of fine grade and also blooded cattle and Poland China hogs. He has his land divided into three farms and has three tenants. He has made many improvements, among them being the building of a good farm residence and other farm buildings, up to 1882, in which year he moved into Luverne. On moving into the city he built a fine dwelling-house on West Main street, where he now lives. He continued his farming and stock-raising enterprises until the spring of 1885, when he built his present store building and engaged in the implement business. He has made himself quite prominent and influential in all business matters since taking up his residence in Luverne, and has connected himself with several of the most important financial enterprises in the county. He was one of the organizers of the First National Bank and is one of its directors and largest stockholders.

The subject of our sketch was born in Wythe county, Virginia, in 1847. His parents were Abner and Malinda (Johnson) Shawver, the former a native of Ohio, and the latter a native of Virginia. In an early day the father moved to Dane county, Wisconsin, and located at Pheasant's Branch, where he resided until his death which occurred in 1854. The father was an extensive land owner and operated several fine farms. He also was engaged largely in the freighting business from Milwaukee to Madison and Sauk City. This was one of the largest enterprises of the kind in the State and our subject's father employed from fifteen to twenty men as teamsters, and during the most of the time kept one hundred head of horses for use on the road in the freighting business. He was a man of considerable means and attained to wide influence in the State in which he resided. In the father's family there were four children, three of whom are now living—Margaret, now Mrs. Henry Oben, of O'Brien county, Iowa, where her husband is engaged in farming; Lydia, married to William Henry, a farmer

of Jasper county, Iowa, and our subject. The educational advantages in the early days of Wisconsin were somewhat limited, and it was only by much effort that our subject succeeded in acquiring a common-school education. Schools, like railroads, in that early day were few and far between, and our subject had to walk a distance of three miles to the nearest school house. He continued with his parents in their home in Dane county until he was about twenty-one years of age. He then rented a farm in Jasper county, Iowa, and for two years continued its operation for himself, at which time he was married and then purchased a farm of 120 acres in the same county, and made that his home for about one year. He then sold out and removed to Rock county, Minnesota, bringing his horses, mules, cattle, etc., with him.

Mr. Shawver was united in marriage to Miss Mary Roger of Des Moines, Iowa. This union has been blessed with four children—Wallace A., now a student in a business college in Quincy, Illinois; Eldora E., Henrietta and Mary L.

Our subject has become one of the best known and most widely respected citizens of Rock county. His financial interests are of extensive nature, and he is actively engaged in numerous of the most important business enterprises of Rock county. Thrifty, industrious, and withal a man of economical habits, he has accumulated a large fortune and is now enjoying the results of an active and successful business career. He is a man of excellent business qualifications, possessed of broad ideas, and enjoys the confidence and esteem of a large circle of business and social friends. He has actively interested himself in all public matters since coming to Rock county and has aided in every way in elevating and improving the administration of local government. While living in Clinton township he held the office of town clerk for five years, and in other ways served his constituents with honor and credit. He is considered as being the most extensive farmer in the county, and employs from ten to twenty men at work constantly on his various farms. In his business in the city he requires three men to assist him the year round. His stock enterprise has been exceedingly profitable, and out of this he has made a large amount of money. He has had as high as one thousand head of stock at one time, and has been the largest shipper of cattle from Rock county to Eastern markets. It can be readily seen that our subject is extensively interested in the financial development of Luverne and vicinity, and throughout his career here he has shown his willingness to aid in all projects tending toward the business development by giving liberally of his means as well as assisting in various other ways. He has become one of the most substantial and respected citizens of Rock county. In politics he affiliates with the democratic party.

———◆·❮◈❯·◆———

JAMES R. CARSON is the able and popular mayor of Pipestone city, Pipestone county, Minnesota, at this writing. The place of his nativity is found in Goshen, Vermont, where he was born July 14, 1846.

The subject of our sketch is the son of David and Maria (Allen) Carson, the former a native of Upper Canada and the latter a native of Vermont. The father was an extensive farmer in the State of Vermont, where he remained until 1857, in which year he sold out and removed to Randolph, Columbia county, Wisconsin. For a number of years he engaged in farming principally, but is now retired from active business, and is living a quiet life in Columbia county. He is a man widely respected in the county in which he lives, and held the office of county treasurer of Columbia county for two years.

For years he was engaged in raising fine blooded horses and sheep, and became one of the substantial and live farmers of the county. He had a family of five children—Polly, who died at the age of fifteen years; James R., Julius A., George G., and Belle, now Mrs. Hughes. The four last named are still living.

The home of our subject's parents remained his abiding place until he reached the age of twenty-one years. Up to this time he had been occupied with work on the home farm, and with pursuing his studies in the district school in Columbia county, Wisconsin. On attaining his majority he purchased eighty acres of land adjoining his father's farm, where he engaged in farming for himself for seven years. In 1876 he sold out his interests in Wisconsin and came to Grand Meadow township, Mower county, Minnesota, where he purchased 160 acres of land and engaged in farming for about five years. At the end of this period he sold eighty acres of his land and came to Pipestone city, where he has since continued to reside. He purchased 160 acres of land in Eden township, Pipestone county, and also became the owner of two lots in the city, upon which he built a fine residence. He has been engaged in diversified financial enterprises, and, since coming to Pipestone, has engaged in buying and selling wheat, grain of all kinds, and also in handling coal. In the last lines mentioned he has done an immense business, and it can be truly said that he handles more grain and coal than any other firm in the city. He is in the employ of Messrs. Hodgins & Hyde, of La Crosse, Wisconsin, with whom he has been engaged for a number of years.

Mr. Carson was married in 1873 to Miss Martha A. Harris, the daughter of William and Alice Harris, of Wisconsin. Mr. and Mrs. Carson have one living child—Neal A. A daughter, Agnes, died when one year old.

In politics Mr. Carson affiliates with the republican party, in which organization he has become exceedingly popular and influential. His abilities as an official have been tested in various ways, and in every instance he has proven his efficiency, and has attended to his various duties ably and with increasing popularity. He has been a member of the village council for some years, and was elected mayor of the city in 1886, which position he has held until the present writing, being the present incumbent. Since coming to the city he has assisted in the most active manner in every project which has had a tendency to elevate and improve the business, social and financial interests of the community. By his public spirit and efficiency in the management of various public projects, he has created a warm sentiment in his favor among the people, and has built up an extensive circle of friends. He is an influential member of the Masonic fraternity.

PHILIP A. JAEGER is an influential and well-to-do farmer and stock raiser of section 34, Dovray township, Murray county, Minnesota. He located in that county in 1878, first settling in Holly township, where he purchased a farm. He lived there for one and a half years and then removed to his present location, where he took a homestead. He was one among the early settlers and the first year engaged in making various improvements, built a house, put up hay, etc. He has since been engaged in general farming and the raising of graded stock. He has taken an active interest in all matters of a public nature and has served his fellow-citizens in various official positions. He has taken a special interest in educational matters and has held various offices in the school district.

Mr. Jaeger was born in the City of New York, May 3, 1844, and removed with his parents when six years old to Milwaukee, Wisconsin, where he remained five years, after which he went to Winnebago county, same State. The parents were John and Mary (Durr) Jaeger, both natives of Germany. They came to America when they were quite young, the father coming when he was about fourteen years of age. In the father's family there were the following-named children—John J. (deceased), Philip A., Mary, Louisa, William, Edward, Lewis, Aaron, Sophia, Albert, Abraham and Ernest. The father was by trade a cabinet maker and after coming west devoted considerable of his attention to farming. The parents still live in Winnebago county, Wisconsin.

The subject of our sketch received most of his education in the city of Milwaukee, completing his educational course at the age of eighteen years. He then engaged in farming until twenty-one years of age, after which he learned the ship-builder's trade at Green Bay. He followed that occupation for some ten years, and then engaged in bridge-building for a year, settling after that time in Shawano county, where he engaged in farming and lumbering for five or six years, during which time he occupied several official positions, such as under sheriff, county supervisor, etc., and was employed as government scaler on the Indian Reservation in said county (Menominee). He then came to Murray county, Minnesota, where he has since resided.

Mr. Philip Jaeger was married to Mary Forrest in January, 1866. She was a native of Illinois, and died in 1868 in Berlin, Wisconsin. Mr. Jaeger was married again in 1870 to Mrs. Lizzie Grimmer, who died in 1877, leaving two children—Olive L. and Winnie M., the oldest being now married and a resident of section twenty-six, Dovray township, Murray county. August 28, 1878,

Mr. Jaeger was married to Miss Mary H. De Vore, a native of Rock Island county, Illinois. Eight years of her life were spent in Sheboygan county, Wisconsin, from whence she removed to Berlin, where she engaged in teaching during her younger days. She was the daughter of Gabriel and Clarissa (Ball) De Vore, both of whom were natives of Ohio. Her father was a cooper by trade, but is now engaged in farming. The parents are both members of the Methodist Episcopal church and are residents of Murray county, where they located in 1879. In her father's family there were five children — Mrs. Jaeger, Mattie, Frank, Abraham and Vina. Mrs. Jaeger learned type setting while in Berlin, Wisconsin, and this, with teaching, was her avocation during fourteen or fifteen years. Mr. and Mrs. Jaeger have been blessed with five children—John P., Clara, William, Edward, Sarah and Alice.

In politics the subject of our sketch affiliates with the prohibition party. He is a man of strong temperance principles, and believes in voting in accordance with his principles. His wife is a consistent member of the Methodist Episcopal church, while he formerly belonged to the Advent church. He is an influential member of the Odd Fellows' fraternity, and is an honorary member of the Farmers' Alliance. Mr. Jaeger is a man of excellent qualities, generous, warmhearted, and public-spirited, and is respected by all who know him.

EDWIN RAY HUMISTON is the present register of deeds of Nobles county, Minnesota. His parents, Caleb and Polly (Todd) Humiston, were natives of Connecticut, and our subject was born in Great Barrington, Massachusetts, May 6, 1827. When he was six years of age the family moved to Hudson, Ohio; where the father carried on a brick-making business for some years. Our subject remained with his parents until he was twenty years of age, then learned the carpenter's trade and followed that business in Ohio until the winter of 1855.

Our subject received a good common-school education in Ohio, and in 1855 came to Dubuque, Iowa, and in the spring of 1856 left that place and removed to St. Peter, Minnesota, where he found employment as carpenter and millwright until the fall of 1871. His home, however, during this time was in Cleveland, Le Sueur county. In the fall of 1871 he left St. Peter and came to Worthington, where he engaged in carpenter work until November, 1888, when he was elected register of deeds on the republican ticket. In January, 1889, our subject entered upon the duties of his office, and up to the present time has been giving excellent satisfaction.

In politics Mr. Humiston affiliates with the republican party. His first vote was cast for Martin Van Buren, the candidate on the free-soil ticket. Since that time he has voted with the republican party.

During the early days of his settlement in Minnesota Mr. Humiston witnessed many exciting occurrences. While in St. Peter, April 12, 1857, he was one of forty men who volunteered to go out and fight the Indians who participated in the Spirit Lake massacre. This little company of men left St. Peter one Sunday at eleven o'clock A. M., starting out in a bad storm on foot. Hurrying along, the morning of the next day they found themselves forty-nine miles distant from St. Peter. They camped late at night and our subject was assigned to the cookship, the company having brought provisions with them. They camped near a deserted house, the inhabitants having left for regions safe from Indian depredations. In this house our subject found a large dish pan nearly full of flour and was mixing it preparatory to the baking of bread. While in the act, a man who had discovered that these new comers were white men, came to the house and told our subject that no provisions found in that house must be eaten as strychine had been put into everything in the house; and this was true as was afterward discovered, strychine being found in the flour, sugar and all other articles, having been put there for the purpose of killing any Indians who might chance that way and partake of the provisions. This was a narrow escape indeed for the entire company, and had not this man discovered what our subject was doing the entire company would have been poisoned. Mr. Humiston drew one month's pay for services on this expedition. At the time of the massacre in 1862 he was living in the big woods of Le Sueur county, and becoming fearful as to the safety of his family he spent the summer as a scout, being familiar with the Indian trails and the entire country. He was with a party on Scott's Lake at the time when two Indians were killed—one escaping. In order for protection in case of necessity they built a small stockade in a corner of his garden.

Mr. Humiston was married May 13, 1858, in Cleveland, Le Sueur county, Minnesota, to Miss Mary A. Davis. This union has been blessed with the following-named children—Frederick, Willis, Henry, John, E. Ray and Mary. Frederick married Gertrude Warren and lives in Worthington, where he is engaged in the hardware business in company with his brother Willis, who married Lillie Glass.

MASON N. CADWELL is a prosperous farmer of Amo township, Cottonwood county, Minnesota. He located on section 14 of that township in 1871, taking up his present claim. He brought his family to the farm in 1872, and has since resided on the place, with the exception of two winters spent in Wisconsin, during the grasshopper raid in southern Minnesota.

The subject of our sketch was born in Allegany county, New York, September 29, 1846, He was the son of George and Melissa Cadwell, the former a native of Allegany county and the latter a native of Cattaraugus county, New York. The father was a farmer by occupation, and died in 1879. The parents were both members of the Methodist Episcopal church, and were loyal Christian people.

The subject of our sketch spent his early life on the home farm, receiving his early training and education in the district schools. At eighteen years of age he went to Jefferson county, Wisconsin, and engaged in agricultural pursuits for seven years. He then spent one summer traveling through Nebraska and Iowa, and then came to Cottonwood county, where he has since lived. Our subject was one of three living children—Marvin, Eva and Mason N.

The subject of our sketch was married, January 18, 1872, to Miss Mary Jane Waite, of Dane county, Wisconsin, and daughter of Martin Waite, a farmer and a native of Cattaraugus county, New York. Miss Waite was also born in Cattaraugus county, New York. In early life she removed to Wisconsin with her parents. Mr. and Mrs. Cadwell have three children—Arthur M., Myra E. and Guy.

Mr. Cadwell, being one of the very first settlers of Amo township, there being but five other settlers in the region when he located here, has found it necessary to engage heartily in public enterprises, and has willingly assisted in these matters for the purpose of building up the affairs of the township. In politics he affiliates with the prohibition party, and has held various official positions, among them being chairman of the board of supervisors, which position he held for three years; township treasurer one year; township clerk, to which he was elected in 1886, and of which position he is the present incumbent, and clerk of school district No. 49. He has held this latter position since the organization of the district, and has given excellent satisfaction, because of the interest and energy he manifests in all educational matters. He is a member of the Grange, and is one of the representative citizens of Amo township. He is a very pleasant neighbor, genial, warm-hearted, and has an agreeable family, and resides in one of the most hospitable homes of the township. He has labored hard on his farm to make it one of the best stock and grain farms in his part of the county, and has provided it with good improvements, and has about eleven acres of a fine grove of trees surrounding his house.

———◦—◦❖◗❖❖◦◦———

WILLIAM H. BUDD. After having spent a long and successful career, engaged in farming, having accumulated some means and gained an enviable reputation for honor and integrity, the gentleman whose name we have just given is now living a retired life in Fairmont, Martin county, Minnesota. He is the son of Abraham D. and Margaret F. (Goble) Budd, both of whom were natives of New Jersey. The place of the nativity of the subject of our sketch is in Roxbury, Morris county, New Jersey, where his birth took place March 28, 1829.

William H. was reared in New Jersey on a farm where his father was born, and where he died on July 31, 1867. He received a good common-school education, and when twenty-one years of age went to Dodge county, Wisconsin and engaged in day labor for a year. Then in March and April, 1851, he took a trip through Western Wisconsin, to within twenty miles of La Crosse; then to Prairie du Chien; then to Iowa, traveling through the northern counties, which then were nothing but a wild prairie. There were but very few settlers, sometimes the houses being from twenty to forty miles apart, and much of the traveling to and fro was done on foot. He returned to Dodge county in the course of a month and a half, and purchased a farm on which he lived until the spring of 1854. He then came to Minnesota and engaged in carpenter work in the city of Mankota for some time. He then went to Kasota and engaged in various employments until December 11, 1855, during a part of which time he was in St. Peter. At the time of his visit to Mankato and St. Peter there were but seven houses in the former and one in the latter place. December 11, 1855, he returned to Wisconsin; had to travel on foot from Kasota to Winona and La Crosse; sold his farm and remained until the spring of 1856, when he went to Chicago, Illinois, then St. Louis, Missouri; to Kansas City; then Lawrence, Topeka and Leavenworth, Kansas, passing through Iowa; on the way back to Mankato, Minnesota. He remained in Kansas but a short time and then returned to the North by the way of Council Bluffs, Des Moines City and Dubuque, reaching Mankota in May, 1856, and engaging as an assistant overseer on the Indian reservation until July 1st of the same year, when he came to Martin county to assist several families in finding a location. Our subject had no team, and had to travel the entire distance on foot. Arriving in Martin county he bought a squatter's right to a claim on which was some native timber, as he expected the families before referred to ere long, and purchased this farm in order to secure wood for them. He paid therefor fifty dollars. He also purchased a team, but was disappointed in that the expected additions to the settlement did not come. He continued to hold his claim, however, a part of which is now within the village limits of Fairmont. He still lives on this land. In March, 1857, the Indian chief Inkpaduta made an attack on the village of Springfield, now Jackson, Jackson county, and, not satisfied with the depredations committed there, the Indians swept down over the country in the vicinity of Fairmont. Luckily for our subject, he was not on his claim, having gone with a neighbor with their ox teams to Iowa for provisions. They were on the return, but were forced to stop for a time, because of the heavy crust that had formed over the surface. The snow was deep and a thick crust had been formed by a rain of sixty-four hours. So our subject had to assist in caring for the oxen, and by the time he returned home the Indians had left the country. In order to find feed on which the oxen might subsist, he was forced to take them further into Iowa, and had to break the crust for four miles before they found a road where the cattle could travel. After reaching a suitable place, he left the oxen and returned to Wisconsin, where he remained a short time. He then came back to his claim in Martin county. He improved this land during that summer, and July 22 they received information of another Indian attack on the settlers toward the northwest—Ft. Ridgely. Our subject, with several neighbors, went about nine miles distant from his claim and built a fort and prepared to fight the Indians. They remained in the fort about one month, and found that the report was false, and they then returned to their claims. In December, 1857, the county was organized, and our subject was appointed one of the first county commissioners by the governor, and in October, 1858, was appointed postmaster at Fairmont. In the spring of 1860 the village of Fairmont was surveyed and platted in the vicinity of our subject's farm. In all these matters he took an active part, and assisted materially in the development

of all projects tending toward the advancement of his locality. He continued in the office of county commissioner until the spring of 1860, and then went to Fillmore county, and worked in Chatfield and Winona during the summer and part of the winter, after which he returned to his Martin county claim. He was elected county commissioner again in 1862, and held the office until February 20, 1864. He has also been clerk of the court, and has held various other official positions. In the fall of 1862 and spring of 1863 he acted as a scout and guide for various parties. February 20, 1864, Mr. Budd enlisted in Company C, Sixth Minnesota Infantry, serving faithfully until August, 1865, when he was honorably discharged. He participated in the battles of Blakeley, Spanish Fort, and numerous skirmishes and battles of minor importance. When he was discharged he returned to his farm and followed agricultural pursuits principally, but also engaged to some extent in work at the carpenter's trade. He has always been a public-spirited, enterprising citizen. He has been a member of the village council two or three times, and has also been village president for some time. He is a member of the Grand Army of the Republic, Phil Kearney post, No. 18, of which he has been quarter master and chaplain. In the fall of 1866 he was elected county commissioner, and served as chairman until 1873.

Mr. Budd was married in Martin county, Minn., March 31, 1864, to Lydia J. Swearingen, daughter of John B. and Jane (Brown) Swearingen, natives, respectively, of Kentucky and Pennsylvania. She was a native of Illinois, and was the widow of Mr. Z. Allen, by whom she had two children—Zilpha and Amy Jane. Mr. and Mrs. Budd have two children—Edith May and Jennie M. The two latter are living with their parents, the two older are married and live near by.

FRANCIS M. RANDALL is one of the thrifty and most reliable farmers and stock raisers of Lake Benton township, Lincoln county, Minnesota. He homesteaded his present excellent farm on section 10, in 1872. At the time our subject came to the county there were but very few settlers, and but very few of those who were here then are now living. Looking back upon his early experiences in this locality, our subject wonders that he had not grown discouraged and removed to find fairer fields and more bountiful results from labors expended. He has met with many hardships and has lost numerous crops. During the years 1874–75–76 his grain was entirely destroyed by grasshoppers. May 11, 1887, his house and its contents were destroyed by fire, and October 17, 1887, his grove was burned. At that time this was the best grove in Lincoln county. Despite all these things, however, our subject has continued manfully at work and has overcome all the misfortunes which have met him. He has gradually grown in wealth and prosperity until to-day he is one of the leading farmers in the county. In 1883 he was met with another misfortune, having his entire crop of wheat, oats, and flax destroyed by a hail-storm, but in spite of these things Mr. Randall is not made of the material which easily gives up. He was full of what is known as "western grit" and outlived and overcame these various troubles by keeping steadily and manfully at work. He deserves great credit for his perseverance and courage, for the hardships through which he has passed have been of such a character as to dash the spirits of the bravest.

Mr. Randall is a native of Sandusky county, Ohio, where he was born October 26, 1846. He is a son of Luke and Elouisa (McFarland) Randall, the former a native of Connecticut and the latter a native of Ohio. The father was of English origin, and the mother of Irish and English descent. The father was a farmer by occupation, and is now residing on a farm in Shoakatan, Lincoln county. In the father's family there were four children —Sarah Jane, our subject, Oliver P. and Olive Louise.

When the subject of our sketch was about two years of age, the family moved to Coles county, Illinois, and two years later settled in Hardin county, Iowa. Eight years later, in 1861, they moved to Kansas, and, after one year's residence there, settled in Madison county, Iowa, and one year later removed to Cass county, Iowa, where they also spent one year. At the expiration of that time they removed to Douglas county, Nebraska. While his father was living there, our subject, Francis M., for five summers crossed and re-crossed the plains in the capacity of a teamster, and during one summer he worked on the Union Pacific Railroad, near Cheyenne, Wyoming Territory. While in that country he suffered many hardships and ran considerable risk of being killed and scalped by the Indians as they very were troublesome at that time; and it was necessary to constantly keep a "sixteen shooter" within reach. After remaining for some years in Nebraska the family came to Lincoln county, Minnesota, and made a permanent settlement.

The subject of our sketch was married March 31, 1873 to Miss Mary Jane Cooley. She was born near Bangor, Somerset county, Maine, December 23, 1854, and was a daughter of James and Sarah Cooley, who were of English and German descent. When Miss Cooley was nine years old the family came West and located in Adams county, Illinois, and one year later removed to Dodge county, Minnesota. She came to Lincoln county in 1872. Her father is now one of the leading merchants of Pipestone, Minnesota. Miss Cooley was one of five children—Sarah Jane, George E., Nelson, Nellie, and Frederick.

Mr. and Mrs. Randall have had six children, three boys and three girls, five of whom are now living—Estella Musetta, Francis Justen, Bertha Mabel (died when fifteen months old), Cora Alice, Clarence Arthur and an infant not named.

In politics the subject of our sketch affiliates with the republican party and is a representative man of Lake Benton township. Since making his location here he has interested himself in the public affairs and has held numerous official positions. He assisted in the organization of the township in 1873, and has been a member of the board of supervisors since 1885. He was clerk of school district No. 2 for some time, and has in every official act proven himself capable and efficient. He is a man of strong, decided opinions, is possessed of the highest character, and is respected by all who know him.

APTAIN CHARLES B. LOVELESS is the gentlemanly and popular proprietor of the Lake View House at Worthington, Minnesota. He is the son of Solomon and Mary Loveless, the former a native of Connecticut, and the latter born in Nova Scotia.

The subject of our sketch has had an interesting and varied career. He was born in a log house in the State of Maine, December 8, 1823. His father was a ship builder, and our subject being thrown somewhat among ships and seamen, imbibed a liking for a seafaring life. At ten years of age our subject became possessed of the idea of adopting the life of a sailor. So, one Saturday night about twelve o'clock, he ran away from home and shipped as a cabin boy on a coasting vessel, and continued in that employment for two years. About this time his father died, and on his death-bed made the urgent request of his son Charles to leave a sailor's life. So our subject, in response to this dy-

ing request, went to learn general blacksmithing, and served an apprenticeship of four years in Schenectady at nine cents a day. Here he was among strangers, and before he found his place to learn the trade, he had spent three or four days in New York City looking for some friends. He had but twenty-four cents in his pocket, and became almost discouraged, yet he was of sturdy make-up, and not easily discouraged. He finally met a Methodist, who was captain of a ship, and he advised our subject to learn a trade. Acting upon this advice Mr. Loveless went to Schenectady, and entered upon his apprenticeship of four years at the blacksmith trade. When that was completed he went to sea again on the old ship North Carolina and served for eight months. He then returned to Schenectady and went into a machine shop where they forged machinery, and while there our subject became very skillful in mounting and finishing molds, etc., being sought after by many parties from far and near who were desirous of obtaining an expert workman. He took a large contract in finishing and putting together stoves, etc., and was thus engaged for five or six years. At the end of this period he went to Boston and engaged in the same business for two years, finishing grates and fancy iron work for local use. He was then in Syracuse for nearly thirty years with the exception of two years spent in Boston and one year spent on a farm. Mr. Loveless' genius has always taken an inventive turn and he has invented several stoves, portable gas works, grates, etc. He commenced inventing in 1854 and has been more or less engaged at it ever since, having produced a number of very useful articles.

When Fort Sumter was fired upon by the Rebels our subject was in Portland, Maine, and at once, fired by patriotic emotions, sold out his patent gas works and commenced recruiting a regiment of cavalry. This was done entirely with his own means and in recruiting the company he used his own conveyance. He succeeded in raising parts of two regiments and commanded Company B, Third Regiment New York Cavalry, being mustered in as captain and commissioned in July, 1861. He served in the most gallant manner for two years, and then returned home and assisted in furthering the work of gathering in recruits for the service. On first starting out with his company, in 1861, he went to the bank in Washington City and withdrew his own money, and with it purchased pots, pans and other camp utensils for the use of his company. After leaving the service he went to New York City and turned his attention to inventing. Among his productions is a gasoline stove, invented in 1864. He organized a company and opened a large establishment and commenced the manufacture of these stoves. His sales in a very short time amounted to $50,000, and during these times, while in Syracuse, New York, his expenses were about $8,000 per year. Perhaps no man in Nobles county has traveled as widely over the United States and Territories as has Mr. Loveless, and his travels have not been confined to this country alone, but he has visited various portions of the British provinces. Very few men have made as many useful and important inventions as he has, and out of these he has at times gathered considerable means. He has been a lover of a good horse during his career, and has kept many fast horses, and spent money lavishly in seeing life and in building up the localities in which he has lived.

In June, 1872, Mr. Loveless came to Worthington, Nobles county, Minnesota, built the Lake View House, and opened a blacksmith shop. For a time he also manufactured carriages and wagons, and his goods were sold all over Southwestern Minnesota. After the hotel was completed he commenced keeping the same and has been in that business ever since with the exception of two years. He has also run a livery in connection with his hotel and operated his blacksmith shop until 1883. In 1885 he visited Philadelphia and organized a stock company for the manufacture of his ventilators and also organized three other companies for the manufacture of his inventions, these companies being made up of prominent business men of the East. Our subject still retains an interest in the company in New York City, where the business reaches large dimensions. Although our subject has been somewhat interested and taken with the grand farming country to be found in the West, he has not invested in any farming lands to speak of. This is explained by the fact that when a young lad he lived with an uncle for two years who made him rise every morning before daylight and had him work hard until dark. This so sickened him of farming that he has never invested to any considerable extent and least of all attempted to operate a farm.

The subject of our sketch was married in New York City, July 5, 1847, to Mary C. Page, a native of Ocean county, New Jersey, where she was born in February, 1822. She was a daughter of Joseph and Annie Page, and died February 9, 1889. This lady was possessed of a gentle, sweet disposition and was loved by all with whom she came in contact. During her life in Worthington she made many warm friends who will remember her for her benevolence toward the poor, for her charity in overlooking the faults of others, and for her generous and kind assistance of all who came to her in time of trouble. She was a lady of high Christian character and always aided liberally in the management of church and religious matters. Mr. and Mrs. Loveless had the following-named children—

Alida, who died in New Jersey; Ella (deceased), Charles, who met his death by drowning in Syracuse; Joseph and William. Joseph married Miss Mary Brayden, of Worthington, and William wedded Miss Belle Allen.

Throughout his life Captain Loveless has been active and public spirited. He has always interested himself in all public affairs, and has with credit held various official positions. His executive abilities, combined with his military spirit, always made him a man to be sought after in the management of affairs in which the presence of a master spirit was needed. Since coming to the village he has been a member of the village council for two terms, and has interested himself in educational matters by assisting in the organization and selection of the school site of the Worthington public schools. While in New York he was foreman of the fire companies of Syracuse for seven years. No man in Southern Minnesota is more decidedly a temperance man than Mr. Loveless, and, believing in total prohibition, he stops at nothing short of a third party movement in bringing this about. In religious matters he has always taken a deep interest, and has assisted liberally in the building up and supporting of the various churches in the city.

———•—◦❦◦—•———

SETH W. THOMPSON is the vice-president and manager of the First National Bank, of Luverne, Rock county, Minnesota. The subject of our sketch came to the city in September, 1887, and accepted the position which he now occupies.

Mr. Thompson is a native of Chautauqua county, New York, where he was born in the year 1836. His parents were John and Pennelia (Bush) Thompson, the former a native of Maine, and the latter born in New York. The parents were farmers by occu-

pation, and engaged in that line throughout the most of their lives.

The subject of our sketch spent his younger days on the home farm, and attended the district schools when not busy with farm work. He remained with his parents until twenty-five years of age, and during eight winters prior to leaving the farm engaged in teaching school. At the age of twenty-five he opened a hardware business in the village of Cattaraugus, New York, and engaged in that line for twelve years. He then removed to Randolph, New York, where he engaged in the hardware business four years, then went to East Randolph, and for two years following he operated a tannery business, and for some years after that time he was connected with a private bank in that county, the firm name being Dow & Thompson. Quitting the banking business, he opened a general mercantile trade and continued in that line for seven years. Then he removed to Luverne, Rock county, Minnesota, where he has since resided. Prior to coming to the county he had invested in considerable land some six miles south of the city. Since making his location he has invested largely in farming lands and in city property, owning at present nearly one thousand acres. Besides general farming he is engaged to some extent in raising blooded horses and cattle. In 1888 he built one of the finest houses in the village, and provided it with all modern improvements. In politics Mr. Thompson affiliates with the republican party, and is an influential member of the Independent Order of Odd Fellows. He is a man of good character, and is one of the wealthy and respected citizens of Luverne and Rock county.

The wedding day of S. W. Thompson occurred in 1859, in which year he was married to Miss Emma Pratt, of New York. Three children have blessed this union—

John F., Charles C. and Carrie E. John F. is assistant cashier of the Seaboard National Bank, in New York City. Charles C. is cashier of the First National Bank of Luverne. Carrie E. married Henry J. Brennan, an officer in the First National Bank of Port Alleghany, Pennsylvania, and a resident of Smethport.

ERASTUS P. LE SUER, a prominent business man of the village of Jasper, Pipestone county, Minnesota, is engaged in the drug trade. He is a native of Jamestown, Chautauqua county, New York, where he was born November 2, 1832.

The parents of the subject of our sketch were Asa and Louisa (Gray) Le Suer, both natives of the State of New York. The father followed the occupation of farming in his native State, and, in 1856, moved with his family to Rochester, Olmsted county, Minnesota. He was the second settler of the city, and engaged for a time in the hotel business. He was also engaged in farming to some extent on 160 acres of land about two miles west of the city. He continued his residence in Rochester until his death, which occurred in 1868. The mother died in 1864. In the father's family there were two children—Helen P., now Mrs. A. C. Covell, of California, and Erastus P. The younger days of our subject were spent with his parents on the home farm, where he remained until sixteen years of age. He was given the educational advantages furnished by the district schools. At sixteen he apprenticed to learn the carpenter's trade, which line of occupation he followed until going to Michigan in the year 1850. Arriving in that State he attended the medical college at Ann Arbor, and graduated in medicine in 1855. He has never practiced his profession, however, but has given his time principally to the drug business. In July, 1856, he went to Rochester, Minnesota, and remained there, engaged in the hotel business, until the destruction of his house by fire on May 9, 1872. In this fire our subject lost about nine thousand dollars. After this stroke of misfortune he removed to Kasson, Minnesota, where he built a hotel and also engaged in operating a drug store and auction store. Remaining in Kasson until 1878, he then sold out his property interests and removed to Canby, Yellow Medicine county, Minnesota, where he built the now popular hotel called the Le Suer House. He continued in this business until in 1884, when he rented his property and engaged exclusively in the drug business. Later he sold out his hotel and store buildings and removed with his stock of goods to the village of Jasper, Pipestone county, Minnesota, where he has since been engaged in business.

Mr. Le Suer was married in June, 1880, to Miss Julia Oleson, a native of Minnesota, by whom he has had one child, Josie M. By a former marriage Mr. Le Suer has three children—Frank, Asa and Earl.

Since coming to the village Mr. Le Suer has occupied a prominent position in business circles and has built up a fine trade. Among his financial interests he is a large stockholder in the Jasper Produce Company. Throughout his career Mr. Le Suer has taken an active interest in all matters which tended to the development of the locality in which he lived. While a resident of Yellow Medicine county he held the position of deputy sheriff for six years, was justice of the peace, village marshal, and also president of the school board. In politics he affiliates with the republican party, and is a leading and influential member of the Independent Order of Odd Fellows. Mr. Le Suer is a careful, systematic business man, and is one of Jasper's prominent citizens.

JOHN B. JOHNSON, a prosperous farmer of Scandia township, Murray county, Minnesota, was born in Skone, Sweden, June 24, 1852, his parents being John and Hannah (Larson) Johnson, natives of Sweden.

Our subject's early life was spent in the home of his parents, where he assisted in farm work and attended the district schools until he reached the age of fifteen years. From that time until 1878 he worked out for farmers in his native land, and in the year just mentioned came to the United States, coming directly to Murray county, Minnesota, and stopping with Hans Pearson in Scandia township for two months. He then went onto a farm owned by Nels Anderson, where he remained during the winter, and in the following spring rented a farm which he operated for eighteen months. He then purchased forty acres of land, built a house, and has made that his permanent residence ever since. He has since added other lands to his farm, and now owns 360 acres, with about 260 acres under cultivation. On this place are a good frame dwelling-house and large granary and a grove of about 10,500 trees. When our subject came to America he was very poor, so poor that he had not a dollar in his pocket, and all that he now owns is the result of hard labor and good management. Besides his land and farm buildings he owns six horses, one colt and seventeen head of cattle. He is a man of earnest, energetic qualities, and is respected for his upright character and good habits. He is a member of the Swedish lutheran church.

Mr. John B. Johnson was married, while still a resident of Sweden, September 10, 1873, to Miss Boel Pearson, daughter of Peter and Anna (Martinson) Hanson. This lady is a native of Sweden, where she was born October 7, 1851. Three children were born to this union in Sweden—Hannah, Nels and Anna. Since coming to America four more children have been added to the family—Ida, Agnes, Emily and Hulda.

SQUIRE B. STEDMAN is the present popular and efficient postmaster of Windom, Minnesota. He was born in Lorain county, Ohio, in the year 1830. His parents were Almeron and Wealthy (Abbott) Stedman, natives, respectively, of Connecticut and Massachusetts. The father was a farmer and lumberman by occupation, and came to Ohio in 1826, where he engaged in farming until his death. He had a family of thirteen children—seven sons and six daughters—all of whom except one grew to man and womanhood.

The subject of our sketch remained with his parents on the home farm and received a good common-school education. He continued with his parents until twenty-one years of age, after which he worked out on various farms in the vicinity of his home for one year. The next season was spent with his father on the home farm, and he then purchased a threshing machine and did considerable work in that line. Soon after he sold out and went to Wisconsin, where he rented a farm for two years. During the first winter of his stay in Wisconsin he worked in the pineries, and at the end of two years returned to Ohio. In the winter of 1855–56 he was married to Miss Thomas. In 1860 he located in Little Canon, Goodhue county, Minnesota, where he engaged in agricultural pursuits and resided nine years. He attained considerable success, and in the spring of 1869 came to Cottonwood county, where he took a pre-emption of 160 acres, on a portion of which is now located the village of Windom. He saw many hardships during the first few years in the county, and for some time had all his grain and garden stuffs destroyed by the grasshoppers. He continued farming until 1880. In 1874 he was elected sheriff of the county. Our subject has always taken an active interest in political matters and has held various official positions, among them being that of chairman of the board of county commissioners and postmaster, being appointed to that position in October, 1885. He has a fine residence in the village, and has surrounded himself with the evidences of prosperity and success. He is a man of excellent character, broad-minded and public spirited and is highly esteemed by all who know him. In politics he affiliates with the democratic party.

On the 20th of January, 1856, Mr. Stedman was married to Miss Angeline H. Thomas, a native of Vermont. This union has been blessed with eight children, six of whom are now living — Frank, Arthur, George, Eli, Eveanlette and Edgar.

DOCTOR J. P. HUMES is a leading physician and surgeon of Winnebago City, Faribault county, Minnesota. Dr. Humes is in every sense of the word a self-made man, one of those strong characters which make many friends. He has built up a large and lucrative practice in Faribault county.

Dr. Humes was born in Crawford county, Pennsylvania, January 16, 1837, and was the son of John C. and Mary E (Griffeth) Humes, natives of Pennsylvania. The father was one of the early settlers of Pennsylvania, and was engaged extensively in farming, continuing his residence in his native State until his death. In politics he was of the democratic faith, and was a leading spirit in the Methodist Episcopal church, in which he was a deacon for many years. His family were of Scotch descent. There were seven children in the father's family four of whom are now living—William W., a farmer on the old homestead; James B., a dentist at Cambridge, Pennsylvania; Julia A., now Mrs. Miller, and Dr. J. P.

The subject of our sketch was reared on the home farm, and was given an academic education in his native State. After completing his course in school he became a pedagogue for some two years in Pennsylvania, and later came to Fulton county, Illinois, arriving in 1856, where he continued one year. In 1857 he settled on a farm of 160 acres a few miles north of Winnebago City, Faribault county, Minnesota. He resided on this land until in May, 1861, and while there experienced all the hardships which usually come to pioneer life. He lived for a time in a board shanty, 12x14 feet, and in 1859 built a frame house, further improving his farm by breaking about eighty acres of land and fencing the entire tract. In May, 1861, he left the farm and returned to Pennsylvania, where he entered a partnership with his brother, James B., in the manufacture of oil barrels. During this time he was engaged in the study of medicine, in which direction he had been reading for some years. He remained in Pennsylvania and carried on his various business enterprises until in August, 1864. He then returned to Winnebago City, and commenced the study of medicine with Dr. Alvin Lockwood. He commenced practice in May, 1866, and in 1867 completed a course at Rush Medical College in Chicago, from which institution he graduated in the spring of that year. Ever since that time he has been actively engaged in the practice of his profession in Winnebago City and vicinity. In 1873, not being satisfied with his medical attainments, he attended a course of lectures at the College of Physicians and Surgeons and also at the University of Medicine in New York City. Returning home he continued his former business. He has built up a large and lucrative practice, and has been very successful in his medical and surgical work. He carries on his farm by proxy, owning at present some 507 acres in Faribault county, and also two thousand acres of land in Carlton county, Minnesota. He has built a beautiful residence in Winnebago City, and has a half block in his grounds.

He takes an active interest in all matters pertaining to the public welfare and has assisted materially in the building up of the financial interests of Winnebago City. He is also interested in religious matters, and is a trustee of the Baptist college, having rendered valuable aid in building that institution. He has been liberally inclined toward other church enterprises, and has assisted in a financial way in the building of all the church edifices in the city. In politics he affiliates with the republican party. He is also a Mason and an Odd Fellow, and is a prominent member of the Minnesota State Medical Society. He is the second oldest resident physician in the county, and is not only one of the oldest M. D.'s, but is one of the most prominent citizens of the county.

Dr. Humes was married in 1867 to Miss Emma McColley, of Winnebago City. This union has been blessed with five children—Alice A., Ella A., Gertrude, Edith and James P.

ISRAEL TURNER. This gentleman is one of the leading financial spirits of the village of Jasper, Pipestone county, Minnesota. He is the president of the Jasper Bank, which was established in March, 1889. Mr. Turner is of English birth, being born March 17, 1843. His parents were Robert and Mary (Timpley) Turner, both of whom were natives of England. The father was an operator in one of the large cotton factories which abound in England.

The subject of our sketch spent his early boyhood days in the parental home, being given excellent educational advantages. He acquired a good education, and also developed fine musical abilities. At the age of sixteen years he engaged as a musician in the British army, continuing about two years and a half. He then joined the navy, and for five years was leader of one of the naval bands. At the close of this five years' service he found employment in the British arsenal at Woolwich, England, in which he continued some two and a half years. During his service in the navy he visited the southeast and southwest coasts of Africa, along which he cruised some two years, thence going to the Brazilian Islands, where he spent three years. The division to which our subject belonged was under the command of Sir Henry Keppell. Captain Speeke and Captain Grant, of the British army were passengers on board of the same ship, "H. M. S. Forte," to Zanzibar, their starting point for the interior of the country. A company of soldiers were also landed at Zanzibar, from whence they struck into the interior, to try if possible to discover the source of the River Nile. After much weary marching and untold miseries and privations, the discovery was made, and the captains named above returned to England by another route, reaching that country before the arrival of the ship. The ship fare, including the oft-heard-of and unconquerable "hard tack," was not in accordance with the taste of our subject, and his physical nature rebelled against the infliction of "hard tack." He could eat it only in small quantities, and in consequence thereof fell away in flesh, and he was forced to purchase his own food. Whenever the vessel stopped at any port he would go ashore and lay in a supply of provisions for his own use. In this way he succeeded in getting through with his naval experience alive. While a member of the military band, he was one of thirty-two musicians, and was one of twenty-four while serving in the navy. Returning to England after his naval service, he then found employment as above stated, in the British arsenal. In 1867 he emigrated to the United States and first located at Cedar Falls, Iowa. While in that city he was in the employ of the Illinois Central Railroad Company, as station and baggage master. This line of employ-ment was followed by him for some three years, when he was promoted to the position of station agent for the same company at New Hartford, Butler county, Iowa, where he remained three years. Then for a period of nine years he held a profitable engagement with the Burling-ton, Cedar Rapids & Northern railroad, as their station agent at Nora Junction, Iowa. After this period he engaged as first agent at Spirit Lake, Iowa, remaining some five months, and from there going to Iowa Falls, where, for a little over fourteen years, he was in the employ of the same company. Removing from that place he went to Mason City, and engaged in the wholesale and retail coal business under the firm name of Turner & Co. This company is one of the largest and strongest of the kind on the Chicago, Milwaukee & St. Paul system of railroads, and the business is still continued under the old partnership name. Removing from Mason City he came to Jasper, Pipe-stone county, in March, 1889, at which time he established his present banking business. He erected a very fine building of the famous Jasper stone, this being the first bank in the village.

The wedding of the subject of our sketch occurred March 19, 1889, on which date he was married to Miss Annie Rhem, a native of Mason City, Iowa, where she was reared and educated.

Mr. Turner is one of the largest capitalists of this part of the county, and, having come to Jasper with a considerable amount of money, will assist materially in building up and improving the village and vicinity. Having been trained in a practical school in the railroad employ as their financial agent, he is fully equipped for the business in which he has embarked, and will, without doubt, meet with a large degree of success. In politics our subject is an independent, be-lieving that it is wisest to elect the best men to office. He is an influential Mason and Knight Templar.

--------◆--◆◆◆◆◆◆◆◆◆--◆--------

REZEAU B. PLOTTS, past assistant engineer United States navy, an in-fluential citizen of Worthington, Nobles county, Minnesota, is the son of Rev. Conley and Anna F. (Frankfort) Plotts, the former a native of New Jersey and the latter born in Philadelphia. Our subject is a native of Mount Holly, New Jersey, where he was born January 29, 1837. Our subject's father was a prominent educator in the Eastern States, and for years was the principal of the schools at Mount Holly, and in Philadelphia was the founder of several school institutes. He was a graduate of Princeton College, and was a man of considerable prominence in educa-tional circles.

The subject of this sketch commenced go-ing to school when he was four years of age, and his younger days were spent almost wholly in obtaining an education. He finished his training in the Central High School of Philadelphia in 1853, his name being now on the roll of honor in that in-stitution, because of his gallant service in the United States navy. The school was of the same grade as most of the colleges in the country, and our subject was able to obtain a classical education. On leaving school he commenced learning the ma-chinist's trade with Reany, Neafie & Levy, in Kensington, Philadelphia. He remained with this firm for some four years, and then employed his time as a journeyman machin-ist whenever he could find work to do in that line. When not able to find work at his trade he taught school in Iowa and Wisconsin, and in the spring of 1859 returned to Williamsport, Pennsylvania, to which place his parents had moved while our subject was learning his trade.

He returned home on account of ill-health, and remained with his parents until the early part of 1860, working a part of the time in the railroad shops of the city. He then went to Norfolk, Virginia, whence, after remaining a short time, he went to Richmond and made that his abiding place until in February, or March, 1861. He left for Washington on the last train for that city before open hostilities between the North and South had cut off all communication. On reaching Washington our subject went to Williamsport and made application for admission into the naval service. July 1, 1861, he was accepted, and ordered to report for duty on the sloop of war "Richmond." In August this vessel left Brooklyn navy yard and cruised for about a month in pursuit of the ship "Sumpter." Then the vessel reported for duty at Pensacola and was sent to blockade the mouth of the Mississippi river, where they relieved the ship "Brooklyn." For some time the vessel was on blockade duty, and October 1, 1861, sailed up to the head of the passes, and remained there until the morning of October 12, when they engaged in battle with the Rebel ram "Manassas." In this engagement the Rebel steamer collided with the "Richmond," and broke a large hole in the side of the ship, and did considerable damage. After fighting for about an hour and a half, the vessels separated, neither having gained a decisive victory. Our subject participated in all the hard-fought engagements while on board the "Richmond," from 1861 to 1863, and was relieved from duty on board this vessel in 1863 and ordered to report to the commander of the "Nipsic." He was with the South Atlantic squadron for about nine months, most of the time lying off Charleston, in the vicinity of which he participated in four engagements. In 1864 he was sent on board the "Octora," in which ship he served during two severe engagements, his vessel leading in the fight in Mobile bay against Fort Morgan. Our subject's squadron continued in the vicinity of Mobile Bay until the close of the war, and Mr. Plotts spent a short time in the hospital as the result of hardships and exposures through which he had passed. Later he was sent to New Orleans, and later was ordered North on sick leave, when he returned home and remained until 1866. He was then ordered on duty again in the naval service, and was sent to League Island, Philadelphia, where he was stationed four years. He was then detached from this service, and, returning home, remained a year and then, March 6, 1872, came to Worthington and settled on land in Elk township and remained until February, 1877. At that date he removed to the village of Worthington, and has since made that his home. He is one of the most public-spirited citizens of the county, and has taken an active part in all public matters. He has been deputy sheriff for five or six years, village recorder six or seven years, and has held various other local offices with credit to himself and satisfaction to his constituents.

In his financial matters Mr. Plotts has been fairly successful, and owns valuable property in the city. He resides in a beautiful Queen Anne cottage, built in 1888, and provided with modern improvements. Mr. Plotts is still attached to the naval service, being retired on pay during peaceful times. He is still liable to be called out for duty at any time. He is a member of the Masonic, Grand Army of the Republic, Post 34, and Ancient Order United Workmen lodges, and of other civic societies.

Mr. Plotts was married in New Orleans, July 23, 1864, to Miss Kate Slavin, daughter of Edward and Anna (Davis) Slavin, natives, respectively, of Ireland and England. Mrs. Plotts was born in Galveston, Texas, June 23, 1845, and died in Worthington, April 2, 1885, leaving the following children—Emily

C., Martha W., Lillie C., Nellie M., Philip E., Manning J. and Walter J., who died in September, 1888. Mrs. Plotts was one of the most prominent and well known of all the old settlers of the county, and was a charter member of Stoddard Post Women's Relief Corps, No. 1, and was also well known for her kindness and charity to those in sickness and distress. She was beloved and mourned by all.

∗∗∗

FRANCIS McQUOID. This gentleman is one of the reliable farmers and stock raisers of Gray township, Pipestone county, Minnesota. He located on section 5 in the spring of 1885. He is largely interested in raising short-horned cattle and hogs of the Suffolk breed, which stock our subject brought from Canada. This is a fine breed of swine and was first introduced into Pipestone county by Mr. McQuoid. He has been thrifty and industrious in the management of his farm, and has one of the best places in the county.

The subject of our sketch was born in the town of Pickering, province of Ontario, Canada, September 23, 1832. He is of Irish descent, his parents, John and Ann (Dunlap) McQuoid, having been born in County Down, in the north of Ireland. The parents both came to Canada before their marriage, but received their education and early training in the land of their birth, the father being seventeen and the mother eighteen years of age when they left Ireland. The father continued a resident of Canada until his death, which occurred in about 1878. The mother died in 1881. They were farmers by occupation, and the mother was a consistent member of the Presbyterian church. In the father's family there were five children— Ann, Francis, Martha, Henry and James, all of whom are living.

The early life of our subject was spent in Pickering, the town of his nativity. Here he received excellent educational advantages, and was able to acquire a thorough course of schooling. At seventeen he left the schools, and gave his attention to work on his father's farm, continuing in this line of employment with his father until he was thirty years of age. On reaching this age he was married, and then engaged in various employments for the purpose of building up and securing a home for himself and family. For the most part he followed the business of farming, and remained in his native country until coming to Pipestone county.

December 24, 1864, Mr. McQuoid was united in marriage to Miss Agnes Weir, a native of the township of Vaughn, province of Ontario, Canada. Her parents were John and Agnes (Temple) Weir, both of whom were natives of Scotland. The parents were married in their native land, and came to Canada in an early day. They brought four children with them—John, James, Jane and a daughter, Agnes, who died before the birth of the wife of the subject of our sketch. Three children have been born to them since coming to Canada— Mungo, Thomas, and Agnes (now Mrs. McQuoid). Of these children, the first Agnes, Jane and Thomas are now dead. When Mrs. McQuoid was about six years old her parents removed to Pickering, province of Ontario, Canada, where she received her early training and education. Her father was a farmer by occupation, and died in 1872. Mr. and Mrs. McQuoid have three children living—Thomas Henry, James and William. Another son, John, died at the age of fifteen years and ten months, in Pickering, Canada. Agnes Temple, a daughter, died at the age of thirteen years and eight months, in the same town in Canada.

The subject of our sketch is a pleasant, sociable gentleman, and is a man held in high esteem by all his neighbors. He is an earnest sympathizer with all matters that tend toward the elevation of politics and morals, and takes an active interest in all affairs of a public nature. His political faith is with the democratic party. As a farmer he has proven an excellent success, and has surrounded himself with the evidences of prosperity, such as a good dwelling house, barns and other buildings so necessary on a well-regulated farm.

——————

CHARLES CHADDERDON is one of the most reliable and prosperous farmers of Great Bend township, Cottonwood county, Minnesota, and resides on an excellent farm on section 15. He was born in the township of Herman, Dodge county, Wisconsin, September 19, 1851. He was the son of Hon. Jonathan and Sophia (Mattise) Chadderdon both natives of New York, the mother born at Middleburgh, in Schoharie county. The father was born March 10, 1808, in the town of Broom, of the same county, and engaged at the carpenter's trade in the State of New York until about 1845, when he removed to Wisconsin, settling on a farm. After nine years' residence there, he removed to Belle Plaine, Scott county, Minnesota, and taking a claim, remained there until 1877 when he removed to LeSueur county, where he lived a retired life until his death, which occurred January 20, 1884. The mother died in Scott county December 24, 1874. The father was a democrat in politics and was one of the prominent citizens of his locality. He took an active part in the local affairs of his government and served one term in the State legislature in the winter of 1859-60. There were thirteen children in the father's family, our subject being the tenth in order of birth.

During his early life the subject of our sketch was given excellent educational advantages and acquired a thorough practical education. He remained with his parents on the homestead until about twenty-four

years of age. He then spent two years studying law at Jordan, Scott county, and in 1878 came to Cottonwood county and purchased the place on which he now lives. It was 160 acres of wild land, having no improvements whatever. Our subject at once commenced operations, planting a grove of trees, etc., and has now one of the best farms in the township.

Mr. Chadderdon was married to Flora C. Nichol, a native of Scott county, Minnesota, March 19, 1879. This lady died August 27, 1879, and was buried at Jordan, her old home. Our subject was again married October 29, 1884, to Miss Ella Harris, a native of Belle Plaine, Scott county, Minnesota, and a daughter of George and Cornelia (King) Harris. Mr. and Mrs. Chadderdon have been blessed with one child, Myrtle C.

The subject of our sketch, as we have already stated, received an excellent education during his early life, having passed through the public schools, and also having attended four terms at Carlton College, at Northfield, Minnesota. He is a man of strong opinions, of progressive ideas, and is one of the most public spirited citizens of the township. He is a man of strong temperance principles, and affiliates with the prohibition party. He takes an active interest in all matters of a religious nature and is an elder in the Presbyterian church. He also belongs to the Ancient Order United Workmen, and various other civic organizations. In public affairs he is one of the prominent citizens, and has been county commissioner for five years, during three years of which he was chairman of the board. He has also been chairman of the township board of supervisors for eight years, and is the present incumbent of that office. He has varied his pursuits since coming to Cottonwood county, and in connection with farming has engaged more or less in teaching school. With the exception of last winter he has taught every winter during the past seventeen years. Mr. Chadderdon is a man of good character, and is esteemed by all who know him.

———❖—❖❖❖—❖———

WILLIAM D. PECK. This gentleman found his location in Pipestone county on section 26, Gray township, in 1878, at which time he filed a "soldier's homestead." He did not settle on his land at once, but returned to his former place of residence, and remained until in March, 1879, which month saw him again on his land in section 26, and since which time he has held continual residence. He commenced improvements by building a house 12x16 feet and a stable 12x32 feet. He continued living in this house for about five years and during the meantime had built a small wing to the house 8x12 feet. Throughout his residence in the township, Mr. Peck has shown himself to be one of the most enterprising and liberal spirited of its citizens. He was one of the organizers of the township and the county. He was the first to hold the position of justice of the peace, and holds that office at the present time, being now on his third term. He has also held the position of pathmaster and has identified himself closely with the best interests of his township. Among the other settlers who lived in the town when Mr. Peck came, were Mr. Smith, Charles Maxfield and others. In June, 1885, Mr. Peck concluded to leave the farm; so, removing to the village of Hatfield, he bought out the grocery business of I. N. Converse. He now has a large stock of miscellaneous drugs, glassware and some hardware and notions. He does a large and extensive trade and is patronized from all parts of the county. He is the only business man in the place and therefore has a monopoly on the trade.

Mr. Peck was born in Harrisburg, Lewis county, New York, June 19, 1830. His parents were David and Eliza (Brownwell) Peck, both of whom were natives of New York, where they were reared and educated and finally married. They made that State their home, engaged in farming until 1860, in which year they removed to Dane county, Wisconsin. Remaining in that county for some two years, they then removed to Mower county, Minnesota, where they remained until their death, the mother dying in about 1875, and the father in 1877. They were both excellent Christian people and leading members of the Methodist Episcopal church. The subject of our sketch was the oldest of seven children, the names of his brothers and sisters being Washington, Charity, Lorenzo, Electa, Lewis, and Nelson. Charity and Electa, the two girls, are now dead.

The subject of our sketch remained with his parents throughout his early life; removing with them at the age of seven years to St. Lawrence county, New York, where he was reared and educated in the common schools. He made the village of Lawrence, in that county, his home until in 1861, when, on September 20, he enlisted in Company F, Ninety-second Regiment New York Volunteer Infantry, his company being attached to the Eighteenth Army Corps. Mr. Peck passed through very honorable service being promoted to the rank of first sergeant the same fall, and being recommended to the office of lieutenant, but owing to the consolidation of his regiment he did not receive this latter office. He was discharged June 10, 1863, at Newburn, North Carolina, as first sergeant under Captain Newton. The subject of our sketch engaged in many hard-fought battles, and spent many weary days in the march to the front. He was at the battle of Fort Anderson, in North Carolina, and participated in a great many skirmishes in the Carolinas and in Virginia. After his discharge he returned to the State of New York, and after one year spent in the vicinity of his native home, he turned his steps westward, locating in Dodge county, Wisconsin, where he remained during one summer. From thence he removed to Mower county, Minnesota, in 1864, remaining a resident there until his removal to Pipestone county in 1878.

Mr. Peck was united in the holy bonds of matrimony July 14, 1851, to Miss Hannah Jenkins, who died in 1860. She was an exemplary member of the Wesleyan church, and at her death left three daughters— Wealthy, Ella and Almeda. Wealthy died at the age of thirteen years. In August, 1861, Mr. Peck was married to Miss Jerusha Rich, a native of the State of New York, where she was reared and given an academic education. She was a lady of large intelligence, and taught school for many years in her native State. By this second marriage Mr. Peck has had no children.

The subject of our sketch is a man of excellent abilities, and is looked upon as one of the leading citizens of the town in which he lives. In religious as well as other matters he takes a leading place, and is an exemplary member of the Methodist Episcopal church, in which society he holds the position of member of the board of trustees. He takes an active interest in the welfare of this religious organization, and occasionally his voice is heard in exhortation and admonition to his brother members and the world around him. While a resident of Mower county, for some six or eight years he held the relation of local preacher in the Methodist Episcopal church. He is a member of the Grand Army of the Republic, Post No. 93, of which he has been chaplain for about a year. In politics he affiliates with the prohibition party, and is heartily in sympathy with all movements which tend to the reformation of the morals and business principles of his fellow-men. Since coming to this county Mr. Peck has been intimately associated with the political interests of the county organization, and has held several positions of trust and responsibility. While a resident of Mower county he held the position of supervisor, clerk, justice of the peace, etc. He was nominated for representative on the Greenback ticket for his district in 1876, and received ninety-three votes out of 103 in his own town. Mr. Peck is a good citizen, and is held in high esteem by all who know him.

MYRON H. OLIVER. This prosperous farmer is located in Verona township, Faribault county, Minnesota, to which place he came in 1867, and purchased a farm of eighty acres on section 17. He has since bought eighty acres more on section 16, and now owns 160 acres. He was born in Orleans county, New York, February 6, 1844.

Our subject's father was John Oliver, a native of the State of New York, from whence he emigrated to Waukesha county, Wisconsin, in 1847. He now resides in the village of Waukesha, and is seventy-four years of age. He has always been engaged in farming until within a few years, when he retired from active business. Our subject's mother's name, before her marriage, was Elizabeth Jane Morse, a native of New York, where she was reared and educated, and where, for some years during her early life, she engaged in the profession of teaching. Her father was Benjamin Morse, a farmer who lived and died in New York. In our subject's father's family there were nine children, seven of whom grew to man and womanhood—Myron H., Lemyra, William, Franklin, Edna, Elizabeth and John. Elizabeth married Henry Johnson, a farmer, and died in 1883, leaving two children.

The early training and education of our subject was received in Waukesha county, where he received the principal part of his education, attending the high school at Fond du Lac for one term. Before twenty years of age he commenced teaching school and continued in that occupation until his enlistment in the Union army in March, 1864, and went to Madison, Wisconsin, but was rejected, and then returned to Fond du Lac county and was engaged in farming during the summer. After harvest he again enlisted, this time in the Twenty-eighth Wisconsin Infantry, and served until the close of the war in 1865. After being discharged he returned to Waukesha county, Wisconsin, and worked his father's farm for a year, remaining in that county for a year and one-half, when, in 1867, he came to Faribault county, Minnesota, as stated in the opening lines of this sketch. He has retained his residence in the county throughout the past years and during grasshopper times. He has been interested to a large extent in educational matters and has taught six winter schools since coming to Minnesota. Mr. Oliver was married in 1871 to Miss Ann Jeffry, a native of Waukesha county, Wisconsin, and daughter of John Jeffry, a farmer and leading citizen of Wisconsin. Mr. and Mrs. Oliver have five children—George, Mabel, Edith, Inez and Ruby.

The political affiliations of the subject of our sketch are with the republican party, and in religious sentiment he belongs to the Methodist Episcopal church. He is a man of good business qualities, and has served in various official positions. Since locating in the county Mr. Oliver has been engaged principally in farming.

⁂

SAMUEL D. PUMPELLY is the present efficient auditor of Lincoln county, Minnesota. He is the son of Benjamin E. and Mary C. (Cochran) Pumpelly, the former a native of Maine and the latter of New Hampshire. The parents were farmers by occupation, and resided for many years in Kentucky. At the breaking out of the Rebellion they were virtually forced to leave their Kentucky home, owing to their intense loyalty, and removed to McLean county, Illinois, where they now reside.

Auditor Pumpelly was born in Mason county, Kentucky, May 20, 1841. His early life was spent on the home farm with his parents, and he was given good educational advantages in the district and select schools. At the age of eighteen he commenced a course of legal studies in the office of Judge Emery Whitaker, of Maysville, Kentucky. After completing his course of studies with that gentleman, and before he was admitted to the bar, the war came on, and he quit the law office, and in September 1861, enlisted in Company A, Sixteenth Regiment Kentucky Volunteer Infantry, as a private, and served honorably and faithfully until February, 1865. He was mustered out at Louisville, Kentucky, bearing the title of captain. For gallant and meritorious service he was first promoted to the rank of orderly sergeant, then to second lieutenant, and later was made first lieutenant. Somewhat later he was commissioned as captain. In September, 1862, he served on the staff of Colonel Cyrus Dunham. This officer had a brigade organized at Louisville, and went to Munfordville, Kentucky, to hold the railroad bridge which was threatened by General Bragg. After two or three days' fighting the brigade was forced to surrender to General Bragg. They were kept prisoners for a short time, and then paroled and sent to Camp Morton, Indianapolis, Indiana. After waiting some two months an exchange was effected, and our subject returned to his regiment at Lebanon, Kentucky. He participated in a great many hard-fought battles, and was a brave soldier. He was with

General Burnside's expedition in the fall of 1863, with whom he went to Knoxville. In January, 1864, the members of his regiment veteranized, and joined General Schofield's Twenty-third Army Corps in front of Dalton. They joined Sherman's army, and went through the great campaign against Atlanta. At the battle of Resaca our subject received a severe wound, being shot in the left side. The bullet passed clear through his body, and he was laid up in the hospital for a long time. As soon as he was able to leave his cot he desired to re-enter the service, but was not constitutionally fit for active duty. In October, 1864, he was made assistant provost marshal at Louisville, and he continued in that position until the close of the war. When hostilities had ceased between the North and South Mr. Pumpelly went to Topeka, Kansas, where he was admitted to the bar both in Federal and State courts. He remained two years, returning then on account of health to Central Illinois, where for eight years he engaged in farming, and in the grocery business. In 1876 he sold out and came to Minnesota, settling on a homestead in Shaokatan township, Lincoln county. He made that his home some eight years and then removed to Lake Benton, having been elected county auditor upon the republican ticket in the fall of 1884. So efficiently did he serve in this capacity and so popular did he become with his constituents that he was re-elected by a handsome majority in 1886 and again re-elected in the fall of 1888. He still owns and operates his farm of 320 acres.

The subject of our sketch was united in marriage in McLean, Illinois, August 28, 1865, to Miss Sarah E. Gibbs, a daughter of James and Mary Salome (Davis) Gibbs, natives of England. This marriage has been blessed with the following-named children—Cora Mabel, Samuel Eaton, Mary Susan and Kate Gertrude.

Since coming to Minnesota our subject has taken an active interest in all matters pertaining to the development and the business resources of the whole country. He has assisted largely in the manipulation of the governmental affairs of the county and township in which he has lived, and has held several positions besides the one mentioned in the opening lines of this sketch. In whatever way he has been called upon to serve his constituents he has proven his efficiency and ability as a business man. His loyalty as a citizen is beyond question and as a friend and neighbor he is held in high esteem by all who know him.

ZEBINA WELD is a prominent citizen of Des Moines River township, Murray county, Minnesota, where he is engaged in farming. He is the son of Zebina and Esther R. (Ridgeway) Weld, natives of Maine. He was born in Athens, Maine, August 15, 1830.

The parental home remained the abiding place of our subject until he was eighteen years of age. Up to this time he had been given a good common-school education and on attaining the age just mentioned he went to Skowhegan to learn the carpenter's trade, continuing thereat for only six months. He then entered a shoe shop to learn the boot and shoe business, but finding this kind of labor too confining for his health he quit that work and went to Brighton, Massachusetts, where he engaged in agricultural pursuits for two years. He was then married, and leaving his wife on the farm with his brother, he went to Chicago and thence to Iowa City, where he located land and worked about a year at the carpenter's trade. His wife then joined him and taught the village school until the following spring when the family moved to the land which the husband had located, built a house and took up their residence. After residing here a short time Mr. Weld was taken with the fever and ague, and selling out his property he removed to Sparta, Wisconsin, where he engaged at work at his trade and also at teaming for some two years. While in Sparta he was quite successful in his business, owning several comfortable houses. His next move was to Plainview, Wabasha county, Minnesota, where he pre-empted 160 acres of land just north of the village, making his home thereon for about seven years. He then purchased a farm and five-acre lot adjoining the village of Elgin. He built the first hotel in this village, and engaged in running it for seven years, when he sold out and moved to Madelia, Watonwan county. Here he purchased a farm and continued in various pursuits for eight years. He then sold out and removed to Murray county in 1878, locating a homestead on the northwest quarter of section 24, where he still lives. He has a fine farm of 160 acres with a well-built and a well-kept dwelling house, and other good buildings, and has about one hundred acres under cultivation. He has a number of head of cattle and sheep and several horses, and in his various lines of business has been very successful. He was one of the first settlers of the township, there being but eight families here when he made his first settlement. He is a man of excellent business qualifications, is possessed of good character, and is highly esteemed by all who know him. Himself and family are members of the Methodist Episcopal church.

Mr. Weld was married in North Anson, Maine, March 1, 1854, to Miss Sarah Bray, a daughter of George and Mary (Bunker) Bray, natives of Maine. This lady was born in Anson, Maine, February 24, 1830. Mr. and Mrs. Weld have been blessed with the following named children—Frank Eugene, who died at eight years of age, Fred Z.,

Robert (deceased), Delburt U., Burt Ivan, Ethel Irene and Ernest G. All of these children reside at home except Fred and Delburt, who own farms in Murray county, on which they reside. In Mr. Weld's father's family there are now living the following named children—George, Zebina, Benjamin G., Charles H., Harriet U. Dyer. Mrs. Weld was one of five children—Dolly C., Robert M. Baxter, Lydia B., now Mrs. Turner, and Sarah B.

An interesting item in Mr. Weld's genealogy is the fact that his grandfather, James Ridgeway, was a soldier in the Revolutionary War, and was one of the party that helped throw the tea overboard in Boston Harbor.

CHARLES G. POOCH resides in Germantown township, Cottonwood county, Minnesota. He was born in Rheinfelt, Germany, September 4, 1836. His parents were John and Lottie (Neams) Pooch, natives of Germany. In 1857 the parents came to America and located for a short time in Ripon, Wisconsin. In the spring of 1859 they removed to Marquette county, and located on a pre-emption.

Our subject followed farming pursuits for several years after coming to this country, and in July, 1861, enlisted in Company I, Seventh Regiment Wisconsin Volunteer Infantry. He served in the Union army until July, 1865; he was discharged July 3, at Milwaukee, where the members of his company were given a grand banquet in honor of their service during the war. Our subject saw considerable service and was in a number of severe battles. He was confined in the hospital for some four or five months, from chronic diarrhœa. He was then granted a thirty day furlough, which was extended thirty days longer and he spent this time at home. Returning at the expiration of his furlough he reported to his regiment for duty. He was once struck under the arm by a piece of shell, which knocked him down and tore the clothes into fragments about where the shell struck. The injury, however, was not very severe and did not confine our subject to the hospital. With the exception of the time mentioned above Mr. Pooch was with his regiment in active service, participating in a great many hard-fought battles. After his discharge he returned to his father's farm in Wisconsin and then purchased a farm in Waushara county, where he resided for six months, this farm being bought in partnership with his brother, John, but at the end of the six months the partnership was dissolved, and our subject went to Green Lake county, where he rented a farm for two years. He then went to Fond du Lac county, and was engaged in agricultural pursuits for a year, after which he went to the city of Ripon, rented a house and engaged at different kinds of employment for another year. His next move was to Westfield, Waushara county, where he purchased a farm, and operated the same for four years. He then, in 1872, left Wisconsin, and came to Germantown township, Cottonwood county, Minnesota, and located on section 6, where he has since resided.

Mr. Pooch was married in Waushara county, Wisconsin, to Miss Amale Borsack, daughter of John and Anna (Wagner) Borsack, natives of Germany. Mrs. Pooch was born in Germany, and came to this country with her parents in an early day. This union has been blessed with the following named children—Bertha, Frank, Herman, William and Edward.

The life of our subject since coming to the county has not been all sunshine, nor has it all been failure. For several years during grasshopper times he raised no crops whatever. Later he has been quite success-ful in gathering in good harvests, and has accumulated considerable means. After the grasshoppers left two crops were destroyed by rust and blight, but, during these hard times, our subject went to other localities to earn money to support his family. Another sad loss visited him during the grasshopper raids. One time, while the family was at church, their home took fire, and everything it contained was destroyed. In spite of these difficulties our subject has been gradually accumulating means, and is now in good circumstances. He owns several head of horses and twenty-five head of cattle, has a good frame house and large barn, and has a nice grove of five acres of trees. In all matters pertaining to the public welfare our subject takes an active interest, and has exerted an influence for good in his township. He has been township clerk during most of his residence here. He has also been school treasurer, justice of the peace, township treasurer, chairman of the board of supervisors, etc. So popular has our subject been with the people with whom he has lived, that, with the exception of one year since locating in the township, he has held some official position. In every instance he has given excellent satisfaction, and has gained the respect of all his fellow-townsmen.

------◆-◆◆◆◆-◆-◆------

FRED H. BALDWIN is one of the leading citizens of Edgerton, Pipestone county, Minnesota. He has been identified with the interests of this village since 1885, at which time he located here and engaged in the grain business. After following that line for about three years he then engaged in handling stock, coal and machinery, in which at present he has an extensive trade. He was born in Essex county, New York, August 12, 1854, his parents being H. C. and A. C. (Stafford)

Baldwin, both of whom were natives of the State of New York. Throughout most of his life the father followed the occupation of farming.

Fred H. Baldwin spent his boyhood days on the farm of his parents and received a good common-school education. He continued his residence on the home farm until he was about nineteen years of age, when he engaged in other pursuits for himself. Two years after his birth his parents removed to Fillmore county, Minnesota, and settled on government land, and it was here that his early life and boyhood days were spent with his parents. In 1878 he removed to Mower county, Minnesota, and settled on a homestead and also took a tree claim adjoining. He lived on this land for about seven years, at the end of which time he "proved up" on the homestead, of which he is still the owner. He also owns the tree claim, but has not submitted his final papers, and he has not as yet received the title thereto from the government. In 1885, he moved into the village of Edgerton, as was stated in the opening of this sketch, and engaged in the grain business, which, after three years, was dropped for the stock, coal and machinery business. In the latter he is still engaged and is doing a large trade.

The subject of our sketch was married in Fillmore county, Minnesota, to Miss Martha Bateman, and daughter of John and Katura Bateman, both of whom were natives of West Virginia. Mr. and Mrs. Baldwin have been blessed with four children—H. Ralph, Lee, Lyle and Irene.

Throughout his life Mr. Baldwin has taken an active interest in all matters which pertain to the welfare of the locality in which he has lived. Wherever he has been he has held local offices and his abilities in this line have been utilized in many different ways. While in Mower county he was township clerk, justice of the peace and township supervisor. At present he holds the office of marshal of Edgerton. In his business relations Mr. Baldwin has proven himself a capable and trustworthy man and enjoys the confidence of a wide circle of friends.

LEVI H. FULLER is a retired farmer and prominent resident of Winnebago City, Faribault county, Minnesota. He was born in Cayuga county, New York, December 23, 1824.

The subject of our sketch was the son of John and. Betsey (Clark) Fuller, natives of Vermont, where they lived until shortly after their marriage. They then located in Chautauqua county, New York, where they engaged in farming, and removing thence settled in Cayuga county, whence they removed to Wyoming county. Later they removed to Wisconsin and engaged in farming in Waukesha county, where they settled in 1856. The father engaged in farming until his death, which occurred in 1877. The mother died in 1875. The father was a democrat in politics in early life, but finally came to believe in the principles enunciated by the republican party. The mother was a consistent member of the Baptist church. They had a family of six children, only four of whom are living—Elizabeth, now Mrs. Hall; Levi H., John W. and Charles R.

Our subject was reared as a farmer's boy and was given the educational advantages furnished by the district schools. He remained beneath the parental roof until he was nineteen years of age and then removed from New York to the State of Wisconsin in 1844 and settled for about three years in Waukesha county, engaged principally in farming. He then removed to Dodge county, where he purchased 120 acres of wild land, built a log house and engaged in farming. After seven years of continuous residence in Dodge county our subject sold out and removed to the township of Merton, Waukesha county, purchasing a farm of 120 acres, and adding forty acres thereto some time later. He continued his residence in Wisconsin until coming to Winnebago City to make his location on the 29th of June, 1888. However, prior to locating in this village he had visited Faribault county in 1882, and had purchased 170 acres of land in the northeastern part, in Winnebago City township. This farm is rented at present. After coming to the village he purchased a residence on Mill street, just west of the high-school building. He has made elegant improvements to his home property, which cost him about $1,400. Throughout his life he has been a man of much prominence, and has always taken an active interest in township affairs, having held various local offices. In politics he affiliates with the republican party, and with his wife belongs to the Baptist church. He is one of Winnebago City's prominent and substantial citizens.

On the 25th of December, 1846, Mr. Fuller was married to Miss Austina Snyder, who was born in Germany in the year 1830. She was the daughter of Casper and Margaret (Welch) Snyder, also natives of Germany. They left their native land on the 2d of May, 1841, and came to America, locating in Genesee, Waukesha county, Wisconsin, where they engaged in farming. Two months after their arrival the father died, and the mother passed from this life in 1875. In the Snyder family there were seven children, five of whom are now living —Anson, George, Acty, Austina, now Mrs. Fuller, and Mary. Mr. and Mrs. Fuller have been blessed with the following named children—Norman E., Genevera, Julia and Edwin M. Norman E. married Miss Emigene Baxter, and is located in Blue Earth county. They have one son, Levi S. Genevera married Mr. A. Lowe, who died in 1887, leaving two children—Orson D. and Roy. Julia married Mr. Muir, by whom she has had one son, Harrison S. Edwin M. is now attending the Rush Medical College in Chicago.

FRANK WORKS is an enterprising and influential farmer and stock raiser located on section 4, Carson township, Cottonwood county, Minnesota. He made his location in the county in August, 1877, first settling in Delton township on section 28, where he homesteaded 160 acres of land. He resided thereon until November, 1888, up to which time he had thoroughly improved his farm and built good farm buildings. At the date just given he removed to his present place, where he has since lived. Our subject was one of the early settlers of Delton township, and took an active part in its public affairs, serving his fellow-citizens in various official capacities. He was clerk of the school district for five years, township constable for three years, and was chairman of the board of supervisors for one year. Wherever he has been he has always taken an active part in public matters.

Mr. Works was born at Columbus Junction, in Louisa county, Iowa, September 1, 1857. His father was Hiram Works, a farmer and carpenter by trade, who was born in Orange county, Vermont, residing in that State until he was twenty-four years of age, when he was married and removed to Ohio. Our subject's mother's name was Prudence Lincoln, a native of Orange county, Vermont. Both parents are still living. Our subject was one of two children, his brother being named Charles.

When our subject was at the tender age of four years his parents removed to Hennepin county, Minnesota, locating at Lake Minnetonka, where they resided some two years. After the Indian troubles had ceased, the family removed to Douglas county, this State, where they resided some five years. Removing thence, they went to Missouri and remaining in that State only six months; returned to Minnetonka Mills, Hennepin county, Minnesota, where they resided four years. The next move was to Douglas county, where they engaged in farming for four years. Then by team they went to Nebraska, selling out their stock; but not being satisfied with that location, they returned to Minnesota and located in Delton township, Cottonwood county, the entire family coming to this location. Since 1877 our subject has remained in the county, and has been engaged in farming. His early education was received principally in the village of Osakis, Douglas county, and was completed in Excelsior, Hennepin county. Mr. Works is a man of excellent qualities, is possessed of a high character, strong, sensible ideas, and is a practical farmer. In politics he affiliates with the republican party, but, being of strong temperance principles, he has voted more or less with the prohibition party. He is a man of excellent principles, and is highly respected.

Mr. Works was married March 18, 1885, to Miss Lizzie Bastian, a native of Germany, and who came to the United States with her parents when she was two years of age. Settling in Illinois, she there received her early training and education. The father was Carl Bastian, who became an early settler of Delton township, Cottonwood county. Mr. and Mrs. Works have three children—Charles L., born April 14, 1886; Nellie, born June 4, 1887, and Myrtle, born September 20, 1888.

K. HABERMAN is a reliable farmer who resides on section 20, of LaCrosse township, Jackson county, Minnesota. The place of his nativity is found in Austria, his birth occurring in February,

1853. Our subject's parents were John and Anna (Heger) Haberman, who were natives of Austria. The mother died in her native land and the father married again and emigrated to America in 1872. He is now a resident of LaCrosse township.

Until twenty years of age the subject of our sketch remained with his parents in his native land. He received a good common-school education and at twenty years of age came to the United States and located for about two months in Wisconsin. He then came to LaCrosse township and located on 160 acres of land. He has worked hard to improve his farm, has built a good house and a large barn and has three acres of a nice grove of trees. Besides his farming he is also engaged in raising cattle and Clydesdale horses. He has met with considerable success and has accumulated some means. He has taken an active part in public matters and is well known and respected throughout the township. In politics he affiliates with the democratic party.

In the year 1873 Mary Ninnerither was united in marriage with Mr. Haberman. Mr. and Mrs. Haberman have six children—Flora, Willie, Carl, Matilda, Mary and Aganie.

PEDER O. SKYBERG. This gentleman is the efficient and popular county treasurer of Rock county, Minnesota. He came to the county in 1872, and settled on a homestead of 160 acres of land in Martin township. He commenced making improvements by building a sod house 14x16 feet. He made his home on the farm until the spring of 1883, at which time he removed to Luverne, having been elected county treasurer in the fall of 1882. After the first year or two of "roughing it" on the farm, he began to accumulate a little means, and commenced branching out in the way of making fine improvements. He broke up a large acreage of land, built good buildings, and planted a fine grove of trees. In 1878 he purchased forty acres of land adjoining his farm, and from that time until coming to the city of Luverne he engaged in general farming. Prior to his election to his present office he held various official positions within the gift of his constituents. For four years he was county commissioner, during one year of which time he was chairman of that body. For six years he held the position of assessor of the township.

Mr. Skyberg is a native of Norway, where he was born on the 18th of April, 1851. His parents, Ole O. and Maren (Peterson) Skyberg, were both natives of Norway. The father was a farmer by occupation, and continued in that business throughout the most of his life until within a few years. He is now living a retired life in his native country. He was a well-to-do farmer, and held various offices in the locality in which he lived. The family were all members of the Lutheran church. The parents had seven sons and four daughters, all of whom are still living, six in Rock county, Minnesota, and five in Solor, Norway.

The early life of the subject of our sketch was spent on the farm of his father. He received a good education in the schools of his native country, and remained with his parents until he was nineteen years of age. Then, in 1870, he left his native country, and came to America, settling in Mitchell county, Iowa, where, for about two years, he worked on a farm, and in the winter months attended school. His next move was to Rock county, Minnesota, where he settled on a farm, as stated in the opening lines of this sketch.

Mr. Skyberg was married, in 1877, to Miss Annie H. Abrahamson, of Winnesheik county, Iowa. This lady was the daughter of Halver and Annie (Austinson) Abrahamson. Her father was one of the leading citizens of the

county in which he lived. Mr. and Mrs. Skyberg have had five children, four of whom are now living—Henrietta, Matilda, George O. and Adeline. Another child, Anna M., died when she was three years old. The family are all members of the Lutheran church.

The subject of our sketch is a republican in politics, and takes an active interest in all the affairs of that organization, being at present chairman of the county central committee. He has been a delegate to the county convention of that party a number of different times, and his influence has always been felt in the councils of his party. Mr. Skyberg is a man of excellent qualities, possessed of good education, thorough and systematic in his business affairs, and has made one of the most gentlemanly and efficient officers the county has ever had. In his farming enterprises he has been quite successful, and has laid up considerable means. He purchased a fine residence in Luverne, in 1883, where he now has a beautiful and commodious home.

SAMUEL P. McINTYRE is a leading and well-to-do farmer of Murray township, Murray, county Minnesota. He has a good farm on section 8. This land was purchased by him in August, 1869, and in 1874 he made his permanent location. He has seen considerable misfortune and much financial loss, having passed through the grasshopper raid and experienced other hardships usually found in pioneer life. He was one of the first settlers of the township in which he lives and became prominent in its affairs. The first year of his settlement he broke ten acres of land, put up a hay barn and built a house in 1875, and also set out about eight acres of trees. Among the official positions which he has held may be named those of clerk and assessor, the former for three years and the latter for one year. For several years he was county superintendent of schools in Murray county, and filled that position efficiently and with great satisfaction to his constituents. He was also county surveyor for four years, holding this office and that of superintendent of schools at the same time. He has taken a prominent part in the affairs of the township and county, and is one of the representative men of Southwestern Minnesota.

Mr. McIntyre was born in Chautauqua county, New York, March 4, 1834. His parents were Amos W. and Laura (Setherland) McIntyre. The father was born in Madison county, New York, where he lived the life of an agriculturist, dying in August, 1879. The mother was born and educated in Vermont. She is still living. In the father's family there were six children.

The subject of our sketch was reared in his native county in the State of New York, until he was twenty-one years of age. He received a good common-school education, and when not in school, assisted his father in work on the home farm. At twenty-one years of age he gave his time entirely to the profession of teaching, having taught three terms before that age. He followed that profession twenty-three years before coming to Murray county, Minnesota, since which time he has taught three terms. Throughout his life he has been occupied principally in teaching school, for which he was educated and prepared by a course at the State normal school, Edinborough, Erie county, Pennsylvania. His early education was of the highest order, and he was well qualified, both by natural and acquired accomplishments, to enter upon the duties of the profession which has occupied his attention through so many years. His high-school course was taken at Chamberlain Institute, in Cattaraugus county, New York. For four terms he attended Waterford acad-

emy, Pennsylvania. In 1856 our subject spent one summer engaged as a civil engineer, surveying in the State of Iowa. While at Fort Dodge he was persuaded by several friends, hunters and trappers, to go to Southern Minnesota and find a location for future agricultural pursuits. Though the country was occupied by Indians, he was assured that they would soon be removed and opportunity given for settlement. The glowing account he then received of the Lake Shetek country was the cause of his location in Minnesota thirteen years afterward. He came to Murray county and located his present farm. His career as a teacher has been one of the most successful, and he has held various honorable and important positions. After completing his commercial course in the Iron City College, of Pittsburgh, he was engaged to become a teacher in that institution, but on account of being taken sick was not able to accept the position. In politics Mr. McIntyre affiliates with the republican party, and is a prominent and influential member of the Masonic fraternity and the Good Templars' lodge.

Mr. McIntyre was married in May, 1863, to Miss Ambrosia P. Chase, a native of Erie county, Pennsylvania, where she was reared and educated. Her early life until her marriage was occupied with teaching. She was a daughter of John B. Chase, a native of, and a farmer in, New York. Mr. and Mrs. McIntyre have had two children—George P. and Edna L., the latter being at present a teacher.

SETH F. HERRICK is a prominent citizen of St. James, Watonwan county, Minnesota, where he is engaged in the hardware business. Mr. Herrick is a native of Chautauqua county, New York, where he was born November 4, 1832.

The parents of the subject of our sketch

were George F. and Julia A. (Maynard) Herrick, natives, respectively, of Vermont and Pennsylvania. In early life the father was a machinist by trade, and later studied medicine and became one of the leading physicians and surgeons of Minnesota. Coming to Minnesota in 1856 he settled in Le Sueur county, where he engaged in the practice of his profession until 1874, when he settled in St. James. After practicing in St. James about two years he went East on a visit, and has not been heard from since. He had a family of three children—Seth F., Sarah, now Mrs. Foote, of St. James, and George H., now a merchant of Owatonna, Minnesota.

The early life of the subject of our sketch was spent in New York and Pennsylvania, where he was given excellent educational advantages. He remained with his parents until he was twenty-three years of age, at which time he was married, and then started for the West, settling in Le Sueur county, Minnesota. He engaged principally in farming for some time, locating on a preemption of 160 acres of land. He engaged in farming for some eight years, when he sold out and invested the proceeds in a saw and grist mill, located on the Le Sueur river two and a half miles from the village of Le Sueur. He operated this business for some four years, and then sold out and engaged as fireman on the Omaha railroad. In September, 1862, while threshing about five miles from Le Sueur, a report came to our subject that the Indians were on the war-path, and were scouring the country, killing all the settlers they could find. Mr. Herrick continued his threshing during the afternoon. The next morning another runner came and told the same story in regard to the Indians. The threshing was then stopped, and our subject started home, a distance of about two miles. He took his family and drove to Le Sueur, where quite a number volunteered to go out

and investigate as to the truth of the reports that were being circulated. Enough men volunteered to fill the wagon driven by our subject, and they then started for Nicollet, a short distance from the village of St. Peter. Here they stopped for the night, and in the morning, their company now numbering four or five wagon loads, they started for New Ulm. After arriving in New Ulm a man came in who stated that there was a family hidden in the tall grass some twelve miles distant, and that one of the women was shot through the arm. About one hundred men volunteered to go out and rescue this family. They discovered the party and returned, but the rescue was not in time. Inflammation set in in her arm, and the woman died before many hours. This company found some fifteen persons who had been killed by the Indians; these they buried, and then returned to New Ulm. The Indians came down on the city, and for one day there was severe fighting. The volunteer soldiers, however, succeeded in keeping the redskins out of the town and in killing a number of their would-be murderers. Quite a number of residences in the outskirts of the village were burned by the soldiers, so that the Indians could find but little shelter when they made their attacks. The next morning the redskins made a fierce attack to capture the village, but without success, and started on up the river. The next day the soldiers and inhabitants of St. Peter all went to Mankato, our subject carrying four wounded persons in his wagon. This was one of the severe and dangerous incidents of our subject's pioneer life in Minnesota. On selling his mill he engaged as fireman on the Omaha railroad for a year and a half, and then took charge of an engine for about eight years, running between St. Paul and St. James. Our subject moved his family to the latter village on the first regular train that ran over the road, and has made his residence in that village ever since. In 1878 he engaged in the hardware business, and now carries a finely assorted stock of hardware, stoves and shelf goods. He is doing a large and profitable business. In politics he affiliates with the prohibition party, and is a man of strong temperance principles. He belongs to the Masonic fraternity, is public spirited and an active participant in all matters pertaining to the public welfare.

Mr. Herrick was married in 1855 to Miss Alma E. Cottrell, of Fulton county, Ohio, and a daughter of Erastus Cottrell. Mr. and Mrs. Herrick are blessed with five living children—Fannie, Clara, Herbert, who married Clara Franks, and now resides in Sioux City; Ellen, now Mrs. A. V. Merrigold, of Sioux City, and Pearl. Fannie married Mr. J. H. Magner, of Sioux City, and has two children —Frederick and David. Clara married Mr. N. F. Phillips, of Minneapolis, and has one child, Burton.

WILLIAM WALLACE RAMSEY, one of the earliest settlers and best known citizens of Lincoln county, is at present living a retired life in the village of Lake Benton. He is a native of Ohio, where he was born June 13, 1831.

The subject of our sketch remained in the State of his birth until he was nineteen years of age, and at that time removed to Adams county, Wisconsin, where he engaged in farming during the summers, and worked in the lumber woods during the winters. Removing from Wisconsin he came to Lincoln county, and during one summer lived at White Walnut Lake. Then he homesteaded his present farm on sections 25-6, in Diamond Lake township. He was the first actual settler of that township, and commenced operations on his farm by building a shanty 8½x14 feet, located on the north side of the lake. This was in 1871, and he lived

in the shanty just mentioned during the following winter, and assisted in the organization of the township. He has identified himself closely with the governmental affairs, and has held numerous official positions, among them being that of school treasurer, which position has been held by him for three terms; also sheriff of the county, which he held for three terms. Besides identifying himself with the political matters of his township, he has also been interested in religious and other work, and has held a stewardship in the Methodist Episcopal church for some time. He is a man of rare business qualities and has served his constituents in the various positions which we have named, with much honor and credit to himself as well as to the thorough satisfaction of all who have had business relations with him. Being one of the early settlers, he experienced many hardships and was an eye witness of much suffering among the people of Lincoln and adjoining counties. During the grasshopper raids which were the cause of so much devastation and suffering in Southern Minnesota, our subject carried provisions for many early settlers from Sioux Falls, Canton and elsewhere. During this time he was associated with T. Lemon and A. E. Burdick, in buying and selling them to various settlers scattered over the country. Our subject carried the first mail sack from the county seat of Lyon county to Lake Benton, where John Snyder was postmaster. During the winter of 1873, an interesting incident is related by our subject which will illustrate some of the many hardships through which the early settlers had to pass, and it must be remembered that this is only one of the many discouragements that come to pioneer life. In the winter of 1873 Mr. Ramsey, in company with Messrs. Wood and Snyder, started out one morning to take a large number of furs to the market at New Ulm. They ate an early breakfast and left home shortly after nine o'clock, and were soon caught in a terrific snowstorm. The storm grew worse as the day progressed, and when night came our subject found that they had not gotten further from home than fifteen miles. After wandering around for a short time they finally came to the conclusion that they were lost, neither of the men knowing which direction to take. The storm grew more and more terrific, and the driving snow became so thick that objects could be seen but a short distance. Not knowing what to do, nor which way to turn, they finally covered themselves with the furs they had brought with them, and in this way succeeded in passing safely through three days and nights. Had it not been for these furs every man of the party would, no doubt, have perished. As it was, our subject had his feet badly frozen, and the others were more or less frost-bitten. This was a terrible experience, and will never be forgotten by those three men and their families.

The subject of our sketch was married, June 9, 1853, to Miss Flora Baldwin, a native of Connecticut. She was reared and educated in Ohio. Mr. and Mrs. Ramsey had nine children, four of whom are now living—Rufus F., Susan, James and Florence. Rufus F., the oldest, was married in March, 1889, to Miss Frankie Compton. He is the first engineer in the Alma City flouring mills. Susan was married, in 1878, to Nelson Ackerman, a well-to-do farmer in Blue Earth county. She has four children—Amy, Ennis, Luther and Mark. James is pleasantly situated on a farm on section 24, Lake Benton township. He homesteaded this land in 1880, and is one of the leading farmers of that township. He was married, in 1880, to Miss Ellen Maynard, by whom he has had three children—Nellie, Myrtie and Alice. Florence has been a teacher in Lincoln county for several years, and in March, 1889, was married to George Duchene, a farmer of Lincoln county.

In politics Mr. Ramsey affiliates with the republican party, and has intimately associated himself with all matters of government. He has held numerous official positions, and has proven himself a capable and trustworthy officer. He is a man of high character, and, wherever known, is highly respected. He has surrounded himself with the evidences of success and prosperity, and has a pleasant and agreeable family.

⚬⚬⚬⚬⚬

AUGUSTUS S. HUSSELTON, a resident of Worthington, Nobles county, Minnesota, is the son of George and Hannah (McCulloch) Husselton, natives, respectively, of Pennsylvania and Maryland. Augustus was born in York county, Pennsylvania, February 27, 1835, and when he was nine years of age the family moved to Danville, Pennsylvania. The father died when our subject was six years of age and the mother married William McClure, a cabinet-maker and carpenter.

When our subject was ten years of age he went into the iron rolling mills in Danville and worked for one year, after which he found employment on a boat. Again he went into the iron mills and continued working there until the spring of 1850 when he went with his mother to Nippenose Valley, Pennsylvania, his step-father having died in 1849. Here our subject worked for his brother Benjamin in a blacksmith shop for three years and attended school during several months of each winter. Three months were then spent by him on a farm, when his mother was again married, this time to Mr. Showers. The next summer our subject left home and worked for a Mr. Shaw on a farm adjoining that of his mother. He went to school during the winter and in the spring of 1854 went down the West Branch of the Susquehanna river engaged in rafting for several months. His next employment was in a saw-mill in Lock Haven and in December, 1854, he was married, after which he engaged in milling for some months.

April 22, 1861, Mr. Husselton enlisted in Company H, Sixth Pennsylvania Reserve Volunteer Corps, and participated in the following battles: Second battle of Bull Run, South Mountain, Antietam, Fredericksburg and Gettysburg. July 4, 1863, after the battle of Gettysburg, our subject's division started in pursuit of Lee's army toward Williamsport, Maryland, from whence they marched to Berlin and then to Manassas Gap, from whence they went to Warrenton. Next, the company marched to Rappahannock Station and remained there some time recruiting. After this they went across the river to Mine Run, falling back toward Centreville and soon advancing near Rappahannock Station, where they were continually harassed by the enemy. Thence the company marched in battle array to Bristow Station, where they camped all winter. In the spring they received orders dated May 3, 1864, to go to Culpeper Court House. May 4 the division crossed the Rapidan and marched twenty-five miles into the wilderness. On the 5th, about 10 o'clock, the sound of fighting could be heard along the line in various places, and soon the firing became general and there was sharp fighting throughout the day. The next day was spent in skirmishing, and on May 7 the division marched all night, although worn and weary from their long march and fighting of the day before. On the 8th of May the fighting again commenced on Lawler's Ridge, our subject being in the pioneer corps and working in the rifle pits during the afternoon. The fighting was intensely severe, and many lives were lost on both sides, these few days witnessing the most severely fought battles of our subject's military career. Mr. Husselton continued on duty in the rifle pits until Sunday morning, May 14, when the

division marched to Spottsylvania and halted until about the 20th of the month. They then marched nine miles across the Mattabony river and had a sharp skirmish with the Rebel forces. The next morning they also had another skirmish with the Rebel pickets and on the 22d crossed the Hay river and on that evening heard that Hancock had driven the Rebels across the stream. On the 23d the division advanced to the North Anna river and engaged in a severe battle with the enemy, after which they went down the river some two miles where our subject was wounded in the right hip, being struck by a shell. He lay on the field all night and in the morning was taken to the field hospital. On the 26th he was taken to Port Royal where he was put onto a boat and taken to Washington, arriving on the 29th of May. He was in the third ward of Finley Hospital. Afterward he was sent to New York City, where he was placed on board a boat bound for Fort Schuyler, where he entered the hospital and remained until June. He then obtained a furlough and went to New York City and remained until the 20th, after which he went to Harrisburg and obtained his discharge. Our subject then concluded to return to his mother's home and went to Morris, Tioga county, Pennsylvania, where he remained until June, 1872. He then came to Worthington, Minnesota, and after stopping a short time returned to the East and brought his family to his new location in October. He moved to his homestead, remained two years and after obtaining his title to the land moved into the village, where he has lived ever since. Since coming to the village he has worked most of the time in the Okabena Mills, first as night watchman and then as engineer until 1882. In that year he engaged in the grocery business, continuing in that line from February, 1882, until September, 1883. He then sold out and engaged in work at the carpenter's trade until the fall of 1887, when he became engineer in the Okabena Mills, continuing in that line until June, 1889.

December 31, 1854, Mr. Husselton was married in Nippenose Valley, Pennsylvania, to Miss Catherine Sechrist, a daughter of Henry and Sarah Sechrist, natives of Pennsylvania. She was born in Jackson township, Lycoming county, Pennsylvania, September 14, 1828. This union has been blessed with the following-named children—Clara, born September 3, 1859, died October 30, 1863; Thomas H., born August 1, 1865; George M., born November 10, 1866; Lettie J., born November 22, 1868, and Hattie, born April 27, 1873, and died November 7, 1878.

━━•❖•❖⟨❖⟩•❖•━━

CHARLES T. HOWE, a thrifty and well-to-do farmer and stock raiser of Pipestone county, Minnesota, is located on the southwest quarter of section 14 in Gray township. He has been industriously occupied in thoroughly improving his farm since 1886. His settlement on the farm, however, was made January 1, 1879, he having filed a soldier's warrant on the land in February, 1878.

The subject of our sketch was born in Ithaca, Tompkins county, New York, February 18, 1846. His parents were John W. and Sarah M. (Hutz) Howe, both of whom were natives of New York. After the parents' marriage they continued to reside in New York State until in 1861, when they removed to Michigan and the father engaged in dealing in horses in Chicago. The mother died in 1884, an exemplary Christian, and was a member of the Methodist Episcopal church. The father died in Chicago in 1885. At the mother's death she was seventy-one years, five months and fifteen days old; the father was sixty-one years old when he died. During a number of years before the father's death he owned a horse

market in Chicago, and engaged extensively in dealing in horses. In the parents' family there were five children—Cordelia, Susan, Mary, Caroline and Charles T.

The parental roof furnished shelter for the subject of our sketch until he was sixteen years of age. Up to this time he had been given excellent school advantages in the common schools in the State of Michigan. When he had reached sixteen years of age he commenced working to learn the profession of engineer, serving an apprenticeship until he was twenty-one years of age. He then received what was known as a grade paper, entitling him to engage in the occupation for which he had fitted himself. December 1, 1864, our subject enlisted as a private in the Thirtieth Michigan Infantry, and was soon after promoted to the rank of corporal, and as such was discharged June 23, 1865. He served under Captain Pigny, his principal duty being that of guarding prisoners at Detroit, where he was discharged. After his discharge from the service, he went to his former home at Grand Rapids, and after remaining a short time, returned to his employment as engineer on the lake steamers. In 1875 he commenced a series of engagements as engineer in steamboats on the large rivers of the United States. His experience in this line of employment has been quite extensive, and of a diversified nature. He has been engineer of vessels steaming on the lakes, on the Delaware and Hudson rivers, and in and about Chesapeake bay. He continued in this line of occupation throughout his life, until in 1886, when he concluded to give his entire attention to farming in Pipestone county. As has already been stated, January 1, 1879, he moved his family from near Grand Rapids, Michigan, to his farm in this county, where they have lived ever since. During the summer of each year, however, up to 1886, Mr. Howe was engaged in the duties of his profession on various Mississippi steamers. The winters were spent by him at his home in this county.

Mr. Howe was married in Lamotte, Michigan, January 28, 1869, to Miss Jennie Maxfield, a native of Lamont, where she was reared and educated. She was the daughter of Iva and Lucinda (Angell) Maxfield, both of whom were natives of the State of New York. After the parents married they moved to Michigan, where her father died in 1874. Her father was a farmer by occupation, and was one of the most reliable and trustworthy citizens of the town in which he lived. The mother is still living, and is a resident of the State of Michigan. Mrs. Howe was one of six children—Matilda, Lemuel, Cornelia, John, Charles and Jennie. Mr. and Mrs. Howe have been blessed with three children, all daughters, and all of whom are living—Maude, Callie and Lottie.

The subject of our sketch is one of the stanch supporters of all matters pertaining to the public welfare, and is always ready to render assistance when the good of his town and locality can be served. In his private business matters he has been eminently successful, his skill as engineer being typical of the thoroughness and skill which he has carried into all departments of his life. He has a fine farm, upon which are found excellent buildings, surrounded with a fine grove of cottonwood, ash, and box-elder trees. He has a comfortable dwelling-house and a large barn 30x56 feet, with eighteen-foot posts, and, taken all in all, he is one of the very best farmers in the county. At present he has about 150 acres of land under cultivation, but he is gradually working into blooded stock, owning some fine Polled-Angus cattle and Hambletonian horses and colts. He has one animal which deserves special mention, it being of three-quarters Hambletonian blood, and from which he expects to raise stock from the noted Flandreau horse, Sun Flower. He has from fifteen to twenty head of well-bred horses. In politics the subject of our sketch is a stanch supporter of the republican party, and is a leading member of the Masonic fraternity. For the past two years he has held the office of supervisor, and has also been a member of the board of school trustees of the district in which he lives.

ROBERT R. JENNESS is one of the most enterprising and wide-awake business men of Windom, Cottonwood county, Minnesota. He located in the village in 1871, since which time he has built up an extensive and profitable mercantile trade.

Mr. Jenness is a native of Vermont, where he was born in the year 1839. His parents were Thomas and Clarrissa (McGlathlin) Jenness, natives of Vermont. The father was a farmer by occupation, and located in Wisconsin in 1855, engaging in farming in Vernon county until his death, which occurred in 1868. The mother is now living in Windom with her son, the subject of our sketch. In the father's family there were four children—John S., now a resident of Vernon county, Wisconsin; Thomas L., of Windom; Robert R., our subject, and Abbie, now Mrs. Masterson, of California.

The early life of the subject of our sketch was spent on the home farm, and he was given good educational advantages in the public schools. At seventeen years of age he left home and went to Missouri, where he engaged in work at the carpenter's trade until the breaking out of the War of the Rebellion. He then returned to Wisconsin and served for two years in the First Wisconsin Cavalry. He was then discharged on account of disability. After his discharge he returned to Wisconsin on a brief visit, and then went to Missouri, returning soon after to Vernon county, Wisconsin, where he engaged in the mercantile business until 1869. He then sold out and located in Wabasha county, Minnesota, where, in company with H. G. Richardson, he engaged in the mercantile business for two years. He then sold out and came to the village of Windom, Cottonwood county. For a short time he worked at his trade and then engaged in the mercantile business in the block on the south side of the public square, where he continued two years. Nine years thereafter were spent in business in the corner store owned by D. Patten & Company, which building he purchased soon after moving into it. In 1885 he built a magnificent brick block, the upper part of which is given for offices. The last few years he has been doing business south of the park and rents his large brick building. He has been extremely fortunate in his business ventures in the county and has accumulated considerable means. He has devoted somewhat of his attention and money to buying and selling lands and purchased a farm of 180 acres, three-quarters of a mile from the center of the village in 1881. He now resides on this farm and has it well provided with good farm buildings. He is engaged in farming and stock raising, and has a number of head of fine graded cattle and horses. He has taken an active interest in all public matters wherever he has been and has occupied a prominent place among his fellow-citizens. He has held the office of county commissioner, which position he holds at the present time, being also a member of the village council. He was postmaster while in Wabasha county and held various other minor official positions. In politics he affiliates with the republican party; and is a leading member of the Masonic, Grand Army of the Republic and Ancient Order of United Workman fraternities. He is a man of excellent business qualifications, of the highest integrity, and is respected by all who know him. Mr. Jenness was married in 1864 to Miss Annie E. Duncan, a daughter of John Duncan, of Kentucky, This union has been blessed with seven children—John E., now in business with his father; Warren M., an engineer; William H., Frederick, Thomas, Lucy and Anna W.

LEWIS FLING is a prominent and well-to-do farmer of Mason township, Murray county, Minnesota. He has an excellent farm on section 8, where he has surrounded himself with the evidences of thrift and prosperity. Mr. Fling was born in the State of Vermont, March 9, 1825, and was the son of Alfred and Sarah (Spaulding) Fling, natives of New Hampshire. The father was a blacksmith by trade, and died about fifteen years ago in Rochester, Minnesota. The mother died soon after.

Lewis Fling left home when he was twenty-one years old. Up to this time he had assisted in work on the home farm, and had attended the district schools. On leaving home our subject obtained a position as guard in the Clinton prison in New York, where he continued two years. Removing thence he located in St. Lawrence county, where he worked at farming for two years. Going westward he located in Ohio and found work at his trade, that of shoemaking, for three years, at the end of which time he came to Madison, Wisconsin. Here he operated a railroad house until about 1860, when he came to the vicinity of Rochester, Minnesota, and engaged in farming until 1871. Thence he went to Murray county, Minnesota, where he now lives. He came overland, driving two teams and forty-one head of cattle. He located the claim where he now lives and engaged in farming and stock raising. He tried to farm during the grasshopper raids, but lost all his crops. Becoming discouraged with his farming operations, he moved to Currie, built a hotel and operated it for ten years. He still owned the farm, however, and at the end of that time he returned to agricultural pursuits, retaining his ownership of the hotel. In the summer of 1888 he moved back to the farm where he now lives. He has 160 acres of fine land, well improved and provided with good buildings.

The wedding day of the subject of our sketch was June 19, 1845. On this day he was married to Miss Ann Hopper, a daughter of Cornelius and Sophia (Case) Hopper, both natives of New York. She was a native of New York State, and in early life received a thorough common-school education. Mr. and Mrs. Fling have been blessed with three children—Alfred C., Emma F. and Minnie E.

Since coming to the township Mr. Fling has taken an active interest in all matters which pertain to the general welfare. He has held various official positions, among them being that of treasurer of Murray county, and also treasurer of his township while a resident of Olmstead county. He is at present one of the board of town supervisors. In politics our subject formerly affiliated with the old whig party, but he has affiliated with the republican party ever since its organization. He was an earnest supporter of President Harrison in the last campaign, and has an excellent recollection of General Harrison's canvass in 1840. A. C. Fling, the son of our subject, has been register of deeds of Murray county for two terms.

----◦--◦-◦⦅⧉⦆◦--◦-◦----

WILLIAM STAUFFER is a retired farmer and reliable and esteemed citizen of Winnebago City, Faribault county, Minnesota. He was born in Chester county, Pennsylvania, April 26, 1826.

The parents of the subject of our sketch were Henry and Susan (Binder) Stauffer, natives also of Chester county, Pennsylvania. Our subject's grand-parents on his father's side were John and Deborah Stauffer, natives of the same place and of German descent. Susan Binder's parents were Abram and Susan Binder, natives of west Canada and also of German descent. They were farmers by occupation on both sides of the house. In our subject's father's family there were eight children, six of whom are now living—Jacob, Joseph, William, Sarah, Maria and Deborah. The parents were members of the Lutheran church and the father affiliated with the democratic party.

The early life of William Stauffer was spent on a farm in Pennsylvania, where he was given a good common-school education and remained with his parents until twenty-five years of age, when he removed to Fayette county, Iowa, in 1851, and settled on 120 acres of government land. He resided in Fayette county for five years and then came to Winnebago township, Faribault county, Minnesota. Soon after coming to this location he settled on 160 acres of land three miles north and one mile west of Winnebago City. There were only six men in the county at this time and our subject with them experienced many privations. He built a primitive log cabin covered with bark and with an earth floor. He broke several acres of land, and commenced raising grain and stock. His nearest market was a long distance off, and the first mill to which he took a grist of grain was 143 miles distant. Our subject continued to improve his farm, building substantial buildings, and has now 540 acres of land under excellent cultivation. This property he now rents. In 1888 he purchased a house and five lots in Winnebago City, and makes this his home.

The subject of our sketch was married January 2, 1851, to Miss Elizabeth L. Miller, of Butler county, Pennsylvania, and daughter of Richard and Mary (Christie) Miller. Mr. and Mrs. Stauffer have twelve living children—Emeline, Henry W., Amelia, Marion, Elizabeth, Amalda, John, Newton, Mary, Edith, Alice and Judson. Emeline married Mr. Thomas Jenkins, and has seven children—Elomore, Fred, Nora, Lorin, Elsie, Grover and Rosa. Melinda married a Mr. Jenkins, and died in 1887. She had two children—Walter and Mira. Henry W. married Mary Miller, by whom he has two children—Clara and Clarence. Amelia married Joseph Spaulding, and had two children—Merritt and Alta. Elizabeth married a Mr. Jenkins, and had four children—Frances, Palmer, Ada and Oscar. Amalda married a Mr. Barns, and had three children—Maggie, Carrie and Lena. Mary married a Mr. Jenkins. Henry W. Stauffer was the first white male child born in Faribault county. He was born February 2, 1857.

The subject of our sketch is a man of considerable prominence in public affairs, and votes with the prohibition party. He is a man of strong temperance principles, and with his wife belongs to the Methodist Protestant church. He is quite a genius in his way, and understands thoroughly the business of contracting and building. He built all his farm buildings with his own hands. He has a fine barn 74x56 feet on his place, and is engaged in stock raising together with farming. The Blue Earth river runs through his farm, making it one of the most desirable stock-raising places in the county. He has an excellent flowing well, forty-seven feet and three inches deep, the water being possessed of mineral qualities and tinctured strongly with iron. In business affairs Mr. Stauffer has been quite successful. He is careful and systematic and withal economical, and has by careful attention to his business accumulated large means. He is a man of excellent character,

and is highly respected by all who know him.

OSCAR T. GILSON, who is now living on section 14, Troy township, Pipestone county, Minnesota, is one of the leading farmers of that part of the county. He was born in Cheshire county, New Hampshire, on the 31st day of May, 1849.

His parents, Frederick A. and Melintha W. (Tuttle) Gilson, were also natives of New Hampshire, as were his grandfather and mother on both sides, but his great-grandfather on his father's side was a native of Massachusetts. The father of the subject of our sketch was born on a farm and spent his early years there, but in his youth learned the blacksmith trade, and afterward went into the business of manufacturing glass, in which business he was engaged in Stoddard for about eighteen years. After this he took charge of a hotel for some three years. Then after living a retired life for some time, he finally engaged in farming, and now lives on the land adjoining his son's.

Oscar T., our subject, spent the first eighteen years of his life attending school, and then for two years helped his father at home, the latter part of the time being spent in his father's hotel at Keene. The following two years were spent in working in a hotel for a man by the name of Starky. Mr. Gilson then returned to Stoddard and engaged in the business of clothes-pin making for one and a half years. After this he went to Salem, Wayne county, Pennsylvania, where he was foreman in a clothes-pin factory for three years. In April, 1876, Mr. Gilson went to Nebraska, where he remained but four weeks, and then went on to Missouri, in which State he remained four months. He then came to Rice county, Minnesota, where he worked on a farm for Major Rice for about eighteen months. In the spring of 1878 he, with his wife and child, and A. E. Woodman and D. B. Whigam and son, came through by ox team to Troy township, Pipestone county, Minnesota, spending fourteen days on the road. They were the first family to settle in Troy township, and there was but one claim shanty in the township at that time. His wife was the first white woman in this part of the county. He located his land and built his house that summer. The sufferings and discomforts of that time can better be imagined than described. The nearest markets were Luverne and Tracy. But they were not long the only settlers in the township, for the very next spring people began coming in.

The subject of our sketch was married on the 10th day of June, 1869, to Mary I. Richardson, a daughter of Albert and Cordelia (Boyden) Richardson. Mrs. Gilson's father was a native of New Hampshire and her mother of Vermont. The mother died when Mrs. Gilson was but three years old, but the father is still alive and living in Missouri. Mr. and Mrs. Gilson have been blessed with two children—Fred A. and Leon A. Fred A. died October 2, 1873, in Pennsylvania; Leon is alive at the present time. Mrs. Gilson began teaching school at the age of fifteen, and has been in the school-room more or less since that time. She is at present teaching in her own township.

Mr. Gilson has held important public offices ever since the town was first organized; he has been school treasurer constantly since the school was started, was town treasurer one term and has been on the board for five years, part of the time as chairman. He was a member of the board when the county was attached to an adjoining county as a township. For two terms he held the assessorship, which office he holds at the present time. He has been elected to every office in the township except that of town clerk. In

early life he had the advantages of a common-school education. In politics he is a democrat, and is one of the enthusiastic supporters of the principles of that party. Mr. Gilson is a man of fine personal appearance, social and hospitable, and takes an active interest in all matters of a public nature.

———◦⋅❁⋅◦———

HON. PETER PETERSON is a general merchant of the village of Slayton, Murray county, Minnesota. He was born in Waldris, kingdom of Norway, December 17, 1846. His parents were Iver and Gertrude (Ingebretson) Peterson, also natives of Norway. When our subject was about eighteen months old the parents left their native land and came to the United States, first locating for three and a half years on a farm in Wisconsin. From there they moved to Winneshiek county, Iowa, locating on government land. There were only about a dozen settlers in that county when our subject's parents made their location there.

Our subject remained with his parents in Winneshiek county, Iowa, for about eleven years, assisting in work on the home farm and attending the district schools. June 7, 1863, he enlisted in Company H, Seventh Iowa Cavalry, and served two years and eleven months. He was a member of the division of the army which operated in the expedition against the Indians throughout Kansas and Nebraska and our subject participated in many engagements with the red men. After his discharge Mr. Peterson returned to the parental home in Winneshiek county, Iowa, and from there went to Freeborn county, Minnesota, whence the same fall he removed to Jackson county, locating on a piece of railroad land. The residence in Jackson county was continued four years, after which our subject, a brother Albert, and his father came to Murray county in 1870, locating on various claims. Our subject continued his residence on his land until 1885, when he sold out and removed to the village of Slayton, where during one summer he engaged in the real estate business. The following spring he purchased a stock of general merchandise, and has engaged in general mercantile pursuits ever since. He now owns the building in which his business is located.

Mr. Peterson was married in the month of June, 1875, in Murray county, to Miss Thea Christianson, daughter of C. and Caroline (Boong) Christianson, natives of the kingdom of Norway. Mrs. Christianson was born in Norway February 4, 1855. Mr. and Mrs. Peterson have been blessed with the following-named children—Ignatius Conrad, Ira Curtiss, Earnest Dean, Clara Gurtrude, Nora Florentia, Ida Maria and Peter Murray. All of these are living except Ignatius Conrad and Nora Florentia.

The subject of our sketch has become one of the most prominent and influential of Murray county's citizens. He has actively participated in governmental affairs, and has held various official positions with honor and credit. For two years he held the office of register of deeds, and also very efficiently represented his district in the lower house of the State legislature, being elected on the republican ticket in 1884 from the district which comprises Murray and Nobles counties. Mr. Peterson has held all the various township offices, and has also been county commissioner for two terms. He is a member of the Modern Woodmen of America and of the Norwegian Lutheran church. Our subject saw much hardship after locating in Murray county, but has weathered all financial and other storms, and has risen to prominence and influence in the county. When he made his location, the census of the county showed 320 residents, and this was depleted somewhat during the grasshopper raids, during which our subject lost

considerable means. He sowed grain every year, and in the meantime turned his attention somewhat to cattle. The third year of the grasshopper scourge he put in 130 acres of wheat, but this was a complete loss, and had it not been for his cattle, he would have become bankrupt. He did not succeed in getting through these severe misfortunes without being burdened by a large debt, but by hard work and careful and systematic habits he has succeeded in placing himself in excellent circumstances. Mr. Peterson is a man of high character, and is respected by all who know him.

CARL S. EASTWOOD is the editor of the Heron Lake *News*, one of the popular and prosperous journals of Jackson county, Minnesota. Mr. Eastwood was born in Wisconsin, August 21, 1858. His parents were Levi and Rachel (Smith) Eastwood, natives of New York and Pennsylvania, respectively.

The subject of this sketch resided with his parents until sixteen years of age; he then commenced doing for himself and found employment in a newspaper office for the purpose of learning the printer's trade. This was at Shell Rock, Iowa. Our subject continued his employment in that village for some time and then went to Mason City, where he was employed on the *Republican* for four years. He then removed to Spirit Lake and became the founder of the *Dickinson County Journal* and operated that newspaper with excellent success for three years. Again changing his field of operations he went to Lakefield, Minnesota, and started the Lakefield *Citizen*. He was also made postmaster of the village and held that position for two years, resigning March 4, 1885, and removing thence to Mankato, Blue Earth county, Minnesota, where for a short time he edited the *Register*, now as then one of the leading newspapers of the city. After six months he sold out to Messrs. Woodard and Geddes. Leaving Mankato, our subject came to Heron Lake, Jackson county, where he became the proprietor and editor of the Heron Lake *News.*

COLONEL HARRISON WHITE, perhaps one of the most influential and best known citizens of Rock county, located in Beaver Creek, in 1877. He built the first store building in the place and engaged in the general mercantile and lumber, coal and grain trade. He also built the first elevator in the place, and in connection with his other lines operated largely as a shipper of grain and live stock. He has continued in these various enterprises ever since, and has built up one of the most extensive trades in Southwestern Minnesota. He has also been engaged to a considerable extent in loaning money and in the real estate business. On the opening of Beaver Creek village, our subject was appointed agent for their lands by the railroad company. Besides his financial interests in the city of Beaver Creek, he also has two fine farms within easy distance, where he carries on general farming and is engaged in raising fine cattle and hogs. Since coming to the city he has taken an active interest in public matters, and has been one of the leading spirits in the affairs of the republican party. He has held various positions of trust, has been president of the village council for four terms, and chairman of the township board. In the political campaign of the fall of 1888, Colonel White was nominated by the republicans of his district for representative in the State legislature. He made a gallant fight for the election, not alone for himself, but for Harrison and Morton and the whole republican ticket. He had many warm friends who worked earnestly for him in this

campaign, friends who held him in high esteem as a man and citizen, and we can do no better than to quote some of the opinions expressed by newspaper writers in favor of the election of Colonel White: "Colonel White is making a gallant fight for election as representative in the legislature. To use his own words, he fought with Sheridan too long to lie down in the fight for the republican party. He accepted the nomination for representative with the odds confessedly against him, but with a resolute courage and indomitable energy characteristic of the man, coupled with the enthusiasm born of his love for the republican party and the old flag, he accepted the responsibility placed upon him by his party, and is bearing the republican banner gallantly. By every consideration of justice he ought to win, and the republicans of this district should come to his support as loyally as he has ever come to the aid of his country or his party when there was any fighting to do. His claims to election are based on a clean record, an upright career, unflinching fidelity to the principles of the republican party, unclouded integrity, abilities of a superior order, and the fullest confidence of those who know him well. Add to this a war record which deserves high rank among the most brilliant and honorable in the annals of the Rebellion, the republicans of Rock county will give Colonel White a magnificent majority. If our Pipestone brothers will give him the support he merits, they will never have cause to regret it."

Colonel White is a native of Boston, where he was born in the year 1841. His parents were William A. and Lucy (Jackson) White, the former a native of Maine and the latter a native of Massachusetts. The father was an importer of dry goods and was engaged extensively in the mercantile trade in company with his brother, Charles A. White.

In 1855 the father moved to the city of New York, where he engaged in the manufacture of American woolen goods. He remained in business in that city until his death, about 1875, and became one of the wealthy and prominent citizen of the East.

The younger days of Colonel White were spent by him in attending school in Boston, Brooklyn and New York. On completing his education he commenced a clerkship in a commercial house of New York City. He continued in that line for about two years, and, on the breaking out of the Rebellion, offered his services to the Union army, and served his country well and ably throughout a long military career. Harrison White came of good revolutionary stock, and when the rebels opened their batteries upon Fort Sumter and the old flag, though he was but nineteen years of age, he promptly abandoned his lucrative position and enlisted as a private in Company G., Thirteenth Regiment New York State Militia, of Brooklyn; which was called out for ninety days, and assigned to McClellan's command. On his return at the expiration of this term he assisted in recruiting and organizing a company of the Sixth New York Cavalry, and was commissioned as lieutenant by Governor E. D. Morgan. He was again mustered into the volunteer service of the United States, this time for a period of three years, and his regiment was assigned for duty to the Army of the Potomac. In August, 1862, Lieutenant White was promoted to the captaincy of his company, and subsequently to the rank of major, while still later, for meritorious services, he was made lieutenant-colonel, and brevet-colonel, the latter commission being conferred both by the governor of New York and the president of the United States, for services at the battle of Five Forks, in Virginia. General Sheridan recommended for Colonel White a third brevet commission "for conspicuous gallantry in action," and

the commission was promptly conferred by President Lincoln. At the close of the active campaign in the East, the Sixth New York, whose ranks had been greatly reduced by the casualties of war, was consolidated with the Fifteenth New York Cavalry, and Colonel White was placed in command of the consolidated regiment. He was ordered by General Grant to Louisville, Kentucky, to protect that country against the incursions of lawless bands of guerrillas, and was assigned to the command of the Second Brigade, First Cavalry Division. The city of New York presented Colonel White's regiment with a beautiful silk flag, upon which the regiment had inscribed the names of seventy-five battles and skirmishes, in all of which Colonel White participated, with the exception of two of minor importance. Colonel White is now in possession of a photograph of the flag which was presented by the city of New York to his regiment. Our subject served under Generals Sheridan, Pleasanton, Buford and Devin in the First Cavalry Division of the Army of the Potomac, and in the same corps with Custer and Kilpatrick. For services in the battle of Cedar Creek, Virginia, General Custer and Colonel White were detailed by special orders from General Sheridan to report to Secretary Stanton the captures by their respective divisions, which amounted to some sixty pieces of artillery, thirteen stands of colors, several thousand stands of small arms and several thousand prisoners, besides wagons, stores and camp equipage. Among his war papers Colonel White has a strong recommendation from General Devin for promotion to a brigadier-generalship, besides several high endorsements from other generals under whom he served, and numerous highly complimentary notices from New York papers.

After his discharge from service in the Union army he returned to New York and located in the town of Mont Clair, New Jersey. He resided in that city, but found employment as a salesman in a lace house in New York. He remained in the East in business until 1877, when he came to the State of Minnesota, stopping for a short time in St. Paul. Shortly afterward, and in the same fall, he came to the village of Beaver Creek, where he has since resided.

Colonel White was united in marriage in the year 1872, to Miss Ella J. Bushnell, a native of Ulster county, New York, and a daughter of Asa B. and Janette (Longendyke) Bushnell. Mr. and Mrs. White have four children—William H., Elsie B., Grant A. and Lucy J.

Being one of the pioneer business men of the city of Beaver Creek, Colonel White has become intimately associated with the financial interests of this locality. Among the business men with whom he has had mercantile relations he is held in the highest esteem and is looked upon as one of the most successful business characters and upright loyal citizens of the community. He belongs to the Masonic fraternity, and is a leading member of John Buford post, No. 165, Grand Army of the Republic, Department of Minnesota, of which he was a charter member and its first commander. Besides being considerably interested in political and financial matters, our subject has not forgotten nor neglected to materially assist in the development of the moral side of his own character and that of the people of the community in which he lives. He has assisted largely in building all the churches in the city, and was one of the organizers of the Presbyterian church, giving liberally toward the erection of the house of worship for that society. He interests himself largely in all the departments of the work of that church and has been superintendent of the Sabbath-school ever since its organization. He is one of the trustees of the church to which he belongs. Col-

onel White has been eminently successful in all the lines of business in which he has engaged, and has proven his capabilities and efficiency in all public and private matters in which his aid has been enlisted. He has become one of the most prominent citizens of Beaver Creek and Rock county.

ANDREW J. LOWRY, one of Pipestone county's representative farmers, located in Elmer township on the 29th of March, 1880. His settlement was made on the northeast quarter of section 32 in the above named township, where he has since lived. He has a fine farm, well adapted to general farming and stock raising, on which is a nice grove of trees and comfortable farm buildings. Since taking up his residence among the pioneers of Elmer township he has taken an active interest in all matters of a public nature, and has been elected by the people to numerous official positions.

The subject of our sketch was born in Berrien county, Michigan, October 6, 1848. The father, John Lowry, was a native of Delaware, in which State he remained until he was about twenty years of age. Removing thence he went to Michigan, where the subject of our sketch was born. The father was a mechanic by trade, and followed that line of employment throughout the most of his life. He died at the age of sixty-six years, in June, 1886. He was a man of the highest integrity, a prominent citizen, and was respected by all who knew him. He was a leading member of the Methodist Episcopal church, in which society he occupied an official position at the time of his death. The mother of our subject was Mary Ann (Mitten) Lowry, a native of the State of Delaware, where she remained until seventeen or eighteen years of age, when, with her parents, she removed to the

State of Michigan. The mother is still living, and is a resident of Wisconsin. In the father's family there were six children, four of whom are living—Bell Richards, now a resident of Wisconsin; Andrew J., our subject; Leonard, married and living in Wisconsin, and Ella Lincoln, who was born on the same day on which President Lincoln was inaugurated. Ella married James Barry and is now living in Wisconsin. James T. died in the fall of 1880. He was a married man and a carpenter by trade. Etta Dell died at the age of sixteen years, in 1878.

Andrew J. Lowry received his education while living at his boyhood's home in Pepin, Wisconsin. His residence with his parents continued until he was about seventeen years of age, when he removed to Michigan and worked out on a farm for some seven or eight years. He then went to Warren county, Illinois, where he was married and took up his residence on a farm and engaged in farming for about five years. At the end of this period he returned to Wisconsin, remaining during the winter. The following spring he came westward and made a settlement in Pipestone county, where he has since lived.

August 15, 1871, is the date of the marriage of Mr. Lowry to Miss Harriet A. Millhollen, a native of Henderson county, Illinois, where she was reared and educated. Her father was Pinkney Millhollen, a miller by trade and an influential citizen of Henderson county. He died some thirty-nine years ago. Mrs. Lowry is one of four children—Henry, David, John and herself. Mrs. Lowry's mother was married the second time to Mr. A. F. Forgey, by whom she had four children—Clark, Elisha Jackson, Adeline, who died in 1875, and Lewis, who died in 1879. Mr. Forgey died some years ago at the age of eighty-four. Mr. and Mrs. Lowry have four children—Elvene, Addie Belle, Lura and Frank Allen, all of whom are living at the home of their parents.

In politics Mr. Lowry affiliates with the republican party. He has been identified with the best interests of the section in which he lives for nearly ten years, and by his sterling qualities of integrity and uprightness has drawn to himself many warm friends. He is a man of good education and sound judgment and in the many positions which he has held in the management of public affairs of the township, has proven himself a citizen of high order and a man to be respected by every one. He is a man of pleasant habits, open-hearted and genial, and his residence is indeed the home of a pleasant and interesting family. Among the offices which Mr. Lowry has held during his residence here may be named those of assessor, which position he held one year in 1885; overseer of highways, holding that position three years, and clerk of the school district No. 17, which he has held since 1884, with the exception of perhaps four months.

DR. T. KIRK is one of the leading physicians and surgeons of St. James, Minnesota. He is a native of Dewitt county, Illinois, where he was born in the year 1857. He is the son of Orage L. and Lucretia G. (Morlan) Kirk, natives of Connecticut. The grandfather of our subject was Samuel Kirk, a farmer by occupation and a resident of Indiana; he was probably of Scotch descent. Our subject's mother was the daughter of John G. Morlan, a native of Pennsylvania, and a wagon and carriage manufacturer. His wife was Lucretia (Gager) Morlan, of Hartford, Connecticut, and for many years a teacher in that State.

The father of our subject was a builder and contractor and followed that line of occupation throughout the most of his life. In 1887 he retired from active business. During his business life he filled a great many important contracts and always kept a large force of men employed. He owned his own brick-yards and manufactured most of the material used in his buildings. He had a family of twelve children, nine of whom are now living : Dr. T., Angeline S., now Mrs. J. M. Dale; Frank, Lucretia, Albert L., George, Leon, William and Harry.

The early life of the subject of our sketch was spent principally in school in Clinton, Dewitt county, Illinois. Completing his educational course he then commenced clerking in various stores, and took up the study of medicine in January, 1878, with Dr. D. W. Admiston. He graduated from Rush Medical College, of Chicago, February 22, 1881, and then engaged in the practice of his profession, coming to St. James, Minnesota, May 15, 1881. Since coming to the village he has built up an extensive and lucrative practice and his professional business calls him on many long rides in all directions from his home town. He owns a beautiful home and office on Main street and is otherwise financially interested in the development of the village. He has always taken an active part in public matters and has held various important official positions within the gift of his fellow-citizens. He is county coroner and is the local physician and surgeon for the St. Paul & Sioux City division of the Omaha railroad. In politics he affiliates with the republican party, belongs to the Masonic fraternity and 'the Minnesota Valley Medical Association.

Dr. Kirk was married in 1886 to Miss Annie M. Clinton, a native of Milwaukee, Wisconsin. She was the daughter of George E. Clinton, a prominent citizen of that place.

———◦◦◦◦◦◦———

JACOB DeMONG, a prominent farmer and stock raiser of Lake Sarah township, Murray county, Minnesota, resides on section 23. He purchased his farm in 1878 and settled thereon in 1879. He now owns two hundred acres of good land under excellent cultivation and well provided with farm buildings. Mr. DeMong has taken an active part in public matters since coming to the township, and has held various official positions, having been township clerk since 1882. He has been chairman of the board of township supervisors and has held various school offices. He has taken quite an active part in educational matters and has taught several terms of school in the township.

Jacob DeMong was born in Schuylkill county, Pennsylvania, December 20, 1854. When one year of age his parents moved to Minnesota, and located in Winona county, where they still live. His parents were John and Elizabeth (Kiefer) DeMong, both of whom were natives of Germany. In 1847 the father came to the United States and for years engaged as a miner in the State of Pennsylvania. In the father's family there were seven children—John, Jacob, Elizabeth, Minnie, Ferdinand, Joseph and Mary. The parents are still living.

In early life the subject of our sketch received a good common-school education and remained with his parents until twenty-three years of age or until he came to Murray county, where he has since lived. In politics Mr. DeMong is an independent and is a member of the Catholic church. He is a well-to-do farmer and is one of the representative citizens of the county. He has always taken an active interest in public matters and has gained a good reputation as an efficient officer.

Mr. DeMong was married December 4, 1884, to Miss Augusta F. Pearsall, a native of Winona county, Minnesota, reared and educated in Murray county. She is a daughter of Powell Pearsall, of whom a sketch is given in another department of this book. Mr. and Mrs. DeMong have one child, Mary Agnes.

DR. JOHN H. TILFORD is one of the leading and most successful physicians and surgeons of Windom, Cottonwood county, Minnesota. The place of his nativity is found in Jefferson county, Indiana, where he was born November 28, 1841.

The parents of the subject of our sketch were Joseph M. and Mary A. (Maxwell) Tilford, natives, respectively, of Kentucky and Indiana. The father left Kentucky when about twenty-one years of age and located in Madison, Indiana, where he engaged in the cabinet-making business. He carried on an extensive trade until 1851, when he removed to the city of Indianapolis, where he engaged in the same business. In 1856 he sold out and purchased the *Indiana State Journal* and engaged in the publication of that newspaper until 1866. Up to this time he had made considerable money, but at this time misfortune came to him in the shape of having to pay a number of notes on which he had signed his name as security. He had also invested heavily in real estate and residence property and was not prepared for the hard times of 1870. His business had to be abruptly closed and he retired to private life. He has always been a prominent man in his State and is one of the leading members of the well-known Harrison club of Indianapolis. Of nine children in the father's family there are six now living—Mrs. Eliza Green, Mrs. Emma Hall, Mrs. Julia Avery, Mrs. Alice Garvey, Dr. John H. and Samuel.

Up to eighteen years of age the subject of our sketch was given educational advantages of a high order. He completed a course in the district schools and entered college. At eighteen he went to the "Northwestern Christian College" in Indianapolis, and attended there for some years. He then engaged in the study of medicine in Indianapolis with Drs. Jamison and Funkhouser, with whom he continued for three years. He then attended medical lectures at Ann Arbor during the winter of 1861–62. In the spring of 1862 he received an invitation from his old preceptor to go to Indianapolis and enter the city hospital to assist in caring for the sick and disabled. He remained several months, and in August of that year was commissioned as assistant surgeon of the Seventy-ninth Indiana Infantry. He went to Louisville, Kentucky, with a portion of the regiment, and throughout the war continued his medical position in the States of Kentucky, Tennessee, Georgia and Alabama. He was always on duty, and during three years never left his command. After being mustered out of the service he returned to Indianapolis, and during the winter of 1865–66 attended a course of lectures at Bellevue Medical College in New York City, and in 1878 ad eundem in Butler Medical College. He then settled in Indianapolis and engaged in the practice of medicine for one year. His next move was to Pittsborough, Hendricks county, Indiana, where he engaged in the practice of medicine for nine years. During this time he graduated from the Indiana Medical College in 1872. On completing his nine years' residence in Pittsborough he removed to Irvington, Marion county, where he engaged in practice for four years. In 1879 he came to Minnesota, locating at Windom, where he has since been engaged in active practice. He has built up an extensive and lucrative business and has been eminently successful in the treatment of the many cases which have come to him. He is a man of excellent qualifications, is highly educated and is a master of the details of his profession. He has performed many remarkable cures and enjoys an enviable reputation both as a physician and surgeon. He has always taken an active part in public matters, and has been a member of the township and school boards and has also been coroner of the county ever since 1879. He is also a leading and influential member of the Minnesota State Medical Society. He has made numerous investments in various kinds of property and has been quite successful. He purchased several lots in the city, on which he has now an elegant residence and where his office is located. He purchased a farm at · Wilder, Jackson county, Minnesota, some time prior to making his residence in Windom. He still owns the farm, on which he has a renter. Dr. Tilford is a republican in politics and belongs to the Masonic, Odd Fellows, Grand Army of the Republic and Ancient Order of United Workmen fraternities.

Dr. Tilford was married in the year 1866 to Miss Luna Meak, a native of Greenfield, Indiana. This lady is possessed of an education of a high order and is a graduate in music, having taught in that profession a number of years in Indianapolis, Noblesville and Greenfield, Indiana. Her father was Cornwell Meak, a former merchant of Greenfield, where he was one of the oldest settlers. He was one of the oldest Masons in the State and was a man of much prominence. He owned three or four farms and engaged extensively in agricultural pursuits. Dr. and Mrs. Tilford have two children—Fred M. and Mattie R.

HON. B. M. LOW. Perhaps no man in all of Murray county is so well known for his intelligence, active public spirit and thorough appreciation of the wants of his locality as is the gentleman whose name heads this article. He came to the county in an early day and has since been identified with all matters which pertain to the improvement and upbuilding of the better interests of the locality in which he has lived. His active participation in public affairs has not been confined to the matters pertaining to his own township, but he has thoroughly acquainted himself and been

associated with all matters pertaining to the welfare of the entire county. Being a man of excellent business qualifications and a character of the highest order, he has been called upon by his fellow-citizens to occupy various important official positions. In every instance he has proven his efficiency and has administered the duties of his various offices with rare fidelity and with increasing popularity. His home is now located on section 10, of Lowville township, said township being named in his honor.

Mr. Low was born in New York, February 3, 1839, and was the son of Jacob and Catharine (Morgan) Low, both of whom were natives of the State of New York. The father followed agricultural pursuits to obtain a livelihood and remained in New York State until 1843, when he emigrated to Wisconsin, locating in the village of Lowville, and making that his home until his death, which occurred in June, 1875. The mother is still living in Wisconsin.

The subject of our sketch spent his early life on the home farm, where he was reared until eighteen years of age. He was given a good common-school education, and when not attending to his school duties assisted his father in work on the farm. Leaving home at the age of nineteen he concluded to test what life had for him, and started out for himself, locating in Madison, Wisconsin, where he learned the jeweler's trade, continuing thereat for six years. He was a loyal, patriotic citizen, and lover of freedom and liberty guaranteed by his government, and disentangling himself from his business relations in September, 1863, he enlisted in Company E, Forty-second Regiment Wisconsin Volunteer Infantry. He served faithfully and gallantly in the Union army, participating in all the engagements of his company until he was discharged in June, 1865. He then removed to Minnesota, residing in Mankato for six months, and in June, 1866, he came to Murray county and located the claim where he now lives.

Mr. Low was married in May, 1868, to Miss Mary McCann, an estimable lady who died in the summer of 1889. Mr. and Mrs. Low had six children, five of whom are now living.

On coming to Murray county our subject at once identified himself with the affairs of local government. Being a republican in politics he assisted in the local organization of that party, and was elected by its franchises to various offices. He was the first clerk of his township, and has also been justice of the peace, and filled the office of county commissioner for two terms. He was then elected as the unanimous choice of the people as a member of the lower house of the State legislature, and is serving his second term in that capacity. Among his fellow legislators Mr. Low enjoys an enviable reputation as a man of strong, clear opinions, firm and fearless in his advocacy of what he deems to be right, and for his high integrity of character as manifested in all his associations, whether of a social or business nature. He is a man of broad and progressive ideas, is a careful observer, and is a quick and accurate reader of human nature. He is indeed a self-made man; having in his younger days acquired but a common-school education, he has throughout the past years been constantly enlarging and developing his thought by careful study and observation. He is a leading member of the Masonic fraternity, and belongs to Jo Hooker Post, Grand Army of the Republic.

LARS FLAGE is a reliable and well-to-do citizen of Highwater township, Cottonwood county, Minnesota. He came to this county in 1873, and located on the southeast quarter of section 18, where he re-

sided some ten years, at the end of which time he removed to the northeast quarter of the same section, making that his home up to the present time.

The subject of this sketch was born in Voss, Norway, November 7, 1845. He was the son of Ole and Julia (Larson) Flage, both of whom were natives of Norway. The father was a shoemaker by trade, and is now a resident of the State of Iowa. The mother died in her native land in 1847.

The subject of our sketch was one of five children—Betsy, Knute, Lars and Sarah (twins) and Mary. Until he was fourteen years of age Lars Flage remained in his native country, being educated in the district schools. In 1860 he came alone to the United States, locating in Dane county, Wisconsin, where he engaged in herding cattle. One year later a removal was made to Winneshiek county, Iowa. Here our subject engaged in agricultural pursuits for a number of years, attending school during the winter months for some time. He received an academic education at Decorah, Iowa, and also attended several other institutions of learning. He followed the profession of teaching for several years in Iowa and Minnesota, and in 1873 located in Cottonwood county. He has taught school three terms in Highwater township, and has always taken an active interest in educational matters. Although deeply engaged in matters pertaining to his private business, he has always had time and spirit to participate in projects pertaining to the general welfare. Affiliating with the republican party, he has been elected to and has efficiently held various positions of trust and responsibility, among them being clerk and supervisor of the township, and also clerk and treasurer of school district No. 38.

Mr. Flage was married February 8, 1886, to Miss Isabel Christoferson, a native of Norway. This lady came to the United

States when she was ten years of age, and from that time on she received her education and training in the State of Minnesota. Mr. and Mrs. Flage have two children—Julia and Oliver.

ELAH S. KING is the editor and publisher of the Jasper *Journal*. Since coming to the village this gentleman has occupied a prominent and influential place, and was the first postmaster in the place. He is an able editor and courteous gentleman, and has built up a large circle of warm friends.

Mr. King is of American birth, being born in Whitewater, Wisconsin, in October, 1864. He is the son of William V. and Antoinette (Porter) King. The father was a native of England and the mother of New York. The father is the present auditor of Jackson county, Minnesota, to which place he came in 1866. He is a man of large ability and wields a wide influence in the county in which he lives. In the father's family there were four children—William P., Nellie, now Mrs. E. W. Davies, of Pipestone; Selah S. and John L.

The subject of our sketch remained with his parents until he was twenty years of age, up to which time he was occupied principally in attending the public schools in Jackson county. At the age just mentioned he commenced learning the art of printing in the city of Pipestone, and after continuing thereat for some time he concluded to find a location and open a paper for himself. On the 27th of July, 1888, he established the Jasper *Journal*. Since that date his paper has been devoted to the interests, financial and otherwise, of Jasper and the surrounding country. In company with Black and Davies, he built his present office late in 1888. July 4, 1888, he was appointed postmaster of Jasper village, the office being established on the 25th of that month. He is one of the stockholders of the Jasper Produce Company, and is otherwise extensively interested in the financial welfare of his town. In politics he is a stanch republican and through his paper ably announces and expounds the principles of the republican party. He holds the office of school clerk, and is becoming one of the most popular business men of Jasper.

EORGE WESLEY DUSTIN. One of the leading and most important business enterprises of Faribault county, and one the loss of which would be keenly felt by the farmers of Verona township, and in fact of the entire county, is the Verona Roller Flouring Mills, located on the Blue Earth river, two miles south of Winnebago City. The gentleman whose name appears at the head of this sketch owns a one-half interest in this enterprise. The Verona Mills were built in 1879, by the father of our subject, at a cost of $9,500. Until its completion the father was the sole proprietor of the mill, and then our subject purchased the same and operated it for six years. At the end of that time Mr. Dustin sold a one-half interest to Mr. Foss, and the partnership was continued for two years. Early in the year 1888 our subject bought the interest owned by Mr. Foss, and in May of that year sold a one-half interest to Mr. A. A. Williams, who is still in the partnership. This mill has seven sets of rollers, kept constantly busy by the excellent patronage received from all parts of the county, its capacity being fifty barrels per day. At present the firm is putting in a steam plant, which will cost about $2,500. This will put the mill in excellent shape, and the owners will be better prepared to take care of the large volume of business that comes to them.

The subject of our sketch was born in Winnebago county, Wisconsin, October 21, 1848. He was the son of Newell Dustin, a carpenter by trade. The father followed that business until 1840, and then turned his attention to milling, engaging in that business in Green Lake county, Wisconsin, where he erected a large mill and operated the same for four years. He then went to Winnebago county, Wisconsin, purchased a farm near Ripon and engaged in agricultural pursuits until 1854. He then sold and again turned his attention to milling, putting up a mill in Juneau county, and continuing in the business for twelve years in one place. At the end of that time, in 1866, he removed to Blue Earth county, Minnesota, erected a large mill near Garden City, and remained there for three years. He then sold out and in 1870 built a mill at Blue Earth City, Faribault county, and operated the business a number of years. In 1879 the father built the mills now known as the Verona Mills, of which George W. Dustin is now the senior proprietor Our subject continued interested in the milling business with his father until the latter's death, which occurred in January, 1885. The father was a member of the Wesleyan Methodist church, and during the early part of his life was a minister of that denomination in the State of Ohio. He was a native of New Hampshire, born December 25, 1801, and was reared and educated in his native State. Our subject's mother's name before her marriage was Ann McMichael, a native of New York, where she was reared and educated and where for some years of her early life she engaged in the profession of teaching. She was a member of the Baptist church, and was an estimable Christian lady. The children of the father's family were George Wesley, Fred W. and Fremont, the latter dying while still an infant.

The native county of our subject remained his home only until he was five years of age, when the family removed to Juneau county, Wisconsin, where our subject received a common-school education. He followed the family in its various moves, finally locating in Blue Earth City, where he completed his education in the public schools of that place, at the age of twenty years. He then commenced working in his father's mill, and, indeed, from the time he was large enough to do any work at all, he has been employed more or less in the milling business, becoming a thorough, practical workman in that line. Going to Faribault county, Minnesota, in the spring of 1870, and settling in Blue Earth City, he followed milling in that place for some time, and also engaged in the same enterprise in central Iowa for about a year. Later he turned his attention to saw milling, and then operated a flouring mill in Dodge county, Minnesota, for one year. Returning to Blue Earth City, he worked in his father's mill for about three years, then engaged in business for himself, purchased his father's interest in the Verona Mills, and has been operating the same ever since. He has carefully watched the business, and has made it a point not to turn out anything but first-class work, and has thus succeeded in making his mill one of the most popular in Southern Minnesota.

George W. Dustin was married, September 12, 1870, to Miss Emma Taylor, born near Menasha, Fond du Lac county, Wisconsin. She was the daughter of Edward Taylor, a farmer and cooper by trade, and who came to Minnesota in 1864. He is still living in Brown county. Mrs. Dustin's mother's name before her marriage was Ellen Roberts. She is also living in Brown county. Mrs. Dustin was one of three children, the other two being Wilson and Janet. To bless the union of Mr. and Mrs. Dustin have been born five children, three of whom are now living—Newell, Cadwallader and Harry. Those deceased were, George, who died at one year of age, and an infant, who died at the age of six weeks.

The subject of this sketch is a man of excellent business qualities, and is one of the leading public spirits of his township and county, affiliating in political matters with the republican party. He has held various official positions, and in each instance has proven his efficiency, and has served his constituents with the highest degree of fidelity. At present he is clerk of the township of Verona, and has held that position since 1885. He is an Odd Fellow, and also a member of the United Workmen, being recorder in the latter lodge.

HENRY W. SINCLAIR is one of the foremost attorneys of Fairmont, Martin county, Minnesota. He is a native of England, where he was born July 1, 1851. His parents were residents of Cumberland, England.

Mr. Sinclair was educated in his native country and made that his home until 1876, in which year he emigrated to America, and came directly to Martin county, Minnesota. For about three years he resided on a farm and occupied his time with agricultural pursuits. At the end of that period he removed to the village of Fairmont, this being in 1880, and for about six years was cashier in the Martin County Bank. While in that position he served his employers faithfully, and built up an enviable reputation as an honorable, painstaking business man. In 1886 he severed his connection with the bank and engaged in the loan and real estate business, and also in the practice of law. He is one of Fairmont's leading public-spirited citizens, and has built up a large and lucrative practice.

The subject of our sketch was married in the year 1878, at Fairmont, to Miss Margaret Wollaston, daughter of Percy and Catharine Wollaston. Mr. and Mrs. Sinclair have had the following named children— Agnes Winnifred, Edith Margaret, John Archibald, Catharine Elizabeth and Nora Frances.

JACOB M. BUTTS is one of the wealthy and most prosperous farmers and stock raisers in Pipestone county, Minnesota. He came to the county in April, 1883, and purchased the whole of section 25 in Osborn township, and commenced making improvements in the way of cultivating his land and erecting large and commodious farm buildings. He built the largest and finest barn in the township, the building being 40x154 feet, his other buildings being of good character and of like pretentious dimensions. He has a large, well-built house, the upright part of which is 24x26 feet, and the wing thereto being 16x20 feet. He has turned his attention largely to the raising of blooded stock, and has some fine specimens of full-blooded Durham cattle, and one-half blood Clyde and Norman horses. He generally keeps from sixty to one hundred head of cattle of the Durham breed. Mr. Butts has one of the finest farms in the county, and has met with excellent success in his farming and stock-raising operations.

The subject of our sketch is a native of Monroe county, Pennsylvania, where he was born August 1, 1835. He is the son of Michael and Catharine A. (Mann) Butts, both of whom were natives of Pennsylvania. The father was a blacksmith by trade, and followed that occupation in connection with farming. In about 1838 the parents removed to the State of Wisconsin, where the father died at about thirty years of age. The mother is still living in Wisconsin, being about eighty years of age. The parents were both exemplary Christian people and were members of the Methodist Episcopal church. They reared a family of eight children, of whom the subject of our sketch was the fourth in order. Their names were—Theodore, Robert, Catharine, Jacob M., Charles, Mary, Rachel and Jerome.

Jacob M. Butts remained beneath the parental roof until he was about eighteen years of age, up to which time he had been given a good common-school education. On attaining the age just mentioned he left home and engaged in farm work for about three years, being employed by neighboring farmers. At the end of that period he took a farm on shares, and conducted it successfully for some years. In 1863 he purchased a farm in Dane county, Wisconsin, and engaged in its operation until 1883, doing a general farming and stock-raising business. He also became quite an extensive tobacco grower, and for some three years made this his principal crop while in Wisconsin. As has been stated in the opening lines of this sketch, in 1883 he left Dane county and settled on his present place in Pipestone county. In August, 1864, our subject enlisted in Company G, Thirty-eighth Wisconsin Infantry, his regiment becoming part of the Ninth Corps. The captain in command of this company was Reuben Beckwith, who continued in command until the close of the war. Our subject was in a number of battles and saw more or less hard service. Some of the engagements in which he participated may be named as follows: Battle of Feeble House, which occurred in October, 1864; Weldon railroad; engagement before Petersburg in the trenches around the city, charging the main works in front of Petersburg, and other smaller battles and skirmishes. He narrowly escaped death by being struck on the head by a piece of shell at the last-named battle. As a result of this blow he was unconscious for some time, but finally recovered and was able to join his regiment. After being discharged from the service our subject returned to his farm in Wisconsin and remained there until coming to Pipestone county.

Mr. Butts was united in marriage December 31, 1857, to Miss Sarah A. Lumus, a native of Ohio. This lady remained in her native State until about fourteen years of age, when, with her parents, she moved to the State of Wisconsin, and resided in Dane county until her marriage. Mr. and Mrs. Butts have been blessed with six children— William, Rosa, Charles, Oscar, Bertie and Fremont. William is now married, and is a resident of Garden City, Kansas, and Rosa is the wife of Frank A. Meacham, a successful and enterprising hardware merchant of Edgerton, Minnesota.

The subject of our sketch holds an influential place among the farmers of the township. He is a man of good executive ability, well educated and possessed of wide practical knowledge. He is energetic and systematic, and to these qualities is traceable his eminent success in farming and stock raising. He is a pleasant man and a good conversationalist, and his surroundings betoken taste and thrift, and in his pleasant home the wayfarer is greeted with a hospitable welcome. In politics our subject affiliates with the republican party, in whose principles he is a firm believer. He is a leading member of the Grand Army of the Republic.

On the 17th of February, 1859, Mr. Butts, in company with six other men, started overland with horses and wagons for Pike's Peak, arriving at Council Bluffs, March 25. Three days later they left Omaha. At Elkhorn river, April 1, there was a foot of snow on the ground. On their way up the Platte river they found streams very high, but they managed to ferry them—using a wagon box for a boat—and reached Fort Kearney April 15. From there our subject crossed the plains and went up into the mountains. Not finding gold as plenty as supposed he returned to the plains and spent some time in hunting buffalo. While he was on the plains the Sioux and Pawnee Indians had a two days' battle over some stolen ponies, in which fifteen of the Pawnees were killed. In June of the same year Mr. Butts returned home and engaged in farming.

Mrs. Butts is a leading member and active worker in the Women's Relief Corps. In fact, figuratively speaking, during the war she was as "good a soldier as ever swung a sword." While her husband was away in the army she carried on farming, took care of the stock, dug potatoes, husked corn, fed hogs, and, when they were ready for the market, drove them to the station from which they were shipped South to feed the army. To dress hogs for their own use, Mrs. Butts formed a company of "War Widows," and they drove their hogs to one place and killed and dressed them, Mrs. Butts being in command. It is true that there were some men left at home, but, as Mr. Butts expresses it, they were of the "home-fire-side-loyal" and "secesh" order, and "no good on earth." The same company that Mrs. Butts had command of scraped lint, dried fruit, dried potatoes and made clothing for the soldiers, meeting every Thursday.

REV. EDWARD H. BRONSON, one of the most highly-esteemed citizens of Luverne, Minnesota, is engaged in the hardware and agricultural implement business. He was a native of Chemung county, New York, where he was born January 27, 1835.

Mr. Bronson is the son of Major T. and Matilda (Hotchkis) Bronson, both natives of Connecticut. The father was a blacksmith by trade, and in 1852 came West to Wisconsin and located in Fall River, Columbia county. In that place he engaged in farming, and was a prominent and influential citizen of that locality. Throughout the most of his life he was a local preacher in the Methodist Episcopal, and later in the Wesleyan Methodist church, being ordained in the latter organization as a traveling preacher. When he was a young man he entered this kind of religious work and accomplished a great deal of good throughout his life. He continued to serve his generation by the grace of God until attaining his eighty-third year, when he passed from this life into the great eternity, where, without doubt, his reward awaited him. Leaving Wisconsin, the father went to Dakota and located at Howard, in Minor county, living with the family of his son, Spencer H., who is editor of the *Advance*. The mother died in Wisconsin in June, 1872. In the father's family there were six children, three of whom are now living—Rev. E. H., our subject; Amanda, now Mrs. Hotchkis, of Howard, Dakota, and Spencer H.

The early years of the subject of our sketch were spent with his parents in the State of New York, where he was given good educational advantages in the district schools. Removing with his parents to the State of Wisconsin, he again attended a public, and later a select school, acquiring a good common-school education. He remained with his parents until he was about twenty-six years of age, having for some years been engaged as a clerk in various stores in the city in which his family lived. In 1862 he enlisted in Company K, Thirty-second Wisconsin Infantry, and at the organization of that company was made first sergeant. Some time later he was promoted to the rank of first lieutenant of his company and continued in the service about three years. For about a year previous to receiving the latter commission he was a recruiting officer in Wisconsin for the Army of the Tennessee. He was mustered out of the service at Milwaukee, after having passed through a severe military experience. Among the battles in which he was engaged were the siege of Atlanta, the various skirmishes in which Sherman's army was engaged on his march to the sea, the battles of Salkehatchie, Jonesborough, and numerous other battles of minor importance.

On the 23d of December, 1864, he was taken prisoner by the Rebel forces under General Lyon, at Nolin Station, Kentucky. He was paroled the same evening and shortly after the close of the war returned to Wisconsin and engaged in the produce business and also in merchandising for some two years at Fall River. In 1867, feeling the call most heavily upon him, he entered the ministry, his first pastorate being in Pardeeville, Columbia county, Wisconsin, later in Greenbush and then at Cambria. In 1872 he removed to Luverne and joined the Minnesota conference. He was the first English speaking clergyman in Rock county and was instrumental in accomplishing a great amount of good among the English speaking people. He established the Methodist Episcopal church of Luverne, with the co-operation of T. P. Grout and James Gillard; also at Beaver Creek he established a Methodist Episcopal church society assisted by E. L. Grout, William Grout, F. Merricot and G. H. and C. R. Hinton. He organized the Methodist Episcopal church at Adrian and one at Ellsworth, where he was assisted by the families of James Birkett and Mr. Ingraham. He established a society of the same church at Ash Creek, in which enterprise he was assisted by Messrs. Joseph Knight, Mitchell, Olds and the Estes family; also at Spring Water assisted by Messrs. Bark, Nobles, Elthorp, Givens and Chapin. He was the pioneer preacher of the southwestern corner of Minnesota, and held the first Methodist services in Pipestone county June 25, 1875. He was in active service in the ministry until 1884, in which year he withdrew from active service, although he has been called upon to supply Jackson, Rushmore, Adrian, Luverne, etc., and frequently to perform the duties of the ministry since in the way of preaching and attending funerals. His ministerial work was given up with great reluctance, but this became a necessity on account of failing health. In an early day he had traveled a great deal and had been exposed to all kinds of weather, all of which combined to undermine his constitution and to break him down in early life. His pioneer experience in establishing Methodism in Rock county was attended with many difficulties and privations. He traveled long distances, forded streams, faced the northwestern winds and experienced blizzards, giving all this service freely and undergoing all these trials willingly for the sake of the good that might be accomplished, and the building up of the church organizations that would benefit the world after he was gone. Soon after coming to Rock county Mr. Bronson secured a homestead at Beaver Creek, which he improved and brought under good cultivation. In 1884 he traded this farm for lots and business property in Luverne. Mr. Bronson has identified himself with all public matters and has served his constituents in various official positions. At present he is the president of the school board and of the city library association. He is a stockholder in the Red Jasper Stone Quarry Company and is also a stockholder in the *Rock County News*, a prohibition paper.

Rev. Bronson was married to Cornelia Silsbee, March 4, 1860. She died of consumption June 9, 1862. He was again married on September 27, 1865, to Mrs. Libbie Grout, of Madison, Wisconsin. This union has been blessed with six children, five of whom are now living—William S., Etheline, Edward M., Jessie, and Ruth. Eleanor died at six years of age on the 23d of December, 1887.

The subject of our sketch throughout the greater portion of his life believed in the principles of the republican party, advocated and defended its doctrines, and stood by its interests. Within a few years, however, he has considerably changed his political belief, and being a strong temperance man and an advocate of temperance principles he has concluded that his affiliations can only be given to the prohibition party. He is a Mason and also a member of the Grand Army of the Republic. Mr. Bronson is a man of high character and is respected as an exemplary citizen by all who know him. Throughout his life he has publicly professed and practiced the principles of the great Master whose teaching it was his desire to promulgate. He has given his life heartily and earnestly to the moral and religious elevation of the people and can look back upon many years spent in a prosperous service on these lines. He has been reasonably successful in his various financial enterprises and has laid up a considerable fortune. He is now engaged in the hardware business and has built up an extensive trade. He has been throughout his life a loyal and active citizen, a consistent Christian man, and is held in high esteem by all with whom he has to do.

ILLIAM C. CAMPBELL, is a' respected citizen of Winnebago City, Faribault county, Minnesota, where he lives a retired life. He is a native of Butler county, Ohio, where he was born March 3, 1821.

The parents of the subject of our sketch were John N. and Phœbe (Clark) Campbell, natives of Pennsylvania. The father was a farmer by occupation, and was the son of Enos Campbell, who served in the Revolutionary War and who was a native of Pennsylvania. The father of our subject was a soldier of the War of 1812 and also served in the Black Hawk War. He removed to Illinois, locating in Sangamon county, in 1828; later removed to Dewitt county, where he lived a retired life until his death in 1887, at the age of ninety-four years. The mother died at ninety-two years of age in 1883. The father was an old line whig, and later joined the republican party. Both parents were devoted members of the Methodist Episcopal church. They had a family of nine children—Israel, Christian, William C., Enos, Brazilla, Lewis, John (deceased), Sallie A. (deceased) and Mary (deceased).

The subject of our sketch spent his early life in the midst of pioneer circumstances in Illinois, receiving his early education in the log school-houses of his district. He remained with his parents until he was twenty-three years of age, at which time his father gave him eighty acres of land and he purchased eighty acres more, making a farm of 160 acres. His father also gave him horses and cattle and established him in good shape on his farm. He engaged in agricultural pursuits in Illinois until 1867, when he came to Winnebago City, Faribault county, Minnesota, and engaged in the grocery business. After following this line for two years he sold out and removed to Granite Falls, where he purchased property and resided for two years. At the end of this time he returned to Winnebago City, and soon after engaged in farming for five years. Again he returned to Winnebago City, and has since made this place his residence. He purchased a fine brick dwelling house on Main street, where he now lives. Our subject enlisted in the Union army during the war as lieutenant of Company C, Forty-first Illinois Infantry, and was in the service five months, going to Paducah, Kentucky, where he was taken sick. On account of severe sickness he was forced to resign his position and return home. Throughout his life the subject of our sketch has been a prominent citizen, and has affiliated with the republican party. He is one of the leading residents of Winnebago City.

Mr. Campbell was married in the year 1843 to Miss Ann Kyle, of Sangamon county,

Illinois, and daughter of Joseph Kyle. Three children blessed this union, only one of whom now lives—Louise, now Mrs. Conklin. Mrs. Conklin has four children—Frederick, Monte C., Lewis and Florence. Mrs. Campbell died in October, 1858. The second marriage of our subject was to Mrs. Catharine Gery, of Clinton, Illinois, a daughter of George Gideon.

JOHN MILTON POORBAUGH is perhaps one of the best known business men of Pipestone county, Minnesota. He is a native of Elkhart, Indiana, born March 17, 1852, and is a son of Philip and Sarah (Shuey) Poorbaugh. The mother died in 1860, and the father, entering the Union army in 1861, left the children orphans, to battle alone with the world. The children, and their ages at this time, were John M., our subject, aged nine years; Frank, aged five; Della, aged seven, and Linna, aged three years.

The father being a farmer, John M. spent most of his time on a farm until he was fourteen years of age. He then went West, to Iowa, and worked on a farm during the first summer. He then went to the pineries, where he worked for one year. Returning then, to Mason City, Iowa, at the age of sixteen, he began learning the mason's trade, and a few years later commenced contracting. To quote Mr. Poorbaugh's own words, he then took "one of the largest contracts he ever had"—certainly an immense one for a boy of sixteen—in Davis county, Missouri. It was to clear twenty acres of heavy timber ready for the plow in three months. When he took this contract he was nearly an entire stranger, without a cent, but he completed the job, employing some twenty-five men, and made considerable money out of it. Mr. Poorbaugh's education was very limited, as he was thrown upon his own re-

sources at an early age, and has been compelled to rely upon his own efforts. Throughout his life, however, thrown as he has been into such active business, his observation and quick perceptions served him in its stead, and he is, in every respect, a self-made man.

On the 7th of September, 1871, he was married to Hattie M. Drinkwater, at Newburg, Mitchell county, Iowa. In 1880 he removed to Pipestone county and settled on a homestead in Sweet township, where he started the Pipestone Nursery, of which he is still the owner. In the fall of 1887 he commenced contracting on the St. Paul, Minneapolis & Manitoba railroad. He did $100,000 worth of work for that company to their entire satisfaction, and holds a flattering recommendation from that corporation. Mr. Poorbaugh is also one of the principal members of the Jasper Improvement Company, which owns some 1,400 acres of land, on which is located the famous Jasper stone quarries, as well as the city of Jasper. At the present writing Mr. Poorbaugh is engaged with contracts on the Burlington, Cedar Rapids & Northern railway, and also in operating the Red Jasper quarries, from which 125 to 170 car loads of stone are shipped per month.

Mr. Poorbaugh's present home is in the suburbs of Pipestone City, where he has a sixty-acre farm, which is finely improved.

Mr. and Mrs. Poorbaugh are the parents of eight children, five boys and three girls, namely—Charles F., Allie A., Stella May, Robert, Carl, John, Della and Dora Bell.

JOSEPH F. SCHWARTZ, a prosperous farmer and stock raiser of Hansonville township, Lincoln county, Minnesota, located on 280 acres of railroad land in 1882. His farm was on section 3 and he has 160 acres under excellent cultivation, provided with good buildings and one of the very best farms in the township. He has a fine barn 40x45 feet and eighteen feet high. He has worked and planned to make his farm one of the finest in the township and his buildings and improvements betoken the high success which has attended his efforts. He has been engaged in general farming and stock raising and cultivates more land and farms more extensively than any other farmer in the township. He has identified himself closely with all public interests and has held various official positions. He was justice of the township for four years; for two years he held the office of supervisor, and is at present assessor and also supervisor. For four years he has held the position of one of the directors of school district No: 36.

The subject of our sketch was born in Otrocin, Bohemia, January 21, 1842. His parents were Frank S. and Josie Schwartz, the father being of French descent. The father was an iron maker by trade and lived and died in his native country, Bohemia. The father died on the 12th day of March, 1879, and the mother died in the old country November 15, 1871. In the father's family there were seven children—Frank, Joseph, Katie, Barbara, Anna, Caroline and Mary.

The subject of our sketch remained with his parents in his native country until he was thirty years of age, at which time he came to the United States, first locating in Pennsylvania. His early life in his native land was spent in assisting his father in work at his trade and in attending the public schools. Advantages for education were of a good character in his native country, and he became well prepared for the duties of life. On coming to this country he located in Pennsylvania and engaged in the mining business for the Pennsylvania Gas and Coal Company, following this occupation for some fifteen years. He then concluded to find a location in the western country. He came at once to Minnesota and made his settlement on his present farm in Lincoln county.

January 21, 1864, in Bohemia, county of Pirglitz, our subject was married to Miss Barbara Staneck, a native of the same province in which our subject was born, Joackinstall. Mr. and Mrs. Schwartz have been blessed with ten children—Charles, Mary, Caroline, Gilhart, Joseph, Jennie, Jeronine, Otto, Anna and Robert.

Since coming to the township Mr. Schwartz has proven himself a capable and trustworthy farmer and citizen. He is a man of excellent character, is an earnest defender of the principles of right and justice. In all public matters tending to the elevation of public interests he takes an active part, and by his public spirit and liberal-heartedness has drawn to himself many warm friends. In politics he is of an independent spirit, affiliating with no particular party, but supporting men rather than parties for positions. He is a leading member of the Masonic fraternity.

WILLIAM W. BARLOW is the present efficient and popular sheriff of Cottonwood county, Minnesota. He made his home here in 1872, settling in Amo township, where he took a soldier's homestead of 160 acres. He made numerous improvements, built a house and granary, and set out a fine grove of trees. He continued on his farm until 1880, when he came to the village of Windom, and operated the Hyat House for one year. He then purchased this property, and rechristened it the Barlow House. This is one of the best hotels in the city, and is still operated by our subject.

Mr. Barlow is a native of the State of New York, where he was born, February 19, 1840. His parents were Rev. Samuel W. and Almira (Wright) Barlow, the former a native of New York, and the latter born in Vermont. The father settled in Delevan, Wisconsin, in the year 1846, and engaged to a large extent in farming, and also was a minister of the Wesleyan Methodist church. He continued his residence in Wisconsin until his death, which occurred in March, 1889. Our subject's mother died in 1844. In the father's family there were seven children—Ruth, now Mrs. William E. Wood; Silas V.; Selinda, now Mrs. J. Shelden; William W., Samuel W., Jr., Josiah W. and James L.

Our subject was reared as a farmer's boy on the old home farm, remaining with his parents until he was twenty-one years of age. He was given good educational advantages, and attended college at Bigfoot Prairie, Walworth county, Wisconsin. He also attended Bryant & Stratton's Commercial College in Chicago, Illinois, in 1861. In August, 1862, he enlisted in Company D, Twenty-second Wisconsin Infantry. He continued in the service until the close of the war, participating in numerous battles. He was taken prisoner at Brentwood, Tennessee, March 25, 1863, and was confined in Libby prison for sixteen days. The rebels took nearly all his clothing from him, and deprived him of all his valuables. He was then sent to parole camp at St. Louis, where he remained two weeks and then returned home on a short visit. He was on provost duty at Murfreesborough for eight months, and then joined General Sherman's army, participating in all the battles of the famous march to the sea. He continued with the army until the close of the war, and went with his regiment to the grand review at Washington, after which he returned home, receiving his discharge at Milwaukee, Wisconsin, June 12, 1865. He enlisted as a private, and for faithful service was promoted to the rank of corporal. When discharged he had a commission as second lieutenant of the company to which he belonged. Returning home after being discharged from further service he took charge of his father's farm, operating the same for two years. He was then married and rented a farm in Walworth county, and engaged in agricultural pursuits until 1872. In this year he came to Cottonwood county, where he has since resided. In 1882 he was elected sheriff of the county, and has held that office ever since. While a resident of the township of Amo he was town clerk for a number of years, and has held numerous other official positions. In politics he affiliates with the republican party, and is a member of the Odd Fellows, Ancient Order of United Workmen and Grand Army of the Republic fraternities, and is one of Cottonwood county's most influential and prominent citizens.

In January, 1867, Mr. Barlow was married to Miss Belinda Mead, a daughter of Kenney and Arzulah (Bush) Mead. This union has been blessed with one daughter, Nellie, who is now attending Hamline University near Minneapolis.

EORGE F. STOW, one of the leading business men of the village of Tyler Lincoln county, Minnesota, established himself in the lumber trade in March, 1885. Since coming to the village he has been one of the active, energetic business characters, and has built up a large and profitable business. He is the son of John G. and Charlotte (Fisher) Stow, natives, respectively, of Massachusetts and Vermont. The family came to Wisconsin in an early day and located in Rock county, where they remained until about 1857 and then removed to Waupaca county. The father died on his farm in Wisconsin, December 21, 1885, and the mother is still living on the old homestead.

The gentleman whose name appears at the head of this sketch was born in Johnstown, Rock county, Wisconsin, February 19,

1850. He resided on the farm of his father in that county until 1857, when with them he removed to Waupaca and there settled on a farm. Our subject remained with his parents assisting in farm work and attending the district schools until he was twenty-two years of age. He received a good common-school education, and on attaining the age just mentioned, commenced teaching school, which profession he followed for about two years, during which time he made his home with his parents. After this period of teaching had expired he removed to the village of Chilton and accepted a position as telegraph operator and station agent for the Wisconsin Central Railroad Company. He continued in this employment from November, 1874, until May, 1882. At that time he came to Tyler and became station agent for the Chicago & Northwestern Railroad Company. He continued in the employ of this company as their agent until in March, 1888, after which time he gave his attention.entirely to his lumber business, which he had established in March, 1885. During his residence in Tyler he filed on a claim in Potter county, Dakota. In order to hold this land, his wife, with the characteristic determination of her sex, went to the claim and resided thereon for six months, at which time our subject proved up and obtained a patent.

Mr. Stow was united in matrimony in Hayton, Wisconsin, December 5, 1877, to Miss Sarah Nicholson, a native of Rochester, New York, where she was born in October, 1859. This lady was the daughter of William and Patience (Love) Nicholson, natives of England.

Since taking up his residence in the village of Tyler our subject has identified himself intimately with all public interests and has held various official positions. He has been village recorder for some time and has held other positions of trust and responsibility. He is also interested in various civic societies,

being an influential member of the Chilton Lodge of Ancient Free and Accepted Masons of Chilton, Wisconsin, and also of the Independent Order of Odd Fellows, Lodge No. 207, of the same place. He is a member of the Temple of Honor and Independent Order of Good Templars of Tyler, and being of a musical turn is one of the prominent members of the Tyler Cornet Band. In his various business enterprises Mr. Stow has attained merited success and has accumulated considerable means. He is careful and systematic in all his transactions, and in whatever direction his attention is drawn, the business with which he is occupied is carried on to success. His connection with the railroad company as depot agent and also with the express companies has always been of the most harmonious and cordial nature, and besides being profitable to himself has been highly satisfactory to the companies, who have given our subject recommendations of the highest grade. Mr. Stow is a man of excellent character and is respected by all who know him.

ANFIN J. BERDAHL, junior member of the firm of Christianson & Berdahl, is one of the leading and most prosperous merchants of Jasper, Pipestone county, Minnesota. These gentlemen were the pioneer merchants of the village, opening their business May 17, 1888.

Mr. Berdahl is a native of Norway, where he was born December 12, 1852. His parents were John E. and Christina (Henjum) Berdahl, natives of Norway. The father was an extensive farmer in his native land and a man of considerable prominence and influence. The family came to America in 1856, settling in Winneshiek county, Iowa, where they lived some four years. Removing thence they settled in Houston county, Minnesota, where the father purchased eighty acres of school land in Black Hammer township. He improved this farm and continued living thereon for a period of six years, at the end of which time he removed to Fillmore county, Minnesota, settling in the town of Amherst. His residence in that town was continued until 1873, in which year he removed to Minnehaha county, Dakota. In the father's family there were nine children, eight of whom are now living— Andrew, Erick, Anfin J., Christina, Martha, Herman, Ole and Christopher.

The subject of our sketch remained with his parents, going with them in their various moves until he was about twenty-four years of age. He had been given ample educational advantages in the common schools and obtained a fair education. At twenty-four years of age he commenced farming on his own account in Minnehaha county, Dakota, continuing his agricultural pursuits until 1887. In that year he rented his farm and moved to Pipestone city, Pipestone county, Minnesota, where he engaged in the general mercantile business with his present partner. After eight months they concluded to move from Pipestone, so, packing their goods, they moved to Jasper village, becoming the pioneer merchants of that place. They put up a store building 22x40 feet, where they have since been engaged in a general trade.

Mr. Berdahl was married in 1878 to Miss Caroline Christenson, of Moody county, Dakota. This union was blessed with three living children—Christian O., John A. and Clara M.

The gentleman whose name appears at the head of this sketch is one of the prominent and successful business men of this part of Pipestone county. In politics he affiliates with the republican party, and both himself and family are members of the Lutheran church. He is a stockholder in the Jasper Produce Company, of which he is the present vice-president. In public matters he takes an active interest and has held several school and township offices.

HANS LAVESSON is the popular register of deeds of Lincoln county, Minnesota. Since coming to the county he has identified himself intimately with the interests of the republican party, and was first elected to his present position on the republican ticket in the fall of 1884. He is now serving on his third term, and throughout his official career he has performed the duties of his office with rare fidelity, and with entire satisfaction to his constituents. So popular has he become that at the two last elections at which he was re-elected, although his name had been brought forward and placed upon the republican ticket as a member of that party, yet the democrats have endorsed him, and assisted in his re-election in 1886–88.

Mr. Lavesson is the son of Lave and Anna Larson, both natives of Sweden. He was born in Skonastift Tornahared, Sweden, July 13, 1848. His parents were farmers by occupation, and he was reared a farmer's boy, receiving the educational advantages furnished by the district schools. Until fifteen years of age he continued his studies in the schools, and assisted his parents on the farm, continuing with them at farm work until he was eighteen years old. He then engaged with an adjoining farmer, and worked out by the year. This line of life was not continued very long, however, for at the end of the year he became convinced that he could make nothing in his own land. So he concluded to emigrate to the United States. This he did, making a location in Wabasha county, Minnesota, where he arrived June 1, 1868. Here he hired out to a farmer for $150 and board for a year, remaining with him for about one year. At the end of that time the wages were raised to $22 per month, but the raising of the wages did him but little good, as he never received any pay. He moved from that place disgusted with the manner in which business was done there, and stopped in Mankato, where he clerked in a dry goods store for some time. Close confinement, however, did not agree with his health, and he was forced to quit that kind of employment. He went to St. Paul and found employment with a liveryman as driver. This was done so that he might have the benefit of out-door work. He remained in the liveryman's employ for four years, and then returned, in 1875, to Wabasha county, where his brother and himself rented a farm and engaged in agricultural pursuits until the spring of 1878. At that time he came to Lincoln county, Minnesota, and took a homestead and tree claim in Ash Lake township. He was one of the early settlers of this locality, and when he came there were only two houses in the township. He retained the ownership of his farm until the summer of 1884, when he sold out for $4,800. Since that time he has been engaged to some extent in buying and selling lands. He has bought and sold, and now owns, three hundred acres of good land, well improved and provided with very fine buildings.

The subject of our sketch was married in Stockholm, Wisconsin, July 25, 1876, to Miss Carrie Pearson, daughter of Peter and Olivia Pearson, natives of Sweden. Miss Pearson was born in Sweden and came to the United States with her parents when she was five years of age. She received her early training and education in Vasa, Goodhue county, Minnesota, where her parents still reside. Mr. and Mrs. Lavesson have been blessed with two children—Charles Elvin and Alice Minnie.

The life of the subject of our sketch since he came to Lincoln county has been intimately associated with all matters pertaining to the public welfare. He has given of his time and means in the furtherance of various projects which tended toward the upbuilding of the general financial interests of the locality in which he has lived. He has interested himself largely in political movements, and has efficiently served his constituents in various official positions. He has been a member of the township board, township clerk, and held the latter office when elected register of deeds. He sent in his resignation as township clerk, but it was not accepted, and he had to hold that position until the following spring election. He has been quite prominent in governmental affairs, and is at present a member of the congressional committee, and has held some official position ever since locating in the county. He has a pleasant family, and, with his wife and children, belongs to the Swedish Lutheran church.

CHARLES W. GILLAM is one of the leading and most substantial citizens of Windom, Cottonwood county, Minnesota. He is a dealer in farm machinery and buys and sells grain of all kinds and is a member of the firm of Thurston Bros. & Gillam, dealers in general merchandise.

Mr. Gillam is a native of Omro, Winnebago county, Wisconsin, where he was born April 10, 1861. His parents were Samuel S. and Cornelia (Clark) Gillam. The father is at present engaged in farming in Cottonwood county. The parents are both natives of New York and are still living. In the father's family there five children—Henry C., William S., Charles W., Edward E. and Albert.

The subject of our sketch was reared on the farm and received the educational advantages furnished by the district school. He remained with his parents, assisting them in farm work, until twenty-one years of age, when he opened a flour and feed store in which he continued for about two years. He then added machinery and commenced buying grain, continuing in this line ever since. He built an elevator in 1887 with a capacity of eight thousand bushels of grain. He is doing a large and extensive business and has a neat office on Ninth street. He is a man of large enterprise, and is one of the city's most enterprising and public-spirited merchants. In 1889 he was elected village recorder, and is also chief of the fire department. He has interested himself largely in real estate investments and owns a considerable amount of land in the county. In politics he affiliates with the republican party, and is one of the most highly respected and substantial citizens of Windom.

CHARLES H. WORKS, who resides on section 28, Delton township, Cottonwood county, Minnesota, is one of the leading farmers of the locality in which he lives. He has taken an active interest in local matters, has filled various township offices and is regarded as an honorable and straightforward man.

JOHN J. HOLDEN is one of the prosperous and influential citizens of Lake Sarah township, Murray county, Minnesota, where he located on section 2, in 1879. He pre-empted his present place, and has resided there ever since, with the exception of four years, from 1880 to 1884, which were spent by him in farming in Lyon county. Mr. Holden was one of the early settlers, and took an active interest in pioneer matters. In 1879 he broke forty acres of land, and the following year set out a fine grove of trees. At present he has a fine farm under good cultivation, and for some time he has owned an interest in a horse-power threshing machine.

In public matters he has always taken an active interest, and was elected assessor, which position he held one year during early days. While in Lyon county he held several official positions, among them being that of assessor, school director and treasurer of his school district. He has been chairman of the board of supervisors' of Lake Sarah township for one year. In county matters he has always taken an active part, and in 1886 was elected one of the county commissioners, which position he still holds, having been re-elected in 1888. He is at present school clerk of District No. 13, which position he has held since 1885. All public matters, and especially educational affairs, meet with his earnest and hearty support.

Mr. Holden was born in Trondhjen, Norway, November 3, 1845. He remained with his parents until he was twenty years of age, and then came to America, locating for four years in Dane county, Wisconsin. While in Dane county, Wisconsin, he worked in a woolen factory, and after four years he went to Goodhue county, Minnesota, and remained until 1876 engaged in farming and in carpenter work. He then purchased a farm in Ellington township, Dodge county, and resided there for seven years, after which he sold out and came to his present place. Referring to his early life, we may see that he received a good common-school education in his native land up to the age of seventeen years, and during this time had learned the dyeing trade.

The parents of the subject of our sketch were Johannes T. and Sarah L. Holden, and there were seven children in the father's family. The parents are still living in their native land.

Mr. Holden was married June 11, 1866, to Miss Karen J. Reberg, born in the same place in which our subject was born. Mr. and Mrs. Holden have seven children— Sophia, Julius, Carl, Lottie, Anna, John and

Matilda. Sophia is married and now resides in Tracy, Lyon county.

The subject of our sketch is a republican in politics, and with his family belongs to the Lutheran church. He stands among the leading and representative men of the county.

JOHN PEARSON is the capable and efficient county auditor of Pipestone county, Minnesota. He located in the county in 1877, and settled on land in Grange and Troy townships, one claim being a homestead of 160 acres and the other a 160-acre timber claim. He moved onto his homestead in 1878, and commenced farming and making improvements by breaking a few acres and building a small house. During the summer of each year until 1885 he made the farm his home, removing thence each winter for the purpose of following business pursuits in other localities. In 1885 he moved into the city of Pipestone, and has since that time made that place his permanent home. He was appointed to his present office in the year 1880 to fill a vacancy, and in 1881 was elected to the office by a large majority. He has held the office ever since, and in 1884 received every vote cast in the county—nine hundred in all. Besides this he has held other official positions, having been treasurer of Grange township in 1879 and 1880, and also supervisor in 1879 ; and is at present a member of the village council.

Mr. Pearson was born near Dayton, Ohio, July 21, 1836. He was the son of Thomas and Nancy (Nock) Pearson, both of whom were natives of Ohio. For many years the father was engaged in farming in his native State, and in 1841 removed to Indiana, first settling in Cass county, and afterward locating in Miami county, in both counties engaging in the occupation of farming. Miami county continued his home until his death, which occurred in 1864. The mother is still living in Wabash, Indiana. In the father's family there were seven children five of whom are now living—Oliver, John, Catharine, Andrew and Susan. Those who died were Nelson and Perry D. The parents were exemplary members of the Baptist church, and the father in early life was an old line whig, affiliating with the republican party from and after its organization. He was an active worker in church and school matters and held several official positions in the township in which he lived.

The boyhood days of the subject of our sketch were spent by him on the home farm where he was given the advantages for education furnished by the district schools. He remained with his parents until 1861, in which year he helped to organize a company of soldiers in Miami county, Indiana, for the purpose of joining the Union army. He accepted the position of lieutenant of the company and stood ready to join in the service. The military hopes of the members of this company, however, were doomed to disappointment. The men had enlisted for three months, but as the quota for three-months men had been filled in Indiana the company was disbanded. This, however, did not deter our subject from again offering his services to the Union army. He enlisted August 29, 1861, as a private in Company D, Thirty-ninth Regiment Indiana Volunteer Infantry, of which he was made corporal, later sergeant, and finally captain. The regiment was afterward mustered as Eighth Indiana Veteran Volunteer Cavalry. The military career of Mr. Pearson extended through four years lacking thirty-five days. He was engaged in the following battles : Shiloh, Corinth, the battle near Nashville, Liberty Gap, Middleton, Nicojack Gap, Gaines Gap, Chickamauga, Peavine Church, Tunnel Hill,

Cheraw Trustle, Stony Face Ridge, Lewis ville, siege of Atlanta, siege of Chattanooga, Solomon's Grove, and many other smaller battles and engagements. It was his misfortune to be taken prisoner at Solomon's Grove, North Carolina, in 1865, being held by the Rebels for twenty days. He was incarcerated in Libby prison and Castle Thunder. He claims to have been fairly well treated with the exception of having to "subsist on short rations" most of the time. His clothes were also taken from him, such as overcoats, blankets, etc., and one Rebel was determined to take our subject's boots, but he declined to give them up to the Rebel, who finally concluded to leave Mr. Pearson in peaceful possession of his footwear. perhaps the result of the little commotion between the Rebel and our subject would have had a different termination had it not been for the fact that when he was taken captive he had charge of a Confederate officer who was a prisoner held by the Union forces. When the Rebel demanded Mr. Pearson's boots this Confederate officer came to his rescue and caused the would-be boot owner to desist. The ground for the officer's objection was, as he said, "When held a prisoner by the Union army and in charge of this man (Pearson) I was treated well, and I now demand for him the same treatment that was given to me." After twenty days of captivity Mr. Pearson was paroled and started for home minus all the buttons of his coat and vest, and minus all moneys which he had with him at the time of his capture.

Mr. Pearson relates many interesting reminiscences of his army life, for but few soldiers saw more active or exciting and dangerous service. He led a cavalry charge while in command of the advance guard on the McCook raid, at midnight, capturing the camp and camp equipage, and routing the enemy. The enemy was prepared to give them a warm reception by having barricades built across the lane and a force behind it. When the Union forces arrived within a few rods the Rebels fired a volley which made one sheet of flame across the lane, and then withdrew. While near Atlanta he had command of a company that was ambushed, and had his horse shot under him. One man and three horses were killed, but the enemy was repulsed. At Missionary Ridge he operated with the cavalry on the flank; was with General McCook on the raid to relieve the prisoners at Andersonville. The command failed to connect with General Stoneman. They traveled four days and nights, fought a battle, were surrounded and defeated, and most of McCook's command and all of Stoneman's was captured. Our subject's regiment cut through the lines and reached the Union forces in safety. He was with General Kilpatrick on the raid around Atlanta. At Lovejoy Station a rifle ball cut his pants, but no further harm was done. In the same battle his company took a battery of two guns in a cavalry charge, the battery firing the last shot when the company was within sixty feet of the muzzles of the cannon. On the same raid he had his saddle stump partially shot away by a grape shot. At Corinth he was on the skirmish line in a thickly wooded valley. The enemy advanced to within about four rods, then opened with a volley. The Union forces in reserve, a short distance in the rear of the skirmishers, supposing the Union boys had all been killed or taken prisoners, opened a heavy volley in the brush. Pearson, with a comrade, took shelter behind a large oak tree, and when the Rebels would fire a volley they would run around on the Rebel side, and when the volley was returned would run around on the Union side. When the battle ended the comrade had four bullet holes in his clothes but was uninjured. In 1862 Mr. Pearson marched with his company from Green river, Kentucky, to Shiloh; Corinth, Mississippi;

then to opposite Chattanooga, Tennessee; then to Louisville, Kentucky; then to Frankfort, Kentucky; and to Nashville, Tennessee; in all about fifteen hundred miles during the summer; and he "stacked arms" with the company every night. At Liberty Gap he and a Confederate soldier exchanged compliments eight times in succession with rifles, across a field, each taking refuge in the corner of a rail fence. The Rebel finally retreated. As the army advanced from Murfreesboro (General Sheridan in the advance) Colonel Harrison was ordered to place his regiment (Thirty-ninth Indiana) a quarter of a mile in advance. The colonel ordered Company D to go a quarter of a mile in advance of the regiment. The captain of Company D ordered Pearson to take four men and place them at intervals of fifty paces apart, one in advance of the other, leaving himself fifty paces in advance of any man in the army. The command was given to "forward march," and thus he marched on to the Rebel camp at Liberty Gap, at the head of Rosecrans' great army. In the fall of 1864 Mr. Pearson was sent to General Kilpatrick's headquarters on detached duty to take command of a company of the provost guards, which position he held through the march through Georgia and North and South Carolina, during which all prisoners and horses were turned over to him. The general had made arrangements whereby he was to become one of the "staff," and act as assistant provost marshal, but he was captured while with headquarters before the necessary papers had arrived to make him a permanent staff officer. He was with General Kilpatrick while reconnoitering at Aiken, South Carolina, when the enemy made a dash on them, driving them back, and, as the general's horse scaled the temporary barricade, the Rebels shot at him (being within fifteen or twenty feet), but missed their mark. Both our subject and the general were res-

cued by the capture of their pursuers. At Solomon's Grove Mr. Pearson was taken prisoner while at headquarters. General Kilpatrick, escaping in his night-clothes, then rallied his men and retook the camp, without either hat, coat, pants or boots. Our subject had one hundred and ninety prisoners in his charge, which were released, and about an equal number of Union prisoners were taken. They were marched forty miles the first day without either breakfast, dinner or supper. During the night he was furnished some corn meal and bacon. He took a sheet of paper, on which he mixed the meal, which was then put in the ashes and baked. He put the meat on a stick, broiled it and then fared sumptuously. During his confinement he was not furnished with any cooking utensils, and used pieces of splinters off of railroad irons for knives; used the top of his hat for bean soup, and slept on the floor without any blankets. The windows of Castle Thunder had neither sash nor glass, and this afforded plenty of fresh air, as it was in March. As they entered Fayetteville, North Carolina, a Rebel rode up to the prisoners and fired into the ranks. One of the men fell, and was left on the street, apparently in a dying condition. Mr. Pearson escaped from the guards twice, but having a sick brother a prisoner, he returned after a spell, to try and release him. The result was they were both marched to Richmond and, after remaining in prison a short time, were paroled. He reached his home in Indiana on the day that General Lee surrendered. Soon after reaching home he was married, and then went to Mankato, Blue Earth county, Minnesota, where for some years he engaged in contracting and building. He followed this line of business until in 1877. He was one of the most popular contractors in Mankato, and built many of the principal buildings in that city, among them being the First National Bank, the Masonic hall, Turner's hall, the city hall, and Pleasant Grove school house, and numerous other store buildings and dwelling-houses of the better class. During this time he employed a great amount of help, and had a force of thirty men under his direction at one time during his business life in that city. In 1877, as has been related before in this biography, Mr. Pearson came to Pipestone county and made his location in Grange township. Throughout his life he has been engaged principally in contracting and building, and is, perhaps, one of the most widely-traveled men in his locality. He has filled contracts in three different States in the West: Iowa, Wisconsin, and Minnesota, and has built numerous very fine buildings. At Sibley, Iowa, he constructed the Emmet Bank building, one of the very finest structures in the county. During the same year he built a large school house at Waterville, and Waseca, both of these buildings being for high-school purposes. Prior to his election to his present office, he performed considerable contracting in the city in which he now lives. He put together the brick work on the Steward block.

Mr. Pearson was united in marriage in 1865, to Miss Lydia M. Wilkerson, daughter of Jacob Wilkerson, of Indiana. This union has been blessed with two living children—Dora, who graduated at Mankato, in 1887, and is now a teacher by profession, filling a position at present in the graded schools in Pipestone City. She taught for some time at Montevideo, Minnesota. Frank E., the other child, is at present a clerk in his father's office, having attended the Sioux Falls University.

Throughout the career of our subject he has been actively interested in all matters of a public nature, and has filled numerous positions of trust and responsibility with credit to himself and honor to his constituents. While in Mankato he served as a member of the city council for two terms of three years each, and otherwise occupied a prominent position in the affairs of that municipality. He invested to some extent in Mankato real estate, and built a comfortable and commodious residence on Lincoln street. Since coming to Pipestone he has purchased a number of city lots, and in 1885 erected a handsome dwelling which cost about two thousand dollars. In his business matters he has been quite successful, and has accumulated considerable means, becoming one of the substantial and most reliable citizens of the county. In politics he affiliates with the republican party, in whose principles he has believed for many years. Our subject is one of the most genial, warm-hearted and sociable officials, and by his courteous conduct and thorough knowledge of the details of his office, he has made hosts of friends and insured for himself re-election to his present position, if he desires it. He is also an influential member of the Grand Army of the Republic, and was the first commander of the post at Pipestone. He served two terms as aid-de-camp to the department commander, and is quarter-master at present, having held that position for three or four years. He is colonel of the Pipestone battalion, and junior vice-commander of the department of Southwestern Minnesota, Grand Army of the Republic Association, which position he has twice held.

⁕⁕⁕

HENRY J. KURTH is a thrifty and industrious farmer of Shaokatan township, Lincoln county, Minnesota. His farm is located on section 8 of that township. He was born in Elgrove, Illinois, March 14, 1855. He was the son of Henry, Sr., and Catharine E. (Wehnes) Kurth. An account of the father's life and death is found in a sketch of Fred H. Kurth in another department of this work. The father was an exemplary citizen and loyal Christian man.

Henry J. continued his residence with his parents until they made a settlement in Lincoln county. He left home at the age of twenty-one years, up to which time he had assisted in work on the home farm and had been given a good common-school education. At twenty-one he entered the employ of Andrew Markman, remaining a short time during harvest and then going to Dakota county, where he rented various farms for a year and a half and then rented his father's farm, operating it one year, and then, after operating other farms in the county, engaged in running a threshing-machine some fourteen years. In 1878 he came to Lincoln county and settled on the place where he now lives, taking it as a homestead and making it his residence ever since. He was one of the first settlers, and has taken an active interest in public matters since making his location. He is a man of excellent principles and is esteemed by all who know him. He is a republican in politics, and among the official positions that he has held may be named those of constable and postmaster, the former being held by him two years and the latter one year.

Henry J. Kurth was married June 6, 1877, to Dora Kauffmann, a daughter of John and Susan Kauffmann. This union has been blessed with six children—George H., Lizzie C., John H., Lena S., Charles W. and an infant.

--------◆-◆-❧◈❧-◆-◆--------

BENEZER C. HUNTINGTON is the proprietor and publisher of the Windom *Reporter*, at Windom, Cottonwood county, Minnesota. He is a native of St. Albans, Vermont, where he was born February 7, 1850. His parents were Simon and Louisa M. (Kellogg) Huntington, natives of Vermont. The father was a farmer by occu-

pation, and, coming to Illinois in 1852, engaged in farming in Winnebago county. In 1856 he removed to Iowa, where he engaged in the drug business and also in manufacturing patent medicine. In 1873 he emigrated to Minnesota, locating in Mountain Lake, Cottonwood county. Here he engaged extensively in farming and stock raising. In the father's family there were five children, three of whom are now living—our subject, Eliza C. and Charles K. A sketch of the father is given in another department of this volume.

The subject of our sketch received his early training and education principally in Iowa, and completed his course in the schools of McGregor. He left the parental home in 1865, and engaged in the business of printing, serving an apprenticeship of three years in various places. He spent some time in the *News* office at McGregor, and also in the office of W. H. Farnham, a publisher of Sparta, Wisconsin, and then spent two years in the *Intelligence* office at Charles City, Iowa. He then returned to McGregor, and worked in the office of the *News and Times* until in April, 1869. He then formed a partnership with Frank Holland and operated a paper at Decorah, Iowa, until September. This newspaper was called the *State Press*, and in September Mr. Holland's interest was purchased by S. S. Haislet. Our subject continued in the business until in the spring of 1870, when he sold out to his partner and removed to Strawberry Point, Iowa, where he purchased a newspaper and continued its operation until June, 1871. At this time he came to Windom, bringing with him a newspaper outfit. He established the Windom *Reporter* in partnership with his father, and they continued its operation until 1882. In that year he purchased his father's interest, and has since been sole proprietor and publisher. Our subject has been engaged in various other occupations, having been a partner of Judge A. D. Perkins in the real estate and abstract business from 1882 to 1885. He has bought and sold lands throughout the county and has been quite successful in making profitable investments. He built his newspaper office in July, 1871, and in 1877 built a nice residence on the north side of the town. In public matters Editor Huntington has always been one of the most active of Windom's citizens. He has affiliated with the republican party and ably conducts his newspaper in the interests of that organization. He was appointed by Governor Pillsbury as one of the State board of immigration in 1877 and was also a member of the republican State central committee in 1877–8. He is an influential Odd Fellow, and is a member of the American Order of United Workmen. He is broad-minded and public-spirited, and is one of the most capable editors in Southern Minnesota.

Mr. Huntington was married in the year 1872 to Miss Julia T. Knowlton, daughter of D. H. Knowlton of Garden Plains, Illinois. Mr. and Mrs. Huntington have been blessed with three children—Aurelia L., Julia G. and Florence A.

———→·‹◆›·←———

HUGH PAUL, who now resides on section 28, South Brook township, Cottonwood county, Minnesota, was born in Liverpool, England, August 14, 1860. His father is Edward Paul, a native of England and a resident of Liverpool. The father came to America some years ago and purchased some twelve sections of land in Southern Minnesota.

Hugh Paul came to America in 1879 and located on the land which his father had purchased some years before. He commenced extensive improvements, his first order for lumber for buildings being thirty-two car loads. From this lumber an elegant frame house was built, forty feet square and two stories high, and also eight barns besides other smaller buildings. This property has been put in excellent shape, and is one of the most perfect stock-breeding establishments in Southern Minnesota. Considerable attention is given to the breeding and importing of English shire horses, Galloway cattle and Shropshire sheep. Among the fine imported horses owned on this farm is Ciciro, No. 3552, a fine chestnut horse, imported from England in June, 1888, and a full brother of the winner of the London sweepstakes in 1889. Our subject has just refused $3,000 for this animal. Another horse worthy of special mention is Bonnie Laddie, a bright bay, two years old, imported in June, 1889. This horse is a brother of the celebrated Darwin, now owned by Messrs. Galbraith Brothers. All the horses on this farm are pure bred and imported, and both as to collective and individual merits may be said to be among the finest in the West. Among the Galloway cattle is found the finely bred "Hero" of Waverstree, born June 25, 1886, and bred by Biggars & Sons, Chapelton, Dalbeatie, Scotland, sire Crusader "2856," dam Chivalry " 8178," 2719, by Blue Bonnet of Peddershill. Another beautiful animal is the imported cow Nancy Lee, 4th, " 8174," 2730, born March 17, 1884, bred by Thomas Biggars & Sons of Scotland, sire Barmoffity Bob " 2266 " and dam Lizzie of Nocklar " 2878," by Neil Gow " 1138 " g. dam Beauty of Nocklar " 2867." Nancy Lee took the first premium at the last Minnesota State Fair. There are other animals of wonderful strength and beauty which deserve more extended mention than can be given in this sketch. Besides the cattle and horses on this farm, our subject has four hundred head of sheep, many of them of the finest blood that can be procured in England.

This great farm is known as the Wavertree farm, and in all comprises a tract of twelve sections of land. It is mostly fine rolling prairie with the Des Moines river running through it from north to south. Its market is Heron Lake, a thriving town on the Chicago, St. Paul, Minneapolis & Omaha railroad, this being the main line between St. Paul and Kansas City, the village being but eight miles distant from the farm. Kimbrae is almost within sight of the farm, being located five miles distant on the Southern Minnesota division of the Chicago, Milwaukee & St. Paul railroad. This monster farm is the wonder and admiration of the entire county and its successful management is due entirely to the ability of Mr. Paul, who has had it in charge for several years. Mr. Paul is a man of excellent qualities, careful and systematic in his business, and is a genial and warm-hearted man, a typical English gentleman. He is laying his plans carefully and systematically to make this farm one of the largest and best horse-breeding establishments in the State of Minnesota.

Mr. Paul was married in the year 1882. This union has been blessed with two children—Edward G. and James Q. Mr. and Mrs. Paul are members of the Presbyterian church, and are leading characters both in religious and social circles. Mr. Paul is a democrat in politics.

—————◆·❧❀❧·◆·❧————

WILLIAM COYLE is a well-known farmer and stock-raiser of Lake Sarah township, Murray county, Minnesota. He located on section 14 of that township in 1878, having purchased his land two years prior to his location. Our subject is a man of large experience and has made a great success of farming. He has paid considerable attention to raising horses and cattle, and has some fine animals of excellent grades.

Mr. Coyle was born in Crawford county, Pennsylvania, January 27, 1831. His parents were Charles and Phoebe Jane (Watson) Coyle, the father a native of Crawford county,

Pennsylvania, where he died in 1869. Charles Coyle was an expert veterinary surgeon and was well known and highly respected both as a citizen and as a surgeon throughout a large scope of country in Pennsylvania. He was one of the best veterinary doctors in that locality. He was a consistent member of the Catholic church. The mother was born in Maryland, whence she moved to Pennsylvania when seven years of age with her parents. She was a member of the Methodist Episcopal church and died in 1866. In the father's family there were ten children—William, George, Joshua, Sina J., Maria, David, J. W., Charles, Lydia and Emma. Only three of these children are now living—William, Joshua and David.

The subject of our sketch received his early training and education in Crawford county, Pennsylvania, where he lived until 1865, in which year he moved to Olmsted county, Minnesota. He purchased a farm in Farmington township, and made that his home until coming to Murray county, in 1878. While a resident of Olmsted county, our subject engaged in the practice of medicine in connection with his farming operations, and while there became quite prominent in the public affairs of his township. He held several official positions with honor and credit.

William Coyle was married, in the year 1856, to Miss Catharine Yager, a native of Erie county, Pennsylvania. This lady died in 1859. Mr. Coyle was married to his second wife, Miss Emily Ette, in 1860. She was a native of Erie county, Pennsylvania, and died in 1862. The present Mrs. Coyle, to whom our subject was married in 1868, was Miss Cordelia Taylor, a native of the State of New York, born in St. Lawrence county, in 1845. She was reared in that county until twelve years of age, and then removed to LaCrosse, Wisconsin, whence, after five years' residence, she removed to Rochester,

Minnesota. Her education was principally received in LaCrosse county, Wisconsin. She was a daughter of James and Amora Ann (Van Wafers) Taylor, the father a native of Ireland, who emigrated to the United States at the age of fifteen years. Mr. and Mrs. Coyle have been blessed with eight children —Frederick, Lorin, Mary, George, Lyman, Maude, Millie and Dock.

The gentleman whose name appears at the head of this sketch is one of the representative citizens of his township, and has held various important official positions. In politics he affiliates with the democratic party, and is in sympathy with the doctrines of the Catholic church. His wife is a member of the Methodist Episcopal church. Mr. Coyle is one of the best business men of the township, and has been school district treasurer, assessor and also township supervisor.

DAVID JONES. This gentleman is a prominent citizen and well-to-do farmer of Shaokatan township, Lincoln county, Minnesota, and resides on section 11. He was born in Wales, in October, 1821. His parents were David and Margaret (Williams) Jones. The only knowledge our subject has of the early life of his father is that he was a milkman in London. Removing from London, the father located in Wales, where our subject was born. The father engaged in farming in that country on a small farm of forty acres, and remained until 1841. His death occurred in 1844. At the time of his death the father was engaged in operating a carding mill, having sold his farm three years before. Our subject's mother died when he was four or five years old.

David Jones left the parental home in 1841, up to which time he had attended school in the winters and assisted his father on the farm. In the year above mentioned the father was married again, and our sub-

ject went to Aberyotwith, a sea-port town, where he was intending to hire out as a cabin boy on some vessel. His father heard of it, however, and he came down to the village and bound him out for five years to learn the cabinet-maker's trade. He remained in that business for five years, and then worked in a wheelwright's shop for one year. He then found employment in iron works and in various other employments until 1848, in which year he came to the United States. Landing in New York City, he went thence to Milwaukee, remaining two years, engaging in various kinds of building during the summers and cabinet-making in the winters. His next location was in Neenah, Winnebago county, Wisconsin, where one year was spent in a chair-making shop. Then, in partnership with two others, he opened an establishment for manufacturing the same line of goods. After one year's prosperous business he purchased the interest of his partners, and operated it alone for six years. He then removed to Clifton, Calumet county, built a saw-mill, and taking in a partner, operated the mill one year, or until the breaking out of the war. His partner then enlisted in the Union army, and his brother then purchased his interest. After a few months the partnership again became broken, as the second partner enlisted, and Mr. Jones rented the mill for three years. After this he sold out and removed to Oshkosh, locating in that place in 1862. Six years were spent by him in the last named city, his time being occupied with the management of a cabinet shop. In 1868 he came to Goodhue county, Minnesota, and purchased a farm, engaging in agricultural pursuits until 1878. In that year he came to Lincoln county, Minnesota, where he purchased the place on which he now lives. He has a fine farm of 360 acres under good cultivation, and provided with good buildings. Since coming to the township he has taken an active interest in all public matters, and has become one of Lincoln county's representative citizens. He has been chairman of the board of supervisors for two years, being the first to hold that office. In politics he is a union labor man.

The marriage of the subject of our sketch occurred March 26, 1852, at which time he was united in matrimony to Elizabeth Jones, a native of Wales. Mr. and Mrs. Jones have been blessed with nine children — David T., John K., Daniel E., Henry W. (deceased), Mary E., Bertie (deceased), Benjamin F., Margaret A. and William W.

WILLIAM S. STORY, a prominent farmer and influential citizen, located on section 4, Amboy township, Cottonwood county, Minnesota, in March, 1881. He has since been engaged in general farming and stock raising. His son Andrew now operates the farm, and our subject is living, to a great extent, a retired life.

Mr. Story was born in Cayuga county, New York, April 23, 1818. His father, Alexander Story, was a native of New York State and was a farmer by occupation. Our subject's mother's name was Abagail (Stevenson) Story, a native of Maryland. In the father's family there were four children—William S., Andrew, Mannassah and Martha Jane.

Our subject was reared in his native county, receiving a good common-school education. Until twenty-five years of age he remained with his parents assisting in work on the home farm. In the fall of 1844, he started for Ohio, where he engaged in farming for two years. Then he returned to his native State, and after a year went back to Ohio, where three or four years were spent in agricultural pursuits. His next move was to Winneshiek county, Iowa, where he remained until going to Sleepy Eye, Brown county, Minnesota, in 1879.

His next move was to locate in Cottonwood county where he has since lived.

William S. Story was married in April, 1849, to Miss Eliza Braudded, a native of Ohio, and who moved with her parents in early life to Indiana, where she was reared and educated. Miss Story was the daughter of John and Ann Clarrissa (Gurly) Braudded. Mrs. Braudded was a native of England, and came to America with her parents at the close of the Rebellion. Mr. Braudded was a native of Indiana. The mother died in that State. The father, after engaging for years in farming pursuits, went to Texas, where he died some years ago. Mr. and Mrs. Story have six children living—Martha, Ella, Andrew, Lincoln, Rose and Lyona. William died at twenty-three years of age. Andrew, the son who is now operating the farm, was married in January, 1889, to Miss Amelia Trach, a native of Wisconsin, and who came to Minnesota with her parents when seven years of age.

In political faith the subject of our sketch affiliates with the republican party. In June, 1885, he was appointed postmaster of Red Rock post-office and has held that position ever since. He has served in various official capacities with rare fidelity, among them being that of supervisor, etc. He is a representative citizen of his township and county and is held in high esteem.

CHARLES SMITH, one of the very first settlers of Gray township and a prominent and leading farmer, made his settlement on section 26, Gray township, Pipestone county, Minnesota, May 2, 1878, settling on a homestead. In the following fall he moved with his family to the place and has made that his residence ever since. He has been prominent in the affairs of the organization and improvement of the township and county, and has assisted in every way in bringing about the era of prosperity, which has dawned upon the people of Pipestone county. He has held many positions within the political gift of his friends and fellow-citizens, and has held the office of justice of the peace, assessor, and township clerk, having been identified with the last office for about five years. He has also been pathmaster for seven years, and treasurer of school district No. 13 since 1883. Among those who settled in the township about the time of the location of our subject were Mr. Campbell, Mr. Clifford, W. D. Peck, H. Dickey and Samuel Avery.

The subject of our sketch is of German descent and birth. He was born in Hesse, Germany, April 4, 1843, and was the son of Jacob and Maria Ann (Wirth) Smith, both of whom were natives of Germany. The father was a miller by trade and in connection with that business was engaged extensively in farming. The father died in his native land in 1846, a prominent man and esteemed by all who knew him. The mother came to the United States in 1867 and located in Grant county, Wisconsin, where she died in 1887, being at that time seventy-seven years of age, and an exemplary member of the Lutheran church. The subject of our sketch was one of four children—Anthony, Jacob, Charles and Vironka. Until he was fourteen years of age Mr. Smith remained with his parents and received a partial education. His training had been received in a religious family and being surrounded with pious influences before he left his boyhood's home he was confirmed in the Lutheran church. At the age of fourteen he came to America, landing in New Orleans, whence he went to Grant county, Wisconsin, and made that his home until in the fall of 1861. In February, 1862, he enlisted as a private in Company H, Sixteenth regiment, United States Volunteer Infantry, at McGregor, Iowa. Soon after he was promoted to the

rank of sergeant, and continued in the service until his discharge, February 12, 1865. Mr. Smith saw much severe service, and his loyalty to his adopted country was well proven in many battles in which he engaged. Among these were the battle of Lookout mountain, where his regiment served under General Thomas; Shiloh, Corinth, which occurred in May, 1862; Stone River, Hoover's Gap, in June, 1863; all the battles and skirmishes in the Tallehoma campaign; Chickamauga, September 19–26, 1863, at which battle he was severely wounded in the head; Mission Ridge, November 24, 1863; Buzzard's Roost, which took place in June, 1864; New Hope Church, in the same month in 1864; Kenesaw Mountain, in July, 1864; Marietta, in the same month; Peach Tree Creek, on the 22d day of same month; Atlanta, where he was engaged in more or less fighting, continuing for a period of three weeks, and Jonesburg, which was the last battle of any note in which our subject participated. After Mr. Smith received his discharge he returned to the State of Wisconsin, and remained until the fall of 1865 in Grant county. At that time he removed to Winona county, Minnesota, where he engaged in the butcher business for about one year. From thence he removed to Buffalo county, Wisconsin, and for a period of one year was engaged in the milling business. Then he removed to Minneapolis, where he engaged in the occupation of milling for about one year. He returned after this period to Grant county, where he stopped for some time engaged in the grocery and butcher business. It was here that he was married in 1868. He continued in the grocery and butcher business with excellent success until 1875, in Lancaster, Grant county. In that year he removed to New Albin, Allamakee county, Iowa, where for one year he was engaged in the butcher business. The following two years were spent by him in the same business in Vernon county, Wisconsin, and at the end of that period he removed to Pipestone county, locating on the farm where he has since lived.

The subject of our sketch was united in marriage August 30, 1868, to Miss Kate Schoenberger, a native of Germany. When she was eight years of age she came with her parents to the United States, settling with them in Crawford county, Wisconsin, where she was reared and educated. Mr. and Mrs. Smith have been blessed with three children—Nettie M., Fred C. and Stella E.

In politics the subject of our sketch affiliates with the republican party. His long war experience and position in the army entitles him to the prominent place he takes in the transactions of the Grand Army of the Republic, Simon Mix Post, No. 95, of which he is the present vice commander. He also stands high in the Odd Fellows fraternity, of which society he is past grand. He has been identified with the Independent Order of Odd Fellows since 1868. The subject of our sketch has seen extremely hard times since coming to Minnesota. When he landed in Pipestone county with his family he had but little in the way of improvement on his farm, and had but thirty-five cents in money with which to carry his family until the spring. However, by good management, and by finding some outside work to do, he managed to get along through the following mild winter without much suffering. For fuel the family used slough grass, and underwent other privations to which pioneer life is subject. The following spring Mr. Smith was forced to go into debt for his seed grain, mortgaging his team to obtain money therefor. Crops came on well during the early summer, but before the harvest was gathered the dreaded grasshopper came and destroyed his first crop. This was very discouraging, but as good fortune would have it Mr. Smith found employment on the railroad, which was then being built through the county, and made enough money to pay off the mortgage on his team. He thus commenced laying the foundation for his present good circumstances. Mr. Smith is energetic and thrifty, and is one of the most practical farmers in the township. He is a good citizen, and holds the esteem of all his fellow-citizens.

JOHN C. KUFUS is a leading and influential business man of Pipestone City, Minnesota. He is an extensive dealer in dry goods, notions, carpets, etc., and has the largest stock in the county. He is also engaged in the flour, feed and seed business, his headquarters for the operation of this line being in the bank building, on Hiawatha street. Mr. Kufus located in Pipestone in 1885 and immediately opened in the mercantile business. His flour and feed store was not opened until in 1888.

The place of the nativity of the subject of our sketch is found in Germany, where he was born August 25, 1845. He is a son of Gottlieb and Fredricke (Dreir) Kufus, both natives of Germany. The father was a house-builder and cabinet-maker by trade and followed that occupation in his native country until in 1847, in which year he came to America and settled in Warren county, Missouri, on a pre-emption of 160 acres of land. While engaged in breaking up his farm and bringing it up to a high state of cultivation, he engaged in work at his trade. He made Missouri his home for some nine years and then came to the State of Iowa and settled at Keokuk. After following his trade in that city for some time, he then came to Juneau county, Wisconsin, and shortly afterward to LaCrosse county, in both of which counties he followed the mercantile business. Moving from Wisconsin, he settled in Sioux Falls, in which city he is now living a retired life, having purchased considerable property and having several houses and store buildings rented, which yield him a large income. He is one of the wealthiest men in that city and is respected and esteemed by all who know him. The mother of our subject died in 1885. In the father's family there were four children, three of whom are now living—Louise, now Mrs. Angel of Sioux Falls ; Horace A., now engaged in the real estate and loan business in Nebraska, and our subject.

John C. Kufus received his early training and education in the States of Missouri and Iowa, remaining with his parents until his marriage. He then opened a restaurant at Wapello, Iowa, where he continued in business until 1884, in which year he removed to Mount Vernon, Dakota. After remaining in that place for about one year engaged in the mercantile business, he then sold out and came to Pipestone City where he has since lived. Since coming to the city our subject has built an elegant dwelling house. which he has provided with all modern improvements. He also purchased a business lot on which the store building used by him for storage purposes now stands. Besides the property interests Mr. Kufus possesses in Pipestone City he also owns two fine farms near Mitchell, Dakota.

Mr. Kufus was married to Miss Mollie M. Rabold, a daughter of William and Minnie (Kuchler) Rabold, both natives of Germany. Her parents came to America in an early day and settled in the State of Iowa, where the father died in 1884. The mother is still living in Wapello, Iowa. Mrs. Kufus was born in Wapello, Louisa county, Iowa, where she received her early training and education and where she was married to our subject. She died in 1887 and was buried in the family burying ground at Sioux Falls, Dakota. Mr. and Mrs. Kufus had four children, all born in Wapello, Iowa, and all liv-

ing at the present time. Their names are—John W., now connected with his father in business; Edwin G., Laurin R. and Talma M.

The subject of our sketch affiliates with the democratic party. Himself and family are attendants of the Methodist Episcopal church. Mr. Kufus has been eminently successful in his business career and has accumulated large means. He has an excellent assortment and a large stock of general merchandise and has built up an extensive trade. He is gentlemanly and intelligent, is energetic, public spirited, and is respected by all with whom he comes in contact. He is one of the solid and substantial business men of the city and county.

<hr/>

JAMES H. HODGMAN is a retired farmer and resides in Winnebago City, Faribault county, Minnesota. He was born in Canada in the year 1822.

The parents of the subject of our sketch were Benjamin and Betsey (Colby) Hodgman, the former a native of Vermont and the latter born in Maine. In early life Benjamin Hodgman went with his parents to Canada, where they engaged in farming. In 1843 he removed to Vermont, and resided there until 1862, in which year he came west to Minnesota, locating at Pine Island, Goodhue county. He followed agricultural pursuits throughout his life, and died in 1865. The mother died in Vermont in 1857. They had a family of ten children, six of whom are now living—Harry, James H., Otis, David, Edwin and Lyman.

The subject of our sketch was reared on a farm, and received his education in the primitive log school-houses so common in the pioneer days. He went with his father to Vermont, and labored on the farm in the summers and worked at lumbering to some extent in the winters. In 1853 he went to Will county, Illinois, and engaged in contracting and building in the village of Lock-port for a year. He then returned to Ver-mont, and in the spring of 1855 located in Rochester, Racine county, Wisconsin. Here he rented a farm, and operated the same for a year. His next move was to Olmsted county, Minnesota, where he settled on gov-ernment land in New Haven township. He owned 320 acres of land, and en-gaged in general farming for six years, after which he removed to Cascade township, six miles from the city of Rochester, and re-sided in that locality until 1877. He then sold out and removed to Winnebago City, where he purchased his present residence and also 160 acres of land near Rice Lake, two miles north of the village. He resided there from September, 1877, until September, 1878, when he returned to New Haven town-ship, Olmsted county, and settled on his timber claim. He engaged in the wood busi-ness, cutting some sixty acres of timber and shipping it to Rochester. He remained some three years, after which one year was spent in the city of Rochester, where he engaged in the furniture business. He then returned to his farm and remained until 1884. He then chartered a car and took his family, household goods, horses, wagons, etc., and went to Portland, Oregon, whence he traveled through Washington Territory and Oregon and along the coast for some two months; then shipping his goods for Ash-land, Jackson county, Oregon, he purchased a house and lot and remained until 1885. He then went to Sacramento, California, for the benefit of his wife's health, as she had been suffering for some years with the rheu-matism. After a two months' stay his next move was to Wichita, Kansas, where the family lived for one year. While residing in that city our subject was engaged in sell-ing pianos and organs. At the end of the year he came again to Winnebago City, where he has since resided.

The subject of our sketch was married in the year 1853 to Miss Diana Colby, of Upper Canada, and daughter of Rufus Colby. This union has been blessed with four children—Jennie L., Willie H., Lee E. and Scott. Mrs. Hodgman died in February, 1889. She was a lady of excellent qualities, and her death was sincerely mourned by a large circle of friends.

In politics Mr. Hodgman affiliates with the republican party, and has served his con-stituents in various official capacities. In Olmsted county he held the office of treas-urer, etc., and in every instance served faith-fully, and to the entire satisfaction of all with whom he came in contact. Since com-ing to Winnebago City he has made many friends and is highly esteemed.

———————

HENRY E. HANSON is the present efficient register of deeds in and for Cottonwood county, Minnesota. He is a na-tive of Fillmore county, Minnesota, where he was born September 18, 1860. He was the son of Elling and Guro (Helgeson) Hanson, both natives of Norway. The parents came to America in an early day, and settled on Rock Prairie, Wisconsin. In about 1857 they came to Minnesota, locating on a farm in Fillmore county. Here the father lived until his death, which occurred in 1860. The mother is now a resident of Ann township, Cottonwood county, Minnesota. They had a family of three children, two of whom are now living—Annie, now Mrs. Eugene Nich-ols, and Henry E., our subject.

Mr. Hanson was reared on a farm, and re-ceived such educational advantages as were furnished in the district schools. In 1871 he came to Cottonwood county with his mother and settled on a farm in Ann township. He attended school for one winter in the village of Sleepy Eye, and taught school for several terms in Ann township and for one term in

Westbrook township. He purchased 160 acres of land, and engaged in farming until 1889, and January 1st moved into the village of Windom to take possession of his present office, to which he had been elected in the fall of 1888. He was elected justice of the peace in 1885, serving four years, and also held the position of township clerk during that time. Since coming to the village he has purchased two lots, on which he has erected a comfortable and commodious home. He has a good farm under excellent cultivation, and has it supplied with good farm buildings. He has been quite successful in raising grain and graded cattle.

Mr. Hanson was married in 1888 to Miss Julia Peterson, a daughter of Paul Peterson, of Cottonwood county. This union has been blessed with one child, Emma P.

In all matters of a public nature Mr. Hanson takes an active and prominent part. He is one of the young progressive men of Cottonwood county, and bids fair to occupy some of the most important positions within the gift of his fellow-citizens. Since taking possession of his office, he has proven himself a man of great efficiency, and has become quite popular. . In politics he affiliates with the republican party, and is a member of the Independent Order of Odd Fellows fraternity, and with his wife belongs to the Lutheran church.

JAMES YOUNG, JR., is a leading farmer of Murray township, Murray county, Minnesota. He homesteaded his land on section 18 of that township, in September, 1869, and was one of the first settlers of the township, and assisted in its organization. He has held various official positions, and in every instance has proven his efficiency, and has become quite popular with his constituents. He was supervisor for three terms, and held various other positions. The first year he built a kind of rude shanty out of poles, thatched with hay. Two months later he went to St. Peter, procured lumber, and bringing this to his farm, built a shanty 12x14 feet. This was his home until he built his present commodious and pleasant residence. The first improvements on his place were of a rude character, consisting of the hay stable and other buildings built in the same primitive manner. He broke some thirty acres of land. The first crop yielded him 132 bushels of wheat. The next season proved a dry one, and from forty acres he reaped a small harvest, and had to haul grain to the Rapidan mill, near Mankato, also to New Ulm and Madelia, New Ulm being his postoffice and market-place for some years. For several years the crops were destroyed, and our subject saw hard times, but this has all been forgotten, and he is now in good circumstances. He is at present engaged in general farming, and gives special attention to raising mules.

The gentleman whose name appears at the head of this sketch was born in the eastern part of Canada, February 9, 1830. At five years of age he went with his parents to Franklin county, New York, and thence to St. Lawrence county, where he remained until he became of age. In the latter county he received his education, and removed thence, locating on a farm in Massachusetts for three years. At the end of that time he returned to his home in the State of New York. After a short period he went to Sauk county, Wisconsin, where he lived four years, then removed to Freeborn county, Minnesota, where he spent eleven years, engaged in farming until coming to Murray county, Minnesota where he has since lived.

On the breaking out of the war Mr. Young felt that it was his duty to answer the call of the president for volunteers to avenge the insults which had been offered the stars and stripes. The fires of patriotism burned in his bosom, and he enlisted February 17, 1862, in Company C, Fifth Minnesota Volunteer Infantry, as a private. He served under Captain Hall, of Albert Lea, and also Captain Timothy J. Sheehan. Mr. Young saw severe service, and fought bravely and gallantly for his country's honor. He participated in the battle of Fort Ridgley, and was for many days in constant battle with the Indians. On account of physical disabilities which had been augmented by his military service, he was discharged in December, 1862, and soon thereafter returned to his home.

Mr. Young was united in the holy bonds of matrimony April 5, 1854, to Miss Luthera Mallory, a native of the State of New York, where she was born February 1, 1831. The place of her birth was in Moira, Franklin county, New York, where she lived until she was twenty-three years of age, and where she received a good common-school education. She was the daughter of Kendrick and Lucinda (Field) Mallory, the former a native of the State of New York, and the latter born in Massachusetts. When her father was quite young the family removed to Massachusetts, where Mr. Mallory was married. They then returned to Franklin county, where he has always remained. The mother died in the State of New York. In the Mallory family there were nine children, eight of whom grew to man and womanhood—Charles, Luthera (now Mrs. Young), Sophia, James, Amanda and Miranda (twins), Alden and Lorin. Mr. and Mrs. Young have been blessed with the following named children— Ida, Lillian, Mary, Addison and Ernest. Ida is now Mrs. R. D. Marlette, her husband being a carpenter of Tracy. Lillian married L. M. Ayers, a publisher of St. Paul. Mary married A. B. Smith, a farmer of Mason township, Murray county.

For many years the subject of our sketch

affiliated with the republican party, but in 1888, being of strong temperance principles, he joined the prohibition movement and is now a member of that party. He takes an active interest in all matters of a religious nature, being a man of pious character, and he and his wife are members of the Methodist Episcopal church.

JOHN L. BENNETT is the efficient and popular postmaster of Lake Benton, Minnesota. He is the son of Justus J. and Sarah (Lang) Bennett, both natives of New York. The Bennetts are of German descent, while the Lang family trace their ancestry to Scotland. The subject of our sketch, John L., was born in Hamburgh, Livingston county, Michigan, January 8, 1840. The parents were farmers by occupation and he resided with them on the home farm, where he was given the advantages for an education furnished by the district schools. He was attached to his home, and remained with his parents, giving them the benefit of his toil, until the breaking out of the war. On the 18th day of August, 1862, Mr. Bennett enlisted in Company E, Twenty-sixth Michigan Volunteer Infantry, and was with that regiment in New York City during the Irish riot. After this disturbance was quelled the regiment was ordered to join the Army of the Potomac at Manassas Junction. Our subject remained with his division of the army throughout the war, and was with them serving on the skirmish line when General Lee surrendered. Our subject was in a great many hard-fought battles and had many narrow escapes. His hardest experience was in the battle of the Wilderness, where he passed through many hair-breadth escapes. He was severely wounded at the battle of Spottsylvania, from the result of which he was laid up from May 11th until August 18th. He was mustered out of service with his regiment at Jackson, Michigan, and shortly after returned to Shiawassee county, where his parents lived. He remained with them until October 4, 1866, when he was married and then moved to Owasso, same State, where he engaged in farming, remaining in that locality until 1872. He then sold out and removed to Hubbardstown and engaged in the grocery business in which line he continued until 1876. He then went to Perry, Michigan, where he worked at the carpenter trade until 1881, in which year he came to Lincoln county and took a 160-acre soldier's homestead and continued his residence on this claim for two and a half years, when he obtained a title from the government and sold out and purchased a furniture store in Lake Benton. This business he still runs in connection with his present position. He was appointed postmaster January 18, 1889.

The subject of our sketch was married October 4, 1866, to Miss Martha Alling, a daughter of Alanson and Bulah Alling, of English descent, and both born in the State of New York. Mr. and Mrs. Bennett have had four children—Rosabelle, J. E., Robert E. and Artie.

Our subject is a man who commands respect wherever he is known. He is an old soldier and can look back over an honorable military career spent in trying to defend the Union. During those times he was a brave and true soldier and served his country well and faithfully, so to-day he is a true and faithful citizen and ably seconds all projects which tend to the protection and building up of the business interests of the village in which he lives.

HENRY E. BRIGGS is the cashier of the First National Bank of Pipestone city. He is a native of England, where he was born in 1856. He was thoroughly educated in his native land and spent two years in Switzerland studying the languages. For two years before leaving England he was engaged in the banking business, and for five years in the wholesale dry goods business. In September, 1880, he came to America, and for a time was engaged in farming near Kingsley, Iowa. In 1882 he came to Luverne, Minnesota, and again turned his attention to agricultural pursuits and also to the raising of stock. He was a large and extensive farmer and operated three sections of land. In 1884 he came to Pipestone and assisted in the organization of the First National Bank of that city. He has large landed interests throughout the county and in Southwestern Minnesota and is considered one of the solid influential citizens of Pipestone. His abilities in a business way have been utilized in various offices, among them being that of village treasurer, which office he held from 1886 to 1888. He is a stanch supporter of the principles of the democratic party, and is an influential member of the Masonic order.

JOHN A. TALBERT, one of the leading farmers of Sweet township, is a resident of section 12. He was born in Columbia county, Wisconsin, March 18, 1859.

The parents of the subject of our sketch were Dr. George E. and Asteline F. (Brayton) Talbert, the father being a native of Virginia and the mother a native of Wisconsin. The father was a man of excellent education, and was thoroughly fitted for the duties of his profession. He was a graduate of the university at Delaware, Ohio, and soon thereafter went to Muscatine, Iowa, where he commenced the practice of his profession. At Muscatine he met his future wife's father, and on his solicitation, in 1856, concluded to remove to Columbia county, Wisconsin, opening business in the practice of his profession in the village of Fall River. He remained in that place until 1860, when he removed to Greene county, Ohio, where he owned a farm, and on which he lived some eighteen months. At the end of this time he returned to Fall River, Wisconsin, and engaged in the practice of his profession until John A. was about eight years old. At this time the father again removed to Ohio, and settled on his farm, remaining there some five and a half years. At the end of this time he again returned to Fall River, Wisconsin, and for two years practiced his profession with excellent success. Removing thence, he settled in the city of Beaver Dam, same State, where he has been engaged in the practice of his profession ever since, and where he has built up an enviable reputation as a physician and surgeon. He is one of the leading citizens of the town in which he lives.

John A. Talbert, whose name appears at the head of this sketch, remained under parental authority until he was about twenty-one years of age, up to which time he had been given excellent school advantages, and had obtained a good education. In 1880 he left his home and came to Minnesota, settling in Rock county, where, during one summer, he worked on a farm, and the following season purchased the farm where he now lives. He built a neat residence in 1884, and has surrounded himself with the comforts indicative of a prosperous farm life.

Mr. Talbert was united in marriage, March 10, 1886, to Miss Emma Rogers, a native of Wisconsin. She is the daughter of William Rogers and wife, both of whom are at present living in Oregon. Mr. and Mrs. Talbert have been blessed with two children; George R. and Ethel May. George R. died when an infant.

The subject of our sketch received a thorough classical education, and was well fitted for any life of business activity into which he might be called. He is a man of broad ideas, sound judgment, and is possessed of a high character. In politics he affiliates with the union labor party. In his farm operations he has been quite successful, and now owns 160 acres of fine land, well improved, and having comfortable buildings thereon.

———————

HON. DANIEL F. GOODRICH, deceased, was one of the prominent attorneys of Faribault county, Minnesota, and resided in the State from 1867 until his death, making his home in Blue Earth City, where he has occupied a prominent position in social and political circles. He was a member of the State legislature, having served in the senate for several terms. He was a republican in politics, and was a member of the Masonic fraternity of Blue Earth City.

———————

JOHN H. CURTIS is a prominent farmer of Shaokatan township, Lincoln county, Minnesota, and owns an excellent farm on section 24.

The place of the nativity of Mr. Curtis is found in Mason county, Kentucky, where he was born October 16, 1829. He was the son of Nicholas and Rebecca (Petticord) Curtis, both natives of Kentucky. The father was a farmer by occupation, and was the son of John Curtis, a native of Virginia, who was also a farmer by occupation.

John H. Curtis assisted his parents on the farm, being favored with but very poor educational advantages. The father died in 1850, and John H. took charge of the farm until 1865. Then he came west, locating in McLain county, Illinois, where he rented and operated a farm until the spring of 1877. He then came to the State of Minnesota, becoming one of the early settlers of Lyon county, where he remained two years. Removing thence in the spring of 1879, he located on his present place on the shores of Lake Shaokatan. He has a fine farm of 148 acres, under good cultivation, and well provided with farm buildings. In politics he affiliates with no particular party, but believes in occupying an independent position. He supports the man best adapted and qualified for the position. He is a man of good character.

In May, 1850, occurred the wedding day of John H. Curtis, when he was married to Miss Sarah Barclay, a native of Kentucky. She died April 13, 1879, and was buried in Shaokatan township. This union was blessed with six children : Alice, Mary Belle, Nicholas, James E., William H. and Charles H., all of whom are living at the present time in Lincoln county.

HON. JAMES B. WAKEFIELD, ex-lieutenant-governor of the State of Minnesota, is a resident of Blue Earth City, Faribault county, where he located in 1856. He was born in Winsted, Litchfield county, Connecticut, on the 21st of March, 1828. He was thoroughly educated in his early life, and was prepared for the legal profession, being admitted to the bar in the State of Ohio in 1851. He practiced two years in Delphi, Indiana, came to Minnesota in 1854, and after two years' work in his profession, settled in Blue Earth City. Mr. Wakefield has trained with the republican party since its organization, has served as a delegate to several national conventions, and has occupied a prominent place in the party affairs of the State. He has been a member of the State senate for three terms, and was speaker of the house during the latter year of a two years' service, and served as lieutenant-governor. He is one of the foremost men in southern Minnesota, and has always been considered one of the most useful and influential citizens of Blue Earth City.

NATHANIEL P. HOAG, a leading farmer and stock raiser of Carson township, Cottonwood county, Minn., located on his present place on section 12, May 13, 1871.

Mr. Hoag was born in Addison county, Vermont, January 22, 1815. His parents were Elijah and Lydia (Varney) Hoag, natives of New York and Maine, respectively. The father was born in Duchess county, New York, and engaged in farming throughout his life. When nine years of age he removed with his parents to Addison county, Vermont, settling in Ferrisburg, whence, after several years' residence, they removed to Lincoln, in the same county. In 1832 the family emigrated to the State of New York, and in 1867 went to the province of Ontario, Canada, locating in the village of Baltimore, where the father died in 1879. The father was a consistent member of the Quaker church. Our subject's mother was reared and educated in the State of Maine, where her people were engaged in farming. Her parents were the first settlers of Vassalborough, in that State. The mother died in 1825. In the father's family there were ten children: Nathaniel P., Richard, Mary, Martha, Abagail, Justin and Hannah by his first marriage, and Jacob, Jane Ann and Lydia by his second marriage.

The early life of our subject was spent in his native county, and he remained with his parents until he was seventeen years of age. Emigrating at that time to Clinton county, same State, he made that his home until July, 1862, when he enlisted in the One Hundred and Eighteenth New York Volunteer Infantry. The colonel of this regiment was Samuel T. Richards, a man of excellent qualities and a good officer. Our subject was mustered into the United States service at Plattsburg, Clinton county, New York, September 1, 1862, and was mustered out on the 14th of June, 1864, as fifth sergeant of his regiment. On leaving the service he at once went to the State of Virginia, where he engaged in lumbering for three years. His next location was in the State of New York, where he remained until the following spring, at which time he came to Cottonwood county.

Mr. Hoag was married April 10, 1877, to Mrs. Jane (Carrington) Baker, a native of the village of Henrietta, Monroe county, New York, where she was born July 7, 1829. When five years of age she went to Ontario, New York, and remained until she was thirteen, when her parents went to Ohio, in which State she received the major part of her education. Miss Carrington married William Baker on the 10th of December, 1850. The family lived a short time in Lafayette and Medina counties, Ohio, then went to Cleveland, thence after two years they emigrated to Wisconsin, locating in Minnesota in September, 1863. Mr. Baker was a farmer by occupation, but was a machinist by trade. He was killed in the Janesville mill, March 13, 1874. Mr. and Mrs. Baker had five children—Nellie, Daniel, George, Helen and Minnie. Helen died at the age of two years; Minnie is now a teacher. Mrs. Hoag's father was William Carrington, a wheelwright by trade, and her mother's maiden name was Jerusha W. Marsh, the father being born in Oneida county, New York, and the mother in Ontario county, same State. The mother is still living and is eighty-five years of age.

In politics the subject of our sketch affiliates with the republican party. He is a man of considerable enterprise and has always taken an active interest in public matters. He has held various official positions. Having been one of the first settlers of Carson township he has been intimately associated with its political affairs, assisting in its organization in June, 1871. He has been clerk of the township, member of the board of supervisors, and director of school district number sixteen, having held the latter position some two years. Mr. Hoag is one of the leading members of the Congregational church, and was ordained a deacon of that society in 1879. He belongs to the Grand Army of the Republic and is one of Cottonwood county's representative citizens.

------◆-◆-◆------

WILLIAM W. GOBLE is one of the prominent residents of the village of Currie, Murray county, Minnesota. He located in the county in June, 1873, and soon after purchased 160 acres of land on section 8, Murray township. He was one among the early settlers of the township, and has taken an active part in all matters of a public nature. The land on which he settled had been homesteaded by a man by the name of Abner T. Marsh. Mr. Marsh had obtained a title to his land and sold out to Mr. Goble. Our subject commenced active operations on his farm, built a log house 16x20 feet, with a lean-to eight feet wide, set out a large number of trees, and made various other improvements. This log house of which we have just spoken became interesting from the fact that in the extensive Indian scare of Southwestern Minnesota it was used by the white settlers as a kind of fort. Mr. Goble remained on his farm until the spring of 1883, when he removed to Tracy, remaining in that village about two years engaged in work at the carpenter's trade. He then came to the village of Currie, where he has since remained.

William W. Goble, whose name appears at the head of this sketch, was born in Erie county, Pennsylvania, September 20, 1836. He received his early training and education in that county, remaining until he was twenty years of age, when, on his birthday, he started to find a location in the West. He stopped in Fond du Lac county,

Wisconsin, and remained there some six or eight months, when he located in Buchanan county, Iowa. After one and a half years spent in farming he returned to Wisconsin and spent two and a half years there, engaged in agricultural pursuits. He then went to the oil regions, engaging in putting down oil wells until 1864. He then returned to Fond du Lac county, Wisconsin, and engaged in farm work for five years. After that time had expired he came to Murray county, Minnesota.

Mr. Goble was united in marriage June 18, 1863, to Miss Samantha J. Finch, a native of Mercer county, Pennsylvania, where she received her early training and education. She died at the age of thirty-two years in the fall of 1882, and was buried in Murray township. She was an estimable Christian lady, and was a member of the Methodist Episcopal church. In January, 1885, Mr. Goble was married to Miss Hettie E. Lester, a native of the State of New York. Mr. Goble had four children by his first wife— Elmer E., Hettie, who died at the age of fifteen years; Lizzie M. and Miron W.

Mr. Goble is a man of the strictest piety, and is an exemplary member of the Presbyterian church, holding the office of elder in that society. For some years he was a member of the Methodist Episcopal church, in which he also held the position of recording steward. In politics he affiliates with the democratic party, and is a member of the Masonic Order, being chaplain of the local lodge. Ever since coming to the county, indeed throughout his life, he has taken an active interest in all matters which pertain to the public welfare, and has held various official positions. He is a man of excellent business abilities, and has been deeply interested in the welfare of all projects for the development of his community. He has been township clerk and also a member of the board of supervisors for some time. He is a man of

excellent reputation and wherever known is highly respected.

PHILIP F. POORBAUGH, a live, energetic business man of Jasper, Pipestone county, Minnesota, is the agent for the Jasper Improvement Company. On the 15th of April, 1888, he came to the place where Jasper village is now located, for the purpose of laying the foundations of that town. For six months he lived in a tent, and commenced booming the village and staking out town lots. He built the Jasper Hotel, which was the first house on the town plat. After running this hotel until in December, 1888, he then sold out and gave his attention more directly to handling village property. In July, 1888, he built the large stone livery stable, and ran a livery in connection with his other business. He also built the first blacksmith shop and also a dwelling-house. He is thoroughly alive to the needs of the village in every way, and aids willingly and largely in making improvements. During this season (summer of 1889) he will build the finest dwelling-house in the village, and one of the finest stone blocks in the county, to be known as the "Bank Block." In social and educational matters our subject has taken a prominent part, and is at present treasurer of the school district, and in May, 1889, by a unanimous vote, he was elected president of the village council.

Mr. Poorbaugh's native place is found in the State of Indiana, where he was born in 1856. A sketch of the life of the father of the subject of our sketch is given in the biography of J. M. Poorbaugh, in another department of this work. The subject of our sketch remained with his parents throughout his boyhood and youth, acquiring a good common-school education in the public schools. At sixteen years of age he apprenticed to learn the mason trade, which line of occupation he followed until in 1887. He was an excellent workman and filled considerable contract work of the Burlington and Manitoba railroads, employing during this time some 250 men. In 1881 he came to Minnesota and located at Pipestone, making that village his headquarters while working on his contracts with the Burlington company. He also engaged to some extent in making real estate investments, buying and selling Pipestone City property. He built a residence in that city and became quite popular among the business men of that place. He owned a homestead and tree claim about nine miles north of Pipestone and lived for some time on the homestead, on which he built a house and made other improvements. His experience on the farm was not of an agreeable character and he soon gave it up for more pleasant as well as more lucrative employment. While on the farm he burned hay for fuel and in various other ways experienced some of the disagreeable features of pioneer life. Again he concluded to try farming, and after living in the village of Pipestone for a short time he purchased a farm of 160 acres six miles west of the city, on which he lived some two years, making excellent improvements. Then he returned to the city of Pipestone, and after one year's residence there came to Jasper village, where he has since lived. Since coming to the village he has had charge of the interests of the Jasper Improvement Company, at which line he has made a remarkable success.

The subject of our sketch was married in 1877 to Miss Annie E. Harrison, of Floyd county, Iowa. This lady is a daughter of Ira and Louisa (Dean) Harrison, her father being a native of Maine, and her mother a native of Pennsylvania. The father was a farmer by occupation and was a man of large prominence in the country in which he lived. He reared a family of nine children. Mr. and Mrs. Poorbaugh have five living children—John E., Nellie L., Sarah A., Bessie E., and Benjamin F.

Mr. Poorbaugh is one of the most alert and wide-awake business men of Jasper village, and it may be truly said of him that he is a "hustler," using a term generally understood by all Westerners. Whatever business he takes hold of prospers in his hands, because it is given his most thorough and active attention. His relations with the company in whose employ he is at present engaged have been of the most cordial character, and his business enterprises have brought him continued financial success. In all matters which tend to the development of Jasper, he renders valuable assistance with both his time and money. In politics he affiliates with the republican party and is one of the representative members of that organization in this part of Pipestone county.

⚹

SETH AUSTIN is one of the most esteemed citizens of Winnebago City, Fairbault county, Minnesota, where he is now living a retired life. The place of his nativity is found in Fort Harrison, Indiana, where he was born, May 17, 1817. His parents were Elijah and Jane (Brink) Austin, natives, respectively, of Connecticut and Pennsylvania. The parents were married in Pennsylvania, April 14, 1793, and had a family of whom two children are now living—Seth and Elijah, who is now a resident of Meeker county.

The father of the subject of our sketch was engaged in the fur business throughout the States of New York and Vermont. Later he turned his attention to agricultural pursuits and became one of the first settlers of Columbus county, Ohio. Later he settled in Fort Harrison, Indiana, where he engaged in farming until late in 1817, when he removed to Edgar county, Illinois, becoming the first settler of that county. He entered some eight hundred acres of government land, paying $2.25 per acre. He continued his residence in Illinois, engaged in stock raising and agricultural pursuits until his death, which occurred October 13, 1846. He was eighty-two years of age when he died, and was one of the wealthiest and most influential men of that locality. He was a man of patriotic spirit, and in early life served in the Revolutionary War, enlisting when he was sixteen years old. The mother died in April, 1829, aged fifty-two years and eight months.

The gentleman whose name appears at the head of this sketch received his early training and education in Illinois. His educational advantages were furnished by the frontier district schools, held in primitive log cabins, some without floors save the bare ground and with greased paper windows. Until twenty-one years of age our subject attended the district schools in winter and at other times assisted his father in work on the home farm. On attaining his majority he went to Wisconsin and for two years worked in the lead mines, after which he returned home and engaged in farming until 1851. His father gave him the home farm on the condition that he provide for the future care of his parents and sisters. In 1851 he moved to Green county, Wisconsin, and engaged in farming, owning six hundred acres of land. He was one of the early settlers of this locality, and during thirty-three years of his residence there became one of the most prominent and wealthy citizens. In 1884 he came to Winnebago City and purchased his present residence property. He had also purchased 320 acres of land some years prior to making his location, and gave a fine farm to each of his sons. Throughout his life our subject has been one of the most active and public-spirited of citizens where he has lived. While a resident of Green county, Wisconsin, he held the position of justice of the peace and also officiated in various other positions.

Mr. Austin was married in 1842 to Miss Elizabeth Wyatt, of Edgar county, Illinois, who died June 23, 1880. As the fruits of this union there are five living children— Elizabeth J., James W., Sidney O., Annie, now a resident of California, and Marion. James married Florence Cotherman, by whom he had two daughters—Adella T. and Leora E. He resides in Winnebago City. Sidney O. married Alice Cotherman, and now resides in Green county, Wisconsin. He has two children—Clarence and Murill. Marion married Emma Cotherman and has one daughter, Florence, and now resides in Winnebago City. The second marriage of Seth Austin occurred April 12, 1883, when he was wedded to Mrs. Eliza Wyatt, widow of John Wyatt, to whom she was married October 1, 1854, and who died in April, 1865, from injuries received in the war. Mrs. Eliza Wyatt was the daughter of Isaac and Mary (Kyle) Betts, natives, respectively, of Pennsylvania and Maryland, and farmers by occupation. Mr. and Mrs. Wyatt had four chidren: William J., who married Lena Morlf, by whom he has had two children— Merta and Roy; Isaac M., who married Nora E. Lawrence and has one child, Hazel J.; Mary E., married to Samuel D. Chyrst, by whom she has had three children—Maude O., Fred J. and Walter C.; and Olive N., who married James Lawrence, by whom she has had one child—Earl A. John Wyatt enlisted in the Union army March 28, 1864, joining Company D, Thirty-eighth Regiment Wisconsin Volunteer Infantry. He was severely wounded by being shot in the shoulder, and from the effects of this wound died in April, 1865. His body was brought back to Wisconsin and was buried in Monroe, Greene county. He rose from the private ranks to that of corporal, and was promoted to the rank of sergeant, but did not live to fill that position. He was a reliable farmer of Greene county before his enlistment.

Three of Mr. Austin's sons died in the service in the Union army. Elijah W. enlisted in the Twenty-second Wisconsin Infantry, and died in the hospital at Nashville, Tennessee, March 22, 1863. Shedrach enlisted in the Fifth Wisconsin Battery, and is supposed to have lost his life on the destruction of the steamboat "North America." Seth enlisted in the Twenty-second Wisconsin Infantry, and died at Jefferson Barracks, Missouri, in 1864. The body of the last son was brought home by the father and interred in an honored grave in Wisconsin. The bodies of the others could not be obtained.

The subject of our sketch has for years affiliated with the republican party, and has always been an active and generous-spirited citizen. He is a man of the highest character, and has for years been a member of the Methodist Episcopal church. Religious matters have always occupied a considerable amount of his attention, and for a long period of time he was a class-leader and steward while residing in Wisconsin. He is now living a retired life in Winnebago City, where he is held in high esteem by all who know him.

————◦━▸━❰❰❱❱━◦━━━

FRANCIS M. DYER is an influential and prosperous farmer and stock raiser, residing on section 26, Lake Side township, Cottonwood county, Minnesota. He made his location in the county in 1871, being one of the early settlers of the township. Mr. Dyer was born in Waldo county, Maine, August 28, 1841. He continued in his native State until he attained the age of twenty-three years, residing with his parents, who were Thompson Dyer and Lucy Bruce (White) Dyer.

The subject of our sketch received a good common school education, and on completing his course of schooling commenced teaching in his native State. He taught but a short time, however, and then engaged in the drug business for a year and seven months. In 1864 he enlisted in the United States Navy, but after being examined was considered unsound. He came to Wabasha county, Minnesota, in November, 1864. He resided in Wabasha county for seven years, engaged in farming and in work at the carpenter's trade, and taught school during the winters. After this period had expired he came to Cottonwood county, and has since been a permanent resident. He has taken an active part in all public matters, and has been a member of the board of supervisors for several years, being chairman of that body for some time. He has held various school offices, and is at present clerk of school district No. 23, having held this position for twelve years. He is a man of large intelligence, and has always taken an active interest in educational matters. He was appointed county superintendent of schools in 1875, and served two years, and again in 1886, serving one year. In politics Mr. Dyer affiliates with the prohibition party. He is a member of the Grange and Ancient Order of United Workmen, and is secretary of the Farmers' Alliance. He is a man of broad, progressive ideas, and is one of Cottonwood county's most respected citizens. He is public spirited, benevolent, and occupies an influential place in the political and social affairs of his county.

Mr. Dyer was married June 29, 1862, to Miss Hattie U. Weld, a native of Cornville, Somerset county, Maine, where she was born January 13, 1843. She was the daughter of Zebina Weld, a native of New Hampshire, and a farmer by occupation. Mr. and Mrs. Dyer have nine children—Willis Frank, Etta L., Hattie U., Abbie May, Clyde M., Blanche O., Elaine E., Grace R. and Merton W. Willis Dyer was married in December, 1887, to Miss Carrie E. Goss, a native of Highland township, Wabasha county, Minnesota. She was the daughter of H. M. Goss, an old settler and farmer of Selma township, Cottonwood county. The Dyers live in a pleasant and commodious home on section 20, and are highly respected.

HON. ERICK SEVATSON, of Jackson county, Minn., is the present representative of his district in the Minnesota legislature. He was born in Norway in the year 1844. In 1864 he came to the United States, and five years later settled in Minnesota. He is engaged in farming in Christiana, Jackson county, Minn., and also conducts a bank at Windom. He is married. He is a republican in politics.

JENS H. CHRISTENSEN, a reliable farmer, of Shaokatan township, Lincoln county, Minnesota, resides on section 17. He was born in Denmark, May 13, 1848, and was the son of Christen Madson and Karen (Jensdaughter) Madson, both of whom were natives of Denmark. The father was a farmer by occupation and had a family of six children. The mother died in Denmark in 1877, where also the father passed from this life February 3, 1878.

The early life of the subject of our sketch was spent in his native land attending school and assisting in work on the home farm until he was sixteen years of age. He then went to work on a farm in Schleswig-Holstein, continuing in that employment for six and one-half years. He then spent a winter in his native place and in the spring joined the army and served six months. Getting permission to return home he went from thence to Schleswig-Holstein, remaining six months, and on the 10th day of May, 1872, took ship for America. Landing in Quebec he passed on to Chicago, from thence going by vessel to Marinette, Wisconsin, where he worked in a saw-mill for two months. Going from thence across the bay into Door county, same State, he engaged in chopping wood for four years after which he purchased a farm of 240 acres, on which he remained until the spring of 1885. He took an active part in matters of a public nature while in Wisconsin and was a member of the board of supervisors for three years and also township clerk for two years. In 1885 he came to Lincoln county, Minn., and purchased the place where he now lives. He has a fine farm of 240 acres and has, perhaps, the best farm buildings in the township. His land is under good cultivation and he has become quite well-to-do. He has taken an active part in public matters and was appointed township clerk the first year of his location in the township. He has held this position ever since and has also been and is a member of the board of school directors. In politics he affiliates with the republican party and has become one of the representative citizens of the county.

November 4, 1876, Mr. Christensen was married to Mary Wisetsky, a native of Bohemia. This union has been blessed with seven children, five of whom are now living—Anna C., Cecilia A., Eacia C., John J. and Louis Albert.

WELCOME D. UNDERWOOD is one of the leading farmers of Lake Sarah township, Murray county, Minnesota. He first came to the county in 1879, but after working a farm during that summer he went to Woodstock, Pipestone county, and homesteaded land in Burke township, where he lived one and a half years. He made considerable improvement, built a house and set out a large number of trees and was one of the first settlers of that township. After a year and a half of residence there he came to Lake Sarah township and purchased his place of 157 acres, this being the same farm that he had worked prior to going to Pipestone county. His place in Pipestone county was adjacent to the present site of the village of Woodstock. Since returning to Murray county he has continued his residence and has been engaged in general farming and stock raising. He is beautifully located on the shores of Lake Maria, and his buildings are surrounded by a natural growth of timber, making it one of the most pleasant locations in the township.

The subject of our sketch was born in Owego, Tioga county, New York, September 1, 1836. His father was Timothy Underwood, a native of Vermont and a farmer by occupation. Removing in early life to the State of New York, the father died in that State some years ago. The mother's maiden name was Hannah Baldwin, a native of Connecticut and still living. In the father's family there were five children—Wealthy, Welcome D., George W., Aurilla and Achsah. When our subject was six years of age the parents removed to Chautauqua county, New York, where they remained. In 1855 our subject was married to Elizabeth Young, of the town of Amity, Erie county, Pennsylvania. He remained in Erie and Chautauqua counties until 1862, when he, with his wife and three children, removed to Wisconsin. September 22, 1865, his wife died, and in 1866, he, with the children, returned to Erie county, Pennsylvania. In 1867 he was married to Rhoda Young, and in 1879 they came to Minnesota as has already been stated. The three children above mentioned bear the names of Mary, Newell and Achsah.

In 1864 our subject enlisted in the Seventeenth Wisconsin Volunteer Infantry and served throughout the war, being discharged in 1865. He was wounded and taken prisoner in March, 1865, and was kept by the Rebels for some thirty days in Libby prison. He participated in the battle of Kingston, North Carolina, where he was wounded; besides various other battles and skirmishes of minor importance.

In politics Mr. Underwood affiliates with the republican party, as did his father before him. He is a man of excellent principles, is genial, warm hearted and public spirited, and is highly respected by all his fellow-citizens.

HASTINGS S. C. MACREDIE, an influential farmer of Murray county, Minnesota, resides on section 9, Slayton township. He is a native of Australia, where he was born March 6, 1856. His parents were George and Charlotta (Murray) Macredie, both of whom were natives of Scotland. The father moved to Australia in 1833, and for a number of years operated sheep ranches. Before going to Australia he followed a seafaring life and was a captain of one of the commercial ships. The grandfather of the subject of our sketch was William Macredie, who was an extensive landed proprietor of Scotland. The grandmother was Miss (Muir) Macredie. Our subject's father returned to Scotland and died in that country, December 13, 1884. His mother died in the same place in April, 1873.

When our subject was about two years of age his parents left Australia and located in France, living during the greater part of the following four years in Paris. When our subject was sixteen the family located on the Clyde, in Scotland, and our subject's education was completed in the city of Edinburgh. Mr. Macredie traveled extensively during his early years, passing back and forth a number of times from France to England and Scotland. He also traveled in Switzerland and Germany, and after completing his education went to Ceylon, India, where he operated a coffee plantation for about three years, also visiting India, Burmah Straits, China and the Cape Colony. Then he was stricken with the terrible jungle fever, and for some time his life was despaired of. Recovering somewhat he was then advised to go to Scotland. This he did and after remaining about a year was married. He then went to his native place in Australia and for about three years engaged in managing one of the stock stations. After the expiration of these three years, in 1882, he came to the United States, landing in San Francisco and going from thence to the State of Minnesota, and soon after locating where he now lives at Slayton, Murray county.

Mr. Macredie was married October 2, 1880, to Miss Janet Donner, by whom he has had three children—Dorothy C., Gwynneth and Marjorie. Mrs. Macredie is a daughter of Edward and Maria Donner, both of whom were natives of England. Her parents resided in their native land until their death, that of the mother occurring in 1882, and the father dying in 18—.

In early life the subject of our sketch was given excellent advantages for obtaining a thorough classical education. He is a man of intelligent, progressive ideas, observant, and a ready reader of human nature. In his extensive travels he has gathered a great amount of practical knowledge of men and affairs, and is well fitted to occupy the prominent place which he fills in his township and county. In politics he affiliates with the democratic party. He has a fine farm of 260 acres, under fine cultivation, and provided with good buildings. He also has a half interest in the Terry livery stable in the village of Slayton.

RICHMOND MORTON is one of the prominent and influential farmers of Pipestone county, Minnesota, located on section 26, Rock township. He made his settlement in that township in the spring of 1880, and has since been identified with the general interests of the township. He was born in Chautauqua county, New York, May 6, 1846.

The parents of the subject of our sketch were William M. and Polly (Sherman) Morton, both of whom are natives of New York. The father was a miller by trade and followed that occupation throughout his life until his death, which occurred in 1870. The mother is still living. In the father's family there were ten children—Lucinda, Marshall, Mary, Angeline, Homer, Olive, Laura, Fannie, John and the subject of our sketch.

Our subject received his early education in the county in which he was born, and remained with his parents during most of the time until he was twenty-three years of age. On reaching that age he came west, locating in Olmsted county, Minnesota, where for a number of years he was engaged in various pursuits. For a time he was engaged in the hardware business, and later, followed farming in company with his brother. During his residence in Olmsted county, he went to Nobles county, same State, and preempted 160 acres of land, on which he remained six months. He then returned to Rochester, Olmsted county, and after remaining a short time, made his settlement in Rock township, as stated in the opening of this sketch. Since coming to the township, he has been engaged in general farming and stock-raising, and has taken an active interest in all matters pertaining to the welfare of the town. His first settlement was made on the southwest quarter of section 8, where he remained some eight years, after which time he settled where he now lives, on section 26.

On the 2d day of February, 1877, Mr. Morton was united in marriage to Miss Essie Hatch, who was also a native of Chautauqua county, New York. When she was two years of age her father's family removed to Minnesota, settling at Rochester, where Mrs. Morton received her education. She was the daughter of Edwin H. Hatch, an influential farmer and dairyman, who now resides in Pipestone. Mr. and Mrs. Morton have three children, all of whom are living —Willis, Daisy and Homer.

Mr. Morton has had considerable pioneer experience in southwestern Minnesota. He was the first settler in Graham Lakes township, Nobles county, where he resided six months, as has already been stated, and where he assisted in the organization of the government of said civil division. Leaving Graham Lake township he returned to Rochester, and soon after, in the fall of 1879, made his entry on his claim in Pipestone county, to which he came in the spring of 1880. In politics our subject affiliates with the republican party, and is a leading and influential member of the order of United Workmen, in which society he holds the position of trustee. In public matters Mr. Morton has always been one of the leaders, and has very creditably and satisfactorily filled several official positions. He has held the office of supervisor one term, and has been treasurer of the township since 1882. He was elected county commissioner (second district) in the fall of 1884 and re-elected in 1886, which term he is now serving. He has held various school offices, and is at present clerk of school district No. 20. He also held the office of treasurer of school district No. 41 for three years. In his farming operations Mr. Morton has been quite successful, and is one of the leading and most well-to-do farmers in the township. He has a pleasant family and a comfortable home.

HON. FRANK A. DAY, of Fairmont, Minnesota, is the present State senator from his district. He was born in the year 1853, and settled in Minnesota in 1874. He was elected to the State house of representatives in 1878; was a member of the republican State central committee in 1884; has been chairman of the Martin county republican central committee since 1876, and a member of the republican congressional district committee for eight years. He resides in Fairmont, where he is an editor and publisher. He is married. He is a republican in politics, and a man of much ability.

GEORGE W. CRANE, a telegraph line builder and repairer, of Worthington, Minnesota, is the son of Whitfield and Salome (Stagg) Crane, natives of Vermont. George W. was born in Addison county, Vermont, March 25, 1835. When he was one year old his parents moved to Potsdam, St. Lawrence county, New York, settling on a large farm. The father died in December, 1844, and the farm was then leased, the family, however, still living on the property. When the lease expired, our subject and his brother, Henry F., being old enough to run the farm, took charge of it and kept the family together until 1863. The names of the children in the father's family were—Henry F., George W., Delia M., Viola E., Byron G. and Elvira R. Our subject was reared on a farm, but, with the other children, was given good advantages for an education.

George W. Crane enlisted, in November, 1861, in Company C, Seventh Vermont Infantry, and served until October 9, 1862. On entering the service he was ordered to Ship Island, in the Gulf of Mexico, where General Butler's expedition was fitted out for the reduction of Forts Jackson and St. Philips. These two forts commanded the approach to the city of New Orleans by way of the Mississippi river. After the reduction of the forts, our subject was taken with his regiment to Camp Paripett; a few miles above

New Orleans, where they remained in camp for some weeks. Thence the regiment went to Baton Rouge, and, after camping there for a few weeks, went to Vicksburg with an expedition under General Williams, consisting of several regiments and Admiral Farragut's entire fleet. Four or five weeks were spent near that city, and while there the Rebel ram "Arkansas" ran through the Union fleet above the city and entered Vicksburg, and the officers of the Union forces being somewhat alarmed and expecting that the Rebel forces was coming in large numbers, the entire command was ordered to fall back to Baton Rouge. Here they bivouacked for a short time, when a force under the rebel general Breckinridge attacked them one morning and there (August 5) ensued the battle of Baton Rouge, in which our subject participated. On the following morning the Arkansas rebel ram appeared above the city and was met and destroyed by the Union iron-clad gunboat "Essex." After this engagement our subject's regiment, together with others, moved to the vicinity of New Orleans and made that their camping ground until October 9, 1862, when our subject was discharged by reason of disabilities. He returned to New York City on the steamer "Potomac" in company with a comrade of the same regiment who had lost an arm in one of the battles. When they reached the city they were directed to the New England Soldier's Relief rooms, where they remained a week and then went to their respective homes. Our subject operated the home farm until 1870 and then went to Swanton, Franklin county, Vermont, where for eight years he was employed at railroad and telegraph work for one of the leading railroad companies. In June, 1878, he removed to Worthington, Minnesota, and again engaged in railroad work, continuing in that line to the present time. Mr. Crane is an influential member of the Ancient Free and Accepted Masons, Worthington lodge, No. 101, and also of the Grand Army of the Republic post. In politics he affiliates with the republican party and by reason of disabilities acquired during the war receives a pension from the government.

March 18, 1865, Mr. Crane was united in marriage in Philipsburgh, Quebec, to Miss Louisa M. Hogle, daughter of Augustus and Eunice (Fordice) Hogle, natives of Canada. Mrs. Crane was born near Philipsburgh, in 1840. The fruits of this union are—May L., now Mrs. Frank Durfee; Frank M., and Nellie, who died in infancy. Frank M. resides in Worthington and clerks in a drug store. Mr. Frank Durfee is a successful hardware merchant of Worthington.

JEREMIAH A. HOUGHTALING, a leading business man of Fairmont, Minnesota, is engaged extensively in the hardware trade. He is the son of Abram and Sarah (Veile) Houghtaling, natives of the State of New York.

Jeremiah Houghtaling was born in Esopus, Ulster county, New York, November 23, 1815. His time, until he was twenty-two years of age, was spent in school and on the farm of his parents. He then turned his attention to boating on the Hudson river, and for a time was employed as a workman on a salary, and later owned an interest in a boat. He followed his employment on the river until 1856, in which year he removed to Ottawa, Waukesha county, Wisconsin, purchased a farm, and resided thereon for two years, engaged in agricultural pursuits. He then sold out and removed to Milwaukee, where he operated a dray line for a short time. In 1859 he moved to Wisconsin, purchased land, and engaged in farming for about eight years. He then returned to the city of Milwaukee and made that his home until 1875, and was employed during this time in the management of a coal yard. In 1875 he came to Fairmont, Minnesota, and engaged in the hardware business. Later he sold a one-half interest in his business to Mr. J. A. Sinclair, and the firm name became Houghtaling & Sinclair. In 1881 our subject sold his half interest in the business to a Mr. Colby, and removed to his farm, where he resided three years. He then returned to the village and bought back a share in the hardware store from Mr. Colby. Mr. Houghtaling took a two-fifths interest, Mr. Sinclair a two-fifths interest and Mr. Colby a one-fifth interest and the business was conducted in this way as Houghtaling, Sinclair & Co., until February, 1887, when our subject purchased Mr. Colby's interest and became the owner of three-fifths of the business. The firm name is now Houghtaling & Sinclair, and they are one of the most substantial and leading firms in the city. They have an extensive stock of goods, have a tin shop in connection and are doing a large and profitable business. They employ two skilled tinners and an apprentice. Besides his village property Mr. Houghtaling owns a fine farm of 360 acres, six miles northwest of Fairmont.

The subject of our sketch is prominent in public matters in the village and has been elected president of Fairmont three different times. While a resident of Wisconsin he was chairman of the township board and was also assessor. His political affiliations are with the democratic party.

Mr. Houghtaling was united in Esopus, New York, December 1, 1836, to Miss Catharine Elting, daughter of Ruloff and Dina (Elting) Elting, natives of Ulster county, New York. Miss Elting was born in New Foltz, Ulster county, New York, April 13, 1819. Mr. and Mrs. Houghtaling have been blessed with the following-named children—Dina (deceased), Abram, Ambrose

(deceased), Sarah Jane (deceased), Magdaline, Victorine (deceased), Kate (deceased), Bruno (deceased), Elmore, Lillian and Richard (deceased). Abram married Barbara Miffley and resides in Fairmont. Magdaline married Byron E. St. John and is now a resident of Martin county. Elmore wedded Mary Wade and resides in the village of Fairmont. Victorine was married to E. G. Comstock, of Milwaukee, and lived in that city until her death.

WILLIAM P. SPAULDING, one of the prosperous and energetic farmers of Verona township, Faribault county, Minnesota, resides on the southwest quarter of section 22. In the year 1856 he came to the county on a tour of inspection, and remained one summer, working out, and before leaving pre-empted a claim on section 15, of said township. He made a few improvements, such as are required by law, and after the summer was ended returned to Portage county, Wisconsin, and engaged in various occupations until the following season. He then returned to his claim in Verona township, sold eighty acres, and then purchased 160 acres of his present place in 1860. From 1863 to 1864 he was engaged in the boot and shoe business at Lake City, Wabasha county, and in 1868 commenced making improvements on his farm. In June of 1870 he located on his place, and made a permanent residence. Being a hard-working and systematic farmer he has succeeded in making his place one of the best in the township. He has provided it with comfortable buildings, dwelling-house, barns, etc., and has one of the choicest locations, his farm being supplied with natural timber, and several springs, also a creek which carries living water through his place during the entire year. He is engaged in farming, and also gives considerable attention to the raising of Cleveland bay and English shire horses, and short-horn cattle. The official history of the township would not be complete without an important place being given to the name of our subject. He has been chairman of the township board for two terms, in 1888 was treasurer, at present holds the office of clerk of school district No. 5, and has for some time been justice of the peace.

W. P. Spaulding is a native of the village of Lewis, Essex county, New York, where he was born May 21, 1835. He was the son of Luke and Rosina (Desmore) Spaulding, both of whom were natives of Vermont. The father was a farmer by occupation, and was a member of the Congregationalist church, being a reputable and representative citizen. The mother during early life was a school-teacher. She is still living at the advanced age of seventy-seven years. In about 1840 our subject's father died, and the mother remarried. Our subject's grandfather was Reuben Spaulding, a native of Vermont and a farmer by occupation.

The subject of our sketch remained in the home of his mother until he was twenty years of age. Up to this time he was given a good education, and spent a considerable time in work on the home farm. Soon after his marriage our subject moved to the State of Minnesota, and came to Faribault county, from whence he went to Lake City, as was stated in the opening lines of this sketch. He is now one of the leading citizens of Verona township.

Mr. Spaulding was married in the year 1866 to Miss Nancy C. Mead, who died in 1880, leaving four children—Elmer, Jessie, Edith and Florence. Our subject's second marriage occurred in 1882, in which year he married Clarissa Oothoudt, a native of the State of New York, and born in the village of Sweden in Monroe county. She was the daughter of Augustus and Sarah (Eletson)

Oothoudt, both of whom were natives of New York. The father was a farmer and an early settler of Minnesota, who still lives, and resides on section 31 of Verona township, Faribault county. During her early life Mrs. Spaulding followed the occupation of teaching. At thirty-six years of age she had taught thirty-four terms of school, having commenced in that profession when fifteen years of age. She was an excellent teacher, and her services were in demand in the schools of Southern Minnesota. She taught in the high schools of Blue Earth City and also at Northfield, where she was engaged for two terms. She was educated at Waupun, Wisconsin, and was married the first time in 1863 to Professor Alvin H. Pelsey, a teacher and for five years a physician. He died in 1874. Mr. and Mrs. Spaulding have two children—Veron and Gladys. Mr. and Mrs. Spaulding are members of the Methodist Episcopal church, and stand high in social and religious circles. Mr. Spaulding is a strong temperance man and affiliates with the prohibition party.

GEORGE F. ROBISON, the present auditor of Cottonwood county, Minnesota, made his location in the county in September, 1870. He is a native of Caroll county, Illinois, where he was born February 2, 1843.

The father of the subject of our sketch was Milus C. Robison, who was born in North Carolina in 1809, of Welsh parents, and, when an orphan about fourteen years of age, in company with two older brothers, emigrated to Illinois, settling in Adams county, where they engaged in farming. In later years he traveled northward to the Galena mines, finally locating a squatter's claim four and a half miles northwest of the present site of Savanna, Illinois, in the year 1827 or 1828. In 1837 he married Catherine, the only daughter of John and Elizabeth Armstrong, who were of Irish and German descent, respectively, and who settled in a very early day on Apple river, a few miles from where it empties into the Mississippi, experiencing much trouble with the Indians. Mrs. Armstrong having on several occasions saved the lives of herself and two children, Catherine and David, by her presence of mind and the exercise of her courage when their house was invaded by the hungry savages during her husband's absence. At the time of the fight, when the few families of whites were quartered in the block-house, at Elizabeth, and the supply of lead was about exhausted, it was Mrs. Armstrong who thought to make bullets of the pewter spoons and platters and who not only superintended the making of the bullets but also loaded several of the guns for the men that stood at the port-holes firing at the attacking Indians.

After their marriage, Mr. and Mrs. Robinson spent the remainder of their lives on the farm first located by him, making there a very comfortable home. He was a farmer of much push and energy, and was widely known and highly respected by the early settlers of northwestern Illinois. He died in 1845, and his wife in 1852. Four children were born to them—three sons and one daughter. The daughter, Elvira, married S. A. Iden, and died in 1870, near Savanna, Illinois. The three sons were volunteers in the War of the Rebellion. John A., the eldest, lost his right arm in the battle of Chickamauga, September 20, 1863, and is now a resident of Savanna, Illinois; Charles T. is now a resident of Custer county, Nebraska, where he is engaged in farming.

The subject of this sketch spent his early days on the home farm, and acquired some education at the district schools. Being left an orphan while young, his opportunities were not the best. He lived with friends until about fourteen years of age; worked by the month a year or two, and then farmed land on shares. The year before the breaking out of the Rebellion he farmed in partnership with his brothers. A portion of the year 1861 our subject attended school at Galena, Illinois, and later attended Mount Carroll Seminary. In February, 1863, he was taken sick, and was obliged to remain out of school the balance of that winter. Returning to the same institution the following winter, he continued there until he enlisted in May, 1864, in Company G, of the One Hundred and Thirty-fourth Regiment Illinois Volunteer Infantry, to serve one hundred days.

He was in the service some five months, among the guerrillas in Kentucky, stationed a portion of the time at Columbus and afterward at Mayfield. He returned with his regiment to Chicago, sick with fever, was taken to the soldiers' home, and was under the doctor's care for two weeks. He was mustered out with the balance of the regiment, on October 25, 1864, while convalescing, and returned to school at Mount Carroll Seminary, remaining, however, only until the Christmas vacation. He then purchased an additional interest in the old homestead and later the interests of all the other heirs. He continued in Illinois until 1870, when he sold out and came to Minnesota, in poor health, spending the summer at Lake City. In September of the same year he came to Cottonwood county and located on 160 acres of land in what is now the town of Carson. He was a member of the board of county commissioners in 1872-3 and 4. Mr. Robison was married in November, 1872, to Miss Mary E. Smith, daughter of Rev. H. H. Smith, then living in Cottonwood county. He improved his farm in Carson and continued his residence thereon until in August, 1877, at which time he sold the farm and moved his family to near Bingham Lake; he then entered the employ of S. H. Soule, for a time assisting in that gentleman's store at Mountain Lake, after which he attended the commercial college in St. Paul for a few months, and then took a trip up to the Red River country and Dakota, thence to Nebraska, selling books and taking subscriptions for newspapers. On his return he located in the fall of 1878 at Windom, where he obtained a position in the post-office, assisting there a portion of each week for about two years and occupying the rest of his time at such employment as came to his hand, working about three months of the summer of 1880 for J. T. Smith of Heron Lake.

Upon the opening of the Bank of Windom in May, 1881, he accepted a position as clerk in the bank. He continued in this business some six years, serving as assistant cashier most of the time. In March, 1888, he was appointed by the county commissioners to fill a vacancy in the office of county auditor, and was elected to that office the same fall.

In politics Mr. Robison affiliates with the republican party. He is a member of the Masonic, Ancient Order of United Workmen, and Grand Army of the Republic fraternities, and is one of Cottonwood county's most prominent officers.

Mr. and Mrs. Robison have five children— Edith E., now a clerk in her father's office; Vivian R., Grace E., Winnifred J. and Archie R.

————•◦••◦⊶◦◦⊷◦◦•◦————

EMBRICK A. ENGEBRETSON is a thrifty and industrious farmer of Mason township, Murray county, Minnesota. He has a fine farm on section 32, where he located his claim in 1879. He was born in the Kingdom of Norway, June 22, 1846. His parents were Andrew and Emily (Erickson) Engebretson, natives of Norway. The father was a farmer by occupation and came to America in 1853. He settled on a homestead in Newburg township, Fillmore county, Minnesota, where he lived until his death, which occurred in October, 1884. The mother is still alive and is residing on the old homestead.

Embrick A. Engebretson left the old country with his parents and came to the United States, residing with them until 1869. He enlisted August 29, 1864, in Company E, Seventh Minnesota Volunteer Infantry, and continued in the service until August, 1865. He then returned to his farm, and in 1869 came by team to Mason township, prospecting for land. He located his claim and went to Jackson, where he spent one winter. In the spring of 1870 he returned to Murray county and found his claim taken by another party. So he located land on section 32, where he now lives. He also owns a farm of 160 acres on section 6, Slayton township. In all he has 322 acres of land.

December 20, 1876, Mr. Engebretson was married to Lizzie Teninson, a native of Norway. This union has been blessed with three children—Adolph, Tilda B. and Edward L.

Since making his location in the county our subject has became one of the most prominent citizens. He has taken an active part in public movements and is able and popular as an official in his township. He has served as supervisor for three years, and for eight years he was chairman of that board. He also held the position of constable for two years, and has been school district treasurer. Our subject is a man of excellent character, courteous and gentlemanly and is highly respected wherever known. Mr. Engebretson is an honored member of the Grand Army of the Republic. He was a charter member of the John A. Logan post, of Slayton, and for two years has held the office of senior vice-commander of that post.

JOHN B. RAMAGE is a pharmacist and one of the leading business men of Lake Benton, Lincoln county, Minnesota. He was born in Kincardine, Canada, September 3, 1851, and was the first white child born in the township of Huron, Bruce county, in which the village of his birth was located. His parents were William and Mary (De-Velling) Ramage, both natives of Canada.

The early life of the subject of our sketch was spent beneath the parental roof, and he was given good educational advantages in the district schools. On attaining the age of thirteen years he commenced work on the lakes, following the occupation of fishing during the summer seasons for five years, continuing his studies in school during the winters of these years. In 1867 he was apprenticed to the proprietor of a jewelry store at Kingston, Canada, to learn that business. Health failed, however, before winter had closed, and during the next summer he engaged in the old business of fishing. In the fall of that year he commenced buying pork, and worked in a pork-packing establishment, having charge of the business during a part of a profitable year's engagement. At the end of this time he commenced clerking in a general store, and for eight months continued therein, when the proprietor failed, and he lost his position. During that winter he attended school, and in the spring of 1870, he went to Lombard, DuPage county, Illinois, where he engaged in agricultural pursuits for some two years. Removing to Chicago he then took charge of a confectionery store and after a short time spent in that line, found employment in a carpet store, continuing therein until in January, 1873. February 22d, he found employment in a drug store at Chebanse, Illinois, and continued in that place for one year, and during the following winter took up the study of medicine. In the spring of 1874 he removed to the State

of Wisconsin, and found employment in various small towns until 1875, when he located in Galesville, where for seven and a half months he found employment on a farm. In the winter of 1876 he became a teamster and followed that business during the winter. He then commenced work by day's work at whatever he could find to do, and finally accepted a position in a flouring mill, where he continued about a year. One year after this was spent in work on a farm at Arcadia, Wisconsin. In the spring of 1880 he came to Pipestone county, Minnesota, and took a pre-emption, on which he lived until the fall of 1883, three months of which time were spent by him in work on the railroad and as a carpenter. In the fall of 1883 he came to Lake Benton and took charge of a drug store owned by Dr. Campbell. For three years he continued a successful and profitable engagement with Dr. Campbell, and at the end of that time he purchased the drug stock and has since conducted a profitable business. In 1886 he passed a creditable examination before the State board of pharmacists, and was granted a certificate granting him the right to engage in that business. Up to the present writing (July 15, 1889) he is the only one in Lincoln county who has passed the examination.

The subject of our sketch was married in Chebanse, Illinois, December 14, 1873, to Miss Austac Whistler, a daughter of Joseph and Sarah (Craven) Whistler, natives of Virginia. Mr. and Mrs. Ramage have been blessed with two children—Leroy C. and Mary Blanche. Mr. and Mrs. Ramage are members of the Methodist Episcopal church, in which they occupy a prominent and influential place. They are exemplary Christian people and are held in high esteem by the citizens of Lake Benton.

The life of the subject of our sketch has been of a somewhat varied nature and he has traveled extensively and engaged in various occupations. Throughout all these lines, however, he has maintained the dignity and integrity of his character and has been respected as a loyal and true citizen wherever he has resided. Active and energetic in all his business relations he has carried these characteristics into public life and has become one of the important factors in the local government of the localities in which he has lived. He has been town clerk for a year and has held other minor positions. He is a member of the Lake Benton Lodge, No. 146, Ancient Free and Accepted Masons.

———◦—❖—❀❂❀—❖—◦———

ELIAS WARNER is a reliable farmer of Highwater township, Cottonwood county, Minnesota, and resides on a fine farm on section 18. He settled on his present homestead in 1872, and has made this his home ever since.

Mr. Warner was born in Stavanger, Norway, May 17, 1847. His parents were Warner and Julia (Guaray) Olson, natives of the same kingdom. The parents came to the United States in 1854, and located in Wisconsin, where they resided until 1871. The father of our subject was a physician of some note in Wisconsin, and died in Green county in 1861. The mother is still living, and now resides with the subject of this sketch. The father's family contained three children—Mary, Elias and Ole. The last named died in Chicago, at three years of age, when the family was on its way to Wisconsin.

Elias Warner was reared in his native country until he was seven years of age, when he came with his parents to the United States. Locating in Wisconsin, he received a good practical education in the village of Browntown, Green county. He made Wisconsin his home until 1871, when he came to his present location in Cottonwood county, Minnesota. Mr. Warner is engaged in general farming and stock-raising on his excellent farm of 280 acres. He is also engaged quite largely in buying and shipping graded stock to St. Paul. Mr. Warner is an energetic and systematic farmer, and has made his farm one of the best in the county. In all matters of a public nature he has always taken a deep interest, and, having assisted in the organization of his township, which was first called West Brook, and later changed to Highwater, he has associated intimately with local politics. He has been chairman of the board of supervisors for two years, supervisor for three years, township treasurer for two years and clerk of school district No. 38 for three years. In politics he affiliates with the republican party, is a member of the order of United Workmen, and is one of the most respected and representative citizens of his township.

Mr. Warner was married March 22, 1872, to Miss Lena Foos, a native of Norway, and a daughter of A. T. Foos, a farmer by occupation. This lady came to America with her parents when she was ten years of age, and located in Fillmore county, Minnesota. Mr. and Mrs. Warner have four children—Albert, Henry, Mary and Lewis.

———◦—❖—❀❂❀—❖—◦———

DR. NEWTON P. SHEPARD, a leading physician and surgeon and prominent citizen of the village of Currie, came to Murray county, Minnesota, on the 9th day of July, 1871. He was one of the first settlers of the village and soon after making his location put up a building on section 12, in Murray township, where he purchased a small tract of railroad land. After remaining a year he returned to Michigan, remaining in that State one year, from whence he came to Currie to engage in the practice of medicine, where he has since resided with the exception of one year, from the fall of 1877 to the fall of 1878, which was spent in Michigan. Dr. Shepard has been the only physician of the village throughout his residence here with the exception of one year, in 1882, when he had a partner, Dr. G. F. Head.

Dr. Shepard is a native of Nobles county, Illinois, where he was born April 10, 1837. When he was four years of age his parents moved to the State of Ohio, where our subject remained until twenty-five years of age. He received a thorough classical education in Lake and Ashtabula counties, Ohio, and left school at the age of twenty. He then commenced the study of medicine with Drs. M. P. Sherwood & Son, of Unionville, Ohio. He remained with this firm for about a year and then engaged in farming and somewhat at carpentering for three or four years. In the meantime he continued his study of medicine and became a graduate of the Eclectic Medical Institute of Ohio. Removing thence he engaged in the practice of medicine in Michigan for a few months and then came to Murray county, as was stated in the opening lines of this sketch.

Dr. Shepard is the son of Daniel S. and Talmira (Phelps) Shepard. The father was a farmer by occupation and was a native of Massachusetts, and the mother was a native of the State of New York. The father died in Michigan. In the father's family there were nine children, of whom our subject was the oldest.

Dr. Shepard, of whom this sketch treats, was united in marriage November 7, 1858, to Miss Eliza Quayle, a native of Painsville, Ohio. This lady died in 1863, leaving three children—Rosa, John and Ralph. Dr. Shepard was married the second time in 1870 to Miss Sabrine Silvernale, a native of Pennsylvania, where she was reared and educated. By this marriage there have been three children—Alice, Louisa and Ray.

The subject of our sketch is one of the best and most efficient physicians and surgeons in Murray county. He has an extensive and profitable practice and has gained an enviable reputation in bringing about radical cures and performing complicated surgical operations. In politics the doctor affiliates with the prohibition party. He is a member of the Masonic fraternity, of which he is the senior warden. He is also chief templar in the Good Templars' society. As a man, a citizen and a physician, Dr. Shepard is held in high esteem.

JOHN ISIDORE BERNARD, one of the early settlers of Pipestone county, located on his present place on section 8, of Gray township, in February, 1880. The first settler of this township was Andrew Gray, who located in 1876 on section 10, his son, Charley Gray, being the first child born in the township. After remaining about eight years Mr. Gray removed to Toledo, Iowa, and has since gone to Nebraska. Among others who located in the township about the time of its organization are C. W. Fenlason, who made his settlement in 1879 on section 14, and in 1886 removed to Colorado. He was the second county superintendent of schools, being elected in 1882, and having held the office of register of deeds from 1880 to 1882. Henry Pease located in the town in 1878, and died in 1888. C. T. Howe, a settler of 1879, still remains in the town. Mr. Bernard has been intimately acquainted with all these early settlers, and relates many interesting reminiscences of early pioneer life. Our subject is engaged in general farming and stock-raising, making a specialty of the Poland-China breed of swine, having as fine specimens of these animals as are found in southern Minnesota. He has been thrifty and energetic in the operation of his farm, and in handling his stock. He commenced at the very bottom of the ladder, being possessed of but very little means when he located in the township; has gradually risen in prosperity and good circumstances, and is one of the representative farmers of the township.

The subject of our sketch was born thirty-five miles from Montreal, Canada, January 29, 1839. His parents were Louis and Mary Bernard. The father and mother were natives of France and followed the occupation of farming throughout the most of their lives. The father died in Canada in 1867. The mother died in 1852.

Mr. Bernard was reared and educated in Canada at the home of his parents, in the the Parish of St. Hermas, county of Two Mountains. After having passed through a course in the district schools, he was sent to St. Thérèse College, forty-five miles north of Montreal, in Terre Bonne county. Through financial difficulties he was recalled home after having passed but four years in the above-named college. At the age of seventeen he moved to Ohio, locating in the city of Cleveland, where he remained for three years, learning the carriage painting trade. Then, in 1861, on the 19th day of April, he enlisted as a private in the Eighth Regiment Ohio Volunteer Infantry. This enlistment was in answer to the president's call for 75,000 volunteers, and it was for a period of three months. After the completion of this time of service he re-enlisted for three years in the Twenty-third Ohio Volunteers, entering the service as a private and continuing in that regiment for one year and a half, when he was honorably discharged on account of sickness. Several eminent men were connected with his regiment, among them being R. B. Hayes, major; lieutenant-colonel, Stanley Matthews; captain, D. C. Howard; and E. P. Scammon, as colonel. Our subject was discharged from service at Fayetteville, West Virginia, in February, 1863. After his discharge he removed to Whitewater, Wisconsin, where he was married and where

he made his home for about three years. In 1866 he removed to LaCrosse county, where for about twelve years he followed the business of painting in the village of West Salem. While here he became quite interested in affairs of local importance, and held various offices in the village in which he lived, such as town clerk, justice of the peace, etc. In 1878 he was assistant sergeant-at-arms of the Wisconsin legislature and held that position during the session of 1878 and 1879. As has been stated in the opening of this sketch, he began looking for a location in the western part of Minnesota and settled on his claim in Pipestone county, April 9, 1880.

Mr. Bernard was married in April, 1865, to Miss Bettie Smith, who was reared and educated in Jefferson county, Wisconsin. Mr. and Mrs. Bernard have but one living child—Ethelyn, who is now Mrs. Franklin B. Bennett, of Pipestone, Minnesota. Their other children died several years ago. Isidore died July 12, 1870; Willie L. died July 5, 1874, and Harry S. died August 26, 1874.

In politics Mr. Bernard is a member of the republican party. His first presidential vote was cast for Abraham Lincoln. He is a man of strong, decided opinions. For two years he held the position of chairman of the board of supervisors; is now on his third term as justice of the peace; is the second president of the Farmers' Alliance of the county, which position he has held for two years; for the same length of time he has also been secretary of the Old Settlers' Association, and is at present secretary of the Live Stock Association of the county; for four years he has been a member of the village board of education, and has held the office of treasurer of this latter board for two years. Thus we see that since Mr. Bernard's residence here he has taken an active interest in all matters which tend to the promotion of the general welfare and prosperity, and his assistance has always been cheerfully rendered in all affairs of a public nature. He is a member of the Grand Army of the Republic, is a pleasant man to meet in social intercourse, and being possessed of a fair education, he is well fitted for the place he occupies before the citizens of the township in which he lives. In every way he is a representative farmer. He has a comfortable home and a pleasant family.

ON. WARRINGTON B. BROWN, of Pipestone, is the present State senator from his district. He was born in Colchester, Chittenden county, Vermont, June 4, 1845. He came to Minnesota in the fall of 1865 and is at present residing in Pipestone City, Pipestone county, where he is engaged in farming; he is married. During the War of the Rebellion he served in Company I, Thirty-eighth Wisconsin Volunteer Infantry, participating in several battles. He was discharged on account of a wound received at the assault on Petersburg, Virginia, April 2, 1865. For six years he served as county commissioner of Pipestone county and during five years was chairman of the board. He was elected to the house of representatives in 1884 and to the State senate in 1886, receiving 2,845 majority over three competitors. He is a republican in politics.

ATHAN BAXTER is a retired farmer and capitalist of Winnebago City, Faribault county, Minnesota. He was born in Bradford county, Pennsylvania, August 2, 1820. He was the son of Chauncey and Nancy (Vroman) Baxter, natives of New York. The father was a leading citizen of his native State, where he was engaged extensively in the lumber business, and also in farming. He had a family of six children, two of whom are now living—Nathan and Celesta, now Mrs. Gilbert, of Wisconsin.

Our subject was reared in Pennsylvania, where he was given a good practical education. He learned the business of handling lumber and also followed farming to some extent until coming to Wisconsin in 1862. He located in Waukesha county, where he engaged in farming and also in the wood business. Here he remained until 1888, having met with large success and having accumulated considerable means. He then sold out his fine farm of two hundred acres of land, and also his valuable city property, and removed to this place, where he has since lived. His coming in 1888 was not the first time he had seen Faribault county, however. In 1887 he had visited this region and had purchased a farm of two hundred acres four miles north of Winnebago City. This he has kept improving, and it is now operated by his son George. Mr. Baxter also purchased a farm of 160 acres three miles north of the village in 1885, and also owns a farm of 160 acres three miles north of Wells that he purchased in 1887. He has another small farm of eighty acres, not far from the city of Winnebago. He is one of the largest landed proprietors in the village, and reaps a large income therefrom. He purchased his residence on Cleveland street in 1888, and is at present making substantial improvements.

Mr. Baxter was married January 1, 1843, to Miss Amelia Decker, a native of Delaware county, New York. She was the daughter of George and Eliza Decker, natives of England and Connecticut, respectively. The father came to America in 1812, and settled in Franklin, Delaware county, New York, where he was married, and reared a family of seven children, three of whom are now living—Fayette, Hannah (now Mrs. Vroman) and Mrs. Baxter. Mr. and Mrs. Baxter have had nine children, six of whom are now living—George E., who married Miss Ada Kilmar, of Janesville, and by whom he had one son—George; Wilbur, who married Miss Ella Hall, of Wisconsin, by whom he had three children—Willie, John and Marion; Osborn, who married Miss Ella Lyman, and has three children—Cora, Elva and Amelia; Emma J., now Mrs. N. Fuller, who has one son—Stewart; Eliza, now Mrs. Gray, and Newton, of Ottawa, Illinois.

The subject of our sketch is a republican in politics, and has affiliated with that party for many years. He is a stanch supporter of the principles of republicanism, and is a man of broad and progressive ideas. He is genial and public-spirited, and is one of the solid and substantial men of the city. Mr. and Mrs. Baxter belong to the Presbyterian church.

UDLEY J. FORBES, a contractor and builder of Winnebago City, is now located on a small farm on section 15 of Verona township, Faribault county, Minnesota. He has a fine residence and through his years of employment as contractor and builder has acquired for himself and family a comfortable home. He came to the county in 1857 and was one of the very first settlers of the vicinity of Winnebago City. The father, Benjamin F. Forbes, first located on section 9, where he remained until 1870, engaged in farming and stock-raising. He then went to Blue Earth City and for a few years engaged in the wind-mill business in partnership with Reuben Waite. The father's next move was to return to his former residence in the township, where he has since lived. He has been closely identified with the official history of his locality and has made an excellent record in various official positions. The father was born in Pennsylvania, was reared and educated in Wisconsin and engaged throughout his life in farming. Dudley Forbes' mother's maiden name was Saphronia Williams, a native of the State of New York.

D. J. Forbes was born in Fond du Lac county, Wisconsin, September 27, 1854. In 1857 the parents removed to Verona township, Faribault county, where our subject received his education. He also attended school at Blue Earth City, and learned the printer's trade, serving an apprenticeship of three years on the Blue Earth City *Post*, established by Williams & Stevens. After this he worked at his trade in different parts of the State until his health failed, when he again commenced study and completed his educational course. He then learned the carpenter's and millwright's trades, at which business he has since engaged, becoming one of the leading and most influential contractors and builders of Faribault county.

For years Mr. Forbes affiliated with the republican party, but being a man of strong temperance principles, he has now joined the prohibition party. He belongs to the United Workmen, of which society he is an earnest working member, and overseer in the lodge at Winnebago City. He is one of the representative and leading citizens of the township and county.

On the 7th day of May, 1876, Miss Alida Lathrop was married to Mr. Forbes. This lady was born in Faribault, Minnesota, and was the daughter of D. Z. Lathrop, a leading farmer of that county. Mr. and Mrs. Forbes have three children—Clara, Naana and Daisy.

ILLIAM A. POTTER is one of the influential farmers and stock-raisers of Amboy township, Cottonwood county, Minnesota. He located in the township in April, 1878, first settling on section 22, where he has since lived. He has 320 acres of land and has one of the best farms in the township. He has always been public-spirited and has with efficiency held various local positions. He has been township clerk since 1880, has been assessor for a year and chairman of the board of supervisors for a year.

Mr. Potter's native place is in Jefferson county, New York, where he was born June 28, 1839. His father was Josiah Potter, a native of Vermont, and who emigrated to New York State when a young man. He was a farmer throughout his life and in 1845 removed to Ohio where he still resides. He is a representative citizen and exerts a strong influence in the political affairs of his locality. He is a leading member of the Methodist Episcopal church. Our subject's mother's name before her marriage was Mary Ann Mills. She was born in New York State and died in 1868; was a member of the Methodist Episcopal church and was a lady of excellent character. Our subject was one of six children : George, who died aged eleven years and eleven months; William A., Sophronia E., Mary Jane, Charles F. and Lucy F.

Until he was six years of age our subject remained with his parents in New York. They then went to Wyandot, Ohio, where he remained until eleven years of age. Hardin county became their next home, where he lived until he became twenty-two years of age. Up to this time he was occupied with work on the farm and with attending the district schools. In November, 1861, he enlisted in Company A, Eighty-second Ohio Volunteer Infantry, and became a member of the Eleventh Corps, his company being commanded by Capt. David Thompson. In 1864 our subject was commissioned first lieutenant of Company K, One Hundred and Eightieth Regiment, and was discharged holding that rank in July, 1865. Mr. Potter was engaged in many hard-fought battles, among them being that of Chancellorsville, Gettysburg, Kingston, Mission Ridge, Look-

out Mountain, Wauhatchie Valley, and many other smaller battles and skirmishes. Our subject was not injured in the war, but was in the hospital sick with the measles for six weeks. After the discharge of our subject he returned to Hardin county, Ohio, and engaged in farming until 1867. He then came to Dodge county, Minnesota, where he resided until 1875, when he removed to New Ulm, where he spent three years in farming, and where for two years he held the office of justice of the peace. His next move was to find his location in Cottonwood county, where he has since lived.

Mr. Potter was married December 20, 1866, to Miss Belle Baker, a native of Pennsylvania. She was the daughter of Joseph Baker, who died when Miss Belle was but six years old. Mr. and Mrs. Potter have seven children—Minnie F., Effie S., Charles I., George W., Claude B., Edward C., and Cora Belle. Minnie and Effie are now married, and reside on section 8 of Amboy township. The former married Warren R. Jeffers, and the latter became the wife of D. E. Noble.

The political faith of our subject is in harmony with the republican party, with which he has affiliated for many years. He belongs to the Ancient Order of United Workmen and Grand Army of the Republic, and is one of the most prosperous and well-to-do citizens of the county. He has a fine farm, and makes a specialty of raising sheep and cattle. He has 650 sheep and a large number of cattle and horses.

⁂

JAMES REID CLEAVELAND is one of the leading farmers and stock-raisers of Lake Sarah township, Murray county, Minnesota. He located on section 20 in June, 1873, homesteading his present place. He was about the fifth settler in the township, the names of the other pioneers being G.

Carman, P. Pearsall, M. Husbrook and M. Cole. Our subject assisted in the organization of the township, and was a member of the first board of supervisors. J. F. Fitch was justice of the peace, and A. L. Dickerman was chairman of the board of supervisors. The subject of our sketch represented his constituents on the second board of supervisors as chairman, and continued that position for six or seven years. He has held various other positions since coming to the township, among them being that of assessor, etc. He has always taken an active interest in matters of a local nature, and has assisted materially in the development and up-building of the general welfare. He has been engaged in general farming and stock raising, and has a number of fine Durham cattle.

Mr. Cleaveland was born in Windsor county, Vermont, August 6, 1825. He is a son of Jediah Cleaveland, a native of Vermont, and a farmer by occupation. The father removed to New Hampshire in an early day, and died in that State. He was a consistent member of the Baptist church, as was also his wife. The mother's maiden name was Harriet Randall, a native of Vermont, where she died when our subject was fifteen years of age. Her death occurred in Royalton. In the father's family there were ten children—William L., Charles D., Norman C., Allen J., Edward H., James R., E. R., Carl, Judson and Harriet E.

The early life of the subject of our sketch was spent in Royalton, Windsor county, Vermont, where he received a good common-school education. At fifteen years of age his father removed to New Hampshire, where our subject engaged in farming pursuits until he was thirty years of age. He held a prominent place among the citizens of the locality in which he lived, and held various official positions. He was collector of taxes, etc., in his locality. After attaining thirty-five years of age he came to Indiana and worked at the carpenter's trade for a year. His next move was to Wabasha county, Minnesota, where he engaged in farming for seven years. From thence he removed to Olmstead county, where he remained eight years, following agricultural pursuits. In all these places he held a prominent place and was township clerk in Wabasha county, and a member of the board of supervisors in Olmstead county. He came to Murray county in 1873 and has made that his home since.

Mr. Cleaveland was married July 14, 1850, in Lyndon, Vermont, to Miss Elmina Taylor, a native of Dover, New Hampshire, where she was born March 2, 1827. She remained in that place until twenty-two years of age, and received an excellent common-school education. Mr. and Mrs. Cleaveland have been blessed with seven children—Edward, who died at five years of age; William D., Stella E., Amelia, Zaidee, Mabel and Hattie B. All the children except Hattie B. are married.

In politics Mr. Cleaveland affiliates with the republican party, and is one of the representative citizens of Murray county. He is a man of good character and is respected by all who know him.

───◆───

JOHN C. CROFOOT is one of the most reliable and substantial farmers of Lincoln county. He is located on a valuable farm on section 30 in Hendricks township. He was born in Hannibal, Oswego county, New York, March 23, 1854. His parents were Benjamin F. and Caroline (Kimball) Crofoot, both of whom were natives of the State of New York. He was a farmer by occupation, and is one of the prominent and influential citizens of his county. Benjamin's parents were Josef and Polly Ann (Chapman) Crofoot, farmers by occupation, and natives of Massachusetts. The subject of our sketch had three brothers and two sisters. Their names were—Anna, Edgar, Emma, Seymore and George.

The subject of our sketch had a strong attachment for his early home, and continued beneath the parental roof for many years. He was given good educational advantages, and when not in school assisted his father in work of the farm. He left home at twenty-one years of age, and went to the city of Auburn, where he found employment for nine months in the manufacturing establishment of D. M. Osburn. Leaving Mr. Osborn's employ he commenced work in the shops of Dodge & Stephenson, and remained with them some two months, after which he returned to his home and worked for his father on the farm for about one year. Then he again returned to Auburn, where he learned the baker's trade, and after following that for a short time worked in a lumber yard for a year. In 1874 he purchased an interest in a mill, which he helped to run during one winter, and in the following winter sold his interest to his partner. In the spring of 1875 he purchased a farm in Oswego county, New York, and rented it, but, seeing that it didn't pay, he sold out. When he was twenty-one years old his father gave him $1,000, but, like a majority of boys, he says, he did not make the best use of it. In the spring of 1876 he started West and came to Lincoln county, Minnesota, where he has since lived. He built the first house in the town of Hendricks, drawing the lumber with cattle a distance of forty miles. He was the first man to carry mail from Hendricks and Shoakatan and the first to carry it from Hendricks to Idlewild, and for a number of years held the contracts for carrying United States mail in this region. While carrying mail in this wild western country, making his trips on foot, he passed through many hardships, and many times

narrowly escaped death from the terrible blizzards. In those early days and terrible storms he has many times passed a whole month without seeing another person, and has seen such storms that for three days in succession he has been unable to reach his barn, only a few feet away. He has also seen some very long winters, and remembers one in which the snow laid on the ground from October 15 until May 12. During this winter the pioneers ground wheat in a coffee mill to get something to live upon, the snow being so deep it was impossible to get to town for provisions. He also dug the first well in the township. He has always taken an active part in township affairs. He helped to organize Hendricks township, and was the first town treasurer, which office he has held for many years, and is the present incumbent. He has also held the office of justice of the peace.

In 1878 Mr. Crofoot accidentally shot himself in the head. He was picked up by Lars Fjeseth and cared for for six months thereafter before he was able to attend to business.

The subject of our sketch was married in 1878 to Miss Sophia Johnson, by whom he has had four children—Benjamin, Pernie, Estella and Pearl.

Since coming to the township our subject has identified himself closely with all matters of a public nature and has assisted in every way possible to aid in the development and growth of the county. He is a man of high character, possessed of broad ideas, generous and public-spirited, and has the respect of all who know him. In politics he affiliates with the democratic party. Being well acquainted with the early settlers of the town and county and with the various localities on the mail route, he is a valuable and available correspondent, and holds that connection with the Lake Benton *News*.

CHARLES F. WARREN, editor and proprietor of the *Cottonwood County Citizen*, of Windom, Minnesota, and one of the leading newspaper men of Southwestern Minnesota, was born at New Boston, Hillsboro county, New Hampshire, May 25, 1829. He was one of three sons of Hon. Parker and Clara (Trull) Warren. Parker Warren was engaged in the mercantile business at New Boston, where he was one of the early settlers. He was of Scotch descent, his early ancestors being of the same family as Dr. Joseph Warren, of Bunker Hill memory. An only brother of Parker's was a wealthy ship owner near Boston, while several sisters had families which are now scattered throughout the eastern States. Parker Warren's wife, Clara Trull, was a native of Massachusetts, like himself. She was one of a family of six sons and six daughters, all of whom married and brought up children, some of whom have occupied prominent State and local positions. Her mother was of the Butler family, of which General B. F. Butler was a member. Parker Warren moved his family to Lowell Mass., in 1839, where the subject of this sketch attended grammar and high school five years, or until the fall of 1844, when the family removed to Wisconsin Territory, and settled on a farm near Beaver Dam, Dodge county, and there successfully battled with the trials of a pioneer life. Parker Warren accomplished much for the material and moral benefit of that community; was a deacon in the Presbyterian church and chorister for many years, and was one of a very few to organize the first church in the country. He was elected representative to the first State legislature in 1849. He died at Augusta, Wisconsin, in 1887, aged about eighty-six years, and his widow is still living there.

Charles F. Warren was engaged in farming, except one year as clerk in the store of his father at Beaver Dam, until 1857.

He spent about one year in business at Mauston, Wisconsin, after several months' travel in Minnesota. In the fall of 1859 he went to Augusta, Wisconsin, with his eldest brother and engaged in farming, opening up a new farm in La Crosse county. In November, 1862, he was married to Miss Henrietta Bulhs, at Fox Lake, Dodge county, Wisconsin, and spent the following winter at the new farm at La Crosse. In the spring he sold out and purchased land in Fillmore county, Minnesota, and moved back to Fox Lake, Wisconsin. In November, 1863, the first son, Henry C., was born, and in February, 1864, the family returned to Augusta for their future home. When President Lincoln issued his last call for "300,000 more," Charles F. Warren deemed it an imperative duty to join the Union forces, and enlisted in the Forty-eighth Wisconsin Infantry, February 10, 1865. The regiment rendezvoused at Milwaukee, and went immediately to St. Louis, where a few days were spent in Benton Barracks, and thence through Missouri to Fort Scott, Kansas, which was the headquarters of the regiment through the summer. In August the regiment was ordered to march across the plains, and was stationed at points along the Arkansas river, guarding the outposts and government trains along the old Santa Fé route far out into New Mexico. In December the regiment started for Leavenworth for discharge and muster out, arriving there on Christmas day, and reached Madison, Wisconsin, January 5, 1866.

In 1867 our subject entered the mercantile business at Augusta, in company with a younger brother, and carried on a fairly successful business for ten years, except for serious losses by fire and other unavoidable circumstances. In the spring of 1877 Mr. Warren left the business to his brother and came out and settled on the homestead near Windom, Minnesota, which he still owns.

While residing at Augusta, Wisconsin, four children were born—Butler Trull, George Francis, Jennie May and Sadie M.

On the 1st of January, 1883, C. F. Warren and his son, H. C., established the *Cottonwood County Citizen*, at Windom, which has met with general favor and has a good circulation throughout this section of the State. It is republican in politics, independent, and bound by no party or clique. In the fall of 1886 H. C. Warren retired from the office and removed to Merrillan, Wisconsin, and was succeeded by Butler T., a younger brother. Charles F. Warren has been honored with several local offices of trust and honor, and is one of the most highly-respected citizens of Windom. He is a member of the Masonic fraternity and Grand Army of the Republic. He is a careful business man, an intelligent and conscientious writer, and has placed the *Citizen* upon a fairly prosperous and remunerative basis. It should have been stated that in 1874 Mr. Warren owned and published a newspaper at Augusta while engaged in other business.

JOSEPH A. BILLINGS is a resident of section 4, Great Bend township, Cottonwood county, Minnesota. He was born in Bradford county, Pennsylvania, June 17, 1834.

The parents of the subject of our sketch were Harry and Polly (Buttles) Billings, the former a native of Massachusetts and the latter born in Connecticut. In about 1852 or 1853 the father came west, locating in Waushara county, Wisconsin, where he resided until 1864. He then removed to Goodhue county, Minnesota, where he died in November, 1868. The mother died in Butler county, Nebraska, January 17, 1888. In the father's family there were twelve children of whom our subject, Joseph Billings, was the eighth child.

Mr. Billings' early life was spent in work on the home farm, where he was given the advantages for an education furnished by the district schools. He remained with his parents until he was twenty-one years of age, and then worked out on various farms until 1861. May 22d of that year he enlisted in Benham Zouaves, a company formed in Berlin, Wisconsin, for the three months' service. The quota for the company, however, was not filled, and it was disbanded without being sent out of the State. Our subject enlisted October 22, 1861, in Company A, Sixteenth Wisconsin Infantry, and was discharged September 26, 1862. He participated in the battle of Shiloh, where he received an injury which caused him to partially lose his hearing. He was in the hospital at Benton barracks, St. Louis, for some time, and after his discharge went to Green Lake county, Wisconsin, where he engaged in farming until 1864. He then came to Goodhue county, Minnesota and purchased a farm of eighty acres and engaged in farming until 1872. He then came by team to Mountain Lake township, Cottonwood county, and located a soldier's claim on section 4. He remained until the memorable grasshopper raid in southern Minnesota, and then returned to Goodhue county and remained one year, coming back at the end of that time to his claim in Cottonwood county and putting in a crop and then returning to Goodhue county, where he remained two years. He then returned to his claim in Mountain Lake township, and resided there until March 1888. Then, having purchased the place on which he now lives some time before, he moved to his present location, where he has lived ever since.

Mr. Billings was married June 17, 1866, to Florence Wait, a native of the State of New York, where she was born November 2, 1849. She was the daughter of B. C. and Mary (Briggs) Wait, natives, respectively, of

New York and Vermont. Her father died June 16, 1873, and her mother is now living in Cannon Falls, Goodhue county, Minnesota. Mr. and Mrs. Billings have been blessed with four children: Milo D., Minnie A., Charles H. and Roy W.

The political affiliations of the subject of our sketch are with the republican party, and he is a prominent factor in the local affairs of that organization. He belongs to the Grand Army of the Republic and Ancient Order United Workmen, and is looked upon as a public-spirited and honorable citizen.

JAIRUS HITCHCOX is one of the most influential farmers of Troy township, Pipestone county, Minnesota. He resides on a fine farm of 240 acres in section 13, on which he settled in the spring of 1886.

The place of nativity of the subject of our sketch is to be found in Onondaga county, New York, where he was born on the third day of April, 1857. His parents were Asahel and Malinda (Davis) Hitchcox, the father a native of New York, where also the mother was born. The father's parents were Samuel and Rosenith (Benedict) Hitchcox. The parents of the subject of our sketch are still living and are residents of Pipestone county.

The subject of our sketch was so endeared to the old homestead that he made that his home until he reached the age of twenty-four years, up to which time he had engaged in work on the farm and attending school during the months of each winter. When he was twelve years of age his parents removed to Illinois, settling in McHenry county, where they lived on a farm. When Mr. Hitchcox left home he rented a dairy farm and shipped his milk to consumers in the city of Chicago. This business was kept up with good success for five years, and in the spring of 1885 he came to Pipestone county, Minnesota, and

located in the city of Pipestone. One year later he located on his farm in section 32, Troy township, where he has since lived. He became owner of the farm in 1883.

Mr. Hitchcox was married January 7, 1880, to Miss Ruth E. Willson, a native of Illinois. This union has been blessed with two children, both of whom are living at present— Myrtle A., and Vera L.

Mr. Hitchcox has been quite successful in his business interests, and has at present one of the finest farms in the county. He is also somewhat engaged in the raising of fine stock. He is a man of excellent tastes in this direction and is thoroughly capable of successful manipulation of the details of his line of business. In politics he is a supporter of the principles promulgated by the republican party, and in all matters of a public nature he takes a deep interest.

EDWIN H. CANFIELD is the present efficient and popular county attorney of Rock county, Minnesota. He located in Luverne in 1881, since which time he has been actively engaged in the practice of the legal profession. In 1885 he was appointed to fill a vacancy in the county attorneyship, and in 1888 was elected to that office. He has become quite prominent in political affairs, and besides the office just mentioned he has also been a member of the school board for three years, at present holding the position of clerk of said board.

Attorney Canfield is a native of Marquette county, Wisconsin, where he was born December 27, 1855. His parents, James F. and Mary E. (Holmes) Canfield were natives of Vermont. When a young man the father came West and settled in Michigan, where for some time he was engaged in the mercantile business. In about 1850 he removed to the State of Wisconsin and for some years engaged in farming. His next move was made in 1866, in which year he located in Olmsted county, Minnesota, where he remained on a farm for four years. At the end of that period he removed to Martin county, and after three years' residence there returned to Olmsted county, remaining until 1881. In that year he came to Luverne, where he now lives a retired life.

The subject of our sketch is the only surviving child of the father's family. He continued with his parents throughout his early life, being given good educational advantages in the common schools. He received a thorough course of study for two and one-half years in the high school and afterwards was given private instruction in the languages for eighteen months. Some three years after the conclusion of his school studies were spent by him in teaching in Olmsted county, during which time he engaged somewhat in the study of law. At the end of this three years' experience in teaching he entered the office of Charles C. Wilson, attorney, remaining with him about twenty months and being admitted to the bar in 1881. Since his admission to practice Mr. Canfield has actively pursued the duties of his profession, most of the time in Rock county.

In 1878 occurred the marriage of the subject of our sketch to Miss Carrie Alma Hill, of Elgin, Minn. Two children have blessed this union—Nina and Arden. The parents of Mrs. Canfield were prominent people of Waseca county, Minn., and resided for a number of years near Alma City, of which locality they were among the pioneers. Alma City was named after Mrs. Canfield.

In 1887 Mr. Canfield purchased 160 acres of land in Mound township, which he has constantly improved ever since. He has also been somewhat engaged in the real estate business, having bought and sold some land in the county. He has been very fortunate in his financial investments and in his legal practice, and has become quite well-to-do. He owns a good residence in the city. Our subject has taken an active interest in all matters which have had a tendency to improve and elevate his fellow-citizens and to develop the various institutions of his city. He was the prime mover in the foundation of the private library which is now the public library of the city and which contains seven hundred volumes. In religious matters he has also taken a prominent stand and has identified himself with all matters pertaining to the moral development of his fellow-man. He has assisted liberally in various church enterprises in the city and was one of the leading founders of the Unity church. In political matters, too, Mr. Canfield has always acted a prominent part. Ever since making his location in the county he has identified himself with the interests of the republican party and has been honored by that organization in various ways. In 1886 he was one of the delegates to the State convention. He is also a member of the Masonic fraternity. As a lawyer Mr. Canfield ranks very high among the members of the bar of Rock and adjoining counties. He is thoroughly qualified for the duties of his profession, and all cases presented to him receive thorough and systematic attention. He is one of the leading trial lawyers of Southwestern Minnesota. Being possessed of excellent legal abilities, and a gentleman of courteous deportment, he has drawn to himself an extensive circle of friends.

PERCY WOLLASTON is the sole proprietor of the Merchants' and Farmers' Bank, and also proprietor of a large general store at Fairmont, Martin county, Minnesota. He was the son of William Charles and Charlotte Jane (Fawcett) Wollaston, natives respectively of Cambridge and Leeds, England. The mother's father was the vicar of Leeds, and both families were occupants of prominent positions in English society and politics.

Percy Wollaston was born in Leeds, England, December 21, 1825. His father was a clergyman, and was master of the grammar school in Leeds for some twenty-six years. Coming from an intellectual family, our subject's early education was in no wise neglected. He was thoroughly educated, and at seventeen years of age went into the country to acquire a knowledge of agriculture. He continued on a farm for two or three years in England, and in 1848 came to the United States, and spent a winter in Charleston, South Carolina. The next summer was spent in the State of New York, where he was engaged in traveling and sightseeing. Early in 1850 he went to St. Catharines, Canada West, and engaged in work in a flouring mill for about a year. Then, in October, 1851, he returned home, and going to London, engaged in the manufacture of carpets. Continuing this business for a year, and then, finding the enterprise not a success, he went to Liverpool and engaged in the shipping business for the White Star Line of sailing ships, trading to Australia. He continued in this employment for ten or twelve years, and then for several years retired from active life, remaining in his native country until 1876, when he came again to America and found his way to the State of Minnesota. He spent about a month in Fairmont, Martin county, and then returned to England and in June, 1876, came again to this country, locating in the village of Fairmont. In the spring of 1877 he built a large frame building on North avenue, now the principal business street, which he opened as a general store in June of that year. In January, 1882, he opened the Merchants' and Farmers' Bank in a small way in the rear of his store. Both enterprises grew steadily, and in 1885 he built an addition on the side of his store for his bank, and, again, in 1888, finding that he still needed more commodious quarters for his increasing business, he added the "Bank building" to the store and built a new brick block adjoining, 40x65 feet in size, half of which is occupied by this bank and the remainder rented for a hardware store.

Mr. Wollaston was one of the pioneer business men of the village and ever since making his location he has earnestly advocated all projects which have tended to develop the business interests of Fairmont. He has done much to establish business and has made many improvements with his own means. When he came to the village there was no mill here, so he erected one, a windmill, which has been recently converted into a steam-mill. There was also no church building at the time of his location, and having been accustomed to church going, he immediately began agitating the project of building an Episcopal church. The matter took definite shape, and ere long an edifice was constructed in which the Episcopal people might worship. This was the means of starting other denominations in building enterprises, and now the village has six churches besides one denomination which holds meetings over our subject's store. Our subject has also been interested largely and actively in educational matters, and has assisted in providing the village with one of the best schools in the State. One of the most elegant residences in southern Minnesota, beautifully located on the lake shore, is the home of the subject of our sketch. Here he owns 380 acres of land, with ten acres of natural timber. His residence is built on an elevation, and is surrounded with the most beautiful grounds in the city, the lawn being smooth and nicely kept and adorned with groups of natural and evergreen trees.

All matters of a public nature have felt the activity of the subject of our sketch. He was the first president of the village council, and has been a member of the council twice since his location in the city. He is a republican in politics, and in religious sentiment is a member of the Episcopal church. He is a man of the highest character, and is one of the most respected citizens of Fairmont.

Mr. Wollaston was married in Oakley, Bedfordshire, England, October 11, 1848, to Miss Catherine Mossop, daughter of Isaac and Agnes Mossop, also natives of England. This lady was born in Cumberland, in that country, October 28, 1826. Mr. and Mrs. Wollaston have been blessed with the following-named children—Catherine, born in Canada, and now the wife of Mr. C. Sharpe, cashier of the Merchants' and Farmers' Bank of Fairmont; William Charles; Charlotte Jane, now Mrs. Clement Roydes; Percy, who married Alice Ramsdale; Margaret Emily, now wife of H. W. Sinclair, an attorney of Fairmont; Francis Henry; George Hyde, who married Lillian Maude Ramsdale; Richard Fawcett, who wedded Mable Ramsdale; Annie and Henrietta, twins, the latter wedding J. A. Sinclair, proprietor of the Fairmont creamery; Lucy, Frederick and Edward L.

————◦❖◦❖◈❖◦❖◦————.

POWELL PEARSALL is a leading farmer and stock-raiser of section 22, Lake Sarah township, Murray county, Minnesota. He located in the county in 1870, and homesteaded his present place. He resides on the shores of Lake Sarah and has a grove of natural timber. Our subject has the honor of being one of the first settlers of the township and of plowing the first furrow ever turned in the township in June, 1870, on section 22. He was the first man to locate with his family in Lake Sarah township. He assisted in the organization of the township and was a member of the second board of township supervisors. He has always taken

an active part in matters of a public nature and has held various official positions. He has been district treasurer of district No. 9 for seven years, has been town supervisor everal times and has always taken an active part in these affairs.

Mr. Pearsall was born in Greene county, New York, in the village of New Baltimore, August 13, 1828. He resided in that place until twenty-one years of age, when he removed to Columbia county, Wisconsin. While in New York State he had been working for himself during most of the time after nine years of age. After coming to Wisconsin he worked at the blacksmith's trade for six years, having learned that trade in New York State. After six years he went to Grand Rapids, Wisconsin, and here engaged in lumbering during the summer and worked in the woods during the winters. In 1864 he left Wisconsin, coming to Winona county, Minnesota, where he resided one year on a farm. Removing thence he settled in Blue Earth county, and in 1870 came to Murray county, as has already been stated.

The father of the subject of our sketch was Samuel Pearsall, a shoemaker by trade. He was born on Long Island and died in about 1860. The mother died in Ohio in 1865. In the father's family there were thirteen children—Matilda, Lydia A., Loman, Fremont, Semantha, Samuel, Powell, William Henry, Jane, Hannah E., John, James I. and Lucy A. Five of these sons served in the Union army during the War of the Rebellion. All the sons are living; all the daughters are dead.

These gentlemen whose names appears at the head of this sketch was married February 5, 1862, in Adams county, Wisconsin, to Miss Mary Jane Hale, a native of Henderson, Jefferson county, New York, where she was born March 1, 1844. At one and a half years of age her parents moved to Kenosha county, Wisconsin, where she was educated in the town of Chester. She was the daughter of O. W. Hale, a farmer. He was born in Jefferson county, New York, and died in McFerson, Blue Earth county, Minnesota, in 1877. Her mother's maiden name was Arthusa Haven, a native of Massachusetts, and still living. There were five children in the Hale family—Larve, Leonora, Ann E. Mary J. and Orville. Mr. and Mrs. Pearsall have two children—Milford M. and Florence A. The latter is married.

For years the subject of our sketch affiliated with the Grange movement in politics, but is now and has been for some time a stanch republican. He is a man of excellent characteristics and is well liked both as a man and citizen by all who know him.

EORGE P. MENNIE is one of the early settlers and best known citizens of Hendricks township, Lincoln county, Minnesota. He is now living on section 26, where he has a fine farm, upon which are comfortable buildings and other improvements, which betoken thrift and hard work. Mr. Mennie was born in the township of Dover, Racine county, Wisconsin, March 22, 1847. He was the son of Peter L. and Margaret (Duffes) Mennie.

The parents of the subject of our sketch were both natives of Scotland. The father was a son of George Mennie, a farmer of Aberdeenshire, Scotland, who died when his son Peter was seven years old, his wife having died about two years previous. Peter L. worked for farmers until he was seventeen years old, and then took passage on a sailing vessel for America, arriving after a voyage of two months. He went to Canada, where he had a brother living, and remained for two years. There he became acquainted with the lady who afterward became his wife. She came to Canada from Scotland

in 1834. They had a very stormy voyage. lasting thirteen weeks, in which the masts of their ship were all blown overboard, and they completed the voyage with jury-masts. Their provisions gave out entirely when they were hundreds of miles from any port, and starvation stared them in the face, until they were supplied by another vessel that answered their signals of distress. John Duffes, the father of Margaret, was a well-to-do farmer. He had $60,000 willed to him in the old country that it was necessary for him to cross the ocean to get; but he had had enough of ocean travel, and never went after it. In 1836 Peter L. Mennie moved from Canada with the Duffes family to Illinois, where they remained two years. "and shook with ague," Peter L. working on the canal in Illinois for two years. In 1838 they removed to Racine county, Wisconsin. The father worked on the Erie canal as a "rip-rapper" for two seasons. He went from there to Mineral Point, Wisconsin, where he worked in the lead mines for two years. He then went to Racine county and bought a farm of eighty acres, and, in 1840, was married at Racine to Margaret Duffes. They resided on their farm for nine years, then sold out and moved to Green Lake county, and there engaged in farming. Their nearest market was Milwaukee—one hundred miles distant—where they had to go for all their supplies of flour. If they did not get goods to bring back for merchants their load of wheat would not pay the expenses of their trip. After a few years what was called "horse boats" (boats propelled by horses) came up the Fox river to Marquette, two miles from Peter L. Mennie's farm, with lumber, and took back wheat. Then times became better for the pioneer settlers of Green Lake county. In 1879 Peter L. Mennie sold his farm, with the intention of retiring, but he got the land fever, and came to Lincoln county, Minnesota, where the most of his children had taken land. He filed a homestead and tree claim on land in section 22, Hendricks township, commuting his homestead entry in 1880. From there he went to Portage City, Wisconsin, where he is now leading a retired life, enjoying the benefits of a long and well-spent career. He has been a man of considerable means, and has always been a representative citizen of the localities in which he has lived. He has served his neighbors and fellow-citizens in various official capacities. In the father's family there were nine children— John D., William G., George P., Mary Jane, Elsie E., Frank L., Ada A., James and Ella M., of whom seven are still living.

George P. Mennie, the subject of our present sketch, remained beneath the parental roof until attaining the age of seventeen. When he was seven years old he went to Marquette, to help drive his father's sheep to be washed. While there, his brothers and himself thought it would be fun to ride on planks in the lake, so they boarded their planks and started. George had two laths for poles to push the plank. He had not gone far when his laths would not reach the bottom and he made a break for shore But the water was nine feet deep and he could not swim. Just as he had given up all hope, he felt something hit his head. He made a grab and got hold of his brother's plank that had come to the rescue. The plank would not hold them both up, but it kept them out part of the time, until the other brother ran nearly half a mile for help. George was so near gone when he was got out that he did not know anything for some time. When he was a little shaver the Indians used to take great pleasure in scaring him. If they saw him away from the house they would get between him and the house, and yell at him to see the little "pale face" run, and then they would run after him. If his father was in the field he

would run to him. There are but few children now that know the pleasure in being chased by Indians. His time was employed in assisting in work on the home farm and attending the district schools. When he was about twelve years old, he was assisting his father to build a fence. He was holding the end of a log on a stone wall while his father fastened the other end. His father let his end fall and broke George's collar bone. His father told him "not to mind it, he could tell folks when he was a man that he *helped to build that fence.*" At seventeen he went to Little Rock, Arkansas, to drive team for the government during the last year of the war, and he then learned what it was to be an employ of Uncle Sam in war times. At St. Louis barracks all that were out at meal time were kept out by the guard until those that were in had got through eating and the tables set again. The guards were German and could not talk English. One night our subject was among the number that were out, and the crowd behind him crowded him up to the guard line. The guard motioned him to stand back, but he might as well have tried to back through a solid wall. The guard then charged him with his bayonet; put it through his pants legs several times; but the pants were heavy, and the point of the bayonet would go past his legs before it would cut the cloth. Finding that he was not doing much damage, he clubbed his gun and knocked George and three or four more down with it. A few days later George with others started for Little Rock on a steamer, on which they were doled out about one-third the rations that they were entitled to. When they reached Cairo the hind end of the steamer came against a barge and all that could jumped for shore. Some of our subject's friends were put in to guard the provisions and his little band of seven filled their satchels. They did not go hungry thereafter until they reached Little Rock, in December, there they stayed for three days without tents or blankets. From there they went to Duvall's Bluffs for the winter,where they were regularly robbed of three-fourths of their rations. They patched out by going to the landing when steamers were unloading and mixing with the laborers that were unloading, and, picking up a box of "hard tack," they would carry it to the levy and drop it on a stone where their comrades were ready to help grab the contents. From the 22d of December, 1864, to January 4, 1865, all they had to eat was the corn that they stole from the pile from which the mules were fed, yet the United States storehouses were full of supplies. What a dreary Christmas and New-Year's feast were spent! The teams never had to go hungry. Our subject was taken sick soon after and sent to Little Rock, where he spent two months. After he had been there about one month he commenced to get better and had a good appetite, but they said that the one little piece of bread and cup of tea were all he could have. The reason they gave was that if they gave enough to eat the sick would want to stay there all the time—so they were literally starved out. In March he was discharged. He then went back home on the steamboat "Albert Lea." At Helena the steamboat was chartered to go to Vicksburg. It took three weeks to reach St. Louis. And when he reached home his father did not know him, he was so poor and thin. He remained at home one year and then went to the lumber woods and hired to go to St. Louis on a lumber raft. One of the pilots used to say that the scenery was worth the trip and it is fine, as they passed through the Dells at Kilbourn which people go to see from all over the United States. When they reached Little Bull falls the river was very high and there had been no lumber run over for days. That night (May 1st) it snowed

six inches and they found their clothes frozen to the lumber in the morning. They then commenced to run the lumber over the falls. It dove so that just below the falls there was not a man in sight—everyone clinging to ropes so as not to be swept away Three were drowned at the falls that day. Mr. Mennie continued to work amid the grand scenery of the lumber woods, and Wisconsin and Mississippi rivers for eight years, making his home at Portage City, after he was married. After these eight years of service in the pineries he returned to Portage City, and made that his ome for about two years. He then came ho Minnesota and settled in Olmsted county, tand engaged in farming for about two years. In 1878 he joined the little handful of early settlers in Lincoln county, and located the claim on which he now lives. Returning to Olmsted county, he remained there until the following spring, then returned for a short time to Lincoln county that he might fulfill the requirements of the law. In the fall of 1879 he moved his family to his land, and made a permanent residence.

The subject of our sketch was married to Miss Alice Wicks, September 6, 1866, at Montello, Wisconsin. This lady was a native of New York State. Her father moved to Green Lake county, when she was two years old. He died the following spring, leaving a wife and six small children in the wilderness to fight for a sustenance amongst hardships that are seldom endured by pioneer settlers. Many times their provisions were all gone, but kind neighbors learning their circumstances helped them to tide over until they could get more supplies. Mr. and Mrs. Mennie have been blessed with seven children—Maud (deceased), Margaret A. (deceased), Herbert (deceased), Jessie C., Earl G., Alice Ione and Madge L. Mr. Mennie has a hospitable home, and a pleasant and agreeable family.

Mr. Mennie's father always allowed his children to keep any money that they earned working for the neighbors at odd spells, when not busy on the home farm. They earned enough to buy them some sheep, working, and also catching quails, so that the three oldest had about $100 apiece when they left home.

During the early life of the subject of our sketch he was given good educational advantages in the district schools and acquired such an education as would fit him for the duties of almost any life. In politics he is an independent, supporting the best candidates for official positions rather than supporting parties. Independent and progressive in his thought, fearless and outspoken in regard to anything which he deems to be right, he has proven himself an important factor in the development and growth of Lincoln county and his abilities have been utilized in various ways in local governmental affairs. He has been chairman of the board of supervisors for one term, was pathmaster one term, and has been clerk of the school board for four years. Being one of the earliest settlers our subject is well known and esteemed for his enterprise and ability as a man and his loyalty and patriotism as a citizen. Possessed of generous qualities and public-spirited he has drawn to himself many friends and is looked upon as being one of most substantial and reliable farmers in the county.

F L. JANES, one of the attorneys of Pipestone City, Minnesota, located in that place January 1, 1884, since which time he has been actively engaged in the practice of his profession. He is a native of Fairfax county, Virginia, where he was born October 18, 1855. His parents were Charles E. and Martha (Reed) Janes, natives of Connecticut. For years the father was a manu-

facturer of paper and other articles and came to Wisconsin with his family, where he engaged in farming. From Wisconsin he came to the State of Minnesota and died in 1878 at Blue Earth City. The mother died about 1865. In the father's family there are four children living—Melville C., Josephine J., Clifford and our subject.

The subject of our sketch spent his early days in assisting his father on the home farm and attending school. He took a course of instruction in the Wisconsin State University at Madison, and studying law for some time was admitted to the bar in Minnesota in 1876. He commenced the practice of his profession at Madelia, Minnesota, and resided there for about eight years. He then came to Pipestone where he has since resided. While in Madelia he was county attorney for two years and resigned that position when he came to Pipestone. He was appointed judge of probate in 1885, and after holding that position for one year resigned.

Mr. Janes was married in the year 1879 to Miss Hattie C. Chase, of Lake Crystal, a daughter of A. J. Chase. Three children have blessed this union—Alexander L., Susie I. and Labelle C.

In politics Mr. Janes affiliates with the republican party and is an influential member of the Masonic fraternity. He is one of the leading attorneys of the county.

H ON. STEPHEN A. MILLER (deceased) was born January 7, 1816, in Perry county, Pennsylvania. After a youth of vicissitude he became a forwarding and commission merchant at Harrisburg, Pennsylvania, in 1837. In 1849 he was chosen prothonotary of Dauphin county, and from 1853 to 1855 was editor of the Harrisburg *Telegraph*. Then he became a flour inspector at Philadelphia, holding the office until 1858, when he removed to Minnesota and opened a store in St. Cloud. In 1861 he was appointed lieutenant-colonel of the First Minnesota Regiment, and acquitted himself with credit at the battle of Bull Run. In September, 1862, he was made colonel of the Seventh Minnesota Regiment, and the same year was nominated by the president and confirmed brigadier-general of volunteers. In 1863 he was elected governor of Minnesota, and in January, 1863, entered upon his duties and served the term of two years. In 1873 he was a member of the lower house of the legislature, and in 1876 was one of the presidential electors. During the last years of his life he was a land agent of the St. Paul & Sioux City Railroad, and was located at Worthington, Minnesota, where he became one of the most influential citizens. His death occurred in 1881.

NICHOLAS BURGER, a prosperous farmer of Delton township, Cottonwood county, Minnesota, is a native of Germany, being born in Baden, in that country, September 10, 1841. His parents, Martin and Kresenzia (Burger) Burger, natives of Germany, were farmers by occupation.

Our subject received his early training on the home farm and was given good educational advantages. He came to the United States in 1861 and learned the butcher's trade in the suburbs of New York City, remaining there until 1862. He then enlisted in Captain Ames' Battery L, Fifth United States Light Artillery, and served until June, 1865, when he was honorably discharged. Mr. Burger participated in fifty-two battles and engagements. He was wounded at Bunker Hill, Virginia, but was only in the hospital a short time. He was kicked by a horse, having sustained a fracture of one of his legs and was laid up from August till November. His company were in the heat of battle at Winchester, Virginia, June 13, 14, 15, 1863, where they were taken prisoners and our subject removed to Libby prison. He was kept there for two days, and then the whole company was moved to Belle Island, where after twenty days they were paroled and then sent to Annapolis, Maryland, where they were soon exchanged. They immediately returned to active service again. After his discharge Mr. Burger went to Chicago and worked at his trade until 1874, when he went to Brown county, Minnesota, and rented a farm, a short distance from Sleepy Eye. Only one year had passed when he came to Cottonwood county and took a homestead where he now lives. He went through the grasshopper suffering from 1874 till 1878.

Mr. Burger was married in Chicago, December 14, 1868, to Miss Matilda Schwieger, daughter of Ferdinand and Fredricka (Moss) Schwieger, natives of Prussia. This lady was born in that country July 6, 1846. Mr. and Mrs. Burger have been blessed with the following named children—Albert, Bertha, Frank, Matilda, Emilia, Helena, August and Martha.

On coming to this county our subject was in straitened circumstances and had but little means. He has, however, by perseverance and thrift succeeded in putting his farm in excellent condition, providing it with good improvements. His pioneer cabin was 12x14 feet, while now he resides in a neat and comfortable one-and-a-half-story house and has other out-buildings of like commodious proportions. Mr. Burger has taken an active interest in public matters and has been township treasurer and chairman of the board of supervisors and school treasurer. He is a man of good character and large influence in the township. He is afflicted with asthma contracted during the war at Belle Island. He has been an invalid ever since and has suffered a great deal. In 1885 he took a trip across the ocean, thinking that this might cure him, but it was a failure and he still suffers greatly.

JOHN AUGUST JAHNKE resides on section 30, Rose Hill township, Cottonwood county, Minnesota. The place of his nativity is found in Germany, where he was born April 26, 1842. His parents, Michael and Mary (Jess) Jahnke, were natives of Germany, and lived in that country throughout their lives. The father died in 1860, having for years been engaged in agricultural pursuits. The mother died in 1889, at a ripe old age.

Until he was fifteen years of age the subject of our sketch resided on the home farm, where he received his education in the district school. On reaching the age just mentioned, he left his home, going to the city to learn the shoemaker's trade. Entering as an apprentice under a very hard and austere master, he completed his trade, learning all necessary to make a master of himself at this trade. At the age of twenty-one he was enlisted in the Prussian army to serve as a soldier for three years. By an accident in disciplining the gun discharged, and the bullet passing through his third finger made a cripple of it. He was then dismissed by the Prussian government, as an invalid, from service, which granted him a pension, though very small, indeed. After that he traveled five years through Germany, where he gained an extensive knowledge of the life of that people, which was afterward of great use to him. He came to America July 3, 1866. Going to Illinois, he located in Chicago, where he found work in a boot and shoe factory for eleven years. Here, in this large and enterprising city, he found ample opportunity for gaining knowledge, which he eagerly sought after. As the separation between capital and labor became more extensive, he entered the labor party and devoted three years to the study of national economy. He strongly advocated the rights of the laboring men, and supported, wherever he could, its progress. He was one of the most active members of this party, and was looked on as the leader by his fellow-men.

Being provoked at the low wages received and dull times, he left Chicago and went to New Ulm, where he resided for two years, when he removed to his present location. He took forty acres as a homestead. The hardships of pioneer life on the prairies are untold. Beginning with no capital, he has greatly increased his property, and has thoroughly improved and provided his farm with buildings surrounded by one of the finest groves and gardens in the county. He is now engaged in raising cattle and horses of higher breed. He has worked hard to make his place one of the best grain and stock farms in the county, and has succeeded admirably in his enterprise, and has added 120 acres to his farm. He is an energetic and successful business man, and has accumulated considerable property, but has met with several reverses of fortune, having lost all he had in the Chicago fire of 1871. Mr. Jahnke is a man of excellent character, great honesty and integrity and is highly respected by all who know him. He has held the offices of his town successfully and never is out of a school office. He is a warm supporter of education, doing all he can to aid its progress. He has helped to build up his district, where they have one of the best schools and some of the most advanced pupils in the county, having secured an able and competent teacher, who has taught many successful terms in this district.

Mr. Jahnke was married August 13, 1865, to Julia Grams, daughter of Andrew Grams, a native of Germany. This union has been blessed with twelve children, seven of whom are living—Mary, Lizzie, Mattie, Rudolph, Alexander, Alma and Sophia. Mary, the eldest daughter, has received an excellent education, having been in the best normal schools of our country, and is now engaged in teaching and has met everywhere with success. Mrs. Jahnke is a Christian woman in the truest sense, a tender mother, devoting herself with great pains to bringing up her children as true men and women and useful citizens of the United States. The family are members of the Lutheran church. The father is not supporting any of the political parties at present, believing both parties wrong as to some of their principles. He is strongly for reform, believing that many evils could thus be avoided, and is in favor of telegraphs, railroads and some other large interests being placed under the government control.

A MUND OLSEN is a substantial farmer of Mason township, Murray county, Minnesota, and resides on section 28. He was born in Egersund, in the kingdom of Norway, March 1, 1839. His parents were Ole and Mary (Nilson) Teninson, both natives of Norway. The father was a farmer by occupation and operated a farm of his own in his native land. The subject of our sketch left his native country at the age of eighteen years. He was given good educational advantages, and during the last six months of his stay at home worked at shoemaking. He came to America when eighteen years old, landing at Quebec, whence, after remaining a few days, he went by boat to Montreal and thence to Chicago, and from there to La Crosse. Soon after he located in Vernon county, Wisconsin, where he remained two years engaged in working on various farms. November 14, 1861, our subject enlisted in Company A, Fifteenth Wisconsin Volunteer Infantry.

He served until the 20th day of December, 1864, when he was discharged at Chattanooga, Tennessee. He fought bravely and gallantly for the Union side, and participated in many hard-fought battles. He was at Island No. 10, and served with his regiment during the entire time of his service with the exception of a short time spent by him in the hospital. His regiment was with the army of the Cumberland. Our subject was wounded at the battle of Chickamauga and was in the hospital for some time. On being discharged he returned to Vernon county, Wisconsin, and engaged in farming until 1870. Then he started out with an ox team and drove through with his family to the place where he now lives. They were three weeks on the way. He settled on his claim as a homestead of 160 acres. He brought $700 and some cattle with him, and thought that he had sufficient to support himself and family. The grasshoppers came, however, and for four years he lost everything. At the end of that time he was in debt seven hundred dollars. During the last ten years, however, he has been gradually getting into better circumstances, and is now entirely out of debt, and has an excellent and well-ordered farm. His first market was at New Ulm, and during the winter of 1880, or the winter of the deep snows, the family ran out of flour, and were obliged to grind their wheat in a coffee-mill. These vexatious and trying circumstances, however, have all been forgotten in the prosperity with which our subject is now surrounded.

Mr. Olsen was married to Bertha M. Teninson, January 28, 1865. This lady was a native of Norway, and was the daughter of Tenis Teninson, who was also born in the old country. Mr. and Mrs. Olsen have been blessed with eight children—Josephine M., Tenis M., Oscar J., Bart, Bargena L., Amelia, Anna M. and Alma.

In politics the subject of our sketch affiliates with the republican party, and is a leading and influential member of the John A. Logan post, No. 162, Grand Army of the Republic, of Slayton. Since coming to the county he has taken an active interest in all matters pertaining to the general welfare, and has held various official positions. In every instance he has proven his efficiency, and has served with increasing popularity. He has been treasurer of the township for two years, and for one year has held the office of treasurer of the school district.

JOSEPH A. BIGHAM is one of the leading and most enterprising citizens of Tyler, Lincoln county, Minnesota, where he is engaged in carrying on an extensive hardware business. He is a son of John C. and Mary (Hannah) Bigham, natives of Ireland. The parents came to this country in early life, and located in Pennsylvania for three years; then moved to Illinois, where they lived one year, removing thence to Minnesota, and they now live in Marshfield township. They have ten children, who have all settled in Tyler, Minnesota. The father has been a farmer throughout his life, and is in prosperous circumstances.

Joseph A. Bigham was born in Mount Morris, Ogle county, Illinois, December 1, 1855. He resided with his parents on the farm, and was given the educational advantages furnished by the district schools until he was seventeen years of age. When he was one year old his parents removed to Wabasha county, Minnesota, where he received his early training and education. The journey from Illinois to Wabasha county, Minnesota, was made by the family with two yoke of oxen and one yoke of cows. On reaching manhood the subject of our sketch commenced farming for himself on rented land near his father's residence. He continued operating this property in partnership

with his brother, Robert A , for about three years, and during the last winter of their lease on this land he attended Bailey's Commercial College in Keokuk, Iowa. On graduating from that institution he returned to Minnesota, and at once engaged in mercantile business in partnership with his brother, Robert A., in Red Wing. This enterprise was not successful, and our subject lost all he had earned while engaged in farming. Then, in the fall of 1878, he came to Lincoln county and took a homestead on the northeast quarter of section 24 in Marshfield township. In the fall he returned to Wabasha county and taught school during the winter, returning to his claim the following spring. He broke some land and lived on the farm for about ten months, when he purchased the land from the government and obtained a patent. He then returned to Wabasha and taught for four months in the same school in which he had engaged before. At the end of this time he came to Marshfield village and purchased a one-half interest in a meat market in partnership with William Evans, in which business he continued for about six months. At the end of this time he sold out, and coming to Tyler studied law in partnership with Andrews & Dean, with whom he continued about a year. He was then admitted to the bar and commenced the active practice of his profession. Shortly after leaving the office of attorneys Andrews & Dean he took a trip to the Yellowstone Park and traveled extensively in the Western country for about two months. During the following two years he engaged in the practice of law and also to some extent in teaching school. The next line in which he engaged was that of purchasing grain for the Winona Mill Company, and after one year's continuance at this business he was honorably discharged on account of there not being grain sufficient to pay for keeping a buyer. Our subject then removed to Walworth county, Dakota, and after remaining three months returned and again commenced buying grain for the Winona Mill Company. He continued with this firm until December, 1887, when he entered the employ of C. R. Seafield, for whom he purchased grain until January, 1889. At this time his proprietor failed in business and our subject was engaged for about two months in settling up his business. He then purchased a hardware store at Tyler, owned by R. D. Cone & Co., of Winona. He has been engaged in this business ever since.

Mr. Bigham was married in Brookings, Dakota, July 4, 1882, to Miss Flora A. Hodgman, a daughter of Edward and Artemetia A. (McCalpin) Hodgman, natives of Vermont and New York, respectively. Miss Hodgman was born in Manitowoc, Wis., September 22, 1866. This union has been blessed with two children—Gertie and Charles Eugene.

Mr. Bigham has been intimately associated with all business projects in the village in which he is located since he first made settlement there. He has aided largely both financially and otherwise in bringing about the present financial and business development of the village, and is looked upon as one of the most substantial citizens of the place. He is a careful and systematic business man and has built up a large trade. In affairs of local government he takes an active part and has been president of the village council for some time and is the present village attorney. He is a member of the Temple of Honor, Independent Order Good Templars and Ancient Order United Workmen. He is a man of the strictest integrity and is respected by all with whom he comes in contact. In the fall of 1889 Mr. Bigham was nominated as a candidate for the Minnesota legislature on the prohibition ticket. He ran away ahead of his ticket, but was defeated by a small majority.

HORACE H. GILMORE is one of the leading and influential farmers of Sweet township, Pipestone county, Minnesota. He has an excellent farm and a pleasant home on section 34, where he located in the spring of 1878. When Mr. Gilmore settled on his farm not a dwelling-house was within sight, and nothing could be seen save the gently undulating prairie as far as the eye could reach. He became one of the organizers of the township and has been intimately identified with all public interests ever since. When he came to the county, what is now the prosperous village of Pipestone, was composed of but two or three buildings—a dwelling owned by Mr. Sweet, Dr. Carr's office, and a small postoffice building, 10x12 feet, then in the course of construction.

Mr. Gilmore was born in Jefferson county, Wisconsin, April 25, 1847. He is the son of Edmund and Sarah (Doty) Gilmore. The parents were natives of the State of Vermont. The father is still living at the age of eighty-four years, and is a resident of Juneau county, Wisconsin. The mother died in Jefferson county, Wisconsin, June 4, 1856. The father's family remained in the State of Vermont until the fall of 1840, when they removed to Jefferson county, Wisconsin, settling on government land and engaging in farming. Here the family remained for a quarter of a century, removing thence to Juneau county, where the father now lives. In the father's family there were eight children.

The subject of our sketch remained beneath the parental roof until he reached the age of thirteen years, up to which time he had assisted in work on the home farm and attended the district school. For about eight months, at this time, he engaged in work for a neighboring farmer, after which returned to the parental home and attended school during the ensuing winter months. The following summer he again found employment on adjoining farms and the next winter attended the district school. The following spring he removed to Juneau county, Wis., and found employment with a lumber firm by the name of T. Weston & Co. He continued a satisfactory and profitable connection with this firm until June 6, 1864, when he enlisted in Company E, Forty-first Wisconsin Infantry. His service in the Union army continued until September 23d of that year, when he was discharged. He then returned to Wisconsin and engaged in the lumber business in the employ of the same firm for which he had worked before he went into the service. He continued with this firm until in the spring of 1878, when he started to come to Minnesota by team. He left his family behind him in Wisconsin, and drove through to Pipestone county, where he homestraded the land on which he now lives. His wife and family came to the township a few months later.

Mr. Gilmore was married November 17, 1874, to Miss Eliza Donaldson, a native of Sauk county, Wisconsin. She was a daughter of J. R. and M. A. (Waddell) Donaldson, the father a native of New York, and the mother a native of Ohio. Her father died in 1860; the mother is still living. Mr. and Mrs. Gilmore have been blessed with two children, both boys and both living—Robert E. and Charles C.

The political faith of the subject of our sketch is with the republican party. Circumstances and educational facilities were such during the early life of our subject that it was almost impossible for him to obtain a thorough education in the schools. He is, however, a close observer, and an eager reader of current events, and by this means has become thoroughly acquainted with the practical side of life. He is a man of excellent judgment and a worthy adviser in all matters pertaining to the public welfare. He is looked upon as being one of the solid and substantial farmers of the township and is respected by all. His farming interests have all prospered in his hands, and, although when coming to the township, he had but a team and wagon, and a few household goods and seventy dollars in money, he has accumulated considerable means and has now a comfortable home, and owns 160 acres of fine land.

EDWARD SPORNITZ is at present the popular and efficient station agent at Verdi village, Lincoln county, Minnesota. He was born in Chatfield, Minnesota, April 11, 1867.

The parents of the subject of our sketch were J. Robert and Elmira C. Spornitz, the former a native of Prussia and the latter a native of New York. The father located in Minnesota in the village of Chatfield, in 1865, and left that place in about 1877, locating in Eyota, of which place he is now a reliable citizen. He is a harness-maker by trade.

The subject of our sketch followed the parents in their various moves, receiving his education in Chatfield and Eyota. He continued residing with his parents, attending school until he was fifteen years old, and then found work on a farm during one summer and fall. He was then struck down with typhoid fever, which left him in a bad condition, as far as health was concerned. He was sick for some two years. He then commenced studying telegraphy at Eyota, where he remained about a year, after which he obtained a position as telegrapher at Elkton, Dakota. After two months he was sent to Kent, Minnesota, and three months later removed to Lake Benton. He became quite an expert operator, and was on the night force for some six months at Lake Benton. From thence he went to Volga, Dakota, as assistant operator, and six months later, February 22, 1888, took charge of the station at Verdi village. In politics the subject of our sketch affiliates with the republican party, and is an influential member of the Independent Order of Odd Fellows. Mr. Spornitz was married November 29, 1888, to Miss Kate Bailey.

JOHN KNOWLES is an enterprising and successful farmer and stock raiser residing on section 20, Amboy township, Cottonwood county, Minn. He located in the county in the fall of 1878, and has become one of its most prominent residents. The place of his nativity is found in Grafton county, New Hampshire, where he was born April 30, 1843.

Our subject's father was Hon. E. C. Knowles, a carpenter by occupation, and a native of New Hampshire, in which State he was reared and educated. For some ten or or twelve years he engaged at railroad carpenter work. He then came to Minnesota, and located in Dakota county, where he farmed for one year, and then went to Rice county, where he lived for thirty years on a farm, after which he removed to Lane county, Oregon. Our subject's mother's name before her marriage was Lucinda Atwood, a native of New Hampshire, and is still living. In the father's family there were eight children—John, Mary, Sarah Jane, Albert P., Ezekiel, Frank, Ella and George Orrin. While living in Rice county E. C. Knowles at one time represented the county in the State legislature.

The early training and education of our subject was received in Grafton county, New Hampshire, where he remained until thirteen years old; then, with his parents, he came to Dakota county, Minnesota, where he remained some two years. His education was completed in the township of Webster, Rice county, in a log school house, when he was twenty years of age. He continued with his father, sharing the benefits of the parental home life, until he was twenty-one years

of age. He had, however, depended considerably upon himself since eighteen years of age. In 1859 he went to Goodhue county two years, and then moved to Rice county, engaging in farming for seventeen years. His next move was to Brown county, where he remained until making his location as one of the early settlers of Amboy township, Cottonwood county. He pre-empted his present place of 160 acres, and has succeeded in making his place one of the best in the township. He has 320 acres of fine land. He has always taken an active interest in public matters, and has held various official positions with honor and credit. He has been township supervisor several times, clerk of school district No. 14 for five years, township assessor, etc. In politics Mr. Knowles affiliates with the republican party, and is a leading member of the Grange, and is one of the representative men of the county.

Mr. Knowles was married August 29, 1872, to Miss Levenia Armstrong, a native of Nova Scotia, where she was born May 27, 1855. Her early training was received in that country until she was fourteen years of age, when she came to Blue Earth county with her parents, who now reside in Washington Territory. Her parents were Charles and Sibyl (Chute) Armstrong, farmers and natives of Nova Scotia. Miss Armstrong was one of nine children—Wallace, Henrietta, Mary, Burton, Edward, Levenia, Hanford, Albert and Ida Belle. Mr. and Mrs. Knowles have seven children—Esther A., Emma Myrtle, Lillie Pearl, Ella Sibyl, E. C., Burton Leon and Hattie Belle.

DEACON D. N. WARE is the pioneer lumber dealer of Winnebago City, Faribault county, Minnesota. He made his location in the city in 1767 and has resided here ever since. He is a native of Massachusetts, where he was born November 4, 1825.

The parents of the subject of our sketch were Daniel and Lydia (Jennings) Ware, natives of Massachusetts. The father was a contractor and builder by occupation and followed that line of business until within fifteen years of the time of his death, when he turned his attention to farming. He died in 1863. The mother died in 1865. Daniel Ware's parents were Daniel and Nabby (Newell) Ware, natives of Massachusetts and farmers by occupation. The latter Daniel's father was Joshua Ware, of English descent. Daniel, senior, was a soldier in the War of the Revolution and served at the battle of Bunker Hill. After his death his wife received a pension on account of this Revolutionary service of her husband. The mother of the subject of our sketch was the daughter of parents born in Massachusetts and who were of English descent.

Deacon Ware was the only child, and until sixteen years of age continued in the family of his parents, being given good educational advantages. He assisted in work on the home farm, and when sixteen engaged in work at the boot and shoe business in Natick, Massachusetts, fourteen miles from Boston. This he continued until he was twenty-eight years of age, then went to Newton, Mass., where he was engaged in the express business. In 1867 he came to Winnebago City, where he has since lived. The following year he built his present excellent and commodious dwelling-house of brick and drew what lumber was used forty-six miles, from Waseca. The lime in this building was drawn from New Ulm, a distance of sixty miles. On coming to the city our subject first intended to engage in farming, but for a time engaged in dealing in real estate and loaned money. On the advent of the railroad our subject engaged in the lumber business and also added wood and coal, having been engaged in these lines ever since. He has been one of Winnebago City's most prominent citizens and has held various official positions, among them being that of village councilman, to which he was elected in 1887-88. Formerly he affiliated with the republican party, but being a strong temperance man, he now affiliates with the prohibition party.

In the year 1846 Mr. Ware was married to Miss Gabriella Fuller, of Massachusetts, a daughter of Benjamin and Suky (Jackson) Fuller, natives of Massachusetts. The parents were farmers by occupation. Mr. and Mrs. Ware have had two sons—Frank N., who married Miss Marion Turner, by whom he had the following children—Alta, Lela and Elsie, and Winfield F. The genealogy of Mrs. Ware's family is traced somewhat as follows: her father, Benjamin, was a native of Massachusetts, and was the son of Benjamin Fuller, whose father was Thomas Fuller, all of whom were prominent men in the State of Massachusetts.

The subject of our sketch has a beautiful home in the southern part of the city, and is one of Faribault county's most esteemed citizens. He is a man of excellent principles, of careful, systematic business habits, and has built up an extensive trade.

----→-◈-◆◈◆-◈-◆----

JOHN A. ARMSTRONG, banker of Winnebago City, Faribault county, Minnesota, is one of the best known and most prominent and influential citizens of Southern Minnesota. He is proprietor of the Winnbago City Bank. He located in the city in 1870 and opened his bank the same fall and in 1877 built his present neat business building.

Mr. Armrtrong is a native of Washington county, New York, where he was born in the year 1834. His parents were Archibald and Nancy (Donaldson) Armstrong, natives of New York State. His parents were of Scotch descent and were farmers by occupation. The father died in 1860 and the mother passed from this life in 1887. They were members of the Presbyterian church in which society they wielded a strong influence and of which the father was a trustee for many years. There were nine children in the father's family—Jane. E., now Mrs. Mack; Archibald, Alice, now Mrs. Robertson; Christa, now Mrs. McFarland; Martha H., now Mrs. Reid; Mary, now Mrs. Beverage; Margaret, now Mrs. McCollum; Isabel, now Mrs. Edie, and John A.

Mr. Armstrong was reared on a farm and received a good common-school education. In early life he also engaged to some extent in the mercantile business and in 1857 came West, locating in the city of Owatonna, Minnesota. He resided in that place for two years and was engaged in the drug and grocery business. He then returned to the East and engaged in the mercantile business in Washington county, New York, for two years, after which he returned to Owatonna in the early part of May, 1861. Our subject was in the city of New York buying goods for his business at Owatonna, Minnesota, when the first gun was fired on Fort Sumter. Coming to Owatonna he remained in business in that city until 1867, when he sold out and removed to Winnebago City.

While in Owatonna he put up several of the best buildings in the place. He built the block now occupied by the First National Bank and also a beautiful home where Pillsbury hall now stands. He also purchased considerable land in the county and was quite successful in his financial investments. Since coming to Winnebago he has taken an active interest in public improvements and owns the finest residence in the village. He is one of the largest land proprietors in the city and owns a number of farms in Faribault and Martin counties. He is a trustee and treasurer of the Baptist college of Winnebago City and is a member of the Presbyterian church. He is public-spirited, generous to a fault, and is one of the most enterprising and prominent men in Faribault county. In politics he affiliates with the republican party.

Mr. Armstrong was married in 1859 to Miss Carrie Carl of Washington county, New York. She died in June, 1874, at Winnebago City, leaving two children—James C. and George C. The second marriage of Mr. Armstrong took place in December, 1875, when he was wedded to Miss Frank Minor, of Winnebago City, and daughter of C. B. Minor. This latter union has been blessed with one child—J. Archibald. Mrs. Armstrong is one of the most estimable and highly respected ladies of Winnebago City, she is a member of the Women's Christian Temperance Union and takes an active interest in all affairs of that organization. She is president of the Young Ladies' Missionary Society of the village and is deeply interested in religious work, having been a teacher in the Sunday-school for a number of years.

JOHN L FERING located on section 2, Highwater township, Cottonwood county, Minnesota, in the year 1869. He located a soldiers' claim of 160 acres and resided thereon for seven years. He then sold out and went to Winneshiek county, Iowa, and engaged in farming for two years, when he returned to Highwater township, locating again on section 2, where he has since remained. During the grasshopper raids our subject was obliged to go to Iowa to obtain means with which to support his family, not being able to obtain sufficient for that purpose on his farm in Cottonwood county. There were but four or five other families in the township when he came, their names being Lott, Fering, Peterson and Erickson. Our subject assisted in the organization of his township and also of school district No. 28.

The gentleman of whom this sketch treats is a native of the kingdom of Norway, his birth occurring August 1, 1841. His father, Lars Fering, was a farmer by occupation, who came to the United States in about 1851, having come from his native country to Canada the year previous. On coming to the States he made Milwaukee, Wisconsin, his headquarters for one year. Then the family removed to Winneshiek county, Iowa. The father is now living in Highwater township. Our subject's mother's name was Caroline Feering, a native of Norway, and who died in 1881.

Until nine years of age the subject of this sketch was reared in his native country. He then emigrated to America with his parents and finally located with them in Winneshiek county, Iowa, where he received his education. Mr. Fering enlisted February 28, 1862, in the Sixteenth Regiment, United States regulars, and was discharged February 28, 1865, at Lookout Mountain, Tennessee. Our subject participated in the following-named battles—Buzzard Roost, Resaca, Marietta, Jonesborough, Chattahoochie river, Kenesaw, Atlanta, etc. Mr. Fering was severely wounded at the battle of Atlanta, in August, 1864, and was in the hospital at Atlanta and Chattanooga for three months, and also a short time at hospital No. 18, at Nashville, Tennessee. After being transferred to Lookout Mountain our subject served with his regiment for three months, when he was discharged, and soon afterward returned to his home in Winneshiek county, Iowa, from whence, after two years' residence, he came to his present location.

Mr. Fering was married in August, 1867, to Miss Richel Iverson, who was born near Stoughtonville, Wisconsin, and reared and educated in Winneshiek county, Iowa. Her parents were Lars and Susan Iverson, who were farmers in Highland township, of the county last above named. Mrs. Fering died in November, 1887, and was buried in Westbrook township. She was a member of the Lutheran church, and her death was greatly mourned by a large circle of loving friends. Mr. and Mrs. Fering had ten children—Lewis, Sever, Laura, Julia, Iver, Christ, Otto, Caroline, John R. and Gertie.

In politics the subject of our sketch is a stanch republican, and with his family, belongs to the Lutheran church. Mr. Fering is a man of wide influence, is a respected and representative citizen, and is a leading member of the Grand Army of the Republic.

EDGAR ORLANDO JENNINGS is one of the prominent and most influential citizens of Lincoln county, Minnesota. He is located on a fine farm on section 32 of Lake Stay township. Mr. Jennings is the son of Eumenus and Lydia (Hoskins) Jennings, the former a native of New York, and the latter a native of Massachusetts.

The subject of our sketch was born in Fort Brewerton, New York, June 8, 1849. His father was a saddler by trade and remained engaged in that business in Fort Brewerton until 1858. Then the family moved, our subject accompanying them, to Lake county, Illinois, where the father purchased a farm and engaged in agricultural pursuits. They continued in that locality, our subject being given good educational advantages, for about three years, when the parents sold out and removed to Freeborn county, Minnesota, locating about five miles west of Albert Lea. Here our subject received thorough instructions in the district schools and assisted his father on the farm until he was twenty-one years of age. He then engaged in work on adjoining farms, continuing in the vicinity of Albert Lea for about three years. He then went north into the pineries and engaged for seven seasons in rafting between St. Paul and St. Louis. At the end of this period he located in Alden, Minnesota, and opened a butcher shop, in which line he continued for about a year, meeting with good success. He then sold out, and in 1878 removed to Lake Stay township, Lincoln county, and settled on a homestead and tree claim, where he now lives. Since 1878 he has been a permanent resident and has occupied his attention principally with general farming and stock-raising. He has associated himself with all projects tending to public development and improvement, and has assisted largely in the administration of local affairs.

Mr. Jennings was united in the holy bonds of matrimony in Albert Lea, March 12, 1877, to Miss Mary G. Wadsworth. This lady was born in Freeborn county, Minnesota, October 19, 1859, and received her early training and education in the city of Albert Lea. She was a daughter of George and Mary (Barns) Wadsworth, both natives of Ohio, and who are both dead. Mr. and Mrs. Wadsworth were among the pioneer settlers of Freeborn county, to which county they came from Cuyahoga Falls, Ohio. Mr. and Mrs. Jennings have been blessed with three children—Guy, Nellie and Bessie.

The business abilities of our subject are of a high character, and have been recognized and utilized in various ways by his fellow-citizens. He has held the office of county commissioner for one year, has been assessor of his township for five years, and for three years has been treasurer of his school district. In all of these positions, and especially in the first, he has proven his capabilities as an official and his loyalty as a citizen. He has aided materially in the various projects for public improvement which have come before the board of county commissioners, and has always championed anything which was in the line of a needed or desirable improvement. His counsels in the deliberations of the honorable body to which he belongs have always been of the wisest and most judicious character, and his influence and work have been highly appreciated. Besides these matters he also takes an active interest in the affairs of the Ancient Order of United Workmen, and is a member of the lodge at Tyler. He has been very successful in his farming operations, and has surrounded himself with buildings and other improvements so essential to the successful management of a large farm. He has a very comfortable and pleasant frame dwelling-house, and has about 140 acres under cultivation. His residence is located on the south side of Lake Stay, about seventeen acres of his land running down into the lake. This is one of the most beautiful lakes in the county, and on account of the abundance of game thereabouts every fall it is the resort for hunters and sportsmen. Mr. Jennings is a man of high character, of excellent systematic business habits, and is held in high esteem by all who know him. When he commenced in life he was a poor young man, with no means, and nothing but his own efforts to depend upon. By hard work and judicious management he has accumulated considerable means, and has risen to a leading position among the farmers of Lincoln county.

ORAN MARTIN SOUTHWELL, deceased, was the son of Martin and Hulda Jane (Candy) Southwell, pioneer settlers of Michigan. These people located in that State in a very early day, and were forty miles from market, having to go that distance to Detroit with an ox team. Oran Southwell was born in Romeo, Michigan, April 10, 1835, and resided in that locality with his parents for a number of years. July 19, 1855, he was married, and the following year removed to Rutland, Illinois, where he resided until February, 1858. Removing thence he located in Winona, Illinois, where his death occurred February 21, 1879.

Mr. Southwell was a loyal citizen, and was a man of patriotic spirit, and in August, 1862, he enlisted in Company H, One Hundred and Fourth Illinois Volunteer Infantry, and was soon afterward elected orderly sergeant of his company. In April, 1863, for gallant service he was appointed as second lieutenant, which position he held during the remainder of the summer and fall of that year. Then came the sudden death of Lieutenant Davidson, and the resignation of Captain Ludington, and our subject was at once appointed to the captaincy of his company, receiving his commission February 22, 1864. He was severely wounded in the knee at the battle of Chickamauga, September 23, 1863. This wound troubled him more or less up to the time of his death. He was also shot through the thigh in the battle of Kenesaw Mountain, June 18, 1864. In consequence of these wounds he tendered his resignation, which was accepted December 20, 1864. He then returned to Wenona, and in April, 1865, he formed a partnership with Dr. Odor and engaged in the drug business. In November, 1867, Isaac Vaughn purchased Dr. Odor's interest and the firm became Southwell & Vaughn. Mr. Southwell resided in that city until his death. He was a man of the highest integrity of character and in business affairs he enjoyed the reputation of being prompt, reliable and correct. He was a leading and consistent member of the Presbyterian church, and held a high position in the Masonic fraternity, of which he was master for years. He was also influential in the Independent Order of Odd Fellows lodge, of which he was vice-grand for some time. He took an active interest in State military affairs, and bent all his energies to perfecting the organization of the Wenona guards, of which he was captain.

He was a man of large intelligence, possessed of broad, practical ideas, and was acknowledged to be one of the leading and most influential citizens of Wenona. In life he was respected, and his presence has been sadly missed by his business associates and many warm friends. The funeral was conducted by the Wenona guards, the procession being formed somewhat as follows: first came the Wenona and visiting lodges of Independent Order of Odd Fellows, then the Wenona and visiting lodges of Ancient Free and Accepted Masons, and then followed the hearse, after which came carriages of relatives and friends.

Mr. Southwell was married July 19, 1855, to Sarah A. Smith, a daughter of Orris and Mary (Morley) Smith. This union was blessed with the following-named children— Flora S., now Mrs. W. J. McAllister; Mary S., now Mrs. A. Moore; Jessie S., now Mrs. W. H. Winter; and Sarah S., now Mrs. T. Lowe.

After the death of Mr. Southwell his widow remained in Wenona about five years. Then she came to Murray county, and, in March, 1884, located in the village of Slayton. Mrs. Southwell was appointed postmistress of the village in December, 1885. She has held the position ever since and has become exceedingly popular. She is a lady of excellent qualities and is well known and highly respected. She is a member of the Presbyterian church.

CARTER DEAN is county attorney of Pipestone county, Minnesota. He came to Pipestone city on the 16th of April, 1880, and has ever since been engaged in the practice of his profession. He has been county attorney ever since November 28, 1880. He is a native of Bureau county, Illinois, where he was born March 22, 1857. His parents were Jonathan P. and Julia A.

(Durland) Dean, natives of New Jersey. His father was a farmer and miller at Lamoille, Illinois.

The subject of our sketch spent his younger days on the farm and was given a good common-school education. He remained at home until he was sixteen years of age and then followed the profession of teaching. He was a teacher in the Clarion graded schools. At eighteen years of age he entered the University of Illinois and remained three years. In 1879 he graduated from the law department of the State University of Illinois, then taught one year in Illinois, and soon after came to Pipestone and made a permanent location. After coming to the county he took an active part in political affairs and became an able assistant in the management of the campaigns.

Mr. Dean was married in November, 1882, to Miss Minnie Lewis, of Lamoille, Illinois. She was a daughter of William and Charlotte (Rix) Lewis, natives of Vermont and Maryland. Mr. and Mrs. Dean have one son, William L.

The subject of our sketch is one of the prominent attorneys and leading citizens of Pipestone county, and has made an excellent official.

JOHN L. CASS is the editor of the *Lake Benton News*. He has ably conducted the various departments of his newspaper enterprise and has built up for himself an excellent reputation as an editor and a large patronage for his newspaper. He has one of the brightest, newsiest sheets to be found in southern Minnesota, and through its columns reaches the minds and consciences of many of Lincoln county's prominent citizens and also prominent people in other and adjoining counties.

Mr. Cass is the son of Andrew and Fannie (Green) Cass, natives of New York. He was born in Richmond, Walworth county, Wisconsin, April 14, 1851. His parents had moved to Wisconsin some time before our subject's birth. When he was a small boy his parents moved to Mauston, Juneau county, where our subject received the most of his education. In August, 1864, the family moved to Owatonna, Minnesota, and puachased a farm near Havana station. Here our subject was given good educational advantages in the district schools and later for a time attended the high school in Owatonna. He then taught school for some six terms and in 1876 he entered the law university at Ann Arbor, Michigan, remaining in that institution for two terms. He then taught one term of school in Michigan, and in the spring of 1877 returned to Owatonna. Entering the political field in the fall he was nominated by the democratic party for clerk of the court. He worked hard and faithfully and only failed to capture the coveted prize by about one hundred votes, although at that time the county was from eight hundred to one thousand votes republican majority. In the winter of 1877–8 our subject taught school near Owatonna and spent some of his time in making collections until April 29, 1879. He then came to Lincoln county and engaged in the practice of law in Marshfield until September 14th, when he made his location in Lake Benton. He resumed his practice of law on a small scale until March 4, 1880, when he was admitted to the bar. After this he made a specialty of the legal profession and built up a large and profitable clientage. March 16, 1887, he purchased the newspaper outfit owned by Charles M. Morse and engaged in publishing a newspaper. Since 1887 our subject has devoted most of his time to his editorial work. Since making his location in Lincoln county Mr. Cass has become one of the most prominent and influential citizens of the county. He has taken an active interest in all public projects and is intimately associated with the affairs of county government and also in the governmental affairs of the township in which he has lived. He has been deputy county treasurer and was county attorney one term by election and one term by appointment. He is a member of Lake Benton Lodge, No. 146, Ancient Free and Accepted Masons, of which he has been secretary for a long time. Mr. Cass has been quite successful in his financial affairs, being possessed of good business qualifications, and has accumulated considerable means. He is an able and fearless writer, and with whatever subject he deals is noted for his discernment and for his decisive words, which cut along sharp lines between what he deems right and the wrong. In political matters he ably seconds and defends the principles of the democratic party and has become quite prominent in the local councils of that organization.

Miss Hannah E. Cass is the owner of the paper, of which Mr. Cass is the editor.

MYRON BARR located in Cottonwood county, Minnesota, settling on section 10, of Lakeside township, in 1870. He was born in Erie county, New York, February 3, 1834.

The gentleman whose name appears at the head of this sketch, is the son of Rufus B. Barr, a native of Shenango county, New York, where he lived until his death, in May, 1887. He was a cooper by trade, in early life, and later engaged in farming, and during the last five or six years of his life engaged in the hardware business. He was a leading citizen, and at his death was seventy-six years of age. He was a consistent member of the Methodist Episcopal church. Myron Barr's mother's maiden name was Mary Blinebury, a native of Dutchess county, New York, and educated in Shenango county. She was an estimable Christian lady, a member of the Methodist Episcopal church, and died in 1862. Our subject's grandfather was Haran Barr, a miller by trade. The grandfather of our subject, on the mother's side, was David Blinebury, a native of the State of New York, where he was engaged in the furniture business. Our subject is one of five living children—Myron, Francis L., Mary Jane, Henry C. and Jasper N.

Until attaining his majority our subject resided in his native State; received a good common-school education, and assisted his father. He apprenticed to learn the milling business for two years, and then purchased timber land in Chautauqua county and engaged in cutting out timber for the railroad. He continued in this line for six or eight years and then went to Pennsylvania, where he lived until 1865, engaged in the same business. He then commenced working at millwrighting, and operated a machine business in Erie county, New York, for two years. This business he has followed to some extent ever since, giving perhaps more of his attention to this than to his farming. After leaving New York Mr. Barr went to North McGregor, Iowa, and was foreman in a lumber yard for a year, then came to Minneapolis, where for one and a half years he was engaged in millwrighting and in working in a sash and blind factory. In 1870 he came to his present place, and settled on eighty acres of land in Lake Side township, commenced making active improvements, setting out a fine grove of trees and preparing to make a permanent home. He has resided on the farm ever since, with the exception of three years, in 1881–82–83, when he was foreman for a lumber company in Cumberland, Wisconsin, for two years, the last year being spent in millwrighting in Hayward, working in a mill that turned out an immense amount of product. He then returned to his present place, where he has since lived.

Mr. Barr was married, June 20, 1861, to

Miss Maggie Boss, a native of Chautauqua county, New York, where she was born December 3, 1843. She was the daughter of George W. Boss, a farmer. Her education was received in the county of her nativity. Mr. and Mrs. Barr have one child, Nellie M., born in 1862, and married to Samuel P. Hyde, now located in Cottonwood county. Mrs. Barr died December 3, 1883. She was missed by a great many friends and relatives. A few months later a son, Frank E. Barr, aged sixteen years, died, leaving the family, as we have already stated, with but one living child.

Mr. Barr is a republican in politics, is a member of the Good Templars society, of which he is chief templar, and is one of the representative citizens of the township and county. He has been township clerk, justice of the peace, and has held various school offices. Our subject is a man of energy, and is always ready to act intelligently, when opportunity presents, for making money. When the Omaha railroad was built our subject opened a boarding-house in Bingham Lake, and, when the road was extended, went to Bigelow, and there engaged in the same business, and the next spring followed the line to Sibley, where he kept railroad quarters until the business dropped off, owing to the completion of the road. Every winter, until 1889, Mr. Barr has operated a force of snow shovelers, and in this way has accumulated some means outside of his farming operation.

ARTHUR L. STOUGHTON is the foreman of the mechanical department of the *Rock County News*, located at Luverne, Minnesota. He is a native of Rock county, Wisconsin, where he was born on the 29th of September, 1855. He is a son of Dr. Guy and Clarinda (Stebbins) Stoughton, natives of Vermont. The father died in 1879, and the mother is still living in Lu-

verne. There are four children in the father's family—Thomas S., John M., Emma S., now Mrs. Gillham, and Arthur L.

The early days of the subject of our sketch were spent in school in Wisconsin, where he attended the State university for two years. At sixteen years of age he commenced learning the printer's trade at Stoughton, Wisconsin, and remained three years, after which he removed to Jefferson, and there spent a short time in the printing business. His next move was to Luverne, to which place he came to take charge of the Luverne *Herald*, the proprietor of which was A. C. Croft, of Stoughton, Wisconsin. Continuing the management of the paper until the following spring, the proprietor then came to Luverne and took charge of the *Herald* himself. For some time our subject remained as foreman in this office, later purchased a half interest in the paper, and subsequently the remaining interest. He continued the publication of the same for about a year, when H. J. Miller purchased a half interest in the business and Mr. Stoughton and that gentleman formed a partnership which continued until 1883. During this time our subject attended the university at Madison in the years 1879 to 1881. In 1883 he turned his attention to mercantile pursuits and followed that business until 1886, after which he was employed in the *Herald* office until 1888. He went to Winona in the fall of that year, and for a time engaged on the Winona *Daily Herald* as superintendent, and, later, as telegraph editor. He had not continued long in Winona when he received a telegram from Luverne asking him to come to that city and take charge of the mechanical department of the *Rock County News*. He accepted this call and has since been located in that city. Our subject is a prominent democratic politician, and is an influential member of the Masonic and Odd Fellows fraternities.

Mr. Stoughton was married in 1879 to

Miss Rose Farry, a resident of Luverne. This union has been blessed with three children—Mabel, Guy and Kate.

━━•❖•❈❉❈•❖•━━

DWIN T. FOWSER is a thrifty farmer and resident of section 4, Slayton township, Murray county, Minnesota. He was born in Lockport township, Will county, Illinois, February 2, 1858. He is the son of Joseph J. and Esther (Ream) Fowser, both of whom were natives of Ohio. In 1854 the parents left their native State and settled in Illinois, locating on section 6 of Lockport township, Will county. There were eight children in the father's family, Edwin T. being the third.

Our subject remained with his parents until twenty-one years of age, up to which time he had been given the advantages for an education furnished by the district schools. He assisted his father in work on the home farm throughout his life, and became a practical farmer. At twenty-one he was married, and took charge of a portion of the father's farm, his brother, Daniel, of whom a sketch is given in another department of this work, having charge of the balance of the home farm. Edwin continued operating this portion of the father's farm for four years, and during the last year of his occupancy moved to another part of the farm, and rented sixty acres more. Two years longer were spent in operating the farm, and, in the spring of 1885, he sold out and removed to Plainfield, where he operated a corn-sheller and thresher during the fall months. In the spring of 1886 he came to Minnesota, and located where he now lives, in Slayton township.

Edwin T. Fowser was married to Sarah Salsgiver, February 4, 1879. This union has been blessed with one child, Pearl E., born April 27, 1887. Mrs. Fowser is a daughter of John and Maria (Wolfe) Salsgiver, both

of whom were natives of Ohio. Later in life her parents moved to the State of Iowa, where Mrs. Fowser was born. The father is still living, and a resident of the State of Indiana; the mother died in 1866.

In early life our subject was given a good practical education, and is one of the most intelligent and progressive citizens of his township. Being a stanch advocate of temperance, he now affiliates with the prohibition party. He has taken an active interest in public matters, and has held various official positions. He has been a member of the board of supervisors for two years, and is at present treasurer of the school district in which he lives. He is a member of the secret order of Modern Woodmen of America, Minnesota camp, No. 169.

━━•❖•❈❉❈•❖•━━

ORENZO L. SWEET, who resides with his son, William W. Sweet, on section 2, Troy Township, Pipestone county, Minnesota, will form the subject of our present article. He has to a great extent retired from the active cares of business, and is reaping the rewards of a long, useful and well-spent life. The genealogy of the Sweet family is traced back to the pioneers of New England and particularly of New York State, but beyond that the thread is lost in the mist of years, and the lineage cannot be followed across the Atlantic. Whether the family is of English, Scotch or German extraction is impossible at this late day to state with any degree of certainty. The traditions and records of the present members of the family run back only three generations from the subject of our present article, and the writer is obliged to use that generation as a starting point upon which to base this sketch.

Elijah Sweet, grandfather of L. L. Sweet, was born in Stockbridge, Massachusetts, on the 29th of November, 1747. He was a soldier in the Revolutionary War, serving as a volunteer in General Schuyler's commands, and won creditable mention in contemporaneous history. An interesting anecdote in his army service was the fact that he was the soldier placed to guard the body of Jane McCrea, the beautiful and accomplished daughter of an American loyalist, who was killed by an Indian escort, July 27, 1777. Elijah Sweet died February 26, 1838. He married Elisabeth Wright, who was born in 1759, and who died July 14, 1838. Their marraige was blessed with the following named children— Elijah, Jr., who is in the direct line of ancestry from our subject, and who is mentioned at length hereafter; Calvin, a soldier in the War of 1812, who died from exposure; William, who died in infancy; Phebe, later the wife of Elder Asahel Holcomb; Electa, who became the wife of John Hemmingway, and Anna, who married Nathaniel Hatch. The father of this family, Elijah Sweet, Sr., was quite a prominent man in pioneer days in the locality in which he lived, as he took and active part in all affairs of a public nature. He participated in the insurrection in Massachusetts raised by Daniel Shay against the court, he siding with the court.

Elijah Sweet, Jr., one of the sons of Elijah and Elisabeth (Wright) Sweet, was the father of our present subject. He was born in Chenango county, New York, January 4, 1774, and upon attaining manhood married Taphene Kinney, who was born October 16, 1780. He died March 9, 1817, and his widow died May 11, 1853. Their union resulted in a family of the following named children— Lovice, who married Elisha Thurston, and who died April 7, 1876; Dimmis, who became the wife of Daniel Bancroft, and who is also deceased; Rhoda L., who married David Strader, and died August 30, 1842; Betsey, afterwards Mrs. Daniel Morehouse, now deceased; Elijah W., who died in infancy; Emily J., who married John Scudder, and died June 14, 1872; Laura, who died in

infancy; Lorenzo Luman, our subject; James K., married Hannah Wright; Rev. William C., a minister, now residing at Etna, Fillmore county, Minnesota, and Elijah P., who married Matilda Wright, and who died January 28, 1880.

We now come down to the personal history of Lorenzo Luman Sweet, whose name heads our present article. He was born in Chenango county, New York, April 16, 1811. His childhood and youth were spent among the rugged hills of that locality, and as those were pioneer days, he underwent the same training in industry, economy and integrity which are so characteristic of the people from that region. He received his education in the common schools of that time, and just before attaining his majority, on the 30th of October, 1831, he was married to Rachel H. Burr. She was born September 5, 1812, in Connecticut. They removed to Pennsylvania, and from there to Wisconsin, where they remained for about eighteen years. In the meantime, in 1845, Mr. Sweet had been ordained to the ministry of the Free-Will Baptist church, and had been filling stations at various points in the States named. In 1860 they removed to Iowa. When the war broke out, although fifty-two years of age, he at once offered his services and tried to enlist, and was soon afterwards mustered into the service in the Thirty-seventh Iowa Infantry, commonly known as the Gray-Beard regiment. At that time four of his sons were wearing the blue in defense of our country, and two of them never returned. In 1864 our subject was disabled by the cars at Memphis, Tennessee, and was discharged the following April. After the war closed he settled at Tipton, Iowa, and there took a prominent part in public matters, and held several offices of trust—for two years revenue assessor, justice of the peace, trustee, etc., attaining a high place in the community, as a man of ability and un-impeachable integrity. He then filled various posts of duty for his church, including Sibley, Rock Rapids and other points, and in 1885 he retired and settled in Lyon county, Iowa. Later he went to McCook county, Dakota, where he remained about two years, preaching statedly, and then, in 1888, settled in Pipestone county, Minnesota, where he makes his home with his son, William W. Sweet, in Troy township. There he is spending his declining years surrounded by members of his family and bearing the respect and esteem of all who know him. He is a member of Simon Mix post, Grand Army of Republic, No. 95.

The marriage of Lorenzo L. Sweet and wife has been blessed with the following-named children—William Wallace, John Orlando, Daniel E., Henry L. R., George A., Dayton M. and Mary E.

William W. was born July 2, 1832, in Otsego county, New York. On the 26th of March, 1858, he married Cordelia Hatch, who was born in 1829, and who died in 1861, leaving one son, Lorenzo R. At the beginning of the war William W. enlisted in the Sixth Iowa Cavalry, and served three years on the frontier in Dakota and Montana. He was with General Sully in his campaigns after the Indians in 1863–64, and participated in the battles at White Stone Hills and in the Bad Lands. After returning from the service he married Nancy Jane McLein, who was born in 1844 in Pennsylvania. This marriage has been blessed with the following-named children—Esther Y., Clara I., William A., Sarah E., Bertha E., Rachel C., Thomas B. L., John G. and Lucy J. In 1879 William W. Sweet moved with his family to Pipestone county, and took a homestead where he now lives. He is an honored member of Simon Mix post, Grand Army of Republic, No. 95.

John O. Sweet, the second son of Lorenzo L., was born in Pennsylvania. He married Lucinda L. Hatch. He now lives in California. His marriage was blessed with one son, Frank J.

It is unnecessary to refer at length to Daniel E. Sweet in this connection, as a biography of him will be found in another department of this work.

Henry Le Roi Sweet was born in Pennsylvania December 10, 1840. He served as a soldier in the Eleventh Iowa Infantry and died in camp hospital May 4, 1862.

George Alonzo Sweet was born in Wisconsin September 13, 1845. He enlisted in the Eleventh Iowa Infantry in January, 1863, and was killed in the battle of Atlanta in June, 1863.

Dayton Marks Sweet was born in Wisconsin July 12, 1849. Upon attaining manhood he married Anna Van Pelt, and their union has been blessed with the following children—Harriet M., Dolly R. and Lizzie. In 1885 they removed to Arkansas, thence to Tipton, Iowa, where Mr. Sweet still lives, engaged in well boring.

Mary Elizabeth Sweet was born April 14, 1852, in Wisconsin. She married James Simmons in 1877 and died October 31, 1880.

This ends the genealogical history of the Sweet family. Their lives have been characterized by integrity and sobriety, and they have been held in high esteem by all with whom they have come in contact as men of worth and also as exemplary citizens. Our principal subject, L. L. Sweet, is a man of much more than ordinary ability. A close observer, of extensive reading and wide experience, he is possessed of an extensive knowledge of men and events. During his residence in Iowa he studied law, was admitted to the bar, and for several years practiced before the courts of that State. A genial, courteous gentleman, he is one of those men whom it is a pleasure to meet.

While in the army he preached nearly

every Sunday to the boys in blue by the request of the chaplain of the Thirty-seventh, and also Thursday evenings performing the duties of the chaplain, except drawing the pay. He was for nine years pastor of a church that he organized in Washington county, Wisconsin; was about three years pastor of a church in Winnebago county, Wisconsin; three years pastor of the Burnett church in Dodge county; and meanwhile attended quarterly and yearly meetings in different parts of the State, often traveling thirty to sixty miles on foot.

HENRY McKINSTRY is one of the prominent and most substantial men of Winnebago City, Faribault county, Minnesota. He is a native of Windsor county, Vermont, where he was born in the year 1842. He is the son of Paul and Harriet, (Lillie) McKinstry, natives of Vermont.

The parents of the subject of our sketch are still living, at a hale old age in Winnebago City. The father is now eighty-two years of age, and with his wife belongs to the Methodist Episcopal church. They are highly esteemed for their many generous deeds and for their earnest religious work in Winnebago City and in the county. They have been members of the Methodist church for many years, in which society our subject's father has held most of the church offices. In his early life Paul McKinstry engaged in farming and came to Minnesota in 1868 and settled at Winnebago City, taking a farm a short distance south of the village. In 1878 he engaged in the mercantile business and followed the same until 1888, when he retired from active life. He is a stockholder in the steam flouring mill and took an active interest in various other financial enterprises and assisted very materially in the building up and improvement of the village. There are four children in the McKin-

stry family—Clarissa, now Mrs. A. P. Hatch, of Ogle county, Illinois; Henry, Azro P. (a farmer and dairyman of Verona, Faribault county, Minnesota), and Ellen, now Mrs. J. F. Winship, of Winnebago City, Minnesota.

Until eleven years of age the subject of our sketch received his training on the home farm, and was then educated at the Newbury Seminary in Orange county, Vermont. At seventeen years of age he commenced teaching school and in 1862 enlisted in Company H, Twelfth Vermont Infantry. He served for nine months and for a time was in one of the hospitals as wardmaster. He was captured by General Mosby on the Rappahannock river and was held prisoner for a short time. At the close of his enlistment he returned home and attended school for some six months in his native county. He then went to Syracuse, New York, and attended a commercial college, taking a thorough course, and also learning telegraphy. He then engaged as operator for the United States Telegraph Company along the Central railroad, later filling the same position for one year in Pennsylvania. He then found a position as book-keeper in a wholesale and retail millinery store in Syracuse, New York, and followed the same for five years. He then went to Boston and engaged in the same business with a wholesale house until 1872, when he came to Winnebago City and for two years clerked in a general store owned by J. F. Winshop. Mr. McKinstry then purchased a stock of boots and shoes and clothing, and has continued in the mercantile trade ever since. He now carries an immense stock of dry goods, clothing, boots and shoes, groceries, etc., and his stock invoices upwards of twenty-five thousand dollars. He is doing an immense and profitable business. His store is 28 by 70 feet and is centrally located. Since coming to the city Mr. McKinstry has interested himself in farming lands and has also made investments in city property. He is a member of the syndicate that built the Syndicate Block, one of the best brick store buildings in the city.

Mr. McKinstry was married in 1868 to Miss Alice D. Packer, of Lowell, Massachusetts, and a daughter of David Packer. This union has been blessed with two children—Ilelen M. and Arthur P.

The subject of our sketch affiliates with the republican party and is chairman of the republican county central committee. He has held various official positions and has been a member of the school board and of the city council. He is a leading Odd Fellow and is a prominent member of the Grand Army of the Republic. Mr. and Mrs. McKinstry are both members of the Methodist Episcopal church, of which he is secretary and treasurer and assistant superintendent of the Sunday-school. Mr. McKinstry is a man of large public spirit, is generous, and is one of the most highly respected and prominent citizens of the city.

J H. TAYLOR, one of the substantial and reliable business men of Jasper, Pipestone county, Minnesota, is the junior member of the firm of J. H. Taylor & Co., proprietors of the Pioneer lumber yard. Mr. Taylor is a native of Jackson county, Wisconsin, where he was born March 20, 1864. His parents, Harvey and Matilda (McAndless) Taylor, were natives of Illinois and New York, respectively. The father followed the mercantile business throughout the most of his life, and died in 1865. The mother is now a resident of Pipestone county. In the father's family there were four children—William K., Frederick, Luella, and our subject.

The early life of the subject of our sketch was spent in the home of his parents. He was given common-school advantages up to the age of sixteen years, when he came with his mother and sister to Pipestone county. On coming to this county he attended school for some time, and then engaged in work on a farm. In 1881 he engaged in work in the lumber yard of C. L. Colman, with whom he continued during one season. At the close of that time he went to Madison, Dakota, where he found employment in a lumber yard as second man. Later he had charge of a lumber yard for Mr. Colman, in Dakota, where he continued for five years. At the end of this time he came to Jasper and established his present business. He purchased five lots east of the railroad depot, built sheds and a fine office. He carries a large line of lumber and building materials, coal and lime. Since coming to the village Mr. Taylor has built up a large business, and is becoming one of the prominent business men of the place. He has made several important improvements, and put up the first pair of hay scales in the village at a cost of about $100. In politics Mr. Taylor affiliates with the republican party. He is an energetic, thorough-going business man, thoroughly alive to the needs of his customers, obliging and trustworthy, and is rapidly growing into the confidence and esteem of his fellow-citizens.

J OHN E. BUELL is a leading citizen and well-to-do farmer of Hope township, Lincoln county, Minnesota, and resides on section 18. He was born in Allegany county, New York, September 18, 1826. His parents were Cyrus and Hannah (Vincent) Buell, both natives of Vermont. The father and mother were of English descent, their parents having been born in England and came to America in the early part of this century. The father was a blacksmith by trade and in connection with that engaged to some extent to farming. He resided in the State of New York until his death, which occurred in about 1834. Our subject's mother was married some time after the father's death and John E. left home when he was eight or nine years old and resided with a brother-in-law until reaching the age of thirteen years. He then came to the State of Michigan, where for six years he engaged in tailoring. At the end of that period he returned to the State of New York and for three and a half years followed his trade, after which he came West to Illinois, locating on a farm in McHenry county.

After two years spent in Illinois our subject was taken with the gold fever, having heard a great deal of the wonderful Eldorado on the Pacific coast. In 1850 he started for California overland and for two years engaged in prospecting and mining for gold. One year was then spent at Sacramento, and he then again engaged in mining for two years, returning at the end of that time to the State of Wisconsin, where he purchased a farm in Adams county. He continued his residence in that county for about eight years when he sold out and migrated to Houston county, Minnesota, where for one year he followed agricultural pursuits. His next move was to Blue Earth county, where he purchased a farm of 160 acres eight miles from Winnebago City. Remaining in that place until 1868, he then located on a claim eight miles from Marshall, Lyons county, where he remained some eight years. While on this farm he passed through some of his most bitter and trying experiences. He lost considerable money in various disastrous occurrences, and passed through the grasshopper times of 1875–76–77. In 1878 he removed to Hope township, Lincoln county, where he has since continued to live. In the town at the time he settled there were only three other parties—John Moore and Tom Robinson, half-breeds, and Thomas Turner.

Mr. Buell was married in July, 1849, to Miss Minerva Calkins, who died about twenty-five years ago, leaving seven children. Mr. Buell was married the second time in July, 1872, to Lorena Gould, a native of New Hampshire.

In politics Mr. Buell affiliates with the republican party and has become quite prominent in the local affairs of that organization. He has taken an active interest in public matters and has held the office of assessor one term and that of school treasurer for three years. In his early life he received a good common school education, and being of a studious turn of mind, has accumulated a large store of general knowledge. He is a man of extensive travels and relates many exciting and thrilling experiences through which he has passed. He is a careful reader of human nature, is an acute observer of passing events and is looked upon as being one of the most intelligent and progressive men of the township. His character is above reproach, and his reputation for honor and integrity is of the highest order.

OLIVER DREW, one of the leading residents of Murray county, Minnesota, resides on section 2 of Mason township. He was born in the State of New York, January 25, 1820. The parents of the subject of our sketch were James and Mercy (Nicholas) Drew, the father a native of Maine, and the mother a native of Connecticut. Throughout the greater part of his life the father was a farmer in the State of New York, where the mother died. The father came West and lived for some time at the residence of his son Oliver and died a few years ago at the advanced age of ninety-five years.

Oliver Drew, of whom this sketch treats, spent his early life with his parents on the farm. He attended school and assited his parents until he was fourteen years old when he left home, and during one season worked on a farm. He then went to live in a doctor's family and attended school during the winter and then apprenticed to learn the tailor's trade, and for fourteen years found employment as a cutter and fitter in various places in the East. At the end of this period he came to the State of Illinois and opened a hotel, which he operated for three years. Then in 1847 he moved to a farm seventy-five miles from Chicago and made that his home until 1850. At this time, being seized with the gold fever, he started overland for California, where he engaged in mining with good success for two and a half years. He cleared over $4,100 and returned to his native State by way of Nicaragua, stopping for a brief time in South America. He opened a general store in Earlville, Illinois, where he remained two years. In 1860 he took a trip overland to Pike's Peak, and prospected in that region for about two years. He returned to the East in August, 1862, and enlisted in Company A, Tenth Regiment Illinois Volunteer Infantry, remaining in the Union army throughout the war. He was discharged in July, 1865, and soon after returned to the State of Illinois, where he lived until 1869. In that year he came by team to Murray county, Minnesota, and settled on a claim, where he now lives. The early experience of the subject of our sketch in this country was filled with the usual hardships which come to the life of the pioneer settler. He passed through the grasshopper raids and experienced the total destruction of three or four crops. He owns 355 acres of excellent land, with five acres of heavy timber on the island in Lake Shetek. Our subject's farm is one of the finest in the county.

Mr. Drew was married August 9, 1856, to Mary E. Atwood, a native of Onondaga county, New York. This union has been blessed with four children—Ellen, Douglas, Clara and Drusilla. Douglas was drowned in Lake Shetek about half a mile from his home, while on a trapping expedition.

Oliver Drew is a man of excellent social and business qualities, and he is one of the most highly esteemed citizens of the township. In politics he affiliates with the democratic party, and among the official positions which he has held may be named that of township treasurer, in which he served ten years, and also school treasurer, in which he has acted ever since the district was organized. His honorable career in the service of the Union army entitles him to the influential position he occupies in the Grand Army of the Republic, John A. Logan Post, No. 162, of Slayton.

Mr. Drew relates many interesting reminiscences of his early life. When he was living in Baldwinsville, New York, he went fishing for cat-fish one night, and was sitting on the railing of the bridge crossing the Seneca river. He fell asleep and fell head first into the river, the water being twelve feet in depth and running very rapidly. He floated about eighty rods down the river and struck an island, and ever after, while living in that town, he went by the name of "Sam Patch." In the historic explosion of Syracuse, New York, he stood within ten feet of a building containing 650 pounds of blasting powder; twenty-five were killed on the spot, and he was one of sixty badly mashed up, but was saved almost by a miracle. These incidents are only two of numerous others which have occurred to him.

<hr>

ALBERT NELSON JEFFERS is one of the foremost citizens of Storden township, Cottonwood county, Minnesota, and resides on section 12. He is a native of America, born in Crawford county, Illinois, August 29, 1843, and was the son of Nelson and Lydia (Allison) Jeffers.

The father of our subject was born at or

near Lexington, Kentucky, in 1819. He died at sixty-six years of age. Removing from Kentucky to Allison Prairie, Crawford county, Illinois, he made that his home for some years, and there married Lydia Allison, and from there removed to Beloit, Rock county, Wisconsin, from whence, after eight years, he emigrated to La Fayette county, Wisconsin, taking 160 acres of land as a pre-emption, and also 160 acres on a land warrant, making 320 acres in all. Here the father lived for twenty-five years, enjoying a degree of prosperity such as is the lot of most farmers in Central Wisconsin. He then removed to Cerro Gordo county, Iowa, where he resided twelve years. When that time had expired he came to Cottonwood county, Minnesota, taking a homestead of 160 acres, and returning to Iowa for a short visit, died there. While in La Fayette county, Wisconsin, in 1868, he was ordained as a minister in the regular Predestinarian Baptist church. He was a man of deep and practical piety, and proclaimed the gospel for some seventeen years. He died in the triumphs of the Christian faith. The mother of the subject of our sketch was the daughter of Daniel Allison, and was born in Crawford county, Illinois, in 1821. She is now living in Cottonwood county. In the father's family there were ten children—Albert N., George Perry, Lyrann, Mary E., Martha, Ida, Laura, Warren R., Owen T., and Lydia, all living but Mary, Martha and Lydia who are deceased. Ida resides in Cerro Gordo county, Iowa, all the others live in Cottonwood county, Minnesota.

The subject of our sketch spent his early life surrounded by the excellent influences of a Christian home. Until eighteen years of age he lived with his parents on the farm and attended the district school. On reaching the age just mentioned he commenced farming for himself and continued thereat for a year and a half. August 17, 1864, he enlisted in Company E, Forty-third Wisconsin Infantry, under Colonel Cobb. He participated in the battle of Nashville, under General Sherman, and in various other battles and skirmishes, and was discharged June 28, 1865, at Nashville, Tennessee. On returning from the war our subject was married and settled on a farm in LaFayette county, where he resided three years. Then he moved to Cerro Gordo county, Iowa, and made that his home until coming to Cottonwood county in 1877. He located 160 acres as a homestead and eighty acres as a tree claim. He has actively proceeded in the improvement of his farm, built a good dwelling-house, and two large barns. He has fifteen acres of a fine grove of trees, some of them being cottonwoods and maples. He is a man of progressive thought in regard to business and believes in diversified farming. In connection with raising grain, he is breeding good stock, such as sheep and Norman horses. He has a great many acres under cultivation and employs five working teams to till his land.

The subject of this sketch, Albert N. Jeffers, was married December 25, 1865, to Sarah Frances Butler, the daughter of Dann and Anna Butler, of Georgetown, Grant county, Wisconsin. The fruits of this union were George Franklin, Anna Mary, Ida Grace, Lydia Hellen, Lydia Luella, Robert Nelson, Sybil Ruth, Ada and Adda (twins). Of these children all are alive with the exception of Lydia Hellen and George Franklin, who are deceased. They all live at home in Cottonwood county, Minnesota. Albert N. Jeffers is an influential member of the Grand Army of the Republic, also of the Independent Order of Odd Fellows, having joined that order in Warren, Jo Daviess county, Illinois, in 1867 and has been a member of this order in good standing up to the present time.

MARTIN J. EASLAND is one of the substantial farmers and prominent old soldiers of Grange township, Pipestone county, Minnesota. He has a farm of 160 acres, well improved, located on section 26, where he has resided since the early part of 1879, being therefore one of the earliest settlers in the township.

The subject of our sketch was born March 6, 1840, in Cleveland, Ohio, and is the son of Kelley and Cynthia (Leet) Easland. The father was a cooper by occupation, and was a native of the State of New York, while the mother was born in Connecticut. The grandparents of the subject of our sketch were James and Mary Easland, natives of the State of New York, the grandfather having been a soldier in the Revolutionary War. Our subject's father died in 1882, and the mother passed from this life August 4, 1885.

The subject of our sketch was warmly attached to his boyhood's home, and he remained with his parents until he reached the age of twenty-one years. Up to this time he attended school at every opportunity, and when not thus engaged, helped his father at the cooper's trade. August 15, 1861, he enlisted in Company I, Thirty-first Illinois Infantry, under Colonel John A. Logan. His service was of the severest kind and was filled with hardships and privations. He was taken prisoner near Brandon, Mississippi, February 9, 1864, and was removed to Mobile, Alabama, where he was incarcerated in a filthy jail with a lot of negroes. One week of misery was spent in this rebel prison, and he was then taken to Cohaba, same State. After enduring prison fare in this place for four weeks, he was then removed to the loathsome Andersonville prison, where he was incarcerated for eight long, weary months. At that time the rebel forces guarding the prison, becoming fearful that General Sherman's army might march upon their headquarters, removed a number of the prisoners, among whom was our subject, to Milan, Georgia. This removal was made because of the proximity of General Sherman's army, and for a time the rebels feared that General Sherman would take possession of that entire country. After remaining at Milan for a short time, our subject was removed to Savannah, where for eight days he experienced the usual terrors of the vile Southern prison. At the end of that time he was removed to Blackshear, Georgia, and from thence in eight days removed to Thomasville, Florida. After nine days of incarceration at the latter named place, he was again taken to the frightful Andersonville prison, in which he suffered untold miseries for nine months; making in all a prisoner of war, thirteen months and fourteen days. Tongue fails to tell of the horrors of the prison in which so many months of our subject's life were spent. This can truly be said, however, that but very few of the inmates of Andersonville, who escaped alive, have ever regained the health they enjoyed before their incarceration. Hundreds and thousands died of the privations, many starved to death, and hundreds were taken away by loathsome diseases contracted in the miasmatic atmosphere in which Andersonville was located. On his discharge, Mr. Easland went to the State of Illinois, locating for a short time in Pekin, remaining there from April 26, 1865, until September, 1866, during this time being under the continuous care of physicians. As a result of his Andersonville life his health was completely broken down and he was prostrated almost beyond hope of recovery. Being ordered by the doctors to come to Minnesota that he might receive some benefit from the atmosphere of this region, he settled in Minnesota, where he remained four years, and during part of which time he held a position in a large saw-mill. Removing from Minneapolis he settled in Clark county, Iowa, where he engaged to some extent in farming. His health, however, had been poor ever since his discharge from Andersonville, and he was able to do but little work. So after a period of six years, already mentioned, which were spent in Clark county, he returned to Minnesota, settling in Steele county, from whence he went in March, 1878, to Pipestone county to find a location. In company with J. L. Humphrey he drove through to Grange township, located his land, and in the fall returned to Steele county. In the following spring he brought his family to Pipestone county, and has been a resident of Grange township ever since.

Mr. Easland was united in marriage to Miss Emma I. Humphrey March 29, 1871. Miss Humphrey was a daughter of H. J. and R. S. Humphrey, both of whom are still living and residents of Grange township. Mr. and Mrs. Easland have been blessed with four children, all of whom are living—Anna I., Samuel L., Burton L. and James W.

The subject of our sketch in early life received a good common-school education, is a man of excellent ideas, and exerts a strong influence in the township in which he lives. He is a good citizen and takes an active interest in all matters pertaining to the welfare of the township at large. He is energetic and industrious, and as far as his health permits, personally superintends the management of his excellent farm. He is known as a man of high character and is respected by all his fellow-townsmen. In politics he affiliates with the republican party. He is a member of the Simon Mix Post, No. 95, Grand Army of the Republic. He has held several official positions, and is at present clerk of the school district in which he lives. For five years he was a member of the board of supervisors, and was clerk of the township for one year.

PETER PAULSON is a prominent resident of section 14, Lime Lake township, Murray county, Minnesota. He was born in Norway, March 10, 1852. His parents were Paul and Dorothea (Johnson) Paulson, both of whom were natives of Norway and farmers by occupation. The parents are now residents of Dual county, South Dakota.

Until fifteen years of age the subject of our sketch was given good educational advantages in his native land. After that time he assisted his father in work on the home farm for about four years, and at nineteen years of age came to America with his parents, landing in Quebec, and going by way of Chicago to Southern Minnesota, and settling in Rushford, Fillmore county. Our subject worked at various employments until 1876, working during the winters in the pineries and in the summer months driving a dray in his village. In 1876 he went to the village of Worthington and worked on the Sioux Falls branch of the Omaha railroad until harvest, when he went to Waseca county, and after a short time spent in the harvest fields, went to his former home in Fillmore county. In 1878 he came to Murray county and located the claim where he now lives. He has worked at various kinds of labor since coming to the farm and in different places, residing on his farm a sufficient portion of the time to enable him to hold it as a homestead. In 1884 he was married and settled for a permanent residence on the farm.

Mr. Paulson was married May 3, 1884, to Anna Hagen, a daughter of Nils and Andrene (Amund) Hagen, natives of Norway. This marriage has been blessed with three children—Nils P., Axel M. and Dagene.

Mr. Paulson is a strong, energetic, systematic farmer, and in his operations has met with good success. In politics Mr. Paulson affiliates with the republican party and has held the office of township treasurer since 1879 and has also been assessor for two terms. He has a fine farm of 160 acres, provided with good buildings. He is a man of good character, and is a consistent member of the Lutheran church.

HANS T. GRAU located on section 4, Lake Benton township, on the shore of the lake from which the township derives its name, in the year 1869. Since that year he has been a permanent resident of Lincoln county and has actively interested himself in all matters of a public nature. During the first two years of his residence here he did but little work on his own farm but engaged himself to adjoining farmers in order to support his family. Our subject was one of the very first settlers of the township, and among those who came about that time were Mr. Taylor, James Gilronan and Henry Brefelt. Mr. Grau assisted in the organization of the township and has materially aided in every enterprise which tended to develop his locality. The first year he built a small shanty 14x10, himself cutting the logs out of which it was built. He lived in this primitive dwelling for some years and then built his present neat and commodious residence, which is 18x26 feet and sixteen feet high. His first stable was built of sods and it accommodated some six or eight head of cattle. He has now good buildings, and the passer-by witnesses on every hand the evidences of prosperity and thrift. He has labored hard on his farm and has brought it up to be one of the best in the township. Our subject is probably the earliest settler now living in the township.

Mr. Grau was born two miles from the city of Christiania, Norway, November 9, 1826. He is the son of Thorval and Rena (Christianson) Grau, both natives of Norway, and farmers by occupation. The father died in the old country when our subject was fourteen years old. The mother remained in that country until her death, which occurred in 1873. The parents were exemplary Christian people, and were members of the Lutheran church. In the father's family there were five children, three boys and two girls: Christ, Hans T., Ole, Mary and Marion.

Hans T. Grau lived on the farm where he was born until coming to America in 1866. He crossed the Atlantic ocean in a sailing vessel and was two months on the way, landing at Quebec. For some time in that city he engaged in railroad work and then came to La Crosse, Wisconsin, where he worked on a farm for some three years. At the end of this period he came to his present place in Lincoln county. Since coming to the county, our subject's life has not been all sunshine nor continued prosperity. In the years 1874-5-6, his crops were all eaten up by the grasshoppers, and his family were well nigh destitute. In order to support them he had to leave home and work on the Wilmar railroad during the summers. He also met disaster in the way of destruction of property by prairie fire, and on account of this had to go to Breckenridge, Minnesota, where he worked for some time. In the fire which destroyed nearly all he had, his wife nearly lost her life while trying to put out the flames. She had her feet badly burned and was laid up on account of this misfortune for some two years.

Mr. Grau was married in January, 1849, to Miss Mary Hanson, a native of Norway, and born in the place of the birth of our subject. Mr. and Mrs. Grau have had four children, all of whom are now dead.

The subject of our sketch is a republican in politics, and has associated himself with the best interests of local government. He has been township trustee for some two years, and has held several other positions of minor importance. He is an exemplary Christian, and a member of the Lutheran church. In spite of the misfortunes that have fallen to his lot, our subject has retained courage and kept on working until he has surrounded himself with comfortable circumstances, and has a well-improved and profitable farming business. Being one of the early settlers he is well known, and where best known is most highly respected all over Lincoln county.

ON. HUMPHREY M. BLAISDELL, a prominent attorney and public man of Fairmont, Minnesota, is the editor of the Fairmont *News*. His parents were Alfred M. and Judith H. (Grey) Blaisdell, natives of Maine. The parents were farmers by occupation, and engaged in that business in their native State throughout their lives.

The place of the nativity of the subject of our sketch is found in the village of Otis, Maine, his birth occurring September 10, 1841. He was reared on a farm, receiving a good education, and resided with his parents until April 25, 1861. At this time he enlisted in Company H, Second Maine Infantry, and served until November, 1862. He participated in the first battle of Bull Run, and had his leg broken by a musket ball; was taken prisoner, and in Libby, Tuscaloosa and Salisbury prisons until June, 1862. In July, 1863, he re-enlisted as sergeant in Company C, First Maine Heavy Artillery, and was on detached duty until the spring of 1864. He then entered the military academy at Philadelphia, Pennsylvania, was examined July 11, 1864, by the board of examiners, of which General Silas Casey was a member, and was commissioned July 21, 1864, as first lieutenant in the Twelfth Regiment, United States Colored Heavy Artillery. He was in command of Company E, of that regiment, during a part of the time, but was principally connected with Company

K, in the department of Kentucky. He was mustered out at the close of the war, April 24, 1866; was examined under general orders from the war department, and passed for a commission in the regular army. He concluded, however, not to follow a military life any longer, and retired from the service and attended school for some time at Bucksport, Maine. He graduated from the East Maine Conference Seminary and read law with Hon. Eugene Hale, at Ellsworth, in that State. He took an active part in local matters, and was a member of the Maine legislature in 1868. In the spring of 1869 he came to Fairmont, Minnesota and engaged in the practice of law, continuing in that profession until the present time. August 9, 1887, he purchased the Fairmont *News*, which paper he has since conducted.

The subject of our sketch is an old-time and honored republican, having assisted in the organization of that party, being one of the warmest supporters of General Fremont. Since coming to Martin county he has made his influence felt in the political history of southern Minnesota, and has exerted a strong influence in local political affairs. His newspaper is one of the largest and best in the county and enjoys an extensive patronage. Mr. Blaisdell is a member of the Minnesota Commandery, of the Loyal Legion and also a member of the Grand Army of the Republic, and has been a member of the staff of Commanders-in-chief Fairchild and Rea.

Mr. Blaisdell was married at the residence of A. B. Stickney, Esq., in St. Paul, August 27, 1871, to Miss Henrietta H. Crosby, daughter of Hon. Josiah and Mary B. (Foss) Crosby, natives of Dexter, Maine, where Miss Henrietta was born February 18, 1850. Mr. and Mrs. Blaisdell have been blessed with the following named children—Josiah C., Alfred and Arthur.

JOHN JANZEN is a leading merchant and proprietor of the oldest mercantile house in the village of Mountain Lake, Cottonwood county, Minnesota. He is the son of John and Annie (Thiessen) Janzen, natives of Germany. The parents were farmers by occupation, and still reside in their native land.

The subject of our sketch was born near Danzig, in West Prussia, March 15, 1850. He resided with his parents on the farm until he was twenty-three years of age, receiving a good common-school education. In April, 1873, he came to the United States, first locating in St. Paul. After two years, he then found employment on various farms. He was not obliged to engage in this kind of employment because his parents were wealthy, and could support him in different style, but he preferred to work in this line and do for himself. He traveled about to some extent in Minnesota and Iowa, and in the summer of 1875 commenced clerking in the general store of S. H. Soule, of Mountain Lake. This gentleman was one of the pioneers of the county. His father opened a farm on the shores of Mountain Lake in 1869. Our subject continued clerking for this gentleman for several years, and April 1, 1881, he entered into partnership with his employer, and continued business until 1884, when he sold out to his senior partner. Our subject then took a trip to Europe, and returned, bringing his brother Abraham with him, locating at Mountain Lake. Immediately after arriving, he purchased Mr. Soule's store, and January 1, 1885, opened the business in his own name. His brother Abraham has been book-keeper and head clerk ever since. In connection with his mercantile trade Mr. Janzen is also doing an extensive real estate and loan business, and is agent for several transportation companies with steamboats plying between Europe and America. Our subject does a large business in the line of conveyancing, and perhaps no man is better known, and, indeed, no man is more favorably known than is the subject of our sketch. He has always proven himself an able supporter of all matters which tended to the improvement of his adopted village, and has taken an active part in matters of a political nature. In politics he affiliates with the republican party and is a member of the Mennonite church. He has been village recorder, township clerk, and is now president of the village. He had charge of the postoffice from 1875 to 1885, and March 28, 1889, was appointed postmaster of Mountain Lake. The subject of our sketch is a man of extraordinary business qualifications. Whatever his hand touches yields success, and, having been fortunate in all his various investments, he has gathered considerable means. He is careful and conservative, and is a wise counselor.

Mr. Janzen was married May 1, 1878, in Cottonwood county, to Miss Anna Goerzen, a daughter of William and Anna Goerzen, natives of Germany. This lady was born in Russia, in September, 1858, and came to America at an early age. Mr. and Mrs. Janzen have been blessed with the following named children—Anna, Catharina, Mary and Helena.

WILLIAM B. GILMORE, Sr., is one of the intelligent and influential farmers of Eden township, Pipestone county Minnesota. His home is located on section 10, where he settled in 1882. Mr. Gilmore is a native of Vermont, where he was born September 2, 1835.

The subject of our sketch is the son of Edmund and Sarah (Doty) Gilmore, both of whom were natives of the State of Vermont. The father is still living at the age of eighty-four years and is a resident of Juneau county, Wisconsin. The mother died in Jefferson county, Wisconsin, June 4, 1856. The father's family remained in the State of Vermont until in the fall of 1840, when they removed to Jefferson county, Wisconsin, settling on government land and engaging in farming. Here the family remained for a quarter of a century, removing thence to Juneau county, where the father now lives. During the gold excitement (in 1852) he went overland to California and remained two years. In the father's family there were eight children, of whom the subject of our sketch was the fourth in order of birth. The grand-parents were Ephraim and Mrs. (Sherman) Gilmore.

Up to the age of twenty-four years the subject of our sketch remained with his parents on the home farm. He was given good school advantages and obtained a good common-school education. When not in school his time was occupied in assisting his father at work on the farm, and he played in the Fort Atkinson Brass Band for twelve years, after his marriage, in 1861, he purchased a farm near that of his father's and commenced farming for himself. In the spring of 1868 he removed to Butler county, Iowa, where he purchased land and engaged in farming until in 1882, when he came to Pipestone county, Minnesota, and settled on the farm where he now lives.

March 11, 1861, Mr. Gilmore was united in matrimony to Miss Mary J. Ellis, a native of New York State. Mrs. Gilmore is a daughter of John and Abigail (Peck) Ellis, natives of Vermont. Mr. and Mrs. Gilmore have been blessed with nine children—William B. J., Alton E., Afton A., Jessie A., Ethel J., Carrie M., Earl C., Elba A. and Lizzie M.

The subject of our sketch is living on a fine farm of 160 acres under excellent cultivation, and upon which are found good farm buildings, and a beautiful grove of timber. Since coming to the township he has identi-

fied himself with all its better interests and his services have never been called for without being freely given. Taking an active interest in the political matters of his town, he affiliates with the republican party and has become one of the prominent leaders of that organization. He cast his first vote for Fremont in 1856. Throughout his life he has been constantly identified with all matters of a public nature, and has held numerous offices of responsibility and trust. While a resident of Iowa he held the office of justice of the peace for four years, held the office of president of the school board, and also that of treasurer for a period of six years. Since coming to Eden township he has been a member of the board of supervisors for four years, during two years of which time he has held the position of chairman of that body. At present he is in the fifth year of official service as one of the school trustees of the district in which he lives. In religious matters he occupies a prominent position before the people and accomplishes a great amount of good. He is an active member of the United Brethren church, and while a resident of Iowa was a licensed minister of that organization and did much active work. Mr. Gilmore is an energetic, painstaking farmer, and has met with merited success in all his financial operations. He is a man of excellent judgment, of unquestionably high character, and has the esteem of all his fellow-townsmen.

HON. SILAS BLACKMUN, an influential resident of Selma township, Cottonwood county, Minnesota, is a native of St. Lawrence county, New York, where he was born October 9, 1835. His parents were Martin P. and Mary A. (Deuel) Blackmun, the former a native of Vermont and the latter born in New York. He resided in St. Lawrence county until 1850 when, with his parents, he moved to Wisconsin, settling on an Indian reservation in what is now Waushara county. They took a claim before the county was surveyed and our subject remained with his parents assisting on the farm until he was twenty-one years of age.

Educational advantages were somewhat limited in the pioneer days of Wisconsin and our subject spent but little time attending school. At twenty-one years of age he purchased a farm and engaged in agricultural pursuits in Waushara county until 1863, when he sold out and removed to Faribault, Minnesota, where during one winter he engaged in teaming. In March, 1864, he located on a pre-emption in Brown county, where he resided three years, and at the end of that time removed to another farm in the same county. In 1874 he came Cottonwood county and settled on 160 acres of land on section 18 of Selma township. He took this piece of land as a tree claim and has made it his home ever since.

Mr. Blackmun was married in Waushara county, Wisconsin, October 26, 1856, to Miss Annie E. Henton, a daughter of William and Mary (Jones) Henton, both natives of Wales. Miss Annie was born in Erie county, Pennsylvania, November 27, 1837. She died February 5, 1858, leaving one child, Theodore C., born September 5, 1857, and died September 23, 1858. The second marriage of our subject took place in the same county in Wisconsin, February 22, 1859, at which time he wedded Miss Elearnor S. Henton, a sister of his first wife. This marriage has been blessed with the following-named children—Walter M., Frank W., Lillie, Lydia, Lucy, Mira and Mabel. Walter M. married Agnes Hudson and resides in Selma township. Frank W. married Alice Luther, and lives on a farm adjoining that of his father. Lillie married Albert Knowles and now lives in Lane county, Oregon. Lydia wedded Perry M. Dickerson and is now a resident of Brown county, Minnesota. The other children are single and are living at home.

The subject of our sketch occupies a prominent position in the political government of his county and State, having participated in political matters during his entire residence here. He was elected to the State legislature on the republican ticket in the fall of 1882, and was re-elected in 1884. He was appointed postmaster of Selma postoffice July 3, 1882, and has held that position ever since, the office being at his residence. Mr. Blackmun has also held nearly all the local township offices and in all his public relations has served his constitutents with rare fidelity and efficiency. He has passed through many circumstances of a trying nature, but is now surrounded with the evidences of prosperity and success and is in good circumstances. In August, 1864, the grasshoppers besieged the country, but did but little damage. The next year the grasshoppers came and destroyed all his crops. In 1873, the year prior to his settlement in Cottonwood county, the grasshoppers came and deposited their eggs and until 1877 the crops were all practically destroyed. In that year our subject had a good crop and began to grow more hopeful. In the following year the crops were again light on account of blight. Since that time crops have been fair and our subject has been successful in accumulating considerable means. He has owned a great deal of land in the county, but has now only 160 acres. Each of his married sons is settled on a quarter section of land on which they live, adjoining his own farm.

CORNELIUS N. BRESSLER, a leading farmer of Diamond Lake township, Lincoln county, Minnesota, purchased a relinquishment of a homestead of section 33, April 19, 1882. On this place he has lived ever since, engaging in general farming with excellent success. There were about five acres broken on the farm when he came into possession, and he commenced adding thereto and making improvements. He was one among the early settlers, and has always been held in high esteem by his neighbors and fellow-citizens.

Mr. Bressler was born in Monroe, Ogle county, Illinois, January 18, 1853. His father was George Bressler, a native of Dauphin county, Pennsylvania, where he resided until after his marriage. He was a carpenter by trade, and followed that occupation until coming West in an early day, making his settlement in Monroe, Ogle county, Illinois. He was one of the first settlers of that section, and made his location when there were no railroads nearer than Chicago. Chicago was his market and to that city he went to sell grain and buy provisions. He was a democrat in politics, and was a member of the Evangelical church. George Bressler's father was a native of Germany, and was a tailor by trade. The mother of the subject of our sketch was Susan Messner, also a native of Dauphin county, Pennsylvania, where she was reared and educated. In the father's family there were ten children —Elizabeth, Sophia, Phœbe, Edward, Sarah, Catharine, Henrietta, George A., Cornelius N., and James Wesley. Elizabeth married Andrew Jackson Montgomery, a hotel proprietor and owner of a restaurant. He died in 1880 in Lake Benton, Minnesota, to which place he had come in an early day. He was a prominent business man of Lake Benton.

The early life of Cornelius N. Bressler was spent in Ogle county, Illinois, where he received his early training and education. He remained in Illinois with his parents on the home farm until he was eighteen years of age, when he purchased an interest in a threshing-machine and made threshing his principal business for a number of years.

He then sold out his interest in the thresher and purchased a one-half interest in a clover huller, operating in that line during three falls. He then traded his interest in the huller for a threshing-machine, continuing in that line for four years. He then sold out and came to Lincoln county in the fall of 1881. He did not make a permanent location until in April, 1882, when he settled on his present place. Throughout his life he has been more or less engaged in agricultural pursuits, having operated a large farm in Illinois in connection with his various machine interests. He also worked more or less at the carpenter's trade with his father and assisted him in the erection of many public buildings in Ogle county, Illinois. While there he also took an interest in musical matters and was a member of the Monroe cornet band for four or five years. Since coming to Lincoln county he has been connected with other enterprises besides that of farming. In 1885 he purchased an interest in a horse-power threshing machine and after conducting that in partnership with another party for two years, became sole proprietor of the outfit. In 1887 he purchased a steam engine, operating his thresher by steam power from that time on. In the fall of 1888 he purchased a new separator, and is now provided with enough machinery to accommodate the threshing orders of a large portion of the county. He has an extensive patronage in this line. In connection therewith he also runs a feed-mill, which he has operated for two years. In this line he has been quite successful and has made a large amount of money. He is fair and trusting in his business dealings and has the confidence of the general public. He is known all over the county as a man of excellent character and as a true and loyal citizen. He has taken an active interest in the public matters of the township in which he resides and has held various official positions. He has been clerk of school district No. 4 for about a year, and is now director of that district in which position he has served his constituency for two years past· In politics he affiliates with the democratic party.

Mr. Bressler was married February 2, 1888, in Lake Benton village, to Miss Lily Louisa Smith, a native of Northfield, Minnesota, where she lived until reaching the age of twelve years. At that time, with her parents, she removed to Lincoln county, where they became pioneer settlers. Her parents are still living in the county.

WILLIAM H. STEVENS is a thrifty and substantial farmer of Murray county, Minnesota, and resides on section 30, of Slayton township. He was born in Eaton county, Michigan, July 14, 1854. His parents were H. G. and Susan (Curtiss) Stevens, the father a native of Ohio and the mother a native of New York. By occupation the father was a farmer in early life, later was a school teacher and store-keeper, and still later a miner. The father died in November, 1878.

The first twenty years of the life of our subject were spent by him in the home of his parents. Up to this time he had been reared as a farmer's boy and had the benefit of the advantages for education furnished by the district schools. At the age of twenty years he engaged for some time with his father in mining, and later rented a farm near Manchester in the State of Iowa. He operated this farm for three years and then worked on a farm in Iowa for two years. Then, in March, 1879, in company with Mr. Lamport, he came to Murray county and soon after located where he now lives. He first went to Currie and remained there a year and then came to his present place.

Mr. Stevens was united in the holy bonds of matrimony January 4, 1887, to Emma M. Beckon, of Murray county, Minnesota, and daughter of J. A. and Mary E. Beckon. This union has been blessed with two children, one girl and one boy.

Having through his life been a man of practical temperance ideas, our subject now affiliates with the prohibition party. He takes an active interest in all matters of a general nature and especially has his influence been felt in the politics of his county. He has been justice of the peace for two years and for four years has been a member of the school board. He is a man of high character and is widely known and respected among the citizens of Murray county.

WENDELIN HECK is one of the pioneer settlers of Pipestone county, Minnesota, who has risen to a position of prominence and influence in Elmer township. He resides on the northwest quarter of section 20, where he made his settlement March 1, 1879. The first settlers of the region in which Mr. Heck located were George F. Wait, F. Kurz and a few others, the gentlemen whose names are given being still residents of Elmer township. Another settler was Henry Paul, who remained until in 1884 and then removed to Wisconsin. Coming to the township in such an early day in its history, Mr. Heck had the privilege of assisting in the organization of its civil government in June, 1879. The counting of the ballots at this election was not as laborious a matter as to-day, there being at that time but ten votes cast to determine the formation of the township. The first two town meetings were held in the house of our subject, which he had built in the spring of 1879. It will be seen that the services of the subject of our sketch, and in fact of all voters in the township, were required to administer the public affairs. Mr. Heck continued his interest in these matters, and in 1881 was elected as one of the school directors of District No. 17, which position he held for one year. He was then elected as treasurer of the same district, and holds that position at the present time. For four years he held the office of township supervisor, and in 1888 was elected chairman of the township board, to which position he was re-elected in 1889.

Mr. Heck was born in Baden, Germany, January 7, 1844. When about eight years of age he came with his parents to the United States, landing in New Orleans, whence they went to Sainte Genevieve county, Missouri, sixty miles below St. Louis. After remaining in that locality for a few years, in 1856, the family removed to Reed's Landing, Minnesota, and, in 1858, a removal was made to Buffalo county, Wisconsin, where the subject of our sketch remained with his parents until in 1879, when he removed to Pipestone county and made a settlement as was stated in the opening lines of this biography. The early life of the subject of our sketch was spent among circumstances which precluded somewhat the obtaining of a thorough classical education. However he was given the advantage of the common schools in which he obtained a fair common-school education. When he was about twenty years of age, February 1, 1864, he enlisted as a private in the Second Cavalry Wisconsin Volunteers. His service continued throughout that year and until November 15, 1865, when he was discharged at Austin, Texas. His military life was of a checkered nature being connected with a number of different commands. For a time he was under Captain Sherman, then under Captain Leroy. The troops to which this regiment was attached were engaged principally in skirmishing and scouting in Mississippi and Tennessee, a small portion of the time being spent in the same line of maneuvers in Arkansas and Louisi-ana. On being discharged from the service Mr. Heck returned to Buffalo county, Wisconsin, where he engaged in farming for two years. Sickness, however, occasioned a cessation of hard work on the farm, and to avoid this he commenced learning the carpenter's trade. He continued in this line until coming to Minnesota in 1879. More or less of his time during his residence in Pipestone county has been occupied in working at his old trade.

April 14, 1868, Mr. Heck was united in the bonds of marriage to Miss Paulina Huth, a native of Pennsylvania, where she was reared and educated. The marriage took place in Buffalo county, Wisconsin. Mr. and Mrs. Heck have eight children—John C., Willie A., Paulina W., Ella Nora, Emily, Anna, Frank and Elmer.

Settlement in a new country is not without its privations and difficulties. Scarcity of schools, long distance from market, many miles from neighbors are among the few trials which have to be met by the first settlers of any locality. These were all met and conquered, or rather lived through, by the subject of our sketch and family. On locating in Elmer township he at once commenced his agricultural operations, breaking twelve acres and building a small house, and thus getting ready for himself, his wife and children a home on the beautiful prairie. The growth of the prosperity of the county has not been without its effect upon the welfare of Mr. Heck. He, too, has grown in wealth, and has surrounded himself with the necessary comforts and appurtenances of a well-managed farm. He has a comfortable home and a pleasant family, and is himself one of the most genial and whole-souled inhabitants of the township. In politics he is an independent, believing that the best ends of government are served by supporting and voting for the best men. This belief he puts in practice by being, in politics, an independent. He is now a member of the Lutheran church, although having been reared a Catholic. He belongs to the Grand Army of the Republic, Simon Mix Post, No. 95.

JULIUS AUGUST FERDINAND SCHWIEGER, of Delton township, Cottonwood county, Minnesota, is the son of Ferdinand and Frederica (Moss) Schwieger, natives of Prussia. Julius was born in Rodgard, Prussia, March 3, 1840.

The subject of our sketch resided in his native land, working on various farms, between the age of ten and seventeen. He continued in his native country until March 28, 1868, when he came to the United States, landing in New York City on that date. He then went to Peotone, forty miles south of Chicago, and employed his time at agricultural pursuits for a year, when he came to Brown county, Minnesota, and took a homestead some two miles south of Sleepy Eye. He made this his home for some nine years, when he sold out and came to Delton township, Cottonwood county, settling on a tree claim on section 22, where he has resided ever since. He has seen hard times, but has gradually overcome them, and is now in good circumstances. The grasshoppers took seven crops, and during these years he had but little grain. His people, however, were in good circumstances, and during these trying times assisted him somewhat. Had he not obtained this assistance he could not have obtained enough for his farm to sustain his family. Mr. Schwieger is a man of good character, and is esteemed by all his fellow-citizens as a man of honor and integrity, and one in whom confidence can be profitably reposed.

Mr. Schwieger was married in Brown county, Minnesota, in December, 1869, to Wilhelmina Gent, daughter of John and Anna (Bastion) Gent, natives of Prussia. This lady was born in that country August 20, 1851, and has borne her husband the following-named children—Augusta (deceased), August, Julius, William, Emma, Charles and John. The family are members of the Lutheran church.

J W. GERBER, one of the solid and financial citizens of Luverne, Minnesota, is engaged in carrying on a large business in hardware, stoves, tinware, oils, paints, copper ware, etc. He made his advent into the city on the 23d of February, 1878, and at once engaged in his present business, in which he has continued ever since. He has now the oldest business in this line in the city. He has built an excellent fire-proof business building, in the rear of the store, which he uses for a tin shop and for storing oils, paints, nails and wire. He also carries on an extensive jobbing trade in powder and sporting goods, carrying the most approved and modernized Winchester stock. In this latter line he is the only one engaged in carrying a wholesale stock in the city. He has an excellent location, a good building and is doing an extensive trade.

The subject of our sketch is a native of Oneida county, New York, where he was born November 12, 1854. He is the son of George P. and Catharine (Paphf) Gerber, the former a native of Germany and the latter a native of France. The father left his native land in 1835, came to America and settled at Whitetown, Oneida county, New York, where for some years he engaged in farming. In 1856 he removed to Durand, Wisconsin, and built the first frame building in that village. Here he engaged in the hotel business until 1865, and then retired from active life, being still a resident of Durand. He made many fortunate and financial moves in his life, and is to-day one of the wealthiest and most substantial citizens of the county in which he lives. In the father's family there were six children, only three of whom are now living—Alonzo, who is now a resident of Portage, Wisconsin; George P., a resident of Durand, same State, where he has been extensively engaged in the real estate business for a number of years. He is one of the substantial men of the village, and owns considerable property, stores and dwelling-houses, which he rents. Our subject is the third son living.

The early days of the subject of our sketch were spent beneath the parental roof in Wisconsin. He received a good high school education in the Durand schools, and at fifteen years of age commenced learning the tinner's trade. Three years of apprenticeship were successfully passed through, after which he engaged as a journeyman tinner until coming to Luverne in 1878. On coming to Luverne, in company with A. Ross, he purchased the hardware stock of J. S. Wheeler, and continued a partnership under the firm name of Gerber & Ross until 1886. At that time Mr. Gerber bought out Mr. Ross' interest, and has continued the business alone ever since. Besides his financial interests in the city, he is also largely interested in farming lands. In 1878 he purchased 320 acres of land in Denver township, on which he has made excellent improvements. He also owns 164 acres in Red Wood county, which he has under good operation. He purchased considerable property and invested in various city enterprises for the purpose of assisting in developing the financial side of Luverne's existence. Every project which has had for its object the maintenance and upbuilding of the city has found in him an earnest and substantial support. He is a stockholder in the Security Bank, and is also largely interested as a stockholder in the red jasper stone quarries of Luverne. He owns considerable stock in the Luverne building and loan association, and also operates well-drilling machines. He makes a considerable specialty of this latter enterprise, and employs a large force of men in operating two machines in the southwestern counties of the State. He has a complete outfit of well augers, drilling machines and hydraulic jetting machines. He has considerable money invested in this business, which is one of the most beneficent and necessary to be found in the county. Farmers and citizens of the southwestern corner of Minnesota would do well to more thoroughly investigate this manner of putting in wells.

The subject of our sketch was married in 1879 to Miss Etta G. Dilley, of Lake City, Minnesota. This lady was a daughter of M. Dilley, a prominent citizen of that place. Mr. and Mrs. Gerber have one son—Herrol W.

In political affairs our subject affiliates with the democratic party. He has held a position on the village council for two years, and has in other ways assisted in the government of his locality. He is a Knight of Pythias, and interests himself actively in the affairs of this civic society. Mr. Gerber is a man of excellent ideas, is a thorough-going, energetic business man, and has become one of the most influential and substantial citizens of Luverne and Rock county.

JOHN TAINTER, one of the prominent farmers of Lincoln county, Minnesota, filed on a homestead and tree claim on section 20, Royal township, March 18, 1878. He made a permanent location on this claim in the fall of that year, and has since made that his residence, where he has been engaged in general farming and stock-raising.

John Tainter was born in Lapeer county, Michigan, October 29, 1845. His parents were Loren and Mary (Norton) Tainter, natives of Vermont and Connecticut respectively. Our subject was reared on the home farm, remaining with his parents in his native State until about 1856, when his father went to Missouri, and our subject and his mother removed to Benton county, Missouri. Here the father had purchased a farm, and our subject made his home with his parents in Missouri until 1862, when they removed to Winona county, Minnesota. Here the family resided on the farm until the fall of 1863, when they moved into the village of Homer, where the father, or one of his sons, had purchased a house and lot, and where the family lived until his father's death, which occurred in January, 1864. Our subject was married in 1867, and continued living with his mother until the spring of 1868, when he settled on a farm in Dodge county which he had purchased in 1867. Continuing his agricultural pursuits in Dodge county until the fall of 1878, he removed to Lincoln county, and settled on his claim, which he had taken in March previous. On starting out for himself in life, our subject had but little to depend upon but his own labors. His father had willed him some land in Missouri, which he traded for a 160-acre farm in Dodge county, Minnesota. Of this our subject deeded sixty acres to his mother and twenty acres to his brother Loren, leaving himself but an eighty-acre farm. In June, 1884, his mother came to Lincoln county, and made her home with our subject. She died January 27, 1886.

John Tainter was married March 26, 1867, in Steele county, Minnesota, to Miss Sarah E. Hitchcock, a daughter of Dwight and Helen J. Kingsley Hitchcock, natives of New York. Sarah E. Hitchcock was born in Badger township, Portage county, Wisconsin, November 21, 1850. When in her fourteenth year she removed from Wisconsin to Minnesota, and lived with her parents at Homer, Winona county, Minnesota. After about a six months' residence there the family removed to Rice Lake, Dodge county, Minnesota, and in 1864 her father took a claim in Steele county, where she was living at the time of her marriage. Mr. Hitchcock died January 17, 1881. Mr. and Mrs. Tainter have been blessed with the following named children—Laura A. Dell, John Edward, Myra Elvira and Mary Leona.

Since coming to Lincoln county the subject of our sketch has held the following offices: County commissioner, to which he was elected in the fall of 1886; township clerk, serving two years; supervisor, two years; chairman of the board of supervisors, two years; school clerk, and in in fact, the only school clerk since the organization. He assisted in the organization of the school district, No. 19, and has taken an active interest in its affairs. He was elected first assessor of the township when it was organized. He is a member of the Ancient Free and Accepted Masons relief lodge, No. 108, of Dodge Centre, Minnesota. He is a pleasant and sociable gentleman, and has an agreeable family.

⁕

WILLIAM M. DAVIS, a real estate dealer and prominent citizen of Fulda, Murray county, Minnesota, is the son of Alban N. and Jane (George) Davis, natives respectively of Kentucky and Ohio. Our subject was born in Jo Daviess county, Illinois, May 13, 1842. When he was thirteen years of age, his parents removed to Faribault, Rice county, Minnesota, whence they moved to Morristown, where they remained two years. Steele county became their next location, where they settled on a pre-emption and where the mother died in 1859. While they resided in Morristown in 1855–56, the majority of the people were Indians, there being three white families to five hundred redskins.

The early life of our subject was spent with his parents in their various locations, where he was given good educational advantages. While his people resided in Morristown he was thrown into the society of Indians and acquired the Indian language. He remained with his parents until in April, 1861, when he enlisted in Company G, First Minnesota Infantry for the three months' service. After the expiration of that time he re-enlisted, October 14, 1861, in Company I, Fourth Minnesota Infantry, and re-enlisted again January 1, 1864, in the same company, from which he was discharged August 9, 1865. He rendered his country gallant service, and was made first sergeant and drill sergeant of his regiment for three years. He was wounded May 22, 1863, in the left knee at Vicksburg, Mississippi, and also in the spine at Mission Ridge, November 25, 1863. He was in all the battles of his regiment, and saw much severe service. After his discharge and on his return home he purchased a farm in the woodlands of Le Sueur county, Minnesota, where he resided for some seven years. He then sold out and came to Murrray county, locating in Bondin township, where he became the first settler. He took a homestead on section 24, where he lived until 1880, when he moved into the village of Fulda. He was the first to build on the original village plat. In 1883 he moved on to the Davis addition and built on the bank of the beautiful lake. He still engaged in farming for some time after moving into the village. Since 1879 he has been engaged, to a large extent, in the real estate business and also in handling farm machinery. He has been a prominent man in public affairs, and has held various official positions, among them being that of township clerk, which he held nine years, assessor one year, chairman of the board of supervisors one year, justice of the peace five years and notary public twelve years. He has been of great assistance in obtaining pensions for old soldiers, for he has always been willing to assist them in every way in his power. He is a man of excellent business qualifications, is warm-hearted and public-spirited, and has always rendered material aid in everything which tends toward the development of his locality. He is well known and highly respected all over the county. The subject of our sketch has been commander of the Grand Army Republic Post of Fulda for five years and has been adjutant for two years.

Mr. Davis was married in Waseca county, Minnesota, April 17, 1864, while on veteran furlough, to Miss Naoma E. Fish, daughter of Benjamin and Minerva E. (Carpenter) Fish, natives of New York and Pennsylvania. Miss Fish was born in Miami county, Indiana, April 9, 1846. This union has been blessed with the following children—Leroy E., Wilba E., George W., Olive Myrtle and Hilbert G.

ROBERT JAMES BUTTS. This prominent settler came to Pipestone county, Minnesota, in the year 1879, settling on railroad land in section 17, Osborn township, where he purchased 160 acres. He at once commenced farming operations and made other improvements in the way of building out-buildings and erecting a good farm house. He has been engaged in general farming and to some extent in stock raising.

Mr. Butts arrived at the house of E. W. Day just as the organization of the township was being completed. He has since always shown his willingness and ability to assist in the furthering of the best interests of the locality in which he resides.

The gentleman whose name appears at the head of this sketch is a native of Northampton county, Pennsylvania, where he was born January 5, 1831. A short sketch of his parents is given in the biography of Jacob M. Butts in another department of this work. His mother is still living, being now eighty-five years of age, and in good health. Our subject remained in the county of his nativity until he was eight years of age, at which time, in company with his parents, he went to Rock county, Wisconsin. His father died when our subject was twelve years old. Robert remained at home until he was twenty-one, up to which time he had been assisting in work on the farm and attending the district school at every opportunity. He thus acquired a good common-school education, and was fitted for the duties of any practical life into which he might be led. At the age of twenty-one he was married and worked an adjoining farm on shares for one year. At the end of this time he removed to Dane county, where he also engaged in working a farm for about a year. He then purchased 160 acres of land in that county, and farmed this land for about two years, at the end of which time he purchased 160 acres more, adjoining his other piece, and made this farm his home until in February, 1864. At this time he removed to Rushford, Fillmore county, Minnesota, and engaged in farming for about a year. February 18, 1865, our subject enlisted as a private in Company K, First Minnesota Heavy Artillery. His company was stationed during the time of his enlistment at Chattanooga, Tennessee, under the command of Captain John Hammond. Our subject was discharged at Fort Snelling, October 10, 1865. After his discharge he returned to Fillmore county, Minnesota, and resumed his agricultural work, at which he continued for about six years. During this time he held a prominent place among the farmers of his locality and was elected twice to the office of treasurer of the school district, holding the same for a period of three years. His next move was to the township of Murray, Murray county, Minnesota, where he

homesteaded 160 acres of land on section 34. He lived on this land for some eight years engaged in general farming and stock raising. In this place his services were also in demand in the public affairs of the township. He held the office of township supervisor for about two terms, was treasurer of the school district for six years, and town treasurer two years. He left Murray county in the spring of 1879, and located in Pipestone county, as was stated in the opening lines of this biography, but still owns his homestead in Murray county.

February 15, 1852, Mr. Butts was united in marriage to Catharine Jane Miller. This lady was a native of Monroe county, Pennsylvania. Her father, Amos Miller, in 1849, settled on a farm in Rock county, Wisconsin, where he remained until the spring of 1858, and then purchased and settled on a farm in Dane county, same State, where he remained until his death, which occurred May 7, 1863, at the age of seventy-three years. Amos Miller and wife had a family of six children —Samuel, Lewis, Catharine, Amos, Anna Margaret and Thomas. Mr. and Mrs. Butts have been blessed with ten children—Amos, Jerome, Elnora, Lorenzo, Amy, Rosella, George Washington, Hattie, Robert and John. Sarah Jane died at three years of age in Dane county, Wisconsin. Amos, Jerome, Elnora and Lorenzo are all married and are residents of the State of Minnesota.

Mr. Butts is a republican in politics, and takes a prominent place in its local councils. He is a member of the Grand Army Republic Post, of which he is the present chaplain, and, during the year 1878, held the office of commander. For a number of years he has been an active member of the Sons of Temperance society, and has been an earnest worker in the promulgation of temperance ideas. In his financial affairs he has been quite successful, and has accumulated a comfortable competency.

He owns several fine farms, in all 480 acres, and his farm is one of the largest in the township. In 1886 he purchased 160 acres on section 17, the same section on which he now lives. Throughout his career our subject has been a hard-working and energetic man, and, in spite of many failures which have fallen to his lot, he has retained courage and kept constantly at work recruiting and building up his fortunes. He relates several instances to show into what straits the fortuns of the pioneer settler may fall. His first crop in Murray county, in 1872, on which he had expended much time and labor was totally destroyed by the grasshoppers. This same experience was passed through the following year and the same insects totally destroyed the second crop. The following year this hard experience fell to his lot again. He had sowed some fifty bushels of wheat, and after the "hoppers" had visited the fields his harvest yielded him 150 bushels. All other grains being destroyed in about the same proportion. The next year the grasshoppers took about half of the oats, and all the barley, but wheat yielded in great abundance, testing sixty-two and a half pounds to the bushel. Still again, the following year, he was met with disappointment, and his wheat crop was a total failure because of the "blight" which took the crops all over the country. The following year, and, from then on, our subject has had good crops, and, in spite of those early discouragements and backsets, has gradually grown in wealth and prosperity. Another interesting anecdote is told of early settlement in Murray county. The first year of our subject's residence there he was instrumental in originating the petition for the organization of the school district. The district was organized, but the following year there were not enough male residents to occupy the offices provided for by law, because of the exodus there had been on account of the grasshopper raids. Mr. Butts held the office of treasurer of the school district, and his wife was one of the trustees and a lady by the name of Youngs, from an adjoining district, was clerk of the board. The first school was held in a shanty, owned by one Williams, on section 4, the teacher receiving $35 as compensation for the term taught. When our subject settled in Murray county on his homestead, in 1871, the nearest neighbor was many miles away, and in September he returned to Fillmore county and brought his family to his prairie home in October. He traded a horse for one hundred bushels of potatoes and seventy-five bushels of wheat and prepared to go to the mill at Ibury. Winter set in quite early, however, and debarred him from taking his trip to the mill, and, from the 1st of December until the following July, the family had to do without mill-ground flour. This trouble, however, was overcome, to some extent, by a primitive method known to most early settlers. Forty bushels of the wheat were ground in a couple of coffee mills, and by this tedious and laborious method sufficient flour was obtained to last the family until the following July, and, strange as it may seem, the family relates that this flour, made in this primitive way, although coarse, was good and wholesome. Mr. Butts says that in July of the following year he succeeded in getting to the mill at Ibury, a distance of some fifty or sixty miles, and on his return with the flour obtained there the family then lived "like white folks." One more incident of the hardships subject of pioneer life through which Mr. Butts passed, and we shall close. On going to Murray county he purchased twenty head of cattle, but on account of the hard times he was forced to sell all but six head in order to furnish subsistence for his family. He also brought four horses and one pony to Murray county on making his settlement there. Winter came upon him and he had no grain for feed, and the horses were starved to death. The pony, however, being possessed of more horse vitality, perhaps, lived through the ordeal and has proven a profitable investment to his owner. From this pony Mr. Butts has raised fourteen head of horses, which has certainly repaid him for the trouble and worry of sustaining the pony's life through the hard winter of 1871–72.

Mr. Butts first joined the Sons of Temperance in Dane county, Wisconsin, and was there elected to several offices in the order, such as conductor, financial scribe, worthy patriarch, etc. He next united with the order at Currie, Murray county, Minnesota, where he held the offices of sentinel, chaplain, etc. While living in Murray county he was a member of the Murray County Agricultural Society, and otherwise indentified himself with matters of a public nature.

ON. H. W. HOLLEY is a retired "railroad man" residing in Winnebago City, Faribault county, Minnesota. He is a native of Jefferson county, New York, where he was born May 5, 1828. Mr. Holley is the son of David and Betsey S. (Randall) Holley, the former a native of New York and the latter born in Massachusetts. The father was a farmer by occupation and followed that line of business throughout his life. He was born in 1802 and died in 1888. The parents were both members of the Episcopal church, and were prominent people of the locality in which they lived. They had a family of two children—H. W. and Ophelia, now Mrs. Bemis, residing on the old homestead.

In early life our subject was given good educational advantages, and attended college at Norwich, Vermont, where he prepared himself for the profession of civil engineering. He started for the West, taking boat at Buffalo and going to Cleveland, Ohio, where he found employment as a civil engineer on the Cleveland & Pittsburgh railroad. He continued in the employ of this company for some four years, and then spent one year in making surveys for the Cincinnati & Parkersburg railroad in Ohio. He then came to Indiana and engaged in surveying in the vicinity of Fort Wayne for some eight months. In 1856 he came to Minnesota and located at Chatfield, Fillmore county, where he published the Chatfield Republican for some four years. He was also appointed receiver of the United States land office at that place and continued to hold that position after the removal of the office to Winnebago City. He continued in the office of receiver of public moneys for eight years at Winnebago City, and also became one of the organizers of the Root River Railroad Company. This corporation built the present Southern Minnesota Railroad to Winnebago City, and our subject was the chief engineer of this company while it was building and until it was sold out to the Chicago, Milwaukee & St. Paul Company. Mr. Holley has since continued his residence at Winnebago City, and has largely interested himself in farms throughout this and adjoining counties. He was proprietor of the town plat of Delevan, Faribault county, around which he also owns a number of farms, and is also financially interested in a number of town sites along the Southern Minnesota Railroad, east of Delevan. He was a member of the constitutional assembly in 1857, and in 1859–60 was a member of the State legislature from Chatfield. Throughout his life he has actively interested himself in all matters of a public nature, and has become one of the most prominent men in the politics of Southern Minnesota. He is considerable of an author, too, having published several works which have become quite popular. He published the "Politicians" in 1876, and a second edition of that work in 1883. In 1886 he issued a book called the

"Heggensville Papers," which had quite a large sale. In 1889 there emanated from his pen a work called "Random Shots at Living Targets," which has become quite popular and has had a large run. In politics he affiliates with the republican party, and is one of the most important factors in the local affairs of that organization.

Mr. Holley was married in 1855 to Miss Eliza Christie, of Ohio, a daughter of John and Martha Christie. Five children have blessed this union—Maud, Kate, now Mrs. Dr. Stauffer, of Winnebago City; Elizabeth, who married A. D. Denne, a merchant of Winnebago City; Harry, who is a civil engineer in Florida, and Mabel.

JAMES H. CLARK is one of the prominent and substantial citizens of the village of Windom, Minnesota, where he is engaged in handling farm machinery and lumber. Mr. Clark's native place is found in Kennebec county, Maine, where he was born in the year 1830.

The parents of the subject of our sketch were Rufus and Jane (Colby) Clark, both of whom were natives of Maine. The father was engaged in the lumber business and also in farming and remained in the State of his nativity until his death. He was a man of much prominence and held various township offices, and was one of the wealthy men of that section of country. He was a member of the Baptist church and took an active part in matters of a temperance nature. The grandfather of the subject of our sketch was Thomas Clark, a native of New Hampshire and a farmer by occupation. He reared a family of twelve children, eight sons and four daughters, eight of whom are now living, the oldest being eighty-eight years of age and the youngest sixty-nine. Rufus Clark reared a family of eight children, six of whom are now living—Lydia A., Carrie M., James H. (our sketch), Abbie A., Charles F. and Emma J.

The early life of the subject of our sketch was spent in various employments. During a great portion of the time he assisted his father, working both at lumbering and at farming. At the age of eighteen years, after having received a good common-school education, he found employment in a shipyard, and continued therein until the spring of 1855. In the year just mentioned he came to St. Croix Falls, Wisconsin, where he worked at millwrighting for one year. Then in company with his brothers, Rufus and Charles, he built a mill at Franconia, Chisago county, Minnesota. This was the first rotary saw-mill on the St. Croix, and our subject and his brothers continued to operate this business until 1866. Then they moved the mill to Taylor's Falls, and added stave machinery to the mill. They remained in that locality until 1878, when our subject sold his interests and came to Windom. He at once commenced in the lumber and fuel business, and continued in that line until 1885, when he put in a large stock of farm machinery. He has a fine office and other buildings, and in the management of his extensive business he employs two men. He is also engaged in raising blooded stock, and owns the famous imported French horse "Ferdinand," weight, eighteen hundred pounds; color, dark dapple-gray; imported in 1885. This animal is one of the finest in Southern Minnesota, and is a descendant of the noted Arab horse "Gallipoli." In all matters of a public nature Mr. Clark is found to be one of the most enterprising and enthusiastic of Windom's citizens. He always aids liberally in the upbuilding of every financial enterprise, and takes an active part in local governmental affairs. He is one of the stockholders and directors of the Windom bank. In politics he affiliates with the republican party, and is a member of the Masonic and Odd Fellows fraternities. He is one of the leading and substantial citizens of Windom.

Mr. Clark was married in 1864 to Miss Carrie Jellison, a native of Maine, and a daughter of Charles Jellison. Mr. and Mrs. Clark have been blessed with three children —Abbie A., now Mrs. L. D. Smith, of Windom, who has one child; Ada F.; Ada L., now Mrs. J. L. Eberle, of Windom, and Justus B., deceased.

JOHN H. THORSNESS is a thrifty and industrious farmer of Verdi township, Lincoln county, Minnesota. He has a fine farm on section 30, well improved, and thoroughly provided with good buildings. Mr. Thorsness was born in Wisconsin, in Dane county, September 24, 1849.

The parents of the subject of our sketch were Hans and Betsey (Randall) Thorsness, both natives of Norway. The father was a farmer by occupation, and a well-to-do and prominent citizen in his native land. He came to America in 1847, locating in Dane county, where he became one of the pioneer settlers. He came to Minnesota in 1864, and died here February 22, 1888.

The State of Wisconsin continued the home of the subject of our sketch for some years. His early life was spent on the home farm in that State, and he assisted his father in farming until he was nineteen years of age. Up to this time he had been given good educational advantages, and, on attaining the age just mentioned, he engaged in agricultural pursuits, in the employ of various farmers in the vicinity of his home for two years. He then went to St. Croix, and worked there, a part of the time in pineries, and a part of the time in saw-mills. Later he rented a farm in Olmsted county, Minnesota, and engaged in farming until 1878, when he came to Lin-

coln county and located the place on which he lives as a homestead. He then returned to Olmsted county and brought his family to his claim, arriving thereon in June, 1878. He has made this township his residence ever since. He at once commenced active operations in getting his farm ready for crops. He succeeded well the first year, but the second brought him his first serious disaster. After his crop was harvested and threshed, his entire crop, together with his barn, was destroyed by fire, having caught from a prairie fire.

Mr. Thorsness was married June 4, 1876, to Silva Thorsness, who was born in Wisconsin. Five children have blessed this union, three of whom are living—Henry, Gilbert and Julius.

The political faith of Mr. Thorsness is attached to the republican party. He is a man of public affairs, and takes an active interest in all public projects. He has held several official positions with efficiency and popularity. He is a man of large experience, careful and conservative in his thought and opinions, and withal, is an industrious farmer, having by reason of thrift and energy brought his farm to a high state of cultivation and accumulated considerable means. He has a pleasant and commodious home, and an agreeable family. His character is irreproachable, as is also his citizenship, and he is held in high esteem.

OLE OPEN is an influential farmer and leading citizen of Lime Lake township, Murray county, Minnesota, and resides on an excellent farm on section 20. He was born in Norway, September 27, 1846. His parents were Nils and Ele (Terdall) Open, both of whom were natives of Norway, and farmers by occupation. They are still residents of their native land.

The subject of our sketch left the parental

home in May, 1869, and came to America. His early life was spent in assisting his father in work on the farm and in attending the district school. On coming to America he located in Lanesboro, Minnesota, where he assisted on various farms during the harvest time. During the winter he worked on the railroad, and the following spring went to Brownsdale, Mower county, where he continued the latter employment until harvest. The various places at which he stopped thereafter for some time were Austin, Wells, Mankato and St. Paul. At these places he worked at various kinds of business, principally at railroad work during certain seasons of the year, and in the harvest fields during harvest time. From St. Paul he returned to Fillmore county, where he worked on a railroad in Fountain during the winter; thence he went to Mankato and St. James, and then to St. Peter. At this latter place he remained during the winter. However, before going to St. Peter, he went over into Murray county, in August, 1871, and located the claim on which he now lives. In the spring of 1872 he came to his land and put up a shanty, and commenced making improvements, soon after finding employment on the Winona & St. Peter railroad, at which occupation he continued until fall. Returning to his claim he spent the winter there, and the following spring he put in his crop, and then left to work at other employments. He continued operating on this plan until 1876, when he made his permanent location on his land. He has seen hard times, passed through the grasshopper raids and experienced other hardships in common with other pioneer settlers. The subject of our sketch is a man of strong characteristics, and has taken an important and active part in the local affairs of his township. In politics he affiliates with the republican party, and has been supervisor of his township for six years. He is a consistent member of the Lutheran church,

and takes an active part in religious matters.

Mr. Open was married to Ellen Olson, November 27, 1876. This lady is a native of Norway and a daughter of Torkil Wesby. Mr. and Mrs. Open have been blessed with six children—Pauline E., Kima O., Tennie N., John E., Eddie A. and Ellis O.

FRED BLOOM, general merchant, has been identified with the interests of the village of Woodstock, Pipestone county, Minnesota, since January 11, 1884. On that date he took possession of the general mercantile business of G. W. Martin, from whom Mr. Bloom purchased his stock. This gentleman is, without doubt, one of the most enterprising citizens of the town and county in which he lives, and has taken a lively interest in all matters of a public nature since taking up his residence among the citizens of Woodstock. He handles an immense stock of general merchandise, and is doing a large and increasing business.

The subject of our sketch was born in Canton Glarus, Switzerland, June 12, 1836. He remained in his native land until 1847, when, with his parents, he migrated to the United States, settling in the town of Washington, Green county, Wisconsin, in which State he remained for twenty-six years, engaged in farming and other pursuits. In February, 1865, he enlisted in Company A, Forty-sixth Wisconsin Infantry as a private, and was discharged May 30, 1865, at Huntsville, Alabama, as third sergeant under Captain I. T. Carr. The military life of Mr. Bloom was spent principally in guarding railroads and army stores at Athens, Alabama. His only wound was received while guarding the roads at the above-named place, the injury, however, was very severe, and our subject has felt its effects throughout the most of his life since the war. After he was discharged from the service he went to

Monticello, Green county, Wisconsin, and engaged in the mercantile business, in which he continued but a short time when he sold out, and in 1867 went to New Glarus. He continued his business in the latter-named city until he was burned out in October, 1872. He then concluded to move to Minnesota, and, in the spring of 1873, settled in Nobles county, of that State, where he engaged in farming until 1882. While in that county Mr. Bloom occupied a prominent and influential place among the residents and farmers. He was a man of good judgment, pleasant and affable in all respects, and became popular as a county official. In 1878 he was elected one of the county commissioners and served three years, during the last year of which term he was chairman of the board.

October 2, 1859, Mr. Bloom was united in matrimony to Miss M. A. Roby, a native of Licking county, Ohio. While still young she removed with her family to Green county, Wisconsin, where she was given a good education. May 18, 1871, Mrs. Bloom died at New Glarus, at the age of thirty-two years. In 1872 Mr. Bloom married Miss Barbary Roby, a sister of his first wife, and also a native of Licking county, Ohio. By his first wife Mr. Bloom had five children—William E, Mary E., A. R., Clara A. and Fred. His second marriage has been blessed with one child—Luther C.

In political faith Mr. Bloom is connected with the republican party, in whose councils he occupies a prominent place. He is also deeply interested in Masonic circles, being a member of the Blue Lodge and Chapter of Pipestone City, of which Chapter Mr. Bloom is the present "Scribe." He is also a member of Stephen Miller Post, No. 139, G. A. R., and is its present commander. He is also postmaster at Woodstock, Minnesota. Throughout his life the subject of our sketch has been thoroughly identified with all matters of public nature pertaining to the government of localities in which he lived. His life has been well spent in the midst of careful business pursuits and in lines of thorough usefulness to his fellow-citizens. Being given the advantages of a good common-school education in his early youth, young manhood found him well fitted for business enterprises in which he engaged. For several years he taught school in Green county, Wisconsin, and while a resident of Washington township of that county was elected clerk of the township, in which capacity he served four years. While a resident of New Glarus he was supervisor for two years, and since coming to the State of Minnesota he has been still more intimately identified with the civil government of localities in which he has resided. Taking his life as a whole, Mr. Bloom has passed many years of usefulness, and has shown himself a good citizen and a man of the highest character.

It will doubtless be of interest to describe their journey from Canton Glarus, Switzerland. The party included sixteen families, March 27, 1847, they went down the Lint canal in a flat boat to Lake Zurich, down said lake in a steamer to Basel; thence in wagons to Paris, France; thence down the River Seine to Havre; thence by sailing forty-eight days landed in New York; thence up the Hudson river to Albany; thence by canal to Buffalo; thence by steamer via the lakes to Milwaukee, where they landed July 4th; thence on lumber wagons one hundred miles to the town of Washington, Green county, Wisconsin.

———◆·◀▨▶·◆———

MISS AGNES E. SAFLEY is the present superintendent of schools of Cottonwood county, Minnesota. She was elected to the position in 1886 and commenced her work January 1, 1887. She is a daughter of Robert Safley, a native of Scotland, who came to Cottonwood county in 1878. Since that time he has been engaged in farming. He was the son of a weaver by trade, and on coming to Cedar county, Iowa, when twenty-seven years of age, Mr. Safley engaged in farming and has made that his business ever since. Miss Agnes' mother's maiden name was Helen Fairbairn, a native of Scotland, where she was married to Mr. Safley May 13, 1842. She passed from this life in 1878. She was a member of the United Presbyterian church. At the time of her death she was sixty years of age, having been born in the year 1818. In the Safley family there were ten children—Joan; Agnes E., the subject of this sketch; John H., James F., Jennie, an infant deceased, Robert B., Frances, Barbara and Walter.

County Superintendent Miss Agnes E. Safley is thoroughly qualified from an educational standpoint for the duties which devolve upon her in the office which she holds. Her early life was spent almost entirely in school, her education being received in the public schools in Iowa, at Cornell college, Mount Vernon, and in the Keokuk Business College, from which she graduated in 1877. She was a popular teacher, especially successful in penmanship, having studied that branch under O. H. Pierce, who is now the president of the Keokuk Business College.

JOHN A. STEGNER is a leading and reliable farmer of Hendricks township, Lincoln county, Minnesota, and lives on an excellent farm on section 34. Mr. Stegner was born in New Jersey, August 6, 1851.

The parents of the subject of our sketch were Conrad and Mary E. (Martin) Stegner, both of whom were natives of Germany. The father was an influential farmer in his native land and came to America in 1846. He was a loyal citizen and served as a soldier in the Mexican War. In 1850 he settled in the State of New Jersey, where our subject was born. Remaining in that State about three years, in 1853 he made a location in Wisconsin. His residence in that State continued until 1860, when he located in Dakota county, Minnesota, and in 1881 removed to Northfield, where he died January 19, 1889. The father was a man of extended experience, a loyal citizen, and was respected by all who knew him.

John A. Stegner left the parental home when he was nineteen years of age. Up to this time he had attended school and assisted in work on the farm. On attaining nineteen years of age he worked out through the summers and taught school during the winter months until he was twenty-four years of age. At this age he was married, and rented a farm in Dakota county, Minnesota. He continued operating that property for about four years and then, in 1879, came to Lincoln county and filed on the place where he now lives.

Mr. Stegner was united in the bonds of matrimony, November 19, 1874, to Miss Mary Jackstetter, by whom he has had six children—William E., Andrew S., Anna E., Irwin H., Fred M. and Paul J., all of whom are living at the present time. Mrs. Stegner is a native of Canada.

The subject of our sketch received a good education in his early life, and attended the college at Northfield for five terms. He was thus well prepared to occupy the duties of any line of occupation into which he might be called. In politics he was a republican until five years ago, since which time he has been a prohibitionist. He has been honored by being placed in several positions of trust and responsibility. He has been justice of the peace ever since the township was organized, and is at present chairman of the board of supervisors, having been a member of that body two terms. He has also taken an active interest in the general affairs of the county, and has identified himself with the interests of the county government. In the fall of 1888 he was elected one of the county commissioners. Mr. Stegner is a man of fine qualities, of excellent character, and is a loyal and upright citizen.

ERDINAND KURZ. This gentleman is one of the leading and most influential farmers and stock raisers in Elmer township, Pipestone county, Minnesota. One of the early settlers of this township, he has been identified with its interests since its organization, and in all matters pertaining to the civil government, and in every way relating to the welfare of the township he has taken an active and leading part. His residence is located on section 20, where he homesteaded his present farm in 1878. Mr. Kurz was one of the organizers of the township, was a member of the first board of trustees, and took an active interest in all matters of that nature.

The subject of our sketch is a native of Germany, being born in Wurtemberg, August 10, 1839. His father, John Kurz, was a native of Germany and a farmer by occupation. He lived and died in the old country. Ferdinand was one of fourteen children, eight of whom are now living. The subject of our sketch remained in his native land, being given excellent educational facilities, until he was about fifteen years of age. He then concluded to emigrate and settle in the United States, and, taking a steamer, after a short voyage he landed in the city of New York, and thence went to Milwaukee, Wisconsin, where he remained until 1866. During his residence in Milwaukee he was engaged in the bakery business for some five or six years. In 1864 he enlisted as a private in the Thirty-fifth Wisconsin Infantry. His service during the

Rebellion was very satisfactory to his superior officers, and he was promoted to the position of sergeant, which rank he held on being discharged in April, 1866. He saw much severe service during the time he spent in the war, was in the service at the siege of Mobile and in a great many battles and skirmishes of minor importance. After his discharge from his regiment, he returned to Milwaukee, remaining a short time, and then removing to St. Paul, Minnesota. After remaining in the latter city for about a year, he then purchased a farm in Dakota county, Minnesota, and made that his home until coming to Pipestone county in 1878. His farm in Dakota county was about fifteen miles from St. Paul, and he was engaged largely in general farming and in stock raising.

In the fall of 1866 Mr. Kurz was united in the bonds of matrimony to Miss Louisa Warweg, a native of Germany. Mrs. Kurz is a lady of fine qualities, being possessed of a good education, and by nature and training well fitted to occupy the position at the head of one of the leading households and influential families in Pipestone county. She is a lady of excellent social tastes, and merits the respect and esteem of all those with whom she comes in contact. Mr. and Mrs. Kurz have no children.

The abilities of the subject of our sketch have been recognized by the citizens of Elmer township ever since he became one among its residents. From the very first organization of the township he has been installed in some public office, being at present township treasurer, which position he has held since the first election of officers in the town. Besides the offices we named at the opening of this sketch he has held the office of director of school district No. 17 for two terms. In politics Mr. Kurz is a representative of the local interests of the republican party, with which organization he has affiliated for many years. He is a member of the Grand Army of the Republic.

———◆◈◆———

CARLISLE FERGUSON is a representative farmer of Murray county, Minnesota, and resides on section 2 of Shetek township, where he located on a homestead June 9, 1872. He has been a prominent resident of that place ever since, and has made valuable and important improvements. He has a fine grove of cottonwood, ash and poplar trees, and his place, in every particular, shows care and thrift in its management.

The gentleman whose name appears at the head of this sketch was born in Mifflin county, Pennsylvania, April 11, 1842. His father, Carlisle Ferguson, was a native of Pennsylvania, where he was reared and educated. He emigrated to Iowa in 1854, and thence came to Minnesota in 1857, locating at Vernon, Dodge county. He engaged in farming until his death, which occurred in 1867. Our subject's mother's name was Sarah Hughes, a native of Bellefonte, Pennsylvania. She is still living, and resides with her son John. In the father's family there are eight living children—Alexander, George, John, Carlisle, Mary Ann, Jane, Martha and Elizabeth.

The early life of the subject of our sketch was spent with his parents in Mifflin county, Pennsylvania, where he received a good common-school education. When thirteen years of age he came with his parents to the State of Iowa, and thence to Minnesota, where he remained until he was eighteen years of age. He then enlisted on the 9th day of October, 1861, in Company K, Third Minnesota Infantry as a private. He served throughout the war, and was discharged at Duvall's Bluff, Arkansas, September 2, 1865. He served his country honorably and faithfully as a private under Captain James Hodges,

who is now a resident of Colorado. Our subject participated in the following principal battles: Vicksburg and Murfreesboro, and also in many other battles and skirmishes. He was taken prisoner July 2, 1862, at the battle of Murfreesboro, and was held by the rebels for two days, when he was liberated on parole and allowed to return home. He has never recovered from the hardships and exposure through which he passed in his army service. He contracted the disease of asthma, from which he has never recovered. After his discharge he returned to Olmsted county, Minnesota, making that his home until 1872. He then came to Murray county, where he has since resided.

During the grasshopper raids in this region our subject was obliged to find other employment in order to support his family. During two seasons he went to Olmsted county and worked at various employments.

Mr. Ferguson was married in Olmsted county, Minnesota, December 23, 1866, to Miss Emma Gould, a native of Clinton county, New York. Early in life she came West, and was reared in Olmsted county. Mr. and Mrs. Ferguson have one child, Lucinda, eleven years of age.

Mr. Ferguson is a man of stanch principles, and affiliates with the republican party. He is a member of the Presbyterian church at Tracy, and is a man of exemplary Christian character. He was deacon of that society for three years. By virtue of his honorable career in the Union army he holds an influential position in the Grand Army of the Republic. He has taken a prominent place in public matters.

———◆◈◆———

JOSEPH S. NARAMORE, a prosperous farmer of Delton township, Cottonwood county, Minnesota, is the son of Samuel and Aurelia (Bardwell) Naramore, natives of Massachusetts. Joseph S. was born in

Goshen, Hampshire county, Massachusetts, May 18, 1827. His father died when he was two and a half years old, and our subject then resided with his mother until he was seven years of age. The mother was then married to Benjamin White, and our subject lived with his uncle, G. Porter, until he was sixteen, when he left the home of his relative and commenced doing for himself.

At sixteen years of age he apprenticed to learn the blacksmith's trade and continued in that line until he was twenty years old, when he moved to Chicopee, Massachusetts, and engaged in work at his trade for a year. Removing thence he followed his old business at Kenosha, Wisconsin, and also engaged to some extent in farming and teaching in Lake county, Illinois. Later he was a salesman in a boot and shoe store for two and a half years in the city of Kenosha; then removed to Lake county, Illinois and engaged in farming and school teaching until the fall of 1855. In this year he removed to Hennepin county, Minnesota, and located in the village of Excelsior, on lake Minnetonka, where he worked at his trade and engaged in farming until February, 1865, when he enlisted in Company D, Second Minnesota Cavalry, and participated in the Indian expedition, serving until December of the same year. After his discharge he returned to Excelsior and worked at his trade until 1872, when he came to Cottonwood county and settled near the village of Mountain Lake. He remained there during two seasons, and then sold out to a Russian and came to Delton township, taking a tree claim on section 12, where he has since lived with the exception of two years during the grasshopper times. During these two years his boys were left to run the farm, and our subject and his wife went back to Excelsior, where he worked at his trade to earn money with which to support his family.

The subject of our sketch was married in Kenosha, Wisconsin, to Miss Hattie Spencer, daughter of Samuel and Martha (Bigelow) Spencer, natives of New Hampshire. Miss Spencer was born in Hinsdale, New Hampshire, January 31, 1830. This union has been blessed with the following named children—Charles Spencer and Fred Albert. Mr. Naramore's family is one of the most influential in Delton township. Mr. Naramore himself is looked upon as being one of the most honorable and influential of its citizens.

Joseph Naramore's son, CHARLES SPENCER NARAMORE, was born in Libertyville, Lake county, Illinois, August 8, 1854. He received a good common-school education at Excelsior, Minnesota, and lived with his parents until he was thirty years of age. At twenty-one years he took a homestead of section 12 of Delton township and improved the place, keeping bachelor's hall thereon for two years while his parents were in Excelsior during the grasshopper times. Besides farming he also dealt in buying and shipping cattle and in other profitable employments.

Charles S. Naramore was married in Delton township, November 27, 1884, to Miss Belle Beaty, daughter of Samuel M. and Anna K. (Caton) Beaty, natives of New Hampshire and Maine, respectively. Miss Beaty was born in Lenark, Carroll county, Illinois, June 20, 1867. By this union there have been two children—Bertie S. and Wilber B., who died March 30, 1889.

Joseph S. Naramore, whose name appears at the head of this sketch, has been one of the most prominent public men in the township. He has been county commissioner two years, township clerk four years, and has held the supervisorship for some time. At present Charles S. Naramore is assessor, school district director, and in all matters tending to the public welfare he always takes an active interest. They have been hard workers and good managers, and although when Joseph Naramore commenced life for himself he had no money and nothing but a suit of clothes, he has gradually grown in wealth and prosperity until to-day he is one of the most solid and substantial citizens in the township. Both the father and son, Charles S., have excellent, well-improved farms.

Joseph Naramore's son, Fred Albert, was born in Excelsior, Hennepin county, Minnesota, February 6, 1863. He is at present engaged in farming on section 12, of Delton township, Cottonwood county, Minnesota. He is unmarried, and resides with his parents.

JULIUS RECK, a thrifty and industrious farmer of Lincoln county, Minnesota, located on section 15, Diamond Lake township, on a homestead in 1878. He also took a tree claim on section 12 and set out about ten acres of trees. The first year he broke forty acres of land and in 1879 had forty acres of a poor crop. This was occasioned by heavy winds which prevailed in the spring, thus blowing the dirt off the seed which had been sown. Among other severe trials through which our subject was called to pass was the destruction of his house by a wind storm in 1879. In 1880 our subject still continued his farming operations, and had a good crop. He was one among the pioneer settlers of the township, and has been actively engaged in bringing his place up to its present high state of cultivation and improvement. The first three years he broke 240 acres on his two claims. In public matters he has been an active participant and has been chairman of the township board of supervisors for some years. He has been treasurer of school district No. 9 for three terms and also of district No. 4 for two terms. For two years he has also occupied the position of justice of

the peace. By constant application to the best interests of his township he has become one of the prominent and influential citizens.

Mr. Reck was born in the city of Wabasha, Wabasha county, Minnesota, June 17, 1858. He is the son of Felix and Philopena (Steutzel) Reck, the father a native of Baden and the mother born in Bavaria, Germany. At the time of the birth of our subject the father was a grain dealer and also was engaged in mercantile pursuits, giving his attention also somewhat to farming. He was formerly engaged in the hotel business, and for years has been a representative citizen of Wabasha county. The father served for three years as a soldier in the German army, in the war between Prussia and Baden. He is still living and is a resident of Wabasha. The mother is also living in Wabasha. In the father's family there were six children—Barbara, Julius, Bertha, Paulina, Bruno and Alfred.

The subject of our sketch remained in Wabasha county until he was twenty years of age. Up to this time he had resided with his parents, who gave him excellent advantages for obtaining an education. When he was twenty years of age he came to Lincoln county and purchased a tree claim as already stated, paying therefor $200. He has since made Lincoln county his home.

Mr. Reck was married December 2, 1884, to Miss Bertha Abram, a native of Prussia. When a year old she was brought by her parents to the United States, and they located in Minnesota. Her parents are now living in Diamond Lake township, Lincoln county, Minnesota. Mr. and Mrs. Reck have one son, Felix.

Mr. Reck affiliates with the democratic party and is a leading member of the Catholic church. He belongs to the Tyler lodge, Ancient Order United Workmen, and takes an active interest in all matters which pertain to the welfare of that society. In public matters the subject of our sketch has always been an intelligent and active participant. He has taken a prominent part in various governmental affairs since coming to the township, and has held various positions of trust. In whatever position he has been called upon to serve his constituents, he has served with efficiency and popularity. He is a man of excellent character, and is held in high esteem by all with whom he has to do.

BENJAMIN W. WOOLSTENCROFT, the proprietor and publisher of the Murray county *Republican*, is the son of Benjamin and Mary Ann (Kerr) Woolstencroft, natives of England and Northern Ireland, respectively. Mr. Woolstencroft was born in Jefferson Barracks, February 22, 1846. He resided on a farm with his parents and attended the district schools until he was seventeen years old. He then enlisted in Company L, Sixth Iowa Cavalry, his enlistment bearing date of November 1, 1862. He served gallantly until May 10, 1864, when he was discharged for disability. He was afterward commissioned as a recruiting officer by the governor of Iowa and was ranked as a first lieutenant. He participated in the battle of Whitestone Hill, September 3, 4 and 5, 1863, and also in a battle with the Indians at Niobrara river.

Our subject had patriotic blood in his veins, having come from good war stock. His father was an old soldier of the Black Hawk War and also served in the Florida and Mexican wars. He held the position of orderly sergeant. After the Civil War was over Benjamin W. Woolstencroft returned to Clayton county, Iowa, to which place his parents had moved when he was a small boy. He remained on the farm until July, 1867, when he came to Nobles county, Minnesota, settling on government land which was then

unsurveyed. He resided here until 1876, assisting in the organization of the county, having been appointed county commissioner by Governor Austin. He was elected first county auditor, but would not qualify. He was county surveyor for eight years in Nobles county. He was also county surveyor for the same length of time in Murray county, which position he now holds. In 1878 he sold out his property in Nobles county and removed to Murray county, where he continued during one winter, about six miles from where the village of Fulda now stands. In the spring of 1879, in the capacity of surveyor, he platted the town of Fulda, and took up his location here. During the first one and a half years he was engaged in bookkeeping for W. H. Johnson & Co., in their general store. At that time he engaged in, the publishing business, in which he has since been occupied.

Mr. Woolstencroft was married in Clayton county, Iowa, December 18, 1866, to Miss Susan Anscomb, daughter of John and Sarah (Rathburn) Anscomb, natives of England and Ohio. Miss Anscomb was born in Monroe, Green county, Wisconsin, April 2, 1848. Mr. and Mrs. Woolstencroft have been blessed with the following-named children—Minnie, Arthur, William, Mark, Belle, John and Lulu. The son Arthur was the first white boy born in Southwestern Minnesota.

The subject of our sketch has been active and public-spirited as a citizen of Fulda. He has held various official positions, among them being that of president of the village council and also of the school board, besides having been county surveyor and holding other county offices. He is a member of the Modern Woodmen of America and also of the Grand Army of the Republic, Zach. Taylor Post, No. 42, of which he has been commander and adjutant for several years. His principal business throughout a great portion of his residence in Minnesota has been that of surveying, and he was the one who surveyed the line of the Southern Minnesota Railroad from Eagle Lake, Nobles county, to the west line of the State.

Mr. Woolstencroft's father was a soldier for twenty-one years and three months, and died in the village of Fulda, February 11, 1887. He was married December 3, 1835, and on the fiftieth anniversary of his wedding day the citizens of Fulda made him a present of a fine gold-headed cane and his wife of a pair of gold spectacles and an easy chair. When the father was on the western expeditions he passed through many hairbreadth escapes, and gathered together many interesting relics, some of which are now in the State historical rooms.

CHARLES EDWARDS is a thrifty and substantial farmer of Hansonville township, Lincoln county, Minnesota, where he is located on section 24, on a fine farm of 160 acres. He has given his attention principally to general farming and stock raising, and in connection therewith has operated a threshing-machine during the last nine years. He made his location in the township in 1879, and has, since that year, been actively engaged in improving his farm. He has set out a large number of cottonwood and box elder trees, and has now a beautiful grove. During the first year he broke up between ten and twelve acres, and this, with six acres broken before he settled on his land, was sown with wheat. His crop yielded eighteen bushels to the acre. He built a small shanty 12x12 feet, and this still forms a part of his dwelling-house. He has, however, added to it and improved it until now he has a very pleasant and comfortable home. He also built a sod stable 14x16 feet, using the building for about a year and building another, and so keeping on improving until he has now provided his farm with all necessary

out-buildings. He was one of the earliest settlers of the township, and has occupied an influential position in all public affairs. He has held several positions of responsibility, among them being that of constable of the township, to which he was elected four years, and supervisor, which position he held one year.

The place of the nativity of Mr. Edwards is to be found in Norway, where he was born in June, 1858. He resided in the old country for some ten years and then with his parents came to the United States, locating in Fillmore county, Minnesota. Ten years of residence there sufficed and our subject came to his present farm in Lincoln county. The educational facilities in his native country and in Fillmore county were of good character and he was able to acquire a good common-school education. On coming to this township he at once took hold of its various enterprises and assisted in its organization in about 1885, our subject originating the petition for its organization. The first township meeting was held at the house of Mr. Westby on section 22.

The subject of our sketch was married January 9, 1881, to Miss Emma Christofforson, a native of Fillmore county. Mr. and Mrs. Edwards have two children—Thea and Clara.

In politics the subject of our sketch affiliates with the republican party and has attained to considerable prominence in the local affairs of that organization. He is also a loyal and consistent member of the Lutheran church, of which he is at present a trustee. In matters of an educational, political and religious nature our subject has been intimately associated with the best interests of the county. He has assisted in every way in developing the farming interests of his locality and has aided in every project tending to its growth and prosperity. He is a thorough-going, hard-working farmer, and is held in high esteem by his fellow-citizens.

HENRY O. WHITEHEAD is one of the foremost citizens of Pipestone county, Minnesota, and lives in a pleasant home on section 18, in Sweet township. He owns a fine farm of 240 acres of land, and has grown in wealth and popularity ever since coming to the county.

The subject of our sketch was born in Ogle county, Illinois, March 7, 1856. He is the son of Job Whitehead, of whom a sketch is given in another department of this work. The mother was Rebecca (Biggers) Whitehead, a native of New York, and at present a resident of Sweet township, where the father is also living. When the subject of our sketch was about nine years of age his parents moved to Cedar Rapids, Iowa, from whence, after a residence of about three years, they moved to Story county, same State, where they engaged in agricultural pursuits. After five years they again moved, this time going to Webster county, same State. and remaining between three and five years. From thence they moved to Lyon county, settling in Rock Rapids, from whence, about five years later, they moved to Pipestone county, Minnesota, where the family has since lived. Up to fourteen years of age the subject of our sketch helped his father on the home farm, and was given good educational advantages.

Mr. Whitehead was married March 19, 1876, in Lyon county, Iowa, to Frances V. Brooks. Her father, John Brooks, was a native of New York, and was a man of prominence in the State in which he lived. For a number of years he was overseer of the United States arsenal at Troy, New York, and during the later years of his life was engaged in the occupation of farming. His death occurred November 19, 1884, in Lyon county, Iowa. The father was a soldier in the Union army for three years. Mrs. Whitehead's mother was Lydia M. (Stebbins) Brooks. She died in Rock county, Minnesota, April 18, 1880. Mr. and Mrs. Whitehead have two children, both of whom are living—Edith P., born April 15, 1879, and Dudley V., born March 31, 1885.

In politics Mr. Whitehead affiliates with the union labor party, having been connected with that organization for some years. Our subject is a man of broad ideas, well-cultivated mind, energetic and careful in his business transactions, and has built up a large circle of warm friends since coming to Pipestone county. He is a good citizen, and takes an active interest in all matters of a public nature. Mrs. Whitehead is a lady of much culture and refinement. She has taken an unusual amount of interest in educational matters, and was elected as the first county superintendent of schools in Pipestone county, but owing to a clause in the laws of the State, at that time, to the effect that a "woman could not hold the office," she was not permitted to qualify.

WILLIAM H. WILSON is engaged in one of the most important business enterprises of Rock county, and is therefore one of Rock county's best known and most trustworthy citizens. He is the proprietor of the Luverne Roller Flouring Mills, located on the Rock river, just east of the city. He came to Luverne in 1876, and for about six years engaged in the hardware business. On first coming to the city, he built his mill, and engaged more or less in its operation. He is one of the most enterprising business men among Luverne's early settlers. He built the first brick building in the city, and indeed the first in the county, in 1878, this building being now used by the Security Bank. This structure was 24x60 feet, two stories high, with good cellar, and cost in the neighborhood of three thousand dollars. The mill, taking into consideration all its improvements, and its equipment with the modern invention now so universally used and known as the roller system, cost some sixteen thousand dollars. Here our subject employs some six men continually, and is engaged in operating an extensive and profitable business. Besides his city business enterprises, he has also invested considerable in lands in the county, and has several choice farms. He is engaged in general farming, and to some extent makes a specialty of Poland-China hogs. Every business project that would help develop the interests of Luverne has met with the hearty support of Mr. Wilson. He became one of the leading spirits in the organization of Rock County Bank, of which he has been vice-president ever since its organization. He was also one of the organizers and is the president of the Security Bank of Howard, Minor county, Dakota. We have already intimated that our subject contributed largely in the building enterprises of Luverne. He has built several business buildings, some of which he has sold and others he rents. He built a very fine residence in 1887 at a cost of about five thousand dollars. This was the finest dwelling house in the city, and is fitted with all the modern improvements.

The place of the nativity of Mr. Wilson is found in Ogdensburg, New York, where he was born in the year 1848. His father was James Wilson, a native of Ireland; his mother was a native of Scotland, and her name before her marriage was Mary Piercey. The father came to America in 1840, and settled in New York State, where he engaged in the occupation of farming. New York remained the home of the parents throughout their life. They had a family of six children, five of whom are now living— William H., John, now a resident of Luverne, and foreman in our subject's mill; Margaret, now Mrs. David Shell of Mitchell, Dakota; Elizabeth, now Mrs. William Kelley, of New York; and James, at present operating the old homestead in St. Lawrence county, New York.

The parental roof sheltered the subject of our sketch until he became sixteen years of age Up to this time he had been assisting in work on the home farm and had attended district school at every opportunity. He thus obtained a good common school education and became well fitted for entering actively upon the duties of active life which have fallen to his lot. At the age of sixteen he went to Ogdensburg, New York, and commenced learning the milling trade, serving an apprenticeship of some six years. Then, in 1870, he came West and settled in Windom, Minnesota, where he engaged in general merchandising. He was the first merchant of that town, and continued his residence there engaged in business until 1876, when he came to Luverne. He built the first store building in Windom, and built another larger store in which he engaged in the mercantile business in partnership with Mr. Hutton, under the firm name of Hutton & Wilson. This business partnership was continued for some time until Mr. Wilson sold out his interest to Mr. Hutton, and came to Luverne. The firm of Hutton & Wilson did an extensive business at Windom, and they were the largest and most substantial dealers in that place.

The subject of our sketch was married in 1881 to Miss Zillah E. Drew, of Luverne, daughter of Charles C. and Sarah Drew. Mr. and Mrs. Wilson have been blessed with one child, a son named Charles.

The political affiliations of the subject of our sketch have been with the democratic party. He is also an influential member of the Masonic and Odd Fellows fraternities. Throughout his business career in Rock county he has proven himself a man of careful, conservative business habits, and also a man of the highest integrity. He has been engaged in diversified pursuits, but in them all, by careful management, has attained merited success, and has made a considerable fortune. In public matters he always takes an active interest, and willingly assists by word and deed, in a financial and in other ways, in every project which tends to the strengthening of the financial status of the town in which he lives. He is a man of excellent principles, honest, upright in every particular, and is respected and esteemed by a large circle of friends.

HAMILTON WELLS is a retired farmer, residing in Pipestone City, Minnesota. He is one of the pioneer settlers of the county, having made his location here on the 26th of March, 1878. He first settled in Grange township, where he homesteaded 160 acres of land, and on which he resided for about two years. While on that land he built a shanty 12x14 feet, and seven feet high, and broke 100 acres, and in every way experienced the usual enjoyments of pioneer life. In 1879 he entered into a contract with the government to carry the mail to. and from Luverne, in Rock county, Minnesota. This engagement was continued for eight years, during the most of which time his residence was in Pipestone City. He made a successful engagement with the government, and during the greater time of his employment on the mail route used two horses, the traffic and governmental matter being so large that one horse was not sufficient. Some years ago he traded his farm for city property, and is now the owner of three houses, other than his own residence, in which he has tenants at present.

The subject of our sketch is a native of Jackson county, Ohio, where he was born on the 3d day of July, 1827. He is the son of Thomas and Mary (McCoy) Wells, natives of Kentucky and Ohio, respectively. The father was engaged principally in farming throughout his life, and in 1846 he removed to Sioux county, Wisconsin, where he followed that occupation until his death. Our subject continued at the home of his parents until he was sixteen years of age, being given good educational advantages in his native State. On attaining the age just mentioned he hired out to work on a farm in Indiana, and remained with one employer for two years. At the end of that time he returned to Ohio and remained another two years, and in 1847 went to Milwaukee, Wisconsin. One year later, in 1848, he went to Sioux county, Wisconsin, and engaged in farming until the breaking out of the war. In October, 1861, he enlisted in Company L, Ninth Illinois Cavalry, and continued in the Union service for three years. In a skirmish with guerillas six miles from Corinth, Mississippi, he was severely wounded, and suffered a long period of disability before his entire recovery. He was engaged in a great many battles and skirmishes. After his three years' services he returned home, and shortly after removed to Iowa, where he engaged in agricultural pursuits for three years in Chickasaw county. At the end of that period he again found his way back to Wisconsin, where for ten years he followed farming, after which he came to Pipestone county, as was stated in the opening of this sketch.

Mr. Wells was married October 17, 1849, to Miss Elizabeth E. Harris, of Harrisburg, Sioux county, Wisconsin. This lady was a daughter of Jonathan and Abigail E. (Crocraft) Harris, her father being an extensive farmer in Sioux county, Wisconsin. Mr. and Mrs. Wells have had four children, three of whom are now living—John W., Henry H. and Charles E. John married Emma Heffel, and is now residing on a farm in Pipestone county; Henry married Miss Ada Chapman, of Berlin, Wisconsin; Charles married Pettie C. Kester, of Reedsburg, Wisconsin. The subject of our sketch has lived a long and useful life. His career has been full of activities and earnest endeavor to build up for himself and family a comfortable fortune. He has accumulated considerable means, and now after a long life has settled down to enjoy the results of his labor. Being an early settler of Pipestone county, he occupies a prominent place in the minds of his fellow-citizens, and has a wide circle of acquaintances. In politics he affiliates with the republican party. His wife is a member of the Methodist Episcopal church, and both take an active interest in all matters which pertain to the social and moral welfare of the public.

ERIC LARRABEE is a prominent farmer of Selma township, Cottonwood county, Minnesota, and is the son of Alvah and Amy (Humphry) Larrabee, natives, respectively, of New York and Vermont. Our subject was born in Winnebago county, Wisconsin, June 10, 1848, to which place his parents had removed in an early day. When Eric was thirteen years of age the parents removed to Freeborn county, Minnesota, locating on a farm of two hundred acres near the city of Albert Lea. Residing on the same for three years, they then sold out and located in Brown county, near the village of Sleepy Eye, on two hundred acres of Sioux reservation land.

Our subject continued residing with his parents until he was a little over twenty-one years of age. He then found employment on various farms, and later learned the mason's trade, which business he followed for some seven or eight months. During this time he took a homestead on section 8 in Butterfield township, Watonwan county. He finally commuted his time and then sold out and took a pre-emption on section 8,

Selma township, Cottonwood county, in which township he afterward took a tree claim. He has resided on this claim ever since, with the exception of two years spent in Brown county, one year on a rented farm and one year working out at his trade. He then returned to his farm, which he had left on account of failure of crops, and has since continued his residence there. He has been quite successful and has a good frame house, barn, and other buildings, and a fine grove of eleven acres of trees. In politics he affiliates with the republican party, is a man of good character, and is widely respected. He has held the office of township clerk, treasurer, and also school director and treasurer of the school district.

Mr. Larabee was married to Miss Allie J. Hall of Waukau, Winnebago county, Wisconsin, on the 23d of March, 1875. They have had three children born to them: Jennie May, born December 14, 1876; Ward W., born May 18, 1878, and Amy O. Larrabee, born November 30, 1884.

REV. DAVID P. OLIN, pastor of the Methodist Episcopal church at Lake Benton, Minnesota, is the son of Rev. Giles and Electa (Palmer) Olin, the former a Methodist Episcopal minister and a native of Wales, and the latter a native of England. In 1866 the parents located at Sparta, Wisconsin, where, two years later, they both died. The parents were exemplary Christian people and died in the triumphs of Christian faith.

Rev. D. P. Olin was born in Montgomery county, New York, December 26, 1852. Removing with his parents to Sparta, Wisconsin, in September, 1865, he was given the educational advantages of the high school, from which institution he graduated in June, 1868. He removed from Sparta to Prairie du Chien, where he resided with Rev. Alfred

Bronson, D. D., for two years, during which time he attended the Prairie du Chien College. Completing his educational course he then entered the employ of G. W. Comstock & Co., proprietors of a soap factory. He continued his engagement with them as traveling salesman for one and a half years, after which he removed to Eau Claire. In that city he accepted a position as bookkeeper and scaler of logs for the Eau Claire Lumber Company. He continued a profitable and satisfactory engagement with this company for three years, after which he went to Red Wing, Minnesota, and established the Red Wing broom factory, in which business he continued for some three and a half years. In March, 1878, he sold out his business and removed to Brookings county, Dakota, where he took a homestead and tree claim and engaged in farming until 1886. He still owns the homestead. In October, 1886, he entered the Christian ministry and was ordained as deacon in October, 1888. His first charge was at Spring Lake, Hand county, Dakota, where he organized a church society and secured sixty-eight members. When he took charge of this work there were but eight persons who had been members of a Methodist Episcopal church. He was given charge of a large circuit or mission field, and succeeded remarkably well in creating an increased religious interest. On his circuit he organized five church societies. This was indeed missionary work of the hardest kind, and in remuneration for his labor he received $198.37 as a total for his year's salary. He was not working, however, for money, and therefore his greatest encouragement and happiness was in the fact that he had succeeded in renewing the religious interest of many people who had severed or lost their connection with church societies to which they had belonged before locating in that country. From Dakota Rev. Mr. Olin removed to Heron Lake, Jackson county, Minnesota, where he was given charge of the Methodist church, having joined the Minnesota conference that fall. He remained at Heron Lake, accomplishing a great amount of good, and building up the church society from a membership of twelve to a membership of thirty-six. Removing thence he was stationed at Lake Benton with charge over Lake Benton and Balaton circuit. He resides in Lake Benton, to which place he came in October, 1888. Rev. Olin is an earnest preacher of the gospel and has succeeded in awakening considerable religious interest in his charge. Besides being a good preacher, a man of good Christian thought, he exhibits in practical life what he defends in his sermons. On taking hold of the charge of which he is shepherd at present he found the church society at a low ebb because of various distressing circumstances which had come to the people in the years previous. He commenced earnestly laboring for his master and the church by the grace of God and much hard work and perseverance has built up and strengthened the church society, increasing the membership at Balaton from twenty-four to sixty-four. Our subject was converted under the ministry of Rev. C. Hobert, D. D., in Red Wing, in February, 1875. His wife and her father were converted at the same time and all were received into the church fellowship on the same day by Rev. Mr. Hobert. The subject of our sketch is a man of excellent Christian character, and living an exemplary Christian life among his people, teaches not only by words but also by actions and actual life the way of holy living. Besides being a good preacher he is a man among men, taking hold of the various interests which circle about his church work and giving them his utmost care and attention, sympathizing with the wants of the distressed, comforting those in sorrow, strengthening the spiritual belief of those who are spiritually downcast. His Christian and gentlemanly bearing are of such a nature as to draw to him many friends in Lake Benton and vicinity.

Rev. Mr. Olin was married by Rev. C. Hobert in Red Wing, July 5, 1875, to Miss Jennie Tyler, a daughter of M. S. and Isabel (Barclay) Tyler, natives, respectively, of England and Scotland. Miss Tyler is a native of Red Wing, Minnesota, where she received her early training and education. Rev. and Mrs. Olin have been blessed with two children—Lottie, born in Red Wing, and Harry, born in Brookings, Brookings county, South Dakota.

———◦—◦⟨⟨⟨◈⟩⟩⟩◦—◦———

PETER O. RAKNESS is the popular and efficient postmaster of the village of Hadley, Murray county, Minnesota. He is also engaged in the general mercantile business and does a large and profitable trade. He was born in Norway, January 9, 1848, and was the son of O. O. and Bertha (Peterson) Rakness, both of whom were natives of Norway. The parents were farmers by occupation and resided in their native land until their death. The mother died in 1850, the death of the father occurring January 19, 1884.

The subject of our sketch left the parental home in 1872. Up to fifteen years of age he had attended the district schools and after that until 1872 he engaged in farming and fishing. In the year just named he sailed to America, landing in New York City, July 1st. Passing thence he came West to Minnesota, locating at the city of Mankato, where he found employment as a mason for Mr. Wilkinson. He continued his residence in Mankato until 1877, when, in March, he went to Oregon, remaining sixteen months, his time being spent in the employ of the Oregon Transfer Company and the Oregon Steam Navigation Company and also with surveying corps, the last three months of his stay in Oregon being spent in salmon fishing in the Columbia river. He then returned to Minnesota, coming to Slayton, Murray county, where he had taken a farm prior to his going to Oregon. Returning to Minnesota he employed his time in working for a surveying corps of the Chicago, St. Paul, Minneapolis & Omaha railroad. After three months he again returned to his farm, where he resided four years. Then selling out all his personal property he went to Madelia and engaged in clerking in a general store owned by Bisbee, Olson & Boynton, continuing with them about a year. He then came to the village of Hadley, Murray county, and opened a general store under the firm name of Rakness & Company, his partner being O. K. Rakness. After nine months this partnership was dissolved and our subject became the sole proprietor. He carries a finely assorted stock of goods, worth somewhat over twenty-five hundred dollars, and is well prepared to meet the wants of his increasing trade. He was appointed postmaster of Hadley village in 1887, which position he holds at the present time. He is a man of excellent business qualifications and has been quite successful in all his financial operations. He is the check payer of the F. H. Peavey Grain Company.

Mr. Rakness was married November 14, 1873, to Johanna Oye, a resident of Mankato at the time of her marriage. This lady was the daughter of Ole and Ingeborg (Tilstad) Oye, both of whom were natives of Norway, where the mother died some years ago and where the father still lives. Miss Oye was a native of Norway, where she was born in the year 1853. Mr. and Mrs. Rakness have been blessed with the following-named children—Bertha, Oscar, Ida, Otto, George, Lena, and Alida.

The political faith of the subject of our sketch is with the republican party, in whose principles he has believed ever since coming to the United States. He has become quite popular in his locality, and being known as an excellent business man, has efficiently filled various official positions. He has been township clerk for four years, justice of the peace for three years, and is a notary public. He is a man of excellent character and is a member of the Lutheran church.

DANIEL B. WHIGAM, a prominent farmer of Troy township, Pipestone county, Minnesota, lives on section 10, which has been his home ever since 1878. The place of his nativity was Lake county, Illinois, where he was born February 18, 1840.

The subject of our sketch is the son of William and Caroline (Wright) Whigam, natives of New York and Vermont, respectively. Captain Daniel Wright, his mother's father, was a native of New York, and was one of the first settlers in Lake county, Illinois, where he built the first log cabin in 1835. Mr. Whigam still has a picture of this old cabin. Mr. Wright lived on this farm until his death, which occurred at the good old age of ninety years. William, a brother of our subject, was the first child born in Lake county. Daniel B.'s father was a native of Brooklyn, New York, and by occupation a sailor until he came to Illinois, which was in 1834 or 1835, where he was one of the pioneer settlers. He died four months before Daniel was born.

The subject of our sketch remained in Illinois until he was nineteen years of age, receiving a common-school education. The four and a-half years following were spent in California, where he followed the business of freighting from Sacramento up the mountains. Then he returned to Illinois and remained on the old homestead for about seven years. In 1871 he came to Faribault, Minne-

sota, where he kept a restaurant until April, 1878. At this time he came to Troy township in company with Major Rice. The journey was made by the good old-fashioned method of ox teams. In June his family followed him. During this summer he built his house, which was the second and at that time the best in Pipestone county. This house has been his home ever since.

August 3, 1863, Mr. Whigam was married to Miss Lucy A. Smith, of Illinois, the daughter of Timothy B. and Lucy P. (Rider) Smith, who came from New Hampshire. This union has been blessed with two children, both living at the present time—Lewis E. and Nellie M. Mrs. Whigam's mother died in 1888, in Troy township. Mrs. Whigam's father spent his last days with his daughter's family, where he died in 1884.

The educational advantages furnished the young in the early days of Mr. Whigam's life were of such a character as to enable him to obtain an excellent common-school education. By careful observation and attentive reading on the current events of the day and of the recent history of our country, Mr. Whigam has become well posted in all matters that pertain to practical life. He is one of the most social of men and is an interesting conversationalist. His life, both in precept and practice, during his residence in this county, has been of such a high character that he has drawn to himself the respect and esteem of all who know him. In matters of a public nature he takes a lively interest, and is one of the very best citizens of the county. In politics he affiliates with the democratic party, and is a member of the Masonic fraternity.

Mr. Whigam states that the most trying time he has experienced since he came to Pipestone county, occurred in the winter of '88. It was about 4 o'clock P. M., and as it had been warm and pleasant all the forenoon, he decided to take his cattle down to the creek and water them. Up to this time he had been carrying water to them all winter. Everything went all right until he had got started home, when the wind suddenly "shifted" and in five minutes one of the worst "blizzards" he had ever witnessed was raging. The cattle could make no headway against it, and he finally lost his way and was obliged to let them go. He went with the wind until he reached a wire fence, which he followed until he came to a neighbor's house a mile from home. From there he took a ball of twine, fastened one end and kept the other in his hand, so in case he should not be able to get home he could return in this manner, after three hours of hard work, he reached his house. The next day they went out for the cattle, but found only one that was alive out of nineteen head, and that one was frozen so badly that it was never able to get around afterward.

WILLIAM A. MILLER, an influential farmer of Prescott township, Faribault county, Minnesota, located on section 6, April 15, 1858. He pre-empted the land on which he now lives and has made it his residence ever since. He has been engaged in farming and stock-raising, and being but two miles from Winnebago City, has an excellent market for all his grain and stock. He has nine acres of a fine grove which for the past five years has supplied the family with fuel. This grove was planted by our subject, and there are now some very large trees. About twenty feet from the door of his dwelling stands a tree some sixty feet in height, its branches spreading fifty feet from tip to tip. In circumference it measures some eight and a half feet, and although having attained such remarkable growth it was planted by Mr. and Mrs. Miller in 1869. It is supposed to be the first tree planted in the township, and when put into the ground was no larger than a walking stick. It was first brought here from Shelbyville by Dr. Humes in 1859, and was used by that gentleman as an ox goad and was given to Mr. Miller, who planted it. Our subject was the second actual settler of Prescott township, Mr. L. W. Brown being the first. During all these years our subject has continued a permanent resident, although having experienced many hardships and severe times. He passed through the grasshopper raids and raised but little grain for two years, and experienced other trials and privations such as are usually found in pioneer life. Faribault was his market place and a trip to that place occupied some five days, Mr. Miller assisted in the organization of the township in 1861, the first meeting being held in the house of Henry McDowell, where there were eleven votes cast for the organization of the civil division. Our subject was one of the first supervisors and afterwards officiated as township clerk, holding various other offices, and has always taken an active part in public matters.

The gentleman whose name appears at the head of this sketch was born in Rockville township, Crawford county, Pennsylvania, November 1, 1833. His parents were of German descent, but were born in America. Until he was twenty-five years of age Mr. Miller remained in his native county, receiving a good practical education, and for some years engaged in farming and lumbering. He was married in 1856, and about two years later came to Faribault county, Minnesota, where he has since lived.

On the 23d day of April, 1856, Mr. Miller was married to Miss Julia Ann Humes, who was born in Woodcock township, Crawford county, Pennsylvania, November 16, 1834. Mr. and Mrs. Miller have six children—Elbert J., Ella A., Bramwell S., Bert B., Matthew, Ozro and Clyde O.

In religious sentiment our subject is a Baptist, and is one of the influential members of that society. A strong temperance man, he has for some time affiliated with the prohibition party in politics and believes in the total destruction of the liquor traffic. He is a well-to-do and prosperous farmer, and is one of the representative citizens of the township and county.

ANDREW E. ERICKSON is a prominent citizen and leading farmer of Lowville township, Murray county, Minnesota, residing on section 23. The place of his nativity is found in Sweden, where he was born August 30, 1838.

The parents of the subject of our sketch were Erick and Saran (Johnson) Anderson, who were also natives of the land of Sweden. They came to America in 1871, and settled in Big Stone county, Minnesota, where the father died in 1888. The mother is still living in Big Stone county.

Andrew E. Erickson was the third of nine children, and he remained with his parents until 1868, when he came to the United States. In his early life he was given good educational advantages, and learned the trade of wagon-making and blacksmithing. On coming to America, he located in Ishpeming, Marquette county, Michigan, where he was employed in wagon-making and blacksmithing for five years. In 1873 he removed to Michigamme, and worked at his trade until 1877, when he opened a general store, stocking it with hardware, furniture, undertaking goods, etc. This business grew to large dimensions and became quite profitable, but it was destroyed by fire in 1885. In the summer of the following year our subject came to Murray county and purchased the land where he now lives. He then returned to the place where he had been doing business for so many years, and

remained until spring. He then brought his family to Murray county, and has made that his home ever since.

The subject of our sketch was married April 24, 1864, to Miss Stina Jonas, a native of Sweden. This marriage has been blessed with the following children—John G., Carl A. and Edward E., all of whom are living at home at the present time.

Our subject is a man of energetic habits, and successfully operates his fine farm of 160 acres, and also runs a steam threshing-machine. He has been quite successful in raising crops and in other business lines, and has accumulated considerable means. In politics he affiliates with the republican party, and has held the offices of township clerk, being at present road overseer and school director. Mr. Erickson is a man of excellent qualities, of character beyond reproach, and is respected by all who know him.

JOHN G. D. WHIPPLE is a prominent and well-known farmer and stock raiser located on the northeast quarter of section 8, Diamond Lake township, Lincoln county, Minnesota. He homesteaded his land April 2, 1877, and was among the first settlers of the township. The first year he broke ten acres of land, and raised sixty-two bushels of wheat, and also forty bushels of corn and forty bushels of potatoes. This crop was raised on ground that had been plowed before Mr. Whipple's settlement. He set out a number of trees the first year and also the second and third years after he came to the township. Among these are to be found fine specimens of cottonwood, ash, willow, in all about an acre near and around his house. He erected a primitive dwelling the first year, 16x16 feet, and has since been adding thereto until he now has a comfortable and commodious house, in which he lives. He took extra pains in building a good straw barn in October, 1877, and this has been so well preserved that it is still used for the accommodation of his stock. Our subject has a fine farm, and has now 120 acres under cultivation, and has the balance for pasture lands. He has excellent living water, and has, indeed, one of the finest farms in the country. On making his settlement Mr. Whipple became an active participant in all public affairs, and assisted in the organization of the township in 1879, the first meeting being held in the Bradley school-house. At this meeting there were from ten to fourteen votes cast.

The subject of our sketch was born in Orleans county, New York, December 7, 1842. He is the son of Austin and Betsey (Dane) Whipple, the former born in Pittsfield, Massachusetts, and the latter a native of New Hampshire. The father was an active and energetic farmer throughout most of his life, but at the time of his death had retired from active business. He died in Naples, Illinois, March 14, 1886, at the age of eighty-one years. The mother of our subject was reared and educated in her native State, and when she was about seventeen years of age came with her parents to Orleans county, New York, where her father engaged in farming. She died in 1879. The parents were both consistent members of the Methodist Episcopal church. In the father's family there were four chidren—John G. D., James, Mary and George. James is now living in Naples, Illinois, where he is engaged in farming and stock raising. Mary died at the age of seven years, and George died when three years old in Orleans county, New York.

The subject of our sketch remained in the county of his nativity until he was thirty-four years of age. During his early life he had received an excellent training and a good education in the public schools. He had assisted his father in work on the home farm, and after our subject's marriage, which occurred in 1867, he took charge of the father's farm, which he rented and operated for some seven years. After that time had expired he came to St. Paul, Minnesota, arriving in that place December 9, 1876. After remaining a short time in St. Paul he came to Lincoln county and located his claim, the family following a month later.

Mr. Whipple was married November 5, 1867, to Miss Lizzie Kennen, a native of Canada, where she was reared and educated until she was seventeen years of age. She then came to the State of New York with a sister and met and finally married our subject at Albion, Orleans county. Mr. and Mrs. Whipple have had four children, three boys and one girl—Ida, Willie, Lewis and Chester, the latter being named after President Arthur. These children have all been thoroughly educated, and Ida has been a teacher in the public schools for three terms.

In the veins of our subject there flowed good Revolutionary blood. He had been taught the principles of good government and had been educated to be a patriotic citizen. On the breaking out of the war our subject's mind was exercised over the welfare of his country, and August 13, 1862, he enlisted in the One Hundred and Fifty-first New York Volunteer Infantry. He continued doing loyal service in the Union army until his discharge, which took place at Washington, June 27, 1865. During part of the time he was under Captain Bowen, and was discharged under Captain Miller. He participated in a number of hard-fought battles and saw much severe service. He participated in the battles of the Wilderness, Spottsylvania, Cold Harbor, after which with his regiment he crossed the James river, remaining at the front besieging Petersburg for some ten days. His regiment was then transferred to the

Shenandoah valley and participated in the battles of Manassas Junction, Winchester, Fisher's Hill and Cedar Creek, these last three engagements being under General Sheridan. He was also in the severe battle of Gettysburg under General Meade. After this our subject's regiment was transferred back to Petersburg, where they continued with General Grant's corps until the close of the war. Gallantly this army charged the breastworks about Petersburg and after accomplishing victory for the Union arms pursued the Rebel General Lee to Appamattox Court House, where he surrendered. Our subject passed through the war without receiving any dangerous wounds. The exposure of his military life, however, undermined his health, and for six months he lay sick in Carver hospital at Washington. After being discharged he returned to New York State, where he remained until the fall of 1867, engaged in working his father's farm.

In commencing the last paragraph we said that military spirit had been inherited by our subject. This is seen from the fact that his mother's grandfather was a captain in the Revolutionary War and her father served in the War of 1812, and her brother, John Dane, served in the Mexican War. By this it will be seen that the military spirit has been continually in the generations of this family, and our subject faithfully and bravely fulfilled the prediction made by the actions of his ancestors when he entered the Union army and fought through the Civil War. Our subject's uncle, Milton Whipple, was a man of large means in New York State and accomplished a great deal in raising money for the Union army and in creating a sentiment in favor of emancipation. He was instrumental in having a monument erected to the old soldiers who went into the service from Riga township, Monroe county, New York. This beautiful and costly monument stands in the burying ground in the village of Churchville. Milton Whipple was a man of large prominence and wide influence in those days; was a representative man in every particular and was held in high esteem.

Since making his location in Lincoln county Mr. Whipple has taken a prominent place among the leading business men of his locality. He has identified himself intimately with the governmental affairs and has served his fellow-citizens in various official capacities. He has been supervisor of the township for several years and was chairman of the board of supervisors for two years. In the spring of 1889 he was re-elected treasurer of the township which position he has held, since 1885. He has been clerk of school district No. 9 since its organization and was one of the leading spirits in the work in having it organized. He is an influential member of the Grand Army of the Republic and holds the office of junior commander of the local lodge. Mr. Whipple is a man of true and loyal citizenship, is possessed of an irreproachable character and is esteemed by a wide circle of friends and acquaintances.

JOHNSON W. STONE, an exemplary citizen and prosperous farmer of Osborn township, Pipestone county, Minnesota, came to this locality in 1879, in company with A. J. Myers and Ed. W. Day. His permanent location was not made in the county at the date just given, however. He pre-empted his land in the southeast quarter of section 20 and then went to Magnolia township, seven miles east of Luverne, Rock county, and lived on a homestead about one and a half years. He then sold out his interest in Rock county, and removed to his present place, where he has resided ever since. He was one of the very first settlers of the township and rendered valuable assistance when the township was organized in 1879.

Mr. Stone was born in Litchfield, Connecticut, May 7, 1835. His father died in 1841 and the mother passed from this life in Susquehanna county, Pennsylvania, in the year 1842. When our subject was about six years of age his father died and he moved with his mother to Susquehanna county, Pennsylvania, where, after his mother's death, one year later, he then found a home with a cousin until he was eighteen years of age. Until this time our subject had been given the advantages of a common-school education, and by studious application to his school duties had become well fitted for any life of business activity. At eighteen years of age, our subject in company with two sisters and an older brother, moved on a farm and engaged in agricultural pursuits. Here Mr. Stone continued his residence for about two years, when, on the marriage of a sister and his older brother, he worked out at farm work by the month. At twenty-two years of age he was married, and for two years thereafter engaged in farming on his own account. He then turned his attention to blacksmithing, and after continuing in that line of employment for some years, removed to Decorah, Iowa, where he employed his time in farming and also buying and selling a number of town lots. One and a half years was the extent of his residence in Decorah. At the end of that time he removed to Saratoga, Winona county, Minnesota, where he remained until he came to Pipestone county, at the time mentioned in the opening of this sketch.

Mr. Stone was married January 1, 1847, to Miss Sarah Birdsall, a native of Pennsylvania, in which State she received an excellent education. Mr. and Mrs. Stone have no children.

In politics the subject of our sketch is a representative republican and takes an active part in the local affairs of that organization. Since coming to the township he has identified himself with everything that pertains to the welfare of public matters and has held several positions of trust and responsibility. Three different times he has been elected to the board of supervisors and has been chairman of that body for two years. He has been one of the side supervisors for three years. His abilities as a public officer have been recognized in other places, and while a resident of Winona county, he held the office of township supervisor, and was also the incumbent of various school offices. In religious matters he takes an active interest, and is an exemplary member of the Baptist church. Since coming to the township our subject has grown in prosperity and has surrounded himself with the evidences of success. He is a man of good character and holds the confidence of his fellow-townsmen.

HENRY P. GOERTZ, a leading merchant of Mountain Lake village, Cottonwood county, Minnesota, is engaged in handling lumber, grain and machinery. He has built up an extensive trade, and has become one of the reliable citizens of the locality. His parents were Peter and Cornelia (Franz) Goertz, natives of Russia and Prussia, respectively. The father was engaged in the grocery and lumber business, and came to the United States in 1875, locating in Cottonwood county, Minnesota, purchasing five acres and a number of lots in the village of Mountain Lake, where he engaged in the general mercantile business. He is one of the prominent citizens of the village and county, and was the first of his countrymen to start in business in the village. In the father's family there were two children —Henry P. and Elizabeth. Elizabeth is now the wife of David Ewart, who is engaged in the mercantile business in Mountain Lake. The father and mother are still living near the village, and are quite well-to-do.

The subject of our sketch was born in Southern Russia in the village of Gnadenfeld, a few miles from the Black Sea, February 28, 1860. He came with his parents to the United States in 1875, and assisted his father in the mercantile business until 1881. Our subject was given a good common-school education, and was well fitted for the practical business of life. In 1881 he and Mr. Erret purchased our subject's father's store, and also engaged in the lumber and grain business soon after, and continued in partnership for some three years. At the end of that time a division of the business took place, and Mr. Ewart took charge of the mercantile department and our subject took the grain and lumber and also engaged in farm machinery business at that time. Our subject has been quite successful in his various business operations and has accumulated large means, being now given to the practice of buying all kinds of goods for cash rather than buying and selling on commission.

The subject of our sketch was married in Mountain Lake, June 20, 1886, to Miss Elizabeth Hiebert, a daughter of Gerhart and Susana (Emms) Hiebert, natives of Germany. Miss Hiebert was born in Berjansk, Russia, January 7, 1866. This union has been blessed with two children—Henry and Peter.

The subject of our sketch has held various official positions with credit and honor, among them being that of township treasurer, school clerk, etc. He is also treasurer of the Cottonwood Creamery Association; treasurer of the Mountain Lake Tow Company; and a member of the village council at present. He is a man of excellent principles and is a member of the Mennonite church. Our subject is one of the most successful business men in the village. He owns a large elevator and other property besides an immense stock of goods. In the beginning of the year 1889 he went in partnership again with Mr. Cornelius Penner, and they started a branch lumber yard at Bingham Lake, Minnesota, and also went in the hardware business with Mr. Ewart again. In 1887, Mr. Goertz purchased a three-acre lot on the south side of the railroad track on which he erected an expensive and most attractive dwelling, and which he is arranging into beautiful lawns, orchard, garden, etc.

Mr. Goertz is a capable business man and is held in high esteem both as a man and citizen by all who know him.

E. HEGGERSTON, one of the prosperous and influential citizens of Ann township, Cottonwood county, Minnesota, resides on section 18. He is a native of the kingdom of Norway, where he was born August 18, 1852. His parents were Erick and Mary (Klomstad) Heggerston. The mother died in 1859 and the father still lives in his native country. In the father's family there were six children, three of whom are now living—Carrie, Ole and E. E.

The subject of our sketch assisted his father on the farm until he was some eighteen years of age, when he came to the United States and stopped for a brief time at La Crosse, Wisconsin. Fillmore county, Minnesota, then became his home for a year, and he came to Ann township in 1872, and took his claim in 1873. Mr. Heggerston is a man of large energy and activity, and is continually in search of something profitable to which he may turn his hand. In the fall of 1881 he went to Todd county, Minnesota, and there worked in the woods during the winter. The next spring he went to Becker county, where he visited an uncle and found employment at various occupations. He next went to Crookston and drove a team of horses to Grand Forks, thence to Laramore, and thence to Stump lake; thence he went to the Cheyenne river, also to Devil's lake, and engaged in traveling through the western country for some three years, finally locating on his original homestead, which had been lying idle while he was away, in Ann township, Cottonwood county, where he has since lived. He is a hard-working, energetic farmer, and has provided his farm with good improvements in the way of a comfortable dwelling-house and commodious barns and other outbuildings. He has a beautiful grove of three acres of trees. During the grasshopper raids he was almost discouraged with farming, and was driven away from home in order to obtain money enough to support himself. These things, however, passed away, and good times have been visiting our subject during the succeeding years.

Mr. Heggerston was married December 17, 1887, to Miss Mary Ellefson, whose parents reside in Walnut Grove, Redwood county, Minnesota. Mr. and Mrs. Heggerston have adopted one child—Mrs. Heggerson's sister —Annie Maria.

In all matters pertaining to the public welfare the subject of our sketch takes an active part. Being a republican in politics, he has been elected to several township offices, such as assessor, justice of the peace, constable, and various school offices. Mr. Heggerston and family are members of the Lutheran church.

MONTREVILLE LAFAYETTE DORWIN, one of the prosperous and influential farmers of Lake Stay township, located on the southeast quarter of section 35 in the spring of 1881. He was the son of La Fayette and Frona (Watson) Dorwin, natives of Vermont. His parents were farmers by occupation, and, leaving the State of Vermont in early life, they removed to Wisconsin, locating near Sparta in about 1864.

Mr. Dorwin was born in Fairfax, Franklin county, Vermont, August 9, 1848. He remained with his parents on the home farm and attended the district schools until he was eighteen years of age. At this time he commenced working out for adjoining farmers and teaming to some extent. This line of employment was continued for some years in and about Sparta, Wisconsin, to which place his parents removed May 1, 1864. Continuing, he engaged in these various lines of occupation until he was twenty-five years of age, he was then married and rented a farm about three miles from Sparta, where he engaged in farming for seven years. Then, in 1881, he purchased and settled on his farm of 156 acres of railroad land on the north side of Dead Coon lake in Lake Stay township. Our subject lives about one-half mile from the site of the former home of Houkak, a brother of the noted Indian chief Little Crow. Houkak's log house stood in this location for years after the Sioux massacre. Little Crow used to visit his brother about twice a year for the purpose of hunting and trapping, and, bringing friends with him whenever he chose, he almost ate Houkak out of house and home. Since making his location in the county, our subject has been quite successful in his operations on his farm, and has accumulated considerable means. He has a fine farm under good cultivation and provided with excellent buildings. He has interested himself to a large extent in public matters and has held several official positions, among them being supervisor, school clerk, which latter office he has held ever since he has been in the township. He is a man of good business qualities, of the highest character, and is esteemed by all his friends and neighbors.

Mr. Dorwin was married in Sparta, Wisconsin, December 25, 1873, to Miss Mary Neuwerth. This lady was a daughter of Mitchell and Mary Neuwerth, natives of

Germany, and she was herself born in that country. Mr. and Mrs. Dorwin have been blessed with the following named children—Harry Orville, Verna Mabel, Orin Newell, Mattie M., Rollin E., Wallace Burton and Laura Irene. Three children were born in Sparta, Wisconsin, and the others were born in Lake Stay township.

WILLIAM H. KENETY is a substantial farmer and citizen of Bondin township, Murray county, Minnesota. He is the son of William and Elizabeth (Conlon) Kenety, natives of Ireland. The father moved to Massachusetts before the birth of William H., and there followed the trade of blacksmithing until 1855, when the family moved to St. Marie, Green Lake county, Wisconsin, where the father bought a farm and put up a blacksmith shop, and followed his old trade in connection with farming.

The subject of our sketch was born in Dedham, Massachusetts, December 17, 1844. His early life was spent in assisting his father and in attending the district school. He remained with his parents until February 5, 1882. Before leaving Wisconsin about nine years were spent in selling farm machinery, as the agent for Bigget & Blackstone. He was then married, and came directly to Fulda, Minnesota, where he purchased eighty acres of railroad land on section 13, on which he built a nice frame house and very fine barn, 20x40 feet, with twelve-foot posts and seven-foot basement. On the north side of the house is a very fine grove of hand-planted trees. Our subject also owns 160 acres as a tree claim on section 28, on which are about ten acres of trees.

Mr. Kenety was married in 1882, in Montello, Marquette county, Wisconsin, to Miss Annie Powers, daughter of Michael and Ellen (Carmody) Powers, who were natives of Ireland. Miss Powers was born in Malone, Franklin county, New York, in February, 1850. When she was a small child her parents moved to Neshkoro, Marquette county, Wisconsin, where the father purchased a farm, about six miles from where Mr. Kenety lived, and where they were still living at the time of her marriage. The day after their marriage they started for Minnesota. This union has been blessed with three children—John, William and Ella. John died September 28, 1886.

Mr. Kenety has always taken an active interest in public matters, as is shown by the fact that he has held many offices of trust and responsibility. Among these may be named that of county commissioner, to which he was elected on the democratic ticket in 1886, and again in 1888. He was also chairman of the board of township supervisors for six years. While in Wisconsin he was township treasurer and tax collector for three years, and also held various school offices. He is a member of the Ancient Order of Hibernians, of Avoca. Mr. Kenety is a man of exemplary character, and is a member of the Catholic church.

EDGAR M. BENTLEY, a leading citizen and business man of Jasper, is engaged in the hardware business, carrying a large and finally assorted stock in his line, and doing a successful business.

The place of the nativity of Mr. Bentley is found in Peoria county, Illinois, where he was born October 1, 1860. His parents, William H. and Hannah B. (Lucas) Bentley, were natives of Greene county, Pennsylvania. The father has followed book-keeping for lumber houses principally throughout his life, and is at present a resident of Peoria, Illinois. He came to that State in about 1842, first settling in Elmwood, where for a number of years he engaged in farming. In the father's family there were five children, all of whom are living—George L., now in Montana; Edgar M., Emma J., Schuyler C., at present a resident of Omaha, and William H., now living in Peoria, Illinois.

The early educational advantages of the subject of our sketch were of good character, and he was able to acquire a good common-school education. . He remained under parental authority until about sixteen years of age, at which time he commenced clerking in a grocery store in Elmwood, where he remained some six years. After this two and one-half years were spent in clerking in a general store at Smithville, Illinois, and thence he removed to Blanchard, Iowa. He remained in Blanchard for one year, engaged in clerking in a drug store, after which he went to Dakota, locating at Colman, where he engaged in the hardware and drug business. After a business career of three years in Coleman, he then sold out and came to Pipestone county, settling in the village of Jasper, where he has since remained. On arriving in the village he purchased a handsome lot on Wall street, and erected a store building 20x40 feet and two stories high. He carries a large line of shelf and heavy hardware, and is doing an excellent and profitable business.

Mr. Bentley was united in marriage in 1886 to Miss Nellie Hoskins, of Colman, Dakota. This lady is a daughter of Thomas E. and Mary (Ramsdell) Hoskins. Mr. and Mrs. Bentley have one son—Ray L.

In politics the subject of our sketch affiliates with the Republican party, and is a leading member of the local lodge Independent Order of Odd Fellows. Since coming to the villiage Mr. Bentley has been intimately identified with all public matters which pertain to its growth and development. He is an active and energetic business man, and, besides carrying his own trade, is largely interested in the Jasper Produce Company, of which he is one of the directors.

ALBERT J. COX, M. D., is one of the leading and most influential physicians and surgeons in Lincoln county, Minnesota. He resides in the village of Tyler, where he is engaged in the active practice of his profession. He is the son of James and Minerva J. (Cook) Cox. His mother was the widow of Zebulon A. Viles, and after Mr. Viles had been dead five years she was married to James Cox, the father of our subject. The doctor's father was a native of Somerestshire, England, and the mother was a native of New York State. Early in their married life they removed to Trempealeau county, Wisconsin, where, March 2, 1862, Albert J., the subject of our sketch, was born.

As soon as the subject of our sketch was old enough he was sent to the district school and was kept therein until he was fourteen years of age, having to attend to his studies both summer and winter. After fourteen he went to school during the winters and assisted at work on the farm during the summers. This was continued until he was eighteen years of age, when, in the fall of 1880, he was sent to the Galesville (Wisconsin) University, from which institution he graduated in June, 1883. He was determined to obtain an education, and being possessed of considerable push and energy, and what is familiarly called in Western phrase " grit " and " stick-to-a-tiveness," he succeeded in earning sufficient money to pay his own way through school. He was in the university about eighty weeks, and the balance of the years spent there he was working at something in order to earn money sufficient to pay his tuition and other expenses. He saw considerable hardship, but bore it all because he was obtaining his much desired education. During a portion of the time he presided over his own "bachelor's hall," being cook, chambermaid and all combined, a great portion of his food being sent to him by his parents. He completed a three years' course in two years, and became a graduate of that institution. After completing his education he returned home and accepted the agency for a subscription book, which business he followed in connection with work on the home farm. He was quite successful in this line, and. in five days' canvassing cleared over fifty dollars. Shortly after returning home he was requested by the county superintendent of schools to attend the teacher's institute and apply for a teacher's certificate. He did so, and wrote for a second grade certificate, and in most of the branches stood one hundred, his lowest grade being eighty per cent. This was a remarkable record, and it was publicly noticed that the doctor passed the best second grade examination of any which appeared before the institute. And had he attempted passing the first grade, as he intended, but did not do so from lack of time, by writing on three more subjects, he could undoubtedly have passed creditably and without doubt would have received the best standing of all the applicants for certificates. He received the papers which granted him permission to teach on Saturday night, and on the Monday morning following he commenced teaching in district No. 9, in the vicinity where he lived and where he had attended school from infancy. He taught in that district for nine months, and during that time commenced the study of medicine with Dr. C. H. Cutter, his father's family physician. He continued his studies for about one year. His teaching was quite remunerative, and he received for his service $30 per month, and at the end of the year he had saved about $270. One great consideration with him, over which he was considerably worried and exercised in mind, was

as to which school of medicine he should adopt for his future practice, allopathy or homoeopathy. He had a bias toward the latter school, and intended all the time of the first year's study to adopt homoeopathy as the guide of his future practice, although during that year he studied with an allopathic physician. He went to Ann Arbor in the fall of 1884 for the purpose of studying homoeopathy, but after hearing the various schools of medicine discussed, and after giving the matter careful thought, and weighing both sides well, he became convinced that there was only one true theory, that of allopathy. Continuing his medical studies at the medical school at Ann Arbor for about one year, he passed the freshman and junior classes, and left the institution with thirteen certificates of excellence in the branches through which he had passed. Returning to the farm, he engaged in work for his father until the fall of 1885. He then entered Rush Medical College, at Chicago, having to borrow money from friends to defray his expenses. He also had to go in debt for the clothes he wore. He gave notes without security in order to obtain means and clothing with which to commence his studies. It is to his credit that it may be stated that all these obligations have been paid and none of the benefactors in those times, none of those friends, have had it to say that our subject defrauded them of one cent. Continuing his studies he graduated from Rush Medical College in the spring of 1886 and came directly to Tyler, Lincoln county, Minnesota, where a location had been found for him by his old preceptor. Here again our subject had to obtain assistance from his friends, who aided him liberally to get his start in his new location. He had to borrow twenty dollars to pay his railroad fare to the place, and had only fourteen dollars when he arrived on the 22d of February, 1886. But it seemed that success was with him and his future was destined to be favored with good fortune. He had not been in the village three days when he had his first patient, and since that time he has been going constantly day and night attending to the wants of his many patients. His professional duties take him into all parts of the county, where he is esteemed and respected as a physician and a man. Soon after coming to the village he borrowed $175, for which he gave his individual note without security, and put in a small stock of drugs in company with J. W. Kendall. This partnership was carried on with large success until the spring of 1889, when the doctor sold out his interest to Mr. Kendall.

Dr. Cox was married in Tyler, June 27, 1887, to Miss Mary J. Bigham, a daughter of John C. and Mary (Hannah) Bigham.

The life of the subject of our sketch since coming to Tyler has been one of continued successes in every direction and in every line in which his faculties have been directed. He is a man of excellent education, and being of a social turn, has become prominent in the social circles of the village and vicinity. In all matters tending to promote the general welfare and to develop the business or society interests of his adopted town he has taken a hearty interest and has aided materially in various ways in the up-building and strengthening of good local government. As a man and citizen he is highly respected, and as a physician and surgeon he stands at the head of his profession and has built up an extensive and profitable patronage.

IRA INGEBRETSON is the popular and efficient postmaster of Lake Wilson, Murray county, Minnesota, where he is also engaged in the general mercantile business, in partnership with his brother. The firm name is Ingebretson Brothers.

Our subject was born in the kingdom of Norway, November 26, 1852. His parents were Andrew and Emily Ingebretson, natives of the same country. The father was a farmer by occupation, and came to America June 23, 1853. Landing in Quebec the family passed through to Spring Grove, Minnesota, arriving there November 1, 1853, being among the first settlers. The family removed to Iowa October 4, 1883, and June 6, 1884, settled in Fillmore county, Minnesota. The father died October 24, 1883, aged fifty-nine years. The mother still lives on the old homestead, having reached her seventieth birthday October 29, 1889. In the father's family there were nine children, four sons and five daughters, our subject being the third in order of birth.

Our subject was attached to his early home and resided with his parents until he attained his majority. He was given good educational advantages, and mastered the course of instruction provided by the district schools. When not in school he assisted in work on the home farm. At twenty-one years of age he started out for himself, and engaged in various kinds of farm labor in the vicinity of his parental home. He continued there until March 28, 1878, when he left by team for Murray county; arrived in Murray county, April 1, 1878, and located a homestead on section 6, Leeds township. He resided on that claim engaged in farming until March 23, 1885. Then, in company with his brother Peter, he established a general store in Lake Wilson, where they have been located ever since. They carry an excellent and finely assorted stock of goods worth somewhat over two thousand dollars. April 13, 1886, our subject was appointed postmaster of the village, which position he has creditably held ever since.

Mr. Ingebretson was married December 18, 1882, to Miss Carrin Simonson, a native of Norway. This union has been blessed with one child—Effie Josephine, born July

22, 1886. Mrs. Ingebretson is a daughter of Hans Simonson, a native of Norway.

Mr. Ingebretson is one of the most public-spirited men of this part of Murray county. He has always been willing to aid, both in word and deed, every project which tended toward the development and improvement of the locality in which he resides. He has assisted in the management of public affairs and has held various official positions, among them being that of supervisor, constable, etc. In politics he affiliates with the republican party. His business qualifications are of a high order and he has met with merited success in all his financial enterprises.

⸺⸻⸺

EORGE W. SNOOK is at present living a retired life in the village of Luverne, Minnesota. He came to Rock county in 1882, bringing with him considerable means, and purchased over two thousand acres of beautiful prairie land. Prior to his coming to Rock county he also invested largely in Dakota lands, where he owns somewhat over one thousand acres. At present his landed interests cover the immense amount of four thousand acres, a great portion of which is under cultivation. Our subject has a great many tenants on his lands and carries on extensive farming of a mixed character.

The subject of our sketch is a native of Maryland, where he was born in the year 1822. His parents, John and Eleanor (Mumford) Snook, were also natives of that State. The father was engaged in farming throughout the most of his life, but was a man of limited circumstances although a man of large influence and was respected by all who knew him.

The boyhood days of the subject of our sketch were spent by him on the home farm, where he continued with his parents until he was about sixteen years of age. Up to this time he obtained somewhat limited educational advantages in the district schools. On attaining the age just mentioned he commenced life for himself. Without a cent of money, and with but very few friends, he took hold of the duties of life which then presented themselves to him with earnestness and the purpose to accomplish life successfully. His first year's labor for himself closed August, 1839, at which time he was located in Clark county, Ohio. The first year's labor of our subject was spent on the turnpike, for which he received sixteen dollars per month. After the first year he engaged in work on various farms and made his first purchase of land with his savings in 1848, in Miami county, Indiana. He purchased this land with the purpose of holding it for higher prices, and this he continued to do until he sold it to excellent advantage. In 1842 he engaged in farming for himself and continued principally at this until 1847 in Miami county, Ohio. Leaving his own farm he commenced working out in different places in Ohio until 1854, remaining in Miami county until 1861. In this year he came to Logan county, Illinois, and purchased a considerable tract of land, soon after making another purchase in McLean county, same State. At this time he engaged extensively in farming and had charge of over 2,000 acres of land, continuing farming in this extensive way until 1882. At this time he made his removal to Rock county, Minnesota, and made the investments referred to in the opening of this sketch. Throughout his life Mr. Snook has been very successful in all his financial ventures and has made a profitable business of farming. He has grown in means and everything to which he has turned his attention has prospered. While in Illinois he assisted in the organization of the First National Bank at Farmer City, in DeWitt county, and while there held several posititions of trust and responsibility within the gift of his fellow-citizens. Among these offices were those of assessor, trustee, etc.

Mr. Snook was married, in 1842, to Miss Mary Fuller, of Clark county, Ohio, a daughter of John and Mercy Fuller. Mr. and Mrs. Snook have six living children—Nancy M., now Mrs. Forest, of McLean county, Illinois; Joseph L., who married Miss Sarah Cushburn, and now resides in Rock county; Walter H., married to Sarah Johnson, and settled in Rock county; Henry Q., who married Emma Barnett, and now lives in Rock county; William W., married to Hattie Dickerson, and now residing in Luverne, and Ella, now Mrs. Humphrey, also of Rock county.

In politics the subject of our sketch affiliates with the republican party. He wields a wide influence in the local affairs of that organization. Our subject is perhaps one of the most notable instances of prosperity and influence in Rock county. He is a man of very large means to-day, and has gathered it not by any sudden revolution of fortune, nor by wild speculations. Throughout his career he has been a man of thought and action, and he has continually acted upon the idea that, if he could not get one dollar per day, rather than remain idle he would work for fifty cents per day. Following this line of thought and action he has been continually active, and has gradually gathered together his means, which, by care and thrift, have doubled many times. He started out in life with but little money and large ideas of what might come to him with care. He knew that a few cents saved each day would, if carefully put away, in time make him a fortune. He has, therefore, been saving. He has abstained from the use of tobacco and liquors of all kinds throughout his life. It has never been his desire to become suddenly rich, but he has taken exceeding good care of every daily opportunity, has lost no time, but has engaged in constant daily toil, and has been economical with all moneys which have come to his possession. He has been upright in all of his business transactions, and he is looked upon as being a man of the highest integrity of character. His life has been one of the most active and also one of the most useful kind. Now, when he is nearing his threescore years and ten, he looks back upon a long career of business success and benefit to his fellow-man. Although so well along in years, to-day he has the look and activity of a man of forty years of age, so well has he preserved his physical organism. Since coming to the county he has been one of its very best citizens; loyal, progressive in all respects, he has made many warm friends, and his removal, when such shall come, will cause many heartfelt regrets among his fellow-citizens in Rock county.

LOUIS ZARN, one of the prominent German farmers, came to Pipestone county, Minnesota, in April, 1879, and was therefore one among the pioneer settlers of Grange township, where he now lives on section 22. Mr. Zarn was born in Germany, October 24, 1842. He is the son of Frederick and Helena Zarn, both of whom were natives of Germany. The father's family came to America in 1849, and first settled a short distance north of Milwaukee, Wisconsin. The mother died in Germany in 1851. The father throughout most of his life was a farmer by occupation, and died near Rochester in 1874.

The parental roof gave shelter to our subject until he was about seventeen years of age, up to which time he had assisted his father in work on the farm and attended district school whenever he could be spared from the farm work. At the age just mentioned he went to Minnesota, locating on a farm near Rochester, where he continued in agricultural pursuits until September 20, 1861, at which time he enlisted in

Company B, Second Minnesota Infantry. He continued in the service throughout the war and was mustered out with his regiment at Fort Snelling in the latter part of August, 1865, his discharge being dated at Louisville, Kentucky, July 11th, previous. The war experience of the subject of our sketch was full of service at the front in the most severe battles in which his regiment participated. His first battle was at Mill Spring, Kentucky, and with his regiment he was engaged in the battle at Shiloh, siege of Corinth, Perryville, battle of Chickamauga, Mission Ridge and Atlanta, and was with Sherman in his famous march to the sea. During the four years of the war service of our subject, he was in the hospital only one week, that being at Nashville, Tennessee. After his discharge from the service Mr. Zarn returned to Rochester, Minnesota, rented a farm, and engaged in farming until April 28, 1879. On that date he started with his wife and three children to come through with two ox teams to Pipestone county. In March of the previous year he had located a claim, but on arriving in Pipestone county, in 1879, he found he had been cheated out of his rights by a man named Bailey, who had filed an entry on the land located by our subject. This being the case Mr. Zarn could not immediately locate, but had to live in his wagons until he finally found a claim on section 22, where he now lives. He at one filed on this land and commenced improvements, building one of the first frame buildings in the township. During the first season he broke about sixty acres of his land and planted some of it to corn, and some of the lighter crops.

Mr. Zarn was married September 28, 1868, to Miss Martha Moulton, a native of New York, and daughter of Henry and Janett Moulton, who were both born in the State of New York. Her parents are both living and residing near Rochester, in Olmstead county, Minnesota. Mr. and Mrs. Zarn have been the parents of seven children, six of whom are living—Willie E., Cora M., Henry F., Bertie A., Walter J. and Janet L. Zora, the second child born to these parents, died in 1871. Willie E., the oldest son, is at present in Washington Territory. Mrs. Zarn's father served for ten months in the army, being a member of Company H, Second Minnesota Heavy Artillery.

In politics the subject of our sketch affiliates with the democratic party, and is a member of the Grand Army of the Republic, Simon Mix Post, No. 95. During his early life Mr. Zarn acquired a good common-school education, and became well fitted for the duties which have fallen to him in his checkered life. He is a man of much industry and energy, and is looked upon with respect by all with whom he has to do. He is a man of good character, and by thrift and industry has surrounded himself with the evidences of prosperity.

JAMES GILRONAN, a prosperous farmer and stock-raiser of Lake Benton township, Lincoln county, is located on section 18. He was one of the earliest settlers of the township, making his location there April 20, 1869. This was before the day of surveyors in that country, and our subject took what was called a "squatter's right" on his land. He is perhaps the earliest settler now living in the township. When our subject made his location in the township, there were but two other parties within ten or twelve miles. One was William Taylor, who had settled on section 7, and another Charles Shindle, who was frozen to death in the winter of 1870–71, while going to Flandreau after a supply of tobacco. The body of Shindle was not found until five or six years later. It was then discovered in Pipestone county. Mr. Taylor was also frozen to death while going from Lake Benton to his home, and his remains were not found until four years later. The early settlers of this region experienced some terrible weather during the first few winters of their settlement in the county. Numbers of people were frozen to death, and besides these already mentioned was a young Mr. Taylor, who was frozen to death while going to Redwood Falls. He was twenty-eight years of age, and a bright and prosperous young man. Charles Taylor was also frozen to death, while going to mill in 1872, and with him were two others, who met their death in the same way. When our subject made his location in the township, he found a couple of log huts on the lake shores, apparently the work of white men. One of these was partially burned down, and our subject took some of the rails from which they were built and used them in putting up a stable. The pioneer experience of our subject was full of hardship and adventure, and he had many narrow escapes from the Indians and winter storms. In 1869 he saw a herd of seven buffalo, and saw one killed by a Flandreau Indian. There were a number of the Indians in the locality at the time, and they had a rare feast at the house of Tom Robinson. Our subject was invited to partake of buffalo roast, but thought it wiser to refuse. He did not have much confidence and did not take much stock in their ways, and concluded to stay at home. Game was abundant in those early days, and our subject subsisted for some time on the various animals that he killed, and fish that he caught. The streams abounded with fish, and antelopes were seen here and there on the prairies. In 1874 there was news brought to the settlement that the Indians were attacking various settlers on the border and setting fire to their homes. This occasioned considerable commotion, and many people were frightened from their homes,

remaining away during the entire summer. These brief reflections on the experiences of early settlement will give the reader an idea of the character of the experiences through which our subject passed. Perhaps no other man in Lincoln county has been so intimately associated with the events of its early history. Coming to the county at a very early day, and being one of the very earliest settlers, our subject has had an opportunity to witness its development from the wild, bleak-looking prairie into a country now dotted over with hundreds of excellent farms and filled with inhabitants who are now enjoying peace and prosperity. Our subject was about the third man to locate in the township, and immediately broke ten acres of land and commenced other improvements, thus laying the foundations for his present comfortable and prosperous circumstances. Our subject assisted in the organization of the county on the second day of November, 1872, the first township meeting being held at the house of John Snyder, on section 7. Snyder came to the county in 1871 and died in 1887. His family still live in the township. Our subject had two brothers, Peter and John, who came with him and settled on sections 7 and 13. The first board of supervisors of the township consisted of William Ross, Thomas Lemon and William Taylor. C. H. Briffett was township clerk. Mr. Gilronan has identified himself most closely with the general interests of the county, and has held various positions of trust and responsibility. Wherever his services have been utilized he has manifested his abilities and has performed the duties of his various offices with great efficiency. In 1886 he was elected county commissioner, and was re-elected in 1888, being the present incumbent. March 12, 1889, he was elected clerk of the township, his first election to this place being in 1874.

The place of the nativity of the subject of

our sketch is to be found in County Cavan, Ireland, where he was born April 18, 1847. Remaining with his parents in his native country until 1865, he then came to America and located for a few years in the State of Connecticut. In 1867 he removed to Minnesota, and in 1869 came to Lincoln county, where he has since resided. The parents of the subject of our sketch were Peter and Mary (McManus) Gilronan. The parents were natives of Ireland, where they engaged in farming throughout their lives. Both of the parents are now dead. In the father's family there were six children.

The subject of our sketch received a good common-school education in his native land, and, being a hard student and a great reader throughout his life, he has gathered an extensive store of general knowledge. He is a man of progressive ideas, of excellent character, and is one of the representative citizens of the township. Himself and family are identified with the Catholic church. In politics our subject affiliates with the republican party.

On the 11th day of May, 1870, Mr. Gilronan was united in marriage to Miss Isabel Taylor, a daughter of the William Taylor mentioned in the opening lines of this biography. She died in August, 1879, leaving the following children—Mary, Eunice, Agnes and James. In March, 1882, our subject wedded his present wife, Bridget Gallagher, who was born in County Cavan, Ireland, in 1856. This union has been blessed with two children—Annie and Jane.

J LOTT resides on section 14 of High Water township, Cottonwood county, Minnesota. He took up his residence here in 1868, and was about the pioneer settler of the township, being the first to take a claim and make a permanent residence. He was practically alone on the prairie, the nearest neighbor on the east being twenty-five miles distant. His son-in-law, Loui Roemer, came with our subject and located in the same locality, on the west half of the same section, remaining one year and then going to New Ulm to work at his trade. Mr. Roemer returned to High Water township, and after six years' residence there went to the northern part of the State. Our subject still remains on the farm; although he has retired from active labor, he yet attends to the management of his business. Since coming to the State farming has been his principal business, but in his younger days he learned the carpenter's trade in Chicago, Illinois. Our subject's residence in Cottonwood county has been of profit both to himself and to all his neighbors. He has always been generous-hearted and public-spirited, and has assisted in every way to advance the interests of his locality. Mr. Lott was born in New Jersey in December, 1818. When he was one and a half years old his parents removed to the State of New York. He was then taken into the home of his mother's father and kept until six years of age. His father having in the meantime remarried, our subject was then taken back to the parental home, and resided with the father for five years. He then commenced taking care of himself, and, being of an independent spirit, although still so young, went to Chicago and resided there and in the adjoining country for some time. He learned the carpenter's trade and also worked to some extent on various farms. When he landed in Chicago there was but one frame building there, and there were but slight signs indeed of the great city which has grown up on the site of what was then a very primitive village. After nine years, residence in and about Chicago, Mr. Lott went to Waukesha county, Wisconsin and remained there for some twelve years, engaged in farming part of the time, and some of the time being spent in work at his trade. His next move was to the Lake Superior copper mines, where he found employment at carpentering for eighteen or nineteen years. He then came to Cottonwood county, Minnesota, and has made that his home ever since. After spending a long time in this county in active farming and in other business, he has retired from active labor, and is now living on what has been gathered as the result of a successful career.

Mr. Lott was married in October, 1841, to Miss Sarah McKown, a native of New Brunswick, where she was born in the year 1819, and reared until six years of age. She then removed to Canada, whence, after being thoroughly educated, she went to Wisconsin, where she was married. Mrs. Lott died January 16, 1889. She was a lady of exemplary Christian character, and was an esteemed member of the Methodist Episcopal church. Mr. Lott has had a family of seven children—John Henry, Edward P., Anelliza, Thomas, Elizabeth M., Joseph and Susana. Of these John Henry, Joseph, Thomas, and Susana are deceased. Edward P. is a lawyer, located on Lake Superior. Coming to the township in such an early day, Mr. Lott has had occasion to assist in the development of various public projects. He was a leading spirit in the organization of the township, and has been supervisor and has also held various school offices. In politics he affiliates with the republican party. Having come to the county in an early day, he passed through many of the experiences which come to all pioneer settlers. Whatever has come to him, however, he has encountered in a manly spirit, has overcome all obstacles, and has finally reached good circumstances and can enjoy his old age in the possession of plenty. During the early days his nearest place for purchasing provisions was New Ulm, a distance of fifty miles, and this village was their trading point for three years. Then Windom began to grow into a little village and our subject could go to that place to obtain provisions. Our subject remembers that many a time he has gone to his trading point with an ox team and camped out on the prairie by the way-side, the trip occupying four days. Mr. Lott is well known throughout the county, and is one of the representative citizens of this township, being respected as a man of integrity by all who know him.

PATRICK GILDEA is a prominent and influential farmer of Cameron township, Murray county, Minnesota, and resides on section 28. He was born in Ireland October 31, 1845, and is the son of Thomas and Mary (Johnson) Gildea, also natives of Ireland. The father was a farmer by occupation, and came to America in 1847, locating in Racine, Wisconsin. After remaining for three years he sent for the rest of his family to join him in Wisconsin. The mother died in Illinois in about 1850. In 1851 the family removed to Sauk county, Wisconsin, and engaged in farming for ten years, when they removed to Prairie du Chien. After two years they came to Minnesota, locating in Rochester, where the father engaged in agricultural pursuits for fourteen years. The family then came to Murray county, and located on a claim in Cameron township.

The subject of our sketch remained with his parents receiving a good common-school education until he was twenty-one years of age. Up to this time he had assisted his father in work on the farm in the vicinity of Rochester. On leaving home he went to Omaha, where he remained during the winter. In the spring he crossed the western plains, hauling government freight to Camp Douglas, Salt Lake City. After three months he went to Boise City, Idaho Territory, and engaged in farming for some ten years. He then took a trip through Oregon and California, going by steamer to Puget sound, and after two months returning to Rochester, Minnesota, on a brief visit to his father's family. He then started out on a trip down the Mississippi river, and at St. Louis purchased an outfit and drove from that place, and located the claim where he lives, in 1878. He was the fourth settler in the township, and built the fifth building.

Mr. Gildea was married in August, 1883, to Miss Mary Nonnenmacher, a native of New York, and a daughter of Andrew and Ernstine (Vill) Nonnenmacher. Her father died some years ago, and her mother is still living in Winona county. Mr. and Mrs. Gildea have three children—Joseph, Mary W. and Gertrude E.

In politics Mr. Gildea affiliates with no particular party, but occupies an independent position, voting for men best fitted for official positions. He takes an active part in all matters of a public nature, and has been chairman of the board of supervisors for five years. He is a consistent member of the Catholic church, and both as a man and a citizen is held in high esteem by all who know him.

CHRISTIAN I. RING, one of Edgerton's most prosperous business men, came to Pipestone county early in 1878, and is at present engaged in the dry goods, clothing, and boot and shoe business. He carries a large stock of goods and has a wide and increasing trade. He was born in Christiania, Norway, June 11, 1848. His parents were Iver H. and Inger (Jacobson) Ring, both natives of Norway, in which country they still live.

The boyhood life of our subject was spent at the home of his parents, who placed him in school until he was fifteen years of age.

At this time he concluded to strike out and do for himself by finding employment as a clerk. He engaged with a firm in Christiania, and continued with them until in 1869, when he emigrated to the United States, locating first at Lansing, Iowa. Here he engaged in work for different farmers for about three years, at the end of which period he again commenced clerking, finding employment in a store in the village of Lansing. He continued a profitable engagement with his employers for a period of three years, when he returned on a visit to his native land, remaining some six months. On returning to the United States he went back to Lansing and again commenced clerking, continuing in that employment in that place for about two years. He then removed to Luverne, Rock county, Minnesota, where he clerked in a store for about three years, removing from thence to Flandreau, Dakota, where he clerked in a branch house for the same firm for which he had worked in Luverne. This firm was by name Landien & Nelson. After six months' stay in Dakota he came to Pipestone City, Minnesota, and found employment for about six months in a lumber yard. He then was placed in charge of the lumber yard of Edgerton, his employer being John Paul, of La Crosse. He continued in charge of this business until the fall of 1888, when he opened in a general mercantile business. He continued running a general store until in March, 1889, when he closed out the grocery business and has since confined himself to handling dry goods, clothing and boots and shoes. He owns a homestead in the county, on which he filed his claim before going to Dakota the first time. He proved up on his claim in March, 1885.

Mr. Ring was married in Lansing, Iowa, March 23, 1885, to Miss Bokina Johnson, who was born about one mile from the city of Christiania, Norway, August 14, 1844, Miss Johnson is the daughter of Carl and

Mary (Olsen) Johnson, both of whom were natives of Norway. Mr. and Mrs. Ring have had one child, which is deceased.

The subject of our sketch has had a practical training in his business and has met with merited success. He also takes a lively interest in public matters and has held many offices, among them being that of village recorder, clerk of the school board and justice of the peace. He is a leading and influential member of the Norwegian Lutheran church. Mr. Ring is a busy, energetic man and is laying the foundation for a large and profitable business. Both as a citizen and as a business man he is held in high esteem by the residents of Edgerton.

EORGE WASHINGTON DAVIS is a leading farmer and stock raiser of Germantown township, Cottonwood county, Minnesota, and resides on one hundred acres of land on section 10. He located in the county in 1886, purchasing his farm of his father.

The subject of this sketch was born in Le Sueur county, Minnesota, March 26, 1865, and was the son of Isaac Davis, a farmer by occupation. George remained with his parents until he was twenty-one years of age, up to which time he had been given a good common-school education. On attaining his majority he engaged in farming, and took a place near Sanborn, Redwood county.

Mr. Davis is a young man of pleasant traits, is intelligent and progressive in his ideas, and is one of the rising young men of Cottonwood county. He is a republican in politics, and is growing in popularity with the members of that party, and has held several of the township offices.

November 23, 1887, Mr. Davis was married to Miss Katie Dellaughter, a daughter of William Dellaughter, a resident of Iowa, and a painter by trade. This lady was born in Le Sueur county, Minnesota, where she received her early education. She completed her education in the schools of Mankato, Blue Earth county, Minnesota. She had two sisters, Emma and Ella. Her mother died when she was seven years old, and the girls, with great difficulty, kept house for the father for three years. The father was then married to Mrs. O'Neal, who had, by a former marriage, four children— Frank, Mamie, Emma and Maud. She was a kind, good woman, and tenderly cared for all the children. Mrs. Davis' father is still living, being now seventy-one years old, and enjoying excellent health.

George W. Davis and wife have one child —Myrtle Ruby, born July 18, 1889.

ERRED L. MARCELLUS, a prominent farmer of Diamond Lake township, Lincoln county, Minnesota, settled on a homestead on section 4 in July, 1872. He was one of the first settlers of this region and when he first made his settlement there was but one house between his and the village of Marshall, some twenty miles distant. This house was occupied by a family by the name of King, who kept a kind of hotel or stopping place for travelers. When our subject located in the township there were perhaps three or four other residents, their names being, Ramsey, Worden, John Stewart and Mr. Snyder. Since making his location in the township our subject has taken an active interest in the affairs of local government and assisted in the organization of the township in the year 1879, the first township meeting being held in Marshfield. He was the first treasurer of the township and has held various other local official positions. The first year of his settlement he commenced making improvements on his farm by breaking about five acres and putting out a grove of trees around his house. He has been engaged since that time in general farming and stock raising and has worked hard to make his place one of the best in the township.

Mr. Marcellus was born in Dundas county, Canada, August 2, 1818. He was the son of Thomas M. Marcellus, a native of Pennsylvania and a farmer by occupation. Thomas Marcellus had a family of nine boys and two girls. He was quite a genius in his way and was able to do almost all kinds of work, being skilled in the tanning and preparing of leather and in the making of farming implements. It was his custom to prepare the leather and make the shoes for the family with his own hands. His son Jacob resides on the old home farm in Pennsylvania. Mr. Marcellus' mother was Elydia Onderkirk, a native of Schenectady, New York. She was married in Dundas county, Canada. In the father's family, as we have already stated, there were eleven children—John, Allie, Peter, Jeremiah, James, Gerred Levi, George, Jacob, Soloman, Robert and Lovina. Of these Thomas, Jacob, Robert and our subject are the only ones left.

The early life of the subject of our sketch was spent by him in his native country in Canada, where he assisted his father work on the home farm. He was given good educational advantages and acquired a good common-school education. He remained in Canada until his marriage, which occurred in 1838, in Dundas county, when he removed to Winchester and engaged for eighteen or twenty years in agricultural pursuits. At the end of that time he removed to Northfield, Minnesota, and rented a farm near Faribault, residing thereon for some two years. He then came to his present place in Lincoln county.

Mr. Marcellus was married in December, 1838, to Miss Dinah Eliza Cassleman, born about one-half mile from the birthplace of Mr. Marcellus. They were reared in the same neighborhood and were schoolmates, acquiring their education in the same school in Canada. She died December 16, 1885, leaving six children—Elizabeth, Elydia, Mary, Lemuel, Louisa and William. Mrs. Marcellus was an exemplary Christian woman, and took an active interest in the work of the Methodist Episcopal church, of which society she was a member. Her children are all now living except Elydia and Louisa. Those living are all residing in Lincoln county in different localities not far from the home of the father. The loss of his estimable and beloved wife has been one of the hardest trials our subject has had to bear since he came to this western country. She was indeed a helpmeet of the truest kind, and constantly endeavored to fill his life with that which would bring peace and happiness. She was a woman of rare domestic tastes, of an equable disposition, possessed of a temperament that drew many friends to her. Respected and liked in life, she was mourned widely in death by a host of acquaintances which she had made throughout Lincoln county.

Mr. Marcellus affiliates with the republican party in politics, and is a consistent member of the Methodist Episcopal church. For many years he has taken an active interest in all religious work, and was class-leader for some years in Canada. He is a man of exemplary character, and is respected by all who know him. As a business man and citizen he stands among the most prominent men of the township. He has a fine farm, a large number of acres under cultivation, and has it provided with excellent farm buildings.

NOAH V. McDOWELL is the gentlemanly proprietor of the Fulda billiard parlors at Fulda, Minnesota. He is the son of Robert and Mary (Wolf) McDowell, natives of Ohio and of Scottish and German descent.

Noah V., whose name appears at the head of this sketch, was born in Fairfield county, Ohio, January 20, 1843. He resided on the farm with his parents, and received a common-school education until he was seventeen years of age, when he started out for himself, and, coming to La Salle county, Illinois, worked for a farmer in La Salle county. In April, 1861, he enlisted in answer to the first call for three months' volunteers in Captain Jaquis'. Company at Ottawa, Illinois. This company was not mustered into service, however, but was disbanded and returned home. November 11, 1861, the subject of our sketch enlisted in Captain William Ford's independent calvary at Ottawa, Illinois. In Februrary, 1862, they were sent to Chicago, where the company remained five weeks, assisting in guarding rebel prisoners. Thence they were removed to Benton Barracks, Missouri, remaining at that place until April 8th. Then they went as escort with General Halleck to Shiloh, but did not reach that point until after the well-known battle by that name. They made this place their headquarters for a short time and then advanced to Corinth, where our subject participated in the famous battle and siege of Corinth. General Halleck being ordered to Washington, our subject's company reported to General Grant in the vicinity of Corinth, acting as his escort until September. The company participated in the preliminary engagements before Corinth, and on the night of the 25th of September had a skirmish with a portion of General Price's army. Falling back, they participated in the second battle of Corinth. They were also in the cavalry engagement at Big Bur Creek, Tuscumbia, Alabama; Buzzard Roost, Tupelo, and many other engagements. In August, 1863, he went to Memphis, thence to Helena, Arkansas. January 9, 1865, they went to Springfield, Illinois, on which date they were mustered out of the service. Our subject rented a farm near that of his father in Livingston county, Illinois, and continued operating this until 1867. He then purchased land, and continued to engage in agricultural pursuits until 1872, when, January 16, he sold out and removed to Nobles county, Minnesota, coming with a four-horse team. He arrived in Worthington February 17, and in a day or two located 160 acres of land as a soldier's homestead on section 10, Bigelow township. He lived on that claim until the fall of 1881, when he sold out and removed to the village of Worthington and opened a railroad boarding-house, in which business he continued until September, 1883. He then purchased a residence and billiard hall, and operated the same until July, 1888. He then moved his stock to Fulda, Murray county, where he has been operating his business ever since. His family still resides in Worthington, where our subject still owns his billiard hall, which is at present rented. Mr. McDowell is a man of good abilities, and is at present engaged in writing a history of his regiment, which was the Fifteenth Illinois Cavalry, organized at Corinth, December 25, 1865, of independent companies. Our subject was appointed historian and secretary of his regiment at their first reunion at St. Louis, September 27, 1887. Our subject was justice of the peace for six years while in Bigelow township, Nobles county, and was also township treasurer for two years. He is a member of the Grand Army of the Republic, Stoddard post, No. 34, at Worthington, and has been a delegate from that post to State encampments, once at Minneapolis and once at St. Paul.

Mr. McDowell was married in Livingston county, Illinois, January 15, 1864, while home on a thirty days' furlough. He was married to Cynthia A. Strange, who was born in Logan county, Illinois, July 5, 1844. This lady was the daughter of John R. and

Mary (Nichols) Strange, natives of Kentucky. Mr. and Mrs. McDowell have been blessed with the following-named children—Mary, Louisa, Andrew, Minnie, Rosa, Martha and John.

------◦-✦-◦❮❰❙❱❯◦-✦-◦------

JOHN D. YOUNG, a leading lumber merchant of Fairmont, Minnesota, is the son of Nicholas and Catharine (Drout) Young, who were natives of Germany. The parents emigrated to America in early life and located in Indiana, where the father engaged for a number of years in buying and selling horses. During the war he had large contracts with the government for furnishing the troops with horses. When our subject was about ten years of age, in 1865, the parents removed to New London, Iowa, where the father engaged in railroad contracting, which business he still follows. After one year's residence in New London the family removed to La Crosse, Wisconsin, in 1866.

The gentleman whose name appears at the head of this sketch was born in Homesville, Indiana, August 21, 1855. When he was a year old the family removed to Reynolds, Indiana, whence, when he was ten years old, they removed to New London, Iowa. In 1866 they went to La Crosse, Wisconsin, and our subject continued a resident of the parental home until the fall of 1878. During his early life he was given a good education, and graduated from the collegiate institution in La Crosse in 1870, after which he went to work for a large milling firm as book-keeper and salesman. He continued with this company until the fall of 1878, and then came to Sherburne, Martin county, Minnesota, and put up the first house in the village, engaging in the lumber business for the La Crosse Lumber Company. He continued his residence in Sherburne for five and a half years and then came to Fairmont and opened a lumber yard for himself, in which business he has continued up to the present time. While living with his father our subject had a varied experience in different lines of business. While a resident of La Crosse he went with his father to Minnesota, and worked for some time as book-keeper and clerk in his father's store on the St. Paul & Pacific railroad line. This was shortly after the Indian massacre, and our subject saw a great many empty cabins along the route, also many signs showing that settlers had been robbed and murdered. Since coming to the village of Fairmont Mr. Young has been heartily engaged in assisting in the building up of the business interests of the village. He has participated in all matters pertaining to the general government, and has held various official positions, among them being that of member of the village council. In politics he affiliates with the republican party. Mr. Young is a man of good business qualifications, and, by careful attention to the details of his trade, has built up a large and lucrative patronage. His parents still live in La Crosse, where a brother, Nicholas H., is depot agent for the Burlington & Quincy Railroad Company. One brother, Edward, resides in Minneapolis. Our subject has three sisters—Kate, Eliza and Maude L., all of whom are living. Eliza is a teacher of painting, and has a large class of pupils in Fairmont. Mr. Young has a very fine residence, furnished in elegant style ; has a hospitable and agreeable family, and is himself a genial, warm-hearted, courteous gentleman.

The subject of our sketch was married September 29, 1880, to Miss Bertha A. Ward, daughter of Reuben M. and Mary S. (Conrow) Ward, natives of New York. This lady was born in Cattaraugus county, New York, March 20, 1859. Mr. and Mrs. Young have two children—Catharine and Mary.

ALEB HEATH, a retired farmer and influential citizen, resides in Pipestone City, Minnesota. He came to the county in 1878, and settled on a homestead of 160 acres in Fountain Prairie township, where he also had a timber claim of 160 acres. He settled on his homestead, built a shanty 12 x 18 feet and one story high, and commenced farming operations by breaking twenty-five acres the first year. He continued his residence in Fountain Prairie township, engaged in general farming, until in 1885, in which year he removed to Pipestone City and settled on sixty-two and a half acres that he had previously purchased of the Milwaukee & St. Paul Railroad Company. This land is within the city limits of Pipestone and is valuable property. Our subject built a neat dwelling-house on this land in 1881. While a resident of Fountain Prairie township our subject moved in an important place among the citizens of that town. In public matters he was at all times looked to for material assistance. For five years he held the office of supervisor of that township and was postmaster at the Heath postoffice, the first office in the township, which latter position he held for six years. He was also a member of the school board and for some time was pathmaster.

The nativity of the subject of our sketch is found in Caledonia, Vermont, where he was born in 1819. He is the son of Archelaus and Sarah (Hall) Heath, both natives of Vermont. The father was a farmer by occupation, and followed that line of occupation throughout the most of his life.

The subject of our sketch remained with his parents during his boyhood days and was given a good education. At sixteen he apprenticed to learn the carpenter's trade at Dover, New Hampshire. He followed this business more or less until within the last five years. Leaving the State of Vermont, he removed to New Hampshire in 1842, and engaged in work at his trade. In 1850 he came Westward, locating in Beaver Dam, Wisconsin, where he purchased a farm, and in connection with farming engaged in work at his trade. In 1878 he came from Wisconsin to his location in Fountain Prairie township, Pipestone county, Minnesota, where he lived until coming to Pipestone City at the date mentioned in the opening lines of this sketch.

Mr. Heath was married in 1840 to Miss Hannah M. Leonard, a native of Glover, Vermont. She was the daughter of Moses and Laura (Chapman) Leonard, the former a native of New Hampshire and the latter of Upper Canada. Her father followed the occupation of farming in the east until coming to Wisconsin in 1872, at which time they went to live with Mr. and Mrs. Heath, with whom they continued until their death. Mrs. Heath received her early training and education in the State of Vermont, where she followed the profession of teaching before her marriage. Mr. and Mrs. Heath have had eight children, four of whom are now living—Viola, Joseph, Moses and Sarah. Viola is now Mrs. Conner, and has three daughters—Edith, Dadah and Hannah. Joseph married Martha Burgess, by whom he has had four children—Olive, Ethel, Milly and Laura. Joseph's present wife was formerly Eunice Bunnell. Moses married Elizabeth Stout, by whom he has had three children—Denver, Herbert and Elizabeth. Sarah married Mr. Smith, of Wisconsin, and now resides in that State.

Our subject and his wife are both members of the Methodist Episcopal church and have led long lives of Christian usefulness. In politics Mr. Heath affiliates with the republican party. Mr. Heath has passed through a long career of activity and usefulness and is now surrounded with the fruits and blessings which are brought by the consciousness of a well-spent life. He is a man who is held in high esteem by all who know him.

PETER NELSON is a well-to-do farmer residing on section 34, West Brook township, Cottonwood county, Minnesota. His native land is Denmark, where he was born February 4, 1850. His parents were Nels and Christena (Nelson) Knutson, both natives of Denmark, where the father still lives and was born in 1811. The mother died in 1883. His father was a laborer, and tried to give his children the advantages of a good education.

Up to fourteen years of age the subject of our sketch attended school and then was obliged to work out. He continued at various employments until attaining twenty-two years of age, when he emigrated to the United States, locating for two years in Mankato, Minnesota; thence he went to Omaha, Nebraska. After a month's stay in that place he went to the State of Iowa, and three months later to Dodge county, Minnesota, which county remained his home for five years. He then came to his present place of residence, taking a homestead of 160 acres of land.

Mr. Nelson was married in June, 1881, to Ingeborg Fosse, daughter of John Fosse, a native of Norway. This union has been blessed with four children: Lars Nikolai, Carl John, Hans Theodore and Annie Christena. The family are members of the Lutheran church.

Our subject has been quite successful in various financial projects, and his careful management of his farm has brought him considerable profit. In connection with raising grain he also raises Durham cattle and Norman horses and Poland China hogs. In this line he has succeeded in producing some of the best animals in the township, and has made it a profitable source of revenue. In public affairs he always takes an active part, and assists in the management of public affairs. In politics he affiliates with the republican party, and has held the office of township treasurer and various positions on the school board. He is a man of high character, and is highly respected by all who know him.

JAMES E. DOAK is an influential business man of Slayton, Murray county, Minnesota, where he is engaged in handling coal, wood, stone, brick, lime, hair, cement, salt, plaster of Paris, etc. He carries a large and complete stock, and is doing an extensive and profitable business.

Mr. Doak is the son of Derius and Martha (Thompson) Doak, both of whom were natives of Maine. The father's family were among the first settlers of New Hampshire, locating in an early day in the village of Londonderry. They came to this county from Ireland, where they resided in the town of Londonderry. They were prominent and influential people of New Hampshire.

James E. Doak was born in Scarsport, Maine, May 24, 1842. During his early life he attended the district school in summer, and, as soon as he became old enough, during the winter he followed a seafaring life. At sixteen years of age he gave his entire time to life on the sea, working on vessels plying between Portland, Maine, and Cuba, and trading in sugar and molasses. When the Civil War commenced our subject was mate of the vessel Augusta, and giving up that position, he enlisted in Company K, Fourth Regiment Maine Volunteer Infantry, his enlistment being dated May 1, 1861, in answer to the first call of the President for volunteers. He served during three years of the war, being discharged July 27, 1864. For gallant and efficient service he was gradually promoted from the rank of private up through all the various offices to second and first lieutenant. He participated in all the battles of his division up to May 24, 1864, when he was wounded at the charge on Taylor's Bridge, twenty miles north of Richmond, Virginia. He was also wounded at Fredericksburg, in December, 1862, and also at Wauping Heights, in September, 1864. After being severely wounded at Taylor's Bridge, and while at home on a furlough, he was discharged from further service. After recovering from his wounds he again engaged in a seafaring life, continuing until 1880. During this period of life on the sea, he served on several vessels plying in the India, Australia, China and California trade. During this time he was master of a ship. In 1880 he quit a sailor's life and was married, after which he engaged in the wholesale tea and coffee business in Boston, Massachusetts. He continued in this line for some three years, and then closed out, and in September, 1885, came to the village of Slayton, Murray county, Minnesota, where he at once opened in his present line, and where he has since remained. Our subject has been an earnest politician throughout his life, and has occupied positions very close to the leaders of the national republican party. Mr. Doak was a resident of the city of New Orleans for a while, and for two years (1869–70) had charge of the river police, receiving his appointment from Governor Warmouth.

Mr. Doak was married in Marlborough, Massachusetts, November 2, 1881, to Emma S. Fay, a daughter of William and Sophia (Fowler) Fay, natives of Marlborough and Northbridge, Massachusetts, respectively. Mrs. Doak's parents were early settlers of Middlesex county, Massachusetts, where they were wealthy and influential people. Her grandfather was one of the prominent men of Marlborough, where he established a banking institution, of which he became president. William Fay, her father, is now president of that bank. Mr. and Mrs. Doak have been blessed with one child : William Fay.

The subject of our sketch has been a very prominent citizen of Slayton ever since making his location, and he has always assisted in developing and carrying out every project which tended toward the improvement of his locality. He is prominent in Grand Army of the Republic circles, and has been commander of the Logan post, No. 162, ever since that post was organized. He is also a member of the Ancient Free and Accepted Masons, and is a director of the camp of Modern Woodmen of America. Perhaps no man in the county has had such a wide personal experience as the subject of our sketch. He has traveled extensively, and has been around the world three or four times. In his sailor's life he visited nearly every part of the civilized world, and has for 173 days at one time been out of sight of land. He is a man of good business qualifications, and has met with merited success in his financial enterprises. He is thrifty and economical, and is highly respected among his business associates.

HANS CASPERSON, one of the reliable citizens and farmers of Royal township, Lincoln county, Minnesota, is the son of Casper and Carrie (Rasmusson) Rasmusson, both natives of Denmark. The parents were farmers in their native land.

Hans Casperson was born in Frinen, Denmark, February 2, 1849. The early educational advantages of the subject of our sketch were not of a very high order, but he was enabled to obtain part of a common school education. The circumstances in which he lived were somewhat straitened, and he was obliged, at twelve years of age, to leave home and commence earning his own living by working on various farms in his native country. He continued at this occupation until 1872, when he emigrated to the United States, first stopping in the vicinity of Albert Lea, Minnesota, where he found employment amongst farmers for four years. At the end of this period he went to Floyd county, Iowa, and followed railroad work for two years, after which he returned to Freeborn county, Minnesota, and for some time followed farming. He then took a contract for building fences and roads and continued at that line for about two years. Then in the spring of 1878 he came to Royal township, Lincoln county, and took a tree claim. He lived on this claim during two summers, but during the winters found employment at Mankato and Rapidan in Blue Earth county, Minnesota. After that, for three or four years he found employment on different farms in Freeborn county, and in 1884 came to his claim and made a permanent settlement.

Mr. Casperson was married in Limestone township, Lincoln county, January 11, 1887, to Miss Ella Hoven, a daughter of Johann Hoven and Ellen (Olea) Hoven, natives of Norway. Mr. and Mrs. Casperson have had one child—Clara, who died in October, 1887.

On coming to Lincoln county our subject had but little means, and had no one to depend upon but himself. He was full of energy and push, however, and commenced actively improving his farm and laying the foundations for future prosperity. He has accomplished much success, and is now in fair circumstances. He has 160 acres of excellent land, about forty acres under cultivation, and seven acres of trees; has a good frame house and barns, and owns a team of horses and several head of cattle. Since coming to the township he had taken an active interest in all matters of a public nature, and has fulfilled his part in the manipulation of local governmental affairs. He was chosen delegate to attend the first county convention held at Marshfield in June, 1881. He

is a man of good business abilities, and has efficiently held several positions. He has held the office of chairman of the board of supervisors for the last two years, and has also been school treasurer for three years. He was elected constable in the spring of 1881, but held that office only a short time, on account of going away. He has also been treasurer of the Farmers' Alliance of this county for some time, and is always interested in the furtherance of any project which has for its aim the benefit and improvement of the condition of the farmers. He is a man of good character, a loyal citizen, and esteemed by all who know him.

GEORGE W. KNISS is engaged in the real estate and loan business in Luverne, Minnesota. He came to the county in June, 1870, and settled in the village of Luverne, where he has resided ever since. He pre-empted land in Clinton township and commenced farming, living on the same for some eighteen months, after which he took a homestead that is now within the city limits of Luverne. He improved all his land and engaged in general farming and stock-raising for a number of years. In company with Judge Hadley, of Luverne, he prepared the first set of abstract books in the county, and they continued as partners in business of this nature for some eight years. In 1880 the partnership just mentioned purchased a one-half interest in the Bank of Luverne, now known as the First National Bank. Our subject was vice-president of the bank which the partnership purchased, and retained his interest and position until 1884, when he sold out. Besides giving his attention to the real estate and loaning business, he has engaged extensively in operating some excellent farming lands. He is now engaged in managing 1,500 acres of land, a great portion of which is improved and upon which are found fine buildings. At the organization of the county he acted as the first county auditor from the 9th day of November, 1870, until the following May, and made out the first election returns of the county. Among the other positions which he has held and in which he has proven himself eminently qualified as an official, are those of deputy register of deeds, which he held two years, and justice of the peace one term. He has been a notary public since 1873, and is so well and favorably known that he does the largest business in the line of drawing papers and taking acknowledgments in the county.

George W. Kniss is a native of Defiance, Defiance county, Ohio, where he was born October 12, 1838. His parents were Jacob and Mernava Kniss, the former a native of Pennsylvania, and the latter a native of Virginia. The father was an extensive leather merchant throughout his life, owned a large tannery and dealt to a considerable extent in boots and shoes. He was one of the wealthy and influential citizens of Defiance. The father died in Ohio in 1849, the mother is still living and is a resident of Luverne. In the father's family there are three children living: Minnie, now Mrs. Dr. H. H. Hurlbert, of Duluth ; our subject, and P. J., of whom a sketch is given in another department of this work.

The early days of the subject of our sketch were spent beneath the parental roof in his native town, where he was given a good common-school education. At the age of seventeen he commenced life for himself as a clerk in one of the stores in his native town. After five years' experience in mercantile trade he enlisted in Company G, Fourteenth Ohio Infantry, in the three months' service under Colonel J. B. Steadman. After this term of service had expired, our subject re-enlisted in Company C, Sixty-eighth Regiment, Ohio Volunteer Infantry, and served four

years and four months. For gallant service he was promoted to the rank of captain of Company H, in which he had enlisted, and of which company he had been promoted to the lieutenancy some time before, which position (captain) he held at the close of the war. He also acted as adjutant for some time, and for nearly a year was commander of a battery of light artillery, and the convalescent camp at Huntsville, Alabama. He was frequently entrusted with the responsibility of perilous undertakings when marching through the enemy's country. His military experience was of an exciting nature, and he passed through many narrow escapes. He was wounded in the left leg at the battle of Champion Hill, in which battle his regiment was connected with the Seventeenth Corps of the Army of the Tennessee, under General McPherson, and in the Third division under General Logan and in General Leggett's brigade. Among the battles in which our subject participated were Pitt's Landing, at Shiloh, siege of Corinth, battle of Hatchie river, Fort Gibson, Raymond, the assault and capture of Jackson, Mississippi, Edwards Ferry, Black River, Champion Hill, siege of Vicksburg, Iuka, Mechanicsville, Washita river, Canton, and in numerous other battles and skirmishes of minor importance. After he was honorably discharged from the service he went to Wisconsin and settled at Portage City in Columbia county. Here for some time he found employment as clerk in a general store, and remained for some two years. He then removed to Yellow River, Wood county, same State, and engaged in lumbering, which line of occupation he followed three years. Thence he removed to Luverne, where he has since resided and where he has carried on a profitable and extensive business.

The subject of our sketch was married in the year 1863 to Miss Lina Older of Packwaukee, Wisconsin. This lady was a daughter of

Jesse and Mary Older, prominent citizens of Wisconsin. Mr. and Mrs. Kniss have been blessed with three children: Lulu B., Myrtle C. and Ralph W.

For years the subject of our sketch affiliated with the republican party, but, being a strong temperance man, on the organization of the prohibition party his attention was directed to its principles, and finally he joined the party, and since then has been working for its victory. He was one of the organizers of the *Rock County News*, a paper operated in the interests of the prohibition party. He is also a Mason, an Odd Fellow and member of the Grand Army of the Republic. He is a man of the highest degree of integrity, and is well known for his business force and progressive ideas, and has an extensive and honorable acquaintance with the settlers of Rock county. He has aided materially in all matters tending to the financial development and other welfare of Luverne and vicinity, and has by constant application to his various business enterprises accumulated considerable means. He is a loyal citizen, a man of high moral character, and is respected by all who know him.

WILLIAM HARRISON came to Pipestone county in the fall of 1879, since which time he has been a resident of section 19, Gray township, where he located on railroad land. During his entire residence here, he has proven himself a man of high character, thrifty and industrious, and has surrounded himself with the signs of prosperity and success. In all public matters he takes an active interest, and has held numerous positions of trust, having been one of the directors of school district No. 25 for two terms, and also a member of the board of supervisors for two years. He

was one among the pioneer settlers of the township, and assisted in its organization.

The subject of our sketch was born in New Jersey, in the town of Phillipsburgh, Warren county, August 29, 1849. His parents were John J. and Catharine (Hauk) Harrison. The father was a farmer by occupation, which line of business he followed throughout the most of his life. In the spring of 1867 the family removed to Wisconsin, where the father died in August, 1872. He was a respected citizen, and a representative man of the locality in which he lived. The mother was a native of the State of New Jersey, where she was reared and educated. She passed from this life when the subject of our sketch was fourteen years of age. William Harrison was one of a large family of children, ten of whom are living: David, Thomas, Elizabeth, John, William, Catharine, Higgins, Williamson, Marshall and Sarah Jane. The names of the deceased children are Jerry, Henry and Effie Ann.

The subject of our sketch received his early education in the State of New Jersey, being given good educational facilities in the county of his nativity. He remained with his father, assisting in work on the farm, until he was about eighteen years of age, when he removed with his family to Wisconsin, remaining in that State one and a half years. At the end of this period he returned to the East and continued his residence in New Jersey, engaged in the hotel business for two and a half years. At the end of that time he returned to Wisconsin, settling in Sauk county, where he remained some time, and then came to Fillmore county, Minnesota. After making the last named county his residence for one and a half years he then removed to Pipestone county, in 1879, where he has been a prominent resident ever since.

Mr. Harrison was married in 1871, on Christmas day, in Baraboo, Sauk county,

Wisconsin, to Miss Elizabeth Palmer. This lady was born near Williamsport, in Lycoming county, Pennsylvania, in July, 1847. When she was eight years of age her parents removed to Sauk county, Wisconsin, where she lived until her marriage. In that county she received an excellent education. Her parents were John K. and Jane (Wilson) Palmer, the father a farmer by occupation, and, at present, living near Augusta, Wisconsin. The mother was born in Lycoming county, Pennsylvania, where she was reared and educated. She is also living, and is an exemplary member of the Methodist Episcopal church. In her father's family there were the following named children: Mary Jane, Elizabeth, William Henry, Emily, Delpha, Rose Ella, Peter and Hannah, seven of whom are still living. Hannah died when she was eighteen months old. Mr. and Mrs. Harrison have been blessed with four children: Mabel, born October 29, 1872; Lela, born March 8, 1874; Mack, born December 18, 1875, and Grover C., born January 21, 1884, and died when two years and five days old. Mabel is attending the high school at Pipestone.

The subject of our sketch has risen to an influential position among the citizens of Gray township, and is one of its representative men. He is a man of excellent judgment and of high character, and has the esteem of all his fellow-townsmen. In politics he affiliates with the democratic party, and has become quite prominent in the local affairs of that organization.

⁎⁂⁎

DAVID M. FAIRBAIRN, a leading and enterprising farmer and stock raiser of Amboy township, Cottonwood county, Minnesota, located on section 22 in May, 1878, where he homesteaded his present place. The subject of our sketch was born in Canada West October 9, 1835. He was the son of David M. Fairbairn, a miller by trade and a native of Scotland, who emigrated to Canada in about 1832. In 1848 he located in Wisconsin and remained there until his death, which occurred April 22, 1873. Our subject's mother's name was Jane (Herd) Fairbairn, who was a native of Scotland, and who died March 8, 1888. There were ten children in the father's family—Jane, Archibald, Elsie, Mary, Janet, David M., Robert H., Esther, William, and James, who died aged one year and six months.

The early training and education of David Fairbairn was received in Canada West. When thirteen years of age he removed to Winnebago county, Wisconsin, remaining in that locality until 1852, when he removed to Waushara county, same State. In 1872 he went to Green Lake county and made that his home until 1878. His life until twenty-two years of age was spent with his parents and he was given a good education in the district schools. On attaining twenty-two years of age he went to California, and prospected along the Pacific coast in Oregon, Washington Territory and other localities, spending some thirteen years. His business was that of mining and freighting. After the length of time just mentioned had expired he returned to Wisconsin on a short visit and then went to Kansas and Missouri, where he remained during the winter looking over the country. Returning to Green Lake, Wisconsin, in the spring he engaged in farming for seven years, and while there became quite prominent in local affairs. He held various official positions; was chairman of the township board for five years and held various other positions. In 1878 he came to his present location in Cottonwood county. He is a hard-working, energetic, and systematic farmer and has been quite successful. He is a man of good ideas and wields a strong influence for good among his fellow-citizens. He has held various official positions and has taken an active part in public matters. He has been justice of the peace, and in various other capacities has proven his willingness to participate in the management of local political affairs. In politics he affiliates with the republican party and has supported that organization from its inception.

Mr. Fairbairn was married July 3, 1872, to Miss Joan Safley, a native of Cedar county, Iowa, and a daughter of Robert Safley, a farmer in that State. Miss Safley was a teacher in her early days and is a member of the Presbyterian church. Mr. and Mrs. Fairbairn have nine children—Agnes D., Robert S., Helen, James L., David A., Jeanie, Mabel, Walter H. and Leonard A.

ARNT LARSON is a substantial farmer and resident of section 20, Lime Lake township, Murray county, Minnesota. He was born in Norway, September 25, 1848, and was the son of Lars and Martha (Runy) Hanson. The parents were natives of Norway, and were occupied with agricultural pursuits.

The subject of our sketch left the parental home in May, 1869, and came to America. His early life was spent in assisting his father in work on the farm, and in attending the district schools. On coming to America he located in Lanesboro, Minnesota, where he assisted on various farms during harvest time. During the winter he worked on the railroad, and the following spring went to Brownsdale, Mower county, where he continued the latter employment until harvest. The places at which he stopped thereafter for some time were Mankato and Lanesboro. At these places he worked at various kinds of business, principally at railroad work during certain seasons of the year, and in the harvest fields during harvest time; also in Fillmore county, where he worked on a railroad in Fountain during the winter.

From thence he went to Mankato and St. James, and then to St. Peter. At this latter place he remained during the winter. However, before going to St. Peter, he went over into Murray county in August, 1871, and located the claim on which he now lives. In the spring of 1872 he came to his land and put up a shanty, this being the first log house in the township. Later he made a permanent location on his farm, after having been during the intervening time engaged in various kinds of labor, spending the winter and early spring on his farm.

Mr. Larson was married to Andrene Nilson, September 4, 1875. This lady was a native of Norway, and a daughter of Nels Braaten. Four children have been born to this union—Lars, Mina A., Nora E., and Charlotta.

The subject of our sketch has been educated in a practical school, and has drawn from his daily life of hard struggle many important and practical lessons. He acquired systematic habits in early life, and has become quite a successful farmer. In politics he affiliates with the republican party, and has been supervisor for six years. Before the village of Avoca was located, our subject was postmaster in his township for two years, and at all times has taken an active interest in public matters, drawing to himself the esteem and confidence of his fellow-citizens. He is a consistent member of the Lutheran church.

JOHN L. STEVENS. This gentleman is one of the reliable citizens of Verdi township, Lincoln county, Minnesota, where he resides on section 32. He has a fine farm under good cultivation, and has it provided with good farm buildings.

Mr. Stevens was born in England, January 21, 1822. He was the son of Matthews and Sarah (Day) Stevens, both of whom were also natives of England. The father was a shepherd by occupation, and followed that line of business in his native country. His family came to America, locating in the State of New York, in the year 1834. Removing thence, they located in the State of Connecticut, where the parents lived until their death.

At the early age of twelve years the subject of our sketch left the parental home and started out to do battle with life for himself. For some time he worked for various employers, receiving as remuneration his board, lodging and clothes. He finally apprenticed to learn the hatter's trade, and entering that employment, continued to engage at it until 1852, when he went to California to prospect for gold. He continued in the mining regions, meeting with varied success, until 1855. He then returned to the State of New York, and after remaining about four weeks went to Jefferson, Wisconsin, where he remained during one winter, going thence to La Crosse county. He engaged in farming in that county, and remained there for ten years, when he removed to Trempealeau, making that his home until 1878. In this year he came to Lincoln county and took a tree claim where he now lives. He broke some twenty acres of land and then went back to Wisconsin, remaining until the spring of 1879. He then moved his family to his claim in Verdi township, where he has lived ever since.

September 1, 1844, Mr. Stevens was united in wedlock to Catherine Stetter, a native of New York. This union has been blessed with eleven children, five of whom are now living—Ann E., Martha J., Ada E., John M. and Adelaid F. Those deceased were Mary L., Charles H., Sarah G., Kate, Ida F. and George A.

In politics the subject of our sketch has affiliated with the republican party ever since its organization and has held various official positions within the gift of his fellow-citizens, among them being that of constable, which he held for two years. He is a member of the Independent Order of Odd Fellows. Mr. Stevens being one of the early settlers of Verdi township, is well known and is highly respected by everyone. He is a man of excellent qualities, is genial and warm-hearted, and is also one of the most public-spirited citizens of the township. Although quite well along in years he has been remarkably well preserved and enjoys the best of health. He is a pleasant, whole-souled gentleman, and carries his three-score years very lightly.

During the war Mr. Stevens enlisted in the Forty-ninth Regiment Wisconsin Volunteer Infantry and served his country faithfully.

GEORGE C. EYLAND, JR., banker, is one of the leading citizens of Woodstock, Pipestone county, Minnesota. He was born February 5, 1853, in the city of New York. His parents were George C. and Serena (Keeler) Eyland, both of whom were natives of the State of New York, both being born in New York City. For many years the father was engaged in the dry-goods business in the city of his nativity, and is now living a retired life in Brooklyn, New York. The parents had a family of eleven children, the subject of our sketch being the second child born to the parents.

The early life of the subject of our sketch was spent in the home of his parents in the city of New York, where he received excellent advantages for obtaining a thorough education. For a number of years he attended the University of the City of New York, from which institution he graduated in 1872. After concluding his studies in school, he then engaged with the firm of Loring Andrew's Sons in the leather business, continuing in their employ for about eight years. He then removed to Buena Vista county, Iowa, having hardware business in Alta and land business in Storm Lake, where he remained until 1883, at which time he removed to Woodstock, Minnesota, and made a permanent settlement. Being given excellent business training during his youth, he was well prepared for the life of business activity which has fallen to his lot since leaving the parental home. On coming to Woodstock in 1883, he embarked in a private banking business, which he established on a solid financial basis in the fall of 1883. In 1885 he incorporated his bank, with a capital of $25,000, and has been identified with the institution up to the present time.

The marriage of the subject of our sketch occurred on July 15, 1885, on which date he was married to Miss Mary E. Bloom, a native of New Glarus, Wisconsin, and daughter of Hon. Fred Bloom, one of the leading merchants of the village of Woodstock. A biography of Mr. Bloom appears in another department of this work. When Mrs. Eyland was some seven or eight years old, she removed with her parents to Nobles county, Minnesota, where she completed a thorough course of education. She is a lady of excellent qualities, and has been a teacher for a. number of years. One daughter has blessed this union: Clara M., born April 10, 1887.

The banking institution with which Mr. Eyland is so honorably connected is one of the leading financial concerns of the southwestern part of Minnesota. Its president is John C. French, Mr. Eyland occupying the position of vice-president and cashier. Mr. Eyland is one of the solid financial men of Pipestone county, and has become thoroughly identified with the financial interests of the locality in which he resides. His business career has been both honorable and profitable, and by his faithfulness to the vari-

ous financial duties which have fallen to his care, and the integrity with which he has administered the affairs of the Woodstock Bank, he has drawn to himself many warm personal friends, and built up an enviable reputation. In social and public matters he takes an active interest, and is looked upon as one of the main stays of the village and county. He is a republican in politics, and has for some time been chairman of the Woodstock republican club. Among the official positions which he has held with honor and credit, are those of treasurer of the township, in which office he is now on his fourth term, and also that of school director of district No. 33, Pipestone county. He is a leading member of the Masonic fraternity, and himself and family are members of the presbyterian church, in which organization he holds the position of trustee. Mr. Eyland is a pleasant, courteous gentleman, is a good citizen, and is respected by all with whom he comes in contact.

❖

FREDERICK MEINZER purchased his present place, the southeast quarter of section 32, Ash Lake township, Lincoln county, Minnesota, in April, 1887. At the same time he purchased 160 acres on the northwest quarter of section 33, and now owns 320 acres of excellent land. He has made this his home since 1887, and has built one of the finest dwelling-houses in the township, the building being 16x24 feet with a wing 16x16. His other buildings, granaries, machinery sheds, etc., all betoken a prosperous farming establishment, and show industry and thrift. His barn is 30x56 feet, the machinery shed 24x30 feet. He engaged largely in farming and also engaged to some extent in stock raising. Before making his location in Ash Lake township Mr. Meinzer resided in the village of Lake Benton for six years, and there took an active part in the affairs of his village and county. In the fall of 1882 he was elected treasurer of Lincoln county and served three terms, delivering up the office to his successor January 1, 1889. He has always served his fellow-citizens in various official capacities, and while a resident of Limestone township was town clerk for a period of two years, being the first to hold that position in the township. He was one of the early settlers in that township, locating there in 1878, 'where he built the second shanty in the township. In 1880 he assisted in its organization, attending the first meeting which was held on section 22. Mr. Meinzer made Limestone township his home for some five years, engaged in general farming and stock raising. The first settler of that township was Jens J. Jerpark.

Frederick Meinzer was born in Baden, Germany, December 6, 1837. He is the son of George Frederick and Christine (Nagel) Meinzer, both of whom were natives of Germany. They were farmers by occupation, and came to the United States in 1848, settling in Racine county, Wisconsin. In 1864 they removed to Houston county, Minnesota, where the father died in January, 1876. He was a loyal citizen, and a consistent member of the Lutheran church. The mother is now living at the advanced age of eighty years. In the father's family there were six children, four of whom are now living—our subject, Philip, Christopher and Louise. Those deceased were Carl and Catharine.

The subject of our sketch was reared in Baden, Germany, until ten years of age, at which time he came to the United States with his parents, and located with them in Wisconsin. Our subject remained in that State until 1862, up to which time he had been spending his time in farm work assisting his father. He received a good common-school education, and January 15, 1862, enlisted in the Nineteenth Wisconsin Infantry, joining the Seventh Army Corps. He entered the service as a private, and was discharged as corporal. He was discharged at Richmond, Virginia, August 9, 1865. He engaged in several battles, among them being Torry's Bluff and the last noted battle of Fair Oaks. Our subject was not wounded in the service, although he passed through many hard-fought battles. After being discharged he came to Houston county, Minnesota. where he remained about a year and a half, then in 1867 he removed to Missouri, and from there returned to Houston county in 1869. He made the latter county his home until coming to Lincoln county in 1878, where he has resided ever since.

Mr. Meinzer was married in October, 1865, to Miss Anna Mary Gerwitz, a native of. Germany. This union has been blessed with seven children: Emelie, Louise, George, Mary, Fred, Charles and Jacob.

Perhaps no man in the township is so well known throughout Lincoln county as our subject. Since coming to the county he has been intimately associated with all affairs of a public nature and has actively identified himself with all projects which tended to the upbuilding of the general welfare. He has held numerous official positions, and in every case has manifested an adaptability and efficiency which have made him popular as a citizen. In politics he affiliates with the republican party, having been a member of that organization since its foundation. He also belongs to the Odd Fellows fraternity, and is secretary of the local organization. He is a member of the Grand Army of the Republic, of which he has been adjutant. He is a representative citizen, and is respected and esteemed by all who know him.

———◦◦❯❮◦◦———

DR. NATHAN D. SATTERLEE, a prominent physician and surgeon of Winnebago City, Minnesota, is a native of Montgomery county, New York, where he was born April 3, 1823. His parents were Nathan Allen and Lucy (Mallery) Satterlee, the former a native of Rhode Island and the latter born in New York. The father was born December 5, 1783, and the mother was born November 15, 1791. The father was a farmer by occupation and served in the War of 1812. The grandfather of our subject was John Satterlee, who was a soldier in the Revolutionary War, serving under General Washington. The grandfather had six brothers who served in the same war. The family originally came from Ireland, in 1748 or 1749, settling in Rhode Island.

Dr. Satterlee's father came to Milwaukee, Wisconsin, June 2, 1848, and later settled at Beaver Dam, where he engaged in farming for four years. He then lived a retired life at Princeton, Green Lake county, Wisconsin, where he died in 1853. The mother died in 1854. In the father's family there were six children, four of whom are still living: Simon P., Clarissa A., Dr. Nathan D. and Joseph.

The subject of our sketch remained with his parents until he was seventeen years of age. Up to this time he had been given a good common-school education, and had been engaged in various kinds of employment. For three years he worked on the construction of the Erie canal. This was after he left home, and he then attended Fairfield Medical College, in New York, and graduated in the winter of 1840–41. He is also a graduate of the Keokuk (Iowa) Medical College. His first engagement in the practice of his profession was in Lewis county, New York, and coming west in 1848, he settled in Beaver Dam, where he engaged in active practice for about thirty years. He then came to Minnesota, locating in Winnebago City, where he engaged in the duties of his profession for five years. His next move was to La Crosse, where he remained two years, after which he returned to Minnesota, locating at different points and finally taking up his residence in Winnebago City, where he enjoys a large and lucrative practice.

Dr. Satterlee was married in 1861, to Mrs. S. M. Wilcox, of Cambria, Columbia county, Wisconsin. He has two children—Rebecca F. and Amanda B.

In politics the subject of our sketch affiliates with the republican party, and is also a member of the Odd Fellows' fraternity. He is the present chairman of the board of health, also a member of the State Medical Association, and is surgeon for the Milwaukee railroad. He is a man of large attainments and has an excellent practice. Dr. Satterlee is one of the heirs to the famous "Hyde estate" in England.

<hr/>

CHARLES H. REIPKE. This gentleman is one of the leading German citizens of Storden township, Cottonwood county, Minnesota. His residence and farm are located on section 26, where he has resided since 1878. Mr. Reipke was born in Hanover, April 21, 1837, his parents being Henry and Caroline (Rinkle) Reipke. The family emigrated to America in 1852 and located for a time in Albany, New York. They made that their abiding place until 1856, when they went to Illinois, making that their home until 1863. In that year they concluded to try their fortunes farther West, and, coming to Minnesota, located in Nicollet county, where the parents still live.

The subject of our sketch was reared a farmer's boy, and assisted his parents on the farm until he was eighteen years of age, and in the meantime was given a good common-school education. At the age just mentioned he commenced learning the baker's trade and followed that line of occupation for some three years, after which he commenced for himself and for two years operated in Albany, New York. Removing thence he went to Illinois, opening a bakery business for himself, and operating the same for four years. His next move was to St. Peter, Nicollet county, Minnesota, where he engaged in the grocery and bakery business for a period of sixteen years. He met with good success and accumulated considerable means. At the end of the sixteen years, Mr. Reipke removed to his present location in Storden township, Cottonwood county, where he located on a homestead of 160 acres, and also took 160 acres as a tree claim. On the tree claim there stands to-day a fine grove of thirty acres of trees, the finest and largest grove in Cottonwood county. Our subject has provided his farm with excellent improvements, building a good house, barn and other outbuildings. He does not confine his attention entirely to the raising of cattle, but also produces a fine grade of Short-horn cattle and Clydesdale and Norman horses.

Mr. Reipke was married in May, 1862, to Elizabeth Miller. This union has been blessed with four living children—Caroline, Rosa, Carl and Henry. Caroline married Gotleib Zinn, and now resides in Minneapolis. Rosa married Henry Troutfeather and resides in Cottonwood county. The family are members of the Luthern church, and occupy a prominent place in the social and religious affairs of the township.

The subject of our sketch is a man of energy and ability, and takes an active part in public matters and affiliates with the democratic party. He is a member of the Odd Fellows' lodge of Windom, becoming a member of the general organization in St. Paul, Lodge No. 12, in 1866.

ON. PIERCE J. KNISS. This gentleman is perhaps one of the best-known and most widely-respected citizens of Rock county, Minnesota. He is the president of the First National Bank of Luverne and is also president of the Jasper Stone Quarry Company of the same town. He made his location in Rock county in June, 1870, and the same fall surveyed the town plat of Luverne. He built a log cabin 16x 18 feet, in which he lived with his family, and also built a real estate office on the village site. Mr. Kniss platted 180 acres of land and laid the foundation for the present prosperous, city with whose interests he has been connected ever since. He established his private bank in 1876, and, later, merged it into the State bank, and in 1886 was mainly instrumental in organizing and establishing the First National Bank, of which he has since been president. This gentleman, perhaps, more than any other in the county, has performed those acts and said those things which gave impetus to the improvement and settlement of Luverne, and which have brought it to its present prosperous condition. He has largely interested himself in every project which has aimed toward the financial development of the city and built up many prosperous and profitable business enterprises. For some years he was engaged in railroad contracting, building seventy miles of the old St. Paul & Sioux City line of road and also fifty miles for the Milwaukee road.

Mr. Kniss was born at Old Defiance, Defiance county, Ohio, on the 16th of November, 1839. His parents were Jacob and Mernava (Taylor) Kniss, the former a native of Pennsylvania and the latter a native of Virginia. Throughout his life the father was largely interested in the leather trade and carried on a large tannery business, being also a boot and shoe merchant. He died in 1849, in Ohio. The mother is still living and is residing with her son P. J. In the father's family there are three living children—Minnie L., now Mrs. Dr. H. H. Hurlbert, of Duluth; George W., of whom a sketch is given in another department of this work, and our subject.

The educational advantages furnished the subject of our sketch in his youthful days were of the highest order. He attended the Delton Academy in Sauk county, Wisconsin, in which institution he matriculated when fifteen years of age. After completing his scholastic course he became a teacher, following that profession in the States of Wisconsin and Illinois. He became a thorough, and by experience, a practical, civil engineer, and spent nine years in surveying and engineering, and for some time was engineer in Wisconsin in connection with the draining of State swamp lands The political career of our subject has been one of the most notable character and he has held many positions of honor and responsibility, having in each instance proven his efficiency and served his constituents to their satisfaction and with credit to himself. The first position to which he was elected was that of chairman of the board of supervisors in 1874, which office he retained for several years. He has been president of the village council, and has held numerous other minor positions. In 1878 he was elected by a unanimous choice of the people as a member of the lower house of the legislature, and was elected to his second term in 1880. He has been quite prominent in the affairs of the republican party, and has represented the local interests of that organization several different times in the State conventions, but is now a prohibitionist in sentiment. He enlisted in Company K, Fiftieth Wisconsin Infantry, entering the service as a private. In May following his enlistment he was promoted to the rank of sergeant, and later became adjutant of his regiment. He was in the service for sixteen months, having enlisted for one year. His regiment was with the division which bivouacked on the Missouri river. The engagements in which he participated were mainly with Rebel bushwhackers, and our subject saw much severe

fighting and had many narrow escapes. His regiment was sent up the Missouri river to Fort Rice, Dakota, to repel the attacks of the Indians and protect the settlers from their ravages. He was in many skirmishes with the red men, and understands the cruelty and fierceness which characterize the Indian method of warfare.

The subject of our sketch was married in 1870 to Miss Mernava Donaldson, of Lindon, Wisconsin. This lady was a daughter of William and Margaret Donaldson, prominent citizens of Lindon. Mr. and Mrs. Kniss have five living children—Lillian M., Everett J., Ella M., Paul D. and Ruth G. The three oldest are at present at Cornell college at Mount Vernon, Iowa.

In company with Judge Perkins, Mr. Kniss organized the Windom Bank in 1881, and also established the first bank at Pipestone City and another at Flandreau, Dakota. He visited California in 1886, purchased lands and set out a large grove of orange trees. At a more recent date he purchased a grove of orange trees already bearing. He has one of the finest residences in the village of Luverne and has embraced an entire block in the grounds about his house. His residence is of brick, fitted with all modern improvements, surrounded with ornamental and shade trees, and he has withal one of the most beautiful homes in the city. Mr. Kniss is the founder of Luverne, and has fathered every movement toward its development since the first day of its foundation. To him more than to any other man is due Luverne's present prosperity and financial strength. Being a man of abundant financial strength he has aided materially in the establishing of nearly every leading business enterprise in the city and county, and whenever his hand has pointed out, or his voice dictated, methods or means by which any organization was to be governed, success has invariably come, and the results have proven the sagacity of Mr. Kniss' judgment. He is a man of broad ideas, and intensely practical, and has therefore become one of the most highly reputed gentleman in the county. His reputation for integrity and business uprightness is without a flaw, and it is well and widely said that Mr. Kniss' word is as good as his written obligation. Coming to the county in the very early day, and locating the city of Luverne, he has watched its needs and has done all he could to help it keep pace with the times.

HENRY COOPER, a substantial farmer of Shetek township, Murray county, Minnesota, took a claim on section 32 in 1872. He is now residing on section 18. He was one of the very first settlers of the township, and has been closely identified with its official history ever since making his location. He is indeed a representative citizen, and is in good circumstances. He came to his present claim in about 1875, since which time he has been engaged in general farming and stock raising. He took a trip to the Pacific coast in the fall of 1888, but soon returned, as there is "no place like home."

The place of the nativity of Mr. Cooper is found in Syracuse, Onondaga county, New York, where he was born in April, 1839. He resided in that village and obtained a good common-school education until he was seventeen years of age. He also attended school for some time in Liverpool, New York. While in New York our subject assisted his father in work at the cooper's trade, and also for some time engaged in boating on the Erie canal. On coming to Wisconsin at seventeen years of age, he then engaged in agricultural pursuits. His first trip to Minnesota was when it was practically a new country, indeed before its organization as a State. Returning to Wisconsin, he remained

in that State until 1862, when he came to Minnesota, and on the next day after his arrival enlisted in the Tenth Regiment Minnesota Volunteer Infantry. He was discharged in 1865, at Memphis, Tennessee. Before going South he participated in two skirmishes with the Indians, at the lower Sioux agency, at the upper Sioux agency, and at the battle of Wood Lake. He had his leg broken and his ankle thrown out of joint at the Winnebago agency. His horse fell on it while he was riding after Sioux Indians in the night. Being ordered South, he participated in the battles of Tupelo, Mobile and Nashville. He passed through many severe experiences, and narrowly escaped being killed a number of times. At Tupelo he was struck on the leg by a piece of shell, and was also sunstruck at this time. Here the bullets fell fast and thick, like leaden hail around him, and when the battle was over he discovered that a bullet had found its way through his hat and another through his coat. After this he was for some time an inmate of the Washington Hospital at Memphis. He was then ordered to report to the commissary department at Fort Pickering, Tennessee. After his discharge he came to Houston county, Minnesota, and lived for a while on his father's farm. His father still resides in that county. Our subject, after a short time, went to Mower county, and after farming for a brief period returned to Houston county. He engaged in farming and also in running a threshing-machine, and in 1872 came to Murray county, where he has since lived.

Mr. Cooper was married, December 25, 1867, to Miss Rosetta Westgate, who was born in the State of New York. Miss Westgate's father was Gifford B. Westgate, a native of the State of New York, and a ship builder, cooper and carpenter by trade. He is still living in Fillmore county, Minnesota. Mr. and Mrs. Cooper have seven children, six boys and one girl—Gifford, John, Alek, Frank, Albert, Floyd and Mabel.

The subject of our sketch affiliates with the republican party, and is an influential member of the Grand Army of the Republic. He is an exemplary citizen and a member of the Methodist Episcopal church. Pioneer life has always had its ups and downs, and our subject has been visited with the various misfortunes which attend the lives of all early settlers. He has had his home destroyed by a terrific hurricane, and had it not been for his forethought, doubtless the whole family would have been killed. One year from the time his house was blown down, his barn, horses and considerable other property were destroyed by fire. Other disastrous strokes of fortune have fallen to his lot, among them being the loss of eleven head of cattle, all of which were stricken with the "black leg." He came near losing his life on one of the long trips he had to make when going to market. Besides all this he went through four years of the grasshopper siege. This was during a very severe storm in the winter. He was driving an ox team, and, losing the main road, wandered about for some time over the snow-clad prairies. Finally the oxen wandered to his brother's place, where he found shelter, but not before he had become very badly frozen. Our subject, however, has kept heart and continued steadily at work and has now surrounded himself with circumstances which betoken a prosperous and successful farm.

———→◦→⟩⟨◆⟩⟨←◦←———

LIAS HOWARD, a prosperous farmer of Murray county, Minnesota, resides on section 28, Shetek township. His location in Murray county was made in July, 1876, at which time he pre-empted the land on which he now lives. He has a fine farm, well located, and provided with excellent buildings. He has turned his attention to a

considerable degree to the culture of fruit trees, and has now one hundred apple trees and a number of currant and gooseberry bushes, etc., having met with good success in this line. Mr. Howard interests himself in the general affairs of his township, and has held various official positions. He has been director of school district No. 1 for some time, besides having held other minor positions.

Elias Howard was born in Oxford county, Maine, December 1, 1833. His parents were Thomas J. and Olive (Bean) Howard, the former a native of New Hampshire, and a mechanic by occupation. Emigrating from New Hampshire, the father settled in Maine, and later located in Ottawa, La Salle county, Illinois, where he died in 1853. The mother was a native of Woodstock, Oxford county, Maine, and is still living. In the father's family there were fifteen children. Those living are—H. B., Silvanus P., Emma, Thomas J. and C. K. Rodney, another son, died in the army, having enlisted in the Second Illinois Battery. He died at the hospital at Bolivar, Tennessee, of diseases contracted in the service. Silvanus enlisted at fourteen years of age and served four years. The father was also in the service as a private in the Union army. Thomas J. also served in the Union army and is now employed in a woolen factory in Dalton, Illinois.

The early life of the subject of our sketch was spent in his native county, where he received his training and an excellent education. He remained in his native place until eighteen years of age. He completed his education at Bethel Hill Academy in his native county. After completing his academic course he went to Massachusetts and found employment for one summer in the Waltham bleaching works. He then went to Sutton, Massachusetts, and worked in the cloth room of the Rhode Island Manufacturing Company for four months. His next move was to emigrate to LaSalle county, Illinois, where for three years he engaged in railroading at Ottawa. He also worked to some extent at the trade of carpentering. Removing thence he located in Wabasha county, Minnesota, where he remained from 1856 to 1875, or until coming to his farm in Murray county.

Mr. Howard was married in the spring of 1858 to Miss Martha Jane Stone, a native of Livingston county, Illinois. Early in her life she removed to Lake county, Illinois, where she received her training and education. Mr. and Mrs. Howard have four children—Cora, at present running a dressmaking establishment at Tracy, Lyon county; Fred, Olive and Alice, who are still living at home. Rodney F., a son fourteen years of age, was killed by lightning in July, 1887.

In politics the subject of our sketch affiliates with no particular party, but always acts and votes on the principle that every person should vote for the man best fitted for the certain position to be filled. Our subject is quite a genius in his way and has done much in the way of building in his township. He has the honor of constructing the first lumber wagon which was built in Murray county. In 1877 this wagon was ironed by Mr. Marsh and Mr. Calkins. The subject of our sketch is a man of good character, honest in all his business dealings, and is held in high esteem by all who know him.

HARVEY JONES settled on the north half of section 36, Osborn township, Pipestone county, Minnesota, in 1886. He has made valuable and important improvements on his farm, and, besides farming, has engaged largely in stock raising. He has made a specialty of the Durham breed of cattle, and has a large herd of fine animals of that stock. His horses are also of good blood. Mr. Jones was born in Iowa county, Wis-

consin, February 6, 1861. His father, W. M. Jones, is of Welsh descent, and is still living at Barneveld, Wisconsin. The father was born in Wales in 1831, and remained with his parents in that country until he was about six years of age, when they emigrated to the United States, settling for some time in the State of New York. In 1848 the family removed to Iowa county, Wisconsin, where they were among the pioneers of that county. The father has lived a long and successful life, and is now a resident of the village of Barneveld, having retired from active business. He is now fifty-eight years of age. The mother of the subject of our sketch was Hannah (Jones) Jones. Both of the parents are members of the Methodist Episcopal church. The parents had a family of eight children—J. W., Harvey, Martin, Sarah, Ruth, Hannah, Mary and Minnie, who died when about seven years of age.

Harvey Jones, whose name appears at the head of this sketch, was reared and given an excellent education in the State of Wisconsin. He attended the Northwestern Business College at Madison, in that State, for three terms, and after this scholastic course was completed he engaged in the mercantile business with his brother, J. W. Jones, in the town of Barneveld. This partnership was continued for a period of four years, when our subject removed to Nebraska, where for two years he followed the line of prospecting. Returning to Wisconsin for one year he engaged in farming, and then came to his present place in Osborn township, Pipestone county, Minnesota.

Mr. Jones was united in marriage March 10, 1888, to Miss Maggie Harris, a native of Barneveld, Wisconsin, where she received her early training and education. She was the daughter of I. Harris, a prominent stock shipper and farmer of Dane county, Wisconsin.

In politics the subject of our sketch affiliates with the republican party, in whose principles he has had a strong belief for many years. Mr. Jones is well educated, is a pleasant, agreeable neighbor, and is one of the reliable citizens of Osborn township.

<hr />

FRED J. CARPENTER is a well-to-do farmer of Lake Side township, Cottonwood county, Minnesota. He made his location in the county in 1872, and in 1888 came to his present location on section 8. The place of his nativity is found in Columbia county, New York, in Hudson City, where he was born July 20, 1848.

The subject of our sketch is a son of Chauncey and D. (Worth) Carpenter, natives of New York State, and whose marriage occurred in the city of Hudson September 2, 1840. They remained in that city until April 1857, when they removed to Green Lake county, Wisconsin, locating in Fond du Lac, where they remained about twelve years. The father died in that city June 25, 1869. He was born July 16, 1810. He was a man of excellent education, and of thorough business qualifications, and followed a mercantile life for many years. The widow came to Minnesota in 1873, and lived with our subject until her death, which occurred November 24, 1878. Her birth took place March 28, 1819. She was an exemplary Christian lady and a member of the Methodist Episcopal church. There were six children in the father's family —Jane, Emily, Margaret, Fred J., Cornelia and Anna. Margaret died November 7, 1858, and Jane died July 24, 1879. The grandfather of the subject of our sketch was Amos Carpenter, a native of the State of New York, and a merchant by occupation. Our subject's grandfather on the mother's side was Walter Worth, a native of New York, and for some time captain of an ocean vessel, in which occupation he lost an arm. Chester Carpenter, an uncle of our subject, was foreman of the jury on the famous Tilton and Beecher trial. He was a flour merchant by trade, and after the trial became a member of Henry Ward Beecher's church.

Fred J. Carpenter was reared in Columbia county, New York, and when about eight years of age emigrated with his people to Wisconsin. He remained under the parental roof until he was twenty-one years of age, and up to this time had been given good educational advantages. He received the principal part of his education in the village of Kingston, Green Lake county, Wisconsin, and after completing his course of schooling engaged in farming for some years. He also engaged in clerking in a general store and in the mill business and later as clerk in a hotel. In 1872 he came to Carson township, Cottonwood county, Minnesota. He still owns 240 acres of land on sections 8 and 9 of that township, which he has thoroughly improved. He resided on that place until 1888, when he came to his present location. Throughout his residence here our subject has taken an active part in all matters pertaining to the public welfare and has actively participated in political affairs. Being a republican in politics he has been with the majority, and has been elected to various official positions. He has been chairman of the board of supervisors for three years, assessor for three years, township clerk four years, and is at present assessor of the township. He has always taken part in educational affairs and has held various school district offices. He is president of the county agricultural society, is a member of the Ancient Order of United Workmen, and is a representative citizen of the county.

Mr. Carpenter was married December 13, 1877, to Miss Clara McNeil, a native of

Minnesota. She was the daughter of Nathan McNeil, a farmer. Mrs. Carpenter died January 29, 1888, leaving three children—Alice May, Hattie Blanche and Frederick Chester.

———◦—◦ᐧ⟨⟩ᐧ◦—◦———

HIRAM B. DANIELSON resides on section 15, Hendricks township, Lincoln county, Minnesota. He made his location on this farm in 1880, and has since been actively engaged in general farming and stock raising. He has identified himself closely with the interests of the township and county, and has held several positions of responsibility.

Hiram B. Danielson is a native of Goodhue county, Minnesota, where he was born April 3, 1859. He is a son of Hans H. and Elizabeth (Anderson) Danielson. The father was a native of Norway, and the mother was a native of Illinois. The father came to America in 1842, first settling in Wisconsin, where he remained until 1856. He then removed to Goodhue county, Minnesota, and has engaged in farming ever since. He is still a resident of that county. In the father's family there were twelve children, Hiram being the second in order of birth. The subject of our sketch remained on the farm of his father assisting in the farm work until he was twenty-one years of age. He received a good common school education in the district schools, and at twenty-one years of age, in the year 1880, came to Lincoln county and purchased a farm of eighty acres, where he now lives. In politics he affiliates with the republican party, and has interested himself in local affairs of his township. He has served as chairman of the board of supervisors two terms, and at present holds the office of township clerk. He is a man of good character, energetic and systematic in his farming operations, and is held in high esteem by all who know him.

Mr. Danielson was married June 25, 1884, to Miss Amanda Sundell, a native of Goodhue county, Minnesota. This union has been blessed with three children—Myra E., Howard H. and Nellie I.

———◦—◦ᐧ⟨⟩ᐧ◦—◦———

ANTON O. LUNDER, a well-to-do farmer and leading citizen of Murray county, Minnesota, resides on section 34 of Slayton township. He is a native of the kingdom of Norway, where he was born March 17, 1855. His parents were Olai N. and Gunell M. (Olson) Lunder, who were also natives of Norway. The father was a farmer by occupation and died at the residence of our subject July 21, 1888. In the father's family there were nine children.

The subject of our sketch left his native land with his parents and emigrated to America at the age of fourteen years. In his native country his early life had been spent in attaining a common-school education, and as much as possible in assisting his father on the farm. Coming to America by steamboat, they landed in Quebec, and from thence went to Lake City, Minnesota, where three months were spent. From thence the family went to Fort Ridgley, same State, and the father settled on a pre-emption, where he remained nineteen years. After this he came to the home of our subject in Murray county, where he died. At the age of twenty-one years the subject of our sketch left the parental home and engaged in various kinds of employment until 1879. He was then married and came to Murray county, where he settled on a homestead and also took a tree claim, and in all owns at present 280 acres of excellent land, under fine cultivation, and provided with excellent buildings.

Mr. Lunder was united in marriage January 15, 1879, to Miss Minnie Evenson, a native of Iowa county, Wisconsin. This union has been blessed with five children—

Gunda O., Hulda M., Goodwin H., Lillie A. and Rudolph.

The subject of our sketch is a man of excellent qualities, is genial and warm-hearted, and is one of the most public-spirited citizens of the township. In politics he affiliates with the republican party, and has held various official positions within the gift of his fellow-citizens. He has been chairman of the board of supervisors for a period of eight years, and still holds the same; has served with rare fidelity and to the satisfaction of his constituents. He was constable for three years and road inspector for the same time. The latter position he still holds. He has represented his township in various republican conventions held during the last eight years.

ㅡㅡㅡ·ㅡ·〉·{ㄷㄷ〉}·〈·ㅡ·ㅡ

LORENZO W. BROWN, one of the prosperous farmers of Faribault county, Minnesota, resides on section 31, of Prescott township, where he owns 360 acres of land. He gives attention to general farming and stock raising, and since the fall of 1856 has been a resident of Faribault county. He first located on section 13, of Verona township, where he purchased 160 acres of land, on which he lived for three years. He built a log house and made improvements and after three years' residence came to his present location, where he has since lived. He has been a hard-working, energetic farmer and has succeeded in making his farm one of the best in the entire county. Our subject was one of the very earliest settlers of the locality, there being but one other man, William Scott by name, in Prescott township. This man was located on section 29, and left soon after our subject came to the township, going to Blue Earth City, from whence he went to California in about 1882. Mr. Brown, being one of the pioneers of the county, assisted in the organization of Prescott township. The first meeting was held on Mr. Scott's place, where thirteen votes were cast. Mr. Brown served on the first board of supervisors and held that office for about eight years. He has been justice of the peace, etc., and has been quite prominent in the official history of his township.

Lorenzo Brown was born in Jefferson county, New York, January 30, 1824. The father was William Brown, a farmer and blacksmith by trade, who was born in Connecticut, near Bridgeport, and was one of the early settlers of the State of New York, in which State he lived until his death. Our subject's mother's maiden name was Lydia Bacon, a native of one of the Eastern States and of Quaker descent. She died when our subject was seven years old. The father married again, taking to wife a Miss Campbell, who died about ten years later, and then the father married a Mrs. Davis, of Ohio. Our subject was the only child by the first marriage. By his second marriage the father had three children—Lydia Angeline, Sophia Evaline and James Madison, the latter now living in Faribault county, Minnesota, to which the place he came in 1860. By his third wife the father had two children— Charles and Adelbert.

Lorenzo Brown received his early training and education in Jefferson county, New York. He remained there until twenty years of age, engaged during the principal part of the time in agricultural pursuits. He then went to Syracuse and engaged as a clerk for Thurber & Co. in the wholesale and retail confectionery business. He followed this for nine years and then engaged in the cigar business, being employed for two years by Messrs. Barton & Co. At the end of this time Mr. Brown concluded to find a location somewhere in the West, and coming to Minnesota after the end of two years traveling through the Southern and Central States, located, as has already been stated, in Verona township.

The subject of our sketch was married in 1851 to Miss Catharine Hook, a native of Switzerland and who was brought to the United States by her parents when she was two years old. This lady died in April, 1881, having lived a long and useful life and having been for years a member of the Presbyterian church. Mr. Brown was married in June, 1883, to Miss Elizabeth Henderson, a native of Dalton, Whitefield county, Georgia. She was a daughter of J. P. Henderson, a farmer, who still lives in Georgia. By his first wife our subject had two children— Edward Therber and Waldwin W. The first died at two years of age, the latter is still living and a resident of Dakota. By his present wife Mr. Brown has one child—Florence M.

The pioneer experience of the subject of our sketch was filled with much that would interest the general reader. Pioneer life at best is filled with hardships, and the life of our subject could not escape those things of a distressing nature which caused many early settlers to become discouraged and leave the country before success crowned their efforts.· During the early times his crops were a failure. Provisions were hard to obtain. Many miles had to be traveled in order to find a market for what little produce was raised; then when once found, poor prices were received. When he first came to the county Mr. Brown bought flour which was brought from Clayton, Iowa, for which he paid from six to eight dollars a hundred. After the first few years crops were better and market points were more easily accessible and prices for produce were better, so that our subject was enabled to accumulate a little means and put his farm in excellent condition. He has now one of the best farms in the county and is in excellent circumstances.

In politics Mr. Brown affiliates with the democratic party and is a leading member of the Presbyterian church. He belongs to the Masonic and Odd Fellows fraternities, being a charter member of the Masonic Lodge of Winnebago and Blue Earth cities. He is now connected with the Lodge at Blue Earth City. He first became a member of the Masonic fraternity in the State of New York. He was master of the first Grange started in Blue Earth City, being made first deputy of that society appointed by the master of the grand lodge. Mr. Brown is a genial, warm-hearted and sociable man, has an estimable family and one of the most hospitable homes in the county.

———⊷⊶⧈⊷⊷———

JEROME CUTLER is a leading farmer and stock raiser, located on section 12, Dale township, Cottonwood county, Minnesota, where he located in the spring of 1871, on a soldier's claim.

The subject of our sketch is a native of Boston, Massachusetts, where he was born March 2, 1837. The father of our subject, Samuel Walter Cutler, was a boot and shoemaker by trade, was born in 1808, and was engaged in business in the city of Boston for many years. He was married there, and after awhile went to Franklin county, Vermont, where he settled and made it his home until his death, which occurred in 1854. Our subject's mother's maiden name was Sarah Mace, born in Milton, Essex county, Vermont, in 1810, where she was reared until the age of twenty-two years. She then went to Boston, where she was married and lived for nearly eight years. She is still living with her children.

The grandfather of our subject on the father's side was Ephraim Cutler. He was a native of Massachusetts, and a farmer by occupation. The grandmother was Persis (Hancock) Cutler. The grandfather on the mother's side was Abram Mace, born in 1770, in New Hampshire, and a miller by trade.

He wedded Prudence Upton, a native of Massachusetts, born in 1787.

The subject of our sketch left Boston with his parents when he was about six years of age, and going to Vermont made that his home until he was twenty-four years old. He received his education in Franklin and La-moille counties, Vermont, attending the Ba-kersfield Academy one term, and in May, 1861, enlisted in Company H, Second Vermont Infantry (Second Brigade, Second Division, Sixth Army Corps). He served faithfully and gallantly in the Union army and was discharged at Brattleborough, Vermont, in 1864. He participated in a goodly number of hard-fought battles, among them being that of first Bull Run, through the Peninsular campaign under McClellan, Fredericksburg, Antietam, Gettysburg, battle of the Wilderness, where he was in the commands of Hooker, Meade and Grant; he was slightly wounded at the battle of Fredericksburg. After his discharge he returned to his old home in Vermont and remained until 1867, when he started for the West, locating in Fayette county, Iowa. He remained in that State until coming to Cottonwood county in 1871, where he has since resided.

The subject of our sketch was one of the very first settlers of the township, and com-menced under difficult and discouraging cir-cumstances. For a time he had to live in a sod shanty, and had to put up with other discomforts. He set out four or five acres of trees and commenced making active im-provements. His son Morris was the second child born in the township, and our subject assisted in the organization of his civil divis-ion in 1874. He has held various important local positions, among them being justice of the peace, township treasurer and assessor, and at present he is clerk of school district No. 11. Mr. Cutler is an energetic, systema-tic farmer, and his integrity of character and earnest work in behalf of the general wel-

fare has won him many friends and warm admirers.

Mr. Cutler was married September 20, 1864, to Miss Emily M. Bailey, a native of Vermont. She was the daughter of Jehial S. Bailey, a carpenter and builder by occu-pation. Mrs. Cutler was an exemplary Christian lady and a member of the Metho-dist Episcopal church. She died May 2, 1889, and was mourned by many friends and loving relatives. Six children were born to Mr. and Mrs. Cutler—Walter L., now in Washington Territory; Alvin B., Jessie E., Morris N., Helen A. and Lucy A.

The subject of our sketch is one of the prominent republicans in his locality, and is a representative citizen. He belongs to the Grand Army of the Republic, of which he is chaplain, and is also a member of the Ancient Order of United Workmen. He has been a member of the Methodist Episcopal church for many years, having joined at the age of seventeen. He has always taken an active part in religious work, and has served re-peatedly as steward, class-leader and Sunday-school superintendent.

———❖———

JOHN C. MARSHALL is the able editor and proprietor of the Edgerton *Enter-prise* of Edgerton, Pipestone county, Minne-sota. This gentleman has conducted this newspaper since the fall of 1887. By his careful management and business push he has built up a large subscription list, and enjoys a large patronage in the line of job printing.

Mr. Marshall is a native of the rock-bound land of Scotland, born in Perthshire, March 17, 1840. His parents, Samuel and Jane (Hill) Marshall, were also natives of Scot-land. When our subject was about four years of age the parents concluded to emi-grate to America. On coming to this coun-try they settled on government land in Dodge county, Wisconsin, where the father built a saw-mill and continued the operation of that line of business in connection with farming for a number of years. In 1860 he built a large flouring-mill, to which he gave his attention principally thereafter. The father is still living in Dodge county, Wisconsin, his mother having died in 1883.

The subject of our sketch was given the educational advantages furnished by the district school, and he was thus enabled to acquire a common school education. He finished his schooling with a course of study in the high school at Horicon, which institution he left when he was about twenty years of age. At that age he commenced learning the milling business, and, in connection therewith, commenced the study of law at home. He rapidly advanced in his legal studies and was admitted to the bar in the month of June 1870. The allurements of the legal profession however failed to capture him, and he gave his attention principally to the milling business. Continuing in the latter line until he was twenty-five years of age, he bought an interest in his father's mill and continued in partnership until in 1884. He then sold out and took charge of the Neosha mill at Neosha, Dodge county, Wisconsin, remaining in that employment for about two and a half years. After this period had expired, he started out on a trip through Colorado, Kansas and Nebraska, and in the fall of 1887 he came to Pipestone, purchased some land, and also engaged in the printing business.

Mr. Marshall was united in the bonds of matrimony, October 9, 1868, to Miss Eleanor C. Young, a native of York State and daughter of Thomas and Louisa (Giles) Young. Her parents were natives of England. Mr. and Mrs. Marshall have been blessed with five children—Samuel T., John, Frank, Lulu and Jessie.

Mr. Marshall is thoroughly educated and widely read, and by his successful management of the Edgerton *Enterprise*, has built up a large circle of friends. He is a man of strong opinions and ably defends the principles of the republican party, to which he belongs. He is a good citizen and enjoys the esteem of his fellow-townsmen. He is a member of Neosha Lodge, No. 108, Ancient Free and Accepted Masons, and also of Oconomowoc Chapter, Ancient Free and Accepted Masons.

JOHN H. COOK is a leading farmer and stock raiser of Ash Lake township, Lincoln county, Minnesota. He homesteaded land on section 34 in 1876 and had also preempted lands in the year 1873. He first commenced his farming operations by breaking about an acre and building a small shanty 12x16 feet in which he lived for about two years. In 1876 he built the shed which he now uses to accommodate his stock. He set out a number of trees in that year, among them being cottonwood, maple, popple and various other kinds. He has worked hard and faithfully to make his farm what it is, one of the best in the township. He has occupied his attention with general farming and stock raising and has been quite successful in accumulating means. He was one of the very first settlers of the township and assisted in its organization in 1879 and held several offices within the gift of the people, among them being that of pathmaster and various others of minor importance. He was the first settler to locate in the southern half of the township and has been fairly successful in his various enterprises. He is of a contented disposition, and being gifted with a happy temperament he is contented in whatever circumstances may happen to come to him.

Mr. Cook is a native of the eastern part of Upper Canada, being born in the county of Dundas, April 17, 1842. He is the son of

William A. Cook, also a native of Canada, where he is still living, engaged in farming and lumbering. He is seventy-six years of age, a loyal citizen and a member of the Methodist Episcopal church. The mother's name before her marriage was Sallie Casselman. She was born in Canada, and died in that country in 1866. She was an exemplary member of the Lutheran church. The subject of our sketch was one of nine children, all of whom grew to man and womanhood—Catharine, Simon, our subject; Caroline, Maria, Norman, George, Sarah and Dinah. Sarah died at the age of sixteen years. The others are all living in Canada.

The subject of our sketch was reared in Canada, where he received the greater part of his education. He made that his home principally until twenty-three years of age. Before that time his parents had started to remove to the United States, but owing to an unfortunate occurrence they were forced to return to their native country. When our subject was about fourteen or fifteen years old his parents went to Jones county, Iowa, where for two years they engaged in farming. Then, selling out, they started with a horse team, by way of Chicago, en route to their native land in Canada. They reached Chicago after a journey of two weeks, and there they loaded their stock and all household goods on a " propeller " and soon after steamed out into Lake Michigan, bound for their old home. About midnight the propeller caught fire from some unknown cause, and the flames could not be stopped. Signals were sent up for help, and ere long a schooner picked up and took on board all the passengers. Horses and wagons, however, and everything of this kind, and also the propeller, were totally destroyed. The schooner was veered around and started for Chicago. Here our subject's family were landed in a terrible plight. Our subject states that all the clothing he possessed, and in fact all that

he had in the world, were his pants, shirt and a wool hat. All the balance had been destroyed by the fire on board the ship. It was quite cold the morning they landed in Chicago, and the sidewalks were frosty, and in the trip to the hotel with the family our subject had to stop several times and put his feet into his hat in order to warm them. In the evening the family got aboard the train and started for the old home in Canada. Before starting, however, they had supplied themselves with the necessary clothing. While on board the burning steamer our subject came near losing his life from the fire. He was only saved, as were also the family, by the early arrival of the rescuing schooner. The suffering at this time was indeed intense, not only physically but mentally as well, and the father was almost crazed by the thought that perhaps his loved ones would be destroyed by the devouring flames, and he said that rather than have them burned he would throw the whole family overboard. On returning to Canada our subject made that his home until he was twenty-three years of age. Up to this age he assisted his father in work on the home farm, and after becoming thirty-three years old he went to the southern part of Illinois, where for three months he found employment in work for a Mr. Sullivan on a 40,000 acre farm. After this brief period he went to Jones county, Iowa, whence, after a short visit to an uncle, he went to Dubuque, Iowa, where he stayed a few days. Removing thence he went on a short visit to Kasota, Minnesota, and after three or four days in that place he went to St. Paul, and from thence to Northfield, in the vicinity of which place he remained five years, working for W. T. Hunter on a large farm. Mr. Hunter's farm was located six miles east of Northfield, and our subject continued a profitable engagement with this gentleman for five years. At the end of this time he located in St. Paul, where for three years he operated a lumber business for Mr. Hunter. He then returned to Northfield, and for one and a half years worked on a farm for Wells Blackman. His next move was to the city of Northfield, where for two or three weeks he worked for D. Sparry, and at the end of this time he came to Lincoln county, where he has since been living, engaged in general farming and stock raising. In politics Mr. Cook affiliates with the republican party, and has taken an active interest in matters pertaining to the welfare of the local organization.

He is a man of the very best character, thorough and systematic as a farmer, pleasant to meet, and is held in high esteem by all with whom he comes in contact. He has an excellent farm, comfortable and commodious home, and has a pleasant family.

Mr. Cook was married November 15, 1875, to Miss Maggie Marcellus, who was born in Canada, January 12, 1856. A biography of her father is found in another department of this work. She came to Minnesota in early life with her parents, and was educated at Northfield. Her marriage took place in Prescott, Wisconsin. Mr. and Mrs. Cook have one child, a girl, born September 24, 1878, named Dinah Irena.

REV. FATHER F. P. KERVICK is the present popular and efficient pastor of the Catholic church societies at Avoca, Fulda, Woodstock and Pipestone. He resides in the village of Avoca. Mr. Kervick was born in Baltimore, Maryland, May 18, 1855. He was the son of John and Mary (King) Kervick, the father a native of Ireland and the mother a native of Ohio. John Kervick came to America with his parents, John and Elizabeth (Dunn) Kervick, in 1823. The family located in Maryland.

The subject of our sketch left his home at the age of seventeen years, up to which time he had been given good educational advantages. At the age just mentioned he entered the St. Charles College, a Catholic institution of learning in the State of Maryland. He continued his studies in that institution, graduating from the classical course in 1877. After his graduation he went to England, where he commenced a course of theological studies. He was ordained a priest of the Catholic church September 25, 1881, at Mill Hill, London, receiving his ordination in the Catholic cathedral. He soon after returned to the United States, and was given charge of the negro missions throughout the South. October 25, 1585, he was transferred to his present charge. He is a man of fine attainments, and is at the head of the St. Francis Academy at Avoca. He has taken an active part in public affairs since coming to the village, and has been president of the village council and also village treasurer. Father Kervick is a man of high scholarly attainments, and, to these being added magnificent natural endowments, he is a man well calculated to successfully take charge of the interests of the Catholic church in this section. He is an excellent pastor, an able preacher, and is beloved by his church people and esteemed by every one who knows him.

ANGUS ROSS is the president of the Security Bank of Luverne, Minnesota. This institution is one of the important financial enterprises in the city, and enjoys an extensive patronage. Mr. Ross came to the county in 1878, and for some time engaged in farming and stock raising, later being engaged in the hardware business in the city of Luverne He engaged in the latter business some five years, and then turned his attention to other pursuits. In 1888, in company with other citizens of Luverne, he organized the Security Bank, of which he is the president.

Mr. Ross was born in Canada in 1844, and is a son of Allen and Belle (McKay) Ross, both natives of Scotland. The father left his native land before his marriage, and came to Canada, where he resided through-out his life. He was a farmer by occupation, and continued in that line until his death. In the father's family there were eight children, six of whom are now living— Walter M., Peter, Angus, John, Robert and Belle. Walter M. is at present a resident of St. Charles, Winona county, Minnesota, where he is engaged in the grain and agricultural implement business. He is a man of much means, and owns several elevators on the Winona & St. Peter railroad. Peter is still a resident of Canada, and is engaged in agricultural pursuits. John resides in Oregon, and his attention is occupied princi-pally in stock raising. Robert resides in Canada, where he is engaged extensively in farming. Belle is now Mrs. Morrison, of Canada.

The early life of the subject of our sketch was spent by him in school in Canada. He remained with his parents in that country until 1865, when he removed to Minnesota, locating at St. Charles, in Winona county, Minnesota. While in that place he attended school and also engaged to some extent in farming. He purchased land southeast of St. Charles and made improvements on the same for a number of years. Later he was engaged in the grain business in that place until coming to Luverne in 1877.

Mr. Ross was married in 1875 to Miss Ella Sinclair, of St. Charles, Minnesota, a daughter of A. C. Sinclair.

Too much can not be said of the executive abilities of Mr. Ross as exhibited in the management of his own private business, and the more intricate affairs of the banking institution with which he is connected. He is a man of excellent abilities and thoroughly understands the details of the institution of which he is the head. To him is due largely the success which has fallen to the lot of the Security Bank. Our subject has also interested himself largely in other financial enterprises and he has purchased more or less city property. In all matters of a public nature and in all projects tending to the development and improvement of Luverne, he has taken an active interest and has aided by his counsels and also by liberal gift of money. In politics he affiliates with the republican party and is also a member of the Masonic fraternity. In his business life, by his thoroughness and unquestionable integrity, he has drawn to himself a large circle of admiring and respecting friends.

ALBERT E. WOODMAN, a leading farmer and representative citizen of Pipestone county, Minnesota, resides on section 14, Troy township. He was born in Rice county, Minnesota, October 26, 1858.

The subject of our sketch is the son of Damon R. Woodman, whose biography appears in another department of this work. His mother was Emma J. (Brown) Woodman, the parents both being natives of Madison county, New York. The father is a prominent farmer of Pipestone county, and is also a resident of Troy township.

The gentleman whose name appears at the head of this biography received his education in the district schools until he attained the age of fifteen years. At this time he commenced attending the high school in Faribault during the winter months, and through the summer attending the district schools. He continued operating this plan for about five years, then in April, 1878, he came to Pipestone county and located where he now lives. His trip to this county from his home near Faribault was made while driving cattle for Major Rice in company with O. T. Gilson and D. B. Whigam, who are both now residents of Troy township. During this trip Mr. Woodman received his initiation into the experiences of pioneer life. His journey occupied fifteen days and it rained during each day, but, notwithstanding the rain, the trip was finally accomplished and the settlement in Pipestone county made. During the first two months he was engaged in freighting for different families, and in company with Mr. Gilson, already mentioned, drew the first load of lumber into Troy township. Until July of that year he worked at various kinds of labor, and in that month returned to Rice county, where he helped his father through the harvest season. When in Pipestone county, in the April previous, he had entered his claim, so in the fall of the year he returned and built a stable on his land and made preparations for putting in crops in the following season. During the winter he found his way to Memphis, Tennessee, where he engaged as timekeeper for the government at the harbor works at Memphis, receiving as compensation seventy-five dollars per month. Four months were spent in this kind of labor, and he then returned to his farm in Pipestone county, Minnesota, remaining thereon until in the fall of 1880. That winter he went to Faribault, where he engaged in the lumber business, returning to his farm the following spring. Working his land during the summer, in the fall he went to Blue Earth county, and engaged in different kinds of employment during the winter. He returned to his farm the following spring and made a permanent residence there, and has lived in Troy township ever since.

Mr. Woodman was united in marriage to Miss Martha Houk, August 9, 1883. Miss Houk was a native of Indiana. Her parents were Levi L. and Jane (Thornton) Houk, the father being a native of Pennsylvania, and the mother a native of Ohio. The mother died October 2, 1883, in Good Thunder, Minnesota, and the father died March 31, 1888, at the same place. Mr. and Mrs. Woodman have three children—Richard L., Belle and Emma A.

Mr. Woodman is a man of excellent abilities. He is thoroughly educated, being a graduate of the Faribault high school. His business knowledge and tact are of a high order, and in all his financial operations he has been eminently successful. He owns 160 acres of fine farming land, and another 160 acres is owned by his wife. In politics Mr. Woodman is a supporter of the principles enunciated by the republican party, and, as a man and citizen, is held in high esteem by all who know him. He is a man of excellent character, a good citizen, and is rapidly growing in wealth and popularity.

SAMUEL S. GILLAM, a prominent and influential farmer of Great Bend township, Cottonwood county, Minnesota, resides on an excellent farm on the shores of Cottonwood lake, on section 24. He was born in Cayuga county, New York, June 26, 1822.

The subject of our sketch is the son of Henry and Hannah (Willet) Gillam, the former a native of Orange county, New York, and the latter a native of Washington county. The parents came to Illinois in 1847, where the father followed the trade of shoemaking until his death, which occurred in about 1848, that of the mother occurring not far from the same time. In the father's family there were eleven children, the subject of our sketch being the youngest.

Up to seventeen years of age the subject of our sketch assisted his father at the shoemaking trade. However, in the meantime he was given good educational advantages and attended the public schools when they were in session. At seventeen years of age he removed to the State of Illinois and engaged in farming for one year. At this time, however, he was taken sick with the fever and ague, and returned to the State of New York, where resided at home with his father until he was twenty-one years of age. He then returned to Illinois, remaining three years when he again returned to New York to the parental home and remained one year. At this time the entire family came to Illinois and our subject found work on a farm in Kendall county, continuing in that line of employment, together with teaching several terms of school, for about five years. A few months were then spent in Monroe county, Wisconsin, after which he went to Milwaukee and remained one year, having charge during that time of the Sabbath school book depository. The climate, however, did not agree with him and he soon removed to Omro, Winnebago county, Wisconsin, where he found work at his trade, and in connection therewith engaged in farming until 1865. January 17th of that year he enlisted in Company A, Forty-eighth Wisconsin Infantry, and was discharged December 30, 1865. After his discharge he went to Winnebago county, Wisconsin, and made that his home until 1869, when he came to Cottonwood county, Minnesota, and took his claim where he now lives. Returning to Illinois he remained in that State during the winter and in the following spring came to Cottonwood county, where he has since lived. He has seen much of hard, pioneer experience, has passed through the grasshopper scourge, and has succeeded in spite of all these back-sets in placing himself in good circumstances, and has surrounded himself with the evidences of prosperity and success.

Mr. Gillam was married August 3, 1853, to Miss Abagail C. Clark, a native of Washington county, New York, and daughter of Hiram and Melinda (Payne) Clark. Her father was a native of Vermont and her mother a native of New York. They emigrated to Illinois in an early day, where they both died. Mr. and Mrs. Gillam have been blessed with five children—Henry C., William S. Charles W., Edward E. and Albert (deceased).

The subject of our sketch is a man of strong temperance principles and affiliates with the prohibition party, having been a strong anti-slavery man. He has always taken an active interest in public affairs, and has held various official positions, among them being that of supervisor of the township, clerk of the same, which position he has held since 1875, being the present incumbent. He has also taken an active interest in educational matters and has been associated for years with the school board. He is a man of good principles and sympathizes with the doctrines of the Methodist Episcopal church. He belongs to the Le Grange Post, Grand Army of the Republic.

FRANK L. MENNIE is one of the leading farmers and stock raisers of Marble township, Lincoln county, Minnesota. He came to Lincoln county in May, 1878, and settled on his present place on section 12. He filed his papers on his claim April 16th of that year. He has resided in Marble township ever since his first settlement, and has been engaged in general farming and stock raising. Our subject was one among the pioneer settlers of the town, and, associated with Mr. Parrott, of whom a sketch is given in another department of this work, our subject organized the township, and served as a member of the first board of supervisors. Of this body Mr. Parrott was chairman, Mr. Mennie clerk and Ole Siverson and Isaac Peterson the other members. In every project which has tended to the development and improvement and better government of the township our subject has taken an active interest, and his abilities have been used in various official positions. He has been township clerk ever since locating in the township, and is at present director of the school district No. 26, which position he has held since its organization.

The place of the nativity of our subject is found in Marquette, Green Lake county, Wisconsin, where he was born July 25, 1854. He is a son of Peter L. and Margaret (Duffes) Mennie, both of whom were natives of Scotland. The father and mother are both living in Portage City, Wisconsin. The father came to America in about 1834, and for a short time resided in the State of Illinois, whence he went to the vicinity of Racine, Wisconsin, locating fourteen miles west of that city, where he lived some eight or ten years. His next move was to Marquette, Green Lake county, that State, whence he moved to Portage, Columbia county. Throughout the most of his life he engaged in the occupation of farming. He is now living a retired life and is enjoying the benefits of a long and well-spent life. He has been a man of considerable means, and was a representative citizen of the localities in which he lived. He has served his neighbors and fellow-citizens in various official capacities. In the father's family there were nine children—John D., William G., George P., Mary Jane, Elsie E., Frank L., Ada A., James and Ella.

Frank L. Mennie remained with his parents in Green Lake county for a number of years, being given a good common-school education, and assisting his father on the farm. He completed his course of education in the R. C. Spencer Commercial College, in Milwaukee, and after his schooling was completed he came to Olmsted county, Minnesota, with his brother George. He resided in Rochester, of that county, for some two years, and then came to Lincoln county,

making his settlement, as stated in the opening lines in this sketch. Mr. Mennie was married October 30, 1878, to Miss Lillian B. Byington. This lady was born in Marquette, Green Lake county, Wisconsin, where she received an excellent education. She was a daughter of M. I. Byington, a harness-maker and carriage-trimmer by trade, and a prominent citizen of the place in which he lived. Mr. and Mrs. Mennie have two children— Edward B. and Ella Irene, both of whom are living at home.

Mr. Mennie experienced all the discomforts and discouragements of pioneer life in making his first settlement in Marble township. Life was commenced here in a shanty, and under many peculiar difficulties known only to the pioneer settlers of a country. His first visit to the township was made by train from Rochester, in the month of April, 1878, at which time he filed on his land, and soon afterward returned to Rochester. During the first years but little could be done in the way of opening farm improvements. After building his shanty, the first year he broke ten acres of land and put in a small crop. The next year he put in ten acres of wheat, and kept slowly increasing through the succeeding years. He has now a fine farm, and a pleasant and commodious home, and has an agreeable family. In politics our subject affiliates with the republican party. Formerly he was a member of the "Temple of Honor," of Wisconsin.

ILLIAM B. STINE is the present clerk of the district court of Murray county, Minnesota, being elected to that office in the year 1886, but did not take the office until 1888. He came to Murray county in November, 1880, and was one of the early settlers of the county.

Mr. Stine was born in Greenville, Tennessee, June 27, 1856. He was the son of

Christian Stine, a tanner by occupation and at present a resident of Murray county, where he located in 1883 in the township of Lowville. The father was born in Greenville, Tennessee. The mother's maiden name was Mary A. Brown, a native of the eastern part of Tennessee, being born in the same place in which her husband was born. They had a family of seven children—William B., our subject; John R., James D., Benjamin D., Jennie, Ida and Hugh E.

William B. Stine remained beneath the parental roof, being the recipient of its hospitalities until he was sixteen years of age, up to which time he had received a good common-school education. From that age on until he was twenty years old he assisted his father in work on the farm. He then learned telegraphy at Lemars, Iowa. He made this his principal business from 1876 till 1886, and during the last seven years was station agent at various places, among them being Rushmore, Nobles county, Minnesota; Mountain Lake, Cottonwood county, and Hadley, Murray county, remaining in the latter place until he was elected clerk of the district court.

Mr. Stine was married May 28, 1882, at Hadley, Murray county, to Miss Minnie Lowe, a native of Canada, where she was born in the year 1863. In 1868 her parents removed to Waverly, Iowa, and thence in 1878 to Lowville, Murray county, Minnesota, where she received the principal part of her education. Later she was sent to Tracy, where she had a thorough course of instruction in the public schools. Mr. and Mrs. Stine have been blessed with three living children—David L., Harry I. and Dura E. Mabel died at the age of two years and fifteen days.

In politics Mr. Stine affiliates with the republican party, and has become quite prominent in the local affairs of that organization. He is a man of push and energy, and is one of the leaders among his fellow-citizens. He is a man of excellent business capabilities and holds his position with ability and efficiency. His character both as a business man and as a citizen is above reproach, and he was made many friends.

HON. HENRY N. RICE, M. D., one of the leading physicians of Martin county, Minnesota, resides in Fairmont, the county seat. A native of Whitley county, Indiana, he was born September 2, 1843, his parents being Daniel B. and Rosana (Nickey) Rice, the former a native of New York and the latter born in Virginia. The early life of the subject of our sketch was spent on the home farm, where he was given the educational advantages for obtaining a common-school education. He remained in his native county until August 2, 1862, when he enlisted in Company B, Seventy-fourth Indiana Infantry. He served throughout the war, being discharged in June, 1865. During his military life he served as a musician in his company, and participated in many severe engagements. He was in the battle of Berrysville, was taken sick with the measles immediately afterwards, and for eighteen months he was very ill, being taken to the Louisville hospital, from whence he went to Quincy, Illinois, and on recovering from his attack of ill health he rejoined his regiment at Dalton, Georgia, and participated in the famous march to the sea. The first battle in which he participated was that of Buzzard's Roost near Snake Creek Gap. He then saw service at the battle of Resaca, where he witnessed the most terrible strife of his entire military experience. From thence the division marched toward Atlanta, and after two months of almost continual fighting reached that place. At Jonesborough he also participated in an extremely hard-fought battle, and was there struck in the shoulder with a bullet, from the results of which he did not recover for some time. In this battle the shot and shell fell so thick and fast that the small trees and brush were mowed down as with a scythe. From Jonesborough the division went onward on a career of success to Savannah, the march occupying sixty days and being one continuous round of skirmishing. At one time the regiment was cut off from all communication with the rest of the army, and several times came very near being destroyed by the rebel forces. They were engaged in destroying bridges along the railroad. They bivouacked at Savannah for some two weeks before communications were opened with the rest of the army, and during this time lived mostly on rice and such provisions as could be gathered up in the immediate vicinity. Marching thence the division reached North Carolina, from whence they removed to Cheraw and engaged in a short battle with the Rebels, capturing a cannon, which was retained by the company, and finally found its way after several years to Fairmont, Minnesota, where, July 4, 1889, it was burst by being too heavily charged. When they came to Raleigh, General Johnston surrendered to Sherman, and from thence the division to which the company was attached marched on to Richmond and then to Washington, where they participated in the grand review. The subject of our sketch was honorably discharged June 9, 1865, and returned home by way of Indianapolis. He engaged in work on a farm through harvest, and in the fall entered the commercial college at Fort Wayne, Indiana, and continued his studies therein until the spring of 1866. Then the family emigrated to Martin county, Minnesota, where the father purchased a farm and our subject settled on a homestead, where he lived some seven years. In 1873 he attended the medical college at Keokuk,

Iowa, and in 1874 commenced the practice of medicine in Fairmont. On locating in that village he at once showed himself a man of much enterprise and public spirit, and willing to take an active part in all movements tending to the general welfare. He became a popular candidate for legislative office and was elected to the lower house of the State legislature in 1875. He was appointed surgeon for the Chicago, Milwaukee & St. Paul railroad in 1880, and still retains that position. He graduated from the Rush Medical College of Chicago in 1886. He is widely known as one of the ablest and most efficient physicians in southern Minnesota. Besides being interested considerably in village property, he is also known as the owner of the "Farm Ranch," one of the finest farms in Southern Minnesota, located on Silver Lake, Martin county, and comprising four hundred acres of land. The farm is well improved and stocked with bronchos and thoroughbred horses. Dr. Rice is a member of the Commandery of the Knights Templar of Albert Lea, is a republican in politics and is one of the foremost citizens of Fairmont.

The subject of our sketch was wedded to Miss Sarah E. Reed, March 15, 1866, in Columbia City, Whitley county, Indiana. This lady was the daughter of Henry and Sarah (Metzker) Reed, natives of Pennsylvania. She was born in Ohio, September 14, 1845. Dr. and Mrs. Rice have been blessed with the following-named children— Estella, Rosana, Stanley, Jenner, Lina and Daisy.

———⋆—⟨⟨✧⟩⟩—⋆———

OTFRED ARVESEN, one of the substantial business men of Jasper village, Pipestone county, Minnesota, is engaged in the lumber trade. He is a native of Norway, where he was born in the year 1865. His parents were Ole P. and Ellen

(Hansen) Arvesen, both natives of Norway. The father is an extensive farmer in his native country, and is also largely interested in ships and ship-building. He has held many pasitions of importance, and is a man of influence and high standing in the country in which he lives. In the father's family there were eleven children, our subject being the sixth, all of whom are living at the present time.

Mr. Arvesen spent his boyhood's days in the home of his parents, being given excellent educational advantages in the municipal schools, from which he graduated when he was about sixteen years of age. After spending a year at home he came to America, and, in the month of April, 1882, located at Manistee, Michigan, without any knowledge of the English language whatever—without a friend or relative in the United States, being the first one of the family to cross the ocean; but with a full stock of good health and strong will, which readily found him employment the ensuing summer months in the pine woods and saw-mills on the Manistee river. In the fall he attended school for a couple of months, and then engaged in "scaling" logs in a shingle-mill during the following summer. Leaving this employment, he again entered the high school in Manistee, and continued his studies for some months. Leaving school he found employment in the lumber office of Louis Sands, where he worked for three and a half years as assistant book-keeper and retail salesman. Then, in July, 1887, he came to Minnesota, and visited relatives in Kittson county. His next move was to Crookston, where he found employment with the Red River Lumber Company on their drives from the Red Lake reservation to Crookston and Grand Forks. His engagement with this company continued for about four months, when the drive was "hung" up on account of the dry season, after which he returned to Kittson county and remained with friends until in February, 1888. Removing thence, he went to Minneapolis and engaged as billing clerk and salesman for the Hall and Ducey Lumber Company, in their wholesale office. On the 11th day of February, 1889, he removed to Jasper, Pipestone county, where he established his present business, having had seven years' practical experience in all branches of the lumber trade, from the stump to the consumer. Although having been in Jasper but a short time, he has already built up quite an extensive trade and gained the confidence of local business men by his push and energy in working up patronage. He has purchased yard-ground and built lumber and lime sheds, and also an office building. In politics he affiliates with the republican party, and is a member of the Lutheran church. Mr. Arvesen is but on the threshold of a useful and prosperous career, and if no disastrous fortunes come to him, he will soon be one of the leading and wealthiest citizens of this part of Pipestone county.

HENRY SIEMUND is one of the prominent farmers of Rose Hill township, Cottonwood county, Minnesota, and resides on a fine farm on section 34. He is of Russian nativity and was born May 23, 1865. His parents were well-to-do people of that country and were by name Henry and Elizabeth (Dietchman) Siemund. The parents emigrated to America in 1875 and after a few days' stay in Kansas came to Rose Hill township, where the mother died in 1878. The father returned to Russia in 1881 and is now a resident of that country. Four brothers and three sisters of our subject are now residents of this country.

The subject of our sketch was reared on a farm; he assisted his father in the support of the family until he had attained the age of twenty-six years, when he located where he now resides, in Rose Hill township. He took 160 acres of land as a homestead and has worked hard and enthusiastically to make his place one of the best in the township. He has provided it with excellent improvements and has a beautiful home. He experienced hard times during the grasshopper raids and was obliged to work on the railroad in St. Paul for two years in order to recruit his circumstances. During several years his crops were entirely destroyed by the grasshoppers. Mr. Siemund and family are members of the Lutheran church of Rose Hill township. In politics he has always affiliated with the republican party and has become quite prominent and influential in the affairs of his township.

Mr. Siemund was married December 8, 1881, to Elizabeth, daughter of Daniel Heben, a native of Austria. This union has been blessed with three children—Mary, Katie and Emiel.

———◦◦◦◦◦———

JACOB WICKERSHEIM, a leading and influential farmer of Ash Lake township, Lincoln county, Minnesota, homesteaded his present farm on the southeast quarter of section 8 in 1878. He was one among the early pioneers of this region and passed through the usual pioneer experiences. He commenced farming in a small way by breaking some thirty-six acres of land and building a small house 12x16 feet and making other trifling improvements. He lived in his primitive dwelling some two years and then built a small addition 10x16 feet and in 1885 built a main part 24x16 feet with fourteen-foot posts, making one of the very best dwelling-houses in the township. He first came to Lincoln county April 27, 1878, and then went back to his home in Faribault, Rice county, for the purpose of reaping his harvest there. He returned to his land in Lincoln county in the fall and made a permanent settlement. In the spring of 1879 he set out a large acreage of cottonwood, box-elder, ash, elm, hackberry and plumb trees and also a variety of fruit trees. He has now one of the nicest groves in the township. At the organization of the township in 1879 our subject took an active part and participated in the first meeting, which was held on section 19 in a little building which was used as a frontier store. He was elected treasurer of the township in 1879, and was the first to perform any official acts in the township. He has held that office with credit and efficiency ever since. He is also treasurer of school district No. 10, which position he has held since the organization of the district. He takes a hearty interest in all matters of an educational nature and is one of the main supports of the various local school organizations. For a year he was director of school district No. 10, and has by word and deed assisted in bringing educational matters to the attention of the people. The first board of township supervisors consisted of our subject, W. W. Townsend, chairman, David Phipps and H. Jacklin. John Courtney was assessor and Mr. Jacklin was justice of the peace.

The subject of our sketch was born in Alsace, Germany, in July, 1836. He was the son of Frederick W. and Catharine (Ortliep) Wickersheim, both of whom were natives of Alsace. In about 1845 the parents brought their family and effects to the United States, locating in Lake county, Illinois, where the father died after twenty years' residence, his death occurring in about 1865. The father was a farmer by occupation, and homesteaded land in Illinois, on which he continued to live throughout his life. He was a prominent member of the Lutheran church, and was an exemplary citizen. The mother died in Wheeling, Cook county, Illinois, in 1868. She was a member of the

Lutheran church, and an estimable Christian lady. In the father's family there were five children, two boys and three girls—Barbara, Ellen, Mary, Frederick and Jacob. Frederick was a well-to-do farmer in Wheeling, where he died some years ago.

Jacob Wickersheim came to America from his native land when he was about nine years of age, and spent the next twenty years of his life on the farm in Lake county, Illinois. He was given good educational advantages in the district schools, and for two years after the period just mentioned he resided in Wheeling, Cook county, Illinois, engaged in handling dry goods and Yankee notions. For some time he followed the road as a peddler, engaged in retailing the goods just mentioned. Coming to Minnesota at the end of the two years spent in Cook county, he spent one and a half years in railroading at Faribault. He then purchased a farm of fifty acres near Roberts Lake, Minnesota, and made that his home for some nine years. Then for six months he was engaged with a brother-in-law in the tombstone and monument business in St. Paul, after which he returned to his farm in the vicinity of Faribault, and selling soon after came to Lincoln county, where he has since lived.

The subject of our sketch was married April 10, 1858, to Miss Louisa Meyer, a native of Alsace, Germany. She came to America with her parents when a small child and located with them in Lake county, Illinois, where she was reared and educated. Mr. and Mrs. Wickersheim have five children—Charles Jacob, William John, Edward Frederick, Mary Louisa and Emma. Charles Jacob is married and a farmer in Ash Lake township. Emma is a school teacher. William John graduated with honors from the Mankato Normal School, May 29, 1889.

The subject of our sketch has taken a prominent interest in all matters which tended toward public advancement, whether in a financial or moral way. He has actively participated in the affairs of local goverment and has served his constituents in various official positions. He is a man of excellent character, of good business qualifications, and is a leading member of the Methodist Episcopal church. He has taken quite an interest in this religious organization and for years has been a class-leader, his son Charles J. being now a class-leader of the local organization. Having come to the county in an early day our subject has passed through many trying experiences, but with all he has been highly successful and has accumulated considerable means. He has a pleasant home and an agreeable family.

EDWARD B. COOK, a well-to-do farmer of Lowville township, Murray county, Minnesota, resides on section 14. He was born in Brome, Canada, March 2, 1845.

The parents of the subject of our sketch were Silas Cook, of New York, and Anna Townsend Cook, born in Brome, Canada. The father was a farmer by occupation, and reared a family of three children, two boys and one girl, our subject being the oldest and only one living at the present time. The father and mother resided in Canada until their death, where, also, our subject's sister, Achsah, died. A brother, William, was killed in the battle of the Wilderness, while serving in the ranks of the Union army. When our subject was some four or five years old his father died, and some time later the mother remarried. She died in about 1854.

Some years after the marriage of his mother the second time, at the age of nine years, our subject went to live with a Mr. Lawrence, and after residing with him for one year, was taken by a Mr. Moffatt, with whom he lived for two years. He then ran away from the latter's home, and returned to that of Mr. Lawrence, continuing with him some five years. At the end of this time he commenced work for himself, engaging in agricultural pursuits on farms in his locality. He continued in his native country until 1871, and then spent two years in New Hampshire, at farm work. He then returned to Canada, and after one year was married and settled down on a farm of his own. After residing on that for two years he rented his farm and went to New Hampshire. One year later he returned to Canada, and in 1883 came to Minnesota, locating on his present farm in Murray county. He has since been a resident of Lowville township. He has 160 acres of excellent land, well improved, and provided with good farm buildings. In politics he affiliates with the democratic party, and has held various official positions, among them being that of supervisor and road overseer. He is a man of good business qualifications, is thorough and systematic, and has been quite successful in his farming operations.

April 24, 1874, occurred the marriage of Mr. Cook to Miss Mary E. Tibbitts, a native of Canada, and daughter of Samuel and Jane (Brunton) Tibbitts, also natives of Canada. In her father's family there were ten children, of whom she was the second in order of birth. Her parents are still living, and are residents of Canada.

JOHN JACOB ZIMMERMAN is one of the prosperous farmers of Grange township, Pipestone county, Minnesota. He owns a fine farm of 240 acres on section 12, on which are good farm buildings. He was born in Baden, Germany, May 22, 1843. Mr. Zimmerman was the son of Nicholas and Catharine (Scheid) Zimmerman, both of whom were natives of Baden, Germany. The father was an overseer in a forest in his native county in Germany, where he lived for a long number of years. His services as overseer extended through a period of forty-five years, and so satisfactory was his work to the government that he was granted a pension after that period. He lived in his native land until his death, which occurred in 1877. The mother died in 1859, in Germany.

The subject of our sketch remained with his parents in the land of his nativity until he attained his majority. Up to the age of fifteen years he was given excellent educational advantages, and acquired a good common school education. At fifteen he commenced helping his father on the home farm, continuing in that line of employment until 1864, when he came to America and settled in Chicago, where he had two sisters and one brother. Employed at different kinds of labor, he remained in Chicago for a period of two years. Then, January 16, 1866, he enlisted in Company G, Eighteenth Regiment United States Regular Infantry. His enlistment was for a period of three years, and he was mustered out of the service January 16, 1869, at Salt Lake City, Utah. Although the War of the Rebellion was concluded some three years before our subject was discharged, yet during that time he saw much hardship and privation in extensive marches in the Southwestern States and Territories. One of the severest tramps he ever experienced was a march of ninety-three days from Fort Leavenworth, Kansas, to Camp Douglas, Salt Lake City. On reaching Camp Douglas he was detailed as one of the gardeners at the hospital, and continued at that post until his discharge in 1869. On being mustered out of the regular service he returned at once to Chicago, where he established himself in the manufacture of cigars; he was there at the time of the great fire. He was not burned out, but he lost a great deal in the hasty removal of his goods. He then broke up housekeeping, and left Chicago for three months, after which he returned and worked in the shop until 1880. At this time he concluded to find a location on a farm somewhere in Southern Minnesota. He came to Pipestone county, and for three years lived on a farm owned by his wife's brother. At that time the owner of the land died, and our subject filed on it as a homestead and tree claim, in all 240 acres, which compose his present farm.

September 12, 1869, is the date of the marriage of Mr. Zimmerman to Miss Ernestina Wilhelmina Buchholz, a native of Germany. The fruits of this union are three children, all of whom are living—Frederick W., Frank H. and Emma Juliana Louisa.

As is well known by all our readers, the educational advantages in Germany are of a high character, and the subject of our sketch, during his early life, was enabled to receive a good common-school education. This, to which are added good, practical ideas, makes him a man of strong influence in the neighborhood in which he lives. In politics he affiliates with the union labor party, and has the interests of the laboring man thoroughly at heart. He was a member of the Druids Society in Chicago. He has creditably held several official positions, among them being that of district treasurer, which office he held for seven years, and in which he is the present incumbent. He is also on his second term as township treasurer. His memories of his service in the regular army are very interesting when related by him to the attentive listener. While at Salt Lake City he had the privilege of visiting the great Mormon tabernacle a number of times, and has also seen the famous prophet, Brigham Young, officiating in the services in the temple.

HALGRUM ERICKSON is an influential farmer of Westbrook township, Cottonwood county, Minnesota, and resides on section 2, where he has a fine farm provided with excellent improvements.

The place of our subject's nativity is in Norway, where he was born November 6, 1850, his parents being Erick and Randi (Olson) Rasmuson, also natives of Norway. The father was a farmer by occupation and lived in his native country until his death, which occurred in 1864. The mother is still living and resides in her native land. Our subject's early life was spent on the farm and he was given a good common-school education until he was nineteen years of age.

At nineteen our subject came to America, locating first in Olmsted county, Minnesota, where he found employment on various farms for three and a half years. He then returned to his native land, where he remained a year and a half. Returning at the end of that time to Olmsted county, he remained three years and then came to Westbrook township, Cottonwood county, where he settled on 120 acres of land which he homesteaded from the government. He made that his residence for two years and then removed to where he now lives, purchasing a farm of eighty acres from his father-in-law. He now owns 340 acres of fine land, on which stands the best house and barn in the township. His farm is well improved and has been brought to a high state of cultivation.

Mr. Erickson was married May 14, 1880, to Annie Chrisson, a native of Norway. This union has been blessed with five children—Erick, Josephine, Ludwig, Hilda and Ole. The family are members of the Lutheran church society of Ann township, our subject assisting liberally in the building of the church edifice in 1884.

Since coming to the township our subject has identified himself with all its best interests and has aided in every interprise which tended to improve the condition of public affairs. He has always taken an active part in political matters and has efficiently held the positions of assessor, chairman of the board of supervisors, supervisor, and treasurer of school district No. 30 for six years. In politics he affiliates with the republican party, and is one of the leading factors in the administration of the local affairs of that organization. Careful in business, honest and upright in all his affairs, generous and warm-hearted, he is well calculated to take a leading place, which he does, among the citizens of his township. He is highly respected both as a man and citizen by all who know him.

EDWARD D. BIGHAM is the able editor and proprietor of the *Lincoln County Journal*, located at Tyler, Lincoln county, Minnesota. He is a son of John C. and Mary (Hannah) Bigham, natives of Ireland. Edward D. was born in Lake City, Wabasha county, Minnesota, January 25, 1860. He lived with his parents on the farm in that county and attended the district schools at every opportunity until he was eighteen years of age. Then the parents removed to Marshfield township, Lincoln county, Minnesota, where our subject lived on the home farm until he was twenty-one years of age, and he was then married and engaged in farming for one year, after which he taught school in the village of Tyler, four months. In the spring of 1882 he concluded to enter the field of journalism and purchased the *Lincoln County Journal*, which he has been operating ever since.

The subject of our sketch was married, May 14, 1881, to Miss Cora E. Hodgman, a daughter of E. and Artemetia (McCalpin) Hodgman, natives of Vermont and New York, respectively. Mr. and Mr. Bigham have been blessed with the following named children—Frank, John, Albert and Mabel.

Ever since he attained his majority, Mr. Bigham has been actively interested in all projects which tended to the improvement and betterment of the affairs of the township in which he has lived. Being possessed of good business abilities he has efficiently assisted in various ways in the administration of local government affairs. He has held the following offices: Deputy sheriff, five years, clerk of the school board, five years, and village councilman, two years. In July, 1883, he was appointed postmaster of Tyler village, and has held that position ever since. He is a man of good education, intelligent, of progressive ideas, and is of valuable aid in the administration of public affairs. He has been one of the foremost citizens of the village of Tyler, and was one of the leading spirits in the drafting of the village laws. In his newspaper business he has met with merited success. He is an excellent writer, and conducts the *Journal* on a basis which commands respect and patronage. In politics he affiliates with the republican party.

OSCAR E. BUSS is a prominent resident and farmer of Moulton township, Murray county, Minnesota. His excellent farm is located on section 20, where he has surrounded himself with many evidences of prosperity. Oscar E. Buss was born in Stephenson county, Illinois, March 21, 1855. His parents were Horace F. and Mercy Buss, both of whom are natives of England. The parents came to America in 1848, and located in Illinois, where our subject was born. In 1869 the family removed to Independence, Iowa, where the father remained until 1885, when he located in Murray county, where he still lives. The mother passed from this life in 1861 in Illinois. In the father's family there were five children, our subject being the third child, and only son.

The subject of our sketch remained with his parents until he reached the age of twenty-two years. During his early life he received the benefits of a good schooling, and obtained an excellent education. When not in school he assisted his father in work on the farm. After he reached the age of twenty-one years he engaged in work on an adjoining farm in Iowa for one year, and then came to Minnesota, locating in Adrian, Nobles county, where he worked at various employments for four years. In 1881 he came to Murray county and located the homestead where he now lives.

Mr. Buss was married March 21, 1880, to Miss Enie A. Penberthie, by whom he had one child, Enie A. Miss Penberthie was a native of Wisconsin. She died March 28, 1884. January 1, 1889, our subject was married to Lizzie Bissett, a native of Scotland.

The farm of our subject is composed of 160 acres of excellent land, which he has under good cultivation, and provided with fine farm buildings. He has been quite successful in his farming operations, and has become quite well-to-do. He has taken an active interest in the local affairs of the republican party, with which he has affiliated for years. He has held various township offices, among them being that of clerk, which position he held for five years. He has also been a member of the school board for some time. He is a man of excellent and pleasant qualities, and is highly respected.

MATTHIAS E. LANG is an influential resident of the village of Lake Wilson. He is a farmer by occupation and owns a fine farm of 160 acres on section 33, Chanarambie township, Murray county, Minnesota.

The place of the nativity of the subject of our sketch is found in Germany, where he was born July 4, 1860. His parents were Casper and Gertrude (Saur) Lang, both of whom were natives of Germany. The father was a farmer by occupation, and had a family of seventeen children, our subject being the fifth in order of birth. In 1869 the family came to America, locating in Mankato, Blue Earth county, Minnesota. They remained in that city until 1878, when they came to Murray county, where both the father and son pre-empted lands. The father settled on section 28, and the son on section 10. The parents are both living, and are at present living on the old homestead.

During his early life the subject of our sketch was given excellent educational advantages, and remained with his parents until he grew to manhood. He followed them in their various migrations and finally located on a farm in Murray county. Our subject was the first to break land in his township, and was one of the most prominent of the pioneer settlers. Until twenty-four years of age he remained beneath the parental roof and then he accepted a position on the Wilson stock farm, where he worked for one year. He then went north to Grant county and took charge of a large wheat farm owned by Mr. Wilson. He operated this business for one year, and was then given charge of several thoroughbred horses owned by the same gentleman, at Lake Wilson. After a short time he became the agent for renting the Wilson lands, in which line of business he has since engaged. He owns a beautiful home in the village of Lake Wilson, on the shores of the lake bearing that name.

The subject of our sketch was married November 18, 1888, to Dosy Drew, a daughter of Oliver and Mary (Atwood) Drew, both of whom were natives of the State of New York. Before Miss Dosy was born, her parents moved to the State of Illinois, where they resided at the time of her birth. They are now residents of Murray county, and a biography of her father is given in another department of this work.

In politics Mr. Lang affiliates with the republican party in whose local counsels he has become quite prominent. He has efficiently filled various official positions, having held the office of supervisor for two years, school treasurer six years, constable one year, and for some time was a road overseer. Thus it will be seen that our subject has taken a prominent part in the public affairs of his locality, and has become one of the leading spirits in all matters tending toward local improvement. He is a man of excellent business qualifications, of the highest character, and is well and favorably known all over Murray county.

HERMAN H. HANEY settled in Pipestone county, Minnesota, in 1878, since which time he has become one of the leading and prosperous farmers of Gray township. He was one among the very first settlers in that township, locating in 1878 on section 2, in the month of October, and continuing his residence on that section until 1888. He was engaged successfully in general farming and stock raising and held a prominent place among the early residents of the township, which place he still retains to-day. He has grown with the growth of Pipestone county and has accumulated considerable means. He was born in the city of Philadelphia, Pennsylvania, January 29, 1855, and was the son of Franz and Dora (Spangenberg) Haney, both of whom were natives of Germany.

In 1848, before their marriage, the parents left their native land and came to Philadelphia, Pennsylvania, where they met and were married, and where they lived for a number of years, removing from thence to Fond du Lac county, Wisconsin, where they are now living, engaged in farming. While in Philadelphia the father followed his trade, that of glove-making. In the father's family there were six children—Amelia, Herman, Lewis, Maria, Frank and Anna.

Mr. Haney's early life was spent at the home of his parents. He received good schooling, and went with them when he was three years of age to the State of Wisconsin. His father's house remained his home until he was twenty-one years of age. Up to this age, what time had not been given to study in school was occupied with work on the farm. On obtaining his majority he concluded to strike out for Western Minnesota and find government land where he might locate and lay the foundation for a successful farm enterprise. He made his settlement in Gray township, as was stated in the opening of this sketch, and has remained a resident ever since. He commenced operations by building a primitive frame house 8x10 feet and an old-fashioned sod stable about 12x14 feet. He has now a comfortable home and good buildings on his farm and to the passer-by there is exhibited signs of prosperity and success.

Mr. Haney was married March 16, 1880, to Miss Mary E. Avery, a native of Oakfield, Fond du Lac county, Wisconsin. Her parents were Jacob and Deborah (Peebles) Avery, natives of New York. In an early day her parents came westward and settled in Wisconsin. The father was a millwright by trade and was killed in a mill in 1885. He was an exemplary man and a leading member of the Baptist church. The mother is still living. Mrs. Haney was one of five children—Newton, Helen J., Jay, Frank and Mary. She received her early training and obtained her education in the county of her nativity, and continued her residence there until she was married in 1880. Mr. and Mrs. Haney are blessed with three living children—Walter, Avery and Dora.

Mr. Haney is a prosperous farmer and an

exemplary citizen, and by his industrious habits and interest in general matters has made many friends and has drawn to himself the respect of all with whom he has to do. In politics he affiliates with the union labor party, and is indeed one of the representative men and farmers of the county.

———•◦•◦❁◦•◦•———

ILBERT B. OLESON, a thrifty and industrious farmer of Lincoln county, Minnesota, is the son of Bore and Olea (Siverson) Oleson, natives of Norway. The family came to the United States in about 1861 and first stopped in Madison, Dane county, Wisconsin, where the father died two weeks after they arrived. In the family there were five children—Gilbert B., Sarah, Betsey, Tonita and Ole.

Gilbert B. Oleson was born in Christianstift, Norway, September 24, 1844, and was reared on a farm in his native country. He was given the educational advantages of the district schools and became well informed in book learning. He came with his parents to America in 1861 and located with them in Madison, Wisconsin. After his father's death, as he was the oldest, our subject became to all practical purposes the head of the family and remained with them, taking care of them until he was twenty-five years of age. He then removed to Chickasaw county, Iowa, where he was married and engaged in farming on land he had purchased some time before. He resided in Chickasaw county for five years, and then sold out and removed to Lac-qui-parle county, Minnesota, in 1872. When he arrived in Lac-qui-parle county he had only fifteen cents in his pocket, and also owned a horse and wagon. He located on a claim in that county and resided there for three years until he was driven out by the grasshopper raids. These destructive insects destroyed all his crops, and growing discouraged he left the claim and removed

to Canby, Yellow Medicine county, Minnesota. Here he started in the hotel business and continued its operation for one year, after which time he took a contract to carry the United States mail from Canby to Maderia, Dakota Territory, distant some fifty-three miles. He fulfilled his contract for a year and then sold out. In Yellow Medicine county he took an active part in public matters and was assessor for two years, being assessor in Lac-qui-parle county for the same length of time. After two years' residence in Canby he came to Royal township, Lincoln county, and settled on a homestead of 160 acres, also taking a tree claim of the same number of acres. His land is the east half of section 18, Royal township. He made his permanent location in that township in the spring of 1879 and has lived there ever since. In the spring of 1880, so rapidly had he grown in public opinion, he was unanimously elected justice of the peace and assessor, which positions he held with great credit and efficiency for some years, being the present justice of the peace of the township. In the fall of 1882 he was elected county commissioner, in which position he has for five years served his constituents with great ability. He was also chairman of the board of supervisors for two years, and was elected township clerk four different times. Since coming to the township he has continuously actively engaged himself in all matters which pertain to the public welfare, and has become one of the leading public spirits in the county. He is a man of rare business abilities, and is heartily in sympathy with the oft repeated phrase "public office is a public trust." He is a man of large intelligence, is genial and courteous in his bearing and conduct and is respected as being one of the most loyal and exemplary citizens of the county and township. The active part he has taken in official matters has inseparably associated his name with the history of

Lincoln county. He is a man of high character, and is highly respected by a wide circle of friends and acquaintances. On coming to the county Mr. Oleson had but little means, but, being of an active and energetic spirit, he has been continually adding to his fortunes, and has now put himself and family in good circumstances. He has an excellent farm of 320 acres, ninety acres under cultivation, a grove of ten acres, and a good frame dwelling house and barn. He has twenty head of cattle, two horses, and a large number of hogs and sheep.

Mr. Oleson was married in Chickasaw county, Iowa, April 30, 1870, to Carrie Marcuson, a daughter of Marcus and Ronag (Tolofson) Oleson, natives of Norway. This union has been blessed with eight children—Bennie, Oscar, Raford, Caroline, Matilda, Anna, Galena and Elmer.

------◆◆◆◆------

URI D. MILLER is a prominent farmer who resides on section 12, Amboy township, Cottonwood county, Minnesota. He is engaged in general farming and stock-raising, and has met with merited success. The place of his nativity is in East Hanover, Lebanon county, Pennsylvania, where he was born December 9, 1856.

The parents of our subject were Jacob and Mary A. (Landis) Miller, natives of Pennsylvania, where they were married May 1, 1846. This State remained their home for six years after their marriage; then they removed to Wisconsin and resided six years, after which they returned to Pennsylvania and resided six years. At the end of this time they returned to Wisconsin. The father enlisted in 1863 in the Twenty-seventh Regiment Wisconsin Volunteer Infantry, serving as a private until his death, which occurred six months after his enlistment, in Little Rock, Arkansas. He was a man of excellent qualities, and was thor-

oughly educated, having been a teacher for a number of years. He was a member of the Methodist Episcopal church, and was a member of that organization for some years. The mother died at Greenbush, Sheboygan county, Wisconsin, in 1879. She was a consistent member of the Methodist Episcopal church, and died in the triumphs of Christian faith. Our subject was one of eight children—Bertha M., Eleanora, Arba Nancy, Ebenezer L., Uri D., Orin D. R., William Romeo and Olivet. The last named married Clinton S. Montgomery, who is a railroad engineer, living in Arizona. She was a teacher by occupation.

The subject of our sketch followed his parents in their various moves, and received his education principally in Sheboygan county, Wisconsin. He assisted his father on the farm, and after his father's death commenced working out in different places in Wisconsin. In the spring of 1877 he came to Lake Crystal, Blue Earth county, Minnesota, and engaged in farming for two years, at which time he homesteaded eighty acres of his present farm in Cottonwood county. He now owns 160 acres. He has been one of the most public-spirited citizens, and has shown his willingness to help in all matters of a public nature. He has held various official positions, and has affiliated with the republican party. He was clerk in school district No. 45 in 1885, and still holds that office. He was supervisor of the township for some six years, and has assisted in various other ways. He is a consistent member of the Methodist Episcopal church, and is now class leader. Formerly he belonged to the Good Templars' society, and was the financial secretary for some time. He is a man of excellent character, and is highly esteemed.

Mr. Miller was married May 1, 1879, to Miss Rara Avis Scherer, a native of Indiana, where she was reared until seven years of age. She was then brought to Blue Earth county, whence, after five years' residence, she removed to Vernon Centre. She is the daughter of Benjamin Franklin Scherer, a farmer. Her mother's maiden name was Martha Ann (Walker) Scherer. Mrs. Miller was educated at Vernon Centre, where she lived for a number of years. She is one of ten children. Mr. and Mrs. Miller have been blessed with four children—Nora, Leonard, Mabel and Loucina.

———◦◦❖◦◦———

JOHN McHARG, one of the leading citizens and farmers of Belfast township, Murray county, Minnesota, was born in Leeds township, Megantic county, Canada, October 6, 1850. His parents were Joseph and Margaret (Hunter) McHarg, natives of the northern part of Ireland and of Scotch descent. In the father's family there were twelve children, of whom our subject was the third in order of birth. The early history of the McHarg family shows that there were three brothers in Scotland. One remained in that land; Joseph came to the United States and John McHarg, the grandfather of the subject of our sketch, located in Ireland, where he engaged in farming. He reared a family of four boys and one girl, one of these children being Joseph, the father of our subject.

In early life our subject was given good educational facilities and he assisted his parents in work on the home farm when not engaged pursuing his studies in school. He remained with his parents until twenty-one years of age and then engaged in lumbering in Vermont. After two years, in 1873, he went to Lawrence, Massachusetts, and worked in the Washington woolen mill during one summer. In the fall he came to Minneapolis and for several years he was employed in a saw-mill during the summer and in the pineries during the winter months. In 1878 he came to Murray county and took a homestead on the northeast quarter of section 28, Belfast township. Here our subject has resided ever since. His parents years ago moved to Canada, where they now live and where our subject has visited them once or twice since taking up his residence in Murray county.

Mr. McHarg was married August 28, 1876, in Westminster church, Minneapolis, to Anna Hardy. This ceremony was performed by Rev. George Sample, assisted by Rev. Wilton. Miss Hardy was a daughter of Robert and Jessie (Shaw) Hardy, natives of Scotland. She was born in Leeds, Megantic county, Canada, April 18, 1850. She lived about two miles from where our subject was born and reared, and their knowledge of each other and their "loves and quarrels" date from their very infancy. They were playmates together in their younger days and their engagement was of four years standing before their marriage. Mr. and Mrs. McHarg have been blessed with the following-named children—Joseph Archibald, born in Minneapolis, March 4, 1878; Robina H., born in Belfast township, Murray county, February 13, 1880; Jessie Shaw, born in the same place February 20, 1885, and a baby born July 8, 1889.

Mrs. McHarg's father, Robert Hardy, was born in Balmoral, Scotland, in September, 1809. He emigrated to Canada, where he died March 13, 1871. The mother is still living and is a resident of Fulda. She was born October 13, 1809, in Aberdeen, Scotland. She has reached the advanced age of eighty years, but is still strong and in good health. In the Hardy family there were nine children, four of whom are living—Robina, born in Edinburgh, Scotland, is now Mrs. Wm. Hogan, of Fulda; Robert, born in the same place; John, born in Canada, and now a resident of Anoka; and Annie, the wife of our subject. Mrs. McHarg's mother's parents were Charles and Betsey (Morrison) Shaw, natives of Aberdeen, Scotland. Mrs. Mc-

Harg's father's parents were James and Katie (Guield) Hardy.

When our subject commenced life for himself he had but little means, his parents not being able to render him any financial assistance. He commenced work with good courage, and by energy and perseverance and economical habits has risen to a front rank among the wealthy and well-to-do citizens of Murray county. Numerous hard circumstances came to him in the early days, among them being the failure of a friend to pay a debt, which caused a heavy loss to fall on our subject. Mr. McHarg now owns a fine farm of eighty acres of land under good cultivation, has several horses and numerous head of cattle, and owns a comfortable frame dwelling-house and farm buildings. He has taken an active interest in public matters, and has held various official positions. He has been court commissioner, is now assessor, and has been school clerk for nine years. He has been chairman of the board of supervisors, and has held some township office almost constantly for the past ten years. He is a man of excellent social qualities and has a pleasant and agreeable family. His wife is a most estimable lady, and presides over one of the most hospitable homes in the township.

ON. PHILO HAWES is the present able and popular mayor of the city of Luverne, Minnesota. He has been largely interested in the real estate and insurance business in this city for some years and has built up a large and profitable patronage. He made his location as a pioneer in this locality in 1867, in which year he took up the first land, where the village of Luverne now stands. He homesteaded 160 acres, and his first residence was a hole dug in the side of the bank, which was covered over and built around the front with medium-sized logs. Here he found his pioneer quarters during several months of 1867, and on the 25th of March, 1868, he brought his family to his new location and built a log house 16x20 feet. This log hut was located near where the Burlington railroad depot now stands. In about 1870 he laid out forty acres of the town plat and commenced making efforts toward building up a little village. At this time, however, his nearest neighbors were forty miles distant. The town of Luverne was named after Mr. Hawes' eldest daughter, who is now dead. Our subject engaged to some extent in farming and followed the same for about four years, during which time he was also engaged as mail agent in conveying the mails from Blue Earth City to Yankton, by what he calls his "pony express." He continued his engagement with the government for about five years, and has made Luverne his home ever since, with the exception of a short time spent in St. Paul and Worthington. The first postoffice in the village was kept in Mr. Hawes' house for five years, he having charge of the business. In about 1870 Mr. Hawes received his first appointment as postmaster and held it until 1873, when his son succeeded him to the position, continuing in the office until 1884. In 1874 Mr. Hawes engaged in the railway mail service on the St. Paul & Sioux City railroad, and made that his principal occupation until 1884. He then returned to his farm and occupied his attention with farming and stock raising until within the last few years. In 1886 he opened a real estate and insurance business in Luverne, and has continued in that line up to the present time. He has been associated intimately with all public projects since the organization of the county, and has assisted ably in the administration of the local government. The second year after the organization of the county he was one of the county commissioners, of which body he was chairman for three years. He has also held many different offices and in each case has proven himself efficient and trustworthy.

Mr. Hawes is a native of Danby, Tompkins county, New York, where he was born December 18, 1830. He is the son of Cyrus and Caroline (Cotter) Hawes, both of whom were natives of Connecticut. The father was a farmer by occupation, and followed that line of occupation throughout the most of his life. The subject of our sketch was reared a farmer's boy, and received his education in the district schools of New York and Wisconsin, having, when twelve years of age, moved with his parents to the latter State, settling in the vicinity of Janesville. After his marriage, which occurred in 1850, and for three years prior to his coming to Minnesota, he was engaged in the mercantile business. In 1853 he removed to Red Wing, and commenced operating a line of stages from that place to Faribault, Zumbrota and other points in the south and southeastern part of Minnesota. He continued in this business for some ten years, and then entered the employ of the Minnesota Stage Company, locating at St. Paul, where he had charge of several routes. He continued a satisfactory and profitable engagement with this company for some nine years. On the breaking out of the Rebellion he determined to cast his lot with the Union forces, so he enlisted as second lieutenant in Company D, Eleventh Minnesota Infantry, and continued in the service until the close of the war. Shortly after being discharged from the service he came to Rock county, where he has since made his principal home. Our subject has been connected for a great number of years with the United States mail service, and has had an extensive and varied experience in that line. In 1856 he had a contract with the government to maintain a mail route from Red Wing to Blue Earth City. This he established and continued for three years.

Next he contracted to transport the mails from Blue Earth City to Yankton, in which line he continued for some five years. This opened mail routes from the Mississippi through to the Missouri river. Besides this he had three shorter routes, one from Jackson to Emmettsville, and other places not far from the first-named village. When he first located in Rock county there were no neighbors, no schools, nor advantages of any kind, and our subject experienced all the privations which come with pioneer life. His market was in Jackson, Jackson county, and the first lumber used in the town of Luverne was drawn by teams from Madelia, a distance of some 125 miles.

The subject of our sketch was married in 1850 to Miss Malvina Hines, of Rock county, Wisconsin. This union has been blessed with three children—Charles O., Eva Luverne and Carrie M. Charles O. married Ellen M. Grout, daughter of Eli L. Grout, of Luverne. They had one son, Edward M. Mrs. Charles O. Hawes died in 1884. Charles O. is now one of the leading merchants of Luverne, being senior member of the firm of Hawes, Houg & Co. He is also connected with the firm of Harroun & Hawes, dealers in books, stationery, etc., of the same village. Eva Luverne married P. F. Kelley, and died some eight years ago. It was after her that Luverne was named.

The subject of our sketch has taken an important place in the affairs of Rock county. Being the earliest settler of the county, he has with interest watched its development, and at every step of the way has aided in its growth to the best of his ability. He has taken an active part in republican politics, and has been a delegate several times to the State and county conventions. He was the commander of the John A. Dix Post, No. 96, in 1888. He has landed interests in the county, and owns considerable valuable city property. He is a man of excellent character, and wields a wide influence among the settlers of his adopted county.

JAMES SHIELDS is a retired farmer of means and influence, who resides in the village of Woodstock, Pipestone county, Minnesota, to which place he came in the fall of 1888. The place of his nativity is found in the North of Ireland, in county Cavan, where he was born in 1834.

The early life of our subject was spent in his native land, where he remained until he was fifteen years of age. When our subject was fifteen years of age he concluded to emigrate to the United States, and taking the ship, he arrived safely in New York City, where he remained for some seven years. He apprenticed to learn the shoemaker's trade under a man named Duffy, and after continuing for some time in that line of employment he engaged in farming, continuing thereat until 1855, when he removed to the State of Wisconsin, settling on a farm in Marquette county. He engaged in agricultural pursuits in Wisconsin for about two years, and then removed to Freeborn county, Minnesota, remaining until the breaking out of the war in 1861. At this time he concluded to give his service to the assistance of his adopted country. He enlisted in the Fourth Minnesota Volunteer Infantry, as a private, and continued in the service of the army for three years and three months. The regiment to which he belonged was attached to Sherman's army in that grand march to the sea. The colonel of this regiment was Mr. Sanborn, who afterward rose to the rank of general. The war experience of the subject of our sketch was of the most severe and exciting nature, and, although he saw many severe battles, he passed through them all with but slight injury, despite the fact that in most of the engagements he was in active

service at the front. Among the battles in which his regiment was engaged were the following : Siege of Corinth, Iuka, battle of Corinth, Fort Gibson, Raymond, Forty Hills, Jackson, Champion Hills, Big Black River, siege of Vicksburg, Altoona and Savannah, besides many other battles and skirmishes of minor importance. Mr. Shields was discharged from the service January 1, 1865, at Savannah, and almost immediately afterward came northward to St. Paul, Minnesota, from whence he went to Freeborn county, same State. Settling down to the quietness of civil life, he engaged in the sawmill business for a period of eight years, after which he removed to Blue Earth county, where, in connection with his milling business, he engaged largely in farming. Pulling up stakes he again removed, this time going to Murray county, this being in the spring of 1879. Looking about for a good location for farming purposes, he settled on a claim on the southeast quarter of section 18, Chanarambie township. Here the subject of our sketch at once identified himself with the interests of the locality in which he had settled. Together with a few Norwegian settlers he assisted in the organization of the above township, and became one of the members of the first board of supervisors, which position he held for some four years. He also was instrumental in the organization of school district No. 30, in which he lived, this being in the year 1880. He gave his best attention to the welfare of the township and became one of its most influential and respected citizens. He owned an excellent farm of 245 acres, two hundred acres of which were under cultivation, and engaged largely in raising cattle. He had a beautiful grove of some eight acres which he had planted himself and which was one of the prominent landmarks of that part of the county.

In June, 1860, Mr. Shields was united in

marriage to Miss Lucy Austin, a native of Ohio. By this union there have been eight children—Irvy, Frank, Mary, Willie, George, Sadie, Bertie and Florence, all of whom are living at home.

Although Mr. Shields' residence in Woodstock is of recent date, he has made many friends by his pleasant and agreeable manners and business integrity. His career has been full of activity and usefulness and he is now retired to enjoy the blessings which come from a career of prosperity. In politics he affiliates with the republican party, of whose principles he is one of the most radical supporters. Having passed through a long and honorable army career, he is one of the leading and influential members of the Grand Army of the Republic. He and his family are members of the Methodist Episcopal church, of which society he holds the position of steward and class-leader. Mr. Shields is a man of strong influence, of high character, and has made numerous warm acquaintances since coming to Woodstock.

——◦→◦•❦❦•◦←◦——

LEWIS JAHNKE, a prominent citizen of Rose Hill township, Cottonwood county, Minnesota, lives on a fine farm on section 30. Germany was the land of his nativity, and he was born August 22, 1839. The parents of our subject were Michael and Mary (Sonburg) Jahnke, also natives of Germany. The parents never emigrated to America, but lived in their native land throughout their lives. The father engaged in farming, and died in 1859.

Up to fifteen years of age Lewis assisted his father in work on the farm and attended public school, and at that age learned the mechanic's trade. He followed this line of business for twenty-three years, and emigrated to America April 1, 1867, locating in Chicago, Illinois, where he worked at his trade for some eight years. He became quite well-to-do, but lost all his property in the great fire in 1871. After his loss he went to Peru, Indiana, where he worked at his trade for a year, returning after that time to Chicago and remaining two years. He then removed to New Ulm, Minnesota, and made that city his home for five years, coming at the end of that period to the place where he now lives. He took a homestead of 160 acres, and has been constantly improving it ever since. He has it provided with excellent buildings, and has a fine grove of four acres of trees. In connection with his farming operations he is also engaged in raising Durham and Holstein cattle, and also Norman and Clydesdale horses. In this line he has met with considerable success, and, with his energy and knowledge of stock raising, he will doubtless soon be one of the most prominent raisers of blooded stock in the county.

Mr. Jahnke was married August 13, 1865, to Miss Emily Grams, a daughter of Andrew Grams, also a native of Germany. This union has been blessed with five children—Owtletie, Mary, Theresa, Clara and an infant now deceased. The members of this family belong to the Lutheran church of Rose Hill township.

The subject of our sketch affiliates with the democratic party and has held various official positions, among them being that of township supervisor, treasurer of the township, and clerk of the school district in which he lives. He is a man of good business qualifications, and in all his dealings with the duties of public office has proven his capability and efficiency. Our subject had considerable military experience in his native land, having enlisted at the age of twenty years in the German army and served three years. He served through the German, Austrian and Prussian War, which lasted from May 1 to October 1, 1866. A few months after his discharge he emigrated to America. Since coming to the township Mr. Jahnke has taken an active interest in all matters pertaining to the public welfare, and has, by his interest in these matters and by his careful attention to his private business, as well as the public duties devolving upon him, gained the respect of his fellow-citizens.

———◆◆◇◆◆———

DAVID L. PHIPPS, a leading farmer and stock raiser of Ash Lake township, Lincoln county, Minnesota, is located on the northwest quarter of section 28. He made his location in Lincoln county in 1876 and was one of the first settlers. He assisted in the organization of the county in 1879 and was elected a member of the board of supervisors for one year. He has served his constituents in various official positions, and in every instance has proven his efficiency as a business man and citizen. On our subject's location in the township he broke thirty-five acres of land, built a neat frame house 16x24 feet, in which he still lives. Among other improvements he made at that time was a sod stable, which accommodated his stock for some years until he built a large new barn in the spring of 1886. He has a large number of cattle and also a number of fine half-blooded Norman horses.

The subject of our sketch was born in Windom county, Vermont, November 9, 1817. He is the son of Charles C. and Anna (Lincoln) Phipps, both of whom were natives of Massachusetts. In early life the parents removed to the State of Vermont, where the father died when our subject was about twenty years of age. The mother died in 1867. The parents were exemplary Christian people, the father being a member of the Methodist Episcopal church and the mother of the Baptist church. Our subject was the youngest of seven children—Theodore Lyman, Hannah, Anna,

Lucinda, Abagail, Eliza and David L. Theodore, Lucinda and Hannah are deceased.

The early life of Mr. Phipps was spent in his native county in Vermont, where he was reared and educated until he was about twenty years of age. He received a good education and assisted in work on the home farm. When twenty years of age our subject purchased a farm of four hundred acres, paying therefor $3,000. He lived on this farm for about four years and then sold out and purchased another of five hundred acres, continuing the operation of this latter place until coming to Minnesota in 1856. He first located in Dakota county, where he preempted 160 acres of land and became one of the first settlers of Lewiston township. For three years he engaged in general farming and stock raising in Dakota county, and then removed to a farm in Northfield township, Rice county. Here he engaged in farming and stock raising for two years, and at the end of this time moved to the city of Northfield and resided there, still continuing the operation of his farm until coming to Lincoln county in 1876.

David L. Phipps was married when twenty-one years of age in June, 1837, to Miss Maria Potter, a native of Vermont, where she was reared and educated. This lady died in 1870. By this marriage there were seven children, only one of whom lived to advanced years—May, born September 15, 1857, in Lewiston township, Dakota county. May married George McCortney, a farmer of Shaokatan township, Lincoln county. Mr. McCortney was born in Faribault, Rice county, Minnesota. Mr. and Mrs. McCortney have one child, Anna Frances. August 22, 1872, David L. Phipps was married to Miss Olia Irene Marcellus, a native of Canada, and daughter of Garret L. Marcellus, one of the early settlers of Ash Lake township. This lady died May 26, 1884, leaving one child, Charley Levi, born in June, 1879·

Mrs. Phipps was an estimable Christian lady and was a member of the Methodist Episcopal church.

The subject of our sketch has become one of the prominent and most well-to-do citizens of the township and has accumulated considerable means as the result of his thrifty and systematic habits. He is a man of excellent abilities and understands thoroughly the details of his occupation. In early life he was given the advantages of a good education and throughout all his life has constantly applied himself to the mastery of the affairs pertaining to the general welfare. He has become well posted on current and historic events and has gathered a large fund of general information. He is a pleasant and courteous gentleman and makes friends wherever he goes. He is a man of highest character, and is esteemed as a warm friend and loyal citizen by all who know him. In politics he affiliates with no particular party, but supports the man best fitted for the office to which he aspires. He has a fine farm of 440 acres under excellent cultivation and provided with good buildings. Perhaps no other man in the township is so deeply interested financially in farming as our subject, as he has a large number of acres constantly under cultivation and has a larger acreage than any other in the county.

FRANCIS DALY, a reliable farmer of Bondin township, Murray county, Minnesota, was born in County Meath, Ireland, in the fall of 1830, his parents being Edward and Jane (Tucker) Daly, natives, respectively, of Dublin and County Meath, Ireland.

The subject of our sketch remained with his parents on the farm and attended the common schools until he reached the age of twenty years, when he came to the United States, first stopping in Long Island, where he worked on a farm for about one year. He then went to New York City and worked out at odd jobs around the docks for a short time. From that time until 1853 his time was spent in various employments, among them being work in a brick-yard, in a rice mill, a soap factory, and as a roustabout on the boat "City of Hartford," after which he returned to the Excelsior Soap Factory in New York City. In 1853 our subject went to Chicago and found employment with Obadiah Jackson in a general store, where he remained one year and then returned to New York and worked for Leavett & Allen, book publishers, with whom he remained until August, 1860. Soon after his return to New York he built a house on Staten Island, and in 1855 was married. After closing his engagement with Messrs. Leavett & Allen, Mr. Daly returned to Ireland, where he remained until May, 1863, engaged in the dairy business. About this time disease got among his cattle and they died off until his business was completely ruined. He then returned to New York and found employment with Messrs. Kiggins & Kellogg in the book business. He remained with this firm until May, 1887, and was head porter and shipper for twenty-four years. During his residence in New York Mr. Daly became the owner of considerable property. He owned a fancy store in Brooklyn and two dwelling-houses, one on Myrtle avenue and the other on Myrtle street. When he acquired this property it was out in the open country, but now the city extends four miles beyond this street. In May, 1887, our subject came to Murray county, Minnesota, and purchased a farm on the southeast quarter of section 21, Bondin township. Our subject has a fine farm of 160 acres, on which are a good frame dwelling-house and barn. Though he has lived in the township but a short time, Mr. Daly has come to be considered one of its wealthy and reliable citizens.

The wedding day of our subject occurred in March, 1855, when he was married to Miss Maria Quinn, a daughter of Patrick and Mary Quinn. Miss Quinn was a native of the town of Athlone, County of Roscommon, Ireland. This union has been blessed with the following-named children—Jane, Edward, John (deceased), Mary, Ellen (deceased) and John.

----◦----•◦••◦•◦◦•◦•◦----

GEORGE BAXTER is a leading farmer of Winnebago township, Faribault county, Minnesota. He is operating a fine farm of 280 acres, which is one of the best places in the township. Mr. Baxter is a native of the village of Troy, Granville township, Bradford county, Pennsylvania, where he was born in the year 1845. His parents were Nathan and Amelia (Decker) Baxter, who are now residents of Winnebago City.

Nathan Baxter was born in Bradford county, Pennsylvania, August 2, 1820. His parents were Chauncey and Nancy (Vroman) Baxter, natives of New York. Chauncey Baxter was a leading citizen of his State and was engaged extensively in lumbering and also in farming. He had a family of six children, two of whom are now living, Nathan and Celestia, the later being now Mrs. Gilbert, of Wisconsin.

Nathan Baxter was reared in Pennsylvania, received a good practical education, learned the lumber business and engaged in farming. He located in Wisconsin in 1862, in Waukesha county, where he engaged in farming and in the wood business. He remained in that State until 1888, at which time he removed to Winnebago City, where he still lives. In 1887 he had visited this region and purchased several farms adjoining Winnebago City. This property he still owns. He has a neat residence on Cleveland street, in Winnebago City, where he is at present making substantial improvements.

Nathan Baxter was married January 1, 1843, to Miss Amelia Decker, who was born in Delaware county, New York, and a daughter of George and Eliza Decker, natives of England and Connecticut, respectively. Her father came to America in 1812, locating in New York, where he was married and reared a large family of children. A brief sketch is given of the children in the biography of Nathan Baxter in another department of this work.

George Baxter, whose name appears at the head of this sketch, spent his early days in school in Pennsylvania. Later the family came West, and our subject found employment at engineering in Muskegon, Michigan. Nine years were spent in this business, part of the time being spent in the shops and a part of the time on the lakes, principally Lake Michigan. Our subject then removed to Oconomowoc, Wisconsin, and operated an engine and threshing machine for some five years. In 1879 he concluded to come to Minnesota, and settled where he now lives. At that time there was nothing but the bare prairie, and settlers were some distance apart. Our subject commenced making improvements on his farm, built a house and granary, living in the latter for some years until he could build his present fine residence. He has two large barns, one 30x40 feet and the other 32x50 feet, with a shed 18x60 feet, all painted and built in excellent shape. He has a large windmill and reservoir. He has set out several acres of trees and has a very pleasant and comfortable home. His farm is under good cultivation and is one of the best in the township.

George Baxter was married in the year 1872, to Miss Etta Kilmer, of Janesville, Wisconsin, and a daughter of James Kilmer. This union has been blessed with one son, George J., aged thirteen years, and now a student in the high school at Winnebago City.

The subject of our sketch is one of the most active and energetic citizens of Winnebago township. He always participates in all matters which tend to the upbuilding of the interests of his locality, and is always alive to its needs. In politics he affiliates with the republican party, as did his father before him. He is one of the most solid and prominent farmers of the township and county.

——◆—❧◆❧—◆——

HOSEA J. HUMPHREY, one of the leading and reliable farmers of Pipestone county, Minnesota, is a resident of section 34, Grange township. He settled in Grange township on a homestead in 1882, and has ever since been identified with the interests of that locality. He was born in Richmond, Chittenden county, Vermont, July 2, 1823. He was the son of James and Orpha (Dow) Humphrey, both of whom were natives of New Hampshire. The father was the son of James and Emma (Hardy) Humphrey, natives of Rhode Island, James Humphrey being the son of John Humphrey, a descendant of English ancestry. The Humphreys throughout their generations have been men of ample means and much influence in the Eastern States, in which the majority of them lived. The mother of the subject of our sketch was the daughter of Isaiah and Abigail (Messer) Dow, who were of French descent. Hosea's mother died in 1861, and his father in 1864, and they were both buried in the town in which our subject was born.

Hosea Humphrey remained with his parents until he reached the age of twenty-two years, up to which time he had for the most part been assisting his father at work on the home farm. He had also been given good educational advantages, and by profiting thereby, he had acquired a good common-school education. When he reached the age above mentioned he went to Massachusetts and commenced learning the carpenter's trade, and, remaining in the State until 1862, he enlisted in Company D, Thirteenth Vermont Volunteer Infantry, serving as a private for about nine months. He then went to work for the government at the carpenter's trade, being employed on government contracts in different places in South Carolina and Tennessee, a portion of the time being spent in Chattanooga, of the latter State. Completing his engagement with the government he returned to Massachusetts, where he continued working at his trade until in 1865, in which year he removed to Steele county, Minnesota. On coming to Minnesota he turned his attention to agricultural pursuits, and, buying a farm, continued this until 1882, when, as has already been stated, he came to Grange township, Pipestone county, and settled on a homestead.

December 4, 1843, is the date of the marriage of our subject to Miss Rosamond Sherman, a native of Waitsfield, Vermont, and daughter of William and Lucy (Wilder) Sherman. Mr. and Mrs. Humphrey have been blessed with two children, both of whom are living—Leslie J., of Dakota, and Emma L, of Grange township.

The subject of our sketch has at all times in his career been an active participant in matters of a public nature. To see this we have but to notice that while in Steele county he held the office of justice of the peace and assessor, and since coming to Pipestone county has been treasurer of the township for four years, and justice of the peace for one term. He is a man of high character and excellent judgment, and is respected by all who know him. He is thrifty and energetic, and has fitted up for himself a comfortable home and an excellent farm. In politics he affiliates with the democratic party, and is a leading member of the Grand Army of the Republic, Simon Mix Post, No. 95, of Pipestone, Minnesota.

MRS. EMELINE GARDNER, widow of the late Allen Gardner, resides on a fine farm on section 8 of Great Bend township, Cottonwood county, Minnesota. She was born in Franklin county, Maine, May 25, 1856, and was the daughter of David and Rosina (Winslow) Moore, natives of Maine. Her father was a ship-builder by occupation during the early part of his life and finally engaged in agricultural pursuits. His parents were John and Emeline (Jackson) Moore, the former being a sailor by occupation. Mrs. Gardner's mother was the daughter of Howard and Mary Winslow, the former's parents being Ezra and Rachel Winslow. Howard Winslow was a local minister in the Methodist Episcopal church, and the family on both sides were prominent and influential people in the East.

Mrs. Gardner was married to Allen Gardner April 9, 1877, and came directly to her home in Cottonwood county. Her husband had located his claim the year before. In all Mrs. Gardner has now four hundred acres of excellent land and one of the finest residences in the county. It is located on the Des Moines river and is one of the most pleasant locations for a home in the township.

Allen Gardner was born in the northern part of Maine, February 28, 1838. He was the son of Allen and Elzina (Doyne) Gardner, natives of Vermont. Allen Gardner engaged in the lumber trade until 1874, when he came to Fillmore county, Minnesota, where he met the lady whose name appears at the head of this sketch. He was one of the first settlers of the vicinity, and was one of the county's most prominent citizens. He was one of the first county commissioners, and had always been prominent in township affairs. He died September 8, 1887, his death being the result of an accident. He was injured by a horse falling on him the last day of August. He lingered until September 8th, when he died. In politics Mr. Gardner was a republican; he was a man of strong will and of sound and decided opinions. He was energetic and systematic, and although when he came to the county he had but little capital, he weathered all the disheartening circumstances, grasshopper raids, etc., and by hard work and perseverance became one of the wealthiest citizens of the township. Mr. Gardner was a member of the Grand Army of the Republic, having enlisted in 1862. He served his country faithfully and gallantly, entitling him to the honorable membership in the Grand Army of the Republic which he held. He was also a member of the Ancient Order of United Workmen, by which society and the former one just named he was cared for to a large extent during his last illness. Mr. and Mrs. Gardner had nine children, of whom the following named are living—Charles W., George W., Laura E., Ethel V. and Emma R. Mrs. Gardner's parents live on an adjoining farm.

ALFRED TERRY is one of the leading citizens of Slayton, Murray county, Minnesota. He is a son of Robert and Amelia Therold (Parsons) Terry, the former a native of England and the latter born in France. The father, Colonel Terry, was a prominent man in the English military service. He was in the English army for some forty-five years, seventeen years of that time being spent in active war. He had command of the English troops that captured the island of St. Martins, and for his gallant and honorable conduct in the battles in connection with this campaign was made governor of the island. Late in life he was retired on full pay and resided in England.

Alfred Terry was born on the island of Malta, December 3, 1842. His education was received at Winchester, England, where he remained until he was nineteen years of age. He then entered the West of England Bank, England, and continued in that institution for five years. At this time he came to America, locating in Lakefield, Canada, where shortly afterward he joined the Canadian volunteers in the Fenian movement. He did not participate in any active warfare, but for nine months was in constant drill preparing for the emergencies of war. After this period had expired he came to the United States, locating in Decorah, Iowa. Here he was employed in farming and various other occupations for about five years, when he removed to Nobles county, Minnesota, where he located on government land. He remained in Nobles county about seven years, during six of which his crops were entirely destroyed by grasshopper raids and hail-storms. On going to Nobles county our subject was in fair circumstances, but owing to these disastrous strokes of fortune, on leaving there at the end of seven years he was badly in debt, and in fact was so poor that he had to walk out of the country, leaving his family until he had earned enough to move them hence. Going to Fulda he opened a small flour and feed store. In connection with this he also engaged in the real estate business, and followed the same two years in Fulda. After two years he went to England on a brief visit, and returning in 1881 he settled in Slayton township, Murray county, making his location before there were any buildings put up on the site of the village. He at once engaged in handling real estate, which has been his principal business ever since. He has done very well in this line, and is now in good circumstances.

Mr. Terry was married in Mankato, February 4, 1875, to Mary E. (Chase) Weston. Mr. and Mrs. Terry have been blessed with two children—Robert Weston and Selina Maria. By her former husband Mrs. Terry had two children—John E. and Andrew I.

Since coming to Slayton, and in fact throughout his entire life in the West, Mr. Terry has actively participated in all public affairs. He is a leading member of the Independent Order of Odd Fellows, and also of the Independent Order of Good Templars and Modern Woodmen of America. He is a member of the Methodist Episcopal church, and is the president of the county Sunday-school association.

WILLIAM OKER is a thrifty farmer located on section 8, Verdi township, Lincoln county, Minnesota. He was born in Prussia, Germany, March 7, 1834. He was the son of Anton and Anna (Konig) Oker. The father was a mechanic by occupation, and died in his native country when our subject was about four years old. The mother died in 1874, at the advanced age of seventy years.

William Oker remained with his parents, being given a common-school education until he was fifteen years of age. At that age he was apprenticed to learn the cabinet-maker's trade, at which he worked some three years. He then engaged as a journeyman cabinet-maker for two years, one year of which was spent in Holland. These various periods brought his life up to the year 1856, in his native land. He was then at the proper age to enter the army. Army life was not in accordance with his tastes, however, and he concluded to emigrate, so, finding an excellent opportunity, he slipped on board a private sailing vessel bound for Brazil. He was on board forty days, and was then landed in New York City on the 15th of October, 1856. He passed through that city en route for Detroit, Michigan, where he remained some three weeks, looking for work. He then hired out to work in a saw-mill on the shores of Lake Michigan. He continued this employment for nine months, receiving $14 a month in the winter and $25 per month during the summer. At the end of these nine months he returned to Detroit, and after one week's stay entered the employ of the Collins Iron Company of Cleveland, Ohio. He went to their works near Marquette and was there employed at the carpenter's trade for two years. At this time he was struck with the gold fever and started for California. In payment for his work for the iron company he received a check of $650. He went to Buffalo, New York, and found that the draft could not be cashed for sixty days, so he decided to go to St. Paul by steamer, but on account of the fact that Lake Pepin was not yet open he stopped at Dubuque, Iowa, for about six weeks. At the end of that time he took the first boat going up the river and landed at Winona. At that place he hired a team and went overland to Rochester, arriving in that city in 1857. Here he found employment at the carpenter's trade, and one year later, in 1858, was married. He purchased a lot and built a house and decided to make that place his home. He engaged in contracting and building for some time and made some money. His dwelling was burned in 1877 and he lost almost everything he possessed. Shortly after he started for Lincoln county, and in February located the claim where he now lives. He then returned to Rochester and the following spring started with his wife and two sons for his farm in Lincoln county. He chartered two cars, filling one with stock and household goods and the other with lumber. He came by railroad as far as Marshall and from thence came to his farm by team. The first two nights the family slept in a quickly-improvised hut made by leaning boards against their wagons.

Soon after he built a shanty and started his sons at breaking. He returned to Rochester, where he had a contract for putting up a building, remaining in that city until fall. He then returned to his farm and with his wife and sons went back to Rochester, where they staid during the winter. The next April the family returned to the farm, since which time they have been permanent residents. Mr. Oker has been a hard working farmer and has labored hard to bring his farm up to a high state of cultivation. He has excellent land, well improved, and has a fine house and barns. In his early life he was given a good common-school education while living with his parents in his native land. In politics he affiliates with the democratic party and has held several positions of trust and responsibility, among these being that of supervisor, which position he held for one year.

Mr. Oker was united in marriage December 19, 1858, to Miss Julia Schmelzer, a native of Germany. Mr. and Mrs. Oker have nine living children—William J., George, Joseph, Julia, Lizzie B., Anna H., Laura K., Frank J. and Edward L.

✦

JOHN A. HYNES, one of the leading and most substantial residents of Delavan township, Faribault county, Minnesota, owns a fine farm on sections 33 and 29. He located on his land on September 14, 1857, and is therefore one of the earliest settlers of his township. He assisted in its organization, which took place in the fall of 1858, the first meeting being held at Bass Lake, on section 16. Fourteen votes were cast at this meeting. The township was duly organized and started on its existence as a civil division. Our subject took an active part in these matters leading up to the organization of his township, and was the first justice of the peace and held an office on the township board. He has always actively engaged in public matters, and has held some official position nearly all the time since coming to the township. At present Mr. Hynes is chairman of the board of supervisors, to which position he was elected in 1889. He has been assessor for a year, clerk for two years, and has been pathmaster of road district No. 8. He has always worked hard for the interests of his township, and has strongly opposed anything which tended to destroy the property of the township or oppress his fellow-citizens. He is one of the most influential men in the township, and was largely instrumental in defeating the project for raising a bonus for the railroad company. He opposed this on the ground that the railroad company would derive sufficient benefit from the freights received and traffic over the road from this township, so that it was not necessary to grant them a bonus for the construction of the road. The early times and the conditions of the settlers of Delavan township are well remembered by our subject, and he often relates how for the first few years he had to go to market in what was then the village of St. Paul. Sometimes he went to Hastings, where he purchased his flour. In that village he bought his first plow. The trip to these points occupied about ten days. Markets, however, have been getting nearer and nearer, and now a crop of grain can be sold and provisions obtained within a very few miles.

The subject of this sketch was born in Ireland, September 22, 1830. His father was Thomas Hynes, a native of Ireland and a farmer by occupation, who came to the United States in 1853, locating in Watertown, Wisconsin. He made that his home until his death, which occurred in 1866. The mother's name was Ann Hayes, who also died in 1866. The parents were exemplary citizens and were members of the Catholic church.

John H. Hynes came to America when he was about twenty years of age. In his native land he had been given a good education, and had assisted his father in various employments, especially in work on the farm. Coming to America he landed in Quebec and from thence went to New York State and on through to Wisconsin. There he was engaged in lumbering on the Wisconsin river for several years, and made several trips down that river in this avocation, both before and after his settlement in Faribault county, Minnesota, in 1857. He found it necessary to go back to the pineries after coming here in order to obtain means of subsistence—and thus he continued making trips on the river "off and on" until 1866, which ended his rafting and river work.

On the 4th of April, 1864, Mr. Hynes was married to Miss Sarah A. Emerson. She was a native of Watertown, Wisconsin, and was the daughter of William Emerson, now a resident of the village just named. Mr. and Mrs. Hynes have had nine children—Mary Ann, Francis, Theresa, Henrietta, Ada, Minnie, Eldon, Joseph and Gracie. The four oldest children were educated in the Winnebago City high schools and are now engaged in teaching. This is an estimable family and the parents are members of the Catholic church.

Mr. Hynes has always been among the first to advance in the improvement of his township and has the honor of building the first brick house in 1869. This is an excellent dwelling 20 x 30 feet with 16-foot posts and with a wing 16 x 26 feet and of the same height. Here the wayfarer finds a pleasant and commodious home and one of the hospitable families in the township. Our subject affiliates with the democratic party in politics and for some years was a member of the Odd Fellows fraternity. Having been a careful, energetic and systematic farmer, he has accumulated large means and is one of the leading and most substantial men in the county. When he landed in Buffalo, New York, fresh from the old country, he had not even a shilling in his pocket. Coming West he took care of what money he earned, and, settling in Wisconsin and later in Minnesota, he engaged successfully in farming, having now over four hundred acres of land and a large amount of valuable stock.

THEODORE M. BROWN. This gentleman is the efficient and popular superintendent of the Pleasant View stock farm, located on section 16, Troy township, Pipestone county, Minnesota. The enterprise over which Mr. Brown exercises control is one of the largest of its kind in Southern Minnesota. The farm is composed of three thousand acres of land, given chiefly to the raising of blooded horses. The subject of our sketch was born November 8, 1841, in Syracuse, New York, and was the son of John E. and Angeline (Bassett) Brown. The father was a native of Scotland, and the mother a native of New York State. The father's father was John A. Brown, an Englishman by birth; the mother was a daughter of Urion D. Bassett, a native of New York and the son of an eminent local artist of Syracuse, New York.

The subject of our sketch had the sad misfortune of being left an orphan at a tender age. When he was but four years old his father died, and he remained with his mother until he was thirteen, when she too died, and he was obliged to rely upon his own slender resources for support and care. He concluded to learn the machinist's trade, and, entering a machine shop, for four years he followed that line of business, when he turned his attention to caring for and handling fine stock. He was at this time a resident of the State of Illinois, being located in Henry county, whither he had come at the age of twelve years.

At seventeen years of age he had attained to such excellence in the handling of blooded stock that he was given charge of a large stock farm in the county just mentioned. He remained in this line of employment until June 17, 1861, when he enlisted in Company H, Nineteenth Illinois Volunteer Infantry. His service with that regiment extended over a period of three years, after which he re-enlisted, joining the One Hundred and First Pennsylvania Volunteer Infantry. Being possessed of an excellent knowledge of military discipline he was detached as drill-master, in care of instructions, in the Army of the Cumberland. During his first enlistment he had charge of the working force of the Pioneer Brigade, Army of the Cumberland. He was mustered out of the service in April, 1865, after having been through all the engagements of his division. He then returned to Illinois and took charge of the working forces of the government between Moline and Rock Island, having in charge somewhat over 1,300 men and 125 teams. So profitable and satisfactory was this employment that he continued his engagement with the government until late in 1871. In this year he again turned his attention to stock raising in Illinois, continuing at this line for some ten years. Then, in 1882 he became foreman of the work on the Northern Pacific railroad bridge at Bismarck, which employment was continued for about four months. He then entered the employ of the proprietors of the Canfield stock and grain farm in Northern Minnesota, one of the largest ranches in the Northwest, composed of about seven thousand acres of land. Continuing his position with this company for about four years, he then for six months took charge of the Barnes' farm, removing at the end of that time to Fargo, in which city he remained for two years. At the end of this period he removed to Pipestone county, and took charge of the large farm of which he is now superintendent, and on which he has since lived.

Mr. Brown was united in marriage, in 1881, in the month of August, to Miss Anna Lambert, a native of Geneseo, Illinois, and daughter of E. Lambert. This union has been blessed with two children—Arthur C. and Raymond R., both of whom are now living.

The executive abilities of Mr. Brown have had excellent opportunity for development and manifestation in the management of the large business in which he is engaged. In every respect he is giving satisfaction to his employers, and has risen in the respect and esteem of his fellow-townsmen. In public matters he takes an active interest, and is able and willing to assist in all matters that further the advancement of the agricultural and financial interests of his township. Although having been given but a limited common school education in his early life, he has, by reading and careful home study, become thoroughly posted on the current events of the day and of the past history of the nation. In politics he affiliates with the republican party.

JOHN Q. PICKET is one of the leading men of Dale township, Cottonwood county, Minnesota. He located in the county October 22, 1873, and has been engaged in farming and stock raising ever since. On coming to the county he commenced making improvements, and with the other early settlers experienced the difficulties which usually encompass pioneer settlements. He takes an active part in public affairs and has held various official positions, among them being constable, supervisor, and various school district offices.

The subject of our sketch was born in Morgan county, Ohio, October 19, 1832.

He was the son of Moses Picket, a farmer by occupation and a native of Virginia. The father moved to Ohio with his parents when he was but a small boy and was educated in Belmont county, where he lived until his death. Our subject's mother's maiden name was Hannah Healy, a native of New York State. When she was still young she came to Morgan county, Ohio, with her parents. She is now dead.

The subject of our sketch remained in his native State until he was twenty years of age, up to which time he had received a good common-school education. His early training being received on a farm he acquired a taste for that occupation, and at forty years of age he came to Cottonwood county, Minnesota, looking for land. He rode through from Ohio with a horse team, and camped out while the weather was pleasant. On coming to the county he located land and has been a permanent resident ever since.

Mr. Picket was married May 5, 1864, to Miss Jane E. Sears, who was born in Morgan county, Ohio, where she was reared and educated. This lady was a teacher in Ohio and was highly educated. Mr. and Mrs. Picket have three children—Mary H., Sadie E. and Thomas M. The family belong to the Protestant Methodist church.

The subject of our sketch is a man of strong temperance sentiments and affiliates with the prohibition party. He has always taken an active interest in public matters and has been postmaster of his township for some four years.

CHRISTIAN J. RAMLO, a prosperous farmer, resides on section 10, Hendricks township, Lincoln county, Minnesota. He is a native of Norway, where he was born July 23, 1853. His parents were James Engan and Mary Ramlo, both of whom were natives of Norway. The father was a farmer in his native land, and followed that occupation until his death, which occurred in May, 1868. The mother is still living in that country. In the father's family there were four children, our subject being the third in order of birth.

The subject of this sketch remained with his parents on the farm in his native country until he was eighteen years of age, up to which time he had been given good educational advantages. When he reached the age just mentioned he concluded to leave his native land and come to America. This he did, and on landing at Quebec started westward, locating in Lansing, Iowa. Here he found work on a farm, which occupation he continued until 1877, in which year he came to Lincoln county and took up the claim where he now lives. He was one of the very first settlers of this part of Lincoln county, and has been intimately associated with its best interests ever since he made his location. He drove through from Iowa by team and on locating his claim commenced active farming operations.

The subject of our sketch was married October 20, 1879, to Miss Gertrude Reppe, a native of Norway. This union has been blessed with five children—James C., Mary C., Elmer M. (deceased), Gena C. and Elmer M.

In his early life Mr. Ramlo was given good educational advantages and acquired a good common-school education. He has therefore been well fitted for the various duties in which he has been engaged. Being one of the early settlers of this locality, he assisted in the organization of the civil township and has held several offices of responsibility. He has been constable for two years, and for two terms has served on the board of supervisors, having also served as treasurer of the school district ever since the township was organized. At present he also holds the position of township assessor. Throughout his life in Lincoln county Mr. Ramlo has

conducted himself in such an upright and conscientious manner as to win for him the commendation of many friends. His character is of the highest, and in whatever position he has been called to serve his constituents he has proven his capabilities and trustworthiness and has won the respect of all with whom he has had to do. Being a man possessed of qualities which were valuable to the public, he has been called upon several times to administer in the closing up of the affairs of several estates. Whenever he has thus served his administration, whether for real estate or personal property, he has given excellent satisfaction and has administered his trust with capability. In politics he affiliates with the republican party.

JOHN N. RIVERS is the present station agent of the Chicago, St. Paul, Minneapolis & Omaha Railroad Company, at Avoca, Murray county, Minnesota. He was born December 10, 1864, in Winona county, Minnesota. His parents were Nicholas and Ann (Assel) Rivers, both of whom were natives of Germany. The father came to America in 1857, and the mother followed him in 1859. They first located in Winona county in about 1860. In the father's family there were eight children, John N., the subject of our sketch, being the third child.

The early life of our subject was spent beneath the parental roof, where he assisted on the home farm, and was given a good common-school education. At sixteen years of age he left home, and engaged in teaching for some two years, and then went to Janesville, Wisconsin. He then commenced studying telegraphy, continuing in that line in Wisconsin until 1884. He then came to Blue Earth City, Minnesota, remaining about five months; thence to Winnebago City, where five months more were spent, and where, during the last month of his stay, he was given the entire charge of the local affairs of the railroad company. He was then transferred to the village of Amboy, whence, after a short time, he went to Lake Crystal. He was then stationed at various places until the latter part of 1885, among them being Winnebago City, Garden City and other towns. In November, 1885, he came to the village of Avoca, as the operator and station agent for the Omaha Railroad Company. He has identified himself with the better interests of the village, and has held various official positions, among them being that of justice of the peace and member of the village council. In politics he affiliates with the democratic party, and is secretary of the Murray county democratic central committee. He has a good common-school education, and attended the State normal school at Winona for two years.

Mr. Rivers was married August 6, 1888, to Miss Anna McGarry. This lady was a native of England, and was the daughter of Thomas and Ann (Welch) McGarry, both of whom were natives of Ireland.

EZRA RICE is one of the leading financial characters of Luverne, Minnesota. He is the vice-president of the Security Bank of that city. He located for a brief time in Rock county in 1868, and in 1871 became a permanent settler, locating on land four miles northwest of Luverne, where he preempted 160 acres of land. He made his home on this pre-emption for about four years, making good improvements and building a house of rough boards and sod. He thoroughly cultivated the farm and set out a large grove of trees, and continued giving his attention principally to the raising of grain and stock until 1873. In the fall of this year he was elected sheriff of Rock county, to fill out the unexpired term of his brother James. He served two successive terms in this office, and then engaged in the grain and machinery business. He continued in this latter line for about six years, at the end of which time he gave his attention exclusively to the grain business, in which he became largely interested financially. He built eight warehouses on the Burlington railroad in 1884, and conducted the business at these places until in June, 1888, at which time he sold out all but two. He still owns a large elevator at Beaver Creek and one at Luverne, both of which are still under his control. He became one of the organizers of the Rock County Bank in 1882, and was a stockholder and director of that institution for some six years. He then severed his connection with the Rock County Bank, and assisted in the organization of the Security Bank on the 8th of May, 1888. He was elected vice-president at that time and is the present incumbent of that office. It can therefore be seen that our subject has taken an active interest in the financial development of Luverne and vicinity, and has become financially interested in a number of important enterprises. Besides this he has taken an active interest in all public matters pertaining to the governmental affairs of the city and county. He has held various offices. In 1883 he was mayor of the city of Luverne.

The gentleman whose name appears at the head of this sketch is a native of Whitley county, Indiana, where he was born December 23, 1845. His parents were Daniel B. and Rosana (Nickey) Rice, the father a native of New York State, and the mother a native of Virginia. The father followed the occupation of farming principally, but, in connection therewith, also carried on an extensive business in contracting and building. He came to Indiana in the early settlement of that country, and continued his residence there until coming to Minnesota in 1866.

He settled in Martin county and is now living in the village of Fairmont. The mother died in Indiana in 1862. In the father's family were seven children, only two of whom are now living— our subject and Dr. Henry Rice, of Fairmont, Minnesota.

The first eighteen years of the life of the subject of our sketch were spent by him on the home farm, during which time he was given the educational advantages furnished by the district schools. In February, 1864, he enlisted in Company E, Seventeenth Regiment Indiana Volunteer Infantry, and remained in the service for ssme twenty months. His military experience was of an exciting and interesting nature. His regiment was attached to General Sherman's army in that wonderful Atlanta campaign. He was also with General Wilson in his raid through Georgia and Alabama. Remaining with his regiment until about September, 1865, he was then discharged at Indianapolis, Indiana. He then attended the commercial college at Fort Wayne, and after completing his studies in that institution, commenced teaching school, and after some years of occupation in that line, he came West and located at Fairmont, Minnesota. He was engaged in various enterprises, among them being farming, milling and merchandising. He continued his residence in Fairmont until coming to Rock county in 1868.

Mr. Rice was married in 1871 to Miss Nettie A. Nichols, daughter of George S. Nichols. This union is blessed with four living children—Blanche, Harriet, Lotta and Cecil.

Mr. Rice is one of the prominent capitalists of Rock county, and besides having interested himself largely in various financial projects in and about Luverne, has also given his attention to large investments in other localities. He has become interested in considerable property in California, Salt Lake City and Sioux Falls, Dakota. In all these projects he has been highly successful and is at present the owner of a large amount of valuable real estate. He own some very fine properties in the City of Luverne, having built an elegant residence in 1884, which he has fitted with all modern improvements and surrounded with beautiful shade and ornamental trees. He has a very pleasant, agreeable family, and is himself a man of excellent social and business qualities. In politics Mr. Rice affiliates with the republican party, is a Mason and a member of the Grand Army of the Republic Post. He is a man possessed of excellent business qualifications, and in whatever lines his attention has been directed he has met with merited success.

———————

HON. JOHN PEMBERTON is one of the prosperous farmers of Osborn township, Pipestone county, Minnesota. He was born in Lancaster, Lancashire county, England, April 30, 1829. He was the son of James and Sophia Pemberton. When he was thirteen years of age he came with his mother and one brother, in 1842, to America, and located in the city of Buffalo, in the vicinity of which place tney lived for about three years. Our subject found work on a farm for a part of the time, and otherwise worked in a cotton factory in the city. He had worked in this line prior to this time, commencing in the spinning department in a factory in England when he was seven years of age, and continuing in that factory until coming to America at the age of thirteen. When he was sixteen years old he came with his mother and older brother to Walworth county, Wisconsin, where they settled on a farm and continued their residence until coming to Pipestone county, Minnesota, in 1881. In Walworth county our subject became a man of much prominence, and, in company with his brother, owned 230 acres of land, well cultivated and well provided with buildings and other appurtenances. They were engaged largely in stock raising, at which they met with considerable success. In public affairs Mr. Pemberton occupied a prominent place, and held numerous positions of responsibility in the township in which he lived. For two years he held the position of treasurer, was supervisor for several years, and was a member of the county board of supervisors, being about the same time elected as chairman of the township board. In the fall of 1877 he was elected as a member of the State legislature of Wisconsin, from the Second district of Walworth county. He served his constituents well and ably during one year, and proved himself an able and conscientious official. For six years he also held the position of director of the township insurance company, and in all matters gave of his means and time liberally for the benefit of his fellow-citizens.

In October, 1857, Mr. Pemberton was united in marriage to Miss Sarah A. Mansur, a native of Maine, where she was reared and educated. This lady was a daughter of Darius Mansur, a farmer of considerable prominence in Wisconsin. Mrs. Pemberton died in the triumphs of Christian faith, December 24, 1881. She was an exemplary Christian lady, and a member of the Methodist Episcopal church. At her death she was fifty years of age. She was buried in the cemetery at Edgerton. Mr. and Mrs. Pemberton were the parents of six children—Ida J., Rose Elizabeth, Minnie A., Charles S., Cassius L. and Arthur J. Ida and Rose are both married.

The subject of our sketch is a stanch republican, having voted with that party ever since its organization. On the organization of the republican party and the nomination of Fremont he joined hands with the supporters of republican principles and cast his ballot for the republican candidate, and since that time he has continually affiliated with the republican party. In February, 1865, he enlisted in the Forty-ninth Wisconsin Volunteer Infantry as a private, and continued through the balance of the war, being discharged as corporal of his company. His discharge was dated November 14, 1865, at Benton Barracks, Missouri. His service was spent principally under Captain A. J. Cheney, who continued as a ranking officer of that company until the close of hostilities between the North and South. Our subject was stationed at St. Louis, and also at Rolla, Missouri, and after being discharged returned home to Wisconsin and resumed his former occupation. He is a member of the Grand Army of the Republic, Post No. 80, of which he is the present adjutant. Mr. Pemberton is a man of good business ability, is thrifty and energetic, and is held in high esteem by all who know him. The circumstances of his early life were such as to practically preclude his receiving an education in the schools. His reading, however, has been extensive, and his self-education has been thoroughly carried on. He is a man of broad ideas, practical and progressive, and is one of the leaders in affairs of a public nature in the township in which he resides. He was elected county commissioner of Pipestone county in the fall of 1883 for three years, and re-elected in the fall of 1886 for four years; was chairman of the board in 1886, and is chairman of the board at the present time.

———————

GEORGE REES is a retired farmer and influential citizen of Lake Side township, Cottonwood county, Minnesota. He came to the county in 1871, and located his present homestead of ninety-six acres on section 30, three-fourths of a mile from Windom.

Mr. Rees was born in Worcestershire,

England, June 5, 1817. He was the son of John Rees, a miller by trade, and a native of England, where he died in 1850. Our subject's mother's name was Mary (Jones) Rees, a native of England, and who came to the United States in 1856, locating with her son, our subject, with whom she lived until her death, which occurred in 1864. Both parents were exemplary members of the Methodist Episcopal church. In the father's family there were eleven children, eight of whom grew to man and womanhood—William, John, Phœbe, George, James, Walter, Mary and Ann.

The early life of the subject of our sketch was spent in his native land, where he received a good practical education until nineteen years of age, in the excellent schools in the vicinity of his parental home. When he reached the age just mentioned our subject engaged in railroading, in which business he continued for eight or ten years. He then followed various occupations until he was thirty-two years old, when, in June, 1849, he came to the United States, locating for a brief time in Newtown, Bucks county, Pennsylvania. After a few weeks he went to New York State, and there engaged in agricultural pursuits for some two years. This period having expired he came West, locating in Winnebago county, Wisconsin, where he lived until 1871. Our subject then came to Cottonwood county, Minnesota, where he became one of the early settlers, there being but five other parties residing in this region at the time of his location.

Mr. Rees was married in April, 1857, to Miss Ruth France, a native of Yorkshire, England, and daughter of Charles France, a farmer, who came to the United States from England in 1821. He settled in Ohio for a few years, and then removed to Winnebago county, Wisconsin, where he died in February, 1865. Mrs. Rees' mother's name was Nancy (Baraclef) France, who died in England. In her father's family there were six children—Edward, Alice, Mary, Martha, Ruth and Jonathan. Mr. and Mrs. Rees have six children—Will, Theodore, George, Mary, Celia and Richard, all of whom are married, and have homes of their own, except one, who lives with the father.

The subject of our sketch has been quite prominent in public matters, and has affiliated with the republican party for some years. He is a man of good character, excellent abilities, and is a consistent member of the Methodist Episcopal church.

MARTIN A. MAZANY, Polak, is one of the leading and reliable citizens of Lincoln county, Minnesota, and is engaged in the mercantile business at Wilno, where he is also postmaster. Mr. Mazany is the son of Ignatius and Mary (Stupanski) Mazany, natives of Cerekwica, State Poznan, County Wongrowiecz, Prussian Poland, where our subject was born October 28, 1860.

The early life of the subject of our sketch was spent with his parents in his native land, where he attended the district school until about eleven years of age. At this time the family emigrated to the United States. There were but two children in the family—our subject and Michael S. Michael S. was born in Slembowo, August 29, 1864. On coming to America with the family he married, and is now a mail-carrier in Dunkirk, Chautauqua county, New York. When the family came to the United States they stopped in Dunkirk, New York, where they still reside. Our subject, Martin A., made that village his home until 1884. In that place he attended English school for some two years and then engaged as a gardener for a railroad conductor, continuing with that employer for about a year. Then for a short time he worked for a Mr. Van Buren, a general insurance agent, as gardener, after which he found employment for four years as fireman and engineer in William Heppner's tannery at Sinclairville, New York. At the end of that time our subject went to Pittsburgh and found employment in a foundry, where he worked for two years. He then engaged as brakeman on the Lake Shore & Michigan Southern Railroad, which line of occupation he followed for about a year. He then removed to Dunkirk and found employment in the Brooks Locomotive Works, where he remained two years. At the end of this period he returned to his employment with the railroad for which he had already worked and continued in their employ about six months, and then commenced an engagement as collector for T. R. Coleman, banker of Dunkirk, New York, continuing with that gentleman until the fall of 1884. At that time he went to South Bend, Indiana, on a brief visit, from whence after two months he went to Stevens' Point, Wisconsin, and spent three months in that place, visiting with a merchant friend. At the end of that time he came to Wilno, Lincoln county, Minnesota, arriving here February 21, 1885. Since coming to the county our subject has identified himself with all interests pertaining to the welfare of the general public and of the business of his own village. He has been quite successful in his various operations, and has accumulated considerable means. He is a man of good character and is respected and esteemed by all who know him.

—————♦•❀❖❀•♦—————

JOSEPH V. MATTHEWS is a farmer by occupation, and resides in Currie, Murray county, Minnesota. He was born in the city of Albany, New York, April 1, 1820. The father of the subject of our sketch was Caleb Matthews, who was born in the State of Vermont, and who emigrat-

ed to New York when he was sixteen years old. He remained in that State for fifteen years, engaged principally in work at the potter's trade. He was not confined in his occupation to the above-named trade, but engaged in various pursuits, among them being that of pump-maker and carpenter, in both of which lines he was quite successful. He finally settled in Chautauqua county, New York, where he died at the advanced age of eighty-four years. He was a respected and representative citizen of the locality in which he lived. The maiden name of the mother of the subject of our sketch was Margaret Salisbury, a native of Schoharie county, New York, where she received her early training and education. She was a resident of the city of Albany at the time of her marriage, and was a consistent and exemplary member of the Free-Will Baptist church. She died some four years after the death of her husband. In the father's family there were twelve children, of whom our subject was the sixth in order of birth. Eleven of these children grew to man and womanhood—Betsey Elizabeth, Margaret A., Sabina, Mary, Joseph V., Benjamin, Hudson, Charlotte, Mariam, Andrew Jackson and William H. Daniel died at the age of six months. Mary married J. Preston, and died in the State of New York at twenty-four years of age.

The subject of our sketch resided in the city of Albany with his parents for a short time and then went to Chautauqua county, where he remained until he was thirty-five years old. In the latter county he received his education in the common schools, and at twenty-one years of age commenced working for himself on various farms. Leaving that State he passed, after a brief stay, from Delhi, Delaware county, Iowa, to Rochester, Olmsted county, Minnesota, locating in the township of Cascade in 1855, and becoming one of the very first settlers of that township. He plastered the first house that was built in the village of Cascade, engaging principally in farming until coming to Murray county in 1872. Wherever he has lived the subject of our sketch has taken an active interest in public matters, and has efficiently filled various official positions. In Olmsted county he was a member of the board of supervisors, of which he was the first chairman, and was also justice of the peace. Since coming to Murray county he has held various positions, and has taken an active interest in matters pertaining to the school district in which he lives. He has a fine farm, provided with good buildings, and the passer-by witnesses the evidences of prosperity and thrift. A man of good education, of charitable ideas, he has taken a prominent place before the people of his county. Coming in an early day, he has experienced all the trials as well as the triumphs which come to the life of the pioneer settlers. He was a member of the first grand jury in Olmsted county, where he also officiated as an officer of the first county fair. His life in Murray county has been full of activity in public affairs. He assisted in the organization of Shetek township and held the offices of supervisor, justice of the peace, chairman of the board of supervisors, and various school offices. He left his farm in 1884 and removed to the village of Currie, where he is now living a retired life. In politics the subject of our sketch affiliates with the prohibition party. He is a loyal member of the Methodist Episcopal church and has been a class-leader in that organization for many years. He is a steward of the church and is also chairman of the executive board. In religious matters he is one of the most active and prominent of Currie's citizens. He is respected as a true citizen and loyal Christian gentleman by all who know him.

Mr. Matthews was united in the bonds of matrimony September 21, 1844, to Miss Clarissa Chipman, a native of Genesee county, New York. This lady was reared and educated in Chautauqua county. Mr. and Mrs. Matthews have six children—James, a farmer; Charles, a real estate dealer in Minneapolis; Marvin, a lawyer of Marshall, Minnesota; Ellen J., now the wife of A. Aendersbe, a butcher and liveryman of Currie; E. T. Matthews, a lawyer at Tracy, Lyon county, Minnesota, and Sidney, who is a law student in the village of Currie.

EORGE W. DOEG, one of the reliable farmers and stock raisers of Verona township, Faribault county, Minnesota, now lives on section 8. He purchased his place in the spring of 1865, at which time he came to the county on a brief visit. He then returned to Wabasha county, Minnesota, where he made his home until 1867, in which year he to came Verona township and settled permanently. He has striven hard to make his farm one of the best in the county, and has a fine grove of trees and also many varieties of fruit trees, apples, etc. He is one of the earliest settlers, and has always taken an active interest in all matters which tended to improve or develop his locality.

Mr. Doeg was born in Alfred, York county, Maine, December 5, 1835. His father was Augustus Doeg, a painter by trade, which business he followed until his death, which occurred in 1876. He spent the most of his early life in New Hampshire, his native State, and afterwards removed to Maine, where he remained until his death. Our subject's mother's maiden name was Hulda Cousins, a native of New Hampshire. She died in about 1864. In the father's family there were six children—Thomas, Samuel, Jane, Sarah, George W. and Almond. The last named served in the Union army and was killed at the battle of Nashville in 1864.

George W. Doeg received his early training and education in his native State, making that place his home until he was twenty-one years of age. He learned the painter's trade and also engaged to some extent in farming, and, on attaining his majority, went to Boston, Massachusetts, where he spent a week visiting a sister who lived in that city. He then went to Chicago, and thence, after a brief stay, he went to a farm a few miles south of the city and commenced work for a farmer. After a short time he returned to Chicago and engaged at the carpenter's trade; four weeks later he started for his home in the East. At Mentor, Ohio, however, he concluded to stop and engage in farming. Making that his home for a year, he then went to Missouri and remained during one winter, after which he returned to Ohio, and a year later was married and settled down to agricultural pursuits in Lake county, Ohio. Two years later he came to Wabasha county, Minnesota, and engaged in farming for six years, and then came to his present place. He has been all through the hard times so well known to the history of Southern Minnesota, namely, the grasshopper times, and understands what the trials of pioneer life mean. In spite of all these discouragements and losses, however, he has succeeded in accumulating considerable means, and has put his farm in excellent condition, supplying it with good farm buildings, and making it one of the best farms in the county.

Mr. Doeg was married in the month of December, 1858, to Miss Emily Carroll, a native of Lake county, Ohio, and born in the village of Mentor. She was a daughter of Samuel D. Carroll, a farmer and cooper by occupation. Mr. and Mrs. Doeg have three children — Albert, Nettie and Mary. The first named is married to a Mr. Adams, a farmer of Verona township. The family are all members of the Methodist Episcopal church.

The subject of our sketch affiliates with the republican party, and throughout his history in Faribault county has actively identified himself with all general interests. He has held various official positions, and has taken an active part in school matters. He is a member of the Odd Fellows fraternity.

WILLIAM H. SMITH, the pioneer butcher of Pipestone county, is at present an honored and reliable citizen of Pipestone City, Minnesota. He built his present meat market on Hiawatha street in 1882, having commenced the butcher business in the city in 1880, in a small building on Olive street. His market is appropriately called the "City Meat Market." He has invested largely in other property in the city, and is the owner of several lots, on which he has built a barn and a large ice house. In connection with his meat market he also carries on a large ice business. In 1880 he took a homestead in Gray township, built a sod house and commenced making improvements. He has prospered in every way, and has now a good frame dwelling-house and outbuildings on his farm.

The gentleman whose name appears at the head of this sketch is a native of Jefferson county, Wisconsin, where he was born in 1840. He is the son of William, Jr., and Martha (Cornish) Smith, the father a native of the southern part of Canada, and the mother a native of Ohio. The father was a mason and cooper by trade, and was the son of William, Sr., and Catharine (Ryan) Smith, the former being a soldier for twenty-one months in the War of 1812. William, Sr., was a farmer by occupation, and coming from Canada in an early day located in Grand Isle county, Vermont, where he engaged in farming, and where he lived until his death. When William, Jr., was sixteen years of age he went to Ohio and engaged in farm work for about seven years, and in 1842 went to the State of Wisconsin, where he engaged in the mason and cooper trades. He remained in Wisconsin until in 1884, when he sold out and came with his family to Pipestone county. He settled in Pipestone city, purchased three lots and built a residence. The mother of the subject of our sketch died in 1870; the father is still living in Pipestone. In the father's family there were nine children, of whom four are now living—Betsey, now Mrs. Benard; William H., our subject; Florence, now Mrs. Wheeler, and Effie.

The subject of our sketch received his early training and education in Jefferson county, Wisconsin. He was given the advantages for an education furnished by the district school and later became a student for some time in a select school. When seventeen years of age he enlisted in Company B, Forty-ninth Wisconsin Volunteer Infantry, as a private. After serving about one year, hostilities were ceased between the North and South, and he was granted his discharge from further service. His military life was principally occupied with doing guard duty in Missouri. At the close of the war he returned to his home in Walworth county, Wisconsin, and for seven years was employed in a livery stable. At the end of that time he turned his attention to work on a farm, continuing thereat somewhat over eight months, after which he was married. He then engaged in railroading on a branch of the Milwaukee & St. Paul road, continuing at that line about nine months. From thence he removed to Buchanan county, Iowa, and turned his attention for one year to agricultural pursuits. Removing thence he went to Lincoln county, Wisconsin, purchased eighty acres of wild land, and, after doing a little clearing and remaining thereon one year, he sold out and removed to Jackson county, where he purchased a

saw-mill. He engaged in handling lumber in this mill for about two years, after which he went to Monroe county, Wisconsin, and for two years turned his attention to the pursuits of the agriculturist. After that period he went to Huron, Dakota, and again engaged in railroading, continuing thereat during one season. At the close of that season's employment he came to Pipestone City, Pipestone county, and took his homestead, and also engaged in the meat business in Pipestone City, as has already been related in the opening lines of this sketch.

The subject of our sketch was married to Miss Orcelia Kenyon, of Cadiz, Wisconsin, a daughter of Oliver and Sallie A. Kenyon, residents of that city. Mr. and Mrs. Smith have been blessed with four children—Nettie B., Edith, Maude and Nathan. Nettie B. is a graduate of the normal school at Mankato. Edith is a teacher by profession, and Maude and Nathan are students in the Pipestone City schools.

In politics the subject of our sketch affiliates with the republican party, and is a member of the Grand Army of the Republic and Good Templars society. Since coming to the city he has been actively engaged in carrying on his successful business. He is an energetic man, and whatever he takes hold of brings merited success. He has a large trade and is doing a profitable business. One among his leading customers is the proprietor of the Calumet hotel, whose meat supplies are all furnished by Mr. Smith. Our subject takes an interest in all public matters and has a wide circle of friends.

SARAH J. WALKER is a resident of Windom, the county seat of Cottonwood county, Minnesota. She is the widow of George B. Walker, who was an influential citizen of the county and a son of Cyrus

Walker. He was born in Abbot, Maine, in 1843.

Mrs. Walker was born in St. Lawrence county, New York, October 16, 1853. Her parents were Simeon and Lorinda (Brooks) Greenfield, both natives of St. Lawrence county, New York. They came to Winona county, Minnesota, in 1857, and made that their home for eleven years. They then moved to Cottonwood county and located on a homestead of eighty acres, afterwards selling this farm and purchasing another not far distant.

At eight years of age the lady of whom this sketch treats went to live with her grandfather, James Greenfield. She remained with him some time and received an excellent education and early training. She was married February 19, 1871, to George B. Walker, this being the first marriage ceremony performed in Cottonwood county. This union was blessed with seven children—Edgar and Edwin (twins); Alfred, George (deceased), Clara, Llewellyn and Harold.

Mr. Walker was an early settler of Cottonwood county, and was the first man to do any plowing in the county after the Indian massacre of 1862. He died April 13, 1887. He was a man of excellent character, public-spirited and generous, and was respected by all who knew him. During the early times Mr. and Mrs. Walker saw many hardships, and for several years had their crops all destroyed by the grasshoppers. Nothing could be made at raising grain, so Mr. Walker traded his horses for cows, and succeeded in making a living with stock. They were able to provide for themselves, and were not obliged to receive assistance from the State.

Coming to the county in an early day, Mrs. Walker has witnessed many changes. She has been of an observant disposition, and has remembered many interesting circumstances which occurred during the early times. Although in straitened circumstances for a number of years in pioneer days, Mrs. Walker now owns a fine farm of 440 acres, located on section 25 of Ann township and section 30 of High Water township. On this farm stands a fine house, excellent large barn and about three acres of a fine grove of trees. There are several acres of natural timber along the creek which passes through the place. Mrs. Walker rents her farm and resides in Windom, where she has lived since July 6, 1887. She is engaged in dressmaking, and is one of the leading dressmakers of the city, having built up a fashionable and profitable trade. She is a lady of excellent character, and is a member of the Methodist Episcopal church. Mrs. Walker remembers the first celebration held in Cottonwood county. The people congregated on a farm adjoining that of her father and there passed the day in celebrating the independence of our country. Mrs. Walker's mother read the Declaration of Independence, this being the first time that instrument was publicly read in the county.

———✦—◆◈◆—✦———

ALLEN FLETCHER CHASE is one of the leading and influential farmers of Lincoln county, Minnesota. His location on the northeast quarter of section 22 in Lake Stay township was made in 1879, but he had filed on this claim in the fall of the year previous. In 1879 he moved his family on the place where he now lives, and proved up and obtained a patent from the United States in 1885.

Mr. Chase is a son of John M. and Eliza (Carney) Chase, the former a native of Vermont, and the latter born in Ohio. Allen was born in Newbury township, Elkhart county, Indiana, March 14, 1844. His early life was spent on the homestead of his parents. With them he moved from Elkhart county, Indiana, to Indian Prairie, St. Joseph county, Michigan, when he was about four years old. Here he was given good educational advantages in the district schools, remaining with his parents assisting in work on the home farm until he was twenty-one years of age. He then commenced running a peddler's wagon for himself, following that line of business for about a year. At the end of that time he engaged in working out on various farms, and followed that line until August, 1864, when he enlisted in Company H, Eighth Regiment Michigan Cavalry, and served until in June, 1865. During his military service he was on scouting duty most of the time, participating in the famous Hood campaign, and being on active duty throughout the entire period. The campaign just referred to was one of the most memorable of the war and was indeed one which will not soon be forgotten by our subject. Here he experinced all the hardships which may come to the life of the soldier in active duty at the front. For three weeks his regiment did not unsaddle their horses and during this time they were kept busy by a continual running fight with the enemy. After the close of the war our subject removed to Ontario, Lagrange county, Indiana, and engaged in farming there until about 1872. One winter of this period, however, was spent in working in a cooper shop, and two years also were occupied with a course of instruction in the collegiate institute at Ontario. In 1872 Mr. Chase came to Brown county, Minnesota, where he purchased a crop already sown. He harvested this crop and the following winter taught school in that county. In the spring he went onto a farm that he had purchased in Renville county, four miles north of Fort Ridgley. Farming on that place for one year he was then driven out by the loss of his entire crop, which was eaten up by the grasshoppers. He returned to Brown county and remained there until the following fall, his wife teaching school at Lone Tree Lake. Mr. Chase also taught school in Renville county. In September, 1874, they returned to Ontario, Indiana, and Mr. Chase taught school during the first winter. The following two summers were spent in work on a farm and the intervening winter he occupied his time in making brooms. One year after this period was spent by him in Houston county, Minnesota, where, in company with his brother Manville T., he opened up and operated a broom factory. In the spring of 1877 he started for Brown county with a team, and after a long and tedious trip through the mud and rainy weather reached a location in that county where he remained one year. The following spring he came to Lincoln county, and his wife returned to the East on an extended visit. Our subject lived a bachelor's life during the summer, and in the fall his wife joined him on the farm in Lincoln county.

The subject of our sketch was married in New Ulm, Minnesota, August 22, 1873, to Miss Ella Ferrand, a daughter of Rev. and Mary N. (Harris) Ferrand, natives of Vermont. She was born in Vermont, October 25, 1849, and came West with her parents in early life. Her mother died in Lincoln county at our subject's home in 1885. Two children have blessed the marriage of Mr. Chase—John B. and Ethel F.

In politics the subject of our sketch affiliates with the republican party, and has been elected to various offices in the gift of his fellow-citizens. He has been chairman of the board of supervisors for seven years, and has also been assessor, clerk and director of the school board, and has been justice of the peace. In all matters of a public nature he takes a prominent position, and has aided materially in various ways in the promulgation of such ideas and in the promotion of such projects as would benefit his fellow-townsmen. For some time he associated with the Farmers' Grange, and did all in his power to build up and improve the general farming interests. As a farmer Mr. Chase is a hard-working, systematic man, and has attained considerable success in every line in which he is engaged. He is a man of stanch character, loyal as a citizen, and has made many warm friends in the township.

In the winter of 1873 Mr. Chase requested Rev. Wilson, of Marshfield, to organize a Congregational church at his house, and the organization was perfected with the following four members: Mr. and Mrs. Chase and Mr. and Mrs. Carpenter. Rev. Dr. Cobb (State superintendent) and Rev. Mr. Simmons (since State superintendent) assisted Mr. Wilson. Since that time church service and a regular Sunday-school has been maintained. New members have been added from time to time, and there is now twenty working members. Ten or twelve members have meanwhile removed to other localities. Mr. Carpenter and Mr. Chase, of course, were chosen deacons, and the latter has from time to time been chosen his own successor. Mrs. Chase is secretary of the church. In connection there is maintained a woman's missionary society, which is in fine working order, and of which Mrs. Chase is president.

HOMAS O. WORNSON, a leading and influential farmer of Lowville township, Murray county, Minnesota, has an excellent farm on section 36. He was born December 8, 1850, and was the son of Ole and Martha (Gunderson) Wornson, both of whom were natives of Norway. The father was a prominent man in his native land, and for twelve years was a lieutenant in the Norwegian army. He came to America in 1860, landing in Quebec, whence he went to Chicago, and then to Rock county, Wisconsin, where he rented a farm for five years. He then removed to Fillmore county, Minnesota, where five years were spent in agricultural pursuits. In 1872 he removed to Murray county, and located a claim on section 6, of Slayton township, where he resided until his death, which occurred in 1880. The mother is still living on the old homestead.

Thomas O. Wornson resided with his parents until the age of eleven years. He then left home while his parents were residing in Wisconsin, and commenced work for himself. For three years he was occupied at farm work, and then rented a farm in Fillmore county, which he operated in company with his father. After the three years spent in Fillmore county, he then followed railroading for two years, and in 1872 came by team to Murray county, and located a claim on section 6, of Slayton township. He continued his agricultural pursuits in that township until 1884, when he sold out and went to Washington Territory and Oregon, looking for a location. Not being satisfied with the country through which he traveled he returned to Murray county, Minnesota, and purchased the place on which he now lives. He has seen hard times, but in spite of these things has accumulated considerable means. He was one of the pioneer settlers of the county, and experienced all the ills through which the pioneer settler usually has to pass.

Mr. Wornson was married to Minnie Christianson, March 23, 1872. She was the daughter of Christian and Caroline (Oleson) Christianson, natives of Norway, where also Miss Minnie was born. Mr. and Mrs. Wornson have been blessed with ten children— Emma, John, Olaf, Alma, Betsey, William (deceased), Sjur Rheinhart (deceased), Cora and Harry.

In politics the subject of our sketch affiliates with the republican party, and has become one among the prominent men in the local governmental affairs. For eight years he was supervisor, and for one year was assessor of Slayton township. Since residing in Lowville township, he has been supervisor, and was a member of the republican county central committee for two years, also town central committee for three years. He is a man of good character, and is a consistent member of the Lutheran church. He takes an active interest in all matters pertaining to education, and has been one of the school directors for some three years.

NATHANIEL P. MINION is a leading farmer residing in Delton township, Cottonwood county, Mindesota. His farm is located on section 34, where, in connection with farming, he also raises blooded stock, with the intention of giving a considerable part of his attention to the raising of Clydesdale horses in the near future. The subject of our sketch was born June 6, 1859, in Canada. His parents were Arthur and Rhoda (Griffen) Minion, the former a native of Ireland, and the latter born in Canada.

The father of the subject of our sketch was born in Ireland in 1811, and in 1831 came to Canada, where he was married. In 1865 he went to Clinton county, Iowa, and engaged in farming until 1871, when he came to Cottonwood county, Minnesota, locating on section 4, of Carson township, where he took a pre-emption. He improved his farm, and became one of the prominent men of the township, being identified with the political history of the county throughout his entire residence there. In 1884 he was accidentally killed on the horse power at a threshing machine, and his death was deeply mourned by a large number of friends, who held him in high esteem both as a man and citizen. The mother is still living in Delton township. In the father's family there were eleven children, our subject being the second youngest.

The subject of our sketch received his early training and education in the country in which he was born and in Iowa, removing to the latter place with his parents in 1865. Our subject was given a high-school education in Iowa, and assisted to some extent on the home farm. After coming to Minnesota he spent a few months in a school in Dodge county, after which he returned to the farm of his parents. He has resided in Cottonwood county ever since, and has become one of its prominent citizens.

Mr. Minion was married March 20, 1881, to Miss Augusta Bastian, a native of Germany. When quite young this lady came with her parents to America, and located in the State of Illinois. Her father was Carl Bastian, a farmer by occupation, and who now resides in Cottonwood county, of which he was one of the early settlers. Mr. and Mrs. Minion have five children: Robert, Frank, Bertha, Lewis and Effie.

The subject of our sketch has a fine location on section 34, where he owns 160 acres of land. He is a hard-working, energetic farmer, and has provided his place with excellent improvements. Throughout his residence in the township he has taken an active interest in all public matters, having been assessor of Delton township for three years. He is public-spirited, liberal in all enterprises which need the assistance of the citizens of the township, and is held in high esteem by all who know him.

CHARLES CHRISTENSON, an influential resident of Iona township, Murray county, Minnesota, is located on an excellent farm of section 30. He is a native of Denmark, and was born July 7, 1852.

The parents of the subject of our sketch were Christen and Catharine (Sorenson) Christenson. The parents were natives of Denmark, and the father followed the trade of blacksmithing in his native country. In 1867 the family came to America, settling in Howard county, Iowa, where they lived on a farm for three years. They then removed to the village of Cresco, where the father died shortly afterwards. The mother removed to Freeborn county, Minnesota, where she died some years later.

The early life of Charles Christenson was spent in the parental home. He assisted in work on the farm and was given a good common-school education. When twenty years of age he commenced work on adjoining farms, working for three years in Howard county, Iowa. He then purchased a team and came to Freeborn county, Minnesota, where for three years he lived on a rented farm. In 1878 he came to Murray county and located his present claim. He was one among the very first settlers, there being only two other families in this neighborhood when he came. There were about five settlers in the northeast corner of the township. Since making his location here he has taken an active part in public matters and has affiliated with the democratic party. He is a man of excellent principles, has a good common-school education, is an able business man and is respected by a wide circle of friends.

The wedding day of Mr. Christenson was on the 18th day of September, 1888, when he was joined in wedlock to Miss Mary J. McDonald, a daughter of R. J. and Elizabeth McDonald. This lady was a native of Minesota, where she has lived throughout her life. She is a lady of estimable character and has an excellent education.

꧁ ꧂

MYRON ORVIS is a prominent citizen of Pipestone county, and is engaged in farming in the city limits of Pipestone. He located in this county in 1886, and purchased a farm in Grange township, where he owned 640 acres, which he has since sold. He purchased the place where he now lives in 1888, and now owns eighty acres in one body at that place. On settling in Grange township he commenced improvements by breaking 114 acres of land and building a stable. On the farm on which he lives at present he has substantial buildings and has made fine improvements. While living in Grange township he took an active part in all public matters and held several official positions, among them being that of school trustee.

The place of the nativity of the subject of our sketch is found in Canada, where he was born in 1838. He is the son of Eleazar B. and Elizabeth (Austin), Orvis, both of whom were natives of Vermont. Shortly after their marriage the parents moved to Canada, where they engaged in farming and remained until their death. They belonged to the society of Friends. They had a family of eight children, seven of whom are now living— Austin, Phœbe, Hulda, Maria, Myron, Andrew and William H. Susan, the second child, is dead.

The subject of our sketch spent his younger days on the home farm and received his early training in Canada. On becoming of age he engaged in farming for himself and followed the same for seven years. At the end of that time he sold out and purchased another farm of one hundred acres near the city of London, where he engaged in farming for about seventeen years. He then sold out and removed to Strathroy, where he resided for two years. Then, in 1886, he came to Pipestone county and made his settlement, as stated in the opening lines of this sketch.

Mr. Orvis was united in marriage, in 1862, to Miss Miriam Linton, a native of Canada. She was the daughter of Isaac and Mary (Stavely) Linton, both natives of England. In about 1840 her parents came to America, and settled in Canada, where the father followed the boot and shoe business until his death, which occurred in 1847. The mother is still residing in Canada. In the Linton family there were five children : Isaac, Eliza, William, Miriam (now Mrs. Orvis) and John. The parents of this family were exemplary Christians and leading members of the Methodist Episcopal church. Mr. and Mrs. Orvis have two children: Charles W. and Mary E., both of whom have been thoroughly educated in a collegiate institution.

The subject of our sketch is a republican in politics, and himself and wife are members of the Methodist Episcopal church, of which our subject is a member of the board of trustees. He is a man of excellent judgment, a systematic farmer, and is one of the substantial citizens of Pipestone county. Of the farm where he now resides he owns eighty acres and his son about 120, Mr. Orvis, Sr., working the place.

ICHARD KENNEN, a thrifty and prosperous farmer and stock-raiser of Ash Lake township, Lincoln county, Minnesota, homesteaded his present land on the northeast quarter of section 28, September 16, 1879. He was one among the early settlers of the township, and took an active interest in public affairs connected with the organization and establishment of the local government. He commenced operations by building a small house, 12x16 feet, with ten-foot posts, and also a sod stable, 10x16 feet. This stable accommodated his stock for about two years, when he put up a good barn. The first work he did during the summer was to put up hay to the amount of about ten tons. He also planted about half a bushel of corn. This was done by cutting holes in the sod with an ax and dropping the corn into the holes thus made. This manner of planting prevented the gophers from destroying the corn before it sprouted. The first year brought our subject his first misfortune. After having stacked his hay, a prairie fire, which had been started by Rev. Mr. Wilson, destroyed his hay and came near destroying his house, too. His dwelling was partly completed, and in order to save it our subject had to plow a couple of furrows around the house some distance away. Mr. Kennen continued improving his farm, and the next year had four acres of a wheat crop, harvesting therefrom twenty-five bushels to the acre. He had also quite a quantity of potatoes and other crops. In 1880 he set out quite a grove of trees, cottonwood, etc., about his house.

Mr. Kennen was born in Upper Canada, September 15, 1852. His parents were James and Sarah (Moffett) Kennen, natives of the northern part of Vermont. They were farmers by occupation, and went to Canada in an early day. The mother died when our subject was about eight years old. In the father's family there were eight children—Anna, Mary, John, Jennie, Lizzie, Maggie, Richard and James. The first three are now dead. The parents were exemplary members of the Methodist Episcopal church.

Richard Kennen's early life, up to ten years of age, was spent by him in Canada, where he received his early education. When he was eight years of age, at the death of his mother, he went to live with his uncle, Richard Kennen, who had a family of twelve children. Our subject lived with this uncle some two years when he began to think that he was in the way. He brooded over this matter for some time and finally concluded to run away. He went to the station and wandered about the trains with his mind filled with an indefinite idea that by means of these cars he might reach some place where he was not in the way. He was told gruffly by several parties to stay away from the train, but he persisted and finally climbed up on the cow-catcher of the engine and rode to a place called Caledonia, where he hired out to a farmer and continued in that occupation for about two years. He was not well taken care of, however, was seriously abused and received no money remuneration for his work. So when two years had expired he went to an adjoining town, having been in hiding during the previous day in a hollow log. Reaching the village he remained in that vicinity for some three years, employed in work on a farm. When three years had expired he went back to where he was born in Canada, and during the summers, for some years, worked on a farm, and in the winter found employment in driving oxen in the pine woods. This occupied his time until coming to Lincoln county, Minnesota, in 1879.

Mr. Kennen was married September 18, 1879, to Miss Mary A. Marcellus. The wedding ceremony was performed by Rev. Wilson, mentioned in the early part of this sketch as having started a prairie fire which proved very destructive to the property of our subject. Mary Marcellus was a native of Dundas county, Upper Canada, where she was born April 8, 1846. She was the daughter of Gerred L. Marcellus, an old settler of Diamond Lake township, Lincoln county, of whom a biography is given in another department of this work. Miss Marcellus was reared in Canada until eighteen years of age, when she came with her parents to Minnesota, locating at Northfield, where she received her education. Mr. and Mrs. Kennen have one adopted son, Albert W. J. Mrs. Kennen is an exemplary Christian lady, and is a member of the Methodist Episcopal church.

—————•—•—❦❀❦—•—•—————

LEMUEL P. RICHARDSON is a leading farmer and stock-raiser of Selma township, Cottonwood county, Minnesota. He is the son of Thomas and Rachel Rebecca

(Smith) Richardson, natives of New York. Our subject was born in Brasier Falls, New York, November 9, 1848.

. When our subject was five years of age, the family moved to Berlin, Wisconsin, the mother dying after they had resided there a year. The father then bound our subject out to a Mr. Randall, with whom he lived a number of years. Mr. Randall lost his wife, married again, and again lost the second wife, and then broke up housekeeping, which obliged our subject to find a home with a brother, E. M. Randall. Our subject resided with this gentleman for two years, and then ran away and returned to his father's home, where he stayed for two years. Three years longer were spent in farm work for two farmers in his locality. He then purchased a team and wagon and came to Selma township, Cottonwood county, Minnesota, in 1871, locating 160 acres of land as a pre-emption. He soon paid for one-half of this land and homesteaded the other half. The first year he was here he did some breaking and the second year had a good crop. The third year the grasshoppers came and partially injured his crops. Since that time he has done fairly well and has accumulated considerable means, becoming quite well to do. In 1876 he sowed no crop, the following summer putting in a small acreage near Sleepy Eye. In 1877 he had a large yield. In 1878 he had heavy straw, but no grain to speak of on account of blight. For his wheat he obtained thirty-five cents a bushel.

Mr. Richardson was married in Sleepy Eye, Minnesota, March 16, 1876, to Miss Edna A. Larrabee, daughter of Alvah S. and Amy (Humphry) Larrabee, natives of New York and Vermont. This lady was born in Winnebago county, Wisconsin, April 27, 1858. Mr. and Mrs. Richardson have been blessed with the following children—Myrtle, Grace, Bert and Celia.

No man in the township takes a more active part in public matters than does our subject. He has been assessor and has held about all the township offices, and has been school clerk ever since the organization of the district. Commencing life as a poor orphan boy, he has by perseverance and continuous labor risen to extensive influence in his township, and has surrounded himself with circumstances betokening prosperity and success in life. On first coming to the township he was six miles from the nearest neighbor, and settled on the bare prairie. His home is now surrounded by a large grove of trees of his own planting. Mr. Richardson is a man of strong opinions, intelligent and progressive in his ideas, and is highly respected.

Richard Kennen is one of the representative citizens of Lincoln county, and is as well one of the most prominent and well-to-do citizens of his township. He has been highly successful in the management of his farm, and has accumulated considerable means. He has excellent lands, under good cultivation, and his farm is well supplied with good buildings. In politics he affiliates with the republican party, and has held several positions of responsibility in the gift of his fellow-citizens. While in Canada he was a member of the Orange lodge and also of the society of Young Britains, and wherever he has resided he has taken a prominent place among the people. He is a man of good character, excellent abilities, and is respected by all with whom he comes in contact.

SIMON F. STILSON is one of the best known citizens of the immediate vicinity of Jasper village, Pipestone county, Minnesota. The most of the town of Jasper is built on the farm owned by Mr. Stilson, and he has therefore been doubly interested in the development of the locality in which he resides. He located on his farm of 160 acres in 1880, and at once commenced making first-class improvements. He is a thorough and therefore a successful farmer, and has surrounded himself with the evidences of prosperity. He is the proprietor of the Stilson addition to the village.

Our subject is a native of Pennsylvania, where he was born in the year 1819. He was reared in the family of a farmer, his father following that occupation during the most of his life. The parents were, by name, Jacob and Marinda (Taylor) Stilson. Our subject came to the State of Indiana in the year 1829, at a time when there were but three white men in a large scope of country in the vicinity of South Bend. Continuing in that locality some five years, he then removed to Illinois. Thence, after a nine years' residence, he returned to Indiana. In 1850 he went to California, where, for four years, he worked in the gold mines and prospected among the mountains. Returning to Indiana he remained a short time, and then came to Minnesota, locating in Fillmore county, where he engaged in farming until coming to Pipestone county in the year 1880.

Mr. Stilson was united in marriage June 8, 1845, to Miss Nancy Henson, a native of Virginia, and a daughter of John and Elizabeth (Smith) Henson. By this union there have been ten children, seven of whom are now living — Martha E., now Mrs. Vickerman; Frances M., John, Mahala (also a Mrs. Vickerman), Alice, James and Schuyler.

The gentleman whose name appears at the head of this sketch is a man of wide influence in the locality in which he resides. His has been a long and checkered career, but it has not been devoid of success, nor of those things which bring honor and respectability in old age. Our subject has lived a long life of usefulness, and now enjoys a high degree of prosperity, which has come to him by virtue of his honorable life. He has been a successful farmer and pioneer of the Western country, and gold-miner of California, and wherever he has been, he has drawn to himself the respect and esteem of all with whom he has associated. He owns an excellent dwelling in Jasper.

EDWARD J. JAEGER, one of the prominent farmers of Bondin township, Murray county, Minnesota, is the son of John P. and Mary A. (Durr) Jaeger, natives of Germany. He was born in Milwaukee, Wisconsin, August 4, 1853.

In 1855, the family removed to Winnebago county, Wisconsin, where our subject remained with them, assisting in work on the farm and being given a good common-school education until he was eighteen years of age. At this time he learned the cooper's trade at Waukau, still returning home to assist his father during the harvest time until he became of age. On reaching twenty-one years of age our subject went with his brother, William W., to Berlin, where they purchased a cooper shop and operated it for five years. He then sold out to his brother and went to Neenah, where he purchased a dwelling and followed coopering until 1884, when he sold out and came to Murray county, Minnesota, and bought 160 acres of land on the southwest quarter of section 12, Bondin township. Here he built a good frame house and barn and has made that his home ever since. He has an excellent farm with about seventy-seven acres under cultivation. He also owns five horses and five head of cattle. When our subject began work for himself he had nothing, but by hard work and economical habits he has acquired all that he now has, and is in very comfortable circumstances. Mr. Jaeger has always taken an active interest in public matters of his township and county and has held the office of township supervisor one year, and chairman of the board of supervisors for one year in Bondin

township. While in Neenah, Wisconsin, he was on the police force. Mr. Jaeger is a man of good character and is an upright and reliable citizen.

November 15, 1876, the subject of our sketch was married to Miss Emma A. Morrison, daughter of John W. and Louisa (Dunton) Morrison, natives of Vermont. Miss Morrison was born in Winnebago county, Wisconsin, October 26, 1853. Her marriage also took place in that county, in the town of Omro. This union has been blessed with three children—Neil, Thadius, and Phillip.

GEORGE L. RICKERMAN, a prosperous farmer of Grange township, Pipestone county, Minnesota, resides on section 22, where he owns a good farm of 160 acres. Mr. Rickerman is of German birth, having first seen the light of day in Baden, Germany, November 12, 1843. His parents were also natives of Germany, and were George L. and Leaner (Calbruner) Rickerman. The family came to America in 1847, landed in New York City, and from thence went by way of the Erie canal and lake route to Milwaukee, Wisconsin. A sad misfortune overtook the family while on this trip in that the mother was drowned at Milwaukee, Wisconsin. The circumstances of her death were somewhat as follows: During the trip she was quite sick while the family were going up the Erie canal. The accident occurred at Milwaukee. It was nearly dark. Little thinking of the awful death that was before her, she started to walk on the dock to the shore. Suddenly the father and family, who were near at hand, heard a scream, and rushing forward found themselves stopped on the edge of the dock from which the mother had been plunged in the waters below. There they stood gazing into the thick darkness, but without result; no sight or sound of the mother could be obtained, and it became so intensely dark that search for the body was given up until the next day. The following day the body of the mother was found, and the family stopped long enough to lay the remains away in their final resting place. The family located at Rome, Jefferson county, Wisconsin, where the father purchased a piece of wild land and engaged in farming. He remained on that farm until his death in 1874.

The subject of our sketch cast his fortune with those of his father until late in the summer of 1864. Up to this time he had been occupying his time with work on the farm and in attending the district school as much as practicable during the winter months of each year. In September, 1864, he enlisted in Company C, Sixteenth Wisconsin Volunteer Infantry, and was discharged in June, 1865. His military life, although short, was full of privations, such as were experienced by nearly all volunteer soldiers. He was with Sherman on the march from Atlanta to the sea. He was sent from the Oka river to Beauford, South Carolina, where he became an inmate of the hospital and where he remained until sent to the U. S. Grant hospital in New York. After six weeks he was again sent to the front and remained with his regiment until the close of the war, being mustered out of the service at the city of Washington. Soon after he returned to his former home in Wisconsin. In 1866 he removed to Monroe county, same State, purchased a farm and engaged in farming on his own account. His residence in Monroe county was continued until 1884, when he went to Mauston, Juneau county, Wisconsin, and engaged in teaming for about four years. He then came to Pipestone county and purchased a farm where he now lives. He has 160 acres of good land and is successfully engaged in general farming and stock raising.

Mr. Rickerman was united in marriage April 23, 1864, to Jane Roassler, a daughter of John N. Roassler. Mr. and Mrs. Rickerman have been blessed with five children— Adelia, Emma, Elmer, Cora and Oliver, all of whom, except Emma, are still living.

The residence of the subject of our sketch in Grange township has as yet been brief, but he has proven himself an exemplary citizen and a man in whom much reliance can be placed. He has a thorough common-school education, is intelligent and widely read, and has a pleasant home. In the details of his farming interests he has been quite successful. In politics he affiliates with the republican party, and is a leading member of the Grand Army of the Republic. He is also identified with the Ancient Order of United Workmen, and has a hearty sympathy with all the movements tending to the betterment of the condition of the laboring man.

------ ◆ ◆ ◆ ------

DENNISON S. GREENMAN is a well-to-do farmer of Shetek township, Murray county, Minnesota, where he located a homestead on section 20, in about 1870. His settlement was made, however, three years previously, in 1867. At this time there were but four other settlers in the county : D. Haddock, Thomas Ireland and Messrs. Aldrich and Marsh. Our subject was the third to locate in the town. He commenced active operations, breaking ten acres and putting up a considerable amount of hay, and residing in a log house which was built by a man by the name of Myers some time before the Indian massacre. Throughout the succeeding years our subject worked hard to make his place one of the best in the township, and at this he has met with success. He owns an excellent farm under good cultivation and well provided with farm buildings. He was one of the very first settlers of the township, and underwent all the usual privations that come to the pioneer life. His market and postoffice were about seventy-five miles distant, at New Ulm. Many trips were made to this place under favorable circumstances, and more often under unfavorable circumstances. Mr. Greenman assisted in the organization of the township, and has held the office of school director of district No. 11 since its organization, holding that position at the present time. He has actively participated in all matters of a public nature, and has held various other local offices with great honor and credit. His farm is beautifully located on the shores of Lake Fremont, where his buildings are surrounded with a large grove of natural timber.

Mr. Greenman was born in Niagara county, New York, May 12, 1832. He was the son of William Greenman, a native of the State of New York, where for some years he followed agricultural pursuits. Removing from New York, the father settled in Illinois, whence, later, he went to Wisconsin, where he died. The mother's maiden name was Jane J. Johnson, a native of Vermont, where she was reared and educated. In the father's family there were ten children—Electa, Henry, Dennison C., James, John, Sarah, Mary, William, Alanson and Samuel.

Our subject followed his parents in their various moves from his native State to Illinois and thence to Wisconsin, receiving the educational advantages furnished by the district schools in those different States. He remained with his parents in Illinois some six years, and then located with them in Walworth county, Wisconsin, whence at the age of fifteen he went to Winnebago county. In March, 1865, he enlisted as a private in Company C, Fifty-third Wisconsin Volunteer Infantry. He was stationed at De Soto, Missouri, and for some time was sick and in the hospital at Fort Leavenworth, Kansas. He was discharged June 1, 1865. After his discharge he returned to Winnebago county, Wisconsin, and in May of the following year came to Murray county Minnesota, where he has since lived. Many misfortunes have fallen to his lot, but he has kept steadily at work, and in spite of all these backsets is now in good circumstances.

Mr. Greenman was married December 29, 1855, to Miss Emily Cook, who was born in Rutland county, Vermont, April 14, 1836. Her parents were Nicholas and Jemima (Maston) Cook, the former a native of Vermont, and the later a native of Maine. Her family emigrated to Wisconsin in an early day, where the father died in 1880. The mother died in Wisconsin in June, 1863. The parents were exemplary Christian people, and at their death were influential members of the Free-Will Baptist church. In the Cook family there were ten children— Mary, Harriet, Levi, Uriah, Caroline, Moses, Elzina, Leonard, Emily and Lydia. All of these are dead now except Emily, Uriah, Moses and Leonard. A biography of Moses is given in another department of this work. Mr. and Mrs. Greenman have seven children —Orville, Ida, Charles, Bert, Frankie, Carrie and Willis. Ida married Douglas Craig, who resided on a farm a short distance north of Tracy, Lyon county, this State.

The subject of our sketch is perhaps one of the best known and most influential citizens of the township. Having made his location in an early day, he has become intimately associated with the history of the township and county, and has always been a willing supporter of all projects which tended toward the development of his locality. In religious matters he is an earnest worker, and with one son belongs to the Methodist Episcopal church, of which society our subject is a class-leader.

MATTHEW M. GUNSOLUS is a reliable and prosperous farmer located in the southwest quarter of section twenty-eight, Osborn township, Pipestone county, Minnesota. Forty acres of this farm is located within the corporate limits of the village of Edgerton. Our subject came to Pipestone county in the fall of 1878, filed a soldier's warrant on his land and has made that his residence ever since. Our subject's family was the second to locate in the township and make a permanent residence. Others had come to the township prior to this time, but only one family had preceded Mr. Gunsolus in making a permanent settlement. Our subject is the oldest living resident settler of the township. His present dwelling-house, which is the best in the township, was built in 1883, and since that time he has been constantly adding to the improvements of his farm. He was one of the organizers of the county and the township, and was one of the leaders in the first township meeting, which was held in the first school-house built in the town. Ever since making his location in the township Mr. Gunsolus has been intimately identified with all matters of a public nature and has filled numerous official positions. His principal occupation has been that of farming, although considerable of his attention has been given to stock raising and dairying. He has a fine herd of Durham and Jersey cattle, and in 1888 his dairy turned out 1,600 pounds of cheese, all of which was disposed of in the home market.

Mr. Gunsolus is a native of Montgomery county, New York, where he was born December 12, 1833. He was the son of Matthew Emanuel and Sarah Jane Gunsolus. The father was a farmer by occupation and made his home in the State of New York throughout most of his life. He died June 13, 1886, in Steuben county, New York. The father was seventy-three years old when he died, and had been for many years a conscientious member of the Methodist Episcopal church. The subject of our sketch and his son attended his father during his last illness in answer to notification by telegram of the father's sickness unto death. The mother passed from this life in 1870. She was sixty-nine years of age at her death. In the father's family there were eight children— John Henry, Susan, George, Catharine, Mary, Tunis, Joseph and our subject. Of these there are but two living at the present time Matthew and his sister Susan.

The boyhood and early life of the subject of our sketch was spent in the state of his nativity at the home of his parents. His father being a farmer by occupation, Matthew followed in the same line of business throughout most of his life spent in New York. He received a good common-school education in the district schools. On reaching manhood he commenced work for himself, principally at farming, and continued his residence in his native State until he was twenty-five years of age, when he started westward on a trip of inspection through Michigan and Wisconsin. Remaining in Wisconsin until the breaking out of the war, he enlisted, in 1862, in the Thirty-third Wisconsin Volunteer Infantry, as a private. His part in the war was important, and all the duties which fell to his lot were well and thoroughly performed. Throughout his service he held the position of a non-commissioned officer, and when discharged was ranked as third sergeant of Company K. He was discharged at Vicksburg, Mississippi, and was mustered out of his regiment at Madison, Wisconsin, having passed a portion of his service under Captain Whicher, and also under Albert S. Sampson. The experience of our subject was of a severe and exciting nature, being spent mostly in hard fighting at the front. He participated in about thirty-eight battles and skirmishes, among them being the battles of Nashville, Kane river, Bolton, siege of Vicksburg, Black River bridge, Cold Harbor, Jackson, Hollow Springs, Pleasant Hill Landing, Tehola, Margo cross roads, Mobile, Spanish Fort, Jerry Run, Safolio river and Blakeley. The last battle in which he was engaged was at Fort Blakeley and the taking of Mobile, in which our subject saw much severe fighting. In the battle of Tehola the Rebel shot fell upon the Union lines like hail, and comrades on the right and left and in front, and, indeed, all about our subject, were struck down by the Rebel bullets. In this battle our subject narrowly escaped death, as it was found afterwards that there were nine bullet holes in his clothing. After his discharge from the service Mr. Gunsolus returned to Fond du Lac county, Wisconsin, and for a short time stopped at Rosendale. From Wisconsin he removed to Waseca county, Minnesota, in about 1865, pre-empted government land and made that his home until coming to Pipestone county in 1878.

Mr. Gunsolus was married on the 9th day of March, 1858, to Miss Mary M. Brooks, a native of Madison county, New York, where she was reared and educated. Mr. and Mrs. Gunsolus have three children, one daughter and two sons—Melissa E., married to Charles E. Hathaway, now a resident of Spencer, Wisconsin; Guy T., married to Miss Josephine Keating, and now a resident of Minneapolis; and Roy E., aged sixteen and still living with his parents.

Our subject is one of the most enterprising citizens of the township, and has always taken a lively interest in matters pertaining to the public welfare. He has always been a stanch republican in politics, and on the organization of that party, voted for its first candidate, John C. Fremont. In the later history of Pipestone county he has been quite prominent in matters pertaining to the official government thereof, and has held several positions of trust and responsibility. At present he is township treasurer, to which office he was elected in 1888. He was the first clerk of the school board in the township, being elected in 1879, one year later being succeeded by Major Runals. He also holds the office of street commissioner, to which he was elected in 1888. In these matters, and also in all those things which tend to the elevation of the morals of his fellow men, he takes an active and influential part. With his family, he is a member of the Methodist Episcopal church, of which society he has held the office of treasurer since its organization. He also holds the offices of trustee and steward of his church. In educational matters he is also a leading spirit, and was one of the promulgators of the plan of erection of the village school house, being a member of the building committee appointed for the purpose of overseeing its construction. He is a stanch temperance man, and has been actively engaged in fighting the saloon element during his entire residence here. In Grand Army of the Republic circles he occupies a prominent place, and has held the office of quartermaster of the post since its organization up to January 1, 1889, at which time he was elected commander, being the present incumbent of that office. Mr. Gunsolus is a man of strictest integrity, has been prospered in all his business operations, and is one of the representative citizens of the township.

———◆◆———

WESLEY E. STODDARD, a prosperous farmer of Amboy township, Cottonwood county, Minnesota, located on section 20, July 1, 1878. His native village was Monroe, Erie county, New York, where his birth took place April 2, 1850. His father was Emory D. Stoddard, a native of Connecticut and a farmer by occupation throughout the most of his life. In the fall of 1863, after having spent some years in New York and Michigan, he came to Blue Earth county, Minnesota, and located near Mankato. He resided on a farm at Winnebago Agency until his death, which occurred in 1872. He was a man of high character, and a member of the Methodist Episcopal church. Our subject's mother's maiden name was Frances Wright; she was born in Massachusetts and died in St. Joseph county, Michigan, in 1858. She was a member of the Methodist church. At the date of the mother's death there were in the father's family five children—Otis, Sarah Frances, Wesley E., George Washington and Darwin. In 1860 the father married Mrs. Eliza (Barns) Robison, and this marriage was blessed with five children—Warren, Elmer, Alice, Emerson B. and Arvilla.

Our subject's parents left New York in about 1854 and went to Newaygo county, Michigan, where the father engaged in lumbering for some three years. At the end of that time, in about the spring of 1857, nearly all his personal property was destroyed by fire. The family then went to St. Joseph county, same State, whence, in the summer of 1863, the family came by team to Blue Earth county, Minnesota. They were on the road some six weeks and during this time camped out along the way. On reaching Blue Earth county, the father made his location as has already been stated.

The subject of our sketch received the main part of his education in Blue Earth county, and at eighteen years of age left home and commenced working out at farm work, spending some two years in Steele county, Minnesota. He then returned to his father's farm and remained nearly a year, after which he went to the pineries in Wisconsin. Four years were spent in lumbering and then our subject came to Minnesota, spending some time in Waseca, Blue Earth and Le Sueur counties, engaged in farming.

In 1878 he went from Le Sueur county to Cottonwood county, and located on his present farm. He has been a hard working man, and has been engaged in farming and stockraising with good success. He has a fine farm of 160 acres and has about thirteen acres of it in a grove of trees—cottonwood, maple, willow, black ash and butternuts. Mr. Stoddard affiliates with the republican party in politics and is one of Cottonwood county's representative citizens. He has been quite successful in his various enterprises since locating in Amboy township; has become quite well to do, and has surrounded himself with evidences of prosperity and success.

DANIEL F. FOWSER is a prosperous farmer residing on section, 4 Slayton township, Murray county, Minnesota. The place of his nativity is to be found in Lockport township, Will county, Illinois, where he was born November 21, 1856. His parents were Joseph J. and Esther (Ream) Fowser, both born in Ohio. The father was a farmer by occupation, and settled in Illinois in 1854, becoming one of the pioneers of that State. He had a family of eight children, of whom our subject was the oldest son.

During the winter months of his early life, our subject attended the district school and at other times assisted his father in work on the home farm, continuing in his birth-place until he was twenty-one years of age. For one year after that time he found employment on the home farm, and at twenty-three years of age was married and took charge of a part of the home farm, his brother, E. T. Fowser, farming a part for four years, after which our subject operated it all alone until 1887. In March of that year the father sold the farm, and the family came to Murray county, Minnesota, where the father still lives. He is now living a retired life in the village of

Slayton. Our subject located on section 4, where he has an excellent form of 160 acres of land provided with what are considered the best buildings in the township. Since making his location here he has engaged principally in farming, but is now turning his attention to raising blooded horses, and also has an interest in an imported shire stallion.

Mr. Fowser was married February 27, 1879, to Miss Henrietta Gardner, a native of Ohio. This union has been blessed with four children—Clayton G., Loyd F., Grace V. and Mabel M. Our subject's wife was a daughter of Martin and Henrietta (Dhuey) Gardner, who were natives of Germany. In their early married life her parents came to the United States and located in Ohio, where their daughter was born, June 13, 1854. Later they removed to Lockport township, Will county, Illinois, where they both died — Mrs. Gardner August 24, 1882, and Mr. Gardner March 30, 1888.

In politics the subject of our sketch affiliates with the republican party, and has served his constituents in various capacities since coming to the township. He is a man of excellent qualities, and is highly respected by his fellow-citizens. He now holds the office of school director in the district in which he resides.

OLE SIVERSON is a thrifty and reliable farmer and stock raiser of Marble township, Lincoln county, Minnesota, and is located on section 24, where he settled in 1870. His settlement was made before the land was surveyed and he filed homestead papers on his farm June 7, 1873. He was the first actual settler in the township, and it was then twenty-two miles to the nearest neighbor. His nearest market was New Ulm, to which place he had to go to obtain flour and provisions. He assisted in the organization of the township and served on the first board of supervisors, being a member of that body for two years. He also served as a member of the second board elected, and is at present treasurer of school district No. 48, which position he has held since its organization. It will be seen by this official record, that Mr. Siverson has taken a prominent place in the history of local government and has accomplished much toward the correct manipulation of local affairs. The first year of his settlement in the township he broke two acres of land, built a log house 14x14 feet, in which he lived some nine or ten years, and at the end of that time he built his present commodious farm-house. The first year he also built a log stable and used this for his stock for some two years. He then built a larger stable of logs and used that for stabling purposes until in 1885, when he built his present good barn. Since coming to the county he has been extensively and successfully engaged in general farming and stock-raising and has accumulated a good fortune.

The subject of our sketch is a native of Christiania, Norway, where he was born January 13, 1842. His parents were Siver and Bertha (Erickson) Peterson, both of whom were natives of the old country. The father died some years ago and the mother is still living in Norway. In the father's family there were seven children—Peter Erick, Rachel, Ole, Mary, Ole and Hans. Mary and Erick are both dead; Mary passed from this life when she was about seven weeks old.

The subject of our sketch remained with his parents in the old country engaged in farming until 1868. He was given good educational advanges and acquired a good common-school education. In 1868 he left his native land, came to America and located in Goodhue county, Minnesota. After working out on a farm in that county for two years, he then came to his present location, where he has since lived. In politics our subject has affiliated for some years with the republican party and takes an active place in the local counsels of that organization. He is a man of good ability, a systematic farmer, and has met with success in all his various enterprises. He is a leading member of the Lutheran church, of which he has been treasurer and trustee for some years.

Mr. Siverson was married in March, 1870, to Miss Kate Sorenson, a native of Norway. This lady came to America when she was sixteen years of age and settled in Goodhue county, Minnesota, where she first met Mr. Siverson. This union has been blessed with ten children— Siver, Charles, Barney, Sophia, Edward, Mary, Martin, Carrie, Lena and another Edward. The first Edward died when four years of age. Mr. Siverson has a pleasant and hospitable home, and is one of the leading farmers of Lincoln county.

---※◆◎◆※---

M ICHAEL CULLEN, one of the most prosperous farmers of Bondin township, Murray county, Minnesota, is the son of Patrick and Mary (Flynn) Cullen, natives of Ireland. He was born in Thell township, County of Sligo, Ireland, September 26, 1852.

When our subject was three years old his father died, but he remained with his mother until her second marriage, which took place when he was seven years of age. From this time until he was seventeen he lived part of the time with her and part with a brother, Martin, occupying his time in farm work and in attending the national schools. At the age just mentioned he came to the United States, first stopping in Brooklyn, New York, where for one year he worked for the city council on public works. He then found employment with Robbins & Appleton, of Bond street, New York, general agents for the American Watch Company, of Waltham, Massachusetts. For one year he acted as porter for this company, and then learned the trade of assaying, smelting and refining of gold and silver, and for nearly seven years thereafter filled the position of assayer and refiner of gold and silver for Messrs. Robbins & Appleton. In the fall of 1875 he was sent by the Walton Gold Mining Company (of which company Messrs. Robbins & Appleton were large shareholders) to experiment on ores with mercury at their mines in Louisa county, Virginia. From there he was sent on a like errand to Enfield, North Carolina. He then returned to New York, and the following June was again sent to the Virginia mines as expert examiner. He remained there until he finished his assays; he then returned to New York and resumed his position of refiner until the spring of 1879, when, on the advice of a physician, he resigned on account of poor health, and came to Minnesota, where his health has been very good. The subject of our sketch came to Murray county, Minnesota, in May, 1879, and took railroad land under contract, on which he lived ten months, and then sold his improvements and moved to a homestead on section 10, Bondin township. He had taken this homestead while residing on the railroad land, and here his residence has since been permanent. When our subject landed in New York he had but little over three dollars in his pocket, but by the labor of his own hands, together with economical habits and good business abilities, he has accumulated a very fair property. He now owns 160 acres of good land, with about ninety acres under cultivation, and provided with a good frame house and barn. He also owns three horses, twenty-three head of cattle and all the machinery he needs. In politics the subject of our sketch affiliates with the democratic party. He is a member of the Ancient Order of Hibernians and of the Catholic church. Mr. Cullen is a man of good character, and is respected and esteemed as a man and citizen. New York

City was the place of the marriage of our subject, where he was united in matrimony, May 16, 1877, by the Rev. Father Keane, in St. Patrick's Cathedral, to Miss Annie Wynne, daughter of John and Mary (Cullen) Wynne. She was born in the village of Keadue, County of Roscommon, Ireland, September 24, 1856. The fruits of this union are five children— Mary, Martin, Charles, John and Michael.

Mr. Cullen was a member of the special commissioners appointed by Governor Hubbard in 1885 to take testimony as to the charge of malfeasance in office preferred by the county commissioners against the clerk of district court of Murray county.

WHEELER NISBET resides on an excellent farm of 160 acres on section 28, Sweet township, Pipestone county, Minnesota. He has been identified with the interests of the township since 1880, and has become quite influential and made many warm friends.

Mr. Nisbet was born in Oneida county, New York State, March 30, 1849. He is a son of William and Catharine (Fox) Nisbet, the former a native of Massachusetts and a farmer by occupation, and the mother a native of New York. The ancestors on the father's side were natives of Scotland, the grandfather having come from that country to America early in the present century. The mother's parents were natives of Germany. The father resided in New York State, engaged in farming, until his death, which occurred August 11, 1869. In the father's family there were seven children, five sons and two daughters. Three of the sons and one daughter are now located in Watertown, Dakota Territory, where they are engaged in farming. One son, Harrison, died in the army, and the other daughter died in New York.

The subject of our sketch remained on the home farm during his early life, and at the time of the father's death took charge of the farming interests of the family. Up to this time he had received a good education, and had rendered assistance to his father at farm work. He was twenty-one years of age when the farm came under his management, and he successfully operated it for about one year. He then came to the State of Minnesota, settling in Pipestone county, where he now lives.

March 20, 1878, Mr. Nisbet was united in marriage to Helen C. Furguson, a native of the State of New York. Her father's occupation was that of a farmer, and they are now residents of Pipestone county, where her father lives on a fine farm of 160 acres.

In politics Mr. Nisbet is a supporter of the principles promulgated by the republican party. He has been a member of the board of supervisors for five years, during three years of which time he was chairman of that body. Mr. Nisbet is a man of good education, is a good citizen, and is respected by all with whom he has to do.

MADS JORGENSON is a prominent farmer of Westbrook township, Cottonwood county, Minnesota, and resides on section 24. The place of his nativity is in Denmark, where he was born in May, 1849. His parents, Jorg and Mary (Mattison) Jenson, were natives of Denmark, and resided in that country until their death, the mother dying in 1856, and the father in 1882. The father was a carpenter by trade, and in connection with that business owned and operated a farm.

The early life of the subject of our sketch was spent in assisting on the home farm, and in attending the public schools. On attaining the age of seventeen years he commenced work for himself, and emigrated to America in 1874, locating in Freeborn county, Minnesota. Here our subject engaged in agricultural pursuits for five years, and then removed to Westbrook township, Cottonwood county, where he purchased another settler's right to the claim of 160 acres, on which he now lives. He has been hard at work improving his farm, and his industry has made his place one of the best in the township. It is provided with a good frame dwelling-house, good granary, barns and other outbuildings. His house is surrounded with a fine grove of trees of three acres in extent. In connection with farming Mr. Jorgenson is also raising Durham cattle. Our subject is a man of strong temperance sentiments, and affiliates with the prohibition party. He is a member of the Baptist church, and stands high in the esteem of his fellow-citizens.

Mr. Jorgenson was married in the year 1873 to Miss Mary Paulson. This union has been blessed with the following children—Annie, Sarah, George, Edward, Walter, Ludvig, Martin Johan, Lanvris and Sine Martina.

CHARLES LANE, a leading farmer of Royal township, located on section 29, March 12, 1881, and since that time has been a permanent resident of Lincoln county, Minnesota. He is a son of Thomas and Charlotte (Williams) Lane, natives of England. The parents were farmers by occupation, and in early life left their native land and came to America, locating in the State of New York.

Charles Lane was born in Brownsville, Jefferson county, New York, May 11, 1838, and spent his early life on the farm of his parents. He was given a good common-school education and resided in his native county until he was married.

The subject of our sketch was married in Henderson, Jefferson county, New York,

February 3, 1860, to Miss Alice P. Eggleston, daughter of Albert and Betsey Ann (Mattison) Eggleston, natives of New York. Miss Eggleston was born in Jefferson county, New York, June 30, 1843. Mr. and Mrs. Lane have been blessed with five children—Mary V., Floyd (deceased), Matthew A., Earl D., and Walter H.

The early life of the subject of our sketch was spent entirely for the benefit of his parents. Whenever he earned anything he turned it into their hands for the support of the family. Therefore, when he left home he had no means whatever. His parents were unable to give him any assistance, and he had to depend on his own efforts to work his way through life. But being possessed of an energetic spirit, economical habits and a determination to carve out for himself success he commenced work and has gradually grown from extremely straitened circumstances to an honorable position among the well-to-do and substantial farmers of Lincoln county. When he made his location in Royal township he found but very few neighbors and had to undergo many hardships and rough experiences so often found in the life of an early settler. There was but little to do save in the way of breaking his ground and preparing it for the first year's crop, and his location was made without a dollar in his pocket and with a family of five children to support. He had scarcely any provisions and no money to purchase them with. A few potatoes, and that few very small, became the staple article of their diet, and our subject had a terrible fit of the blues for some time. However, he soon found a friend who was willing to give him a little help in the way of work, and our subject eagerly took hold of whatever he could find to do. Perseverance and continual work accomplished the end he desired, and although those hard times are often remembered with something of bitterness, yet at the same time it proved an experience which cultivated in him those habits that have materially assisted in building up his present good circumstances. Society there was none in those early days, as neighbors were far distant. Markets were also long distances away, and our subject relates many instances when he has gone to market with an ox team a distance of some eighteen or twenty miles. Mr. Lane has met with some financial reverses, and has lost stock and grain to the amout of at least five hundred dollars since locating in the county. His severest and saddest loss, however, was the death of his son Floyd, who had almost attained to manhood and was the pride of the family. This young man died after a brief illness of only eighteen hours. Although these hardships, misfortunes and losses have been of a very severe nature, time has contributed largely to the healing of the wounds, and our subject's family have been steadily growing in prosperity, until to-day they are among the most well-to-do farmers in the county. Mr. Lane is a man of careful, systematic habits, is a thorough farmer, and last year raised a crop which netted him something over a thousand dollars. He has now a fine farm of 160 acres, well provided with a good frame dwelling-house and other out-buildings. He has three yoke of oxen, three cows, and numerous head of young cattle, as well as various kinds of farm implements, so necessary on a large farm.

———————

LEARNED COBURN is a reliable and well-to-do farmer of Belfast township, Murray county, Minnesota. He was born in East Montpelier, Vermont, April 2, 1852. His parents were James A. and Abbie (Dagget) Coburn, natives of Vermont. The parents were farmers by occupation and were well-to-do people of the locality in which they lived.

The early life of the subject of our sketch was spent on the home farm with his parents. He was given a good common-school education and when sixteen years of age attended the academy at Barre, Vermont. The principal part of two winters was spent in that institution. The balance of the time until he was twenty-one years old was spent by him in the home of his parents. He then lived with his mother's people for two years, and assisted them in operating their farm, receiving as compensation a part of the products of the harvests. At the end of these two years he went to North Montpelier and opened and started a cheese factory in company with Marcus Peck, of Brookfield, that State. After operating this factory for two years our subject sold out his interest to his brother, Arthur D., and then purchased a farm in the vicinity of Barre. He engaged in agricultural pursuits for four years, and then, selling out, took a trip through the far west, seeking a new location. He spent two months in Montana and then returned as far as Fargo, Dakota, making up his mind to locate there. In the spring of 1883 he took his family to that city and intended to reside there and work at the carpenter trade. Times, however, were somewhat dull and little work could be obtained. Remaining until fall he then came to Murray county, Minnesota, and took charge of the farm of his uncle, Lewis L. Coburn. This farm was composed of between forty-seven and forty-eight hundred acres of land. Our subject built several buildings on this farm and rented small portions to various parties. He is now located on 700 acres of this property where he has excellent buildings, a large frame house and three barns, one 48x100 feet, another 48x48 feet and the third 18x32 feet. The house is 24x36 feet, all thoroughly finished and nicely painted. He has the land on the section in which these buildings are located, and is also general manager of the entire farming interests of his uncle. He received a good salary for managing this immense business.

Mr. Coburn was married in Calais, Vermont, September 3, 1873, to Miss Corrie E. Bennett, born in the place of her marriage, February 20, 1854, and a daughter of Charles S. and Caroline E. (Le Barron) Bennett. Her parents were natives of Vermont and farmers by occupation. Mr. and Mrs. Coburn have been blessed with the following children—Charles Fred, Blanche May, Cassius Lee (who died at Fargo) and Anna Bessie.

Being possessed of excellent business qualifications, and of broad, progressive ideas, our subject has become one of the leading spirits in all matters pertaining to the public welfare of his township. He takes an active part in political matters and has held various offices. He is a man of excellent education, and after quitting his course in the academy in the East, taught school for some four terms. He is a member of the lodge of Ancient Free and Accepted Masons of Fulda, and has been worshipful master to that lodge ever since its organization in July, 1886. He is quite prominent in the counsels of this civic society, and has represented his lodge at two sessions of the grand lodge. He has taken the Royal Arch degree, and January 8, 1889, he had the thirty-second degree in that order conferred upon him.

CHARLES M. PEASE is one of the most highly esteemed and reliable farmers of Burke township, Pipestone county, Minnesota. He homesteaded his present farm on section 18, in 1884, since which time he has been occupied in thoroughly improving his land. The subject of our sketch was born in Whitewater, Walworth county, Wisconsin, December 9, 1862. When he was about two years of age the parents removed to Freeport, Illinois, where they lived some ten years. Here Charles received the foundation of his education, being given good educational advantages in the district schools. Later he went to DeWitt county, in the same State, where he completed his education at the age of eighteen years. At this time he removed with his parents to Pipestone county, Minnesota, where he has since lived.

Charles M. Pease is the son of Henry W. Pease, one of the first settlers of Gray township, Pipestone county. The father located on section 24, of that township, in May, 1878, and continued his residence in the county until his death, which occurred in Pipestone city, January 28, 1888. His death was brought about by pneumonia after he had been sick but about ten days. The father was one of the most prominent citizens of the township, and assisted in the organization of the same in the spring of 1879. He was a strong republican in politics, and was a justice of the peace for one year, having also held other offices within the gift of his fellow-citizens. In religious matters he was an enthusiastic worker, and was a member of the Methodist Episcopal church. He was ordained as a minister in that organization at the annual conference held in St. Paul in 1874. He held several charges and continued his ministerial work for about eight years. He was a man of high Christian character, a good preacher, and accomplished a great amount of good in the various fields of labor to which he was sent. His last charge was the Luverne circuit, which he left in 1880. The father was a native of the State of New York, where he was born January 11, 1827, the place of his nativity being in Charlotte, Chittendon county. In that locality he was reared and educated, and remained until he was twenty-two years of age. He was given the privileges of the district school, and acquired a thorough common-school education. His father was a farmer, and his early life was spent more or less at farm work. In 1840 Henry W. Pease removed to Illinois, where he remained for some years. Removing thence, he settled in Wisconsin, and, after a few years' location there, returned to the State of Illinois. He made Illinois his home, until he came to Minnesota, in 1873, in which year he located in Minneapolis and found employment as a carriage painter. The following year, in 1874, he commenced his ministerial duties, in which he continued some eight years, as has already been related. In 1878 he located in Pipestone county, where he lived principally until his death.

Henry W. Pease was married May 14, 1848, to Miss Louisa L. Macomber, who was a native of Essex county, New York, where she was reared and educated. The fruits of this marriage were ten children, seven of whom are living—Eugene, Fred, Charles M. (whose name appears at the head of this sketch), William, Abraham, Leonard and Mamie. The father was a man of excellent character, and stood high in the esteem of his fellow-townsmen. He was a Royal Arch Mason.

Charles M. Pease is one of the representative citizens of his township. He is a young man of acknowledged ability and highest integrity. He has been quite successful in his farming operations and has accumulated considerable means. He takes an active part in public matters, and holds the esteem of all who know him.

G EORGE GATES is one of the leading residents of Moulton township, Murray county, Minnesota, and has an excellent farm located on section 30. The place of his nativity is Schoharie county, New York, where he was born January 23, 1817. His parents were Oldham and Mehit-able (Hatfield) Gates, the father a native of Massachusetts and the mother a native of New York. Throughout his life the father was by occupation a farmer. He died in New York State in 1828. The mother died in Wisconsin in 1876.

After the death of his father our subject removed to Jefferson county, New York. He then lived with his grandparents four years, after which he went to live with an uncle, with whom he lived until attaining his majority. Early in 1838 our subject entered the Gouverneur Wesleyan Seminary, in St. Lawrence county, New York. He attended this school summers and taught school winters until 1840, when he received a diploma from that seminary. This diploma was signed by Jesse T. Peck, its honored principal, and since one of the most able and honored bishops of the Methodist Episcopal church. In 1840 our subject removed to Watertown, New York, and engaged in teaching school, remaining in that vicinity for five years. In 1845 he removed to Wisconsin, and remained in Racine one year, then settling on Hart Prairie, Walworth county, Wisconsin. During 1846 he bought some government land in Fond du Lac county, but remained in Walworth county until 1849. During this year he settled on his farm in Fond du Lac county, and made that his home until 1866, when he came to Fillmore county, Minnesota, purchased a farm, and, in connection with its operation, engaged in teaching during the winter months. In 1878 he located a farm in Pipestone county and then returned to Fillmore county, remaining there until 1880. He then came to his farm in Pipestone county and made that his home until 1883. His family joined him on the farm in 1882, and in 1883 he located on the place where he now lives in Murray county.

Mr. Gates was married April 14, 1850, to Adeline M. Phelps, a daughter of Milo and

Wealthy (Kellogg) Phelps, natives of the State of New York. In early life her parents moved to the State of Ohio, where she was born, September 25, 1825. Mr. and Mrs. Gates have been blessed with five children, three of whom are now living. They have twelve grandchildren.

In politics the gentleman whose name appears at the head of this sketch affiliates with the republican party. During the last presidential campaign he was one of the most earnest supporters of President Harrison, having had the honor of voting for his illustrious ancestor. Our subject is a man of advanced age and is wonderfully preserved. His mind is yet strong, as is also his physical organism. He is a man of extensive knowledge, having in early life obtained a thorough education, and having added thereto by careful reading. His character both as a citizen and as a neighbor is beyond reproach and he is held in high esteem by all with whom he has to do. He is a stanch supporter of all temperance movements, and is a member of the Sons of Temperance. He has taught school thirty-six winter terms.

WHEELOCK HUBBELL is a prosperous farmer who resides on section 4 of Rose Hill township, Cottonwood county, Minnesota. He was born December 16, 1857, in the State of Wisconsin.

The parents of the subject of our sketch were Silas and Eliza (Clement) Hubbell, natives of Canada, who moved to Wisconsin in 1838, locating in Rock county and engaging in farming. The next move was to Dodge county, whence they went to Winneshiek county, Iowa. The father died in Spring Valley, Minnesota, in March, 1887.; the mother is now living, and is a resident of section 4, Rose Hill township. Our subject was one of nine children—Abner (de-

ceased), Maria, Ella, Charles O., Ira, John, Annie, Wheelock and Amos E.

Mr. Hubbell was reared as a farmer's boy and attended the common schools during the winter months of each year until he was sixteen years of age. He then commenced learning the trade of blacksmithing in the shop of his brothers, Charles and Ira. After learning the trade he removed to Lansing, Iowa, where he remained a year, after which he went to Winneshiek county, whence he came to his present place. He has a fine farm, part of which was taken as a tree claim and part as a pre-emption in 1878. He also owns a comfortable house and good barns. Three years of his time since coming to Minnesota was spent in Windom, where he worked at his trade. At present he has a blacksmith shop on his farm and works more or less at his trade in connection with his farming. Mr. Hubbell is a man of strong opinions, of progressive ideas, and is one of the active public men of the township. He is a genial, warm-hearted gentleman, and is respected and esteemed by all his fellow-citizens.

Mr. Hubbell was married in Frankville, October 12, 1879, to Miss Bessie Allen, daughter of H. B. Allen, now a prominent resident of the village of Swan, Marion county, Iowa. Mr. and Mrs. Hubbell have two children—Grant A., born October 13, 1880, and Roby May, born November 5, 1887.

Z BAILEY, a retired citizen and influential resident of the village of Verdi, Lincoln county, Minnesota, was born in the State of Massachusetts, October 30, 1834.

The parents of the subject of our sketch were George T. and Martha (Smith) Bailey, both of whom were natives of England. The father was a shoemaker by trade, and followed that occupation throughout his life.

His parents were also natives of England. In 1833 the father came to America, settling for a time in Massachusetts, from whence he removed to Hudson city on the Hudson river, in about 1835. This place was made their home until in about 1844. At this time the mother died, and the father and family for some years lived a kind of roving life, spending brief periods in various places in the Eastern States. In 1848 the father went to Corning, in New York State, where he purchased property, built a house, and has remained until the present time.

The subject of our sketch remained in New York State until he was twenty-one years of age, up to which time he had been moving about with his father and had received his education in the common schools. He then came to the State of Wisconsin, locating in the vicinity of Melrose, where he purchased a farm of one hundred acres and engaged in agricultural pursuits until 1877. He then came by team to the State of Minnesota, arriving in Marshall, Lyon county, whence he went to Verdi township and took a homestead on section 32. Here he followed the life of an agriculturist for some three years, broke a number of acres of land and put it under good cultivation. After this time had expired he sold out and removed to the village of Verdi, where he established a grocery business. This business he continued to operate until early in 1889, when he sold out to Messrs. Cleveland & Merrill, who are now engaged in its operation. Since this time the subject of our sketch has retired from active business life, and has been enjoying the results of a long life of thrift and industry. The life of our subject has not been devoid of military experience, and he was willing to prove his loyalty to his native land by enlisting in the Union army. August 14, 1862, he joined Company F, Twenty-fifth Wisconsin Volunteer Infantry, and continued

in the service until the 28th of December, 1863. He participated in the siege of Vicksburg, and saw service in numerous other severe engagements. He was afflicted to a great extent with dropsy and rheumatism, and spent some time in various hospitals. He was in Benton Barracks, Missouri, for some time, whence he was honorably discharged.

Mr. Bailey was united in the bonds of matrimony June 13, 1857, to Catharine J. House, a native of Cortland county, New York. This lady was a daughter of George House, a native of New York. This union has been blessed with the following named children—Mattie, Frankie, Dora, Katie, William, and Mary (now deceased).

While a resident of Verdi township, our subject took an active part in all public matters. He affiliates with the republican party, and has with credit and honor filled various official positions. He was the first chairman of the board of supervisors, holding that position for two terms. He was treasurer of the township for one term, and is at present justice of the peace, having held the latter position for ten years. He has been postmaster of Verdi for some five years. By virtue of his military career and honorable discharge he has held an influential position in the Old Abe Post, No. 39, Grand Army of the Republic, of Lake Benton, of which he has been commander. Mr. Bailey is a man of broad ideas, of thorough and varied experience in the practical things of life, and is possessed of an extensive store of general knowledge. In his early life he received a good common-school education, to which he has been constantly adding by private study and extensive reading. He is well posted in the general history of the country, and is in considerable demand as an orator on 4th of July occasions. Being possessed of excellent practical ideas, he takes a leading place in the business affairs of his village and wields a strong influence for the improvement and welfare of his village. He is a man of high character, and is widely respected as a man and citizen.

OHN J. MIHIN is a well-to-do farmer residing on section 32, Lowville township, Murray county, Minnesota. He was born in McHenry county, Illinois, August 23, 1856. His parents were Michael and Mary (Hourigan) Mihin, both of whom were natives of Ireland. The father followed agricultural pursuits in his native land until 1849, when he came to America, locating in the State of New York. Some time later and before the birth of our subject, he moved to the State of Illinois. In about 1861 the family removed to Winona county, Minnesota, where they were among the pioneer settlers in that locality and where the mother died a few years later. Remaining in Winona county until 1866, the father then removed to Wabasha county, where he engaged in farming until 1872, when he located on a homestead in Murray county. He is at present residing with his son John J.

The subject of our sketch remained with his parents throughout his early life, following them in their various moves and engaging with them in farming in Winona and Wabasha counties. In these localities he was given a good common-school education, and continued his residence there until his marriage. After the age of fourteen years, however, he did not spend much time with his parents, but resided in their immediate vicinty. After his marriage he came to Murray county and located the claim on which he now lives. He has taken an active part in the public matters of his township, and has affiliated with the democratic party. He has filled many official positions, among them being that of supervisor and school director. He is a man of good business qualifications, has 240 acres of land under good cultivation, and provided with good farm buildings.

Mr. Mihin was married, November 21, 1881, to Miss Katie Ryan, a daughter of James and Ellen (Welch) Ryan, natives of Ireland. Miss Ryan's parents came to America in an early day, locating in Minnesota, where she was born. Three children have blessed this union —Mary E., Clara A. and John F.

Mr. Mihin was nominated for sheriff by the democratic county convention in the fall of 1888, and received a large vote, but was defeated, the county being republican by too heavy a majority to overcome.

AMUEL AVERY, a thrifty and energetic farmer and stock raiser, is located on an excellent farm on section 28, Gray township, Pipestone county, Minnesota. He homesteaded his land in 1879, and by careful attention to the details of his occupation he has made his farm what it is, one of the best in the township. He was one of the early settlers, and has been identified with the interests of his locality ever since his location. He assisted in the organization of the township, and was one of the first supervisors, which office he has held twice since. He has also been assessor for two terms, and also treasurer of district No. 25 since its organization. He was instrumental in having his school district set off, and has always been willing to serve in any official capacity where his services were needed.

Mr. Avery was born in Lewis county, New York, January 13, 1824. His parents, Joseph and Clara (Truax) Avery, were natives of the same State. In early life the parents settled in Lewis county, and made that their home for thirty-five years, rearing and educating their family in that place. The father was engaged in diversified occupations; he was a farmer, and besides that was engaged in running a saw-mill and owned a lime-kiln. He continued in these occupations throughout his life until his death, which occurred in 1869. The mother died in 1865. She was an exemplary Christian and a member of the Methodist Episcopal church. The subject of our sketch was one of eleven children, and was the fifth in order of birth. The names of the children in the parents' family were Jacob, Lydia, Sallie Ann, Mary, Samuel, Deborah, George, Martha, John, Elizabeth and a child that died when quite young.

The subject of our sketch was reared and educated by his parents in the county of his nativity in New York. He remained with his parents, serving them, and being given good educational advantages until he had attained the age of twenty-one years. At this age he was married, and engaged in work for himself, principally following the carpenter's trade, but to some extent engaged in the occupation of farming. After his marriage he settled in Oswego, remaining there a few years. After this he removed to Winnebago county, Wisconsin, where he settled on a farm, and, as we have already stated, engaged to a great extent in work at the carpenter's trade. He continued this line of work until the opening of the war, when he enlisted in the Forty-eighth Wisconsin Volunteer Infantry as a private, being soon after promoted to the rank of corporal, and as such being discharged January 6, 1866. The war experience of the subject of our sketch had to do with many different localities, and he was moved from place to place, guarding army stores and rebel prisoners, and later being sent out on the plains to assist in protecting the settlers from Indian raids. His company was under the command of Captain Charles Felker, who was in command most of the time while our subject was in the service. For a period he was with his regiment in Kansas, guarding property at Fort Scott.

From thence he was removed to Fort Riley, marching thence to Fort Lenard, on the western plains, where he was engaged in watching the treacherous Indians. He was discharged at Madison, Wisconsin, and after turning over his arms to the government at Fort Leavenworth, Kansas, he returned to Winnebago county, Wisconsin. He made that county his home until he came to southern Minnesota and settled in Pipestone county, as was stated in the opening of this biography.

In June, 1845, Mr. Avery was united in marriage to Sarah Jane Rea, a native of Oswego county, New York. Miss Rea was reared and educated in Lewis county, New York, in the vicinity of the early home of her husband. Mr. and Mrs. Avery have two children—Erwin, a mechanic, who is married and a resident of Wisconsin, and Delciett, now married to G. D. Gamble.

Since coming to the township, Mr. Avery has been identified with its best interests, continually and in every way has assisted to the utmost extent of his means and ability in the management of public affairs. He has drawn to himself the good-will and esteem of all his fellow-townsmen and has made many warm friends. He is a man of excellent ideas, energetic and practical, and ranks among the representative citizens of Pipestone county. He is a leading member of the Grand Army of the Republic.

GEORGE L. MACOMBER resides on section thirty-four, Great Bend township, Cottonwood county, Minnesota. He was about the first settler in the township, making his location in May, 1871, at which time he took a soldier's homestead. He did not at once take up his residence on his claim but for a time resided in Windom. For four years he was county superintendent of the schools of Cottonwood county, and during this time resided in the county seat.

The subject of this sketch was born in Durham, Androscoggin county, Maine, November 28, 1848. His father, Hon. Leonard Macomber, was a farmer and an influential citizen of Maine, and was born in the same county in which our subject was born. The father was a prominent public man and was a member of the Maine legislature for one term. Our subject's mother's name before her marriage was Ann Eliza Swett, a native of Turner, Maine, and a teacher by profession during her early life. This lady is a sister of Hon. Leonard Swett, who was a prominent lawyer of Chicago, and the friend and law associate of Abraham Lincoln. Our subject was one of two children—Joseph and himself.

George L. Macomber was reared in his native county and given a good common-school education. He also took a course in the State college, and after completing his studies therein at about twenty-one years of age he came to Minnesota, and took his claim in Cottonwood county, where he has since lived. In November, 1863, our subject enlisted in the Thirtieth Maine Infantry, under Captain Noyes, who commanded Company E. Mr. Macomber served faithfully until August 22, 1865, when he was discharged and returned to his home in Maine.

Mr. Macomber was married December 26, 1880, to Miss Anna T. Thurston. This lady was born in Marquette county, Wisconsin, and was brought by her parents to Minnesota when she was about a year old. She was the daughter of Rev. J. M. Thurston, one of the pioneer Baptist ministers of southern Minnesota, coming to Garden City in 1860, now a resident of Windom. Miss Thurston attended the Pillsbury college and acquired a classical education. Mr. and Mrs. Macomber have three children—Minnie, Ruth and George.

In politics Mr. Macomber affiliates with the republican party, is one of the prominent and representative citizens of the county, and especially influential in the township in which he lives. Our subject does not confine his attention wholly to the raising of grain but is a systematic and intelligent breeder of blooded stock. He has at present about 600 head of grade Cotswold and Merino sheep, and also about forty head of fine Holstein cattle. Since locating in the county Mr. Macomber has actively participated in all matters pertaining to the public good and has held various official positions with credit to himself and satisfaction to his constituents.

ISAAC VANDERWARKER, a thrifty and prosperous farmer of Alta Vista township, Lincoln county, Minnesota, is a son of Isaac and Elizabeth (Terhune) Vanderwarker. The parents were both natives of New York and were prominent farmers of that State.

Isaac's birth-place was in Saratoga county, New York, where he was born September 19, 1819. Our subject was born in the same house in which the births of both his father and grandfather took place. He remained on the farm with his parents until he had attained twenty-two years of age. Up to this time he had attended the common schools and had been given a good common-school education. On attaining this age he commenced working for himself by renting a farm and engaging somewhat in teaming in New York. He continued in this business for about five years, and then in the spring of 1856 went to Marquette, Michigan, where he had charge of twenty-seven teams hauling iron ore on a tram railroad. Following this line of business for about six months he then came to Freeborn county, Minnesota, and settled on a homestead, where he engaged in farming until 1879. He then sold out his interests in Freeborn county and came to Alta Vista township, Lincoln county, Minnesota, where he took a homestead and tree claim on section 28. He proved up on his homestead on May 12, 1885, and on the tree claim in 1887.

April 6, 1862, he commenced his military service in the Union army by enlisting in Company K, Fourth Minnesota Infantry. On the 20th of April he went on board a steamboat at St. Paul and with his regiment went to Benton Barracks at St. Louis, Missouri. From there his regiment was ordered report at the front. This they did, and our subject participated in all the battles of his regiment until the fall of 1863. His military experience had been of a severe and trying nature, and in the fall of 1863 he was transferred to the invalid corps and sent to St. Louis. Here a number of those who were with him were organized into a company, and, our subject among them, were sent to Washington, where they remained until April 5, 1865. Our subject was honorably discharged from further service and returned to his home in Minnesota.

The subject of our sketch was united in the bonds of matrimony in Clinton county, New York, November 19, 1845, to Miss Clorinda D. Stokes. This lady died February 15, 1861, leaving the following named children—Elizabeth, Helen, George, Mary, Clara and Agnes. Elizabeth married Christopher Bingham, and now resides in Alta Vista township. Helen married George Scofield, and is a resident of California. George married Sarah Cole and now has charge of a large railroad shop in the State of Michigan. Mary is now the widow of Hugh Robertson and resides in Alta Vista township. Clara is still single and lives with her father. Agnes is living with friends in California. Mr. Vanderwarker's second marriage took place on September 15,

1865, in Preston, Fillmore county, Minnesota, where he was married to Miss Carrie Smith. This lady was a daughter of Daniel and Eliza (Bullis) Smith, the former a native of Vermont and the latter of New York. By this marriage there have been three children —Minnie, Clarence and Frank. Minnie married G. A. Bronson, one of the most successful and best known photographers in the city of St. Paul. Clarence and Frank are still at home.

Throughout his eventful career Mr. Vanderwarker has been a man who has proven of general utility in the localities in which he has lived. Possessed of progressive ideas and of excellent business qualities, he has assisted ably and efficiently in the administration of local government. Among the positions which he has ably filled have been those of township treasurer and treasurer of the school board, of which he has also been director, in Freeborn county. Since coming to Alta Vista township he has also actively interested himself in public affairs, and has been chairman of the board of supervisors for about six years. He was also elected as justice of the peace, but on account of ill-health did not qualify. Since coming to this county he has been quite successful, and has accumulated considerable means. He is systematic and thorough in all his farm work, and has surrounded himself with the evidences of prosperity and success. Having been broken down in health during his service in the war, he is entitled to and receives a pension of four dollars per month. This is but a pittance, and is no remuneration for the hardships our subject experienced during his military life. Mr. Vanderwarker has a fine farm, has about 140 acres under cultivation, and owns considerable stock, besides many useful implements of farm machinery. As a loyal citizen he stands above reproach; and is much respected in the township.

ROBERT HERREN, a well-known retired capitalist of the village of Luverne, in Rock county, Minnesota, made that his home in July, 1873. When he settled in the city he engaged in the lumber business in partnership with U. F. Hinds, with whom he continued until 1885, at which time the business was closed out and the partners retired from active life. These gentlemen were the pioneer lumbermen of Rock county, and had in their employ a number of teams drawing lumber from Worthington to Luverne. They also engaged farmers to bring lumber to their yards on their return trips from Worthington, which was then the only marketing place for wheat for Rock county farmers. This partnership also invested largely in farm lands, purchasing four farms of 160 acres each, and one of 120. On this land they carried on general farming in connection with their lumber business in the city. After coming to Rock county our subject became the individual owner of a farm of forty acres, one mile west of the city, which he improved and held until the fall of 1888, at which time he sold out to good advantage.

The subject of our sketch was born in Herkimer county, New York, December 25, 1816. His parents, Isaac and Catharine (Frayer) Herren, were also natives of New York State, where they engaged for many years in agricultural pursuits. Later in life the parents moved to Ashtabula county, Ohio, this being in 1832. They continued farming operations in Ohio until the father's death in 1856. The father was a loyal and patriotic citizen and soldier in the War of 1812. In the father's family there were ten children, six of whom are now living—Robert, Abram, Catherine (now Mrs. Frayer), Henry, Laura (now Mrs. Lyman), and Sarah (now Mrs. Brown). The Herren family is understood to be of Scotch-Irish descent, and the Frayers of German descent these people coming from the old country and becoming settlers of America in a very early day.

Mr. Herren, whose name appears at the head of this sketch, received his early education in New York and Ohio, where he remained in the home of his parents and was sent at every opportunity to the district schools. He remained with his parents until he was about eighteen years of age. At that time he commenced learning the cooper's trade. He soon mastered the details of that work and engaged in the management of a shop, employing from three to six men, making all kinds of materials usually turned out by a first-class cooper shop. He followed this business for a few years, and then, in 1852, being seized with the "gold fever," as many other Easterners were, he went to California and remained in the gold diggings for about two years. Our subject was one of those who were reasonably successful in their prospecting. The first year he engaged in working a mine and then turned his attention to the mercantile business. At the end of these two years spent in California he returned to Ohio, sold out his home and moved thence to Columbia county, Wisconsin, where he engaged in the grain trade for a few years. He then engaged in the lumber business for about two years, and at the end of that time went to Connecticut, where he had charge of a large company of men doing work on railroad construction. Some three months were spent by him in this employment, and he then returned to the State of Wisconsin. On his return to Wisconsin he sold out all his property there and came to Luverne, where he has since lived. He has been actively engaged in improving his business and residence property, and has a fine home which he built in about 1879 in the north part of the city. His residence is on a beautiful and prominent location near the court house, and his grounds being higher than most other places his residence has become one of the most prominent landmarks in the city.

The subject of our sketch was married March 1, 1838, to Caroline Hill, of Harpersfield, Ashtabula county, Ohio, where she was born April 24, 1818. This lady was the daughter of Edward and Jemima (Deneson) Hill, both of whom were natives of New York. Her father was engaged in farming to some extent and also in the boot and shoe business. The parents moved in early life to Ashtabula county, Ohio, and engaged in agricultural pursuits until a few years before their death. In her father's family there were seven sons and three daughters, two of whom are now living—Marvin Hill, of Chicago, and Mrs. Herren, who was the youngest of the family. Mr. and Mrs. Herren have a family of five children—Edwin R., Adelle E., Julia M., Herbert E. and Addie E. Edwin R. married Annie Yeomans, by whom he has had four children—Frances B., Annie L., Edith M. and Julia E. Adelle married Mr. T. B. Coon, by whom she has had one child—Eveline. T. B. Coon is the cashier of the Kilbourn City Bank of Wisconsin. Julia M., now Mrs. Hulburt Manchester, is a resident of Unionville, Lake county, Ohio. Herbert E. married Miss Susie Guiwits. Edwin R. gave his services to the Union army during the War of the Rebellion, and enlisted in Company D, Fourth Regiment Wisconsin Volunteer Infantry, being commissioned as lieutenant of that company. Later he was promoted to the rank of captain, and was discharged as major. He was severely wounded at the battle of Port Hudson, where he was shot in the knee pan, and was obliged to have his limb amputated. After his discharge from the service he returned to his home in Wisconsin and engaged in mercantile business. He is now in the lumber business at Stevens' Point, Wisconsin.

Since coming to the county our subject has become one of the most prominent citizens therein. He has actively interested himself in all matters relating to the proper government of his county, and has taken an active part in the affairs of the democratic party. His excellent business abilities have been thoroughly tested in the administration of public affairs. He has held several offices, among them being that of register of deeds, to which he was elected in 1884; president of the village council, which position he held one year, and one year as member of the town board. Mr. Herren is one of the best known and most highly esteemed citizens of Rock county. In whatever line of business he has engaged, his transactions have been characterized by thorough and constant integrity, and he has built up an enviable reputation as a business man. Being himself possessed of but limited school education, he has successfully carried out the idea of thoroughly educating his family, and his children were all given excellent school advantages. Mr. Herren is a man of progressive ideas, well posted on current affairs, and by his thorough and systematic attention to the details of his business matters, has gathered a large and increasing fortune.

EDWARD WALSHE, a thrifty farmer of Murray township, Murray county, Minnesota, located on section 3 in 1885. He purchased a good farm of 240 acres, and has since been engaged in farming and stock raising. He has taken a prominent part in the public affairs of his township, and has held various official positions. In every instance he has served with rare fidelity and faithfulness. Among the positions which he has held, may be named that of chairman of the board of supervisors, on which he is now serving his third term. He always takes a lively interest in educational matters, and has become quite prominent among his fellow-townsmen.

Edward Walshe was born in Kilkenny, Ireland, January 15, 1857. He made that place his home until eighteen years of age, and there received a good common-school education. On attaining the age just mentioned he came to the United States, in 1876, locating at Boston for three years, where he engaged as agent and collector for the Burkhardt Brewing Company. His next move was to go to Canada, where he finished his education in the University of Ottawa, graduating from the same in 1883. He then returned to Boston and re-engaged with his old employers for a year. He then came West and purchased his present place in Murray county.

The subject of our sketch is unmarried. In politics he affiliates with the democratic party, and is a consistent member of the Catholic church. He is a man of the highest character, and possessed of good business qualifications; is genial, warm-hearted and public-spirited, and is highly respected by all with whom he comes in contact. He is a man of good education, and ably assists in the administration of the various social, religious and public matters of his township, and is indeed one of Murray county's representative citizens.

JACOB F. GRANT, an influential farmer of Lake Side township, Cottonwood county, Minnesota, is engaged in farming and stock raising on section 28. He first located in Carson township, this county, in 1869, and made that his home for four years. He was one of the first settlers of the township, and assisted in its organization in 1872. He was a member of the first board of supervisors, and served one year. He was also elected treasurer of the township. He has at all times taken an active part in matters

pertaining to the public welfare. In 1874 our subject exchanged his place in Carson township for his present farm, on which he is now living. He has 240 acres of excellent land, three or four acres of a nice grove of trees, and has surrounded himself with the evidences of prosperity and success. He is also engaged in raising cattle of the Aberdeen Angus stock. Since coming to Lake Side township Mr. Grant has taken an active interest in political matters, and has held various official positions, having been a member of the board of supervisors since 1883. He is also director of school district No. 10, and has been treasurer and clerk of the school district for some time. Mr. Grant was born in Canada West, in Stormount county, September 11, 1845. His father, George J. Grant, was a native of the same county and was a farmer by occupation. He was born in May, 1809, and died in March, 1888; he was of Scotch descent, and was an influential citizen of Canada. Our subject's mother's maiden name was Margaret Shaver who was also a native of Stormount county, Canada, where she was born in 1811; she is still living on the old homestead. Our subject was one of ten children—James W., George P. (deceased), Mary Margaret (deceased), Catharine A., Rachel E. (deceased), Jacob F.; Sarah A. and Jane A. (twins), who died when they were about fourteen years of age; Maria B. and John G.

Our subject was reared in Canada until he was twenty-one years of age, receiving a good education. He aided his father on the farm, and on attaining his majority went to Brown county, Wisconsin, where he engaged in lumbering four or five years. He then located in Carson township, Cottonwood county, Minnesota, as has already been stated.

Mr. Grant was married in March, 1872, to Miss Emma V. Greenfield, a native of New York. She was a daughter of S. Greenfield, an old settler of Lake Side township, Cottonwood county. She was an estimable Christian lady, and was a member of the Methodist Episcopal church; she died in 1873. In March, 1876, Mr. Grant was married to Miss Mary C. Geddes, a native of Albany, New York. This lady was reared in Wisconsin until she was about fourteen years of age, and thence she removed to Blue Earth county, Minnesota, where she completed her education. Mr. Grant had one child by his first wife—Emma J., and has five children by his second wife—George W., Charles F., John G., James Allen and Fred Ray.

The pioneer life of our subject on coming to Cottonwood county was attended with many difficulties and affairs of a trying nature. For several years during the grasshopper raids he raised no crops whatever, and for mail and groceries had to go by way of ox teams to Madelia, Watonwan county, a distance of thirty-five miles. In politics Mr. Grant affiliates with the republican party, is a member of the Ancient Order of United Workmen, and is in sympathy with the tenets of the Presbyterian church. Throughout his residence in Cottonwood county he has been a man of action and has intelligently participated in all matters of a public nature.

※

ANTON H. DRUEKE is at present one of the leading merchants of the village of Avoca. He was born in Prussia August 15, 1854, and is the son of John and Theresia (Sasse) Drueke, natives of Germany. The father was a well-to-do farmer in his native land. The subject of our sketch came to America with his parents in 1864, and located in Mankato, where his father was killed by a boiler explosion. The mother still resides in Mankato. The subject of our sketch left the parental home in 1880, up to which time he had been employed in work

on the farm and in clerking. In 1880 he came to the village of Avoca and opened a general mercantile business, which he now runs. He carries a large and finely assorted stock of goods, worth between six and seven thousand dollars. He is also engaged in buying and selling grain, and handles all kinds of farm machinery and agricultural implements. He is a man of excellent character, is pleasant and courteous, and has built up a large and profitable trade. In politics he affiliates with the republican party, and has held various official positions. He has been chairman of the board of supervisors for some three years, president of the village council, and is at present postmaster of Avoca.

Mr. Drueke was married in Mankato, March 31, 1880, to Miss Mary Aachen, a native of Iowa. Four children have blessed this union—Rose M. (deceased), Harry P., Isabel and Theresia M.

※

WASHINGTON Z. HAIGHT is one of the influential business men of Winnebago City, Faribault county, Minnesota. He is dealing extensively in the Halliday standard windmills and pumps. He also handles gas-pipe, hose, creamery supplies, wood and tile well-curbing, feed mills, mill machinery, water wheels, steam engines, belts, horse hay-forks, scales, hardwood lumber, etc. He also does repairing work on the various kinds of goods which he carries in stock. He is also the proprietor of Haight's patent well augers and drills and non-leaking pump valves.

The subject of our sketch is a native of Jefferson county, Pennsylvania, where he was born March 25, 1839. He was the son of Nelson and Harriet N. (McCabe) Haight, natives of New York. The father was engaged in the lumber business in Pennsylvania for years and came to Minnesota in 1853, settling at Caledonia, Houston county, Minnesota. He settled on 160 acres of government land, and first built a log house 16x24 feet. He commenced making improvements and accomplished a great deal. He moved to Faribault county in 1864, and settled in Lura township on a homestead of 160 acres. He made substantial improvements and lived on that farm until within a few months of his death, when he made his home with his son, our subject. He died in 1881. The mother is still living and is a resident of Lura township, where she resides with her daughter, Mrs. Laura V. Tabor. In the father's family there were twelve children, eight of whom are now living — Mary E. (now Mrs. Deming), Milicent (now Mrs. Kirkman), Washington Z., Louisa (now Mrs. Armstrong), Laura V. (now Mrs. Tabor), Marquis de Lafayette, Caroline M. (now Mrs. Boyn), and Jenet (now Mrs. Lindahl). The parents were members of the Methodist Episcopal church, and were consistent Christians throughout their lives. The father was for years a class-leader and steward of the Methodist church, and accomplished much toward the building up of that society. In politics he affiliated with the republican party throughout the latter years of his life.

The subject of our sketch was reared on the home farm, and received a good common-school education. He resided with his parents until he was twenty-five years of age. Prior to this, however, for some years he had had charge of the home farm. After leaving home he engaged in the agricultural implement business at Wells, Faribault county, Minnesota, and soon afterward invented a peat machine. He continued in Wells some three years, and succeeded in manufacturing a large quantity of peat and selling several of his machines, which he manufactured during 1871 and 1872. He next engaged in boring wells at Easton, Faribault county, and invented a well-boring machine in 1876, commencing the manufacture of this machine at Easton. In 1878 he removed his entire plant to Winnebago City, where he purchased seven lots on the corner of Main and Mill streets, and where he erected his present business buildings. He employs from ten to fifteen men in his own business, besides others whom he has engaged in putting down wells with his patent well-machines. He has had a large and profitable business, and is well known as a successful worker in his line. He owns considerable property, and has a good dwelling-house on Mill street, near his place of business. Since coming to the city he has taken an active interest in all matters of a public nature, and has assisted materially in developing the present financial interests of Winnebago City. He is one of the members of the executive board of the Baptist college, and is also a member of the board of directors of the public schools. He belongs to the Methodist Episcopal church, in which society he holds the position of steward. He is a member of the Driving Park Association, and is one of its stockholders. Formerly he was president of the Farmers' Warehouse Company, of the city. In politics he affiliates with the republican party, and is an influential member of the Independent Order of Odd Fellows. He has been quite successful in his business affairs, and is one of the prominent and most substantial business men in the county.

Mr. Haight was married in 1865 to Miss Clarissa A. Woodard, of Caledonia, Minnesota, a daughter of Sheldon Woodard. Seven children have blessed this union, five of whom are now living—Milo M., Warren W., Hiram H., Eddy E. and Forest F.

THOMAS MORRILL, one of the prominent farmers of Pipestone county, Minnesota, resides on section 4, in Troy township. He was born in Chittenden county, Vermont, September 25, 1822.

The parents of the subject of our sketch were natives of New Hampshire and Vermont, their names being James and Eunice (Fitch) Morrill. The father was a farmer by occupation, and was engaged largely in agricultural interests in his native State until his death, which occurred some time in the 50's. The mother is also dead, her demise occurring soon after the death of her husband. The parents left Vermont in 1833, removing to St. Lawrence county, New York, where the father purchased a large tract of land and engaged in farming.

Thomas Morrill remained with his parents during the early years of his life, working on the farm and attending school, in which he was given advantages for obtaining a fair education. His life with his parents continued until he reached the age of twenty-three years, when he came westward, locating in Mukwanago, Waukesha county, Wisconsin, where he soon found employment at farm work, and in which line he continued for a few years. He remained in Wisconsin until 1849, when he returned to Vermont and New York State to visit friends, remaining with them until in the spring of 1850. In the latter year, in company with his brother-in-law, C. T. Loveland, he came to Wisconsin, locating in Dodge county, where Mr. Loveland purchased a large farm. Thomas remained in his brother-in-law's employ, sharing in the profits of the farm, until in the fall of 1851, when he concluded to find land for his own use. Removing to the western part of the State he settled on 160 acres of State land in La Crosse Valley, where he continued his farming operations for a number of years. His work was not confined to agricultural pursuits exclusively, but he found time to engage somewhat in contracting and building. He constructed a large dam across the La Crosse river for M. Palmer, the dam remaining intact until this day, although having been built in the years

1852 and 1853. He remained in Wisconsin until sometime in 1880, when he removed to the western part of the State of Minnesota, settling where he now lives in Troy township, Pipestone county. Since coming to this State he has confined his business operations almost exclusively to farming, and has now 160 acres of excellent land under a high state of cultivation, ten acres of which is near the city of Pipestone.

Mr. Morrill was united in marriage in 1854, to Miss Matilda A. McEldowney, the wedding day being on July 4, of that year. This union was blessed with five children, all of whom are living at the present time. Mrs. Morrill died in October, 1868, in La Crosse Valley. In 1869, Mr. Morrill was married to Matilda (Brayton) Taylor, widow of W. H. Taylor, by whom she had six children, all living at the present time. By the latter marriage Mr. Morrill has had no children. Mr. Morrill's two daughters by his first wife are both married, one to J. T. Parker and the other to F. Whitman, a telegraph operator located at Palatine, Illinois, twenty-five miles west of Chicago. One son, Frank, is a blacksmith, and a resident of Pipestone, Minnesota. Andrew, another son, is a civil engineer by profession and is in the employ of the B. & M. Railroad Company, with headquarters at Lincoln, Nebraska. The other son, Elgin A., is living with his father on the farm. A daughter of Mrs Morrill is one of the teachers in the public schools of the city of Pipestone.

Mr. Morrill came to this county with but very little of this world's goods, having but three horses and about $240 in money. By careful attention to the details of his farming operations and by thrift and economy he has accumulated a considerable fortune, and is to day looked upon as one of the substantial and representative citizens of the township and county in which he lives. In personal appearance he is finely-formed man, is genial, warm-hearted and hospitable, and is esteemed and rested by all with whom he has to do. The educational advantages in the early days which were spent by him in his native State were not of the highest order, but he was enabled to obtain a good common-school education, and by much reading and careful observation he has accumulated a large fund of information, upon which he has a faculty of happily drawing whenever occasion requires. In politics he is a stanch republican, and has the satisfaction of knowing that the party with which he has affiliated so long was successful in electing Benjamin Harrison as president, for whose grandfather Mr. Morrill cast his vote in 1840. By virtue of his stanch qualities of integrity and executive ability he has, at various times, been placed in official positions by his friends and the voters of the county in which he has lived. While in Wisconsin he held the office of assessor for four years, that of treasurer one year, and was also supervisor for one year. In Pipestone county he has held many positions of trust and responsibility within the gift of the voters of his township, having been township treasurer hnd overseer of highways for some years. In whatever way Mr. Morrill has turned in his business interests he has always met with success and is proud of the fact that what he owns to-day is clear of all indebtedness.

FREDERICK W. SCHWIEGER is one of the prosperous farmers of Delton township, Cottonwood county, Minnesota. He was born in Prussia, October 4, 1837, his parents being Ferdinand and Frederica (Moss) Schwieger, natives of Prussia.

When our subject was nine years of age, he commenced working for different neighbors in his native country. He followed this line of employment for four or five years, and was at home during the winters, when he attended school. This continued until he was fourteen years of age, when he engaged in work as a farm hand for some five years. He then found work in Missay City in a store. Three years later he went to Stettin City, where he found work in a large store for ten years. Then he kept a store for himself for a year, when he sold out in 1866 and came to the United States, first stopping in Chicago, where he remained about six weeks. He then went into the country and worked for a farmer, from August until the following March. He then found employment with another farmer and continued with him for two years, when he rented a farm in Will county, Illinois, operating the same for about seven years. He then came to Delton township, Cottonwood county, Minnesota, and took a homestead on section 22. He now owns 240 acres, with about 160 acres under cultivation. He has a good farm, well stocked, and provided with machinery and all kinds of necessary improvements. All the early settlers of this region passed through the hard times of 1873–78, and our subject was not an exception to the rule. His crops were destroyed by grasshoppers and blight during these years and but little crop was raised on his farm. January 13, 1881, his house was destroyed by fire and all the contents were burned, our subject not even saving his hat, boots or coat. There was no insurance on the property and it was a total loss. In spite of these things, our subject has kept sturdily on accumulating, until he has a fine farm and is in good circumstances. He is one of the foremost citizens of the township, and always takes an active interest in public matters. He has been school director for two years and also supervisor for some length of time.

Mr. Schwieger was married in Will county, Illinois, in February, 1870, to Miss Sophia

Tode, who died November 20, 1874, leaving two children—Emma and Albert. Mr. Schwieger was married the second time in the same county, in 1875, to Miss Mary Storbeck, a daughter of Heinrich and Loise (Strotman) Storbeck, and a native of Mecklenburg-Schwerin. Mr. and Mrs. Schwieger have had three children—William, Sophia (who died some years ago), and Sophia.

WILLIAM E. DEAN is one of the leading and most able attorneys of Lincoln county, Minnesota. He located in the village of Tyler in 1879, since which time he has been actively engaged in the practice of his profession. He devotes a considerable portion of his attention to loaning money and to buying and selling lands. He has made many warm friends by his careful and successful attention to the various details of his large business. He is the son of Edwin and Rebecca (Low) Dean, natives of Maine. Mrs. Dean was the daughter of Judge Low, a very prominent jurist of the State of Maine.

Attorney Dean was born in Belvidere, Illinois, in the year 1853. His parents were farmers by occupation and he was reared a farmer's boy, being given the educational advantages furnished by the district schools. At fourteen he was sent to the graded schools in the city of Belvidere, and continued his studies therein for about four years and then engaged in the profession of teaching, following that occupation during two winters, and then coming to Lincoln county in 1873. His coming to Lincoln county was for the purpose of finding a farm for himself. He took a squatter's claim and built a house, but remained only a short time, and removed to Albert Lea, Minnesota, where he studied law some two years. While there he made several trips on foot to his claim; his circumstances being

so limited that he did not have the means to travel by railway or hire a team. He remained in Albert Lea for three years; during two years of which time he studied law, and taught school during one year. He went from Albert Lea to Iowa City, Iowa, in 1876, for the purpose of attending the law department of the Iowa State University. He continued in that institution until a short time before the close of his last term, when he was taken seriously ill and was removed to the home of his parents. He was not expected to live for some time, but good nursing finally brought him through, and he regained his wonted good health, and then removed to Marshall, where, after studying law for a short time, he was admitted to the bar in 1877. He then returned to his claim, where he opened a land office and did a good business until in 1878, when he proved up on his land and moved into Marshfield, which was then the county seat of Lincoln county, Minnesota. He engaged in the practice of law in that place until in the fall of 1879, when he removed to Tyler, where he has since resided.

Mr. Dean was married in Tyler, September 26, 1881, to Miss Mary Starr, a daughter of Isaac and Ellen (Hannah) Starr, natives of Pennsylvania. Mrs. Dean was born in Pennsylvania and died May 1, 1889. The marriage just chronicled was blessed with two children—Albert Low and William E.

The life of the subject of our sketch has been cast among many difficulties and hardships, all of which he has conquered. He received a good common-school education in his youth, and being a careful student and a close observer, he has accumulated a vast fund of general knowledge. He is, indeed, a self-made man, having received but very little assistance and less encouragement while prosecuting his legal studies. He is a leading citizen of Tyler and vicinity, and occupies a high position as an attorney in the esteem of his fellow-citizens. Since coming to the village he has identified himself with local governmental affairs, and has held the office of judge of probate for one term, besides having held numerous minor positions. He is a member of the Independent Order of Odd Fellows, Lake Benton Lodge, No. 77, and also of the Temple of Honor and the Ancient Order of United Workmen.

---·─·◦·❦◈❦·◦·─·---

BRIGHAM FOSTER is a reliable farmer of Shetek township, Murray county, Minnesota. He located on the southwest quarter of section 10, of that township in June, 1872. He was one of the early settlers, and assisted in the organization of that township in which he has held some of the most important official positions. He has been chairman of the board of supervisors seven years, and justice of the peace for three years. He was county commissioner from 1878 to 1881, and was treasurer of his township for some years during the early days. He has always taken an active interest in all public matters, and originated the first petition for the organization of school district No. 16, of which he was one of the first directors, and which position he held some eight years. He saw hard times during the first four or five years of his residence here, passing through the grasshopper scourge of 1873–77. He had many acres of grain destroyed during those years, and in order to support his family had to leave home and work at various kinds of employment in Wabasha county, this State. In 1873 he began putting out trees, principally cottonwoods; and now has a beautiful grove of five acres about his house. He has turned his attention somewhat to the raising of small fruits and has a large variety of currants, and red and black raspberries, etc.

Mr. Foster's parents were Enoch and Eliza (Gates) Foster, both of whom were natives of Cheshire county, New Hampshire, where they were reared and educated. They resided in that county until 1830, and then removed to Niagara county, New York, locating in the village of Somerset. In about 1844 the family removed to Michigan, where the father died in 1871. He was a farmer by occupation and an influential citizen. The mother died in 1872.

Mr. Foster was born in Somerset, Niagara county, New York, March 25, 1831. He remained in that place until thirteen years of age, when, with his parents, he removed to Jackson county, Michigan. Here he completed his education, and remained four years assisting his father in work on the home farm. In 1848 they settled near the village of Quincy, in Branch county, Michigan. In 1853 our subject went to Douglas county, Illinois, but in 1854 returned to Michigan, where he joined his father on the home farm. Returning to Douglas county he remained a year, and in October, 1856, went to Wabasha county, Minnesota. In December, 1863, he enlisted in the First Battery, Minnesota Light Artillery, as a private, being discharged as a corporal in July, 1865, at St. Paul. He served under Captain William Z. Clayton. He served his country bravely in the following named battles: Peach Tree Creek, Atlanta, and Bentonville, and numerous other battles and skirmishes of minor importance. After his discharge from the service he returned to Wabasha county, and made that his home from 1865, to 1872. He then came to Murray county, and located as was stated in the opening lines of this sketch. He has been engaged in general farming and stock raising, and has met with large success. Mr. Foster was married in December, 1857, to Miss Mary A. Cook, a native of Vermont. This lady removed, in 1840, to the State of Illinois, and received her education in the village of Wauconda, Lake county. She was a daughter. of Andrew C. and Mary (Oaks) Cook, natives of Vermont. Her father was a farmer by occupation and a representative citizen of the locality in which he lived. Mr. and Mrs. Foster have had six children: Robert C., Frank, Andrew Enoch, Seymore R., Nellie and Kitte May. Robert C., Frank and Nellie are married, and reside in homes of their own. The balance of the children live with their parents.

The subject of our sketch has been highly successful in his financial operations, and has become one of the most prosperous and well-to-do citizens of the township. He is a man of strong, decided opinions, is intelligent, energetic, and public-spirited, and is one of Murray county's representative citizens.

MADISON McCOLLUM, an industrious and influential farmer of Lake Stay township, Lincoln county, Minnesota, is the son of Thomas and Mary (Mc-Donald) McCollum. The father was a native of Kentucky, and the mother was born in Tennessee. They were well-to-do farmers, and were people of influence and respectability in the locality in which they lived.

The subject of our sketch was born in Wayne county, Kentucky, January 19, 1832. His boyhood days were spent on the home farm, and his educational facilities were furnished by the district schools. He remained with his parents until he was about twenty-one years of age, when he started out for himself, and came to Minnesota in the fall of 1852. He stopped for a short time in Dakota county, on what is now the site of West St. Paul. The first winter of his stay in Minnesota he procured a claim some six miles above Mendota, at a place called Black Dog Village, where he and his father lived some five or six years. At the end of that period they removed to Scott county, and he

purchased a farm, on which they lived until 1878. He then sold out his interests in Scott county, and came to Lake Stay township, where he has resided ever since, with the exception of the winter of 1888–89, when he and his wife went East on a visit. It had been some years since our subject had left the Eastern States, and he concluded to visit the old home and birthplace. They left Lincoln county in October, and after a long and enjoyable visit among relatives they returned in April, 1889. On coming to Lincoln county, Mr. McCollum settled on the northeast quarter of section 2, Lake Stay township, where he took a tree claim and where he is now living surrounded with the evidences of thrift and prosperity. While a resident of Scott county our subject enlisted in Hatch's battalion, Company B, in the spring of 1863. He served with that battalion until being mustered out of the service in June, 1865. He enlisted as a private and served as a commissary sergeant for some time, also as a corporal and orderly sergeant. He was well fitted for a military life and took kindly to military discipline. One peculiar and ludicrous incident is related by him of the military experience and of the difficulties some experienced in controlling the soldiers. While stationed at Fort Abercrombie he had charge of a squad of men commissioned to take several barrels of whiskey to Georgetown on the Red river. The boys were very desirous and almost determined to sample the "goods" that they had with them, but after much trouble, much coaxing, and finally stern measures, our subject succeeded in reaching his destination with the rum intact and shortly afterward turned it over to its proper owners. It was out of his charge but a short time when it was tapped by some one and this was the signal for a general and glorious drunk. The result of this was seen in several brawls and in a tragedy. Indians and teamsters and some soldiers were all very drunk, and in fights which ensued a teamster was shot by an Indian and a soldier was smothered in his bunk. Neither of these white men belonged to our subject's squad. The above incident shows that our subject had good control over his men.

Mr. McCollum was married in Scott county, Minnesota, in May, 1856, to Mrs. Mary Cordell, neé McDonald, a daughter of James and Elizabeth McDonald. This lady was the widow of Charles Cordell, by whom she had two children—Sarah, now Mrs. Franklin McKennett, a resident of Dakota county, Minnesota, and Emeline, now Mrs. James Casterline, a resident of Oregon, where the husband died some time ago. Mr. and Mrs. McCollum have been blessed with the following-named children—Daniel, John and Amanda. Daniel is single, and living with his parents. In the spring of 1889 he returned from Oregon, where he had gone to look for a place in which to locate. He did not like that country as well as southern Minnesota, and so concluded to return to his father's farm. John married Miss Emma Mendoles, and is living on a farm near that of his father. Amanda married Charles Sinks, of Wilton, Wisconsin.

The residence of our subject in Lincoln county has not been devoid of interest in public matters. He has interested himself in local affairs, and has been county commissioner for four years, in which position he has served his constituents ably and efficiently. He has also been assessor and township supervisor, and in his official business relations he has always proven himself a man of rare capabilities. In politics he affiliates with the republican party. A staunch supporter of all those things which he believes to be right, and therefore a loyal citizen, a good friend and neighbor, he has made many warm acquaintances in the township and county. He lives on a fine farm and tree

claim, upon which he proved up in July, 1888. He is surrounded with comfortable circumstances, and has a pleasant home.

———♦◦❀◦♦———

ALBERT QUACKENBUSH, a farmer and prominent citizen, is located on section 12, Murray township, Murray county, Minnesota. He located in the year 1870 on a homestead in Slayton township, where he resided some six years, after which he removed to the French farm in Shetek township, where he engaged in farming and trapping for about two years. Then he came to section 12, Murray township, where he preempted his present place. From the very first our subject has striven hard to make his farm one of the best in the township. He has succeeded quite well, and has his land under good cultivation and provided with excellent farm buildings. He owns 320 acres where he now is, and also 160 acres in Slayton township, which latter was his first homestead. He has about five acres of a beautiful grove located about his buildings. In this grove are to be found about eight thousand trees—box elders, ash and willows.

Mr. Quackenbush is a native of Onondaga county, New York, where he was born January 13, 1844. He was the son of Jacob Quackenbush, a native of Germany, who emigrated to New York when a young man. The father was a cooper by trade, and on coming to America engaged to a large extent in farming. He died in 1881. The mother's name before her marriage was Miss Case. She died when our subject was about two years of age. The father was married again to Miss Joan Hocom. In the father's family there were six children—John, Jeston, Gaston, David, Albert and Agnes.

The early life of the subject of our sketch was spent by him in his native county, where he received a good education, working as much as possible on the home farm.

He remained with his father until he was nineteen years of age. Then, in January, 1864, he enlisted in the Twenty-fourth New York Cavalry, serving until the close of hostilities, being discharged in 1865 at Clouds Mill, Virginia. He participated in the following named battles—Wilderness, Cold Harbor and Spottsylvania, and was under fire at Petersburg for nine months, before which fortifications he was dismounted, and was doing infantry duty. The captain of his regiment was named Taylor. After his discharge our subject returned to the State of New York, and made that his home until the fall of 1871. He then went to Michigan, whence after about six months he went to Wisconsin, and thence on to Murray county, Minnesota, where he has since lived. In politics Mr. Quackenbush affiliates with the democratic party, and takes an active interest in the public affairs, and has become one of the representative citizens of the township. He is a man of good education, high character, and is highly respected by all who know him.

Mr. Quackenbush was married July 17, 1874, to Miss Ann Noyes. This lady was born in the State of New York, where she was reared and educated. This union has been blessed with five children—Josephine, Eldora, William, Ray and Della.

HEINRICH GIESELMAN is an influential and well-to-do farmer who resides on section 32 of Southbrook township, Cottonwood county, Minnesota. He was born in Germany, April 15, 1839, his parents being Ans and Charlotte (Brant) Gieselman, also natives of the fatherland. They were well-to do people in that land and are still living. In the father's family there were two children—Heinrich and William.

The subject of this sketch emigrated to America in September, 1870, and after about a month went to Jackson county, Minnesota, and engaged in various pursuits for nearly half a year. He then bought his present farm of 160 acres of land of a Mr. Benson of Heron Lake. At the time of the purchase there were no improvements on the farm and it was nothing but wild prairie. It is now provided with excellent buildings and other improvements that betoken success and prosperity. Surrounding his dwelling our subject has three acres of a fine grove of trees. In connection with his farming he is also engaged in raising a fine grade of stock.

Mr. Gieselman was married in September, 1881, to Mrs. Gertrude Morgmarode, by whom he has had four children. Mrs. Gieselman had two children by her former husband. The names of all the children are as follows—Jo, Frank, Henry, John, Willie and Adam. The family are members of the Catholic church at Heron Lake. Mrs. Gieselman was the daughter of John Morgmarode, and was also a native Germany. Her father died in that land and her mother emigrated to America.

STELLA PERRIGO, M. D., is one of the leading physicians and surgeons of the homeopathic school in Pipestone City, Pipestone county, Minnesota. This lady came to Pipestone county for the purpose of practicing in her profession in 1882, and made her headquarters in the town of Osborne, where her sister, Mrs. R. E. Thomas, resided. In 1884 she became an actual resident, settling on Liberty Hill farm, in Osborne township, where her husband, Myron H. Perrigo, settled on a homestead of 160 acres. They continued improving this land until moving to the city of Pipestone in 1888. Mrs. Perrigo graduated at the Hahnemann College and Hospital in Chicago, in 1884. She is the only homeopathic physican in the county, as well as the only lady physician therein.

Dr. Perrigo is a native of Walworth county, Wisconsin, and is a daughter of Peter and Mariah (Eastman) Himebaugh.

In 1889 she purchased property in the city of Pipestone, where she has a fine residence. She has been quite successful in her medical practice, and is known as a successful physician far and near. She makes many extensive rides on professional business throughout Pipestone and adjoining counties and even into Dakota and Iowa. She is a lady of thorough education and well qualified for the duties of her profession.

Dr. Perrigo has connected with her in her practice her nephew, Fred A. Perrigo, a son of William H. Perrigo, of Milwaukee.

In July, 1889, she was elected county physician for Pipestone county, which position she now holds.

MRS. EMILY ADELIA GOWIN, a resident of Delton township, Cottonwood county, Minnesota, is the daughter of Thomas P. and Rachel Rebecca (Smith) Richardson, natives of New York. Mrs. Gowin was born in that State April 10, 1847. Her father was a farmer by occupation, and when she was eight years old the family moved to Berlin, Wisconsin, where they remained a short time, and where her mother died. After the death of her mother the father broke up housekeeping, and the children scattered for about a year. Then the father married Almira Fairbanks, and, gathering the children together, provided them with a home, with the exception of an elderly son, Lemuel. After her father's marriage our subject lived with him until September 26, 1866. At this time she was married, in Waupun, Wisconsin, to John Gowin, who was the son of David and Mercy Ann Gowin, natives of New York.

After Mrs. Gowin's marriage she settled, with her husband, in Fond du Lac county, Wisconsin, where they resided until the fall of 1870. They then moved to Dodge county, Minnesota, renting a farm until 1873. It was in this year that they came to Selma township, Cottonwood county, and settled on a homestead on the northwest quarter of section 8. March 5, 1888, Mr. Gowin was working in a saw-mill in Antigo, Wisconsin, when he was struck by a log and killed almost instantly. He had gone to this place to find employment during the winter. His crops had been destroyed, and he was obliged to find other work to support his family. His wife and children were at this time on the claim in Selma township. After her husband's death Mrs. Gowin remained on the farm about two years, when she took a homestead on section 4 of Delton township, where she has since lived. She is a good manager, and thoroughly understands the farming business; has about fifty acres of land under cultivation, and has the farm provided with good buildings.

Mr. and Mrs. Gowin had the following-named children—Milton, Adeline, Clarence and Calista (twins), Harriet, Rosie, Grant, Mary and Charles, all living but Calista, who died when about six months old. Adeline married Samuel Hudson, and is now residing in Selma township.

JOHN P. BOULTON is one of the leading and well-know farmers of Alta Vista township, Lincoln county, Minnesota, and is located on section two. He is the son of William and Mary (Leslie) Boulton, natives of England. The parents resided in England throughout the most of their lives.

Our subject's native place is in Westmoreland, England, where he was born May 2, 1837. He remained with his parents, obtaining a good common-school education until he was about seventeen years of age. He then learned professional engineering and followed that occupation, engaged in opperating stationary and locomotive engines for some twenty-four years, twelve years in England and twelve years in the United States. In 1868 he came to America and located for a time in the State of New Jersey. After one year's residence in that State he removed to Plymouth, Pennsylvania, where he remained for a few years. Removing thence the family located at Shenandoah, remaining in that place for about nine years, when, in the spring of 1880, they came to Minnesota and located on section two in Alta Vista township, Lincoln county. He paid $1,000 for 160 acres of land, and has since been engaged in the successful operation of the same. Since coming to the township Mr. Boulton has occupied himself principally with farm business and has been highly successful in all his operations. He has engaged to some extent in raising stock and has a fine farm, well improved and well supplied with buildings. He is a man of the highest integrity of character, and is looked upon with respect and confidence by all his fellow-citizens. He is a man of good ideas, and having in early life obtained a good common-school education, is well prepared to assist in various ways in the management of local township affairs. He has served his fellow-citizens in various official capacities, and among other offices has been treasurer of the school district for sometime. In politics he affiliates with the democratic party, and has become prominent in the local counsels of that organization.

Mr. Boulton was married in Ulverston, England, in 1865, to Miss Mary Pennington, a daughter of Christopher and Anna (Tyson) Pennington, natives of England. Mr. and Mrs. Boulton have been blessed with two children —Robert and William. The members of the family belong to the Catholic church.

ENJAMIN B. THOMPSON, a prominent citizen and furniture dealer of Fulda, Murray county, Minnesota, is the son of William R. and Betsey (Berry) Thompson, the father a native of Farnum, England, and the mother born in Vermont.

The parents were well-to-do citizens of the State of Vermont, and the father before coming to the United States, was a quartermaster of the military barracks in Quebec, Canada, in the War of 1812. The Berry family is one of considerable note in the early history of America, the grandfather of Betsey Berry having come to America in the ship Mayflower. The father of Betsey Berry was a major in the War of the Revolution, and his uniform now hangs in the museum of the State of Maine. The mother of our subject died February 19, 1841, and the father was murdered in Boston, Massachusetts, January 2, 1853, and was robbed of $12,000. This family were possessed of an intensely military spirit and served their country bravely and gallantly. Major Berry was one of only eight survivors of his regiment, First Vermont Infantry. He died March 14, 1833, at the age of ninety-nine years eleven months and sixteen days.

The gentleman whose name appears at the head of this sketch was born in Bingham, Somerset county, Maine, March 17, 1833. He was reared in that State, remaining with his parents until eight years old and with relatives on various farms until he was sixteen years of age. His mother died when he was eight years old and he was then bound out to work for relatives. At sixteen years of age he purchased horses and wagon and commenced peddling various kinds of dress and dry goods and Yankee notions all over Maine and New Brunswick. He engaged in various kinds of employment, part of the time purchasing horses in Canada and shipping them through to the United States. After running his wagon for about eight years he was married, and commenced running a boarding-house in Vassalborough, Maine. He was thus engaged for eight years, and then, in 1862, went to Mauston, Juneau county, Wisconsin, where he engaged in carpenter work until 1863. He then went to Johnsonville, Tennessee, and joined a construction corps, being given charge of a division. After seven months his health failed, and he returned home. His work in the South was in perilous circumstances, and while at Johnsonville the Rebels fired on the Union fortifications, and many cannon balls went through the building where our subject and his corps were at work. After returning to Wisconsin he commenced work at his trade, which he followed until March 15, 1880, when he came to Fulda, Murray county, Minnesota, where he still engaged in work at his trade for a year. He then opened a furniture store, which he has since conducted. Mr. Thompson is a man of excellent qualities, possessed of a generous, open-hearted disposition, and has made many warm friends in Fulda and adjoining country. He has been quite successful in his business operations, and has accumulated considerable means.

Mr. Thompson was married in Searsport, Maine, in September, 1856, to Miss Mary E. Chase, by whom he had two children—C. E. and F. H. She died July 25, 1862. Mr. Thompson was again married, March 14, 1868, at Lindina, Juneau county, Wisconsin, to Miss Cloe M. Trumball, a relative of the Harrison family, her mother being a second cousin of William Henry Harrison. Miss Trumball was the daughter of Gilbert and Lois (Heath) Trumball, natives of New York. She was born in November, 1850, in Concord, Erie county, New York. This union has been blessed with the following-named children— Willie A., Calvin L., Mary L., Cora M. and Ella H.

NELSON MINET, one of the leaders in the public affairs of Grange township, Pipestone county, Minnesota, resides on section 24. The place of the nativity of Mr. Minet is to be found in the State of Vermont, where he was born August 5, 1843. The names of his parents were John and Mary (Martin) Minet, both of whom were natives of Canada. The father was a farmer by occupation, and in an early day removed from Vermont to Wisconsin, where he now lives. He is a man of prominence and influence in the town where he lives. The mother died in Wisconsin in 1886.

Work on the home farm occupied a considerable portion of the attention of our subject until he was fifteen years of age. He was, however, given the advantages for education furnished by the district schools, and being a ready student he acquired a good common-school education. When he was fifteen years old he left the parental home and commenced working in the pineries in Wisconsin, engaging in that employment during the winter months and in the summer of each year finding employment on the river. This line of life was continued until August 22, 1862, when he enlisted in the Tenth Wisconsin battery of light artillery, serving throughout the war and receiving his discharge June 25, 1865. He was first under Captain Beebe, who was the ranking officer of this company, and when the time of the enlistment of the company expired, our subject was transferred to the Twelfth Wisconsin Battery Light Artillery. Ater an honorable service in the war he returned to Wisconsin and engaged in work in the pineries and on the Mississipi river after the plan he had followed before he entered the service. This kind of life was continued with success until 1874, when he entered the railroad employ as a brakeman, which occupation he followed for two years. At this time he took to himself a wife and purchased a farm in Juneau county, Wisconsin, on which he remained engaging successfully in agricultural pursuits until coming to Pipestone county in 1878. He drove through by the primitive method of a team and covered wagon, located his land and remained until fall, making some improvements. At this time there was not a house to be seen anywhere in the township, and the first house was built that season by a man by the name of Clarey. This gentleman is now dead. Our subject commenced making improvements on the farm by breaking some of his land and building a small house. In the fall he returned to Wisconsin and after remaining in that State during the winter came with his family to the farm in Pipestone county and made a pernament settlement.

October 16, 1871, the subject of our sketch was united in the holy bonds of matrimony to Margaret Clews, a native of Norway. This union has been blessed with four children—Harry N., Harvey D., Charles B. and Stella M., all of whom are living at the present time.

Mr. Minet is undoubtedly one of the leading farmers of Grange township, and stands well up among the representative farmers of Pipestone county. He is a man of excellent character, intelligent, and takes an active interest in all matters that pertain to the public welfare. He has a good farm and has surrounded himself with good buildings and the necessary appurtenances of a well-ordered farm. In politics he occupies a leading position in the local affairs of the republican party, in whose principles he firmly believes, and with which he has affiliated for a long term of years. Among the official positions which he has held within the gift of the citizens of the township in which he lives, are those of assessor and road overseer, he having been the incumbent of the first office for a period of four years

and the latter for three years. His volunteer service during the War of the Rebellion entitles him to the leading position which he occupies in the councils of the Grand Army of the Republic, Simon Mix Post, No 95. Mr. Minet is an excellent citizen and is respected by all with whom he comes in contact.

————

HOWARD M. GOSS, an enterprising farmer, residing in Selma township, Cottonwood county, Minnesota, is an influential and prominent citizen. His birthplace is found in Randolph, Orange county, Vermont, where he first saw the light, March 7, 1840. His parents were John C. and Elizabeth (Moulton) Goss, both natives of Vermont. Our subject's father was engaged in the boot and shoe trade in his native State until 1852, after which he followed agricultural pursuits for two years, and then moved to Kingston, Green Lake county, Wisconsin, where he purchased a farm on which he lived for one year. He then rented land for three years, during which time he was engaged in the boot and shoe business in Kingston. In the fall of 1858 the family moved to Highland, Wabasha county, Minnesota, and settled on a homestead of 160 acres, where they remained until the fall of 1874, when they again removed to Selma, Cottonwood, county, Minnesota, where John C. Goss, the father, died in 1877.

The parental home remained the abiding place of our subject until 1861, when he enlisted October 3d, in Company G, Third Minnesota Infantry. He served faithfully and gallantly for three years and was discharged November 16, 1864, at Devall's Bluff, Arkansas. The last year's service was spent at Little Rock, Arkansas, in the commissary department. Among the battles in which our subject participated was that of the taking of Little Lock. He was captured by

General Forrest's forces at Murfreesboro and held prisoner for two days, when he was paroled and sent to Benton Barracks, St. Louis, and exchanged. Soon after he participated in an Indian expedition in Minnesota and then returned South. After his discharge he returned to his father's farm in Minnesota and resided with him for two years. Soon after leaving the service he purchased a farm, and, although living with his father, operated in his own interests. Mr. Goss resided in Wabasha county until 1871, when he sold out and removed to Selma township, Cottonwood county, settling on the 160 acres of land on section 34. Here he has remained ever since and has made comfortable improvements in the way of a large frame house with a fine dairy room and ice house attached thereto. He has a fine barn and a nice grove of eleven acres of trees. Although having passed through a great many misfortunes in the way of loss of grain during the grasshopper raids and also by rust and blight, our subject has accumulated considerable means and has now a prosperous-looking and valuable farm. He has been a man of considerable prominence in county politics and has affiliated with the republican party. He is a man of strong principles and is highly esteemed. He has been county commissioner for four years, township clerk three or four years, chairman of the supervisors for five years, justice of the peace twelve years, and school clerk since the organization of the district in 1874. He is a member of the Ancient Order of United Workmen, Independent Order of Odd Fellows and Grand Army of the Republic.

Mr. Goss was married in Highland, Wabasha county, October 19, 1866, to Miss Julia Knudson, daughter of Christopher and Carrie (Grove) Knudson. Julia Knudson was born in Norway, December 28, 1844.

Mr. and Mrs. Goss have been blessed with the following-named children—Francis (deceased), Carrie, Ruth, Francis and Dana. Carrie is now Mrs. Willis Dyer, and has one child, Ivan. She lives in Lakeside township, Cottonwood county.

WILLIAM PARROTT. This gentleman is one of the representative and substantial farmers and stock raisers of Marble township, Lincoln county, Minnesota, where he homesteaded land on the southeast quarter of section 2, on the 16th of April, 1878. Several other parties came from Wisconsin with Mr. Parrott to make a location in Lincoln county. Among these were George Mennie, William Mennie, Frank L. Mennie, and two others, who did not locate in this locality but went through to Dakota. Mr. Parrott was one of the early settlers of the township and passed through all the experiences of pioneer settlers. He originated the petition for the organization of the township in 1880 or 1881, and the first township meeting was held in the house of Ole Siverson. There were about thirteen votes cast at this meeting. Our subject was chairman of the first board of supervisors, which position he still holds. He has also held other positions of trust and has in every case shown himself to be a capable and trustworthy man. He was the first assessor of the township, which position he still holds. He has also held the office of clerk of school district No. 26 since its organization. He has been actively interested in all educational matters and originated the petition for the organization of the district just named. On coming to the township he broke up ten acres of land and in the year following built a house 16x22 feet. He resided in this building some five years, and then constructed his present comfortable dwelling house, which is 18x26 feet in size.

The first year he also built a small sod stable 14x24 feet, and which, after using for two years, was discarded for a building of more prosperous and pretentious appearance. Since his location in the township our subject has been engaged in general farming and stock raising, having accomplished considerable success in every department of his busy life.

Mr. Parrott was born in Green Lake county, Wisconsin, June 13, 1852. He was reared and educated in that county and made that his home until coming to Marble township in 1878. He remained at home with his parents until about sixteen years of age, after which he worked out on various farms for four years, and continued to work at farming until coming to Lincoln county.

The subject of our sketch was the son of Charles P. and Catharine (Small) Parrott, the father a native of London, England, and the mother a native of Ireland. The father emigrated to America from his native land in 1847 and located in Green Lake county, Wisconsin, where he became one of the early settlers. He underwent many hardships in that early day, and had to go many miles to obtain supplies for his family. Milwaukee was the grain market, and it was to that city that the pioneers had to haul their wheat. The father was married in June, 1850. He continued his residence in Wisconsin for a long number of years and became a prominent and influential citizen. He held various offices in his township, and for twenty-six years was clerk of the same. In the father's family there were eleven children—Mary Ann, William, Rose, Charles, John, Maggie, Kate, Aggie, Lizzie, James and Minnie.

The gentleman whose name appears at the head of this sketch was married September 13, 1872, to Miss Elsie Mennie, a native of Green Lake county, Wisconsin, where she received her early training and education and resided until her marriage. She was a daughter of Peter Mennie, a prominent farmer of that locality. Mr. and Mrs. Parrott have three children—Frank, Mabel and Nellie.

In politics the subject of our sketch affiliates with the democratic party. For some years he was a member of the Temple of Honor, and served that organization in the capacity of usher for some years. Mr. Parrott was one of the very first settlers of the town, and his little girl, Nellie, was the first American child born in the township. Our subject has been conducting his farming affairs on a systematic basis, and has surrounded himself with signs of success and prosperity. He is a man of excellent character, intelligent and liberal-spirited, and holds the esteem and respect of all with whom he has to do.

* * *

JOHN A. JOHNSON is at present one of the leading liverymen of the village of Slayton, Murray county, Minnesota. He was born in Sweden June 24, 1852, his parents being Swen P. and Fredericka C. (Cromick) Johnson, also natives of Sweden. Swen P. Johnson was a farmer and left his native country for America some time after our subject's birth. He located finally in St. Peter, Minnesota, where the mother died February 22, 1874. In 1875 the father came to Murray county and located on a homestead, where he lived until 1879. Then having attained a ripe old age, he retired from active life, and has since been living with his children.

The subject of our sketch came to America with his parents, landing in New York, December 13, 1868. They went directly to St. Peter, Minnesota, where the father rented a farm. The subject of our sketch resided with his father on the farm until he was eighteen years of age, attaining that age while his parents resided in the vicinity of St. Peter. After this he worked at various kinds of employment until 1876, when he obtained a position in the insane hospital in St. Peter. Here he was employed for nine years, until August, 1886. After the nine years had expired he worked at various kinds of employment, and about the first of November, 1887, he came to Slayton, where he opened a livery stable. He has since operated this business with excellent success. Mr. Johnson is one of the reliable and influential citizens of the village. He is a man of excellent character and both as a business man and citizen is held in high esteem. He is a republican in politics.

May 28, 1882, Mr. Johnson was married to Miss Anna Rinkel. This union has been blessed with three children—Ruth H., Clifford H. and George A.

JOSEPH STRINGER is a resident of Alta Vista township, Lincoln county, Minnesota. He is the son of John and Mary (Spencer) Stringer, natives of England. When our subject was about thirteen months old the parents came to the United States and located for a time in Illinois. Removing thence they went to Waukesha, Wisconsin, and made that their home until 1863. They then removed to Pepin county, where they still remain. The subject of our sketch was born in London, England, March 7, 1850. With his parents he came to America and after locating a short time in Illinois came to Wisconsin, in which State he received a good common-school education. He remained with his parents assisting in work on the home farm and attending school until he was nineteen years of age. However, at seventeen he had commenced working for adjoining farmers, earning money for his own use. One summer before attaining this age he was away from home working in the lumber business along the river. In May, 1878, he went to Marshall, Lyon county, Minnesota, and engaged in running a breaking team until harvest time. At that time he went to Mankota and engaged in working in harvest fields and through the threshing season, coming to Lincoln county in the fall of that year. He took a homestead on section 20, Alta Vista township, and then returned to Medo township, Blue Earth county, where he remained until the following spring. Then, in April of 1879, he returned to his claim in Lincoln county and has made that his permanent residence ever since, with the exception of about two weeks, which were spent in a short visit to friends in Wisconsin. He now owns a fine farm of 240 acres, on which are found excellent improvements in the way of fences and outbuildings which are so necessary in the operation of a good farm. He has an excellent frame dwelling-house, a good barn 32x60 feet, with fourteen-foot posts, with a good stone basement eight feet in height. He has about 150 acres under cultivation and has a fine grove of trees of his own planting.

The subject of our sketch was married in Blue Earth county, Minnesota, in July, 1880, to Miss Libbie Emerson, a daughter of Juduthan and Lucy (Higgins) Emerson.

The subject of our sketch started out in life for himself a poor young man, having nothing but his own brain and sturdy efforts upon which to depend, and with which to carve out a fortune. He is a man of upright habits, energetic and thrifty, and in all his business relations has been largely successful. Whatever he has to-day is the result of his own hard labor and good management. In politics he affiliates with the democatic party and has taken an active interest in the political affairs of his township. He was town clerk for one and a half years and held the office of justice of the peace for some time. He is a man of good character and is respected by all who know him.

ARNI SIGVALDSON, is one of the substantial farmers of Limestone township, Lincoln county, Minnesota. He is a native of Iceland and was born in Vopnafjord, May 12, 1847. His parents were Sigvald and Arnfrid (Johnson) Sigvald, both natives of Iceland. The parents were farmers in that land and were well-to-do and prominent people.

The subject of our sketch remained with his parents engaged in work on the farm until he was twenty-one years of age, at which time he engaged in work for the minister and continued for some five years attending to one of his farms. He obtained a good common-school education in his native land and came to the United States in 1873. He first settled in Milwaukee, Wisconsin, where he worked in a railroad round-house for three and a half years. He then went to Madison, in the same State, and attended the Norwegian Lutheran Academy for some six months. After this he went to Bear Lake, Michigan, and for five months found employment in a saw-mill. From thence he removed to Winnipeg, Manitoba, and during the winter engaged in clerking in a general store. In the spring of 1878 he again moved, this time locating for about a month in Marshall, Minnesota, after which he came to Lincoln county and settled on a homestead and tree claim on section 20, Limestone township. He has made his residence on this section ever since and proved up on his homestead in 1883.

Mr. Sigvaldson was united in marriage June 8, 1878, to Miss Gidrun Arason, a daughter of Ara and Gudrun (Asmundson) Arason, both of them being natives of Iceland. The fruits of this union are—Skapti Aron, Thora Jonina, Gudrun Julia, Mary Jakobina and Frank.

The subject of our sketch has taken an active interest in the public affairs of his township and has held several offices. He was the first supervisor of the township and continued in that position until 1884, at which time he was elected clerk, of which position he is the present incumbent. He has also been justice of the peace since 1884, and is the clerk of the school board and has been for two years. He is a man of good character, a loyal citizen, and a member of the Iceland Lutheran church.

ELI GILBERT, a thrifty farmer of Moulton township, Murray county, Minnesota, resides on section 8. He was born in the State of New York, November 9, 1849. Until twelve years of age he attended school in the vicinity of his home and then moved to Fond du Lac, Wisconsin. He remained in the State of Wisconsin until the spring of 1875, in which year he removed to Freeborn county, Minnesota, where he followed agricultural pursuits until 1878. He then came to Moulton township, Murray county, and became one of its pioneer settlers. He has been thoroughly identified with all the interests of his locality and has assisted materially in the various public improvements which have been from time to time projected in his township.

Mr. Gilbert was married October 1, 1874, to Mary E. Hart, a native of Wisconsin, and daughter of Herman P. Hart. This union has been blessed with five children, four of whom are now living.

In early life the subject of our sketch was given good educational advantages and became well posted in the learning to be obtained from the district schools. In politics he is an independent, affiliating with no particular party, but supporting the man he thinks best qualified for the position. He has taken an active part in public affairs and has held various official positions, being at present treasurer of his township. He is a man of high character, and is widely known and highly respected as a citizen and neighbor.

PETER O. VINE is a leading citizen of Alta Vista township, Lincoln county, Minnesota. He is the son of John S. and Catharine (Schofeldt) Vine, natives of the State of New York. The parents were well-to-do farmers in that State, and when our subject was two years of age they removed to Green Lake county, Wisconsin, where they are still living in good circumstances, and respected by all who know them.

The place of the nativity of the subject of our sketch is found in the State of New York, where he was born in the year 1844. He removed with the parents to the State of Wisconsin, and remained with them, assisting in work on the home farm, and attending the district school until he was twenty-one years of age. Two years prior to attaining his majority, however, he had been engaged in working more or less for neighboring farmers, and had been saving money for the purpose of buying a farm for himself. On attaining his majority he purchased a farm in Green Lake county, and made that his home until 1879. In that year he rented his farm and came to Lincoln county. The first winter he came to Marshfield, then the county seat. In the following spring he came to section 22, Alta Vista township, and took a homestead of 160 acres, proving up on this land in 1886.

The subject of our sketch was married in Marquette, Wisconsin, in December, 1875, to Miss Corina R. Larson, daughter of Ingebret and Cloe (Smith) Larson, the former a native of Norway, and the latter of New York. This lady was born in Lenawee county, Michigan. Mr. and Mrs. Vine have been blessed with two children—Vernon V. and Oakley W.

Mr. Vine, although of a retiring disposition, and not desirous of pushing himself forward in public affairs, has always been ready to take an active part in the administration of matters pertaining to local government. He has served in various official positions, and in every capacity has proven his efficiency; and has served his constituents to their entire satisfaction. He has held the office of assessor for three terms, and is at present clerk of the township. He is a man of excellent character, and as a loyal citizen and an active benefactor in all general development he has no peer in the township. His wife is a member of the Society of Friends, and is an estimable Christian lady. The subject of our sketch started out in life with nothing but his own hands to depend upon, and with them has carved the way to prosperity and comfortable circumstances. He has created for himself and family a comfortable and pleasant home. Besides the 160 acres he owns in this township he also has a tree-claim of 160 acres in Limestone township, upon which he proved up some time ago. May 25, 1887, he completed his comfortable frame dwelling-house.

———————

CHARLES W. EMBURY, the subject of the present sketch and a prosperous farmer, came to Pipestone county, Minnesota, in December, 1878, locating on a homestead of 160 acres in the southwest quarter of section two in Gray township. He has been a hard-working man and with his own hands has improved his place and made it what it now is,—one of the best farms in the township. He has been engaged in general farming and stock raising and in all his labors has met with good success. He was one of the very first settlers in Gray township and assisted in its organization in 1879. The other settlers who resided here at that time were L. D. Peck, Andrew Gray, Mr. Gleason and Herman Haney, who resided in the northeastern part of the township.

The subject of our sketch was born in St

Armand, Canada East, April 5, 1842. His parents were Charles and Hannah (Brill) Embury, both of whom were natives of Canada East and who now live in Steele county, Minnesota, where they located in about 1876. The father has been a farmer throughout most of his life, and both the father and mother are exemplary members of the Methodist Episcopal church. The parents had a family of seven children, six boys and one girl: Russell John, Catherine E., Charles W., Samuel B., Carmi H., William L. and Edwin R.

The boyhood and youth of the subject of our sketch were spent in school in the place of his nativity. When he was eighteen years of age he removed with his parents to Rice county, Minnesota, where he remained some nine years working for his father on the farm. At this time our subject started out for himself, and, coming to Blue Earth county, purchased a farm and engaged in general farming for a number of years. Then, in December, 1878, he removed to Pipestone county, and made his settlement as was stated is the opening lines of this sketch.

Mr. Embury was united in marriage to Miss Delphine Everson, April 5, 1886. This lady was born in Bergen, Vernon county, Wisconsin, February 22, 1854, and in that State received her early training and a good education. Her parents were LaFayette and Harriet (Morley) Everson, both of whom were natives of New York. Early in life they removed to LaCrosse, Wisconsin, where they met, and later, on November 29, 1852, were married in Vernon county, Wisconsin. For many years her father was engaged in the pursuit of the agriculturist, and during the past fifteen years has been a resident of the city of La Crosse. The parents were well-to-do, and wherever they have lived have been honorable and esteemed citizens. In the father's early life he was a resident

of Ohio, where he received his education and early training. While the mother was still young her people removed to Pennsylvania, where she was reared until coming to Wisconsin. Mrs. Embury was married the first time in 1873 to Alfred D. Hewett, a native of Pennsylvania, who died in 1881. He was a farmer by occupation, and by him Mrs. Embury had three children—Irving, Earl and Amy. Mr. and Mrs. Embury have been blessed with one child—Alta Hannah, born January 28, 1887.

The subject of our sketch is one of the reliable and trustworthy citizens of the township in which he resides, and takes an active interest in all matters which pertain to the welfare of the county. He is thrifty and industrious and has a well-improved farm, every foot of which he cultivates with the exception of the ground upon which his buildings stand. In politics he affiliates with the republican party, and has become one of the leaders in the local affairs of that organization. He is a representative citizen and enjoys the respect and esteem of all with whom he comes in contact.

Charles W. Embury, the subject of this sketch, is a great-grandson of Rev. Phillip Embury, the first Methodist minister that preached the gospel in America.

THORB TORJUSON, one of the leading men of his nationality in Westbrook township, Cottonwood county, Minnesota, resides on section 22. He is a native of the kingdom of Norway, where he was born October 10, 1847. The parents of our subject were Torgus and Martha (Torbjorn) Einertson, natives of Norway. The parents emigrated to America in 1862, locating in Wisconsin for several years. They then came to Olmsted county, Minnesota, and thence to Westbrook township, Cottonwood county, where they now live. Our subject's father was a blacksmith by trade, and is now engaged in farming. In the father's family there were nine children, four of whom are now living—Torjus, Ole, Ellen and our subject.

On attaining his majority, our subject commenced doing for himself, up to this time having resided with his parents, having been given good educational advantages. At twenty-one years of age he commenced working in different lines in Olmsted county, and a year later came to his present location in Westbrook township, where he took a homestead of 160 acres. He has made excellent improvements, and has a grove of eight acres of trees surrounding his house.

In politics the subject of our sketch affiliates with the Republican party, and is a member of the Lutheran church. Since coming to the township he has taken an active interest in all matters of a public nature, and has held various township offices, such as supervisor, constable and township clerk, having held the latter position for several years. He is a man of push and energy, and being possessed of good character, is looked upon with much respect by his fellow-citizens.

OSWELL BOOMHAUER is a prosperous citizen of Murray township, Murray county, Minnesota, living on a homestead on section 18, where he settled in 1867. He has engaged in general farming and stock-raising with large success. When the subject of our sketch came to the township there were other settlers, he being about the fifth to make a location in the township. Moses Cook, Abner Marsh, Captain Aldridge and Jo Aldridge were the parties whom our subject found in the township when he came. The first year Mr. Boomhauer broke about five acres of land, built a straw barn, and put up a log house, the latter being burned after two years, when he erected his present house. Mr. Boomhauer assisted in the organization of the township and throughout its history has been one of the most interested of its citizen in all matters pertaining to the public welfare. The first public meeting was held on section 7, and our subject became a member of the first board of supervisors. He also served in the capacity of township treasurer, which position he held for some time.

The parents of the subject of our sketch were John and Submit (Whitcomb) Boomhauer, the fathers of both the parents being natives of the State of New York. The father was a farmer by occupation and was a well-to-do citizen of the place in which he lived. In the father's family there were thirteen children — Abigail, Fineta, Roswell, Sarah, Sena, Maria, Emily, Miranda, Elizabeth, Mary Ann, John J., Lucy Jane, Simon Peter and Margaret.

The gentleman whose name appears at the head of this sketch was born in Schoharie county, New York, March 1, 1822. He resided in his native county until 1867, and received his early training and education in his native place. For some time he engaged in farming and took an active interest in all matters pertaining to the public welfare in the State in which he was born. On coming to Murray county he made his present location and has ever since resided in Murray county. He has seen many hardships, among them being the destruction of all his crops for four years by the grasshoppers. In order to support his family he had to work out and hunt and trap. One crop was destroyed by hail. All these hardships, however, are now forgotten, as our subject realizes the prosperity and success which have attended his efforts since those early days. He has an excellent farm under good cultivation, and has a large number of cattle and other stock.

Mr. Boomhauer was united in matrimony April 8, 1846, to Miss Angeline Silvernale. This lady was a native of Albany, New York, and was a daughter of Nicholas and Maria (Owens) Silvernale, both of whom were natives of Columbia county, New York. Her parents are still living and are residents of the State of Michigan. When Miss Silvernale was two years of age her parents removed to Schoharie county, New York, and made that their residence for ten years, removing thence to Bradford county, Pennsylvania, where she resided until her marriage. She received an excellent education. In the Silvernale family there were seven children—Angeline, now Mrs. Boomhauer; Margaret, Hattie, Abram, Barney, Sabrine and Calion. Mr. and Mrs. Boomhauer have thirteen living children—John, Calvin, Abram, Barnet, Charles, Albert, Lagrand, Ann, Harrietta, Sabrine, Loretta, Emma and Nellie.

In politics the subject of our sketch affiliates with the democratic party and is a leading member of the Methodist Episcopal church, in which society he holds the office of trustee. He has been a prominent man in the affairs of his town, and has held various official positions with credit to himself and with satisfaction to his constituents. He is a man of high character and is esteemed by all who know him.

ICHABOD B. SMITH is a leading resident of Sweet township, Pipestone county, Minnesota. His home is located on a fine farm on section 28, where he settled in 1878. The subject of our sketch was a Maineite by birth, being born in Somerset county in September, 1835.

Our subject's parents were Daniel and Sarah (Dunker) Smith, both natives of Maine and farmers by occupation. The grandfather, Ichabod Smith, was born in Burwick, Maine,

September 10, 1778, was a blacksmith by trade, and was a prominent citizen in the State of Maine, where he spent his life. He died at Moosehead Lake, Maine, January 15, 1857. Daniel Smith lived and died in his native State, his death occurring October 20, 1887. He was a man of rare qualities and was beloved by all with whom he came in contact. The paper in speaking of his death, said: "The deceased was one of nature's noblemen, honest, benevolent, and liberal to a fault. No person ever appealed in vain to 'Uncle Daniel' for a favor which was in his power to grant." During a long residence in Anson township, Somerset county, Maine, he lived such a humane, benevolent, upright life that he was mourned far and wide by hundreds of warm friends and loving relatives. The mother died September 8, 1886.

The boyhood days of our subject were spent on the farm of his father in Somerset county, where he was given good advantages for receiving a common-school education. When fifteen years of age he commenced working more or less for neighboring farmers in the vicinity of his father's home. Remaining in his native county until April, 1858, he removed to Juneau county, Wisconsin, where he engaged at different kinds of labor until 1861. September 9th of that year he enlisted in Company H., Tenth Wisconsin Volunteer Infantry, and remained with that company until March 3, 1863, when he was discharged from further service. His war experience was of a most trying and exciting kind. It was full of exposure to danger and to sickness, and in consequence of these things, at the date of his discharge, he was completely broken down in health and had to return home to recuperate. On recovering somewhat of his wonted good health he concluded to again offer his services to the Union army. June 15, 1864, he re-enlisted in Compay E, Forty-first Wisconsin Volunteer Infantry, and continued in the service until September 23d, of that year, when he received his discharge. He at once returned to his home in Wisconsin and engaged in various kinds of light labor, such as his broken-down state of health would permit, until 1878. That year, in company with John Clark and Horace Gilmore, he started out with teams to drive through to Pipestone county, Minnesota. In this primitive manner of traveling they accomplished their journey after a few weeks and settled in Sweet township, where they were the first settlers. The subject of our sketch at once located on a homestead, where he has since lived engaged in general farming and stock-raising.

Mr. Smith was married February 13, 1865, to Miss Margaret A. Donaldson, a resident of Wisconsin. The fruits of this union are four children, three of whom are living at the present time: Daniel, Pearlie H. and Mary E. Ichabod R. died when eight years of age.

Mr. Smith is a man of high character and is respected by all citizens of the township in which he lives. He is a man of generous and benevolent characteristics and carries these traits into every department of his life. His career has been visited with many difficulties and sad misfortunes, but through all of these trils he has risen to his duties with a manly fortitude such as should characterize a worthy son of an honored sire. Of his father's family there were four sons in the Union army during the Rebellion, our subject being the only survivor. In politics Mr. Smith is a leading member of the democratic party and belong to the Grand Army of the Republic, Simon Mix Post, No. 95.

RICHARD LAHART, an influential citizen of Cottonwood county, Minnesota, is the son of John and Bridget (Pollard) Lahart, natives of Ireland. Our subject was born in County Tipperary, parish of Ballingerry, Ireland, November 1, 1829. His early life was spent with his parents on a farm, in which occupation they were engaged for many years. Until 1852 he remained in his native country and then came to the United States, stopping first for about a year in Onondaga county, New York. He then went to Allegheny county, remaining about a year, engaged in the lumber business. His next move was to Illinois, where he found employment as a foreman on a railroad, continuing in that line until the cholera broke out among the railroad employes in 1854. He then ceased this work and went to Chippewa Falls, Wisconsin, and engaged in lumbering until 1858. He then came to Wabasha county, Minnesota, and filed on a tract of government land. He lived on his claim until the spring of 1861 when he sold out and rented a farm until 1870. Then he moved to Delton township, Cottonwood county, and filed on a piece of land as a pre-emption. He afterwards changed this to a homestead. This land was on section 34, where he has lived ever since, and where he is now surrounded with the evidences of prosperity and success. While in Wabasha county his home was in Plainview, and his family remained in that town until a year after our subject located in Delton township.

Mr. Lahart was married in Wabasha county, December 22, 1859, to Miss Bridget Granahan. This union has been blessed with the following-named children—John F., Mary Jane (now dead), Thomas E., James W., Charles R., David A., Ellen. Mary, Louisa and Katie. John F. married Maggie Cail, and resides in Minneapolis. He is engaged in the wheat business and owns four elevators in Dakota.

The interest that our subject has taken in political matters is shown by the fact that he has held various township offices, and in each instance has proven a satisfactory and honorable official. He has been township supervisor, school director, etc. With his family he belongs to the Catholic church. Our subject is now in good circumstances, although he has passed through many trying conditions which have brought him considerable loss financially. Several crops in the early days were destroyed by the grasshoppers, and our subject was obliged to leave home in order to obtain money for his family's support. He shoveled snow on the railroads during the winters, and at one time was obliged to obtain seed grain from the State. Since those days, however, he has been doing quite well, and owns a fine farm of 160 acres which is free from incumbrances, with almost the entire acreage under cultivation. He has a fine frame house, a large barn 30x60 feet, with ten-foot posts and a stone basement. He was penniless when he commenced work for himself, and had nothing to depend upon but his own exertions. He has succeeded well in his work and has accumulated considerable means. Whatever he has has been gained through his own exertions.

JOSEPH PICKERING, a thrifty and industrious farmer of Lake Stay township, Lincoln county, is the son of Enoch and Fannie Pickering, both natives of England. The mother died when our subject was a small child, and the father came to America in about 1844, locating in Dodge county, Wisconsin, where he settled on a farm.

Joseph Pickering was born in Stavotshire, England, May 3, 1836. He remained with his father's family until fifteen years of age, coming with them to America in 1844. At fifteen he left home and never returned again, engaging in various lines of common labor until he was twenty-five years of age. He then rented a farm in Goodhue county, Minnesota, and engaged in agricultural pursuits for one year. August 12, 1862, he enlisted in Company F, Sixth Minnesota Volunteer Infantry, and served in the Union army until August 19, 1865, when he was honorably discharged. In 1862 his regiment was ordered on an expedition to Fort Ridgley. They went to that place and after remaining a short time they marched to Birch Cooley to reinforce Company A of this regiment and ninety citizens who were engaged in a battle in that region. The members of Company F heard the firing and other sounds of battle between Company A and the Indians, and started out to assist them. After traveling two or three hours and not being able to find the battle-field on account of the cessation of the firing, they returned to the vicinity of the fort. During the night they were surrounded by the Indians and in the morning a fierce battle took place. Company F, double-quicked through the Indians' lines and found their way into the camp of Company A, where they witnessed a terrible sight. All of the company had been killed or wounded except eighteen men, and these were on the point of despair and were ready to surrender to the Indians. After this raid, Company F returned to Fort Ridgley. The company traveled over much territory on their return trip. This was done for the purpose of picking up the living and wounded settlers and burying the dead. About three months of the following winter were spent by Company F in the village of Glencoe, and after that time had expired they went to Fort Snelling and made headquarters there until spring. They were then ordered to Redwood Falls and there concentrated for the summer campaign against the Indians. Going to Big Bend on the Missouri river, they then returned to Fort Snelling, after having been gone for four months. From Fort Snelling they took a course across the country to Preston lakes, where they built winter quarters and remained until spring. Returning to Fort Snelling they took boats and started down the river to Helena, Arkansas, remaining in that vicinity for three months, then being sent to St. Louis. Remaining in the last named city until March, they were then ordered to report at New Orleans, and after two weeks' stay in the barracks at that city were sent to Dauphin Island, Georgia. After camping in this vicinity for five or six weeks they were then sent on an expedition to Spanish Fort and Fort Blakeley, where they were engaged in besieging the position of the enemy for some three weeks. After the capitulation of the Rebel forces the division to which Company F. was attached was sent to Montgomery, Alabama, where they remained until they received orders to be discharged. After his discharge our subject came to Minnesota and found a location for two years at Pine Island in Goodhue county. His next move was to the State of Wisconsin, where he remained until April, 1879, engaged in farming. He then came to Lincoln county and settled on his homestead of 160 acres on the northeast quarter of section 30 in Lake Stay township. He has remained in that township ever since and is engaged in general farming and stock raising.

The marriage of the subject of our sketch occurred in Dodge county, Wisconsin, in January, 1858. He was married to Miss Abagail Nash, who died some years ago, leaving one child, Elizabeth, now Mrs. Franklin Hall. The second marriage of Mr. Pickering occurred March 2, 1874, in Trempealeau, Wisconsin. On that date he was wedded to Miss Betsey Comstock, a daughter of Rufus and Hannah Comstock, natives of New York. This union has been blessed with three children—William James, Bertie Elmer and Mabelle.

In politics the subject of our sketch affiliates with the republican party and has become quite prominent in the councils of that organization. Five different times he has been elected a delegate to the republican county convention and has served his constituents with fidelity and efficiency in various official positions. He has held the office of township supervisor, and has assisted in various other ways in the upbuilding of the political affairs of the town and county. He is a member of the republican county central committee, and is also a member of the Old Abe Post, No 39, Grand Army of the Republic of Lake Benton. Perhaps no man in the township has done more toward improving the general interests of farming and the public welfare than our subject. He is widely known and wherever known is respected as a citizen of loyal character, a farmer of thorough and systematic habits, and as one of the most influential of Lincoln county's citizens. He has an excellent farm supplied with good buildings and all necessary improvements, and has a pleasant and interesting family.

FRANK D. LINDQUIST is a prosperous merchant and one of the most influential citizens of the village of Dundee, Murray county, Minnesota. He is the son of Frederick and Ellen (Clancy) Lindquist. The father was born in Sweden, the mother born of Irish parents in New York. She died June 24, 1882.

Frank D. Lindquist was born in Carver county, Minnesota, March 3, 1862. When about nine years of age his parents moved to Murray county, Minnesota, and located on a farm in Belfast township, where they remained until the spring of 1888. Our subject was the owner of this farm, having purchased it after the death of his mother in 1882. In the spring of 1888 he sold the farm to his father and came to the village of Dundee, where he built a store and residence, and engaged in the general mercantile business. In October, 1888, he brought his family to the village, where they are pleasantly and happily domiciled.

Frank D. Lindquist was married in Windom, January 5, 1886, to Miss Rosa Gallagher, a native of Trempealeau county, Wisconsin, where she was born September 24, 1864. Her parents were Daniel and Mary (Drugan) Gallagher, natives of Ireland. Mr. and Mrs. Lindquist have one child, Minnie Myrtle. While a resident of Belfast township, of which he was the second settler, our subject served in various official capacities, and in every instance proved his worth and acceptability. He is clerk of the township, which office he has held for several years, school treasurer, assessor, and held the office of justice of the peace for six years. Besides his mercantile interests in Dundee, our subject is also financially interested in various other locations, owning 160 acres of land on section 24 of Belfast township, and also a one half interest in 160 acres on section 1, Graham Lake township, Nobles county, Minnesota. The village of Dundee is located on a portion of this land. Besides being in the mercantile business in Dundee, our subject also has a large trade in lumber and building materials. Mr. Lindquist is a man of excellent business abilities, and has met with merited success in his various financial enterprises.

Mr. Lindquist received an excellent education. He attended the Mankato Normal School during the winter of 1878-79. He taught one term of school in Belfast township during the winter of 1887-88.

———◦❖◦❘⟨❖⟩❘◦❖◦———

CHESTER N. LEWIS, a leading farmer and stock raiser of Lake Side township, Cottonwood county, Minnesota, located on section 20 in 1870. He was one of the early settlers of his locality, and on coming here commenced active operations on his farm. In 1870 he built a sod shanty, living in this for several years, and then built a more substantial and commodious dwelling. He was a member of the first board of supervisors of the township.

The subject of our sketch is a native of Saratoga county, New York, where he was born October 12, 1823. His father was Simeon Lewis, a native of Rhode Island, and a farmer by occupation. He emigrated to New York State when he was twenty-one years of age, and made that his home until his death. He was born March 25, 1776, and died in 1860. He was an influential citizen, and a Baptist in belief. Our subject's mother's name was Lucy (Rose) Lewis, born in Springfield, Massachusetts, in 1778. While still in her teens she moved to the State of New York, and was married near Saratoga Springs. She died at seventy years of age. She was an estimable Christian lady, and took an active interest in religious matters. There were twelve children in our subject's father's family—Warren, Simeon, Jesse, Matilda, Gideon, Lucinda, Sebastian, Elvira, Elias, Benjamin, Esther Ann and Chester N.

The subject of our sketch was reared in Saratoga county, New York, until 1866. He received a good common-school education, and remained with his parents until he was twenty-four years of age. In 1866 he removed to Minnesota, locating in Quincy township, Olmsted county, where he resided until 1870. In that year he came to Cottonwood county, where he has since lived.

Mr. Lewis was married December 8, 1847, to Miss Sarah F. Townsend, a native of Massachusetts. The marriage took place in Galway, Saratoga county, New York. Miss Townsend was a lady of high culture, and was engaged for some years as a teacher. Mr. and Mrs. Lewis have one adopted child, Thomas. Soon after their marriage Mr. and Mrs. Lewis adopted a girl, who is married and living in Olmsted county. She wedded Frank Thompson.

The subject of our sketch was formerly a whig in politics, but now affiliates with the republican party. He is a man of estimable character, and belongs to the Methodist Episcopal church.

――――◆―❖◆❖―◆――――

WARREN McCARTER is one of the leading and influential farmers of Grange township, Pipestone county, Minnesota. His farm is located on section 22, where he has a pleasant, commodious home. He was born February 19, 1835, in Tioga county, Pennsylvania. His parents were Elisha B. and Mary (Morrison) McCarter, both of whom were natives of Pennsylvania. The mother died in 1837, and the father died in 1866, both of whom passing their last days in Tioga county, Pennsylvania. The father was a farmer by occupation and a leading and influential citizen of the county in which he lived. The subject of our sketch left the parental roof in 1851. Later he went to La Crosse county, Wisconsin. Up to the time of leaving home he had been given the advantages for education furnished by the district school, and had assisted his father in work on the home farm until 1850. In that year and during the most of 1851 he engaged in work in a blacksmith shop learning the blacksmith trade. On coming to Wisconsin he adopted the plan of working in the pineries during the winter and in the summer working on the Mississippi river. Continuing this method of life for about two years he went to Olmsted county, Minnesota, where he was one of the first settlers. He pre-empted government land and settled down to the occupation of farming, in which he engaged until October, 1861. While a resident of Olmsted county he experienced many of the difficulties and hardships usually passed through by the first settlers of every country. His nearest market was Red Wing, about fifty miles away, and there were but few neighbors and they were miles away. In the fall of 1861 he enlisted in Company K, Third Minnesota Volunteer Infantry, and served throughout the war, being discharged September 19, 1865. The first battle in which he was engaged was at Murfreesboro, where he was taken prisoner by the Rebels and removed to McMinville. He was paroled and taken from that place to Benton Barracks, Missouri, whence he returned to his home in Minnesota. Soon after he went to Fort Snelling and joined the command of General Sibley, and was with him through his fall campaign against the Indians, being a member of the squad which captured the thirty-eight Indians who were hanged at Mankato, Blue Earth county, a few months later. He returned to the South in December, 1862, and was with his original company throughout the remainder of the war; saw service at Fort Hinman, from whence he went to Vicksburg, near which his regiment was stationed when the city surrendered to the Union army. From thence the regiment went to Little Rock, Arkansas, and served at various points and in numerous battles and small skirmishes. He was discharged from the service September 19, 1865, being mustered out at Fort Snelling, Minnesota. He at once returned to Olmsted county, and remained there engaged in farming until 1879. In that year he came to Grange township, Pipestone county, located his claim and then returned to his home in the eastern part of the State. In the spring of 1880 he brought his family and made a permanent settlement on his land in Grange township.

Mr. McCarter was married to Nancy Huyler, in October, 1855. Miss Huyler was a native of Pennsylvania, and a daughter of George and Sarah (Furman) Huyler, who were also natives of Pennsylvania. This union has been blessed with six children, four of whom are living—Emma L., Merton J., Bertha A. and George H.

In politics the subject of our sketch affiliates with the republican party, of whose principles he is a warm supporter. By virtue of an honorable war record he occupies a leading position in the Grand Army of the Republic, Simon Mix Post, No. 95. He has been chairman of the town board of supervisors for one year, and in all his relations in life, whether public or private, he has conducted himself in an honorable and efficient manner. He is a man of broad ideas, and is respected by all.

THEODORE EICKHOLT is a prominent farmer of Selma township, Cottonwood county, Minnesota. He was born on the river Rhine, in Prussia, June 10, 1824, his parents being Herman and Hermina (Voss) Eickholt, natives of Prussia.

The subject of this sketch resided with his parents on their farm until he was twenty years of age. Until fourteen he was given a good common-school education, and when twenty he enlisted in the Prussian army, serving two years. In 1848 he was again called to the ranks and served three months during the riots in his native country. After his first two years' service he went to live with his mother, his father having died in 1842. He resided with his mother until 1847, when she died, and our subject remaind with the other children on the homestead. In 1849 our subject came to America to avoid being pressed into the Prussian service again. On coming to this country he took out naturalization papers, and, after a brief time, returned to Prussia. He had been home but a short time when he was taken by the police before the governor of the province to be forced into the army of that country. He was told by friends that the police were looking for him, but, feeling assured that his claim as an American citizen would be honored, he did not seek to avoid the officers. On being taken before the governor he claimed American citizenship, and was ordered to show his papers, which he did. He was then told that he could remain in the country five days, when he stated that he could not finish his business in that time. He was then told that he could have ten days, and again he objected that he could not possibly finish his business in that time. He was then told that he could have eleven days and no more, and if caught in the country after that time he would be considered subject to military duty. For some time he lived close to the Prussian line, and every night would go to the side where he was not subject to the police authority. Five policemen arrested him once, but he told them that he did not live on that side of the line, but was only there during the day time, remaining at home on the other side every night. He was annoyed a great deal, but managed to remain in the country until 1854, when he prepared to start to this country. After getting ready to start, a minister friendly to the king and in high favor at court, wanted to go part of the way with our subject to assist him in escaping. This offer was made by this minister on the ground that our subject had not been treated properly by the government authorities. Our subject succeeded in taking ship and getting to this country. He first located in Columbia county, Wisconsin, where he purchased 160 acres of government land. He resided there until 1864, when he was drafted into the Union service. He furnished an eight-hundred dollar substitute, and in the spring of 1865 sold out and removed to Effingham, Illinois, purchased a farm and remained three and a half years. On going to that place he had a good team, wagon and various other articles of personal property and $1,400 in money. He remained in that country until he lost everything he had on account of failure of the crops. His next move was to return to Sauk county, Wisconsin, where he rented a farm, remaining some two years. Concluding, however, that but little was to be made by remaining in that country, he sold out and removed to Winona county, Minnesota, where he rented a farm and operated it for one year. After putting in his crops he came to Selma township, Cottonwood county, and homesteaded his present place, building a stable and cutting considerable hay. In October, 1871, he found his stable and hay had been destroyed by fire. Our subject continued farming, meeting with various discouragements. When the grasshoppers first came to the country he had eight acres of wheat in good condition. This was entirely destroyed by the grasshoppers, as were his crops through the following three years. In 1877 he raised a large amount of grain. He sowed thirty bushels of wheat, and threshed over five hundred bushels. Mr. Eickholt has a fine farm of 320 acres, a nice frame house, and has a large barn. His land is under good cultivation, and well improved. In politics Mr. Eickholt affiliates with the democratic party, and is one of the leading citizens of the township.

Mr. Eickholt was married in Columbia county, Wisconsin, in September, 1857, to Miss Mary Klein, daughter of Henry and Elizabeth (Neder) Klein, natives of Prussia. This lady was born in Erfert, Prussia, August 27, 1841. Mr. and Mrs. Eickholt have been blessed with the following-named children— Herman, Christian, Hermina, Werner, Gerhard, Mary, Bertha, Gertrude and Theodore. Werner died October 5, 1881. Gerhard died November 26, 1881. August 2d of the same year Hermina was taken sick with the typhoid fever, and at one time the whole family, with the exception of Mrs. Eickholt and a babe, were sick with the dread disease.

They were without help and all alone, as the neighbors were afraid to visit them, with one exception, H. M. Goss, who came three times a week to see if the family were in need of anything. The family had a terrible siege of sickness for several months, and there was not a night from August until January 15, 1882, when the lamps were not burning. January 15th was the first night during all that time that some one did not sit up as a nurse all night. After the family got well Mrs. Eickholt took sick, and was sick for three years. All were under Dr. C. A. Greene's care. Christian took sick in 1878, and was sick six years. Herman married Lizzie Renner. Hermina married Manus Brown. Christian wedded Mary Thorson.

----◦--◦◦◦◦--◦---

MAJOR FRANCIS WOODARD, a leading and well-known citizen of Lincoln county, located on the southwest quarter of section 20, of Lake Stay township, in November, 1881. Since coming to the township he has taken an active interest in all matters of a public nature, and has served his fellow-citizens in various ways. He is a man of much native ability, and being possessed of a good education, wields an extensive influence in his town and county. He is a son of William and Martha (Doolittle) Woodard, the former a native of Vermont, and the latter a native of New York. His parents were farmers in Erie county, New York, where they lived until their death. The father died in 1863, the mother in 1869.

Our subject was born in Evans township, Erie county, New York, February 7, 1840. He was given good educational advantages in the district schools and remained with his parents on the farm until he grew to manhood. When about nineteen years of age he was married, and after the death of his parents engaged in working the home farm until 1871. He then sold out his interests in New York State and moved to Faribault, Minnesota, and engaged in teaming and also to some extent in farming. His removal to and location in that city was for the purpose of giving his children good educational facilities. He purchased property and otherwise interested himself in the public enterprises of that city. He made Faribault his home until 1880, in which year he removed to Balaton, Lyon county, Minnesota. His trip overland from Faribault to Balaton was made by team, and was about the hardest two weeks' experience that our subject ever passed through. The roads were in terrible condition, mud everywhere, and apparently unfathomable in depth, and some days the little company could not proceed more than six or seven miles. During this trip the weather was extremely unsettled and the rain fell during a great portion of the time. However, they were fortunate enough to find houses to sleep in every night except one. After passing through this hard experience and getting a first taste of pioneer life they lived in Balaton, and our subject rented a farm, which he worked one season. The first winter found the early settlers but little prepared for the intense cold and heavy snow storms. About the middle of October, one of those terrible blizzards, so well known in Western Minnesota, swept over the country, and Mr. Woodard could not have his threshing done until late in the winter, and when he prepared to thresh out the grain, he found that the stacks had blown so full of snow and ice that it was impossible to do anything with it. It was worthless for the grain and was too icy and full of snow for fuel. The grain was threshed, however, during the winter. This was a hard time, and will be remembered as one of the most bitter winters experienced by the early settlers. The family—not this family alone, but all families in that region—were without fuel. Provisions were scarce and hard to procure, and they were forced to burn railroad fences and posts and whatever else they could pick up or tear down on the prairies. Before the spring opened, and before the snow had begun to disappear, our subject moved to another farm a few miles distant, and in the fall purchased the right to a claim in Lake Stay township, Lincoln county, where he chanced to be with a part of his family on a visit. He then concluded to return to his place near Balaton. During this trip he was destined to meet with another experience which in after years could be related as an interesting pioneer reminiscence. They started on their return to the farm near Balaton, and some time after night had set in reached Coon Creek, a swollen stream, which they had to cross. Fearful for the safety of his wife and two children, whom he had with him, our subject started the team into the water. The rushing stream nearly threw the horses off their feet and the water came up over the front end of the wagon, and it was only by dint of careful driving that the family got through in safety. However, this was done and they had suffered nothing save a terrible fright and very wet clothes. They did not return to their claim until the following spring, but continued improving it and getting it ready for occupancy and cultivation. On coming to the county our subject was in poor circumstances, but by careful and systematic management of his farm he has grown in wealth and prosperity, and is now one of the leading and substantial citizens of the township. He has cultivated his farm thoroughly and has reaped excellent harvests. His land is well fenced and provided with excellent buildings. He has nine head of good horses, a herd of twenty-seven cattle and a number of hogs, and has his farm well supplied with the necessary and needful machinery. Since making his location here our subject has identified himself closely with the best interests of the town and county, and his abilities as a business man have been utilized in various official positions. He has held the position of township clerk and has been justice of the peace during most of his residence in the township. While in New York State he also efficiently filled several school offices, continued in some official position during his entire residence there after attaining his majority. He has also been one of the school directors and road overseer since coming to Lake Stay township. The subject of our sketch is a man of pleasant qualities, of excellent character, and is highly esteemed. In politics he affiliates with the prohibition party.

Mr. Woodard was married March 9, 1859, in Pontiac, to Miss Ann Eliza Page, a daughter of John and Ann Eliza (Tucker) Page, natives of Vermont. Mr. and Mrs. Woodard have been blessed with the following-named children—Ida Melissa, Willis Howard, Orlando Francis, Lily May, Albert Horatio, Helen Bessie and Horace Belden, the last two being twins. Ida married Elbert Hamm, and now lives one-half mile from Balaton. Orlando F. and Lily May are both teaching school.

———·◦·——

WASHBURN LEWIS came to Murray county, Minnesota, in the spring of 1870 and located a farm on section 10 of Murray township. He has an excellent prairie farm and is engaged in general agricultural pursuits. He was about the first settler in the township and is perhaps the first Norwegian settler in Murray county. He assisted in the organization of his township and also in the location of the county seat at Currie. Among the various positions which he has held, for he has taken an active part in public matters, may be named that of supervisor, which he held for one term.

His residence since 1870 has not been wholly permanent. Two years of this time were spent in Kandiyohi county, where he ran a boarding house. The balance of the time has been spent in Murray township. He has an excellent farm of 160 acres, under good cultivation, provided with good farm buildings. He has been quite successful in his farming operations, and in spite of the grasshopper raids of four years through which he passed he has become quite well-to-do and has brought himself into good circumstances.

Mr. Lewis was born in the southern part of the kingdom of Norway. At ten years of age he left his native land and with his parents came to the United States, locating in Green county, Wisconsin, where they lived for three years on a farm. Then Mower county, Minnesota, became their home, where they engaged in farming for thirteen years. During this time our subject had assisted his parents on the farm and attended the common schools at every opportunity. However, his educational advantages were not of the best character, and whatever he possesses to-day is mainly attributable to his own private study and home instruction. He enlisted in September, 1864, in the First Minnesota Heavy Artillery as a private. He served until the close of hostilities between the North and South, and then received his discharge at St. Paul. During the most of his time in the service he was stationed at Cameron Hill, Tennessee. On leaving the service he returned to Mower county, where he lived for a while with his parents. In 1870 he came to Murray county, where he has resided ever since. The subject of our sketch is a man of considerable public spirit, and takes an active interest in public affairs. Possessed of good character he is highly respected by all who know him. He is a consistent member of the Lutheran church.

Mr. Lewis was married in the spring of 1870 to Miss Emma Goeson, a native of Norway. This lady came to America with her parents when she was ten years of age, and located in the State of Iowa, in Fayette county, where her parents lived on a farm. She was reared in Iowa, where she was given a good common-school education. Mr. and Mrs. Lewis have had five children—Lauris G., (who died at three years of age), Gilbert B., Lauris G., Julia B. and Oliver Alfred.

———◆◦✦◦◆———

ROBERT A. VAN NEST is a prosperous farmer located on section 17, Lake Side township, Cottonwood county, Minnesota. He was born in Minneapolis, Minnesota, January 31, 1862, and is the son of Hiram and Rachel C. (Blaisdell) Van Nest, natives, respectively, of Ohio and Maine. The parents were married in Minneapolis early in 1861, and still reside in that city. The father is a speculator and farmer and is engaged in raising blooded stock, giving most of his attention, however, to speculation. He has been and is a prominent man in that locality. The subject of our sketch was one of three sons—Robert A., John H. and Charley Elliott, the latter being named after the eminent physician, Dr. Elliott, of Minneapolis.

The gentleman whose name appears at the head of this sketch was thoroughly educated in his younger days in the city of Minneapolis. He also attended the medical college in New York City, and graduated from that institution in 1887. He also attended the State University of Minnesota and the McGill University, in Montreal, Canada, and received a thorough classical education. For one year after completing his educational course, he was engaged in business at Minneapolis. He came to his present location in August, 1888, where he has since resided. He has one of the finest farms in the State of Minnesota, comprising 2,240 acres, and given principally to stock raising. Generally our subject has three hundred head of cattle, and buys and sells continually. He has three large barns on his farm, one of which will hold four hundred head of stock. His horse barns are 40x90 feet, 30x150 feet and 40x50 feet. He has a sheep barn eighteen feet wide and 150 feet long. He has one of the largest and most pleasant farm-houses in the township, in which are contained eighteen rooms. Besides the monstrous farm our subject owns in this township, he has two other farms in Great Bend township, these latter being rented out. Besides being engaged in raising grain our subject also takes a great fancy to the raising of blooded horses, and has a number of fine specimens of the Norman breed. He has also numerous shorthorn cattle and Berkshire hogs, some of them among the best in the State. In politics Mr. Van Nest affiliates with the republican party, and has taken an active part in all public matters. In the spring of 1889 was elected supervisor of Lakeside township.

Mr. Van Nest was married, November 1, 1888, to Miss Emma Filteau, a native of Chicago, but reared and educated in Minneapolis. She was the daughter of Charles Filteau, a native of Canada and a bridge builder, residing at present in Minneapolis. Her father built all the bridges on the main line of the Omaha railroad through the State of Minnesota. He is a representative citizen of Minneapolis.

———◆◦✦◦◆———

WILLIAM T. W. ERREDGE, one of the reliable farmers of Pipestone county, located on section 32, in Gray township, April 1, 1882. There were but few settlers in that region at that time, and Mr. Erredge was one of the first settlers in the south half of the township. The claim on which he located had been filed upon by another party whose right Mr. Erredge bought. out. He at once commenced his improvements, there being about twenty-seven acres broken on the place. He built his dwelling-house soon after making his location. He also built a large combination granary and stable 14x18 feet and two stories high. On each side of this was a wing, 14x18 feet which were used by him for stabling his horses and cattle. Since coming to the township he has been engaged in general farming and stock raising, and has steadily increased in wealth and prosperity.

Mr. Erredge was born in the City of London, England, April 13, 1825. He is a son of George and Sophia (Read) Erredge, both of whom were natives of England, the father being born in the town of Brighton and the mother born in Somersetshire. The father followed the occupation of butchering throughout the most of his life in the city of London, in which place he located in 1819. He died in that city in July, 1858. The mother's death occurred December 4, 1833. The subject of our sketch was one of eleven children, only three of whom grew to man and womanhood—Eliza, our subject, and Henry.

The gentleman whose name appears at the head of this biography was reared in London, in which city he received excellent educational advantages. He remained with the father's family until he was sixteen years of age, and after that time, until he was twenty-one years old, he clerked in several dry goods, grocery and drug stores. When he attained his majority, in the year 1845, he came to the United States, landing in New York City after a voyage of five weeks and four days. Leaving New York, he came directly to Waukesha county, Wisconsin, remaining in that locality until he came to Pipestone county in 1882. While in Wisconsin he was engaged principally in farming, but in connection therewith also engaged somewhat in threshing. In that State he became quite prominent in local affairs and held several offices in the township in which he lived.

Mr. Erredge was wedded December 29, 1857, to Miss Sarah Donnelly, a native of Charleston, Massachusetts, where she was reared and educated. She came West with her parents to Wisconsin in 1848, and resided in Waukesha county till her marriage. She was the daughter of Peter D. and Mary (McGlaughlin) Donnelly, both of whom were natives of Ireland. The father followed the occupation of farming in Wisconsin until his death, which occurred January 21, 1870. The mother died August 9, 1850. They were members of the Catholic church and people of excellent character and wide influence in locality in which they resided. They had a family of seven children—Mary, Peter, James, Sarah, Ellen, Catharine and Francis. James lost his life by drowning, at Charleston, when he was two years of age. Sarah is now the wife of the subject of our sketch. Catharine and Francis are the only remaining living children. Mr. and Mr. Erredge have been blessed with five children—Richmond W., now married and a ressdent of Gray township; Lillian S., now Mrs. I. Dressler, of Elmer township, this county; George H., who lives at home with his parents; Francis J., a clerk in the city of Pipestone, and Mary Ellen, who still lives at home.

In his political faith Mr. Erredge affiliates with the democrat party. He is a man of broad ideas, energetic and intelligent, and is one of the representative citizens of the township. His farming operations have been carried on with merited success, and he has placed himself and family in comfortable circumstances. In all matters of a public nature he takes a lively interest and has the welfare of his township and county thoroughly at heart. His family are all members of the Episcopal church, in which society they are held in high esteem and exert a wide influence. He has shown his ability as an official in the management of the affairs of numerous local offices. He has been overseer of highways for two terms, and is at present township treasurer.

AMOS PORTER located on section 14, Lake Stay township, Lincoln county, Minnesota, in the fall of 1882. He owns a good farm and is well-to-do and influential. He is a son of Justus K. and Sibyl A. (Harding) Porter, natives of Connecticut and New York. Mr. Porter was born in Watertown, Wisconsin, October 26, 1851.

The early days of the subject of our sketch were spent on the home farm. He assisted in work on the farm and attended the district school until he was sixteen years of age. Two years longer he continued on the farm helping his father in the farm work. At eighteen he entered the Northwestern College at Watertown and continued his course of studies for about two years. When about twenty years old he went to New York, and in company with his brother-in-law, A. H. Carpenter, built a steam grist-mill and engaged in operating the same for about one and a half years. He then sold out and returned to Wisconsin, and resided with his parents until he was twenty-six years of age. During several winters he taught school and engaged in various occupations. In 1878 Mr. Porter was married, and then engaged in farming for two and a half years. When this period had expired he moved to the city of Watertown and engaged in running an engine for two and a half years, part of this time being spent in work for a brickyard and part of the time for a railroad company. When this time had expired he came to Lincoln county and made his location on his present farm, where he has lived ever since.

The subject of our sketch was married April 10, 1878, to Miss Anna Schuleman, a daughter of Frederick Schuleman, a native of Germany. This lady was born in Watertown, Wisconsin, in April, 1854. She received her early training in that city, and made that her home until her marriage in 1878. Mr. and Mrs. Porter have been blessed with the following-named children— Emily, Josephine E., Elsie, Anna, Mary M., Lois Sibyl and Frederick L.

In politics our subject affiliates with the republican party. He has interested himself in various public enterprises, and has officiated in several official positions in the gift of his township. He has been justice of the peace ever since he came to the township, was town clerk for one year, town treasurer one year, and has held the office of school clerk since 1882. He is a man of strong, decided character, is a hard-working, thorough-going farmer, and is respected by all who know him. He is a loyal patriotic citizen, and interests himself in all matters of a public nature. He is a consistent member of the Congregational church, and belongs to the Independent Order of Odd Fellows of Watertown, Wisconsin. He has been quite successful on his farm, and the passer-by witnesses the evidences of thrift and prosperity on his well-regulated place.

CLINTON WILSON, JR., the proprietor of a livery and sale stable at Fulda, Murray county, Minnesota, is the son of Clinton and Sarah (Shinkle) Wilson. The father was a native of Clark county, Kentucky, where he was born October 30, 1806; the mother was born in Ohio, September 4, 1807. Our subject, Clinton, Jr., was born in Sangamon county, Illinois, November 29, 1841, after the death of his father, who was killed by lightning. After the death of the father the mother kept house for her husband's parents for some years.

The subject of our sketch remained with his mother at the home of his grandparents during his early life, employing his time during the summers in farm work and in the winters attending the district school. In 1859 our subject removed with his mother to her farm, where he remained until August 12, 1862, at which time he enlisted in Company C, One Hundred and Fourteenth Illinois Volunteer Infantry. He was severely wounded May 20, 1863, but recovered and served till the end of the war and was honorably discharged with his regiment at Springfield, Illinois, August 12, 1865. He then returned to Sangamon county and remained three years. In 1866 he was married and engaged in farming. At the end of the three years just mentioned he removed to Montgomery county, Illinois, where he engaged in farming for four years, from whence he came to Murray county, Minnesota and took a homestead of 160 acres on section 14, Bondin township. He remained on this homestead until the fall of 1879, during the last two years of which time he was postmaster. He then moved into the village of Fulda and the postoffice was discontinued in the township. In Fulda he was engaged in mercantile pursuits for four years and was also postmaster, which position he held until Cleveland was elected. At the end of the four years he closed out his store and went into the livery business. He keeps a large and first-class livery and is doing a profitable business. The subject of our sketch takes an active interest in civic matters and holds a membership in the Ancient Free and Accepted Masons, the Modern Woodmen of America and the Grand Army of the Republic of Fulda. Mr. Wilson is a republican in politics and takes an active interest in the local affairs of his township. He was treas-urer of the village of Fulda for three terms and was also township treasurer one term. Our subject was in Murray county at the time of the grasshopper raids, which begun in 1873 and lasted four years. During this time the people of that region were obliged to receive some aid from the State in order to live. Part of the time there was not flour enough in the township to make one biscuit. There was little real suffering, but the people had to live on short rations and very coarse food during a large part of the time. For coffee they were often obliged to use wheat or barley. Since that time our subect has been doing very well indeed, and is now in good circumstances.

Mr. Wilson was married in Sangamon county, Illinois, October 18, 1866, to Miss Rebecca J. Bales, daughter of Moses and Catharine Bales. She was born in Madison county, Ohio. Mr. and Mrs. Wilson have been blessed with eight children—Dora M., James A., William O., Leona, C. Earl, Nellie, Maude and Myrtle.

———————

WALTER M. BLACKMUN, a farmer of considerable prominence and a leading citizen, is located on section 18 of Selma township, Cottonwood county, Minnesota. He is the son of Silas and Eleanor (Hinton) Blackmun, natives of New York. Walter M. was born in Waushara county, Wisconsin, in 1859. When he was five years of age his parents moved to Brown county, Minnesota, where he lived until 1874.

Up to 1874 our subject resided with his parents and was given good educational advantages. In that year he came to Selma township, Cottonwood county, with his parents and continued living with them until 1883, when he moved to his farm of 160 acres on section 18. He has a comfortable frame house, a good frame barn and granary and has 160 acres under cultivation. He also owns 160 acres on section 2 of Delton township, which he holds as a tree claim. He has altogether 270 acres under cultivation. Mr. Blackmun is a man of considerable ability and is looked upon as being one of the substantial citizens of the township. He is township treasurer and has held that office for three years; has been assessor two years, justice of the peace two years, and has successfully administered the details of these various offices. In his business life he has been continually fortunate and has accumulated considerable means.

July 23, 1882, Mr. Blackmun was married at his father's house to Miss Agnes E. Hudson, daughter of Charles and Sarah (Blackman) Hudson, natives, respectively, of Canada and New York. She was born in Waushara county, Wisconsin, April 9, 1863; came to Faribault county, Minnesota, at three months of age and was educated there. Mr. and Mrs. Blackmun have had the following children—Raymond and Willie Clyde.

━━━•→•┤◁◈▷├•←•━━━

WILLARD S. FRENCH, who now resides on section 10 of Slayton township, Murray county, Minnesota, was born in Saint Clair county, Michigan, February 7, 1843. He was the son of Marcus L. and Louisa M. (Storrs) French, both of whom were natives of New York. The father was a farmer by occupation, and was the son of Enos and Mahetable French, farmers of New York.

The early life up to eighteen years of age of the subject of our sketch was spent beneath the parental roof. Up to this time he had been given good educational advantages, attending the district school during the winter months of each year. During the summers he assisted his father in work on the home farm. At the age of eighteen, in company with his father and two brothers, he made the first trip overland by the Northern

route to Montana in company with a train of emigrants numbering some seventy-five men. This trip occupied from the 20th day of May till the 10th of August, and they went by way of Fort Benton. Our subject, his father and brothers built the first house in Bannock City, and after this engaged in mining for gold. The father and brother returned to the State of Minnesota after one year in Montana. Willard remained in that locality for three years. Then our subject prospected for a year and a half in Alder gulch, from whence he went to Confederate gulch and there mined for one year. He then came to the State of Minnesota, stopping near St. Peter, where his family lived. He remained about two years in that locality and then in company with Captain Aldridge, whom he met at New Ulm, came to what is now Slayton township, Murray county, where our subject now lives. Mr. French was the second settler in the township, the first being Soloman Lester, the latter having been the first settler and the first to build in the township. Mr. French built the second house, and at once identified himself with the interests of his locality. In matters of a political nature he does not take an active part, but has held various official positions.

The subject of our sketch was married March 8, 1870, to Miss Matilda Bell, a daughter of Charles R. Bell, whom the Indians killed near Fort Ridgely, while on duty at that post, during the summer of 1862. Mr. and Mrs. French have been blessed with seven children, five of whom are living—two sons—Arthur B. and Jay E., and three daughters—Ruby A., Ella V. and Nadine L.

Being a man of excellent business qualifications, Mr. French has been called upon to serve in various official capacities by his fellow-citizens. He was one of the first county commissioners, and was appointed the county's agent to purchase the various books used by the first officials. For one term he very efficiently served as deputy sheriff, and has been justice of the peace for several terms. He is exceedingly popular all over the county, as will be noticed by the fact that, although a democrat in politics, he has oftentimes been elected to office by the franchises of republicans. He is a man of good education, sound common sense, and is overflowing with practical ideas. His character is irreproachable, and he is held in high esteem.

———————

W̱ILLIAM LOCKWOOD located in Edgerton, Osborn township, Pipestone county, Minnesota, in September, 1878, and is therefore one of the earliest settlers of that locality. He homesteaded his present place on section 22 in 1883. On the opening up of the village of Edgerton, Mr. Lockwood put up a store building and engaged in the mercantile business. For a year he owned a store at Woodstock, but he sold out there to a firm name Ellthorp & Ware. Since 1878 he has been more or less engaged in the mercantile business at various places. His farm property are of great value and are well located near the village of Edgerton. Besides the land he owns on section 22, he has 80 acres inside the corporation of the village on section 21; 160 acres on the southwest quarter of section 23, and 80 acres on the southeast quarter of section 15. Besides his property interests in Minnesota he is financially interested in other localities and owns considerable property. He owns a one-half interest in a store building in Crowley, Louisiana, in partnership with C. S. Howard. The subject of our sketch has one of the finest farms in the entire county, and perhaps the best in the township. In late years he has been turning his attention largely to the breeding of thoroughbred cattle. His cattle are principally Herefords, and he is the owner of a fine full-blooded bull which cost $1,600. He has some fine horses of the Norman and Morgan stock, and shipped a stallion of each of these breeds to his property in Louisiana. He has a small herd of Hereford cattle, all nicely formed, excellent animals. The passer-by sees very fine buildings on Mr. Lockwood's farm. He has two large barns, one 80 x 30 feet, and the other 20 x 75. His dwelling is one of the very best in the township, well-built, convenient and commodious.

The subject of our sketch was born in Oswego county, New York, November 8, 1849. He received his early training and education in the county of his nativity, and at about fourteen years of age found employment on the Erie canal for two summers, and for one season thereafter was engaged as deck hand on one of the lake steamers. At the end of this time he came to Baraboo, Wisconsin, and engaged for two years in farming. He then engaged in the selling of pumps and fanning mills, and followed this line of business for three years, in the employ of a firm in Baraboo. At the end of this time he engaged in this line of business for himself in the towns of Durand and Mondova, continuing in the business for a period of four years. He then removed to Fountain City, and engaged in the stage business, having a contract with the United States for carrying mail. After one year had expired he removed to Independence, Wisconsin, and engaged in the hotel and livery business for a short time. His next move was to Rushmore, Minnesota, and, after remaining there a short time, he came to the village of Edgerton, where he made his settlement and opened business as was stated in the opening lines of this sketch.

December 20, 1874, Mr. Lockwood was united in matrimony to Miss Ida M. Burdett, a native of Waukau, Winnebago county, Wisconsin. This lady is a daughter of Mr. and Mrs. F. W. Burdett, natives of Worcester, Mass. When she was eight years of age her parents removed to Concord, Minnesota. She was educated in the city of Eau Claire, Wisconsin. Mr. and Mrs. Lockwood have one child, a son—Lee William.

In politics the subject of our sketch is a loyal supporter of the principles of the republican party. He belongs to the Masonic fraternity, and his wife is a member of the Congregational church. Ever since coming to the township Mr. Lockwood has been identified with all movements which have tended to the social and financial welfare of his fellow-citizens, and in all matters of a public nature he takes an active part. He is a pleasant, affable gentleman, a man of high character and thorough business integrity, and is esteemed by all with whom he has to do. His business qualities are of a high order, and he has been called upon to exercise them in the administration of the affairs of various public offices. He is at present treasurer of Osborn township and has held various offices in the school district. He is an upright, honorable man, and enjoys an enviable reputation among the citizens of Pipestone county.

ROYAL C. WEEDEN is a thrifty farmer residing on section 5, Murray township, Murray county, Minnesota, where he purchased land of the railroad company in 1879. In 1880 he made a permanent location.

The subject of our sketch was born in Washington county, New York, in March, 1826. He was the son of Cogswell W. Weeden, a native of Rhode Island. The father removed to the State of New York at a very early date, and made that his home throughout life.

The early training and education of the subject of our sketch up to the age of fifteen years was received in Easton, Washington county, New York, where he resided with his parents. He then left home and went to New York City and engaged in clerking in a dry goods store for some three years. After spending some time on the New Jersey railroads he returned to New York City and found employment at clerking for three years. Returning to his native home and remaining a short time, during a portion of which he was pursuing a course of study in the Stillwater Seminary, in Saratoga county, New York, he then went to Union village, where he completed his education under the instruction of Judge Lowry, principal of the public schools. He graduated from the high school, and again returned to New York City and found employment as clerk for three years. Passing from thence he went to Chicago and engaged for two or three years as a clerk in the house of J. B. Farwell & Co. Mr. Weeden enlisted in the First Regiment Wisconsin Volunteer Infantry as a private on the breaking out of the war. At the end of three months he was discharged and re-enlisted in the Fourteenth Regiment as a fife major and leader of the band. He continued in the service until the close of the war, when he was honorably discharged. He participated in the battle of Shiloh, where he was wounded. The wound he received was very severe, and his health was not regained for six months after his discharge. Leaving the service he returned to Wisconsin, settling on a farm in Dodge county for a few years. His next move was to Rockford, Illinois, where he was inspector of internal revenue for five years. He then came to his present place, where he has since lived. Mr. Weeden is a prominent citizen of Murray county, and has taken an active part in the local affairs of the republican party. He is a prominent member of the Masonic and Odd Fellows fraternities, and also associates with the United Workmen. He is a man of good abilities, well known and highly respected by his fellow-citizens.

Mr. Weeden was united in the bonds of matrimony in December, 1852, to Miss Harrietta O'Gearn, a native of Wilton, Saratoga county, New York, where she was reared and educated. In early life this lady was a teacher by profession. Mr. and Mrs. Weeden have no children.

———◦—❁◦❁—◦———

AMES WILLMANN is one of the leading Norwegian farmers and substantial citizens of Limestone township, Lincoln county, Minnesota. He is the son of Tobias and Tena (Knuteson) Willmann, both natives of Norway. The subject of our sketch was born in Bergenstift, Norway, February 24, 1853. He remained with his parents on the farm and attended school until he was twelve years of age. At this age, in 1865, he came to the United States with his parents, and first settled fourteen miles east of Dodgeville, Wisconsin. He continued living with his parents until 1866 or 1867, but worked for neighboring farmers during most of the time up to that year. At that time the family moved to Fillmore county, Minnesota, and our subject went with them and continued in that locality until 1879, with the exception of about two years, during which period he was in the Wisconsin pineries. In March, 1879, he came to Lincoln county, Minnesota, and took a homestead of 160 acres on the northeast quarter of section 34. He has made this his home ever since, proving up on his land in June, 1884.

Mr. Willmann was united in the bonds of matrimony in Fillmore county, May 25, 1879, to Miss Julia Berg, a native of that county, where she was reared and educated. Her parents were Andrew and Christine (Berg)

Berg, both of whom were natives of Norway, Mrs. Willmann was born in Fillmore county, February 12, 1860. The names of the children in the Willmann family are—Anna, Ida Tobias, Amanda and Betsey.

When our subject settled in Lincoln county he had but very little means, and for some few years had to live in straitened circumstances. His family occupied a dwelling which was part a dugout and part boards. This primitive method of living was continued for some time, and was then replaced by a good, substantial dwelling, more in harmony with the success and prosperity which had attended the labors of our subject. He has been quite successful in raising grain, and has surrounded himself with the necessary appurtenances of successful farming. He owns three horses, eight head of cattle and has all the necessary machinery. He has a fine farm and has about seventy acres under cultivation. Since making his location in the township he has taken a prominent interest in public affairs, and has held the offices of town supervisor and clerk of the school board. He is a man of the strictest integrity, and is a member of the Norwegian Lutheran church.

———◦—❁◦❁—◦———

OHN NELSON is a reliable farmer of Belfast township, Murray county, Minnesota. He is the son of Nels and Kaisa Ler, both of whom were natives of Sweden. When our subject was three or four years old the mother died in her native land.

John Nelson was born March 3, 1836, in Wermland, Sweden. On the death of the mother he was bound out to a neighboring family and continued with them until thirteen years of age. He then employed his time at the shoemaking trade for about six months, and then went to his father's home and found employment in a saw-mill until about 1855. He then emigrated to Norway, and staid there until 1866, engaged in various kinds of labor, among them being work in a grist-mill, on various farms, and as general carrier about the harbors of Christiania, Norway, where he lived. August 22, 1866, he left his native land and came to America, first stopping in Rolla, Missouri, and from thence, after three weeks' stay, he went to Hannibal, where he found employment with the Hannibal & St. Joseph Railroad Company. Two months were spent in the employ of General Scofield, and then our subject went to Glasgow, same State, where he took the steamer for St. Louis. From thence he went to Washington and worked at macadamizing various highways until spring. From thence, coming to Chicago, he continued mason work for some time, and then commenced at work in loading various boats with lumber and wood. His next employment was in a brickyard nineteen miles from Chicago. In 1867 he went to Evanston and worked at drilling stone, assisting the masons in completing the Methodist University of that place. He did not remain long, however, but soon went to Clairmont, Fayette county, Iowa, where he followed the stone business until winter set in. McGregor was his next objective point, and from there he went to St. Louis, where he obtained a free pass over the Iron Mountain Railroad, and then worked on their railroad until Christmas, and then went to St. Mary's Landing to procure a boat. In this he failed, and then went to Cairo and next to Grand Levee, Louisiana, where he found employment for three months. He then returned to his family in Clairmont, Iowa, and worked for a while at the mason trade. His next location was at a point midway between Elgin and Clairmont, where he worked in a saw-mill, getting out lumber and staves and headings for the Clairmont grist-mill. He continued in this until the spring of 1870, when he came to Murray

county in the summer and took a pre-emption on the southeast quarter of section 24. He has made this his home ever since, and has been engaged in general farming and stock raising, together with blacksmithing and repairing. He has 174 acres of land, about 100 acres under cultivation, and has a frame dwelling-house 12x24 feet with an addition 12x24.

John Nelson was married in Norway to Maron Amelia Anderson, January 1, 1864. She died in Murray county in 1882, leaving five children—Adolph, Anna, William, Emmett and Lewis. May 6, 1883, Mr. Nelson was married again in Cottonwood county to Miss Brit Sogge, a daughter of Goodmund Sogge. This lady was born in Norway in August, 1843.

The subject of our sketch was the first settler of Belfast township, and has taken an active interest in all matters pertaining to the public welfare ever since making his location. He has been township supervisor, and has held other positions. His early life in the county was filled with many hardships, among them being the destruction of his crops by the grasshoppers by which he lost four crops. During these years he was obliged to find work at different occupations in order to support his family. For some time he worked in the pineries, and again he went to the harvest fields outside of the grasshopper belt working on three different railroads. He is a man of good character, and is highly respected by his fellow-citizens.

DE WITT A. DAY is a prosperous farmer of Lake Side township, Cottonwood county, Minnesota. He resides on section 4, where he located in 1873. He has passed through all the vicissitudes and trying circumstances common to the life of all pioneer settlers, but these things have been forgotten to a great extent and our subject is now surrounded with the signs of prosperity and success. In matters of a public nature Mr. Day has always been an active and enterprising citizen, and has held various official positions; he has been assessor during four successive terms, and has been a member of the board of supervisors for three terms; for two years he was treasurer of the school district, and has taken an active interest in educational matters. In his farming operations he has been quite successful and is carrying on an extensive business in grain and stock raising.

Mr. Day was born in Franklin county, New York, May 5, 1839. He was the son of Orrado Day, who was a native of Massachusetts, and a farmer by occupation. In early life he removed to Franklin county, New York, where he was married and resided for some years. In 1862 he came to Wisconsin and remained one year, after which he returned to New York State, where he lived until after the close of the Civil War. He then came to Minnesota, locating in Wabasha county, where he died in 1871. He was an influential citizen and a member of the Methodist Episcopal church. DeWitt's mother's maiden name was Eliza Allen, a native of New York, and who died when our subject was four years of age. Our subject's father married Phœbe Allen, who was also a native of New York State, and who died in 1859. In the father's family there were twelve children, ten of whom grew to man and womanhood—Orrin, Louisa, Rodney, Anna, James, Rhoda, Phœbe, Cynthia, Charles and DeWitt A.

Until twenty-four years of age our subject spent the greater part of the time in New York. He received a good education in the district schools, and assisted his father in the work on the farm. At twenty-four years of age he came to Waupun, Wisconsin, where he stayed a short time, and then

enlisted August 15, 1862, as a private in Company A, Thirty-second Wisconsin Infantry, and was discharged June 11, 1865. Mr. Day participated in numerous battles, among those being Tallahatchie, December 3, 1862; Holly Springs, December 16, 1862; Parker Cross Roads; Coliersville, November 3, 1863; Moscow, the following day; LaFayette, December 27th; siege of Atlanta, in August, 1864; Jonesborough, August 31. 1864; Saltpatchie, February 3, 1865, and Bentonville, North Carolina. Our subject was also engaged in many skirmishes and battles of minor importance. On being discharged from the service he came to Wabasha county, Minnesota, and engaged in farming for seven years. He then removed to his present location, where he has resided ever since. In politics Mr. Day affiliates with the republican party. He is a member of the Independent Order of Odd Fellows, Ancient Order of United Workmen and Grand Army of the Republic fraternities.

Mr. Day was married January 17, 1866, to Miss Eliza E. Jackson, a native of Franklin county, New York, where she was reared and educated. Mr. and Mrs. Day have three children—Emma B., a teacher; Bert R. and Susie W.

—————◆◈◆—————

JAMES FRANCIS HOSFORD located permanently on his present excellent farm on the southeast quarter of section 8, Lake Stay township, Lincoln county, Minnesota, in the spring of 1881. He first came to his claim when nineteen years of age, and made a few improvements. The farm had been located and claimed by his father a short time before. Our subject worked on the claim during the summer of 1878, and in the fall returned to Dakota county, from whence he had come to Lake Stay township. The following spring he returned to his claim and engaged in making improvements thereon until in the fall, when he went to the Wisconsin pineries. Continuing in work there until spring, he again returned to the claim, and has made his home there ever since. This claim was owned by Mr. Hosford's father, and our subject made a special effort to become the possessor of it. In the fall of 1884 he purchased the farm of his father, he having proved up on it some time before.

James F. Hosford was born in Dakota county, Minnesota, November 8, 1859. His parents were Caleb and Margaret (Strathern) Hosford, the father a native of New York, and the mother a native of Scotland. The parents were farmers by occupation, and were well-to-do and influential people in Dakota county. The early days of the subject of our sketch were spent by him on the home farm. He was given good educational advantages in the district schools, and remained beneath the parental roof until he was nineteen years of age. He then came to his father's claim in Lake Stay township, Lincoln county, and after working that during the summer returned to Dakota county in the fall, returning to his claim, as stated in the opening of this sketch.

Mr. Hosford was united in marriage in Lake Stay township, December, 1884, to Miss Ella K. Christianson, a daughter of Seivert and Onny (Johnson) Christianson, natives of Iceland. This lady was born in Iceland, and came with her parents to this country while still young. She is a lady of good qualities and received a good common-school education. Mr. and Mrs. Hosford have been blessed with two children—Margaret and Alva.

On starting out for himself, at the age of nineteen years, our subject had but little money, and had no one to depend upon but himself. His capital was his hands and his efforts. He took hold of the duties of life which presented themselves to him manfully, and determined, if possible, to lay the foundations for a successful life and to obtain a competency. He has been quite successful in all business enterprises, and in whatever way he has turned his attention he has met with prosperity. He has worked hard, but success has crowned his efforts, and to-day, instead of being a poor man, he is possessed of a good farm, well improved, and is a man of prominence in his township and county. He has a good quarter-section of land, with about sixty-five acres under cultivation, five horses and seven head of cattle, besides all implements necessary to successful farming. He has a comfortable frame dwelling-house, and has a pleasant and agreeable family. He has been honored by being placed in various official positions in his township. He has been township treasurer for two years, township supervisor and assessor for one year, and clerk of the school district for four years. Mr. Hosford is a man of good qualities, public-spirited and benevolent, and has the esteem of all with whom he has to do.

HALSEY E. LAMPORT is an influential farmer and resident of section 30, Slayton township, Murray county, Minnesota. The place of his nativity was Mishawaka, Indiana, where he was born August 13, 1849, and his parents were A. M. and Roxy (Ferris) Lamport. The father was born in Ovid, Cayuga county, New York; the mother in Manchester, Dearborn county, Indiana. In early life the father was a shoemaker by trade, but on account of ill-health he finally engaged in farming in Indiana, and followed that occupation until his death, which occurred November 17, 1874. The mother is still living and resides in Decatur, Michigan. In the father's family there were seven children, our subject being the third in order of birth.

The early life of our subject was spent

under parental authority in his native county in Indiana. He was given good educational advantages in the district schools, and did not leave home until he was twenty-one years of age. At that age he went to Toledo, Ohio, and found employment as baggageman for one of the railroad companies. Following this employment for fifteen months he then came west to Manchester, Iowa, where he hired out on a farm for two years. He then rented a piece of land and operated it for another two years. In 1879 he came by team to Currie. For one year he lived on the shores of Lake Shetek. He then purchased a settler's right to the place where he now lives. Since coming to the township our subject has taken an active interest in general matters, and has served in the official capacities of justice of the peace for two years, township clerk for three years, and has held various other positions. He is a man of strong temperance sentiments, and in politics affiliates with the prohibition party. He is a man of excellent abilities, and is widely respected as a man and citizen.

The wedding day of the subject of our sketch occurred March 16, 1876, at Manchester, Delaware county, Iowa, when he was married to Eva E. Stevens, a native of Eaton county, Michigan.

———————

JACOB GORECKI is a substantial farmer of Limestone township, Lincoln county, Minnesota. He is the son of Stanislof and Mary Wiland Gorecki, both of whom were natives of Germany. His parents were well-to-do and were influential people in their native land.

The subject of our sketch was born in Konietz county, Tuchlka, Germany, July 26, 1849. He remained with his parents and received a common-school education in his native land, and when old enough commenced working out as a common laborer. He continued in his native country until 1868, when, in company with his parents, he came to the United States, crossing the ocean in a sailing vessel, and arriving in New York City May 1, 1869. For some three months after he reached this country our subject engaged in work on various farms, and at the end of that time removed to the vicinity of Chicago, where for a time he engaged in farm work. His next move was to go to Sag Bridge, where he worked in the stone quarries for eleven years. This period of employment was spent under one boss. Our subject being thrifty and economical, laid by considerable money. At the end of this period of service he purchased a farm and engaged in farming for himself in Cook county, Illinois. He remained on this farm for six years and then sold out and came to Lincoln county, Minnesota, and purchased 115 acres on section 19 in Limestone township, where he has since lived. He has a good frame house and frame stable and granary and has provided his farm with all the appurtenances necessary to its successful operation. During the eleven years in which he engaged in quarry work in Illinois he drove team for six years, and at various times has traveled considerable. He has visited Cairo, Illinois, Dubois and other places in that State, and also has journeyed to various localities in the State of Michigan. Throughout his career he has been successful in all his various enterprises. Besides being a quarryman and teamster in the quarries in which he worked, he also had experience as engineer for a water pump, also for four months worked for a railroad in Illinois, so that, take it altogether, our subject has passed through varied experiences, but through it all has been economically inclined, and has saved considerable money.

Mr. Gorecki was married in Cook county, Illinois, January 14, 1876, to Miss Rose Glads, daughter of Charles and Margaret (Chemiel) Glads, natives of Germany. This lady was born in the same place as her husband, in 1840. She remained in her native country some years, until coming to America with her parents, where she received her education. The fruits of this union are Anna, Theresa, Joseph, Martha, Mary and Helena.

The subject of our sketch has been a dutiful son, and has had his parents with him during his entire residence in this country. His father died October 15, 1886, at our subject's home in Lincoln county. The mother is still living. On coming to the United States our subject was in very limited circumstances. He is now comfortably settled on his farm, and is one of the most substantial and well-to-do citizens of the township. Since making his location here he has taken an active interest in all matters of a public nature, and has been a consistent member of the Catholic church. He has held the offices of town supervisor and town treasurer. Besides operating his farm, which he has done successfully, he has also been agent for a self-operating washing-machine, and has given more or less of his attention to making sales of this article throughout the township. Mr. Gorecki is a man of true loyal character, is a good citizen, and is held in high esteem by all with whom he has to do.

--------◆-◈◆◈◉◆◈-◆-------

MRS. MARIANNE E. JACKSON is a resident of section 8, Lake Side township, Cottonwood county, Minnesota. She is the widow of William H. Jackson, who purchased 160 acres of land on this section in 1871. He died May 15, 1873.

William H. Jackson was a native of Franklin county, New York, where he was born in 1828. He was reared in his native State, receiving his education in the common-schools, and at thirty four years of age went to Canada, where he engaged in the mercan-

tile business for some time. Returning to his native county in New York, he remained until 1869, and then went to Wabasha county, Minnesota, locating at Plainview and becoming a foreman in a warehouse for a few years. In 1871 he went to the Eastern States, from whence he came to Cottonwood county, April 13, 1872. Mr. Jackson was a man of high Christian character and was loved and respected by all who knew him. He belonged to the Odd Fellows' fraternity, and was a public-spirited and benevolent citizen. He died at the age of forty-four years and was buried in the State of New York. Mr. and Mrs. Jackson have one son, Samuel Warren, now aged about twenty years.

Mrs. Jackson, whose name appears at the head of this sketch, is a native of St. Lawrence county, New York, where she was born, May 24, 1833. Her parents, Samuel and Avis Kingston, were natives of Ireland and farmers by occupation. The parents were members of the Methodist Episcopal church, and were exemplary Christian people. Mrs. Jackson received her education in an academy at Potsdam, St. Lawrence county, New York, and also at a ladies' seminary, and at common-schools in Brasher. Having fitted herself for an educational life, Mrs. Jackson engaged in teaching school and has taught altogether some thirty-eight terms. She is a lady of excellent qualities, and is held in high esteem by all who know her. She is benevolent and charitable and is a member of the Methodist Episcopal church.

After coming to Cottonwood county Mr. Jackson opened a store where the village of Bingham Lake now stands and had an interest in the same for some time. He labored hard to bring his farm to a high state of cultivation and succeeded in making it one of the best. Mrs. Jackson now owns two hundred acres of land where her residence is located, on section 8, and also owns eighty acres on section 16.

JOSEPH H. PARKER settled in Pipestone county, Minnesota, in 1879. The year before, however, he had homesteaded his present place on section 20, Gray township, but his permanent settlement was not made until 1879. He was one of the first settlers to take land in the township and assisted in the organization both of the township and county in 1879.

Our subject was born in Burlington county, New Jersey, July 29, 1855. His parents were Isaac and Phœbe (Skirum) Parker, natives of New Jersey, where they were married and where they lived throughout their lives. The mother died in 1867, and was a member of the Methodist Episcopal church and an exemplary Christian. The father is still living in New Jersey, where he has been engaged in vegetable farming for many years. Joseph Parker was one of seven children, being the second in order of birth—Elizabeth, Joseph, Mary, Lily, Emma, Charley and Phœbe. The last child died when it was seven months of age. Mr. Parker remained with his parents in his native place until the death of his mother, which occurred when he was eleven years of age. Up to this time he had received but little schooling, and what education he had been given was not of a high order. At eleven years of age, on the death of his mother, he hired out to a farmer for a period of six years, receiving but little therefor in the way of money wages. He was, however, given fair advantages for receiving a common school education, which he did by dint of hard study and careful attention to his school duties. At the end of the six years above mentioned he hired out for wages, and continued at farm work until he came to Pipestone county, in 1878. On coming West from his native State he stopped for two months in Sioux City, Iowa, and on landing in that place had but fifty cents in cash to commence life with as a stranger in a busy city. He found employment in the nursery of George H. Wright, and after continuing for some time with him came to Pipestone county by team with Charles Wright. After remaining two years on the farm in Pipestone county he found employment on the farm of Sweet & Nichols, with whom he continued some five years. He did not return to his place until in 1885, since which time he has been a resident of his farm, and has been actively engaged in its operation.

Mr. Parker was married December 4, 1884, to Miss Ella Morrill, who was born in Wisconsin, June 13, 1860. She was a daughter of Thomas and Matilda A. (McEldowney) Morrill, her father being a native of Vermont and her mother of Pennsylvania. Her mother died in 1868, leaving a family of five children—Frank, Andrew, Ella, Edgar and Emma. The mother was a member of the Baptist church, and a thorough Christian lady. The father was married to his second wife in May, 1869, she being Miss Matilda B. Taylor, a native of New York City. Mr. Morrill is at present a resident of Pipestone county, and a biography of his life is given in another department of this work. Mrs. Parker was reared and educated in Wisconsin, where she taught some four terms of school. She received a good education, and is a lady of high intelligence. Mr. and Mrs. Parker have one child, a son, Joseph Howard, born September 23, 1888. Mrs. Parker is an influential member of the Presbyterian church, and is an estimable Christian lady.

In politics the subject of our sketch affiliates with the democratic party, having been a defender of its principles for many years, his father being a democrat before him. During his residence in this county Mr. Parker has formed many warm acquaintances, and has built up a large circle of friends, who believe in his ability and worth both as a man and as a citizen. In matters of a public nature he takes an active interest, and his assistance in these regards is never asked for in vain. He is a member of the society of American Mechanics, and is a leading and representative citizen of the township in which he lives.

JOHN B. DISCH is a leading and influential citizen of Fenton township, Murray county, Minnesota. He resides on a farm on section 34, where he has surrounded himself with many evidences of prosperity and thrift.

The place of nativity of the subject of our sketch is found in Switzerland, where he was born May 15, 1828. His parents were John B. and Tresie (Vencine) Disch, both natives of the same country. The father was a shepherd among the Alps and lived in his native land until his death, which occurred in about 1832. The mother died'in her native land in the fall of 1886.

John B. Disch left his home at the tender age of six years and went to Germany, where for ten years he found employment on a farm in Wittenberg. He then returned home and remained there one winter, after which he went back to Germany, locating at the same place and apprenticing to learn the tailor's trade. At the end of two and a-half years he went to Italy and there followed his trade for two years, returning at the end of that time to his native place. He then served his time in the army, and in 1852 came to America in a sailing vessel. He was forty-two days crossing the ocean, and landing in New York City he took the train for Cleveland. About fifty miles from the latter place he found employment on a railroad and worked in that line for two months, and then went to Cincinnati, where he engaged in work at his trade. For one and a half years he lived in Newport, just across the Ohio river from Cincinnati. From that point he went to Indianapolis, Indiana,

and there engaged for two years in work at his trade. From thence he went to Madison, Wisconsin, and worked at his trade for three years, and then returned to Indianapolis. He was then married and soon after returned to Madison, whence, after two months, he went to Prairie du Chien, same State, and operated a clothing store for two years. Then selling out and going to St. Paul, he engaged in work at his trade for another two years, after which he went to Stillwater, where still another two years were spent in work at his trade. Then in partnership with Mr. Jo. Walf he opened and operated a wholesale liquor store. After two years this partnership was dissolved and our subject engaged in the retail liquor business. He continued at this business for some time and then had all his property destroyed by fire. After this he purchased a lot, built a house and ran a hotel and retail liquor store for some time, when he sold out the saloon and operated a restaurant for six or seven years. He was again the victim of a severe loss by fire, all his buildings and property being destroyed. However, he again opened up in business and erected a new building on the site of his hotel. This new building was three stories high, and was known as the "Mansion House." Our subject still owns the property. In August, 1877, Mr. Disch went to Worthington, and under the direction of Captain Minor, a prominent real estate man of that village, came to the place where he now lives and took 320 acres of land. He has since purchased 160 acres adjoining, and now owns a fine farm of 480 acres. Shortly after he returned to Stillwater and remained until 1881, when he removed his family to the farm in Murray county and made a permanent settlement. Our subject has an excellent farm under good cultivation and provided with fine buildings. He was one of the first settlers of the township and has striven hard to make his farm one of the best in the township. In politics he affiliates with the democratic party and is a consistent member of the Catholic church. He is a man of good character and is respected by all.

Mr. Disch was married July 10, 1856, to Dortha Walder, a native of Switzerland, of which country her parents were also natives. They lived in that place until her death. Mr. and Mrs. Disch have had the following-named children—Mary L. (deceased), Anna T., Rose M., John B., Nicholas A., Thomas, Louis O., Mary L., Joseph F., and Dortha M.

ALVIN H. CARPENTER located in Lake Stay township, Lincoln county, Minnesota, April 28, 1877, and has since made his home on the northwest quarter of section 10, where he owns a fine farm under good cultivation. His parents were Caleb and Susan (Haynes) Carpenter, both of whom were natives of Vermont. Alvin was born in Strongsville, Cuyahoga county, Ohio, March 23, 1830.

The early life of our subject was spent on the home farm, where he remained with the parents until he was nineteen years of age. He was given good educational advantages in the district schools, and also attended a select school for some time. On attaining nineteen years of age he commenced work by the month on various farms in Dane county, Wisconsin, to which place he had removed quite early in life. He continued in Dane county for about two years, engaged in working out, and at the end of that time he purchased a farm and operated it for about a year. Removing thence he went to the mining country near Denver, Colorado, and after remaining during the summer, in the fall returned to Wisconsin, where he spent the winter, and then in the spring of the next year disposed of what property he had in Wisconsin and Ohio, and went to California, engaging in farming in that State for four years. Then for the two years following he engaged in work in the mines, returning to his parents in Ohio at the end of that time. On his return he purchased his father's farm, and one year later was married in Watertown, Wisconsin, and bringing his bride back to his farm in Ohio, they made that their home for about six years. At the end of that period our subject removed with his family to Randolph, Cattaraugus county, New York. Arriving in that place he purchased a saw and planing mill and carpenter shop, and continued doing almost all kinds of woodwork for about four years. During the greater part of this time he was in partnership with Messrs. Leech & Billings. He remained in that business until the establishment was burned out, and then removed to Jefferson county, where he rented a farm and engaged in its operation for two years. His next move was to Minnesota, and coming to Lincoln county he settled on a claim, where he has lived ever since. He proved up on his homestead in July, 1887. The vicissitudes which have visited the life of Mr. Carpenter have been of various kinds and some of them of an exceedingly severe nature. While in California he was quite successful in his various business enterprises and accumulated considerable means. On his return to Ohio he purchased his father's farm with the money he had saved while in California. When he purchased the mill in New York he had to mortgage his farm, and when the mill, upon which there was no insurance, was destroyed by fire, our subject lost all he had, and did not possess enough money to pay the freight on his household goods when he reached Wisconsin on his way to his present home in Minnesota. He succeeded in completing the journey and made his location, and since that time has been eagerly and systematically endeavoring to replenish his depleted fortunes. He now owns a fine farm of 160 acres, with about sixty acres under cultivation, has four horses and sixteen head of cattle, and is well supplied with various kinds of farm implements. He has good buildings and has surrounded himself with signs of thrift and industry. Since coming to the township Mr. Carpenter has identified himself closely with all the interests of his locality. He has assisted both by word and money in the various public enterprises which have been brought to the attention of the people. In the political government of his township he has also taken an active interest, and being possessed of good business abilities, has in every way served his constituency well and efficiently. He has held various official positions, among them being the office of justice of the peace, assessor, supervisor, treasurer and director of the school district. For seven or eight years he has been postmaster of Lake Stay postoffice. He is a loyal citizen, a good friend and neighbor, has many warm friends and acquaintances, and is a consistent member of the Congregationalist church.

December 20, 1868, was the wedding-day of the subject of our sketch. On that day Mr. Carpenter was married in Watertown, Wisconsin, to Miss Mary J. Porter, a daughter of Justus K. and Sibyl (Harding) Porter, both of whom were natives of New York State. This happy union has been blessed with the following named children— Nellie Susan, Alice Elizabeth, May Lily (who died January 23, 1889), and Justus A.

DANIEL C. DAVIS is an influential citizen of Bingham Lake, Cottonwood county, Minnesota, where he has resided since 1871. He was the first permanent settler in the village, and, in company with R. P. Matthews, established all the corners on the town site. On coming to the village Mr. Davis opened a general store and operated the same for about three years. He then commenced handling stock, in which line he has been engaged ever since, in connection with farming. He raises thoroughbred sheep and keeps constantly over two hundred head. Ever since coming to the county our subject has taken an active interest in all matters of a public nature and has held with credit various official positions. He was treasurer of the township for two years, and efficiently filled the office of county commissioner for three years. He has always been a member of the school board and has taken an active part in educational matters.

Mr. Davis was born in St. Lawrence county, New York, July 29, 1844. His father, George W. Davis, was a farmer and a lawyer by profession. He was a native of Vermont, where he was reared and educated. He studied law while still a young man and followed that line for some years. He was a custom officer at Hogansburgh, Franklin county, New York, from the time of Lincoln's first administration to that of Grover Cleveland. He is now living a retired life in New York. Our subject's mother's maiden name was Caroline Jackson, a native of Vermont, where she was reared and educated. The parents were farmers and are still living. Our subject was one of five children— Daniel C., James B. (deceased), Martha A., George E. and Laura A.

Receiving his early training and education in his native State, our subject remained there until he was twenty years of age. He then came west to Peshtigo, Marinette county, Wisconsin, where he engaged in lumbering during one season. Removing thence he went to St. Johnsville, Illinois, where he engaged in handling horses for two years. He then removed to Plainview, Minnesota, and in 1871 came to his present location and engaged in the mercantile business. In politics Mr. Davis affiliates with the republican party, and from 1872 to 1886 was postmaster of Bingham Lake. He is an influential citizen, a prosperous merchant and is esteemed by all who know him. He is a member of the Odd Fellows' fraternity.

Mr. Davis was married in October, 1872, to Miss Minnie S. Rich, a native of Vermont, but reared and educated in Minnesota. Her parents were pioneer settlers of Wabasha county, this State. They are now in the hotel business in Volga, Dakota. Mrs. Davis was for years a teacher. Mr. and Mrs. have had one child, Harry D.

COLONEL SAMUEL McPHAIL is perhaps one of the best known and most influential citizens of Alta Vista township, Lincoln county, Minnesota. He is the son of John and Hannah (McAdams) McPhail, both natives of Scotland.

The native place of our subject, Cōlonel McPhail, is in Russellville, Logan county, Kentucky, where he was born May 2, 1826. His parents moved to East Carroll parish, Louisiana, and located on a cotton plantation when our subject was about eight years of age. Here our subject lived with his parents and went to school until he was twelve years of age, and from that time until reaching sixteen years he was assisting his father in his various duties as a city and topographical engineer. The father was an able surveyor and a man of extensive learning and instilled much of his learning into the mind of his son. The father's life was full of varied experiences and covered an extensive territory. For years he was engaged in surveying rivers and harbors and State lines, in all of which our subject rendered him valuable assistance. When Samuel attained the age of sixteen years he was sent to Baton Rouge, where he entered the State military school. Remain-

ing in that institution for about two years he was then assigned to General Zach. Taylor's command at Point Isabel, Texas. From that point our subject marched with the troops to Palo Alto, where they engaged in their first severe battle May 8, 1846, this being six days after our subject was assigned to duty. After the battle of Palo Alto the command started out on the march and the following morning engaged in a battle at Resaca de la Palma. Forty days later found our subject in the heat of the Mexican campaign on their way toward Camargo, where they stopped thirty days for refreshments and to prepare for their march to Monterey. Having arrived before the last-named city they commenced their siege of the same in September, 1846, the enemy capitulating on the 23d day of that month. Eight days later the regiment returned to Camargo to escort a supply train. The route, however, was changed by orders from headquarters and the regiment started under instructions to march across Mexico to Camargo, thence to Matamoras, thence to Topeca, and from thence they sailed to Vera Cruz and joined General Winfield Scott's forces. They remained until after the siege of that city, which lasted from the 9th of March until the 23d. On April 2d they started for the City of Mexico and were met by the forces of Santa Anna, who gave battle and checked the march of the United States troops at Cerro Gordo, April 18, 1847. They then marched to the City of Mexico and were present at four hard-fought battles before the city. After the surrender of the City of Mexico his regiment was stationed at the City of Tolucco until peace was declared in 1848, when his regiment returned to the United States *via* Vera Cruz.

In 1849 Colonel McPhail visited the Pacific Coast, returned in 1850 and came to Minnesota. In 1851 he made a claim in what is now Houston county, and was the original proprietor of Caledonia, the county seat. On the opening of the Civil War he reported for duty to General Lyon at St. Louis arsenal and was sent to Cairo, Illinois, and was then put on extraordinary duty, in which he visited General Pillow's command at Memphis, Tennessee, where, having been once in General Pillow's command in Mexico, he was enabled to procure a pass from him, which permitted him to pass all the Confederate lines. He has this pass yet in his possession. By this pass he was enabled to visit General Cheatam's command at Columbus, also Holland's Ram, the "Turtle," and to give much valuable information to General Prentiss, then at Cairo. He was in the battle of Fort Donelson, in February, 1862. He returned to Minnesota in 1862, and was sent by Governor Ramsey, with a colonel's commission, to command all the mounted forces of Minnesota. He took forty men at Fort Snelling, marched all night and reported to General Sibley at St. Peter, Minnesota. Remained in St. Peter one day and night and was then sent by General Sibley to the relief of Fort Ridgely. They left St. Peter near sundown, marched fifty miles that night with 150 citizen-volunteers, and arrived at Fort Ridgely at sunrise next morning.

The next movements were those which immediately preceded the

BATTLE AT BIRCH COULIE.

As so much has been written concerning this, we give, in Colonel McPhail's own language, the events leading up to the battle:

"I received orders from General Sibley to take what mounted men I had and move immediately in the direction of the Lower Sioux Agency, the General saying, 'I will send three companies of infantry and some artillery with you. You will ascertain the whereabouts of Major Brown's command and relieve him if he be in trouble. You will move cautiously; keep on the prairie as much as possible, and avoid every possibility of an ambush.'

"I immediately mounted what men I had, the number being just seventy-two. These were citizen-volunteers; many of them mere boys (but of the best of mettle). They were principally armed with shot-guns brought from home. Not one-half of this number had saddles. With this command I moved out about three miles and halted until the detachment of infantry and two mountain howitzers came up, under the command of Major McLaren, of the Sixth Regiment Minnesota Infantry. This perhaps was a halt of half an hour. My command then moved on the mounted men in front, until we reached the forks of the road, about eight miles from Fort Ridgely. Here we made a short halt to determine which road to take, as we were all in a strange land. While here we heard two or three shots, but were undetermined as to the direction they came from. We finally took the right hand road, as the left led us directly into the woods and deep ravines. We moved on until arriving at the east branch of Birch Coulie creek, a deep ravine with some underbrush. Here one of the companies of the Sixth Regiment was deployed and skirmished the deep ravine, the column following closely. We then moved forward about half a mile and discovered men to our left in front. At first they appeared to be walking as if in search of something. They spread out and moved to our left and rear, in the direction of the ravine we had just crossed. Some of the boys shouted 'they are Brown's men,' and started to meet them; when about 400 yards from the command the Indians raised out of the grass and fired on them, wounding one horse. We were then in sight of what proved to be Major Brown's camp, which was on the west side of the west branch of Birch Coulie creek, and only the top of a few Sibley tents were visible. At this time only some thirty or forty Indians had been in sight. My command was then formed into a hollow square, mounted men in front, the infantry holding both flanks and the rear, the the wagons in square. One howitzer was to the front, the other to the rear. We moved in this plan some three hundred yards and halted to see if I could make out what the camp was. Lieutenant Sheehan and myself could not make out whether they were Sibley tents or Indian tepees. I called a half-breed, Quinn by name, and he was undetermined in the matter. By this time fully two hundred Indians were in sight, moving slowly to our left and rear. Feeling that it would be madness to attack the Indians in the ravines and brush with the command I had, Lieutenant Sheehan bravely offered his services to carry dispatches to General Sibley. My command was then on the open prairie between the east and west branches of Birch Coulie creek. Lieutenant Sheehan left on his perilous journey. I watched with anxiety to see him raise the hill on the east side of the creek, but failing to see him, I became concerned for his safety, having heard shots fired in the direction of the crossing. Then William Wilkins, a lad from Rice county, offered to go. I made some objections as to his age, but he had the mettle, and I requested one of the boys to let him have a saddle, he having none, when the brave little fellow mounted, and away he went, crossing the ravine half a mile above the road, came out safely, and, as far as I could see him, he was sailing in the air in the direction of Fort Ridgely. I then held a consultation with Major Mc-Laren. I told him I had decided to withdraw to the east side of the creek and go into camp. The Major at first objected. I then explained to him that it was not our safety that concerned me, but that reinforcements would have to cross the Coulie, perhaps in the night, to reach us. I gave the order, and the command withdrew to the east side of the Coulie, went into camp and awaited the arrival of General Sibley, who arrived about midnight."

At about 4:30 A. M., on the morning of September 2d, the Indians made an attack on the detachment of troops which was encamped on the west side of the west branch of Birch Coulie. This command had taken the usual precautions, although no immediate fears were entertained. Their first warning was a shower of bullets pouring into the encampment, and a fearful and terrible battle ensued, which, for numbers engaged, was one of the most bloody of any in which our forces were engaged during the war. The loss of men in proportion to those engaged was extremely large; twenty-three were killed outright, or mortally wounded, and forty-five were so severely wounded as to require surgical aid; while scarce a man remained whose clothing had not been pierced by the enemy's bullets. The advance of Colonel Sibley's forces from the east side of Birch Coulie soon relieved the command.

In 1863 Colonel McPhail commanded the cavalry in the Indian expedition under General Sibley, and had three hard-fought battles—Black Mound, Dead Buffalo Lake and Stony Lake. In the first of these his cavalry "played Indian," and took thirty-one of the red men's scalps.

After the Minnesota cavalry was mustered out, in 1863, Colonel McPhail went on duty in the Army of the Potomac until the spring of 1864. When he returned he built a stockade fort at Redwood Falls, and located and laid out the town of Redwood Falls. He continued in this place engaged in selling lands and in other lines of business until 1875, when he came to Lincoln county and settled on a tree claim. He received his patent in the spring of 1887. This claim was not taken because of any desire of our subject to make a home, but he took it at the solicitation of the government officials, who desired him to make an experimental tree claim. He commenced his operations with the understanding that in case the tree experiment failed he was to have the land as a homestead. He made a great success in the growth of trees, and as to the kinds best adapted to the Minnesota climate. He has ever since been located in Lincoln county, and has attained large success in his experiments on his land.

Colonel McPhail was united in marriage in St. Louis, Missouri, May 2, 1850, to Miss Martha Kingston, a daughter of John and Mary (Atkinson) Kingston. This lady was a sister of the well-known John Dickenson, and was a native of Lebanon, Illinois. Her father was a native of Kentucky, and was well-to-do and respected by the citizens of the place in which he lived. Mrs. Kingston McPhail died a number of years ago, leaving two children—Etta (now Mrs. G. W. Anderson, a resident of St. Paul) and John (who resides at Tacoma, Washington Territory). The second marriage of Colonel McPhail took place in Grant county, Dakota, September 22, 1885, at which time he was wedded to Miss Minnie Baker, a daughter of August and Caroline (Miller) Baker, natives of Germany. This lady was born in West Prussia, March 30, 1860. Colonel and Mrs. McPhail have been blessed with one child, Logan, named after the illustrious general and statesman.

The subject of our sketch is perhaps the most widely traveled man in Minnesota. He has visited nearly every State in the Union, and in his military character has marched overland through the great territory at the west of the Mississippi river. Possessed of an excellent education and having imbibed the spirit of adventure from his father, who before him was a man of extensive travels and wide knowledge, he was well fitted for enjoying his varied experience in the great western country during his military life from 1846 until 1867. Wherever he has been, his qualities as a thorough-going, active, energetic man have been always identified and utilized. In his military career he served his country with loyalty and fidelity and no duty was ever placed upon him but was entered into with heartiness that bespoke successful accomplishment. His military conduct was of such a gallant nature that it was continually commended by his superior officers, and the promotions he has received have been granted him because of military conduct. In civil life he has been just as prominent as in military life. He is at present county attorney of Lincoln county and has held that position for sixteen years. While in Caledonia, Minnesota, he was judge of the county court, and while in that position exhibited excellent abilities as a judicial officer. He has also held numerous positions of minor importance. He is a member of the Ancient Free and Accepted Masons, Franklin Lodge, No. 25, and also of the Naphtella Chapter, No. 4. In politics he is, as he avers, a straight republican, and always supports the ticket put forth by that party. It is well to notice that in his military career his promotions were gradual and betokened a continual daring spirit and a hearty interest in the successful outcome for the Union arms in the Civil War. He was promoted successively through the offices of second and first lieutenants, captain, major, lieutenant-colonel, and finally colonel. This is no honorary title given by courteous friends and neighbors, but it is a title which has been earned by participation in many hard-fought engagements and for military conduct at the front in the thick of battle. Being a man of public character, and indeed one of the early settlers of Lincoln county, our subject is perhaps one of the best known and most respected citizens of this part of Minnesota.

He is a man of strong, decided opinions, caustic and decisive speech, is feared by his foes, and respected by a wide circle of friends. Our subject has had the honor of raising the first oranges in Minnesota on his experimental tree claim. On his claim he has also a real coffee tree growing, besides many other curiosities as well as plants and trees which most people think cannot be grown successfully in this northern climate.

⁓⁓⬦⬧⬦⬧⬧⬦⬦⁓

HON. JACOB ARMEL KIESTER, an early settler in Blue Earth City, the county seat of Faribault county, Minnesota, was born in Mount Pleasant, Westmoreland county, Pennsylvania, on the 29th day of April, 1832. His great-grandparents, on both the paternal and maternal sides, were Germans, and came from the old world and settled in eastern Pennsylvania before the American Revolution. His grandparents, Conrad and Sussana Kiester, emigrated to western Pennsylvania in their youth, and located in Westmoreland county when that region of country was yet quite new. Here the father of the subject of this sketch, David Kiester, was born. David Kiester married Miss Lydia Armel in 1831, and their children were—Jacob A. and Daniel B. Kiester. Lydia Kiester died in 1883 at the age of seventy-one years, and David Kiester died in 1888 at the age of eighty-one. David Kiester resided all his life at Mount Pleasant, Pennsylvania, of which place he was for many years chief burgess and justice of the peace. He was a man of fine education and extensive reading, always taking a large interest in politics, and was a prominent and consistent church member from his youth until his death, and was ever highly respected for his unquestioned integrity and ability.

Jacob A. received his education in the common schools and at Mount Pleasant and Dickinson colleges in Pennsylvania, pursuing with the exception of several studies, the usual college course, but did not graduate. He also spent four years of his youth in learning the mercantile business and book-keeping with an uncle, Jacob Armel, for whom he was named. He commenced the study of the law while yet in college, and removing subsequently, temporarily, to the city of Madison, Indiana, continued his legal studies in the office and under the direction of Hon. S. C. Stevens, formerly one of the associate justices of the Supreme court of that State. He was admitted to the bar at Madison in 1854. Some time after his admission to the bar, he returned to Pennsylvania, still continuing his legal studies, having in the meantime his eye on the West as a promising opening for a young attorney. In 1857 the great "tidal wave" of immigration was directed to Minnesota, as it had been for several years previous; and, in the spring of that year, Mr. Kiester came to Minnesota, intending to locate at St. Paul, but the Capital removal bill having been passed, removing the Capital to St. Peter, he went thither. But the removal bill proved a failure and finding that property was held at exorbitant figures at that place he concluded to visit the Blue Earth valley. Arriving at Blue Earth City, he found only a few log cabins, but a country surrounding the place which he believed would at no distant day be one of the most productive, wealthy and populous sections of Minnesota. In this he was not disappointed. Here he concluded to locate for the time being at least, and here he has made his home ever since. He engaged in the practice of the law, being the second attorney to locate at this village. In April, 1857, he was the plaintiff's attorney in the first law suit instituted and tried in the county. Judgment was rendered in behalf of his client. He was soon chosen county surveyor, which office he held for two terms. A number of important county roads which exist to this time were surveyed by him, and also the boundary lines of many farms and several additions to Blue Earth City and other work done pertaining to the business of surveyor. He was also elected register of deeds of the county, the most important county office in those days, in the fall of 1857, and this office he held for eight consecutive years, but declined a re-election. In consequence of being register of deeds, he became also the principal conveyancer for many years in the south half of the county, and which continued to be the fact long after he retired from that office. He was elected a member of the State legislature and served in the session of 1865, representing a district embracing a large part of Southwestern Minnesota. Soon afterwards he was appointed county attorney of Faribault county and held the office a large part of a term. In 1869 he was elected judge of the probate court, which office he still holds, being elected twice with but slight opposition, and for eight consecutive terms without opposition, and by the unanimous vote of the electors. Though so long in this office the remarkable circumstance has occurred, that no appeals have ever, as yet, been taken from his decisions. He was for some years a member of the board of education of Blue Earth City independent school district and was for two years president of the board. He has also held other local offices from time to time.

Mr. Kiester was married in 1859 to Miss Caroline Billings, daughter of Levi Billings, one of the early settlers in Faribault county. They have had six children, one of whom is now dead. Those living are Charles C., May F., Grace L., Oliver A. and Gertrude.

The first temperance society in Faribault county was a Good Templar's lodge, organized at Blue Earth City in 1860, of which

Mr. Kiester was the first worthy chief, and held this office several terms.

Mr. Kiester was made a Mason in 1859 and was worshipful master of Blue Earth City Lodge, No. 57, in 1876 and 1877. He was mainly instrumental in securing for this lodge the largest Masonic library (and the first) in Southern Minnesota. It is a library of purely standard Masonic books. He was district deputy grand master in 1882 and 1883, and was grand orator of the Grand Lodge of Minnesota in 1885, and was subsequently twice senior grand warden, and twice deputy grand master, and in 1889 was chosen grand master of Masons in Minnesota.

Mr. Kiester and family are communicants of the Protestant Episcopal church, and he has for some years been lay reader of the parish. His political connection is with the republican party, in the organization of which, in Faribault county, he was the first mover in calling the first county and legislative conventions in 1857, and which organization he has continued to this day. He was also at one time a member of the Republican State Central Committee. He was an earnest supporter of the Union cause during the great Rebellion. He follows fearlessly the dictates of his own conscience and gives to religious, educational and fraternal institutions his hearty support. He has always taken an active part in all public enterprises of a local character and devoted much time and labor to securing a railroad for Blue Earth City. His tastes have always been of a studious and literary character, and he is a diligent reader of the current sciences and literature of the times. He has, since when quite young, been a frequent contributor to various newspapers and periodicals, usually under some *nom de plume*. For a number of years he employed his leisure hours in writing a complete history of Faribault county, its first quarter of a century being volume first, which is now substantially finished, and which will be published at no distant day. One of the townships in Faribault county was named for Mr. Kiester.

＊＊＊＊＊＊

FREMONT S. GIBSON. This gentleman has been a prominent factor in the later growth and development of Rock county, Minnesota. Until recently he has been proprietor of the Beaver Creek Roller Flouring Mills, which were destroyed by fire April 9, 1889, and he is still a resident of Beaver Creek, Minnesota.

F. S. Gibson is a native of Essex county, New York, where he was born September 23, 1856. He is the son of Rev. William and Hannah (McKee) Gibson, natives of Essex county, New York. The father was engaged largely in farming during the most of his life, but since twenty-one years of age he has been connected with the Methodist Episcopal church as an exhorter and minister. The father moved to Floyd county, Iowa, in 1865, where he remained until 1887, when he removed to Beaver Creek, where he has had charge of the Methodist Episcopal church for two years. He connected himself with the Minnesota conference, and holds a ministerial relation with the church at Heron Lake. The father was a stanch abolitionist before the war, and enlisted in 1862 in Company G, Eleventh New York Cavalry. He served for one year, and then, on account of ill-health, resigned and returned home, holding the rank of second lieutenant. In the spring of 1864, health being somewhat restored to him, he again enlisted in the Second Regiment Harris Light Cavalry, of New York, remaining with that regiment until the close of the war. He held the office of quartermaster and acted as drillmaster for the regiment during his later service. His military career was of an exciting nature, and he was engaged in fourteen severe battles during the last year's service. He was with General Sheridan in the Shenandoah Valley and in Sheridan's raid around Richmond, and on to Appomattox, and was wounded April 6, 1865, at the battle of Harper's Farm, or Sailor's Creek, Virginia. At that engagement his horse was shot from under him, and as the horse fell Mr. Gibson was caught beneath its body. From the effects of this accident he has never fully recovered, In the father's family there were ten children—John H., Catherine M., William T., Fremont S., George A., Emma G., Sarah F., Ida M., Frank E. and Charles Edward.

The early life of the subject of our sketch was spent with his parents on the home farm. He was given good educational advantages in the district schools. He remained with his parents until his marriage, after which for two years he engaged in farming in Chickasaw county, Iowa. He then went on the road and occupied his time by selling fruit trees for one year, after which he came to Rock county, Minnesota, and settled at Luverne. Until 1885 he engaged in handling farm machinery in Luverne and in that year sold out and removed to Beaver Creek, where he opened a private bank and operated the same for about a year. Then he organized the State Bank, with a capital of $25,000 and accepted the position of president of the institution. About the same time he organized the mill company, of which he was made president. It had a capital of $20,000. In September, 1888, he purchased all the rights of the milling company. In November, he sold out his bank stock and retired from his connection with the bank. He then gave his entire time to caring for the extensive and important interests which clustered around his milling enterprise. The mill had a capacity of one hundred barrels of flour per day, had fourteen sets of rollers and was thoroughly and completely fitted with all modern milling improvements. This was continued until April 9, 1889, when, as stated, it was destroyed by fire, loss, $25,000; insurance, $17,000. He has been interested in various business enterprises in the county and purchased considerable property, being now the owner of three fine farms in Rock county. His name is indissolubly associated with the business history of Southwestern Minnesota, as he has assisted very materially in advancing the interests of Rock county. He built a fine brick business building at Beaver Creek in 1887, which cost over $4,500.

In matters of a public nature, Mr. Gibson has taken a prominent part and has affiliated with the republican party since he could vote. He was president of the school board, is a member of the Odd Fellows fraternity and is one of the substantial and prominent citizens of the county.

Mr. Gibson was united in marriage in 1877, to Miss Saphronia R. Clark. This lady was a daughter of William and Catherine (Souers) Clark, and is a native of Detroit, Michigan. She is a lady of excellent qualities and is highly educated. Mr. and Mrs. Gibson have had one child, Daisy M.

ALVIN M. BOOMHOWER is a farmer and stock raiser residing on section 26, Holly township, Murray county, Minnesota. He came to this county with his father's family in 1866, his father locating a farm two miles west of the village of Currie, where he still lives. A biography of the father is found elsewhere in this work.

The subject of our sketch was born in Schoharie county, New York, May 3, 1851. At twelve years of age he came west with his parents, locating first in Dodge county, Minnesota, remaining there for some four years. He then came with them to Murray county. In about 1869 our subject went to Alma City, Waseca county, Minnesota, where

he received a good practical business education. He then returned to Murray county and located on a homestead three miles from the village of Slayton, making his residence on that land for some five years. He was then married and resided on a farm near the village of Currie, after which he came to his present place on section 26, of Holly township. He has a fine farm of 240 acres, and is engaged in general farming and stock raising. He has one of the best farms in the township, and his buildings are well protected by a grove of cottonwood, walnut and willow trees.

Mr. Boomhower was married in March, 1882, to Miss Carrie A. Quackenbush, a native of Wisconsin. She is a daughter of Justin Q. Quackenbush, a farmer by occupation and one of the first settlers of Murray county. Mr. Quackenbush died in 1884. The subject of our sketch is a republican in politics. He is a member of the Sons of Temperance.

JOB WHITEHEAD is one of the earliest settlers of Pipestone county, Minnesota, and is now one of the most influential and well-to-do citizens of Sweet township, where he resides on section 2. He was born in Tiffin, Ohio, April 6, 1831. His parents were Johnathan and Lucy (Hatch) Whitehead, both of whom were natives of Ohio. The father was by occupation a tanner and currier and was an influential citizen of the locality in which he lived. In about 1839 the parents removed to Ogle county, Illinois. The parents were professed Christians of the Methodist persuasion, but, as it will appear in this biography, young Job did not adhere to the religion of his fathers. Living most of his time on the frontier he learned to love that freedom of action and thought that are characteristic of him.

The subject of our sketch remained with

his parents throughout his early life, and with them went to Illinois, where he received his early education, such as could be had on the wide unsettled frontier, by going two or three miles to school, three or four months in the year. He was about ten years old when his parents moved to Ogle county, Illinois, then an unsettled county eighty miles west of Chicago, and there, upon the wide prairie, with the chance of education above mentioned, he lived on a farm with his parents, and when supplies must be had would haul their wheat and produce to Chicago across unbridged streams and sloughs; and at night the "starry world above his head; his wagon box and blanket for his bed:"

> "Then like the lamb when tired of play
> Lay down and slept the night away."

Under such conditions, watching the forces of Nature and their phenomena, it taught him those lessons of liberty and justice so little practiced under our present form of government, which pretends to protect the individual in his natural rights—the earth, the air, the water and the sunshine—but steals them all away by legislation and transfers them into the hands of a privileged class, yet still demands obedience to the powers that be, claiming they are ordained of God.

In 1853, at the age of twenty-one, he married Rebecca Biggers, seventeen years old, daughter of Clark Biggers. After their marriage the young couple rented a farm and commenced keeping house with as little means perhaps as any one ever did before or since. Eight years after this marriage the anti-slavery war broke out between the North and the South; although willing to peril life and health in the cause of human rights, he did not enlist, although openly denouncing the crime of human slavery, black or white. His father and mother were earnest abolitionists of the Garrison school, and the young boy must have nursed in those principles of humanity and liberty that have been the ruling force in his character through life. This biography would not be complete or truthful to leave out of this record the folly, the virtue and vice, the hopes and fears, the joys and sorrows, that make up the sum of human life and the subject of this sketch has had more than his share of some of them. In 1860 he purchased eighty acres of land six miles southwest of Rochelle, Illinois, by contract to pay in four annual payments, and then commenced the struggle to make a home on the wide, unbroken prairies of Illinois. Having good health and an unlimited amount of energy it seemed a very easy thing to do. He had not yet learned that a few gold gamblers of the world controlled the price of his products and labor by controlling the money volume and transportation. At this time, in 1856, was born to them a son—Henry Owen.

> "Like rays of light in darkness drear
> Comes childhood's innocence to cheer,
> To nerve the arm and heart to bear,
> The heavy burdens of our care,
> Or we would sink beneath our load
> Nor dare the roughness of life's road."

After taking off one crop, building and breaking up, he found the proceeds were not enough to pay the cost of interest and labor, to say nothing of principal. He saw that debt must accumulate and without some unusual streak of fortune must eventually take the place, and he sold the improvements, settled up his business and hired his board at six dollars per week, including his wife and child. He had yet to learn that man was born to an inheritance of a certain amount of unoccupied land without money or price. Land should be as free to man as the air he breathes. If not he is a slave! Who owns the land, owns him that tills the land. Man can not be free until he has the right to go onto a piece of unoccupied land, improve it, sell his labor to whoever wants to buy and go somewhere else and do the same. After boarding his family about one year he concluded to try again to buy a home. He bought eighty acres in the same county and here was born their second son, William Wallace; and three years after his birth, in 1863, feeling very uncertain of paying for the farm, he sold out and moved to Cedar Rapids, Iowa. His parents also came to Cedar Rapids to live with him. He first moved his household goods by wagon; a long and tedious journey, creeping along over the muddy and hilly roads with one small team of mules. However, he reached the place in safety, rented a house, got dinner and stood waiting for his parents and family to come on the train. They came and were somewhat surprised to find they were so comfortably settled. Now, what to do was the question, as father, mother, wife and children must have a living, and every dollar had been spent in rent and house fixtures and a team of horses; but with health and strength he thought there must be some way to do it, so the next morning found him in hot pursuit of something to do to keep the wolf of want from the door. But after searching the city from one end to the other and finding no employment of any kind, although answering a dozen advertisments and each time disappointed, night found his courage giving way. The next morning found him more fortunate; he bought twenty acres of timber from Mr. Beaver, of Cedar Rapids, and bargained to pay for it by delivering sixteen cords of good body wood, to be corded in Mr. Beaver's yard, which he commenced to deliver immediately. This timber was growing on three very high hills and had to be cut and rolled down in the valley before it could be loaded on a wagon. Very few would have undertaken such a contract—it looked almost

impossible of accomplishment at the time. But Mr. Whitehead had already learned that there was more faith in immediate action, and that hard blows would accomplish much more than to have "the faith of a small mustered seed" said to "remove mountains." So he immediately commenced work on his contract, and by making some ingenious arrangements for loading, also shortening the distance to town, he then could make five or six dollars per day. He also kept two or three boarders, and it seemed as though they were on the road to success. In a little over a year having cut and hauled all the timber, from which he made altogether $1,500, and not finding any more team work, he rented a farm of a Mr. Gibson, on Crab Apple creek, eleven miles northeast of Cedar Rapids and moved there with his family, having laid up clear of all expenses $350. He determined to make farming pay better than the hard lifting and chopping in the hot summer. He adopted the rule to do whatever he found to do in the best possible manner, and left nothing undone that might add to his success. When he came to plant his corn, to facilitate the cultivation he determined there should be no crooked rows and marked it out as straight as a rope could be drawn. It was Mr. Gibson's pride to refer his neighbors to his renter's corn rows by saying in conversation " as straight as Whitehead rows of corn," and travelers would be heard to say, " Oh! they are the straightest rows of corn I ever saw."

In the fall, when he came to market his crop, which proved to be an average one, he found the price of wheat to be fifty-five cents per bushel; oats eight cents a bushel and corn fifteen cents per bushel, which would not pay the cost of production. Then he began to despair of ever being able by honest labor to make a home. He again sold out to the first emigrant going west, and gave immediate possession by moving out that afternoon, and packed up his household goods, and left them in the care of Mr. Gibson, to be forwarded to any point that he might afterward direct. Previous to this sale he had been making some experiments in tanning glove leather, which he had partly learned from his father, who was a practical tanner and currier. Having made some important discovery in that direction, he determined to use them to his advantage. Tanning a few skins and making a full set of glove patterns, and printing a few thousand recipes, he then returned to Ogle county, Illinois, his former home, to spend the winter and give his wife a chance to visit her sisters and friends, upon his return to Illinois, finding there was a ready sale for his recipes and patterns, he immediately went to work, first offering his old friends one-half the proceeds for carrying him around, which was very liberal, as the sales would sometimes reach as high as thirty dollars a day. His plan was to take any kind of produce, and sell it in the first market, and so passed a very profitable and pleasant winter, and the next spring, in 1866, he moved to Story county, Iowa, near the college farm, and bought forty acres of unimproved land, and paid $400 cash for it, having saved from his sales $800, and now was the possessor of forty acres of land and $400 to improve it with. His first business was to build a house, looking around among the carpenters he found one who agreed to furnish lumber, lath and plaster, and build the house in a good, workmanlike manner for $400. In the meantime he had sent to Mr. Gibson for his household goods, which came in due time. By making gloves and mittens, it enabled him to break and fence the land with a good post and rail fence, paint the house and set out six thousand small trees. At this time he invented and patented a vehicle to run without horses, by combined levers and springs. He made a small model that cost him $75, and sent it

to Washington. Munn & Co., of New York City, were his agents, and he received a letter from them offering to put up a full-sized vehicle for $1,000, but, acting upon the advice of some wealthy friends he did nothing further with it. At this time was born to them, in 1869, a third son — George Ulysses, and it now seemed as though his efforts to secure a home had been successful and nothing could add to his comfort or happiness. A snug little home, three interesting children; free from the burden of debt, close to market and good schools—reasonable mortals would have been content. But Mr. Whitehead thought he must have more land. With three boys growing up, it looked as if he must secure a home for them if possible. Having received a good offer ($1,400) for his little home, he sold out and moved to Webster county, on the Des Moines river, and bought 160 acres, timber and prairie land, unimproved, for $7.00 per acre. He commenced to improve by building 200 rods of ditch and about 500 rods of good post and rail fence—the first open fence built in the settlement, as the farmers let their hogs and cattle all run out. But Mr. Whitehead could not see the propriety of putting more value in a fence than the farm was worth, and eventually they all adopted the open fence, but not without a fight in the courts. But soon, in place of the crooked worm rail fence, appeared the straight post and rail or board fence, which added safety to the road and beauty to the farm. The first summer he rented land adjoining him. The second year his crops were all destroyed by a terrible hail storm, and he lost a span of work horses that cost him $400; and two valuable colts. Having lost two years of labor and $600 in horses, the wolf of want again looked in at the door. At this time (1871) was born the fourth child, a daughter named Lulu. In 1870 Dudley Whitehead, brother of Job Whitehead, had moved to

Lyon county, Iowa, eighty miles north of Sioux City, and located a colony and laid out a town on the Rock river known as Rock Rapids. It was in an unsettled and wild country, but unsurpassed in loveliness and fertility, and from the glowing descriptions sent to him from his brother, and from the fact that he had determined to buy no more land, he was induced to go and see it for himself. In the summer of 1872 he made a visit to his brother at Rock Rapids, and was so well pleased with the country that he sold out, and in the fall of the same year moved to Lyon county, Iowa, and made a settlement on Little Rock river, fifteen miles east of Rock Rapids, by taking the last eighty acres of homestead land in the county. He immediately commenced improvements by building, planting fruit and other trees, as he had always done on the six other farms which he had bought and improved with so much hard labor. And here, in Lyon county, Iowa, was multiplied to him all the evils fourfold which he had heretofore passed through. That section of the country was visited in 1873 with countless millions of grasshoppers. It was as though all the grasshoppers in the world, including those of Egypt in Pharaoh's time, had come. They covered the surface of the earth, and ate up everything but the grass, and packed the earth so full of eggs that the plow would leave them on the surface like sown oats. And for three years they devoured the land and left the inhabitants in want and despair. The subject of this sketch was left in utter destitution, with a large family, and was forced to tramp hundreds of miles to find employment. No one but a parent can understand the feelings of hopelessness and despair that fill the heart when leaving home and loved ones in the uncertainty of relieving their wants or of ever seeing them again. Mr. Whitehead remained in Lyon county for about eight years, being engaged in different kinds of employment, generally in farming for himself. In 1874 was born their fifth child, a daughter, named Evalina. In the same year, with his brother, Dudley, he came to Pipestone county, and in April of that year located the claim where he now lives. His brother located on the quarter section where the Milwaukee depot now stands. The subject of our sketch did the first breaking in the entire county, and has been identified with the interests of this locality ever since. In 1878 he brought his family to his new home, where they have lived ever since, occupying a prominent and leading place in the social movements of the town in which they reside.

In politics Mr. Whitehead is a union labor man, heartily indorsing the principles of the Cincinnati convention, and will support no man for office that does not believe in and advocate those principles. He believes in free homes for all mankind; they must not be subject to taxation, judgments nor executions; that national banks are more dangerous to our liberties than foreign foes; that our money should be a full legal tender paper money, without redemption; that the amount be increased to one hundred dollars per capita; that the supreme court of the United States is a dangerous and unnecessary power, as is also the senate of the United States, composed of millionaires, lawyers and bankers; and that the people—the government—should own and control the railroads. In short, he believes that the productions belong to the producers, as does the sunlight, the air, the water and the earth, which is man's inheritance—the free gift of nature.

Mr. Whitehead has lived a long life of usefulness, and with an incredible amount of work has improved and built up eight good homes, with houses, fences, fruit and other trees for some other happy inmates. And by careful attention to his business matters, by thrift and energy, together with economical habits, has made for himself a comfortable home, with trees and fruits and flowers, and now enjoys the happiness usually brought by a long and well-spent life. He is a man of high character, and has the respect and confidence of all his fellow-townsmen."   * *

CHARLES H. BENNETT. This gentleman is one of the most enterprising business characters of all Pipestone county, and he has done more in the upbuilding of the financial and other interests of Pipestone City and vicinity than any other resident. He is energetic and full of practical ideas, and he has assisted in financial and all other ways possible in the development of the financial institutions of his locality. He has been looked up to for years as one of the mainstays of the business element of the city, and has built up for himself a widespread and enviable reputation. He is at present engaged in operating a very fine drug business and also in dealing in city property in Pipestone City. He came to the county in the latter part of August, 1873, with a view to starting a town. At that time he found himself in a treeless, uninhabited county, and had a choice of fine locations. In April of 1874 he came to where Pipestone City now stands, bringing with him a load of lumber from Luverne, in Rock county. Of this he built the first habitation in the city or county, just across the street, east from where the old Calumet hotel stood. After building his shanty he ate his dinner, and looked upon this day's work as the commencement of his town enterprise. He at once returned to Le Mars, Iowa, at which place he was engaged in the drug business, and where he had settled in 1869. In that city he was one among the first settlers, building the first store on the town site, and shipping in the first bill of goods over the Illinois Central Railroad in 1869. From this time he commenced making trips by team to Pipestone City, making some half-dozen visits each year. He continued in this way until in 1876, when he made a permanent location where is now the site of Pipestone City. He had made some improvements prior to this time. In 1874 he had forty acres of land broken, being the first breaking in the county, part of which was on the town plat, and the balance where the large groves are now found west of the city. These groves are beautiful landmarks, at present there being two of them of twenty acres each just west of the city. Some of these trees are forty feet high, were the first to be set out, and are now the finest and largest in the county. On coming to this location in 1876, he at once commenced making further improvements. He had the original town plat of Pipestone City laid out in July of that year, and had interested with him in the enterprise a gentleman by the name of D. E. Sweet, who is now a resident of Louisiana. After this brief view of the establishment and early history of what is now the prosperous city of Pipestone, it can be readily seen and understood that Mr. Bennett was foremost as founder of the city, and to him as much, or more than any other man, is due its present welfare and prosperity. Throughout its history there has never been any project tending to the development of Pipestone but has found in Mr. Bennett a warm and valuable friend.

The gentleman, whose name appears at the head of this biography, is a native of Union City, Branch county, Michigan, where he was born July 2, 1846. His parents were Isaiah and Emily (True) Bennett, natives, respectively, of Vermont and New Hampshire. In his younger days the father was a Methodist clergyman in New York State, and later was a pioneer clergyman and merchant in Michigan. He interested himself largely in the development of the State in which he had located, and became one of the founders of the cities of Jackson, Ann Arbor, and Union City. At the birth of our subject, he was a resident of Union City, where he was engaged in the general mercantile business. In 1851 the father organized an expedition which went overland to California, returning after an absence of some two years. In 1857 he removed with his family to Dubuque, Iowa, and there lived a retired life until his death, which occurred November 27, 1865. The mother is still living and has reached the advanced age of eighty-two years. She is at present living with her son, Charles, the subject of this sketch. In the father's family there were six children, four of whom are now living—General William T. Bennett, now a resident of Australia; Major Orson W. Bennett, now a resident of Union City; Charles H., and Annie E., now the wife of Silas B. Wright, a banker, insurance and real estate broker of De Land, Volusia county, Florida. The sons of this family have always been loyal and patriotic citizens, and all volunteered and served in the late War of the Rebellion, and were honorably mustered out at its close.

Charles H. Bennett, the subject of our sketch, remained with his parents through his early life, being given excellent educational advantages in the schools at Union City, Michigan, and also in the high school at Dubuque, Iowa. After completing his education, he accepted a clerkship in a drug store in the city of Dubuque, in which employment he remained for two years. Leaving that city he then went to Philadelphia, Pennsylvania, where he again engaged in the drug business as a student with Professor W. M. Proctor, and attended lectures given at the Philadelphia College of Pharmacy. He con-

tinued in this city, following the drug business and engaged in the study of pharmacy, for some two years, after which he removed to Chicago and there filled the position of prescriptionist in leading drug stores. While in Chicago he enlisted in Company D, Ellsworth Zouaves, One Hundred and Thirtyfourth Illinois Infantry. This was in April, 1865, and he continued in the service for some seven months in Missouri and Kentucky. He was with the Union forces that cleared the rebels and guerrillas out of western Kentucky, and that drove the rebel general Price out of Missouri when that general started through the State on his last raid. Closing his military career he returned to Chicago and engaged with Wilson Brothers, jobbers, importers and manufacturers of gents' furnishing goods. He was one of the first salesmen that this firm ever employed, and he continued a satisfactory and profitable engagement with them, resigning to engage in business on his own account in Charleston. In 1866 he removed to Sioux City, Iowa, and entered the employ of Charles Kent, who operated a large drug store. During the years 1866–67 he had entire charge of this business. Then he removed to Le Mars, then a paper city, as has been already stated, in 1869, and became the pioneer drug merchant and business man of that city. Continuing in Le Mars principally for some eight years, he then sold out his stock and business property and removed to Pipestone City. Besides his city investments he has also become largely interested in farming lands, and now owns some four hundred acres, partly surrounding the present town site. Fifty-five acres of this land was laid out in the original town plat. He has built two stone store buildings—the Syndicate and the Bennett blocks—which are considered equal to any of the magnificent buildings of the city. They are fitted with plate and stained glass fronts, high ceilings, hard pine floors, bronze fittings, wood finish, and are erected in ornate and modern styles of architecture; besides being almost fire-proof. They are conspicuous monuments of energy and taste, and of the abiding faith of Mr. Bennett in the future of the city. His first wood office building was put up after the construction of the pine shanty already mentioned; it was constructed in June, 1876, the lumber being hauled by team by him from Worthington, about fifty miles distant. This building was then used as an office, and is now a part of the residence of Mr. Bennett. Later a wood store building was erected by our subject, and used by him for his drug business for some ten years. Mr. Bennett has been one of the most public-spirited citizens of the county, and has given liberally of his means to assist in its development. He gave some four thousand dollars' worth of property toward the building of the original Calumet hotel. The proprietors of this hotel, the finest in Southwest Minnesota, were the Close Brothers. Prior to this, Mr. Bennett donated twenty-eight acres of land to the Chicago, Milwaukee and St. Paul Railroad Company, for the magnificent sum of one dollar, this land being granted for right of way and depot grounds in the city limits. Altogether, he has presented many thousand dollars' worth of property to the four different railroad companies which now enter Pipestone city for a meagre consideration. He has deeded to these railway companies grounds on which the four railroad depots are located. In early days of the town he also gave business and residence locations to parties who have built thereon.

The subject of our sketch was united in matrimony October 6, 1877, to Miss Adelaide B. George, of Warner, New Hampshire. This lady was the daughter of Gilman C. George, and is a lady of excellent education and rare social and domestic qualities. She has exhibited marked poetic genius, and her name appears as a contributor in various leading publications.

In politics Mr. Bennett affiliates with the republican party, and is a leading and influential member of the Grand Army of the Republic, Simon Mix Post, No. 95, being past commander of the local organization. He has interested himself largely in the welfare of the old soldiers, and was appointed the first agent in the county for the State Soldiers' Home Board. He has frequently represented the post in department, and in 1888 in the Columbus National Grand Army of the Republic encampments, and was the originator of the movement which resulted in the Minnesota legislature, in 1889, appropriating $12,000 for publishing 10,000 copies of a history and roster of Minnesota Soldiers of the Rebellion, and presenting each survivor a copy. Our subject has held many positions of trust and responsibility within the gift of his fellow-citizens. He was elected the first county attorney at the organization of the county, was the first town clerk, and one of the first members of the city council. Wherever he has lived his services have been demanded in various official positions, in all of which he has proven his capability and efficiency. While a resident of Iowa he held the position of justice of the peace, which office he has also held since coming to Pipestone county. He is at present one of the board of Pipestone county commissioners, and actively interests himself in all matters pertaining to the welfare of the county. He is honorably connected with the Old Settlers' Historical Society of Pipestone county, of which he is the historian. This society meets once a year at Pipestone City, enjoys an annual banquet and indulges in reminiscences of pioneer days. He is also secretary and one of the board of trustees of the Presbyterian church. Mr. Bennett is one of the solid and substantial citizens of Pipestone City and county, and is, without doubt, one of the most progressive and enterprising men to be found in southern Minnesota. He has always been willing to assist in public projects, and has ever held out liberal financial and other inducements for any and all business institutions that would add to the growth and prosperity of his locality.

ALVIN T. SHATTUCK, a leading citizen and wagon-manufacturer of Worthington, Nobles county, Minnesota, is a native of Bath, Steuben county, New York, his birth occuring October 15, 1844. His parents, Daniel and Harriet (Emerson) Shattuck, were natives of New York. The father was a carpenter by trade, and followed that occupation throughout the most of his life.

Calvin T. was given a good common-school education and lived with his parents until he was eighteen years of age. He then enlisted in Company F, One Hundred and Sixty-first New York Volunteer Infantry, and served gallantly and faithfully throughout the war. His first engagement was near Port Hudson, Louisiana, the next at Fort Donelson, and then followed Mansfield, where he saw much severe fighting. Then came the battles of Sabine Cross Roads, and Alexandria on the Red river in Louisiana, besides numerous sharp skirmishes. Mr. Shattuck served in the Union army until October 28, 1865, when he was mustered out of the service with his regiment at Fort Jefferson. He returned to his home in New York and for several years engaged in carpenter work. April 20, 1872, he landed in Worthington and followed his old trade for a while, and then engaged in farming for three years, on a soldier's homestead that he had taken on section 2, Dewald township, Nobles county. At the end of these three years he returned to the village, and working in the flouring mills, for three

years, after which he went to the Black Hills with a load of poultry and flour, being gone about four months. Returning to Worthington he engaged in carpenter work until 1880. He then bought out a stock of groceries and operated a store for two years. He then sold out and engaged in manufacturing wagons, which line he has followed ever since, except six months spent at the Hot Springs in Arkansas.

The subject of this sketch is a prominent citizen and has the confidence of all with whom he has to do. He is a member of the Grand Army of the Republic post of Worthington and also of the Independent Order of Good Templars. He is a genial, warm-hearted man and is possessed of a high moral character.

Mr. Shattuck was married in Bath, Steuben county, New York, in April, 1866, to Mary Elida Dunlap, a daughter of Edwin and Sarah Ann (Fenton) Dunlap, natives of New York. Mrs. Shattuck was born near Madison, Wisconsin, May 23, 1846. This union has been blessed with the following-named children—Minnie and Dollie. The latter died April 13, 1886.

REV. D. GRIFFIN GUNN, one of the leading ministers and ablest divines of the Episcopal church in the Northwest, is a resident of Wilder, Jackson county, Minnesota. Mr. Gunn is a native of North Carolina, and was born in Caswell county, March 13, 1845.

When he was one year old his people emigrated to Alabama, locating in Lowndes county, where they resided some nine years. Their next move was to Brandon, Mississippi, where our subject remained until he was sixteen years of age and where for two years he attended the State Military School. He spent four years in the Confederate army; returned to Mississippi and completed his literary education by taking a private course in one of the best schools in the State. He then pursued a course of studies in the theological seminary of the Episcopal church at New York City. Leaving that institution in 1874, he then took charge of the Saint Ambrose church, continuing its pastor for four years. Our subject then turned his steps westward and located in Windom, Cottonwood county, Minnesota, where he built the Church of the Good Shepherd and was pastor of the same for some three years, then going to Worthington, Nobles county, Minnesota, he headed a project which resulted in the building of a neat church edifice over which Mr. Gunn had charge for about a year, on the expiration of which time he returned he returned to his former charge in Windom. Remaining in charge of the Windom church for two years, he then turned his attention to a college enterprise mentioned in another part of this sketch. In the meantime, however, Mr. Gunn was instrumental in building good churches in Slayton, St. James, Madelia and Lake Crystal.

In 1885 Mr. Gunn laid out the site of the present prosperous little village of Wilder, where he now resides and where he owns some fourteen residences, besides numerous unimproved lots. Adjoining this village is the Breck farm and commercial college, of which our subject was the founder. Of this institution Bishop Whipple is president and our subject is secretary and attorney-in-fact. The history of this educational enterprise will be found in another department of this volume.

Mr. Gunn is a genial, warm-hearted gentleman, is a progressive and energetic business man and citizen, and is and able and interesting preacher. His management of the various important enterprises that have engrossed his attention since he chose the Northwest as his abiding place, is indeed commendable, and the eminent success that has crowned his work shows him to be a man of more than ordinary talent and ability. Mr. Gunn is a member of the Masonic fraternity, of the Independent Order Odd Fellows, and also belongs to the Good Templars Society.

Mr. Gunn was married December 19, 1865, to Miss Kate M. August, a native of Vicksburg, Mississippi. She was the daughter of A. N. August, a merchant of Vicksburg and a major in the Confederate army. Miss August was educated in the Clinton Institute of Vicksburg. Mr. and Mrs. Gunn have been blessed with eight children—Lizzie, Griffin, Katie, Daniel, Fannie, Albert, Alford and Henry Benjamin Whipple.

THE WILDER FARM COLLEGE was founded by Rev. D. G. Gunn, of Wilder. The donors of the property at Wilder were Colonel John L. Merriam, Amherst H. Wilder and Mrs. Carrie Thompson, all of St. Paul, Minnesota. The idea of founding a college of industry, to meet the wants of the middle class, was conceived by Mr. Gunn, while in New York City in 1880, but the project was not carried into effect until 1885, when Mr. Gunn and family moved on the ground and built the first house—now used as a cheese factory, R. H. Rucker being superintendent and manager. Then he began the foundation upon which has been finished recently the Farm College, for young men and women. The college was opened in September, 1887, by Rev. Charles Ware and Mrs. S. B. Ware, and the work begun with eighteen pupils, and closed after a successful term. The second year was opened by Eugene Rucker, B. S., in September, 1888, and closed with success—and thirty-six pupils. The third year opened in September, 1889, and is destined to close with over one hundred pupils. The officers of the college are as follows: Eugene Rucker, B. S., principal; William A. Dryden, B. S., superintendent; Edward P.

Coleman, B. S., secretary; F. M. Wallace, B. S., master of accounts; Eugene Dryden, librarian; Miss Thurston, musical directress; Miss Taylor, oratory; George H. Drury, janitor, and Mrs. M. F. Drury, matron. The college is something new in the plan of teaching, and is destined to revolutionize educational work. There is no end to the possibilities of such a work. The trustees of the college are: Rt. Rev. H. B. Whipple, D.D., LL.D., president ex-officio; Rev. James Dobbin, vice-president, Faribault, Minnesota; Rev. D. Grifflin Gunn, secretary, Wilder, Minnesota; Rev. Frank Millspaugh, Minneapolis, Minnesota; George H. Christian, Minneapolis, Minnesota; Harvey Officer, St. Paul, Minnesota; Sylvester M. Cary, St. Paul, Minnesota; Victor M. Watkins, treasurer, St. Paul, Minnesota.

CHARLES MYLIUS is president of the First National Bank of Pipestone, Minnesota. He was a native of England, where he was born in the year 1848. He was the son of Henry and Fannie (Ripley) Mylius, both natives of England. The father was a man of considerable wealth and was engaged extensively in the operation of his landed estates.

The subject of our sketch remained with his parents during his early life and was given an excellent classical education, becoming a graduate of the Victoria University. After he had completed his education he engaged in the banking business in his native country until coming to America in 1883. His first settlement was made at Le Mars, Iowa, where he engaged in banking. After one year's residence in that city he came to Pipestone and opened a private bank, which was continued until the organization of the First National, of which our subject was made president. The First National Bank opened for public business March 4, 1889. Since coming to the city Mr. Mylius has been ac-

tively engaged in improving his various property interests, building the famous Calumet Hotel and bank in 1888. This structure is one of the finest in the State and is exceedingly well planned and built in the most approved modern style. From the ground up, it is the most elaborate in all its details and was built at a cost of some thirty thousand dollars. The Calumet is one of the finest hotels in the State outside of St. Paul and Minneapolis. Besides this fine property our subject erected the finest dwelling-house in the city in 1886, and has beautified his residence grounds by setting out shade and ornamental trees. Besides having invested largely in city property Mr. Mylius has also interested himself extensively in farming lands and at present owns 640 acres in one body, which he uses as a grain farm. He also owns large tracts of land in adjoining counties. A brother of our subject, Edward H. Mylius, is engaged in operating the bank of Mylius Brothers & Co., at Adrian, Nobles county, Minnesota.

The business career of the subject of our sketch has been of the most successful character, and in all his various financial ventures he has met with continued and merited success. Receiving an excellent education in practical business life as well as in the schools of his native country, he came to Pipestone well fitted for the financial life which has fallen to his lot. He is a man of energetic and systematic habits and whatever occupies his attention is handled with thoroughness and dispatch. He has become one of the wealthiest and most substantial citizens of Southwestern Minnesota, and enjoys the utmost confidence of those with whom he has business transactions. He takes an active interest in all matters which tend toward the development of the city and county. He is a leading member of the Masonic fraternity, and in politics is of a conservative turn of mind.

WILLIAM JACOBSEN is engaged in the loan and real estate business in Luverne, Minnesota. He is one of the best known citizens of the county, having made his location here in an early day, and having been intimately associated with all business developments ever since. He came to Luverne in March, 1873, and engaged in the mercantile business, building a business block on Main street, where he continued in trade for some eight years. His first building was the first east of the old Luverne House, and five years of the time mentioned above were spent in that building. He then built just east of the Security Bank building, and for three years carried on his business there. He then sold out to Messrs. Landen & Nelson. In connection with his mercantile business he also engaged somewhat in farming and stock raising, in which lines he has continued ever since. May 2, 1882, he organized the Rock County Bank, of which he was president for some six years. He erected the bank building in 1882, and became one of the most important factors in that enterprise. He was one of the organizers of the Security Bank and also of the Bank of Valley Springs, Minnesota, of which he was president. He has been identified with the financial interests of some of the most important business institutions of the town and county, and has built up a large fortune for himself as a result of his own energetic labors and business capability.

The place of the nativity of the subject of our sketch is found in Norway, where he was born in 1844. His younger days were spent in school, and he was given a thorough course in an agricultural and business college in his native land. Until he came to America in 1866 he was connected with various farming enterprises in Norway. On coming to America he first located in Allamakee county, Iowa, where he was employed on a farm in the summers and attended school during the winters for some two years. Then for a time he taught school and afterward accepted a position as a clerk in a store at Waukon, Iowa, continuing thereat for some four years. At the end of that period he went to Lansing and engaged in the same business for some six months. Removing thence he went to Madison, Wisconsin, and took a course in a business college in that place. From thence he went to Chicago and engaged in clerking for the well-known firm of Field, Leiter & Co., with whom he remained for a few months. Returning to Waukon in the fall, he remained until spring and then came to Rock county, Minnesota, making his location in the village of Luverne.

Mr. Jacobsen was married in 1877 to Miss Milla Erickson, of Luverne, a daughter of Andrew and Maria Erickson. Five children have blessed this union—Effa, William, Leonard, Walter and Nora.

The subject of our sketch is a stanch republican in politics, and is a member of the Masonic fraternity. He has a beautiful home in the northwestern part of the city, fitted with all modern conveniences and surrounded with beautiful shade and ornamental trees. He has a pleasant and agreeable family, and occupies a prominent place in the social circles of the city. Mr. Jacobsen has associated himself with all enterprises which have tended toward the improvement and development of the financial resources of Luverne and vicinity. As has been already stated he has been closely connected with the organization of several of the local banks, and not only of this village but also of adjoining towns. He has been engaged to a considerable extent in putting up business buildings and residences in the city, and has done as much, if not more, than any other man toward making the city what it now is. The growth of Luverne has been rapid and important, and our subject has always proven a willing supporter of all projects which aided in this improvement. He is one of the wealthiest and most substantial citizens, and is respected and esteemed by all with whom has to do.

HON A. D. PERKINS is the popular and efficient judge of the Thirteenth Judicial district of the State of Minnesota. He resides in Windom, Cottonwood county, Minnesota.

Judge Perkins is a native of Erie county, New York, where he was born March 24, 1847. His parents were Horace and Eliza (Horton) Perkins, both of whom were natives of Erie county, New York. The subject of our sketch remained with his mother until he was thirteen years of age, up to which time he had attended the district school, and worked on the home farm. For two years after leaving home he engaged in farm work, the first year at $4 per month, and the second at $5.50 per month. During the winters he attended school, working in various families for his board. The third year he entered the employ of a farmer, who compelled him to sleep in an outhouse, where he was so exposed that he took a severe cold, being obliged to return home after one month's service. When he was sufficiently recovered he took a three months' course in penmanship, and then his mother arranged matters so that he could take a course in the Griffith Business Institute, at Springfield, Erie county, New York. He continued in this institution for three years, and then engaged in various occupations for himself. He went to the oil region near Oil Creek, Pennsylvania, where he continued some two years. He then returned home with the intention of taking up the study of law, or entering an apprenticeship in a machine shop. He went to a point twenty miles from Buffalo, and not knowing what else to do, looked over a machine shop in that place, and finally entered the employ of Strickland & Co. Soon after he purchased twenty-five dollars' worth of law books, and started for home, at this time being nineteen years of age. He made an arrangement to work for his step-father (his mother having married Mr. Wood in 1856) one day in the week for his board. The balance of his time was devoted to the study of law. After one year spent in this way he wrote to Mr. Boies, a lawyer of Hamburg, in regard to studying law in his office. The business of this gentleman had been purchased by a Mr. Calkins, and the letter falling into the latter gentleman's hands, our subject some time after made an arrangement with him to study law and work for his board. He remained with that gentleman for about two years, during which time he pursued his studies earnestly, and with great diligence. He also taught one term of school. Then, feeling great need of a better education, he returned to Griffeth Institute. In the meantime he fell into the company of a young man was on his way to the West. An agreement was made between them that if this young man could find a suitable location in the far West our subject was to drop everything and join him. Word was received and Mr. Perkins came to Alma, Buffalo county, Wisconsin, in the spring of 1868. He then opened a law office and became connected with the county newspaper. At the end of six months, not being satisfied with the newspaper investment, he bartered his interest for lumber, and shipped it. He then made an arrangement with U. F. Sargeant, an attorney at Plainview, to which place he went and engaged in the practice of his profession. His next location was at Madelia, Watonwan county, where he opened a law office and entered the political arena as a candidate for county attorney. He was not successful in this move, however, and soon after located in Windom. Since March, 1872, he has been a resident of that place. Perhaps no man in the county has proven such a public-spirited citizen as Judge Perkins. He has taken an active interest in public affairs and has rendered valuable assistance in the administration of the affairs of county government. The first office to which he was elected was that of county attorney in 1872, at the same time being elected to the office of judge of probate, and holding these offices for a number of years. In 1897 he was elected as a member of the upper house of the State legislature, serving in that capacity for four years. He was a presidential elector in 1884, and cast his ballot for James G. Blaine. He was appointed district judge of the Thirteenth Judicial district of Minnesota in 1885, and was elected to that office in 1886. His district is composed of six counties—Cottonwood, Jackson, Nobles, Rock, Murray and Pipestone. In the administration of the judicial affairs of his office Judge Perkins has proven himself a man of rare capabilities and possessed of a mind of remarkable legal acumen. He is a man of large experience and thorough cultivated thought and is well equipped both by natural and acquired endowments to fill the important judicial position which he now holds. In 1881, in partnership with P. J. Kniss, of Luverne, Judge Perkins founded the Windom Bank, and after three months purchased Mr. Kniss' interest and took in Erick Sevatson. The bank was incorporated as a State institution in May, 1885, with a capital or $40,000. Judge Jerkins is a stanch republican in politics and is a member of the Masonic fraternity. He has a beautiful residence in the north part of the village of Windom, where he now resides.

Mr. Perkins was married in 1871 to Miss Florence A. Burcher, of Plainview, Minnesota, daughter of Rodman and Esther (Davidson) Burcher, natives of Wyoming

county, New York. Her parents came West in 1855 and settled near Plainview. Mrs. Perkins is a lady of refinement and is an excellent musician. Judge and Mrs. Perkins have been blessed with four children, three of whom are now living—Eliza A., Trueman A. and Ray B.

CHARLES WHITMAN. This gentleman is perhaps one of the best known citizens of Lincoln county, in which he holds the official position of sheriff. He is an active, public-spirited citizen, and has taken an active interest in all matters pertaining to the local government. He has a host of friends, and has proved one of the most efficient sheriffs Lincoln county has ever had. Mr. Whitman was born in Tompkins county, New York, December 20, 1838, and is the son of Gaylord G. and Mary (Dunham) Whitman, both natives of Wales.

Our subject was reared on a farm and was given the advantages of a good common-school education. He remained with his parents, assisting in work on the home farm until he was twelve years of age, when he started out for himself. For some three years he engaged in various kinds of employment, among them being lumbering and working on a canal in New York State. In the spring of 1856 he came to Minnesota and engaged in work for various farmers in Winona county. On the breaking out of the war he concluded to join the Union army and prove by actual military service his devotion to his country. In February, 1863, he enlisted in the Second Minnesota Battery, and served until the close to the war. He was with General Sherman at Atlanta and from thence went with General Thomas' corps to Nashville in pursuit of Hood. He participated in a great many hard-fought battles but came through without injury. After his discharge in 1865 he returned to

Winona county and engaged in farming on land that he had purchased before entering the Union service. He continued his residence in Winona county until March, 1881, when he sold out and came to Lincoln county, where for seven years he was manager of a ranch owned by Weeks & Sanborn. In the fall of 1886 he was elected sheriff of the county by a handsome majority on the republican ticket and was re-elected in the fall of 1888.

Mr. Whitman was married in Fillmore county, Minnesota, November 21, 1878, to Miss Susan E. Wood, a daughter of Robert and Susan (Gates) Wood, the former of English birth and the latter born in Massachusetts. Miss Wood was born in Marlborough, Massachusetts, May 18, 1855, where she lived with her parents until in about 1862, when they removed to Winona county, Minnesota. In Massachusetts her father was engaged in the boot and shoe business, but on coming to Minnesota he located on a farm and engaged in agricultural pursuits. Mr. and Mrs. Whitman have been blessed with two children—Madge and Gail.

Sheriff Whitman is one of the strongest official characters in the county. His official acts have all been conducted with caution and yet with dispatch. He is a man of excellent character and is a stanch supporter of the principles of the republican party. By virtue of an honorable military career he holds an influential position in the "Old Abe" Post, No. 39, Grand Army of the Republic, of Lake Benton. His wife is a member of the relief corps, "Old Abe" Post, No. 48, of which she is senior vice-president. Mr. Whitman is a member of the Rising Sun Lodge, No. 38, Ancient Free and Accepted Mason of St. Charles, Minnesota. Since making his location in the county our subject has proven himself a man of excellent business qualifications and has successfully engaged in various business enterprises, accumulating in these different lines considerable means.

HANS CHRISTIAN ANDERSON, who resided in Selma township, Cottonwood county, Minnesota, is the son of Andres and Anna Mary Elizabeth (Hansdotter) Anderson, both of whom were natives of Denmark. Hans was born in Odense, Denmark, December 3, 1848. The father died when Hans was not quite a year old and our subject lived on the farm with his mother until he was fourteen years old. He then went to herding cattle for various neighbors, and followed that line for one and a half years. He then commenced learning the blacksmith's trade and worked at that business for three and a half years, after which he turned his attention to agricultural pursuits for about a year. His next business was to engage in work for a civil engineer in making ditches and drains. Our subject was thus engaged for some three years. After this time he worked in a brick-yard for three years. He was then married and engaged in the iron works at Odense for some four or five years. November 15, 1879, he came to the United States, stopping some six months in Minneapolis, Minnesota. In the spring he commenced work on the railroad and worked some four years during the summers, the winters being spent in work in the woods. Coming to Watonwan county, our subject built a little home in Nelson township, where he lived one year. During this time he was working on the railroad, and after the year had expired, he sold his farm and purchased 160 acres on section 10, in Selma township, where he has since lived. He has a comfortable frame house, has about 110 acres under cultivation and is in good circumstances. Mr. Anderson is a man of excellent principles, is respected and esteemed by all, and is a member of the Lutheran church.

Mr. Anderson was married March 25 1875, in Odense, Denmark, to Miss Sophia Grauberg, a daughter of Nels Gust and Lizzie Grauberg. Mrs. Anderson was born in

Petiolongas, September 2, 1842. Mr. and Mrs. Anderson have been blessed with the following-named children—Hannah E., Clara C., Olivia, Nels, Christian, Augustus, Carda A. H., Eda M. and Pete A.

JOHN McKENZIE is one of the leading and ablest attorneys in Lincoln county, Minnesota. He has a large practice and all legal matters that come to his hands receive the most careful and thorough attention. He was born in Buffalo, New York, September 20, 1862.

The subject of our sketch is a son of John and Harriet (Maybe) McKenzie, the former a native of Canada and the latter born in Michigan. The father lost his life by drowning when our subject was about two years old. John was then taken into the family of his grandparents, with whom he lived until he was eighteen or nineteen years of age. While living with them in Sanilac county, Michigan, on a farm, he attended the district school until he was twelve years of age. At this age he was sent to an academy at Port Sanilac, where he continued his studies six or seven years and then graduated from that institution. Coming westward he located in Yellow Medicine county, Minnesota, where he taught school for about a year, after which he attended Carleton College at Northfield for two seasons, pursuing special studies. His next move was to Marshall, Minnesota, where he studied law with A. C. Forbes, Esq., for about a year. While teaching he had also carefully pursued a course of legal studies and had spent some time in a law office in Canby. In June, 1886, he was admitted to the bar at Marshall. Mr. McKenzie had pursued a careful and thorough course of study in law and had become well prepared for the practice of his profession. His examination for admission to the bar was most satisfactory to his friends and reflected credit on himself by virtue of its excellence. The newspaper referred to his admission to the bar as follows: "Mr. John McKenzie passed a very creditable examination and surpassed the most sanguine expectations of his friends. Judge Weber and the examining committee of attorneys who were present speak in the highest terms of Mr. McKenzie, and admit that they were agreeably surprised at John's knowledge of legal lore." This examination was a little on the order of a competition, as there were three candidates for admission. Each was therefore put upon his mettle to out-do the others and answer correctly the many perplexing questions that were put to them by their examiners. Our subject was about as well prepared for the examination as was the committee who conducted it. The correctness of his answers to the questions put to him was certainly commendable, and when the ordeal was over it was found that Mr. McKenzie stood highest of the three who appeared before the examiners. The next move made by our subject was to locate in New Ulm, where he entered the office of Hon. John Lind, continuing with him during the summer of 1886. That fall he came to Lake Benton and took the place of Forbes, Davis and McKenzie, attorneys, which business he now conducts under his own proprietorhip. Since coming to the village Mr. McKenzie has proven himself one of the most active and public-spirited citizens, and has labored hard and earnestly in every project which tended to the building up and development of the locality. He has made many friends by his uprightness of character and is loyal in his attention to various offices of local government. As a lawyer the people have nothing but words of praise and commendation for him. He is painstaking and thorough in his management of the details of every case placed in his hands.

Mr. McKenzie was married in Canby, Minnesota, in January, 1887, to Miss Kate A. Gilruth, a daughter of James and Ellen (Osler) Gilruth, natives of Scotland. One child has blessed this union, Harriet Ellen, born in Lake Benton.

WILLIAM W. GRAY is one of the thrifty and prosperous citizens of Pipestone county, Minnesota, and is located on section 34, of Grange township. He was born in the State of Vermont in Washington county, May 19, 1836. His parents, David and Mary (Wilson) Gray, were also natives of the Green Mountain State, where they lived until their death. The father was a wheelwright by trade and followed that occupation throughout the greater part of his life. He was a good mechanic and was esteemed and respected in the neighborhood in which he lived.

The subject of our sketch remained beneath the parental roof until he was about twenty years of age, up to which time he had been given a good common-school education, and had assisted his father in work at his trade. On reaching that age he removed to the State of New York, where, during one summer, he engaged in work on a farm with an uncle. The same fall he removed to Genesee county, Michigan, where he remained but a few months, and from whence he went to Grand Rapids, same State. In the latter city he made an engagement to work in the lumber woods, which he did during the coming winter, and the next summer found employment in a brickyard. He then went to Chicago, and about sixty miles west of that city found work in the harvest fields, continuing his employment on a farm there for about two years, and then returning to Chicago. He then found employment in a sash,

blind and door factory, in which he remained for about two years. On the breaking out of the Rebellion he offered his service to the Union army, and in October, 1861, enlisted in Company B, Fifty-fifth Illinois Infantry, and was discharged September 24, 1862. At the battle of Pittsburg Landing, early one Sunday morning, he was severely wounded and was removed to the hospital at Mound City, thence being taken to Cairo, and thence to Chicago, where he remained a year before he was able to perform any work. Removing thence he went to Fort Wayne, Indiana, where for one year he had charge of the machinery department of a sash, door and blind factory. Returning to Chicago, he again found employment in the same shop in which he had previously worked. All but one of the following five years were spent in Chicago, the one excepted being spent by him in his native State, where he remained among friends and relatives. Returning to Chicago he again found work with his old firm and continued a profitable engagement with them for about five years, continuing his residence in Chicago until 1879. In that year he came to Pipestone county, Minnesota, and homesteaded his present farm of 160 acres in Grange township.

Mr. Gray was married August 3, 1869, to Miss Clara E. Shaffer, by whom he had one child, Estella. Mr. Gray came to the county early in 1879, and in July was followed by his wife and child. Soon after their arrival the wife died, September 26th of that year. Mr. Gray was afterwards married to Mary B. Scribner.

The subject of our sketch is a most exemplary citizen, and is looked upon as being one of the reliable farmers of the township. He is a man of excellent judgment, of good education, and takes an active part in public affairs. In politics he affiliates with the republican party and is a leading member of the Grand Army Republic, Simon Mix Post, No. 95.

⁃⬥⬦⬥⬦⬥⬦⬥⁃

JAMES P. MORSE is a prominent furniture dealer of Slayton, Murray county, Minnesota. He is the son of Benjamin and Anna (Tilley) Morse, natives, respectively, of Maine and New Brunswick, Canada. Mr. Morse was born in Sheffield, New Brunswick, October 13, 1814. When about eight years of age he removed with his parents to St. Johns, where the father engaged in work as a ship-builder.

The early life of our subject until thirteen years of age was spent with his parents, and he was given a good common school education. On reaching thirteen years of age, his mother died and he had to look out for himself more or less until he was sixteen years old. He was then bound out to learn the millwright trade and served an apprenticeship of five years, after which he commenced work at that trade for himself in his native county. Until 1864 our subject remained in his native country working at his trade for various firms. For two years he was employed by his brother Thomas as workman on sectional docks. He was also foreman in building the St. Louis bridge and had charge of forty-five carpenters for two and a half years on this structure. After this until 1872 he engaged in work at his trade throughout the Western States, building mills, elevators, etc. In 1872 he went to Clarence, Missouri, and engaged in manufacturing and selling furniture, operating this business in that city until 1886. He then came to Slayton and opened his present furniture store. Since coming to this place he has sold his Missouri property and invested the proceeds in a comfortable home and large stock of goods in Slayton. Our subject has taken an important part in the general history of the various localities in which he has lived, and especially since coming to Slayton has actively assisted in the pushing forward of various public projects. Among the various positions which he has held may be named that of councillor while in his native country, and also various local offices in Missouri and Minnesota. He was a leading member of the Presbyterian church for some sixteen years before coming to Slayton, but since his location here is associated with the work of the Methodist Episcopal society. Mr. Morse is a pleasant, intelligent gentleman and is held in high esteem.

The subject of our sketch was married in Sheffield, New Brunswick, August 3, 1836, to Miss Mary Flumer, daughter of John and Sarah (Stewart) Flumer, natives of New Brunswick. This union has been blessed with the following-named children— Lydia, who died at the age of seventeen years; Anna (also deceased), Alethas, John P., Jane, Irene, Ellen (deceased), James, and Helen (deceased). Irene married Mr. John Reave and is now residing in Slayton, where her parents reside with her. Mr. Reave is at present clerk of the Illinois legislature. For one year he was private secretary for Hon. Mr. Farwell, a leading dry goods merchant of Chicago.

⁃⬥⬦⬥⬦⬥⬦⬥⁃

GEORGE N. LAING is the present judge of probate of Cottonwood county, Minnesota, and a leading attorney of Windom, Minnesota. Mr. Laing came to the village in 1881 and since that time has been engaged in the practice of his profession. He is a native of Ontario, Canada, where he was born November 16, 1850. His parents were Samuel W., and Charlotte (Miller) Laing, natives, respectively, of New Jersey and Canada.

Mr. Laing was reared as a farmer's boy and was given the advantages of such an education as was provided by the district schools. After leaving home he visited various parts of the United States, going to New Jersey, later returning to Canada, and then locating in Sparta, Wisconsin. He commenced the study of medicine with Dr. D. C. Beebe and continued with that gentleman for two years. Later he went to Madison Wisconsin, and studied law in the office of Professor Carpenter, also entering the law school in that city. He graduated from the school in 1881, and shortly after came to Minnesota and located in Windom. He has been elected to various official positions, has been village recorder and was elected judge of probate in 1882, '84, '86, and 1888. He has been one of the most prominent citizens of the village, and has been president of the school board and chairman of the republican county committee. He is at present chairman of the republican committee of the Thirteenth Judicial District. In 1887 he was appointed as one of the committe of three to revise the probate laws of Minnesota. For two years he labored hard in this direction and the revised laws were adopted by the legislature at the session of 1889.

Mr. Laing affiliates with the republican party and takes an active interest in various civic societies, such as the Masonic and Ancient Order of United Workmen, of both of which he holds the position of master.

In June, 1886, Mr. Laing was married to Amy Warbusse, daughter of Elias H., and Violet Warbusse, of Philadelphia, Pennsylvania. This union has been blessed with one son, Dewitt B.

ROBERT SCARF is one of the most prosperous merchants of Pipestone, and is engaged in the wholesale and retail drug business. He made his location in the city in 1879, and immediately opened in his present line, since which time he has been a permanent resident. He has a large and finely assorted stock of drugs, paints, wall paper, books and stationery, and has an excellent business location on the corner of Olive and Hiawatha streets.

The gentleman whose name appears at the head of this sketch is a native of Vermont, where he was born in the year 1846. His parents were William and Eliza (Hamilton) Scarf. The parents were well-to-do farmers in Vermont, and made that State their home throughout life, both of them dying in 1855. The subject of our sketch was the oldest of four children, the names of the others being William, Henry and George B. After the death of the parents William and Henry were taken into the home of the mother's brother, Thomas Hamilton, and our subject and George B. were bound out to a farmer, with whom they were to serve until they reached their majority. Our subject, however, only remained with his master ten months, at the end of which time he engaged in work at the printer's trade, continuing in that line of employment for two years, during 1859 and 1860. After that time had expired he engaged in farm-work for eighteen months, and then enlisted in Company E, Twenty-seventh Iowa Infantry, this being in 1862. He continued in the service throughout the war, being discharged in February, 1866. When discharged he was corporal of his company. During the last two and a half years of his military service he was a mounted scout in the South, and saw much severe service and passed through many exciting adventures in Southern raids. After the close of the war he returned to McGregor, Iowa, in which State he had lived before the war. On returning to McGregor at once engaged in the grocery business, in which line he continued for about a year, going from that point to Julesberg, Colorado, and from thence, after a four months' residence, to Cheyenne, Wyoming, where he remained two and a half years. His next move was to Nebraska, where he purchased railroad land and remained sometime. Later he returned to Iowa, and soon after went to Lyle, Minnesota, and engaged in the drug business. He made Lyle his home until coming to Pipestone in August, 1879.

In 1872 our subject was united in marriage to Miss Nellie Cook, of St. Ansgar, Iowa. This union has been blessed with three children—Zillah L., Henry A. and Ralph H.

The business career of our subject has been one of continued success. His business has been of a varied and complex nature, but into all the various lines he has carried his characteristic push and systematic habits, and as a necessary consequence has achieved success. He has always interested himself in public matters, and has aided materially in the development of the locality in which he resides. In politics he has affiliated with the republican party and has held numerous offices, among them being that of justice of the peace, member of the school board, etc. He is an influential member of the Grand Army Republic, Masonic and Odd Fellows fraternities. In religious as well as business matters he is actively interested, and is a consistent member of the Methodist Episcopal church, in which society he has been one of the board of trustees for a period of six years. The drug business of the subject of our sketch has reached large dimensions, and as a wholesaler he supplies scores of smaller drug stores throughout Southwestern Minnesota. He also carries a fine line of jewelry and musical instruments, and in this trade has built up a large patronage. Being a man of push and energy and large means, he has become one of the prominent business men of the city and county. Systematic in his business habits, and thorough in every particular, whether in public or private life, honest and reliable in all relations, he has

gathered to himself a large number of warm friends and patrons.

STEWART YOUNG is the present popular and efficient county auditor of Rock county, Minnesota. His location in Rock county was made in April, 1872, at which time he settled in Magnolia township on a pre-emption of 160 acres. Somewhat later he homesteaded 160 acres adjoining his pre-emption. His first improvement was a house, 14 x 24 feet, with six-foot posts, battened, and then sided up with sods. The roof of this primitive dwelling was covered with tarred paper and then sodded over. He lived in this house until 1886. He improved his 320 acres of land and engaged in general farming and stock raising. He was assessor of his township for three terms, and was chairman of the board of supervisors for one term. He was elected to his present position in the fall of 1886, and the same fall moved into the village of Luverne where, in the spring of 1887, he bought a lot and built a fine residence in the northwestern part of the city. He has now a beautiful home fitted with all modern improvements, and has his ground ornamented with various kinds of shade trees.

The subject of our sketch is a native of Tompkins county, New York, where he was born January 2, 1844. He is the son of Matthias and Elizabeth (Meligan) Young, both natives of New Jersey. After his marriage the father moved to Tompkins county, where he engaged in farming and where he still lives. He is a man of wide influence and is now living a retired life. The mother died in 1854. In the father's family there were eleven children, eight of whom are now living. Our subject, the oldest son, was reared on the home farm and received his education in the district schools. When he was nineteen years of age he enlisted in

Company D, One Hundred and Fortieth Regiment, New York Volunteer Infantry, and served as a private for two years. He was wounded three times, twice at the battle of the Wilderness, where he was shot in the right foot and in the left hand, and again at the battle of Hatcher's Run, where he was wounded in the right thigh. His first wounds were quite severe; he was shot through the palm of his hand and had a portion of his fore-finger shot away. His hand has bean of little service to him since. He remained in the Union army until the close of the war, having participated in a large number of battles, prominent among them being Mine Run, Wilderness, Weldon railroad, South Side railroad, Hatcher's Run, and many other skirmishes. He enlisted in July, 1863, and was discharged at Wilmington, Delaware, in June, 1865. After being discharged he returned to Tompkins county, New York, and engaged in farming until 1868. He then removed to Dakota, settling twelve miles northwest of Sioux City, where he purchased a farm of eighty acres. He lived in that locality until the spring of 1872, when he came to Rock county, as already stated.

The subject of our sketch was married in December, 1866, to Miss Sarah A. Colegrove, of Newfield, Tompkins county, New York, where she received her early training and education. This lady was a daughter of James and Mary (Brooks) Colegrove. Her father was a farmer by occupation. Mr. and Mrs. Young have been blessed with two children—Roscoe E. and Nora.

Political matters in connection with the affairs of the republican party have commanded the attention of our subject to a large extent. Throughout his residence in Rock county he has taken an active interest in the affairs of that party, and has been a delegate to the county conventions of that organization. He is a leading member of the Masonic fraternity, and is at present adjutant in the John A. Dix Post, No. 96, Grand Army of the Republic. He is a man of excellent ability, and makes an official of a high order. He is gentlemanly and courteous in all his dealings with the public, and is becoming more popular with every year's service in his present position. He is a man of the highest integrity· and holds the esteem of all with whom he has to do.

ALBERT JOHNSON. Since coming to Limestone township, Lincoln county, this gentleman has been engaged in general farming and stock raising, and has become quite well-to-do. He is a hard working and systematic farmer, and has an excellent farm under good cultivation. Mr. Johnson is a native of the southern part of Iceland, where he was born September 1, 1856. His parents, John and Solveg (Johnson) Siverson, were also natives of Iceland, where they were engaged in farming.

The subject of our sketch remained with his parents on the farm until 1879, at which time he came to the United States, and made his location in Lincoln county, settling on a homestead on the southeast quarter of section 6, Limestone township. He has associated himself with all projects tending to the development of the farming interests of his locality, and has held the office of school clerk for some time. He is a member of the Iceland Lutheran church, and, as a man, is held in high esteem by all his neighbors. He has 160 acres of excellent land, about sixty acres under cultivation, a good comfortable dwelling-house and other buildings. When he came to the township he had about four hundred dollars in money, and by careful attention to the details of his farming operations and stock raising he has become a man of means and prominence.

The subject of our sketch was married in Iceland, in October, 1877, to Miss Augusta Grinsom, who was also a native of that country, where she was reared and educated. The fruits of this union are Winnifred, Jennie, Bertha, Patrina Christina Sigerborg and Elizabeth.

REDERICK P. BROWN is a leading citizen of Blue Earth City, Faribault county, Minnesota. He is at present running an abstract office in that village. He is a native of the kingdom of Norway, where he was born, August 12, 1838. His parents were John N. and Annie (Halverson) Brown, natives of Norway. The father was one of Norway's most loyal citizens, and was a captain in the navy throughout his life. He died in 1842. In 1853 the mother brought her family to America and settled in Dane county, Wisconsin, later living with her daughter, Mrs. Salver, of Austin, Minnesota. She died in 1885.

The subject of our sketch came to America in 1854. After nine years of age he followed a seafaring life until his emigration to the United States. His education was received in his native land, and, on coming to this country, he located in Wisconsin, where he engaged in farming for some two years. He then began clerking, and in 1861 came to Rochester, Minnesota, where he engaged in clerking until 1866. He then came to Blue Earth City and opened in a mercantile business, in which line he continued until 1872. He was then elected register of deeds and continued to hold that office until 1887. He was one of the most popular officials which the county has ever had, and succeeded in manipulating the details of his office to the satisfaction of all. While register of deeds he prepared a set of abstract books for the county, and in 1887 on leaving the office of register of deeds, he gave his

entire attention to abstract work. He is a man of large means, and owns a farm of some four hundred acres besides considerable property in the village. He also owns an interest in the business of the mercantile firm of Hagen & Brown, and has a fine residence in the city.

Mr. Brown was married in 1863 to Miss Lena Wilson, a native of Norway. In a very early day her father came to Wisconsin, locating in Dane county, from whence they removed to Vermillion county, Dakota, where the father lived until his death. Mrs. Brown is one of nine living children. Mr. and Mrs. Brown have seven living children—Anna, Nordahl, Lovina, George, Hattie, Frank and Harry.

In politics the subject of our sketch affiliates with the republican party, and occupies a prominent place in the local affairs of that organization. He is a member of the Masonic fraternity, and, with his wife, belongs to the Lutheran church. He is one of the substantial and influential citizens of the town and county.

SHEPARD LEE is a well-to-do farmer of Selma township, Cottonwood county, Minnesota, and resides on a fine farm on section 32. He was born in Pickering, Victoria county, Canada, March 11, 1837. His parents were Jonathan and Euphemia (Barclay) Lee, the former a native of New York, and the latter born in Canada. The mother was of German descent, born in Canada of German parents. The parents were farmers throughout their lives, and were early settlers of the locality in which they lived.

The subject of our sketch resided with his parents on their farm in the heavy pine timber of Canada until he was nineteen years of age, when he went to work for himself by taking jobs of clearing land, and engaged in this occupation until he was twenty-four years of age. He then came to Columbia county, Wisconsin, and rented a farm, remaining one year, and then going to Dodge county, whence, after two years engaged in farming, he went to Goodhue county, Minnesota, in 1860. Here he purchased a farm and made his home for ten years. Selling out at the end of this period, he removed to Selma township, Cottonwood county, and located a homestead of eighty acres on section 32. The first two years he did not raise enough to support himself and family, and had to leave the farm and go to the woods in the vicinity of Mankato, where as a chopper he earned his living. After two years he returned to the farm and engaged in farming, with poor success, until 1880. In that year he had eighty acres of land sown to crop, but the ground was so wet he could not harvest it, and he was again obliged to leave home. This time he went to Cumberland, Wisconsin, and remained three years, in the meantime renting his farm. While in Wisconsin he was engaged in working in the big woods, and also at the carpenter's trade and at any other kind of work he could find to do. Since his return at the end of the three years he has had good crops, and at the present writing has seventy-five acres of wheat and forty acres of oats, with a prospect of an excellent harvest. He has 160 acres of fine land provided with good buildings.

Mr. Lee was married in Sanilac county, Michigan, July 4, 1860, to Miss Elizabeth Watson, daughter of Charles and Frances (Ellsworth) Watson, natives of England. She was born in Canada January 13, 1842. Mr. and Mrs. Lee have had the following children—George W., Emily A., Jane E., Nathan, who died at two months of age, Charles H., who died February 5, 1887, Frank L., John W., William J., Alice, Marion and Albert. Emily married William Trusdall. Jane married Frederick Knapp. George, the oldest son, has a homestead of 160 acres in Selma township.

———————

HENRY H. RAPH is a resident of section 10, Grange township, Pipestone county, Minnesota. He was born in Northampton county, Pennsylvania, March 17, 1837. He was the son of David and Margaret (Ruggles) Raph, natives of Pennsylvania, and who removed from that State to Dane county, Wisconsin, when our subject was about ten years old. Soon after coming to Wisconsin the mother died, and the father returned to Pennsylvania, in which State he died the following year. There were six children in the father's family, but after this double bereavement they became scattered, and our subject has lost all trace of them.

Being left an orphan at an early age, our subject has had to make his own way in the world, with no help whatever from kith or kin. At the age of eleven he was put to work with a farmer in Wisconsin. This man was a disagreeable character, and our subject acquired a bitter dislike for him, and at the age of thirteen years ran away, and for four years worked for another man, but at the end of this time he returned to the home of his first employer and continued with him for five years. Then, at the age of twenty-one years, he was married, purchased a farm and settled down to follow agricultural pursuits. Eight years of a prosperous life were spent in Wisconsin, and at the end of that time he traded his land for a farm in Goodhue county, Minnesota, to which place he moved and remained until 1878. In that year he lost his land by reason of defective title. He then came to Pipestone county and settled on the land where he now lives, returning to Goodhue county to work during the winter months.

He has been quite successful in bringing his farm to a high state of cultivation, and has built good buildings thereon. He is a man of large energy and perseverance, and despite of the failures and misfortunes which have fallen to his lot, he has risen above them and acquired considerable means.

Mr. Raph was married January 1, 1857, to Miss Adeline Cornwall. This union has been blessed with five children, four of whom are living—Mattie I., Arthur B., Elida M. and John C.

The subject of our sketch, by attending school during the winter months during the early part of his life, acquired a good common-school education, and is to-day one of the leading and substantial farmers of Grange township. In politics he is a republican.

DANIEL SHELL, one of the leading business men of Southwestern Minnesota, is a resident of Worthington, the county seat of Nobles county. He is an old settler of that locality, and has for many years been identified with the business interests of that region. He has also taken an active interest in all matters of a public nature, and has filled various official positions. A man of large means, liberal and public-spirited, he has taken a leading part in all matters or moves calculated to benefit his town or county, and his name is indissolubly connected with the history of the growth and development of Nobles county and Southwestern Minnesota.

GUSTAV M. WARNER is a leading hardware merchant of Sherburne, Martin county, Minnesota. He was born in Green Lake county, Wisconsin, July 20, 1854. His parents, Conrad and Susan Warner, were natives of Germany, and came to this country in early life, settling in Wisconsin. They removed thence in 1862, locating in Mower county, Minnesota, where they purchased a farm and engaged in agricultural pursuits.

Mr. Warner remained with his parents, coming with them to Minnesota in 1862, and helping the father on the farm throughout his early life. His educational advantages were somewhat limited, and the knowledge he obtained was mostly gathered by evening study at home. In 1877 he purchased a farm in Mower county, and operated it until the fall of 1879. In the spring of 1880 he removed to Martin county and purchased 160 acres of land in Waverly township, for which he paid $3.35 per acre. He lived on this place, keeping bachelor's hall and improving the land until 1884. In the fall of that year he sold his farm and personal property, and removed to the western part of the State, going also into Dakota in search of a location. He was not satisfied with the condition of the land in that country, and in January, 1885, returned to Martin county, purchased property in the village of Sherburne, and opened a hardware store, in connection with which he also operated a tin shop. Since that time he has been permanently located in the village, and has built up an extensive trade. He owned and ran a threshing-machine every fall while he was engaged in farming, and as there were but few machines in the county he was kept busy until obliged to quit work by the cold weather. In this way he made the money with which he started his present business. In politics our subject affiliates with the prohibition party. He is a man of excellent moral character, and is esteemed by all who know him.

On the 8th day of March, 1882, the subject of this sketch was married in Frazer township, Martin county, to Miss Amelia Bursack, daughter of William Bursack, a native of Germany. This lady was born in Green

Lake county, Wisconsin, January 18, 1859. This union has been blessed with one child, M. Estella, born in Sherburne, January 14, 1887.

USTOF BERGSTROM is one of the leading and representative citizens of Selma township, Cottonwood county, Minnesota. He is the son of Andres and Christine (Gensdotter) Bergstrom, natives of Sweden. Our subject was born in Linshippings stift, Sweden, April 2, 1857.

Mr. Bergstrom lived with his parents during his early life, and was given a good common-school education until fifteen years of age. He resided with his father until attaining twenty-three years of age, when he came to the United States, locating for a year in Brown county, Minnesota. He then went to Mankato and worked on the railroad for a year, after which he returned to Brown county and rented a farm, which he operated for two years. He then came to Salem township and purchased 160 acres on section 10, where he has lived ever since. He has worked hard to bring his farm up to its present good state of cultivation; to surround himself with prosperity, and with the evidences of success. He has succeeded well, and is now comfortably located in a substantial frame dwelling-house, and has his farm provided with other buildings and improvements. He is a man of good character, and is respected by all who know him.

May 26th, 1882, Mr. Bergstrom was married to Miss Ingret Matilda Nelson, a daughter of Nels and Sophia Nelson, natives of Sweden. This lady was born in Selmor, Sweden, May 11, 1857. The marriage has been blessed with the following-named children— Fannie, Minnie, Charles, Agnes A. and Mary. Fannie, Charley and Minnie are deceased. This family has met with considerable misfortune, and during one year had a great deal of sickness. Two children died in that year. Our subject also lost that year eleven head of cattle, and was in such straitened circumstances that had it not been for the help of friends and neighbors he could not have obtained sufficient food to preserve the lives of his family. He found friends, however, who assisted him to outlive this dark period. He has overcome those evil circumstances, and is now enjoying prosperity and success.

RANK TERRY, a leading business man of Slayton, Murray county, Minnesota, is engaged in operating a first-class livery. He is the son of George S. and Georgianna (Le Broy) Terry, natives of Hampshire, England.

Frank Terry is also of English birth, being born in Hampshire of that country, December 22, 1866. He lived on the farm with his parents until their death, the father dying in his native land in November, 1878, and the mother in November, 1882. Until fifteen years of age our subject received a good common-school education, and was then apprenticed to the proprietor of a training stable, with whom he served over a year. In 1883 he emigrated to America, locating on a farm for a short time in the vicinity of St. James, Minnesota. In the fall of that year he came to the village of Slayton, and during the winter worked at whatever he could find to do. In the spring of 1884 he found employment in the creamery, at which employment he continued until fall. In the late winter he commenced an engagement in the livery barn of A. Moore, continuing with him most of the time until fall. Then, in company with Mr. Mobray, he engaged in hunting prairie chickens and shipping to foreign markets. This occupation proved quite successful and highly profitable, as they killed and shipped over fifteen hundred chickens, most of them going to the city of Minneapolis. During the winter that followed he went to his native land on a brief visit, remaining there from December until July, 1886, in which month he returned to Slayton. He then built his livery barn, purchased his horses and has been engaged in operating a livery business ever since. He has first-class outfits and is well prepared to supply the traveling public with desirable and fair-priced livery outfits. He is a pleasant, obliging gentleman, and has made many friends during his residence in Slayton.

HON. DANIEL McARTHUR is the esteemed probate judge of Lincoln county, Minnesota, where he has a large number of warm friends. He is the son of Donald and Catharine (McDonald) McArthur, who were born in the highlands of Scotland. The parents of the subject of our sketch were farmers by occupation, and in early life came from their native land to America, stopping in Canada.

Judge McArthur was born in Ontario, near Toronto, Canada, September 8, 1832. He resided with his parents on the home farm, and attended the district schools, acquiring a good common-school education. During his early life he attended school nearly all the time, but on becoming old enough to work on the farm he was sent to school during the winter months, and during the summers assisted in the farm work. He remained with his parents until he was about twenty-one years of age, when he commenced working at the carpenter's trade, continuing for three years at this occupation during the summer months and attending school for some time in the winter. After this period had expired he commenced working on a farm, and in the spring of 1857 came to

Minnesota and located on a pre-emption in Olmsted county. He remained on this farm, with the exception of the time spent in the Union army, until 1880, when he removed to Lake Benton. In August, 1862, Judge McArthur enlisted in Company F, Ninth Minnesota Volunteer Infantry, as a private. Part of his regiment was sent to Glencoe, whence, after one month had expired, they were sent to Fort Ridgely, making that fort their headquarters until 1863. The regiment was then ordered South to participate in active proceedings at the front. Our subject saw an exciting military career until June 10, 1864, when he was taken prisoner. He was kept by the Rebel forces until October 16, 1864, when he escaped to the Union lines. His escape from his Rebel captors was made by jumping from the cars while he was being taken from one prison to another. He was sixteen days tramping through the marshes and hiding in the woods, shunning every sign of human life, and suffering untold distress from hunger and thirst. After sixteen days he succeeded in finding his way back to the Union lines, where he joined his regiment. He continued in the service until August 25, 1865, when his regiment was mustered out at Fort Snelling. Mr. McArthur then returned to his home in Olmsted county, resumed farming, and continued his residence there until 1880. In 1878 he started for the western part of the State for the purpose of looking up a place in which to locate. He selected a piece of land in Lincoln county, filed on it as a soldier's homestead and improved it until 1880, when he moved his family from his home in Olmsted county to his claim near Lake Benton. He has purchased other lands adjoining, and now has 240 acres. He continued his residence on it until the fall of 1886, then the family moved to the village of Lake Benton, where the following spring he built a nice residence.

Judge McArthur was married in Goodhue county, Minnesota, in February, 1858, to Jane Martin, daughter of Thomas and Jane (Annett) Martin, natives of the lowlands of Scotland. This union has been blessed with three children — Katie J., Daniel T. and Gilbert W., all born in Olmsted county.

The subject of our sketch has taken an active interest in all matters pertaining to the local government since coming to the county. In fact his abilities are of such a high order in this particular that it has been almost impossible for him to escape the responsibilities of official position. Without solicitation he has at various times been called upon to serve in various responsible places for the benefit of his fellow-citizens. He affiliates with the republican party. Among the offices which he has held may be named the following: Village recorder, chairman of the board of supervisors, which position he held for four years, and justice of the peace, which office he has held ever since his location in the county, with the exception of one year. He is at present justice of the peace and probate judge. In the latter position he has succeeded in winning the respect and admiration of his fellow-citizens by virtue of his rare fidelity to the interests of the various kinds of business which come to his hands. Many difficulties of an intricate and delicate nature are presented to him for adjudication and in all these he has manifested a desire to fulfill the spirit of the laws and to deal out impartial justice to all parties concerned. Having been connected with the department of justice for many years, he has become well versed in the law. He is a man of the highest integrity of character, is a loyal citizen, a warm friend and obliging neighbor, and has planted himself firmly in the respect of his fellow-citizens. He is a member of the Independent Order of Odd Fellows, lodge No. 77, of Lake Benton, and

was the first commander of Old Abe post, No. 39, of the village.

JOSEPH BRISTOL is a resident of Sweet township, Pipestone county, Minnesota, and owns a fine farm on section 12. He is one of the well-to-do and influential farmers of the county, and is held in high esteem by his fellow-citizens. He was born September 6, 1846, in the State of New York. The parents of our subject were David and Miss (Robinson) Bristol, natives of New York. About three years after the birth of our subject the family removed to Rock county, Wisconsin, where the father rented a farm and engaged in its operation for a number of years. Later he removed to Dane county, same State, where he followed agriculture until his death, in June, 1856. The mother remarried, and went to California in the spring of 1859, where she died the following spring.

The subject of our sketch remained with his father on the farm, and received his education in the common schools of Wisconsin. When the mother went to California, Joseph settled in Marshalltown, Iowa, and remained about one year, engaged in different kinds of occupation. He then returned to his native State, settling in Camden, Oneida county, where he found employment in a large mill, and continued in that line of work until August 5, 1862. At that date our subject enlisted in Company B, One Hundred and Seventeenth New York Infantry. He continued throughout the service, and was discharged at Raleigh, North Carolina, June 8, 1865, being mustered out at Syracuse, New York, June 22d of the same year. Much severe service was seen by our subject. After his discharge our subject returned to Camden, New York, and remained about a month, after which he removed to La Crosse, Wisconsin. Arriving in that place, he turned his attention to carpenter work, and continued at that line until 1869, in which year he removed to St. Charles, Minnesota, and engaged in running a threshing-machine. St. Charles remained his home but a few years, after which he concluded to try to better his fortunes by finding a location somewhere on a farm. So he fitted up a team and wagon and started out for Southwestern Minnesota, arriving in Pipestone county and locating the claim where he now lives on the 20th of May, 1878. He at once commenced breaking his land, and remained until June 23, when he returned to St. Charles and again resumed the threshing business. May 9th of the following year he brought his family to his farm, and has since remained.

Mr. Bristol was married, November 15, 1870, to Miss Ellen Larson. This union has been blessed with one child—Julia, now living at home.

Coming to the township in an early day, Mr. Bristol has had the privilege of witnessing the remarkable growth of this county in wealth and prosperity. With the growth of the township our subject has also grown in wealth, and now has an excellent farm, on which are found good buildings. He has a pleasant home and a bright and agreeable family. In all matters pertaining to the general welfare of the township, his assistance has never been asked in vain. He is an intelligent and whole-hearted gentleman, and is one of the most agreeable persons to meet in the township. In politics he has identified himself with no particular party, but believes in supporting the best men. He has held several positions in the government of the township, and has at all times proven a satisfactory official. For the past five years he has been a member of the town board, and during two years of that time has held the position of chairman. He is a leading and influential member of the Grand Army of the Republic, Simon Mix Post, No. 95.

A. W. ANNIS, an attorney and mayor of the village of Windom, Cottonwood county, Minnesota, is a native of Port Huron, Michigan, where he was born August 8, 1854. His parents were Rev. G. N. and Melissa (Willitts) Annis, natives of New York and Ohio, respectively. The father was highly educated, and was a minister of the Baptist church, commencing his labors in that denomination at thirty years of age. He is now living in Washington Territory.

The subject of our sketch followed his parents in their various moves to the States of Michigan and Minnesota. He was thoroughly educated in his youth and young manhood, and took up the profession of teaching, being principal of the Madelia schools for three years after coming to this State, and came to Windom in 1881, taking charge of the schools of that village for two years. He has given a number of years to educational work, and has had charge of some of the leading schools in the State of Minnesota. After leaving the school in Windom, Mr. Annis went to Dakota, with the intention of establishing himself in the mercantile business. After spending a summer he altered his plans, went to Ann Arbor, Michigan, and graduated from the law department of that institution in 1885. In July of that year he returned to Windom, opened a law office, and also became principal of the schools for one year. For the same length of time he was in partnership with Mr. J. S. Ingalls, since which time he has been conducting his business alone. He has built up an extensive practice, is a man of the strictest integrity, and is esteemed both as a business man and exemplary citizen. In politics he affiliates with the republican party, is an Odd Fellow, and is one of the prominent attorneys of the county.

Mr. Annis was married in 1888 to Miss Ella F. Chadwick, daughter of Edwin and Helen M. Chadwick, of Galesburg, Michigan. Mrs. Annis died March 18, 1889, leaving one child, Earl C.

BENJAMIN H. SORENSON is a thrifty farmer of Alta-Vista township, Lincoln county, Minnesota, where he owns a farm on section 8. Mr. Sorenson is the son of Soren and Karen (Jorgen) Zahl, natives of Norway. The parents were influential people in their native land, and were engaged in the occupation of farming.

The subject of our sketch was born in the northern part of Norway, at Holgeland, January 12, 1840. He remained with his parents on the farm, receiving a good common-school education until he was seventeen years of age. Though the parents lived on a farm, and engaged somewhat in farming, this was not their sole business. Considerable of their attention was given to fishing. When our subject reached the age of seventeen he engaged in clerking in a general store in his native country, and continued his employment there for about six years. He then became a fisherman by occupation, and engaged in that line for about seven years. At the end of this period he concluded to try his fortunes in the new world. He came to America in 1869, and located for a time in Goodhue county, Minnesota, where he engaged in working on a farm for about a year. Then in 1870 he came to Lincoln county, and located a homestead in what is now Alta Vista township. When he first came to the county the land where he located was not surveyed, and he could not file on his property for two years, at which time the survey was made. He owns a fine farm of 240 acres, with about seventy acres under cultivation, has a good barn 30x50 feet in size with sixteen-foot posts, a good frame dwelling-house, and also a frame granary 16x26 feet, with an addition four-

teen feet in width, which he uses as a machinery shed. These buildings are all nicely painted, and show excellent care and attention.

The subject of our sketch was married in Norway, in September, 1864, to Ragnhild Siversen. This union has been blessed with the following-named children—Saras K. and Bernard M. Saras K. was married to Miss Diana Christianson, a daughter of Christian and Almira Sorenson. This marriage occurred December 19, 1888.

The subject of our sketch was the first settler of Alta Vista township, and since making his location has become well-known for uprightness of character and loyal citizenship. He has contributed generously of his time and means in the furtherance of projects tending to public improvement. His son is clerk of the school board, and the family occupy a prominent place among the citizens of the township. In politics our subject affiliates with the republican party.

JOHN P. HAUG is a member of the firm of Hawes, Haug & Co., general merchants of Luverne, Minnesota. Mr. Haug made his location in this city in August, 1880, and for some seven years engaged in clerking. At the end of that period, in connection with the gentleman named above, he opened his present business, at which he has since been engaged. They have an excellent and fully assorted stock of goods, and are carrying on a large business.

Mr. Haug is a native of Norway, where he was born November 27, 1859. His parents were Peter J. and Marthan (Peterson) Haug, both natives of Norway. The father was an extensive farmer of his native land, and a prominent member of the Lutheran church. In the father's family there were seven children—Jens, John P., Martin P., now a manufacturer; Petra, now Mrs. Satrug; Andrew,

Ole and Carl, the last three being at present in Luverne.

The subject of our sketch received his early training on the home farm, and was a graduate of what is known as the middle schools of Norway. After his school days were over he was employed as a clerk in an office for some time, and came to America in April, 1880. He first visited Wisconsin and other parts of the West before coming to Luverne, where he located in August of that year. Our subject is a republican in politics, belongs to the Masonic fraternity, and is an influential member of the Lutheran church. The firm of which he is one of the leading members possesses an extensive patronage. Our subject has been one of the most active business men in the village, and by his energetic business habits has made many friends among the merchants of the city. He is a man of gentlemanly bearing, of high character, and is becoming one of the most respected merchants of the place.

ANDREW MILNE is the president of the Star Manufacturing Company, proprietors of the foundry and machine shops of Winnebago City, Faribault county, Iowa. The company is composed of Andrew Milne, president; W. J. Milne, secretary, and James Bennett, treasurer. This company manufactures articles of iron, brass, etc., and all kinds of castings are made to order, and they also manufacture and deal in engines, boilers, mill machinery, steam and water fittings, leather and rubber beltings, sleighs, wagons, etc. The company was incorporated in 1886, and is doing a large business, keeping an average of five men at work constantly, and using somewhat over a ton of iron a week.

The gentleman whose name appears at the head of this sketch is a native of Edinburgh, Scotland, where he was born in 1837. His parents were William and Margaret (Gearns) Milne, natives of Scotland. The father was a blacksmith by trade, and later in life became an overseer in a woolen mill. He went to Canada in 1842 and died in 1852. The mother died in the same year. They had a family of eight children, four of whom are now living—Euphemia, now Mrs. Stewart; Jane, now Mrs. Hamilton; James and Andrew.

When he was five years of age our subject came with his parents to Canada, where he received his education and resided with his parents until he was fourteen years of age. He then commenced learning the blacksmith's trade, serving an apprenticeship of five years, and attending night school in order to obtain a better education. After this period of time had expired he accepted a position on the Grand Trunk railroad, and was employed as foreman of a gang of laborers running a steam shoveler. He continued at this until 1857, when he came to Whitewater, Wisconsin, and worked at blacksmithing for the Central Railroad Company for a time. The company failed and our subject found work as foreman in the wagon and plow shops of Winchester, DeWolf & Co., for eight years. He then commenced operating a machine shop at Fort Atkinson, under the firm name of Powers, Milne & Co. He continued in this line until 1874, when he removed to New Richmond, same State, and engaged in the hotel business. Later he turned his attention to blacksmithing and located at Shell Rock, Washburn county, where he finally found work with the Shell Rock Lumber Company and continued with them some five years. One year thereafter was spent in Iowa, and he then, in 1886, came to Winnebago City, where he has since resided. Since locating here he has purchased a fine residence in the city, and has become otherwise interested in various investments. He has always been a man of activity in public matters and has held various official positions, having affiliated for years with the republican party. While at Shell Rock, Wisconsin, he was the first chairman of the county board, and was also chairman of the Shell Rock township supervisors for some time. He is a member of the Masonic fraternity, and with his family attends the Presbyterian church.

Mr. Milne was married July 14, 1858, to Eunice Williams, of Cold Springs, Jefferson county, Wisconsin. She was a daughter of Ezra Williams, a prominent citizen of that place. Mr. and Mrs. Milne have been blessed with three children—Euphemia J., now Mrs. Turris (who has three children—Essie, Ella and Maude); William J. and Maude M.

SIMON HANSON, a leading merchant and influential citizen, operates a general store in Hadley, Murray county, Minnesota. He was born in Norway, October 14, 1849. His parents were Hans and Julia (Engebretson) Simonson, both natives of Norway. The father during his early life was a stockman, and later engaged in farming in his native land. He came to America with his family in 1861, landing at Quebec, whence he went to Wisconsin, and thence, after a brief stay of four months, to Fillmore county, Minnesota. Here he purchased land and engaged in farming for eleven years. Then in 1872 he removed to Murray county and took a claim on section 10 of Leeds township, where he now lives. The father was one of the first settlers of the township, and became one of its most prominent citizens.

The subject of our sketch was given a good common-school education in Norway up to the time of his coming to America with his parents in 1861. He continued with them on the home farm occupied in farm work and attending the district schools in the win-

ters until he was twenty-three years of age. He then left home and worked in various parts of the State until he was twenty-eight years old. He was then married and took a homestead about a mile from the village of Hadley. Here he engaged in farming until 1887, in which year he removed to Slayton and with a partner opened a general store. After ten months this partnership was dissolved and Mr. Hanson came to Hadley village and opened the store which he now runs. He has an excellent stock of goods worth about two thousand dollars.

Mr. Hanson was married December 9, 1877, to Miss Ida Peterson, a native of Norway, and a daughter of Ira and Gertrude (Engebretson) Peterson. Her parents now reside in the village of Slayton. Mr. and Mrs. Hanson have been blessed with four children—Henry, Gertie, and Charles and Stella (twins.)

Since making his location in Murray county, our subject has taken an active part in all public affairs and has served his fellow-citizens in various official positions. Affiliating with the republican party he has been elected by the constituents of that organization to the offices of justice of the peace, supervisor, chairman of the board of supervisors, and road overseer, holding the latter office five years. He is a man of excellent character and belongs to the Lutheran church.

JOSEPH SAVAGE, a resident farmer of Delton township, Cottonwood county, Minnesota, is the son of Patrick and Rose (Brodigan) Savage, natives of Ireland. Joseph was born in County Louth, Ireland, October 20, 1828. When eleven years of age our subject commenced work in a cotton factory, and was thus engaged for twenty-five years, first commencing that work in a factory in Droghady, Ireland. His engagement in that line of business was continued for the number of years just stated in various places in the old country and in America. When about seventeen years of age he came to America, and found employment at his trade in Lowell, Massachusetts, after which he removed to Putnam, Connecticut, remaining in that city for fourteen or fifteen years. At the end of this time he visited various places in the South as an expert, adjusting machinery in cotton factories. Being thus engaged until the spring of 1861, he then went to Markesan, Green Lake county, Wisconsin, where he engaged in work on a farm. His next move was to Winona, Minnesota, and thence he went to Mankato, and various other places. He finally settled in Brown county, Minnesota, where he took a homestead and resided about fifteen years, when he sold out and removed to Delton township, Cottonwood county, where he took a tree claim on section 24 in 1878, where he has since lived. While a resident of Mankato he went South in the government employ, and while in Decatur, Alabama, was pressed into the service as a deck hand on board a gunboat. Before he was taken on board the boat he had charge of the mail along a railroad which was destroyed by the Union army. He carried the mail for a time on a hand-car, and also carried passengers occasionally, and quite often made the sum of twenty-five dollars per day from passengers who had to pass along the route.

Mr. Savage was married in Putnam, Connecticut, August 5, 1850, to Miss Esther Riley, daughter of Barnard and Mary (Doyle) Riley, natives of Dublin, Ireland. This lady was born in Dublin on Palm Sunday in the month of April, 1831. She died in Cottonwood county, November 6, 1885. This union was blessed with the following-named children—Joseph, who died in 1854; Mary Ann, married to William Williams, and now residing in Iowa; Rose J., married to Edward

Hilton, and now residing in St. Paul; Catharine, married to James Quinn, and a resident of Los Angeles, California; Esther, married to Alphonzo Charboneau, head waiter of the Merchants Hotel, St. Paul; John P., Margaret, Ellen, Joseph, Nicholas, Alice and Theresa. While a resident of Connecticut our subject sent for his parents and his family, thirteen in all, and paid their passage to America, and assisted them in getting comfortably settled in this country.

<hr/>

ALEXANDER McNAUGHTON is a resident of section 26, Altona township, Pipestone county, Minnesota. He is a well-known and prosperous farmer, and owns an excellent farm of 160 acres. Mr. McNaughton is a Canadian by birth and was born in that country, February 6, 1851.

The parents of our subject were Peter and Janet (McIntyre) McNaughton, both of whom were born in Canada. The parents were well-to-do farmers of that country, and resided there throughout their lives, the father dying some years ago.

The early life of the subject of our sketch was spent on the home farm. He was a dutiful son and assisted his parents in every way possible to improve their farm and lay by means to protect them in their old age. He was given a good common-school education and remained beneath the parental roof until he was twenty-six years of age. At that time he went to Chicago and worked at the cabinet-maker's trade for about six months in that city. He then returned to his home in Canada and remained about two years, removing thence to Eau Claire, Wisconsin. He remained in that city and vicinity for about five years, occupied with work at the lumber business. Then, May 7, 1878, he came to Pipestone county and took his claim in Altona township. When he first came there was but one house in the township, that being the dwelling of Morris Rouche, who lived about three miles from where our subject located. Mr. McNaughton put up the second shanty in the township and made his home on his farm throughout the season, breaking five acres of land and making other improvements. He then went back to Wisconsin and after remaining in that State about five months, returned to his claim and has remained ever since with the exception of five months in the summer of 1879, which were spent in Wisconsin.

Mr. McNaughton was married March 1, 1888, to Miss Nora Hickey, of Canada. Her parents now live in St. Mary's, Canada.

The subject of our sketch has taken a great interest in the affairs of the local government since coming to the township and has held various positions of trust. He has been chairman of the board of supervisors one term, and has served as a member of the board for four terms. He has also been assessor of the township for some years. In politics he affiliates with the republican party. Mr. McNaughton is a man of good business qualities, is respected for his honesty and uprightness of character, and exerts a wide influence among the citizens of his township. He has a good farm of 160 acres and has a pleasant home.

HON. M. K. ARMSTRONG is the president of the Bank of St. James, established in 1878. He is a native of Erie county, Ohio, where he was born September 19, 1832. Coming to Minnesota in an early day, he has been one of its most prominent citizens, and has held important positions. He was appointed surveyor of Watonwan county, and later held the same office in Mower county for two years. In 1859 he went to Yankton, Dakota, and surveyed numerous claims for early settlers. He was elected to the first legislature of Dakota, and

served for ten years. He was elected Territorial treasurer in 1864 and held the position for two years. During a period of ten years he was secretary of the Biographical and Historical Society of Dakota, and while occupying that position wrote a history of Dakota. He was appointed secretary of the peace commission to treat with the Indians in 1868–69. He was a member of the senate of the Territory during the same years. In 1870 he was elected Territorial delegate to congress, and served two terms, from 1871 to 1875. In 1878 he located in St. James, Watonwan county, Minnesota, where he engaged in the banking business. He is a democrat in politics and is one of Watonwan county's most prominent citizens.

JOHN G. MILLER, one of the foremost business men of Lakefield, Jackson county, Minnesota, is the son of Eli and Mary Ann (Brown) Miller, natives of Pennsylvania. Our subject was born in the same State, his birthplace being opposite Harrisburg in Cumberland county, where he first saw the light June 24, 1834.

When our subject was thirteen years old he was bound out to Benjamin Morrison, a machinist, and remained under his charge until 1849, when the indenture of apprenticeship was mutually annulled. At this time he moved with his father's family across the Alleghany mountains, locating in Wayne county, Ohio, in September, and shortly afterward our subject ran away, joining a company on its way to California. His father caught him, however, before he had gone very far and brought him back to the family fold. John continued his residence with his father until 1851, and then found employment in the neighborhood, working on various farms until 1855. He then removed to Mercer county, Ohio, where he taught school and worked at the carpenter's trade until 1864. However, in the years 1863 and 1864, he made two trips to Canada in the interest of the State and under orders from Governor Todd. In these matters pertaining to the welfare of various State enterprises our subject was highly successful, and merited the commendation which he received from his superior officers. In 1864 he removed to Princeton, Bureau county, Illinois, and there entered the employ of the Chicago, Rock Island & Pacific Railroad Company, continuing a profitable engagement with this company until 1875. He then made an engagement with the Peoria City Plow Company and the Mathiesen & Hegeler Zinc Works, of La Salle, Illinois, and removed overland to Jackson county, Minnesota, in company with his son-in-law, B. D. Froelinger. He located on section 6, of Belmont township, and resided on this farm on the Des Moines river for one year. During this time the village of Lakefield was surveyed and platted, and coming to the village, Mr. Miller engaged in contract work until August, 1880. At that date he brought his family to Lakefield, where they still live. For a short time after bringing his family our subject engaged in work at his trade and then put in a stock of machinery, which business he has been conducting ever since with merited success. He is agent for the Walter A. Wood Farm Machinery Company.

In September, 1858, in Mercer county, Ohio, Mr. Miller was married to Miss Barbara Waples, daughter of Casper and Margaret Waples, natives of Bavaria, Germany. Miss Barbara was born in Mercer county, Ohio, February 11, 1841. Mr. and Mrs. Miller have been blessed with the following named children—Charlotte Frances, Margaret Alice, William T. S., George B. McClellan, Katie Gertrude and Charles Francis. Charlotte married Bernard D. Froelinger, and now resides in Marshall county, Illinois.

In politics the subject of our sketch affiliates with the prohibition party, and is also a man of strong prohibition principles, believing in the entire destruction of the liquor traffic. He has been quite prominent in local governmental affairs, assisted in the organization of school district No. 38, of which he has been a trustee for five years; has been postmaster for two years; was justice of the peace for six years, and has been village justice since the incorporation of Lakefield. In connection with his other business he has also pursued the study of law, and has practiced to some extent before the minor courts. He has not been admitted to the bar, but intends presenting himself for that purpose some day in the near future. He is a member of the Independent Order of Good Templars, and is a man highly respected and esteemed by his fellow-citizens.

⚬⚬⚬⚬⚬

BENJAMIN F. VORIES, a leading attorney of Fairmont, Martin county, Minnesota, is the son of John H. and Ellen (Jacobs) Vories, natives, respectively, of New Jersey and Virginia. Our subject was born in Marshall county, Indiana, December 31, 1853, to which State his parents had removed in early life.

When our subject was about ten years of age his father died, and he with three other sons lived on the farm with the mother, until they commenced doing for themselves several years later. Our subject attended the district school, and was also provided with the advantages furnished by a private school in his locality. On completing his education in the schools of his township, he turned his attention to the profession of teaching, and engaged thereat for some three terms. He then attended the Union Christian College in southern Indiana, and graduated therefrom after a four years' course of study. He then returned home, and after a short time went into a law office in Plymouth, studying with the firm of Capern & Capern, and continuing with them for some three years. He was admitted to the bar in the village in which he had studied in May, 1878, at a term of court over which Judge Keath presided. In June of that year he came to Minnesota, and after traveling about for some time settled in Fairmont in August, but, owing to ill health, he remained but a short time, and on leaving returned to Indiana. In December he again came to Fairmont, and formed a law partnership with M. E. L. Shanks, Esq. They remained in partnership until Mr. Shanks was elected county auditor, at which time the firm was dissolved. Since then our subject has continued in business alone, and he has built up a large and lucrative practice.

No attorney in the county has taken a more prominent part in public affairs, and no other man has risen to a higher degree of popularity. He is one of the best attorneys in southern Minnesota, and handles all cases that come to him with a remarkable vigilance and success, and has in all official positions to which he has been called, served with the highest degree of efficiency. He has been a member of the village council for five years, and has also been attorney for the corporation for several terms. In the fall of 1884 he was elected county attorney, but, being a candidate again in 1886, was defeated by F. S. Livermore by but thirteen votes. In 1888 he was elected again to the office of county attorney on the democratic ticket, although the county is republican by a heavy majority. To illustrate the popularity to which Mr. Vories has attained, it is but necessary to say that although the county was republican by 682 majority, yet when he was a candidate for county attorney the last time in 1888, he was elected by a majority of 337 votes; and this in the face

of the fact that his opponent stumped every district in the county while our subject made not a single speech. He is a member of the Ancient Free and Accepted Masons, Lodge No. 64, of Fairmont, and also of Chapter No. 50, Apollo Commandery, of Albert Lea.

CAPTAIN MONS GRINAGER, deceased, was, during his life-time, one of the leading men of Southwestern Minnesota. He was born in Hadeland, in the kingdom of Norway, October 7, 1832, and died in the city of Minneapolis, State of Minnesota, January 30, 1889. In the year 1853 he immigrated to America, coming directly to St. Paul. In 1854 he removed to Decorah, Iowa, where he remained until 1859. He then settled on a farm at Bath, Freeborn county, Minnesota. In December, 1861, he recruited a company, consisting chiefly of Scandinavians from Iowa and Minnesota, and joined the Fifteenth Regiment of Wisconsin Infantry. His company became Company K of that regiment; he was chosen captain, and served as such with honor and credit during the war, participating in ten regular battles, besides many skirmishes. Captain Grinager was severely wounded and made prisoner in the battle of Stone River; but he escaped and lay concealed in an old building at Murfreesboro, Tennessee, for several days without food or surgical attendance, until the arrival of the Federal troops. At the battle of Chickamauga, all his superior officers being disabled, Captain Grinager commanded the regiment, and was specially mentioned for gallant services. At the close of the war, Captain Grinager returned to his farm in Freeborn county, Minnesota. In 1874 he was appointed by President Grant register of the land office at Worthington, Minnesota. He was re-appointed by President Hayes in 1877 and by President Arthur in 1882. He resigned this office in 1886, and accepted the vice-presidency of the Scandia Bank of Minneapolis, removing with his family to that city, where he was identified with other important business interests. Captain Grinager was honored in 1888 by his party by being placed at the head of the republican electoral ticket of Minnesota, and by being made vice-president of the National Republican league. He was elected a companion of the Minnesota Commandery of the Military Order of the Loyal Legion, May 2, 1888, and his funeral services were participated in by the sorrowing companions of the order.

Captain Grinager was justly honored by thousands of citizens of the State of his adoption, and tenderly loved by a large circle of personal friends. He was, in war, the true type of a brave and self-sacrificing volunteer soldier—in peace a shining example of honest, industrious, patriotic citizenship. He conscientiously performed the duties of official position, and in all relations of life, as husband, father, associate and friend, he was a model of faithfulness and integrity.

LEXANDER C. FLETCHER is a leading farmer and stock raiser located on section 32 of Lake Benton township, Lincoln county, Minnesota. He located on this claim in 1879, purchasing the homestead right of another party. He has thoroughly improved his farm at considerable cost, and has made his place one of the finest in the township. He has over 217 acres of land, on which is found excellent water and soil of the very best quality. Mr. Fletcher was one of the very first settlers of Lake Benton township and since making his location here has been actively engaged in operating his farm, and has met with merited success in all its departments.

The place of the nativity of the subject of our sketch is found near Brooklyn, five miles from Carbondale, Susquehanna county, Pennsylvania, where he was born April 19, 1828. Making his home with his parents in that locality until he was seven years of age, they then removed to Oneida county, New York, where they remained some two or three years. Removing thence they lived for some three years in the village of Seneca Lake, in Chemung county. Our subject made his home with his parents until he attained the age of twenty years, at which time he removed with them to Lake county, Illinois, and there engaged in working out on various farms. In the year 1850, together with his brother-in-law, he went to California to prospect and work in the mines. He remained in that State for some five years, engaged principally in mining, and after that period returned to Lake county, Illinois, to visit his parents. On arriving in that locality he found that his people had disposed of all their property and removed to Winona, Minnesota. Our subject followed the family and located in the vicinity of the city of Winona. Here he continued to live until coming to his present place in 1879. Throughout his varied career our subject has been a prominent man in the various localities in which he has lived. He is possessed of more than ordinary abilities and has served in various official capacities. He has held the office of township supervisor, township clerk, and various school offices. He has always been interested in the financial and social development of the citizens of the locality in which he has resided, and has taken an interest in political and civic matters of various kinds. While in Winona he joined the Prairie Lodge, No. 7, Independent Order of Odd Fellows.

Mr. Fletcher was united in the holy bonds of matrimony, June 1, 1858, to Miss Rhoda Gilbert, a native of England. This lady came to America when twelve years of age with her parents and located in the Western

States. Mrs. Fletcher died in August, 1888, leaving seven living children—Fannie L., now Mrs. William Brattle, of Lake Benton; William G.; George, who married in 1887; Helen, who married to John Bassett; Hattie, now Mrs. A. Wair, a resident of Minneapolis; Hughes, a farmer of Marshfield township, Lincoln county; Lulu, single and a resident of Winona, and Abbie, now in the district schools near her father's home. Fannie and Hattie are both graduates of the Winona normal school.

The parents of the subject of our sketch were Joshua and Mary Louise (Gear) Fletcher. The father was a native of Massachusetts, and throughout his life gave his attention to a large extent to agricultural pursuits. He was also a shoemaker by trade and followed that line of business in connection with his farming. In early life he came West, located in Wisconsin and later in Winona, Minnesota, where he died. The mother of our subject was born in New York State, where she received her early training and education. She was married in Susquehanna county, Pennsylvania, and coming West with her family, died in 1867, in Winona. The mother was a loyal Christian woman and a consistent member of the Presbyterian church. In the father's family there were ten children, all of whom grew to man and womanhood—Charles, Edmund, Harriet, Catharine, Alexander C., Albert (deceased), Frank (deceased), George and Mott. The mother's people made settlement on land where the city of Winona now stands.

Our subject came first to Lincoln county with his two sons, George and William, who took land for themselves, built a small house 12x16 feet, and then returned to Winona, where they remained during the winter. They sent a man to build the house and the sons took charge of the work on the place. Crops were very good, and the next year our subject broke one hundred acres and also set out a fine grove of trees. He has a beautiful location and has a pleasant and commodious dwelling house. Since he came to the county, his crops have been generally very fair, and he has accumulated considerable means. Being one of the early settlers and being possessed of an enterprising spirit, he has held several offices within the gift of the people. For four years he served officially on the board of county commissioners, and is at present justice of the peace. In the latter position he has served about four years and has administered all affairs which have come to him with rare judgment and impartiality to all concerned. He has also held various school district offices in his district. In politics Mr. Fletcher affiliates with the republican party and is at present a member of Lodge No. 77, Independent Order of Odd Fellows. Since coming to the township he has in various official transactions proven his reliability as a man and a citizen, and has made many warm friends.

DAMON R. WOODMAN is one of the leading and most hospitable and influential citizens of Troy township, Pipestone county, Minnesota. His fine farm is located on section 11, where he has resided since 1879.

Mr. Woodman was born in Madison, Madison county, New York, March 25, 1829. He is the son of Isaac and Rokana (Richmond) Woodman, both of whom were natives of the same county. Isaac's parents were natives of Rhode Island, and his father was a soldier in the Revolutionary War, in which he served during the greater part of seven years. When Damon was about seventeen years old his parents left Madison county and removed to Bureau county, Illinois, where the father engaged in work at the carpenter's trade. In 1854 the parents removed to Rice county, Minnesota, locating near the city of Faribault, where they were among the pioneer settlers. The father died in April, 1861, and the mother died in June, 1869.

Damon R. left New York with his parents when he was seventeen years of age, and removed to Bureau county, Illinois. During his early years he was given excellent school advantages and obtained a good common-school education. On coming to Illinois he assisted his father in work at the carpenter's trade, which line of business he followed for some five years. He then concluded to turn his attention to agricultural pursuits, rented a farm and continued its operation for some two years. In 1854, when his parents removed to Minnesota, he came with them and settled on government land, remaining in Rice county until 1879. At that time he started out by team to find a location in Southwestern Minnesota. He came to Pipestone county and located on the land where he now lives. He came to this county alone in the fall of 1879, and his family followed him the next spring.

December 14, 1853, Mr. Woodman was united in marriage to Emma J. Brown, a native of Madison county, New York. Her parents were natives of the same county and are now dead. Mr. and Mrs. Woodman have been blessed with three children—Ella R., now married and residing in San Francisco, California; Albert E., a farmer on land adjoining his father's farm; and Lucy M., who still lives at home.

Mr. Woodman is a republican in politics, and is a leader in all matters which tend to the local advancement of that party. He takes an active interest in all things of a public nature, and has the esteem and confidence of his fellow-townsmen. He has an excellent farm of 116 acres under a high state of cultivation, and is also engaged to some extent in stock raising. He is a man of excellent social qualities, pleasant and agreeable in conversation, hospitable and charitable to a very great extent, and is a man possessed of such magnetic temperament that he draws many friends about him. His home is one of the happiest in the township and his family one of the most pleasant and agreeable.

HANS PETER LEWIS is a prominent dealer in general merchandise in Fulda, Murray county, Minnesota. He is the son of L. E. and Ann C. (Tieg) Lewis, both natives of the kingdom of Norway, and farmers by occupation. The mother died in Norway in July, 1886; the father is still living in that country.

The gentleman whose name appears at the head of this sketch was born in Holland parish, Norway, August 29, 1851. He resided with his parents on the farm, receiving a good common-school education, until about fifteen years of age, after which he helped his father in the farm work. In the spring of 1871 he came to the United States and first located in Grant county, Wisconsin, where during three seasons he worked on a farm. In the spring of 1872 he went to Jackson county, Minnesota, with his brother Christian, with whom he stopped for a short time. Moving thence he went to Windom and clerked in a lumber yard, and about Christmas went to Lake Crystal and attended school until spring, returning to his employment in the lumber yard for a short time thereafter. He then went to Baldwin, Wisconsin, and clerked in a general store for 1½ years, and continued his clerkship in various stores for several parties until the spring of 1878, when he went to Heron Lake, Minnesota, as book-keeper and clerk for J. T. Smith, continuing with him until August, 1880. He then came to Fulda and took charge of a branch store, over which he continued control until 1883, when Mr. J. M. Jackson purchased an interest therein and took charge of the business. Our subject continued clerking for Mr. Smith until the fall of 1884, when he opened a general mercantile business for himself. He has one of the largest stocks in the village and is doing a large and profitable trade. He is a man of public spirit, and has actively participated in all general matters. He has been village recorder almost throughout his entire residence here, and in the spring of 1889 was elected president of the village council. His brother, Christian, is a resident of Jackson county, where he is county sheriff. Mr. Lewis is a member of the Ancient Free and Accepted Masons, and was the first member initiated in Fulda Lodge, No. 170. He is a man of excellent character and is a consistent member of the Lutheran church.

Mr. Lewis was married in Heron Lake, May 1, 1880, to Miss Julia E. Rhude, daughter of O. and Rachel Rhude. Mr. and Mrs. Lewis have been blessed with two children —Roy V. and Florence E.

JUDGE J. G. REDDING is one of the leading lawyers of Windom, Cottonwood county, Minnesota. He was born at Beaver Dam, Wisconsin, in the year 1849 and was the son of George W.; and Johanna (Gleed) Redding, the former a native of Vermont and the latter born in England.

Our subject's early life was spent on the farm and he attended the district school during the winter months until he was seventeen years of age. He then became a student at Hamline University, where he pursued his studies for three years. He then engaged in teaching school and later studied law for two years and was admitted to the bar in 1871. He came to the village of Windom in 1882. Since that time he has

steadily gained in popularity and in the esteem of his fellow-citizens. He was elected clerk of the court in 1882, and on the completion of that term became judge of probate. He has also been county attorney and has otherwise prominently assisted in the affairs of local government. In politics he affiliates with the republican party, is a member of the Independent Order of Odd Fellows and Ancient Order of United Workmen.

Judge Redding was married to Ella Lambie of Plainview, Minnesota, in the year 1883. Both himself and wife are members of the Methodist Episcopal church. By a former wife Mr. Redding had three children—J. Gleed, Annie and Paul.

NELS NELSON is a member of the firm of Nelson Brothers & Company, leading merchants of Luverne, Minnesota. This firm carries an immense stock of goods, including dry goods, carpets, clothing, boots and shoes, hats, caps, crockery, groceries, etc. They have an elegant double store one hundred feet long, each room being twenty-five feet wide. They employ five clerks and do an immense business, it sometimes being necessary to double their clerical force. Our subject first commenced business in Luverne on Main street, one block from where he is now located. His store was then twenty by forty feet, and the business was then conducted under the firm name of Landin & Nelson. This firm did a large general business and remained in that location for four years, at the end of that time purchasing the general stock of William Jacobsen and removed their goods to their present location on the 12th of May, 1880.

The place of the nativity of the subject of our sketch is found in Norway, where his birth took place on the 8th of February, 1848. His parents, Nels and Carrie (Larson) Nelson, were also natives of Norway. Mr.

Nelson, Sr., was reared on a farm, and engaged in that occupation in his native land until coming to America in 1858. His first settlement was made in Winneshiek county, Iowa, where he purchased land three miles north of the village of Camden. Here the father continued farming until his death in 1875. He was an active member of the Lutheran church, and lived a consistent Christian life. The mother is now residing in Luverne, living with her son and daughter. In the parents' family there are six living children—Lars Nelson, now engaged in an extensive farming and stock raising business in Dakota; Carrie, now Mrs. C. Gunderson, of Calmar, Iowa; Nels, our subject; Gurena, now Mrs. F. C. Mahoney, of Luverne, a member of the firm of Nelson Brothers & Company; Bertie, now Mrs. Cartrande, of Dakota; and Samuel B., also one of the members of the firm.

Our subject received a good common-school education between the ages of ten and nineteen years, and during that time spent the intervals in farm work. At nineteen he commenced clerking in a general store in Camden, Iowa, to which place he had gone with his parents from his native land in 1858. He continued in the employ of one firm in that city for seven years, at the end of which time he came to Luverne and started in business as mentioned in the opening lines of this sketch. He also owned a branch store at Flandreau, Dakota, which he established in 1878, operating the same for four years. His successful business traits have been more or less succeeded to by his numerous clerks, a number of these having become successful merchants at different points. One is a merchant at Luverne, another at Lisbon, Dakota; another at Grafton, same territory; another at Fall River, Dakota; and another in business at Flandreau. The firm have also a branch store at Beaver Creek, and our subject is inter-

ested in several other mercantile enterprises in different parts of the State of Minnesota. He is actively engaged in assisting in the building up of the financial enterprises of Luverne, and was one of the organizers of the First National Bank, which started out under the name of the Bank of Luverne. Our subject has been a director of this financial institution since its organization. He is also one of the stockholders of the Red Jasper Quarry Company, of Luverne. In matters pertaining to the local government of the town and county in which he lives, Mr. Nelson has taken an active interest and has held several official positions. He has been a member of the village council one year, chairman of the council board for four years, and has also been a member of the school board for some time. He built his elegant residence, where he now lives, in 1884. In politics our subject affiliates with the republican party, is a leading member of the Masonic fraternity, and is one of the most prominent and substantial citizens of Luverne.

AZRO P. McKINSTRY, one of the leading dairymen of the State, located in Verona township, Faribault county, Minnesota, his present home, in the year 1870, and purchased a farm of 178 acres. He has been engaged extensively in the dairy business and has raised a large number of Holstein and Jersey cattle, keeping constantly from sixty to seventy-five head. He is probably engaged more extensively in dairying than any other farmer in the county. His farming operations are on rather a small scale, his object being to raise only sufficient wheat, oats, etc., for his own use. His farm is located three miles from the thriving village of Winnebago City, which point Mr. McKinstry largely supplies with dairy products. He built and made a success of the first "silo" in the county.

Mr. McKinstry was born in Bethel, Vermont, in July, 1844, and was the son of Paul and Harriet (Lillie) McKinstry, natives of Vermont. The parents are still living at a hale old age, and reside in Winnebago City. The father is now eighty-two years old, and, with his wife, belongs to the Methodist Episcopal church. They are highly esteemed for their many generous deeds and for their earnest religious work in Winnebago City and in the county. They have been members of the Methodist Episcopal church for many years, and our subject's father has held most of the church offices in that denomination. In his early life Paul McKinstry engaged in farming, and came to Minnesota in 1868, and settled at Winnebago City, taking a farm a short distance south of the village. In 1878 he engaged in the mercantile business and followed the same until 1888, when he retired from active work. He is stockholder in the steam-flouring mill, and took an active interest in the various other financial enterprises, assisting very materially in the building up and improving of the village. There are four children in the father's family —Clarissa, now Mrs. A. P. Hatch, of Ogle county, Illinois; Henry, a merchant in Winnebago City; our subject, and Ellen, now Mrs. J. F. Winship, of Winnebago City.

Until he was eighteen years of age, Azro P. McKinstry remained a resident of his native place. He attended the public schools, and learned the saddlery business. He enlisted in the Tenth Vermont Volunteer Infantry in August, 1862, and served as a private throughout the war, being discharged at Burlington, Vermont, in 1865. He served gallantly and faithfully and participated in a large number of battles. He was wounded at Cold Harbor, and was in the hospital for six months. After his recovery he again went to the front and served until the close of the war. On his discharge he engaged in work at his trade for a year, and then operated a shop of his own for three years at Northfield, Vermont. He then removed to a farm and engaged in agricultural pursuits in the vicinity of Bradford for two years. At the end of that time he came to his present location, where he has since resided.

The marriage of the subject of our sketch occurred January 4, 1867, on which date he was wedded to Miss Laura Belle Rogers, a native of Newbury, Vermont, and a school teacher during her younger days. She was a daughter of Oliver B. Rogers, a farmer and influential citizen of Newbury. Mr. and Mrs. McKinstry have four children—Harry, Ned, Florence and Mabel.

Throughout his residence in Faribault county, Mr. McKinstry has proven a valuable and public-spirited citizen, and has held various official positions, among them being that of chairman of the board of township supervisors, etc. He is a strong temperance advocate, and is a member of the prohibition party. He belongs to the Methodist Episcopal church, and also to the United Workmen. He is one of Faribault county's most prominent and representative citizens.

❧

BENJAMIN TARBOT is one of the leading farmers of Rose Hill township, Cottonwood county, Minnesota, and resides on a beautiful farm on section 30. He is of Russian birth, born October 24, 1857. His parents, Peter and Catharine (Oust) Tarbot, were natives of that country, and were engaged in farming until their death, living and dying in their native land.

The subject of our sketch was reared as a farmer's boy and assisted his father in cultivating the soil when not in school. He was given good educational advantages up to the age of seventeen and then left his parents and emigrated to the United States. Four weeks were spent in the State of Kansas and then our subject concluded to come farther north. Going to St. Paul, Minnesota, he came thence to Mountain Lake, Cottonwood county, thence to Heron Lake, Jackson county, and thence came to his present location, pre-empting one hundred and one acres of land. During the grasshopper times he was compelled to change his claim to a homestead. He has since made it his home, and has succeeded well in his farming operations. He has seen hard times as well as the other early settlers, and during the grasshopper raids was compelled to cease farming and work at other employments in order to obtain a livelihood. He is a man of good character, energetic and systematic in his business operations, is a republican in politics, and with his family belongs to the Lutheran church, and is highly esteemed both as a neighbor and citizen.

Mr. Tarbot was married July 4, 1882, to Catharine Avia, daughter of John Avia, a native of Austria. This union has been blessed with five children—Matilda, Lena, John, Henry and Edwin.

———◦━❦━◦———

JOHN G. JOHNSON, a public-spirited and influential citizen of Lowville township, Murray county, Minnesota, has an excellent farm on section 36. He was born in Norway, July 3, 1863.

The parents of the subject of our sketch were Gilbert and Anna (Engebretson) Johnson, both natives of Norway. The father was a farmer by occupation and reared a family of eleven children, our subject being the oldest. The family came to America in 1866, landing at Quebec, whence they went to Fillmore county, Minnesota, where the father purchased a farm. He continued his residence thereon until 1872, and then removed to Murray county, locating a claim on section 2, of Leeds township. He resided on that claim until about 1884, when he sold out and purchased land on section 36, of Lowville township, and resided there until his death, which occurred in 1888. The mother is still living on the home farm.

The home attachments of our subject were of such a congenial nature that he remained with his parents until he was eighteen years of age. He was given good educational advantages and acquired a mastery over the branches of a common-school education. At times when not in school, he assisted his father in work on the farm. At eighteen he went to Adrian, Nobles county, and worked one season, when he returned to the vicinity of his father's home and engaged in farming for two years. He then went to Dakota and worked a farm one summer, returning after that time to his father's home in Murray county. Then he rented a farm and operated it until 1888, when he purchased eighty acres of land on the section where he now lives. He is a man of excellent character, careful and practical in his business affairs, and has been quite successful. He is public pirited and affiliates with the democratic party, also belonging to the Lutheran church. He has taken an active part in all public matters and has been clerk of the township for some time. His character is of the highest order, and he is respected by all who know him.

———◦━❦━◦———

GEORGE E. CLEVELAND is one of the reliable business men of the village of Verdi, Lincoln county, Minnesota, where he is engaged in the general mercantile business in partnership with G. Merrill, under the firm name of Cleveland & Merrill. He was born in Koos county, New Hampshire, June 26, 1857.

The parents of the subject of our sketch were M. C. and Eliza J. Cleveland, the father being a native of Vermont, and the mother a native of Massachusetts. The family lived on a farm, the father locating in New Hampshire about thirty-five years ago. There were six children in the father's family, George E. being the oldest.

When seventeen years of age the subject of our sketch left his native State and came to Rochester, Minnesota, with his parents. Up to this time he had assisted on the home farm, and been given good educational advantages. Two years were spent by the family in Rochester, whence they came to Murray county, locating near Tracy. Here the father was frozen to death January 7, 1873, in the great "January blizzard." The subject of our sketch remained with the family, taking charge of its affairs and managing the home place. He remained on the farm for about four years, and then with the family went back to Rochester, remaining four years. Our subject was then married, and returned to the old farm in Murray county. After remaining one year he then came to the "Morris ranch" in Pipestone county, and making that his home for three years, then came to Verdi village, where he found employment with G. W. Van Dusen & Co., buying grain. He is still engaged with that company, and carries on a mercantile business in connection therewith. He formed his present partnership with Mr. Merrill in June, 1888. The firm carries a large stock of excellent goods worth somewhat over two thousand dollars.

Mr. Cleveland was married, November 20, 1878, to Frances J. Heilig. This union has been blessed with five children—Ira, Arthur, Grover, Lloyd and William. In politics the subject of our sketch affiliates with the democratic party, and takes an active interest in the local affairs of that organization. He has held several official positions, among them being that of constable, which position he held for three years. He is at present postmaster of Verdi village. Mr. Cleveland

is a man of good business capabilities, and is highly esteemed as a man and citizen. He is a prominent member of the Independent Order of Odd Fellows.

WILLIAM B. FRY, a well-to-do farmer located in Delton township, Cottonwood county, Minnesota, is the son of Jeremiah and Hannah (Edson) Fry, natives respectively of New York and Vermont. William B. Fry was born in New Hartford, Connecticut, March 7, 1829. His father was a minister of the Reformed Methodist church, and owned a farm where he made his home.

The subject of our sketch resided with his parents until he was about twenty years of age. He was thoroughly educated, and taught school for some time before he left the parental roof. His first business after leaving home was in the mercantile trade; he kept store for a short time in McGrawville, New York, and then returning home, remained with his father on the farm for about a year. He then removed with his father to Connecticut, where he engaged in the mercantile business, remaining about three years. He then sold out and removed to Wisconsin, settling about ten miles from Milwaukee, where he taught school for several terms. He then went to McHenry county, Illinois, and then rented a farm, which he operated for three years. In August, 1862, feeling the stirrings of patriotism within him, he enlisted in the service of his country in Company D, Ninety-fifth Regiment Illinois Volunteer Infantry, and served faithfully and well until in March, 1864. He was then discharged on account of wounds received in the battle of Vicksburg, May 19, 1863, this being the last battle in which he participated. Our subject was with his regiment from the time of his enlistment until he was wounded. He was then not able to do duty, and remained in the hospital for some time. For a year and a half after he was wounded he was not able to sit up all day. He has never fully recovered, and still carries the bullet in his body. He receives a pension of twelve dollars per month. After his discharge our subject returned to McHenry county, Illinois, but was not able to do any work for some time. That fall he went to Connecticut on a brief visit to his parents, remaining with them until February, when he again returned for a short time to McHenry county, Illinois. He then located in Fond du Lac county, Wisconsin, and for eight years worked his mother-in-law's farm. In 1873 he removed to Madelia, Watonwan county, Minnesota, where he purchased a farm, engaging in agricultural pursuits for two years. He then sold out and came to Delton township, Cottonwood county, where he purchased a farm of eighty acres on section 14, this being his present place of residence. He also took a tree claim of 160 acres on section 14, but did not succeed in getting his trees to come up to the requirements of the timber culture act. His son, Edson R., has filed on this piece of land as a tree claim.

Mr. Fry was married in Fairwater, Wisconsin, March 12, 1865, to Miss Catharine Staple, daughter of David and Susanna (Robins) Staple, natives respectively of Maine and Massachusetts. This lady was born in Wellington, Maine, August 25, 1833. Her father died in May, 1862, leaving a wife and the following children—Lucinda, now the widow of Warren Johnson; Julia, now Mrs. A. Bradbury; David (deceased), Daniel, Joseph, Samuel, Catharine, and Susan, now dead. Mr. and Mrs. Fry have been blessed with the following children—Edson R., Willie E., G. Elmer, Florence R., Edith L. and Fred N.

Since coming to the county Mr. Fry has taken quite an interest in public matters, and has held various official positions. He

has been justice of the peace, township clerk, township treasurer and assessor, having held some office nearly all the time since locating in the township. He is a member of the Free-Will Baptist church, and is a loyal Christian gentleman and an enterprising citizen. He has passed through many trying times, and in early days had much of his crops destroyed by grasshoppers, and in other ways damaged. He is now in good circumstances, however, and is comfortably located on a good farm.

MATTHIAS J. BECKER is a prominent and substantial farmer of Altona township, Pipestone county, Minnesota. His farm is located on section 34. Mr. Becker was born in the State of New York, June 3, 1861. His parents were John J. and Catharine (Williams) Becker, both natives of Germany. John J. was the son of Matthias Becker, who was a shoemaker by trade and a native of Germany. The elder Matthias came to America with his wife and family and located in the State of New York, where they spent the most of their lives. John J. was reared in that State and was married there. Our subject's father was a farmer by occupation and was quite well-to-do and influential in the community in which he lived. He had a family of ten children, of whom Matthias was the eldest. In 1869 the father removed his family to Rice county, Minnesota, and purchased a farm on which he still lives.

Matthias J. Becker remained with his parents, assisting in the work of the home farm and attending the district schools until 1879. He then came to Pipestone county for the purpose of improving his father's place, which the father had located in 1878. Our subject continued his residence on his father's farm until 1882, when he homesteaded the place, the father surrendering his prior right. Later the father purchased a farm of 160 acres adjoining this place, and our subject operated both places. He is not married, but has a brother and sister living with him on his farm. Coming to this country with but little means, our subject has by thrift and economy saved considerable means and has placed himself in good circumstances. He has an excellent farm with sixty acres under cultivation and engages in general farming and stock raising. He is a man of good qualifications, having been well educated in his youthful days, and has been a constant and eager reader of the accounts of passing events. In politics he affiliates with the democratic party, and takes a prominent stand in local matters. He is noted for his integrity of character, and is respected by all.

THOMAS LEMON, a prominent farmer of Lake Benton township, Lincoln county, Minnesota, homesteaded his present place on sections 34 and 35 in 1872. He commenced operations the first year he came by breaking twenty acres and building a log house some 16x20 feet. This log house is still a portion of his dwelling, but he has improved it considerably and has built an addition 8x24 feet. He has also adorned and beautified his place by planting trees, among them being cottonwood and elm. He has a fine farm, and the passer-by is greeted with many evidences of prosperity and thrift. Our subject was one among the early settlers of this township, there being but three or four residents in the locality when he made his location here. He assisted in the organization of the township, and was a member of the board of supervisors for two years. He has also held other official positions; has always taken an active interest in local affairs and has proven himself a valuable addition to the company of settlers in Lake Benton

township. His farming operations have not always been met with success, but he has kept heart in the face of all troubles, has borne up courageously under all losses, and continued manfully at work replenishing his depleted circumstances. He lost much by grasshopper raids in 1874–5–6, and has been a loser to a large extent by diseases among his stock. Despite all these he has kept sturdily at work and has accumulated considerable means, becoming one of the reliable and substantial farmers of the township.

The subject of our sketch is a native of Ireland and was born in May, 1846. He remained with his parents in that country until he was nineteen years of age, at which time he came to the United States, locating eighteen miles from Winona, at Money Creek. Here he remained until coming to his present residence in Lake Benton township. The subject of our sketch received a good common-school education in his native land and assisted his father in work about the home place until coming to America.

Mr. Lemon was married in June, 1864, to Miss Ellen Jane Miller, also a native of Ireland. When this lady was seventeen years of age she left her native country and came to America, locating in Wisconsin, where her marriage took place, in the city of La Crosse. Mr. and Mrs. Lemon have seven children—William C., James, Eliza, John, Stella, Rufus and Blanche.

Mr. Lemon is one of the foremost citizens of his township and ever since making his location here has proven one of its greatest benefactors. He has heartily engaged in every project which has tended toward the financial or other development of his locality, and has assisted in various capacities in the administration of local government. In politics he has affiliated for some years with the republican party, in whose principles he earnestly believes. He is a man of excellent character, systematic and thorough-going as a farmer and has met with merited success. He has a pleasant home and an agreeable family.

JOHN M. DICKSON is one of the representative and influential citizens of Fulda, Murray county, Minnesota. He is the president of the Bank of Fulda, one of the leading financial institutions of the county.

He was born in Fox Lake, Wisconsin, February 24, 1858, and is a son of John and Jane (Marshall) Dickson, natives of Glasgow, Scotland. In an early day the parents came to America and became pioneer settlers, about sixty miles west of Milwaukee, Wisconsin. From this point they had to go to Milwaukee for provisions, that city being their nearest railroad station. Here they marketed all their wheat and other grains, and did all their trading.

The subject of our sketch spent his early life among the pioneer settlements of Wisconsin, and as schools were few and far between, his early life was not supplied with the best facilities for receiving an education. Later, however, he was given good educational advantages. At the age of nineteen he commenced work for himself, and in partnership with his brother, Peter, shipped cattle to eastern markets. After one year in Wisconsin he went to Heron Lake, Minnesota, and engaged in the mercantile business, but after eighteen months removed to Fulda, Murray county, and operated a store for one and a half years. He then sold out his mercantile business and opened his present bank, in which line he has been engaged ever since. On first coming to Heron Lake he was in the employ of J. T. Smith, for about a year buying flax. Since coming to Fulda, and indeed throughout his life, the subject of our sketch has proven himself one of the most public-spirited citizens of the county. He has taken an active part in general matters and has as-

sisted in various ways in building up the locality. He has been prominent in politics in this county, has been president of the village council, school-director, and has held various other minor offices. He is a member of the Ancient Free and Accepted Masons, Fulda Lodge, No. 170, first becoming a member of the order when twenty-one years of age, in Fox Lake, Wisconsin.

Mr. Dickson was married in Le Sueur county, Minnesota, September 15, 1885, to Miss Esther Jones, a native of that county. Her parents died when she was only two years of age and she was reared by her sister, Mrs. R. T. Roberts. Mr. and Mrs. Dickson have one child, Marshall.

FRANKLIN L. PLANK, one of the early settlers of Troy township, Pipestone county, Minnesota, is now residing on section 24. He came to this county when it was nothing but a wild unbroken prairie, selected his land, and soon after settled thereon and made a permanent home. Many settlers have come and gone since he first landed in the township, and through all these changes he has been one of the permanent factors in the improvement and building up of the agricultural and financial interests of the locality in which he lives.

Mr. Plank was born in Wolcott, Wayne county, New York, September 30, 1846. He is the son of Lewis and Mary (Park) Plank, both natives of New York. The mother died when Franklin was but eighteen months old; the father is still living and is a resident of Anoka, Minnesota. Mr. Plank's ancestry is traceable to English origin, his great-grandfather being a native of England. His grandfather and mother were both natives of Connecticut. The great-grandfather was a soldier in the Revolutionary War, having come to this country some time before that war was commenced. The grandfather was a soldier in the War of 1812. The Planks throughout their generations have been mostly given to the occupation of farming, and have been men of excellent character and considerable wealth.

Mr. Plank resided in the place of his nativity until the year 1863, up to which time he had been attending school and working on the home farm. December 9, 1863, he enlisted in Company G, Ninth New York Heavy Artillery, and continued in the service until the close of the war, being discharged October 28, 1865. At the battle of Petersburg he was severely wounded by a shot through the leg. He was taken to Conehead hospital and from thence to City Point, where for a long time he suffered much pain from his wounded limb. While in the hospital he had the pleasure of shaking hands with President Lincoln, who went through the hospital shaking hands with all the wounded soldiers. Mr. Plank was afterwards removed to the hospital in Washington, where he was still confined when President Lincoln was assassinated. After his discharge he returned home and remained until 1868, in which year he came to Illinois, where he worked on a farm in Winnebago county. During the late summer and fall months he was engaged in running a threshing machine, and continued these lines of work until the fall of 1871, when he removed to Waterloo, Iowa. Arriving in that city he found employment in an elevator and after continuing in that line of employment until sometime in 1872, he came to Minnesota, looking for a location. He first went to Wilmar, Kandiyohi county, and not liking the lay of the country, he went to Anoka, where he remained until 1878 working at the lumber business. In that year he went to Beaver Creek, Rock county, and in that place hired a team and proceeded overland to Sioux Falls, and from thence, returning to Beaver Creek by way of Pipestone county, he located his claim in Troy township, after which he returned to Anoka. He returned to his claim in August and built a shanty 10x12 feet, and entered upon the enjoyments of pioneer life. Since that day his residence has been permanent.

August 29, 1880, the subject of our sketch was married to Miss Josephine G. Rice, daughter of Major Rice. Mr. and Mrs. Plank have had two children—Mabel A. and George W.

Too much cannot be said of Mr. Plank as regards his prominence in the public matters of Troy township. He is a man well versed in the practical things of life, is a good reader of human nature, and by being observant has educated himself in a practical way so that he is looked upon as being one of the leaders among the citizens of the town in which he lives. His early education was received in the common-schools and he also attended the Leavenworth Academy in New York for sometime. His experience during the War of the Rebellion entitles him to the prominent position which he occupies in the Grand Army of the Republic, Simon Mix Post, No. 95. Mr. Plank is a man of fine personal qualities, is pleasant, and sociable and has formed many warm friendships in Pipestone county.

CHARLES M. RENSHAW is a thrifty farmer of Fenton township, Murray county, Minnesota, and resides on section 8. His native place is found on the island of Jamaica, where he was born at the American mission station, May 8, 1845. He was the son of Rev. C. Stewart and Mira (Orum) Renshaw. The mother was a native of Philadelphia. In early life the father served in the United States navy, and later became a missionary of the Congregational church.

The gentleman whose name appears at the head of this sketch left home at the age of sixteen years. Up to this time he had been given a good common-school education. November 19, 1862, he enlisted in Company I, Thirty-first Massachusetts Volunteer Infantry. He served faithfully throughout the entire war, being discharged December 20, 1865. After leaving the Union service he went to Pittsfield, Massachusetts, where he remained some eighteen months learning the carpenter's trade. Seven months were then spent by him in traveling and he then went to Apple River, Jo Daviess county, Illinois, arriving in September, 1868. He engaged in contracting and building at that point until 1871, when he was married and went to Chicago in answer to a call from Potter Palmer for men to assist in cleaning up the debris left by the great fire. He remained in that city until 1873, and then started on a trip through Illinois and Wisconsin, selling sewing machines. After some time he returned to Apple River and made that place his headquarters for about a year. He then went back to his old trade of contracting and building, and engaged in that business until 1882, when he changed his location to the village of Nora in the same county, where he engaged in the same work. Here he remained until May 17, 1886, when he took a contract to build a store for S. B. Rockey in Chandler. Coming to Murray county he found a beautiful country, and located his claim. He has made his home in the county ever since. The subject of our sketch has been one of the most prominent citizens of the county, and by virtue of his excellent capability as a business man he has risen to high esteem in the minds of his fellow-citizens. He has a thorough classical education, and was for some time a cadet in the military academy at Annapolis. In politics he affiliates with the republican party, but being a stanch temperance man he is in sympathy with any movement for bringing about the prohibition of the liquor traffic.

He has served his constituents in various official positions, having held the office of supervisor, and being at the present time township clerk: He is a member of the Grand Army of the Republic.

Mr. Renshaw was married October 26, 1871, to Miss Mary Lemont. Mr. and Mrs. Renshaw have been blessed with nine children, seven of whom are now living, three boys and four girls.

HON. JOHN F. SHOEMAKER, one of the best known and most highly respected citizens of Luverne, Minnesota, was born in Chemung county, New York, in 1838. He is the son of Samuel and Sarah (Law) Shoemaker, natives of Pennsylvania. The father was an extensive farmer in the State of New York, and came west in 1846, settling in Kankakee, Illinois. He resided in Illinois engaged in farming until his death, which occurred in 1848. The mother is still living in that State. The father was of German descent, and was one of the prominent and influential farmers of the locality in which he lived. In the father's family there were seven children, five of whom are now living—Charles D., engaged in contracting and building in Illinois; Matilda, now Mrs. H. W. Blackburn, of the same State; Hannah, now Mrs. William Jackson, of Nebraska; John F. and Samuel H., editor and publisher of the DeWitt *Observer*, of DeWitt, Illinois. Elizabeth married George Haverill, of Iowa, and died at the age of thirty-six years. Catherine died when four years of age.

The boyhood days of our subject were spent on the farm in New York, and in 1846 he came with his parents to Illinois, and made his home on the farm of his parents until two years after his father's death. He received a good common-school education. Two years after his father's death he com-

SOUTHWESTERN MINNESOTA.

menced working out on adjoining farms, and continued in this way until 1851. In that year he went to live with his step-father, with whom he continued three years, and during much of that time he made a specialty of attending school, thus acquiring the finishing touches of a common-school education. At the end of the time just mentioned he commenced learning the carpenter's trade, and continued in that line of business until 1869, with the exception of three years, during which he served in the Union army. He commenced contracting when he was seventeen years old at McGregor, Iowa, and for a number of years employed from twelve to fifteen men. Mr. Shoemaker enlisted in Company L, Seventh Iowa Cavalry, and first held the office of corporal. After serving a short time in that rank he acted as quartermaster sergeant for several months. He was then appointed second lieutenant, and later received his commission as first lieutenant, holding this latter office until the close of the war. He was discharged at Sioux City, June 22, 1866, after having had a severe service in the Indian War in Dakota and Montana. While in the service he held other positions besides those mentioned. By appointment he held the rank of post adjutant at Fort Randall for two months. He was also quartermaster and commissary at Fort Ponka, Dakota, for six months, and for some time was in command of a company at that fort. His regiment was engaged in a severe one-day's battle in the Bad Lands in Dakota, in the vicinity where the Northern Pacific railroad now crosses these lands. After his service and honorable discharge he returned home to McGregor, Iowa, and engaged in work at his trade until 1869. He then came to Rock county, and pre-empted 160 acres of land, homesteading 170 acres, and purchasing 200 acres adjoining, making in all a farm of 530 acres. He settled down to make a spe-

cialty of farming. Within a few years he had broken four hundred acres and fenced a good portion of his farm, building a good dwelling-house. He has continued farming, and has also occupied somewhat of his attention in the raising of fine graded Short-horn cattle. At present he has about one hundred head of Durhams. His land and home are in Mound township, some three miles from Luverne. The Burlington & Northern railroad runs through a portion of his farm. He has also the good fortune of having the fine, red jasper stone quarry on his place, of which there is an unlimited supply. Since coming to the county our subject has identified himself closely with the interests of the locality and has, with honor and credit, held several official positions. From 1872 to 1878 he efficiently filled the position of county treasurer, and had the honor of being the first treasurer of the county. On the organization of the county Governor Austin appointed him as one of the commissioners to locate the county seat. Of this body our subject was made chairman and became mainly instrumental in locating the county seat where it now stands. He assisted in the organization of the township in which his farm is located in 1872, and since that time has held the office of town clerk and was also overseer of highways for some time. In 1886 he was elected as an independent candidate to represent his district in the lower house of the legislature. He served two years, and again in 1888 was elected to the same office on the independent ticket by a nice majority.

The subject of our sketch was married in 1859 to Miss Catharine McDermott, of Clayton county, Iowa. This union has been blessed with four living children—Hattie, Minnie, Charles H. and Gertrude. The two oldest daughters were thoroughly educated and prepared for the profession of teaching, in which Minnie is still engaged.

As has already been intimated Mr. Shoe-maker is independent in politics, associating himself with those principles and those move-ments with which he thinks is to be found the highest degree of safety for the govern-ment. In matters of a social nature he takes a lively interest, being a man of excellent conversational abilities and possessed of ex-tensive general knowledge. He is also a member of several civic societies, among them being the Masonic, Odd Fellows, and Grand Army of the Republic, being a mem-ber of the John A. Dix Post, of Luverne. Financially Mr. Shoemaker is one among those most largely interested in the develop-ment of Luverne and Rock county. All pro-jects tending toward the upbuilding of the business interests of Luverne and vicinity meet with his approval and earnest and hearty support. He is one of the stockholders of the Rock County *News.*

NDRES QUEVLI is one of the lead-ing men of Windom, Minnesota, where he carries a large stock of drugs and merchandise. He is a native of the kingdom of Norway, where he was born in the year 1832. His parents were Crist and Mary Quevli, farmers by occupation in Norway. The father served in the War of 1814 be-tween Sweden and Norway. He had a family of three children—Mary, now Mrs. Hamkingson, of Norway; Annie M., now Mrs. Hempstead, of Jackson, Minnesota, and Andres.

The early life of our subject was spent in his native land, where he received a good common-school education. He remained with his parents until he was of age, when he took charge of the home farm and resided thereon until 1870, when he came to the United States. He located in Minnesota, purchasing a farm of eighty acres and homesteading eighty acres in Jackson county. He resided in that county, engaged in general farming, for some six years, when he removed to Windom, Cotton-wood county. On coming to this village he purchased a store building north of the pub-lic square and put in a large and extensive stock of dry goods. Somewhat later he built an addition to his store and added a stock of drugs, hardware, clothing, etc. He has taken an active interest in all public matters and has held various official positions. He has been a member of the school board and the village council, and while in Jackson county was supervisor of his township. In politics our subject affiliates with the repub-lican party, and, with his wife, belongs to the Lutheran church. He has been a prominent man in religious matters and has held most of the offices of the organization to which he belongs. He is liberal-minded, public-spirited and always assists generously in the further-ing of any project which tends toward the development and improvement of his locality.

Mr. Quevli was married in Norway to Goreni Quevli, who died in 1884, leaving six children—Crist, a physician at Tacoma, Washington Territory; Nels, a druggist of Lamberton, Minnesota; Mary, Andrew, Annie and Martha. Mr. Quevli was married the second time to Mrs. Lena Larson, a native of Norway.

ENRY ENKE is a thrifty farmer and prominent citizen, located on section 22, Verdi township, Lincoln county, Minne-sota. He is a native of Minnesota, having been born in the city of Rochester, August 10, 1857. His parents were John C. and Anna M. (Schmelzer) Enke, both of whom were natives of Germany. The father came to America in 1853 and first settled in the State of Pennsylvania. His next location was made in Iowa, whence he removed to Minnesota, locating in Rochester in the winter of 1855. Up to this time, throughout his life, the father had been engaged in work at the mason's trade. In August, 1865, he removed to Omaha, Nebraska, and worked at his trade some two years, removing thence to Missouri Valley Junction, Iowa. He made that his home until 1871, when he returned to Rochester, Minnesota, and remained there until 1878. He then concluded to find a location in some western county, and came to Lincoln county and located his claim, soon after returning to Rochester, and remaining in that city until the next July, when he returned to his farm and made a permanent settlement.

Henry Enke remained with his parents, following them in their various migrations, until the year 1880, up to which time he had been given good educational advantages and had received a good common-school education. In 1880 he went to Lake Benton and engaged in work at the mason's trade, which he had learned from his father. He lived in Lake Benton for two years, and then returned to the farm, where he employed his time for three years. After another period spent in Lake Benton, he returned again to the farm, where he has since remained. He took his present claim as a pre-emption in 1879, having also taken a tree claim in 1878. At present he has a fine farm of 160 acres, under excellent cultivation and well provided with buildings.

Mr. Enke was married June 5, 1881, to Dora C. Eddy. This union has been blessed with five children—Hattie M., Lutie, Charles, Freddy (deceased) and an infant.

In early life our subject was given excellent educational advantages and became well qualified to enter upon the duties of any life to which he might be called. He is a man of much intelligence, possessed of good business capabilities, and has been a prominent factor in the public affairs of his township.

In politics he belongs to the democratic party, and is a member of the Odd Fellows fraternity. Mr. Enke is a man of good character, and is esteemed by all who know him.

----·--◆--❧◆❧·--◆·--·

WILBER POTTER is a prosperous farmer and prominent citizen of Delton township, Cottonwood county, Minnesota. His parents were David and Nellie (Gaffin) Potter natives, respectively, of New York and Connecticut. Our subject was born in Hoosick, New York, November 26, 1808. He resided on the farm with his parents, assisting in work thereon until he was eighteen years of age. He then learned the boot and shoe trade and followed that business for about ten years, making his home with his parents. He lived with them until their death. He was the only child, and when he had obtained means wherewith to purchase a home of his own the parents lived with him.

After the death of his parents our subject did not continue the shoe business, but soon engaged in farming in the vicinity of Alexandria for three or four years. At the end of that time he sold out and removed to Cattaraugus county, same State, and purchased a farm on which he lived for about five years. He then sold out and went to Rockford, Illinois, residing there a few months. His next move was to a place midway between Janesville and Beloit, Wisconsin, on the Rock river, where he purchased a claim and on its being brought into the market by the government, filed papers, and made it his residence for four years. Removing to the township of Union he purchased another farm where he lived eight years. This land is now the site of the prosperous village of Evansville. Our subject's next move was to Columbia county, Wisconsin, where he purchased a farm and resided some two years. Thence he went to Waupaca county, and purchased village property in the village of Weyauwega and engaged in the cabinet business for some three years. He then traded his business for eighty acres of land and settled in Cedar Lake. He commenced hotel keeping and continued thereat for some seven years, during which time he was postmaster of the village. His next move was to Winnebago county, where he operated a farm for some eight years. He then concluded that he might find a better location in the State of Iowa and went to Winneshiek county, in that State, making that his home some three years. In 1873 he came to Cottonwood county, Minnesota, and became one of the earliest settlers of Amboy township, his nearest neighbor being five miles distant. The postoffice of Red Rock was in his care and kept in his house for many years. This office was on the line of the mail route from Windom to Lamberton, which our subject was instrumental in having established. After his eight years of residence in Amboy township, Mr. Potter removed to Delton township, settling on 160 acres on section 14. Mr. Potter throughout his life has been one of the most active participants in all public matters, and has always taken an active part in political matters. He is a man of good business qualifications, and has held various township offices. While in New York he was supervisor and constable, and in Wisconsin supervisor, postmaster, township treasurer, and was also one of the county commissioners who established the road from Beloit to Janesville, this being the first road laid out through that region and was before Wisconsin became a State. He took a census of Amboy and Storden townships in Cottonwood county in 1880, and has actively participated in public affairs. He is a man of advanced years, and yet remarkably well preserved, both in mind and body. Possessed of good ideas and of the highest character, he is esteemed and highly respected by all who know him.

Mr. Potter was married in Wyomingville, New York, in the year 1827, to Eliza N. Green. This lady died in Union township, Wisconsin, in 1849, leaving the following-named children — Albert, Peter, William, Harvey (now deceased), and Julia, who married Edson Hall, and now lives in Oil City, Pennsylvania. Mr. Potter's second marriage was to Miss Maria Mily, and occurred in Watertown, Wisconsin, August 1, 1850. Miss Mily was a daughter of Walter and Catharine (Kraner) Mily, natives of Ireland. She was born in Ireland, June 15, 1832. The second marriage of our subject was blessed with the following-named children— David W., Hattie E., Charles C., Alice S. (now deceased), Adelbert S., Allen B. (deceased), and Estella M. David W. married Gertie White, and now lives in Washington Territory. Hattie married S. T. Watson, and is a resident of California. Charles C. is a veterinary surgeon in Ellendale, Dakota. Estella married Charles H. Works, a sketch of whom is given in another department of this work. Albert married Lucretia Doty, who died, and later he married Caroline Stall. He is a prominent lawyer in Wisconsin. Peter resides on a farm in Wisconsin. William is a resident of Montana, and is a carpenter and miller by trade.

GUSTAF ANDERSON is one of the thrifty and industrious farmers of Altona township, Pipestone county, Minnesota. He resides on section 26, where he owns a fine farm of 160 acres, which he took as a tree claim in 1880.

Mr. Anderson was born in Sweden, July 15, 1851, and was the son of Andrew and Stenia (Johnson) Johnson, both of whom were natives of Sweden. The father continued living in his native land until his death, which occurred in 1862. The mother is still living in Sweden. The father was a farmer and carpenter by occupation.

The subject of our sketch left the land of his nativity in 1868 and came to the United States. Up to this time he had lived with his parents and had attended the common schools. Arriving in New York City he went thence to Red Wing, Minnesota, where he found employment on a farm for some time. Then, in the fall, he went to Dunn county, Wisconsin, and purchased a farm on which he lived until March, 1880. He then came to Pipestone county, Minnesota, and made his location in Altona township. Here he has resided ever since. His brother, Alfred W., of whom a sketch is given in another department of this work, came to the township in 1878, and is still a resident.

The subject of our sketch was married April 9, 1876, in Wisconsin, to Matilda Anderson. This union has been blessed with three children—Walter, Charles and John, all of whom are living at the present time.

Mr. Anderson has been a prominent citizen of the township ever since he first made his settlement here. He has assisted in public matters and has held the office of road overseer for three terms. In politics he affiliates with the republican party and for many years was a member of the Lutheran church. He is a man of exemplary character and is highly respected.

PETER KRALL is one of the most prominent and well-to-do farmers of Lincoln county, Minnesota, and is one of the most public-spirited men in the county, having identified himself with all public matters since taking up his residence in Marshfield township. He lives on the west half of section 22. He is a man of good education, intelligent and progressive ideas, and is a forcible and popular public speaker. His abilities have been utilized on various occa-

sions in the way of making public addresses, and, as a 4th of July speaker, his services are often demanded.

Peter Krall was born near the city of Cologne, Germany, April 8, 1833. His parents were John and Dora (Scherfjen) Krall, natives of Prussia. The subject of our sketch remained with his parents on their farm until he was twenty-eight years old. He was given educational advantages in the common schools until old enough to attend a normal school, when he was sent to the city of Broehl for the purpose of attending the normal institution in that place. He continued his studies for four years, and then, in 1853, came to the United States and first located in Milwaukee, Wisconsin. Here he worked in a vinegar factory for one year, and then his father purchased a farm near Watertown, Wisconsin, and our subject and his sister Kate moved to the farm to take charge of it while the father remained in Milwaukee. Our subject continued his operations on this place for four years and then purchased a farm for himself in the vicinity of La Crosse, where he remained four years. He then sold out and went to Belvidere, Goodhue county, Minnesota, purchased a farm and engaged in agricultural pursuits for seven years, at the end of which time he sold out, removing in the spring of 1877 to Lincoln county. He had located his claim in Marshfield township the year before, and when he arrived in 1877 he commenced making improvements. His nearest neighbors were three miles distant, and there were only seven other families in the township when he made his settlement. He located a homestead and a tree claim, both of which he still owns. He proved up on his homestead in 1883.

The subject of our sketch was married in La Crosse, Wisconsin, January 10, 1862, to Miss Christina Rothers, who died in 1869, leaving four children—Anthony, Kate, Peter and Sophia. Mr. Krall was married the second time, in Belvidere township, Goodhue county, February 10, 1873, to Mary Gonjers, widow of Peter Charley, by whom she had one child, whose name was Nicholas. Mr. and Mrs. Krall have eight children—Annie, Sibela, Mary, John, Matthias, Josephine, Rosa and Lena.

Mr. Krall has taken an active interest in matters pertaining to local government, and has held several official positions in the locality in which he has lived. While in Wisconsin he held the office of justice of the peace, and has held that position since coming to Minnesota. He has been a justice for over twenty years. He has also been township supervisor, assessor, school treasurer, and in these positions, and in every other public capacity, has served his constituents with rare fidelity and efficiency. He is a man of strong, decided opinions, of the highest integrity and is highly respected. In school and religious matters he interests himself quite extensively and is a consistent member of the Catholic church. He has a good farm, well-improved and provided with good buildings. Besides his farming and stock raising he also owns and runs a steam-thresher.

ROLLIN S. GOODELL, who now lives on section two of Troy township, Pipestone county, Minnesota, is one of the foremost farmers of that section of country. He is a native of Madison county, New York, where he was born August 12, 1847.

The parents of our subject were George W. and Harriet (Cooper) Goodell, also natives of New York. The father's parents were natives of Massachusetts, and those of the mother claim nativity in New Hampshire. The family is of Scotch descent, the great-grandfather being a native of Scotland. The father of our subject died in Orleans county, New York, in 1874, where he had lived for many years, being a man of large influence and respected by all who knew him. The mother is still living and is a resident of Rochester, New York. In the father's family there were seven children, the subject of our sketch being the third in order of birth. The family were mostly engaged in the occupation of farming in New York.

The early life of the subject of this sketch was spent in the home of his parents, where, up to the age of nineteen years, he had received a good common-school education, and had assisted his father in the operation of the home farm. During his early life our subject had the pleasure of hearing many speakers then very famous throughout the country, among them being Garret Smith, whom he heard several times in his eloquent pleas for equal human rights. Early in the year 1867 our subject removed with his parents to Orleans county, New York, where they engaged in farming, our subject remaining with them until November, 1868. In that year he removed to the State of Michigan and worked in the lumber woods during the ensuing winter. Thence he removed to Iowa, this being in April, 1869. During the eighteen months spent there he had the pleasure of seeing the golden spike driven at the junction of the east and west lines of track of the Union Pacific railroad. Most of this time he was engaged in farming, and leaving that State he returned to Orleans county, New York, where he was married and remained nine years. Then, in the spring of 1879, he followed the "course of empire westward" again to the State of Iowa, locating on a farm and remaining until the following year. He then removed to Rock Rapids, Lyon county, Iowa, and engaged in farming until 1882, removing thence to Luverne, Rock county, Minnesota. After one year's work on a farm in that county he came to Pipestone county. Ten months of his life were then spent in Sweet township, and at the end of that time he removed to Troy township and settled on the farm where he now lives.

The date of the marriage of Mr. Goodell was January 11, 1871, on which day he was married to Emily A. Marcellus, a native of New York, and a daughter of John and Abigail (Hagedorn) Marcellus. Her parents were natives of the Mohawk valley, in New York State, and their parents were natives of Holland. Mrs. Goodell's parents are still living and are residents of New York. This union has been blessed with three children— Mabel N., Ida N. and George W., all of whom are living at the present writing.

The hospitable home of Mr. Goodell is one of the finest and most commodious dwelling-houses in the township, and the wayfarer who may, belated on his travels, come to this home, is always sure of a cheerful and pleasant reception. Our subject has, by his active interest in public matters, taken a deep and lasting hold on the respect of his fellow-townsmen, and by his careful business traits has accumulated considerable means. He was given good school advantages in his younger days and attained a first-class common-school education. In politics he is a warm supporter of the principles of the republican party, with which he has affiliated for many years. He is a leading and influential member of the Masonic fraternity.

<hr>

HARVEY S. KELLOM is a prominent and substantial farmer of Great Bend township, Cottonwood county, Minnesota, and resides on a farm on section 27. He was born in Hillsboro county, New Hampshire, May 10, 1834.

The parents of the subject of our sketch were Ruel and Clarissa (Brockway) Kellom.

Ruel was a carpenter by trade and followed that line of occupation in New Hampshire until his death. Ruel was the son of Daniel Kellom, who was a prominent citizen. He served in the Revolutionary War, and died in New Hampshire at the age of 100 years. Daniel Kellom's wife lived to the age of 103 years. Our subject's mother was the daughter of Asa Brockway, who died in Des Moines township, Murray county, Minnesota, August 11, 1885. The mother was born March 1, 1800. Our subject's father was born in 1786 and died in West Concord, New Hampshire, in 1882. In the father's family there were ten children, four sons and six daughters, Harvey, our subject being the eighth child.

The subject of our sketch attended school in the place of his nativity until he was nine years of age, when he went into the home of his aunt, Annie Ayers, who resided on a farm. He remained there about six months, and in the fall returned home and attended school during the winter. The following year he worked for a farmer by the name of William Trevis, who resided in Deering township. From that time on for several years he worked on different farms during the summers and attended school during the winters. He received but small wages for his work, sometimes $2.50 and sometimes $3 per month. His employment was also diversified; for a while he clerked in a hotel in North Chelmsford and received $25 and board for the year, having the privilege of attending school during three months. He remained in this line some three years, receiving as compensation for his last year's work the munificent sum of $40. He then returned to his parents and attended school during the winter and then went to work for the firm of Farrer Brothers, manufacturers of wooden ware. He received $12 a month and boarded himself. He continued in the employ of this company for some seven years, finally receiving $2.50 per day for his labor. Three years of this time were spent in Burlington, Vermont, and six months at Manchester, New Hampshire. He was then married and removed to Wisconsin in 1835, renting a piece of land near Beaver Dam. He engaged in farming one season on this place and then rented a place of 160 acres, operating the same for two years. He then rented another farm of eighty acres, operated it one year and then bought ten acres of land on which he built a home. The next year he purchased forty acres, making fifty in all, on which he lived for some two years. In the spring of 1861 he started with two yoke of cattle in a lumber wagon for Blue Earth county, Minnesota. He did not reach his destination, however, but stopped in Oakwood township and bought a farm of eighty acres for which he paid $350. He lived in a tent for some three months and then built a house, and continued working this place for six years. During this time he had been quite prosperous, and he purchased an adjoining farm of 160 acres, and also eighty acres in Plainview township. In 1867 he sold his land and moved to Plainview, where he purchased a house, and the next year engaged in the dry goods business, also carrying a stock of ladies' boots and shoes and millinery. He operated in this line until 1883, and in the meantime, in 1879, he purchased a section of land lying in sections 7 and 27 of Great Bend township. He had 140 acres of land broken on section 27, and continued active improvements in an agricultural line, going back and forth between his farm and Plainview, in order to attend to his business in the latter city. In 1883 he moved his family to his farm, and has since made that his home. He opened a millinery store in Windom, which his wife operated until March 1, 1889, and the business was then sold. In 1888 our subject purchased 320 acres of land, and sold 160 acres, leaving his farming acreage, at the present time, 1,800 acres. He is a man of large means, and has accumulated his property as the result of hard work and persistent endeavor along these various business lines. He still owns three stores and lots, and also a fine residence and five lots in Plainview. Also another dwelling house and lot on Main street in the same place. He has always persistently aimed toward making his farm and various other properties the best in the vicinity, and in this he has succeeded, and is remarkably well located, and has fine improvements.

Mr. Kellom was married to Lucy N. Brockway, August 23, 1855, in Manchester, New Hampshire. Lucy Brockway was the daughter of Elbridge G. and Abagail O. Brockway, natives of New Hampshire. Miss Brockway was born in Clairmont, New Hampshire, April 8, 1836. Her father was born in 1809, and died in April, 1845. Her mother was born in 1816, and died in 1861. Elbridge G. Brockway was the son of Jonathan and Lolly (Proctor) Brockway, the latter living to the hale old age of one hundred and six years. Jonathan Brockway was a soldier in the Revolutionary War, and lived and died in New Hampshire. Mrs. Kellom's mother was the daughter of Tillis and Betsey (Young) Brockway, the former a native of New Hampshire, where he was born in 1780, and the latter a native of Nova Scotia; the former dying in July, 1847, and the latter passing away at the age of eighty years.

Mr. Kellom is a man of strong religious and temperance sentiments, and affiliates with the prohibition party. He is a member of the Patrons of Husbandry, and also of the Independent Order of Odd Fellows fraternity. He attends the Methodist Episcopal church, and is one of the leading and influential men of Cottonwood county.

OTTO KAUPP is one of the most successful and prominent business men of Blue Earth City, Faribault county, Minnesota, where he is engaged as a dealer in general hardware, iron, tinware, stoves, etc. Perhaps no man in the county has been as important a factor in its various political affairs as has Mr. Kaupp. He was appointed postmaster April 1, 1887, and was elected township collector in 1876, county treasurer in 1877 and president of the village council in 1882. He was township clerk from 1883 to 1885, and was treasurer of the village from 1885 to 1886. He has always been active and public-spirited in all matters pertaining to the general welfare, and has assisted liberally in the development of home enterprises.

Mr. Kaupp is a native of the kingdom of Wurtemberg, Germany, where he was born December 1, 1842. He was the son of A. Matthias and Josephine (Heid) Kaupp, who were also natives of Wurtemberg. The mother died when our subject was quite a small child ; the father died in 1856. They had a family of five children—Sebastian, George, Albertine, Otto and Agate.

From six to fourteen years of age the subject of our sketch spent most of his time in school in his native land. After his father's death he worked for two years at various lines of employment, and in 1858 he took ship for America. He came at once to Mankato, Blue Earth county, Minnesota, and engaged in farming until 1860, in which year he began learning the tinner's trade. He served an apprenticeship of three years and then worked as an expert tinner. He then came to Blue Earth City and opened in his present business, starting in a small way and gradually building up his business to its present extensive and profitable dimensions. He has perhaps the largest stock of goods in the county, and does a business second to none. He has interested himself largely in landed property, and has purchased various farms in the county, and owns a fine residence in the village east of the court house. His home cost about $4,500 and is beautified with many ornamental shade trees. His place of business is located on Main street, and he keeps four men constantly employed.

Mr Kaupp was married October 29, 1868, to Miss Mary McLaughlin, of Blue Earth City, and daughter of Owen McLaughlin. Mr. and Mrs. Kaupp have had five children —George M., Mary A., Margaret A., Seraphine M. and Otto A. (deceased). In politics the subject of our sketch affiliates with the democratic party, and, with his wife and children, belongs to the Catholic church. He has always taken an active interest in the general affairs of not only his county, but of the State as well, and has taken an active part in the affairs of his party. He has become one of the most solid and substantial men of Blue Earth City.

JOSEPH K. MILLER, a thrifty and reliable farmer of Shaokatan township, Lincoln county, Minnesota, resides on section 22. He was born in Lycoming county, Pennsylvania, September 4, 1835. His parents were Michael and Elizabeth (English) Miller, both natives of Pennsylvania. The father's father was also named Michael, and was a miller and farmer by occupation. When the subject of our sketch was about eight years of age his father was drowned. The mother is still living. About a year after the death of his father, Joseph Miller went to live with his grandparents, and remained with them until the death of the grandfather, which occurred when our subject was about eighteen years old. Up to this time he had assisted his relatives in work on their home farm, and had been given good educational advantages. After this he stayed two years with an uncle on a farm. Then ten years were spent in working. in the lumber woods of Pennsylvania. In the spring of 1867 he came to Fillmore county, Minnesota, rented a farm, and engaged in farming until the spring of 1872. After this he went to Brookings county, Dakota, going by team, and remaining until the fall of 1878. In the meantime, however, in 1875, he had filed on the claim where he now lives. In 1878 he made his location in Lincoln county, and has been a resident ever since. At the time of his location there were but three other families in the township. The subject of our sketch has taken an active interest in political matters since coming to the township. He has been treasurer of the school district for three terms, and held other offices. Wherever he has been he has taken an active part in matters of a public -nature, and while in Brookings county, Dakota, was a member of the board of county commissioners.

The wedding day of the subject of our sketch was November 20, 1860. At that time he was married to Adelia Day. This union has been blessed with nine children—Janet, Laura, Harry, Lizzie, Wilda, Ida, Earnest, Pearl and Grover. Mr. Miller is prominent in the local affairs of the democratic party, with which organization he has affiliated for some years. He is a man of good business qualifications, and as a citizen and neighbor is held in high esteem by all who know him.

———————

ALBERT G. BRANDT, a well-to do farmer of Delton township, Cottonwood county, Minnesota, is a native of Scranton, Luzerne county, Pennsylvania, where he was born February 26, 1859. His parents were Gustav and Louisa (Smidt) Brandt, both natives of Prussia. They were farmers by occupation and came to America in an early day.

The subject of our sketch resided with his parents on their farm until he was well along in years. When he was eight years of age the parents moved from Pennsylvania to Olmsted county, Minnesota, where they rented a farm for two years. Thence they went to Winona county, rented land for three years and then, thinking to find a better location, came to Cottonwood county in 1870, locating on a homestead in Selma township, where the parents still live. Our subject continued with his father until he was about twenty-five years of age, when he took a homestead on section 20 of Delton township on the 1st of August, 1885. He improved this farm and has made it his residence since the spring of 1886. He is a man of good character, and is one of the prominent young men of the locality.

Mr. Brandt was married in Selma township, this county, February 22, 1885, to Miss Matilda Kaping, daughter of Fred and Sophia (Kilson) Kaping, both natives of Prussia. This lady was born in Nicollet county, Minnesota, March 2, 1861. Mr. and Mrs. Brandt have one child, May.

———————

ALFRED W. ANDERSON is a thrifty and prosperous farmer residing on section 24 of Altona township, Pipestone county, Minnesota. He is the son of Andrew and Stenia (Johnson) Johnson, both natives of Sweden. The father was a farmer and carpenter by occupation, and died in his native land in 1862. The mother is still living in Sweden.

Alfred W. Anderson was born in Sweden, April 22, 1856. He remained with his parents throughout his early life, being given a good common-school education. Until fifteen years of age he remained beneath the parental roof, and then found employment on a farm until 1873. In that year he came to Minnesota, landing in New York City, and going thence to Eau Claire, Wisconsin, in the vicinity of which place he found employment at farm work for about a year and a half. Removing thence he went to Rusk Station, and after working for a farmer for about six months returned to the vicinity of Eau Claire, and found a place in the village of Spring Brook, where he did chores and attended school. This plan he adopted during the following winter and the next summer worked at lumbering. Through the latter part of the season he found employment in various harvest fields near River Falls, and in the fall went to the village of Knapp and engaged in hauling logs during the winter. Then, in company with his brother Gus, he purchased a piece of land and continued in farming in that vicinity and employed in other occupations until 1878. Then, in May, himself and his brothers Gus and Fred, and August Lindahl, came to Pipestone county, Minnesota, where our subject located his present claim in Altona township. He at once commenced working this, and broke the very first furrow in the township. He experienced considerable hardship but has succeeded in overcoming them all and in laying up considerable means. His early market was Luverne and from that point he had to haul all his supplies. He has remained in the county ever since his first location with the exception of about three years, which where spent mostly in work in the Wisconsin pineries.

March 10, 1880, Mr. Anderson married Miss Ruth S. Flick, at River Falls, Wisconsin. The names of the children resulting from this union are as follows—Grace M., Mabel C., Edwin C., Delbert T. and Lilla M.

Since coming to the township Mr. Anderson has affiliated with the republican party, and has assisted actively in the development and upbuilding of public affairs. He has served his consituents in several official positions, in all of which he has proven his capabilities as a business man and his loyalty as a citizen. He is a man of excellent char-

acter and is held in high esteem. He has a fine farm of 320 acres under good cultivation and provided with excellent buildings.

CHARLES C. CHRISTMAN is a leading and influential merchant of Fulda, Murray county, Minnesota. He was born in Ohio, January 2, 1836. His parents were Hiram and Elizabeth (Peal) Christman, natives of Pennsylvania.

When our subject was but a small babe his parents removed to Milwaukee, Wisconsin, near which place they remained four or five years, removing thence to Chicago, when that city was still in its infancy. Not liking the location, the family remained but a short time, and then removed to Calumet, Illinois, whence they went to Richmond, McHenry county, and there remained, engaged in farming for twenty-one years. Here our subject attended the district schools until he was about eighteen years of age and then attended the high schools at Rockport, and resided with his parents until he reached the age of twenty-seven years. He was then married and removed to Le Sueur county, Minnesota. Our subject had made his location in Le Sueur county in 1855, taking a pre-emption, on which he lived long enough to obtain a title. He engaged in teaming and farming until September, 1864, when he enlisted in Company C, First Minnesota heavy artillery and served until July of the following year. He was sent to Chattanooga, and other points in the South, but did not participate in any battles. He returned home after his discharge, and remained until 1866, when he removed to Davis county, Missouri. Here he engaged in farming and teaching school for nearly three years, after which he removed to Le Sueur county, Minnesota, and engaged in farming until in April, 1877. He then came to Murray county and took a homestead of 160 acres of land, on section 10, of Bondin township, where he resided until 1887. Renting his land for a short time, he soon sold it and lived on a rented farm until the spring of 1888, when he traded his land for property in Fulda and for a stock of general merchandise.

Mr. Christman was married in Le Sueur county, July 8, 1860, to Miss Frederica L. M. Dunlevy, a daughter of William and Jane A. (Scott) Dunlevy, natives of New York. This lady was born in the State of Vermont, November 17, 1841. This union has been blessed with the following named children— Albert, Alice, and Belle, an adopted daughter.

The subject of our sketch is a man of good business qualifications, and is highly respected both as a business man and citizen.

ASA A. START is a leading farmer of Dale township, Cottonwood county, Minnesota. He resides on section 12, where he located in 1871, and where he has lived ever since. He was born in Bakerville, Franklin county, Vermont, May 7, 1836.

The father of the subject of our sketch was born in the same town in which his son was born. Asa's parents were George S. and Mary (Colton) Start. The father was a distiller by trade, and lived in Vermont until his death, which occurred in 1865. The mother was a daughter of Emeius Colton, a farmer of Franklin county, Vermont. She was educated in Shelden, Vermont, and is still living in that State, at the age of eighty-one years. She was born January 14, 1806. The father was born December 17, 1803. The grandparents of our subject were Moses and Margaret (Gould) Start, the former a native of New Hampshire, where for many years he was engaged in farming. Our subject was one of seven children, five of whom are living, he being the third in order of birth.

Asa A. Start was reared in Franklin county, Vermont, where he remained until he was twenty-one years of age. He assisted his father on the farm, and received a good common-school education. After he was twenty-one years of age he went to Massachusetts, where for eighteen months he was on a farm. He then removed to Delaware county, Iowa, where he attended Almora Institute for about a year. He then returned to Vermont, and enlisted, in July, 1862, in Company I, Tenth Vermont Volunteer Infantry. His regiment was part of the Third Army Corps and Third Brigade of the Army of the Potomac. Our subject was on reserve detached duty on the upper Potomac river for some time. He did not participate in any very severe battles, but was in a number of skirmishes. He was somewhat disabled, and was in the hospital for a year, first at Alexandria, opposite Washington, in what was called the Methodist church hospital. Our subject's discharge was granted at Burlington, Vermont, April 26, 1865. One and a half years were spent in that State, and then he came to Nebraska, where he engaged in the grain business for three years. He then emigrated to Fayette county, Illinois, where two years were spent in agricultural pursuits. At the end of that time he came to Cottonwood county, locating on his present place, where he has lived ever since. He was one of the first settlers, there being but one other complete family in the township when he came. This was the family of John Harvey. On making his location, our subject at once commenced to improve his farm. He built a sod shanty, and the second year set out a grove of trees. He passed through the grasshopper raids, raising but little grain, and experienced various other hardships and discouragements usually found in pioneer life. He has passed successfully through all these trials, however, and by dint of hard work and perseverance has become quite well to-do and accumulated considerable property. He has always taken an active interest in public matters, and being a republican in politics, has held many offices. He has held all the township offices except that of constable, and has been treasurer of school district No. 11 for three terms. He has the honor of being one of the first justices of the peace, holding that office for two years. He was chairman of the board of supervisors for eight years. He is a United Workman, a member of the Grand Army of the Republic post, and is a member of the Masonic fraternity. He is a man of strong, progressive ideas, well educated, thoroughly up to the times, and is looked upon as one of the leading and most influential citizens in the township.

Mr. Start was married, March 22, 1862, to Miss Helen Cutler, a native of Boston, Massachusetts, but reared and educated in Vermont. Mr. and Mrs. Start have six living children—Elmer A., Gilman C., Luella A., Mabel, Herbert E. and Mary. Those deceased were—George Byron, died at thirteen years of age, and an infant.

WILLIAM J. STEGNER is one of the reliable farmers of Hendricks township, Lincoln county, Minnesota, where he is located on a fine farm on section 32. The birth-place of our subject is found in Wisconsin, where he was born May 5, 1856, being the son of Conrad and Mary (Martin) Stegner. The parents were well-to-do farmers and occupied a prominent position in the locality in which they lived.

The early life of the subject of our sketch was spent with his parents on the home farm in his native State. He was given good educational advantages and acquired a good common-school education. He remained beneath the parental roof until in 1875, when he went to Minneapolis and found employment there as a coachman, at which he continued for about four years. Then in 1878 he came to Lincoln county, and located his present claim. He concluded not to make a permanent location at that time, and so returned to Minneapolis and remained for a few months. Then in the fall of 1878 he returned to his farm and built what he calls a "$7 shanty," after which he returned again to Minneapolis, remaining in that city until the following spring. At that time he made a permanent location on his farm where he has been actively engaged in general farming ever since. During several winters, however, he returned to Minneapolis and found employment for brief periods.

Mr. Stegner was married March 28, 1882, to Louisa Zimmerman. This union has been blessed with six children—Alice, Lidia (deceased), Robert, Ruth, Wilbur B. and Winnifred S., the last two being twins.

In politics the subject of our sketch is a member of the prohibition party. He is a strong temperance man, and because of these sentiments cast his vote with that party. He is a man of excellent principles and tries to act out those principles in daily life. His active interest in matters relating to the public welfare has made him many friends. He is a member of the German Evangelical church. In his farming operations he has been quite successful, and although coming to the county a poor man, he has met with such success that his farm plainly manifests good circumstances to the most casual observer. He has a good home and has supplied his farm with good buildings.

JOHN GILRONAN is an influential farmer of Altona township, Pipestone county, Minnesota. He has an excellent farm on section 22, where he has resided since the fall of 1879. Mr. Gilronan is a native of Ireland, where he was born February 19, 1849. His parents were Peter and Mary (McManus) Gilronan, both natives of Ireland and farmers by occupation. The grandfather's name was also Peter Gilronan, a native of Ireland and a farmer by occupation. The father of our subject continued his residence in his native country until his death which occurred in 1887. His mother died in 1881.

John Gilronan came to America April 12, 1868. His early life had been spent in his native country, where he was given good educational advantages in the public schools. Until coming to this country he assisted his father in work on the home farm. Leaving home and arriving in New York City on the date just mentioned, after a week's stay in the city he went to Wabasha county, Minnesota, where he engaged in work for a farmer for about a year. In 1869, in company with his two brothers, Peter and James, he came to Lake Benton, Lincoln county, for the purpose of looking up land. They found only four white men in that vicinity, and as they looked over the county on every side nothing was to be seen but the wild, unimproved prairie. They remained during the summer and had considerable sport shooting game, with which the country abounded. During that season our subject saw a herd of buffalo on the prairie a short distance from where Lake Benton now stands. Late in the season our subject went to Rochester and remained in that vicinity for about a year. He was not satisfied with the location of this city, however, nor with the looks of the country thereabouts, and in 1871 he went to Lansing, Mower county, where he remained during the winter of that year. Again he returned to Rochester and made that his home for about a year, after which he went to Rock Island county, Illinois, where he engaged in work on a farm for two years. At the end of that time he returned to Rochester and engaged in work on various farms for some time. He then purchased a farm and made his residence in Olmsted county until the spring of 1879. He then came to Lake Benton, Lincoln county, and soon after located his present farm as a pre-emption. He remained on this land during the summer and improved it to some extent, in the fall returning to Olmsted county for his family. Returning to his farm in Altona township he has remained here ever since.

The subject of this sketch was united in marriage January 10, 1876, to Miss Selina Ringey. This marriage has been blessed with six children, five of whom are living—Mary, Josephine, John G., Rosa and Thomas H.

Mr. Gilronan affiliates with the republican party and is a man of good business qualifications having served his fellow citizens in various official capacities. He has been chairman of the board of supervisors for two years, and member of the school board for six years. In his farming operations he has been highly successful and has thoroughly improved his farm and provided it with good buildings, and has surrounded himself with the evidences of thrift and prosperity. He is a man of good character and is respected by all who know him.

⁂

DANIEL H. GEORGE is a prosperous farmer of Troy township, Pipestone county, Minnesota, and resides on an excellent farm located in section 2. He was born March 8, 1834, in Northampton county, Pennsylvania.

The ancestors of our subject were mostly of American birth, and his parents were Daniel and Nancy (Dalrymple) George, the father being a native of the place in which our subject was born, and the mother a native of New Jersey. Daniel George, the father of our subject, was born January 17,

1793, and the date of the mother's birth was September 12, 1801, their marriage occurring January 27, 1820. Removing to Illinois the father died in 1865; the mother passed away in 1847 while residing in Pennsylvania.

Daniel H. George, whose name appears at the head of this sketch, remained under the parental roof until he attained the age of seventeen years, up to which time he had engaged in work on his father's farm. The winter months were spent in attending the district schools, where he obtained a good common-school education. At the age of seventeen he commenced to learn the trade of carriage and wagon-making, serving a regular apprenticeship of three years. He then went to Bath, in his native county, where he worked as a journeyman wagon-maker for five years. In 1857 he went to Warren county, New Jersey, and opened a business for himself. He continued conducting a prosperous business in that county until 1867, when he removed to Will county, Illinois, rented his father's farm, and engaged in agricultural pursuits until 1865. He then concluded to re-engage in work at his trade, and removed to Lemont, Illinois, where he engaged in manufacturing for himself until the fall of 1873. At that time he again engaged in farming, renting a farm in that county, on which he remained until 1886. In the spring of that year he came to Pipestone county, Minnesota, and located where he has since lived. He is engaged quite extensively in farming operations, and, besides his own land, rents a farm on section 3.

Mr. George was married December 17, 1857, to Susan A. Butler, and this marriage has been blessed with seven children—Ida, William H., Lizzie, Harry E., Rollin D., Bertha and Irwin E., all living at the present time. Three children died in infancy.

The subject of our sketch is a man of sterling qualities, honest and upright in all his dealings, and by careful attention to the details of his work has accumulated considerable means. He takes an active interest in all matters pertaining to the public welfare, and has gained the confidence of his neighbors and fellow-citizens. In politics he affiliates with the republican party.

B A. SWARTWOUT is a well-to-do farmer who resides on section 29, of Springfield township, Cottonwood county, Minnesota. He is a native of the State of New York, where he was born August 13, 1841. His parents were Harry and Ann (Van Hanig) Swartwout, natives of Saratoga county, New York. The father was a farmer by occupation, and during the early years of his life engaged in work at the carpenter's trade. In the father's family there were four children. The mother died in 1853 and the father in 1859 in New York.

The subject of our sketch was much attached to his home and continued his residence with his parents until seventeen years of age. Up to this time he had been given good educational advantages in the public schools in the locality in which he lived. Leaving home at the age of seventeen he went to Battle Creek, Michigan, where he spent a couple of years visiting among friends, after which he engaged in farming for four years. When this period had expired he purchased 120 acres of land and held it for six months, and then sold out at a good advance over the purchase price. Going from thence to Cincinnati, Ohio, he remained four months, and then took a trip through Iowa, Kansas and Missouri, looking for a location. He then returned to Michigan and remained for some time until he came west in company with A. S. Talmage. Forming a partnership with this gentleman he purchased 960 acres of land, where he now lives. He has a fine farm of extensive dimensions, thoroughly improved and provided with excellent buildings.

Mr. Swartwout was married March 30, 1869, to Miss Amanda Angell, a native of Michigan. Her parents are still living in that State.

Ever since coming to Cottonwood county Mr. Swartwout has taken an active part in all matters pertaining to the public welfare. He has assisted materially in the development of all moves which have tended to the upbuilding of the agricultural and financial interests of the locality in which he lives. In politics he affiliates with the republican party, and has been a member of the board of school directors for eight years. He belongs to the Ancient Order of United Workmen, and is a man of good character, being held in high esteem by all with whom he has to do.

━━━━◦━◦━❮❮❮◗❯❯❯━◦━◦━━━━

ULMER F. HINDS is a well-known and respected capitalist, who is living a retired life in Luverne, Minnesota. In company with Robert Herren he opened the pioneer lumber yard in the city in June, 1873, under the firm name of Hinds & Herren. For three years a great portion of their building materials was hauled by team from Worthington, and they also hired farmers to bring lumber to Luverne, on their return trips from Worthington, to which point they went to sell their grain. This partnership was continued for some ten years, the business stand being first located on Main street, where the postoffice now is. In about 1885 our subject sold out his business interests, and has since been living a retired life.

Mr. Hinds is a native of Kennebec county, Maine, where he was born October 23, 1828. He was reared on a farm and received an education such as is usually given to farmers' sons. For some time before he left home he engaged in the lumber business, continuing in that line until the spring of 1852. He then went to California, and for four years was there engaged in the lumber business. In 1856 he returned to his early home, and one year later moved to Kilbourn City, Wisconsin, where in company with Mr. Drinker, he built a large steam saw mill. Here he did an immense business, sawing some fifteen thousand feet of lumber per day. For thirteen years he engaged in this profitable enterprise and then sold out and returned to his native State, where he lived a retired life until 1873. As has already been stated, in that year he came to Rock county, Minnesota, and made a permanent settlement in Luverne.

The subject of our sketch is the son of Benjamin and Ann (Wheeler) Hinds, natives of Maine. Throughout his life the father was engaged extensively in farming and lumbering. He was the son of Benjamin Hinds, a native of Scotland, and one of the pioneer settlers of Maine. Benjamin Hinds, senior, built the first saw mill on the Kennebec river, and engaged in lumbering for many years. Our subject is one of five living children—William, now in Colorado; Elizabeth, now Mrs. Crosby, of Maine; Benjamin, a resident of New York State; Ulmer F., and Susan, now Mrs. Burnham, of Furgus Falls.

Mr. Hinds was married in the year 1857 to Miss Maria Winn, of Benton, Maine. She was a daughter of Japhet and Annie (Simpson) Winn, natives of Maine. Her father was a blacksmith by trade, and later engaged in the mercantile business.

Since making his location in Luverne Mr. Hinds has built up an enviable reputation for business integrity and uprightness of character. In whatever line he has engaged, and in whatever way he has turned his attention, he has met with merited success, and has gathered a large fortune. After many years of hard work and business activity he is now living a retired life, enjoying the fruits of his labors. His life has been one of activity, and he has traveled quite extensively throughout the United States. He has made two trips to California, and has visited various other parts of the country, both in the way of business and in search of pleasure. In all matters pertaining to the government of the village and county, he has taken an active interest, and has been honored by being elected to several positions of trust. He has held the office of town treasurer with credit to himself and satisfaction to his constituents. He has been one of the largest land-holders in the county, but has sold a great portion, having the care of but little at present. He has done his share toward improving the city of Luverne, and has built business buildings and other dwelling-houses, putting up a fine residence where he now lives in 1876. Being one of the pioneers of Rock county, and having passed through all the experience usually met with by the early settlers, he takes an active interest in all matters related to the county's early settlement, and is known and esteemed by all others who came to the county in an early day. In politics our subject affiliates with the republican party, and is a leading and influential member of the Masonic fraternity.

⊷⊶⊷⊷⋖⋛⋗⊷⊷⊷⊷⊷

WEBSTER KUTCHIN is the able editor and proprietor of the Lake Benton *Republican*, of Lake Benton, Lincoln county, Minnesota. This gentleman is the son of Thomas T. and Amanda Kutchin, the former a native of England and the latter born in Pennsylvania. The parents were well-to-do farmers by occupation and were held in high esteem in the State in which they lived.

The subject of our sketch was born in Pottsville, Pennsylvania, October 24, 1845.

He lived on the farm of his parents and attended the district schools until he was twenty years of age. His first occupation after leaving home was working at the printing business in Fort Atkinson, Wisconsin. He continued that employment in that place for about two years and then removed to Fort Howard, same State, where for some time he was employed in work on the Fort Howard *Monitor*. Thence he removed to Tracy, Minnesota, and became the founder of the Tracy *Gazette*, of which, during a term of three years, he was the editor and proprietor. At the end of that time he sold out to William Todd, and then removed to Dakota, where he founded a paper called the *Gazette*. For three years he continued in the management of that journal, building up for it a large patronage and an enviable reputation. He then sold out and removed to Brookings, Dakota, where he purchased the Brookings County *Sentinel*, continuing the proprietorship of this paper for one year, when he sold out to Whiting Brothers and came to Lake Benton, where he established his present paper. From Brookings he brought a newspaper outfit, as at that place he had owned sufficient material to establish two papers.

Editor Kutchin was married in Waupun, Wisconsin, June 18, 1884, to Miss Marion L. More, daughter of Dr. D. W. and Sarah (Jenkins) Moore, prominent residents of that place.

Perhaps no citizen in Lake Benton is more widely known or wields more influence in Lincoln county than does the subject of our sketch. His life since coming to the county has been of the most irreproachable kind, and not only that, but he has been actively interested in all matters which pertain to the betterment of his locality, and by this interest has made a host of friends. Being of a genial disposition, a pleasant conversationalist and well posted on current events and in the past history of our country, he becomes at once an instructive and pleasant companion and friend. He is a man of excellent qualities and has been quite successful in his various business ventures. For his newspaper he has built up a large circulation and has a profitable patronage in other lines.

MILO T. DeWOLF is one of the prominent and prosperous business men of the village of Windom, Cottonwood county, Minnesota. He made his location in the county in 1871, coming from Oswego county, New York. On coming to the county he first located in the township of Amboy, where he pre-empted land on section 34. He resided there until grasshopper times, when he moved to Blue Earth county, where he remained three years engaged in work on a farm for monthly wages. Then for a brief time he was engaged in the mercantile business in the village of Lake Crystal in partnership with John W. Horlbert. After six months had expired our subject engaged in the butcher business, continuing therein for one and a half years. After this he returned to Cottonwood county and opened up a farm of 2,240 acres for R. Barden. He contined in the management of this extensive farm for three years and then purchased a quarter section on section 16. Since that time he has been the owner of one thousand acres of land and now owns four hundred acres. He has been more or less engaged in the stock business in connection with raising grain, and for the past three years has been engaged in the mercantile business in Bingham Lake, where also he is engaged extensively in handling hay. Mr. DeWolf was one of the early settlers of his township and became one of its most prominent men. In 1881 he was elected county commissioner and served three years.

He is at present chairman of that body. He was treasurer of the township for eight years and is at present school district treasurer, having held that office for ten years. He has always taken an interest in matters pertaining to the political welfare of his locality. In whatever capacity he has been called upon to serve his constituents he has proven his efficiency and acceptability. He is at present residing in the village of Windom, the county seat of Cottonwood county.

Mr. DeWolf was born in Oswego county, New York, October 7, 1847. His parents were William and Melissa (Place) DeWolf, natives of New York State. The mother died in June, 1868, and the father is still living.

The subject of our sketch spent his early life with his parents, and remained beneath the parental roof, receiving a good common-school education, until he was twenty-four years of age. He also taught school several terms and after that engaged in clerking in a store for a year. He then came west and located in Ogle county, Illinois, where he engaged in agricultural pursuits for some time. Removing thence he located in Pleasant Grove, Olmsted county, Minnesota, and from thence came to Cottonwood county, where he located his farm. He then returned to the State of New York, where he was married and then located permanently in Minnesota.

Mr. DeWolf was married to Miss Louisa Gardner, a native of Oswego county, New York. This lady received an excellent education in Hartford, Connecticut, and taught school for a number years in her early life. Mr. and Mrs. DeWolf have three children—Blanch, Archie and an infant unnamed.

The subject of our sketch has become one of Cottonwood county's most prominent citizens. He is a man of energy and strong opinions, and whatever business he takes hold of moves on to success. He has met with large profit in his various business ventures and has accumulated large means. He is a republican in politics and is a member of the Ancient Order of United Workmen, belonging also to the local Grand Lodge. He is a director of the Cottonwood County Bank. He is a man of excellent character and is held in high esteem.

HENRY SMITH is the efficient and popular sheriff of Murray county, Minnesota. He resides on a farm on the southwest quarter of section 30 of Belfast township.

Mr. Smith was born October 3, 1856, in Green Lake county, Wisconsin. He is of Irish descent, his parents, John and Mary (McDevitt) Smith, being natives of Ireland. Our subject's early life was spent on a farm, and until fourteen years of age he was educated in the common schools. When about nineteen or twenty he started out for himself and worked in the pineries in the State of Wisconsin. He worked in the woods and on the river until 1880, when he came to Murray county and purchased the right to the tree claim on which he now lives.

Mr. Smith was married in Fulda, June 7, 1888, to Miss Mary Nevin, who was born in Austin, Minnesota, March 25, 1866. This lady was the daughter of James and Bridget (Joice) Nevin, natives of Ireland. The marriage of Mr. Smith has been blessed with one child—Frances Jane.

Mr. Smith has been identified with the local interests of the republican party. He was elected sheriff of Murray county on the republican ticket, in the fall of 1884, 1886, and again in the fall of 1888. He has proven an able and efficient officer, and has served his constituents to their entire satisfaction. When he began life for himself he had no means whatever, and had naught to depend upon but his own efforts. He now owns a fine farm of 160 acres, with about forty-five acres under cultivation, ten acres of a fine grove of trees, a good frame dwelling-house and barn, besides considerable stock. He has been quite successful in his farming operations, and is provided with all necessary farm machinery. He is a member of the Ancient Order of Hibernians, and is a consistent member of the Catholic church.

DR. HARRY W. MERRILL, one of the leading physicians and surgeons of Pipestone, Minnesota, made his location here February 29, 1884, and immediately engaged in the practice of his profession, in which he has accomplished eminent success. He is a native of Osage, Mitchell county, Iowa, where he was born December 2, 1856. His parents, James H. and Mary A. (Chase) Merrill, were natives of Maine. The father was a builder and contractor by trade and followed that line of occupation in Portland and other cities in his native State. In 1854 the father came to Iowa, after having spent some time engaged in the contract business in Georgia, Alabama and Mississippi. After coming to Iowa he settled at Osage, Mitchell county, where he engaged in contracting and building until 1872, when he removed to Maywood, Illinois. For two years in that city he engaged in his old business and then accepted a position as foreman for the Chicago Road Scraper and Ditcher Company, remaining with that company until 1886. He is still living in Maywood, having retired from active business. Throughout his career the father has been a man of large public enterprise and has interested himself extensively in public affairs of the localities in which he has lived. While in Mitchell county, Iowa, he served his county as sheriff for two terms, and was a member of the school board for some years, holding that position where he now lives in Illinois. In the father's family there were two children—Dr. Harry W. and a sister, Hattie E.

The educational advantages furnished the subject of our sketch during his early life were of a good character and he acquired an excellent education. For some years he attended the public schools in Osage and later in that city attended the Cedar Valley seminary, remaining in the city until 1872. In that year he removed with his father's family to Maywood, Illinois, where for two years he attended schools. He then went to work for H. W. Small, a commission broker of Chicago, and remained with that gentleman for one year. At the end of that time he engaged as traveling salesman in Ohio for the Chicago Scraper and Ditcher Company. After one year spent in the employ of this company he then engaged with his uncle, F. A. Merrill, in the livery and feed stable business at Maywood. Two years later he found employment with a publishing company at Chicago, with whom he continued at work on a periodical called the *Interior*, until 1882. During the last two years of this service he was engaged in reading medicine to some extent, entering the Rush Medical College late in 1881 and graduating from that institution in February, 1883. Soon after he commenced the practice of medicine in Algonquin, McHenry county, Illinois, remaining there until coming to Pipestone in 1884.

The marriage of the subject of our sketch occurred in 1884, in which year he was wedded to Miss Alice C. Thompson, daughter of H. E. Thompson, now of Pipestone. This marriage has been blessed with one child, a son named John W.

Since coming to Pipestone county, Dr. Merrill has built up a large practice and an enviable reputation as a physician and surgeon. He is a member of the Southwestern Minnesota Medical Society, of which he is at present the president. In public matters he takes an active interest and renders substantial assistance in every project relating to the development of Pipestone city's best interests. In 1886 he was elected county coroner, and has held that position ever since. He is a man of excellent abilities, a well qualified and expert physician and surgeon, and is esteemed by all who know him.

PETER D. HALSEY, one of the early settlers of Pipestone county, has been identified with the interests of Troy township since June, 1879. He now resides on section 6 of that township. He was born in the State of New York, June 23, 1850, and is the son of William and Ann (Harrison) Halsey, both of whom were natives of Massachusetts. The father's parents were natives of France and the mother's parents were of English birth. The father was a blacksmith by trade and followed that line of employment throughout the most of his life.

The subject of our sketch remained with his parents until he was ten years of age and then commenced working out for neighboring farmers. This line of employment was continued for about seven years, at the end of which time he removed to Sauk county, Wisconsin, where he found work on a farm for about eighteen months. He then removed to Minnesota, settling in Olmsted county, and remaining there on a farm for about eight months. During this time, however, he visited various parts of the State, and finding the vicinity of Mankato an eligible place of residence he removed to Blue Earth county and resided near Mankato for about four years. Five years following were spent by him on a farm near Winnebago Agency, same county, and June 2, 1879, he removed to Pipestone county, and settled on his present farm. He came by team, having started with a yoke of oxen to drive through to Nebraska. On coming to Pipestone county he was struck with the lay of the land and concluded to stop and locate. He did so and has resided in Troy township ever since.

Mr. Halsey was united in the bonds of marriage in October, 1860, to Miss Hattie Whipple, who died later. On the 13th of February, 1878, Mr. Halsey was again married, to Laura McNeal. By his first marriage Mr. Halsey had four children—Lynford W., Nellie M., Fred E. and Minnesota M. All living at the present time.

Circumstances were such during the early life of Mr. Halsey that he was not able to obtain much schooling, but by home study and careful observation he has stored his mind with an abundant knowledge of the practical side of things. He is a close observer and is one who profits by his observations. In the affairs of the town in which he lives he takes a prominent part, and has held several minor official positions. He has been a member of the town board for two years and has occupied a position on the school board for six years. In politics he is a firm believer in the principles of the republican party, with which he has affiliated for a number of years. In his business interests he has attained marked success and has gathered a comfortable fortune.

JOHN GROSS, one of the leading farmers and stock raisers of Pipestone county, Minnesota, resides on section 22 of Gray township. He came to the county March 22, 1879, and located his present homestead. He is one of the thorough and energetic farmers of the town, and has improved his farm by constant cultivation, and erected good farm buildings. On settling on his land he built a small stable, and made that his dwelling until he built his present good house. Mr. Gross is a practical farmer, and has met with considerable success in all his farming operations.

The subject of our sketch was born in Northampton county, Pennsylvania, January 3, 1830. His father was a farmer and stock raiser, and was also named John Gross. He was also a native of Northampton county, and made that place his home throughout life, dying in 1861. The mother passed from this life in 1875. In the father's family there were twelve children, our subject being the eighth in order of birth.

Mr. Gross remained with his parents in his native county throughout his early life, and received his education in the district schools. In 1851, determining to strike out for himself, he removed to Stephenson county, Illinois, and made a two-years' residence in that locality. He then started with a company of prospectors for Pike's Peak, and followed that line of occupation during one summer, returning after that time to Ogle county, Illinois, where he resided seven years, engaged in general farming and stock raising. After that period had expired he removed to the State of Iowa, locating in Story county, where for two years he engaged in the butcher business, after which he began clerking in a dry goods store, continuing in that line for five years, and continuing in Story county engaged in various enterprises for seven years longer. Then, in 1879, he removed to Pipestone county, Minnesota, where he has resided ever since.

The marriage of Mr. Gross occurred August 4, 1850, on which day he was united in matrimony to Miss Eliza Rockel, a native of Northampton county, Pennsylvania, where she was reared and educated. Mr. and Mrs. Gross have had twelve children, eight of whom are now living—Ellen and Jane (twins), Lucy, John, Allen and Curty (twins), Emma and one unnamed. Daniel, a son aged twenty-two years, died in October, 1886; William and Addie (twins), and an infant, also died in early life.

The subject of our sketch was one of the early settlers in Gray township, and, with the growth of his neighborhood in prosperity, he has gathered a comfortable amount of means, and is now well situated. He interests himself in public matters, and especially in those things which pertain to the welfare and prosperity of his town. Throughout his career he has been closely identified with religious work. In politics he affiliates with the republican party, but is not very closely allied to that party, believing in supporting the best candidate. As a citizen and neighbor he is held in high esteem by the residents of the town in which he lives.

MATTHIAS DRESSEN, a reliable farmer of Marshfield township, Lincoln county, Minnesota, located on the northwest quarter of section 10 in the spring of 1877. He is the son of Matthias and Kate (Schaffer) Dressen, both of whom were natives of Prussia. The parents were farmers by occupation, and resided in their native country throughout their lives. They died in about 1852.

Matthias was born in the city of Cologne, Germany, October 18, 1828, and spent his early life with his parents on the farm. When he was about twenty-four years of age the parents died, and our subject entered the service of the Prussian army, continuing his military life in his native country for about three years. He then came to the United States in 1854, and first stopped in Rochester, New York, where he found employment on a farm for about four years. Again the spirit of roving took possession of him, and he came westward, stopping for about three years in Iowa City, Iowa, where he engaged in teaming. His next move was to Louisa county, same State, where for a

year he worked on a farm. Removing thence he made Red Wing, Minnesota, his headquarters, purchased a farm and lived thereon from 1861 until 1877, when he came to Lincoln county, settling on his tree claim. He has given a great portion of his time to making a success of trees which he has set out on his tree claim. Although in many instances growing trees on the western prairies has been fruitless, our subject has succeeded in raising a fine grove. Mr. Dressen has one of the best farms in Marshfield township, and has provided himself with a good dwelling-house and other buildings necessary to the successful operation of a well-regulated farm. He has a large cattle barn, and also a large horse barn, and not far distant stands a large granary, all these building being in excellent repair and nicely painted. Besides being engaged in general farming our subject makes a specialty of raising fine blooded hogs. Since coming to the township our subject has served efficiently in various official positions, having been township treasurer for three terms, and supervisor for two terms. He is a member of the Catholic church, and takes an active interest in matters of an educational nature. On coming to the township our subject was possessed of but little means, and had to depend on his own efforts for obtaining sustenance and accumulating a fortune. He has been thrifty and systematic in his habits, and has successfully operated his farm, being now surrounded with the evidences of prosperity and success. He has a nice home, and a pleasant and agreeable family.

Mr. Dressen was married in New York, March 15, 1854, to Anna M. Flagel. Mr. and Mrs. Dressen have been blessed with the following-named children—Henry, Theodore, Mary, John, Charles, Kate, William, Theresa, Gretchin, Anna, Peter, Susan, Lizzie, Matthias (deceased) and Phillis (deceased). Henry and Theodore are married, the latter to Miss Kate Myer. Mary married Michael Scholer. Kate married Edward Butman.

————◆❖◆————

HENRY HEINEMAN owns a good farm on section 26, Storden township, Cottonwood county, Minnesota. He is a native of Germany, where he was born February 8, 1834. His parents were Henry and Elizabeth (Kools) Heineman, also natives of Germany. The parents emigrated to America in 1857 and located in the State of New York. They both died some years ago. They were farmers by occupation and were influential citizens of the State of New York.

Until twenty-four years of age the subject of our sketch assisted his father in work on the farm, and also attended the district school acquiring a good practical education. At the age just mentioned he commenced working for various employers and occupied his time in various pursuits until 1861. In that year he enlisted in Company I, Twenty-seventh New York Volunteer Infantry, under Colonel H. W. Slocum. He participated in the battle of Bull Run, in the Peninsular Campaign, the two battles about Fredericksburg, and various other battles of minor importance. Mr. Heineman was sunstruck on the march between Washington and Fair Oaks Court House, but was not seriously injured. He was discharged in 1863, and shortly afterwards returned to his home in New York and commenced work, continuing thereat until 1873. At that time he removed to Minnesota, taking up his abode in St. Paul, where he engaged in various employments for four years. From thence he removed to his present homestead of one hundred and sixty acres, where he has since lived. He is an energetic, hard-working farmer and has striven to make his place one of the best in the township. He has taken pride in putting it under good cultivation and in putting up good buildings. He has

five acres of a good grove of trees. In connection with his farming operations, he also is raising blooded stock and always has some choice animal for sale.

Mr. Heineman was married September 23, 1864, to Mrs. Elizabeth Bass, a widow with three children. Mr. and Mrs. Heineman have been blessed with one child—Otto. The Heineman family are pleasant and agreeable people and have a cheerful and hospitable home. They are members of the Lutheran church.

In politics the subject of our sketch affiliates with the democratic party. He is an influential member of the Grand Army of the Republic, LaGrange Post, No. 76, of Windom. His history in the township has been one of activity in public matters. He has held various official positions, such as chairman of the township board, treasurer and clerk of school district No. 52. He is at present a member of the board of supervisors. Mr. Heineman is a man of broad ideas, strong principles, and is esteemed by all who know him.

————◆❖◆————

GODFREY KIKUL resides on section 18, Rose Hill township, Cottonwood county, Minnesota. He is a native of Russia, where he was born November 17, 1857. The parents of our subject were Fred and Elizabeth (Hachabaum) Kikul, both natives of Germany. The parents brought their family to the United States in 1877, and returned to their native country in 1881, where they still live.

The subject of our sketch followed his parents in their various migrations, leaving his native land with them and coming to America in 1877, and continuing his residence in his father's family until he was twenty-two years of age. At that time our subject pre-empted 177 acres of land where he now resides. This was afterward changed to a homestead, and our subject has been actively engage in making excellent improvements. He has one of the best farms in the township, and is acknowledged to be one of the most systematic and successful farmers in his region. Besides raising grain, he is also engaged quite extensively in raising Galloway cattle and horses of fine blood. In this line he shows his accurate knowledge of stock raising and is producing some of the finest animals of their kind in the county. He has always taken an active interest in public matters and affiliates with the republican party. With his family he belongs to the Lutheran church of Rose Hill, and assisted quite largely in building the edifice in 1884. Mr. Kikul was married to Mary Rupee, daughter of Jacob Rupee, August 9, 1881.

FRANK A. HYKE, one of the leading business men of Luverne, Minnesota, is a dealer in flour, feed, grain, wood, coal, etc. He is one of the prominent business men of the city, and has built up an extensive patronage. He made his location in Rock county in 1871, in which year he settled in Luverne and engaged in the harness business. He was one of the very earliest pioneers of the county, and has continued his residence here ever since his first settlement. He continued in the harness business until 1878, in which year he purchased a farm of 160 acres in Springwater township, and engaged to some extent in farming. Prior to selling out his harness shop, however, he engaged to some extent in his present business. He has the honor of being the pioneer wheat and grain buyer of Rock county, and made the first shipment of grain from Sioux City, Iowa City, Le Mars, and other points to Luverne over the Omaha railroad when that road was first built into the city. For some time prior to the building of the road he had a train of teams hauling grain to Worthington, Nobles county, and returning with lumber and goods to Luverne. On the advent of the railroad our subject purchased a large grain warehouse near the track, and used that until 1884, in which year he built a large elevator on the B., C. R. & N. Railroad, where he now keeps from two to six men constantly at work and does an extensive business. He has been one of the benefactors of the city, and has been actively interested in all projects tending to the improvement of the village. He has built several stores and other buildings and has purchased quite a number of farms in the county, having four under operation at the present time. Throughout his residence here he has been doing an immense business and has had "many irons in the fire," in farming, mercantile, grain, and other business—no matter how largely he has been interested, he has kept a continual personal oversight of his affairs. He is a stockholder in the First National Bank, the Bank of Beaver Creek, and has interested himself largely in the building and loan association of his adopted city, and in many ways his financial interest in the growth of Luverne is shown.

The gentleman whose name appears at the head of this sketch was born in Bohemia in the year 1850. His father was Frank Hyke, also a native of that country, and now a resident of Winneshiek county, Iowa, where he is engaged in farming. When our subject was but a small boy his parents came to America and settled at Rochester, Racine county, Wisconsin. After remaining in that locality for some years they removed to Iowa.

Mr. Hyke received a good education in the common schools in Racine county, Wisconsin, and after getting pretty well along into his "teens" commenced a three-years' apprenticeship to learn the harness business. After that time had expired he then engaged as a journeyman harnessmaker, working some three months for Mr. Codman, of whom he learned his trade. At the end of that time he went to Burlington, Wisconsin, where he worked for a short period. He then went to Decorah, Iowa, where he engaged at his trade for two and a half years. Removing thence he settled in Charles City, Iowa, where another two and a half years were spent. His next move was to Luverne, where he has since lived. In 1874 occurred the wedding of our subject. The union has been blessed with six children—Ida M., Charlotte, Ethel, Clarence R. D., Eva and Beatrice. In politics the subject of our sketch affiliates with no particular party, but believes that the best ends of government are served by electing the best men to office. Since coming to the city he has built up a large and extensive patronage in his various business enterprises, and is to-day one of the best-known and most highly respected citizens of Luverne, and, indeed, of Rock county.

LARS I. FJESETH is the present efficient treasurer of Lincoln county, Minnesota. He is the son of Ingebret and Gorina (Larson) Fjeseth, both natives of Norway. The parents were well-to-do farmers in their native land where they still live.

The subject of our sketch was born about seven miles from Throndhjem, Norway, September 17, 1844. He was reared on the farm of his father, with whom he continued until 1867. He was given good educational advantages in the district schools until he was fifteen years of age and for about one year attended a private school. When not in school he assisted his father on the farm. He remained with his parents until his marriage, which occurred in 1867. Shortly after that event our subject came to America, locating in Allamakee county, Iowa,

where he engaged at farm work for about a year. He then purchased a farm and operated it successfully for about six years, at the end of which time he sold out and moved to the village of Quindahl in the same county. Here he engaged in general merchandising for about two years and then sold out, coming directly to Lincoln county, Minnesota, where he settled on a homestead and tree claim in Hendricks township. He proved up on the homestead some years ago and still owns both farms. In 1888 he rented his farm and moved into the village of Lake Benton. In November, 1888, he was elected county treasurer on the republican ticket, receiving a handsome majority.

The subject of our sketch was married March 20, 1867. This union has been blessed with seven children, three of whom are now living—Hannah, Albert and Gertrude. Those deceased were Albert, Sr., Albert, Jr., Gertrude, Sr., and Benedict.

Since coming to Lincoln county, our subject has taken an active interest in the affairs of the republican party and has become quite prominent in the local councils of that organization. While living in Kendricks township he occupied various official positions, among them being that of township supervisor, clerk, justice of the peace and chairman of the town board. He has also held the position of school clerk, and during most of the time since he came to this county he has held two official positions. Before the township was organized he was assessor of the territory now comprised in nine townships in the northern part of the county. Mr. Fjeseth and family are members of the Norwegian Lutheran church. The subject of our sketch is a man of excellent qualities, both of mind and heart, and administers the affairs of his official positions with rare fidelity. As a man and citizen he is highly respected and has made a host of friends since locating in the county.

ILVANUS BARROWS is one of the most substantial citizens and well-to-do farmers of Chanarambie township, Murray county, Minnesota. He resides on an excellent farm on section 34. He was born in Vermont, January 1, 1852, and was the son of Oscar A. and Julia (Gray) Barrows. The father was a farmer by occupation and was a patriotic citizen, serving his country during the War of the Rebellion. In the spring of 1866 he left Vermont and came to Olmsted county, Minnesota, where he remained with his family for some eleven years. He then removed to Mower county, where he engaged in farming for three years, and at the end of that time, in 1879, he came to Murray county, and resided for about eight years with his son, the subject of our sketch. In 1887 the father removed to Slayton, where he still resides. The mother is dead.

Silvanus Barrows left the parental home at the age of twenty-two years, up to which time he had been assisting his father in work on the home farm and attending the district schools. At twenty-two he worked in partnership with his father until the spring of 1878, when he came by team to Murray county, locating the claim where he now lives. He owns a fine farm of 480 acres. He built one of the first houses in the township and made the first improvements. Being one of the earliest settlers he was a leading spirit in the steps taken in the organization of the township.

Mr. Barrows was married to Susia A. Dudley, March 2, 1879. She was a native of Wisconsin. Mr. and Mrs. Barrows have been blessed with four children—Oscar, Elsie L., Archie L. and Estella.

In politics Mr. Barrows affiliates with the republican party and is becoming one of the leading factors in that organization in Murray county. He is a man of excellent business qualifications, and has been called to serve in various official capacities for his fellow-citizens. He was chairman of the township board of supervisors for some two years, and was a member of the board for one year. He was township assessor for two years, and in the fall of 1888 was elected county commissioner, which position he ably fills at the present time. Mr. Barrows is a genial, warm-hearted, public-spirited citizen, and is widely known and highly respected.

PROF. EUGENE RUCKER, B. S., principal of the Farm College and Business Institute at Wilder, Jackson county, Minnesota, is a native of Olmsted county, Minnesota, where he was born April 19, 1862. His parents were Robert Henry and Saram Ann (Housten) Rucker, both natives of Ohio. The mother died in 1865, and the father is engaged in business in Jackson, Minnesota.

The subject of this sketch made his home principally with his father until he was twenty-two years of age. When he was ten years old the family emigrated to Pottawattamie county, Iowa, and in 1886 removed to Dawson county, Nebraska. Our subject was given a good common-school education during his early life, and attended the Western Normal College at Shenandoah, Page county, Iowa, graduating from that institution July 29, 1886. Then, in company with a class-mate, he went to Nebraska and took a pre-emption. November 26, 1887, he returned to Minnesota, and for a short time stopped in the city of Mankato. Then, for five months, he took charge of a school in Jackson county, and in November, 1888, became connected with the school at Wilder, and is now principal of the college mentioned above. He has been elected for a period of three years, from August 1, 1889. Mr. Rucker is a very efficient teacher and has given eminent satisfaction. Both as a teacher and citizen he enjoys the confidence and respect of his fellow-citizens. In politics he affiliates with the prohibition party, and is a member of the Odd Fellows fraternity.

Prof. Rucker was married to Miss Lizzie A. Bailey, a native of Carroll county, Illinois, and daughter of Ira L. and Eugenia (Ruppe) Bailey. Her parents were farmers who settled in the State of Illinois in an early day. Mrs. Rucker was educated in Shenandoah, Page county, Iowa, at the Western Normal College, graduating from that institution. She taught some four years in Iowa, and one and a half years in the primary department of the Shenandoah public schools. Prof. and Mrs. Rucker have two children—Muriel Virginia, born January 6, 1888, and Mildred Antoinette, born June 20, 1889.

TABOR C. RICHMOND, a prominent farmer of Lake Side township, Cottonwood county, Minnesota, resides on an excellent farm on section 26. He was born in Barnard township, Windsor county, Vermont, April 21, 1844.

The parents were farmers by occupation, and the father, Gilbert Richmond, who now resides in Bingham Lake, Cottonwood county, is a native of Vermont. The mother's maiden name was Sarah Imus, a native of Essex county, New York. Our subject was one of four children, of whom one died in the Union army and one in infancy. Two children are living—Tabor C. and O. T.

The subject of our sketch was reared in Windsor county, Vermont, until he was eight years of age, when his parents emigrated to the State of New York, and after two years' residence there removed to Wisconsin, where our subject remained until coming to his present location, in 1870. The early education of our subject was not neg-

lected; he was given excellent advantages in an academy in Essex county, New York. After completing his education in Wisconsin, he engaged in buying and selling cattle, and also in the milling business. On coming to Cottonwood county he engaged in farming, in which line he has been engaged ever since.

Mr. Richmond was married March 12, 1864, to Miss Almira Kibby, a native of Essex county, New York, and educated in Rosendale, Fond du Lac county, Wisconsin. She was the daughter of Anson Kibby, a mason by trade. Mr. and Mrs. Richmond have been blessed with five children—Elizabeth, Sarah, Gilbert, Nellie and Tabor, the two oldest being engaged in the profession of teaching.

On the breaking out of the war the subject of our sketch manifested his patriotism by enlisting April 22, 1861, in the Third Regiment Wisconsin Volunteer Infantry. He served as a private in many hard-fought battles, and was discharged February 8, 1863, at the West Philadelphia hospital. He was engaged in numerous battles, among them being Winchester, Cedar Mountain, Second Battle of Bull Run, South Mountain, Antietam, Banks' retreat out of the Shenandoah valley, and was severely wounded September 16, 1862, in the battle of Antietam. From thence he was taken to the hospital, and was confined there until February 8, the date of his discharge. On receiving his discharge, he returned to Wisconsin, and remained until 1870, when he located on his present place. No man in the township has taken a more active part in public affairs than has our subject. He has been treasurer of the township for several terms, having assisted in the organization of both the county and township. He was a member of the board of supervisors, and has held various other positions. In politics he affiliates with the republican party, and has been warden of the Masonic fraternity, in which society he is an influential member. He is well known throughout the county, and is recognized as one of the most influential citizens. He is a man of good character, and is public-spirited in all matters of a general nature.

⸺⟶⟨⟨⟩⟩⟵⸺

S͘ J. ABBOTT, of Delavan, Faribault county, is one of the best known lawyers in Southern Minnesota. He is an old settler in that locality, and, having always taken a prominent part in public matters, he has attained a reputation which extends over a good share of the State. A strong and active republican, and one of the ablest of Minnesota's stump orators, his name is indissolubly associated with the political history of the State. An eloquent speaker, an able lawyer, and a genial gentleman, his "friends are legion."

⸺⟶⟨⟨⟩⟩⟵⸺

ROBERT CAMPBELL, one of the early settlers and well-to-do citizens and farmers of Pipestone county, Minnesota, located on his present place on section 29, Gray township, in 1879. He has been a resident of that section ever since, and has engaged in a general farming and stock-raising business. He was one of the organizers of the county and also of the township in which he lives, and has held several positions of trust within the gift of his fellow-citizens. Mr. Campbell looks back to those early times, and recollects many names of pioneer settlers. It may be interesting to note some of these names, and learn somewhat of their settlement and later life. This information will be, of course, to some extent imperfect, but it is given in the expectation that it may interest some of the friends of the parties whose names are presented. Among those early settlers were Mr. Peck, who still resides in the county; Charles

Smith, also living in the county; H. Dicky, Henry M. Pease, who died in 1888; Samuel Bailey, who died in 1886 in this county; A. W. Fenlason, who located in 1879, and remained until 1887; Herman Haney, still residing in the county; Horace Milley, who located in the county and remained until 1881, when he removed to Minneapolis; Charles Embury, who still resides in the county; J. I. Bernard, who is still living in the county; Joseph Parker, who came in 1878, and still remains; Marshall and William Harrison, two brothers, who were among the early settlers, and who still remain; William Lobdell, who came in 1879, and still remains; William Clifford, who located in 1878, and is still a resident, and A. Smith, who still remains, having also located in 1878. Mr. Fenlason, mentioned above, was the county superintendent for two terms.

The subject of our sketch was born in Burlington, Vermont, October 4, 1843, and was the son of Robert and Helen (McLansbery) Campbell, natives of Argyleshire, Scotland, where they were reared and educated. They were married in their native country, and came to America in about 1837, settling at Burlington, Vermont, where they lived until about 1854. Up to this time the father had been engaged largely in mason work. In the year just named the father started on a tour of prospecting in the State of Ohio, going by way of the lakes, and was probably lost in some storm, as he was never seen or heard of afterward. After this sad occurrence the mother moved her family to Allegheny City, Pennsylvania, where she lived for two years. Removing thence the family settled in Clinton Junction, on the Northwestern railroad in Wisconsin. They made that place their residence until 1865, up to which time our subject and a brother-in-law had worked a farm together. The mother is still residing in Wisconsin.

Mr. Campbell received his education in Vermont and Wisconsin, and at seventeen years of age enlisted in the Fourth Wisconsin Battery as a private, being promoted shortly to the rank of lieutenant, and as such was discharged July 7, 1865. Mr. Campbell was only engaged in one battle of any note, that being the fight at Chapin's farm in 1864. He was, however, engaged in many skirmishes, deporting himself with honor wherever and in whatever duty he was engaged; being with a cavalry company, most of his time was spent in sharp skirmishes. Our subject was at Fortress Monroe during the time that McClellan was in the peninsular campaign in 1862. After his discharge our subject returned to Wisconsin, and after remaining for three months removed to Saratoga, Winona county, Minnesota, where he spent about three years engaged in agricultural pursuits. After this period he engaged in farming for about nine years near Blooming Prairie, Steele county, same State, at the end of that time removing to his present place in Gray township, where he has lived ever since.

The marriage of Mr. Campbell occurred March 25, 1878, at which time he took to wife Miss Ella Peck, a daughter of W. D. Peck, a merchant of Hatfield, Pipestone county. Miss Peck was a lady of excellent qualities and highly educated, having received her education in Austin, this State. Mr. and Mrs. Campbell have four children, two boys and two girls, all living,—Bruce, Eva and Ethie (twins), and William Duane.

Mr. Campbell has occupied a prominent place in the history of his township since he took up his residence among its citizens. Its best interests have always found in him an able abettor, and he has at all times proven himself willing to assist in public affairs. His services have been utilized in many instances, and in every case he has proven himself competent and able. Among

these offices may be named that of treasurer, which position he held for two years; chairman of the board of supervisors, one year; township assessor, four years, and several other minor positions. He is a man of excellent character, an exemplary citizen, and is indeed one of the representative men of the township in which he lives.

DR. ABNER H. TWISS, an influential farmer of Des Moines River township, Murray county, Minnesota, is a native of Windsor, Vermont, where he was born April 18, 1832. His parents were Peter and Harriet (Gaggett) Twiss, both of whom were natives of New Hampshire.

The subject of our sketch went from Vermont to Peterborough, New Hampshire, when four years of age, where he resided on a farm, being given a good common-school education until he was fourteen years old. At that age, in company with his uncle Benjamin Twiss, he went to Groton, Massachusetts, where he remained one year, learning the butcher business. Eighteen months thereafter were spent in that business in the employ of J. Graves. At the end of that time he went to Boston, Massachusetts, working as a cutter for eighteen months in the "Quincy market" of that city. His next move was to Rockford, Illinois, where he entered the employ of T. D. Diamond, with whom he continued eighteen months at his trade. He then went to Picatona, Winnebago county, and, in company with Zenas Palmer, engaged in the butcher business for three years. He then sold out and removed to Derand, where, in company with W. M. Arnold, he engaged in buying and selling cattle and in operating a meat market for three years. Selling out at the end of that time he went to St. Louis, rented one of the stalls in the city market place, and engaged in operating a meat market for five years.

His next move was to Alton, Illinois, where he found employment with John Smith, who had a contract to furnish a division of the Union army with meat supplies. Three or four months were then spent in Cairo, after which he returned to his work for Mr. Smith, with whom he continued two and a half years. Being taken sick at the end of this time, he removed to St. Louis, from whence he went to St. Paul, where he engaged in manufacturing ox bows. From thence he went to various localities in Wisconsin, engaged in purchasing hickory timber. He was then married and for six or seven years thereafter engaged in various lines of business in Wisconsin. At his marriage he removed to Viroqua, from whence he went to Trempealeau county, where he took a homestead. After six years' residence there he sold out for ten thousand and fifty dollars, and removed to Dunn county, locating at Knapp Station, where he manufactured bob sleds and sled runners for two years. June 10, 1878, he came to Murray county and took a pre-emption on section 10, where he has since lived. He has an excellent farm—has about one hundred acres in crop this season. He has a good house twelve by twenty feet with an addition twelve by sixteen, and also a stable fourteen by sixteen which accommodates a number of cattle and several head of horses. Our subject is a man of excellent ability, and is at present devoting his time to the practice of medicine. He has rented his farm and has built up a large patronage as a physician. His commencement in this line was modest and unassuming, but he has gained considerable popularity, and has built up a large business, having now all the practice he can possibly attend to. He has performed numerous remarkable cures in various very severe cases. Our subject is a man of large experience, is public-spirited and is esteemed by all who know him. Both as a man and a citizen he stands high in the respect of his fellow-citizens. Dr. Twiss was married in New Amsterdam, Wisconsin, March 21, 1865, to Miss Louisa Mosier, daughter of Peter and Sarah (Aimes) Mosier. Miss Mosier was a native of Syracuse, New York, where she was born November 4, 1845. This union has been blessed with the following children—Etta M., Inez and Frank, who was burned to death at the age of eighteen months. Etta married Charles Clark and Inez wedded Charles Rigle.

PETER JACOBS is a leading farmer of Marshfield township, Lincoln county, Minnesota, having located on the northeast quarter of section 4 in the spring of 1879. His parents were John and Mary Jacobs, both natives of Prussia. The parents resided in their native country until about 1856, when they came to the United States, and stopped in Chicago. They are still living.

Peter Jacobs was born on the river Rhine near the city of Trier, Germany, March 4, 1848. He resided with his parents in his native land until he was eight years of age, when the family came to the United States and settled in Chicago. He lived with them in that city and was sent to the public schools until he was thirteen years old, at which time he left home and began life for himself. His first business was packing staves and shingles in Michigan, where he remained about three years. Returning then to Chicago, he lived with his parents for some time, and learned the cooper's trade. In 1864 he enlisted in the Union army, becoming a teamster in General Saunder's division. He continued in the service until March 22, 1865, and then, being honorably discharged, returned to Chicago, and engaged in work at his trade for two years. He then engaged in gardening, in which line he continued for about two years, returning at the end of this

time to his old trade, and continuing about a
year thereat. He then opened a grocery
store, and engaged in that business for about
nine months, when he sold out and went to
Minneapolis, Minnesota, where he worked at
his trade. One year later he returned to
Chicago, finding work at the cooper's trade
for about a year, when he went to Stirling,
Illinois, and after one year's location there
went to Winona, Minnesota. But three
weeks were spent in Winona, and then our
subject went to Wabasha, and remained one
year engaged at work at his trade. From
Wabasha he removed to Minneapolis, and
after four months returned to Wabasha,
making that his home until he was married
in 1878. He then came to his present place
in Marshfield township, Lincoln county,
where he has resided ever since.

February 20, 1878, Mr. Jacobs was united
in marriage to Miss Louisa Pilsticer. Mr.
and Mrs. Jacobs have been blessed with four
children—Mary, Lena, Clara and Frank, all
of whom are residing at home at the present
time.

As the traveler passes through Marshfield
township he will see no more thrifty-looking
farm than the home of Mr. Jacobs. Since
making his location on his present farm he
has actively engaged in making good improvements, and has succeeded well in accomplishing his object. He has an excellent
farm and has good buildings, his dwelling-
house being very pleasant and commodious.
He is a man of much energy, and is a thrifty
and successful farmer. Besides his general
farming operations he is also engaged in
stock raising, in all of which he has met with
continued success, and has accumulated considerable means. He is a man of prominence
and influence, and is widely respected by all
with whom he has to do. Possessed of a
good character, honest and fearless in his
expressions as to what he believes to be right,
his opinions are heeded, and he is an important factor in the management of the public
affairs of his township. He has held the
offices of school treasurer and township
treasurer.

PAUL F. SHERMAN. This gentleman
is one of the leading general merchants of the village of Jasper, Pipestone
county, Minnesota. He is a native of Aroostook county, Maine, where he was born in
May, 1855.

The parents of the subject of our sketch
were John and Zena Sherman, natives of
Maine. The father was a farmer by occupation, but in connection therewith was also
an extensive operator in the lumber business. In 1865 the parents removed to Minnesota, settling for a time in the city of
Shakopee, Scott county, where the father
engaged in the manufacture of wagons. In
1877 he removed to Amaret, Lyon county,
where he has since been engaged in farming.
The mother died in 1862, leaving two children, our subject and John F., also a resident of Jasper.

The subject of our sketch followed his
parents in their various moves and in the
city of Shakopee was given excellent advantages for receiving a common-school education. He continued his studies in school
until about fourteen years old, at which
time he found work as a clerk in one of the
stores of that village. For five years he
continued his clerkship and then attended
the high school of that place two years, after which he removed to Sioux Falls, Dakota,
where he settled on 320 acres of land and
engaged in farming. He thoroughly improved this land and owned a large number
of cattle and horses. He took a prominent
part in the affairs of that locality and held
several offices, among them being that of
assessor for four years, and being also a
member of the school board during the en-

tire time of his residence there. During his residence in Dakota he also took an active interest in the workings of the Farmer's Alliance, and held the office of secretary of the local organization for some time, being one of the organizers of that society. He was the secretary of the first meeting held by the alliance and was afterwards appointed as a delegate to attend meetings in various counties throughout the territory. He interested himself also in insurance matters and became a general solicitor and traveling agent for the Farmer's Mutual Protective Association of Plankington, Dakota, continuing that relation with said company for about four years. In 1888 he went to Amaret, Lyon county, Minnesota, and put in a stock of general merchandise, continuing in business in that place until April, 1889, at which time he closed out a part of his goods and brought the remainder to Jasper. On arriving in this village he purchased the store building on Wall street, where he is at present located, doing an excellent business.

Mr. Sherman was married in 1888 to Miss Mamie Chisholm, of Hartford, Dakota, and a daughter of Robert Chisholm. Mrs. Sherman is a lady of excellent social qualities and is highly educated. She is an excellent musician and has the honor of bringing the first piano to the village of Jasper.

In politics the subject of our sketch is an earnest supporter of the principles of the republican party. He is a man of excellent business capacity and is rapidly becoming one of the prominent business men of the village. He is a large stockholder in the Jasper Produce Company. Throughout his career he has been quite successful in all his business and has accumulated considerable means. He is a man of push and energy, and by virtue of these qualities will succeed at whatever he turns his attention to. He is held in high esteem by all his fellow-citizens. He has a large and finely assorted stock of goods and is doing an excellent business and has an excellent and increasing trade.

HENRY GRALING, a citizen of Germantown township, Cottonwood county, Minnesota, is the son of John and Margaret (Hutteroth) Graling, both natives of Germany. Our subject was born in Prussia, October 2, 1836, and resided with his parents on the farm until 1847, when they came to the United States.

On coming to this country the Graling family first stopped in Wyoming county, New York. There they purchased a farm and engaged in agricultural pursuits for some years, our subject remaining with his parents until he was twenty-four years old. After his marriage, Henry Graling engaged in farming, and also taught school for some time. For some years he was engaged in buying and selling butter, cheese, etc., and remained in New York State until 1871. In this year he removed to Minnesota and located in Fillmore county, where he lived one year. He then came to Germantown township, Cottonwood county, and located a homestead of 160 acres, also a tree claim of the same amount, this being the north half of section 30. Our subject still resides on the homestead, but some time ago gave the tree claim to his son John. When our subject came to the township in the spring of 1873 there were but few settlers here. He at once commenced operations, breaking and seeding about ten acres of land, and made other improvements. His crop, however, was destroyed by the grasshoppers. The next year the same story was repeated and continued during four seasons. The fifth crop our subject tried to raise was a good one and yielded an excellent harvest, some going twenty-seven bushels to the acre. Rust and blight destroyed the next two crops, but since that time our subject has been quite successful, and has reaped fair harvests. During the grasshopper raids Mr. Graling was compelled to leave home in order to obtain means on which to support his family. He received a little flour from the State, and went into the woods and engaged as a chopper for several winters. These were hard times, and our subject's family have been driven almost to desperation, having come at one time to the point when every mouthful of flour and bread in the house had been used, and they had to obtain provisions from a neighbor on which to breakfast. This was on the return of our subject from one of his trips. The next morning, after breakfast, he went to the railroad station and got the provisions that he had sent home some time before, but which had not been delivered to his family.

The subject of our sketch. was married in Wyoming county, New York, July 29, 1858, to Miss Catharine Lesinger, daughter of Michael and Barbara (Engel) Lesinger, natives of Alsace, France. This lady was born in Alsace January 18, 1839, and in 1847 came with her parents to the United States. Mr. and Mrs. Graling have had the following-named children — Elizabeth (deceased), Emma, John, Henry (deceased), Lutcher (deceased), Martha, Catharine (deceased), George (deceased), and Laura (deceased). Emma married Lewis Roemer, and is now a resident of Highwater township, Cottonwood county, Minnesota. John is now living on the tree claim spoken of heretofore.

Mr. Graling is one of the leading citizens of the township, and is always actively interested in matters of a general nature. He is at present assessor and school clerk, and has been justice of the peace of his township, clerk, and has held some town office nearly all the time since locating in the county. He is a man of good principles, and is a consistent member of the Reformed Dutch church. When he commenced life for himself he had but little means, and had nothing to depend upon but his own energies. He is now in good circumstances, has 160 acres of land, with 110 acres under cultivation, has good buildings, and has a goodly amount of stock.

DR. MITCHELL MIKKELSEN is a physician and surgeon of Delavan, Faribault county, Minnesota. He is a native of Dane county, Wisconsin, where he was born in the year 1850.

The parents of Dr. Mikkelsen were both natives of Norway and were Knudt and Carrie Mikkelsen. The father was a farmer by occupation and came to America early in 1850, settling in Dane county, Wisconsin. After a short time spent in that county he removed to Juneau county, and engaged in farming until 1864, when, with his family, he came to Lowry township, Faribault county, Minnesota, and settled on 160 acres of government land. The father is still living and is residing on the farm on which he settled in 1864. In the family there were six children, five of whom are now living— Dr. Mitchell, Ole, Helen, Erick, Martha and Knudt A.

Coming from Wisconsin to Faribault county when fourteen years of age, our subject received the principal part of his education in the schools of that county. He was reared on a farm and commenced the study of medicine in 1875 with Dr. Winch, of Blue Earth City. He studied medicine for two years and graduated at Keokuk, Iowa, in 1877. After practicing medicine for a number of years he went to Chicago and graduated from the College of Physicans and Surgeons in 1884. He has been engaged in the practice of his profession in the village of Delavan ever since his first graduation. He has built up a large and extensive practice in Delevan and the adjoining country, and is called one of the best physicians in the county. He is studious and enthusiastic in his pursuit of fresh truths in the line of his professional business and has performed many delicate and complicated surgical operations. He is a member of the State Medical Society and is president of the board of pension examiners.

Dr. Mikkelsen was married to Miss Ella Heffron in 1879. This lady was a daughter of N. L. Heffron, of Blue Earth City. Two children have blessed this union, one now living—Willie B.

In politics Dr. Mikkelsen affiliates with the republican party and also belongs to the Masonic fraternity. His practice has been very lucrative during the last ten years and he is the owner of one of the finest residences in the village, located on Second and Thompson streets. The doctor's practice is not confined to the village in which he lives, but he has calls from long distances to attend the sick in adjoining counties. Both as a professional man and citizen Dr. Mikkelsen is held in high esteem.

ILBERT H. HENTON, a thrifty and respected citizen of Luverne, Minnesota, is engaged in blacksmithing and is also a carriage-maker. Mr. Henton is a native of Erie county, Pennsylvania, where he was born March 13, 1843. He is the son of Thomas and Maria (Cohoon) Henton, the father a native of Wales and the mother born in New York. The father came to America when he was seventeen years old and settled in Erie county, Pennsylvania, and for the first few years engaged in working out on farms. Later he purchased a farm and commenced work for himself, engaging in that occupation some seventeen years. He then sold out his interests in that State, and in 1852 came to Wisconsin, settling in Columbia county, in the town of Otsego, where he engaged in farming until his death in 1883. The mother still resides in that place. In the father's family there were eleven children who grew to man and womanhood—William, now a resident of Sioux Falls, Dakota; Mary, now Mrs. Goodwin, of Harper Creek, Pennsylvania; Lucinda, who died in Wisconsin; Theodore, now a resident of that State; Gillson, a resident of Luverne; Wallace, who was shot and killed at the battle of Bull Run; Cyrus, now a resident of Beaver Creek, Rock county, and who also served in the Union army, being shot in the breast in the second battle of Bull Run; Gilbert H.; Emily, now Mrs. James, of Otsego, Wisconsin, and Henry, who died in the same State.

The boyhood of the subject of our sketch was spent on the home farm. He was given the privilege of attending the district schools and acquired a good common-school education. At seventeen years of age he enlisted in the Thirteenth Regiment Wisconsin Light Artillery, and continued as a private in that regiment for sixteen months. He was then promoted to the rank of lieutenant, and for seventeen months, or until the close of the war, he continued in that rank. He was engaged in many light skirmishes and some quite severe battles. On the close of the war he returned home, and from thence went to Tama county, Iowa, locating in the city of Toledo. In that place he learned the trade of blacksmithing and carriage making with his brother William, with whom he served three and a half years. He then returned to Wisconsin and opened a shop for himself at Fall River, Columbia county, where he remained three years. At the end of that time he removed to Beaver Creek, Rock county, Minnesota, this being in 1872. He at once settled on a homestead of 160 acres and engaged in agricultural pursuits for some eight years. He first built a sod house, and experienced other difficulties and hardships usually met with by the pioneer settlers. In later years he built a nice dwelling-house, set out a fine grove of trees and otherwise improved his farm. In 1880 he removed to the village of Luverne and purchased six lots and built a good dwelling-house and barn and blacksmith shop. He also made other improvements and prepared himself for doing a large business. At present he employs two men besides himself and is doing a large and profitable trade.

Mr. Henton was married in 1866 to Miss Helen M. Randall, of Fall River, Wisconsin. This lady was a daughter of Israel and Celia (Watson) Randall. Mr. and Mrs. Henton have had five children, four of whom are now living—Fred E., Eva M., Bertie D. and Hattie L. Marion is the name of the one deceased. Mr. Henton is a consistent member of the Methodist Episcopal church, of which organization he became a member at Fall River, Wisconsin, in 1870. His wife joined the same church in 1871, and since that time has been a leading church worker. The children are all members of the same church.

The subject of our sketch, since his conversion, has taken an active interest in all matters of a religious nature. He helped to organize and establish the Methodist Episcopal church at Beaver Creek, and was a member of that society for eight years, during which time he held the offices of district steward and recording secretary, and was always secretary of the quarterly conference. While at Beaver Creek, in company with the brethren and minister, he came to Luverne, and assisted in the establishment of the Methodist Episcopal church in this city, and since taking up his residence in Luverne he has always been a prominent worker in the denomination. He has held the office of Sunday-school superintendent and district steward for a number of years, and has also been one of the members of the official board, holding the relation of trustee and steward therewith. He has assisted liberally in the support of financial enterprises of the church society and was largely instrumental in the building of the present elegant church edifice. He has a pleasant home and a hospitable family and is highly esteemed by all who know him. In politics he affiliates with the republican party and has held several positions of trust and responsiblity, having been a member of the city council for some two years. He is also an influential member of the Grand Army of the Republic.

———————

CHARLES E. OLIVER, a representative citizen of Faribault county, is engaged in agricultural pursuits on section 16 of Verona township. He was born in Waukesha county, Wisconsin, October 23, 1850. His father was James Oliver, a native of the State of New York, where he was born in the year 1811. In about 1848 the father emigrated to Wisconsin and made that his home until his death, which occurred in 1888, at the age of seventy-seven years. He was an exemplary Christian and was a member of the Wesleyan Methodist church. Our subject's mother's name was Maria Cain, a native of the Empire State, and who is now residing in Columbia county, Wisconsin. The subject of our sketch was one of six children—Edwin, John, Francis, Charles E., James and Elizabeth.

Charles E. Oliver received his early training and education in the county of his nativity. He made that his home until he was fourteen years of age and then removed to Columbia county, where he completed his education, and from whence he removed at eighteen years of age. He attended the high school at Beaver Dam, Wisconsin, and became thus amply equipped for the practical duties of life. After completing his education he commenced working by the month, and followed that line for four or five years, and then took a farm and worked it on shares for several years. He then came to Faribault county, Minnesota, where he has resided ever since. He has labored hard and faithfully on his farm and now has one of the most valuable and productive places in the township.

On the 25th day of December, 1879, Miss Lizzie Sherman was united in marriage with Mr. Oliver. This lady was a native of Columbia county, Wisconsin, and was a daughter of Heman Sherman, a farmer and a prominent citizen of Wisconsin. He settled in Columbia county in about 1850. Mr. and Mrs. Oliver have been blessed with two children—Laura and Millie.

The subject of our sketch being a man of strong religious principles, has for years been a member of the Free-Will Baptist church, of which he is a trustee. His political faith is in the principles promulgated by the republican party, and as a member of that organization he has exerted a strong influence in the official affairs of the township. He has been treasurer of school district No. 5 since 1881, and has also served three years as clerk of the township; for one year was chairman of the board of supervisors and has been assessor of the township since the spring of 1889.

FRANCIS SELLECK is a thrifty farmer who resides on section 32, Hendricks township, Lincoln county, Minnesota. This gentleman was born in Canada, April 7, 1845, and was the son of Joseph and Jane (Tarrett) Selleck. Joseph Selleck, the father, was a native of Vermont, and throughout the most of his life engaged in the occupation of farming. He removed to Canada

in early life and there met and married Jane Tarrett. The father was drowned on the field of the famous "old wind-mill" battle. He was an officer in the army and was a man who was in high repute among all who knew him. The mother was a native of Ireland and came to Canada with her parents when she was fifteen years of age. She is still living.

The early life of the subject of this sketch was spent with his parents. He assisted in work on the home farm and was given the advantages of the district school. Being of a studious disposition, and having good advantages, he therefore obtained a good common-school education. On reaching twenty years of age he left home and came west, locating about twelve miles from La Crosse, where he remained some eight months. Returning at the end of this time to his native place in Canada he remained some five years. Then again severing his friendships and family ties, he returned to La Crosse and engaged in farming some six years. Then in the spring of 1878 he came to Lincoln county, and located the place where he now lives. He built a small cabin and then returned to Wisconsin and remained about a year in Trempealeau county. Then in the spring of 1879 he removed his family to his farm in Lincoln county, of which he was one of the early pioneers.

The marriage of the subject of our sketch occurred November 18, 1870. On that date he was wedded to Miss L. Perry, by whom he has had three children—John F., Charles H. and Albert E.

The subject of our sketch, being one of the early pioneers, was intimately associated with all movements toward the organization of the township government. Being a stanch republican in politics, he was called upon to serve his constituents in several official relations. He has been a member of the board of supervisors and his influence has been felt for good in all local political affairs. He is a thrifty and energetic farmer and has accumulated considerable means. He owns a fine farm of 320 acres of land, under good cultivation, and provided with comfortable buildings. He is a man of good character, is a loyal citizen and has a pleasant and agreeable family.

OTIS T. RICHMOND, a well-to-do farmer and stock-raiser of Lakeside township, Cottonwood county, Minnesota, resides on section 34, where he located in 1871. He was one of the first settlers of the township and throughout his history here has been one of its most public-spirited citizens.

Mr. Richmond was born in Utica, Winnebago county, Wisconsin, June 21, 1857. He was the son of Gilbert R. and Sarah (Imus) Richmond, natives of New York State, and at present residing in Bingham Lake. In the father's family there were four children— Tabor C., Byron J., Charles and Otis T. Byron J. and Charles are both deceased.

When eight years of age the subject of our sketch moved with his parents from Winnebago county to Delhi, where they resided three years. It was there that he received the principal part of his education. He resided in Wisconsin until coming to Minnesota, and since 1871 has been a resident of Lakeside township. He is successfully engaged in farming and in the raising of a good grade of stock. He has worked hard to make his farm one of the best in the township, and has it now provided with excellent improvements. He has to-day 240 acres of land, and is looked upon as one of the leading and most prosperous farmers in this region. In politics Mr. Richmond affiliates with the republican party and has always taken an active interest in matters pertaining to the general welfare. He has held various official

positions, among them being that of supervisor four years and treasurer of school district No. 23 for six or seven years. He has always taken a deep interest in township affairs and exerts a wide influence for the benefit of public institutions.

September 19, 1884, Mr. Richmond was married to Luella Young, a native of Jefferson county, New York. This lady came to Cottonwood county with her parents when she was but eleven years of age. They were early settlers of the county. Her father was Richard Young, a farmer who died in 1872. In her father's family, there were five children. Mr. and Mrs. Richmond have one child, Byron.

PETER N. OSTROM, a thrifty and reliable farmer of Scandia township, Murray county, Minnesota, is the son of Nels and Bengta (Johnson) Peterson, natives of Sweden. He was born about one mile from Christianstad, Sweden, August 7, 1844.

At the early age of eight years our subject began to earn his own living, first by herding, receiving as compensation a very few clothes, and all the wooden shoes he needed. No money was received until he was fifteen years of age, and was able to do a man's work. For the first year's work for wages he received nine dollars, but after that got better pay. He worked out in Sweden until coming to America, on the 2d day of May, 1866. Leaving his native land, after three or four days, he reached Liverpool. After spending a week in that city he sailed for New York. During his passage there was cholera on board, there being about 130 deaths in less than a week. As a consequence the ship was quarantined at New York for forty-two days. July 27, 1866, our subject landed in St. Paul, Minnesota, and went on immediately to Afton, where his brother Nels was living, and for whom he worked for one year. This brother had sent him money with which to pay his passage to the United States. After the close of this year's work he worked around in different places until 1868, when he purchased land in Nicollet county, and lived with his brother Nels, who purchased a half-section near his farm. He improved this farm and other land near by, which he rented, and made it his home until 1872, when he removed to his present place on the northeast quarter of section 10, Scandia township. He had filed on this land the fall before. When our subject came to the township he found three other families who had settled here when he filed on his land. In the spring he came to his place, built a sod house, and broke seven acres of land, which he put into wheat, and from which he harvested twenty-one bushels. He succeeded in raising a little wheat during each year of the grasshopper raids. Since those early times he has been prosperous in his farming operations, and now owns 302 acres of excellent land, on which he has a very nice frame house one and a half stories high and 18x26 feet, with an addition, 16x16 feet. He also owns six horses, one colt and twenty-eight cattle; also. a one-half interest in an imported French draft-horse, which cost $1,600. Our subject is a man of influence in the political affairs of his locality, and has been township clerk, county commissioner for six years, town treasurer, and has also been school treasurer and school clerk.

Mr. Ostrom was married in Nicollet county, Minnesota, February 9, 1870, to Ellen Pearson, daughter of Pear and Ingar (Isaacson) Pearson, natives of Sweden. She was born in Sweden, February 9, 1853. Mr. and Mrs. Ostrom have no children of their own, but have adopted two children—Ellen and Gusta, children of Mrs. Ostrom's brother, Peter W. Peterson, who died February 2, 1885. March, 27, 1887, Mrs. Peterson died, and they took another child, Amelia. March 10, 1881, Mrs. Ingri Swenson was frozen to death, leaving a child two and a half years old, which our subject took to bring up. This child was called Sigfrid M. Swenson.

------◆◆◆◆◆------

WILLIAM HARRISON came to Pipestone county in the fall of 1879, since which time he has been a resident of section 19, Gray township, where he located on railroad land. During his entire residence here he has proven himself a man of high character, thrifty and industrious, and has surrounded himself with the signs of prosperity and success. In all public matters he has taken an active interest, and has held numerous positions of trust, having been one of the directors of school district No. 25 for two terms and also a member of the board of supervisors for two years. He was one among the pioneer settlers of the township, and assisted in its organization.

The subject of our sketch was born in the town of Phillipsburgh, Warren county, New Jersey, August 29, 1849. His parents were John J. and Catharine (Hauk) Harrison. The father was a farmer by occupation, which line of business he followed throughout the most of his life. In the spring of 1867 the family removed to Wisconsin, where the father died in August, 1872. He was a respected citizen and a representative man of the locality in which he lived. The mother was a native of the State of New Jersey, where she was reared and educated. She passed from this life when the subject of our sketch was fourteen years of age. William Harrison was one of a large family of children, ten of whom are now living—David, Thomas, Elizabeth, John, William, Catharine, Higgins, Williamson, Marshall and Sarah Jane. The names of the deceased children are—Jerry, Henry and Effie Allie.

The subject of our sketch received his early education in the State of New Jersey, being given good educational facilities in the county of his nativity. He remained with his father, assisting in work on the farm, until he was about eighteen years of age, when he re-moved with his family to Wisconsin, remaining in that State one and a half years. At the end of this period he returned to the East and continued his residence in New Jersey, engaged in the hotel business for two and a half years. Then he returned to Wisconsin, settling in Sauk county, where he remained for some time, and then came to Fillmore county, Minnesota. After making the last named county his residence for one and a half years, he then removed to Pipestone county in 1879, where he has been a permanent resident ever since.

Mr. Harrison was married in 1871, on Christmas day, in Baraboo, Sauk county, Wisconsin, to Miss Elizabeth Palmer. This lady was born near Williamsport, Lycoming county, Pennsylvania, in July, 1847. When she was eight years old her parents removed to Sauk county, Wisconsin, where she lived until her marriage. In that county she received an excellent education. Her parents were John K. and Jane (Wilson) Palmer, the father a farmer by occupation, and at present living near Augusta, Wisconsin. The mother was born in Lycoming county, Pennsylvania. She is also living, and is an exemplary member of the Methodist Episcopal church. In her father's family there were the following-named children — Mary Jane, Elizabeth, William Henry, Emily Delpha, Rose Ella, Peter and Hannah, six of whom are still living. Hannah died when she was eighteen months old. Mr. and Mrs. Harrison have been blessed with three children — Mabel, Lelea and Mack. Mabel, who was born October 29, 1872, is attending the high school at Pipestone.

The subject of our sketch has risen to an influential position among the citizens of Gray township, and is one of its most representative men. He is a man of excellent judgment, of high character, and is esteemed by all his fellow-townsmen. In politics he affiliates with the democratic party, and has become quite prominent in the local affairs of that organization.

WILLIAM P. REMPEL is the senior member of the firm of W. L. Rempel & Brother, dealers in grain, flax seed and farming implements, in St. James, Watonwan county, Minnesota. This firm has also large farming interests throughout the county, and the gentlemen composing it are considered among the most substantial and influential men in the locality.

The subject of our sketch is a native of Russia, where he was born August 25, 1856. He is the son of Peter W. and Annie (Penner) Rempel, natives of Russia. The father was a merchant in his native land and followed the mercantile trade throughout his life, dying in 1869. His father was William Rempel, a native of Germany, who was engaged in the ship business, moving to Russia in early life and there engaged in farming, residing in that country until his death. Our subject's mother's father was Peter Penner, a native of Russia and a farmer by occupation. The grandparents on both sides of the house reared large families. The mother of our subject came to America with her family in 1876. She had nine living children — Mary, now Mrs. Folk; Peter, who married Minnie Hann; Jacob, wedded to Mary Loeven; Annie, now Mrs. John Wawatysky; William P., Bernard, John, who married Mary P. Epp; Katie, now Mrs. Frank Schroeder, and David. The parents and family were members of the Mennonite church.

The subject of this sketch received his early education in his native land and worked in his father's store for some two years. He came with his mother to America and settled in Watonwan county, Minnesota, purchasing lands in Butterfield township, where our subject has large farming interests. He remained at home some five years after coming to this country, and then, in 1881, located in the village of St. James. He engaged in the grain business, renting a building for the first year. The second year the firm purchased a small storehouse for which they paid three hundred dollars. They operated their business in that place for two years, when their transactions became of such an extensive character that it was necessary to rent two other buildings. In 1884 the firm built their present elevator, it being the only one in the village and having a capacity of twenty-five thousand bushels of grain. Their other storehouses have the same capacity. They operate their elevator and warehouse with a ten horse-power engine, and are so popular and reliable that they handle most of the grain in this section of the country. The Rempel Brothers also have a lumber yard at Butterfield, where also they have an elevator of twenty-five thousand bushels capacity. They also own a warehouse at Bingham Lake, where they purchase grain, having there a capacity for storing ten thousand bushels. They have also warehouses at Slayton and Hadley, Murray county, the former of which has ten thousand bushels capacity and the latter six thousand. This firm keeps six men constantly employed and is doing an extensive and profitable business. Mr. Rempel is one of the most public-spirited citizens of St. James and vicinity, and has held various official positions with rare fidelity to the interests of his constituents. He has been township supervisor and assessor in Butterfield township, and has been a member of the village board in St. James for a year. He is a member of the Mennonite church and affiliates with the republican party. He is one of the most reliable and most highly esteemed citizens of St. James.

WILLIAM F. HAGEDORN, a leading farmer of Marshfield township, Lincoln county, Minnesota, located on the northwest quarter of section 33 in 1879. He has since been a prominent resident and has taken an active part in all matters of local importance. He is the son of William and Wilhelmina (Lutz) Hagedorn, both of whom were natives of Germany. The parents were farmers by occupation and resided in the old country until about 1869, when they came to America.

The subject of our sketch was born in Waxfeld, Prussia, May 23, 1849. He remained with his parents on the farm, being given a good education, until he was nineteen years of age. He then came to America, first stopping for a short time in Rochester, Minnesota, where he worked at the mason's trade, which business he had learned in the old country. He continued at Rochester, Olmsted county, some four years, and then removed to Potsdam, same county. He made the latter place his home for seven years, engaged during this time in work at his trade. He then came to Lincoln county and purchased eighty acres of railroad land since which time he has bought forty acres more adjoining; his father also gave him forty acres, and he now owns an excellent farm of one hundred and sixty acres, all well improved. His farm is well supplied with a good dwelling-house, two barns and a granary, and to the passer-by all things betoken thrift and industry. Mr. Hagedorn is a man of genial qualities and is enterprising and public-spirited. He is well known and highly respected in the locality in which he lives. He is a careful manager, and this, connected with hard and systematic labor, has brought to him merited success, and he is now in good circumstances.

Mr. Hagedorn was married in Rochester, September 21, 1872, to Miss Catharina Chlausen, who died in 1879, leaving two children—Charles and Mary. Our subject's second marriage was to Wilhelmina Fink. This union has been blessed with one child, Emma. Mr. Hagedorn has a pleasant, agreeable family, and the members thereof belong to the Lutheran church.

JOHN A. OLSON, a thrifty and industrious farmer of Ellsborough township, Murray county, Minnesota, was born in Helsingland, Sweden, June 23, 1837. His parents were Ole and Karen Arneson, of Swedish birth. His parents were farmers by occupation and were well-to-do people in their native land.

The subject of our sketch remained with his parents, attending school and assisting on the home farm, until he was sixteen years of age. He then commenced working by the month on adjoining farms, and followed that kind of employment until the spring of 1869, when he came to the United States. His first eight months were employed in work in a coal mine in McHenry county, Illinois. Sixteen months thereafter were spent by him in agricultural pursuits. Removing thence he went to St. Paul, Minnesota, and engaged in work on the railroad until the fall of 1871, when he came to Murray county and took a homestead of 160 acres on section 2, of Ellsborough township. After he had filed on his claim he commenced work on the railroad and employed his time in that business for two years. Then three years were spent on the farm. His crops, however, did not yield him very much income. The first four crops were entirely destroyed and he had hard work to make both ends meet. The

fifth crop was fair and he harvested fifteen bushels to the acre. Two seasons his crops were so entirely destroyed by hail that he got only six bushels per acre. During the succeeding years he has met with considerable success in his farming operations and has become quite well-to-do. The spring of 1889, however, again saw misfortune in that about thirty-five acres of wheat were destroyed by the heavy winds, the wind blowing off the soil and uncovering the grain. This land he afterward sowed to barley. The subject of our sketch has surrounded himself with the evidences of prosperity, has good outbuildings and a comfortable frame house. He has taken an active interest in public matters and is highly respected by his neighbors and fellow-citizens.

Mr. Olson was married April 12, 1878, in Ellsborough township, to Agnetta Holtlian, a native of Gudbrandsdalen, Norway, where she was born April 19, 1845. She was the daughter of A. and Kristina Amunson, both natives of Norway. Mr. and Mrs. Olson have no children of their own, but have adopted Andrew Albian, a son of H. and Kate Olson.

LORENTZ V. ACKERMANN is a resident of section 18, Grange township, Pipestone county, Minnesota. This gentleman is a farmer by occupation, and is one of the representative and respected citizens of the township in which he resides. He was born in Germany August 10, 1854. He is a son of Bartholomew and Magdaline (Schmidt) Ackermann, natives of Germany, where they remained until 1857. In that year they came to America and settled in New York State, where they engaged in farming for a period of eight years. In 1863 they came westward, settling in Minneapolis, where they now live.

The parents of our subject were in humble

circumstances, and could furnish but slight advantages for the intellectual improvement of their children. The son whose name appears at the head of this sketch left the parental home at the age of nine years, and worked out for his board and attended school. The desire for an education sprung up within him, and he followed this course of life until he was eighteen years of age. He had come to this country with his parents in 1857, and when eighteen years old removed to the vicinity of Faribault, where he engaged in work on a farm for about one year. He was then married, and moved into the city of Faribault, where he worked at whatever could find to do. For two years he found employment in a commission house, and later worked for a short time on a farm, returning again to the commission business. Ceasing the latter employment he again found work on a farm and continued in this line until 1878, when, in company with John Meyer, he drove through by team to Pipestone county, located his farm and broke some twenty acres of land. Then, in August, he returned to his family, returning by the way of Windom, where he worked for a few weeks, and from thence went on to Faribault. In the fall of that year he brought his family to his new location, where he has since remained. During the first years of his location in the county he laid the foundations for future prosperity and usefulness, and has by careful industry grown in prosperity, and has made himself a comfortable home. During the first year of his residence here he had the misfortune to lose one of his thumbs by the accidental discharge of a gun.

In March, 1873, Mr. Ackermann was married to Maria Meyer, and this union has been blessed with eight children, all of whom are living—John W., Catharine, Tracy, Magdaline, Frances, Elizabeth, Ludwig B. and Charles L.

By dint of perseverance our subject acquired a good common-school education during his early years, and life finds him well prepared for its duties and responsibilities. He is a man of excellent character, is genial and sociable, and is respected by his fellow-citizens. In public matters he takes a leading interest, and has served his township in various official positions, having been one of the members of the first board of supervisors, and being at the present time chairman of that body. For one term he was township assessor, and for several terms he has been pathmaster. He is the present incumbent of the office of treasurer of the school district, to which position he was elected in 1882. In politics he is a republican.

JOHN W. WERNER is a well-to-do farmer of Germantown township, Cottonwood county, Minnesota. He was born in Radeidz, now Harmsdorf, Germany, April 20, 1853. His parents, paul and Louisa (Stearns) Werner, were also natives of Germany, and were farmers by occupation.

Until he was sixteen years of age our subject resided in his native land, and obtained a common-school education. He then came to the United States, landing in New York city, from whence he went to Princeton, Wisconsin, near which place his parents located. Our subject worked at various employments in Wisconsin for seven years, and at the end of that time went to Rochester, Minnesota, where he engaged with a farmer for three years. In 1879 he came to Germantown township, purchased a squatter's right to eighty acres on section 8, which he then took as a homestead. He also purchased eighty acres on the same section, and has made this home ever since. When he left Germany he had to borrow sixty dollars with which to pay his passage to the United States. After he had been in this country one year, himself and brother Fred paid the passage of the parents and a sister, Charlotte. For the past two years the parents have been living with their son, the subject of this sketch.

Mr. Werner was married July 22, 1884, to Miss Minnie Griese, daughter of August and Louisa (Lentz) Griese, natives of Germany. This lady was born in Germany, March 25, 1859, and came with her parents to this country in early life.

The subject of our sketch is a hard-working, energetic farmer, and understands thoroughly the details of the business in which he is engaged. He has been highly successful, and carefully attends to all his interests. He has finally surrounded himself with the evidences of prosperity and success, and is now acknowledged to be one of the leading men of the township. He has a good frame house on his farm, a small stable, and has 112 acres under cultivation, and also operates a tract of railroad land adjoining his farm. He has served his fellow-citizens in various official positions, and is at present chairman of the board of township supervisors.

ABRAHAM JAYCOX is one of the thrifty and reliable farmers of La-verne township, Rock county, Minnesota, being located on a fine farm on section 13. He came to the county and made his location in June, 1876, settling where he now lives on eighty acres of railroad land. He at once commenced improvements by building a small shanty and breaking considerable land. He has since purchased 120 acres on section 14 and now owns an excellent farm of two hundred acres. In 1886 he turned his attention to raising Jersey cattle and has at present some fine animals of that breed. He finds that the Jersey blood does remarkably well in the dairy business, which he has car-

ried on for a number of years. Besides his cattle he also owns a large number of very fine blooded horses.

The gentleman whose name appears at the head of this sketch is a native of Putnam county, New York, where he was born September 18, 1829. His parents were John and Elizabeth (Carson) Jaycox, both natives of the same county. The father was a farmer by occupation and continued in that line of business throughout the most of his life. He had a family of thirteen children, eight of which are now living—David P., Abraham, Isaiah, John, William H., Mary, Martha and Servia.

The subject of our sketch came to the State of Minnesota April 5, 1856, first settling in Fillmore county, where he was engaged in farming for some twenty years, with the exception of three years which were spent in the Union service. He enlisted August 15, 1862, in answer to the call for 300,000 men, in Company E, Seventh Minnesota Volunteer Infantry, and served for three years and three days. His military experience was full of exciting adventures and many narrow escapes. During the first year of his service he was in the Indian war in Minnesota, and was one of the soldiers that stood guard at the hanging of the thirty-eight Indians at Mankato, December 26, 1862. From Minnesota his regiment went south to St. Louis, where they remained the following winter, thence going to Paducah, Kentucky, and from thence to Memphis, Tennessee. From thence they marched to Tupelo, Mississippi, and here had a severe engagement of two full days with the Rebel General Forrest. The division then turned into Tennessee and moved toward Nashville and about December 14 and 15, 1864, had a hard-fought battle with General Hood. Thence the company marched to east Mississippi, thence to New Orleans and thence to Spanish Fort, where they were engaged in severe fighting for ten days. The division then went to Blakeley, Alabama, and after considerable skirmishing went to Montgomery. Our subject returned home on the 10th of August, 1865, and eight days later was mustered out of the service. In 1876 he sold out his farming interests in Fillmore county, and moved to Rock county, where he has since been engaged in operating his extensive farm.

The subject of our sketch was married in the year 1852, to Miss Nancy Le Forge, daughter of William and Susan (Fretenburg) Le Forge. The parents were natives of New York, and the father was engaged in work on steamers on the Hudson river from Albany to New York. He held the position of first mate on one of the principal steamers until he was fifty years of age, entering that service when he was a young man. The parents lived and died in New York State. Mr. and Mrs. Joycox have ten living children— Catharine J., now Mrs. W. D. Allen; Carson, who married Hattie Wood; Flavia, now Mrs. William Wheeler; Mary S., now Mrs. M. Gillard; Abram L., Minnie, Saram, Ada A., Nancy P. and James.

Mr. Joycox is one of the early settlers of Rock county and throughout his entire residence has taken an active interest in all matters pertaining to its growth and development. He has been interested in its political growth and in its good government, and has held numerous positions of trust and responsibility. He is the present chairman of the board of township supervisors, which position he has held for the past six years; during the past eleven years he has been a member of the board. In his farming operations our subject has met with deserved success and has surrounded himself with the evidences of prosperity. He is a man of good character, excellent natural endowments, and is respected by all who know him.

$\mathbb{A}$LBERT E. SPRINGER is a dealer in lumber, doors, sash, blinds, building materials, etc., in Delavan, Minnesota, and is agent for O. L. Coleman.

Mr. Springer is a native of Lee county, Illinois, where he was born December 28, 1856. His parents were Michael and Caroline Springer, natives of Germany. Shortly after their marriage the parents came to America and located in Lee county, Illinois, where the father engaged in farming. He was in the lumber business before he left his native land. In 1862 the family came to Faribault county and settled on 130 acres of land about one-half mile northwest from the village of Delavan. They were among the earliest pioneers of this locality, and their nearest neighbors to the east were twenty-two miles distant. The father first put up a shanty 12 x 14 feet, with seven-foot posts, and a small gable roof, and made this his home for some years. Later he built a fine house and barn, and kept continually adding new and valuable improvements. The father has been quite prominent in matters of a public nature, and has been a member of the school board and supervisor for a number of years. He is a republican in politics and yields a strong influence in party counsels. In the family there were four children: Herman L., Albert E., Charles and Millie.

Reared on a farm, our subject was given the advantages for an education furnished by the district schools. He attended one term of school in the village of Delavan, and made his home principally with his parents until twenty-eight years of age. During several years prior to this age he had been engaged in different kinds of business. For some time he had operated a threshing-machine. He had also bought and sold horses. At twenty-three years of age he purchased a farm one mile west of the village, this farm comprising two hundred acres. He improved this property and now has it in the hands of a renter. In 1885 he moved his family to the village and took charge of Mr. Coleman's lumber interests. He is one of the most successful and energetic business men in the village, and has made an honorable record, both in public and private life. In politics he affiliates with the democratic party; he is an Odd Fellow, and is also a member of the village council and school board. He is one of the well-to-do and substantial citizens of this part of Faribault county. Mr. Springer was married in the year 1885 to Miss Nellie Dobie, a daughter of Joseph Dobie, of Sterling, Blue Earth county, this State. One child has blessed this union—Ethel.

--- ✦ ⟨✦⟩ ✦ ✦ ---

JOHN C. JONAS is one of the leading republicans of the southern part of Pipestone county, Minnesota, having his residence in the village of Trosky. He is one of the substantial and solid business men and has large financial interests in the township in which he lives. He settled in the village of Trosky in 1886, coming from Traer, Iowa, where he had been engaged in dealing in horses, and in loaning money.

Mr. Jones is a native of Stephenson county, Illinois, where he was born June 22, 1859. His parents were Thomas and Saloam (Rench) Jonas, the former a native of France, and the latter born in Holland. The father remained in his native country until he reached young manhood, when he came to the United States, settling in Buffalo, New York, where he married and lived for a number of years. His business was that of loaning money, and he lived a prosperous life until his death in 1881, when, on the 15th of April, he died at. McConnell's Grove, Stephenson county, Illinois, to which village he had come in 1839. He was a man of wealth and wide influence and left many friends to mourn his death. The mother is still living at McConnell's

Grove, and is seventy-seven years of age. In the father's family there were ten children, all of whom are living—Fred, Margaret, Elizabeth, Jacob, Sophia, Mary, Henry, Addie, John C. and Magdaline.

The subject of our sketch remained with his parents on the farm until he was about twenty-four years old, up to which time he had received a good common-school education and had assisted on the farm. On reaching that age he removed to Black Hawk county, Iowa, where he purchased 240 acres of land, and where he engaged in agricultural pursuits for about three years. He then sold out and purchased a breeding establishment at Traer, in Tama county, Iowa. After one year's operation of that business he sold out most of his stock and removed the remainder to Trosky, where he has since lived. He is now engaged in breeding fine Percheron and Norman horses, and owns some of the finest stock and best bred animals in the State. He is also engaged largely in loaning money, and in these lines he transacts a large and increasing business.

December 24, 1883, was the date of the marriage of Mr. Jonas to Sarah Jane Hake, who was a native of Stephenson county, Illinois, being born October 27, 1858. She was the daughter of William and Lovina (Ready) Hake, both natives of Ohio. Her father died in 1865, having spent the most of his life in the occupation of farming. The mother is still living. Mrs. Jonas was reared in Stephenson county, where she received excellent educational advantages. This union has been blessed with two children—Pearl, born December 10, 1886, and a babe, born February 18, 1889.

It may be of interest to the progeny of the subject of our sketch to give a brief history of each member of his father's family. Frederick, the oldest son in the family, is a resident of Mount Pleasant, Iowa, where he is engaged in pattern-making for a wheel and scraper company. Margaret Jonas was married to Richard Ditmire, a farmer and influential citizen of Stephenson county, Illinois. Elizabeth Jonas married 'C. Coleman, a farmer, living in Illinois. Magdaline is now Mrs. D. Cross, and resides in Stephenson county, Illinois. In the same county resides Sophia, who was married to William Hopper. Henry Jonas married Miss Friedley, and is at present living in West Point township, Stephenson county, Illinois. Jacob is residing on the home farm. Addie married John Reybolt and is located in Stephenson county. Mary was married to John France, who is a resident of Freeport, Illinois, and a prominent carpenter and builder of that place.

John C. Jonas is a man of excellent business capacities, having met with eminent success in all the business enterprises in which he has embarked. He is a man of strict integrity, careful and methodical in his business habits, and carries these characteristics into all the details of his life. At whatever lines of business he has been engaged he has made many friends by his push and energy. In politics he affiliates with the republican party, and has held various local offices.

HANS P. PAULSON is a leading farmer and stock raiser of Lincoln county, Minnesota, located on section 8 of Ash Lake township, where he settled in the spring of 1878. He was one of the very first settlers of the township, and broke some sixteen acres of land on his homestead the first year. This first year was spent by him in setting out trees of various kinds, and during that time he lived in what is known as a "dug-out." He occupied this as a dwelling for one year, and' then built a frame shanty twelve by sixteen feet, and continued residing in that until 1884, when his house and everything it contained was de-stroyed by fire. Kind friends, however, came to his aid, and he was assisted in various ways, so that he was able to proceed with his farming operations. He soon recovered from his temporary loss and has been steadily growing in prosperity ever since. Although very poor when he came to the township, he is now one of its most prosperous and substantial men. He has a comfortable house and other farm buildings, owns 142 acres of land, a great portion of which is under cultivation. In the official matters of his township he has been an active participant. He assisted in the organization of Ash Lake township in 1879, and was a member of the board of supervisors for six years, being chairman of that body for one year. At present he holds the office of treasurer of school district No. 12. Coming to the township when everything was new, our subject has had plenty of opportunity to watch its development and advancement. He was the second man to make a location, the first being Mr. Nelson, who settled on section 6.

Mr. Paulson was born in Falster, Denmark, April 28, 1852. His parents were Chris and Maria (Knutson) Paulson, natives of the same place in which our subject was born. The father was a common laborer, and is still a resident of the old country. The mother died in 1882. In the father's family there were the following-named children—our subject, Dorothea, Paul, Dorothea, Helen and Maria. Both Dorotheas are dead.

The early life of the subject of our sketch was spent by him in the place of his nativity. He assisted his father in various kinds of labor, and was given good educational advantages in the public schools. On attaining twenty years of age he left his native land and, crossing the ocean in twelve days, landed at Castle Garden, from whence he removed to Lake Superior, where he found work in the iron mines for one year and half. He then found employment in the copper mines, and continued in that employment for six months, after which he came to Minneapolis, Minnesota, and, remaining there three months, went thence to St. Croix county, Wisconsin. He resided in that locality until coming to Lincoln county in 1878.

Mr. Paulson was married in St. Croix county, Wisconsin, to Miss Caroline Hanson, daughter of Berg B. Hanson, a merchant of Baldwin, St. Croix county. This lady was born twenty miles from Manitowoc, Wisconsin, where she was reared and educated. Mr. and Mrs. Paulson have seven children— Augusta Mary, Clara Barentyne, Helen Matilda, Henry Theodore, Albert George, Emma Sophia, and Hannah Margaret.

Perhaps no man in this part of Lincoln county is as well known and as popular in public circles as is the subject of our sketch. He has continually and actively interested himself in all matters which tended to the uplifting and renovating of governmental affairs, and has held various official positions. In different capacities he has been called upon to serve his constituents and has proven his efficiency, and has grown in popular favor. Besides his connection with matters of a political nature, being a republican in politics, he is also intimately associated with the welfare of the Baptist Church Society. On these lines he is one of the most enthusiastic and earnest of workers. Being formerly a Lutheran, he now holds a membership in the Baptist church. He is well posted on a large variety of subjects, is a good talker, and seems to have a special adaptability to winning men to believe in the Christian religion. He is peculiarly gifted in this particular, and has accomplished, and is accomplishing, a great amount of good in the township in which he lives. Besides being a representative man in religious circles, he also holds the esteem and respect of all his neighbors as a thorough-going and sys-

tematic farmer. In these lines he has been very successful, and has accumulated considerable means.

PETER JOHNSON, a reliable farmer, resides on section 10, Scandia township, Murray county, Minnesota, and is the son of John and Bengta (Nelson) Pearson, natives of Sweden. He was born in Skon, Sweden, January 22, 1850.

Our subject left the parental home at eleven years of age, up to which time he had attended the common-schools and assisted his parents in farm work. From that age until about fifteen he worked out, and then returned home, where he remained for one year, after which he again left the home of his parents never to return. Until 1870 he remained in his native land working for farmers, and then came to the United States, coming directly to Minnesota, where he stopped in St. Peter and worked on the railroad. This work was begun on the 13th of May and continued until November 15th of the same year. Three months were then spent in work for a farmer, after which two months more were spent on the railroad. After a short rest another two months were spent in railroad work. The following two months were again spent in farm work. He was then married and moved onto his wife's farm in Nicollet county, Minnesota, and operated that until 1886, when they sold out and moved to Murray county, where our subject purchased 160 acres of land on the southeast quarter of section 10, Scandia township, which has remained his home ever since. Since that time he has added 120 acres of land and now owns 280 acres of excellent land with 156 acres under cultivation, while his daughter, Mary Abram, owns 160 acres on section 9. He has been very successful in his farming operations and has a comfortable frame house and good frame barn. The subject of our sketch has always taken an active interest in local political affairs, and has been chairman of the board of supervisors for some seven or eight years. He has also efficiently filled the offices of township treasurer and school treasurer. He takes an interest in religious matters and is a member of the Swedish Lutheran church.

The wedding day of Mr. Johnson occurred on the 22d of September, 1872, at which time he was married in Nicollet county, Minnesota, to Miss Inger Tolson, a native of Sweden, her birth-place being the same town in which her husband was born, the date of her birth being April 11, 1840. At the time of her marriage to Mr. Johnson she was the widow of John Adrams, by whom she had two children—Gustaf and Mary. Mr. and Mrs. Johnson have been blessed with six children—Alfred, Herman, Anton, Emily (deceased), Aaron and Hino.

ANIEL J. DENHART made his settlement in Elmer township, Pipestone county, Minnesota, in March, 1883, locating an excellent farm on section 14. He now owns 240 acres of land, and is engaged extensively in general farming and in the raising of Short-horn and Holstein cattle. He also owns several thoroughbred horses of the Clydesdale stock. Since coming to the township Mr. Denhart has been an active participant in the administration of the affairs of local government, and has held several positions of trust and responsibility. He has been chairman of the board of supervisors for three years, and has also been clerk of school district No. 19 since his settlement in the township.

The subject of this sketch is a native of Somerset county, Pennsylvania, where he was born January 22, 1853. His father, John D. Denhart, was a farmer by occupa-

tion, and was a native of Germany. When twenty years of age he left his native land and came to the United States, locating in Pennsylvania, where he lived for several years. He died at the home of our subject, at the age of seventy-four years, in 1876. The mother was Nancy Helm, who is still living, and makes her home with her children. In the father's family there were twelve children, eight of whom are still living—Jacob, Henry, Dorothy, Eva, John, Frank, Daniel and Joseph.

When our subject was about three years of age the family removed to Stephenson county, Illinois, and it was in that State that Daniel received his early training and was given the advantages for obtaining a good common-school education. He remained with his parents and attended the district schools until he was twenty-one years of age. On attaining his majority, he worked at the carpenter's trade, and also spent an apprenticeship as a stone and brick mason. He continued in these lines of employment until 1881, and in the meantime, in 1878, went to Washington Territory and followed his trades there. Returning to Illinois in 1881, he engaged in the mercantile business, but his health failed, and he started out in search of a location on a farm; visited Southern Minnesota, and found his present location in Pipestone county, where he has since been engaged in the occupation of farming.

In September, 1876, occurred the marriage of our subject to Miss Christa McHose, a native of Stephenson county, Illinois. Mrs. Denhart is a pleasant, sociable lady, well educated, having attended and graduated from the high school at Orange City, Illinois. She is a daughter of William McHose, a prominent and influential farmer of Illinois. In her father's family were thirteen children—Anna, John, Rebecca, Oliver, Sarah, Susan, Christa, Ella, Eva, Endisses, George, Mary and Thomas. Mr. and Mrs. Denhart have four children, all of whom are living—Daisy, William, Florence and Raymond:

In his political faith Mr. Denhart is a follower of the democratic principles, and since coming to Pipestone county has been identified with the religious interests of the Methodist Episcopal church. Prior to his settlement in this county he was a member of the United Brethren church. In social and religious matters he is a man of much influence and prominence. Since his residence here he has held the position of trustee in the above-named organization, and for one year was clerk of the district conference. At present he also holds the office of steward, to which he was elected for three years. Our subject has been trained in a practical school, and in spite of the many difficulties which have confronted him at various times in his life, he has risen to a position of wealth and responsibility in the county in which he lives. He is a man of excellent habits, is a good citizen, and is respected by all who know him.

———————

THOMAS THORSON is the efficient register of deeds of Watonwan county, Minnesota, and is also president of the village council of St. James, where he resides. He is a native of Rock county, Wisconsin, where he was born in the year 1852. His parents were natives of Norway, and were Thore and Rachel (Evans) Thorson.

The parents came to America in 1842, and became pioneer settlers of Rock county, Wisconsin. They engaged in farming, and continued residents of that county until 1854, when they came to Houston county, Minnesota. For several years they engaged in farming, and then removed to Iowa, later settling in Fillmore county, Minnesota. In 1869 they came to Watonwan county, and were pioneer settlers of Rosendahl township, where the father is now engaged in operating a fine farm of two hundred acres. There are seven living children in the father's family— Mary, now Mrs. Haugen; Thomas, Nels, Caroline, now Mrs. Gerlinger; Samuel, Belle, now Mrs. Troman, and Knute. The father of our subject has been a prominent citizen in his township, and has held various official positions, among them being that of school director and road supervisor. He belongs to the republican party, and is a member of the Lutheran church.

The subject of our sketch was reared as a farmer's boy, but was given a good education. He attended the Normal School at Mankato for some years, and taught some eleven months in Watonwan county. He remained with his parents principally until he was twenty-one years old, when he rented a farm in Rosendahl township, operating the same for one year. His next move was to engage as a clerk in St. James for a year. In 1875 he was elected to the office of register of deeds, and has held that office ever since. He has been one of the most popular and efficient county officials that the county has ever had. He was elected justice of the peace in 1882, and held the office until 1889, when he refused to accept a re-election. In 1889 he was elected president of the village council, of which he is the present popular incumbent. In connection with his other work he is engaged to a large extent in buying and selling lands throughout the county. He built a fine residence in the village in 1884, and in 1888 built the house where he now lives. In politics he affiliates with the republican party, and is a member of the Masonic Lodge, of which he has been secretary for four years. No man in the village is more actively interested or takes a livelier part in matters pertaining to the public welfare than does this gentleman. By money and counsel he always aids liberally in the upbuilding of any project which tends toward general improvement, and he is looked upon as one of the solid and most influential citizens of the county. Mr. Thorson was married, in the year 1884, to Miss Alice Duryea, a daughter of Daniel H. Duryea, of St. James.

THOMAS SCOTT, an influential farmer and stock raiser of Carson township, Cottonwood county, Minnesota, is at present located on section 32. He came to the county in 1871, locating on section 6 of Lake Side township, where he pre-empted land. He resided there until the spring of 1889, when he came to his present farm. He has an excellent piece of farming land and is also engaged in raising Durham cattle. Our subject was among the early settlers of Lake Side township and his taken an active interest in county matters since making his location.

Mr. Scott is of Irish birth, being born in County Donegal, August 12, 1843. His father, Edward Scott, was a surveyor and teacher and held the office of postmaster for some time. He was a representative man in Ireland and died in that country in 1860. Thomas' mother's name was Isabel Beatie, born in Ireland in January, 1811. She came to America, September 13, 1866, and lived for three years in Boston, after which she came to Minnesota, and has since lived with her son. She is a loyal Christian lady and belonged for years to the Church of England. In the father's family there are six living children—Jane, Lizzie, Sarah, Thomas, William and Alexander. The deceased were John, Susan, Margaret and Wilhelmina I.

Our subject remained in his native country until he was twenty-one years of age, up to which time he has been given a good common-school education, and for five years had been a mail-carrier. On attaining his majority, in June, 1864, he came to the United States, and located in Massachusetts until 1870. He then came West, traveling in Wisconsin and Iowa for about a year. His next move was to come to Cottonwood county, Minnesota, where he has remained ever since. He has passed through many trying circumstances and saw much trouble during the grasshopper raids but kept steadily at work, gradually building up the good circumstances with which he is now surrounded. While the grasshoppers were here our subject had to go elsewhere during the fall and winter and work to obtain enough money to enable him to return to his farm and remain until the harvest.

Our subject has been looked upon with great favor in his township and is considered one of its representative citizens. He is a republican in politics and constantly advocates and supports all matters which tend to the building up of the general welfare.

MICHAEL C. MAHONEY was the first actual settler of Burke township, Pipestone county, Minnesota. On his advent into the county there was naught to be seen but the wild, rolling prairie, and he had ample chance to choose and find a location, which he did, locating his farm on section 8, where still lives. Mr. Mahoney made his settlement January 25, 1878, and was the first to break sod in the township, which he did in April of that year. He broke about sixty acres of land, built a sod shanty, and laid the basis for the prosperity and good fortune which have come to him through the ensuing years. He lived in the sod hut for about two years, and then erected a more comfortable and commodious dwelling and surrounded himself with the signs of prosperity. Mr. Mahoney participated in the first steps toward the organization of the township, the first meeting being held in John Shey's shanty, where they discussed the name of the township. One declared that it should be named after the first settler, but Mr. Mahoney declined that honor and suggested that it be called Erin, which title was decided upon. However, on the return of the papers from the State secretary, it was found, to the surprise of the organizers, that the name was changed to that of Burke, this being their second choice, the reason being that there was already one Erin township in the State. Mr. Mahoney was the chairman of the first board of supervisors, which position he held for three years, and throughout all his residence he has been closely identified with the interests of its government and with the prosperity and welfare of the township at large. He has held numerous positions of responsibility, and in every instance has proven himself capable and efficient.

The place of the nativity of our subject is to be found in the town of Mallow, County Cork, Ireland, where he was born in 1843. He remained in his native country until about seventeen years old, up to which time he obtained a good common-school education. At that age he emigated to America, and, within sixty days after landing in New York City, enlisted in the Ninety-ninth Regiment National Guards, and remained in the service throughout the war. During this time he was engaged principally as a marine engineer on the Monitor, and after his discharge from the service, came to Chicago to erect pumping engines for the water works of that city. He remained in that city some two years after the great fire of 1871, in which he lost some $2,500 worth of personal property, tools, money, etc. In 1873 he came to the State of Minnesota, and was appointed master mechanic of the roundhouse at Waseca, in which he remained some six months, removing thence to Rochester, near which city he purchased lands, paying therefor twelve hundred dollars. After two years spent on this farm he sold out for sixteen hundred dollars, and removed to Pipestone county, locating on section 8, where he has since lived.

Mr. Mahoney was married in 1863 to Miss nah Umbrille, a native of County Kerry, Ireland. Mr. and Mrs. Mahoney have one child—Kate. In September, 1884, death took four children out of this family in one week from diphtheria—Minnie, aged fourteen years; Willie, seven years of age; Bridgie, four years old, and Mattie, two years old.

In politics Mr. Mahoney trained with the democratic party until the nomination of Mr. Blaine for president, at which time he became a republican, and since which time he has continued his affiliation with that organization. Our subject is a man of strong characteristics, is an earnest advocate of temperance reform, and is energetic and active in anything that may elevate the moral tone of the commonwealth. While a member of the board of county commissioners, which position he held from 1887 to 1888, it was mainly through his instrumentality that the liquor license in the county was placed at fifteen hundred dollars. To Mr. Mahoney is largely due the credit of accomplishing the thorough and efficient work in the line of temperance which has been in Pipestone county during the past few years. He has been vice-president of the old settlers' association for two years. In 1887 he was one of the leading spirits and the vice-president of the committee which had in hand the preparations for the celebration of the 4th of July. Mr. Mahoney has come to be looked upon as a kind of father by the younger generation which is growing up to take the places of the present burden-bearers. In his farming operations he has met with large success and has accumulated a comfortable competency. He is a man in whom all have confidence and whose judgment is a criterion to be followed by all who know him.

PATRICK CRONIN purchased his present farm on the southwest quarter of section 9, Marshfield township, Lincoln county, Minnesota, in 1878. He located on his land in 1879, and has since been a resident of the township. He is a son of Patrick and Bridget (Brennen) Cronin, both of whom were natives of Ireland.

Mr. Cronin was born in Ithaca, New York, March 2, 1855. His parents came to America some years before. When he was only a small boy his parents removed to Wisconsin, and for years the father engaged in working on different railroads in that State. The family finally located near Rochester, Minnesota, where they purchased a farm, and where the parents now live. Our subject made his home beneath the parental roof until he was twenty-five or twenty-six years of age. Up to this time he had been given good educational facilities in the district schools, and become well prepared for the practical duties of life. On attaining the age just mentioned, in about 1878, he came to his present location in Lincoln county, and purchased his farm. The following year he moved to the place and commenced making improvements. He now owns three hundred acres of excellent land, and has a good two-story dwelling-house, and a fine barn forty-six by forty-eight feet. He takes excellent care of his buildings, and keeps them all thoroughly repaired. The house and barn are well painted, and evidence care and thrift. Mr. Cronin has taken an active interest in local affairs since coming to the township, and has held several official positions. In every instance he has proven his trustworthiness and capability and has served his constituents with honor and credit to himself and satisfaction to them. He has been assessor for three years and was also township supervisor for some time. He is a consistent member of the Catholic church, and is held in high esteem as an exemplary citizen by all who know him.

Mr. Cronin was married in Rochester, Minnesota, February 28, 1882, to Miss Mary Lawler, a daughter of John and Elizabeth (McElligott) Lawler, both of whom were natives of Ireland. The fruits of this union are the following-named children—Martin, John, Hannah and Cecelia.

NICHOLAS WEBER is a leading citizen and prominent resident of Currie, Murray county, Minnesota, where he located in April, 1879. He is engaged in manufacturing wagons, and also deals in machinery. In November, 1879, he built a shop and commenced work at his present business. The extent of his means when he came to the county was very limited, and besides engaging in wagon-making, he also followed the carpenter's trade somewhat, in order to support his family. He has been quite successful in his business and does a large and profitable trade.

Nicholas Weber was born in Luxemburg, Germany, May 13, 1853. His parents were Peter and Anna Catharine (Farthel) Weber, natives of Germany and farmers by occupation. The father died in his native country when our subject was about four years of age. The mother is still living in the fatherland. The names of the children in the father's family were Anna, Mary, Michael, John, Elizabeth and Nicholas. All these are still living; those deceased being Catharine, John, Peter, Mary and Magdaline.

Nicholas Weber remained in his native land until he was seventeen years old. He received a good common-school education and was reared a farmer's boy. In March, 1871, he came to the United States, landing at Portland, Maine, whence he came to Minnesota, locating in Houston county.

Here he engaged in wagon-making for eight years, a portion of the time being spent in the employ of Nick Beck, Scott Reeves and Thomas Abbots. The last two years of this time were spent in work for himself. When the eight years had rolled by he came to Murray county and made a permanent location in the village of Currie. In politics the subject of our sketch has affiliated for some time with the democratic party and is a loyal and consistent member of the Catholic church. For two years he has been librarian of his church and was one of the first trustees, which position he holds at the present time. Mr. Weber is a man of excellent character, and is widely known and highly respected. He has good business capabilities.

Nicholas Weber was married February 21, 1876, in Caledonia, Houston county, Minnesota, to Miss Anna M. Schiltz. This lady was a native of Germany and came to the United States when sixteen years of age. Mr. and Mrs. Weber have been blessed with the following-named children—Josephine, Mary, Helen, Frank, and Anna Maria, who died March 16, 1881, at the age of five years.

DR. WILLIAM J. TAYLOR is one of the leading physicians and surgeons of Pipestone, Minnesota. He came to the city in 1874 at a time when there was but one shanty in the place. He did not make his location at that time, but came on a brief visit with Rev. E. A. Bronson. At that time the doctor was a resident of Dane county, Wisconsin, to which place he had moved in 1852, but on his coming to Pipestone county on this trip he took up a homestead and also a tree claim in Gray township, part of which is now in the village of Pipestone. He returned to Wisconsin, and in 1875 again came to Pipestone county, bringing teams, lumber, etc., and at once

proceeding to make improvements. He broke up considerable land, built a stable and a shanty and remained here some three months. In April, 1876, he removed his family to his claim, and has been a resident of the county ever since, with the exception of one year during the grasshopper times. This was in 1876 when, on the 10th of August, he removed to Luverne and engaged in the practice of his profession for about one year. Then he returned to this county and settled on his claims. He has improved a large part of his land, having some 250 acres under cultivation. He keeps a large amount of stock and does a general farming business.

Our subject is a native of Cattaraugus county, New York, where he was born April 18, 1844. He is the son of Jesse and Effie (Bayles) Taylor, the former a native of England and the latter of Vermont. The father came to America in 1815 and settled near Rochester, New York, where he engaged in farming. He afterwards removed to Cuba, Allegany county, where he also followed agricultural pursuits. Removing thence, he settled in Wisconsin in about 1852 at the town of Middleton, Dane county. Here he engaged in farming until 1881, when he sold out and removed to Pipestone, where he is now living a retired life. In the father's family there were three children—Elizabeth, now the wife of Rev. E. H. Bronson, of Luverne; Dr. W. J. and Orville J., an attorney of Sioux City, Iowa.

The early life of our subject was spent principally on the farm of his father. Until eighteen years of age he alternated between farming and the district school and was able to acquire a good common-school education. On the 20th of August, 1862, he enlisted in Company K, Twenty-third Wisconsin Volunteer Infantry, and remained in the service until the 27th of July, 1865. His military career was full of hardships and many narrow escapes. He participated in many battles, among them being the siege of Atlanta, the last battle of Jonesborough, and was with General Sherman on his march to the sea. During this grand march our subject was employed mainly as a forager until he went to Goldsborough. After his honorable discharge our subject returned to Middleton, Wisconsin. Here he engaged in teaching and also attended the state university at Madison. He took a scientific course in that institution and obtained a thorough education after which he taught school in Dane county until 1871. In that year he entered the drug store in the city of Middleton and remained a year, after which he went to Chicago and entered the Rush Medical College and after his graduation from that institution came to Pipestone county, Minn., since which time he has been actively engaged in the practice of his profession.

The subject of our sketch was united in marriage in the year 1869, to Miss Sanford, of Middleton, Wisconsin, where she was educated and received her early training. She was a daughter of J. D. Sanford, a resident of the place just named. Dr. and Mrs. Taylor have been blessed with five children—Orva, Luella, Maude, Mary, and Jennie.

Since coming to the city our subject has associated himself with all projects tending to the business improvement of the village, and besides assisting in making public improvements, he has built for himself a drug store block which was constructed in 1884 on Olive street. He is a member of the Masonic chapter and is also honorably associated with the Southwestern Medical Society and also with the Odd Fellows fraternity. He is a leading and influential member of the Grand Army of the Republic. Since coming to the county the doctor has been actively engaged in his medical practice and has built up an enviable reputation as a physician and surgeon. He has performed many difficult operations and has brought about many radical cures and is therefore looked upon as being one of the very best physicians and surgeons in Southwestern Minnesota. As a business man he is careful and conservative and has met with large success in whatever he has engaged. He is a man of excellent character, possessed of broad ideas, intelligent and courteous, and has a wide circle of friends extending throughout the entire county.

CHARLES TESMER located in Germantown township, Cottonwood county, Minnesota, in 1872, in which year he took a homestead on section 4, where he still lives.

The subject of our sketch was born July 12, 1850, in western Prussia, Germany, his parents being David and Christina (Schmid) Tesmer, also natives of Germany. When our subject was fourteen years of age he learned the tailor's trade, and worked at that business for some two years. It was too confining, however, and he was obliged to give it up. He then found employment on a farm and worked in that line for three years. Then, in 1869, he came to America, stopping for some time in New Ulm, Minnesota. He could find no work, however, of any profitable character, and in the winter he went to Waseca, where he hired to an Irish farmer for $10 per month, and employed his time in splitting rails until spring. For this work he never received his pay, and concluded that this was not a good country to live in, and made plans to return to Germany. These, however, were defeated by his procuring work on the railroad. He followed this business until 1872, when he came to Germantown township, where he has since lived.

November 6, 1872, Mr. Tesmer was married to Miss Anna Semro, daughter of David and Hattie (Schmid) Semro, and who was born in West Prussia, Germany, April 20, 1852. Mr. and Mrs. Tesmer had known each other in the old country for years, and the lady came to America to marry Mr. Tesmer. She died April 14, 1885, leaving the following-named children—Carl, Adolf, Benjamin and Mary. Mr. Tesmer was married the second time April 28, 1886, in Germantown township, to Minnie Ohlman, daughter of David and Elizabeth Ohlman. This lady was born in Germany July 8, 1854. She was the widow of Fritz Bohne when she married her present husband.

Perhaps no man in the county has had such hard trials to encounter as the subject of this sketch, and perhaps no man has fought them so manfully and overcome so well. During grasshopper times, when everything was destroyed for several years by this terrible scourge, our subject could raise no grain, and had to go long distances from home in order to earn money on which to support his family. The only assistance which he ever received from the State was a bushel of seed wheat. After five years of continued losses and discouragements, and more or less debt, our subject was almost discouraged, and was heartily sick of Minnesota, occasioned somewhat by the annoying impudence of his creditors. He has, however, kept sturdily at work, and and has finally overcome these difficulties, and has surrounded himself with evidences of prosperity. He is at present in good circumstances, has a pleasant frame dwelling-house, a large barn and granary, owns four horses and eighteen head of cattle, and has one hundred and ten acres of land under cultivation of his own farm, and also fifty acres under cultivation on railroad land adjoining. Mr. Tesmer is a man of good character, and and is highly esteemed by all who know him.

EDWIN GILHAM is the present sheriff of Rock county, Minnesota. He is a resident of the city of Luverne. Mr. Gilham is a native of Macoupin county, Illinois, where he was born in 1845.

The parents of the subject of our sketch were Josiah and Margaret (Lester) Gilham, both natives of Illinois, where they followed the occupation of farming. In about 1847 the parents removed to Wisconsin, and occupied their time in farming and mining. The mother died in Wisconsin in 1866. In 1877 the father removed to Rock county, Minnesota, and made his home with our subject until his death, which came early in 1889. In the father's family there are seven living children—Marcelia, Lillie C., Edwin, Saphronia, Pelay N., Delia, Elias A.

The boyhood days of the subject of this sketch were spent by him on the home farm, where he was given a good education. He remained with his parents until he was about fifteen years of age, and then commenced work on a farm in Iowa, where he remained about two years. His next move was to enlist in December, 1863, in Company E, Fifth Regiment Iowa Cavalry. He remained in the service throughout the war, and was discharged August 18, 1865. He was engaged in many battles under General Thomas and General Willson, in Tennessee, Georgia, Alabama and Kentucky, his regiment being attached to what was known as the Western Division. After his discharge he returned to Dubuque county, Iowa, engaged in mining, and remained in that county until the following year. In August, 1866, he removed to Sioux Falls, Dakota, and there, in company with a friend, engaged in trapping for about a year. Removing from Sioux Falls to several adjoining places he remained in Dakota until March, 1868, and then came to Luverne, taking a contract from Philo Hawes to carry the mail from that point to Yankton by way of Sioux Falls. He fulfilled his share of the contract for about nine months and then sold out. At the end of this time he located in Yankton, where he remained principally until 1873, in which year he came to Luverne and engaged in farming on 160 acres which he had homesteaded in 1871. He continued farming on this land, just west of the city, until he was elected sheriff in 1878. He has held the office since that date, being the present incumbent. Four years prior to his election he was deputy sheriff under Sheriff Rice.

The subject of our sketch was married in 1872 to Miss Eva G. Miles, of Yankton, Dakota.

Our subject passed through many interesting experiences on first coming to the vicinity of Luverne in the fall of 1866 and the spring of 1867. During these times he hunted elk along the Rock river and was engaged extensively in trapping. He carried his operations through an extensive scope of country between Sioux Falls and Flandreau and Pipestone. There was then not a shanty or house of any description in all Rock county, and when he engaged for Mr. Hawes in carrying the mail there was but one house between Luverne and Sioux Falls, while from that city to Yankton, a distance of fifty-two miles, there was not a house to be seen. Our subject has become one of the popular officials of Rock county, and has gained a strong hold on the esteem and confidence of his fellow-citizens.

⚬—⟶·❖·⟨❀⟩·❖·⟵—

OLE ASLAKSON, an influential farmer, of Scandia township, Murray county, Minnesota, was born in Christian stift, Norway, February 2, 1846. His parents were Oslak and Anna (Ammonson) Olson, both of whom were natives of Norway.

The subject of our sketch spent his early life in the mountains of his native land, and much of his time during the winters, until he was sixteen years of age, was spent in hunting in the woods and mountains. During these mountain trips he had many narrow escapes. He received a good common-school education, and when sixteen years of age engaged in work in a tannery for one year. He then found employment on board an ocean vessel and followed a seafaring life for some eighteen months. Returning to his home in Norway, he remained a short time, and then found work in the copper mines for another eighteen months. In 1869, to avoid being a soldier, he came to the United States, first stopping in Madison, Wisconsin, where for six months he engaged in farming pursuits. He then came to Nicollet county, Minnesota, chopped wood during the winter, and in the spring rented a farm, which he operated two years. He did very well during these two years, and rented the farm for another two years. The third year, however, his grain was destroyed, as were also his crops the next year. He then moved to the village of St. Peter, and for four years engaged in work at the carpenter's trade, after which he came to Murray county and settled on a homestead on the southeast quarter of section 14, Scandia township. He at once commenced active improvements on his farm, built a sod house, in which he lived until 1888. He has now a neat frame dwelling-house and a good frame barn, thirty-six by forty feet. He has 160 acres of excellent land, with 100 acres under cultivation, and owns quite a number of head of horses and cattle. He is a man of good business qualification, and has identified himself with all matters of a public nature ever since his location. He has accumulated considerable means, and holds the respect of all who know him. He has been school clerk, school treasurer, and has been constable of the township for nine years.

Mr. Aslakson was married in Norway, on Easter day, in the year 1869, to Miss Thura

Knutson, daughter of Knute and Margaret (Viglickson) Thergerson. This lady was a native of Norway, and came to America in early life. Mr. and Mrs. Aslakson have had the following-named children—Alick, Anna Mary, Anna, Lena E. (deceased), Amelia (deceased), and Lena Elizabeth.

ARNEST TOPEL, a resident of Marshfield township, Lincoln county, Minnesota, is the son of Edward and Caroline (Kagler) Topel, natives of Saxony, Germany. The parents remained in their native country until 1840 and then came to America, locating in the State of Wisconsin. The father died in Centreville in that State, in 1862, and one and a half years later the mother married Frederick Cook, who owns a farm near Sheboygan, Wisconsin.

The birthplace of the subject of our sketch is found in Sheboygan, Wisconsin, where he first saw the light of day July 1, 1849. Removing with his parents to Centreville, when he was two years of age, he lived there with the family for six or seven years. After the father's death, and on the marriage of the mother the second time, our subject went with the family to the farm of his stepfather near Sheboygan. He remained with his mother until he was fourteen years old, and then left home and went into the pine woods, where he found employment and worked during thirteen or fourteen winters. In the summers during that time he worked in a shingle mill, and sometimes for farmers throughout northern Wisconsin. In 1871 Mr. Topel was married and removed to Ludington, Michigan, where he resided for about two years and then removed to Clark county, Wisconsin, renting a farm and engaging in agricultural pursuits for about a year. The year following was spent in work in a mill and in the pineries, and then

our subject's wife returned to the home of her parents and remained with them for some time. In 1879 Mr. Topel came to Lincoln county and located his farm as a tree claim on section 4, Marshfield township, settling on one hundred and sixty acres on the northwest quarter of that section. He continued on the farm, taking care of himself and leading a bachelor's life for two years, when his wife joined him, and since that time they have made it their home. Mr. Topel has been quite successful in his various farming enterprises and has laid by considerable means. He has good farm buildings, has a number of head of horses and cattle, and has his land under excellent cultivation. His life in Marshfield township is not without its unfortunate side, and he has met with considerable financial loss and other discouragements. October 31, 1883, when our subject was away from home, the wife went to the well, a few rods from the house, to get water, and on looking back to the building she saw that it had caught fire. She hastened back to save the children, who were both in the burning building—Edward, two and a half years old, and Earnest, one year old, were frightened almost into spasms. One was lying on the floor, screaming for his mother, and the other did not know what to do. Mrs. Topel caught up the one and threw it out of the house, but Edward had concealed himself somewhere so that she failed to find him. The house was completely destroyed, including everything that it contained, and Edward perished in the burning building. Mrs. Topel was very severely burned. Nearly all her clothing was burned from her body and her face was so badly scorched that she was almost unrecognizable. Besides the loss of the house and the more touching and sad loss of the child Edward, all the fruits of that harvest were destroyed, as it had been threshed and put into one of the rooms of the house. On escaping from the house

Mrs. Topel found her clothing burning, and in order to save herself had to roll on the ground to put out the fire. In spite of these backsets and misfortunes Mr. Topel has kept heart and has been continually applying himself to the details of his farming enterprise and has put himself in good circumstances. He has a good farm, provided with excellent buildings, and under good cultivation. Since coming to the township he has taken an active interest in all matters of a public nature and has assisted actively in the local government.

Mr. Topel was married in Sheboygan county, Wisconsin, May 22, 1871, to Miss Amanda Howard, daughter of Elias and Catharine (Jennings) Howard, natives of New York. Miss Howard was born in Wisconsin, August 8, 1850, and received her early training and education in that State. Mr. and Mrs. Topel have been blessed with the following-named children—Henry, Edward, Earnest and George; all of these, except the oldest, being born in Minnesota. Henry was born in Wisconsin.

Mr. Topel is a man of exemplary character, is a loyal citizen, and his family are all members of the Lutheran church.

—◦—◦—◦⦅⟨⦆⟩◦—◦—◦—

ADAM BARTLEY is a prosperous and influential farmer of Carson township, Cottonwood county, Minnesota, and resides on the northwest quarter of section 14. He located on this claim June 3, 1871, and for the first six weeks camped out in his wagon until he could make improvements on his land. He built a sod house and continued his residence on the farm until the fall of 1880, when he went to Iowa, and remained a year. He then returned to his farm, and has since resided thereon.

Mr. Bartley was born in Canada West, September 11, 1844. His father was also a native of Canada, and is now living, at the age of ninety-four years, on a farm twenty miles distant from the place at which he was born. Our subject's mother's name before her marriage was Catharine Marquette, a native of Canada, and still living. In the father's family there are thirteen living children—Henry, Rosana, George, Aurilla, Catharine, Carrie, Adam, Michael, William, Lucinda, Margaret, Reuben and Phœbe Ann.

Our subject was reared as a farmer's boy; the educational advantages he received were furnished by the district schools of his native country. He remained beneath the parental roof until he was twenty-four years of age, when he was married, and engaged in farming, coming to Iowa in February, 1869. In May, 1871, he came to Cottonwood county, Minnesota, and located the land on which he now lives. He was one of the very first settlers of the township, assisted in its organization, passed through varied trying circumstances of early days, and has witnessed the growth of the township from the bleak, almost bare prairie, to the land now dotted with productive farms and pleasant homes. On coming to the county our subject had but little means; the extent of his money was forty cents, and his personal effects included a few household goods and a team of horses. He traded the horses for two yoke of oxen, and with this outfit plowed his ground and prepared it for the crop. He has been quite successful in his farming operations, and has accumulated considerable property. He has a number of cattle of the Durham grade, 117 head of sheep, and nine horses. He keeps about sixty head of cattle. Our subject assisted in the organization of the township in 1871, associating in this enterprise with the other early settlers, who were Messrs. Robinson, Smith and Hanson. In politics Mr. Bartley affiliates with the republican party, and is one of the representative men of the county.

Mr. Bartley was married November 25, 1867, to Miss Elizabeth Story, born in Canada West April 22, 1844. She was the daughter of Benjamin Story, a native of Scotland; her mother was of English birth. In an early day the family came to Canada, where they reared four children. Her mother died in 1882, being over sixty years of age. The father left Canada and came to Sac county, Iowa, where he now lives a retired life on a farm, and is over eighty years of age. In the Story family there are six living children—Belle, Robert, Elizabeth, Martha, Frank and Mary. Mr. and Mrs. Bartley have been blessed with the following children—Adam, Catharine and Lizzie.

———··≻·❦⊙❦·≺·❀··———

SARDIS H. TURNER, one of the prominent farmers of Osborne township, Pipestone county, Minnesota, made his location on the southwest quarter of section 8, March 16, 1878, taking his place as a homestead. On reaching his new home he at once commenced active operations, breaking some ten acres of land and erecting a sod shanty in which he lived for a number of years. In 1884 he built a comfortable dwelling-house, and has continued to make other improvements, until now his farm is provided with good buildings and everything necessary to comfort and successful management. The first year our subject had five acres of corn and the grasshoppers succeeded in harvesting the crop before he did, thus causing the loss of all the time and labor which he had bestowed in seeding and cultivating. Ever since he has resided in the township our subject has exhibited considerable enterprise in building up the welfare of his locality and has surrounded himself with a large circle of friends. He was one among the earliest settlers and assisted in the organization of the township in the spring of 1879.

He served as township treasurer and was one of the first to hold that position. There were but few in the township when our subject made his location here. Among these were A. D. Kingsbury, A. A. Dodge, George Spalding, E. W. Day, M. N. Gunsolas and Mrs. Ann Day.

The place of the nativity of the subject of our sketch is to be found in Lewis county, New York, where he was born February 5, 1837. His father was Henry Turner, a native of Onondaga county, New York, and a blacksmith by trade, which occupation he followed throughout the greater part of his life. He came to Wisconsin in an early day and for several years engaged principally in farming. His death occurred in the fall of 1878, at which time he was seventy-seven years old. He was an exemplary Christian and a member of the Baptist church. The mother of our subject was Rosella B. Edwards, a native of Vermont, where she was reared and educated. Early in her life she emigrated with her parents to Jefferson county, New York, where she met and married Henry Turner. She died February 9, 1889, at the age of seventy-eight years. She was an estimable Christian lady and had her name enrolled in the church records of the Baptist church. Our subject was one of thirteen children, of whom he was the fifth in order of birth. The names of these children were Mary M., George E., Jane, John S., Sardis, Charles M., Almon R., Alzo D., Melvin, Melvina C., Arletta, Lucetta R., Rosetta. Those deceased in the father's family were Jane, Almon, Melvin and Lucetta.

While Sardis H. was still quite young the parents removed to Rodman, Jefferson county, New York, where our subject received his early training and education, remaining in that locality until he was about seventeen years of age. He was of an exceedingly studious turn of mind, and ad-

vanced rapidly in his studies, receiving a certificate granting him the right to teach at
the age of thirteen years. When he attained
the age of seventeen years the parents removed to Jefferson county, Wisconsin, this
being in the fall of 1854. Here our subject
engaged in teaching school during the winter
of the first year's residence and worked on a
farm during the summer months. In the
fall of 1855 he removed to Portage county,
same State, where he spent a number of years
working on a farm—working on a farm during
the summers and teaching school during the
winter months of four years. During this
time he was married, and after the period of
teaching just mentioned he engaged in working on a farm for two years. In November,
1863, he enlisted in Company H, First Wisconsin Cavalry, as a private. Among the
battles in which our subject engaged were,
Cleveland, Lost Mountain, Hopkinsville,
Kentucky, West Point, Georgia, Carters-
ville, and numerous other skirmishes and
battles of minor importance. After his discharge at Nashville, Tennessee, in July, 1865,
Mr. Turner returned to his home in Wisconsin and resumed teaching and farming and
remained in Portage county until in the fall
of 1875. At that time he located in Saratoga, Winona county, Minnesota, where he
remained engaged in various pursuits, principally that of teaching, for three years.
When that time had expired he removed to
his present place in Osborne township, Pipestone county.

The marriage of the subject of our sketch
occurred April 7, 1861, in Belmont, Portage
county, Wisconsin. He was married to
Miss Mary Jane Smith, who was born in
Aroostook county, Maine, in 1842. This
lady received her early training and education in the county of her nativity, where she
remained until about twelve years of age, at
which time she removed with her parents to
Dane county, Wisconsin, where she com-

pleted her education. Later she moved with
her parents to Belmont, Wisconsin, where
she remained until her marriage. Miss
Smith was a daughter of Stephen and Martha
J. (Lincoln) Smith, both of whom were
natives of New Brunswick, the father being
born in St. Johns in 1818, and the mother
born in Frederickton in 1821. The parents
were farmers by occupation and reared a
large family of children—Thomas N., John
L., Theodore L., Dorinda N., Martha Ann,
Jeronia and Annetta, twins; Cordelia,
George Washington, Amanda, Hannah Jane.
Annetta, Thomas and Martha Ann are now
dead, the last named leaving a husband and
three children at her death. Her parents
were exemplary members of the Free Will
Baptist church. Mr. and Mrs. Turner have
five children—Edward Allen, Myron Aldro,
Dora May, Marion and Martha A. Dora
May married George Straw, May 16, 1886,
and is now living in St. Paul.

The subject of our sketch is a man of progressive ideas and of high moral character.
Believing in the renovation of political parties he has cut loose from his old affiliation
with republicanism and is now an earnest
supporter of the principles and policy of the
prohibition party. He is a thorough temperance man and believes in placing the government in the hands of the temperance
people. Our subject has been identified
with the interests of Osborne township, and,
indeed, of the whole county for a number of
years, and being one of the pioneer settlers
is held in high esteem by the citizens of the
township in which he is located. Among
the positions of trust which he has held in
the township may be named that of treasurer, to which office he has been elected several times, being the first incumbent of that
position in the town. In his farming operations Mr. Turner has been very successful.
He is at present engaged in farming and
stock-raising business, giving special atten-

tion to Durham cattle and blooded horses. He owns some of the best animals of the Durham stock in the county.

---❖❖---❖❦◈❦❖---❖❖---

ZEBEDIAH W. MARSH is a leading and influential citizen of Shetek township, Murray county, Minnesota. He homesteaded his present place on section 21 in 1871. He was one of the first settlers of the township—the other early settlers being D. Greenman, E. C. French, W. F. Silvernale, David Haddock, T. Conner and Mr. Armstrong. Our subject assisted in the organization of the township, and originated the petition to organize the first school district in the county in the year 1873. By appointment he served one year as county sheriff, and was then elected to that position for two terms. He has also been county commissioner for one year, and has been treasurer of school district No. 1 from its organization up to the present time. He has also held the offices of justice of the peace and township treasurer, and is holding the latter office at the present time. It will thus be seen that Mr. Marsh takes an active interest in all matters of a public nature, and in every instance he has given excellent satisfaction in the administration of the duties of his offices. On coming to the county in the fall of 1871 our subject put up hay, rented a house on the lake shore and made that his home during the winter. He busied himself with getting out logs for a house for himself, which was put up in June, 1872. He broke six acres of land, and planted it to corn. Later he broke twelve acres more, and the following year set out two acres of trees. He has been quite successful in raising trees, and has now a beautiful grove. He has made his residence in Shetek township since his location, with the exception of four years which were spent by him in work at the blacksmith's trade in Currie; his family,

however, remained on the farm. These four years were the years of the grasshopper raids, and no crops could be raised. Our subject experienced many hardships during his early settlement, but these have all been forgotten in the prosperity and good circumstances with which he is surrounded to-day. His nearest market during those early days was New Ulm and Heron Lake, the distance to New Ulm being seventy-five miles, and the trip to that place occupying four days.

Mr. Marsh was born in St. Lawrence county, New York, in the village of Gouverneur, May 1, 1837. He remained in his native county until he was seven years of age, and from thence removed to Ashtabula, Ohio, where he resided for twelve years. Here he received his education and early training, and at nineteen years of age came to Winona county, Minnesota, locating in Saratoga township. His occupation up to this time and while in Ohio was principally that of a sailor, this line of occupation being engaged in for some five seasons. He resided in Winona county, engaged in farming and teaming until 1861, and then enlisted in the Second Minnesota Volunteer Infantry as a private. In June, 1862, he was discharged as an orderly sergeant, and in August of that year re-enlisted as a second lieutenant in the Seventh Minnesota Infantry. He continued in the service throughout the war, being discharged in August, 1865. He participated in many hard-fought battles, and served his country bravely and well. Our subject was engaged in many fights with the Sioux Indians of Dakota. He was at the battles of Big Mound and Dead Buffalo Lake. He also served for several years in the operations of the Army of the South, and participated in the battles of Somerset, Tallahatchie River, Big Blue River, Tupelo, Nashville, where our subject commanded his regiment through a two-days' battle. He was discharged at Fort Snelling in 1865, and then returned to

Saratoga township, Winona county, Minnesota, where he remained until 1871, engaged in farming. While in that county he occupied a prominent position and held various offices, such as constable, for two years, and deputy county sheriff, for two years. In the fall of 1871 he came to his present location, as related in the opening lines of this sketch.

Mr. Marsh was married September 30, 1863, while on a furlough, to Miss Mary Jane Jasper, a native of Newton, Union county, Pennsylvania. This lady was reared and educated in West Philadelphia. Mr. and Mrs. Marsh have been blessed with five children—Millionette, Ella M., Clyde, Walter and John. Millionette married Everett Greenman, and is now residing in Shetek township. She was thoroughly educated, and taught twelve terms of school in Murray county prior to her marriage.

The subject of our sketch is a man of broad ideas, is possessed of excellent business capabilities, and is highly esteemed as a true and loyal citizen. He is a man of great energy, is independent in thought, and in politics affiliates with no particular party, but supports the man best fitted for the position. He belongs to the Masonic fraternity, and is an influential member of the Grand Army of the Republic.

———◆—◈❨◆❩◈—◆———

LFRED BLENKIRON is a prosperous farmer and influential citizen, living on section 31, Springfield township, Cottonwood county, Minnesota. The place of his birth was in Yorkshire, England, where he first saw the light June 30, 1855. The parents of our subject were John and Anna (Southerland) Blenkiron, the former a native of England, and the latter born in Scotland.

The subject of our sketch remained in England until he was nineteen years of age, up to which time he had received a good common-school education. At that age he went to the island of Ceylon, where he engaged for six years on a coffee plantation. At the expiration of that time he returned to England for two years, when, in 1881, he came to America, and soon came to Cottonwood county, locating on the place where he now lives. In connection with A. B. Keir, our subject purchased 640 acres of excellent land, where he is now engaged in farming. Since coming to the township Mr. Blenkiron has shown his capability as a public-spirited citizen, and has assisted in various ways in the administration of local affairs. In politics he affiliates with the democratic party, is a member of the Ancient Order of United Workmen, and belongs to the Episcopal church.

Mr. Blenkiron wedded Mary Elotia Moore, December 8, 1884. This union has been blessed with two children, both of whom are now deceased.

———◆—◈❨◆❩◈—◆———

ERNT TORESDAHL is the leading member of the firm of Bernt Toresdahl & Company, proprietors of the Minneapolis Store of Pipestone, Minnesota. This firm carries one of the largest and best assorted stocks of goods in the city, consisting of dry goods, notions, hosiery, fancy goods and gents' furnishing goods. Their store has become quite popular with the denizens of Pipestone, and the company enjoys a large and profitable trade. Our subject located in the city in May, 1888, at which time he brought his immense stock of goods from the city of Minneapolis, where he had been doing business for some two years. The place of the nativity of Mr. Toresdahl is found in Norway, where he was born in 1860.

The subject of our sketch is the son of Swan and Mary (Larson) Toresdahl, both natives of Norway. The father was an influential man in his native land and was engaged extensively in farming, and also in the stock business. He operated quite largely in shipping horses from Norway to England, and is still living, engaged in that business. The mother died in 1865. In the father's family there were five children, three of whom are now living—Asbijoren, Bernt and Gurene. The first named came to America in 1884 and settled in Wright county, Iowa, where he is engaged in farming. The grandfather of our subject was Asbijoren Toresdahl, an influential farmer of Norway. He was a soldier for seven years in the war between Denmark and Norway and Sweden, and was wounded by being shot in the arm in one of the prominent battles.

The parental home remained the abiding place of our subject until he was thirteen years of age, up to which time he had been given more or less educational advantages in the place of his nativity. When thirteen years old he was sent to school at Staranger, where he remained two years, continuing his educational course. At the end of that period he engaged as a clerk in a dry goods and notion house, remaining with his employer for about five years. 1880 found him on his way to America. He first settled in Sheldahl, Iowa, where he accepted a position as clerk in a drug store. About eighteen months were spent in that employment, and then he went to Eagle Grove, Wright county, where he clerked in a dry goods house for three years. Removing thence he stopped in Randall, same State, where for one year he found employment in a dry goods house. He went thence to Minneapolis, as clerk in a dry goods and clothing house. After eight months of clerking he opened in the same line that he now carries and continued in business in that city for about two years, at which time he brought his present stock of goods to Pipestone.

After coming to Pipestone he took in John Grun as a partner, under the firm name of Bernt Toresdahl & Co.

The subject of our sketch was married in 1888 to Miss Julia Egland, of Iowa. This lady was a daughter of Knute Egland, a native of Norway. This marriage has been blessed with two children—Hiram C. and Martine.

Since coming to America the subject of our sketch has been one of the stanch supporters of the republican party. He is also a member of the order of Knights of the White Cross. Matters of a public nature interest him, and he always aids in those enterprises by word and deed, giving of his means whenever it is necessary to further the projects of public importance. In his mercantile business he has been quite successful, having accumulated considerable means. He has an excellent stock of goods and enjoys a large and increasing trade.

———⋅◦⋅✦⋅◦⋅◦⋅———

KNUTE TORGERSON is a leading farmer and stock raiser of section 16, Highwater township, Cottonwood county, Minnesota. He made his location on his present place in 1872, coming with the family of his parents. They settled on section 22 of that township, and the father remained there until his death, which occurred in 1882. The father was a native of Norway, and came to the United States in 1856, settling in La Crosse county, Wisconsin. Throughout his life he was a farmer by occupation, and a member of the Lutheran church. Our subject's mother's name was Gro Knutson, a native of Norway, and now a resident of section 22 of Highwater township. In the father's family there were seven children, of whom our subject was the third youngest—Julia, Torg, Jennie, Bessie, Knute, Ole (deceased) and John (deceased).

The subject of our sketch is a native of

La Crosse county, Wisconsin, his birth occurring August 4, 1863. He was reared in La Crosse county until he was nine years of age. He then came to Cottonwood county and received a common-school education in the district schools. He remained with his parents until he was seventeen years of age, and then commenced work for himself. In 1885 he bought his present farm of eighty acres, and has since been operating the same in his own behalf. Since attaining his majority he has taken an active interest in all public matters, and was elected assessor of Highwater township in 1886, which position he still holds. He was also chairman of the township board for one year. His father being one of the early settlers of the township, he assisted in its organization, and interested his son, our subject, in the affairs of the government. Our subject has been clerk of the township, and, by careful and capable attention to the details of the various offices which he has held, has made himself well known to the people, and has gained their respect and esteem. In politics he affiliates with the republican party, and, with his family, belongs to the Lutheran church. He is a man of excellent principles, and a man of the highest integrity.

Mr. Torgerson was married June 2, 1885, to Miss Susie Seim, a native of Norway. When she was a year old her parents came to America, locating for a few years in the State of Iowa. From thence they went to Fillmore county, Minnesota, where Miss Susie completed her education. Her father was Ole Seim, and now lives in Murray county. Mr. and Mrs. Torgerson have three children —Alice F., Olaf W. and Albert O.

JOSEPH A. SHAVER, a leading business man of Rock county, Minnesota, is the manager of the C. P. Crosby lumber yard, at Beaver Creek. He is a native of Colum-

bia county, Wisconsin, where he was born in 1859.

The parents of the subject of our sketch were Benjamin W. and Julia A. (Hall) Shaver, both of whom were natives of the State of New York. The father has been engaged in the livery business throughout the most of his life. He came west to Wisconsin in an early day, and remained in that State until 1872, in which year he removed to Kasson, Minnesota, and engaged in the same line of business—that of operating a livery. He remained in Kasson for two years, and then removed his family to Faribault, Minnesota, where he continued his old business until going to Cedar Falls, Iowa, in 1883. He has changed his location a number of times, but has finally found a permanent location in Cedar Falls, where he is now engaged in the livery business. He was a man of strong patriotic sentiments, and served in the Union army during 1864 and 1865. In the father's family there were four children—George, Joseph A., Emiline and Zelia.

The subject of our sketch remained with his parents during his early life, receiving his education and training in Kasson and Faribault. Prior to 1884 he assisted his father in the livery business, and in that year came to Beaver Creek and opened the lumber yard, of which he is the present manager.

Mr. Shaver was married November 29, 1888, to Miss Mary V. Bailey, of Luverne, Minnesota, daughter of Joseph N. and Kate (Strong) Bailey.

Mr. Shaver has earnestly taken hold of the business affairs of Beaver Creek village, and has assisted in the organization of various financial enterprises. He was one of the organizers of the roller flouring mills, and continued his interest in the same until after the mill was gotten under good headway. He then sold out. He has purchased a house and lot in the village and has a beautiful home. In politics he affiliates with the republican party, and was elected one of the board of village trustees in 1888. He is a man of excellent business principles, a loyal citizen, and is one of the prominent business characters of the locality.

JACOB G. HIEBERT is one of the leading general merchants of the village of Mountain Lake, Cottonwood county, Minnesota. He is the son of George and Susan (Emm) Hiebert, both natives of Germany. The parents came to America in 1876 and settled in Mountain Lake township on a farm about three miles from the village of Mountain Lake. The parents are still living on that farm. The father was a miller by trade, and while in his native country operated a large flouring mill. In the father's family there were the following children—Jacob, Eliza, George, David, Susan, John and Peter. These children were by his first wife, who died in 1881. The second marriage of the father was to Gertrude Nichols, by whom he had four children—Helen, Gertrude, Anna and Mary. The daughter, Eliza, is the wife of H. P. Goertz, a prominent business man of Mountain. Lake, and of whom a sketch is given in another department of this work.

Mr. Hiebert was born in the village of Perdenia in Southern Russia, May 15, 1863. He remained with his parents in their native land until in 1876, when they came to the United States, locating in Cottonwood county. Our subject resided on the farm with his father and assisted him in its operation until 1886, when he commenced clerking for David Ewert, a merchant of Mountain Lake village. He continued with that gentleman for nearly two years, and then opened in the furniture business for himself, continuing in that line for about a year, when he sold out his furniture stock and engaged in the general mercantile business, having been engaged in this line ever since. He is doing an excellent business and has built up a large trade. His father and J. J. Balzer are in company with him in this business. In public matters our subject takes an active interest and has become one of the prominent and substantial business men of the village.

JOHN LAVESON, a leading farmer and stock raiser of Ash Lake township, Lincoln county, Minnesota, owns an excellent farm on the northwest quarter of section 14, where he homesteaded in 1880. There were no improvements on the property when he settled, and it is now provided with an excellent dwelling-house and other buildings, barns, granaries, etc. The barn is 26x50 feet, with fourteen-foot posts, and with a shed on the west side. The dwelling-house is substantially built of good materials, and is 16x24 feet, with a kitchen 14x16 feet and fourteen-foot posts. The granary is well built, and is 14x28 feet, having a shed 8x36 feet on the west side and also one on the north end 14x14 feet. Mr Laveson came to Lincoln county in 1879, about a week before Christmas. He first located on section 2, where his brother was then living. In the spring of 1880 he took the homestead where he now lives. He at once commenced active operations, improving his farm, breaking about five acres of land, and erecting a shanty 10x12 feet, in which he lived until 1885, when he built his present comfortable and commodious dwelling. The first year he built a stable 14x16 feet, with a straw roof, and used this for his stock for some two years. To this he has been continually adding and making improvements, until he has the best barn and farm buildings in the township. The second year of his settle ment he had a good crop, and has continued in general farming up to the present time. He has taken an active interest in public matters, and has been treasurer of school district number 30.

Mr. Laveson was born in the southern part of Sweden, March 12, 1840. He was the son of Lave Larson, a native of Sweden, in which country he was engaged in farming until his death, which occurred in 1883. The mother's name before her marriage was Anna Nelson, a native of Sweden, in which country she still lives. In the father's family there were seven children, five boys and two girls—Sesa, Pete, Hannah, Nels, our subject, Andrew and Hans.

John Laveson remained on a farm in his native country, where he received a good common-school education throughout his early life. He did not leave his native land until he was thirty-one years of age, when he came to the United States, landing at Castle Garden, June 19, 1871. Soon after coming to this country he went to Mankato, Minnesota, from whence, after five weeks' stay, he went to Wabasha county, same State, and lived on a rented farm until 1879. He then came to Lincoln county and made his location, as related in the opening lines of this sketch. He was among the early settlers of the township, and has become one of its prominent men. Our subject is still unmarried. In politics he affiliates with the republican party, and has been a stanch supporter of the principles of that organization ever since coming to the United States. Besides taking an active interest in all public matters, he has also actively interested himself in the religious affairs of the Lutheran church, of which he is at present a deacon and trustee. He takes an active part in the affairs of this society, and has been a trustee since its organization. He has been quite successful in his various financial operations since making his location in Lincoln county, and he is now one of the most substantial of its citizens.

F. PRIDE is a member of the firm of Francisco, Pride & Wing, millers of Blue Earth City, Faribault county, Minnesota, and proprietors of the Blue Earth City roller mills.

Mr. Pride is a native of Peoria county, Illinois, where he was born in the year 1856. He is the son of Charles G. and Delia M. (Hendricks) Pride, natives of Pulaski, New York. The parents were farmers by occupation and settled in Peoria county, Illinois, in 1854, removing to Waseca county, Minnesota, in 1865, in both of which places they engaged in farming.

Our subject remained with his parents until twenty-seven years of age. He was given a good common-school education in early life and assisted his father in farm work. He was married when twenty-seven years of age to Miss Rosetha A. Styles, of Wisconsin, by whom he had one child—Elsie M. In 1884 he removed to Henderson, and from that time on engaged in milling in various places, coming to Blue Earth City in September, 1885. In politics he is an independent, and belongs to the Masonic fraternity. Mr. and Mrs. Pride are members of the Presbyterian church.

JOHN SWAN is a prosperous and reliable farmer, of Scandia township, Murray county, Minnesota. He is the son of Swen and Pernella (Nelson) Pearson, natives of Sweden, where our subject was born, in the city of Stockholm, June 24, 1858. Up to fifteen years of age his life was spent in the home of his parents, where he received a good common-school education. From that age until twenty he was away from home, except for occasional visits, employing his time in working for farmers. At the age just mentioned he returned home, and after remaining about two years came, in 1881, to the United States, stopping first in Niagara county, New York, where he worked by the month at farm work from the 25th of July until the 8th of the following November. At that time he came to Murray county and staid with Ole Miller for three weeks, at the end of which time he moved onto a farm owned by his brother Peter, remaining until spring. The next summer was spent in work for Mr. Fehring, and in the fall he moved back to his brother's, where he remained until February 22. The next day he was married and moved to his wife's farm, remaining on that place until 1886, and then moved into the village of Lake Wilson, and after keeping a hotel in that place for one year, returned to the farm, which has remained his home ever since. The farm which our subject's wife owned was a fine one of 200 acres, with about one-half of it under cultivation. Our subject also owns considerable stock. Mr. Swan is a member of the Swedish Lutheran church, and being a man of good character, is highly respected by all who know him.

February 23, 1883, is the day on which our subject was married in Scandia township, to Fredreka Clare, daughter of Henry Clare, a native of Germany, where she also was born in the year 1850. Before her marriage to Mr. Swan, Miss Clare had been married to August Bosch, who died, leaving her a widow with three children—Jennie L., Earnest C. and Lotta. Mr. and Mrs. Swan have been blessed with one child—Elida.

JACOB KLAASSEN is a prominent farmer and stock raiser, located on section 18 of Carson township, Cottonwood county, Minnesota. He located in this county with his parents in 1875. The parents settled on section 12, where they still live. The parents of our subject were of Russian birth, and remained in that country until 1875, when the father came to Cottonwood county, Minnesota, bringing with him four sons and one daughter. He was a farmer by occupation in his native country, and has followed that line of occupation since coming to America. Our subject's mother's name was Mary Johnson, also a native of Russia, and who died in that country when our subject was four years old. The father was married again to Sarah Wiens, a native of Russia, and who is now living in Cottonwood county.

The subject was born in Russia and was educated and reared in his native country until he was seventeen years of age. At this time he came with his father to the United States, and located with him on section 12 of Carson township, as already stated. He lived with his parents for four years, and in 1879 was married and then purchased his present farm of eighty acres, on which he has lived ever since. He has made good improvements on his farm and is engaged in general farming and stock raising. With his father he was one of the early settlers of the county, and took pride in setting out trees about his place.

December 4, 1879, Mr. Klaassen was married to Miss Mary Loeven, a native of Russia, who came to America when she was eighteen years of age. She was reared and educated in her native land and was the daughter of David Loeven, a school teacher and also a farmer for two years before coming to America. In 1876 her parents came to the United States, settling in Carson township, where the father engaged to some extent in farming. He is also a local preacher, and attends to the ministry in his church in connection with his other duties. Mr. and Mrs. Klaassen have four children—David, Mary, Nelson and Anna.

Perhaps no man in the township takes more active part in public affairs than does the subject of our sketch. He is always ready and willing to share in the establishment and upbuilding of general interests, and always takes an active interest in political matters. Being a republican in politics, he has been chairman of the board of supervisors for about a year and a half, at the end of that time resigning his office to attend to other duties. For three years he was assessor of Carson township, and has been road overseer and supervisor for some years. In every official capacity he has proven his integrity and efficiency, and is esteemed by all who know him. He has labored hard and energetically on his place to make it one of the best in the township, and his success is evinced by the excellent buildings he has thereon and the high state of cultivation to which he has brought his land.

⁕

JAMES HINES homesteaded his present place on section 22, of Fountain Prairie township, Pipestone county, Minnesota, in 1879. The year before he had visited this part of the country in company with nine others, and at the time located his land, broke two acres, built a small shanty and remained a short time. Commencing on his farm in a small way, building small buildings, he has kept increasing in means and making improvements until he now owns good barns and out-houses and a comfortable dwelling-house. He has met with several disasters since coming here, having had a large barn burned in 1882 and losing, among other things, eight hundred bushels of grain, some stock, farm machinery, etc. At that time he also lost by fire his dwelling-house. Despite these unfortunate occurrences, and others which have come of late years, he has by careful management accumulated considerable means. He has been fortunate in having excellent crops and this has done much toward replacing the losses which have come to him in the various ways referred to. Among those who came to the township with Mr. Hines may be named Mr. Malony, Charles Chaffey, Mr. Hirschy, Patrick Sweeney, E. Link and C. Sizer. Our subject and Mr. Hirschy are the only ones of that company remaining in the township. Our subject assisted in the organization of the township and was deeply interested in the proper commencement of the public affairs of his civil division. The first meeting was held on section 21, on land which was then in the possession of Mr. Hines. Mr. Sizer was the first clerk and Mr. Heath the first chairman of the board of supervisors, Mr. Link being a member of that board. Patrick Sweeney was the first assessor, and Mr. Heck township treasurer. Mr. Hines has been identified with the official history of the township in various ways, and his abilities have been called into play in the office of township treasurer, which he held for three years, and also in that of treasurer of school district No. 24, which position he held for two years. With the growth of the general prosperity of the township Mr. Hines has also grown in wealth, and is now acknowledged to be one of the leading and most substantial farmers in the township. He is one of the largest farmers and owns six hundred acres of land, and besides his extensive farming has also invested largely in Norman and Percheron horses. His lands are located in different localities, eighty acres being on section 8, of Grange township, forty acres on section 3, of the same town, 160 acres on section 21, of Fountain Prairie township, and the balance on section 22, of the latter township.

Mr. Hines is a native of Ireland, where he was born April 16, 1850. His father was Thomas Hines, a farmer by occupation, who died in 1876, in Steele county, Minnesota.

When our subject was about six years old the parents came to America from Ireland, their native land, and settled in Walworth county, Wisconsin: After remaining there some six or seven years they then removed to the central part of the State, locating in Adams county. Eight or nine years were spent in that locality, after which they removed to Steele county, Minnesota, where the mother still resides. In the father's family there were five sons and four daughters, three of the sons being soldiers in the Union army during the War of the Rebellion; John served in the Twenty-second Wisconsin Infantry; Thomas enlisted in the Second Wisconsin Cavalry, and died at Helena, Arkansas, from diseases contracted in the service; Dennis joined the Thirty-eighth Wisconsin Infantry and came out with his life, although being severely wounded in one of his knees. Those living in the father's family are Mary, Hannah, Maggie, Elizabeth, John, Dennis, William and James.

The subject of our sketch received his education and training principally in the State of Wisconsin, where he was given excellent educational advantages in the district schools, and acquired a good common-school education. He moved about with his parents in Wisconsin at the various times above mentioned, and received his education principally in Adams county. On attaining early manhood he commenced work in the pineries, following that employment throughout the months of each winter and working on the river during the summer months. This plan of employment occupied his time for some fourteen or fifteen years, when he came to Pipestone county in 1879, as was stated in the opening lines of this sketch.

The wedding day of the subject of our sketch occurred December 28, 1882, on which day he was married to Miss Anna Malony, a native of Wisconsin. Mr. and Mrs. Hines

have three children—Maggie, Thomas and Elizabeth.

The subject of our sketch affiliates with the democratic party, and is a consistent member of the Catholic church. Since coming to the township Mr. Hines has exerted himself in every possible way to build up the best interests of his locality. In all matters it can truly be said that Mr. Hines is one of the best citizens of the township. He is a man of exemplary character, and has a wide circle of friends.

———•◦•◦◦◦◦•◦•———

PETER G. DALY is a leading farmer of Marshfield township, Lincoln county, Minnesota. He is the son of John W. and Johanna Daly, both natives of Ireland. The parents left their native country and came to America in early life, settling in Canada, where they lived for some time. Some time in 1857 they left Canada and came to the United States. The father found employment in the Eastern States in work on various railroads. In about 1865 the family located in Olmsted county, Minnesota, where they have lived ever since.

The subject of our sketch was born February 26, 1855, on a farm about midway between Montreal and Quebec, Canada. He was reared a farmer's boy and received his education in the district schools. He came with his parents to the United States, and finally, in 1865, located with them in Olmsted county, Minnesota, and continued to reside with them until he was about twenty-five years of age. In 1878 he came to Lincoln county and purchased railroad land, which he has continued to improve ever since. In 1879 he came to the farm and staid through one season, and the following winter returned to the home of his parents. Until 1885 he came to his farm and worked during the summers and returned to the home of his parents during the winters. In that year he was married, and, coming to his farm, has made it his permanent residence ever since.

Mr. Daly was married January 7, 1885, at St. Bridget's church, in Olmsted county, Minnesota, to Miss Hannah O'Conner. This lady was a daughter of Thomas and Mary (Lawler) O'Conner, both natives of Ireland. The fruits of this union have been—John Francis, who died when six months old, and Thomas William.

The subject of our sketch had but little means when he first located in Lincoln county. He has worked steadily and systematically, however, and, being of an economical disposition, has succeeded in placing himself in good circumstances, and has provided his large farm of 320 acres with excellent buildings and other good improvements. He has a good frame dwelling-house and excellent barns. Since coming to the township he has taken an active interest in all matters of a public nature, and has assisted largely in all matters which pertain to the general welfare. He has been interested in the local government and has held several official positions, among them being that of township clerk, which he held four years, and also clerk of the school board. Mr. Daly is a man of excellent character, thrifty and industrious, and is widely known and highly respected.

JOHN B. BERNARDY, who now resides on section 2 of South Brook township, Cottonwood county, Minnesota, is a native of Belgium, where he was born October 30, 1845. He is the son of Matthias and Mary Katharina (Kanife) Bernardy, both of whom were also natives of Belgium. The parents lived and died in their native land. They had a family of three children—John B., Peter and Katie.

The subject of our sketch was the only one of the family who emigrated to America. He was reared on a farm, in his native land, and assisted his father until he was seventeen years of age. At that age he went to France for a short time, and then returned home, and came to America, May 10, 1865. He first located at Port Washington, Wisconsin, and there engaged in work for a farmer for some time. He visited various places after that, among them being Appleton, Wisconsin, and Sandy Point, Michigan, working in a spoke factory in the former place, and also working to some extent at the mason's trade, and in the latter place working in a saw-mill. He then went to Peoria county, Illinois, and worked on a farm for a short time, thence going to Appleton, Wisconsin, where he learned the carpenter's trade. His next move was to Waterloo, Iowa, and thence to Illinois, visiting from that time on, Kansas City, Baxter Springs, Neosia, Missouri, and Fort Smith and Fort Sill, Indian Territory. In the last-named place he was engaged as a reserve soldier by the government. In the other places he was engaged in work at the carpenter's trade. Ten months thereafter were spent in Chicago, and then fifteen months were spent by our subject in his native country, returning to America, September 4, 1874. He then came to Cottonwood county, Minn., and preempted 160 acres, afterwards changing it to a homestead, where he now lives. During the grasshopper times our subject was compelled to go elsewhere to earn money enough to provide food and clothing. He has improved his farm since those days, and has now one of the best places in South Brook township.

Mr. Bernardy was married April 25, 1879, to Josephine Peltzel, daughter of Joseph Peltzel, a native of Austria, but who emigrated to America May 13, 1875. Her father died in Nobles county, Minnesota, June 4, 1889; her mother still lives in that county. Mr. and Mrs. Bernardy have six children—Mary, John, Joe, Frank, Charley and Lewis. All the members of the family are members of the Catholic church of Heron Lake.

The subject of our sketch is a man of excellent business qualities, and has been eminently successful in the prosecution of his farming operations. He is engaged extensively in farming, and also raises fine Holstein cattle and gives considerable of his attention to the raising of Norman and English draft-horses. The last year he took two car loads of stock to Chicago and one to Omaha. In politics Mr. Bernardy has afflliated for some time with the democratic party, having cast his first vote for Seymour and Blair. Our subject is a man of excellent character, and is highly esteemed by all who know him.

MOSES COOK, of whom this sketch treats, is a reliable farmer of Shetek township, Murray county, Minnesota. He came to this region first in 1866 on a hunting and fishing expedition. Liking the country, in the fall he came and homesteaded land on section 24 of Mason township. He made that his home for about five years, engaged in farming. He assisted in the organization of that township in about 1868, and thoroughly identified himself with the government of the township. He was a member of the school board and held other offices. He made excellent improvements on his farm. Then two years were spent by him in Missouri, and after this time, in 1874, he returned to Murray county, locating in Shetek township, where he has since lived. Besides engaging in farming he has followed the well business for some two or three years.

Moses Cook was born in Rutland county, Vermont, July 8, 1829. His father was Nicholas Cook, a farmer and a native of the State of Vermont; he died in about 1879. Our subject remained in the State of his nativity, working on a farm until he was eighteen years of age. He then came to Winnebago county, Wisconsin, where he remained two years, after which he found work in the pineries in Waupaca county, and employed his time in cooking, chopping, teaming and running on the river for some sixteen seasons. At the end of that time he came to Murray county, Minnesota, where he has since resided, with the exception of the two years spent in Missouri. He was one of the first settlers, and has been closely identified with the history of the county and township.

Mr. Cook was married in June, 1873, to Miss Effie Bull, a native of Canada. Leaving Canada with her parents she went to the State of Iowa and from thence, when a girl, came to Minnesota with her parents. Mr. and Mrs. Cook have one child—Ova, thirteen years of age.

Our subject has become quite prominent as a citizen and as a worker in religious lines. He is a man of stanch principles and is a member of the prohibition party. While a resident of Mason township he was a class-leader for some time. During his residence here our subject has engaged to a considerable extent in fishing, and has had many interesting and enjoyable experiences in that kind of sport. At one time, in one day, out of Bloody Lake he caught 201 pickerel, ranging from two to five pounds. This was done with a spear and decoy hook. Again, our subject and John Boomhower caught five hundred pounds of buffalo fish with their hands. Some of the fish weighed as much as twenty-three pounds. These fish were caught in a small slough north of Lake Sarah. During the early days our subject experienced hard times, and had to apply himself to various kinds of work in order to provide for himself and family. He had considerable experience in hunting and trapping, and the next year after coming to the township caught in one night seventy-nine musk rats, which, in the market, netted him from three to eight cents apiece. The principal business of our subject has been that of general farming and stock raising. He has always met with more of less success and is now nicely located on an excellent farm, where he has provided himself with good farm buildings.

———•◦•‹‹◦››•◦•———

DR. LEE H. BUGBEE, one of the popular young business men of Pipestone, Minnesota, is a dentist by profession, and is actively engaged in the practice of that art. He located in the city in 1883, where he has since continued in business. He is a native of Pomfret, Windsor county, Vermont, where he was born April 26, 1860.

The parents of the subject of our sketch were Austin and Betsey A. (Stewart) Bugbee, the father being a native of Vermont and the mother of New Hampshire. The father was reared on a farm, in which line of occupation he has continued throughout his life, being now engaged in that business in Sharon, Vermont. He has been a man of extensive influence in his native place and and has held several offices, among them being that of select man, town clerk and justice of the peace. The mother died in 1864. In the father's family there were three children—Clara M., now Mrs. Frank Tacher; Elsie I., now Mrs. Ira B. Johnson; and Dr. Lee H. Our subject has, however, two half-sisters—Carrie A. and Minnie A. Austin Bugbee was the son of Rufus and Eliza (Henry) Bugbee, the former a native of Vermont and the latter born in Canada. Rufus was a farmer throughout his life, which was spent principally in the State of Vermont; he died in 1874, and his wife died

in 1876. Rufus had a family of whom four children are now living—Austin, Edwin, Justin and Herman. Rufus was the son of Abial Bugbee, a native of Connecticut and a farmer by occupation. Abial Bugbee settled in Vermont before it became a State and lived in that country until he died. He was a man of patriotic spirit, a colonel in the Revolutionary War and a soldier in the French and Indian War for a number of years, holding the military title of colonel. The Bugbee family are of Welsh descent. Betsey A. Stewart, the mother of our subject, was the daughter of Hazen and Harriet (Elliot) Stewart, both natives of Grafton, New Hampshire, near which place they were engaged in farming. Hazen Stewart removed to Vermont when he was a young man and made that State his home until his death, in 1886, his wife's death preceding his by some thirteen years. Mr. and Mrs. Stewart had a family of five children, three of whom are now living—Dr. C. L., Dr. H. E. and Maria. Hazen Stewart was the son of Gardner Stewart, a native of Scotland, who came to America with his parents when he was young and settled in New Hampshire.

The subject of our sketch was reared on the home farm until he was twelve years of age. Up to this time he had been given some advantages for obtaining an education in the common schools. On attaining the age of twelve years he worked out on adjoining farms and to some extent in sawmills, continuing in these lines of employment until he was twenty-one years of age. During this time the winter months had been spent in school and he had obtained a good common-school education. On attaining his majority he commenced reading medicine with his uncle, Dr. C. L. Stewart, continuing in that gentleman's office for one year. He then entered the office of Dr. Abbot, a dentist, with whom he continued some eight months. He then came to Gilman, Iroquois county, Illinois, where he studied dentistry with Dr. I. B. Johnson, continuing with him some six months. From thence he removed to Dell Rapids and Egan, Dakota, where he engaged in the active practice of dentistry. · Remaining a few months in those places, he then came to Pipestone and established himself in business, continuing his branch office at Dell Rapids and Egan, Dakota, for some time. Our subject is the only resident dentist in the county and has built up a large and increasing practice.

In September, 1885, Dr. Bugbee was united in marriage with Miss Lillie E. Hood, of Sharon, Vermont, and a daughter of Amos and Betsey Hood. Mrs. Bugbee died in January, 1887, at Pipestone, and was buried in the beautiful cemetery near that city. She was an exemplary Christian lady and was a member of the Baptist church, in which she occupied a prominent place. In every way possible to her she rendered assistance in the work of that society. For some time she was a member of the church choir and was a member of the Ladies' Aid Society.

Dr. Bugbee is a stanch temperance man, and besides being a member of the Good Templars' Society, is an ardent supporter of the principles of the prohibition party. In social and religious circles he exerts a wide influence and is a member of the Baptist church of Pipestone. In company with Dr. Merrill our subject built his present elegant office building on Hiawatha street.

⚬—⚬—⟡—⟨⟨⟡⟩⟩—⟡—⚬—⚬

WILLIAM L. TAYLOR, one of the substantial farmers of Mountain Lake township, Cottonwood county, Minnesota, is a native of Westfield, Chautauqua county, New York, where he was born February 12, 1832. His parents were of Scotch

descent and were born in Ireland. Their names were Thomas and Jane (Cosgrove) Taylor.

The subject of our sketch resided on a farm with his parents and attended the district schools until he was twenty-one years of age. He then commenced working at the carpenter's trade in the vicinity of his home in New York State, to which State the parents had come in early life. After a year our subject removed to Belvidere, . Illinois, and worked at his trade there and at Rockford for two years. In September, 1856, he went to Winona, Minnesota, where he was married the following year. In the spring of 1858 he removed to Wabasha county, and March 12th pre-empted government land and resided thereon for six years. In the mean time, however, he engaged to some extent in work at his trade in the city of Rochester. After the six years had expired he sold his farm and purchased property in that city. In 1873 he came to Cottonwood county, trading his Rochester property for farming land on sections 13 and 14 of Mountain Lake township. He has now about two hundred acres of land, with one hundred and twenty acres under cultivation, five acres of a fine grove of trees of his own planting, and good farm buildings. Our subject has devoted his time to farming ever since coming to the township, with the exception of four years during the grasshopper raids, during which time he worked at his trade in various localities. Our subject has taken a prominent interest in all matters of a public nature, has been chairman of the board of supervisors four years, and has also been county commissioner and school treasurer. He is a man of strictly temperance principles, and is an old-time republican. He is a member of the Methodist Episcopal church.

Mr. Taylor was married September 15, 1857, to Miss Julia Griffing, daughter of

Charles D. and Zelinda C. (Dennison) Griffing, natives of Kentucky. Miss Julia Griffing was born in Ashworth, Kentucky, September 13, 1836. This union has been blessed with the following-named children—Edith J., Mary A., Clara I., Lettie M., John H. and William E. Edith married William McMahill, and resides in Blue Earth county, Minnesota. Mary married J. B. Jones, and is now a resident of Garfield county, Washington Territory.

HEINRICH LEDER, a resident of Mountain Lake township, Cottonwood county, Minnesota, is the son of Christof and Caroline Leder, natives of northern Germany. He was born in Dohnsen, Germany, July 23, 1831. His early life was spent on a farm with his parents. Until fourteen years of age he attended the public schools and then assisted his parents in work on the farm until 1855. In this year he came to the United States, first locating at Cape Girardeau, 150 miles below St. Louis, where he worked at his trade, that of a stone mason, during the winter. In the spring he came to St. Paul and during the summer worked at the mason's trade, and in the fall and winter was engaged as a plasterer. This he followed until the fall of the next year. He then went to Le Sueur county, Minnesota, and bought eighty acres of land, on which he lived until 1871. He then sold out and came to Cottonwood county, purchasing 160 acres of land in Mountain Lake township. He also took a homestead of eighty acres on the same section where he now lives. He has made valuable improvements and has a comfortable frame house and commodious and substantial stable.

Mr. Leder was married near Cape Girardeau, December 25, 1855, to Christine Hamann, daughter of Henry and Sophia (Gravae) Hamann, natives of Germany. This lady was born in that country December 8, 1835. Mr. and Mrs. Leder have been blessed with the following-named children—Albert, John, Emil, Henry, Frederick, August, William, Philip, Caroline, Sophia, Charles and Christian. All of the children are living except Albert, Emil, August, Sophia and Christian. Albert and Emil were frozen to death, the former being thirteen years old and the latter eleven. These two sons were with their father drawing wood on the 12th of February, 1872. They were hauling wood from the timber nine miles distant, and had drawn it all home except one small load. The two boys desired their father to let them go after this last load. The winter weather had been very severe and the father feared to let them go alone for the wood. He did not want to go himself, as he could earn two dollars a day shoveling snow on the railroad. The boys, however, insisted and finally overcame his scruples, and he agreed to let them carry out their plans. On thinking the matter over, however, he again hesitated, fearful lest his sons might be lost in case a storm came up, and withdrew his consent, but again they persuaded him and insisted that it was best to go at once, for by waiting a few days longer the roads would be drifted full of snow. He again reluctantly gave his consent, and started for his work on the railroad. He had not gone far, however, until he became so worried over this matter that he returned to the house and advised the boys not to proceed on so dangerous a journey. They were very anxious, however, to carry out their plan of going for the wood, and he withdrew his objections and allowed them to proceed as they desired. Mr. Leder went to his work and labored with a heavy heart during the morning hours. After noon he consulted with one of his fellow-workmen, related the circumstances, and told him that he felt so badly that he could not work, and believed he would return home. The fellow-laborer told him that there was no danger, as his brother had gone to the same place for wood, and would probably be with the boys. So Mr. Leder, resting a little more quietly and trying to drown his fears, continued work until about the middle of the afternoon, when a terrible snow storm came up. He was compelled to quit work and return home. Night came on and his sons did not put in an appearance. Morning dawned and still the sons were absent. Determined to find the boys if possible, the father started out to procure help, but was driven back by the intense severity of the storm. The following day he obtained assistance and started to find the whereabouts of his sons. He found the sled about three miles from home, but apparently the boys had unhitched the horses and allowed them to wander off by themselves. The team was tracked some distance to a large slough, where they were found stuck fast in the snow and frozen solid. The little party then followed the track of the boys for some eleven miles and found them locked in each others' arms, frozen to death. Apparently they had in their wanderings passed near a neighbor's house but did not succeed in reaching shelter. This was one of the saddest losses that has ever fallen to the lot of Mr. Leder, and he has never quite got over the loss of his sons. His son John married Helenus Chauler, and resides on a farm in Brown county.

The subject of our sketch has passed through many hard experiences since coming to Cottonwood county. He has lost considerable by grasshopper raids, and also by storm and fire. In 1881 the roof blew off his stable, and two horses were frozen to death, besides several head of cattle were so badly frost-bitten that they died a short time after. In June, 1879, our subject and his family were attending religious services when his house took fire and was burned to the ground. Everything in the shape of household goods was destroyed, and worse than all there was no insurance on the building or contents. This was a heavy loss and took a great deal of courage for our subject to continue in this country and try to recover his lost fortunes. He has kept sturdily and manfully at work, and has been gradually building anew his lost fortunes until to-day he is quite well-to-do and surrounded with the evidences of prosperity and success. He is a man of excellent character, and is energetic and public-spirited. He is esteemed by all who know him.

HOMER C. WING is a member of the firm of Francisco, Pride & Wing, proprietors of the Blue Earth City flouring mills of Blue Earth City, Faribault county, Minnesota. He was born in Cass county, Illinois, in the year 1858, and was the son of Benjamin and Cynthia (Smith) Wing, natives of New York and Illinois, respectively.

Our subject was reared on a farm and was given good common-school education. His early life was quite varied in its experiences, and he resided in numerous locations, and engaged in milling business in Hokah, Minnesota, and also in Minneapolis. On coming to this city he entered his present partnership, and purchased the Blue Earth City mills. Our subject has charge of this property, and has proven one of the most successful of managers.

Mr. Wing was married in 1883 to Miss Frances L. Styles, by whom he has had three children—Ethel B., Lulu and Perry L.

AY LaDUE, one of the prominent citizens of Luverne, Rock county, Minnesota, was born in Chautauqua county, New York, April 7, 1827. His father, Joshua LaDue, was one of the pioneer settlers of that county.

The subject of our sketch remained under the parental roof throughout his early life, receiving a fair common school education. In 1847 he engaged in the mercantile business in company with F. P. Ishenwood in Fredonia, New York. The firm did business in that city for some five years. In 1850 Mr. LaDue went to Sherman in the same State, and in company with A. D. Leet commenced in the mercantile business in that city. In 1853 he was appointed postmaster, and held that position until the fall of 1857, when he resigned, with a view of making Minnesota his future home. In 1858, in company with A. D. Leet, he commenced business in Rochester, Minnesota, and continued a resident of that city until 1862. At this time the partnership was dissolved and the stock closed out. On account of ill-health Mr. LaDue then started out on the road with a team and began carrying a wholesale stock of notions. He continued in this line for I. R. Johnson & Co. for some five years, and then engaged with the old and popular house of Whitfield Brothers & Co., of New York City. For some twenty years he represented this firm.

Mr. LaDue was married in 1850 to Miss Jennie Buell, a native of New York State. This marriage has been blessed with the following-named children — Clarence M., Lemont, Mabel, John J. and Albert. The son, John J., is engaged in business in Luverne, and Albert is employed in the Rock County Bank, of that place.

Mr. LaDue is quite an extensive farmer, owning some seven hundred and ten acres of land, lying just southeast of the city. He has this under excellent cultivation and thoroughly improved. He owns some forty-two head of horses, many of them of excellent breed. He also has 140 head of cattle, among them being a number of full-blooded Durhams. Associated with him in his farm enterprise he has his two oldest sons.

JACOB TOBERT, a resident of section 20, Rose Hill township, Cottonwood county, Minnesota, is a native of Russia, and was born March 5, 1850.

The parents of the subject of this sketch were Peter and Catharine (Oust) Tobert, natives of Russia. The father was a farmer, and lived in his native land until his death, which occurred in 1865. The mother is still living in that country. The grandfather of our subject was governor of the southern province of Russia for three years, and the family were quite prominent in Russian affairs.

Up to twenty-three years of age Jacob Tobert assisted his father on the home farm. He received a good common-school education, and was married in 1873, after which he worked on a farm for some three years. He then emigrated to America, the land of equal rights, of which he had heard so much. Coming to Minnesota he rented a farm near Heron Lake, and from thence came to his present residence in Rose Hill township. He took a pre-emption of 160 acres, and during grasshopper times changed it to a homestead. He has some of the best improvements found on any farm in the township, and is one of the most systematic and careful farmers in the region. He gives his attention principally to the raising of grain, but has several head of cattle and horses. He is a man of large experience, has a well-trained mind, and is highly esteemed by all who know him. In politics he is a republican, and is a stanch member of the Lutheran church.

Mr. Tobert was married January 15, 1873, to Miss Maria, daughter of H. Staodaten, a native of Russia. This union has been blessed with seven children—Maria (deceased), John (deceased), Catharine (deceased), Paulina, Leonard, Henry and Phenia. Mrs. Tobert died October 15, 1883. She was a lady of estimable character, and her death was mourned by a large circle of friends.

JOHN E. JOHNSON, a thrifty and reliable farmer of Scandia township, Murray county, Minnesota, was born in Ostre Toten, Norway, November 28, 1856, his parents being Even and Agnette (Anderson) Johnson. In the father's family there were the following-named children — Frederick, now in Monroe county, Wisconsin; Martha, now the wife of Jonas Lindblom; our subject and Even E.

Previous to coming to America in 1869, our subject remained with his parents in Norway and attended the common schools between the ages of eight and twelve years. On coming to the United States at the date just mentioned, the family lived on a rented farm fourteen miles from St. Peter for two years, and then came directly to Murray county, where they took a homestead on the northeast quarter of section 22, Scandia township. The first year they built a dug-out house in which they lived until 1877. Some land was broken the first year, and he and his father went to Cottonwood county and worked on the Northwestern railroad until haying time, when they returned to the claim and put up some hay and then went with an ox team to St. Peter, one hundred miles distant, to get provisions. They were on the road about two weeks. The next spring our subject went to St. Peter for pro-visions, and was away from home for five weeks as there was so much rain that some of the streams were so swollen that he could not possibly cross them, but had to go about fifty miles out of his regular course. Several of the streams he crossed were so high that he had to tie the wagon-box to the wagon and swim the oxen. This was a very trying journey and one which no one would care to repeat a second time. When he started, his people had twenty-five pounds of flour. This, of course, was gone long before his return, and as their neighbors were as destitute as they were, none could be borrowed. During this time the family would have actually suffered from hunger if it had not been that his brother Even killed some wild fowls and found some of their eggs, on which the family managed to subsist until our subject's return. In 1873 they raised a small crop, and then for four years the grasshoppers destroyed nearly everything, so that they had only just about enough wheat to make flour for the family. Since that time they have had good crops and have done very well indeed. Our subject now owns a fine farm of 160 acres with about eighty acres under cultivation, a comfortable frame house and frame barn 24x48 feet in size. He also owns considerable stock. Our subject got a post-office established on his farm and of this he was postmaster until the village of Balaton was started, when the office was removed to that place. Our subject has been quite active in local political affairs, and has held the office of town clerk for ten years, was justice of the peace for several terms, and was school clerk for six or eight years. He is a man of good character, and is an exemplary member of the Norwegian Lutheran church.

May 12, 1884, our subject was married in Tracy, Minnesota, to Miss Carrie Olson, daughter of Martin and Gunhilda (Johnson) Olson, natives of Norway. She was born in Western Toten, Norway, August 29, 1862.

This union has been blessed with two children—Earl Milford and Amy Georgiana.

HELGA THORSEN, who resides on section 30 of Ann township, Cottonwood county, Minnesota, was born in the kingdom of Norway, April 9, 1850. His parents, Thor and Mary (Helgeson) Asleson, were both natives of Norway, The father died in his native land January 13, 1872, and the mother emigrated to America in 1874, locating in the city of Chicago for a short time. She then came to Ann township, where she now lives with her son, the subject of this sketch.

Helga Thorsen assisted his father in work on the home farm until he was twenty-two years of age. He was given a good common-school education, and on attaining the age just mentioned, he came to America, and for a short time worked in a furniture factory in Chicago. Six months after locating in Chicago he went to Indiana, where a half year was spent in chopping in the big woods. His next move was to return to Chicago, and from thence he went to Kendall county, Illinois, where for a year he engaged in agricultural pursuits. He then came to Ann township, Cottonwood county, Minnesota, and located on his present farm of 160 acres. This was in the year 1874, and our subject took his farm first as a pre-emption, afterwards changing it to a tree claim. He has made excellent improvements, and has nearly eleven acres of the finest grove in the township. Among the trees may be found soft maple, elm, white willow, ash and cottonwood. He has also an extensive variety of fruit trees, consisting of apples, plums, and also a large line of berries. He has one of the finest farms, and withal the best improved in the entire county. In connection with his farming operations he is also engaged largely in raising stock. During the early years of his settlement in the county he experienced many backsets in his various enterprises, having his crops destroyed for several years by the grasshoppers. In 1875 his crops were all destroyed, and he was compelled to work in the woods in order to obtain a livelihood. He returned to his farm in the spring of 1876, and seeded forty-six acres. This year also the grasshoppers took the crop, and there was not a bushel harvested from this entire acreage. During the fall he went to Goodhue county, and worked during the harvest season, in order to obtain sufficient means to keep him through the winter. The next spring he plowed twenty acres of ground, and put it into grain, and had an enormous harvest. He had twenty-nine and a half bushels to the acre on one piece. From that time the crops were better, and our subject commenced gathering means, and is now in comfortable circumstances. Mr. Thorsen is a man of good character, honest and industrious, and attends the Lutheran church. In politics he affiliates with the republican party, in the principles of which organization he has believed since making his location in the United States.

GEORGE A. CARNEGIE. This gentleman is one of the leading business men of the city of Pipestone, Minnesota, where he is the proprietor of a first-class feed, sale and livery stable. He located in this city in 1883, and after remaining about six months went to Woonsocket, Dakota, at which place he owned a livery stable and a farm. After remaining in that place about one year he then sold out his interests in that locality and returned to Pipestone, where he has since been engaged in the livery business. On arriving in the city he purchased his present stables just south of the new Calumet hotel. His business is the oldest of the kind in the city and he has made himself popular with the traveling public, as well as local residents.

Mr. Carnegie is a native of Canada, where he was born in 1850. His parents, John and Jane (McGowan) Carnegie, were both natives of Scotland. During their early life they came to Canada, where they were married. The father was a goldsmith by trade and made that his principal occupation throughout life. He is now a resident of Jasper village, Pipestone county, Minnesota, to which place he came in 1888. He is now engaged in operating a jewelry store in that place. When the family first came to Minnesota they located in Fillmore county, where for some time the father was engaged in farming and operating a steam saw-mill. Remaining in Fillmore county until the breaking out of the war, the father then enlisted in the service and served during the continuation of hostilities. After the close of the war he removed to the village of Dresbach, Winona county, Minnesota, on the Mississippi river, where he owned a large steam saw-mill. Remaining in that village for two years, he then went to Hokah, Minnesota, where he engaged as foreman in a large machine shop for somewhat over a year. At the end of that time he returned to his farm in Fillmore county, making that his home for some years. His next move was to Wells, Faribault county, where he built the machine shops of the Southern Minnesota Railroad Company. After two years' residence in Wells he again returned to his farm in Fillmore county. In 1888 he located in Jasper village, as has already been stated. In the father's family there were nine children, eight of whom are now living—Christa, James, Margaret, George, Alexander, John, Frank and Sarah.

The principal part of the early life of our subject was spent on the farm of his father, in Fillmore county, this State. He was given good school privileges and acquired a good common-school education. Until fifteen years of age he remained at home, and at that age went to Howard county, Iowa, and engaged in farm work. He made this his principal business until 1884, since which time he has confined his attention exclusively to the livery business. He first purchased a farm of eighty acres in Fillmore county, in 1878, and after farming that land for one year sold out. On returning to Minnesota from Iowa he settled on a farm in Rock county, where he homesteaded 160 acres in Rosedale township. Here he resided, following agriculture, for seven years, at the end of which time he came to Pipestone City, and thence to Dakota, as was before stated. In 1884 he returned to Pipestone, and has since been successfully operating a well-equipped livery. Since coming to the village Mr. Carnegie has become quite popular as a liveryman. He has made several investments in city property with good success, having purchased several lots on which he built houses and then sold out at good advantage, making a very satisfactory profit on his investments. He also traded property for a dwelling house in the city, which he rents.

Mr. Carnegie was married in 1883 to Mrs. Nellie Colburn, by whom he has had two daughters—Mabel J. and Nellie. In politics the subject of our sketch affiliates with the republican party and is one of the most active business men of the city.

———————

JOHN HOFFMAN is a leading and substantial farmer of Royal township, Lincoln county, Minnesota, and is the son of Charles and Mary (Stalsman) Hoffman, natives of West Prussia.

The place of the nativity of the subject of our sketch is found in West Prussia, where he was born June 21, 1852. His parents were farmers by occupation, and our subject was reared a farmer's boy. He was given good educational advantages in the district schools, in which he continued his studies until fourteen years of age. At the age of seventeen he learned the tailor's trade, and when eighteen came to the United States, first stopping at Chicago, Illinois, where he worked at his trade for twelve years. At the end of that time he came directly to Lincoln county and purchased 280 acres of railroad land in Royal township. He came to the county in the spring of 1883, and has since been a permanent resident.

John Hoffman was married in Chicago, February 12, 1878, to Celia Pekorski, a daughter of John and Mary Pekorski, natives of West Prussia. This lady was born in the same place, in April, 1861. Mr. and Mrs. Hoffman have been blessed with the following-named children—Bennie, who died in Chicago; Mary, Frank, Stanislaus, Vina and Francis. The family occupies a prominent place in the social affairs of the township, and are leading members of the Catholic church.

Since coming to the township Mr. Hoffman has identified himself with all matters which have tended to the improvement of various public enterprises, and has served his constituents in various official capacities. His farming operations have been attended with fair success, although he has not made as much money here as in Chicago. However, he has a very nice farm, has a good frame house one and a half stories high, a large barn 18x60 feet in size, and has about 155 acres of land under cultivation. He has considerable stock, and is giving considerable of his attention to raising good cattle. The business abilities of Mr. Hoffman are of good character, and, whatever he turns his hand to, meets with more or less success. Possessed of excellent character, genial and public-spirited, he has won his way into the esteem and respect of all his fellow-citizens.

CHARLES ELG is a reliable and enterprising farmer of Selma township, Cottonwood county, Minnesota. He is a native of Sweden, being born in Kromnoberg, November 5, 1860. His parents were Andrew and Augusta Elg, natives of the same country, where the father was engaged in blacksmithing. The parents were in well-to-do circumstances, and gave our subject a good common-school education up to fourteen years of age. From that time until 1880 our subject worked in his father's blacksmith shop.

In 1880, thinking that they might better their condition in the new world, the Elg family left their native land and came to the United States, locating within a brief time on section 14 of Selma township, Cottonwood county, Minnesota. The father took a homestead of 160 acres, and our subject made his home with his parents, assisting in work on the farm, until 1888. He then purchased eighty acres on section 13, and now has fifty acres in crops. On this eighty the father and son are in partnership, and are conducting an active farming business. Our subject has two brothers and two sisters—Oscar, Henneng, Alma and Sigri, our subject being the oldest in the family.

Since coming to the county Mr. Elg and his father have labored hard to put their farms under good cultivation, and have thoroughly stocked and improved them. They have several head of horses and a large herd of cattle, and have just completed a neat and commodious frame dwelling-house on the homestead, and have besides this a granary and good stable. In spite of the fact that they have met with various losses by hail, etc., since coming to the county, and that they were poor when they made their location, they have gradually worked into good circumstances, and have now an excellent farm, provided with comfortable and valuable improvements. Our subject has taken an active interest in public matters, and has always assisted in political affairs of his township. He is a member of the board of school directors. He is a young man of good character, pleasant and agreeable, and is one of the most energetic and business-like farmers in the township.

GUY S. STEDMAN is engaged extensively in farming on section 6, of Cameron township, Murray county, Minnesota. His native State is Iowa, where he was born June 29, 1854.

Mr. Stedman's parents were C. A. and Elizabeth (Robinson) Stedman, the father a native of Vermont, and the mother a native of Pennsylvania. The parents came to the State of Iowa in about 1852, where the father was a teacher and lawyer by profession. He engaged to some extent in farming for a number of years in connection with his other business. In the father's family there were eight children, our subject being the fourth in order of birth.

Until fifteen years of age our subject assisted his father in every way possible, and was given a good common-school education. Two years longer he continued his residence under the parental roof, and then left home to carve out his fortunes for himself. He engaged in work at the brick-maker's trade, in which line he continued until twenty-three years of age. He then rented a farm, and engaged in its operation for two years. In 1879 he came to Murray county by team, and took a pre-emption on section 20 of Cameron township. After a two years' residence there, he sold out and took a homestead, on which he now lives, on section 6.

Mr. Stedman was married August 17, 1875, to Mary J. Gable, a native of Ohio. Her parents are still living and residing in La Crosse, Wisconsin. Mr. and Mrs. Stedman have been blessed with eight children, six of whom are now living.

The subject of our sketch is a man of strong temperance principles, and affiliates with the prohibition party. He is a man of excellent character, and is one of Cameron township's most public-spirited citizens. He has held various township offices, among them being that of assessor, supervisor, each of which he held for three years, and also school director.

DR. EZRA M. CARR, one of the leading and most popular physicians of Pipestone county, located in Pipestone City, March 15, 1878, where he has ever since been actively engaged in the practice of his profession. In reality he is the pioneer physician of the county. Since his location here he has made many long rides to attend to patients. During the early days, as he was the only physician in the county, he was sometimes called to travel sixty miles to attend a case. He became well known and popular throughout the entire southwestern part of Minnesota. Having spent a successful career in his profession and having performed many radical cures and difficult operations he has built up an enviable reputation and is still sometimes called to ride forty miles to see a patient.

Dr. Carr is a native of Canada, where he was born June 12, 1838. His parents were James H. and Laura (Rose) Carr, the father a native of Washington county, New York, and the mother born in Canada. The father was a millwright by trade and at an early date settled at Madison, Wisconsin. Later he removed to Eau Claire, where he resided until his death in 1884. The mother is still living in the last-named city. In the father's family there were nine children, six of whom are now living—Dr. Ezra M., Mary, now Mrs. Childs; Hannah, now Mrs. Olds; Martha, now Mrs. Jenkins; Laura, now Mrs. Johnson, and Wesley. James, another son, was a soldier in the War of the Rebellion and died in Andersonville prison. Ezekiel served in the Union army and died from the effects of wounds at Madison, Wisconsin, to which place he had returned at the close of the war.

The parental home remained the abiding place of our subject until he was nineteen years of age, up to which time he had been given good educational advantages in the public schools of Wisconsin. He attended the university at Madison and took a scientific course, graduating with the degree of B. S. Prior to this he had served three years as an apprentice to the trade of millwrighting. After his graduation he read medicine at Madison and also taught school during the summer months in Missouri and Wisconsin. He attended lectures at Mc-Donald's College at St. Louis during each winter and graduated from that institution in 1859. He then went to Texas and engaged in the business of selling tobaccos until the breaking out of the war. Returning to Wisconsin he commenced the practice of medicine in the northeastern part of the State, continuing in that locality until 1863, in which year he commenced work for the United States government in the quartermaster's department, in which he continued about a year. He was then transferred to duty in the hospital, in which he successfully practiced for eleven months. From thence he returned home and after a short time went to Indianapolis, Indiana, where he practiced for three years and was to some extent engaged in the mercantile business. In 1870 he removed to Minnesota, first stopping at Minneapolis, where he opened an office and engaged in practice. Remaining in that city until 1878 he then came to Pipestone and built on the place where he now lives on Olive street, his house being the sixth building put up in the city. He has invested to some extent in other properties and now owns another dwelling-house in the city.

In 1865 Mr. Carr was married to Miss Jennie Bell, of Madison, Wisconsin. One child has blessed this union—Ida B.

The subject of our sketch has been one of the most intelligent of Pipestone's benefactors. He has rendered material aid in many ways in the development and advancement of the city's interests. He is one of the best known and most widely respected citizens of Pipestone. The political affairs of the municipal and county government have attracted more or less of his attention and he has held several positions of trust and responsibility. He has been court commissioner, register of deeds of the county, village recorder, and is at present county physician. In his profession the doctor is at present a prohibitionist. He is a leading and influential member of the Masonic and Odd Fellow fraternities and occupies a prominent position in the Southwestern Minnesota Medical Society. In his profession Dr. Carr has met with remarkable success in all its departments. He is a skilled surgeon and a physician of undoubted ability. Thoroughly educated, a gentleman in every sense of the word, energetic and public-spirited, he has firmly planted himself in the respect and esteem of his fellow-citizens.

ANDREW O. ANDERSON is an influential farmer who resides on section 24 of Ann township, Cottonwood county, Minnesota. The place of his nativity is to be found in the kingdom of Norway, where he was born November 2, 1837. His parents were natives of Norway, their names being Ole and Isabel (Hoganson) Anderson. In the father's family there were nine children—Hogan, Ole, Thomas, Anton, Andrew, Isabel, Rachel, Helen and Andrew O. The parents emigrated to America in 1840, finding a home in Racine county, Wisconsin, where they resided until their death. The father was a farmer by occupation and was a well-to-do and influential citizen of his township.

The early life of the subject of our sketch was spent on the home farm, where he was given good educational advantages in the district schools. At the age of twenty-one years he went to Beloit and worked at the blacksmith's trade for about a year. A year and a half thereafter were then spent with his parents, and then he engaged in black-smithing, following that occupation for two years. In the spring of 1860 Andrew went to Nevada, where he remained for two years in different lines of business. He then went to Missouri, whence, after a year's residence, he went to Illinois, into which State he took a drove of cattle. One month later he went back to his old home in Wisconsin and lived with his parents for some three years. Then, in the spring of 1871, he came to Minnesota, finding a location in Cotton-wood county, where he now lives. He took a homestead of 160 acres, and has since been actively and energetically engaged in improving the same, having provided it with an excellent frame house and other good buildings. He has three acres of an excellent grove of trees. Our subject's life since coming to Cottonwood county has not been all success, nor has it all been failure, but he has met with his share of backsets and hardships such as usually come to pioneer life. For several years the grasshoppers ravaged his fields and destroyed nearly all his crops, obliging our subject to go elsewhere to earn a living. For several years he raised no grain whatever, and finally, after the disappearance of the grasshoppers, he was met with success in raising grain, and since that time has placed himself in good circumstances. In connection with his farming operations he is also engaged in raising stock,

and has several head of good horses and cattle, and also a large herd of fine sheep.

The subject of our sketch was married December 26, 1875, to Julia Narveson, a native of Norway. Some years ago her parents emigrated to the United States, and her father is now a resident of Ann township. Mr. and Mrs. Anderson have been blessed with one child, Oscar Arnold, born August 6, 1877. This family ranks high in the esteem of the citizens of Ann township. They are consistent and influential members of the Lutheran church.

The political faith of the subject of our sketch is fixed in the principles promulgated by the republican party. He is a man of much public spirit, and always takes an interest in affairs pertaining to the general welfare. He has held several township offices, among them being that of clerk and treasurer.

———◦◦❦◦◦———

REV. HENRY JAJESKI, the present able and efficient pastor of the Catholic church at Wilno, Lincoln county, Minnesota, is the son of Henry and Catharine (Wisniewski) Jajeski, natives of Poland. In about 1867 the parents left their native land, emigrating to the United States, and finding a location in Winona, Minnesota. Here the father engaged in buying wheat, and became one of the prominent and influential citizens of that place.

Rev. Henry Jajeski was born in Pomerania, Poland, November 27, 1859. When he was about eight years of age he came with his parents to the United States, locating with them in Winona, Minnesota, where he was given excellent educational advantages in the Catholic school, operated and conducted by the sisters of the Catholic church. He continued his studies in that institution for two years, and was then sent to St. John's University, in Stearns county, where, after a thorough course of study for five years, he was graduated from the classical course in the year 1878. For some years he had been training his mind and directing his life toward the Catholic clergy. In order to be thoroughly fitted and prepared for work in this line, after his graduation at St. John's, he went to Grand Seminary, in Montreal, Canada. For five and a half years he pursued his studies in that institution, and, graduating therefrom, was ordained a priest in the Catholic church December 25, 1883. A few weeks later he was given charge of the churches at Minnesota Lake, Wells and Mapleton, in the southern part of Minnesota. He remained one year on this charge, accomplishing great success, and added considerable to the strength of his church in these localities. At the expiration of the year's service he came to Wilno, where for three years he had charge of the church, and also one at Tyler and at Lake Benton. After three years had elapsed he was made pastor of the church at Wilno, over which he has since presided. His church has a membership of some 160 families, all of whom are devotedly attached to their beloved pastor. He is a man of the highest attainments, having been thoroughly educated both in literature and theology, and is well fitted for the successful management of the manifold duties which devolve upon him as the pastor of a large and increasing congregation. Besides his education attained in school, he is also peculiarly fitted for his high calling by excellent natural endowments. He is a genial, courteous gentleman, and, both as a man and pastor, is held in the highest esteem. He is a thorough scholar, and in his pulpit ministrations calls assistance from a wide range of diversified knowledge and study. He is a deep thinker, a careful and clear reasoner. He is a powerful speaker, and by the force of his eloquence carries conviction into the minds of all who hear him. Believing thoroughly in the principles on which his church is founded, he calls to his aid in their defense and proclamation a resistless array of thought clothed in ripe, scholarly words. His position among his fellow-citizens, too, is without reproach, and he is acknowledged as one of the most exemplary citizens, as well as one of the truest representatives of his exalted calling. Being possessed of a wide acquaintance among the people of Lincoln county, he is accomplishing a great amount of good and building up and strengthening the church organization over which he presides as pastor.

※

FRANZ TOEVS, a prominent resident of Mountain Lake township, Cottonwood county, Minnesota, was born in Prussia, April 3, 1812. His parents were Frank and Elizabeth (Dick) Toevs, natives of Prussia. The mother died when our subject was about seven years old, the father died in 1833.

Mr. Toevs remained with his father throughout his early life, and when he had reached young manhood he commenced clerking in a store in Marionberg by Dantzig, where he continued eleven years. At twenty-eight years of age he went to Russia and became the proprietor of a large farm, and also owned and operated a large lumber yard in the village of Pordoneu. He went to this place with a colony of Germans, who had been induced to settle there by the Russian government who desired to have some civilizing and enlightening influence among the Russian natives of that locality. They were promised exemption from military duty; but after they had improved the country materially and assisted in the civilization and building up and improving of the Russian inhabitants, the law was so changed that these Germans were obliged to either leave the country within ten years or be subject to military duty. Our subject, with hundreds of others, became dissatisfied with this state of affairs and this manifest injustice which was about to be meted out to himself and his fellow-Germans, so he sold out and emigrated to the United States with a small colony, settling in Cottonwood county, Minnesota, August 9, 1875. Our subject was the leader of the colony, and, coming to his new location, purchased a section of land. He now only owns a quarter section, however, having given the other three quarters to three sons. His own place is very finely improved and provided with a good large barn and other buildings, and a well-built and commodious dwelling-house. He has a beautiful grove of his own planting, has a thrifty apple orchard, and has raised more fruit from his apple trees than is needed for the use of his own family.

The subject of our sketch was married in Prussia, in 1839, to Miss Augusta Johnson, who lived only about seven months after her marriage. Mr. Toevs' second marriage occurred in Pordoneu, Russia, April 9, 1840, on which date he was wedded to Sarah Wall, who died April 10, 1850. Mr. Toevs was married again June 10, 1850, in Pordoneu, to Susana Avaikantin, daughter of Jacob and Susana (Weines) Avaikantin, natives of Prussia. This lady was born in Russia, November 10, 1816, and, when our subject married her, was the widow of Peter Enns, by whom she had five children, all dead except Peter and Margaret, the former married and a resident of Russia. Margaret married John Enns, and resides in Kansas. Mr. Toevs by his third marriage had two children—Frank and Katie (deceased). Frank married Margaret Isaak, and resides in Cottonwood county. Mr. Toevs' third wife died October 19, 1855, and our subject was married February 21, 1856, to Miss Elizabeth Dick, daughter of Nicholi and Anna (Hildebrand) Dick, natives of Russia, where she was born March 19, 1836. This last union

has been blessed with the following named children—Nicholi, John, Peter (deceased), Jacob, George, Peter, Henry (deceased), Anna, Elizabeth and Henry. Nicholi married Anna Dick, and now resides in the village of Mountain Lake, where he is engaged in Sunday-school mission work. John married Augusta Enns, and is engaged in the machinery business in Mountain Lake. Jacob wedded Lena Lohrenzend, and now resides on a farm in Watonwan county.

The subject of our sketch is one of the most prominent citizens of Mountain Lake township, and has been one of the most active and public-spirited men of his town. He is a man of considerable means, and is an influential member of the Mennonite church.

———————

WILLIAM D. BITLEY is a prominent farmer and stock raiser, located on section 9, of Lake Sarah township, Murray county, Minnesota. He came to his present location in 1878, where he has since lived.

Mr. Bitley was born in Saratoga county, New York, in the village of Monroe, July 14, 1853. His father was James Bitley, a farmer by occupation, and a native of New York. He died when our subject was seven years of age. The mother's maiden name was Julia Spraker, who died when our subject was seventeen years old. In the father's family there were twelve children—Maria B., Edward, Caroline, Mary, Elizabeth, Belle, Fanny, Benjamin, James (who was burned to death), Agnes and William D.

The subject of our sketch was reared in his native county, in the State of New York, until he was seventeen years of age, when, on the death of his mother, he went to Branchport, in the western part of Yates county, where he resided fourteen years with the family of an uncle. He attended school during a portion of this time, and obtained a good, practical education. Remaining in the State of New York until 1877, he came west to Minnesota, purchasing his land in Murray county. He remained in the city of Faribault for a brief time during the following winter, and then went back to the State of New York, where he remained a year, after which he came to his present location.

March 13, 1889, Mr. Bitley was married to Miss Maggie White, a native of Marquette county, Wisconsin. This lady was given an excellent education, and during several years taught school.

Mr. Bitley is one of the representative citizens of Lake Sarah township, and by virtue of his careful, systematic and economical habits has accumulated considerable means. In religious belief he is in harmony with the Universalist church.

* · ◆ · ❘◆❘ · ◆ · ·

LE O. KNUDSON, one of the leading and most influential farmers of Ann township, Cottonwood county, Minnesota, resides on section 24. He was born April 30, 1854, in the kingdom of Norway.

The parents of the subject of our sketch were Ole and Bertha (Halverson) Knudson, who emigrated from Norway to America in 1873, locating for a brief period in Wisconsin. The same year they came to Houston county, Minnesota, and thence removed to Fillmore county, where they remained four years and in which county the mother died. Our subject and his father then went to Redwood county, from whence they came to Ann township, Cottonwood county, where our subject has resided ever since. The father afterwards removed to Pope county, Minnesota, where he now lives on a homestead.

The subject of our sketch followed his father in the various moves throughout the

West, finally locating in Cottonwood county, as stated. He has a fine homestead of one hundred and sixty acres, on which he has good buildings and five acres of a nice grove of trees. He is engaged in farming, and in connection therewith also raises a good grade of horses and cattle. In his early life he received a good common-school education, and has taught four terms of school. For two years he was agent for the text-books used in the public schools.

Mr. Knudson was married March 31, 1884, to Miss Ella Erickson, a native of Norway. This union has been blessed with one child—Lillie.

The subject of our sketch has affiliated for some years with the republican party, and has held various official positions within the gift of his fellow-citizens. He has been a delegate to the republican county convention several times and has always taken a lively interest in matters of a political nature. He has been township clerk and justice of the peace for several years. The former position he still holds. He was postmaster of the West Brook postoffice of Cottonwood county for some five years. Mr. Knudson is one of the representative farmers of his nationality in the county, and among his people, and in fact among all citizens of the county, he wields a strong influence for the upbuilding and promotion of public interests. He is a man of excellent characteristics, is well liked both as a man and citizen, and is looked upon as one of the leading spirits of the township and county.

· · ◆ · ❘◆❘ · ◆ · ·

DANIEL E. SWEET, one of the very first settlers in Pipestone county, and one of the founders of Pipestone City, was born in Pennsylvania, April 10, 1838, and was the fourth son of Lorenzo L. and Rachel Burr Sweet. He went to Wisconsin with his parents, and in 1860 to Iowa. He married Amarancy Hatch, who died in 1870. They had one child, which died in infancy. Daniel Sweet enlisted in the Eleventh Iowa Infantry when the war broke out, and was promoted to the office of color-sergeant, in which capacity he served until the close of hostilities. He then settled in Cedar county, Iowa, where he remained until the spring of 1872, when he removed to Lyon county, Iowa. In the spring of 1874 he came to Pipestone county, Minnesota, and entered as a claim land which afterward became a part of the original plat of Pipestone City. He was an active, energetic man, and was a prominent factor in the early growth and development of both city and county. He held a number of important offices during his residence here, including those of postmaster, county surveyor and probate judge. He remained in Pipestone until November, 1886, when he removed with his family to Jennings, Louisiana, where he still lives, having charge of a line of steamboats.

⎯⎯◆⎯❦⎯◆⎯⎯

AMELIUS E. WOODRUFF is a prominent farmer of Mountain Lake township, Cottonwood county, Minnesota. He is the son of Lyman and Laura (Lee) Woodruff, natives of New York. The father was a farmer by training, but was engaged to some extent in iron mining and contracting. He moved to Minnesota in 1863, and settled in Merriam Park, where they engaged in farming for five or six years. The parents are still living.

Mr. Woodruff, whose name appears at the head of this sketch, was born in Essex county, New York, July 26, 1841. He resided with his parents during the most of the time until he was twenty-eight years of age. He was given a good common-school education, and assisted his father in various lines of business for several years until 1866, when he came

to Minnesota. After five or six years spent in farming with his father at Merriam Park, Mr. Woodruff became the manager of a farm owned by Mr. Culver, at Farmington, near Minneapolis. After one year spent in this employment, our subject accepted a position as foreman of a construction crew on one of the railroads leading into Minneapolis. Continuing in this business for two years he went to St. Paul, and took the contract for grading one of the principal avenues. After this was completed he came to Cottonwood county, and took charge of a large tract of land for Messrs. Merriam and Wilder. This farm was composed of 3,500 acres in one body, and also about four sections near Windom. When our subject came to this locality there was nothing to be seen but wild prairie. He has utilized his genius in improving the farm, and providing it with good buildings. He has now about 850 acres under cultivation, has 250 head of cattle and fifty horses. Our subject is one of the most successful farm managers in southern Minnesota. . He is an apt student of human nature, and is one of the most successful managers of men that we have ever seen. He constantly employs a large force of help, and also has charge of Governor Merriam's farm in Martin county. Mr. Woodruff is one of the most enterprising and public-spirited citizens in the township. All matters of a public nature receive his sanction and earnest support. Whatever tends to the general improvement meets with his hearty assistance, and he takes an active part in all matters of a political nature. He has been chairman of the town board of supervisors, and justice of the peace, in which latter office he has administered the law with rare fidelity to right and justice. He is held in high esteem by all with whom he has to do.

Mr. Woodruff was married in Essex county, New York, in September, 1868, to Miss

Loretta Ware, daughter of Silas and Emily Ware, natives of New York. One child was born to this union, Addie, who died in April, 1870.

VEN E. JOHNSON, a thrifty farmer of Scandia township, Murray county, Minnesota, is the son of Even and Agnette (Anderson) Johnson, natives of Norway. He was born in Ostre Toten, Norway, May 29, 1863.

When our subject was six months old his parents came to the United States, arriving in St. Peter, Minnesota, July 4, 1869. There the family lived with Hans Peterson Roli for a time, and then moved to a farm in Nicollet county, owned by a Mrs. Hanson. This farm the father rented and worked for one year, and then worked another farm on the same section for another year ; then came to Murray county in April, 1871, and took a homestead on the northwest quarter of section 22, Scandia township, where they now live. Our subject followed his father's family in their various migrations, and remained with them until the spring of 1889, when he moved to his own farm, on the southeast quarter of section 16, Scandia township. This farm consists of 120 acres, and was purchased by our subject in 1885, since which time he has continued to improve it, and in the spring of 1888 put up a frame house and barn. He has about seventy acres under cultivation. Mr. Johnson and his father's family were here during the grasshopper raids, and saw very hard times. The first year he and his mother were here alone, the father and brother, John E., being in Nicollet county at work. The family had no flour during the most of one summer, and had to live on game and eggs that they found, that had been laid by the wild fowls. There were only two settlers in sight at this time, and they were as badly off for food as were our subject's fam-

ily. Mr. Johnson has taken an active interest in local politics, and has been township assessor for two years in succession, during 1886 and 1887. He is a good citizen and a member of the Norwegian Lutheran church.

The subject of our sketch was married December 27, 1888, in Scandia township, to Miss Anna M. Anderson, daughter of Otto and Brita (Peterson) Ottosen, natives of Norway. She was born in Fillmore county, Minnesota, June 15, 1865.

NELSON A. HERRICK is a leading farmer and stock raiser in Hansonville township, Lincoln county, Minnesota. He located on a homestead on section 4, in the spring of 1881, purchasing his right to the land on which he settled from Mr. C. Eggen, who is now dead. Eggen came to the county in the fall of 1879, built a small house 12x12 feet in size, and made some other improvements. Mr. Herrick reached his farm on the 21st of September, his wife and family following him in October. He has since been a resident of the township, and has become one of the substantial and most respected citizens. He has been engaged extensively in farming, and has improved his farm by building good buildings, and setting out a large number of trees. He has worked hard and faithfully to bring his farm up to what it now is, one of the best in the township. Altogether he has two hundred acres of land, and besides his general farming he keeps from fifteen to twenty head of Holstein cattle. Mr. Herrick has identified himself closely with all public interests of his locality, and has held the office of town clerk since the organization of the township in 1884. He was also treasurer of the school district, which position he has held since the foundation of the district, Mr. Herrick being the one who originated the petition for its organization. So concerned was he in regard to the allowance of this petition and the establishment of the school district that he went before the board of commissioners personally to see that his petition was allowed. Besides having been interested in township matters, he has also taken an active part in county matters, and has assisted materially in the development of its general interests.

Mr. Herrick was born in Lower Canada, fifty miles east of Montreal, September 17, 1850. He was the son of Lemuel D. and Edna (Preston) Herrick, both of whom were natives of Virginia. The father was reared and educated in that State, and in early life removed to Canada. The parents were both members of the Free-Will Baptist church, and exerted a wide influence for good in the community in which they lived. The subject of our sketch was one of eight children, five of whom grew to manhood—George W., Hiram A., Nelson A., Luther L. and Dorson J. The parents remained in Canada but a few years, and then removed to Marquette county, Wisconsin, where they lived from 1851 until 1864. In the latter year they removed to Black Hawk county, Iowa, remaining there, engaged in farming, until 1879. Removing thence they located in Yellow Medicine county, Minnesota, where the father died June 2, 1880, at the age of sixty-seven years. The mother is still living in that county.

The subject of our sketch followed his parents in their migrations to various places throughout the northwestern country, and was given the advantages of a good common-school education. He assisted his father on the farm, and remained at home until twenty-eight years of age. His education was principally received in Waterloo, Iowa, and when not in school he worked on his father's farm. Prior to this age, in 1873, he was married, and continued his residence

with his parents until 1878, when he removed to Lincoln county.

Mr. Herrick was married February 17, 1873, to Miss Elizabeth Hoyt, a native of Columbia county, Wisconsin, where she was born in the year 1850. This lady was the daughter of Gilman H. Hoyt, a prominent farmer of Wisconsin, and a native of Virginia. He died in 1885. Mrs. Herrick was thoroughly educated in the town of her nativity, and made that her home principally until her marriage. Mr. and Mrs. Herrick have been blessed with five children—Bertha Edna, Cloe Elizabeth (deceased), Rosetta Mable, Luella and George Arnold.

The subject of this sketch is a prominent republican in politics, and takes an active part in the interests of the local organization. He is a man of systematic habits, careful and frugal in all his business affairs, and has accumulated considerable property. He has a pleasant and hospitable family, and is surrounded with the evidences of prosperity and success. Mr. Herrick is a loyal citizen, and to all matters which have had a tendency to elevate and bring prosperity to the public generally, he has given his hearty support. He is a man of excellent character and is respected by all who knew him.

AXEL R. LAGERWALL is another of the well-to-do farmers of Scandia township, Murray county, Minnesota, and is the son of Ranghaldt and Ingakarin (Falk) Samuelson, natives of Sweden. He was also a native of that country, where he was born October 21, 1841, in Aster Galten Lanhapinglan.

The first fourteen years of our subject's life were spent with his parents in his native land, after which he left home to earn his own living, and worked for farmers until the year 1869, at which time he came to the United States, coming directly to Minnesota.

He first stopped in Austin, arriving in that place on the 7th day of June. The first three weeks he was unable to find work, the next three being spent in railroad work. Four months were then spent in farm labor. The winter of 1879–80 was spent by our subject in the city of Austin at various kinds of employment, such as cutting ice, chopping wood, etc. When spring came he kept a boarding shanty on the railroad between Brownsdale and Lanesboro. This occupation was continued until the following October, when he came to Mankato, and found work until spring. He then moved to the village of St. James and kept boarders who were working for him, he having contracted to do one mile of grading. In the fall of 1871 our subject first came to Scandia township, where he settled on a homestead on section 30, remaining until the following spring. He then took a contract for building one mile of railroad between Sleepy Eye and Springfield. After finishing this he built one mile above Tracy, and then worked by the day with team for five weeks. He then returned to his claim, where his family had been living in his absence. The greater part of his time since has been spent on his farm, though he has done some railroad work. Mr. Lagerwall owns a fine farm of 160 acres, with eighty-five acres under cultivation. He has a good frame house; owns five horses and considerable stock. Our subject was one of the early settlers, and together with the other pioneers saw very hard times. During his first winter he started for Windom, eighty-five miles distant, to get provisions. He was stormed in for one day near Currie, and then succeeded in reaching Lew Mason's, where he was snowbound for three days and two nights. He then gave up trying to reach Windom at that time and started for home. When he reached the house of August Bosch, five miles from his own home, his team gave out and another stop had to be made. The snow was so deep and so badly drifted, that he could not get with his team to within half a mile of his house. He was living in a cellar at that time, and when he reached the place he found his wife snowed in, and all he could see was about six inches of stovepipe. His wife had been unable to get out of the house for five days when her husband opportunely came to her rescue. He found her nearly dead. About the second year of our subject's residence in the county the grasshoppers began their raids. But little was left by these insects of the first crop and none of the second. The third year a little grain was left, and the fourth a little more. The fifth year our subject thought that he would get the better of them, so he made a roller, and after they hatched out rolled this over the ground, thus killing most of them, so that he had very little trouble with them after that. These were terrible times, but their bitterness is largely relieved by the good times which have followed. Our subject is now in very comfortable circumstances, having done very well in his farming operations since the grasshoppers left. Mr. Lagerwall is a public-spirited citizen and takes an active interest in political matters. He has held the office of school treasurer for twelve years, and has also been a constable, township supervisor, an auctioneer, etc. Our subject's parents have lived with him during the most of the time since he came to Minnesota, though some of their time is spent with his brothers.

In the village of Currie occurred the marriage of our subject to Miss Gustava Johnson, a native of Sweden, she being born April 3, 1841, in the same place in which her husband's birth took place. Mr. and Mrs. Lagerwall have been blessed with the following named children—Axel, Alma Olivia (deceased), Ida Matilda, Hannah Sophia, Earnest (deceased) and Carl Earnest.

JAMES McCREADY is one of the reliable and prosperous farmers of Limestone township, Lincoln county, Minnesota. He is the son of David and Isabel (Fields) McCready, natives of the northern part of Ireland. The parents were well-to-do farmers, and were of Scotch descent.

The subject of our sketch was born in County Monaghan, in the northern part of Ireland, March 23, 1829. When he was about three years old his grandfather Fields took him and kept him in his family until he was nine years of age. Then his parents brought him to the United States, locating in St. Lawrence county, New York, where they arrived in August, 1839. The father purchased a farm in the woods, and our subject remained with his parents until he was sixteen years of age. He then commenced working out, but made his home principally with his parents until he was twenty years of age. He received a good common-school education, and after reaching twenty years of age left home, but for four years all the money he earned, with the exception of enough to clothe himself, was given to his parents. In 1853 he was married, and rented a farm, which he operated until 1869. In that year he moved to Minnesota, and arrived in Rushford, Fillmore county, April 22, where, after remaining two days, he met his brother, who came with a team and took him to his farm at Saratoga, Winona county. He remained in that locality until the month of November, at which time he removed to Elmira, Olmsted county, where he purchased a farm, on which he lived until the spring of 1880. He then sold out and came to Lincoln county, settling on a pre-emption of 160 acres upon which he had filed a year previous. He at once commenced his farming operations, did some breaking and put up what was known in early days as a "shak," into which his family moved when they came. He took a tree claim, filing on a quarter section for

his son, and then returned to Olmsted county for his family. While he was gone his pre-emption was "jumped," so he had to obtain a relinquishment of the tree claim of his son, and made his settlement on that. He made his home here for about five years, and then changed his entry on his land from a tree claim to a homestead. He has continued his residence here ever since, and has been quite successful in all his operations.

Mr. McCready was married in the city of Ogdensburgh, October 6, 1853, to Miss Anna M. Harper, Rev. M. Miller, pastor of the Presbyterian church of that place, officiating at the ceremony. Miss Harper was a daughter of Robert and Margaret Harper, natives of Ireland. She was born in County Cavan, Ireland, April 25, 1825. The fruits of this union are—David, who married Miss Sarah Benson, a native of Ireland; Mary E., now Mrs. Charles F. Thibbetts, a resident of Lyon county, Minnesota; and Alma J., married to William G. Hunter, a wheat buyer at Marshall, Minnesota.

The subject of our sketch is a systematic farmer, and has brought his farm to a high state of cultivation. He has put up good buildings, and has surrounded himself with the evidences of prosperity. In public matters he has taken an active interest, and has been chairman of the board of supervisors for five years. In politics he affiliates with the republican party, and is a consistent member of the Presbyterian church.

HANS NELSON HAMMERO. This gentleman is one of the leading farmers of his nationality in Cottonwood county, and is located on section 14 of West Brook township. He is of Norwegian birth, and is the son of News and Mary (Christianson) Hanson, who have always lived in their native country, Norway. The father was a farmer by occupation and was a well-to-do citizen of Norway.

Our subject assisted his father on the farm until he was twenty-five years of age and then worked as a fisherman, which business he followed for some time. In 1880 he emigrated to the United States, locating at Highwater, Cottonwood county, Minnesota, for a short time, and then going to Lyon county. In thirty days he returned to Cottonwood county, and resided in Highwater for some six months. At that time he came to his present location, taking 118 acres as a homestead. He has been one of the most successful farmers of the township and has accumulated considerable means. He is energetic and industrious, and has labored hard to make his farm a profitable investment. He has made good improvements on his land, and has just finished a fine new house which cost somewhat over two thousand dollars. He gives considerable attention to the raising of Short-horn cattle and Norman horses, and has met with considerable success in this line. He has always been one of the prominent citizens of the township and has taken a leading part in all matters of a public nature. Being a man of strong temperance sentiments, he affiliates with the prohibition party, and is working for the prohibition of the liquor traffic. He is a man of excellent qualities, genial, warm-hearted, sociable, and is highly esteemed by all who knew him. He is a member of the Baptist church.

Mr. Hammero was married in the year 1875 to Miss Nekkoline Nelson, a native of Norway.

———◦—❖—◦❰◈❱◦—❖—◦———

CHARLES HEATHFIELD is a leading resident of Fountain Prairie township, Pipestone county, Minnesota, and resides on a fine farm on section 34, where he is engaged in general farming and stock raising.

He was born in East Kent, England, January 5, 1828. His parents were John H. and Amy (Burbridge) Heathfield, both of whom were natives of England. The father was a farmer by occupation, and came to America in 1853. He died in Wisconsin in 1877, the mother having passed away in Oneida county, New York, in 1858. In the father's family there were two children—James and our subject.

Charles Heathfield passed the early days of his life under parental authority in his English home, remaining in his native country until he had attained his majority. He had received an education of a high order, his school life closing when he was about fifteen. At that time he commenced serving a seven-years' apprenticeship to learn the mason's trade. At twenty-one years of age he came with his parents to America, locating in the State of New York. He followed his trade until his enlistment in the Union army, in July, 1861. He joined the Third New York Volunteer Infantry. After passing through this period of service he was discharged at Washington. He then removed to Sauk county, Wisconsin, where, in 1865, he re-enlisted in the Forty-ninth Wisconsin Infantry, being discharged September 9, 1865, at Benton Barracks, Missouri. He was engaged in many hard-fought battles, and saw much service at the front. Among the battles in which he participated were those of Bull Run, South Mountain, Gettysburg, and Chicamauga, besides numerous skirmishes and battles of minor importance. After his discharge he returned to Wisconsin, where he engaged principally in hop-raising until 1879, in which year he came to his present place.

Mr. Heathfield was married November 18, 1851, to Miss Jane Giles, who was also a native of East Kent, England. This union has been blessed with nine living children—Julia, Libbie, Laura, William, Charles, Nelson, Lelia, Elmer and Mary Emma, the first three of the children being now married, and the rest single; Lelia is a school teacher by profession.

On coming to Pipestone county, Mr. Heathfield at once identified himself with the public interests of the locality. He was one of the leading spirits in the steps taken toward the organization of the civil division, attending the first township meeting, which was held in the spring óf 1879 at the house of E. E. Rink, who still resides in the county. At that meeting there were nine votes cast. Mr. Heathfield and Moses Heath are perhaps the oldest settlers remaining in the township. In politics our subject is a stanch republican, and has held the offices of school district treasurer for two years. He is also a leading member of the Grand Army of the Republic, Post No. 96, and is associated with the order of Odd Fellows, to which he has belonged for many years. Since coming to the township he has been engaged in general farming to some extent and also in stock raising. He has greatly improved his farm property, and has put up good outbuildings and a comfortable dwelling-house, and has set out a fine grove of trees. Our subject is looked upon as being a representative citizen and enjoys the respect and esteem of a large circle of friends. He is a man of good judgment, of sound moral qualities, and is a safe guide in all matters pertaining to the individual or public welfare.

JOHN HANSON is one of the reliable and influential farmers of Ann township, Cottonwood county, Minnesota, and is located on a fine farm on section 36. The place of his nativity is found in Norway, where he was born January 1, 1833.

The subject of our sketch was the son of Hans and Mary (Johnson) Alfson, both of whom were natives of Norway. The father died in his native land at the age of fifty years. The mother was born in 1811 and emigrated to America in the spring of 1866. She located in Dunn county, Wisconsin, where she remained three years. She then located in Cottonwood county, Minnesota, where she has since lived. She is at present residing in Highwater township. The parents were farmers by occupation and reared a family of eight children, three of whom are living—Andrew, Mary and Hans; all the children emigrated to America.

Until he was about eighteen years of age John Hanson assisted his father on the farm and attended the public schools. At eighteen he commenced learning the carpenter's trade and work at that business for some eight years. He was then married and emigrated to America, locating in Lafayette county, Wisconsin. After a two years' residence he went to Dunn county, same State, and engaged in work at his trade for five years. At the end of that time he concluded to change his occupation and engaged in farming, following that business for some four years. He then sold out his interests in Wisconsin and came to Highwater township, Cottonwood county, Minnesota, where he lived ten years. He then sold out and purchased one hundred and twenty acres of school land where he now lives in Ann township. He has built a fine house, good barn, and has thoroughly improved his farm. He has a fine grove of two acres of trees and owns about ten acres of heavy timber. His farm is well adapted to stock raising as well as agricultural pursuits and living water is to be found on his place the "year round."

The subject of our sketch was married in February, 1875, to Catharina Olson, who came to America from Norway, her native land, with her parents and a brother and sister. They located in Cottonwood county, Minnesota, where the parents both died. Mr. and Mrs. Hanson have been blessed with six children—Helen, Ole, Lewis, Ida, Clara and John. Lewis is now in Washington Territory, and the rest of the children are all at home.

The subject of our sketch is one of the leading citizens of his township and is a man of good moral character, being a consistent member of the Lutheran church. In politics he affiliates with the republican party and takes an active interest in all matters of a public nature. He assisted in the organization of the county, at which time there were sixty-five votes cast. He has held various township offices, such as township clerk, supervisor and school clerk of district number three. He is one of the thrifty, energetic farmers of the township, and in spite of the losses through which he passed during the grasshopper raids, when there was nothing raised for some four years, he has succeeded in accumulating some means and is now in excellent circumstances. He has always taken care of his own property and during those hard days succeeded in providing for his own sustenance, not having to apply to the government for aid in any year. In connection with his farming, Mr. Hanson also engaged in raising stock, and has some fine animals on hand. He has sold several cows for forty-five dollars apiece, this being but a sample of his herd. Mr. Hanson is one of the most liberal and progressive-minded citizens of the township.

———❖——❖❧❖❖—❖———

WILLIAM WILLIAMS is located on the northeast quarter of section 20, Lake Stay township, Lincoln county, Minnesota, where he located April 15, 1877. He is the son of Josiah and Catharine (Buzzard) Williams, both of whom were natives of Pennsylvania. The parents were farmers in that State and occupied an influential position in the township in which they lived.

William Williams was born in Westmore-

land county, Pennsylvania, September 6, 1835. He resided with his parents on the home farm until he was nearly twenty-four years old. During his earlier days he had been given good educational advantages and acquired a good common-school education. He remained in Pennsylvania in the county in which he was born until about a year after his marriage, which occurred February 13, 1859. After a two years' residence in Armstrong county he then went to Venango county, same State, and engaged in teaming in the oil country for two years. He then removed to Jefferson county, where he worked in a saw-mill for about a year. The next move was to Reed's Landing, Wabasha county, Minnesota, where he found employment at day work in various occupations on the river. He continued this for about twelve years and then removed to Buffalo county, Wisconsin. For about three years in that county our subject engaged in the wood business and at the end of that period came to Lincoln county, settling on the homestead where he now lives.

Mr. Williams was united in matrimony in Armstrong county, Pennsylvania, February 13, 1859, to Miss Susan J. Shaw, daughter of John and Rachel (Husk) Shaw, both natives of New Jersey. Miss Shaw was born in Armstrong county, Pennsylvania, April 6, 1841, being reared and receiving her education in the county of her birth. Mr. and Mrs. Williams have been blessed with the following-named children—Normia Fulvia, Parthena Frenkalet, Philetus Leland, Shelby Bryer, Orlande Speaden, Ambrose Writner, Artemus Thumlo, Ralston Virgil, Ava Irene, Amy Delina and Earl Waldo, all of whom are living except the first two.

On coming to this county Mr. Williams had but little means and has seen hard times. He has, however, kept courageously at work, and by systematic and thorough attention to his farming duties has accumulated considerable property, and is now in good circumstances. On coming to the county he had nothing but a span of horses and a wagon, this being the extent of his property interests. He now owns 160 acres of fine land with about 130 acres under cultivation, has nine horses, considerable stock, and all necessary farm machinery. He was among the very first settlers of the township and therefore experienced all the usual hardships which have to be borne by the pioneer settlers. There were but two other families in the township when he located; the names of these families were Dean and Wells. For two or three years after locating in the township these families had to experience many trying things. It was almost impossible to obtain fuel in the shape of coal or wood and they had to burn hay. Provisions also were very scarce, and in order to obtain them they had to go a long distance to market. Our subject's family passed through all these trying circumstances, and because of these things prize more highly the good circumstances which surround them now. Our subject managed to obtain an ownership of over a one-half interest in a threshing machine, which he engaged in running during several years of his early stay in the township. In this way he provided for his family, and he has often said since that had it not been for this enterprise his family would have suffered much more than they did. One winter they could not obtain any flour for some months, and had to grind wheat in a coffee-mill. After the wheat was ground, it was then run through a sieve, and this sifted meal was used for baking purposes. This was about all the family had to live on, as their potatoes had been destroyed by the severe frost. This was one of the hardest winters through which our subject and his family had to pass. Since coming to the county Mr. Williams has been a hearty supporter of everything which tended to elevate the condition of his fellow-citizens or develop the general interests of the township and county. He is a man of good business characteristics, and therefore has been put forward by his fellow-citizens to take hold of the duties of various official positions. He has been chairman of the board of township supervisors for two years, was one of the school directors for eight years, was treasurer of the township for seven or eight years, and was also road overseer for some time. He has been president of the cemetery association for four years. Mr. Williams is a loyal citizen, an exemplary Christian man, and is a member of the Congregationalist church.

LOUIS HIRSCHY, a leading farmer and reliable citizen of Fountain Prairie township, came to Pipestone county, Minnesota, in the year 1878, locating on his present land on section 18, on the 20th day of March. Mr. Hirschy has the honor of putting up the first "permanent shanty" which was erected for dwelling purposes. Into this he moved in the month of April and continued his residence during the breaking season. He broke about twenty acres of land and in the fall went to the big woods, where he remained during the winter. Returning the next spring he put the twenty acres into crops of wheat and oats, raising therefrom an excellent harvest. He has continued his residence there ever since. On coming to his land in the spring of 1879 he built a good frame house to take the place of the shanty which had been built the year before. This building is still used by him as a residence. Our subject is one of the very first settlers of the township, there being but one or two others who came in the spring of 1879, one of these being Michael Gilfillan, who put up a small shanty on section 8, and remained during the summer, going to the big woods in the fall, and again returning to his claim in the spring of 1879, but at the end of that season going to Lincoln county, where he still lives. Mr. Hirschy was one of the leaders in the movement towards the organization of the township in 1879, and was also conspicuous in the organization of the county. He was a member of the first board of township trustees. Our subject was not at the first meeting, but after it was over was notified that he was elected to a position on the board of supervisors and instructed to go to Mr. Connor's house and qualify, but on going to this place he found but two women in the house and therefore withdrew and did not qualify. After remaining for some three years on the farm, Mr. Hirschy removed to the village of Lake Benton, where for three years he was engaged in the retail liquor business. He then sold out and returned to his farm. He has three hundred and twenty acres of land, of which two hundred and fifty acres are broken and under cultivation. He is engaged largely in farming, and also in stock raising, owning a large number of Clydesdale and English shire horses and Short-horn cattle. In his business enterprises he has been quite successful and has accumulated considerable means, at present owning one of the finest farms in the township.

Louis Hirschy was born in Dayton, Ohio, January 28, 1857. His parents were Samuel H. and Margaret (Felker) Hirschy, the father being a native of Switzerland and the mother born in Saxony, Germany. In early life the father was a farmer and day laborer and by frugality and economy he accumulated considerable means, and is now engaged in the mercantile business in Wabasha, Minnesota. The parents both emigrated to this country when they were young. In the father's family there were three children—Louis, Charles and Clara.

Mr. Hirschy's early days were spent in Wabasha, Minnesota, to which place his par-

ents came when he was quite young. He attended the district schools, and completed his education at Prairie du Chien, Wisconsin, in about 1875, having attended college there. After completing his course in college he returned to his parents and for four years remained principally at home. Then he came to Pipestone county and settled on his present place, where he has since lived. In politics our subject affiliates with the republican party, in whose counsels he has become one of the leading local spirits. He is a member of the Odd Fellows fraternity, and has passed through all the degrees of the local organization. In public matters he has always been an earnest supporter of all things which tended to improve the general welfare, and since the organization of the township he has taken a prominent place in its political government. The name of the township originated from the fact that there is a spring of living water on the prairie on our subject's farm. Mr. Hirschy is an exemplary citizen, is energetic and public-spirited, and is esteemed by a wide circle of friends.

In 1885 Mr. Hirschy was married to Miss Maggie Hartigan, a native of London, England. This lady came to the United States when quite young, settling for some time in New York, from whence she removed to the State of Minnesota. This union has been blessed with two children—Samuel and Charles.

FRANK F. BURDETT, of Edgerton, Minnesota, is the son of Frederick and Augusta (Hapgood) Burdett, natives of Massachusetts.

The subject of this sketch was born in Worcester, Massachusetts, on July 23, 1850. When he was about six years of age his parents moved to Winnebago county, Wisconsin, settling in the village of Delhi, where his father was engaged in teaching music.

Until about sixteen years old our subject remained at home with his parents, attending the district schools. He then went to Eau Claire, where he attended the seminary of that place for two terms, after which he attended the commercial college of the same place for some time. After his graduation from that institution he went to Nobles county, Minnesota, where he took a homestead and remained on it, engaged in farming for some ten years, after which he sold out and, in September, 1880, came to Edgerton and engaged in the mercantile business. He has a very fine double store, with one room devoted to groceries and boots and shoes and the other to dry goods and readymade clothing.

April 13, 1875 in Nobles county, Minnesota, occurred the marriage of Mr. Burdett to Miss Alice Lytton, a daughter of John N. and Lucy (Gleason) Lytton, natives of North Carolina. This marriage has been blessed with the following-named children—Fred Ernest, and Gussie, both born in Nobles county, and Frank, born in Edgerton. The last named child died at the age of seven months; the others are living at the present time.

Mr. Burdett is a public-spirited citizen, and has always taken an active interest in the political affairs of his town and county. He has held the following offices with satisfaction to his constituents and with credit to himself: Member of the village council, holding that position at the present time; and treasurer of the Farmers' Co-operative Association of Edgerton. At present our subject is the only merchant in the village. At the time of his location here, however, there were three others, but they have now gone. As a result of this Mr. Burdett has a large trade and is a prosperous business man. He owns his store building and also a residence in the village. He is a man of good character, of excellent business ability and is one of the most prominent and respected citizens of Edgerton and vicinity.

EDWARD J. ARNESON, an influential farmer of West Brook township, Cottonwood county, Minnesota, is a resident of section 10. The place of his nativity is found in the kingdom of Norway, where he was born July 10, 1851.

The parents of the subject of our sketch were Arnt and Hannah (Hanson) Arneson, also natives of Norway, and residing in that country throughout their lives up to the present time. The father is a fisherman by occupation, and reared a family of five children, three of whom are now living—Hans, Anna and Edward J.

The subject of our sketch assisted his father in his fishing operations up to the age of twenty-two years, when he emigrated to America. Up to twelve years of age he attended the public schools and received a limited common-school education. On coming to America he located a farm in West Brook township, and then went to Goodhue county and worked through the harvest, going from thence to Wisconsin, where he worked in a saw-mill for a short time. He then returned to West Brook township, and spent the winter on his farm, going back to Wisconsin in the spring and remaining in that State for three years, working during the summer months in a saw-mill and during the winters in the woods. He then came to his present location and settled on 160 acres as a homestead. He is a hard-working farmer, and has striven constantly to make his place one of the best in the township. He has succeeded quite well in this enterprise, and has put his land under an excellent state of cultivation and provided it with a good dwelling-house and outbuildings. He has four acres of a fine grove of trees about his house. In connection with his farming he is engaged in stock raising to a considerable extent and with good success. He has nineteen head of fine cattle and several Norman horses. In politics Mr. Arneson affiliates with the republican party, and always takes an active interest in matters pertaining to the public welfare. He is a man of good character, and is much respected.

Mr. Arneson was married in July, 1881, to Luna Peterson, a native of Norway. This union has been blessed with four children— Alfred, Martin, Theodore and Hannah.

———◦◦——

Allen G. Lincoln is a prosperous farmer living on section 32 of Sweet township, Pipestone county, Minnesota.

The subject of our sketch is the son of Oliver and Almira (Denton) Lincoln, the former a native of Vermont and the latter born in New York. They were the parents of thirteen children—nine boys and four girls, Allen being the eighth child. The father was a mechanic by occupation and was the son of a farmer of Vermont. The mother's father was also a farmer. The parents both died in Michigan in 1886.

The native place of our subject is to be found in Genessee county, New York, where he first saw the light of day October 23, 1850. During the first sixteen years of his life Allen G. Lincoln remained at home assisting his father and attending the common schools. At that age he started out for himself and came to Iowa, where for three years he worked on a farm in Butler county. He then rented a farm in that county for one year, after which, in 1871, he came to Minnesota and took a homestead in Rock county, where he followed agricultural pursuits for some four years. The village of Luverne became his next abiding place, where, in partnership with James Gillard, he opened a hardware store and for two years engaged in that business. He then

sold out, and in May, 1878, came to Pipestone county, and took 160 acres of land, where he now lives, as a pre-emption.

The marriage of our subject occurred April 23, 1870, at which time he wedded Miss Julia Gillard. Mr. and Mrs. Lincoln have been blessed with five children—Freddy O., Edward A., Lettie M., Ovid H. and Gracie S. all living at the present time. Mrs. Lincoln's parents are still living, and are residing in Rock county.

In politics the subject of this present sketch affiliates with the republican party, and has always taken an active interest in the affairs of that party, as well as in all matters tending to the general welfare of his town and county. For seven years he was one of the school directors, was town treasurer of Eden township, Rock county, for five years, and was also constable for one year in that county. Mr. Lincoln is a man of excellent character, is an energetic and enterprising farmer and holds the highest respect and esteem of a wide circle of friends and neighbors.

———◦◦——

Angus Grant is an influential and well-to-do farmer and stock raiser of Lake Sarah township, Murray county, Minnesota. He located here in 1878, and purchased 120 acres on section 9, where he still lives. He improved his place and made it his home for two years, then went east and, coming back some time later, sold his farm and took charge as superintendent of a farm of twelve hundred acres, with his residence on section 9. This is one of the largest farms in the township, and in fact in the county, and our subject is giving his attention largely to the raising of blooded stock, such as full blooded Short-horn cattle and Norman horses. This is in company with his brothers, D. and D.W. Grant, who are railroad contractors. The improvements on this farm are among the best in the township, if not the best. They have two large barns, one forty-six by one hundred feet and the other thirty-two by 250 feet. The house on which our subject lives is twenty-four by thirty feet with an addition eighteen by twenty feet.

Mr. Grant was born in Upper Canada, May 24, 1856. He was reared in that country until nine years of age, when his parents moved to central Ohio, where they staid ten years, and where our subject received a good common-school education. Then, with his parents, he removed to Rice county, Minnesota, and located on a farm where they resided four or five years. Then our subject commenced railroading on the Northern Pacific railroad, and continued in this line for five or six years. He then took a trip to California and Washington Territory in search of a location. Not liking the country, however, he returned to Minnesota and soon after located on his present place.

The father of the subject of our sketch was William Grant, a farmer and lumberman. He was born in Canada and died in Ohio. He was a man of considerable means and was highly respected. The mother's maiden name was Catharine McDonald, a native of Canada and who died in 1887 in Rice county, Minnesota. She was a consistent member of the Methodist Episcopal church.

Mr. Grant was married in August, 1879, to Miss Anna Mills, a native of Rice county, Minnesota. This lady was given an excellent education in the St. Mary's seminary at Faribault. Mr. and Mrs. Grant have been blessed with three children—Rosie, Donald and Goldie Maud. Mrs. Grant is the daughter of John Mills, a native of New York State. Her father was a lawyer and died when Mrs. Grant was six months old. Her mother is still living.

Perhaps no man in Murray county has charge of such important interests financially as the subject of our sketch. He has a great number of men under his supervision and yearly puts in a large acreage of grain besides raising many head of horses and cattle. In the management of his immense farming business he has been met with merited success and has accumulated considerable means. He is a man of excellent principles and is highly respected by all with whom he has to do.